FLORIDA CAMPING

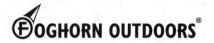

FLORIDA CAMPING

The Complete Guide to More Than 900 Tent and RV Campgrounds

THIRD EDITION

Marilyn A. Moore

AVALON
TRAVEL

FOGHORN OUTDOORS
FLORIDA CAMPING
The Complete Guide to More Than
900 Tent and RV Campgrounds

Third Edition

Marilyn A. Moore

Text © 2003 by Marilyn A. Moore.
All rights reserved.
Illustrations and maps © 2003 by
Avalon Travel Publishing.
All rights reserved.

Avalon Travel Publishing is a division of
Avalon Publishing Group, Inc.

Some photos and illustrations are used by permission
and are the property of the original copyright owners.

ISBN: 1-56691-573-2
ISSN: 1095-1814

Please send all feedback about this book to:

ⒻOGHORN OUTDOORS®
Florida Camping
Avalon Travel Publishing
1400 65th Street, Suite 250
Emeryville, CA 94608, USA
atpfeedback@avalonpub.com
www.foghorn.com

Printing History
1st edition—1998
3rd edition—November 2003
5 4 3 2 1

Editor: Kathryn Ettinger
Series Manager: Marisa Solís
Researchers: Tom Dubocq, Sally Deneen, Robert McClure, Joanne Moore
Copy Editor: Jill Metzler
Proofreader: Donna Leverenz
Graphics Coordinator: Amber Pirker
Illustrator: Bob Race
Production Coordinator: Darren Alessi
Cover Designer: Jacob Goolkasian
Interior Designer: Darren Alessi
Map Editors: Olivia Solís, Naomi Adler Dancis
Cartographers: Darren Alessi, Mike Morgenfeld, Olivia Solís
Indexers: Kathryn Ettinger, Nyree Sarkissian, Amy Scott

Front cover photo: © Christina Lease

Printed in the United States of America by Worzalla

Contents

SPECIAL TOPICS

- Little Lake George
- Moses Creek
- Pellicer Creek
- Rodman Reservoir

- St. Augustine Beach
- St. Johns River
- Vilano Beach

Including:
- Crystal River
- Fore Lake
- Lake Bryant
- Lake Eaton

- Lake George
- Ocala National Forest
- Ocklawaha River
- Orange Lake
- St. Johns River

Including:
- Halifax River
- Hontoon Island
- Lake Monroe

- Lake Woodruff National
  Wildlife Refuge
- Rose Bay
- St. Johns River

Including:
- Arbuckle Creek
- Billy Lake
- Bull Creek
- Crews Lake
- Dead River
- Eagle Lake
- Econlockhatchee River
- Haines Creek
- Hudson Beach
- Kissimmee River
- Lake Apopka
- Lake Beauclaire
- Lake Bonnet
- Lake Cypress
- Lake Deaton
- Lake Eustis
- Lake Garfield
- Lake Griffin
- Lake Harris
- Lake Hart
- Lake Hatchineha
- Lake Jackson
- Lake Jesup

- Lake Juliana
- Lake Kissimmee
- Lake Kissimmee
  State Park
- Lake Lowery
- Lake Marian
- Lake Panasoffkee
- Lake Pearl
- Lake Pierce
- Lake Rosalie
- Lake Saunders
- Lake Smith
- Lake Tohopekaliga
- Lake Whippoorwill
- Mud River
- Mullet Lake
- Outlet River
- Peace River
- Rock Springs Run
- Tsala Apopka Lake
- Wekiva River
- Wekiwa Springs State Park
- Withlacoochee River
- Withlacoochee State Forest

Florida Regions Map

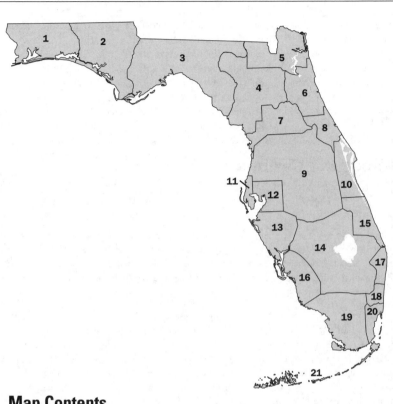

Map Contents

How to Use This Book

Foghorn Outdoors Florida Camping is divided into 21 regional chapters. Maps at the beginning of each chapter show where all the campgrounds in that region are located.

You can search for the ideal camping spot in two ways:

1. If you know the name of the specific campground where you'd like to stay, or the name of the surrounding geographical area or nearby feature (town, national or state park or forest, lake, river, etc.), look it up in the index and turn to the corresponding page.

2. To find a campground in a particular part of Florida, turn to the map at the beginning of that region. You can identify entry numbers in the area where you would like to camp, then refer to the chapter table of contents to find the page numbers for those campgrounds.

About the Ratings

We've rated the parks in this book on a scale of 1 to 10. Some overlap exists between the following categories. This is not rocket science.

1 to 4

Ratings from 1 to 4 apply to mobile home parks or RV campgrounds in a city or on a busy suburban highway, near strip shopping centers, housing developments, or an otherwise non-nature setting. You stay in these facilities because they're convenient for something else you want to do, such as shopping or visiting relatives. Your neighbors may be living there year-round. Amenities are basic.

3 to 7

A rating of 3 to 7 applies to an RV resort or mobile home park with lots of amenities, such as a swimming pool, recreation hall, shuffleboard courts, and more. These parks are in rural or suburban settings but are more recreation oriented. In addition to travelers, campers are snowbirds, year-round retirees, or people who are interested in living in the area because of its proximity to tourist attractions or the "Florida lifestyle." Alternately, it's a campground with basic necessities, but it gets a higher rating because of its location in a setting of great natural beauty. For instance, an older private campground in a deeply wooded setting may not have the deluxe features of a new "resort," but it's highly acceptable for campers who need to stay there because the state campgrounds are full or because they are looking for convenient locations to hiking, biking, canoeing, or popular tourist attractions.

7 to 9

Places with great trees and outdoor activities nearby or right on site earn a rating between 7 and 9. Camping in these spots is a joy. Some RV parks are included because they include such resort features as golf courses, tennis courts, or boating opportunities, or are so centrally located to tourist attractions that they combine features of both destination parks and easy-access locations to nearby Florida attractions.

10

This is camping nirvana. For nature lovers, the scenery or remoteness are hard to match in Florida; there are possibilities of seeing wildlife or rare natural areas, and close proximity to a stream, lake, river, or other water is likely. A very few RV parks make this grade on the basis of their resort-style on-site amenities, professional management, and general appeal to visitors of all kinds who want to be near Florida's finest attractions.

About the Maps

This book is divided into several chapters based on established regions; an overview map of these regions follows the table of contents. At the start of each chapter, you'll find a map of the entire region. Campgrounds are plotted on these maps by their map numbers.

The maps in this book are designed to show the general location of each campground. Readers are advised to purchase a detailed state map, particularly before heading out to any campground when venturing into the wilderness. Nautical charts are needed for some boat-in campsites—please do not attempt to go without them. We've also listed websites where they are available; often you can download detailed maps, particularly of remote backwoods or wilderness areas, for general orientation.

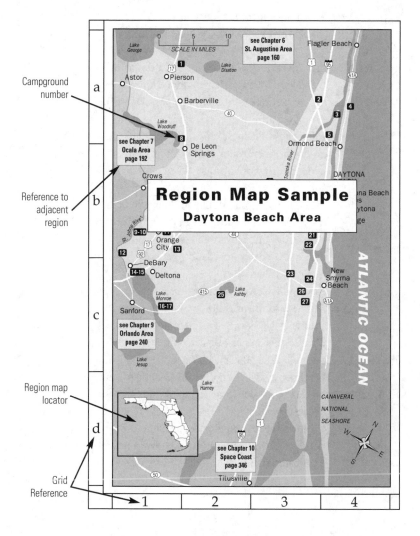

About the Campground Profiles

Each campground in this book is listed in a consistent, easy-to-read format to help you choose the ideal camping spot. From a general overview of the setting to detailed driving directions, the profile will provide all the information you need. Here is an example:

Map number and camp-ground name →

General location of the campground named by its proximity to the nearest major town or landmark →

Icons noting activities and facilities at or nearby the campground

Rating, on a scale of 1–10

Map the campground can be found on and page number the map can be found on

1 SOMEWHERE USA CAMPGROUND

Rating: 10

South of Somewhere USA Lake

Somewhere Area map, page 4

Each campground in this book begins with a brief overview of its setting. The description typically covers ambience, information about the attractions, and activities popular at the campground.

Campsites, facilities: This section provides the number of campsites for both tents and RVs and whether hookups are available. Facilities such as restrooms, picnic areas, recreation areas, laundry, and dump stations will be addressed, as well as the availability of piped water, showers, playground, stores, and others amenities. The campground's pet policy is also mentioned here.

Reservations, fees: This section notes whether reservations are accepted, and the rates for tent sites and RV sites. If there are additional fees for parking or pets, or discounted weekly or seasonal rates, those will also be noted here.

Directions: This section provides mile-by-mile driving directions to the campground from the nearest major town.

Contact: This section provides an address, phone number, and Internet address, if available, for each campground.

About the Icons

Listings in this book feature symbols that represent the recreational offerings on-site or within a short distance of the campground. Other symbols identify whether there are sites for RVs and/or tents, playgrounds, natural springs, or any wheelchair-accessible facilities. Wheelchair accessibility has been indicated when it was mentioned by campground managers, and concerned persons should call the contact number to ensure that their specific needs will be met. The icons are not meant to represent every activity or service, but rather those that are most significant.

— Hiking trails are available.

— Biking trails or routes are available. This usually refers to trail biking, although it may represent road cycling as well. Refer to the text for that campground for details.

— Swimming opportunities are available.

— Fishing opportunities are available.

— Boating opportunities are available. Various types of vessels apply under this umbrella activity, including motorboats and personal watercrafts (Jet Skis). Refer to the text for that campground for more details, including mph restrictions and boat ramp availability.

— Springs are located nearby. Refer to the text for that campground for more information.

— Pets are permitted. Campgrounds that allow pets may require an additional fee or that pets be leashed. Campgrounds may also restrict pet size or behavior. Refer to the text for that campground for specific instructions or call in advance.

— A playground is available. A campground with a playground can be desirable for campers traveling with children.

— Wheelchair access is provided, as advertised by campground managers. However, concerned persons are advised to call the contact number of a campground to be certain that their specific needs will be met.

— RV sites are provided.

— Tent sites are provided.

Our Commitment

We are committed to making *Foghorn Outdoors Florida Camping* the most accurate, thorough, complete, and enjoyable camping guide to the state. With this third edition, you can rest assured that every camping spot in this book has been carefully reviewed and accompanied by the most up-to-date information. During the preparation of this guide, some fees may have gone up, and some camping destinations may have opened, closed, or changed hands. If you have a specific need or concern, it's best to call the location ahead of time. In addition, public campgrounds under government jurisdiction are being revamped and improved. During this time of renovations, approximate temporary closing times are listed, but it is always a good idea to call to check the current status since these programs can run into unexpected roadblocks.

If you would like to comment on the book, whether it's to suggest a tent or RV spot we overlooked, or to let us know about any noteworthy experience—good or bad—that occurred while using *Foghorn Outdoors Florida Camping* as your guide, we would appreciate hearing from you. Please address correspondence to:

Foghorn Outdoors Florida Camping, Third Edition
Avalon Travel Publishing
1400 65th Street, Suite 250
Emeryville, CA 94608, U.S.A.
email: atpfeedback@avalonpub.com
If you send us an email, please put "Florida Camping" in the subject line.

COURTESY OF VISIT FLORIDA

Introduction

Introduction

Many of us have discovered camping is the perfect escape from the pressures of modern life. It's a way to spend quality time with your family or mate, make new friends, learn new skills, and rediscover the soul-restoring qualities of nature. You can use a camping park as your home base for anything that satisfies your psyche—from active sports like trail biking and canoeing, to more quiet pursuits like antiquing and bird-watching.

You can camp as a cheap way to travel to Disney World or tour the state. Florida is also a favored destination for RVers escaping the winter winds and seeking social and leisure lifestyles. Driving vacations are less hassle: No airport security, no delayed flights, no expensive restaurant bills, plus you get to bring your own pillow (and whatever other personal belongings you wouldn't bring on a plane).

RV industry associations and RV manufacturers say that more and more people are discovering the joys of camping and the moving lifestyle, particularly since air travel and fears about foreign travel are pressing upon us now. Thankfully, since the first edition of this book was published in 1998, dozens of new campgrounds have opened and thousands of acres of wilderness have been made publicly accessible. We can't speak more highly of the state of Florida's continuing efforts to acquire and preserve new lands for the public, through the Save Our Rivers program and others. At the same time, many commercial parks have closed, falling victim to the developer's bulldozer and being converted into housing subdivisions or shopping centers. Some older private parks have simply filled to capacity, and many of their sites are now occupied by full-time RVers in retirement. Even newly built parks are filling up quickly, as they sell the Great American Dream of second-home ownership: a patch of land on which to park your rig that you can rent out to itinerant travelers when you've gone back home to Canada, Northern states, or elsewhere.

In this age when your everyday life can follow you anywhere you go, when you have to monitor (and respond to) cell phones, personal digital accessories, and voice mail, it seems more important than ever to unplug now and then. To hit the road—and disconnect—at least for a little while.

History

You're not alone, and here's a bit of historical perspective: Ever since the Model T was invented, Florida has been a camping mecca, drawing thousands of people seeking adventure and sunshine.

As early as 1916, the first "snowbirds" were packing up homemade house cars or trailers and heading south for the winter. Experts estimated that one-half of the 50,000 trailers on the road in the United States were hauled to Florida during one winter in the 1930s. Sunshine State hoteliers and boardinghouse owners howled that their business would drop. But the hotels remained crowded, and trailer parks began to spring up all over the state to accommodate RVs. It helped that the campers' money was as green as everyone else's.

Those early campers formed their own version of the Good Sam Club, calling themselves the Tin Can Tourists of the World. Founded in a Tampa campground in 1919, the group grew to 30,000 members by 1938. Its goals were to provide members with "safe and clean camping areas, wholesome entertainment, and high moral values," according to Florida state archives. Their official emblem? A tin can soldered to the radiator cap of a member's car.

The origin of the tin can moniker isn't clear. It may have referred to campers' preference for canned foodstuffs (forget the freeze-dried food; it hadn't been invented). Or it could have been a reference to the Tin Lizzie, as Model T Fords were called.

The Tin Can Tourists gathered at parks around the state, usually in Tampa, Sarasota, Ocala, and Eustis. During the summer, they met at a campground in Michigan. Their favored Florida migration route: Dade City (Pasco County) at Thanksgiving and Arcadia (DeSoto County) for Christmas, where they celebrated with a community Christmas tree and a Santa Claus for the children, according to *The WPA Guide to Florida,* a book written during the Great Depression.

In 1931, the city of Sarasota opened a municipal trailer park that quickly became winter headquarters for the Tin Can Tourists. During its first season, 1,500 people in 600 trailers set up camp. Five years later, the population had grown to 7,460 people and nearly 3,000 cars, as noted in *So This Is Florida* (written by Frank Parker Stockbridge and John Holliday Perry; published in 1938).

The Sarasota Tourist Park was located on 30 acres wooded with Australian pines at a railroad crossing and Ringling Boulevard. The park even hosted the Tin Canners' annual convention, featuring a parade of new models and equipment—basically, a 1930s-style RV show.

Ocala and Arcadia also had municipal trailer parks in the 1930s, but the millionaire's city of Palm Beach allowed trailers to park for one hour only.

Conveniences at a park in Bartow in Polk County sound much the same as today's: water, electricity, hot and cold showers, laundry facilities, a recreation hall, shuffleboard courts, and horseshoe pits. The price? Stockbridge and Perry tell us that camping cost $1.30 by the week for two people, plus 25 cents for each additional person. (Campground owners got that extra-person charge started early, didn't they?) Fees at other parks ranged from $1 to $5.

Camping in those days presented much the same spectacle as today. You would have seen dusty cars and trailers with license plates from all over the United States. Campers caught up with old acquaintances and made new friends. They played shuffleboard and cards, or they congregated in the recreation hall. They cooked in the open and hung laundry out to dry. And when dusk came, they lounged outdoors to watch the sun set.

So take a moment, as you embark on your camping adventure, and think back to the Tin Can Campers. Americans have been enjoying the great outdoors of Florida in their own individual style for a long, long time.

Current Trends

This third edition of *Foghorn Outdoors Florida Camping* will bring you up-to-date. We've added about 75 new, never-before-listed parks. In addition, some parks listed in previous editions now have different names. (They are not listed as new parks, but their new owners' investment in renovations and your camping enjoyment is usually noted.)

Things move quickly in Florida, a state that always seems to be on the cutting edge of national trends. Consider the following:

• The Internet has changed the way people camp. New RVs now come equipped with desk areas for computers. Some campgrounds brag that they are "modem friendly" or place web-accessible computers in their recreation halls so travelers can check their email and keep in touch with home. State parks, national parks, and public agencies that administer public lands post maps on their websites that you can download for general orientation and other details. On the negative side, countless gigabytes in commercial cyberspace are devoted to pseudo RV directories. Use these online directories at your own risk; they are often totally out of date. Once online, they make minimal effort to recheck the information on a regular basis.

In some places, you can camp right on the beach.

- Full-time camping has become a reality for many people. Recessionary times, early retirement bonuses and layoffs, or just plain old wanderlust have converted many a former working stiff into a roadmaster. The full-time camping lifestyle (estimated at about $1,500 a month in expenses) is more economical than ever.
- Middle-class parents, perhaps recalling the long drive-across-America trips they enjoyed as children, see camping as a budget-stretching way to take their own kids on Disney World vacations or to Florida beaches. The kids themselves, toughened by outdoors Scouting activities and the rage for "extreme sports," are happy to go, at least until they reach the age where they no longer go want to go anywhere with their parental units.
- Our fast-paced modern lives have ignited a thirst for getting out of the city and into a more natural setting. The RV industry has noticed and is now producing both bigger, fancier RVs for affluent retirees and smaller, lighter, more efficient trailers and pop-tops for family campers.
- Older people are no longer "senior citizens." They're "active retirees searching for an active lifestyle." Many RV parks now have tennis courts, golf courses, exercise rooms, and full-time activities directors. Of course, the heated swimming pool and spa, shuffleboard courts, and stocked fishing ponds are still ubiquitous, as is the recreation hall with bingo, potluck suppers, and ice-cream socials. These parks have become the wintertime home address for both the affluent RVer and penny-pinching retiree. Oddly, we notice that a waning trend is the once *de rigueur* horseshoe pit, while the bocce ball and *pétanque* courts are holding their own.
- Florida state parks previously banned pets, making these award-winning natural beauties inaccessible to many travelers. Now most parks allow you to bring dogs, provided they have proof of vaccination against rabies and behave on a leash. Tip: If you travel with a pet, you must carry proof of rabies vaccination. State parks also are now under a convenient, systemwide reservation system, relieving the uncertainty of being greeted with the equivalent of a "no vacancy" sign.
- Some RV parks are getting more luxurious—and falling under corporate chains. A handful of RV parks are selling not just resort-style living or condominium lots, but "RV portes"—a luxury garage for the vehicle with attached housing. Several parks now offer "super" sites with spas, patio furniture, and barbecue grills. The jury is still out on this feature.

But one thing hasn't changed: Every camper in Florida is different. This book was written to help all of you, no matter where you fall on the spectrum of roughing it.

We recognize that one person's idea of the perfect vacation is traveling in a fully equipped, modern RV complete with microwave and satellite dish. Another would scoff at such luxuries, preferring a tent in the woods and cooking over a backpacker's stove. One camper's notion of heaven is hearing the bellow of an alligator deep in a cypress swamp; another would consider wading in waist-deep swamp water something like living out a horror movie. Some campgrounds are as luxurious as country clubs, whereas others are little more than a clearing in the forest.

Campers in Florida approach the experience with vastly diverging goals and expectations: to get out of the cold for the winter; to visit friends and family; to tour theme parks; to explore the state's natural wonders; to snorkel, canoe, hike, fish, ride horses, and bicycle off-road; or to scuba dive in a below-ground cavern or bubbling spring. Still others may plan to do a little of everything.

But Florida is a big state. It's a hard day's drive from the state line to South Florida, and six hours traversing Florida from east to west. Even if you've decided where you're going, where will you stay on the way? What will you find when you get there?

We'll answer those questions—whether you're piloting a huge motorcoach or crammed into a tiny Toyota with a tarp and a sleeping bag, whether you need a place to plug in the TV or level ground to pitch a tent, whether you want shade trees to ward off the broiling sun or wide-open space to park a long, long trailer.

Maybe you need a convenient stop on the highway as you travel toward Florida's vast wilderness areas. Perhaps you just want to hunker down for the winter in a deluxe resort with like-minded people. Possibly, you're only interested in finding a cheap place to stay while you visit tourist attractions.

All 873,000 of you who drive to the Sunshine State each year with your camping gear, or the 200,000 Floridians who own recreational vehicles, will find the kind of campground that suits you best in *Foghorn Outdoors Florida Camping*. Why? Because this book is the only guide that includes almost every campsite in the state—more than 116,000 of them. They're part of 923 campgrounds, RV parks, and backcountry sites stretching from Pensacola to Key West.

If you're a wilderness lover heading for the Everglades by car from the northern state line, you have a lot of mileage to cover. You don't want to waste time on the way, but who wants to sleep in a parking lot? Tent-friendly, wooded campgrounds are noted in these pages.

If you've got your pop-top trailer in tow and the kids in the backseat, Disney World beckons (and Universal Studios, and a myriad of other tourism attractions clustered around the Big Mouse). Where can you stop? We'll direct you to family-friendly spots.

If you're a retired couple heading for warmer climes, do you know which RV parks welcome folks for the winter season? We'll tell you.

Other details will help you make your choice, too. Are the mosquitoes worse by the lake? Is it hard to back a trailer into the spots at Campground A? Will you have to pitch your tent, and then sleep, on gravel at Campground B? Are there showers with hot or cold water? Outhouses or restrooms? Is electricity available? (In Florida, even die-hard tent campers often use box fans on summer nights.)

We hope to give you the insights you'll need to help you choose a campground where you and your companions will be happy.

Ready? Let's hit the road. Fire up the ignition on the Class A motorcoach. Hitch up the Airstream or the Scamp (our favorite), or whatever trailer suits your appetites. Throw the cooler in the back of the car. Snatch up your propane bottles or your backpack, and strap on the bike racks. We're going to show you Florida in a way that no other guidebook does.

Florida's Top Campgrounds

Can't decide where to camp this weekend? Check out our picks for the state in several categories:

Top 10 Easily Accessible Beachfront Campgrounds

Anastasia State Park, St. Augustine Area, pages 166–167
Bahia Honda State Park, Florida Keys, page 603
Cape San Blas Camping Resort, Panama City Area, pages 83–84
Fort Pickens Campground, Pensacola Area, pages 51–52
Grayton Beach State Park, Panama City Area, page 73
Gulf Beach Campground, Sarasota/Bradenton Area, page 414
Henderson Beach State Park, Pensacola Area, page 59
Long Key State Park, Florida Keys, pages 599–600
St. Andrews State Park, Panama City Area, page 78
St. Joseph Peninsula State Park, Panama City Area, pages 82–83

Top 10 Campgrounds for Families

Arcadia's Peace River Campground, Sarasota/Bradenton Area, pages 410–411
Disney's Fort Wilderness Campground, Orlando Area, pages 299–300
Encore SuperPark–Daytona Beach North, Daytona Beach Area, pages 221–222
Encore SuperPark–Orlando, Orlando Area, page 300
Kathryn Abbey Hanna Park, Jacksonville Area, pages 152–153
Lion Country Safari KOA, Greater West Palm Beach, pages 511–512
Markham Park, Greater Fort Lauderdale, pages 523–524
River Ranch RV Resort, Orlando Area, pages 332–333
River Valley RV Resort, Orlando Area, pages 337–338
Suwannee River KOA, Tallahassee Area, page 99
Suwannee Valley Campground, Tallahassee Area, page 103

Top 10 Island Retreats

Anclote Key State Preserve Boat-In Sites, St. Petersburg Area, pages 371–372
Boca Chita Key Boat-In Sites, Greater Miami, page 590
Canaveral National Seashore, Space Coast, pages 347–348
Cayo Costa State Park Boat-In Sites, Fort Myers/Naples Area, pages 484–485
Dry Tortugas National Park, Florida Keys, pages 608–610
Fort De Soto Park Campground, St. Petersburg Area, pages 380–381
Hontoon Island State Park, Daytona Beach Area, pages 227–228
Little Talbot Island State Park, Jacksonville Area, pages 150–151
Long Point Park, Space Coast, pages 362–363
Peanut Island, Greater West Palm Beach, pages 509–510

Top 10 Campgrounds with Natural Springs

Gemini Springs, Daytona Beach Area, pages 230–231
Ginnie Springs Resort, Gainesville Area, pages 132–133
Ichetucknee Springs Campground, Gainesville Area, pages 131–132
Kelly Park (Rock Springs), Orlando Area, pages 282–283
Manatee Springs State Park, Gainesville Area, pages 139–140
Otter Springs, Gainesville Area, page 140
Rainbow Springs State Park, Ocala Area, pages 203–304
Salt Springs Recreation Area, Ocala Area, pages 207–208
Vortex Spring RV Park, Panama City Area, pages 64–65
Wekiwa Springs State Park, Orlando Area, pages 284–285

Top 10 Luxurious Campgrounds

Roughing it? Not here. These parks can't be called campgrounds, really. They're more like resort hotels.

Bluewater Key RV Park, Florida Keys, pages 605–606
Clerbrook Resort, Orlando Area, page 290
Deer Creek RV Golf Resort, Orlando Area, pages 306–307
Disney's Fort Wilderness Campground, Orlando Area, pages 299–300
Grand Lake RV & Golf Resort, Ocala Area, page 193
The Great Outdoors Resort, Space Coast, page 352
River Ranch RV Resort, Orlando Area, pages 332–333
Seasons in the Sun Motorcoach Resort, Space Coast, page 350
Silver Lakes RV Resort and Golf Club, Fort Myers/Naples Area, pages 501–502
Topsail Hill State Preserve, Pensacola Area, page 60

Top 10 Bicycling Areas

Everglades National Park, The Everglades, pages 534–572
The Tallahassee and Gainesville areas, pages 87–125, 129–144
Most Florida state parks, see individual listings
National and state forests, see individual listings
O'Leno State Park, Gainesville Area, page 133
Paynes Prairie Preserve State Park, Gainesville Area, page 136
Pine Log State Forest, Panama City Area, pages 71–72
River water management district lands, see individual listings
The White Springs/Suwannee River area, Tallahassee Area, pages 101–104
Withlacoochee State Forest, Orlando Area, pages 242–251

New Campgrounds Added to This Book (since 2001), by Area

Daytona

Harris Village and RV Park, page 224

International RV Park and Campground, page 225

Tiger Bay State Forest, page 224

Florida Keys

Blue Fin-Rock Harbor, pages 597–598

El Mar RV Resort, pages 607–608

Fort Myers/Naples

Caloosahatchee Regional Park, pages 481–482

Citrus Park, page 495

Gulf Waters RV Resort, page 489

RiverBend Motorcoach Resort, page 482

Gainesville

Big Oaks River Resort and Campground, page 143

B's Marina and Campground, pages 143–144

Ranch Motel and Campground, pages 136–137

Lake Okeechobee

Big Lake Lodge and RV Park, pages 440–441

Camp Florida Resort, page 431

The Marina RV Resort, page 447

Primrose RV Park, pages 444–445

Robin's Nest RV Resort, page 448

Windsor Manor RV Park, page 441–442

Miami

The Boardwalk, page 588

Ocala

Emeralda Marsh Conservation Area, pages 205–206

Ocklawaha Prairie Restoration Area, page 206

Rock Crusher Canyon RV and Music Park, page 202

Silver River State Park, pages 197–198

St. Johns River Campground, pages 214–215

Sunnyhill Restoration Area, page 205

Wildwoods Campground, page 216

Orlando

Adams Marina and RV Park, page 270

Andy's Travel Trailer Park, pages 267–268

Camp Mack's River Resort, page 330

Clarcona Horseman's Park, page 295

Cypress Gardens Campground, page 324

Encore SuperPark—Orlando, page 300

Lake Glenada RV Park, page 344

Lake Mills Park, page 298

Lake Pierce Eco Resort, page 321

Lakemont Ridge Home and RV Park, pages 327–328

Lakeside Stables, pages 341–342

Mullet Lake Park, page 297

Reflections on Silver Lake, page 339

Settler's Rest RV Park, page 265

Sun Resorts, page 294

Sunburst RV Park—Port Richey, pages 258–259

Panama

Emerald Coast RV Beach Resort, pages 75–76

Long Leaf RV Park, page 63

Panama City Beach RV Resort, pages 77–78

Raccoon River Campground, page 76

Pensacola

Bayview RV Campground, page 57

Cedar Lakes RV Park & Campground, page 47

Destin RV Beach Resort, page 59

Eagle's Landing RV Park, page 46

Mystic Springs, pages 41–42

Mystic Springs Airstream Park, page 41

Pensacola/Perdido Bay KOA, page 51

Space Coast

F. Burton Smith Regional Park, page 355

Seasons in the Sun Motorcoach Resort,
page 350
Willow Lakes RV and Golf Resort,
pages 349–350

St. Augustine

Acosta Creek Harbor, page 181
Black Creek Ravines Conservation Area,
page 161
Caravelle Ranch Wildlife Management Area,
page 182
Graham Swamp Conservation Area,
page 178
Half Shell Resort, pages 182–183
Harley Paiute's Campground & Marina,
pages 185–186
Jennings State Forest, page 162
Port Cove RV Park & Marina, pages 186–187

St. Petersburg

Palm Harbor Resort, page 372

Tallahassee

Bear Creek Tract, pages 91–92
Fort Braden Tract, page 92
Suwannee River Hideaway Campground,
page 123

Tampa

Alafia River State Park, pages 391–392

Treasure Coast

Fort Drum Marsh Conservation Area,
page 464
Outdoor Resorts at St. Lucie West,
pages 466–467
South Fork St. Lucie River Management
Area, pages 468–469
West Jupiter Wetlands Management Area,
page 473

West Palm Beach

Peanut Island, pages 509–510

Top 20 Most Unusual Campgrounds

Buttgenbach Mine Campground/Croom Motorcycle Area, Orlando Area, pages 249–250, is nirvana for motorcyclists, dirt bikers, and all-terrain cyclists.

Campgrounds with intermediate and advanced mountain biking areas include Alafia River State Park, Greater Tampa, pages 391–392; Markham Park, Greater Fort Lauderdale, pages 523–524; and Quiet Waters Park, Greater Fort Lauderdale, page 517.

Falling Waters State Park, Panama City Area, page 67, has Florida's only waterfall.

Florida Caverns State Park, Panama City Area, pages 68–69, has beautiful caves.

Kissimmee Billie Swamp Safari, Lake Okeechobee, pages 456–457, offers a taste of how the Seminole Indians once lived. Sleep in a chickee hut. Or take a swamp buggy ride into the wilderness, and you may see American bison, panthers, and antelopes.

Lion Country Safari KOA, Greater West Palm Beach, pages 511–512, is part of a wildlife park where lions roam free in the nation's first cageless zoo.

Manatee Hammock, Space Coast, pages 352–353, is one the closest campgrounds from which to watch space launches at Kennedy Space Center; several others also make that claim in the Space Coast chapter. The truth is you can see space launches take flight from campgrounds as far away as Kissimmee. It just depends on how good a view you want to get.

Mike Roess Gold Head Branch State Park, St. Augustine Area, pages 162–163, has a mini-canyon.

Miller's Marine Campground, Tallahassee Area, page 125, rents houseboats from which you can go upstream from the Gulf of Mexico on the Suwannee River.

O'Leno State Park, Gainesville Area, page 133, has a river that goes underground and reappears three miles later.

Pioneer Park of Hardee County, Lake Okeechobee, page 427, has a small wildlife refuge including bears and a cougar.

Quiet Waters Park, Greater Fort Lauderdale, page 517, has a "rent a camp" package that includes permanent tents mounted on wooden platforms, plus boatless water-skiing (skiers are pulled by cable across a lake).

Rock Crusher Canyon RV and Music Park, Ocala Area, page 202, has a big-time concert venue. Top-name artists like Willie Nelson and others perform here in an amphitheater.

Seven nudist campgrounds will give you the chance to get an all-over suntan: Hidden River Resort, Jacksonville Area, page 157; Lake Como Club, Orlando Area, page 264; Riviera Naturist Resort, Pensacola Area, page 48; Seminole Health Club, Greater Fort Lauderdale, page 524; Sunnier Palms Nudist Campground, Treasure Coast, page 466; Sunny Sands Nudist Resort, Daytona Beach Area, page 221; and Sunsport Gardens, Greater West Palm Beach, page 511.

Skydive City, Orlando Area, page 264, has a campground where you must be prepared to parachute.

Suwannee Valley Campground, Tallahassee Area, page 103, has a dog activity area.

Torreya State Park, Tallahassee Area, pages 87–88, has mountains. Well, OK, steep hills.

Tresca Memorial Park/Advent Christian Village, Gainesville Area, page 129, and **Orange Blossom Fellowship Community,** Orlando Area, pages 338–339, are oriented to Bible study and a Christian lifestyle.

Wallaby Ranch Flight Park, Orlando Area, page 305, is for hang gliders.

Wishful Thinkin' Farms, Sarasota/Bradenton Area, pages 403–404, is roughing it at a real working horse ranch.

Best Campgrounds (Rated 10), by Area

Daytona
Gemini Springs, pages 230–231
Hontoon Island State Park, pages 227–228

Everglades
Picnic Key Boat/Canoe Sites, page 538
Tiger Key Boat/Canoe Sites, page 537

Florida Keys
Bahia Honda State Park, page 603
Bluewater Key RV Park, pages 605–606
Dry Tortugas National Park, pages 608–610
John Pennekamp Coral Reef State Park, pages 595–596
Long Key State Park, pages 599–600

Fort Lauderdale
Markham Park, pages 523–524

Fort Myers/Naples
Cayo Costa State Park Boat-In Sites, pages 484–485
Koreshan State Historic Site, page 493
Silver Lakes RV Resort and Golf Club, pages 501–502

Gainesville
Manatee Springs State Park, pages 139–140
O'Leno State Park, page 133
Paynes Prairie Preserve State Park, page 136

Jacksonville
Fort Clinch State Park, pages 148–149
Little Talbot Island State Park, pages 150–151

Lake Okeechobee
Fisheating Creek Campground, page 429

Miami
Boca Chita Key Boat-In Sites, page 590

Ocala
Encore RV Park—Ocala, page 194
Encore SuperPark—Crystal River, pages 199–200
Rock Crusher Canyon RV and Music Park, page 202
Silver River State Park, pages 197–198

Camping Tips

Ten Things You Should Know About Camping in Florida

Here are some things we've learned in the course of researching this book and during our many years of camping in Florida:

1. When to Come

You can camp in Florida at any time—the weather's fine! On the other hand, it depends on who you are and what kind of experience you're looking for.

When are parks least crowded? For the purposes of most out-of-state visitors, Florida has two seasons. North Florida, particularly along the Gulf Coast in the Panhandle, sees its "high" season in the summer months when school is out. South and Central Florida campgrounds are busiest in the winter months, mainly mid-December through April.

Most campgrounds are open 12 months of the year. However, some that are oriented to snow-bird visitors, usually retirees, do close down in the long Florida hot summer, generally May through October. Even if they don't close, that would be the "slow" season for this type of park.

2. Reservations

Most private campgrounds recommend that you make reservations, as we've noted in the listings. Often, they require a nonrefundable deposit ranging from $25 to $100 or more, depending on the length of your stay.

Overnighters, beware: We advise that you don't make reservations for an overnight stop unless you are absolutely certain you wish to stay in a particular place. If you're just traveling through, many private campgrounds will squeeze you in overnight even without a reservation. Just call ahead and tell them how big your rig is.

Using this method, you may not get the choicest spot, it's true. One private campground near Sarasota put us in a utility right-of-way under the telephone and electric poles. Our view was of the back of some mobile homes, the perimeter fence, and the trash receptacle. But hey, we were there for only one night and just passing through on the way to someplace nicer.

For state parks, definitely make a reservation. Reservations are now handled by ReserveAmerica; call 800/326-3521. Previously, in most parks, only half the sites were available by reservation, and the rest were first-come, first-served. The old policy added to a lot of heartache and a kind of gambling mentality if you were planning a trip on a weekend when all the sites that could be reserved we full. For state parks, using the reservation system is almost mandatory now if you're sure you're going to be arriving at a particular park that night. In a pinch, call the park directly.

But making reservations at private campgrounds can have its pitfalls. Consider this tale: On a scorching-hot summer weekend a few years ago, we made reservations at a private campground in the Florida Keys. We drove south, chose a site as instructed by the office, unhitched the trailer, and plugged in the electric cord. Then we switched on the air-conditioning. Nothing. We jiggled the circuit breaker. Nope. We took the air conditioner apart trying to find a short circuit. Nada. Now the sweat was rolling down hot little faces. It was 90 degrees in the shade, and there really was no shade to speak of. After an hour of trying, it was clear there was to be no air-conditioning—and that we were not going to stay. We departed, but our $25 deposit was lost.

Snowbirds

You're the exception to the rule on reservations. If you've come to Florida to stay for the winter or for several weeks, make a reservation early. Parks fill up fast during their big season. Many visitors return to the same park year after year, and this is the best way to guarantee you'll get the site you want.

If it's your first time in the area, you might scout for a park where you'd like to stay next winter. Try a few days at several places to get a feel for the crowd, the activities, and things to do in the area. Then make your reservation for the following year. Many parks accept reservations as early as the preceding spring, so you'll have to act quickly.

State Parks

Most of the best campgrounds in Florida are in state parks, where demand is high on weekends and holidays. We advise you to make reservations, especially at the more popular places.

Under the new system, state parks now accept reservations 11 months in advance of stay. (It used to be just 60 days in advance, which meant marking your calendar exactly 60 days before your planned visit, then calling first thing in the morning to reserve a spot.) Again, call ReserveAmerica at 800/326-3521. This company has a contract with the state park service to book your spot, at least as of 2003.

3. Tents

Based on our research, roughly one-half of the campgrounds in Florida prohibit tent campers. It seems unfair at first glance, but it's just basic free-market economics. Consider that the bread and butter of most private parks is the retired, long-staying RVer who has invested thousands of dollars in a rig and wants to mix with like-minded folks. Other parks set aside a separate tenting area, which may make you feel like a second-class citizen. An optimist would tell you to consider yourself lucky. You won't be bothered by the hum of loud air conditioners, generators, or TV sets from the RV section.

An alternative for the tenting crowd is to look beyond the private campgrounds. This book lists plenty of out-of-the-way backcountry wonders where you'll feel well removed from the settled world that greets most RV campers. Florida's award-winning state parks all accept tents, as do many county parks.

You can also try the water management districts and wildlife management areas for the quiet, secluded tent camping of your dreams. One native Floridian we know treasures his winter trips

---

Wilderness Etiquette

"Enjoy America's country and leave no trace." That's the motto of the Leave No Trace program, and we strongly support it. Promoting responsible outdoor recreation through education, research, and partnerships is its mission. Look for the **Keep It Wild Tips,** developed from the policies of Leave No Trace, sprinkled throughout this book. For a free pocket-sized, weatherproof card printed with these policies, as well as information that details how to minimize human impact on wild areas, contact Leave No Trace at P.O. Box 997, Boulder, CO 80306, 303/442-8222 or 800/332-4100, website: www.lnt.org.

to the Three Lakes Wildlife Management Area in Central Florida. When we checked it out on a casual visit, we were astounded to see three wild turkeys scampering out of an oak hammock to take cover in tall blond grasses and a bobcat dashing into saw palmetto thickets. Understandably, many people consider tent camping the only way to go.

We're particularly fond of state parks, which seek to maintain a setting as it looked when the first Europeans arrived in Florida the century after Columbus. But if you really want to get away from city lights, check out the little-known state forests and water management districts, as well as the primitive areas offered by the national parks and national forests. Some county parks are real gems, too.

Rugged types who don't mind giving up niceties such as electricity and running water also can consider the hunter domains overseen by the Florida Fish and Wildlife Conservation Commission. Even if you're not a hunter, you're likely to see wild animals in these public areas. In most cases, we've noted the times of the hunting season, which are generally in the late fall through early winter at short intervals. Keep in mind that the starting and ending dates vary from year to year. Check with the Florida Fish and Wildlife Conservation Commission at 850/488-4676 or www.floridaconservation.org to make sure that your trip does not overlap with hunting periods.

4. RV Restrictions

If you think the only rule limiting RVs is the length of your rig and the size of the available site, then think again. A few Florida RV parks don't allow pop-top campers, truck campers, vans, converted school buses, or RVs more than 20 years old. Some now restrict visitors to class A motor homes, or recreational vehicles more than 36 feet long.

5. Pets

Many Florida state parks now allow pets in their campgrounds. You must have proof of the pet's rabies vaccination and carry it with you. A $2 charge per pet applies. In addition, pets must be kept on a leash at all times and must be well behaved.

A few state parks, particularly those near beaches, may allow your pet in the campground but not on the beach.

Pets are allowed in most private parks, national forests, many county-run campgrounds, Florida Fish and Wildlife Conservation Commission campsites, many water management district sites, and U.S. Army Corps of Engineers sites.

In a few fish camps and remote areas, dogs don't need to be leashed, but leashes are the rule just about everywhere else.

Some places charge an extra fee of $2 or so per day per pet. Many RV parks restrict the size and weight of the pets they will allow (under 20 pounds, for example). Others prohibit specific breeds, such as pit bulls, rottweilers, or German shepherds. One campground in the Panhandle told us pets are allowed, except for potbellied pigs. We guess you'll have to leave your potbellied pigs in the kennel at home.

Most parks have other requirements, such as walking your dog in a special area. It's fair to say that nearly all require you to clean up after your dog. They may even put all the pet owners in a special section. Of course, do not leave your pet unattended or tie him or her up to your RV while you hit the golf course or run down to the grocery store.

Which leads us to another point: Never leave your pet locked in your car. Even with the windows cracked, the temperature inside a car can quickly reach fatal levels in hot Florida.

Keep It Wild Tip: Plan Ahead and Prepare

• Find out about any regulations or environmental issues concerning the area you plan to visit ahead of time.
• Obtain necessary permits.
• Pack food in reusable containers to reduce waste.
• Avoid heavy-use areas, which puts strain on the land and its resources.

6. Children

At many private RV parks, children are not welcome. Our listings note when this is the case.

Some parks are willing to bend the rules if you look like a reasonable person and promise not to let your kids go unsupervised in the common areas, such as the swimming pool or restrooms. Others, even those that are strictly targeted to retirees, allow grandchildren to visit for, say, two weeks during the course of a year.

Then there are those parks that say they allow children but give you the third degree: "How big are the kids?" Some places frown on babies or small children, perhaps because they cry at night. Others are OK with little ones but dislike teenagers. Said one campground manager in Panama City: "Kids are OK, as long as they're not Spring Breakers."

Sometimes, it's clear that the rules are intended to keep out the working poor. There's a touch of elitism in a regulation that allows retirees to stay as long as they can pay, but wants no school-age children on the grounds for more than two weeks.

But like irresponsible pet owners who have made it difficult for everyone else, some lax parents have made it tough for other families. We were shocked when one campground owner near North Port cautioned us, "We allow kids, as long as you don't go off and leave them here alone for days." Huh? We certainly don't suggest such negligence unless you want the child and welfare investigators asking questions.

7. Age Restrictions

You've reached voting age, so you're an adult, right? Not necessarily. You may not be old enough. Not only do some campgrounds ban children, but there may be other complicated rules as well. Some require at least one camper to be over the age of 55; others say all visitors must be over 65. Yes, in Florida, a trailer park is not always a trailer park; it's a "retirement community" or an "adult resort." As many Baby Boomers are passing the age of 50, one wonders the fate of these rules. We note now as we go into the third edition, that some parks have dropped the adults-only age to 35-plus. Hey, some social demographer could write a paper on that one.

8. Rates

Let's start with the free places and work upward. Florida Fish and Wildlife Conservation Commission sites, spots along the Florida National Scenic Trail, and water management district sites do not charge campers, or exact fees as small as $5 per carload. Also, primitive camping within national forests is free. Check the listings for details.

The least-expensive parks are national and state forests, state parks, and county parks. State parks charge $2 extra for electricity and add a surcharge for beachfront campsites.

Most private RV parks charge competitive rates, usually around $25 to $30 per night for two people. At deluxe resorts, charges can go as high as $70. In most places, cable TV service and sewer hookups are included in the base rate. (Since the second edition of the book, many rates are up 10 to 15 percent.)

Then there are add-ons. Private parks usually charge a fee for each additional person, normally $1 to $3 each. Sometimes, discounts are given for children under 12. Extra people can cost as much as $8 to $15 in a handful of places.

Also, some private operators charge extra for use of air-conditioning, electric heaters, and washers or dryers (usually $2 daily). A few parks ask for $2 extra for cable TV.

More desirable sites (closest to the beach, for example) go for a higher rate. And rates "in season" will be higher than those in slow times of the year. Finally, some campgrounds charge even more when there's a special festival or other crowd-drawing attraction, such as Biketoberfest in Daytona Beach.

On the other hand, national parks, county parks, and others offer discounted rates to folks over 65 or the disabled. You'll be required to provide proof of age or disability. (Under federal policy, disability is proven by showing proof of medically determined permanent disability, or eligibility for receiving benefits under federal law.)

Snowbirds who store their RVs on site after the season ends can save money. After the sixth month, they do not pay the local tourist tax, which varies by location, but can be as high as 11 percent. In addition, most parks charge only nominal fees for storing a rig during the summer.

Just as an FYI: If you don't mind traffic noise, you can also camp for free in some Wal-Mart parking lots and those of a restaurant chain called Cracker Barrel. You'll need to ask the manager for permission to stay overnight. Some Moose lodges also allow RVs to hook up in their parking areas. Campground owners, naturally, don't like this trend, considering it competition. For our part, Florida offers too many pretty places for us to consider staying in a parking lot.

9. Using the Facilities

If you're not in a self-contained RV, you're going to have to face the communal restrooms and showers. Many parks brag that their facilities are sparkling clean. That may be, but we've found plenty that gave us pause. The drains don't drain, the hot water runs out, or you're forced to listen helplessly to endless palaver from your neighbors. Bring soap, shampoo, toothbrush and toothpaste, and other niceties in a separate bag; sometimes, a flashlight is needed for the walk. Don't forget a towel and a change of clothes. Most campgrounds perform a daily cleaning routine about 11 A.M., and that's it for the day. If you must take a shower at night, you'll likely find you have to wait your turn, and by then, things aren't so sparkling, or the water is tepid. Mornings are quieter, and you're more likely to have hot water. Get up early.

10. The Florida Effect

Things change here. From the time Henry Flagler's railroad came marching down the east coast, change has been a constant in Florida. Hurricanes and wildfires roar through, eradicating buildings, washing out streets, and even eliminating big sections of forest.

Mobile home parks on the city/suburb edge get supplanted by subdivisions, sometimes in a matter of weeks. One example is the All-Star Resort in Perdido Key, near Pensacola. Just two years after it opened with brand-new, sparkling facilities, winning our highest ranking of 10, it was torn down, reportedly for a condominium. Well, it was right on the beach—the most valuable property there can be in Florida. All this, and much more, can affect whether the information in this book is up-to-date. Although we've made every effort to be sure the data are current and accurate, give us some wriggle room to account for the "Florida Effect."

Change can be a good thing—the state of Florida runs a remarkable, proactive land acquisition program to preserve natural areas, and thousands and thousands of acres are added each year. Public access points and available facilities are subject to change, and new areas may be open after we go to press. If you have a specific need or concern, it's a good idea to call the responsible agency ahead of time. We've also listed websites for the larger state land resource management areas (see the Resource Guide). Browse their websites often to see if new lands are open for hiking, camping, boating, or other activities. Often, you can download maps or recreation guides from these websites as information is updated through the coming months.

Climate and Weather Protection

Camping in Florida rewards you with many surprises: Sunsets over the Gulf of Mexico, watching the golden orb drop into the horizon with a refreshing iced tea in your hand and a gentle sea breeze rustling your hair. Snorkeling in the Florida Keys just 20 steps from your beachfront tent. A herd of deer snooping around your campsite in the woods. Hiking in a shady pine forest, canoeing down the Peace River, casting a line into the surf, going to sleep on an island so secluded that you can only get there by boat. Mountain biking on lonely forest roads where you suddenly come across an abandoned homestead from the 1920s.

It can also be a shock—with sudden downpours that Floridians call "palmetto pounders"; gale-force winds that rock your trailer and blow down your tent; mosquitoes, gnats, no-see-ums, spiders, and roaches; or broiling-hot days with sticky humid nights.

Cold

When most folks think of Florida, they think warm weather and sunny skies. (We'll get to that soon.) The truth is that Florida's climate is amazingly diverse—and subject to dramatic change. Even people who've lived in Florida a long time sometimes overlook this fact.

One spring break several years ago, we set out from Miami on a weeklong camping trip. In Miami, the temperature was near the 80s during the day and in the mid-70s at night, and we thought we'd packed all the personal gear we could possibly need—shorts, T-shirts, swimsuits, and sunglasses. By the time we reached Lake City in northern Florida at the end of that first day, skies had turned cloudy and then stormy, as the leading edge of a cold front dipped south.

Florida's Average Daily Maximum Temperatures

	Jan.	March	May	July	Sept.	Nov.
Daytona Beach	68	75	84	90	87	76
Miami	75	79	85	89	88	80
Orlando	71	78	88	92	90	78
Pensacola	60	69	83	90	86	70
Tampa	70	77	87	90	89	78

Source: National Weather Service

Dinnertime in the campground was uncomfortable. Temperatures had dropped into the 60s and the wind had picked up.

It sounds ridiculous to think about wind-chill factors when there's no snow on the ground, but we had no long pants and no long-sleeved shirts, and we were cold! That Arctic front never traveled south of Orlando, but tell that to our shivering kids as we bundled them up into the car and headed for the nearest Kmart to buy blue jeans and sweatshirts.

Yes, Florida is hot in the summertime. But from October through May, the weather can vary significantly, depending on your location. North Florida—from the Panhandle east to Jacksonville—even has changing seasons. (See the temperature chart, earlier in this chapter.)

By the standards of most people who live outside of Florida, though, winters are mild, offset by an occasional cold front that may bring freezing or near-freezing weather. And those fronts last for just a couple of days. Many visitors don't seem to mind them, and they don't let the weather interrupt their outdoors pursuits. We've seen Canadians and Europeans accustomed to colder climes basking on the beach in 50-degree weather—giving truth to the old saying that you can tell who the tourists are because they have tans in the winter.

Even without a weather report, you can often tell what's going to happen. A cold front usually sweeps south in a broad band. As the cold collides with the warm air, cloudy skies and swift winds are formed, sometimes accompanied by rain. As the front continues south, the skies often clear. You'll see crisp, sunny days and clear, starlit skies at night. Keep an ear on the radio weather reports throughout the year.

On any outing in the winter, bring at least a long-sleeved shirt and a pair of long pants. A heavy jacket or windbreaker is also a good idea, even if you just leave it in the car. On one trip, when the mercury dipped into the 20s at night in O'Leno State Park near High Springs, we appreciated having saved our down jackets from long-ago mountaineering days out West.

Watch the weather reports and read the weather maps before you leave. If a cold front is a possibility, bring enough warm clothing to last for a couple of days. And don't forget to pack

---

The Dangers of Dehydration

Dehydration doesn't just mean that your body is in need of water. It also means that you're in danger of a rising body temperature, nausea, and, in hot weather, suffering from heat-related illness. The solution? Replace your body fluids by drinking lots of water—8 to 10 cups per day—and up to one gallon if the weather is warm or if you're really active.

If you're feeling thirsty, you are mildly dehydrated. But if you're experiencing headaches and dry mouth—and your urine output is under two cups over 24 hours—chances are your case is serious. Replace electrolytes (salt, potassium, and bicarbonate) by drinking fruit juice or an energy drink such as Gatorade. If these drinks or purified water are not available, then drink whatever liquid is at hand. That's right, even if the water may be contaminated; avoiding or treating serious cases of dehydration is worth the risk.

Although physicians once recommended that hikers take salt pills, they now believe that regular diets, including dehydrated foods that campers often consume, provide enough salts without supplements.

for everyone in your party, particularly children. When they get cold and miserable, it's hard for anyone to have a good time.

Heat

Yes, it's hot here. But as you can see from the temperature chart, it's often cooler in the hottest summer months than in many places, say, in the landlocked Midwest. Ocean breezes and frequent rains oblige us with extra relief, and you can always jump into the nearest pool or river to cool off. If you're really desperate to get out of the heat, you can stop at a movie theater or a mall.

Still, it's nice to have air-conditioning during summer, both in your car and in your RV. Tenters can buy an inexpensive box fan to stir the air on hot, still nights. (We've actually seen a couple of tent campers with window air conditioners; they set them up on concrete blocks and poked the business end through an opening!) Backpackers, of course, have to make do.

Which brings us to a discussion on the dangers of heat. You need to be concerned about three things (listed here in order of seriousness): heat cramps, heat exhaustion, and heatstroke. The key to preventing all three is to drink plenty of liquids. Limit exercise in the hottest part of the day. Wear a hat. Look for shade. (After you've been in Florida awhile, you'll just instinctively cross the street to walk on the shady side.) Wear lightweight, light-colored clothing that reflects sunlight. Avoid getting sunburned, which makes you feel hotter and impedes the body's thermostat.

Heat cramps, usually painful spasms in the leg or abdominal muscles, are the first symptom that you're not handling your environment properly. It means that you're lacking salt, probably caused by losing more water (through sweat) than you're gaining. Stop exercising, get out of the sun, and drink salted water (one teaspoon of salt to a quart of water). Do NOT drink caffeine or alcohol because they make symptoms worse and are dehydrating. Massage the cramps gently.

Heat exhaustion comes on when your personal cooling system starts to shut down, usually after prolonged activity in hot, humid weather. Skin may become cold, pale, and clammy. You may become weak and may even vomit. Your body temperature will be normal or slightly lower. At these signs, lie down in the shade. Remove any restrictive clothing and raise your legs above your head to encourage blood flow. Drink salted water.

Heatstroke, also called sunstroke, is really dangerous. Usually, the skin is hot and dry. You will not sweat, and your internal body temperature may be 106 degrees or higher. Dizziness, vomiting, diarrhea, and confusion are also symptoms. If any of these symptoms occur, call 911 or go to a hospital without delay. If you are in the backcountry (or on the way to the hospital), remove your clothing. Lower your body temperature with cool water or sponges, fans, or air conditioners. Do NOT consume any liquids.

> **Each year, about 175 people in the United States die from heat-related causes. Men are more susceptible than women; children, the elderly, and people who are sick or overweight also are frequent victims. Know your limits, and don't overdo it.**

Rain

Be prepared for drenching downpours. Rain gear is essential year-round. Summer (May through October) is the rainy season, but thunderstorms and heavy rain are possible at all times of the year. Can you imagine 18 inches of rain in 24 hours in the middle of October? How about March? We've seen it happen.

Florida rains are rarely the gentle drizzling kind that last all day. They burst upon you with an intensity that may surprise people who have no experience with the subtropics. Fortunately, the skies often clear within a couple of hours, but by then several inches of rain may have drenched you to the skin. Driving is dangerous in these conditions, and flash flooding may occur.

Make sure everyone in your party brings a poncho, available at discount stores for less than $5. Or bring a nylon jacket purchased at a discount store, or even something as elaborate as Gore-Tex rain pants and jackets from an outdoors shop. The pricier (but hotter) rain pants are worth considering. We find lightweight, fast-drying nylon expedition pants helpful. One of us wore expedition pants while chest-deep in the Everglades and found that they dried quickly after climbing back into the canoe. Inexpensive shorts are practical in most cases. For other helpful gear, see the Backcountry Camping section in this chapter.

Besides personal rain gear, your camping equipment should be up to snuff for storms. Not all tents are created equal. If the rain fly on your model isn't big enough to keep water off the walls, then consider buying a large waterproof tarp to use as a second, backup rain fly. To keep dew, dampness, or rain out, it also helps to lay a ground tarp, which could be something as simple as a poncho or a shower curtain, under the tent.

Examine the seams of your tent for potential leaky points. Find any? Use a seam sealant such as McNett Outdoor's Seam Grip, Kenyon's Seam Sealer, or Seam Lock—all are polyurethane glues that plug tiny seam holes. Keep a patch kit in your tent sack. Both items are available at camp stores.

You don't have to be confined to a tent or RV during a storm. In a summer rain, sitting inside is extremely warm, and the humidity makes it feel even warmer. Even worse is having to retreat to your car when it's pouring outside.

Here's something that works in all but the most blustery weather: a plastic tarp rigged with lines and poles. Put it over the picnic table, and you can still sit outside, cook dinner, read a book, or play board games. We've used poles fashioned from metal electrical conduit; they can be screwed together for height and break down into portable sizes for traveling. At the end of each pole is a cork from a wine bottle with a nail embedded in it; the nails slip into the holes on the edges of the tarp. Ropes staked to the ground in a triangular pattern keep the poles standing. (Never tie anything to trees, however, because you may damage them.)

Sun

Many private campgrounds in Florida don't have tree canopies; or you may be assigned to a site as leafless as the desert. After you've spent all day swimming or hiking in the hot sun, you'll crave a chance to get into the shade. Fortunately, you can bring your own.

A sunroom or screen tent comes in handy to keep the broiling sun at bay. These 8-by-10-foot rooms go up just like a tent; some are big enough to slip over the campground picnic table. They cost about $200 at sporting goods or RV supply stores. The kind with screens around them also keep out bugs.

You don't need to spend that much money, though. Our homemade tarp tent (see previous Rain section), which cost about $30, worked fine everywhere but along the shore when the winds were stronger than 25 knots. Our biggest problem was during one windy trip at Long Key State Park in the Florida Keys: The sand wouldn't hold traditional tent stakes, but we resolved this by buying "sand hogs," heavy metal anchors that look like corkscrews topped with a triangular piece of flat iron.

Too much sunshine is a real health concern in Florida. Studies say that native Floridians with fair complexions and light-colored eyes run an extremely high risk of getting skin cancer. But no matter where you were born or what you look like, sunscreens are a must to prevent sunburn, which can cause problems later in life. In addition to skin cancer, excess exposure to sun can lead to cataracts, premature aging, and even damage to your immune system. Be especially careful with children, who will resist secondary applications of sunscreen after the first dip in the water. Plus, they often lose (or won't wear) hats.

You can buy sunscreens almost everywhere in Florida, from grocery stores to gas stations. Purchase the highest-rated sunscreen you can find; an SPF of 15 is considered the minimum recommended protection. On a prolonged outdoors trip, SPF 15 is not adequate for kids unless you want to be reapply it every hour or two.

Unfortunately, not even sunscreens may be enough to prevent melanoma, the most malignant and deadly form of skin cancer. Many dermatologists today recommend use of sunscreens in combination with two other caveats: Limit sun exposure, particularly between 11 A.M. and 1 P.M., and wear protective clothing, such as hats, long sleeves, and long pants.

Even on rare days when skies are overcast, you can still get a harmful sunburn. Ultraviolet rays are particularly dangerous when you're in a boat or at the beach; they reflect off the water or the sand, doubling their effects.

Most people are uncomfortable without sunglasses. If you forgot to bring a pair, cheap sunglasses ($5 to $10) are readily available in convenience stores, gas stations, and drugstores. But be forewarned: Unless the glasses promise 100 percent UV protection, they could do more harm than good, in some cases doubling the amount of UVA rays your eyes would experience without sunglasses. You can spring for a better pair from sunglass kiosks in shopping malls. Don't forget to get a pair for the kids, and be prepared to replace them often.

You'll also want to invest in several tubes of lip protection balm. Some brands have sunscreens in their formulas. Soothe painful, sun-scorched lips with Bag Balm or Vaseline. (We have seen Bag Balm literally cure horrible swollen lip damage within hours.)

For backpackers, it's best to limit hikes to mornings or late afternoons, which is when you'll be most likely to see more wildlife anyway. Bring plenty of water; consider one gallon per person per day, if practical.

Boaters, canoeists, and kayakers should wear wide-brimmed hats, available at Army-Navy surplus stores or outdoors shops. Backpackers might make do with baseball caps, but remember to use sunblock, particularly on your ears and neck. Bicyclists have the problem that they must wear helmets, but helmets don't provide sufficient sun protection. Slather on that sunscreen repeatedly, especially on the neck under the chin and areas you don't normally think will get burned. Look for a sunscreen that resists sweat, or you end up with the double whammy of irritated eyes from the sweat plus the sunscreen. Use a bandanna or sweatband under your bike helmet for a little control.

Hypothermia

Being exposed to wet, cold weather for an extended period can be fatal—even at 50 degrees. In fact, cases of hypothermia are a lot more common than you would expect in the Sunshine State. In part, that's because Florida's sunny reputation makes some campers blasé. A few years ago, rugged Army Rangers training in the Panhandle were severely stricken; some even died. They spent 10 wet hours in air that did not dip below 50 degrees.

So the first line of defense against hypothermia is the expectation that it could happen. Remember that being cold and wet at the same time can be deadly. Keep your clothes dry at all costs, and stay out of the wind. In short, remain warm and dry.

If you start to shiver, you could be on the way to hypothermia. Never ignore shivering. Get warm and dry however you can. Make a fire. Go into a building, if one is available. Get out of the wind and into dry clothes.

The second wave of symptoms may include uncontrollable shivering, slow or slurred speech, incoherence, uncoordinated movements, stumbling, exhaustion, and drowsiness.

If a person has entered this second stage of hypothermia, some exercise will help by burning calories and raising the internal body temperature. But remember, as those calories are burned, they must be replaced. A good choice is warm soup (not hot because blazing temperatures can shock a cold body and cause a heart attack). Another good choice is snacks with quick energy release such as candy or an energy bar.

Do not let anyone with such symptoms go to sleep! Get the person out of the wind and rain, take off all wet clothes (no need to be shy when you may be dying), and put on dry clothes. Administer warm drinks. Dry clothes and a warm sleeping bag are best until the victim recovers.

If the sufferer is only semiconscious, leave his or her clothes stripped off and get him or her into a sleeping bag with another naked person. The best treatment then is skin-to-skin contact. In no case should the victim be left in wet clothing because it tends to wick heat away from the body.

For more information on what to wear, see the clothing information in the Backcountry Camping section in this chapter.

Lightning and Severe Weather

Florida is home to some of the most extreme thunderstorms in the country, so you'll want to keep a close eye on the weather.

We have found it worthwhile to fork over a few bucks for a special NOAA Weather Radio. (NOAA is the National Oceanic and Atmospheric Administration, which runs the National Weather Service.) For as little as about $40, you get access to continuous-loop weather reports that are updated throughout the day. Weather on demand, in other words.

The radios are permanently tuned to the free NOAA service, and the only investment is the initial cost. Advisories are continuous, and bad weather alerts are broadcast as soon as they are issued. The information is immediate, more complete and thoroughly detailed, unlike the intermittent and brief weather reports on local radio stations. Weather radios are sold at Radio Shack, electronics and sporting goods stores, marine shops, and outdoors stores.

For up to $200, you can also get weather radios that, even when left in their inactive mode, will chirp to life and let you know when a weather alert has been issued in your area. These devices are particularly important if you're bound for a boat-in backcountry campsite.

A weather radio can provide good service even if you're camping in more urban conditions. Several years ago, a line of tornadoes rolled across Central Florida, flattening a campground near Kissimmee. Much was made of the fact that campers didn't have warning. There was talk of installing tornado warning sirens to alert folks that they should leave their RVs and take cover in a secure building on the grounds. The talk has come to little, so you are responsible for monitoring severe weather.

You're more likely to experience lightning than tornadoes. Lightning strikes more than 1,000 people a year in the United States, often in Florida. In fact, Florida is considered the lightning capital of the nation. Most victims are standing when they are hit. The electricity enters the head first, knocking them unconscious. Nerves and blood vessels speed the electricity through the body.

The good news is that you have some warning, or an inkling that something is up. People who are struck often see lightning or hear thunder in the distance and try to squeeze in one more round of golf or hook another fish. When you hear thunder, take precautions immediately. If you're in a field or on open water, make for cover right away. Do not stand under a solitary tree or clump of trees. Nor should you stand near a fence or metallic objects. Ideally, you will find shelter in a building or car. If you're outdoors away from civilization, try to head for a forest. Do not stand under the tallest tree, but rather seek out the shortest. If you are caught in the middle of a field, lie down far away from objects that might attract lightning.

Of Bugs, Beasts, and Toxic Plants

We don't want to scare anyone. You're not likely to encounter many of these critters, but you ought to be aware that they are out there.

Alligators

Alligators are unlikely to hurt you, with a few important exceptions.

The myth of dangerous alligators is largely just that—a myth. Think about the reports you've heard of alligators attacking people. You hear, what, maybe one every few years? The very fact that such encounters make such big news is a clue to their rarity. In Florida, far more people are killed by lightning than by alligators.

One of our friends once waded through alligator-infested, chest-deep waters for long stretches on two consecutive days. It makes for a great story, but in fact he was largely unconcerned. The reason? He was in the middle of the Everglades, where gators have precious little contact with humans. And when Clyde Butcher, the famous photographic chronicler of Florida's outdoors, lowers his burly body into the waters to shoot his stunning black-and-white photos, he says he doesn't worry one bit about alligators snapping at his bare legs or any other part of him.

Which brings us to one big exception. With hundreds of people moving to Florida every day, more and more of the alligator's territory is being invaded. This is not usually a problem—at

While alligators are most often associated in visitors' minds with the Everglades, the truth is they are ubiquitous throughout Florida. As long as they are not fed by humans, they are shy creatures, and alligator attacks are fairly rare.

least from the human point of view—until people start feeding the beasts. A fed gator is a dangerous gator. It's as simple as that. Under normal circumstances, an alligator does not view an adult human as food. Once the marshmallows start flying, however, all bets are off.

Crocodiles, which are found in extreme southern Florida, are endangered and shy creatures, which—unlike their African counterparts—pose no threat to humans. You won't see many of them.

So if you suspect an alligator has been fed—if he starts edging toward you, for instance, indicating he has lost his natural shyness—get the heck out of there, and by all means don't put your hand near his mouth.

Also, old, sick alligators may go after a person, particularly a child. Because of their size, children make a better target. Alligators six feet or longer present the greatest danger to kids. Those under four feet generally are not a problem. When you swim in freshwater in Florida, keep an eye out for large gators. Also, avoid swimming at dusk or at night, when they often are feeding. They might not recognize you as a human until it's too late.

Don't let your pets near any body of freshwater in Florida. Pets, also because of their size and posture, may be viewed as eligible fare for the dinner hour. A child splashing in the water with his dog can be a lethal mix.

Poisonous Toads

The nasty little South American import known as *bufo marinus* secretes a toxic substance and is chiefly a threat to pets. If you handle a greenish gray toad with brown bumps that look like a bad case of warts, be sure to wash your hands thoroughly afterward. Don't let children or pets play with them. A dog who has handled a bufo in his mouth may foam at the lip, cough, and gag. Try to get a hose or water bottle to wash out the dog's mouth.

Snakes

Most snakes in Florida are not poisonous. Like alligators, they are a largely overblown menace in the backcountry, especially when you consider how few people are killed by them. Still, we don't want to minimize their threat, because a snakebite is serious. At the very least, it will ruin your camping trip. As a rule, stay away from all snakes. Even a nonpoisonous snake can strike and break the skin.

Bear in mind that snakes, poisonous and nonpoisonous, are more scared of you than you are of them. Be careful where you plant your feet and hands when you are outdoors, and never, ever reach into a pile of wood. To gather firewood, use a downed branch to move individual pieces of wood to where you can see them and confirm they are not harboring a snake (or a scorpion or a spider, for that matter).

If bitten, forget the old wisdom of scratching an X on the spot and sucking out the venom. Doctors have found the sucking method to be ineffective, impractical, and messy, as well as potentially dangerous for the good Samaritan sucking the venom. The new wisdom: Stay calm and get medical help as soon as possible. Realize that most bites turn out to be dry bites, meaning no venom was injected.

If you're near your drive-up campsite when the bite occurs, simply get in the car and travel calmly to an emergency physician. If you're

The Eastern diamondback rattler can grow to eight feet long.

in the backcountry, walk out slowly; don't run because the venom may spread through your bloodstream more quickly. Better yet, sit down and get medical help to come to you. The U.S. Army advises its soldiers to lie quietly, move no more than necessary, and don't smoke, eat, or drink any fluids. Remove any jewelry from the bitten extremity because rings, bracelets, and the like may become a tourniquet if swelling occurs. If a limb was bitten, don't elevate it—keep the extremity level with the body. If you don't know what type of snake struck, then try to remember what the reptile looked like so you can describe it to a physician.

You may fashion a splint out of a tent stake or something similar in the meantime. Loosely tie it with a sock, T-shirt, or another piece of clothing. It should be tight enough to stop the flow of blood near the skin, the Army advises. But don't tie it tight enough that it becomes a tourniquet—or you'll risk losing the limb. If swelling is occurring quickly, place an inch-wide constricting band about two inches above the bite, suggests the Cooperative Extension Service of Mississippi State University. Remember: Make it loose enough that you can slip a finger underneath. Don't place a constricting band on a joint.

There are four types of poisonous snakes to worry about:

Rattlesnakes

Florida is home to several species of rattlesnakes, including Eastern diamondbacks, which can grow up to eight feet long. Usually found in woodpiles and in the ubiquitous clusters of saw palmetto that dot Florida woodlands, they are an excellent reason to stay on hiking trails and watch your step around downed wood.

One time in the Big Cypress Swamp, a troop of about 25 Boy Scouts was hiking along a trail that was blocked by a fallen log. The guys and their scoutmasters all stepped over the log—until the 22nd or 23rd boy noticed a rattlesnake wedged under it. The laggards chose an alternate path.

Water Moccasins

Also known as cottonmouths, these snakes are mottled brown and black pit vipers with cotton-white coloring on the inside of their mouths. If you're lucky, though, you'll never see the inside of one's mouth. That's a sign of warning! These snakes are usually found in or near the water. If you're swimming in freshwater, stay away from clumps of vegetation, particularly if enough of it is growing above the water's surface for a snake to hide. And watch where you are stepping when you're at the shoreline.

As a boy, one of our friends was swimming in front of a dock on Lake Placid when his father commanded him to get out of the water immediately. Ignoring his father's objections, he swam around to where he could use the ladder at dockside—right next to a clump of vegetation where two big, fat cottonmouths were sunning themselves. He still remembers that cotton-white color.

Coral Snakes

These snakes have smaller injectors and inject less poison than the aforementioned pit vipers, but their venom packs more punch and rapidly affects the nervous system. Fortunately, they are not very aggressive. They're usually found under rocks or debris on the ground.

Coral snakes have black snouts and their bodies are ringed entirely with red, yellow or off-white, and black bands. Several nonpoisonous snakes, such as the scarlet king or the milk snake, look like coral snakes. Remember that coral snakes have black noses; the imitators have yellow or red noses. Although other nonpoisonous snakes have the same coloring, on the coral snake the red ring always touches the yellow ring. (Here's an old saying: "Red touch black, venom lack; red touch yellow, bad for fellow.")

Copperheads

These snakes are pit vipers without rattles that live in dry upland areas in the Panhandle and grow up to four feet long. You can recognize them by their copper-colored head and the reddish hourglass on the body. Their venom is not as potent as rattlers'.

Raccoons

We know raccoons look cute. Heck, the former Florida governor Lawton Chiles even compared himself with an old "he-coon" in a close-fought election campaign. But stay away from these masked marauders because some carry rabies.

And don't feed them. We've been invaded on more than one picnic by raccoons rampaging across the table expecting a handout. It's tough to scare off the little buggers once they know people have food. Also take precautions against raccoons stealing food while you sleep. It's best to store food and water in your car or RV. If you're roughing it in the backcountry, you may want to keep food in the tent with you.

Raccoons are experts at opening unsecured coolers.

Or, if you have a hard-sided cooler, store food and water inside and secure it with numerous loops of rope, tied tight. You need the rope because raccoons are clever enough to open some coolers. Use thick rope, not twine, so they can't chew their way through.

Bears

Although they once roamed most of the state, black bears in Florida now number fewer than 1,500 and are confined to scattered pockets. The biggest pockets are in the Big Cypress National Preserve and Osceola, Ocala, and Apalachicola National Forests, as well as the surrounding areas.

So rare are bears today that state biologists have to put electronic collars on the animals and drive 150 miles in a single day at times to find them. Females typically range 10 miles or so in a day, while the larger, 250- to 350-pound adult males will go farther.

These secretive, shy, little-seen mammals come out mostly at night and tend to be found around thick clumps of trees and underbrush. They consider the tender shoots of saw palmetto thickets a bear's answer to ice cream. You're extremely unlikely to encounter these officially designated "threatened" animals. The worst possibility is to unexpectedly come up against a mama bear and her cubs, usually in the summer or fall.

If you're camping where bears are likely to be, place all food inside backpacks or nylon stuff sacks and hang the bags from a tree limb. Here's the process: Look for a sturdy tree limb that extends at least eight feet from the trunk of a tree. Throw a length of rope over the limb. Tie one end of the rope to a sack of food. Pull on the other end of the rope to haul the bag, pulley-style, into the air so the bag hangs 10 feet or higher above the ground. Then wrap the other end of the rope a few times around the tree trunk and tie it tightly.

Wild Hogs

Descended from domestic pigs that escaped from early settlers, wild hogs are a major nuisance. They root around in the ground, leaving big, plowlike ruts in their wake, destroying natural areas. They can be very dangerous when cornered. In many designated hunting areas, they are the only animal for which there is no bag limit. Spareribs all around, we say!

One of our researchers and his family were confronted with a wild hog in the campground at Myakka River State Park. The animal was rooting around, looking for food underneath the picnic table when they returned to camp. Feeling cornered (the picnic table was next to a wet marshy area), the hog grew agitated. Clearly, trouble was on the way. The family was lucky because they climbed onto the picnic table and the hog soon ran off.

If you see a wild hog, head the other way immediately and start looking for an escape route. Climb a tree, get into a car, or head inside a building. Merely backing away will usually defuse the situation. In any case, do not knowingly approach a hog. It will feel threatened and could charge.

Bees, Wasps, and Yellow Jackets

These insects can be a serious problem—even a fatal one for people who are susceptible. Obviously, you should never disturb their nests on purpose. Remember when you're walking in the woods that these insects strive to keep their nests dry. So don't poke your hand into a hollow log (good advice on numerous counts) or places where nests could be hidden.

In our experience, yellow jackets are the most aggressive of the three, followed by wasps, then bees. Unlike bees, which lose their stinger after one piercing, wasps and yellow jackets can return to sting you repeatedly.

If you are being attacked, run! If you are stung, watch for signs of allergic reaction: swelling, wooziness, shortness of breath, fainting, cramps, or shock. Should any of these symptoms seem to be occurring, head for the nearest emergency room.

As a stopgap measure, consider treating stings with a semiliquid mixture of water and baking soda. If you know you are allergic to such stings, be sure to bring along an antidote when you go camping.

Mosquitoes

Well, what would Florida be without mosquitoes? A lot more pleasant, that's what we say. But that's impossible and, besides, it wouldn't be the same mosaic of ecosystems that we've come to enjoy. That's right—skeeters have their place in the ecological web.

Think of a camping trip without the soothing croaks of mosquito-eating frogs. What would the Florida outdoors be like without skeeter-munching dragonflies darting across hiking trails? And mosquito larvae are a major food for fish.

Mosquitoes are drawn by carbon dioxide—what we all exhale—so you can't very well avoid them altogether. Mosquitoes are worst in summer, of course, and are generally more of a problem in southern Florida than northern Florida. Most, but not all, mosquitoes prefer to bite at dusk. Some also swarm at night. All avoid direct sunlight, though, because it dries them out and kills them.

With rare exception, mosquitoes are merely pests. The exception is when they transmit disease. Although malaria has been wiped out (except in some Third World countries), you can contract encephalitis, which causes brain inflammation, through mosquito bites. More recently has been the spread of potentially fatal West Nile virus by mosquitoes. It's uncommon, yet it makes sense to avoid mosquito bites as much as possible.

In urban areas, so-called sentinel chickens are deliberately put out to be bitten by mosquitoes, then tested to see if the disease-carrying insects have done the deed. For years little evidence of disease transmission existed, but in recent years a few outbreaks have been reported.

What do we do to protect ourselves? We rub poison all over our bodies! Sad to say, but insecticides are the most effective way to keep skeeters away. We prefer formulations containing DEET—particularly when facing the 47 types of mosquitoes in Everglades National Park. Avon's Skin So Soft can be helpful, although it is not marketed as an insecticide and hence has not been tested as one. (Some people assume it's safer than DEET, but as far as we know, no one has checked.) The standard advice is to wear long sleeves and long pants, although we find this fairly uncomfortable in the summer when mosquitoes are most numerous.

Make sure to cover any exposed skin with insecticide. In our experience, skeeters are particularly attracted to the ankles, arms, neck, and—while you sleep, if you're careless enough to let one into your tent or RV—face.

If possible, escape to your tent or RV at dusk. Another nicety is a dining fly enclosed by mosquito netting, although this is obviously impractical for backpackers and canoeists. Mosquitoes also tend to avoid smoke and heat, another great argument for having a campfire. Make a big, hot, smoky one, then sit back and enjoy.

Roaches

We hate roaches. But they are as much a part of the Florida landscape as the air. You'll find roaches in five-star hotels, luxury homes, and even cars. Folks here call them "palmetto bugs."

There's not much you can do about roaches if you're tent camping, except push them out of your way. In an RV, clean up Florida-style after every meal: Sweep the floor, wipe the counters, and get rid of crumbs. And please, don't spray the campsite with Raid. We were in a county park near Tampa having dinner at the picnic table when our neighbors decided to declare chemical war on bugs. Not very neighborly when the wind is blowing.

Ticks

Ticks are one of the more serious insect threats because they can spread Lyme disease. A vaccine is now available if you're really worried about Lyme disease or expect to be regularly exposed to ticks.

You'll tend to find ticks on your body if you've been in the deep woods, although they can appear in a standard commercial campground, too. You're most likely to encounter them if you're crashing through little-disturbed, low-lying brush during a hike. Stay on the trail to minimize this threat.

Keep It Wild Tip: Respect Nature

- Treat our natural environment with respect. Leave plants, rocks, and historical artifacts where you find them.
- Observe wildlife from a distance. Never feed animals, and always keep food in critter-proof containers and dispose of it properly.
- Let nature's sound prevail. Avoid loud voices and noises. Keep radios at a low volume.
- Control pets at all times.

Get into the practice of surveying your skin any time you've been in the deep woods. If possible, have a camping mate look over your back, neck, and scalp. Don't forget to check under your clothes; we've discovered ticks in unmentionable areas! If you find a tick, it will look like a brown wart. What has happened is that the tick has been sucking on you all day, with its head burrowed in your flesh, and its body has become engorged with your blood.

Don't take the advice of some standard guides that prescribe covering the little bugger with gas, Vaseline, or some other toxic substance. The theory is that the tick will come out because it's short on oxygen. Another bird-brained idea is to burn the tick out by touching its back end with a cigarette. In our experience, these solutions don't work. Usually the tick dies and you're left with a dead tick partially burrowed into your flesh.

Our remedy: Take a pair of tweezers and very carefully—as if you were a surgeon—burrow down around the tick's head, which is embedded in your flesh. Give a gentle pull, or two or three, until the tick comes out. You'll have to yank it out. The primary danger is crushing the tick's head or blood-engorged body. This can release its body fluids and the nasties they carry, so try hard not to let it happen. If you screw up and the tick's head remains embedded in you, go in again with the tweezers (after washing them in alcohol) and try to get it out. Check to see if the mouthparts broke off in the wound, and if so, seek medical attention. No matter what happens, wash the area thoroughly with alcohol. If the area becomes infected or a welt develops, then consult a doctor. You can buy a tick removal kit at many camping stores.

More on Lyme disease: A few days or weeks after a bite, you may suffer flulike symptoms, headaches, a stiff neck, fever, aching muscles, and malaise. A rash usually develops at about the same time. The rash generally looks like an expanding red ring with a clear center (a kind of bull's-eye), but it can vary from a blotchy appearance to red throughout. See a doctor if you're suffering symptoms. A blood test will help determine if you have Lyme disease instead of just an allergic reaction to tick saliva. If you start taking antibiotics soon, the disease can be cured. If you don't get medical help, later possible complications can spell trouble: recurring acute arthritis (usually of the knees, hips, or ankles), heart palpitations, tingling in the extremities, and lethargy.

It should go without saying, but don't forget to check children and pets for ticks after spending any time in the woods.

Ants and Scorpions

The worst of the ants is the fire ant, imported from South America. In northern and central Florida, you'll see the big piles they call home. Just stay away from them. Red ants also inhabit southern Florida, and although their piles are not as obvious, you can avoid them if you're careful.

If you get bitten, wash the affected area with soap and water or rubbing alcohol. Do not scratch open the white-headed blister that may form, because you risk an infection. If you are bitten numerous times, consult a doctor or go to an emergency room.

Scorpions are rare and are not a life-threatening problem in Florida. Ditto for centipedes. You're most likely to find them in woodpiles, but they've been known to turn up in people's tents. Check your shoes before putting them on in the morning; shoes are a favorite hiding place. If you are stung, it will hurt but won't kill you. Wash the wound, then see a doctor.

Chiggers

The term "chigger" is a common name used to describe the larval stage of parasitic mites. These minuscule insects can ruin an otherwise perfect camping trip. Much like a mite, they are impossible to see. But you'll know if you have them because they will start burrowing into your skin—usually your softest skin, often in private areas—and you will experience an incredible itching and small, red welts.

The best remedy for chiggers can be obtained from a doctor, although a good soap-and-water treatment may suffice. Another remedy is to seal the skin from contact with air: You can use home remedies such as nail polish, calamine lotion, Vaseline, cold cream, or baby oil. But you'll get more relief by using something that includes antihistamines, such as Caladryl, or hydrocortisone salves and creams, according to Iowa State University's Entomology Department. Or ask a pharmacist to suggest a local anesthetic or analgesic.

To avoid chiggers, stay away from Spanish moss. The gray-green moss commonly hangs in long intertwined curly strands from the branches of old oaks in Central and North Florida. It sways elegantly in the breeze until it falls in clumps onto the ground. So don't roll around on the forest floor. (Darn! That's our favorite part.)

Poison Ivy and Other Plant Pests

Poison ivy is the bane of adventuresome Florida campers. It can be such an innocent mistake to stumble into one of these itch machines. Our main advice is to stay away from any plant with which you are not familiar, particularly because Florida's version doesn't look identical to the poison ivy Northern visitors know.

Locally, poison ivy comes in many forms—bush, ground cover, and vine. It has a special affinity for sabal palms. Remember: "Leaves of three, let it be." The leaves are a forest green, or perhaps a little lighter, and vaguely heart- or arrow-shaped. You can usually see beads of the poison, which often have hardened into little, black, wartlike eruptions on the leaves themselves. You may see white berries accompanying poison ivy—or you may not, depending on whether or not the plant is in bloom.

"Leaves of three, let it be": A brush with poison ivy can spoil a camping trip.

Keep your dog on the hiking trails. Otherwise, the next time you snuggle up to your four-legged buddy after his or her romp in the woods, you may find yourself scratching because the itchy sap has been transferred to you.

Many other plants in Florida are irritants at best, poisonous at worst. Among them are periwinkle, yellow allamanda, crape jasmine, oleander, crown of thorns, lantana, pencil tree, Brazilian pepper, and poinsettia. Even lime or mango trees can lead to problems; oil from the lime peel and mango skin and tree sap sometimes causes blistering and reddening.

Backcountry Camping (Plus a Few Hints for Car Campers)

Most of Everglades National Park is waterlogged, and many visitors see less than 10 percent of the park because they stick to the windshield tour and maybe stroll on a few boardwalks. A few, though, venture through the former Indian canoe trails, bootlegger hangouts, and just plain satisfying bays, inlets, and saw grass plains where a sunset is a spiritual experience.

The hale and hearty are well advised to try some overnight trips into Florida's backcountry, either by canoeing, kayaking, or backpacking. Or, if you're a little less fit, some remote spots can be reached by motorboat. By heading into the backcountry, you can see some of the most jaw-droppingly beautiful parts of Florida. An added benefit, we think, is that you can usually do it with little or no company in the nation's fourth most populous state.

We're particularly fond of Everglades National Park for canoeing trips, although many fine adventures are possible elsewhere, from the Panhandle to Southwest Florida.

For backpacking, your best bet is often the Florida National Scenic Trail, which eventually is supposed to cover approximately 1,300 miles from the Gulf Islands National Seashore near Pensacola to the Big Cypress National Preserve east of Naples. About 1,000 miles of the trail already have been completed, and we've listed some special camping spots along the way.

Here we also must put in a plug for the Florida Trail Association, a dedicated group of volunteers that maintains the trail and is usually in the process of building a new leg of it somewhere. It's worthwhile and satisfying work. The association's headquarters is in Gainesville; call 352/378-8823 or 877/HIKE-FLA; website: www.florida-trail.org. Some fine backpacking is also available on spur trails in state parks and national forests.

Whether you're hoofing it, paddling, or motorboating, you'll need specialized equipment.

Food

If you're in a pop-top camper or even a motor coach, your menu is pretty much whatever you wish. We like spaghetti, hamburgers, salads, and soups, just like at home. But if you're going on an overnighter by canoe or motorboat, you're not really in that much of a different situation from someone tenting in a commercial campground. You could bring along a bulky Coleman stove, a cooler, hot dogs, water jug—the works. But if you're strapping on a 40-pound backpack or going out for an extended stay, you'll want to plan your menus carefully. You can buy the freeze-dried offerings sold in camping stores, but they're fairly expensive.

To save money, at least on some meals, don't neglect the light, easy-to-make stuff you can get right off the supermarket shelf. Consider ramen noodle soup, Lipton Cup-a-Soup, instant oatmeal in single-serving pouches, macaroni and cheese, and the small cans of tuna, clams, and the like that go great on top of crackers. Fresh fruit and vegetables generally keep well, too. Some coffee or tea bags come in handy. Whole books have been written about meals for the trail, and we won't try to replicate them here.

Plan ahead, bearing in mind that you may be caught unexpectedly without a fire for some reason, and bring extra food. Surplus food is crucial if you get lost or hurt and have to stay out extra days.

Do-It-Yourself Jerky

Try making your own beef jerky before you leave home. It's delicious, fairly cheap, lightweight, and compact. It's also easy. Here's the method recommended by former authors of the book Sally Deneen and Robert McClure: Buy lean steak (flank steak works best) and remove all fat and gristle. Cutting across the grain, slice it into pieces about one-quarter inch thick. Marinate it in whatever you like. We use a healthy dose of Worcestershire sauce, a somewhat smaller amount of soy sauce, and a little sesame oil (just a splash for flavoring; you can substitute browned sesame seeds if you like). Add red pepper flakes or Tabasco and some Mrs. Dash or other seasonings. We're garlic freaks, so we always include some of that. Marinate the beef 12 to 24 hours—the longer you marinate it, the tastier it will be.

Then just plop the strips onto a cookie sheet, leaving at least an inch between each strip. Bake at 125 to 150 degrees Fahrenheit if your oven thermometer goes that low; if not, just set it on low. Leave the door cracked. You are not so much cooking the meat as you are drying it out. That's the point—to get rid of all the moisture. As with the marinating process, this will often take 12 hours or more. Keep checking the strips every half hour or so after about eight hours. It's ready when all the moisture is gone, yet the meat is still chewy. If the ends start to get so dry that they break off in crystal-like pieces, you've overcooked the jerky. (Don't worry, though; some of the thicker pieces are probably still OK. This is one reason to cut one or two extremely thin pieces; they're sort of like the canaries in the coal mine, warning you that it's time to pull the rest of the batch out.)

A tasty concoction that is easy to make is gorp. Buy granola or another oat-based cereal. Lots of breakfast cereals can be substituted, but stick to the granola-type ones; Cocoa Puffs will not suffice. To the cereal, add a few things: dried fruit (raisins are traditional, but there's no law), nuts (we like peanuts, but suit yourself), and small pieces of candy. Chocolate chips are traditional, although we've seen gorp made with all kinds of things, including M&Ms and Hershey's Kisses. Mix it all up and divide it into sandwich bags. Gorp is eaten by the handful during rest breaks along a hiking trail. We keep a small bag handy so we can snork some down at even the shortest break. The candy provides quick energy. The nuts provide fat, which you will burn slowly. And the oats give your body that midrange energy burn you'll need to keep going. The fruit? It tastes good. Probably helps keep you regular, too.

Some people travel light, like the ranger we met at Olympic National Park who carried a Tupperware container of chocolate bars and graham crackers in his daypack. Some people travel cheap, like the pair of hiking retirees we met on their latest of several trips to the bottom of the Grand Canyon who said they buy all their food at the supermarket (and are sure to include some dessert). For more food ideas, we like the food-on-the-trail tips found in *Backpacker* magazine.

Utensils and Dishes

Although we once shared a camp with a guy who lugged along a miniature espresso maker, you don't really need a lot of kitchen accessories. Bring only what you'll use. We prefer a mess

kit that folds down for compact, lightweight carrying, along with
a similar small saucepan apparatus and perhaps a pot holder.
Plus, you'll need silverware, maybe a spatula, and a large metal
mug you can sit on the stove for fast cups of tea (it doubles as a
soup bowl).

And what about the washing up? Susan Windrem, one of our
best friends from car-camping days, swears by a few drops of
ammonia in a bucket or bowl. She even washes her hands
in it before starting to cook or handle food. The little bit
of ammonia presumably kills germs in the water and
caked-on food. It's not a bad idea if you can stand the
smell. Just don't use a lot, and bring some hand lotion
for afterward.

Stoves

In most backcountry locations, you'll need a camper's stove, which
can be purchased at outdoors shops and through catalogs. Even
at those campsites where ground fires are allowed, you'll still
want to bring along a stove. There's little fun in waiting half
an hour or longer while you make a fire and boil water for a
cup of tea or some soup when you first reach camp, tired, cold, and hungry. Florida's unpredictable downpours can render dead, downed wood
useless. Plus, campfires make for notoriously messy cleanups when
the meal is done.

Some campers spend hours debating the merits of various
lightweight, collapsible stoves. From that, we will refrain. We
prefer the MSR Whisperlite, burning white gas, because it's
light and folds down to a small size. We know someone who
traveled to China and other far-flung points
with the MSR Internationale so he could use
all types of fuel he might encounter.

To find the perfect stove for you, turn to
consumer guides, such as the annual gear-
rating edition of *Backpacker* magazine. But

Stoves are
available in
many styles and
burn a variety of fuels. These are three typical examples. Top: **White gas stoves** are
the most popular because they are inexpensive and easy to find; they do require
priming and can be explosive. Middle: **Gas
canister stoves** burn propane, butane,
isobutane, and mixtures of the three. These
are the easiest to use but have two disad-
vantages: 1) Because the fuel is bottled,
determining how much fuel is left can be
difficult. 2) The fuel is limited to above-
freezing conditions. Bottom: **Liquid fuel
stoves** burn Coleman fuel, denatured alcohol, kerosene, and even gasoline; these
fuels are economical and have a high heat
output, but most must be primed.

the important thing is to find your own favorite stove and make sure you know how to use it before you hit the trail. Always try out the stove before you leave home—even if it worked on previous adventures—if it's been in storage for more than, say, a week. You don't want to find out the hard way that your stove no longer works.

Most campers we know use white gas for their stoves. Do so with extreme caution. It is highly flammable and even explosive under the wrong conditions. Butane is another possibility, although we admit we have little experience with it. It appears to us to be bulky and heavy, but butane has its adherents. Their chief claim is that butane lights easily. Avoid kerosene. Aside from being smelly, it is hard to find in some places. Remember that these fuels are not interchangeable. Carefully read the instructions that come with your stove.

For car camping, the hardy Coleman stove with propane can't be beat. A two-burner stove can handle the demands of a pasta dinner, or side dishes when you're cooking meat on a grill. Table-top grills, also powered by propane, are available for as little as $50. Trouble is, once you get all that heating equipment on the picnic table, will you have space to eat? It's all in the organization and planning.

Water

We don't worry about water quality much in most campgrounds because it's city water. But much of the water in natural Florida is just plain nasty. It's not dangerous, but it contains a lot of gunk, usually humus or some other by-product of rotting matter. So try to bring along all the water you will need. If you're canoeing or traveling in a motorboat, this should not be much of a problem. (Carry water in a raccoon-proof container, though, if you're in brackish or salt water. Raccoons in these places are perpetually thirsty—and clever. The crafty critters will gnaw through anything that is not thick enough, including those gallon jugs of water you buy at the supermarket. It's best to store water and food in a hard-sided cooler that is tied shut with numerous loops of rope.)

Water filters are a wise investment since all wilderness water should be considered contaminated. Make sure the filter can be easily cleaned or has a replaceable cartridge. The filter pores must be 0.4 microns or less to remove bacteria.

Backpackers can try to carry enough water for a day or two, but you won't want to skimp on liquids if you're trudging around in Florida's heat. This calls for a water purifier, which also can be purchased at outdoors shops and through catalogs. Again, some backcountry campers spend hours debating the merits of various models. We won't. Just make sure you know how to use the purifier before you hit the trail, and check to make sure it's still in working order before you leave home. It's prudent to bring along an extra filter in case the one you're

Keep It Wild Tip: Campfires

- Fire use can scar the backcountry, so take extreme precaution when preparing to build and maintain a fire.
- Where fires are permitted, use existing fire rings. If a fire ring isn't available, then use a lightweight stove for cooking.
- For fuel, gather sticks from the ground that are no thicker than the diameter of your wrist. Don't break branches off live, dead, or downed trees because this could cause personal injury and scar the natural setting.
- When leaving, put out the fire completely, pack out all trash from the fire ring, and scatter the ashes away from the site. Forest fires *can* be started by campfires that are not properly dismantled.

using gets clogged. One note of caution: Purifiers do not turn saltwater into fresh, nor do most of them remove industrial pollutants.

What if you have no water? And no purifier? In many places in Florida, you can dig down a few feet and find water. After you dig a hole, let the water sit for at least an hour. This allows the dirt to settle. Then scoop out some water and pour it through a handkerchief to sift it further. Repeat this process until you fill a pan, then boil the water for four minutes. This treatment will eliminate any of the nasties that may send your stomach cramping and your body running to the bathroom. Cryptosporidium, a single-cell parasite, most commonly causes watery diarrhea, but also can bring on nausea, dehydration, abdominal cramps, and fever lasting for several days, starting two days to nearly two weeks after infection. Giardia causes many of the same symptoms.

In a real pinch, you can purify water with iodine tablets—no backpack is complete without them. But your first taste of this "water" will remind you why you should invest in a good purifier. Iodine will not kill all illness-causing microorganisms, and too much of it can be dangerous to your health. The effectiveness of the tablets depends on how long you let the water sit—sometimes up to half an hour—and the temperature and organic content of the water.

Clothing

You shouldn't wear cotton because when it gets wet, it can be deadly. Of course, many people do camp in blue jeans. Our advice is to opt for nylon expedition pants and a waterproof shell. If you insist on cotton, make sure you always have at least one dry pair of pants and extra shirts in a waterproof bag. That way, if you're forced to make camp early because of inclement weather, you can change into dry duds.

When it's cold, layer your clothes. Usually a T-shirt, overshirt, and light jacket will be enough. But in North Florida and even the southern part of the state in the winter, you'll sometimes want to give yourself four or more layers, including a decent jacket or even a winter coat. Don't forget a knit cap or other hat; much of your body heat is lost through your head.

In an RV, where you have closets, bringing extra clothes is not so much of a space issue as it is when you're on the trail. The important thing is to be prepared for any kind of weather, and be sure that you've considered everyone in your party. And don't count on a campfire to keep warm; most counties have outlawed ground fires because of the risk of starting a conflagration you didn't intend. In wintertime, forest areas are tinder-dry, and forest fires are a danger. (And don't light a fire on top of your picnic table, as we saw in one Florida Keys campground.)

If you're going to be canoeing or hiking in cold weather, consider a layer of underwear made of synthetic fabrics that wick moisture away from the body. On top of that, you'll want an insulating layer. Good choices are jackets of down, woolen pants, or more synthetics. On top of that, use a waterproof shell layer to keep your other clothes dry.

About the materials: Down-filled gear is great, until it gets wet. Then it's almost useless. Cotton is even worse—being naked may be preferable in some cases because at least you're dry. Wool retains some of its insulating properties even when wet. Synthetics offer some of the best combinations but are generally pricey.

For warmer times, go ahead and pack that bathing suit. You never know when you might want it.

Rain Gear

Words to live by: Bring it. Use it.

Bring a poncho because it also can function as a tarp, be used as a ground cover, and serve probably a dozen other uses. Also consider some kind of waterproof jacket or shell. Used in combination with rain pants and a poncho, this can help you stay pretty dry in Florida.

We eschew expensive rain pants in favor of nylon expedition pants. They're light enough for a hot Florida afternoon, though they afford reasonable protection against the wind when wet. Also, they dry out quickly once you're out of the rain.

Boots

It is hard to underestimate the importance of good boots to a backpacker. Choose them carefully, break them in before you reach the trailhead, and cushion your feet with a good pair of backpacking socks—which often cost about $10. Lightweight silk sockliners, also available at outdoors shops, can prevent blisters from forming.

Remember that your boots and socks are a team; make sure they fit together well. The fit should be snug but not overly tight. Also make sure the boots support your ankles adequately. If these precautions fail and blisters develop, pull out the moleskin. Cut it into pieces big enough to cover your blisters so you can slip on dry socks and continue your hike in relative comfort. Moleskin is available at drugstores.

There's nothing wrong with bringing high-ankle hiking boots to an RV park or more nature-oriented campground. They'll keep your feet dry and warm, and you'll generally avoid twisted ankles on uneven terrain. If you have to trek to the restrooms in the middle of the night, they provide ease of mind as you walk through piles of leaves.

Keep It Wild Tip: Sanitation

- If refuse facilities are available, use them to help concentrate impact.
- If no restroom is available, deposit human waste into a "cat hole" dug six to eight inches deep and at least 75 paces (200 feet) from any water source or campsite. Fill the cat hole with soil when finished.
- Use toilet paper sparingly. When finished, either *carefully* burn it in a *controlled* fire or, better yet, pack it out.
- To wash dishes or your body, carry water at least 200 feet away from the source and use small amounts of phosphate-free biodegradable soap. After washing, strain water using a cloth (to remove food particles) and scatter away from site.
- Scour your campsite for even the tiniest piece of trash and any other evidence of your stay. Pack out all waste, even if it's not yours.
- Never litter.

Compass, Map, and GPS

Some people bring along global positioning systems (GPS) in the backcountry, and one of us wishes to heaven he had had one during three days lost in the Everglades. GPS is a nice insurance policy for a few hundred bucks. You'll need to spend some time learning to use it first, though; don't just throw it in the rucksack and take off. Also, remember that a GPS is no substitute for a working compass, detailed maps or charts, and a firm grounding in the art of orienteering.

Camping Gear Checklist

Personal Items
Bathing suit
Feminine hygiene products
Hat with a broad brim to keep sun off
  your face, ears, and neck
Hiking boots or sneakers
Insect repellent
Rain gear: jacket, poncho, rain pants
Pants, long (airy weave in summer,
  thicker in winter)
Personal prescription medicine
Sandals or flip-flops
Shirt, long-sleeved (airy weave in sum-
  mer, thicker in winter)
Shorts
Soap
Sunglasses
Sunscreen
Toiletries
Towels
Water shoes

Camping Gear for Backpackers
Bandanna or handkerchief
Camping knife
Can opener
Compass
Dishes and silverware
Dish soap (preferably biodegradable)
First-aid kit

Flashlight
Food
Fuel
Hatchet
Matches in waterproof container
Sleeping bag (we get by with 20-
  degree bags, but you might want
  something with a lower rating if
  you plan to do much winter camp-
  ing, particularly if you'll be north
  of Orlando)
Stove
Tarp or screen-room tent
Tent
Toilet paper
Whistle

Nice to Have, When Appropriate
Bag for dirty clothes
Bicycles
Board games, deck of cards
Books, magazines
Camera, with flash and extra film
Canoe or inflatable boat
Extra propane or stove fuel
Fishing rod and tackle
Folding chairs
Lantern
Laundry detergent
Tool kit for the car, RV, and other needs

COURTESY OF PENSACOLA CONVENTION & VISITOR INFORMATION CENTER

Chapter 1

Pensacola Area

Pensacola Area

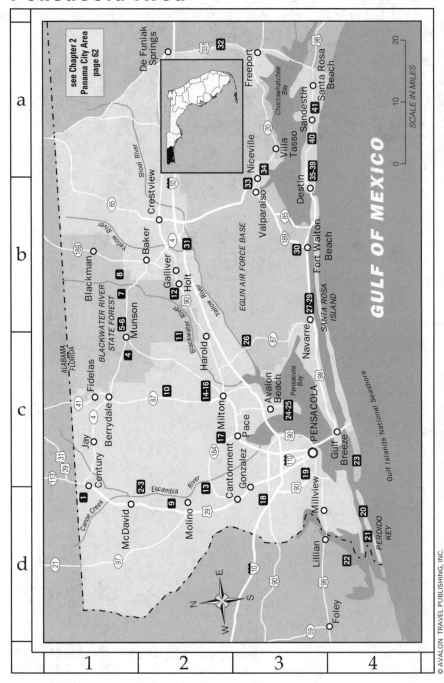

see Chapter 2
Panama City Area
page 62

SCALE IN MILES

GULF OF MEXICO

De Funiak Springs

Freeport

Santa Rosa Beach

Sandestin

Villa Tasso

Niceville

Crestview

Baker

Galliver

Holt

Blackman

Munson

Fidelas

Berrydale

Jay

Century

McDavid

Molino

Milton

Pace

Cantonment

Gonzalez

Avalon Beach

Navarre

Fort Walton Beach

Destin

Valparaiso

PENSACOLA

Gulf Breeze

Millview

Lillian

Foley

PERDIDO KEY

Gulf Islands National Seashore

SANTA ROSA ISLAND

Pensacola Bay

EGLIN AIR FORCE BASE

BLACKWATER RIVER STATE FOREST

Shoal River

Yellow River

Blackwater River

Escambia River

Canoe Creek

Choctawhatchee Bay

ALABAMA
FLORIDA

32
41
40
35-39
33
34
30
31
8
7
5-6
4
12
11
26
27-29
10
14-16
17
24-25
23
19
13
18
9
2-3
1
20
21
22

© AVALON TRAVEL PUBLISHING, INC.

1 LAKE STONE CAMPGROUND

Rating: 6

In Century just south of the Alabama border

Pensacola map, grid d1, page 40

Majestic pines throw dappled shade over large, grassy sites set on a peninsula extending into an irregularly shaped artificial lake. The shimmering waters of Lake Stone (sometimes called Stone Lake) encircle this quiet, family-style campground favored by an older clientele and by locals for weekend getaways. Some campsites slope down to the water, and guests can fish from their sites—when there is water, that is. A nearby boat ramp is part of the county-run park. A couple of years ago, the lake had been drained, but it is back in business now with "pretty good fishing."

Campsites, facilities: All 76 RV and tent sites have water, electricity, and picnic tables. Restrooms, showers, a playground, and two dump stations are provided. Restaurants and grocery stores are located about three miles away. Children are welcome. Leashed pets are permitted.

Reservations, fees: Reservations are not accepted. Sites are $11.05 per night. Campers age 60 and older pay $6.69 nightly for a site. Credit cards are not accepted. Maximum stay is 45 days.

Directions: From U.S. 29 on the south end of Century, turn west on State Road 4 (across from the courthouse). Drive 1.5 miles to the park, at left. The entrance is the second driveway.

Contact: Lake Stone Campground, 801 West State Road 4, Century, FL 32535, 850/256-5555.

2 MYSTIC SPRINGS AIRSTREAM PARK

Rating: 6

North of Molino, just south of McDavid, off of U.S. 29

Pensacola map, grid d2, page 40

Got an Airstream trailer, or traveling with someone who does? You're welcome here except on rally weekends, when the park can be full. This wooded, 10-acre park on the banks of the Escambia River is shaded by old oaks laden with Spanish moss. With the closing of Land Yacht Harbor near Melbourne, this is one of only two Airstream parks in Florida that we know about (the other one is near Christmas, Florida; see Christmas Airsteam Park in the Orlando chapter).

Campsites, facilities: There are 58 sites with full hookups. Some are pull-through; some have 50-amp service. A recreation pavilion and communal kitchen are available. Children are welcome. Leashed pets are permitted.

Reservations, fees: Reservations are recommended. Sites are $9 to $11 per night. Credit cards are not accepted.

Directions: From I-10, take Exit 10B onto U.S. 29 northbound. Drive about 23 miles north. Turn right on Mystic Springs Road and drive .7 mile.

Contact: Mystic Springs Airstream Park, 591 Mystic Springs Road, McDavid, FL 32568, 850/256-3280, website: www.geocities.com/mystic-springs.

3 MYSTIC SPRINGS

Rating: 7

North of Molino, just south of McDavid, off of U.S. 29

Pensacola map, grid d2, page 40

Right next door to Mystic Springs Airstream Park (see campground above), the Northwest Florida Water Management District is building a small reservation-only campground and picnic area on the west side of the Escambia River. Call to see if it's open. You won't need an Airstream to park here.

Campsites, facilities: Open on weekends only, this campground will accommodate a few RVs and tents. Call for more information. Children are welcome. Leashed pets are permitted.

Reservations, fees: Reservations are required.

You must get a $20 permit from the water management district in advance, and the place is open for weekend use only.

Directions: From I-10, take Exit 10B onto U.S. 29 northbound. Drive about 23 miles north. Turn right on Mystic Springs Road and drive .7 mile.

Contact: Northwest Florida Water Management District, 81 Water Management Drive, Havana, FL 32333, 850/539-5999.

4 COLDWATER RECREATION AREA
🏃 🏊 ⛽ 🐎 🚐 ⛺

Rating: 9

In Blackwater River State Forest west of Munson
Pensacola map, grid c1, page 40

Hankering for a trail ride amid oak, juniper, and soaring pine trees? This campground is restricted to horseback riders and to groups needing four or more campsites. Four horseback riding trails diverge from Jernigan Bridge near the campground. There's also a swimming area and canoe launch at the bridge. This area is sometimes used for major bird dog field trials. Sixty new paddocks have been added, so as many as 132 horses can be accommodated. Horses are not allowed in the creek.

Campsites, facilities: There are 69 RV and tent sites with water, electricity, picnic tables, and fire rings. A maximum of two tents or one RV is permitted on each site. Restrooms, showers, a dump station, an amphitheater, two corrals, stables, and outside paddocks are on the property. Kennels for 124 dogs and a dining hall/pavilion accommodating 110 people are available for an extra charge. Children are welcome. Leashed pets are permitted. Proof of a current negative Coggins test is required for each horse.

Reservations, fees: Reservations are required. Sites are $13 per night for five people, or $7 for people 65 and over or who are disabled. Proof of age or 100 percent disability is re-

quired for the discount. Credit cards are not accepted. The maximum stay is 14 days.

Directions: From Milton, drive 15 miles north on State Road 191. At Hardy Road, turn west and drive 5.5 miles to the park.

Contact: Blackwater Forestry Center, 11650 Munson Highway, Milton, FL 32570, 850/957-6140, fax 850/957-6143.

5 KRUL RECREATION AREA
🏃 🏊 ♿ 🚐 ⛺

Rating: 9

In Blackwater River State Forest west of Bear Lake and east of Munson
Pensacola map, grid b1, page 40

A hiking trail begins at the campground and ends at Bear Lake. The Sweetwater Trail (leading to a wheelchair-accessible 2,900-foot boardwalk and a suspended bridge) is accessible by wheelchair for .5 mile. The campground also has a seven-acre swimming lake.

Campsites, facilities: There are 45 sites with water and electricity and five primitive tent sites. A maximum of two tents or one RV is permitted on each site. Restrooms, showers, picnic tables, fire rings, and a dump station are available. Children are welcome. Pets are not permitted.

Reservations, fees: Reservations are not accepted. Sites are $13 per night for five people, or $7 for people 65 and over or who are 100 percent disabled. Proof of age or disability is required. Credit cards are not accepted. The maximum stay is 14 days.

Directions: From Munson, drive .75 mile east on State Road 4. The campground entrance is on the north side of the road.

Contact: Blackwater Forestry Center, 11650 Munson Highway, Milton, FL 32570, 850/957-6140, fax 850/957-6143.

6 BEAR LAKE RECREATION AREA
🚶🚴🛶🐎🚐🔺

Rating: 9

In Blackwater River State Forest
east of Munson

Pensacola map, grid b1, page 40

Located just east of the Krul Recreation Area (see previous campground), this spot is set on the shores of Bear Lake. Anglers can enjoy the 107-acre lake, but they can't bring boats with outboard motors. The fishing pier is wheelchair accessible. Mountain bikers can use a six-mile-long dirt trail. The Sweetwater hiking trail connects to the four-mile Bear Lake Loop Trail, and then to the 21-mile Jackson Trail. The closest stores for supplies are in Munson, 2.5 miles west of the campground.

Campsites, facilities: There are 40 sites, eight for tents only. Each site has water, and 20 have electricity. Three sites are pull-through; RVs as long as 35 feet can be accommodated. A maximum of two tents or one RV is permitted on each site. Restrooms, showers, picnic tables, fire rings, a dump station, and a boat ramp are provided. Children are welcome. Leashed pets are permitted.

Reservations, fees: Reservations are not accepted. Sites are $12 per night for five people, or $7 for people 65 and over or who are 100 percent disabled. Proof of age or disability is required. Credit cards are not accepted. The maximum stay is 14 days.

Directions: From Munson, drive 2.5 miles east on State Road 4. The campground entrance is on the north side of the road.

Contact: Blackwater Forestry Center, 11650 Munson Highway, Milton, FL 32570, 850/957-6140, fax 850/957-6143.

7 HURRICANE LAKE RECREATION AREA

Rating: 9

In Blackwater River State Forest
north of Baker

Pensacola map, grid b1, page 40

Campsites overlook Hurricane Lake, a 318-acre impoundment that is popular for fishing. Half the sites are on the north side; the others are on the south. Outboard motors are not permitted on the lake. A canoe launch with access to the Blackwater River and a six-mile hiking trail are near the campground. Blackwater River State Forest is known for its longleaf pine/wire grass ecosystem, which once covered 60 million acres in the Southeast. Don't be alarmed if you see scorched areas: State foresters use fire to control hardwoods and to promote the flowering of wire grass. Fire also helps protect the habitat of the endangered red-cockaded woodpecker. Look for bogs of carnivorous pitcher plants. Throughout the forest, you'll find unpaved roads good for mountain biking. Horse trails are threaded through the western portion of the forest.

Campsites, facilities: There are two campgrounds here: One on the north side and one on the south. The north side has 13 RV and tent sites with water and electricity, plus five sites with water only. RVs longer than 35 feet cannot be accommodated; none of the sites is pull-through. A maximum of two tents or one RV is permitted on each site. Restrooms, showers, picnic tables, fire rings, a dump station, and a boat ramp are on site. The south campground has 18 primitive sites with restrooms only. Children are welcome. Leashed pets are permitted.

Reservations, fees: Reservations are not accepted. Sites are $13 per night for five people, or $7 for people 65 and over or who are 100 percent disabled. Proof of age or disability is required. Credit cards are not accepted. The maximum stay is 14 days.

Directions: From Baker, drive six miles west

on State Road 4. Turn north on Beaver Creek Road and proceed about 8.5 miles. At Bullard Church Road, turn east and follow the signs to the campground.

Contact: Blackwater Forestry Center, 11650 Munson Highway, Milton, FL 32570, 850/957-6140, fax 850/957-6143.

8 KARICK LAKE

Rating: 9

In the far eastern part of Blackwater River State Forest north of Baker
Pensacola map, grid b1, page 40

Take a refreshing dip or cast your line for fish in 65-acre Karick Lake. Boats with outboard motors are prohibited. The fishing pier is wheelchair accessible. One major attraction is the campground's location at the eastern terminus of the 21-mile-long Jackson Trail, which meanders through the state forest, crossing the Blackwater River at Peaden Bridge. The campground, set in a hardwood forest, is actually two in one; half of the sites sit on one side of the lake and half on the other.

Campsites, facilities: There are 30 sites, 15 with water and electricity in the northern section and 15 with water only in the southern section. A maximum of two tents or one RV is permitted on each site. Restrooms, showers, picnic tables, fire rings, a dump station, and a boat ramp are provided. Children are welcome. Leashed pets are permitted.

Reservations, fees: Reservations are not accepted. Sites are $13 per night for five people, or $7 for people 65 and over or who are 100 percent disabled. Proof of age or disability is required. Credit cards are not accepted. The maximum stay is 14 days.

Directions: From Baker, drive eight miles north on County Road 189 to the campground entrance on the east side of the road.

Contact: Blackwater Forestry Center, 11650 Munson Highway, Milton, FL 32570, 850/957-6140, fax 850/957-6143.

9 LAKESIDE AT BARTH

Rating: 4

On U.S. 29 north of Pensacola near Molino
Pensacola map, grid d2, page 40

Frequented mostly by locals, this place offers country camping near the city. The area north of the paper mill town of Cantonment is off the well-worn tourist track, and you'll discover rolling hills of pine forests, tiny communities that are little more than crossroads, and people who say, "yes, ma'am" and "no, sir" in the Southern way. Nestled on 80 wooded acres, the campground has grassy sites with lots of shade. The swimming lake is .5 acre in size; the fishing lakes are five and eight acres. Pick up groceries in Cantonment.

Campsites, facilities: All 28 full-hookup, pull-through sites are for RVs and tents. A primitive group camping area accommodates some tents. Restrooms, showers, a playground, a covered pavilion, two man-made fishing lakes, and one swimming lake are available. Children are welcome. Leashed pets are permitted.

Reservations, fees: Reservations are not necessary. Sites are $13.50 per night for two people, plus $2 for each additional person. Credit cards are not accepted. RVers can stay as long as they like, but tenters are limited to two weeks.

Directions: From I-10 at Pensacola, take Exit 10B heading north on U.S. 29 and drive 16 miles. After you cross State Road 97, continue two miles to Barth Road. Turn east (right) and drive one mile to the campground.

Contact: Lakeside at Barth, 855 Barth Road, Molino, FL 32577, 850/587-2322.

10 ADVENTURES UNLIMITED OUTDOOR CENTER

Rating: 7

North of Milton
Pensacola map, grid c2, page 40

Billing itself as a getaway from city life, this

privately run resort/canoe concessionaire overlooks the confluence of Wolfe Creek and Coldwater Creek at Tomahawk Landing. It's a sprawling, 88-acre, canoeing-oriented complex with large cabins for groups, a small inn, small cottages, "camping cabins," and group activities for family reunions, birthday parties, and youth retreats. Canoeing and tubing package trips and hayrides are available, as are challenge rope courses for team building. On the property you'll find an old dam and millpond, a historic cemetery, and two riverside beaches. Adventures Unlimited also arranges one- to three-day-long canoe trips. Canoes equipped with camping equipment are available (with reservations).

Campsites, facilities: There are 10 RV sites with water and electricity and 10 primitive tent sites. Restrooms, showers, picnic tables, and fire rings are provided. A game field, volleyball court, limited store, small playground, cabins, canoes, and inner tubes (for tubing on the river) are available. The four-room Schoolhouse Inn was once a school that served a tiny community nearby. Families and groups are welcome. Pets are not permitted.

Reservations, fees: Reservations are recommended. Sites are $20 per night for four people, plus $3 for each additional person. One tent is permitted per site. Major credit cards are accepted.

Directions: From Milton, drive 12 miles north on State Road 87. Turn east at the Adventures Unlimited sign. Drive four miles to the campground, which is just south of the confluence of Coldwater Creek and Wolfe Creek.

Contact: Adventures Unlimited Outdoor Center, 8974 Tomahawk Landing Road, Milton, FL 32570, 850/623-6197 or 800/BE-YOUNG (800/239-6864), fax 850/626-3124, website: www.adventuresunlimited.com.

11 BLACKWATER RIVER STATE PARK

Rating: 10

In Blackwater River State Forest

Pensacola map, grid c2, page 40

With just 30 sites, this campground fills up fast in the busy summer months, but it's worth the effort if you require a more developed campground than those nearby. The 590-acre state park is located on the south side of Blackwater River State Forest, the largest state forest in Florida at more than 200,000 acres. The tea-colored river, a popular stream for canoeing and kayaking, flows through the park. Don't expect white water; the river is quite shallow in places and the bottom is sandy. Canoe concessions are located nearby. The closest is Blackwater Canoe Rental at 10274 Pond Road in Milton, located on the state park access road; phone 850/623-0235 or 800/967-6789; website: www.blackwatercanoe.com. The big sandbars on each bend in the river are strikingly white in contrast to the darkness of the water; stop now and then to swim or soak up some rays on the broad ivory banks. In the summer, you may glimpse a Mississippi kite, a graceful, hawklike bird with gray underparts and a pale head, winging overhead. At other times, look for river otters, deer, turkey, and bobcats as you drift lazily downstream.

Campsites, facilities: There are 30 sites with water, electricity, picnic tables, and fire rings. Wheelchair-accessible restrooms and showers are available. Children are welcome. Pets are allowed with proof of vaccination.

Reservations, fees: Reservations are recommended; call ReserveAmerica at 800/326-3521. Sites are $8 per night for four people, plus $2 for each additional person, $2 for electricity, and $2 per pet. Major credit cards are accepted. The maximum stay is 14 days.

Directions: From I-10 at Milton, use Exit 31 on State Road 87 northbound. Travel .5 mile, then turn east on U.S. 90. Drive five more miles to Harold and turn north on the state park access road. The campground is three miles away.

Contact: Blackwater River State Park, 7720 Deaton Bridge Road, Holt, FL 32564, 850/983-5363, fax 850/983-5364, website: www.floridastateparks.org.

12 EAGLE'S LANDING RV PARK

Rating: 6

Near Holt east of Milton
Pensacola map, grid b2, page 40

The owners describe this sunny park as the perfect overnight stop. It's certainly close to the interstate, and convenient to shopping and outdoor recreation throughout the area. This 10-acre park has 60 grassy sites, 24 of which are available for seasonal stays. Tents are allowed at the management's option.

Campsites, facilities: There are 60 pull-through sites with full hookups and picnic tables. Sites are a whopping 85 feet long and 35 feet wide, and some have 50-amp service. Restrooms, showers, laundry facilities, a recreation room, dog-walk area, and telephone service are available. Children are welcome. Leashed pets are permitted.

Reservations, fees: Reservations are recommended. Sites are $15 to $17 per night for two people, plus $2 per extra person over age four. Major credit cards are accepted. Long-term rates are available.

Directions: From I-10, take Exit 45 and go north .25 mile to the park entrance on the left.

Contact: Eagle's Landing RV Park, 4504 Log Lake Road, Holt, FL 32564, 850/537-9657, fax 850/537-9625, website: www.campingandcampgrounds.com/eagle.htm.

13 ESCAMBIA RIVER WATER MANAGEMENT AREA

Rating: 8

Along the Escambia River
Pensacola map, grid d2, page 40

Locals like to hop in a boat and head out here for a few days, picking camping spots atop the natural levees created by rivers and streams. Covering a whopping 53 square miles and hugging the banks of the Escambia River for approximately 30 miles, this beautiful floodplain is packed with hardwoods such as shaggy-limbed cypress, gums, and oaks, as well as stands of Atlantic white cedar and willow oak. (The timber was logged in the past but has substantially regrown.) Because the area is so huge, you'll usually be alone. A boat or canoe is the best means of getting around. Hunters head to these parts from November through January, so wear bright orange clothing when you're on land. Small-game hunting continues through early March, and turkey hunters show up in March and April, but these folks should not be a threat to campers. (Even so, wear an orange hat or vest if you feel uncomfortable.) Look for spotted softshell turtles and rambunctious river otters along the Escambia. The land flanking the waterway once teemed with deer, but they were largely hunted out of existence and only now are making a comeback. Turkeys and squirrels are plentiful. For wildlife viewing, spring is the best season to visit. You'll see quite a few birds migrating north after spending the winter in the tropics. Fishing in the Escambia River and its tributary creeks is also popular.

Campsites, facilities: There are virtually unlimited opportunities for hikers and boaters to enjoy primitive camping in this 2.5-mile-wide swath of land extending along both sides of the Escambia River north from Escambia Bay to about two miles south of the Alabama border. Five designated primitive camping areas can accommodate an indeterminate number of campers, but you are allowed to camp anywhere you find dry land. There are no facilities. Bring water and camping supplies. Pack out trash. Children and pets are permitted.

Reservations, fees: Reservations are not necessary. Camping is free.

Directions: There are numerous places to access this land. In the southern end, boat launches are available where U.S. 90 and County Road 184 cross the Escambia River. In the northern end, boat launches are available at the end of several dirt roads. Contact the water district for more details. Hikers can access a trail by heading west on County Road 184 across the Escambia River, proceeding about two miles, and then turning right onto a dirt road. The trailhead is located where the dirt road veers sharply left. The trail heads north, then loops east to the river, a distance of about three miles. It's a good idea to call the water district ahead of time to check on access and flood conditions.

Contact: Northwest Florida Water Management District, Division of Land Management and Acquisition, 81 Water Management Drive, Havana, FL 32333, 850/539-5999.

⑭ CEDAR LAKES RV PARK & CAMPGROUND

Rating: 5

Near Milton

Pensacola map, grid b3, page 40

Opened in 2000, this park sits on 16 acres and features two three-acre, spring-fed lakes surrounded by woods. It's an all-ages park, but older campers are preferred. Lots are shady, and the sunsets are beautiful. Campers can fish in the lakes. The park is continually being improved and enlarged.

Campsites, facilities: There are 18 RV sites for overnighters, with seven to 14 available for seasonal visitors. Almost all sites are pull-through, with no length restrictions; the sites have full hookups or water and electricity. Eight tent

sites are set apart from the RVs. Restrooms, showers, laundry facilities, and telephone service are available. Also on the premises are lakes, a small clubhouse (for potluck dinners, card games, and the like), and a dog-walk area. Children are allowed. Leashed pets are permitted.

Reservations, fees: Reservations are recommended. Sites are $16.50 per night for two people, plus $3 per extra person. Credit cards are not accepted. Long-term rates are available.

Directions: From I-10, take Exit 28 south to County Road 184 (Hickory Hammock Road) .75 mile away. Turn east and drive one mile to Coachman Road. Then go south to the park entrance on the left.

Contact: Cedar Lakes RV Park & Campground, 4312 Coachman Road, Milton, FL 32583, 850/626-9291, website: www.cedarlakesrv-park.com.

⑮ MILTON/GULF PINES KOA (FORMERLY GULF PINES RV RESORT)

Rating: 7

Off I-10 near Milton

Pensacola map, grid c2, page 40

This convenient, easy-on, easy-off RV park offers respite to travelers passing through and to visitors seeking to explore the Panhandle area from a base with fancier amenities than are available at most spots near here. The wooded park has a store, playground, miniature golf, pool, and recreation room.

Campsites, facilities: There are 96 pull-through RV sites with full hookups, picnic tables, and optional phone service, plus 20 tent sites. Restrooms, showers, a dump station, laundry facilities, a pool, a clubhouse, miniature golf, playground, a store, and a dog-walk area are available. All areas are wheelchair accessible. Children are welcome. Leashed pets are permitted.

Reservations, fees: Reservations are recommended. Sites are $26 to $29 per night for two people, plus $3 per extra person. Major credit cards are accepted. Long-term (up to six months) or seasonal stays are available.

Directions: From I-10, take Exit 31 at State Road 87 and drive north 300 feet to the campground.

Contact: Milton/Gulf Pines KOA, 8700 Gulf Pines Drive, Milton, FL 32583, 850/623-0808, fax 850/623-6618, website: www.miltonkoa.com.

16 CEDAR PINES CAMPGROUND
≈ 🏠 ♿ 🚐 ⛰

Rating: 5

North of Milton
Pensacola map, grid c2, page 40

More than 200 huge oak trees provide shade at this pretty campground near Blackwater River State Forest and Whiting Field Naval Air Station. Groceries and other supplies can be obtained within three miles. From here, you're just 31 miles from Brewton, Alabama, if you want to add another state to your "been there" list. Closer to home is the big town in this area, Milton, which once went by the names Scratch Ankle and Hard Scrabble.

Campsites, facilities: There are 40 RV sites with full hookups and cable TV, and four tent sites with water and electricity. Thirty-four sites are pull-through, and all can accommodate double slide-out RVs. Many sites have patios or picnic tables. Restrooms, showers, laundry facilities, a clubhouse, a pool, and a dump station are available. The restrooms, clubhouse, and library are wheelchair accessible. Children are welcome. Leashed pets are permitted.

Reservations, fees: Reservations are recommended. Sites are $18 per night for two people, plus $1 for each additional person. Credit cards are not accepted. Long-term stays are allowed.

Directions: From U.S. 90 in Milton, drive four miles north on State Road 87. The park is on the east side of the road.

Contact: Cedar Pines Campground, 6436 Robie Road, Milton, FL 32570, 850/623-8869, fax 850/623-1520, website: www.cedarpines.com.

17 RIVIERA NATURIST RESORT
≈ 🏠 ♿ 🚐 ⛰

Rating: 5

Northwest of Pace and Milton
Pensacola map, grid c2, page 40

Set on 16 shady, wooded acres, this family-oriented resort offers a haven for those who like to camp in the buff. Nudity is required—weather permitting. Guests are clothed when practical (in cold weather); nude when possible (other times). Identification is required because management doesn't want to encourage curiosity seekers. Cameras are not allowed without permission.

Campsites, facilities: This nudist campground has 29 grassy RV spaces, 10 with full hookups available for vacationers; primitive tent sites are nearly unlimited. The resort has picnic tables, restrooms, showers, a swimming pool and Jacuzzi, a volleyball field, horseshoes, *pétanque* (a French game similar to cricket), and a .5-mile nature trail. An area is set aside for suntanning. Children are welcome with parents. Leashed pets are permitted.

Reservations, fees: Reservations are recommended. Sites are $22 to $28 per night. Major credit cards are accepted. The maximum stay is one month during the summer and three to five months during the winter.

Directions: From I-10 at Pensacola, take Exit 17. Turn east on U.S. 90. Drive 6.5 miles to County Road 197A/Woodbine Road. Turn north on Woodbine Road and go two miles, then turn east on Guernsey Road. The park is .4 mile away, on the north side of the road.

Contact: Riviera Naturist Resort, P.O. Box 2233, 5000 Guernsey Road, Pace, FL 32571, 850/994-3665, fax 850/994-1906, website: www.sunburst-rivieraclubs.com/riviera.html.

18 TALL OAKS CAMPGROUND

Rating: 2

On the west side of Pensacola
Pensacola map, grid d3, page 40

Set on five acres shaded with azalea, magnolia, and live oaks, this campground caters to overnight travelers, as well as long-term visitors. A shopping center .25 mile away offers citified essentials—groceries, a hair salon, and a restaurant, for instance. Within a five-minute drive are golf courses, a hospital, and the Five Flags Speedway. The urban location is convenient to Pensacola attractions such as historic Seville Square, where you'll find quaint restaurants, bars, and shops, and the National Museum of Naval Aviation. (The museum, one of the world's largest dedicated to air and space technology, displays the first airplane to cross the Atlantic and all manner of military aircraft. It also salutes the famous Blue Angels, the U.S. Navy's precision flight demonstration team based in Pensacola.)

Campsites, facilities: There are 70 sandy RV spaces with full hookups and an open wooded area for primitive tent sites. Picnic tables are provided at about half the sites. Amenities include restrooms, showers, laundry facilities, vending machines, a pay phone, and a dump station. Children are welcome. Leashed pets are permitted.

Reservations, fees: Reservations are not necessary. Sites are $12 to $18 per night. Major credit cards are accepted. Long-term rates are available.

Directions: From I-10 eastbound, take Exit 5 onto Alternate U.S. 90/Nine Mile Road. Drive one mile east, then turn south on Pine Forest Road and continue to the park on your right. From I-10 westbound, take Exit 7 onto State Road 297/Pine Forest Road. Drive north for .5 mile to the entrance.

Contact: Tall Oaks Campground, 9301 Pine Forest Road, Pensacola, FL 32534, 850/479-3212.

19 MAYFAIR MOTEL AND RV PARK

Rating: 2

In west Pensacola
Pensacola map, grid c3, page 40

Shopping and restaurants are on hand, and you can swim in the motel's pool (next door). The park's urban location is convenient to Pensacola's historical attractions and the National Museum of Naval Aviation (for description, see previous campground); the beach is within a 15-minute drive. There's a lot to see and do in Pensacola, a city that considers itself to have been ruled by five countries since its founding in the 1500s: France, Britain, Spain, the Confederacy, and the United States. Three historic districts lie to the southeast of the campground: The North Hill Preservation District is a residential area where the city's wealthy once lived in grand homes; the Palafox Historic District embraces the commercial district and the industrial waterfront; and the more-trendy Seville Historic District has museums, parks, and old buildings housing restaurants and shops.

Campsites, facilities: There are 24 RV sites with full hookups; 10 are available for overnighters and 14 for seasonal visitors. Restrooms, showers, a dump station, and laundry facilities are provided. No pull-through RVs, please. Children are welcome. Leashed pets are permitted.

Reservations, fees: Reservations are recommended. Sites are $20 per night. Major credit cards are accepted. Long-term stays are OK.

Directions: From I-10, exit on State Road 297/Pine Forest Road and drive 3.5 miles south to U.S. 90/Mobile Highway. Turn east on U.S. 90 and look for the campground/motel complex.

Contact: Mayfair Motel and RV Park, 4540 Mobile Highway, Pensacola, FL 32506, 850/455-8561, fax 850/455-0090.

20 BIG LAGOON STATE PARK

🏃 🚵 🛶 🚐 🏕 ⛱ ♿ 🚍 ⛰

Rating: 10

On Perdido Key southwest of Pensacola

Pensacola map, grid d4, page 40

The campground at this 698-acre state park is located along a series of sandy ridges with tall slash pines towering overhead. Most sites have thick foliage screens between them that afford good privacy. Bird-watchers will be delighted here because the wind-whipped sandpine scrub, gnarled slash pines, and swampy salt marshes harbor loons, grebes, cormorants, great blue herons, and many other species seen daily. During the fall, this is one of the last resting places for birds migrating south across the Gulf of Mexico. You may also see gray foxes, raccoons, skunks, and opossums. Hikers can improve their chances of spotting these animals by walking the one-mile boardwalk; there's also the 3.5-mile "Girl Scout Cookie" hiking trail looping through the park. Two swimming areas are on Big Lagoon, near the Intracoastal Waterway. Boating, canoeing, windsurfing, and fishing opportunities are abundant because the park is encircled almost completely by water. If you're hankering for seaside fun on the Gulf of Mexico, registered campers are permitted to use the white-sand beach at Perdido Key State Park, located five miles west, at no additional charge. Special events are held here throughout the year, including a bluegrass festival in May, concerts on holiday weekends, and Christmas and Halloween celebrations.

Campsites, facilities: The state park campground has 49 sites with piped water and electricity; an additional 26 sites have no electric hookups. Picnic tables, grills, restrooms, showers, a playground, and a dump station are provided. The park also has a boat ramp, three nature trails, an amphitheater, and two swimming areas. Campsites 8 and 9 are wheelchair accessible, as are the restrooms, boardwalks, and some picnic pavilions. Beach wheelchairs are available upon request. Children are welcome. Pets are allowed in the campground with proof of vaccination.

Reservations, fees: Reservations are recommended; call ReserveAmerica at 800/326-3521. From March 1 through August 31, sites are $12 per night for four people, plus $2 for each additional person and $2 for each pet. Between September 1 and February 28, sites are $10. Major credit cards are accepted. The maximum stay is 14 days.

Directions: From Pensacola, drive 12 miles west on State Road 292 to Perdido Key. Turn east on State Road 292A/Gulf Beach Highway and drive .5 mile to the park entrance.

Contact: Big Lagoon State Park, 12301 Gulf Beach Highway, Pensacola, FL 32507, 850/492-1595, fax 850/492-4380, website: www.floridastateparks.org.

21 PLAYA DEL RIO RV PARK

🚵 🚣 🛶 🚐 🏕 ♿ 🚍

Rating: 9

On Perdido Key

Pensacola map, grid d4, page 40

This resort-style park's location on Perdido Key and the white-sand Gulf of Mexico beaches can't be beat no matter where you wind up parking your rig. Fronting on the Ole River with a view of Ono Island, this park offers boat dockage for campground guests' boats—and even a free paddleboat and kayak for their use. Bird-watching and various boating tours are available, and the beach is across the street via a short path. Fish off the dock or try your hand at catching crabs from the dock.

Campsites, facilities: There are 28 RV sites for rigs up to 45 feet. Some sites have concrete pads; all have full hookups, cable TV, and phone availability. Restrooms, showers, a dump station, laundry facilities, fishing dock, community room, barbecue grills, and picnic area are on site. The restrooms, laundry, community room, and boat docks are wheelchair accessible. Children are welcome. Leashed pets are permitted.

Reservations, fees: Reservations are recommended. Sites are $20 to $45 (highest rates are from March 1 through September 14) per night for two people, plus $2 per extra person. Major credit cards are accepted. Long-term stays are allowed.

Directions: From I-10 westbound, take Exit 72 south onto State Road 297 (Pine Forest Road). At Blue Angel Parkway, turn right and head south to Sorrento Road (Highway 292), which changes names to Perdido Key Drive after the Intracoastal Bridge. The resort is 4.5 miles on the right. From I-10 eastbound, take Alabama State Road 59 south through the Alabama towns of Foley and Gulf Shores. At Alabama State Road 182, turn left and continue east. The road changes names to Florida Highway 292, then to Perdido Key Drive.

Contact: Playa del Rio RV Park, 16990 Perdido Key Drive, Perdido Key, FL 32507, 850/492-0904 or 888/200-0904, fax 850/492-4471, website: www.playadelrio.com.

22 PENSACOLA/PERDIDO BAY KOA

Rating: 6

West of Perdido Key
Pensacola map, grid b3, page 40

Despite its name, this campground is actually in Alabama across Perdido Bay from Florida. We include it because it's less than a mile from the Florida state line and might be an option if the other parks are full. The owners call it "snowbird heaven."

Campsites, facilities: There are 50 full-hookup sites available for overnighters and seasonal visitors; 10 tents can be accommodated. Restrooms, showers, a dump station, laundry facilities, and telephone service are available. On the premises are a heated pool, a boat dock, a clubhouse, shuffleboard courts, a dog-walk area, and boat access to Perdido Bay and the Gulf of Mexico. Children are welcome. Leashed pets are permitted.

Reservations, fees: Reservations are recom-

mended. Sites are $25 per night for two people, plus $3 per extra person and $2.75 for cable TV. Major credit cards are accepted. Long-term rates are available.

Directions: From Perdido Key, drive west on U.S. 98 and cross the bridge to Alabama. Turn left (south) on State Route 99 to the park.

Contact: Pensacola/Perdido Bay KOA, 33951 Spinnaker Drive, Lillian, AL 36549, 251/961-1717, website: www.koa.com/where/FL/01102.htm.

23 FORT PICKENS CAMPGROUND

Rating: 10

Within Gulf Islands National Seashore on the western end of Santa Rosa Island
Pensacola map, grid c4, page 40

Sea oats on the sand dunes wave gently in the breeze, and the powder-white beach beckons campers to kick off their shoes and take a dip in the warm Gulf of Mexico waters. Campsites are split among six loops; tenters are accommodated in loops B and D, and they'll enjoy the luxury of having the fewest neighbors. The campground is within walking distance of one of the world's best beaches. Ride your bike up and down the main road for views of the Gulf, or try surf casting at water's edge. At night, store your ice chests inside to foil curious raccoons. Note that the campground is very busy during the summer months. In fact, the vacation season in Florida's Panhandle is the reverse of Central and South Florida. Here, the big "season" is summer, not winter.

West of the campground is the massive complex of Fort Pickens, built in 1834 to defend Pensacola Bay and its naval yard. As technology changed warfare over the years, alterations were made to the fort, and the Army pulled out in 1940. The fort also served as a prison that at one time held Geronimo, the famed Apache chief. Bring a flashlight: Some of the passageways are not well lit. Guided tours of the fort are available.

Campsites, facilities: This National Park Service campground offers 168 sites with water and electric hookups and 42 tent sites without electricity. Picnic tables, grills, restrooms, showers, and a dump station are provided. There's also a campground store, an interpretive nature trail, and a bike trail. Two sites are wheelchair accessible. Children are welcome. Leashed pets are permitted. Only one RV or two tents are allowed on each site.

Reservations, fees: Reservations are accepted through the National Park Service reservations system; call 800/365-2267 or see www.reservations.nps.gov. Sites are $20 per night for six people (or immediate family members), plus the park entrance fee of $8. Major credit cards are accepted. Overnight stays are limited to 44 days per calendar year, with no more than 14 days between March 1 and Labor Day.

Directions: At the dead end of U.S. 98 in Pensacola Beach, drive west on Fort Pickens Road/State Road 399 for eight miles to the park entrance.

Contact: Gulf Islands National Seashore Park Headquarters, 1801 Gulf Breeze Parkway, Gulf Breeze, FL 32561, 850/934-2600, 850/934-2621, or 800/365-2267 (reservations).

24 PELICAN PALMS RV PARK

Rating: 5

Southeast of Milton
Pensacola map, grid c3, page 40

A good base for exploring the canoeing, cycling, hiking, and fishing opportunities nearby, this park is three miles from a PGA golf course and other courses. It's also a convenient overnight stop from the interstate that welcomes tenters. Tall pines dot the park. Sites are level and grassy.

Campsites, facilities: Thirty-one RV sites are available; 23 are pull-through and all have full hookups. Six sites have 50-amp service, and 10 have picnic tables. Tenters can choose from 10 spots, some with water and electricity. Restrooms, showers, a dump station, laundry facilities, a recreation room, and a pool are on site. Recently added are a small store and book exchange. Children are welcome. Leashed pets are permitted.

Reservations, fees: Reservations are not usually necessary. Sites are $19 per night for two people, plus $2 per extra person. For $2, add 50-amp service. Major credit cards are accepted. Stay as long as you like.

Directions: From I-10, take Exit 26 and drive south on County Road 191 for .1 mile. The park is on the east side of the road.

Contact: Pelican Palms RV Park, 3700 Garcon Point Road, Milton, FL 32583, 850/623-0576, website: www.pelicanpalmsrvpark.com.

25 BY THE BAY RV PARK AND CAMPGROUND

Rating: 7

On the eastern side of Escambia Bay, just south of the I-10 bridge
Pensacola map, grid c3, page 40

In the fall, mallards waddle around a pond in the center of this six-acre campground set in a secluded wooded area on Escambia Bay. Just three miles from the interstate, the peaceful country park is convenient to Pensacola and makes a good stop for overnighters traveling through the area. If you'll be staying more than just one night, though, you may want to swim or fish in the bay. Note that the campground roads are dirt, not paved.

Nearby is the Garcon Point Peninsula, a stretch of wild land administered by the Northwest Florida Water Management District (850/484-5125), where bird-watching, hiking, beach walking, surf fishing, and nature study are popular pursuits. This is one of several places in the state where you can see carnivorous vegetation—pitcher plants that lure passing insects with a display that looks like a blossom, and then, chomp! Also, if you head to Garcon Point in the spring or summer, you're likely to see rainbow-colored displays of wild-flowers. The point separates Escambia Bay from East Bay. Animals of interest here include the marsh rabbit and southeastern kestrel, along with deer and wading birds. Swamps, wet prairies, and pine and hardwood forests make up most of the landscape, rounded out by beachfront and salt marshes. Head south from Avalon Beach on County Road 281 or County Road 191 to reach Garcon Point.

Campsites, facilities: There are 35 sites with full hookups; RVs up to 45 feet can be accommodated among some of the sites, and eight of the sites are pull-through. Four tent sites are available with water and electricity. Each site has a picnic table. Restrooms, showers, and laundry facilities are provided. Children are welcome. Leashed pets under 30 pounds (no aggressive dogs) are permitted.

Reservations, fees: Reservations are recommended. Sites are $20 to $24 per night for two people, plus $2 for each additional person. For full hookups, 50-amp service, and waterfront sites, add $2 for each amenity. Credit cards are not accepted. Long-term rates are available.

Directions: From I-10, take Exit 22 and go south on Avalon Boulevard for two miles. Turn right on Pearson Road and follow it as it winds around and becomes Michael Drive. The campground is at the end of the road.

Contact: By the Bay RV Park and Campground, 5550 Michael Drive, Milton, FL 32583, 850/623-0262. Mailing address: 4281 Highway 90, Pace, FL 32571.

26 YELLOW RIVER WATER MANAGEMENT AREA

Rating: 8

Along the Yellow River off I-10
Pensacola map, grid c3, page 40

Sandwiched between I-10 and the northern boundary of Eglin Air Force Base (see campground in this chapter), this tract administered by the Northwest Florida Water Management

District is a place where, if you're lucky, you might see a secretive, nocturnal Florida black bear. Look for mountain laurel and, in spring, the showy blossoms of the spider lily. Realistically, the only way to get around the area is by boat or canoe. The landscape is quite varied: With 18 types of habitat ranging from tidal marsh to high, dry xeric uplands, it is one of the water district's most varied parcels of land.

Campsites, facilities: Primitive camping is allowed throughout the area, but there are no designated campsites and no facilities except for eight boat ramps. Bring water, food, and camping supplies. Pack out trash. Children and pets are permitted.

Reservations, fees: Reservations are not necessary. Camping is free.

Directions: There are numerous boat ramps on the river. One of the easiest to reach is the Sigler Lake ramp off I-10. From I-10 at Holt, take Exit 11 and head south on County Road 189. It will become a dirt road that ends at the river. Another boat ramp is accessible by exiting I-10 at State Road 87 (Exit 31) and heading south. Cross the river and look for the Broxson boat ramp on your left.

Contact: Northwest Florida Water Management District, 81 Water Management Drive, Havana, FL 32333, 850/539-5999.

27 EMERALD BEACH RV PARK

Rating: 8

On U.S. 98, between Fort Walton Beach and Pensacola
Pensacola map, grid b3, page 40

The park slopes gently down to the water and a 300-foot sandy white beach. This area is marketed by local tourist councils as the "Emerald Coast," a reference to the emerald green waters offshore. Although you won't find much shade here, seven lucky RVers can overlook Santa Rosa Sound. Everyone is parked close together, but campers in big rigs don't seem to mind; they are more interested in fishing, boating, and swimming. The location of the park is central to Fort Walton Beach (14 miles east) and to Pensacola (18 miles west).

Campsites, facilities: There are 71 RV slots with full hookups; 37 are pull-through. Restrooms, showers, a dump station, a pool, and shuffleboard courts are available. Children are welcome. Leashed pets are permitted.

Reservations, fees: Reservations are recommended. Sites are $35 to $44 per night for two people, plus $2 per extra person. Major credit cards are accepted. Long-term stays are OK.

Directions: From Navarre, drive 1.5 miles east on U.S. 98. The park is on the south side of the road.

Contact: Emerald Beach RV Park, 8885 Navarre Parkway, Navarre, FL 32566, 850/939-3431, website: www.emeraldbeachrvpark.com.

28 NAVARRE BEACH CAMPGROUND

Rating: 8

On U.S. 98, between Fort Walton Beach and Pensacola

Pensacola map, grid b3, page 40

Tall pines give shade and atmosphere to this manicured, resort-style family campground that boasts its own beach and a fishing pier on Santa Rosa Sound. Recently added is a computer room with high-speed access. The managers also are planning to add a hot tub and "super sites" with 80-amp service for 40-foot plus rigs; call to see if they are ready. Children under 12 must be accompanied by an adult at all times, and all kids swimming in the pool must be supervised by a grown-up. The park's maxim: "Do unto others as you would have them do unto you." Navarre Beach is still relatively quiet, although development sprawls along the U.S. 98 corridor and shopping centers, fast-food eateries, and the other accoutrements of modern life are rapidly moving in.

Campsites, facilities: All 130 sites have full hookups and cable TV. Six tent sites are avail-

able. Restrooms, showers, two laundry facilities, a dump station, a game room, a fishing pier, a pool, horseshoe pits, shuffleboard and basketball courts, a store, cabin rentals, and a playground are available. Campfires are permitted at a communal fire pit. The bathhouse and pavilion are wheelchair accessible. Children are welcome. Small pets are permitted at the discretion of the management; for example, no "potbellied pigs" would be admitted.

Reservations, fees: Reservations are recommended. Sites are $34 to $46 per night for two people, plus $2.50 for each additional person. Major credit cards are accepted. Long-term stays are allowed.

Directions: From the Navarre Beach Bridge, drive one mile east on U.S. 98.

Contact: Navarre Beach Campground, 9201 Navarre Parkway, Navarre, FL 32566, 850/939-2188, fax 850/939-4712, website: www.navbeach.com.

29 MAGNOLIA BEACH CAMPGROUND

Rating: 7

East of Navarre

Pensacola map, grid b3, page 40

Swim on the park's sandy beach or cast a line for a seafood dinner from the long pier. Some sites overlook Santa Rosa Sound, which gets less boat traffic here than in other locations. From this five-acre park, you can combine your seaside delights with the wilderness. Just drive up State Road 87 toward Blackwater River State Park and the surrounding state forest for canoeing and other adventures.

Campsites, facilities: This campground has 50 RV sites with full hookups. Restrooms, showers, laundry facilities, and a 600-foot-long fishing pier are provided. You can tie your boat up to the pier to load or unload passengers or gear, but the boat cannot be left there longer than that. The water around the pier is somewhat shallow, and jumping and diving are not permitted. Children are welcome, but those under 12 must be supervised at all times. Pets under 15 pounds are permitted on a leash.

Reservations, fees: Reservations are suggested. Sites are $19 to $25 per night for two people, plus $2 per extra person. Credit cards are not accepted. Long-term rates are available.

Directions: From Navarre, drive three miles east on U.S. 98. The park is on the south side.

Contact: Magnolia Beach Campground, 9807 Navarre Parkway, Navarre, FL 32566, 850/939-2717 or 877/375-4600, website: www.magnolia beach.com.

30 PLAYGROUND RV PARK

Rating: 3

On the north side of Fort Walton Beach
Pensacola map, grid b3, page 40

Although located beside a busy highway with strip shopping centers and heavy commercial activity, this park offers shady, wooded sites and is nearly always full. It's convenient to Eglin Air Force Base, and beaches are only six miles away.

Campsites, facilities: This mobile home community and apartment complex has 65 RV sites with full hookups and cable TV. Eleven sites are pull-through. Restrooms, showers, laundry facilities, and a dump station are available. Children are welcome. Small, leashed pets are permitted.

Reservations, fees: Reservations are accepted only a few days in advance. Sites are $24 per night for two people, plus $2 for each additional person over the age of six. Credit cards are not accepted. Long-term stays are OK.

Directions: From the junction of U.S. 98 and State Road 189 in Fort Walton Beach, drive north on State Road 189 for four miles. The park is on the east (right) side of the road.

Contact: Playground RV Park, 777 Beal Parkway, Fort Walton Beach, FL 32547, 850/862-3513.

31 RIVER'S EDGE RV CAMPGROUND

Rating: 8

South of Holt
Pensacola map, grid b2, page 40

Sprawling across 144 acres on the banks of the Yellow River, this campground is heavily wooded and peaceful, suitable as a destination park or as an overnight spot. Even the biggest rigs can be accommodated on the extra-large pull-through sites. The campground provides 24-hour security. While you're here, fish from the river's edge or on nearby Log Lake and hike the one-mile nature trail. An old, quaint, un-passable bridge spans the Yellow River. Blackwater River State Forest is close by. Supplies are available in Crestview, about 10 miles east of the park.

Campsites, facilities: Of the 110 RV sites, most have full hookups. Twenty primitive tent spots are set apart from the travel trailers. Picnic tables, fire pits, restrooms, showers, laundry facilities, a dump station, a boat launch, playground, clubhouse, pavilion, and camp circle are on the grounds. Children are welcome. Leashed pets are permitted.

Reservations, fees: Reservations are recommended. Sites are $15 per night for two adults, plus $2 for each additional person. No credit cards are accepted. Long-term stays are OK.

Directions: From I-10 near Holt, take Exit 45 and drive south on State Road 189 for 1.5 miles to the park.

Contact: River's Edge RV Campground, 4001 Log Lake Road, Holt, FL 32564, 850/537-2267.

32 LAZY DAYS RV PARK

Rating: 2

East of Niceville in Freeport
Pensacola map, grid a2, page 40

This roadside RV haven attracts snowbirds in

the winter and travelers passing through year-round. Oaks and maples shade some sites; other spots at the 8.5-acre park are open and sunny. The beach is 10 miles away. Points of interest in the area include Eden State Gardens, Seaside, Grayton Beach, and Destin.

Campsites, facilities: There are 25 full-hookup RV sites with optional cable TV and telephone service. Picnic tables, restrooms, showers, a dump station, laundry facilities, a game room, and horseshoe pits are available. Children are welcome. Pets are allowed on a leash. Pop-top trailers are not allowed.

Reservations, fees: Reservations are recommended. Sites are $20 per night for two people, plus $2 for each additional person over age five. Credit cards are not accepted. Long-term rates are available.

Directions: From I-10 at De Funiak Springs, take Exit 85 and head south on U.S. 331 for 17 miles. Or, from U.S. 98 west of Panama City, drive seven miles north on U.S. 331 to the park.

Contact: Lazy Days RV Park, 18655 U.S. 331 South, Freeport, FL 32439, 850/835-4606, website: www.lazydaysrv.net.

33 EGLIN AIR FORCE BASE

Rating: 8

South of I-10 and between Pensacola and De Funiak Springs

Pensacola map, grid b3, page 40

One of the largest swaths of wilderness in Florida is controlled by the Department of Defense (DOD). Although most people don't think of the military as being in the wild woods business, the DOD has been an admirable caretaker of the grounds in recent years. For instance, the military went so far as to take special steps to save endangered red-cockaded woodpeckers by planting trees and protecting the rare birds' homes from fire.

What you give up here in lack of amenities you get back in an astounding variety of natural settings for camping. They include sites on the Choctawhatchee and East Bays, which may be favored by saltwater anglers; six sites on ponds suitable for freshwater fishing; one on Metts Bluff overlooking the Yellow River; one at Gin Hole Landing, where boaters can launch onto the Yellow River; and others beside small creeks or bayous. Swimmers can take a plunge in the Gulf of Mexico, which is only a short drive away.

Wild animals you might spot include deer, coyote, wild turkey, wild hog, quail, rabbit, or, if you're exceptionally lucky, the secretive black bear. But remember also that hunting is allowed. The general gun season, when you'll want to be sure to wear orange-blaze vests and hats (or avoid the area altogether), varies from year to year but generally occurs on specific dates such as weekends between Thanksgiving and mid-January. Call ahead for the dates. Seasons for small-game and turkey hunters follow, but these present less of a threat to campers. Still, ask about hunting dates and bring along the orange-blaze outerwear. Also, if you come at these times, don't be surprised if you're sharing a campsite with hunters. Some areas of the base are closed to hunting, and others are designated for hunting only by bow and arrow.

Campsites, facilities: Primitive campsites are scattered across about 446,000 acres square miles. Children are welcome. Pets are also permitted, but they must be restrained and are supposed to stay at least 50 yards outside your campsite. Supplies and restaurants are available in Niceville and Valparaiso, on the base's southern boundary.

Reservations, fees: Permits are required and may be obtained in two ways: (1) Writing to Eglin Air Force Base at Natural Resources Division, AFDTC/EMN, 107 Highway 85N, Niceville, FL 32578. Include a photocopy of a valid driver's license for the main person in your camping party, as well as updated address information and phone number if different from that on the driver's license; or (2) Dropping by the office, which is open 7 A.M. to 4:30 P.M.

Monday through Thursday, 7 A.M. to 6 P.M. Friday, and 7:30 A.M. to 12:30 P.M. Saturday. The office is closed Sundays and holidays. The cost is $5 for five consecutive nights for up to 10 people.

Directions: From I-10 near Crestview, take Exit 56 and head south on State Road 85 for about 15 miles to the base's Jackson Guard in Niceville.

Contact: Eglin Air Force Base, Natural Resources Division/Jackson Guard, 107 Highway 85 North, Niceville, FL 32578, 850/882-4164, website: www.eglin.af.mil/newcomers/leisure.htm.

34 FRED GANNON ROCKY BAYOU STATE PARK

Rating: 9

Near Niceville

Pensacola map, grid a3, page 40

This park on the edge of the Eglin Air Force Base territory has another military link: It was named after a colonel who helped develop the 357-acre parcel of land after the state acquired it from the U.S. Forest Service. Most visitors to the area focus on the beach, even though it's fairly narrow and not your typical postcard bathing beach. There are plenty of other water-oriented delights here in a forest setting of tall sand pines. Swimmers, boaters, canoeists, and anglers can explore the treasures of Rocky Bayou, which opens into Choctawhatchee Bay; there's also a freshwater lake on the property. (You'll need the appropriate fishing license depending on whether you try your hand at fresh or saltwater fishing.) Ten campsites overlook the bayou. It'll take you about 25 minutes to explore each of the three nature trails. If you choose only one, then pick the Sand Pine Trail, which leads along Puddin Head Lake and through the woods. Incidentally, the town of Niceville was once named Boggy, but folks didn't think that sounded too appealing.

Campsites, facilities: There are 42 RV and tent sites in this state park, offering water and electricity, picnic tables, grills, and fire rings. Restrooms, showers, a dump station, a boat ramp, a pavilion, and a playground are available. Two campsites and the boat ramp are wheelchair accessible. Children are welcome. Pets with proof of rabies vaccination are allowed.

Reservations, fees: Reservations are recommended; call ReserveAmerica at 800/326-3521. Sites are $8 per night, plus $2 for electricity and $2 for pets. Major credit cards are accepted. The maximum stay is 14 days.

Directions: From I-10 near Crestview, take Exit 56 and drive south on State Road 85 for 15 miles. Turn east onto State Road 20 in Niceville and drive nine miles to the park.

Contact: Fred Gannon Rocky Bayou State Park, 4281 Highway 20, Niceville, FL 32578, 850/833-9144, website: www.floridastateparks.org.

35 BAYVIEW RV CAMPGROUND

Rating: 4

In Destin

Pensacola map, grid b3, page 40

Located across from Destin's main boat launch, this park offers boat storage for guests and is set in a quiet neighborhood. A miniature lighthouse welcomes campers who set up their tents or RVs under large shade trees.

Campsites, facilities: This tiny park has 12 RV sites with full hookups, as well as several tent sites. Restrooms, showers, and laundry facilities are available. Children are welcome. Leashed pets are permitted.

Reservations, fees: Reservations are recommended. Sites are $25 per night for two people, plus $2 per extra person. Major credit cards are accepted. Long-term rates are available.

Directions: From the U.S. 98 bridge in Destin, drive east 1.6 miles. Turn north on Beach Drive and continue 1.3 miles to the park on the left.

Contact: Bayview RV Campground, 749 Beach Drive, Destin, FL 32541, 850/837-5085, website: www.bayviewdestin.com.

36 DESTIN RV RESORT

Rating: 7

In Destin

Pensacola map, grid b3, page 40

Just a five-minute walk from Destin's celebrated white-sand beach, this full-service RV resort is proud of its location in "the world's luckiest fishing village." Each year, anglers catch more billfish in Destin than in all of the other Gulf ports combined; they also hook king mackerel, cobia, and other game fish. There's even a fishing museum here. Charter boats and guide services are widely available, and the fleet is said to be the largest in the state. If you're not into deep-sea fishing, the campground pool is open year-round, and the game room, which is stocked with books, games, and a color TV, is air-conditioned. Jet Skis, pontoon boats, speedboat tours, and ultralight flights are available at Boogies Water Sports near the Destin bridge; other places rent sailboards. Shopping, restaurants, automobile and RV service centers, and attractions are located nearby. Many sites in this campground are pull-through, making parking a breeze.

Campsites, facilities: There are 112 RV sites with full hookups, cable TV, and telephone service; 58 spots suitable for tents have water and electricity. Picnic tables, restrooms, showers, laundry facilities, a dump station, a pool, a game room, horseshoe pits, a playground, a volleyball field, shuffleboard courts, and a convenience store are provided. The management reserves the right to refuse vehicles that are "not in conformance with the overall quality and appearance of the park." Children are welcome. Leashed pets are permitted.

Reservations, fees: Reservations are recommended. Sites are $18 to $28 per night for two people, plus $2 for each additional person. Major credit cards are accepted. Long-term stays are OK.

Directions: From the U.S. 98 bridge in Destin, drive six miles east. The park is .5 mile east of Matthew Drive; turn south on Regions Way to enter.

Contact: Destin RV Resort, 150 Regions Way, Destin, FL 32541, 850/837-6215, 850/837-5698, or 888/815-8388, fax 850/837-9345, website: www.destinrvpark.com.

37 CRYSTAL BEACH RV PARK

Rating: 7

In Destin

Pensacola map, grid b3, page 40

If you want to be close to the beach, this 3.6-acre park is just across the two-lane road from the Gulf of Mexico. Best of all, the highway along here has been closed to through traffic, so pedestrians have easy access. The park—a local fixture for more than four decades—is mostly sunny and open but is dotted with some trees. Destin-area attractions include the U.S. Air Force Armament Museum, Eden State Gardens, the Indian Temple Mound Museum, and the Gulfarium (a marine-life park with trained porpoises, sea otters, exhibits, and the like).

Campsites, facilities: All 75 RV sites have full hookups and cable TV. Restrooms, showers, laundry facilities, a dump station, a pool, a meeting hall, a limited store, and beach access are available. Management says that most areas are wheelchair accessible. Children are welcome. Leashed pets are permitted.

Reservations, fees: Reservations are recommended in the summer and fall. Sites are $25 to $37 per night for two people, plus $3 for each additional person over the age of 10 and $2 for 50-amp electrical service. Major credit cards are accepted. Long-term stays are OK.

Directions: From the U.S. 98 bridge in Destin, drive a little more than five miles east to Matthew Boulevard. Turn south and go two blocks to Scenic Highway 98. Turn left. The park is one block ahead on the left.

Contact: Crystal Beach RV Park, 2825 Scenic Highway 98, Destin, FL 32541, 850/837-6447, website: www.beachdirectory.com/crystalbeach.

38 DESTIN RV BEACH RESORT

Rating: 6

East of Destin

Pensacola map, grid b3, page 40

This brand-new motor coach resort offers luxury sites for sale, but overnighters can try them out for size. They get private beach access, fancy landscaping and lighting, and an intimate park of just 36 sites.

Campsites, facilities: There are 36 full-hookup sites with professional landscaping and cable TV. Restrooms, showers, laundry facilities, and telephone service are available. On the premises are a heated pool, two luxury rental units built above the office building, brick-paved driveways, and a path to the beach. Children are welcome. Leashed pets are permitted.

Reservations, fees: Reservations are recommended. Call to see if sites are available. Rates vary depending on the specials that are being offered; the primary focus here is on lot sales.

Directions: From U.S. 98 and MidBay Bridge Road (Highway 293), drive east on U.S. 98 about five miles. Turn right on Miramar Beach Drive to the park at the beach.

Contact: Destin RV Beach Resort, 362 Miramar Beach Drive, Destin, FL 32550, 850/837-3529, website: www.destinrvresort.com.

39 HENDERSON BEACH STATE PARK

Rating: 10

In Destin

Pensacola map, grid b3, page 40

Opened in March 2000, this is one of the newest campgrounds in Florida's award-winning state park system. Since opening, Henderson Beach State Park has doubled the size of its campground with the addition of another loop along the Gulf of Mexico. The park has 6,000 feet of white-sand shoreline (with a boardwalk from the campground to the beach) and 208 acres

of sand pine, scrub oak, and other vegetation. Why is the sand so white? It's composed of quartz and silicon dioxide polished by countless years of wave action. You can scuba dive just one mile offshore, or swim in the Gulf, or cast a line from the surf to while away the day. Restaurants and shopping are within one mile. The campground has its own beach area separate from the day users' beach.

Campsites, facilities: Sixty sites accommodate RVs and tenters. Each site has water, electricity, picnic tables, and grills. Twenty-two sites are pull-through; some sites have 50-amp service. Restrooms, showers, and a dump station are available. Most areas are wheelchair accessible. Clotheslines and tent lines must not be tied to trees; poles are provided for this purpose. Children are welcome. Leashed pets are permitted.

Reservations, fees: Reservations are recommended; call ReserveAmerica at 800/326-3521. Sites are $17 per night for two people, plus $2 per extra person, $2 for electricity, and $2 for pets. Major credit cards are accepted. The maximum stay is 14 days.

Directions: From Destin, drive east on U.S. 98 to the park entrance.

Contact: Henderson Beach State Park, 17000 Emerald Coast Parkway, Destin, FL 32541, 850/837-7550, fax 850/650-0290, website: www.floridastateparks.org.

40 CAMPING ON THE GULF HOLIDAY TRAVEL PARK

Rating: 8

East of Destin

Pensacola map, grid a3, page 40

If you've come to Florida to visit the beach, you'll love this renovated park, where you can book a site directly on the fabled white sands of the Gulf of Mexico. As the owners say, "You can't get much closer than this!" Beachfront spots, naturally, are the most dear, but shady, grassy sites and sites with concrete pads are convenient to the water and the oceanfront walkway. The campground "beach patrol" will help you park your rig, and the management offers "express check-in" for many reserved visitors. New bath houses and a 3,500-square-foot activity center were recently built.

Campsites, facilities: There are 212 RV sites with full hookups and cable TV; some have telephone service. Picnic tables, grills, restrooms, showers, laundry facilities, a dump station, a heated pool, a gift shop, rental cabins, and a playground are provided. Children are welcome. Leashed pets are permitted, though not on the beachfront campsites.

Reservations, fees: Reservations are recommended. Sites are $30 to $65 per night for five people. Phone service costs $1 a day extra. Major credit cards are accepted. Long-term stays are OK from September through May.

Directions: From the U.S. 98 bridge in Destin, drive east for 10 miles to the park on the south side of the road.

Contact: Camping on the Gulf Holiday Travel Park, 10005 West Emerald Coast Parkway, Destin, FL 32541, 850/837-6334 or 877/226-7485 (reservations), fax 850/654-5048, website: www.campgulf.com.

41 TOPSAIL HILL STATE PRESERVE

Rating: 10

In Santa Rosa Beach

Pensacola map, grid a3, page 40

If you own a large RV, this 140-acre private-campground-turned-state-preserve is where you'll want to be. One of the most deluxe RV parks in Florida, Topsail has resort-style amenities such as a heated swimming pool, fishing lakes, professional landscaping, oversized lots, and immaculate grounds. Even the restrooms are heated and air-conditioned, according to sea-

son. The park is tucked into a pine forest near sandy beaches and upscale shopping centers. Free shuttle service is available to the beach.

Longtimers remember this park as Emerald Coast RV Resort, but the neighboring 1,639-acre state preserve—Topsail, home to one of the world's last remaining populations of the endangered Choctawhatchee beach mouse—took it over, and it is now part of the state park system. Tiny wildflowers bloom most months at the preserve, which features wispy savannas, cypress domes, coastal dune lakes, and, of course, the feature from which it derives its name, a 25-foot-high lakeside dune.

Campsites, facilities: All 156 RV sites have full hookups. Cable TV and telephone service are available. Picnic tables, grills, restrooms, showers, laundry facilities, a dump station, a pool, a recreation center, tennis courts, a lake, boat and canoe rentals, rental cabins, a driving range, horseshoe pits, and shuffleboard courts are on site. Tents are not allowed. The restrooms, office, and beach boardwalk are wheelchair accessible. Children and leashed pets are welcome.

Reservations, fees: Reservations are recommended; call ReserveAmerica at 800/326-3521. Sites are $32 per night for two people, plus $3 for each additional person. Major credit cards are accepted. Long-term stays are OK.

Directions: From I-10 at De Funiak Springs, take Exit 85 and head south on U.S. 331 for 26 miles to U.S. 98. Turn west (right) and drive five miles to County Road 30A. Turn south (left) and drive .2 mile to the park entrance on your right.

Contact: Topsail Hill State Preserve, 7525 West Scenic Highway 30A, Santa Rosa Beach, FL 32459, 850/267-0299, fax 850/267-9014, website: www.floridastateparks.org.

COURTESY OF FLORIDA STATE PARKS

Chapter 2

Panama City Area

Panama City Area

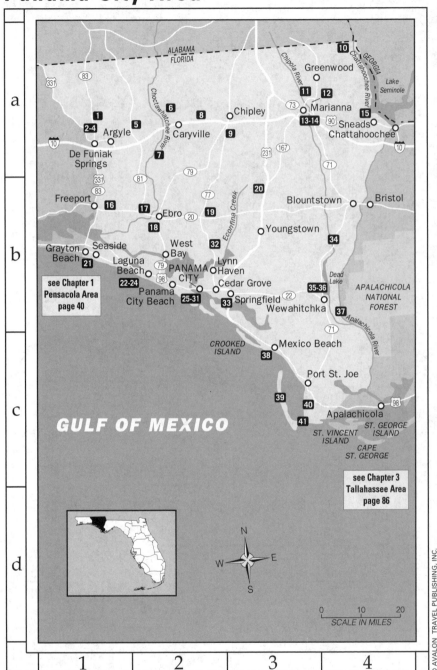

ALABAMA
FLORIDA

GEORGIA

[10]

Greenwood

Chattahoochee River

Lake Seminole

[331] [83]

[11] [12]

[1]
[2-4]
Argyle

[5]

[6]

[8]

Chipley

[73]

Marianna

[90]

Sneads

[15]

[13-14]

Chattahoochee

[10]

Caryville

[9]

[231]

[167]

[71]

De Funiak Springs

[7]

[81]

[79]

[77]

[20]

Blountstown

Bristol

Freeport

[16]

[17]

Ebro

[19]

[20]

Econfina Creek

Youngstown

[34]

[18]

[32]

West Bay

Grayton Beach

Seaside

[21]

Laguna Beach

[79]

[98]

PANAMA CITY

Lynn Haven

Cedar Grove

Dead Lake

APALACHICOLA NATIONAL FOREST

see Chapter 1 Pensacola Area page 40

[22-24]

Panama City Beach

[25-31]

[33]

Springfield

[22]

Wewahitchka

[35-36]

[37]

Apalachicola River

[71]

CROOKED ISLAND

[38]

Mexico Beach

Port St. Joe

GULF OF MEXICO

[39]

[40]

[98]

[41]

Apalachicola

ST. VINCENT ISLAND

ST. GEORGE ISLAND

CAPE ST. GEORGE

see Chapter 3 Tallahassee Area page 86

N
W   E
S

0   10   20
SCALE IN MILES

1   2   3   4

© AVALON TRAVEL PUBLISHING, INC.

1 SUNSET KING RESORT

Rating: 8

North of De Funiak Springs on Kings Lake
Panama City map, grid a1, page 62

Set on 580-acre Kings Lake, this park caters to anglers and campers who like lots of on-site amenities, such as miniature golf, croquet, basketball, volleyball, badminton, and much more. Kids can play in the fenced playground. Swim in the lakeview pool, or fish off the 75-foot lighted pier. The lake is stocked regularly with black bass, shellcracker, crappie, and bream; in 1987, it yielded bass weighing in at more than 17 pounds.

Campsites, facilities: This park has 100 full-hookup RV sites and 10 additional spots for tenters. Rigs up to 45 feet in length can be accommodated. Cable TV, picnic tables, grills, restrooms, showers, a dump station, a clubhouse, a pavilion, a pool, a boat ramp, boat docks, a playground, a game room, miniature golf, horseshoe pits, a store, and laundry facilities are on site. Owners Roger and Kimberly Roy have made Internet service available in the clubhouse. The clubhouse and bathhouse are wheelchair accessible. Children and pets are welcome.

Reservations, fees: Reservations are not necessary, but the peak season at the park is February through March and November through December. Sites are $18 per night for two people, plus $1 per extra person. Cable TV is $1 extra. Major credit cards are accepted. Long-term stays are OK.

Directions: If westbound: From I-10 west of De Funiak Springs, take Exit 70 and drive north on State Road 285 for .4 mile. Turn right onto U.S. 90 and drive 8.5 miles east. When you reach Kings Lake Road, turn north and follow the signs to the park. If eastbound: Take I-10 Exit 85 and turn right on Highway 331. Drive two miles to U.S. 90 and turn left. Continue five miles on U.S. 90 until you reach Kings Lake Road. Roads leading to the park are paved.

Contact: Sunset King Resort, 366 Paradise Is-land Drive, De Funiak Springs, FL 32433, 850/892-7229 or 800/747-5454, fax 850/892-7998, website: www.sunsetking.com.

2 LONG LEAF RV PARK

Rating: 3

Near De Funiak Springs
Panama City map, grid a1, page 62

Weary travelers on I-10 will find this park convenient, though it offers no pool or recreation room. It has long pull-through spaces on gravel roads just 3.5 miles south of the interstate. Overnighters are welcome. Shopping and restaurants are close by.

Campsites, facilities: There are 25 partially shaded RV sites, all with water and electricity. Nineteen sites have full hookups. All have picnic tables. Tents are not allowed. Restrooms, showers, laundry facilities, and telephone service are available. Most areas are wheelchair accessible. On the premises is a dog-walk area. Children are welcome. Leashed pets are permitted.

Reservations, fees: Reservations are recommended. Sites are $18 to $20 per night for two people, plus $2 per extra person. Credit cards are not accepted. Long-term rates are available.

Directions: From I-10, take Exit 85 onto U.S. 331 and drive 3.5 miles south.

Contact: Long Leaf RV Park, 5687 U.S. 331 South, De Funiak Springs, FL 32435, 850/892-7261.

3 BASS HAVEN CAMPGROUND

Rating: 5

North of De Funiak Springs on Juniper Lake
Panama City map, grid a1, page 62

Rigs up to 30 feet long can be accommodated in this 1.5-acre park on Juniper Lake, which is famed for its bass fishing, and the locals nurture the belief that the world-record largemouth bass will come from its waters. But there's more to do around here than fish: Take a 15-minute drive to Vortex Spring or explore the city of De Funiak Springs, which has dozens of spectacular Victorian homes that circle a spring-fed lake; it's said to be one of two perfectly round lakes in the world. Around the turn of the century, this town was famous as the home of the Winter Chautauqua, a cultural and philosophical movement that brought lecturers and speechmakers here to the still-standing Chautauqua Auditorium. Also nearby is the Chautauqua Winery (850/892-5887), the largest winery in Florida; tours are available. If you're feeling really energetic, take a drive north to the highest point in Florida—345 feet above sea level. It's just an imperceptible bump flagged with a sign and a granite marker, but you can say you bagged another peak. From De Funiak Springs, drive north on U.S. 331/State Road 285 about 20 miles until State Road 285 forks off to the northeast. Continue on State Road 285 about two miles; the marker is in a pine woods with a small picnic area.

Campsites, facilities: The campground has 19 full-hookup RV sites and six tent sites set apart from the RVs. On the premises are picnic tables, restrooms, showers, a dump station, a boat ramp, boat docks, boat rentals, horseshoe pits, a volleyball field, a store, and laundry facilities. Children and pets are welcome.

Reservations, fees: Reservations are not necessary. Sites are $14.95 per night, plus $1 for cable TV. Credit cards are not accepted. The maximum stay is six months.

Directions: From I-10 at De Funiak Springs, take Exit 85 and drive north on U.S. 331 for two miles, then turn east onto U.S. 90 and go several blocks through town. At State Road 83, turn left and drive 2.5 miles north. At Juniper Lake Road, turn west (left) and follow the signs to the park.

Contact: Bass Haven Campground, 350 Bass Haven Drive, De Funiak Springs, FL 32433, 850/892-4043.

4 JUNIPER LAKE CAMPGROUND

Rating: 5

North of De Funiak Springs on Juniper Lake
Panama City map, grid a1, page 62

Juniper Lake is considered to be one of the area's finest fishing lakes for bass. In fact, those in the know are so confident that they believe a world-record largemouth bass will be pulled from here someday. Will you be the lucky angler? Stay a few days at one of the campsites right on the lakeshore of this 4.5-acre park and give it a try. Under new ownership, the park has recently undergone improvements to the laundry room, restrooms, electrical wiring, and landscaping.

Campsites, facilities: This park has 18 RV sites with full hookups and cable TV and 15 spots for tenters. Overnighters are welcome, and 50-amp service is available. On the premises are picnic tables, restrooms, showers, a picnic area, a clubhouse, covered boat slips with electricity, johnboats for rent, three docks, and laundry facilities. Children are welcome. Leashed pets are OK.

Reservations, fees: Reservations are suggested. Sites are $15 per night. Credit cards are not accepted. Long-term stays are OK.

Directions: From I-10 at De Funiak Springs, take Exit 85 and drive north on U.S. 331 for two miles, then turn east onto U.S. 90 and go several blocks through town. At State Road 83, turn north and drive 2.5 miles. At Juniper Lake Road, turn west and follow the signs to the park.

Contact: Juniper Lake Campground, 363 Black Bass Boulevard, De Funiak Springs, FL 32433, 850/892-3445, fax 850/892-9136, website: www.juniperlakervcampground.com.

5 VORTEX SPRING RV PARK

Rating: 10

In Ponce de Leon
Panama City map, grid a2, page 62

For decades, Florida pitchmen have exploited the legend of Spanish explorer Juan Ponce de

Leon, romanticizing his quest to find a fountain of youth in the flowery paradise he discovered on Easter Sunday in 1513 and named La Florida. Historians, however, portray him as a gold-hungry despot who arrived in the New World on Christopher Columbus' second voyage, then conquered the Carib Indians. He was hunting for hidden riches, not just a fountain, when he was mortally wounded by an Indian arrow at Charlotte Harbor in 1521. Nonetheless, his name has been attached ever since to Florida's myriad springs—natural wonders with supposedly curative powers that have drawn countless visitors and are now a resource for the state's thriving bottled water industry.

The family-run Vortex Spring camping resort, on the outskirts of the city of Ponce de Leon, capitalizes on another angle: scuba diving and underwater caving. The centerpiece of this 480-acre private campground is a spring and underwater cavern that spews 28 million gallons of water daily at a constant temperature of 68 degrees Fahrenheit. The spring basin, crystal clear and 48 feet deep, is shared by catfish, freshwater eels, rare shadow bass, and a vegetarian piranha named Paco. The limestone cavern, restricted to cave-certified divers, meanders farther for 100 yards to a depth of 115 feet. The daily diving fee is $25 per person, which includes air fill. On the surface, the spring spills into Blue Creek, which is good for snorkeling, canoeing, or a paddleboat ride. The swimming area has a small water slide, a nine-foot diving platform, a slide for small children, and an old-fashioned rope swing. The campsites are grassy and semishaded; wood for campfires is sold at the store, along with other supplies.

Near the campground is a 443-acre park named after you-know-who: Ponce de Leon Springs State Park, on State Road 181A, .5 mile south of U.S. 90. Two springs are surrounded by a wall built in 1926 when the waters were a "fountain of youth" attraction; they produce 14 million gallons daily that flow into the Choctawhatchee River. No camping is permitted, but there's a swimming beach with a bathhouse, a picnic area, and a couple of nature trails. Admission is $2 per car. For more information, call 850/836-4281.

Campsites, facilities: This park has 22 RV sites and 26 tent sites. Seven have full hookups and are pull-through; 22 have water and electricity. Additional tent sites are primitive. Each developed site has a picnic table, grill, and fire ring. On the premises are restrooms, showers, scuba diving facilities, a campground store, and a spring for swimming. Snorkel gear, paddleboat, canoe, kayak, and inner tube rentals are available. A go-cart park is a mile from the campsites. Children are welcome. Pets are discouraged, but small leashed pets are permitted.

Reservations, fees: Reservations are recommended, particularly during holidays. Sites are $15.50 to $23 per night for two people, plus $5 for each additional person. Major credit cards are accepted.

Directions: From I-10 east of De Funiak Springs, take Exit 96 to State Road 81 and drive five miles north to the park at right. Turn right at the sign and drive .5 mile to the campground.

Contact: Vortex Spring, 1517 Vortex Spring Lane, Ponce de Leon, FL 32455, 850/836-4979 or 800/342-0640, fax 850/836-4557, website: www.vortexspring.com.

6 CHOCTAWHATCHEE RIVER WATER MANAGEMENT AREA BOAT-IN SITES

Rating: 7

Near Caryville, along the Choctawhatchee River

Panama City map, grid a2, page 62

Before the railroads, the Choctawhatchee River was a vital waterway linking antebellum plantations at the Alabama border to the docks downstream at Choctawhatchee Bay on the Gulf of Mexico. Today, it's a scenic waterway and much of the riverbanks are owned by the water management district.

The banks are high and heavily wooded, with large sandbars that make good camping spots. The drill here: Bring a johnboat with a little kicker of a motor, launch at the boat ramp, then travel downriver—passing cypress, tupelo, gum, ash, and hickory trees along the way—to scope out the banks for a good place to pitch a tent. As for fine spots, "we can't promise too many," says George Fisher of the Northwest Florida Water Management District. When the river is high, it's hard to find a good piece of dry land. The east side of the river, off State Road 179, is laced with a hiking trail and dirt roads open to backpackers and horseback riders. The river and several lakes are open to boaters and anglers. Wear bright orange clothing during the hunting season, from November through early March, lest you be mistaken for a deer or wild hog.

Note: It's not advisable to bring a canoe because the river here flows swiftly.

Campsites, facilities: Boaters can access an indeterminate number of primitive tent camping areas with no facilities or drinking water. Trash must be packed out. Children and pets are permitted.

Reservations, fees: Reservations are not necessary. Camping is free.

Directions: From I-10 east of Ponce de Leon, take Exit 104 and proceed north on County Road 279 to Caryville. Turn left onto U.S. 90 and travel about two miles west, then turn right onto State Road 179A. Go about five miles north to the crossroads of Cerrogordo (if you hit the hamlet of Baker Settlement, you've gone too far) and turn right onto the unnamed road leading to Cerrogordo Landing. About one mile ahead is the boat ramp.

Contact: Northwest Florida Water Management District, 81 Water Management Drive, Havana, FL 32333, 850/539-5999.

7 CHOCTAWHATCHEE RIVER WATER MANAGEMENT AREA HIKE-IN SITES

Rating: 4

South of Caryville
Panama City map, grid a2, page 62

This is rustic with a capital R, so only adventurers need read on. Backpacking is possible in the eastern part of the property near State Road 284, an area that's loaded with wildlife. This river floodplain will likely be inundated with water at times, so check ahead on conditions. Wear bright orange during hunting season, from November through early March. Boats and canoes are best launched on the west side of the river.

Campsites, facilities: Backpackers can camp along the Choctawhatchee River. There are no facilities. Children and pets are permitted.

Reservations, fees: Reservations are not necessary. Camping is free.

Directions: From I-10 east of Ponce de Leon, take Exit 104 and drive south on County Road 279. Continue south on State Road 280 and drive about five miles to the intersection of County Road 284 at Hinson's Crossroads. A dirt road into the preserve is on the west side of County Road 284, about four miles south of Hinson's Crossroads. For boat and canoe launching: From I-10 at Ponce de Leon, take Exit 96 and drive south on State Road 81. Turn east on the dirt road extension of County Road 183 and drive to the river.

Contact: Northwest Florida Water Management District, 81 Water Management Drive, Havana, FL 32333, 850/539-5999.

8 NORTHWEST FLORIDA CAMPGROUNDS

Rating: 4

In Chipley
Panama City map, grid a2, page 62

Under new ownership, this quiet, 18-acre park

caters to overnight campers and RV caravans on I-10, as well as vacationers headed to Panama City beaches. Five acres of woods shield you from the highway, and the campsites have been recently renovated. An unusual feature is a music pavilion used for concerts and special gatherings. On the grounds of the park is an 1888-built log cabin. The town of Chipley boasts buildings that date back to the early 1900s, and the local chamber of commerce offers a walking tour. Also in Chipley is an antique mall.

Campsites, facilities: This campground has 95 pull-through RV sites with water and electricity; 45 have full hookups. Twelve have 50-amp service. On the premises are restrooms, showers, laundry facilities, a rental cabin, a dump station, a recreation room, horseshoe pits, and a volleyball court. Children are welcome. Leashed pets are permitted.

Reservations, fees: Reservations are not necessary. Sites are $15 to $18 per night for two people, plus $1 for each additional person. If you want to use an electric heater, there is an additional charge of $2 per day. Credit cards are not accepted.

Directions: From I-10 at Chipley, take Exit 120 north onto State Road 77 and drive two miles. Turn west onto U.S. 90, then drive 1.25 miles. Turn north on Griffin Road and proceed to the park.

Contact: Northwest Florida Campgrounds, 677 Griffin Road, Chipley, FL 32428, 850/638-0362, fax 850/638-0372, website: www.northwestfloridacampground.com.

9 FALLING WATERS STATE PARK

Rating: 8

Near Chipley
Panama City map, grid a3, page 62

This 155-acre park is a fine overnight camping spot with a unique attraction: Florida's only waterfall. Sure, it's no Niagara, plunging just 67 feet into a cylindrical sinkhole where it

vanishes into the limestone. The site, though, has a prehistoric feel, lush with ferns and ancient hardwoods. Slash pines shade the campground, and there's a trail leading to the swimming lake. The trail continues past the site of an oil well drilled by wildcatters in 1919. It produced a dribble of crude and was capped three years later. Just above the falls, a whiskey still produced spirits for frontier railroad crews in the 1800s. The waterfall itself powered a gristmill for several years. Timbers from the old mill are on display.

Campsites, facilities: This state park has seven campsites for RVs and 17 for tents, all with water and electricity, picnic tables, and fire rings; seven are pull-through sites. There are restrooms, showers, a dump station, a swimming lake, and a playground. Children are welcome. Pets are permitted with up-to-date vaccination records. The picnic area is wheelchair accessible.

Reservations, fees: Reservations are recommended; call ReserveAmerica at 800/326-3521. The fee is $8 to $10 per night for four people, plus $2 per extra person or per pet. Electricity costs $2 extra. Major credit cards are accepted.

Directions: From I-10 at Chipley, take Exit 120 onto State Road 77 and drive south for three miles to the park.

Contact: Falling Waters State Park, 1130 State Park Road, Chipley, FL 32428, 850/638-6130, fax 850/638-6273.

10 NEAL'S LANDING

Rating: 2

On the Chattahoochee River, near the Georgia border
Panama City map, grid a4, page 62

Sites are shady and spaced far apart from each other in this campground operated by the U.S. Army Corps of Engineers. Visitors have access to a boat ramp on the Chattahoochee River but will find that it's typically very busy, attracting boaters and anglers from three states:

Georgia is across the river to the east, and Alabama is just a hop, skip, and jump to the north. (Note that the bathroom facilities serve both the campground and the boat launch.)

Campsites, facilities: Eleven sites are for RVs or tents; none has electricity. Each site has a picnic table, a grill, and a lantern hanger. Restrooms, showers, a dump station, and a boat ramp are available. Children and leashed pets are welcome.

Reservations, fees: Reservations are not accepted. Sites are $5 per night for up to eight people. There's a self-pay station at the entrance. Credit cards are not accepted. Maximum stay is 14 days.

Directions: From the west side of Sneads at the junction of State Road 271 and U.S. 90, drive 22 miles north on State Road 271. At County Road 164, turn right (northeast) and drive 1.3 miles. At State Road 2, turn right (eastbound) and drive .9 mile. The campground is on the south side of the road, just before the bridge and the Georgia state line.

Contact: U.S. Army Corps of Engineers, Resource Management Office, Lake Seminole Site Office, P.O. Box 96, Chattahoochee, FL 32324, 229/662-2001, website: www.sam.usace.army.mil/op/rec/seminole/campgrnd.htm.

11 UPPER CHIPOLA RIVER WATER MANAGEMENT AREA

Rating: 7

Along the banks of the Upper Chipola River and its tributaries

Panama City map, grid a3, page 62

If you're into primitive camping, then you'll want to come here for solitude instead of heading to the more popular Florida Caverns State Park (see next campground). Just remember that there are no facilities. These 7,374 acres span 18 miles along the Chipola River, so the area is subject to flooding. A trail runs alongside much of the river. Trees in the area include iris, basswood, and Florida maple. In

some places, little shade is available right next to the water. You might catch sight of deer in the forested lands set farther back from the river if you're up early or out in the evening at twilight. Also keep your eyes peeled for southern brown bats flitting about at dusk and the occasional Barbour's map turtle lumbering around the shoreline. In the spring, you can feast on the succulent purple-black boysenberries that grow in briar patches here. In November and December, you may encounter deer hunters, so wear bright orange clothing if you are hiking. Turkey hunters show up in March and April. The best access is by boat.

Campsites, facilities: Primitive camping is available on some 7,400 acres stretching from the Alabama border to Florida Caverns State Park. There are no official campsites, but you'll find no shortage of places to set up housekeeping for up to 14 days. No facilities are provided. Bring water and camping supplies. Pack out trash. Children and pets are permitted.

Reservations, fees: Reservations are not necessary. Camping is free.

Directions: There are only a few places to launch a boat here. Our suggestion: Head north on Highway 71 from Marianna and turn left at the small settlement of Greenwood (by the Junior Food Store) onto County Road 162/Fort Road. When you pass the bridge over the Chipola River, double back on the dirt road to the river. For more information, contact the water management district.

Contact: Northwest Florida Water Management District, 81 Water Management Drive, Havana, FL 32333, 850/539-5999.

12 FLORIDA CAVERNS STATE PARK

Rating: 10

North of Marianna

Panama City map, grid a4, page 62

Caves in Florida? You bet. Be sure to take the 45-minute ranger-led tour to see the stalactites, stalagmites, columns, flowstones, and draperies that were formed tens of thousands of years ago. Although not as large as Kentucky's Mammoth Cave, the Florida Caverns are arguably just as interesting; there's even a "wedding cake" formation in one chamber, where some couples have celebrated their nuptials. The state park and the caverns were developed in the 1930s by the Civilian Conservation Corps, which built trails and passages and installed lighting to make the caverns accessible to the public. This is the only cave in Florida that the public can enter without a scientific research permit. Tours are first-come, first-served; if your only reason for coming is to see the caves, then go directly there to buy your ticket ($2.50 to $5) because they sell out fast. The rest of the 1,300-acre park has much to offer: a swimming area at Blue Hole, a boat ramp on the Chipola River, canoe rentals, hiking and equestrian trails, and forests of American beech, southern magnolia, spruce pine, white oak, and some plants more typical of the Appalachian Mountains.

Campsites, facilities: There are 32 sites for RVs and tents, all with water and electricity, picnic tables, grills, and fire rings. Restrooms, showers, a dump station, a boat ramp, a playground, and a snack bar are provided. Three tent-only sites can be had. The camping area and visitors center are wheelchair accessible. Children are welcome. Pets are permitted with proof of vaccination.

Reservations, fees: Reservations are recommended; call ReserveAmerica at 800/326-3521. Sites are $8 to $12 per night for four people, plus $2 for electricity and $2 for each additional person and per pet. Major credit cards are accepted.

Directions: From I-10 at Marianna, take Exit 142 and drive north on State Road 71 for 1.8 miles to U.S. 90. Turn west and drive 1.5 miles to State Road 166. Turn north and drive three miles to the park entrance.

Contact: Florida Caverns State Park, 3345 Caverns Road, Marianna, FL 32446, 850/482-9598, website: www.floridastateparks.org.

13 ARROWHEAD CAMPSITES

Rating: 5

In Marianna on U.S. 90

Panama City map, grid a3, page 62

Arrowhead Campground borders on Mill Pond, a spring-fed, seven-mile-long lake where one angler caught a world-record shellcracker. The campground has tall pines and elms and plenty of stuff for kids, including a swimming pool, a playground, and a game room. A whopping 180 sites are pull-through. Even though the park recently opened an RV sales and supply store, the woods and lake provide for pretty views.

Campsites, facilities: There are 244 RV and tent sites with full hookups, cable TV, and picnic tables. Restrooms, showers, laundry facilities, a dump station, a game room, a pool, a playground, a boat ramp, boat docks, canoe rentals, and five cabins are available. An RV supplies store recently opened on site. Children are welcome. Leashed pets are permitted.

Reservations, fees: Reservations are recommended. Sites are $16 per night for four people, plus $2 for each additional person. Major credit cards are accepted. Long-term stays are OK.

Directions: From I-10 at Marianna, take Exit 142 heading north on State Road 71 for 1.8 miles. At U.S. 90, turn left and drive .2 mile west. The park is on the right, on the lake.

Contact: Arrowhead Campsites, 4820 U.S. 90 East, Marianna, FL 32446, 850/482-5583 or 800/643-9166, fax 850/482-4713, website: www.arrowheadcamp.com.

14 DOVE REST RV PARK

Rating: 4

South of Marianna

Panama City map, grid a3, page 62

With many pull-through sites near the highway, this 26-acre campground offers easy on-and-off access for even the weariest interstate traveler. It's convenient to Florida Caverns State Park, restaurants, and shopping. The park is divided into two sections: one is sunny, and the other is shaded by some of the park's 300 trees. A Wal-Mart is one-half mile away.

Campsites, facilities: All 110 pull-through RV sites have full hookups and cable TV. About 76 are available for overnighters, and 24 for seasonal stays. Primitive tent camping is permitted throughout the park's 26 acres. Restrooms, showers, laundry facilities, a dump station, a basketball court, a recreation hall, and horseshoe pits are on site. Restaurants are .5 mile away. Children are welcome. Leashed pets are permitted.

Reservations, fees: Reservations normally are not necessary. Sites are $20 per night for two people, plus $2 for each additional person. Credit cards are not accepted. Long-term rates are available.

Directions: From I-10 at Marianna, take Exit 142 and drive south on State Road 71 for .5 mile.

Contact: Dove Rest RV Park, 1973 Dove Rest Drive, Marianna, FL 32448, 850/482-5313.

15 THREE RIVERS STATE PARK

Rating: 9

North of Sneads

Panama City map, grid a4, page 62

Camping here is a lakeside affair in a forest of pines and hardwood trees, but most visitors come to fish, not explore the forest. Three Rivers State Park is so named because it is located at the junction of the Chattahoochee and Flint Rivers, which merge to form the Apalachicola River, and Lake Seminole. The 683-acre park fronts two miles of shoreline on Lake Seminole, which is a popular place for catching largemouth and smallmouth bass, catfish, and bluegill. Commonly seen around the lake are alligators and alligator snapping turtles; in the woods, you may encounter white-tailed deer. A shady, two-mile-long nature trail loop winds along the lakeshore. The fishing

pier is 100 feet long, so don't worry if you don't have a boat or choose not to rent one from one of the nearby marinas.

Campsites, facilities: There are 65 sites for tents or RVs; 21 have electric hookups. Each site has water, a picnic table, a grill, and a fire ring. Restrooms, showers, a dump station, a boat ramp, and a fishing pier are available. Children are welcome. Leashed pets with proof of rabies vaccination are accepted.

Reservations, fees: Reservations are recommended; call ReserveAmerica at 800/326-3521. Fee is $8 per night for four people, plus $2 for electricity and $2 for each additional person or per pet. Major credit cards are accepted. The maximum stay is 14 days.

Directions: From the west side of Sneads at the junction of State Road 271 and U.S. 90, drive two miles north on State Road 271. Turn north (right) at the sign for the state park.

Contact: Three Rivers State Park, Route 1, Box 15-A, Sneads, FL 32460, 850/482-9006.

16 THE OUTPOST RV PARK

Rating: 2

East of Freeport

Panama City map, grid b1, page 62

Located on Black Creek near the Choctawhatchee Bay, this small rural store has 10 sites available for anglers, hunters, and overnighters. A boat ramp makes water access easy, and bait and tackle are available at the store.

Campsites, facilities: Ten RV sites with full hookups and 50-amp service are available. There are no restrooms or showers. A store, a boat ramp, a dock, and canoe rentals are available. Children are welcome. Small leashed pets are permitted.

Reservations, fees: Reservations are recommended. Sites are $18 per night for two people, plus $2 per extra person. Credit cards are not accepted. Long-term stays are permitted.

Directions: From the intersection of State Road 331 and County Road 3280 in Freeport, drive

east five miles on County Road 3280. Look for the store on the right side of the road.
Contact: The Outpost RV Park, 4576 County Road 3280 East, Freeport, FL 32439, 850/835-2779, fax 850/835-2628.

17 CHOCTAWHATCHEE RIVER WATER MANAGEMENT AREA SOUTHERN BOAT-IN SITES

Rating: 8

Along the Choctawhatchee and East Rivers
Panama City map, grid b2, page 62

This pristine, wildlife-packed area features some of the best fishing in Florida for bass, bream, and catfish. It's also popular for hunting deer, squirrels, and raccoons. It can be difficult to find dry ground where you can pitch a tent when the rivers run high, so contact the water district or the Florida Fish and Wildlife Conservation Commission (850/265-3676) to check conditions. Sometimes you can sleep on ancient beach dunes where water filters quickly through the sand, leaving a dry, shady hammock atop a rise—a nice place to pitch a tent.

Campsites, facilities: There are no established campsites, but primitive camping is allowed throughout the area. Aside from several boat ramps, there are no facilities. Bring water, food, and camping supplies. Pack out trash. Children and pets are permitted.

Reservations, fees: Reservations are not necessary. Camping is free.

Directions: There are seven boat ramps in and around this property. Probably the easiest to reach is where U.S. 20 crosses the Choctawhatchee River just west of Pine Log State Forest and the tiny town of Ebro. The water management area stretches along the Choctawhatchee and East Rivers from U.S. 20 to just east of Choctawhatchee Bay.

Contact: Northwest Florida Water Management District, 81 Water Management Drive, Havana, FL 32333, 850/539-5999.

18 PINE LOG STATE FOREST

Rating: 10

South of Ebro
Panama City map, grid b2, page 62

Grassy, wooded sites form a half circle around a five-acre swimming lake fringed with slash pines and hardwoods. If the weather is clear, you'll see spectacular sunsets over the water. Swimming is allowed (at your own risk) in the eastern lake only; signs warn of submerged objects. You can fish on all lakes and streams in the forest, but only carry-in boats and electric motors are permitted in the two lakes near the campground. A ranger's residence is within view, which makes for a secure feeling when there are few other campers about. Pine Log is the only developed campground in the 6,911-acre state forest, one of Florida's first. Acquired in the 1930s, it was clear-cut at that time, but replanting has created an enchanting place, thick with slash, longleaf, and sand pines, as well as oak, cypress, red maple, sweet gum, juniper, and magnolia trees. Horse trails and several miles of hiking trails, including an eight-mile section of the Florida National Scenic Trail, are nearby, and the forest roads are good for mountain bikes. Although the Florida trail is open only to foot traffic, the Crooked Creek Trail welcomes mountain bikers. It's a nine-mile, single-track, figure-eight loop (you can also do just 4.5 miles) opened by the division of forestry in conjunction with the Panama City Flyers Bicycle Club. The trail is closed during the first nine days of hunting season. Call ahead or see the kiosk at the parking area located on State Road 79 for the exact dates. At other times during the hunting season, cyclists should wear fluorescent orange and use extreme caution.

Campsites, facilities: Twenty campsites have electricity, water, picnic tables, grills, and fire rings. Restrooms, showers, a dump station, and two lakes are on site. Children are welcome. Leashed pets are permitted.

Reservations, fees: Reservations are not taken. Sites are $13 per night for five people. There's a self-pay station at the campground entrance. Credit cards are not accepted. The maximum stay is 14 days.

Directions: From the intersection of U.S. 20 and State Road 79 in the town of Ebro, drive south on State Road 79 for 1.3 miles. Use the second state forest entrance, marked Environmental Road, and watch for signs indicating camping. Turn west on the dirt road and travel about .5 mile to the campground.

Contact: Florida Division of Forestry, 715 West 15th Street, Panama City, FL 32401, 850/872-4175, fax 850/872-4879, website: www.fl-dof.com/stateforests/pine_log.htm. For hunting and fishing information, contact the Florida Fish and Wildlife Conservation Commission, 3911 Highway 2321, Panama City, FL 32409, 850/265-3677 or 800/955-8771.

19 ECONFINA CREEK WATER MANAGEMENT AREA

Rating: 9

West of Fountain along Econfina Creek
Panama City map, grid b2, page 62

Wow! It's hard to find this place—"middle of nowhere" doesn't do justice to the remoteness—but it's well worth the drive. You'll find scenic springs, limestone bluffs, ravines, and lots of wild animals. The ground is made of limestone deposited eons ago by dying sea creatures when this part of Florida was under an ancient ocean. Today, that limestone is easily eaten away by the tannic acids that flow from dead leaves and other vegetation. The process creates huge sinkholes, solution holes, and other paths that allow water to seep through the ground to the Floridan Aquifer, the source of northwest Florida's drinking water.

Look for unusual plants such as oak leaf hydrangea, ash, pyramid magnolia, St. John's wort, and liverwort. Resident animals include rare snails, the brightly colored summer tanager bird, the alligator snapping turtle, the gopher tortoise, the endangered fox squirrel, and a large population of warblers.

The Econfina Creek Canoe Trail begins at Scotts Bridge in northern Bay County and follows the river south to Walsingham Park, the Econfina Creek Canoe Livery, a canoe launch at Highway 20, and last to the Highway 388 bridge. To obtain a rental canoe or learn about water conditions, call the Econfina Creek Canoe Livery (850/722-9032). The Northwest River Water Management District says you can paddle for 26 miles; contact the district for a map, or get information from the canoe livery listed here. By the way, Econfina is pronounced "Ee-con-fine-ah."

Horseback riding and bicycling also are permitted on the trails. Hunters head to these parts from mid-November to about January 1, so wear bright orange hats or vests.

Campsites, facilities: Ten primitive camping areas have no facilities. Three areas are designated for groups of 10 campers. Trash must be packed out. Children and pets are welcome.

Reservations, fees: Reservations are not necessary. Camping is free.

Directions: One drive-in camping area, Walsingham, and two hike-in areas, Anise and Ashe, are accessible off a dirt road heading east and then south from Porter Lake Road in southeast Washington County. Two drive-in sites, Bluff and Longleaf, and two other hike-in sites, Devil's Hole and Sea Shell, are located off a network of roads leading north from Highway 20 about two miles east of Econfina Creek. (The hiking distance required is quite short, less than .25 mile.) To find a canoe launch, head north from the hamlet of Fountain on U.S. 231 and turn left (west) onto Scott's Bridge Road. You'll see the launch site when you reach Econfina Creek. Call the water district for good maps. Also consider purchasing a U.S. Geological Survey topographic map.

Contact: Northwest Florida Water Management District, 81 Water Management Drive, Havana, FL 32333, 850/539-5999.

20 PINE LAKE RV PARK

Rating: 5

North of Fountain

Panama City map, grid b3, page 62

Retired campers and full-timers are preferred at this 45-acre rural park, which has a stocked fishing lake on the property and is near 150-acre Compass Lake. Feed the fish and the ducks, or cast a line for dinner. Most sites are pull-through, and the staff is proud to offer easy, safe access for any size RV.

Campsites, facilities: Adult campers will find 150 RV sites with full hookups and picnic tables. Restrooms, showers, laundry facilities, a dump station, and horseshoe pits are available. Tents and pop-up trailers are not allowed. Children may visit campers and are accepted as guests if they happen to show up with grownups, but park management clearly prefers adults because of the lack of child-friendly facilities. Leashed pets are permitted.

Reservations, fees: Reservations are recommended but usually not necessary. Sites are $18 per night for two people, plus $2 for each additional person. Major credit cards are accepted. Long-term stays are OK.

Directions: From I-10 west of Marianna, take Exit 130 onto U.S. 231. Drive south for 15 miles. The park is just south of the intersection with State Road 167.

Contact: Pine Lake RV Park, 21036 U.S. 231, Fountain, FL 32438, 850/722-1401, fax 850/722-1403, email: rvbeaver@aol.com.

21 GRAYTON BEACH STATE PARK

Rating: 10

East of Destin

Panama City map, grid b1, page 62

Set on a stretch of coastline with spectacular beaches, this park is a notch above the rest. The beach here is on a peninsula ringed with marshes and the emerald waters of the Gulf of Mexico, and is protected by barrier dunes covered with sea oats. The sand is so white that it resembles snow. Use lots of sunscreen at the swimming beach because the white sand reflects ultraviolet rays and increases the chance of sunburn. Saltwater and ocean breezes have fashioned the trees into bonsai-like shapes; you may see mature sand pines that resemble bushes. The intimate little campground is slipped into a pine scrub woods near a lake. Both freshwater and saltwater fishing are possible, and the boat ramp is in protected waters on Western Lake. Buy supplies before you arrive; there's not much around here except for Seaside, a planned resort community famed for its architecture. Just two miles east of the state park, Seaside's new Victorian-style buildings are often photographed for magazine advertisements or used as movie backdrops. They're a bit Disneyesque in their perfection.

Campsites, facilities: There are 37 sites with water, electricity, picnic tables, and grills. Restrooms, showers, a dump station, and a boat ramp are available. Children are welcome. Pets are prohibited.

Reservations, fees: Reservations are recommended; call ReserveAmerica at 800/326-3521. Sites are $8 to $14 per night for a single family of four people, plus $2 for each additional person and $2 for electric hookups. Major credit cards are accepted. The maximum stay is 14 days.

Directions: From I-10 at De Funiak Springs, take Exit 85 and go south on U.S. 331 for 26 miles. At U.S. 98, turn left and drive two miles east to County Road 283. Turn south and drive three miles. At County Road 30A, turn eastbound and go .5 mile to the park.

Contact: Grayton Beach State Park, 357 Main Park Road, Santa Rosa Beach, FL 32549, 850/231-4210, website: www.floridastateparks.org.

22 PEACH CREEK RV PARK

Rating: 6

East of Destin
Panama City map, grid b1, page 62

Set in a wooded area, the park is located on Peach Creek with access to the Choctawhatchee Bay and River and is only two miles from Eden State Park. Grayton Beach State Park is just five miles away.

Campsites, facilities: There are 14 full-hookup RV sites, with half available for overnighters. All have 50-amp service and picnic tables. Restrooms, showers, a dump station, laundry facilities, and telephone service are available. On the premises are a boat ramp, a campground store, propane sales, canoe and boat rentals, a dog-walk area, and a nature trail. Most areas are wheelchair accessible. Children are welcome. Leashed pets are permitted.

Reservations, fees: Reservations are recommended. Sites are $20 per night for two people. Major credit cards are accepted. Long-term stays are OK.

Directions: From the intersection of U.S. 98 and Highway 331, drive east four miles. The campground is located one mile east of the intersection with County Road 395.

Contact: Peach Creek RV Park, 4401 Highway 98 East, Santa Rosa Beach, FL 32459, 850/231-1948.

23 PANAMA CITY BEACH CAMPGROUND AND RV RESORT

Rating: 4

On Panama City Beach's Miracle Strip
Panama City map, grid b1, page 62

Surprise! Tenters are welcome here, and the tent area is shady. For a beachside park, this one also has more breathing room (18 acres) and greenery (tall slash pines, grassy areas) than most. You can fish or watch the ducks swim in Lake Robbie Drive, but confine your swimming to the pool. Some people may consider being right next door to the amusement park an advantage, whereas others will dislike the noise.

Campsites, facilities: In addition to 180 full-hookup RV spots, the campground has an area accommodating 20 tents with electricity and space for primitive camping. Restrooms, showers, picnic tables, laundry facilities, a dump station, a pool, a playground, a recreation room, horseshoe pits, a volleyball field, and a small fishing pond are on site. Children are welcome. Leashed pets are permitted; pet owners must clean up messes.

Reservations, fees: Reservations are required in summer. Sites are $21.50 to $28.50 per night for four people, plus $4 for each additional person. Major credit cards are accepted. Long-term stays are permitted. One bathhouse is wheelchair accessible.

Directions: From the intersection of Alternate U.S. 98/Front Beach Road and County Road 392 in Panama City Beach, travel west on Alternate U.S. 98 for 2.3 miles. The park is just east of the Miracle Strip Amusement Park.

Contact: Panama City Beach Campground and RV Resort, 11826 Front Beach Road, Panama City Beach, FL 32407, 850/235-1643.

24 MIRACLE STRIP RV AND MOBILE HOME PARK

Rating: 1

On Panama City Beach's Miracle Strip
Panama City map, grid b2, page 62

Walk to the beach or to the many shops, restaurants, and tourist attractions of the Miracle Strip commercial area; the park is down the street from a large amusement park. Freshwater anglers can test their luck on Lake Flora behind the park (and next to Wal-Mart). There's not much shade.

Campsites, facilities: Primarily a mobile home park (52 units), the 11-acre facility has 30 sites available for RVs up to 40 feet long. Restrooms, showers, a lake, and a clubhouse are on the premises. Families with children are welcome. Leashed pets under 20 pounds are permitted.

Reservations, fees: These first-come, first-served sites run $25 per night for two people, plus $3 per extra person over age 16. Credit cards are not accepted. Long-term rates are available.

Directions: From the intersection of Alternate U.S. 98/Front Beach Road and County Road 392 in Panama City Beach, travel west on Alternate U.S. 98 for two miles. The park is on the north side of the road, next to Wal-Mart.

Contact: Miracle Strip RV and Mobile Home Park, 10510 Front Beach Road, Panama City Beach, FL 32407, 850/234-3833.

25 PINEGLEN MOTORCOACH AND RV PARK

Rating: 9

In Panama City Beach

Panama City map, grid b2, page 62

Nicely secluded from the hurly-burly atmosphere of the beachfront, this modern but nature-blessed park boasts a covered gazebo for picnics along one of the three stocked fishing lakes. Tall pines shade the campground, which is close to the beaches, amusement parks, shopping, and restaurants.

Campsites, facilities: This park offers 60 RV sites with full hookups or water and electricity, picnic tables, grills, and cable TV. Sixteen sites are pull-through, and 30 have 50-amp service. Restrooms, showers, a dump station, laundry facilities, and telephone service are available. On the premises are a screened-in pool, a clubhouse, a dog-walk area, and three stocked fishing lakes. The bathhouses, laundry room, and pool area are wheelchair accessible. Children are welcome. Leashed pets are permitted.

Reservations, fees: Reservations are recommended. Sites are $22 to $31 per night for a family of two adults and four children up to age 12, plus $2 per extra person over 12 years old. Major credit cards are accepted.

Long-term (up to six months) or seasonal stays are allowed.

Directions: From U.S. 98 at the intersection of State Road 79, drive east on U.S. 98 about four miles. The park is on the north side across from a large furniture store.

Contact: Pineglen Motorcoach and RV Park, 11930 Panama City Parkway, Panama City Beach, FL 32407, 850/230-8535, fax 850/230-2554, website: www.rvflorida.com.

26 EMERALD COAST RV BEACH RESORT

Rating: 9

West of Panama City Beach

Panama City map, grid b2, page 62

Manicured to near perfection, this big-rig resort caters to families and snowbirds who want a beachside destination vacation on a quiet street yet near shopping and entertainment. Palms and pines cast shade over the paved roads and sites. The managers describe it as "upscale," and the park has won awards for its cleanliness and neatness. All campsites are lighted. Even the restrooms are heated or air-conditioned.

Campsites, facilities: There are 138 full-hookup RV sites with concrete pads, picnic tables, and cable TV. Restrooms, showers, laundry facilities, and telephone service are available. On the premises are a new heated pool, a clubhouse, horseshoe pits, shuffleboard courts, a dog-walk area, and miniature golf. Movies, pancakes, cook-outs, bingo, cards, arts and crafts, and local tours provide entertainment. Children are welcome. Leashed pets are permitted, but not German shepherds, Doberman pinschers, rottweilers, or pit bulls.

Reservations, fees: Reservations are recommended. Sites are $32 per night for two people, plus $3 per extra person. Major credit cards are accepted. Long-term rates are available.

Directions: From I-10, take Exit 17 southbound on State Road 79 about 35 miles to the junction with U.S. 98. At U.S. 98, go east 6.6 miles.

Turn right on Allison Avenue (Pack-Rat Storage is on the corner) and drive one block to the park. From Panama City at the bridge, head west on Alternate 98 for 1.5 miles and follow the directions above.

Contact: Emerald Coast RV Beach Resort, 1957 Allison Avenue, Panama City Beach FL 32407, 850/235-0924 or 800/232-2478, fax 850/235-9609, website: www.rvresort.com.

27 RACCOON RIVER CAMPGROUND
≈ ♨ 🏠 🚸 ♿ 🚐 ⛺

Rating: 5

In Panama City Beach

Panama City map, grid b2, page 62

Set centrally near the beach, this cleanly kept park backs onto a pretty lake. Ask for sites 76 through 98 to be closest to the waterfront views of the lake and woods. The tenting area is also near the lake—a bonus. A small bridge leads to a wooded area for quiet walks.

Campsites, facilities: There are 143 full-hookup RV sites and 18 tent sites with electricity. Additionally, primitive tenters can be accommodated in a field near the pool. All developed sites have picnic tables, cable TV, and concrete pads. Forty-three are pull-through. Restrooms, showers, laundry facilities, and telephone service are available. On the premises are two heated pools, a fenced-in playground, a clubhouse, store, and recreation hall. Most areas are wheelchair accessible. Children are welcome. Leashed pets under 20 pounds are permitted, but not in the tent area or if you have a pop-up camper.

Reservations, fees: Reservations are recommended. Sites are $24 per night for four people, plus $4 per extra person and $2 for air conditioners or using a 50-amp site. Major credit cards are accepted. Long-term rates are available.

Directions: From Panama City Beach at the bridge over St. Andrews Bay, head west on U.S. 98A for about one mile. Turn right at

County Road 392A/Hutchison Boulevard and continue west about .5 mile to the park on your left.

Contact: Raccoon River Campground, 12209 Hutchison Boulevard, Panama City Beach, FL 32407, 850/234-0181, fax 850/234-1090.

28 CAMPER'S INN (FORMERLY PANAMA CITY BEACH KOA)
≈ 🏠 🚸 🚐 ⛺

Rating: 4

In Panama City Beach

Panama City map, grid b2, page 62

Set in the most commercial part of Panama City Beach, this park is across the street and about a block's walk from beaches and the Gulf of Mexico, although there's not much of a view. T-shirt and souvenir shops, amusement parks, bumper cars, a dog track, bars, and strip clubs are the milieu. But there's plenty to do without leaving the campground, from playing ball to swimming in the two pools. Small children and nonswimmers must be supervised in the pool areas. Camping supplies, gifts, toys, groceries, and rental bikes are available.

Campsites, facilities: RVs and tents can be accommodated in this 240-space mobile home and RV park, of which about 99 are available for RVs and 15 for tents. There's a tent-only area with water available; seven tent sites also have electricity. Adjacent to the tent area are 10 pull-through RV sites. Full hookups, cable TV, restrooms, showers, picnic tables, laundry facilities, and a dump station are available. Also on site are a pool, a recreation hall, a playground, a volleyball area, basketball and shuffleboard courts, several stores, cabins for rent, and a gasoline station. Planned activities include potluck dinners, karaoke, dances, cards, and bingo. Children are welcome. Leashed pets are permitted.

Reservations, fees: Reservations are recommended. Sites are $18 to $36 per night for two people, plus $4 for each additional person over the age of 10, and $2 for cable TV.

Major credit cards are accepted. Long-term rates are available.

Directions: From the intersection of U.S. 98 and County Road 3033/Beckrich Road in Panama City Beach, drive south on County Road 3033. Turn east on County Road 392 and drive .7 mile. Continue for two miles on Thomas Drive to the park.

Contact: Camper's Inn, 8800 Thomas Drive, Panama City Beach, FL 32408, 850/234-5731 or 866/872-2267.

29 MAGNOLIA BEACH RV PARK

Rating: 6

In Panama City Beach on St. Andrews Bay
Panama City map, grid b2, page 62

Many campsites are shaded by tall oaks and magnolias, which is remarkable for a developed bayfront RV park in the Panama City area. Fourteen spots overlook St. Andrews Bay, the pool, and the fishing pier. If you're traveling with kids, the managers may let you have one of the sites across from the pool, the better to keep an eye on your brood. (Tip: Reserve ahead for those sites.) This tranquil spot is for those who prefer to be removed from the honky-tonk, theme-park atmosphere of Panama City's Miracle Strip but who still want to stay close to the beaches. It's a snowbird destination, complete with winter activities; the Spring Break crowd is unlikely to be staying at this seven-acre park. The bay also gives boaters access to Gulf of Mexico fishing grounds.

Campsites, facilities: All 91 RV-only sites have full hookups, cable TV, and picnic tables. Restrooms, showers, laundry facilities, a dump station, a pool, a boat ramp, a fishing pier, a club room, propane, and a store are on site. Groceries and restaurants are two miles away. Children are welcome. Leashed pets are permitted.

Reservations, fees: Reservations are recommended. Sites are $18 to $26 per night for two people, plus $1 for each additional person over age eight. Major credit cards are accepted.

Directions: From the intersection of U.S. 98 and County Road 3031/Thomas Drive in Panama City Beach, head south on Thomas Drive. At the fourth traffic light, turn left (east) onto Magnolia Beach Road. Drive two miles on Magnolia Beach Road until the road dead-ends at the park.

Contact: Magnolia Beach RV Park, 4100 Magnolia Beach Road, Panama City Beach, FL 32408, 850/235-1581, website: http://interoz.com/magnoliabeach.

30 PANAMA CITY BEACH RV RESORT

Rating: 9

In Panama City Beach
Panama City map, grid b2, page 62

Located just outside St. Andrews State Park, this is a deluxe way to be near that park's marvelous beaches. The park is brand-new and caters to motor coaches and other big rigs.

Campsites, facilities: There are 69 large, full-hookup RV sites with professional landscaping to accommodate even the biggest vehicles. Everything is manicured and new. Instead of concrete walkways, all driveways and paths are covered with pretty paver blocks. More than 800 palms, magnolias, wax myrtles, and oaks have been planted, and the lighting is designed to accent the greenery.

Restrooms, showers, laundry facilities, and telephone service are available. On the premises are a heated pool, exercise room, a recreation hall, walking paths, a store, beach access, and four luxury rental units. Lots are for sale. Children are welcome. Leashed pets are permitted.

Reservations, fees: Reservations are recommended. Sites are $30 per night, but prices are subject to change. Major credit cards are accepted.

Directions: From the intersection of U.S. 98 and County Road 3033/Beckrich Road in Panama City Beach, drive south on County Road 3033. Turn east on County Road 392 and drive

.7 mile. Continue for 2.5 miles on Thomas Drive to the park.

Contact: Panama City Beach RV Resort, 4702 Thomas Drive, Panama City Beach, FL 32408; (866)-637-3529, website: www.panamacity rvresort.com.

31 ST. ANDREWS STATE PARK

Rating: 10

East of Panama City Beach
Panama City map, grid b2, page 62

Famed internationally for its clear waters and blinding white-sand beaches, this 1,260-acre state park gets hard use from tourists and locals, especially during the summer. Camping is split between the Pine Grove and Lagoon Campgrounds; both overlook Grand Lagoon, a narrow body of water separating the park from the rest of the barrier island. Some sites are directly on the water, and slash pines offer shade. The best swimming is on the gulf side of the park, where big rolling sand dunes separate the road from the beach. You can snorkel there or in a protected pool behind a rock jetty. Fishing is from the jetty, the beach, two piers, or by boat; among the fish caught here are dolphin, bluefish, flounder, Spanish mackerel, sea trout, redfish, and bonito.

Two short nature trails give hikers an opportunity to see alligators and birds in a salt marsh. Also in the park is a turpentine still that shows how early settlers derived the solvent from pine trees, a practice that became a major industry at the turn of the century. World War II–era circular cannon platforms still stand in the park, which was used as a military reservation at the time. Across from the park is Shell Island, which is reachable by park shuttle in the spring and summer or by boat year-round; it's a 700-acre oasis that remains almost untouched by development. Unfortunately, this park is so close to major tourist areas and the urban area that it can get crowded.

Campsites, facilities: There are 176 sites with water, electricity, picnic tables, and grills. Restrooms, showers, a dump station, two fishing piers, a boat ramp, a store, picnic areas, and swimming beaches are available. Children are welcome, but pets are not allowed.

Reservations, fees: Reservations are recommended; call ReserveAmerica at 800/326-3521. From October 1 through February 28, sites are $10 per night for four people, plus $2 for electricity and $2 for a waterfront location. From March 1 through September 30, sites are $17 per night, plus the extra charges mentioned. Major credit cards are accepted. The maximum stay is 14 days.

Directions: From the intersection of U.S. 98 and County Road 3031/Thomas Drive in Panama City Beach, turn south on County Road 3031. Drive five miles to the dead end at the beach and turn left. The park entrance is just ahead.

Contact: St. Andrews State Park, 4415 Thomas Drive, Panama City, FL 32408, 850/233-5140.

32 DEER HAVEN RV AND MOBILE HOME PARK

Rating: 2

In Southport
Panama City map, grid b2, page 62

Located near Deer Point Lake, this park offers boaters access to the Gulf of Mexico and saltwater and freshwater fishing. It's convenient to Panama City Beach but distant enough to avoid the traffic jams, or as owners Steve and Kena Staton say, "convenience and country living without the congestion." Grocery stores, bait and tackle, laundry facilities, and restaurants are located one mile away. Children are allowed, but there is no playground and the clientele is mostly adult.

Campsites, facilities: Set on four acres, this park has 39 trailer and mobile home spaces, with 21 spots available for RVs up to 40 feet long. Each site has a concrete patio. Full hookups, cable TV, telephone service, restrooms, showers, a recreation room, and a horseshoe pit are on site. Children are welcome. Small house pets are allowed.

Reservations, fees: Reservations are recommended. Sites are $15 per night for two people, plus $2 for each additional person. Credit cards are not accepted. Long-term stays are permitted.

Directions: From the intersection of U.S. 231 and County Road 2321 north of Panama City, drive west on County Road 2321 for seven miles. The park is on the south side of the road.

Contact: Deer Haven RV and Mobile Home Park, 2812 County Road 2321, Southport, FL 32409, 850/265-6205, email: deerhaven-park@cs.com.

33 GULF-OAKS RV PARK

Rating: 1

In the community of Parker near Panama City

Panama City map, grid b3, page 62

Most sites are nestled under tall oak trees at this park that fronts on 300 feet of navigable waters, as well as a saltwater bayou. Gulf-Oaks targets overnighters and long-term residents but is far from the traditional tourist attractions of Panama City Beach. Tyndall Air Force Base, located 1.25 miles to the east on U.S. 98, doesn't allow the public to camp in its campground, but it does permit hikers to use nature trails that traverse through a freshwater swamp and pine flatwoods.

Campsites, facilities: This 2.7-acre urban park has 30 RV sites with full hookups, cable TV, telephone access, and a dump station. There are no restrooms or showers. Children and leashed pets are allowed.

Reservations, fees: Reservations are recommended. Sites are $15 per night for two people and $2 per extra person. Credit cards are not accepted. Long-term stays are permitted.

Directions: From the intersection of U.S. 98 and Business Route U.S. 98 in Parker, travel north for .5 mile on U.S. 98 to the park on the east side of the road.

Contact: Gulf-Oaks RV Park, 5612 East U.S. 98, Lot 25, Panama City, FL 32404, 850/874-0827.

34 SCOTTS FERRY GENERAL STORE AND CAMPGROUND

Rating: 5

South of Blountstown

Panama City map, grid b4, page 62

Nearly hidden under the highway bridge over the Chipola River, this canoeing-oriented campground is slipped into a hardwood forest sloping down to a little boat dock. It's a shady spot with an open-air pavilion, but you may hear road noise from the bridge. The campground rents canoes and charges $2 for use of the boat launch; the affiliated store sells hunting and camping supplies, bait, and gasoline. For a fee, you can rent covered picnic tables, some of which are large enough to accommodate a group. Two miles south of here is The Junction, which sells groceries, hardware, tackle, ammunition, and liquor; rents out videos; and operates an indoor flea market.

Campsites, facilities: The 25 campsites have water and electric hookups and picnic tables. Restrooms, showers, a boat ramp, a pavilion, rental cabins, and a store are on site. Children are welcome. Leashed pets are permitted.

Reservations, fees: Reservations are not necessary. Sites are $15.50 per night for two people, plus $3 for each extra person. Major credit cards are accepted. Long-term stays are OK.

Directions: From Blountstown, drive south on State Road 71 for 11 miles. The park is on the west (right) side of the road, just before you cross the bridge.

Contact: Scotts Ferry General Store and Campground, 6648 State Route 715, Blountstown, FL 32424, 850/674-2900.

35 PARKER FARM CAMPGROUND

Rating: 1

On the northwest side of Wewahitchka
Panama City map, grid b4, page 62

Little more than an open, grassy field in the countryside, this no-frills campground is located next to the North Florida Motor Speedway, which claims to be the fastest dirt track in the nation. It also adjoins a field for flying remote-control airplanes, with a three-day Labor Day Weekend "fly in." Restaurants and groceries are available within one mile.

Campsites, facilities: All 16 RV sites have full hookups, and two of the sites have optional telephone service. A dump station can be used for a $2 fee. There are no showers or restrooms. Alcoholic beverages are prohibited. Children are welcome. Leashed pets are permitted, but they must be kept inside your rig. The owner says that all areas of the park are wheelchair accessible.

Reservations, fees: Reservations are not necessary except on Labor Day weekend. Sites are $14 per night for two people, plus $2 for each additional person over age 12. Credit cards are not accepted. Long-term stays are OK.

Directions: From the junction of State Roads 71 and 22 in Wewahitchka, drive west on State Road 22 for .3 mile. Turn north on County Road 22A and drive three miles to the park.

Contact: Parker Farm Campground, 440 Parker Farm Road, Wewahitchka, FL 32465, 850/639-5204.

36 DEAD LAKES PARK

Rating: 9

North of Wewahitchka
Panama City map, grid b4, page 62

This park's eerie beauty and its name stem from the thousands of bleached tree trunks rooted in the lake water. The trees drowned when a sandbar formed in the Apalachicola River, blocking the mouth of the Chipola River and flooding 12,000 acres of swamp. Before this event, there were twin lakes that the Indians called "water eyes," or Wewahitchka, a name that was adopted by the nearby town. Two other ponds in the park were dug in 1936 and held a fish hatchery until 1951. Half a century ago, turpentine was tapped from the pines, and honey, harvested by bees from the hardwood tupelo trees, was barreled for medicinal purposes. Spanish moss that draped the trees was a commodity used for packing and furniture stuffing. Such commerce is history today, and the Dead Lakes area is primarily a recreational retreat surrounded by swamp and flatwood forests. These vistas made the silver screen in Peter Fonda's 1997 movie, *Ulee's Gold,* a critically acclaimed drama in which Fonda played a beekeeper. The bees in this area really do produce a succulent honey called "Tupelo Gold."

The campsites are shaded by native longleaf pines and carpeted with wire grass. There's a hiking trail for viewing wildlife, and the boat ramp provides access to the Dead Lakes and the Chipola River. The tree trunks create an obstacle course for those in canoes and fishing boats. You can hook bass, bream, and carp in the old hatching ponds as well as in the lakes, where the drowned forest makes casting a real challenge. Formerly called Dead Lakes State Park, the land was acquired in 2002 by Gulf County, which is undertaking numerous improvements to the campground, the boat ramp, and other facilities.

Campsites, facilities: There are 22 sites for tents and RVs up to 40 feet long, all of which have water and electricity. Each site has a picnic table, a grill, and a fire pit. The maximum RV length is 35 feet. Facilities include restrooms, showers, a dump station, and a boat ramp. Children are welcome. Pets are allowed with proof of vaccination.

Reservations, fees: Reservations are not necessary. Sites cost $10 per night.

Directions: From Port St. Joe, take State Road

71 north for 24 miles to Wewahitchka. Drive one mile north of town and turn east on Gary Rowell Road. Continue .5 mile to the park. From Panama City, take State Road 22 east for 25 miles to State Road 71 and turn north. Go one mile to Gary Rowell Road, turn east, and proceed to the park.

Contact: For information about Dead Lakes Park, contact Paula Ramsey Pickett of the Gulf County Tourism Development Council at 850/229-7800; email: info@VisitGulf.com. The park is located at 510 Gary Rowell Road, Wewahitchka.

37 APALACHICOLA RIVER WATER MANAGEMENT AREA

Rating: 6

Along the Apalachicola River

Panama City map, grid b4, page 62

When Florida was a backwater, the Apalachicola River was the equivalent of a superhighway. Water was the means by which folks got around the Sunshine State before the advent of railroads and automobiles. Today, these 35,000 or so acres along the river are virtually deserted. The isolated upland islands of this large alluvial floodplain are considered unique. River flows are variable and are controlled by the U.S. Army Corps of Engineers at the Jim Woodruff Dam, a two-hour drive north of here. Nevertheless, the Apalachicola is navigable and is a favorite with powerboaters and fishers. Canoeists are less enthusiastic because of the open water and traffic.

Bird-watching is good, with 99 species known to swoop into the area. Hawks, swallow-tailed kites, and Mississippi kites all can be seen soaring high overhead, particularly in the spring. Bald eagles and alligator snapping turtles are common. If you're really lucky, you'll see a Florida black bear. Horseback riding and hiking are popular in the section between the Florida and Apalachicola Rivers—the part most accessible by car—which is known as Florida River Island. The place is loaded with wild animals, including deer, turkey, rabbit, and bobcat, which become targets for hunters starting in mid-November and lasting until late April. Particularly during the general gun seasons—around Thanksgiving and from mid-December to mid-February—wear bright orange clothing when hiking or horseback riding.

Campsites, facilities: Three primitive camping areas with no facilities lie at the northern end of this tract. There are 17 boat ramps and a network of dirt roads and hiking trails. Pack in water, food, and camping supplies; pack out trash. Children are welcome. Pets are permitted.

Reservations, fees: Reservations are not necessary. Camping is free.

Directions: Numerous boat ramps are located off dirt roads leading west from State Road 379 or east from State Roads 71 and 22A. For camping, take State Road 379 north from Sumatra and make a left onto Forest Service Road 188, which leads to a network of dirt roads. At the northern edge of the water management area, on the Florida River, is an unnamed primitive campsite. Farther south, not far from a horse-trailer parking area, is the Greenback Lake site. Even farther south, near the Florida River, is the Acorn Lake site. Touring this remote country requires a compass and good maps, such as those available from the U.S. Geological Survey or in the free "Apalachicola River Wildlife and Environmental Area" pamphlet put out by the Florida Fish and Wildlife Conservation Commission.

Contact: Northwest Florida Water Management District, 81 Water Management Drive, Havana, FL 32333, 850/539-5999. Florida Fish and Wildlife Conservation Commission, 3911 Highway 2321, Panama City, FL 32409, 904/265-3676.

38 EL GOVERNOR RV CAMPGROUND

Rating: 2

In Mexico Beach
Panama City map, grid c3, page 62

Set in the center of Mexico Beach, a family-oriented community of vacation homes and waterfront motels on the Gulf of Mexico, this RV park has a small creek and a good location across the street from the water. Don't expect much shade, greenery, or water views, which are blocked by the motel. Charter boat services, fishing guides, and boat storage and dockage are available in town. There are two similar campgrounds in the area: Islander RV Park, on the west side of town, and Rustic Sands Resort, on 15th Street north of U.S. 98.

Campsites, facilities: This campground has 57 RV sites (10 pull-through) with full hookups. Restrooms, showers, picnic tables, laundry facilities, and a dump station are on site. Children and leashed pets are permitted.

Reservations, fees: Reservations are recommended. Sites are $16.50 per night for four people, plus $2 for each additional person. Credit cards are not accepted. Stays up to six months are allowed.

Directions: Drive through Mexico Beach on U.S. 98. The park is in the middle of town at the corner of 17th Street, across from the big El Governor Motel.

Contact: El Governor RV Campground, 1700 Highway 98, Mexico Beach, FL 32410, 850/648-5432.

39 ST. JOSEPH PENINSULA STATE PARK

Rating: 10

Near Port St. Joe
Panama City map, grid c3, page 62

Surrounded by water on three sides, this secluded, woodsy state park boasts one of the best beaches in Florida, with broad expanses of sugar-white sand, dunes studded with sea oats and struggling grasses, and trees twisted by the wind. Once again in 2002, "Dr. Beach," a university professor who rates these things, has named this beach America's No. 1. You can swim in either the Gulf of Mexico or St. Joseph Bay. The water is clear enough for snorkeling; be sure to use a dive flag. On the bay side, you may see bay scallops, octopus, and three types of crabs (hermit, fiddler, and horseshoe). Canoes are available for rent.

When you can tear yourself away from the water, try hiking on nine miles of heavily forested trails. Bike riders will find paved roads with little traffic inside and outside the park. Here's a tip: Buy groceries in Port St. Joe, 22 miles away, and bring wood along for a campfire; supplies in the community of vacation homes on the peninsula are limited. Sprawling over 2,516 acres, the park dominates the northern tip of the peninsula, which has seen little development since the Army used it for training during World War II. More than 200 species of birds have been seen here. In the fall, campers may see hawks heading south or monarch butterflies flying to their winter home in Mexico. There's plenty of other wildlife; even a black bear has been spotted—look in the campground office for a photo of the creature.

Campsites, facilities: The state park has 119 campsites, including 99 with electric hookups. Each site has water, a picnic table, a grill, and a fire ring. On the premises are restrooms, showers, a dump station, a boat ramp and basin, beaches, a playground, and rental cabins. Some campsites and the picnic area are wheelchair accessible. Children are welcome. Pets are not allowed.

Reservations, fees: Reservations are recommended; call ReserveAmerica at 800/326-3521. Sites are $8 to $15 per night for four people, plus $2 for each additional person and $2 for electricity. Major credit cards are accepted. The maximum stay is 120 days.

Directions: From Port St. Joe, travel east on

U.S. 98 to State Road 30. At the fork, veer right and proceed south on State Road C-30 for six miles, then turn right onto State Road 30-E and drive eight miles west to the park.

Contact: St. Joseph Peninsula State Park, 8899 Cape San Blas Road, Port St. Joe, FL 32456, 850/227-1327, fax 850/227-1488, website: floridastateparks.org.

40 PRESNELL'S BAYSIDE MARINA AND RV RESORT

Rating: 5

South of Port St. Joe

Panama City map, grid c3, page 62

All sites in this 7.5-acre boating-oriented campground are on the waterfront, with sweeping views of St. Joseph Bay and St. Joseph Peninsula. Fishing guides, boat rentals, and charter services are available at the marina. You can swim in the bay, but the clear water is shallow and there's no real beach—just grass flats frequented by wading birds. An 18-hole golf course is located .25 mile away.

In the 1830s, this stretch of coastal highway was the most populous—and notorious—burg in all of Florida: the city of St. Joseph, population 12,000, is where the state's first constitution was penned. St. Joseph had a racetrack, nice hotels, bawdy houses, and a reputation as the "wickedest city in the Southeast." With a new railroad linking it to the Apalachicola River, St. Joseph boomed, thanks to King Cotton. Its harbor was described as "a forest of spars and masts" because it was cluttered with ships transporting 150,000 bales of cotton a year. A catastrophe killed the townspeople of St. Joseph in 1841, when a South American sailing ship arrived with yellow fever in its hold. Within a few weeks, St. Joseph was a ghost town. Three years later, a hurricane-generated tidal wave washed away what was left.

After a century, commerce was resurrected thanks to a Savannah scientist named Dr. Charles H. Herty, who invented a cheap way to make newsprint, paper sacks, and corrugated boxes from the slash pine trees that grow like weeds in northwest Florida. U.S. 98 was lined with trailers and shacks sheltering laborers who built the first paper plant at Port St. Joe. The paper mill has closed, which is bad news for mill workers yet good news for campers. The pungent aroma that sometimes wafted through campsites on St. Joseph Bay was the perfume of wood-pulp brew—the smell of money.

Campsites, facilities: All 24 RV sites have water and electricity. On the premises are restrooms, showers, a boat ramp, a limited store, rental trailers, bait and tackle, boat rentals, and a small play area. Children are welcome. Leashed pets are permitted.

Reservations, fees: Reservations are required in July and August and recommended the rest of the year. Sites are $14 to $17 per night for four people, plus $2 for each additional person. Major credit cards are accepted. Long-term stays are OK.

Directions: From Port St. Joe, drive one mile east on U.S. 98 to County Road 30-A. At the fork, veer right and proceed south on County Road 30-A (a.k.a. C30-A) for 2.1 miles to the park.

Contact: Presnell's Bayside Marina and RV Resort, 2115 County Road 30-A, Port St. Joe, FL 32456, 850/229-2710, website: www.presnells.com.

41 CAPE SAN BLAS CAMPING RESORT

Rating: 10

Near Port St. Joe

Panama City map, grid c3, page 62

Not only does the San Blas campground rival the state park down the road, it is also superior in some respects. For starters, it has a pool and a beach, and the campsites are nestled in dunes, making them cozy, albeit a bit challenging for maneuvering motor homes.

(Because of this, RVs 38 feet and longer should keep going to the state park.) Another plus is for the hearing impaired: the owners are well versed in sign language.

The resort's biggest advantage is its easy reach—via canoe or boat only—to lush St. Vincent National Wildlife Refuge, a 12,000-acre island. The island was named by Franciscan friars when the Spanish were in charge. It was later purchased by Dr. R.V. Pierce, a patent medicine manufacturer who stocked it as a hunting preserve with deer, boar, geese, and quail. In 1948, the island's owners added an eclectic menagerie—zebra, ring-necked pheasant, oriental jungle fowl, and giant Asian sambar deer. When the federal authorities took over some 20 years ago, the exotic critters were evicted, except for a small, elusive herd of sambar, which roam here to this day. The refuge is abundant with other furred and feathered wildlife, including white-tailed deer, feral pigs, turkeys, bald eagles, and pelicans. Endangered red wolves are being bred for transplanting onto the mainland. This resort is a haven for hunters, anglers, and hikers, with 14 miles of palm-lined beach on the gulf and bay, plus 80 miles of sandy roads criss-crossing the interior. Pack a picnic lunch and plenty of drinking water, and spend the day playing Robinson Crusoe; camping is prohibited without a hunting permit. A few warnings: there are no restrooms, lots of ticks and flies, and a few poisonous snakes. And beware of strong currents when crossing the .25-wide Indian Pass between St. Vincent and San Blas.

Campsites, facilities: The camp has 32 RV sites with water and electricity, including 11 with additional sewer connections; tight curves restrict vehicle size to 38 feet. There are 14 tent sites in a separate area. Each site has a picnic table and fire ring. On the premises are restrooms, showers, laundry facilities, a dump station, a swimming pool, canoe rentals, a playground, a volleyball net, a basketball hoop, a horseshoe pit, and a small store offering limited groceries, bait, and tackle. A 24-hour modem station for laptop computers is situated right outside the office. Children are welcome. Leashed pets are permitted.

Reservations, fees: Reservations are recommended. Sites are $18 to $24 per night for two people, plus $2 for each additional person. Major credit cards are accepted. Stays are limited to 90 days.

Directions: From Port St. Joe, travel east on U.S. 98 to County Road 30-A. At the fork, veer right and proceed south on County Road 30-A (a.k.a. C30-A) for six miles, then turn right onto Cape San Blas Road. Go 1.5 miles west to the park on the south side of the road.

Contact: Cape San Blas Camping Resort, P.O. Box 645, Port St. Joe, FL 32457, 850/229-6800, website: www.capesanblas.com/capecamp.

COURTESY OF VISIT FLORIDA

Chapter 3

Tallahassee Area

Tallahassee Area

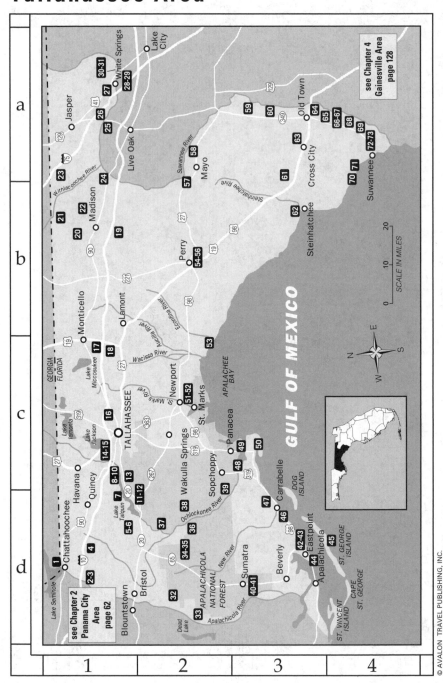

see Chapter 4
Gainesville Area
page 128

GULF OF MEXICO

SCALE IN MILES
0   10   20

GEORGIA
FLORIDA

APALACHEE
BAY

DOG
ISLAND

ST. GEORGE
ISLAND

CAPE
ST. GEORGE

ST. VINCENT
ISLAND

APALACHICOLA
NATIONAL
FOREST

see Chapter 2
Panama City
Area
page 62

Lake Seminole

Withlacoochee River

Suwannee River

Steinhatchee River

Econfina River

Aucilla River

Wacissa River

St. Marks River

Ochlockonee River

New River

Apalachicola River

Dead Lake

Lake Miccosukee

Lake Jackson

Lake Iamonia

Lake Talquin

© AVALON TRAVEL PUBLISHING, INC.

1 EAST BANK CAMPGROUND, LAKE SEMINOLE

Rating: 8

On Lake Seminole north of Chattahoochee

Tallahassee map, grid d1, page 86

This park is actually in Georgia, but the easiest way to get to it is from Chattahoochee, Florida, and its boundary is only a couple of blocks north of the Sunshine State. An engineer's eye for detail is evident; each neatly kept campsite even has a special metal post for hanging camp lanterns, and one site (number 9) was designed for campers in wheelchairs. Sites are laid out in several pods on a gentle slope overlooking Lake Seminole, a 37,500-acre reservoir formed by damming the confluence of the Chattahoochee and Flint Rivers upstream of the Jim Woodruff Lock and Dam. Boating, fishing, water-skiing, and swimming are the things to do here. Anglers may hook lunker, largemouth, scrappy hybrid, striped, and white bass, or catfish, crappie, and bream. Canada geese spending the winter in the area paddle around the edge of the lake near the campground.

Campsites, facilities: There are 78 sites in this U.S. Army Corps of Engineers campground on Lake Seminole. Two primitive sites are set aside for tent camping only. All other sites have water and electricity; about 10 of those are for tents only. Picnic tables, grills, and fire rings are available. Restrooms, showers, a dump station, laundry facilities, a boat ramp, shuffleboard, and horseshoe pits are on the grounds. Children are welcome. Leashed pets are permitted.

Reservations, fees: Reserve your spot at least four days in advance of your arrival at 877/444-6777 or www.reserveusa.com. Rangers say, however, that there are almost always spots available, so reservations are not strictly necessary. Sites are $12 to $16 per night for up to eight people. Major credit cards are accepted by the reservation system. The maximum stay is two weeks, although you may request a two-week extension.

Directions: In Chattahoochee, from the junction of U.S. 90 and State Road 269, drive four blocks west on U.S. 90 to Bolivar Street and look for the campground sign. Drive north on Bolivar Street for 1.4 miles to the campground entrance.

Contact: U.S. Army Corps of Engineers, Resource Management Office, Lake Seminole, P.O. Box 96, 2382 Booster Club Road, Chattahoochee, FL 32324, 229/662-2001. The campground phone number is 229/662-9273, website: www.sam.usace.army.mil.

2 TORREYA STATE PARK

Rating: 10

North of Bristol

Tallahassee map, grid d1, page 86

Perched atop 150-foot bluffs above the Apalachicola River, Torreya (pronounced "tory-ah") State Park is unique in Florida. In addition to the unusual terrain of deep ravines and hills, the park is noteworthy in that it supports trees and plants normally seen in Georgia's Appalachian Mountains. Wildlife and birds are plentiful, and at summer's end, the hardwood forest puts on a brilliant autumnal display. It's also one of just a few places in the world where the rare Torreya tree grows. Once common across the river bluffs, the Torreya is nearly extinct today because it is prone to at least 30 pathogens that attack just before it goes to seed. Only about 100 are left. (To see one, go to site number 29; as you face the site, the tree is on your right, about 18 feet ahead.)

Also in the park is the Gregory House, an 1849 plantation home originally built across the river. The Civilian Conservation Corps, which built the park in the 1930s, moved the house—a feat that will boggle your mind. They dismantled the building, floated it across the river, and rebuilt it here. Earlier in history, the river bluffs were home to a Civil War gun battery, and archaeologists have found evidence of many Indian settlements.

The main campground is on top of one of the bluffs, and a few sites have sweeping views of the valleys beyond. Several short trails lead down to wooded ravines, good spots for exploring and picking up dead branches for your campfire. Take only fallen and dead limbs from the ground.

Torreya State Park is a great place to limber up for hiking in more hilly terrain out of state. Break in those boots on 15 miles of trails; Florida flatlanders will be startled by how steep those slopes are. Hike for 45 minutes or make a day out of it.

Campsites, facilities: There are 30 sites for RVs and tents. Each site has a picnic table, grill, and fire ring. In addition, two primitive backpacking sites are available (see next campground). Park facilities include restrooms, showers, a dump station, hiking trails, and a museum. You can also rent a yurt (a type of circular tent), which has air-conditioning and heating. It sleeps five people. The picnic area is wheelchair accessible. Children are welcome. Pets are prohibited.

Reservations, fees: Reservations are recommended; call ReserveAmerica at 800/326-3521. Sites are $8 per night for four people, plus $2 for each additional person and $2 for electricity. Major credit cards are accepted. The maximum stay is six weeks.

Directions: From I-10 west of Quincy, take Exit 174 and head west on State Road 12 for about 11 miles. At County Road 1641, turn north and drive seven miles to the park. Or, from U.S. 20 in Bristol, drive north on State Road 12 for eight miles, turn left on County Road 1641, and drive seven miles west to the park. The route is well marked, with signs pointing the way.

Contact: Torreya State Park, HC 2, Box 70, Bristol, FL 32321, 850/643-2674, website: www.floridastateparks.org.

3 TORREYA STATE PARK BACKPACKING SITES

Rating: 9

North of Bristol
Tallahassee map, grid d1, page 86

If you're warming up for a trek on the Appalachian Trail or in some other more mountainous locale, this is a great place for a shakedown trip. Backpackers can hike as many as 15 miles of steep hills and ravines to the Rock Bluff and Rock Creek campsites. Not up to it? The Rock Creek site is just .8 mile into the woods. Hardier campers can take the long way around (seven miles) to get there. The preferred site is Rock Bluff, just 1.25 miles in. Along the way, you may hear the sharp trill of bald eagles or glimpse deer, foxes, bobcats, raccoons, and all kinds of snakes.

Some caveats: You must stick strictly to the trail and camp only at designated sites. Hunters are common in the lands adjacent to the park, and much of the property is not fenced. During the hunting season (usually November through January), wear brightly colored clothing.

Campsites, facilities: Rock Bluff and Rock Creek are two primitive backpacking areas with ground grills, a few benches, and outhouses. Each area can accommodate 12 people on four sites. Water is available in nearby streams, but it must be treated before drinking; better to bring your own. Pack out all garbage. Children are welcome. Pets are prohibited.

Reservations, fees: You must register with the park ranger at least one hour before sunset. If you can't find a ranger, then go to the pay phone at the workshop; a personal phone number is listed there. If you still cannot make contact with a ranger, then the only place you are allowed to stay is at the main campground. Backpacking costs $3 for adults and $2 for those under age 17.

Directions: From I-10 west of Quincy, take Exit 174 and head west on State Road 12 for about 11 miles. At County Road 1641, turn north and drive seven miles to the park. Or, from U.S. 20 in Bristol, drive north on State Road 12 for eight miles, turn left on County Road 1641, and drive seven miles west to the park. The route is well marked, with signs pointing the way.

Contact: Torreya State Park, HC 2, Box 70, Bristol, FL 32321, 850/643-2674, website: www.floridastateparks.org.

4 CHATTAHOOCHEE/ TALLAHASSEE WEST KOA

Rating: 6

Off I-10 south of Chattahoochee
Tallahassee map, grid d1, page 86

Convenient for overnight travelers, this KOA could become a base camp for exploring nearby attractions in Chattahoochee, such as Lake Seminole. Three Spanish missions were built here in the 1600s, and Native Americans were present as far back as 1450. Andrew Jackson was in command at a federal arsenal here during the Indian wars. That fortification later became a prison, then a mental institution. The Florida State Hospital is still a major employer. East of here is the town of Havana, Florida, which has antique shops that draw hundreds of tourists every weekend. Note that the campground pool is open from mid-March through mid-October only.

Campsites, facilities: There are 46 RV sites with water and electric hookups, picnic tables, and grills. Six of the 10 tent sites have electricity. Restrooms, showers, laundry facilities, a dump station, a convenience store, a pool, a playground, a horseshoe pitch area, video rentals, and cabins are available. The main building, pavilion, and restrooms (except showers) are wheelchair accessible. Children are welcome. Leashed pets are permitted.

Reservations, fees: Reservations are recommended. Sites are $24 per night for two people, plus $2 for each additional child or $3 per adult, and $3 for electricity. Major credit cards are accepted. Long-term stays are OK.

Directions: From I-10 at Chattahoochee, take Exit 166 southbound on County Road 270A and drive one mile to the park entrance on the east side of the road.

Contact: Chattahoochee/Tallahassee West KOA, 2309 Flat Creek Road, Chattahoochee, FL 32324, 850/442-6657 or 800/KOA-2153, website: www.koa.com.

5 WHIPPOORWILL SPORTSMAN'S LODGE

Rating: 4

On Lake Talquin south of Quincy
Tallahassee map, grid d1, page 86

This tiny campground is part of a fishing- and hunting-oriented motel on Lake Talquin. Sites are shady and can accommodate rigs up to 40 feet long. Launch your fishing boat from the paved boat ramp; you can tie it up at the covered docks after your trip. Unpaved roads for exploring by bicycle surround the park. Pick up groceries in Quincy, which is 15 miles away; some limited supplies are available at the lodge. The restaurant was recently expanded and hosts a shrimp boil every Friday night.

Campsites, facilities: There are seven RV sites with full hookups and picnic tables. Restrooms, showers, laundry facilities, horseshoe pits, a boat ramp, boat and canoe rentals, trailer rentals, covered boat slips, a fishing pier, a convenience store, and a restaurant/waterfront pub are on site. The fishing pier, stores, and restrooms are wheelchair accessible. Children are welcome. Leashed pets are permitted.

Reservations, fees: Reservations are recommended. Sites are $15 per night for two people, plus $5 for each additional person. Major credit cards are accepted. The maximum stay is three months.

Directions: From I-10 at Quincy, take Exit 181 southbound on State Road 267 for eight miles. Turn east at Cook's Landing Road and drive three miles until the road dead-ends.

Contact: Whippoorwill Sportsman's Lodge,

3129 Cook's Landing Road, Quincy, FL 32351, 850/875-2605, fax 850/875-3345, email: fishtalquin@aol.com.

6 PAT THOMAS PARK

Rating: 7

On Lake Talquin south of Quincy
Tallahassee map, grid d1, page 86

Tailored to overnight and short-term campers, this peaceful park is located on an oak-shaded hill sloping down to Lake Talquin, which surrounds it on three sides. Launch your fishing boat or canoe from the boat ramp near the campground. A full-time park ranger lives on the premises. Restaurants, supermarkets, and laundry facilities are available 10 miles north in Quincy. Bait and tackle and limited groceries can be obtained within one mile. The park is a popular daytime spot for locals all week long; they fish for the day at the piers, then go home, or hold family reunions and other gatherings in the new picnic pavilion.

Campsites, facilities: This two-acre county park has 15 RV sites with full hookups and 15 tent-only sites with water and electricity. On the premises are showers, restrooms, picnic tables, grills, fishing piers, a dump station, a boat ramp, and a playground. Most areas are wheelchair accessible. Children are welcome. Dogs are prohibited.

Reservations, fees: Reservations are recommended. Sites are $5 to $10 per night for two people, plus $1 extra for each additional person (small children are free). Credit cards are not accepted. The maximum stay is 14 days.

Directions: From I-10 at Quincy, take Exit 181 southbound on State Road 267 for nine miles. Turn east at the sign for Hopkins Landing and drive one mile until the road dead-ends at the park.

Contact: Pat Thomas Park, 949 Hopkins Landing Road, Quincy, FL 32351, 850/875-4544 or 850/875-8699.

7 INGRAM'S MARINA

Rating: 4

On Lake Talquin south of Quincy
Tallahassee map, grid d1, page 86

If you're hooked on fishing, you'll appreciate this angler-oriented camp, which sprawls over a hill on the edge of Lake Talquin. Interior roads are unpaved and uneven, but plenty of oak trees provide shade. Some boats can be docked in covered slips on a protected inlet. Bait and tackle and limited groceries are available here. It's near popular hunting areas.

Campsites, facilities: This fish camp has 55 RV sites with full hookups and 10 sites for tents with water and electricity. On the premises are showers, restrooms, cabin and boat rentals, a boat ramp, docks, groceries, bait and tackle, and laundry facilities. All areas of the park are said to be wheelchair accessible. Children are welcome. Leashed pets are permitted.

Reservations, fees: Reservations are recommended. Sites are $15 per night for two people, plus $1 for each additional person. Major credit cards are accepted. Long-term stays are permitted.

Directions: From I-10 at Quincy, take Exit 181 southbound on State Road 267 for eight miles. Turn east at Cook's Landing Road and drive three miles until the road dead-ends at the park.

Contact: Ingram's Marina, 354 Lois Lane, Quincy, FL 32351, 850/627-2241, website: www.ingramsmarina.com.

8 HIGH BLUFF CAMPGROUND (FORMERLY JOE BUDD)

Rating: 8

On Lake Talquin south of Quincy
Tallahassee map, grid c1, page 86

Improvements are coming to the High Bluff Campground, which is located near one of Florida's premier deer-hunting spots in the Joe Budd Wildlife Management Area, within the Lake Talquin State Forest. Hunters and anglers now tend to dominate the sole camping area—a mowed pine- and oak-dotted field on the shore of Lake Talquin. Soon, the campground will have two vault restrooms, potable water, and 32 designated campsites, and it will be open year-round, not just during hunting season.

What sets Joe Budd Wildlife Management Area apart is its plentiful deer and the rolling hills and creek bottoms that contrast with much of pancake-flat Florida. Boaters will notice less development surrounding the upper portion of 12-mile-long Lake Talquin, compared with the ampler evidence of humans around the lower lake. As one of only two sizable reservoirs in Florida, 8,850-acre Lake Talquin offers rewards: largemouth and white bass, speckled perch, and bream. But watch out, or else your fishing line or boat motor—not the fish—may be what gets snagged. Dead standing trees jut hazardously from the water. The trees are remnants from when the Jackson Bluff Dam was built on the Ochlockonee River in 1927.

Campsites, facilities: A clearing by the lake with a fishing pier accommodates 20 to 25 parties of primitive campers. Trash must be packed out. A county-run boat ramp is nearby. Dogs are permitted on a leash. Plans are to construct 32 campsites with picnic tables and fire rings.

Reservations, fees: Reservations are not accepted. Camping permits are not needed, but hunting requires a permit. Sites are $5 each for up to six people and $1 per extra person.

Directions: From I-10 west of Tallahassee, take Exit 192 and go west on U.S. 90 for 2.1 miles, then turn left at State Road 268. Travel 2.4 miles, passing Central Road and veering left onto Peters Road. After the pavement ends (in less than one mile), turn left at High Bluff Road. Continue 2.5 miles to the campground.

Contact: Lake Talquin State Forest, 856 Geddie Road, Tallahassee, FL 32304, 850/488-1871, fax 850/922-2107, website: www.fl-dof.com.

9 BEAR CREEK TRACT

Rating: 6

**In the Lake Talquin State Forest
south of Quincy**

Tallassee map, grid b3, page 86

A primitive campground provides a base for backpacking, hiking, and bicycling in Lake Talquin State Forest. This area is closed to hunters year-round, so you can go about your fun with a relaxed mind. A series of nature trails threads through the Bear Creek Tract, and the campground is nestled below tall pines on a small creek. You'll have to hike in (no bicycles allowed) from the parking area about 2.5 miles away. The hike is described as moderately strenuous with narrow footing along steep inclines in some areas. For the less athletically inclined, a "Living Forest" nature trail at the parking area provides educational and interpretive information from "talking trees."

It's worth noting that about two miles south of the main Bear Creek parking area, cyclists will find the Lines Tract Off-Road Bicycle Trail. The main trail, about seven miles long, is for beginners to intermediate-level riders. You'll find low clearance obstacles, logs, and tight turns around trees. The trail is for two-way traffic, but a counterclockwise direction is recommended. Off the main trail are several more technical loops. To get to the Lines Tract, from the Bear Creek Tract, continue south on State Route 267 and turn west on Cooks Landing Road to the parking area. In the rest of the forest, bicycles are allowed on open forest roads, but not on hiking trails.

Campsites, facilities: There are sites for 10 two-person tents with fire rings. Sites are designated by white bands on the trees. A four-person or family-sized tent is equivalent to two two-person tents. No water or electricity is available. Human waste must be buried six inches deep, at least 100 feet away from the camping area and water sources, and out of sight of the trail. No alcohol is allowed. Children are welcome. Leashed pets are permitted.

Reservations, fees: A state forest use permit is required in advance of your stay. Sites are $5 per night. The maximum stay is 14 days.

Directions: From I-10, take Exit 181 south on State Route 267 for about four miles. The parking area for Bear Creek is on your left.

Contact: Lake Talquin State Forest, 856 Geddie Road, Tallahassee, FL 32304, 850/488-1871, fax 850/922-2107, website: www.fl-dof.com.

10 FORT BRADEN TRACT

Rating: 6

In the Lake Talquin State Forest four miles west of Tallahassee

Tallassee map, grid b3, page 86

Closed to hunters year-round, this area is for hikers and horseback riders. Set within Lake Talquin State Forest on the south side of the lake, this primitive area has an 11-mile circuit hiking loop and a separate 11-mile loop for equestrians. A primitive group camp is located about .5 mile from the main parking lot, and two primitive campsites are on the lakefront. You'll have to hike in to all. The views of the lake are worth the effort.

Campsites, facilities: If you're not traveling with a group, you'll want to choose from the two primitive sites on the lake, about two miles from the parking area. There are sites for three two-person tents with fire rings. Sites are designated by white bands on the trees. A four-person or family-sized tent is equivalent to two two-person tents. No water or electricity is available. Human waste must be buried six inches deep, at least 100 feet away from the camping area and water sources, and out of sight of the trail. No alcohol is allowed. Children are welcome. Leashed pets are permitted.

Reservations, fees: A state forest use permit is required in advance of your stay. Sites are $5 per night. The maximum stay is 14 days.

Directions: From Tallahassee, take State Road 263 to the intersection of State Road 20, then follow State Road 20 west for seven miles. Pass the intersection with Coe Landing Road and continue about .5 mile to the parking area on the north side of the road.

Contact: Lake Talquin State Forest, 856 Geddie Road, Tallahassee, FL 32304, 850/488-1871, fax 850/922-2107, website: www.fl-dof.com.

11 HALL'S LANDING

Rating: 6

On Lake Talquin near Tallahassee

Tallahassee map, grid d2, page 86

Here's a tent-only, primitive campground with hot showers. Offering a large sodded area for tents, this roomy spot has a long boardwalk along the lake with three observation areas.

Campsites, facilities: There are 10 tent sites with drinking water but no electricity. Facilities include restrooms, showers, a cooking grill, and a campfire pit. The day-use area has five picnic shelters, a wheelchair-accessible lakeside boardwalk, a picnic area and pier, two fishing piers and boat docks, a fish-cleaning station, and a boat ramp. Children are welcome. Leashed pets are permitted.

Reservations, fees: Reservations are not accepted. Tent sites are free. RVs are not permitted. The maximum stay is 10 days, or 30 days per calendar year.

Directions: From Tallahassee, take State Road 263 to the intersection of State Road 20, then follow State Road 20 west for 14 miles. The park is on the north side of the road, on Lake Talquin.

Contact: Leon County Parks & Recreation Department, 2280 Miccosukee Road, Tallahassee, FL 32308, 850/488-0221, website: www.co.leon.fl.us/parks/camping.asp.

12 WILLIAM'S LANDING

Rating: 4

On Lake Talquin near Tallahassee
Tallahassee map, grid d2, page 86

Located four miles west of Coe's Landing (see next campground), this campground is slightly larger than that facility and has a recreation field. It's popular with large groups of picnickers. There's no dump station or electricity.

Campsites, facilities: There are 10 campsites for RVs and six for tents. Drinking water is available, but there are no hookups. Facilities include restrooms, two picnic shelters, two fishing piers and boat docks, two fish-cleaning stations, and a boat ramp. Children are welcome. Leashed pets are permitted.

Reservations, fees: Reservations are not accepted. Camping is free. The maximum stay is 10 days or 30 days in a calendar year.

Directions: From Tallahassee, take State Road 263 to the intersection of State Road 20, then follow State Road 20 west for 11 miles. The park is on the north side of the road, on Lake Talquin.

Contact: Leon County Parks & Recreation Department, 2280 Miccosukee Road, Tallahassee, FL 32308, 850/488-0221, website: www.co.leon.fl.us/parks/camping.asp.

13 COE'S LANDING

Rating: 6

On Lake Talquin near Tallahassee
Tallahassee map, grid c1, page 86

This is one of three campgrounds operated by Leon County along Lake Talquin, a haven for anglers just north of Apalachicola National Forest. (It's the only county park that accepts reservations, and park managers brag that each campsite has been located so that everyone has a view of the lake.) Most of the lakeshore is publicly owned and open to hikers. Talquin, which covers 8,850 acres, was formed by damming the Ochlockonee River in 1927. The dam broke once, in 1957, and was rebuilt. The lake is managed by the Florida Fish and Wildlife Conservation Commission, which stocks it with largemouth and striped bass, bluegill, and crappie. Swimming is prohibited.

Nearby is the northern starting point of the Tallahassee–St. Marks Historic Railroad State Trail, a 16-mile paved route for bicycling, in-line skating, horseback riding, and hiking. The trail follows an abandoned railbed that was used to transport timber, cotton, and passengers to the Gulf of Mexico for 140 years. It begins at a parking lot at the intersection of U.S. 319 and State Road 363, and it ends in St. Marks at the edge of the St. Marks National Wildlife Refuge in Wakulla County. For bicyclists seeking a more rigorous challenge, turn off on a spur about 1.25 miles south of the Tallahassee end to the Munson Hills Off-Road Bicycle Trail through the Apalachicola Forest.

The Munson Hills are rolling sand dunes left from the shoreline one million years ago and now are rooted with longleaf pine forest. The sometimes muddy bike trail dips through wetland hammocks of oak, cherry, and sassafras trees that are home to gopher tortoises, salamanders, deer, and the endangered eastern indigo snake. Bicyclists have two options: the 7.5-mile Munson Hills Loop or the Tall Pine Shortcut, which cuts the loop to 4.25 miles.

Campsites, facilities: There are 17 sites for RVs (tents are not allowed) with electricity and water. Facilities include restrooms, showers, a dump station, two picnic shelters, two fishing piers and boat docks, a fish-cleaning station, and a boat ramp. Children are welcome. Leashed pets are permitted.

Reservations, fees: Reservations are accepted; call 850/350-9560 or 866/350-9560. Camping is $12.10 per night. The maximum stay is 10 days or 30 days in a calendar year.

Directions: From Tallahassee, take State Road 263 to the intersection of State Road 20, then follow State Road 20 west for seven miles. The park is on the north side of the road, on Lake Talquin.

Contact: Leon County Parks & Recreation Department, 2280 Miccosukee Road, Tallahassee, FL 32308, 850/488-0221, fax 850/487-3072, website: www.co.leon.fl.us/parks/camping.asp.

14 BIG OAK RV PARK

Rating: 4

In Tallahassee

Tallahassee map, grid c1, page 86

"Very convenient," the management says of Big Oak. Indeed, this RV park puts you just 10 minutes from the governor's mansion and the nerve center of state government. Tallahassee is dotted with RV parks for that very reason; with a part-time legislature, don't be surprised if your neighbor with the big, flashy rig is a state senator on official business or a high-powered lobbyist here to buy a few rounds at Clyde's, Tallahassee's premier political watering hole.

Like most of Tallahassee, Big Oak is shaded by large trees, and it has the feel of bygone motor courts, which were popular before the advent of motel chains. From here, it's a short hike—across a busy highway—to fast-food restaurants, a couple of supermarkets, and an ATM. Just minutes away are a major shopping mall, movie theaters, and all the cultural fare and political intrigue of the Sunshine State's capital. The city has three marked scenic routes directing motorists along canopied roads and country lanes to museums and historic sites: the Native Trail, which takes about four hours, and the Cotton and Quail Trails, which take three to 3.5 hours each. For information and maps, call the Tallahassee Area Convention and Visitors Bureau at 800/628-2866.

Campsites, facilities: There are 72 RV sites with full hookups; 12 are pull-through. On the premises are restrooms, showers, laundry facilities, shuffleboard courts, and a horseshoe pit. Children are welcome. Leashed pets are permitted.

Reservations, fees: Reservations are accepted. Sites are $25 per night for two people, plus $2 for each additional person. Major credit cards are accepted. Long-term stays are OK.

Directions: From I-10 in Tallahassee, take Exit 199 onto U.S. 27 and drive 2.5 miles north to the park, on the west side of the road.

Contact: Big Oak RV Park, 4024 North Monroe Street, Tallahassee, FL 32303, 850/562-4660, website: www.bigoakrvpark.com.

15 LAKESIDE TRAVEL PARK AND CAMPGROUND

Rating: 2

In Tallahassee

Tallahassee map, grid c1, page 86

A laid-back spot on the western outskirts of Tallahassee, this 10-acre campground offers a small pond and oak-shaded sites. It's located near good fishing on Lake Talquin and the campuses of Florida State University and Florida Agricultural and Mechanical University. It's also within .5 mile of Wal-Mart, McDonald's, Steak 'n' Shake, and, among other businesses, a car lot. The park has a split personality; more-permanent guests reside in one area while overnighters sleep in another. Plenty of open sites are usually available, except on big football weekends when the Florida State Seminoles play at home against their Gainesville rivals, the University of Florida Gators.

Campsites, facilities: There are 65 RV sites with full hookups; 20 are pull-through. The park has restrooms, showers, laundry facilities, a dump station, and a fishing lake. Within .5 mile are a grocery store and restaurants. Children and leashed pets are welcome.

Reservations, fees: Reservations are taken. Sites are $20 to $25.30 per night for two people, plus $1 per extra person. Major credit cards are accepted. Long-term stays are OK.

Directions: From I-10 at Tallahassee, take Exit 196 onto State Road 263 (Capital Circle) and drive 1.5 miles south to U.S. 90. Turn west and drive one mile to the park. Alternatively, take

I-10 Exit 192, then go east four miles on U.S. 90 to the park, at right.

Contact: Lakeside Travel Park and Campground, 6401 West Tennessee Street, Tallahassee, FL 32304, 850/574-5998.

16 TALLAHASSEE RV PARK

Rating: 4

East of Tallahassee

Tallahassee map, grid c1, page 86

This park on the east side of Tallahassee has easy access to the interstate and the city. Lighted, paved interior roads and big, grassy sites are comfortable for parking even the largest RVs. The park is shaded with large pines, magnolia, and dogwood, and is neatly landscaped with flowers and shrubs. Across the street is a nine-hole golf course and driving range. South of the park off U.S. 319 is Apalachicola National Forest and an attraction for Civil War history buffs: the Natural Bridge State Historic Site, where a five-day battle raged in the final weeks of the war. It ended with a rebel victory when a militia of old men and boys defeated seasoned Union troops, giving Tallahassee the distinction of being the only Confederate capital never to fall into Yankee hands. To get to the site, take U.S. 319 to State Road 363 and turn south. Continue four miles to Woodville, then turn east on Natural Bridge Road and drive six miles to the park. It's a great spot for picnics and for seeing Natural Bridge, where the St. Marks River disappears into a cavern and runs underground for 150 feet before resurfacing.

Campsites, facilities: This park has 73 RV sites with electricity, water, and picnic tables; 66 of those sites have sewer hookups. Big rigs are welcome because many sites are pull-through. On the premises are restrooms, showers, a dump station, a large recreation hall, and a pool. Management says all areas are wheelchair accessible. Children are welcome. Leashed pets are permitted.

Reservations, fees: Reservations are recommended. Sites are $25 per night for two people, plus $3 for each additional adult. Major credit cards are accepted.

Directions: From I-10 at Tallahassee, take Exit 209A onto U.S. 90 and drive .5 mile west to the park.

Contact: Tallahassee RV Park, 6504 Mahan Drive, Tallahassee, FL 32308, 850/878-7641, and fax 850/878-7082, website: www.tallahasseervpark.com.

17 A CAMPER'S WORLD

Rating: 3

Near Monticello off I-10

Tallahassee map, grid c1, page 86

Campers on the move will appreciate the easy interstate access this five-acre park has to offer. The sites are spacious and shaded by tall pines and landscaped with flowers and shrubs. It's far enough away from the highway to cut the traffic noise a few decibels. The exit also is not as congested as those closer to nearby Tallahassee and Lake City.

Campsites, facilities: There are 33 RV sites with full hookups (30-amp and 50-amp service) and picnic tables; 24 are pull-through. Big rigs and slide-outs are welcome. On the premises are restrooms, showers, laundry facilities, a dump station, a pool, a playground, and modem hookup for laptop computers. Children are welcome. Leashed pets are permitted.

Reservations, fees: Reservations are accepted. Sites are $20 to $22 per night for two people, plus $2.50 per additional person. Major credit cards are accepted. Long-term stays are OK.

Directions: From I-10, take Exit 225 north onto U.S. 19 and drive .2 mile to the park entrance on the west side of the road.

Contact: A Camper's World, 397 Campground Road, Lamont, FL 32336, 850/997-3300.

18 TALLAHASSEE EAST KOA

Rating: 6

South of Monticello off I-10

Tallahassee map, grid c1, page 86

Recognized with a top rating from KOA, this wooded campground has seen many physical improvements in the past couple of years. The entrance road has been paved, cottages have been added, and campers can enjoy free continental breakfast. Parking and hooking up are no hassle because all of the sites are pull-through. There's plenty of space for the kids to play, a pond to toss in a fishing line, rings to build campfires, and a game room with a fireplace.

Campsites, facilities: There are 68 pull-through RV sites with water and electric hookups, 40 of which have sewer connections. The park has a separate section for tents. Facilities include restrooms, showers, a laundry room, a dump station, a convenience/country crafts store, a pool, a fishing pond, a game and meeting room, a playground, and rental cabins. Firewood, modem hookups, mini-storage, and propane are available. The pool is available from late spring through the end of fall. Children are welcome. Leashed pets are permitted.

Reservations, fees: Reservations are taken. Sites are $26 per night for two adults, plus $1.50 for each extra child and $2.50 for adults. Major credit cards are accepted. Long-term stays are OK.

Directions: From I-10 near Monticello, take Exit 225 onto U.S. 19 and head south for .25 mile. Turn right on County Road 158B (Nash Road) and drive 2.4 miles, then turn north on County Road 259 and drive .25 mile to the park.

Contact: Tallahassee East KOA, Route 5, Box 5160, Monticello, FL 32344, 850/997-3890 or 800/KOA-3890, fax 850/997-1509, website: www.koa.com.

19 MADISON CAMPGROUND

Rating: 5

Near Madison

Tallahassee map, grid b1, page 86

Set in a wooded area near the Suwannee River, this campground is part of the Deerwood Inn motel complex, which has a pool with a luau hut, a floodlighted miniature golf course, one tennis court, and a game room with pool tables and video games. You're likely not to be crowded by other campers, the owners say, and the park's location near the interstate makes it an ideal stopover. Nearby is historic Madison, the county seat, where pre–Civil War cotton plantations once flourished. The explorer Hernando de Soto came through here in the 1590s, and a Spanish mission called Santa Helena de Machaba was founded northwest of the town. Madison County remains a quiet agricultural community.

Campsites, facilities: This park has 80 pull-through RV sites (39 with full hookups) and 10 tent-only sites set apart from the RVs. Water and electricity are available at all sites. You'll find restrooms, showers, picnic tables, grills, some fire rings, a dump station, and laundry facilities. A recreation room, a pool, a playground, a game room, a miniature golf course, a tennis court, horseshoe pits, shuffleboard courts, and a volleyball area are available. Children are welcome. Leashed pets are permitted for a $2 fee.

Reservations, fees: Reservations are not necessary. Sites are $16 to $18 per night. Major credit cards are accepted. Long-term stays are OK.

Directions: From I-10 east of Madison, take Exit 258 and head south on State Road 53 for .2 mile to the park.

Contact: Madison Campground, Route 1, Box 3095, Madison, FL 32340, 850/973-2501, fax 850/973-3805.

20 YOGI BEAR JELLYSTONE CAMP RESORTS

Rating: 8

Near Madison
Tallahassee map, grid b1, page 86

Opened in 2000, this campground targets overnighters and destination travelers. It's a fun place for kids with lots for them to enjoy, including a 60-foot-high circular water slide that speeds them down to a lake surrounded by a white-sand beach. The surroundings are wooded and natural, as befits this beautiful area of Florida. Giving a new meaning to "planned activities," this park holds paintball contests and the like, and during late summer 2002 sponsored a "Jellystone Survivor" event patterned on the popular reality TV show.

Campsites, facilities: Campers can choose from 100 RV sites and eight tent sites, which are separated from the RV section. RV sites have full hookups or water and electricity. All sites have picnic tables and grills. Sixty-five sites are pull-through. Restrooms, showers, a dump station, laundry facilities, and telephone service are available. On the premises are a three lakes, a pool, a playground, a campground store, a nature trail, a snack bar, boat rentals, a clubhouse, putt-putt golf, and a dog-walk area. Most areas are wheelchair accessible. Children are welcome. Leashed pets are permitted.

Reservations, fees: Reservations are not necessary. Sites are $25 per night for two people, plus $4 per extra person. Major credit cards are accepted. Long-term stays are permitted.

Directions: From I-10, take Exit 258 and drive south on State Road 53 about 150 yards. Turn right on Southwest Old Saint Augustine Road. Pass the Deerwood Inn; look for the Jellystone campground signs on the left.

Contact: Yogi Bear Jellystone Camp Resorts, Route 1, Box 3199J, 1151 Southwest Old St. Augustine Road, Madison, FL 32340, 850/973-8269 or 850/973-8546, fax 850/973-4114, website: www.jellystoneflorida.com.

21 SIMS BOATING CLUB AND CAMPGROUND

Rating: 6

On Cherry Lake just south of the state line
Tallahassee map, grid b1, page 86

Looking for quiet, lakefront camping? This family-oriented park offers oak-shaded and sunny sites overlooking one-mile-wide Cherry Lake, a favorite water-skiing and fishing destination for locals. The family-owned boating club requires an annual campground membership fee, but for campers and boaters looking for a regular weekend retreat or summer getaway, $300 isn't much to pay.

Campsites, facilities: There are 36 full-hookup overnight RV sites and a tenting area set apart from the vehicles. All sites have electricity, picnic tables, and cable TV. Restrooms, showers, a dump station, a boat ramp, and a dock are available. Children are welcome. Pets are prohibited.

Reservations, fees: An annual campground membership fee ($300) is required. Sites are $7 per night. Credit cards are not accepted. Special rates are available if you want to leave your rig on site, but full-time living is not encouraged.

Directions: From I-75 in Georgia, go southbound on State Road 145 to Pinetta, Florida, about 11 miles. At the Pinetta Baptist Church, turn west on Northeast 172nd Avenue and drive to the dead end. Turn north on County Road 18 and follow it to the fork in the road. Veer left on Northeast 25th Street, which dead-ends at Sims Boating Club and Campground. From Madison, Florida, drive north on State Road 591 and go left on Northeast 172nd Ave; follow previous directions.

Contact: Sims Boating Club and Campground, 2092 Northeast Cherry Lake Circle, Madison, FL 33340, 850/929-2414.

22 MADISON BLUE SPRINGS STATE PARK

🏊 〰️ 🏕️ ♿ 🚐 ⛰️

Rating: 8

East of Madison and north of Lee on the Withlacoochee River

Tallahassee map, grid b1, page 86

This fantastic park is undergoing changes. It was closed in 2002 and now is being developed into a state park. Call ahead to see if the park has reopened to the public; it's possible that it will be opened upon your request while all the plans are being worked out. In any case, it will be worth the wait.

Several camping areas in Florida share the name Blue Springs, but here the water really is blue, almost turquoise. Nature trails wind along the unspoiled riverbanks, and the woods are laced with horseback-riding trails. Previously, this 67-acre wooded park was a popular destination for scuba divers and snorkelers who explored the first-magnitude spring or nearby caverns along the Withlacoochee River. A swimming beach let nondivers get their feet wet. Canoes and dive gear were available for rent. Divers have traveled from as far away as Australia to explore the 6.5 miles of caves. Cave divers had to be fully certified; an open-water basin with an underwater platform was great for checkout dives. Only 26 springs nationwide pump more than 100 million gallons of freshwater per day—and this is one of them.

Campsites, facilities: There were 15 RV sites with water and electric hookups in two separate areas. About 50 tents could be accommodated on primitive, wooded sites overlooking the Withlacoochee River. Restrooms, showers, picnic tables, and some fire rings were provided.

Reservations, fees: Call for updated information.

Directions: From I-10 east of Madison, take Exit 262 northbound on County Road 255 about five miles. Drive through the town of Lee. At State Road 6 on the north side of town, turn east (right). Go about five miles to the park.

Contact: Check www.floridastateparks.org for updates, or call Suwannee River State Park at 386/329-3721 to see if the park can be opened for your party upon request.

23 JENNINGS OUTDOOR RESORT

🏊 🛶 🚐 🏕️ 🚴 ♿ 🚐 ⛰️

Rating: 3

Off the northernmost exit in Florida on I-75

Tallahassee map, grid a1, page 86

Jennings is a rural park with paved sites set among some oaks, convenient to the interstate. There is a fishing pond on site (catch-and-release; no license required), and you can take out paddleboats and canoes. Most campers spend a night or two at this 30-acre park, although some stay for months. Drive just 10 miles and you can take a dip in Blue Springs, one of the super-fun, super-cool, refreshing places in North Florida where clear water bubbles up from the bowels of the earth. You also can reach the dark, mysterious Okefenokee Swamp in one hour or so. Stephen Foster Folk Culture Center State Park is about a half hour away. The biggest town nearby is Lake City, about 40 miles to the south. Osceola National Forest near Lake City is another place to explore. But the buzz is about the roller coasters found three highway exits north at the animal-oriented theme park Wild Adventures in Valdosta, Georgia. For hours, call 229/559-1330.

Campsites, facilities: This park has 102 pull-through RV sites with full hookups and 10 tent-only sites. On the premises are showers, restrooms, picnic tables, a dump station, a pool, a fishing pond, boat/canoe rentals, paddleboats, a recreation hall, a playground, horseshoes, shuffleboard, limited groceries, RV supplies, propane, and laundry facilities. Restaurants are close by. Children are allowed, but the rules remind parents: "It is your responsibility to entertain and discipline your children. If you disagree, choose another campground." Leashed pets are permitted.

Reservations, fees: Reservations normally are

not necessary. Sites are $19 per night for two people, plus $2 for each additional person and $2 for cable TV. Major credit cards are accepted. Long-term rates are available.

Directions: From Valdosta, Georgia, travel 18 miles south on I-75. If you are coming from the south, it's the last exit in Florida (Exit 467) onto State Road 143. The campground is right off the highway.

Contact: Jennings Outdoor Resort, 2039 Hamilton Avenue, Jennings, FL 32053, 386/938-3321, fax 386/938-3322.

24 SUWANNEE RIVER STATE PARK

Rating: 10

Northwest of the town of Live Oak at the confluence of the Suwannee and Withlacoochee Rivers

Tallahassee map, grid a1, page 86

One feature of this 1,800-acre park is an overlook that offers a panoramic view of the Suwannee and Withlacoochee Rivers and surrounding wooded uplands. When the water is low, springs can be seen bubbling up from the riverbanks. Today the river is sentried by canoeists—the park is the starting point for the Suwannee River Canoe Trail, which flows to the Gulf of Mexico. Catfish, bass, and panfish can be pulled from the river. The campground is set in a densely wooded forest of slash pines, and at night the only sound you may hear is the lonesome wail of a freight train headed to the big city.

Established in 1936, Suwannee River State Park was one of the first parks in the state system, and it is steeped in American history. A short hike from the ranger station brings you to the ruins of earthworks built by Confederate soldiers to protect the railroad bridge over the river and trainloads of beef, salt, and sugar headed to rebels based in Georgia. Five thousand Union troops sent from Jacksonville to take the bridge were beaten back in a bloody five-hour faceoff near Olustee on February 20, 1864—Florida's only major Civil War battle.

Later, paddle-wheel ferries plied these waters when the Suwannee was a commerce route, a highway to Gulf ports for a prospering logging industry. The pioneer village of Columbus here was little more than the railroad bridge, a ferry landing, and a sawmill operated by George F. Drew, who became Florida's governor in 1876. All that's left of the settlement is the old Columbus Cemetery, which is accessible from a trail in the park. The disproportionate number of infants buried there is silent testimony to how tough it was to survive in the wilds of Florida.

Campsites, facilities: There are 30 campsites with electricity and water, picnic tables, grills, and fire rings. A boat ramp, canoe rentals, a playground, and several short hiking trails are in the park. Children are welcome. Pets are permitted.

Reservations, fees: Reservations are recommended; call ReserveAmerica at 800/326-3521. Sites are $8 to $10 per night for up to eight people, plus $2 for electricity and $2 for each pet. No more than two tents or one RV are permitted on each site. Major credit cards are accepted. The maximum stay is 14 days.

Directions: From I-10 west of Live Oak, take Exit 275 northbound and drive six miles on U.S. 90 to the park, on the right side of the road.

Contact: Suwannee River State Park, 20185 County Road 132, Live Oak, FL 32060, 386/362-2746, website: www.floridastate parks.org.

25 SPIRIT OF THE SUWANNEE MUSIC PARK

Rating: 8

North of Live Oak on the Suwannee River

Tallahassee map, grid a1, page 86

This music-oriented campground is nestled on 600 acres of forest draped in Spanish moss. Among the things that make the place special are the three pickin' sheds used for impromptu jam sessions and the grassy meadow that becomes a stage for weekend rock 'n' roll, blues, and bluegrass festivals, plus special activities for Halloween, Thanksgiving, and other holidays. A horse camping area has recently opened, and there are 22 miles of trails available for equestrians. The park is open to the public, but management is now selling memberships that include free camping and use of the park, park models, and wedding packages.

An on-site concession rents bicycles and outfits canoeists for day trips or overnight paddling expeditions. Also available are about 18 miles of walking and bicycling trails along the Suwannee River, Rees Lake, and through the Bay Swamp. The restaurant features a Southern-style menu and holiday dinner specials. Square dancing, bingo, card playing, and Sunday church services are held in the common areas.

Nearby is Suwannee Spring. Sulfury water issues from this big hole in the ground, but it drew the likes of the Firestones and other rich northerners who came to visit the large tourist hotels of the Jacksonville area at the end of the 1800s and the early part of this century. Smelly? Maybe. But people back then believed it could cure what ailed them, be it kidney problems, rheumatism, or gout. Railroad baron Henry Flagler built a spur route to bring the curious, making it one of Florida's earliest tourist attractions. Several hotels were built here, but the last one burned down in 1925. The Suwannee River Water Management District has purchased the land around the spring and is working to reverse erosion and other problems caused by years of overuse.

Campsites, facilities: This unusual campground has full-hookup sites for more than 180 RVs, water and electric sites for 600 others, plus tent camping areas that can accommodate more than 2,000 tents. Cable TV, picnic tables, grills, a pool, a river beach, a fishing dock, a game room, a boat ramp, a restaurant, an amphitheater, a music hall, an open-air concert stage, cabins, rental trailers, stables, canoe rentals, horseshoes, miniature golf, and nature trails are on site. A horse camping area has 68 water and electric sites with easy access to rental stalls, stables, and pens. Children are welcome and are kept busy with crafts and other activities programs. Up to two pets under 20 pounds are allowed; they must be kept on a six-foot leash and are prohibited in concert areas.

Reservations, fees: Reservations are recommended two weeks in advance on holiday weekends and are accepted one year ahead for big events. Sites normally are $18 to $25 per night for four people, plus $2 per extra person over age four. The pet fee is $10 each. Camping rates rise during special events. Major credit cards are accepted. Maximum stay is six months.

Directions: From I-75 north of Live Oak, take Exit 451 and drive 4.7 miles south on U.S. 129 to the park. Or, from I-10 at Live Oak, take Exit 283 and head 4.9 miles north on U.S. 129.

Contact: Spirit of the Suwannee Music Park, 3076 95th Drive, Live Oak, FL 32060, 386/364-1683 or 800/428-4147, fax 386/364-2998, website: www.musicliveshere.com.

26 HOLTON CREEK CONSERVATION AREA

Rating: 9

Southwest of Jasper and northwest of Live Oak on the Suwannee River at Highway 249 and Highway 751

Tallahassee map, grid a1, page 86

The biggest draw along these three miles or so of riverfront acreage is Holton Creek, which boils up from one of North Florida's famous "first-magnitude" (read: "really big") springs. The limestone ground—laid down eons ago when this area was covered by an ancient sea—is pockmarked today with sinkholes and other depressions. The property contains a variety of habitats, although the three most common are sand hills, upland forests, and frequently flooded bottomland forests.

Two of the biggest cypress trees in the state are located here, along with the largest collection of old-growth bottomland forest remaining in the area. The juxtaposition of high uplands and undisturbed wetlands is hard to find anywhere else, even way out here in the backwoods of North Florida. That diversity is one of the reasons why the Suwannee River Water Management District bought the land.

Campsites, facilities: This is primitive camping along the Suwannee River. There are no designated campsites, but you can find your own spot, often on sandbars or the riverbanks. No facilities are provided. You are only allowed to camp here if you are canoeing or boating on the Suwannee River or hiking on the Florida National Scenic Trail. Trash and all other waste must be packed out. Children are permitted, as are leashed pets.

Reservations, fees: If you'll be arriving by canoe or boat, you need to obtain a permit, also known as a Special Use License, from the Suwannee River Water Management District. Camping is free.

Directions: The closest upstream canoe launch is at Gibson Park, at the intersection of Highway 751 and Highway 249. From Live Oak, follow Highway 249 north about 12 miles to the boat launch. There are several hiking entry points; download a map from the website of the water management district.

Contact: Suwannee River Water Management District, Public Use Land Coordinator, 9925 County Road 49, Live Oak, FL 32060, 386/326-1001 or 800/226-1066 (within Florida), website: www.srwmd.state.fl.us.

27 STEPHEN FOSTER FOLK CULTURE CENTER STATE PARK

🏃 🚴 🛶 🐕 ⛺ ♿ 🚐 ⛰️

Rating: 9

In White Springs on U.S. 41 by the Suwannee River

Tallahassee map, grid a1, page 86

The Suwannee got its name from Seminole Indian words meaning "black, muddy water," but the river was made famous in the American standard "Old Folks at Home." The man who wrote the tune, Stephen Collins Foster, a Yankee from Pittsburgh, had little to do with the river other than liking its name. The popular composer had never actually seen the Suwannee, but it sounded better than South Carolina's Pee Dee River. Foster's family had lost their home there when he was a child, which left a lifelong impression of loss and longing. The story goes that Foster asked his brother for help in replacing the Pee Dee with a more lyrical river name. Many people today know Florida's state song as "Way Down Upon the Suwannee River."

The state park itself is way down upon the Suwannee River on 650 acres. It's one of the state's most unusual parks, combining outdoor recreation, American history, and cultural arts programs. A tribute to Foster, the state park has the feel of a well-manicured antebellum plantation, so often the setting for Foster's reminiscing lyrics. The idea for the Foster memorial originated with the son of Josiah K. Lilly, an Indiana pharmaceutical manufacturing tycoon. The land was donated to the state by Lillian Saunders, who was a local member of the Florida Federation of Music Clubs. It opened in 1950.

A museum on the grounds displays memorabilia of Foster's life, antique pianos, and mechanical dioramas depicting the themes of his other works, like "Camptown Races" and "Oh Susanna." A tube-bell carillon—touted as the world's largest—regularly chimes a repertoire of Foster favorites and echoes through the campground at 10 A.M., noon, 2 P.M., and 4 P.M. Tours are offered daily at 9 A.M., 11 A.M., 1 P.M., and 3 P.M. The state park hosts numerous events, such as the annual Florida Folk Festival, a Memorial Day weekend event featuring music, dance, crafts, food, and storytelling; a Christmas festival; and the "Jeannie" ball and women's vocal competition in the fall, which takes its name from Foster's "Jeannie with the Light Brown Hair." The Nature & Heritage Tourism Center, offering information on travel and leisure destinations in Florida, is also on site here, as is a gift shop and craft square, where artisans demonstrate their work throughout the year.

The state park makes a fine home base for exploring the picturesque countryside. White Sulphur Springs, on the riverbank at the Foster Center, has lured visitors since the 1700s, when Native Americans considered the sulfurous waters to be sacred and curative. In 1906, it was part of a spa that attracted Teddy Roosevelt and other famous tourists.

You'll find lots of shade under moss-draped oaks, and a bit of peace alongside the meandering Suwannee. Fishing is popular from the steep banks of the river, and a new canoe launch has been built, allowing easy access from within the park. Hiking is available along a 4.5-mile nature trail and a 4.5-mile section of the Florida National Scenic Trail that runs alongside the river. Mountain bikers have fun on the nature trail but are not allowed on the Florida Trail, which is reserved for hikers. Nearby are 33 miles of trails in the Big Shoals Public Lands. Big Shoals is a 3,700-acre preserve along the Suwannee river that features the only whitewater rapids in the state. However, the water levels fluctuate, and during the dry months of winter, the water is too low for white water.

Campsites, facilities: The campground has been expanded to 45 campsites for RVs and tents. Some sites accommodate big rigs in pull-through sites. All sites have water, electricity, fire rings, grills, and picnic tables. Restrooms, showers, laundry facilities, and a playground are available. Concession stands, craft shops, a museum, a carillon bell tower, and an amphitheater for musical events are situated within the park. Entry to the museum, carillon tower, and craft square is free for registered campers. Most areas are wheelchair accessible. Children are welcome. Pets are permitted.

Reservations, fees: Reservations are recommended; call ReserveAmerica at 800/326-3521. The campground is open Memorial Day weekend for participants in the Florida Folk Festi-

val only. Sites are $12 per night for four people, plus $2 for electricity. Group, weekly, and monthly rates are available. Major credit cards are accepted. The maximum stay is 14 days. Walk-in campers are accepted for a maximum two-day stay.

Directions: From Lake City, head north on U.S. 41 about 18 miles to White Springs. You'll see the entrance to the state park and culture center after you pass two traffic lights. From I-75, take Exit 439 eastbound on State Road 136. Travel three miles to U.S. 41 and turn north (left). The park is just ahead on the left. From I-10, take Exit 301 and drive north on U.S. 41 about nine miles to the park entrance on the left.

Contact: Stephen Foster Folk Culture Center State Park, P.O. Drawer G, White Springs, FL 32096, 386/397-2733 or 386/397-4331, website: www.floridastateparks.org.

28 SWIFT CREEK CONSERVATION AREA

Rating: 5

On the Suwannee River just south of White Springs

Tallahassee map, grid a1, page 86

Logged just a decade or so ago, this timberland is now growing back after being purchased by the Suwannee River Water Management District. It is quite convenient for those who don't want to hike or canoe very far. By wilderness standards, though, it's pretty puny at 269 acres and situated right next to the town of White Springs. The water district purchased the land to buffer the river from the town in an effort to preserve high water quality.

Campsites, facilities: This is primitive camping along the Suwannee River. There are no designated campsites, but you can find your own spot, often on sandbars or the riverbanks. No facilities are provided. You are only allowed to camp here if you are canoeing or boating on the Suwannee River or hiking on the Florida National Scenic Trail. Trash and all other waste must be packed out. Children are permitted, as are leashed pets.

Reservations, fees: If you'll be arriving by canoe or boat, you need to obtain a permit, also known as a Special Use License, from the Suwannee River Water Management District. Camping is free.

Directions: One boat ramp where you can launch a canoe is at Highway 41 Bridge Park in White Springs, on the right side of U.S. 41 just north of the river. It's immediately adjacent to the conservation area. This is also where you can pick up the Florida National Scenic Trail into the conservation area. Upstream from here is a boat ramp at Turner Bridge Park, about 25 miles east of Jasper. From Jasper, take County Road 6 east to the river.

Contact: Suwannee River Water Management District, Public Use Land Coordinator, 9925 County Road 49, Live Oak, FL 32060, 386/326-1001 or 800/226-1066 (within Florida), website: www.srwmd.state.fl.us.

29 SUWANNEE VALLEY CAMPGROUND

Rating: 10

On the Suwannee River in White Springs
Tallahassee map, grid a1, page 86

Here is a favored destination for RV caravans, camping clubs, and family groups that takes advantage of the spacious pull-through sites and a large recreation center for group activities. The campground is located on 36 oak-shaded acres on the banks of the Suwannee River and appeals to all age groups and types of campers. Off-road bicycling, canoeing, and hiking are nearby, and the Florida National Scenic Trail skirts the campground. There's a playground and wading pool for the kids, and the laundry room is equipped with many washers and dryers. A dog activity area allows you to let your pet off its leash to run and play. Steak and chicken cookouts are held every Saturday night.

Campsites, facilities: The campground has 119 pull-through sites with full hookups and grills. There's a separate tent area in a meadow with 40 sites. Restrooms, showers, a recreation hall, swimming and kiddie pools, horseshoe pits, basketball and shuffleboard courts, laundry facilities, canoe and kayak rentals, a dog activity area, rental cabins, and a convenience store are provided. The clubhouse is wheelchair accessible. Children are welcome, as are leashed pets.

Reservations, fees: Reservations are recommended. Sites are $19 per night for two adults and two children, plus $2 per extra person. Hookup to 50-amp service is an additional $2, and modem/phone service is $3. Major credit cards are accepted. Long-term stays are OK.

Directions: From I-75, take Exit 439 and travel 2.5 miles east on State Road 136. Turn right just before a bridge onto White Springs Road. Go .1 mile, then turn left onto Stephen Foster Road and drive .5 mile to the park. Or, from I-10, take Exit 301 and drive eight miles north on U.S. 41. Turn left on State Road 136. Turn left after the bridge onto White Springs Road. Go .1 mile, turn onto Stephen Foster Road, and drive .5 mile.

Contact: Suwannee Valley Campground, Route 1, Box 1860, White Springs, FL 32096, 386/397-1667, fax 386/397-1560, website: www.suwanneevalleycampground.com.

30 BIG SHOALS CONSERVATION AREA

Rating: 9

On the Suwannee River east of White Springs
Tallahassee map, grid a1, page 86

Florida's only real white-water rapids are found on the Suwannee River next to this land, which is owned by the Suwannee River Water Management District. Both the water district tract and the adjacent state forest are named for the Big Shoals rapids. Canoeists should portage around them. The shoals, limestone deposited millions of years ago when this area was covered by vast oceans, can almost provide a bridge across the river in periods of low water. The terrain in the adjacent conservation area and state forest is quite varied, ranging from dry, high ground that supports an ecosystem of longleaf pine and wire grass, to dark, low cypress swamps. In the spring, wild azaleas, dogwood, and wild tupelo provide a riot of color. Ticks can be a problem. This is one of the least-developed stretches of the Suwannee. Hiking is available in the conservation area and the state forest next door.

Campsites, facilities: This is primitive camping along the Suwannee River. There are no designated campsites, but you can find your own spot, often on sandbars or the riverbanks. No facilities are provided. You are only allowed to camp here if you are canoeing or boating on the Suwannee River. Trash and human waste must be packed out. Leashed pets are permitted, as are children.

Reservations, fees: If you'll be arriving by canoe or boat, you need to obtain a permit, also known as a Special Use License, from the Suwannee River Water Management District. Camping is free.

Directions: To reach the nearest canoe launch, take Highway 135 north from White Springs. Turn right on Godwin Bridge Road, the first paved road after you cross Four Mile Branch, about 3.5 miles outside town. Follow that road about one mile to the end, where you can launch your canoe into the river. You'll have to portage around Big Shoals about one mile downriver.

Contact: Suwannee River Water Management District, Public Use Land Coordinator, 9925 County Road 49, Live Oak, FL 32060, 386/326-1001 or 800/226-1066 (within Florida), website: www.srwmd.state.fl.us.

31 KELLY'S RV PARK

Rating: 6

Near White Springs
Tallahassee map, grid a1, page 86
This tidy campground has paved streets and spacious, wooded sites on 20 acres, with a secluded spot for tent camping. Visitors with pets in tow will find an area set aside for dog walking. A nature trail hooks up with the state's Gar Pond and Shoal Trails, which are excellent for hiking and off-road biking. A public boat ramp is within .5 mile of the campground.

Campsites, facilities: This park offers 56 RV sites with full hookups and picnic tables, and a separate area with 20 tent sites. On the premises are restrooms, showers, laundry facilities, a nature trail, horseshoe pits, and a clubhouse. Children are welcome. Leashed pets (no attack breeds) are permitted.

Reservations, fees: Reservations are recommended November through March. Sites are $18 per night for two people, plus $2 for each additional person. Major credit cards are accepted. Long-term stays are OK.

Directions: From I-75, take Exit 439 and proceed east on State Road 136 into White Springs, then turn south on U.S. 41. The park is 1.5 miles down the road. Or, from I-10, take Exit 301 and drive 5.5 miles north on U.S. 41.

Contact: Kelly's RV Park, Route 1, Box 370, White Springs, FL 32096, 386/397-2616.

32 CAMEL LAKE

Rating: 7

South of Bristol in Apalachicola National Forest
Tallahassee map, grid d2, page 86
Camping at the remote northwestern corner of Apalachicola National Forest will be unavailable through late 2003 or early 2004 while renovations are made to the day-use area. After it reopens, it's a great destination or starting point for backpackers because it has a trailhead for the Florida National Scenic Trail, which meanders east from here through the forest for about 60 miles. The site is in a grassy, open area dotted with longleaf pines, and slopes down to Camel Lake, which has a swimming area.

Small boats are permitted, with a 10-horse-power limit on motors. Backpackers departing from here need to tote drinking water or be prepared to purify or filter standing surface water. The next spigot is 28 miles away at the Porter Lake campground near the Ochlockonee River Bridge.

Along the way, the trail passes through the ruins of Vilas, a turpentining settlement along the Apalachicola Northern rail line. You can camp beside the trail unless it's hunting season, generally mid-November through early January; then you must camp at the developed campgrounds. From Porter Lake, the hike continues 29 miles to the southeast corner of the national forest, at U.S. 319, approximately one mile west of Medart. This eastern section is considerably wetter and tougher to travel, especially after heavy rain, when the swamp water can be waist deep in the Bradwell Bay Wilderness. Check with the ranger in Crawfordville (850/926-3561) before venturing there. Wear safety orange during hunting season and carry a compass. Detailed trail maps are available from the U.S. Forest Service.

Campsites, facilities: Six campsites are for tents and self-contained RVs. Facilities include restrooms, a swimming beach with outdoor showers, a boat ramp, and a picnic area with tables and grills. Drinking water is available. Children are welcome. Pets must be leashed in the camping area.

Reservations, fees: Reservations are not accepted, but call the forest office to see if the campground has reopened. Camping is $5 per vehicle. Stays are limited to 14 days per month.

Directions: From Bristol, take State Road 12 south for 11 miles. Turn left on Forest Service Road 105 and drive two miles east to the park.

Contact: Apalachicola National Forest, Apalachicola Ranger District, P.O. Box 579, Highway 20, Bristol, FL 32321, 850/643-2282, website: www.southernregion.fs.fed.us/florida/recreation/apalachicola_rec.htm.

33 COTTON LANDING

Rating: 6

West of Sumatra in Apalachicola National Forest

Tallahassee map, grid d2, page 86

This campground offers a more rustic alternative to nearby Wright Lake, with fishing and boating on Kennedy Creek, which feeds into the Apalachicola River. See the trip notes for Wright Lake and Hickory Landing (campgrounds in this chapter) for a description of the area. Campers, be advised: there's no drinking water at Cotton Landing. Canoeing is not recommended because of the boat traffic on the Apalachicola River.

Campsites, facilities: This rustic camping area has room for about 10 tents or RVs. Camping is primitive; no drinking water or hookups are available. There are chemical toilets and a boat ramp. Children are welcome. Pets must be leashed in the camping area.

Reservations, fees: Reservations are not accepted. Camping is $3 per vehicle. Stays are limited to 14 days per month.

Directions: From Sumatra, take County Road 379 northwest for 3.2 miles. Turn west on Forest Service Road 123 and continue 2.8 miles. Turn west on Forest Service Road 123B and drive .7 mile to the campground.

Contact: Apalachicola National Forest, Apalachicola Ranger District, P.O. Box 579, Highway 20, Bristol, FL 32321, 850/643-2282, website: www.southernregion.fs.fed.us/florida/recreation/apalachicola_rec.htm.

34 PORTER LAKE

Rating: 7

South of Telogia in Apalachicola National Forest

Tallahassee map, grid d2, page 86

Porter Lake is a good stop for canoeists on the Ochlockonee River. It's on a short branch about 10 miles downstream from Pine Creek Landing (see campground in this chapter) on the west side of the river. This is also a trailhead for the Florida National Scenic Trail, which meanders through the national forest. For more information, see Camel Lake (see campground in this chapter).

Campsites, facilities: The primitive camping area has room for about four tents and RVs. A hand pump for spring-fed drinking water is provided. Children are welcome. Pets must be leashed in the camping area.

Reservations, fees: Reservations are not accepted. Camping is free. Stays are limited to 14 days per month.

Directions: From Telogia, drive south on County Road 67 for 16 miles, then turn east on Forest Service Road 13 and drive three miles to the campground.

Contact: Apalachicola National Forest, Apalachicola Ranger District, P.O. Box 579, Highway 20, Bristol, FL 32321, 850/643-2282, website: www.southernregion.fs.fed.us/florida/recreation/apalachicola_rec.htm.

35 WHITEHEAD LAKE

Rating: 6

South of Telogia in Apalachicola National Forest

Tallahassee map, grid d2, page 86

This is one of the larger primitive campgrounds on the Ochlockonee River's west bank, a good spot for fishing and launching boats, with no horsepower limit on boat motors. For campers traveling the river, it is 14 miles downstream from Pine Creek Landing and provides an alternative to making camp at Porter Lake, a few miles upriver.

Campsites, facilities: This primitive camping area has room for 10 tents or RVs. Hand-pumped drinking water, chemical toilets, and a boat ramp are available. Children are welcome. Pets must be leashed in the camping area.

Reservations, fees: Reservations are accepted.

Camping is $3 per vehicle. Stays are limited to 14 days per month.

Directions: From Telogia, drive 16 miles south on County Road 67. Turn east on Forest Service Road 13 and drive 1.5 miles. Turn south on Forest Service Road 186 and drive 1.5 miles to the campground.

Contact: Apalachicola National Forest, Apalachicola Ranger District, P.O. Box 579, Highway 20, Bristol, FL 32321, 850/643-2282, website: www.southernregion.fs.fed.us/florida/recreation/apalachicola_rec.htm.

36 HITCHCOCK LAKE

Rating: 6

South of Telogia in Apalachicola National Forest

Tallahassee map, grid d2, page 86

This campground is touted for excellent fishing and boating on the Ochlockonee River. For canoe campers paddling downstream, it is located on the west side of the river, 27 miles from Pine Creek Landing, roughly across from Mack Landing on the east side.

Campsites, facilities: There are 10 primitive sites with no hookups or drinking water. The campground has a boat ramp. Children are welcome. Pets must be leashed in the camping area.

Reservations, fees: Reservations are not accepted. Camping is free. Stays are limited to 14 days per month.

Directions: From Telogia, drive south on County Road 67 for 23 miles, then turn east on Forest Service Road 184 and drive 1.5 miles to the campground.

Contact: Apalachicola National Forest, Apalachicola Ranger District, P.O. Box 579, Highway 20, Bristol, FL 32321, 850/643-2282, website: www.southernregion.fs.fed.us/florida/recreation/apalachicola_rec.htm.

37 PINE CREEK LANDING

Rating: 5

In Apalachicola National Forest on the Ochlockonee River

Tallahassee map, grid d2, page 86

By RV standards, this is a rugged camping spot, set at the end of a dirt road with no drinking water, not even a communal spigot. The camp is popular with local hunters, who leave their trailers behind upon returning to the workaday world. But to the trained eye, the campground has superb potential: miles of logging trails for hiking and mountain biking in relative solitude except from November to January during hunting season. But the big plus of Pine Creek Landing is its boat ramp on the Ochlockonee River—a prime portal for canoeing to Ochlockonee River State Park through 50 miles of the vast Apalachicola National Forest. Established in 1936, the federal forest stretches 54 miles from Tallahassee and covers 631,260 acres of pineland, hardwood forest, hammocks, savannas, and dry ridges. Wildlife is as varied as the landscape: 190 species of birds, nine kinds of bats, coral snakes, various rattlers, alligators, flying squirrels, marsh rabbits, red and gray foxes, weasels, mink, otters, skunks, bobcats, deer, feral hogs, and, occasionally, a black bear. The Ochlockonee River slices the forest in two, with the Wakulla County District on the east side.

From Pine Creek Landing, you can meander downstream with the river current pushing your canoe at two to three miles per hour, and wind up at Ochlockonee River State Park in two or three days without trying too hard. Possible obstructions include floating logs. Occasionally, the river is low in spots, requiring a portage. The best time for canoeing is from February through May, when the weather is cool and not too buggy. Camping is available at five established sites south of Pine Creek Landing, with two tucked away on creeks along the eastern riverbank. Both usually are

marked on the river and are easily accessible from highways in Wakulla County. The other three sites are on the west bank, accessible from Liberty County.

But don't feel that you're limited to designated sites. Camping is permitted throughout the forest, except during hunting season—generally mid-November through early January. For obvious reasons, camping is restricted to designated campgrounds when hunters are out and about. Year-round, no permits are required for camping or making campfires. But for your own safety, file your planned itinerary with someone trustworthy or with the district ranger before venturing into remote areas of the forest.

Campsites, facilities: There are 10 primitive sites for tents and self-contained RVs. Bring water, food, and supplies. No facilities are available. Children are welcome. Pets should be leashed in the camping area.

Reservations, fees: Reservations are not accepted. Camping is free. The maximum stay is 14 days per month.

Directions: From Tallahassee, drive 18 miles west on State Road 20. At Bloxham, turn left on State Road 375 and go south for 12 miles. Head west on Forest Service Road 335/Piney Creek Road and drive one-half mile to the campground. The boat ramp is one mile west of the camp.

Contact: Apalachicola National Forest, Wakulla Ranger District, 57 Taft Drive, Crawfordville, FL 32327, 850/926-3561, fax 850/926-1904, website: www.southernregion.fs.fed.us/florida/forests/apalachicola.htm.

38 MACK LANDING

Rating: 9

In Apalachicola National Forest near Sopchoppy

Tallahassee map, grid d2, page 86

Mack Landing sits on a bluff in a hardwood forest about 27 miles downstream from Pine Creek Landing (see previous campground) and is popular with anglers. A steep, paved boat ramp leads to a creek that feeds into the Ochlockonee River, and space is available to tie boats to trees on the riverbank. The sites are casually laid out and spacious.

Campsites, facilities: The 10 primitive sites will accommodate tents or self-contained RVs. Each site has a picnic table and fire ring, but no electricity or water. There are vault (nonflush) toilets and a boat ramp. Bring water, food, and supplies. Children are welcome. Pets should be leashed in the camping area.

Reservations, fees: Reservations are not accepted. Camping is $3 daily. The maximum stay is 14 days per month.

Directions: From Sopchoppy, drive west and then north on State Road 375 for 10 miles. Turn left on Forest Service Road 336/Mack Landing Road and drive one mile west to the camp.

Contact: Apalachicola National Forest, Wakulla Ranger District, 57 Taft Drive, Crawfordville, FL 32327, 850/926-3561, fax 850/926-1904, website: www.southernregion.fs.fed.us/florida/forests/apalachicola.htm.

39 WOOD LAKE

Rating: 6

In Apalachicola National Forest near Sopchoppy

Tallahassee map, grid d2, page 86

This small campground located about 12 miles downstream from Mack Landing (see previous campground) provides anglers and boaters with a gently sloping ramp for launching into a creek that runs into one of the most interesting stretches, in terms of wildlife, of the Ochlockonee River, as it twists through Liberty and Franklin Counties, passing Ochlockonee River State Park some 10 miles downstream.

Campsites, facilities: The primitive sites will accommodate tents or self-contained RVs. There are no amenities. The boat ramp may be unusable in low-water conditions. Children

are welcome. Pets should be leashed in the camping area.

Reservations, fees: Reservations are not accepted. Camping is free. The maximum stay is 14 days per month.

Directions: From Sopchoppy, take U.S. 319 south for four miles. Turn west and then north on County Road 299 and drive three miles. Turn west onto Forest Service Road 338 and drive two miles to the camp.

Contact: Apalachicola National Forest, Wakulla Ranger District, 57 Taft Drive, Crawfordville, FL 32327, 850/926-3561, fax 850/926-1904, website: www.southernregion.fs.fed.us/florida/forests/apalachicola.htm.

40 WRIGHT LAKE

Rating: 8

Near Sumatra in Apalachicola National Forest

Tallahassee map, grid d3, page 86

Set in tall pines on the west side of Apalachicola National Forest, this secluded park has spacious campsites beside a spring-fed lake lined with moss-draped cypress and live oak. Staffers consider it the KOA of the Apalachicola forest, thanks to its amenities compared with the typical primitive camps elsewhere in the forest. There's a beach for swimming and fishing, a lakeside picnic area, and an interpretive trail for hiking. The camping area is along the 31.5-mile Apalachee Savannahs Scenic Byway, which you can pick up in Sumatra by heading north on State Road 379. The highway, suitable for bicycling, is a showcase of flat and rolling terrain and wet lowlands abundant with magnolia, cypress swamps, and stands of native longleaf pine. Grassy savannas are speckled with wildflowers such as orchids, pitcher plants, and sundews. Stop often, keeping an eye out for red-cockaded woodpeckers, wild turkeys, bobcats, alligators, and possibly a black bear.

South of Wright Lake, off of State Road 65 on Forest Service Road 129, is the Fort Gadsden Historic Site, overlooking the immense Apalachicola River, a waterway once plied by steamboats, ferries, and barges linking Georgia and Alabama to Gulf ports. The fort is a nice stop for a picnic beside oaks covered with resurrection ferns. Interpretive exhibits, meanwhile, help resurrect the site's gruesome military history. The first fortification here was called Fort Blount, built by British troops. They abandoned the fort after the War of 1812, but not before helping a colony of Choctaw Indians and runaway slaves set up cannons to fire upon American warships. On July 24, 1816, the fort was attacked by troops under the command of General Andrew Jackson, who ordered the slaves returned to their "rightful owners." A red-hot cannonball hit the fort's gunpowder magazine, killing all but 60 of the 334 occupants, women and children included. Two of the uninjured survivors, one Native American and one black, were executed. Jackson rebuilt the fort while fighting Spanish forces in 1818. It was renamed for James Gadsden, an American diplomat and Jackson's aide-de-camp during the campaign. A Florida county also bears Gadsden's name.

Campsites, facilities: There are 20 sites with water, electricity, and fire pits for RVs or tents. Each site has a pad for an RV and a cleared area for a tent. The park has restrooms (with flush toilets), hot showers, a dump station, picnic tables, grills, and a swimming lake. A boat ramp is nearby at Hickory Landing. Children are welcome. Pets should be leashed in the park but can run free in the forest.

Reservations, fees: Reservations are not taken, but you can call the ranger district to see if a spot is available. The fee is $8 nightly per vehicle. Credit cards are not accepted. The maximum stay is 14 days per month.

Directions: From Sumatra, take State Road 65 south for two miles. Turn west on Forest Service Road 101 and drive two miles. Turn north at the sign for the park and proceed .25 mile.

Contact: Apalachicola National Forest, Apalachicola Ranger District, P.O. Box 579, Highway 20, Bristol, FL 32321, 850/643-2282,

website: www.southernregion.fs.fed.us/florida/recreation/apalachicola_rec.htm.

41 HICKORY LANDING

Rating: 8

Near Sumatra in Apalachicola National Forest

Tallahassee map, grid d3, page 86

Hickory Landing is the no-frills neighbor of the Wright Lake campground, with secluded sites nestled in hickory trees and oaks. The landing has a mineral spring (by the boat ramp) but no showers, swimming, or electricity. The boat ramp opens onto Owl Creek, which feeds into the Apalachicola River. It's fine for powerboating and fishing, but not so great for canoeing because of the boat traffic.

Campsites, facilities: There are 10 primitive sites for tents and self-contained RVs. Drinking water is available, as are chemical toilets, picnic tables, grills, and a boat ramp. Children are welcome. Pets should be leashed in the camping area but can run free in the forest.

Reservations, fees: Reservations are not accepted. Camping is $3 per vehicle. The maximum stay is 14 days each month.

Directions: From Sumatra, take State Road 65 south for two miles. Turn west on Forest Service Road 101 and drive 1.5 miles, then turn south on Forest Service Road 101B and drive one mile to the landing.

Contact: Apalachicola National Forest, Apalachicola Ranger District, P.O. Box 579, Highway 20, Bristol, FL 32321, 850/643-2282, website: www.southernregion.fs.fed.us/florida/recreation/apalachicola_rec.htm.

42 SPORTSMAN'S LODGE

Rating: 3

In Eastpoint

Tallahassee map, grid d3, page 86

This fishing-oriented resort includes a motel, a

marina, and waterfront, oak-shaded RV sites along East Bay. You can fish from the dock or hook up with a charter captain for deep-sea trolling in the Gulf of Mexico or for inland freshwater fishing. It's close to Apalachicola, as well as the white-sand beaches of St. George Island. The complex is a short walk from the town of Eastpoint, an old fishing village with restaurants and a small food store.

Campsites, facilities: A handful of the 74 full-hookup RV sites are available for overnighters and seasonal visitors. The rest are occupied by full-timers or people who leave their rigs on site and use them on the weekends and holidays. On the premises are charter boats, docks, and a marina. There are no showers or restrooms. Groceries, bait, fuel, and ice are available about 1.5 miles away. Children are welcome. Leashed pets are permitted.

Reservations, fees: Reservations are recommended. Sites are $15 per night. Major credit cards are accepted. Long-term stays are OK.

Directions: From Apalachicola, cross the John Gorrie Memorial Bridge. Make the first left. The park is 400 yards up the road.

Contact: Sportsman's Lodge, 99 N. Bayshore Drive, Eastpoint, FL 32328, 850/670-8423, fax 850/670-8316.

43 GULF VIEW CAMPGROUND

Rating: 8

Near Eastpoint

Tallahassee map, grid d3, page 86

The name says it all: Gulf View is a restful spot with a fabulous vista of St. George Island and the water. Its grassy campsites are shaded by towering slash pines on a gentle hill sloping down to the highway, and you can swim or fish from the seawall across U.S. 98 (although relatively few people do). The eight-acre park also is convenient to the resort community on St. George Island. Snowbirds dominate in winter, when license plates often hail from Ohio, Michigan, Indiana, New York, and Canada.

Campsites, facilities: Of the 45 RV and tent sites with full hookups, about 30 are available for overnighters and seasonal visitors; most sites have picnic tables. Restrooms, showers, and laundry facilities are available. Children are welcome. Leashed pets are permitted.

Reservations, fees: Reservations are suggested in winter. Sites are $19 per night for two adults and two children under age 12, plus $1 per additional person. Credit cards are not accepted. Long-term stays are OK.

Directions: From Apalachicola, take U.S. 98 east for eight miles to the park.

Contact: Gulf View Campground, 897 U.S. 98, Eastpoint, FL 32328, 850/670-8970, fax 850/670-8857, email: justme@gtcom.net.

44 APALACHICOLA BAY CAMPGROUND

Rating: 4

In Eastpoint

Tallahassee map, grid d3, page 86

By Florida standards, this park is great for campers on the move, a convenient overnight stop for travelers, especially during the peak summer season, when other campgrounds directly on the Gulf of Mexico are filled. It has shady sites and a pool, but alas, no beach. The park is the first one you reach as you begin traveling east on U.S. 98, a scenic highway that hugs the Gulf Coast and is dotted with picturesque fishing hamlets and expensive vacation homes. It also is on the outskirts of Apalachicola, a favorite getaway for politicians from Tallahassee, the state capital.

For centuries, Apalachicola has been famous for seafood, especially its oysters—don't pass through without slurping down a few. Ancient Indians first feasted here on the shellfish. The teeming fish life and natural harbor also drew Spanish explorer Hernando de Soto. More than 450 years ago, he established a base of operations for a disastrous expedition from the Apalachicola River to Georgia, Alabama, and the Mississippi River, where de Soto, starving and sick, died.

Apalachicola's next footnote in history came some 300 years later with the arrival of John Gorrie, a physician with a chilling legacy: he's credited with inventing air-conditioning. While living here, Gorrie experimented with ways to artificially cool air so that sufferers of malaria and other fevers would be more comfortable. In 1851, he was awarded the first U.S. patent for mechanical refrigeration. Gorrie also served as Apalachicola's postmaster and mayor before his death in 1855. The landmark Gorrie bridge just outside the Apalachicola Bay Campground was named after Florida's ice man.

Campsites, facilities: There are 48 full-hookup RV spots and 11 tent sites with water, electricity, and picnic tables. Cable TV is available at the roomy RV sites. Twenty-eight sites are pull-through and can accommodate 40-foot RVs even pulling another vehicle. On the premises are restrooms, showers, laundry facilities, a dump station, a pool, cabins, and a playground. All areas are wheelchair accessible. Children are welcome. Leashed pets are permitted.

Reservations, fees: Reservations are recommended. Sites are $20 per night for two people, plus $3 per extra person. Credit cards are accepted. Long-term stays are OK.

Directions: From Apalachicola, take U.S. 98 east for five miles, crossing the John Gorrie Memorial Bridge (a.k.a. Apalachicola Bay Bridge) that leads to St. George Island. The campground is 300 yards east of the bridge, on the south side of the road. Look for the large, lighted campground sign.

Contact: Apalachicola Bay Campground, P.O. Box 621, 118 Highway 98, Eastpoint, FL 32328, 850/670-8307.

45 ST. GEORGE ISLAND STATE PARK

Rating: 10

On St. George Island

Tallahassee map, grid d4, page 86

Again and again, this barrier island makes the lists of the finest beaches in the United States. That's a big reason why the campground here is so extremely popular and a jewel of the Florida state park system—there are nine miles of beaches and sand dunes with the texture of powdered sugar. The 1,962-acre park, a combination of beachfront, sandy dunes, salt marsh, and pine and oak forests, was acquired by the state in 1963 and was opened to recreation in 1980. It's a haven for wildlife, with osprey nesting atop dead pines, and ghost crabs, salt-marsh snakes, and diamondback terrapin turtles residing on the bay. Migratory birds rest here in the fall and spring; the feathered guests include snowy plover, tern, black skimmer, and willet. Fishers reel in flounder, redfish, sea trout, whiting, and an occasional Spanish mackerel. (A saltwater fishing license is required.)

Prior to 1965, when the causeway was finished, St. George Island was way off the beaten path. In the 1900s, its forests were tapped for turpentine; the scars are still visible on the larger slash pines. During World War II, the beach dunes were used for training exercises in preparation for D day, the invasion at Normandy. Today, St. George Island is subject to invasion, with its resort village drawing hordes of vacationers in the summer. It's tough to get a site here during the peak summer season and on long weekends. Fortunately, there are alternative campgrounds on the mainland; that way, you can still visit the park for long walks on the beach, shelling, sunbathing, swimming, splashing in the surf, and fishing and boating on the Gulf or St. George Sound. Another alternative is the primitive campsites at the park's Gap Point, a 2.5-mile hike along a nature trail from the developed camping area. The park is also popular with bicyclists.

Campsites, facilities: There are 60 RV sites with water and electricity, picnic tables, and campfire rings. Primitive tent sites also are available for hikers. The park has restrooms, showers, a dump station, two boat ramps, a boardwalk, and beaches. Children are welcome. Alcohol is not permitted. Pets are allowed with proof of vaccination.

Reservations, fees: Reservations are recommended; call ReserveAmerica at 800/326-3521. Sites are $8 to $14 per night for four people, plus $2 for each additional person and $2 per pet. Major credit cards are accepted. The maximum stay is 14 days.

Directions: From Apalachicola, take U.S. 98 east for six miles, then turn south on the St. George Island toll bridge. Drive eight miles to the island traffic circle, then turn east on East Gulf Beach Drive. The park is located at the end of the road.

Contact: St. George Island State Park, 1900 E. Gulf Beach Drive, St. George Island, FL 32328, 850/927-2111, fax 850/927-2500.

46 CARRABELLE PALMS RV PARK

Rating: 7

In Carrabelle

Tallahassee map, grid d3, page 86

Gulf breezes kiss this well-kept, sunny campground, but the sites are somewhat crowded, as is the case in many waterfront parks. Across the road is a public beach for fishing and swimming in the gulf waters.

Campsites, facilities: RVs and occasionally tents are accepted at these 48 full-hookup sites with picnic tables; plans are in the works to add more campsites. Restrooms, showers, a dump station, a small store, a modem hookup for laptop computers, and a recreation hall are available. A public beach is located across the street. Children are welcome. Leashed pets are permitted.

Reservations, fees: Reservations are recommended. Sites are $18.50 to $20.50 per night

for two people, plus $2 per additional person. Major credit cards are accepted. Long-term stays are OK.

Directions: From Apalachicola, take U.S. 98 east for about 20 miles to Carrabelle Beach, then look for the park across from the beach.

Contact: Carrabelle Palms RV Park, 1843 Highway 98 West, Carrabelle, FL 32322, 850/697-2638.

47 HO-HUM RV PARK

Rating: 7

East of Carrabelle

Tallahassee map, grid d3, page 86

For beachfront living, this three-acre park welcomes older RVers who can relax in the park swings and gaze out over the water. The sites are numbered and laid out in rows on hard-as-a-rock shell roads along 400 feet of beachfront, and recently the owner has planted palm trees to frame the view. All sites enjoy spectacular views of the Gulf and are swept by sea breezes. The farthest your site can be is 250 feet from water's edge, but some sites are 15 feet away. Snowbirds come in winter, playing cards and bingo; in summer, the crowd turns to anglers. While children are permitted, there's not much for them to do, and the park tends to be peopled by a few overnighters and mostly seasonal visitors who stay for a week or two or the entire winter. The proprietors report that their place is becoming increasingly popular among birders; migratory birds swoop onto an island one mile offshore. Campers pull their boats up on the sand, which also is fun for wading and shelling. At night, hook up the cable TV, if you must, but keep the volume low enough to hear the surf breaking on the shore.

Campsites, facilities: All 50 sites have full hookups and picnic tables. On the premises are restrooms, showers, a recreation room, a 250-foot fishing pier, modem hookup for laptop computers in the laundry room, and cable TV. Children are allowed; they must be accompanied by an adult at all times. Leashed pets are permitted.

Reservations, fees: Reservations are recommended. Sites are $20 to $22 per night for two people, plus $2 for each additional person and $5 for cable TV. Major credit cards are accepted. Seasonal rates are available.

Directions: From Apalachicola, take U.S. 98 east for 22 miles to Carrabelle. The park is four miles east of Carrabelle, on the gulf side.

Contact: Ho-Hum RV Park, 2132 Highway 98E, Carrabelle, FL 32322, 850/617-6625 or 888/88-HO-HUM.

48 OCHLOCKONEE RIVER STATE PARK

Rating: 9

South of Sopchoppy

Tallahassee map, grid c3, page 86

Nestled between Apalachicola National Forest and the St. Marks National Wildlife Refuge, this 392-acre state park is an ideal base camp for exploring the vast northwest Florida wilderness on foot or via canoe. Advisory to campers: Bring plenty of bug repellent in summer; beware of ticks, chiggers, and wasp hives in low-hanging oak branches, and think twice about refilling your water tanks from the park's spigots—the well water, while potable, had a straw-colored tinge when we camped here (hence the park's Indian name: Yellow Water).

The place is teeming with wildlife, including deer, fox squirrels, bobcat, and overly friendly raccoons. It's not unusual to see endangered red-cockaded woodpeckers, which nest in the upper cavities of old pines suffering from heart rot. The woods are periodically cleaned by controlled burning, which produces a bonus for nature lovers: explosions of wildflowers in summer months. The park also sports small grassy ponds, dense swampy bay heads, and oak thickets. From the park boat ramp, mariners can launch saltwater fishing trips to Ochlockonee Bay and the Gulf of Mexico, which are five miles downstream, or ply the Ochlockonee and Dead Rivers and Tide Creek in search of largemouth bass, bream, catfish, and speckled perch. (State fishing licenses are required.) For canoeists, the park marks the end of the Ochlockonee River Lower Canoe Trail, a 50-mile route along the Wakulla County line through Apalachicola National Forest.

Campsites, facilities: There are 30 campsites for tents and RVs, all with water, picnic tables, fire rings, and electricity. Four sites are pull-through. Facilities include restrooms (wheelchair accessible), showers, a dump station, canoe rentals, and a boat ramp. Children are welcome. Leashed pets are permitted with proof of rabies vaccination.

Reservations, fees: Reservations are recommended; call ReserveAmerica at 800/326-3521. Sites are $9 to $11 per night for eight people, plus $1 for each additional person and $2 for electricity. Major credit cards are accepted.

Directions: From Tallahassee, take U.S. 319 south for 25 miles to Sopchoppy. Continue four miles south on U.S. 319 to the park, which is on the east side of the road.

Contact: Ochlockonee River State Park, P.O. Box 5, 429 State Park Road, Sopchoppy, FL 32358, 850/962-2771, fax 850/962-2403.

49 HOLIDAY PARK AND CAMPGROUND

Rating: 6

In Panacea

Tallahassee map, grid c3, page 86

This seaside resort is a straight shot from Tallahassee, with plenty of space for big RVs, including pull-through sites. The park sports oak trees, waterfront sites, and fantastic views of the Gulf of Mexico and the Panacea bridge. An open-air pavilion and hefty barbecue pit are available for parties. You can walk to nearby seafood restaurants. There's a nice, quiet beach and a long pier jutting into Ochlockonee Bay; a public boat ramp is nearby, and Wakulla Springs is a convenient drive away.

Campsites, facilities: This campground has 75 RV sites with full hookups, picnic tables, and cable TV. Some tent sites are available in a designated area. Facilities include restrooms, showers, a laundry room, a gift shop, a pool, a beach, a fishing pier, a recreation room, a playground, horseshoe pits, and shuffleboard and volleyball courts. All areas are said to be wheelchair accessible. Children are welcome. Leashed pets are permitted.

Reservations, fees: Reservations are accepted. Sites are $22 to $31 per night for two people, plus $5 for each additional person. Major credit cards are accepted. Long-term stays are OK.

Directions: From Tallahassee, take U.S. 319 south for 25 miles to the intersection with U.S. 98 in Panacea. Take U.S. 98 west for nine miles to the park.

Contact: Holiday Park and Campground, 14 Coastal Highway, Panacea, FL 32346; tel./fax 850/984-5757, website: www.holidaycampground.com.

50 ALLIGATOR POINT KOA CAMPGROUND RESORT
🚲 🛶 🚐 🐕 ♿ 🚐 ⛺

Rating: 7

In Panacea
Tallahassee map, grid c3, page 86

This sunny park sits on a small peninsula jutting into the Gulf of Mexico and is a convenient getaway destination from Tallahassee. Most sites surround several large ponds, and many face the Gulf. It's a good spot to launch fishing trips, for shelling on the beach, and for enjoying the sunset.

Campsites, facilities: This campground has 114 RV sites, all with full hookups, cable TV, and picnic tables. Twenty-five sites are available for tents. There are restrooms, showers, laundry facilities, a dump station, a convenience store, a pool, a playground, bicycle and paddleboat rentals, a horseshoe pitch area, and a clubhouse. Camping cabins or cottages are available for rent; park models

are for sale. Children are welcome. Leashed pets are permitted.

Reservations, fees: Reservations are recommended in the summer and on holidays. Sites are $36 per night for two people, plus $5 for each additional adult (children are free). Major credit cards are accepted. Long-term stays are OK.

Directions: From Tallahassee, take U.S. 319 south for 25 miles to the intersection with U.S. 98 in Panacea. Take U.S. 98 west for 13 miles to the junction of State Road 370. Turn south and drive to the park.

Contact: Alligator Point KOA Campground Resort, 1320 Alligator Drive, Panacea, FL 32346, 850/349-2525, fax 850/349-2067, website: www.alligatorpointkoa.com.

51 NEWPORT RECREATION PARK
🚲 🛶 🚐 🐕 ♿ 🚐 ⛺

Rating: 3

In Newport south of Tallahassee
Tallahassee map, grid c2, page 86

Located off the beaten path, this no-frills campground makes a base for exploring the St. Marks River, spectacular Wakulla Springs, and the St. Marks National Wildlife Refuge, a 64,248-acre preserve that sprawls along 40 miles of Apalachee Bay and stretches from the Ochlockonee River (pronounced "o'clock-nee") on the west to the Aucilla River on the east. Its salt marshes, hardwood and pine forests, and palm and live oak hammocks are popular for hiking, fishing, canoeing, mountain biking, and hunting. The park provides a camping destination for backpackers and bicyclists coming from Tallahassee. It is a few miles from the terminus of the Tallahassee–St. Marks Historic Railroad State Trail, a 16-mile paved route. For information, call the trail headquarters at 850/922-6007.

Downriver, where the St. Marks joins the Wakulla River, lies the San Marcos de Apalache State Historic Site, hallowed ground steeped in military lore. In 1528, Spanish explorer Panfilo de Narvaez arrived here from Tampa and built the first ships made by white men in the New World. His carpenters caulked their yellow-pine hulls with pitch and fiber from palmetto palm fronds. The vessels didn't get far. They sunk when de Narvaez tried to retreat to Mexico. (He was among the drowned.) In 1677, the Spanish considered the rivers' confluence a strategic location and built a pine fort, which promptly was sacked and burned by pirates.

A stone fort called San Marcos built in 1739 was occupied by both the Spanish and the British over the next 80 years, until Florida was ceded to the United States. In the 1850s, stone from the old fort was used to build a military hospital for victims of yellow fever. San Marcos also played a role, albeit minor, in the Civil War: It was taken by Confederate forces in 1861 and renamed Fort Ward, then blockaded by a Union squadron for the rest of the conflict. Today, a museum sits on the foundation of the old hospital; ancient Spanish and Confederate earthworks are visible at the site, as is a military cemetery.

Another nearby point of interest is Wakulla Springs, a three-acre wonder touted as one of the world's largest and deepest freshwater springs, with as much as a billion gallons a day flowing out. It's located in Edward Ball Wakulla Springs State Park, about 20 miles west of Newport, and can be viewed from glass-bottomed boats. The spring is teeming with fish, and the mouth of a cavern yawns 100 feet below—complete with a few fossilized mastodon bones. The remains of nine other Ice Age mammals have been discovered as far as 1,200 feet into the cave. Wakulla Springs has no camping facilities, but it's especially worth a side trip for bird lovers. During the winter, the park attracts thousands of migrating waterfowl, including American wigeon, hooded merganser, and American coot. Feathered locals include limpkin, purple gallinule, anhinga, and bald eagle. For more information, contact Wakulla Springs State Park at 550 Wakulla Park Drive, Wakulla Springs, FL 32305, 850/224-5950.

Campsites, facilities: There are 41 campsites, 15 suitable for self-contained RVs and the rest for tents. Each site has a fire ring. Some sites have electricity and water. Park facilities include restrooms, showers, a dump station, and a boat ramp. All areas of this county park are said to be wheelchair accessible. Canoes and boats can be rented nearby. Children are welcome. Pets are permitted.

Reservations, fees: Reservations are recommended. Sites are $10 to $15 per night for up to five people. A maximum of two tents is allowed per site. Credit cards are not accepted. Stays are limited to two weeks.

Directions: From Tallahassee, take State Road 363 south for 12 miles, then turn east on U.S. 98/319. Drive through Newport to the park.

Contact: Wakulla County Parks and Recreation Department, 79 Recreation Drive, Crawfordville, FL 32326, 850/926-7227, fax 850/926-5251. The park telephone is 850/925-4530.

52 ST. MARKS NATIONAL WILDLIFE REFUGE

Rating: 8

In southern Wakulla County between U.S. 98 and Apalachee Bay/the Gulf of Mexico
Tallahassee map, grid c2, page 86

This is strictly for hard-core backpackers. Camping is allowed only along a section of the Florida National Scenic Trail that passes through the scenic refuge, which is alive with the sounds of chirping birds. Only hikers who plan to complete the entire 35-mile route through the refuge are allowed to camp along it. The refuge is run by the U.S. Fish and Wildlife Service, which generally does not permit camping on its Florida lands but does so in this case to accommodate through-hikers on the trail.

Although the route is quite flat, you'll find it challenging in one very important aspect: When you reach the St. Marks River, a refuge official told us, there is no bridge, but you must cross the river. Most backpackers flag down a passing boat and persuade the boater to provide ferry service. One suggestion is to call Shield's Marina (850/925-5612) ahead of time and make arrangements for pickup. The marina is across the river and sees a lot of boat traffic. The other alternative is to swim, but no one recommends that. The trail passes through varied terrain—sunny pine flatwoods dotted by fan-shaped saw palmetto; pine uplands studded with turkey oaks; dark, shady bottomland hardwood areas filled with trees such as gum and maple; sun-washed freshwater marsh; and mixed areas of pines, hardwoods, and cabbage palms. It's not uncommon to see deer and turkey. Lucky hikers might spot a Florida black bear or a bobcat. Hundreds of species of birds either live in or pass through the refuge.

Campsites, facilities: There are five primitive hike-in campsites along the Florida National Scenic Trail. No facilities are provided. Bring water, food, and camping gear. Children are allowed. Pets are prohibited.

Reservations, fees: Campers must obtain a permit from the wildlife refuge. You should apply as far ahead as possible by phone, mail, or fax. However, you can be granted a permit at the wildlife refuge office, which is about one-third of the way through your hike. There is rarely competition for these campsites. Sites are $1 per night per person. Credit cards are not accepted.

Directions: The eastern trailhead is at the point where U.S. 98 crosses the Aucilla River. The western trailhead is near Medart on State Road 319. Refuge officials can provide more specific directions when they issue the camping permit.

Contact: St. Marks National Wildlife Refuge, 1255 Lighthouse Road, P.O. Box 68, St. Marks, FL 32355, 850/925-6121, website: http://saint-marks.fws.gov.

53 ELITE RESORTS AT ECONFINA

Rating: 4

South of Lamont on the Gulf of Mexico
Tallahassee map, grid c2, page 86

This private campground is next to the 3,377-acre Econfina River State Park's boat ramp and rents canoes so campers can explore it. Permanent residents live at about 20 sites set off to one area, whereas overnighters stay in another area, sleeping beside two ponds. The 27-acre park has fishing guide services and a store is available. In the state park, you'll find hiking and horseback trails, pine and oak forests, and a salt marsh. Upstream, the river, which flows almost two miles to the Gulf, offers challenging canoeing waters on the stretch between Lamont and the County Road 257 bridge. Bugs can be a problem in this area, so come prepared. The park recently built a swimming pool, but the main attraction is fishing.

Campsites, facilities: There are 29 full-hookup RV sites and 20 to 30 primitive tent sites, all with picnic tables and fire rings. Restrooms, showers, a pool, a clubhouse, horseshoes, volleyball, a small playground, a limited store, bait, tackle, canoe rentals, and a boat ramp are available. Children are welcome. Leashed pets are permitted.

Reservations, fees: Reservations are recommended. Tent sites are $14 for two people, plus $5 per extra person. Full-hookup sites are $22 per rig; if a tent for sleeping is added to that site, then add $5 per tenter. Children under 12 camp for free. Major credit cards are accepted. Long-term stays are OK.

Directions: From I-10 west of Greenville, take Exit 233 and head south on County Road 257 for approximately 25 miles, crossing U.S. 19/98. Continue south for another five miles on County Road 14 until it ends at the park.

Contact: Elite Resorts at Econfina, 4705 Econfina River Road, Lamont, FL 32336, 850/584-2135, fax 850/838-2164.

54 SOUTHERN OAKS RV CAMPGROUND

Rating: 5

South of Perry

Tallahassee map, grid b2, page 86

Southern Oaks RV Campground is a good base camp for exploring the undiscovered Big Bend area, one of the few places in Florida without a convenient interstate highway. The major road that runs through this area is U.S. 19/98, going roughly east-west through Taylor, Dixie, and Levy Counties. Here in Perry, you'll be less than one hour's drive from the beach, freshwater and saltwater fishing, hunting grounds, and wilderness areas, as well as many historic and archaeological sites. Unspoiled rivers, many of them great for canoeing or houseboating, run south toward the Gulf.

Begin your exploration of the area in Perry, which is known as the forest capital of Florida. More than 90 percent of the land in Taylor County is owned by the timber industry. Stop by the Forest Capital State Museum (850/584-3227) for a better understanding of the business and modern forest management practices; there's also a "cracker" homestead typical of those where early settlers lived. (Crackers were so-called because they cracked whips to drive their cattle.)

Campsites, facilities: All 100 RV campsites have full hookups, with optional cable TV and telephone service. Eighteen tent sites are also available. On the premises are picnic tables, restrooms, showers, a dump station, horseshoe pits, a pool, a Jacuzzi, fire rings, and laundry facilities. The bathhouse, laundry room, clubhouse, and store are wheelchair accessible. Children are welcome. Leashed pets are permitted.

Reservations, fees: Reservations are recommended. Sites are $20 per night for two people, plus $3 for each additional person. Major credit cards are accepted. Long-term stays are welcome.

Directions: From I-10 at Greenville, take Exit 241 and drive south on U.S. 221 for 23 miles

to Perry. Continue south through Perry on U.S. 19/98 to the park.

Contact: Southern Oaks RV Campground, 3641 Highway 19 South, Perry, FL 32347, 850/584-3221 or 800/339-5421 (reservations only).

55 TOWN AND COUNTRY CAMPER LODGE

Rating: 3

South of Perry

Tallahassee map, grid b2, page 86

Groceries and restaurants are available within one mile of this trailer park. The campsites are grassy and have concrete patios. The Gulf of Mexico is 20 miles to the south.

Campsites, facilities: There are 25 RV and tent sites in this park, which also has 29 mobile homes. All sites have full hookups, cable TV, and telephone service. On the premises are picnic tables, restrooms, showers, rental trailers, and laundry facilities. The bathhouse and laundry room are wheelchair accessible. Leashed pets and children are welcome.

Reservations, fees: Reservations are not necessary. Sites are $11.50 per night for two people, plus $2 for each additional adult and $1 per child. Credit cards are not accepted. Long-term stays are OK.

Directions: From the intersection of U.S. 19/98 and U.S. 27 in Perry, drive south on U.S. 19/98 for 2.5 miles to the park.

Contact: Town and Country Camper Lodge, 2785 Highway 19 South, Perry, FL 32348, 850/584-3095.

56 WESTGATE MOTEL CAMPGROUND

Rating: 2

In Perry

Tallahassee map, grid b2, page 86

Campers stay on pine-shaded acreage behind the motel, which is located in the town of Perry.

Shopping is close by, and the motel pool and other facilities are available to guests of the RV park.

Campsites, facilities: The 60 RV sites have full hookups, cable TV connections, and picnic tables. Restrooms and showers are located in the motel building. A pool, laundry facilities, a dump station, and RV supplies are available. Children are welcome. Leashed pets are permitted.

Reservations, fees: Reservations are not necessary. Sites are $21 per night for two people, plus $2 for each additional person and $2 for cable TV. Major credit cards are accepted. Long-term stays are OK.

Directions: From the intersection of U.S. 19/98 and U.S. 27 in Perry, drive south on U.S. 19/98 for one mile.

Contact: Westgate Motel Campground, 1627 South Byron Butler Parkway, Perry, FL 32348, 850/584-5235, fax 850/584-3037, website: www.westgateusa.com.

57 BLUE SPRING PARK
🏊 🚤 🎣 🏕 🚐 ⛺

Rating: 7

West of Mayo

Tallahassee map, grid b2, page 86

Set on a bluff on the Suwannee River, this small county park is popular with locals on hot summer days when the cool waters of the spring are most refreshing. Nearby is yet another spring, Yana Springs. Sites in the wooded, no-frills campground are small. Canoes can be launched from the boat ramp, but it's a bit steep for bigger boats. Additional sites were added recently, and other improvements are in the works for the future.

Campsites, facilities: This Lafayette County park has 25 campsites with water and electric hookups, as well as a primitive camping area for about 85 tents. You'll find only a pit toilet in the campground; a public bathhouse with showers and flush toilets requires an approximately .25-mile walk or bicycle ride to the main park. A boat ramp and a little, old playground

are also on site. Children are welcome. Leashed pets are permitted in the campground but not the main park.

Reservations, fees: Sites are first-come, first-served. Fee for two people is $12 nightly at sites with water and electricity, $6 nightly at primitive sites. Add $1.50 for each additional person. A park entrance fee of $1.50 per person may apply. All fees are subject to change. Credit cards are not accepted. Maximum stay is 14 days.

Directions: From the town of Mayo, drive west on U.S. 27 for 4.8 miles. At County Road 251B, turn right (north) and proceed 2.1 miles. Turn right (east) on a dirt road at the sign for the park.

Contact: Blue Spring Park, 799 Northwest Blue Spring Road, Mayo, FL 32066, 386/294-1617.

58 JIM HOLLIS' RIVER RENDEZVOUS
🏊 🚤 🎣 🏕 🚐 ⛺

Rating: 8

East of Mayo

Tallahassee map, grid a2, page 86

A spectacular canopy of old-growth oaks hung with lacy Spanish moss greets guests at Jim Hollis' River Rendezvous, which caters to scuba divers and canoeists who want resort-style amenities. Most folks are accommodated in the rental trailers or the bunkhouse, but there's lots of room in the hilly, shady campground. Sites overlook the Suwannee River, which rings with the sounds of paddlers enjoying themselves on sunny weekends. Sometimes a retreat and youthgroup destination, the park offers scuba-diving courses and a full-service dive shop where you can refill your tanks. Nearby are half a dozen springs and caverns suitable for experienced divers; Peacock Springs State Park is six miles north of Mayo. Alcohol may be consumed only at your campsite or lodgings.

Campsites, facilities: The resort has 15 RV sites with water and electricity, nine full-hookup sites, and 100 primitive tent spots set apart from the RVs. On the premises are showers, restrooms, fire rings, a game room, a bunkhouse, a sauna and steam room, cabins, motel rooms, two Jacuzzis, a boat ramp, boat and canoe rentals, a playground with a trampoline, a gun range, horseshoes, volleyball, pavilions, pool tables, a restaurant, a spring for fishing and swimming, and laundry facilities. Scuba-diving gear is available for rent. Children and leashed pets are welcome.

Reservations, fees: Reservations are recommended. Sites are $5 per night per adult and $2 per child age 12 and older. Add $7 for full hookups or $5 for water and electricity. Major credit cards are accepted. Long-term stays are OK.

Directions: From Mayo, drive south on U.S. 27 for three miles. Turn left on Convict Springs Road. When the road turns to grated dirt (in about one mile), continue another mile to the park. Alternatively, from Branford, drive north on U.S. 27 for 12.7 miles. Turn right on Convict Springs Road. Proceed two miles to the park.

Contact: Jim Hollis' River Rendezvous, Convict Springs Road, Route 2, Box 635, Mayo, FL 32066, 904/294-2510 or 800/533-5276, fax 904/294-1133, website: http://jimhollis.com.

59 GORNTO SPRINGS PARK

Rating: 6

North of Old Town
Tallahassee map, grid a3, page 86

Tucked on a rise of oak trees and saw palmetto, this out-of-the-way campground is one of three Dixie County–operated parks on the west side of the Suwannee River. These parks are suitable for canoeists and people who want to get far away from city life. You can swim in the river or launch your canoe and paddle all the way to the Gulf of Mexico. Yes, there is a spring next to the riverbank at Gornto (sometimes spelled "Guaranto"), and swimmers in the hot summer months appreciate the cool water. The campground, which is not attend-

ed, is a bit run-down, but the bucolic setting more than makes up for it.

Campsites, facilities: This small, riverside county park has 24 campsites evenly divided for RVs and tents with some picnic tables, flush toilets (no showers), and a boat ramp. Electricity is available at 10 sites. Bring your own water. Children are welcome. Pets are prohibited, as are alcoholic beverages and firearms.

Reservations, fees: Reservations are not accepted. Sites are $8 per night, plus $4 for electricity. Credit cards are not accepted. The maximum stay is 14 days.

Directions: From U.S. 19/98 in Old Town, drive north on County Road 349 for 12 miles. Turn east on County Road 353, drive .5 mile past Rock Sink Baptist Church, make a sharp right, and follow the pavement until it ends. Continue on the limerock road about two miles to the park.

Contact: Dixie County Commissioner's Office, P.O. Box 2600, Cross City, FL 32628, 352/498-1206.

60 SUWANNEE RIVER KOA

Rating: 10

Near Old Town
Tallahassee map, grid a3, page 86

"We are not a condo campground! We are a camper's campground!" That's the motto of the owners of this KOA, who pride themselves on their wooded, back-to-nature setting. The 18-acre family park runs 1,400 feet along the oak-shaded bank of the Suwannee River; a dock offers boaters and anglers easy access to the river, where you can canoe, water-ski, and snorkel. Little of the surrounding area has been touched by developers, so this destination campground combines good amenities with wilderness ambience. Teens and older kids will delight in the game room; the big pool is another draw. If you need help launching your boat, the staff will do it for you with a campground truck. They'll also deliver firewood to your site. A grocery store is located two miles away in Old Town, but you'll have to drive to Chiefland for most shopping needs. A large picnic pavilion on the river is suitable for family reunions and big groups. Hike a grassy trail along the riverbank. From Old Town, you can bicycle the Nature Coast State Trail, a paved path reclaimed from old rail beds that will ultimately stretch 31 miles.

Campsites, facilities: There are 80 RV sites and, in a separate section, 20 tent sites. All sites have picnic tables, electricity, water, and cable TV; 55 have sewer connections. Restrooms, showers, laundry facilities, a convenience store, and a dump station are provided. You'll also find a pool, a game room, a boat ramp and dock, canoe rentals, cabins, a playground, horseshoe pits, shuffleboard courts, a volleyball area, and shuffleboard courts. Children are welcome. Leashed pets are permitted.

Reservations, fees: Reservations are recommended on holidays. Sites are $18 to $22 per night for two people, plus $3 for each additional adult and $2 for children ages 12 to 17. Major credit cards are accepted. Long-term stays are OK.

Directions: From U.S. 19/98 in Old Town, turn north on County Road 349 and drive 1.5 miles. Turn right on KOA Road and continue .5 mile to the park.

Contact: Suwannee River KOA, P.O. Box 460, Old Town, FL 32680, 352/542-7636 or 800/562-7635, email: carl.muller@att.net.

61 STEINHATCHEE RV REFUGE

Rating: 8

Northeast of Steinhatchee

Tallahassee map, grid a3, page 86

This refurbished, nature-oriented campground adjoins a 25,000-acre wildlife preserve and the Steinhatchee River. Oaks and pines shade the sites, some of which have hunters' travel trailers parked year-round so they can run down here for the weekend when the season opens.

You can rent a canoe at the campground, paddle several hours, and wind up in the fishing village Steinhatchee on the Gulf of Mexico. You can arrange shuttle service with the campground or paddle back upstream. An airfield was recently added, and the owners were planning to open another park across the road.

Campsites, facilities: Out of a total of 100 RV sites, 50 are available for overnighters and 25 for seasonal visitors. Twenty tent sites are set apart from the RV area. The RV sites have full hookups, or water and electricity. Restrooms, showers, a dump station, and laundry facilities are available. On the premises are a restaurant, a convenience store, bait and tackle, canoe rentals, a clubhouse, a dog-walk area, and a nature trail. Children are welcome. Leashed pets are permitted.

Reservations, fees: Reservations are recommended. Sites are $8 to $18 per night for two people, plus $2.50 per extra person. Major credit cards are accepted. Long-term stays are permitted.

Directions: From Perry, drive southeast 27 miles. The park is located in Tennille, at the intersection of U.S. 19/27 and State Road 51.

Contact: Steinhatchee RV Refuge, Box 48, Perry, FL 32348, 850/589-1541 or 800/589-1541, website: www.steinhatcheeoutpost.com.

62 WOODS GULF BREEZE RV PARK

Rating: 6

In Steinhatchee

Tallahassee map, grid b3, page 86

Campers are shaded by huge oak trees in this 10-acre riverfront campground set in the fishing village of Steinhatchee (pronounced "steenhatchee"). During the 1870s, Steinhatchee was a small port for moving rafts of cedar logs down the coast, but today it's a hot spot for commercial and recreational anglers. You'll find lots of seafood restaurants, fishing guides, and charter services here. Launch your boat from the campground ramp. You can also swim in the Steinhatchee River. The river's mouth meets the Gulf of Mexico in this town and flows through miles and miles of uninhabited wilderness; canoes are available for rent at Steinhatchee Landing (352/498-3513), a resort where former President Jimmy Carter stayed in 1996. Several other businesses in the area also rent RV spaces, including the following: Ideal Fish Camp and Motel (352/498-3877), Pat Johnson's Fish Camp (352/498-3159), Pace's Fish Camp and Marina (352/498-3008), Keaton Beach Marina (352/578-2299), Craig's Seagull Fishcamp (352/498-3909), and Edward's Fisherman's Rest (352/498-3421).

Campsites, facilities: The campground has 46 full-hookup RV sites, most with cable TV. Another 10 spots are for tents. Picnic tables, restrooms, showers, grills, a dump station, cabins and rental trailers, a boat ramp, boat rentals, and laundry facilities are available. Children and leashed pets are allowed.

Reservations, fees: Reservations are recommended. Sites are $23 to $28 per night for two people, plus $3 per extra person. Major credit cards are accepted. Long-term stays are OK.

Directions: From Perry, drive southeast on U.S. 19/98 for 28 miles. At State Road 51, turn right and continue nine miles south to Steinhatchee. Turn west on Riverside Drive and go about one mile. After you pass Roy's Restaurant, look for Second Avenue North and turn left into the park.

Contact: Woods Gulf Breeze RV Park, Second Avenue North/P.O. Box 213, Steinhatchee, FL 32359, 352/498-3948, fax 352/498-9428, website: www.woodsgulfbreeze.com.

63 SHADY OAKS RV AND MOBILE HOME PARK

Rating: 5

Near Old Town

Tallahassee map, grid a3, page 86

Tall oaks spread their branches over the RV lots, providing coolness and shade for overnighters and seasonal visitors. What's there to do other than visit local springs or go down to the Gulf of Mexico at Steinhatchee or Horseshoe Beach? Besides bingo and potluck dinners in the recreation hall, campers like to play indoor shuffleboard on a long, narrow table.

Campsites, facilities: There are about 30 sites for RVs and 10 tent sites separate from the 50 or so mobile homes in this park. All have full hookups and cable TV. Restrooms, showers, laundry facilities, a dump station, a recreation hall, a pool, a basketball hoop, a playground, a limited store, horseshoes, shuffleboard, and a pond are on site. Children are welcome. Leashed pets are permitted.

Reservations, fees: Reservations are recommended. Sites are $16 per night for two people, plus $2 per extra person. Cable TV costs $1 per day. Credit cards are not accepted. Long-term stays are OK.

Directions: From Cross City, drive two miles east on U.S. 19/98, then turn left at the second blinking light and proceed to the park.

Contact: Shady Oaks RV and Mobile Home Park, Route 3, Box 490, Old Town, FL 32680, 352/498-7276.

64 ORIGINAL SUWANNEE RIVER CAMPGROUND

Rating: 6

East of Old Town

Tallahassee map, grid a3, page 86

Tall oaks cast shade on this waterfront park, which is set on a small peninsula with canal access to the Suwannee River. Boats can be tied up near the campsites in protected waters; boat ramps are nearby. You can fish in the canal from the campground dock or toss in a line all around the 12.5-acre, horseshoe-shaped campground; it's nearly surrounded by water. Several sites are pull-through. Under new ownership, the park offers plenty of space so you won't feel crowded next to your neighbor. Boats are available for rent.

Campsites, facilities: Seventy sites with full hookups accommodate RVs, while 10 sites are for tents. About 20 sites are open for overnighters. Restrooms, showers, laundry facilities, a dump station, boat docks, boat rentals, and a clubhouse are available. Children are welcome. Small, leashed pets are permitted.

Reservations, fees: Reservations are recommended. RV sites are $21 per night for two people, plus $2 for each additional person. Kids under age eight stay free. Credit cards are accepted. Long-term rates are available.

Directions: From Old Town, drive three miles south on U.S. 19/98. See the park just before you cross the river.

Contact: Original Suwannee River Campground, HC 3, Box 63, Old Town, FL 32680, 352/542-7680, fax 352/542-0046, email: osrcampground@inetw.net.

65 OLD TOWN CAMPGROUND

Rating: 5

South of Old Town

Tallahassee map, grid a3, page 86

Owners Linda and Joe Navatto have made improvements to this oak- and pine-tree-shaded park that welcomes adult vacationers. Since purchasing the property in 1999, they built two new bathhouses, added a miniature golf area and volleyball field, and upgraded the grounds. If a camper had a sudden health problem, an emergency medical technician (Joe) may be available to assist. The park is situated just three miles from the Suwannee River.

Campsites, facilities: There are 24 RV sites for overnighters and 10 for seasonal stays; about 20 tents can be accommodated in a separate area. Fifteen sites have full hookups and 10 have water and electricity. Picnic tables, restrooms, showers, laundry facilities, cable TV, telephone service, a pavilion, miniature golf, a volleyball field, and horseshoe pits are available. Most areas are wheelchair accessible.

Children under age 16 are not welcome. Leashed pets are permitted.

Reservations, fees: Reservations are recommended. Sites are $10 to $16 per night. Credit cards are not accepted. Seasonal stays are allowed.

Directions: From U.S. 19/98 in Old Town, drive about two miles south on County Road 349 to the campground on the east side.

Contact: Old Town Campground, P.O. Box 522, Old Town, FL 32680, 352/542-9500, fax 352/542-9914, website: www.gocampingamerica.com/oldtown.

66 HINTON LANDING

Rating: 7

South of Old Town

Tallahassee map, grid a4, page 86

Hinton Landing is the nicest of the three Dixie County parks west of the Suwannee. The river flows past your doorstep, perfect for canoeing, and the setting is wooded and peaceful. There's an open-air pavilion with three picnic tables on the high riverbank, a parking area for boat trailers, and two new docks, including one that is wheelchair accessible. Don't expect fancy restrooms, though.

Campsites, facilities: This Dixie County park has 10 sites with nonpotable water, picnic tables, and flush toilets (no showers). Some sites have electricity. Most of the park can be used by someone in a wheelchair, including the floating dock, county officials say. Children are welcome. Bring drinking water. Pets are prohibited, as are alcoholic beverages and firearms.

Reservations, fees: Reservations are not accepted. Sites are $8 per night, plus $4 for electricity. Credit cards are not accepted. The maximum stay is 14 days.

Directions: From U.S. 19/98 in Old Town, drive three miles south on County Road 349. Turn east on County Road 346A and go two miles. Turn south on County Road 317 and drive .25 mile to the park.

Contact: Dixie County Commissioner's Office, P.O. Box 2600, Cross City, FL 32628, 352/498-1206.

67 SUWANNEE RIVER HIDEAWAY CAMPGROUND

Rating: 8

South of Old Town

Tallahassee map, grid a4, page 86

A 1,500-foot boardwalk that meanders through the wetlands and ends at the Suwannee River is the centerpiece of this park on 108 wooded acres. It's the perfect choice for the camper who needs more developed amenities than Hinton Landing (see previous campground) but seeks the tranquillity and peace of being near the river and in the woods. A clubhouse and two miles of hiking trails are planned for future development.

Campsites, facilities: There are 40 RV sites with full hookups, including 30-amp and 50-amp electrical service and cable TV. Fourteen sites are set aside for tents. Restrooms, showers, laundry facilities, and telephone service are available. On the premises is a picturesque 1920s-style general store. Children are welcome. Leashed pets are permitted.

Reservations, fees: Reservations are recommended. Sites are $12 to $16.50 per night for two people, plus $2 per extra person over age 12. Fifty-amp service costs $2 additional. Major credit cards are accepted. Long-term rates are available.

Directions: From U.S. 19/98 in Old Town, drive three miles south on County Road 349. Turn east on County Road 346A and go one mile to the park entrance on the right.

Contact: Suwannee River Hideaway Campground, P.O. Box 1135, Old Town, FL 32680, 352/542-7800, website: www.riverhideaway.com.

68 NEW PINE LANDING

Rating: 4

South of Old Town

Tallahassee map, grid a4, page 86

These tiny sites are clustered around a boat ramp on the Suwannee River in a wooded residential neighborhood of stilt homes. This park is too small for most trailers. Come well stocked; groceries can be purchased about 15 miles to the northwest in Cross City or in Chiefland, 25 miles to the northeast. An attendant lives one block away.

Campsites, facilities: There are five sites for tents and one for a small RV, with electricity, picnic tables, and grills. Bring drinking water. Restrooms (no showers) and a boat ramp are available. Children are welcome. Pets are prohibited, as are alcoholic beverages and firearms.

Reservations, fees: Reservations are not accepted. Sites are $8 per night, plus $4 for electricity. Credit cards are not accepted. The maximum stay is 14 days.

Directions: From U.S. 19/98 in Old Town, drive five miles south on County Road 349. Turn east on New Pine Landing Road (just south of Old Pine Landing Road) and drive 1.5 miles to the campground.

Contact: Dixie County Commissioner's Office, P.O. Box 2600, Cross City, FL 32628, 352/498-1206.

69 YELLOW JACKET CAMPGROUND

Rating: 8

South of Old Town

Tallahassee map, grid a4, page 86

Under new ownership since 2001, improvements to this lovely 40-acre campground are ongoing. Standing on the banks of the Suwannee in this shady, secluded campground, you'll see little but wilderness up and down the river for about one mile in either direction. You can fish for bass or bream in several private ponds or on the river; there are also 85,000 acres of public hunting lands adjacent to the park. Campers tend to be families, and some bring bicycles to tool around the place. If you have a small trailer, ask for a riverfront site. As many as 300 more sites are to be added during the next couple of years.

Campsites, facilities: About 66 RV sites have water and electricity; several dozen tent spots have water only. More sites are planned. Picnic tables, fire pits, restrooms, showers, 10 remodeled cottages, a playground, and a boat ramp are available. Children are welcome. Leashed pets are permitted.

Reservations, fees: Reservations are recommended. Sites are $16 to $25 per night for a family of four, plus $6 for each additional person. Prices are subject to change without notice. Credit cards are accepted. Long-term stays are OK.

Directions: From U.S. 19/98 in Old Town, drive south on County Road 349 for 9.1 miles. Turn left (east) at the sign and drive one mile to the park.

Contact: Yellow Jacket Campground, HC1 P.O. Box 220, Old Town, FL 32680, 352/542-8365, fax 352/542-0223, website: www.yellow-jacketcampground.com.

🔟 HORSESHOE BEACH PARK

Rating: 7

On the Gulf of Mexico south of Cross City
Tallahassee map, grid b4, page 86

Campsites are clustered around a sunny circular gravel drive overlooking the Gulf of Mexico in the little fishing community of Horseshoe Beach. Mudflats covered with old oyster shells make swimming difficult, but you'll have great views of the water and several uninhabited spoil islands (sandbars or oyster beds that are visible at low tide). A few seafood restaurants are in town; watch the shrimp boats head home every afternoon with their catch.

Campsites, facilities: All 14 RV sites and five tent spots in this Dixie County park have water and electricity; a few have picnic tables. Restrooms with showers are available. Children are welcome. Pets are prohibited, as alcoholic beverages and firearms.

Reservations, fees: Reservations are not accepted. Camping costs $8 per night, plus $4 for electricity. Credit cards are not accepted. The maximum stay is 14 days.

Directions: From Cross City, drive south on County Road 351 for 15 miles. Turn right on Eighth Avenue in Horseshoe Beach and continue to the park, which is also called Butler Douglas Memorial Park.

Contact: Dixie County Commissioner's Office, P.O. Box 2600, Cross City, FL 32628, 352/498-1206.

🔳 SHIRED ISLAND PARK

Rating: 9

On the Gulf of Mexico south of Cross City
Tallahassee map, grid a4, page 86

Although not an island in the traditional sense of the word, Shired Island (pronounced "shirred") is surrounded by swamp and wetlands. At these prices, it offers one of the best deals in Florida for an island camping experience. The water vistas are spectacular; all around you are the marshy islands of the Lower Suwannee National Wildlife Refuge. Swim in the warm, shallow waters of the Gulf of Mexico but don't expect white-sand beaches; the sand is more coarse and dark along this stretch of the Big Bend. Many campers set up near one of the six covered picnic pavilions at this county park and use them as outdoor living rooms. A boat ramp is nearby. Bring everything you need because stores are 20 miles away in Cross City.

Campsites, facilities: There are 17 RV sites and five tent sites with nonpotable water, electricity, picnic tables, and grills. Restrooms with concrete floors accessible for wheelchairs are available, but not showers. Bring drinking water. Children are welcome. Pets are prohibited, as are alcoholic beverages and firearms.

Reservations, fees: Reservations are not accepted. Camping costs $8 per night, plus $4 for electricity. Credit cards are not accepted. The maximum stay is 14 days.

Directions: From Cross City, drive south on County Road 351 for seven miles. At County Road 357, turn left (south) and go 11 miles to the park. Don't turn at the boat ramp.

Contact: Dixie County Commissioner's Office, P.O. Box 2600, Cross City, FL 32628, 352/498-1206.

72 MILLER'S MARINE CAMPGROUND

Rating: 8

In Suwannee

Tallahassee map, grid a4, page 86

There's a campground here, but the real emphasis is on fishing and houseboating. Miller's Marine rents these floating homes (at least 44 feet long) so you can explore the marshes at the mouth of the Suwannee River where it empties into the Gulf of Mexico. Or travel upstream 70 miles to get a glimpse of what it may have been like when stern-wheelers cruised north at the turn of the century. Fishing boats are also available; anglers catch drum, redfish, sea trout, and tarpon near East Pass. The campsites, which are barely large enough to accommodate a big rig, overlook a river marsh and a canal leading to the Suwannee. Covered boat docks are available at this 16-acre complex, but you are not permitted to park your boat trailer at your site. **Campsites, facilities:** All 34 sites have full hookups and cable TV. Six spots are for tents. Restrooms, showers, a dump station, a marina, a boat ramp, cabins, houseboats, picnic tables, and boat rentals are available. Limited groceries are located within 1.5 miles. Children are welcome. Leashed pets are permitted.

Reservations, fees: Reservations are recommended. Sites are $22 per night for two people. Major credit cards are accepted. Long-term stays are OK.

Directions: From U.S. 19/98 in Old Town, drive south on County Road 349 for 23 miles to the park. Turn left at the bridge in Suwannee and follow the sign to Miller's Marine on Big Bradford Road.

Contact: Miller's Marine Campground, P.O. Box 280, Suwannee, FL 32692, 352/542-7349, fax 352/542-3200, email: suwanneee@inetw.net.

73 ANGLER'S RESORT AT SUWANNEE

Rating: 6

In Suwannee

Tallahassee map, grid a4, page 86

"People come here to fish," says the owner, and everything here is geared to the serious angler. The campsites are set in a shady oak grove near the marina, cottages, and rental units. Open water is about one mile away. Covered boat slips ($5 per night), gas, bait, tackle, and fishing guides are available.

Campsites, facilities: Twenty-two full-hookup sites for self-contained RVs are available. There are no public restrooms or showers. Boat docks, a boat ramp, rental units, a small store, and a café are on the premises. Children are welcome. Leashed pets are permitted.

Reservations, fees: Reservations are recommended. Sites are $20 per night for two people, plus $2 for each additional person. Major credit cards are accepted. Long-term stays are OK.

Directions: From U.S. 19/98 in Old Town, drive south on County Road 349 for 23 miles to the park on the east side of the road.

Contact: Angler's Resort at Suwannee, P.O. Box 77, Suwannee, FL 32692, 352/542-7077.

COURTESY OF VISIT FLORIDA

Chapter 4

Gainesville Area

Gainesville Area

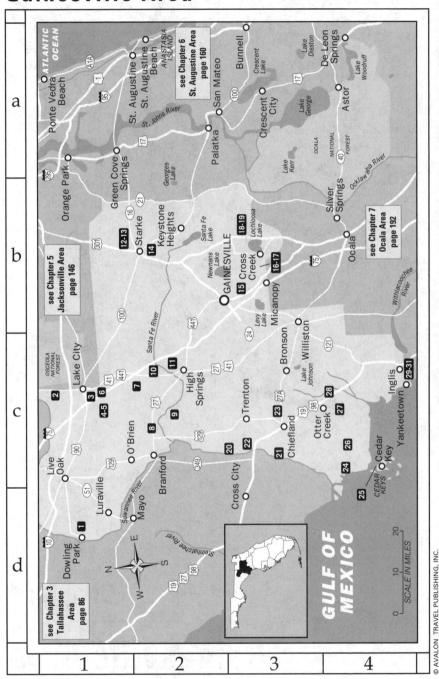

◼ TRESCA MEMORIAL PARK/ ADVENT CHRISTIAN VILLAGE

Rating: 6

Southwest of Live Oak

Gainesville map, grid d1, page 128

The campground is part of the Advent Christian Village, a 1,000-acre nondenominational retirement community set on the serene Suwannee River. But it is not strictly for seniors—there's also a church youth camp, and children are welcome in the campground. Outdoor recreation amenities abound, including hiking, fishing, and canoeing. There's also exercise equipment in the fitness center. The campground is oriented toward churchgoers, with conference facilities available for conventions, family celebrations, and personal retreats; alcoholic beverages are prohibited. Pastoral and counseling staff are on call. Each year, the village hosts a cultural series featuring theater, music, and dance.

Campsites, facilities: A retirement community, a youth-oriented church camp, and an RV campground all in one, this park offers 15 RV sites and limited tent-only sites. Eleven pull-through RV sites have full hookups and cable TV; telephone service can be arranged. On the premises are restrooms, showers, a dump station, two pools, a boat ramp, a dock, canoe rentals, a playground, exercise equipment, horseshoe pits, shuffleboard and tennis courts, a volleyball area, hiking trail, laundry facilities, and medical clinic. Nearby are a grocery store, a post office, a barber shop, and beauty salon. Twenty-four-hour security is provided. Children are welcome in the RV park. Pets are permitted.

Reservations, fees: Reservations are not usually necessary, but you can be assured of a spot by calling 800/371-8381. Sites are $19 per night for full hookups; $14 for dry camping. Long-term stays are permitted.

Directions: From I-10 west of Live Oak, take Exit 258 southbound on State Road 53 for 17 miles to State Road 250. Turn east and drive three miles to the park.

Contact: Tresca Memorial Park/Advent Christian Village, P.O. Box 4345, Dowling Park, FL 32060, 904/658-5200 or 800/647-3353, fax 904/658-5279, email: registration@acvillage.net.

◼ LAKE CITY KOA NORTH

Rating: 3

In northwest Lake City off I-10

Gainesville map, grid c1, page 128

Located on the outskirts of Osceola National Forest, this 20-acre park is grassy and mostly shaded. Still, it's convenient to the interstate, and you'll find the KOA amenities you've come to expect, plus free coffee in the morning. Additional features include a pool and two small ponds, where campers fish or feed ducks. The dirt interior roads lead to grassy sites and are named for alphabetical letters (B Road has no sewer hookups). It's about 3.5 miles to shopping and restaurants on U.S. 90 in Lake City.

Campsites, facilities: This park has 30 RV sites for overnighters and 20 available for seasonal visitors, plus a few tent sites. Most RV sites have full hookups; the rest have water and electricity. All sites have picnic tables. Cable TV is available. On the premises are restrooms, showers, laundry facilities, a pool, a playground, shuffleboard, volleyball, basketball, firewood, propane, and rental cabins. Children are welcome. Leashed pets are permitted.

Reservations, fees: Reservations are recommended for full-hookup sites with cable TV. Sites are $22 to $24 per night for two people, plus $2 per additional person over age three. Major credit cards are accepted. Long-term stays are OK.

Directions: From I-10, take Exit 301 onto northbound U.S. 441, then drive one mile to the park.

Contact: Lake City KOA North, Route 16, Box 243, Lake City, FL 32055, 386/752-9131 or 800/562-9141, fax 386/529-9414, website: www.koa.com.

3 INN AND OUT CAMPGROUND

Rating: 3

In Lake City off I-75

Gainesville map, grid c1, page 128

Lake City is a popular layover for traveling campers in a hurry to refuel, restock supplies, and reenergize before hitting the highway again in the morning. This park sits atop a hill overlooking the bustling intersection of I-75 and U.S. 90—convenient to restaurants, a large Wal-Mart shopping center, RV repair services, and even a bowling alley and movie theater. Two more perks are that Inn and Out has its own gas station and convenience store on the premises. For late-night arrivals, an attendant is on duty 24 hours. Grassy sites sit aside paved interior roads. The park has expanded, and it's somewhat easy to tell which part is the original park: the new acreage is totally sunny, whereas the original park has some shady areas.

Campsites, facilities: There are 95 RV and tent sites with full hookups. Seventy-eight sites are pull-through; 55 sites have cable TV. Restrooms, showers, laundry facilities, a dump station, a pool, a gas station, and a 24-hour convenience store are available. Children are welcome. Leashed pets are permitted.

Reservations, fees: Reservations are recommended but not always necessary. Sites are $20 per night. Major credit cards are accepted. Long-term stays are OK.

Directions: From I-75, take Exit 427 and head east on U.S. 90 for .25 mile, then turn south into the park.

Contact: Inn and Out Campground, 4490 W. Highway 90, Lake City, FL 32055, 386/752-1648.

4 WAYNE'S RV RESORT

Rating: 2

In western Lake City off I-75

Gainesville map, grid c1, page 128

This 40-acre park, shaded by pines and oaks, is convenient to the interstate as well as restaurants and suburban shopping centers on U.S. 90. If you dally on your way down the road, dip into the two swimming pools, let the kids burn off steam in the campground, and do your laundry. An "adult lounge" keeps non-parents secluded from the kids.

Campsites, facilities: The 78 RV sites are set apart from a tent area of 24 water-and-electric sites. Most RV sites have full hookups, cable TV, and are pull-through; the rest have water and electricity only. The park has a pool, a playground, shuffleboard, volleyball, picnic tables, laundry facilities, limited groceries, propane, a dump station, restrooms, and showers. The restrooms, store, and pool area are wheelchair accessible. Children are welcome. Leashed pets are permitted.

Reservations, fees: Reservations are recommended. Sites are $16 per night for four people, plus $3 for each additional person. Major credit cards are accepted. Long-term stays are OK.

Directions: From I-75, take Exit 427 and head west on U.S. 90 for .2 mile to the second stoplight. Turn south on County Road 252B.

Contact: Wayne's RV Resort Inc., Route 21, Box 501, Lake City, FL 32024, 386/752-5721, fax 386/754-3864, website: www.waynesrvresort.com.

5 CASEY JONES CAMPGROUND

Rating: 3

South of Lake City off I-75

Gainesville map, grid c1, page 128

The well-kept, grassy park has quick access to I-75. Restaurants and a convenience store are nearby. Restrooms are kept clean and stocked, and the proprietors are friendly and helpful. Overnighters may find this spot appealing because it's easy to get in and out of, but a remarkable number of snowbirds have decided to spend winters here on a sunny hill above the interstate. Asked why, one RVer in a new fifth wheel explained he'd had a heart attack on his last stay here and spent a month in a hospital in nearby Lake City. After enduring another winter in the Northeast, his wife told him, "Let's just go back to Casey Jones."

Campsites, facilities: The campground has 69 pull-through RV sites and 20 tent-only sites. Each RV site has full hookups, cable TV, and a picnic table. Facilities include restrooms, showers, a laundry room, a dump station, a playground, and a recreation room. Children are welcome, but the park tends to draw retirees. Leashed pets are permitted.

Reservations, fees: Reservations are recommended but not required. Sites are $18 per night. No credit cards are accepted. Long-term stays are OK.

Directions: From I-75, take Exit 423 onto State Road 47 heading east for .1 mile. Turn north at the stoplight and travel .2 mile to the park.

Contact: Casey Jones Campground, Route 15, Box 4000, Lake City, FL 32024, 386/755-0471 or 800/226-5559.

⑥ LAKE CITY RV PARK

Rating: 1

South of Lake City off I-75
Gainesville map, grid c1, page 128

This one-acre park provides a shady layover for interstate travelers, but there are no restrooms or showers. Groceries, restaurants, and laundry facilities are available off the interstate on the way to the campground.

Campsites, facilities: All 10 sites have full hookups and cable TV. A dump station is available, but there are no restrooms or showers, so campers must be self-contained. Children are welcome. Leashed pets are permitted.

Reservations, fees: Reservations are not necessary. Sites are $10 per night. Credit cards are not accepted.

Directions: From I-75, take Exit 427 and head east on U.S. 90 to U.S. 41. Drive two miles south to the campground.

Contact: Lake City RV Park, Route 10, Box

399, 2314 Southeast Main Boulevard, Lake City, FL 32025, 386/755-0110.

⑦ E-Z RV PARK

Rating: 1

South of Lake City off I-75
Gainesville map, grid c2, page 128

Guests at this pine- and oak-shaded park enjoy some easy pull-through sites big enough to accommodate 42-foot rigs, as well as convenient access to gas stations and restaurants. Lots of overnighters stay here, but long-term campers toss horseshoes, play basketball, use the grill, or browse the aisles of antiques at the shops next door. O'Leno State Park is nearby.

Campsites, facilities: Half of these 28 RV sites are pull-through, full-hookup spots; the rest have water and electricity only. Restrooms, showers, picnic tables, horseshoes, basketball, a barbecue area, and a dump station are available. Need a hair cut? A barber shop and beauty salon are on premises. Children are welcome. Leashed pets are permitted.

Reservations, fees: Reservations are not necessary. Sites are $17 per night for two people, plus $2 per additional person and $3 for 50-amp service. Credit cards are not accepted. Long-term stays are OK.

Directions: From I-75, take Exit 414 westbound onto U.S. 41 for .1 mile, then turn north on Otis Howell Road and proceed .1 mile to the park.

Contact: E-Z RV Park, Route 2, Box 6015, Lake City, FL 32024, 386/752-2279.

⑧ ICHETUCKNEE SPRINGS CAMPGROUND

Rating: 9

Near Fort White off I-75
Gainesville map, grid c2, page 128

Rustic, forested Ichetucknee Springs Campground covers 20 acres, complete with a tavern serving up pizza, nachos, and other munchies. The emphasis is on family fun; there's even an annual New Year's Eve party. Groups can rent the entire campground during off-season. But the main attraction is next door: Ichetucknee Springs State Park, a mecca for the leisurely sport of river tubing. Deepwater springs pump 233 million gallons a day into the Ichetucknee River, creating a gin-clear waterway so remarkable that the main spring was declared a National Natural Landmark in 1972. The waters draw thousands to the park each year for tubing, an endeavor that requires little in the way of skill, energy, and equipment—just an old inner tube or float for lounging. You'll drift 3.5 miles past limestone outcrops under a canopy of oak and cypress. Occasionally, an alligator or snake can be spotted, and caution is advised. Tubing is permitted from 8 A.M. until sunset.

Launch at one of three drop sites: at the north entrance, the south entrance, or a midpoint drop-off open only at peak periods. From the south entrance, the river ride lasts 60 to 90 minutes. A free shuttle tram, which operates from May through September, returns tubers to the starting point. The ride from the north entrance is the longest lasting—from two to three hours—and so popular that the park limits the trip to 750 tubers a day. Return shuttle service also is available. Inner tubes can be rented at the campground and dropped off at the end of the ride.

A few pointers: Start early to avoid the crowds. Stick together because it's easy to get separated. Children and nonswimmers should wear flotation vests. Bring along a pair of old sneakers or other footwear for the walk to the shuttle trams. A few rules: Food, drink, alcohol, tobacco, and disposable items are prohibited on the river. Climbing and jumping from riverbanks, trees, and docks is strictly forbidden. Respect the environment and your fellow tubers—avoid stirring up the river bottom with swim fins.

Campsites, facilities: There are 16 RV sites with electricity and water, and 21 tent sites. Some of the tent sites are large enough to accommodate as many as 15 tents. Restrooms, showers, a dump station, a tavern, two game rooms, a volleyball field, a basketball court, and horseshoe pits are on site. The campsites, bathrooms, showers, and tavern/restaurant are wheelchair accessible. Canoes, inner tubes, and snorkeling equipment may be rented. Children are welcome. Leashed pets are permitted.

Reservations, fees: Reservations are recommended. Sites are $10 per night, plus $4 for each adult and $2 for each child. Credit cards are not accepted.

Directions: From I-75 southbound, take Exit 423 onto State Road 47 and drive south for 14 miles to Elim Church Road/County Road 238. Turn west and drive 3.5 miles to Breckenridge Lane. Turn right at the park. From I-75 northbound, take Exit 399 onto U.S. 441, then merge with U.S. 27 north for 2.5 miles and go west on Elim Church Road. Go west for 3.5 miles to Breckenridge Lane and look for the park sign on your right.

Contact: Ichetucknee Springs Campground, 245 Southwest Breckenridge Lane, Fort White, FL 32038, 386/497-2285.

⑨ GINNIE SPRINGS RESORT

🏕️ 🚵 🏊 🛶 🌊 🚐 ⛺

Rating: 9

Near High Springs
Gainesville map, grid c2, page 128

For active campers, this is one of Florida's most attractive campgrounds, offering everything from mountain biking to canoeing, kayaking, and diving. The park covers 200 acres of wilderness along a two-mile stretch of the lazy Santa Fe River and includes seven crystal springs, all bubbling away at a constant water temperature of 72 degrees Fahrenheit. Rent or bring your own rubber raft (get free air refills here) for a refreshing hour-long float down the Santa Fe on a hot summer day. For really adventurous visitors, the park offers instruction in underwater cavern and cave exploration.

Campsites, facilities: Fifty-five RV sites have water and electricity and are set apart from nearly 300 tent sites (which have spigots). All sites have picnic tables and grills. Group sites are available. Restrooms, showers, laundry facilities, a restaurant, a rental cottage, and a country store are located on the premises. Also available is a full complement of recreational sports services, including scuba diving and underwater cave exploration for certified divers. Canoes, kayaks, inner tubes, and diving equipment can be rented here. Children are welcome. Pets are not permitted.

Reservations, fees: Reservations are recommended for RV sites. Sites are $28 per night for two people and $14 for each additional person. Younger children camp for free. Electricity costs an additional $4 per site. Major credit cards are accepted. Long-term stays are OK.

Directions: From I-75, take Exit 399 onto U.S. 441 five miles north to the town of High Springs. At the first stoplight in High Springs (at the Hardee's), turn left. Continue through the next stoplight, at the center of town, and go approximately .5 mile farther to the turnoff for County Road 340/NE 182nd Avenue. (You will see a sign on top of a pole indicating that this is the turnoff for Ginnie, Blue, and Poe Springs.) Turn right onto County Road 340 and go approximately 6.5 miles, to the sign indicating the turnoff to Ginnie Springs (NE 60th Avenue). Turn right and drive approximately one mile to the Ginnie Springs entrance.

Contact: Ginnie Springs Resort, 7300 Northeast Ginnie Springs Road, High Springs, FL 32643, 386/454-7188, fax 386/454-2085, website: www.ginniespringsoutdoors.com.

10 O'LENO STATE PARK

Rating: 10

North of High Springs off I-75

Gainesville map, grid c2, page 128

Always magical, this place is especially so in the cooler months when it's quiet and un-

crowded. The park encompasses 6,400 acres of hardwood forest flush with deer and other wildlife, miles of service roads great for mountain biking, and a historic wooden suspension bridge built by the Civilian Conservation Corps in the 1930s. The black-water Santa Fe River meanders through the forest, then actually goes underground at the "river sink" and reappears three miles later. Hike along one of the many nature trails to the spot where it disappears, but don't expect drama; the water gathers in a wide lake and seeps into the ground so slowly that algae grows across the top.

You can swim or canoe on the river, a tributary of the Suwannee; canoes are available for rent. Rangers say the river is an unpredictable fishing spot, but you may see alligators and turtles while trying your luck. Campsites are split between two areas: the Dogwood Camp and the Magnolia Camp. The heart of the park is an assortment of 1930s-era buildings and newer cabins at the point where the bridge crosses the river. Near this spot in the mid-1800s stood a lumber town perhaps called Keno (as in the game of chance) and later known as Old Leno. All that remains is a mill dam and an old road. Groceries, laundry facilities, and restaurants are available six miles from the park.

Campsites, facilities: This state park campground has 61 sites with water, electricity, picnic tables, grills, and fire rings. Restrooms, showers, a dump station, a playground, and hiking and horseback-riding trails are available. Children are welcome. Pets are prohibited.

Reservations, fees: Reservations are accepted. Sites are $18 per night for four people, plus $2 for each additional person and $2 for use of electricity. Major credit cards are accepted. Maximum stay is 14 days.

Directions: From I-75 southbound, take Exit 414 onto U.S. 441 and drive five miles south to the park. From I-75 northbound, take Exit 399 onto U.S. 441 and drive 15 miles west and north to the park.

Contact: O'Leno State Park, Route 2, Box 1010, High Springs, FL 32643, 386/454-1853.

11 HIGH SPRINGS CAMPGROUND

Rating: 7

East of High Springs near I-75
Gainesville map, grid c2, page 128

With tall oaks, a natural setting, and a secluded location, this place will remind you more of a state park than a privately operated campground. Sites are shaded and thoughtfully laid out; 18 are pull-through, and even big rigs can be accommodated. This makes a good overnight spot for I-75 travelers—indeed, most guests are overnighters—but it's also a good base for exploring High Springs' antique shops, the museums of Gainesville 17 miles to the south, and the O'Leno, Ichetucknee Springs, and Paynes Prairie State Parks. Groceries and restaurants are located within four miles of here. The campground is located on the oldest federal highway or road in Florida, built in 1824 on the route taken by Franciscan missionaries in the 1590s. (Three of the missions they built were within 15 miles of this campground.) It was also one of the major north-south trails used by Florida Indians; Hernando de Soto became the first European to set foot on it back in 1539.

Campsites, facilities: There are 45 RV sites with full hookups, plus five tent areas; most have concrete picnic tables and fire rings. Restrooms, showers, laundry facilities, a dump station, a pool, and a playground are available. All areas are said to be wheelchair accessible. Children are welcome. Leashed pets are permitted.

Reservations, fees: Reservations are not necessary. Sites are $15 to $18 per night for four people, plus $2 for each additional person. Credit cards are not accepted.

Directions: From I-75 north of Alachua, take Exit 404 and drive west on County Road 236 for .1 mile. Turn north onto Old Bellamy Road and drive 1,000 feet to the campground, on the left.

Contact: High Springs Campground, 24004 Northwest Old Bellamy Road, High Springs, FL 32643, 386/454-1688, email: hscamping @aol.com.

12 BRADFORD MOTEL AND CAMPGROUND

Rating: 2

North of Starke
Gainesville map, grid b1, page 128

This urban park is set in a partially wooded area behind a motel and near restaurants and shops. Just north of the campground is the little burg of Lawtey. Go slowly because it's known as a speed trap. Starke is a good starting point for exploring this off-the-tourist-track area, which is famous for extra-sweet strawberries, timber (half of Bradford County is heavily forested), lake fishing, hunting, and agriculture. Outside of Florida, Starke may be more familiar as a newspaper dateline when there's an execution at the Florida State Prison in Raiford. On execution days, reporters and protesters pour into Starke, the nearest big town.

Campsites, facilities: There are 28 full-hookup campsites, including five for tents. Restrooms, showers, a laundry room, and a dump station are on the grounds. All sites have cable TV with HBO programming. Children and leashed pets are welcome.

Reservations, fees: Reservations are recommended. Sites are $16 per night for two people, plus $2 for each additional person. Major credit cards are accepted. Long-term stays are OK.

Directions: From I-75, take Exit 414 northbound on U.S. 441 for .25 mile. Turn east on State Road 238 and drive 13 miles to the town of Lake Butler. Continue east on State Road 100 for 15 miles into Starke. Turn north on U.S. 301; the park is on the north side of town.

Contact: Bradford Motel and Campground, 1757 North Temple Avenue, Starke, FL 32091, 904/964-5332, fax 904/964-2026.

13 KINGSLEY BEACH RV PARK AND RESORT CAMPGROUND

Rating: 8

Near Lawtey next to Camp Blanding Wildlife Management Area

Gainesville map, grid b1, page 128

Once upon a time, kids plunged down the giant water slide and three smaller slides to splash into the enclosed pier at this campground's next-door neighbor, Strickland's Landing. That property was sold for a housing development, and the campground was closed in 2002. Now the park has reopened with a splash, modeling itself on a resort where campers will want to stay six months or longer. Historically, folks came from miles around to boat and fish at spring-fed Kingsley Lake, a two-mile-long, round lake that's great for snorkeling, scuba diving, and water-skiing; it's so round that it used to be called the Silver Dollar. The slides are gone, but the beach beckons swimmers. Hunters drive a short distance east to stalk turkey, deer, and other animals in season at the 55,195-acre Camp Blanding Wildlife Management Area.

Campsites, facilities: There are 360 sites with full hookups. Restrooms, showers, a store, a restaurant, boat ramp, and game room with pool tables and weekend entertainment are available. There is no swimming pool, but the beach more than suffices. Snorkeling and scuba equipment, paddleboats, and kayaks are for rent.

Reservations, fees: Reservations are recommended. Sites are $25 a night for up to six people; there is a $10 charge for each additional person. Long-term visitors are encouraged.

Directions: From Green Cove Springs, travel 18 miles west on Highway 16. The park is just past Camp Blanding Wildlife Management Area.

Contact: Kingsley Beach RV and Resort Campground, 6003 Kingsley Lake Drive, Starke, FL 32091, 904/533-2006, fax 904/533-9333, website: www.kingsleybeach.com.

14 STARKE KOA

Rating: 6

South of Starke

Gainesville map, grid b2, page 128

The largest and most developed campground in Bradford County, this KOA offers easy access to several fishing lakes nearby and to Gainesville, Jacksonville, and Kingsley Lake. The new owners, the four-generation Steffen family who took over in November 1999, have a full schedule of activities planned for their guests, including bingo, potluck dinners, Sunday morning breakfasts, and hobo stew dinner around the campfire. Nearly 75 people came for turkey and all the trimmings on one recent Thanksgiving Day. Note that the pool is not open January through March. The Starke golf course is nearby.

While you're in Starke, don't miss visiting the Camp Blanding Museum and Memorial Park, which displays weapons and World War II artifacts in a refurbished barracks and recalls a turning point in local history: Starke was pretty sleepy until the Second World War—it had only 2,000 residents when the National Guard camp east of here was expanded to accommodate 90,000 GIs. Also in Starke are several restored turn-of-the-century homes and commercial buildings; pick up a driving brochure from the Starke-Bradford County Chamber of Commerce. The chamber also can provide brochures detailing fishing at the Camp Blanding Fish Management Area, Lake Santa Fe, Lake Hampton, Lake Altho, and Sampson and Rowell Lakes.

Campsites, facilities: There are 127 sites with full hookups, cable TV, and picnic tables, plus a primitive tent camping area accommodating 20 tents. Restrooms, showers, laundry facilities, a pool, a recreation hall, and a store are available. The clubhouse, restrooms, and recreation hall are wheelchair accessible. Children are welcome. Leashed pets are permitted.

Reservations, fees: Reservations are recommended. Sites are $26 per night for two people,

plus $3 for each additional person. Rates are likely to be higher during the annual Gatornational drag races in March. Major credit cards are accepted. Long-term stays are OK.

Directions: From the intersection of U.S. 301 and State Road 100 in Starke, drive south on U.S. 301 for 1.5 miles to the campground.

Contact: Starke KOA, 1475 South Walnut Street, Starke, FL 32091, 904/964-8484 or 800/KOA-8498, website: www.starkekoa.com.

15 PAYNES PRAIRIE PRESERVE STATE PARK

Rating: 10

Near Micanopy south of Gainesville
Gainesville map, grid b3, page 128

Did you ever expect to see bison in Florida? At Paynes Prairie, wild bison still roam this 21,000-acre park, once called the "great Alachua Savannah." Wildlife more commonly observed are sandhill cranes, hawks, and wading birds. Hook up with a ranger-led nature walk, or venture out on one of the many trails. Foot traffic only is allowed on the 2.5-mile La Chua Trail and the short (.3-mile) Wacahoota Trail. Hikers, mountain bikers, and horseback riders share the path as they travel through 6.5 miles of shady hammock, pine flatwoods, and old fields on the Chacala Trail. At Cone's Dike, hikers and mountain bikers have access to the 8.24-mile trail that heads out into the marsh; wear a hat because there is no shade. Cyclists can also use the paved park road from the campground to the visitor center, where an observation tower provides views of the vast prairie.

Anglers and canoeists have access to Lake Wauberg at a boat ramp near the camping area. Common catches are bream, bass, and speckled perch. On the north side of the park at the Boulware Springs Trailhead is the terminus for the 17-mile Gainesville-to-Hawthorne walking, biking, and horseback-riding trail. The campground is 10 miles south of Gainesville, home to the University of Florida and the Flori-

da Museum of Natural History. Don't miss seeing Devil's Millhopper State Geological Site on the north side of town. There's a 120-foot-deep sinkhole with a stairway to the bottom; on the way down, you'll see plants and animals similar to those in the Appalachian Mountains.

Campsites, facilities: There are 35 RV sites and 15 tent sites, all with water and electricity. Picnic tables, grills, fire rings, a dump station, a boat ramp, a visitors center with an observatory, and 25 miles of hiking, horseback-riding, and bicycling trails are in the park. The campground and visitors center are wheelchair accessible. Children are welcome. Pets are prohibited.

Reservations, fees: Reservations are recommended; call ReserveAmerica at 800/326-3521. Sites are $11 per night for four people, plus $2 for each additional person and $2 for electricity. Major credit cards are accepted. The maximum stay is 120 days.

Directions: From I-75, take Exit 374 eastbound for .5 mile to U.S. 441 in Micanopy. Turn north on U.S. 441 and drive one mile to the park.

Contact: Paynes Prairie Preserve State Park, 100 Savannah Boulevard, Micanopy, FL 32667, 352/466-3397, fax 352/466-4297, website: www.floridastateparks.org.

16 RANCH MOTEL AND CAMPGROUND

Rating: 2

In Hawthorne
Gainesville map, grid b3, page 128

Close to everything and friendly are how the owners of this motel/RV park complex describe their property. The motel has only 12 rooms, so the RV park is a dominant feature, not an afterthought. With 15 fishing lakes within three miles, the park attracts anglers and seasonal visitors.

Campsites, facilities: There are 35 RV sites (12 pull-through) with full hookups. Five tent sites have water and electricity. All sites have picnic tables. Restrooms, showers, laundry facilities, cable TV, and telephone service are available. Most areas are wheelchair accessible. Children are welcome. Leashed pets are permitted.

Reservations, fees: Reservations are recommended. Sites are $18 to $20 per night for two people, plus $2 per extra person over age three. Credit cards are accepted. Long-term rates are available.

Directions: From the intersection of U.S. 301 and State Road 20 in Hawthorne, drive .75 mile south on U.S. 301 to the park.

Contact: Ranch Motel and Campground, P.O. Box 806, 8010 Southeast U.S. Highway 301, Hawthorne, FL 32640, 352/481-3851, fax 352/481-3562.

⒘ TWIN LAKES FISH CAMP

Rating: 4

Just north of Cross Creek, halfway between Gainesville and Ocala

Gainesville map, grid b3, page 128

Located on Cross Creek, which flows into Lake Lochloosa and Orange Lake, the campground has lots of shade and greenery. The fishing until recent years was great, although lately, drought has caused the water to drop so low that the park was forced to drop its guide service. Still, there's much to draw you here: You can photograph an eagle on the wing or watch a sunset over the water. Cross Creek is famous as the home of Marjorie Kinnan Rawlings, Pulitzer Prize–winning author of *The Yearling.* You can tour the home at the Marjorie Kinnan Rawlings State Historic Site, 1.5 miles from the campground. The Cracker-style house comprises three separate structures connected by screen porches and open verandas, all designed to take advantage of cooling breezes. The house is closed to the public on Mondays, Tuesdays, and Wednesdays and during August and September. Restaurants are nearby, and even the Yearling Restaurant has reopened after a decade-long hiatus to offer a variety of

dishes from seafood to venison. The park is near the rails-to-trails bike path and Micanopy's fall antiques and arts and crafts festivals.

Campsites, facilities: The 15 RV sites have full hookups; five tent sites come with water and electricity. Picnic tables, restrooms, showers, a dump station, laundry facilities, cabins, and snacks are available. All areas of the park are said to be wheelchair accessible. Children are welcome; in the wintertime, most campers are retired snowbirds. Leashed pets are permitted.

Reservations, fees: Reservations are recommended. Sites are $15 per night for two people, plus $2 for each additional person. Credit cards are not accepted. Long-term stays are OK. The campground is closed Christmas Day, Easter weekend, and Thanksgiving Day.

Directions: From I-75, take Exit 374 eastbound for .5 mile on County Road 346 into Micanopy. Continue east for five miles until County Road 346 dead-ends at County Road 325. Turn south and drive three miles. The campground is one mile north of the hamlet of Cross Creek.

Contact: Twin Lakes Fish Camp, 17105 South County Road 325, Hawthorne, FL 32640, 352/466-3194, email: fishlakes@aol.com.

⒙ GATOR LANDING GOLF CLUB AND CAMPGROUND

Rating: 6

South of Hawthorne

Gainesville map, grid b3, page 128

Set on 800-acre Little Orange Lake, this resort boasts a 130-foot fishing pier, water sports, and a nine-hole, par-37 golf course. Sites are for sale, and about 115 new sites were being added during 2003. Oversized sites are 40 by 70 feet.

Campsites, facilities: This new resort has 35 overnight sites and 20 sites for seasonal stays. Tenters can choose from 12 sites in an area set apart from the RV area. All sites have water and electricity, and 15 have full hookups. Restrooms, showers, a dump station, a pool, a dock, a lake, a dog-walk area, and a boat ramp are on the premises. Children are welcome. Leashed pets up to about 50 pounds are permitted; no rottweilers, Doberman pinschers, or pit bulls are allowed.

Reservations, fees: Reservations are recommended. Sites are $14 to $20 per night for two people, plus $1 per extra person and $1 for 50-amp service. Credit cards are not accepted. Long-term stays are allowed.

Directions: From the intersection of U.S. 301 and State Road 20, drive south on U.S. 301 across the railroad tracks. Take the first left and go 1.3 miles on Holden Park Road.

Contact: Gator Landing Golf Club and Campground, 8815 Holden Park Road, Hawthorne, FL 32640, 352/481-5547 or 800/379-7066.

19 LOCHLOOSA WILDLIFE CONSERVATION AREA

Rating: 7

Surrounding Lochloosa Lake
southwest of Hawthorne
Gainesville map, grid b3, page 128

Not too far of a drive from author Marjorie Kinnan Rawlings' historic home/museum at Cross Creek, this 27,327-acre conservation area offers rustic camping on the shore of Lochloosa Lake. More than 20 miles of meandering trails can be used for hiking, bicycling, or horseback riding. Along the way, you might spy some of the rare or endangered resident critters, such as black bear, sandhill cranes, wood storks, and fox squirrels, among others. Seasonal hunting is allowed in nearly half the area. Much of this land was owned by Georgia-Pacific Corp. until 1995, when the St. Johns River Water Management District bought it to protect the environmentally sensitive watershed and preserve the shoreline. A fishing pier was recently added. After all, this is all part of the Orange Lake basin, and nearby angler-haven Orange Lake (to the west, on the other side of Cross Creek) was deemed an Outstanding Florida Water by the state in 1987. Don't be too surprised if you

see some forestry work going on in this conservation area; through the sales agreement, Georgia-Pacific is allowed to continue operating here, although with some restrictions.

Campsites, facilities: Tents only are permitted at this primitive camping area. An observation deck is provided, and four boat ramps here or nearby provide access to the area. There are no restrooms or other facilities. Bring food, water, mosquito repellent, and everything you'll need. Children are welcome. Leashed pets are permitted. Camping is not allowed during hunting season.

Reservations, fees: Sites are first-come, first-served. Camping is free. If your party has at least seven people, get a free permit and reserve at least one week ahead at 386/329-4883. Maximum stay for all campers is seven days.

Directions: From Hawthorne, go south on U.S. 301 to the entrance at right. The entrance is less than two miles north of Highway 325 and a little more than eight miles south of the Gainesville-Hawthorne State Trail. Alternatively, if you're arriving from the town of Cross Creek, drive nearly six miles southeast on County Road 325, turn north (left) onto U.S. 301, and continue less than two miles to the entrance at left.

Contact: St. Johns River Water Management District, Division of Land Management, P.O. Box 1429, Palatka, FL 32178-1429, 386/329-4500 or 800/451-7106, website: www.sjrwmd.com.

20 HART SPRINGS GILCHRIST COUNTY PARK

Rating: 8

Near Trenton
Gainesville map, grid c3, page 128

Bordering this sprawling 400-acre park is the Suwannee River, a beautiful spot with bubbling springs and a beach for swimming and snorkeling. Fishing is good along the riverbank for trout, bass, bream, and catfish; there's also a boat ramp. A half-mile-long boardwalk that is wheelchair accessible meanders along the river's edge for a view of alligators, turtles, herons, and the occasional manatee. The campground is nestled under spreading oaks. The park is staffed around the clock by an attendant who lives here. Improvements were made in winter 2002 to double the park in size.

Campsites, facilities: There are 70 full-hookup RV sites with concrete pads and 50 grassy tent sites with water, electricity, picnic tables, and grills. Restrooms, showers, volleyball courts, a boat ramp, a snack bar, and both open-air and closed pavilions for group activities are available. Most areas are wheelchair accessible. Children are welcome. Pets and alcohol are prohibited.

Reservations, fees: Reservations are not necessary. Sites are $11 per night for four people, plus $2 for each additional person and $2 for electricity. These rates are subject to change. Credit cards are not accepted. Long-term stays are OK.

Directions: From I-75 north of Gainesville, take Exit 387 onto State Road 26 and drive west for 32 miles, through Trenton, then turn right on County Road 341 and head north for five miles. Head west on County Road 344 for .7 mile to the park.

Contact: Hart Springs Gilchrist County Park, 4240 Southwest 86th Avenue, Bell, FL 32619, 352/463-3444, email: www.gilchristchamber@svic.net.

21 MANATEE SPRINGS STATE PARK

Rating: 10

Near Chiefland west of U.S. 19/98

Gainesville map, grid c3, page 128

One of the gems of Florida's state park network, Manatee Springs encompasses 2,373 acres of heavily wooded hammock dressed in Spanish moss beside the lower Suwannee River. A nature trail and boardwalk lead to the scenic, meandering waterway; at the end is a boat

dock, a launch pad for canoeing and fishing expeditions. And more natural wonders await within the park's boundaries: Manatee Springs is a fantastic swimming and snorkeling hole where 117 million gallons of crystal-clear water bubble to the surface every day, then wash down a 1,000-foot run to the Suwannee and the Gulf of Mexico, 23 miles downstream. Occasionally, manatees can be seen from the banks, especially during the winter months. Certified divers can explore underground caverns that link a series of sinkholes. Divers must register at the ranger station. More than eight miles of trails for hikers and mountain bikers wind through the park. Keep on the lookout for red-shouldered hawks and have an ear cocked at night for the eerie hoots of barred owls. Just one word of warning about this pretty place: Ticks and chiggers can be a nuisance during the summer months. First aid is available at the ranger station.

Campsites, facilities: The park has 94 RV and tent sites with water, electricity, fire grills, and picnic tables. On the premises are showers, restrooms, a dump station, playgrounds, a snack bar, a canoe rental concession, nature trails, horseshoe pits, and volleyball courts. One camping area is wheelchair accessible, but the restrooms are not. Golf, groceries, restaurants, and laundry facilities are located within six miles. Children are welcome. Pets are allowed with proof of vaccination.

Reservations, fees: Reservations are recommended; call ReserveAmerica at 800/326-3521. Sites are $11 per night for four people, plus $2 for each additional person, for electricity, and per pet. Major credit cards are accepted. The maximum stay is 14 days.

Directions: From U.S. 19/98 in Chiefland, turn west on State Road 320 and drive six miles to the park.

Contact: Manatee Springs State Park, 11650 Northwest 115th Street, Chiefland, FL 32626, 352/493-6072, fax 352/493-6089, website: www.floridastateparks.org. Additional information can be obtained from Suwannee Basin

GEOpark, 11650 Northwest 115th Street, Chiefland, FL 32626, 352/493-6072.

22 OTTER SPRINGS (FORMERLY ELITE RESORT AT OTTER SPRINGS)

Rating: 9

Northwest of Fanning Springs
Gainesville map, grid c3, page 128

This lovely place boasts one mile of frontage on the east bank of the Suwannee River and two natural springs. Formerly known as Elite Resort at Otter Springs, public access was cut off in 2001, and plans were made to develop the site for a water bottling plant. However, after public protest, the state has now intervened. The Suwannee River Water Management District plans to finalize the purchase of this valuable site in late 2003. Call to see if the park has reopened. These 780 acres of woods have access to the Suwannee River for boating, canoeing, and fishing. One spring empties into the Suwannee after a mile-long run through the park; the other is about 30 yards in size.

Campsites, facilities: Originally, there were 185 RV sites and several dozen sites for tents, plus restrooms, showers, laundry facilities, a pool, a recreation room, and other amenities. It's unclear at this writing how the property will be developed or changed, but the state has a history of intervening and rescuing valuable environmental lands like this.

Reservations, fees: Call to see if the park has opened.

Directions: From the intersection of U.S. 19/98 in Fanning Springs, drive north one mile on State Road 26. At State Road 232, turn left and continue about two miles to the entrance. The second mile is unpaved road.

Contact: Suwannee River Water Management District, 9225 County Road 49, Live Oak, FL 32060, 386/362-1001 or 800/226-1066 (toll free in Florida), website: www.srwmd.state.fl.us.

23 BREEZY ACRES CAMPGROUND

Rating: 4

Near Chiefland on Alternate U.S. 27
Gainesville map, grid c3, page 128

This quiet, sunny park in the countryside caters to seniors, with coffee-and-doughnut socials on Saturday mornings and cozy potluck dinners on Wednesday nights.

Campsites, facilities: You'll be out in the country sleeping at one of the park's 50 large, grassy RV sites with full hookups. On the premises are showers, restrooms, laundry facilities, a dump station, a recreation room, horseshoe pits, and shuffleboard courts. Children are not permitted. Leashed pets are allowed.

Reservations, fees: Reservations are recommended. Sites are $13 per night for four people, plus $1 for each additional person and for using air conditioners. Credit cards are not accepted. Long-term stays are OK.

Directions: From U.S. 19/98 in Chiefland, turn east on Alternate U.S. 27 and drive seven miles to the park.

Contact: Breezy Acres Campground, 10050 Northeast 20th Avenue, Chiefland, FL 32626, 352/493-7602.

24 SHELL MOUND COUNTY PARK

Rating: 9

Outside Cedar Key
Gainesville map, grid c4, page 128

This little treasure is a favorite for locals and is often overlooked by travelers exploring nearby Cedar Key. Here you can camp beneath gnarled oaks in the heart of the Lower Suwannee River National Wildlife Refuge, a 52,000-acre parcel of dry scrub, bottomland hardwoods, cypress swamp, and coastal marshes. It is teeming with more than 250 species of birds, reptiles, and mammals, including American bald eagles, eastern indigo snakes, Atlantic Ripley turtles, gopher tortoises, bobcats, red foxes, and white-tailed deer. The refuge stretches for 26 miles along the Gulf of Mexico and offers plenty of paved roadways, scenic overlooks, and trails for animal lovers who want to observe wildlife. For more information, contact the refuge manager at 352/493-0238 or see detailed maps and trail guides at http://lower-suwannee@fws.gov. Adjacent to the nine-acre campground is a prehistoric Indian mound. Throughout the park you'll have spectacular views of the Gulf and marshes.

Campsites, facilities: Eight RV sites and six tent sites have water, electricity, picnic tables, and campfire rings. Another three tent sites are primitive. Restrooms, showers, a boat ramp, and a dump station are available. Children are welcome. Leashed pets are permitted. Alcohol is forbidden.

Reservations, fees: Reservations are accepted; call the campground host at 352/543-6153. Sites are first-come, first-served. The fee is $5 per night for two people, plus $1 for each additional person. Primitive tent sites are $3.50 per person. Credit cards are not accepted. Stays are limited to seven days.

Directions: From U.S. 19/98 at Otter Creek, turn southwest on State Road 24, drive 22 miles to County Road 347, and turn right. Drive 2.3 miles north to County Road 326 and turn left, then proceed 3.2 miles west to the campground.

Contact: Levy County Parks and Recreation Department, P.O. Box 248, Bronson, FL 32621, 352/486-5127 or 352/543-6153 (campground host).

25 CEDAR KEY SUNSET ISLE PARK (FORMERLY SUNSET ISLE PARK)

Rating: 6

In Cedar Key

Gainesville map, grid d4, page 128

Shady sites and beguiling sunsets on a marsh at the edge of the Gulf of Mexico are featured at this campground behind the Sunset Isle Motel. The new owners have greatly expanded this park and are working on more improvements. It's just 1.3 miles from the center of Cedar Key, so you could cycle, walk, or take a street-worthy golf cart into town.

Cedar Key, also known as Margaritaville North, is a colony of artists and salty fishermen who would make balladeer Jimmy Buffett feel right at home. Reminiscent of Key West, quaint Cedar Key is home to a history museum and plenty of seafood restaurants, art galleries, and, yes, touristy T-shirt shops—it's just a lot less crazy and crowded than its sister city in the Florida Keys.

Like Key West, Cedar Key is steeped in seafaring lore. Spanish colonists built fortifications near the existing city, and Cedar Key was a bustling port and railroad terminal up until the Civil War. Until the turn of the century, it prospered by harvesting slabs of cedar for pencils, until all the cedars were felled. Now fishing and tourism are mainstays of the economy. Offshore, accessible only by boat, is the Cedar Keys National Wildlife Refuge, a dozen islands that host a seabird rookery and an 1850s lighthouse. Rental boats are available at the downtown marina. To the south, the 30,000-acre Waccasassa Bay State Preserve, also accessible only by boat, offers more opportunities for fresh and saltwater fishing, bird-watching, and canoeing—or for simply savoring unspoiled vistas of windswept black rush marsh and cypress hammocks; for information, call 352/543-5567. Little has changed since the 18th century, when pirate Jose Gasparilla plied the currents offshore, plundering Spanish merchant ships. Legend has it that he buried treasure a dozen miles north of here, at the mouth of the Suwannee River.

Campsites, facilities: There are 53 RV sites with full hookups and 12 or more sites for tents. Restrooms, showers, a recreation room, and a pool are available, as are motel rooms. You can fish from five docks, or watch the sunset; one dock even has a fireplace. Children are welcome. Leashed pets are permitted.

Reservations, fees: Reservations are recommended. Sites are $35 per night for waterfront lots; or $30 for water views, and the second night drops to $20 to $25. The extra fee charge for more than two people is $4. Tent camping is $16 for two people plus $3 per extra person. Major credit cards are accepted. Long-term stays are OK.

Directions: From U.S. 19/98 at Otter Creek, turn west on State Road 24 and drive 24 miles. The park, which is part of a motel facility, is on the north side of State Road 24 as you enter Cedar Key.

Contact: Cedar Key Sunset Isle Park, P.O. Box 150, Cedar Key, FL 32625, 352/543-6124, website: www.cedarkeyrv.com.

26 RAINBOW COUNTRY RV CAMPGROUND

Rating: 5

In Sumner off U.S. 19/98
Gainesville map, grid c4, page 128

You'll find a mix of sunny and shaded sites at this family-oriented campground, which is located just six miles from the beaches, docks, restaurants, and shopping in the historic village of Cedar Key. Next door is an antiques shop, bait, tackle, and groceries. The typical camper is a Floridian on a weekend getaway; the 12-acre park doesn't tend to attract many snowbirds. Perched on the edge of expansive wildlife preserves, this is a perfect spot for artists and shutterbugs whose favored subjects are panoramas of marshland dotted with palms.

Campsites, facilities: This park has 62 RV sites, 42 with full hookups, and 50 sites for tents. Each site has water, electricity, and a picnic table. On the premises are showers, restrooms, a dump station, laundry facilities, limited groceries, rental campers, a community kitchen with potluck dinners, a game room, a recreation room, bocce ball, horseshoes, and basketball hoops. Children are welcome. Leashed pets are permitted.

Reservations, fees: Reservations are recommended. Sites are $12 to $15 per night for two people, plus $1 to $2 for each additional person. Kids under three are free. Major credit cards are accepted. Long-term stays are allowed.

Directions: From U.S. 19/98 at Otter Creek, turn southwest on State Road 24 and drive 14 miles to the campground.

Contact: Rainbow Country RV Campground, 11951 Southwest Shiloh Road, Cedar Key, FL 32625, 352/543-6268.

27 SHADY OAKS CAMPGROUND

Rating: 2

South of Otter Creek off U.S. 19/98
Gainesville map, grid c4, page 128

Shady Oaks is described as "edge of woods quiet," which aptly sums up this place on the road to Cedar Key. The campground is wooded and grassy, with deer and wild turkeys occasionally wandering through. Like the critters, you are on your own: pick out a site, slip $10 in the self-service payment box, hook up your rig, and kick back. "Just holler" across the fence if you want to meet owner Wayne Fouts. There are no restrooms, and the nearest phone is .75 mile away at Martin's convenience store on the corner of State Road 24 and U.S. 19/98, which is open from 6 A.M. to 6 P.M. daily except Monday.

Campsites, facilities: The 13 RV sites have full hookups and picnic tables. There are no restrooms or showers. The closest groceries and restaurants are 13 miles north in Chiefland. Children are welcome. Leashed pets are permitted.

Reservations, fees: Reservations are not necessary. Sites are $10 per night. Credit cards are not accepted. Long-term stays are OK.

Directions: From U.S. 19/98 in Otter Creek, turn west on State Road 24 and drive .75 mile to the campground.

Contact: Shady Oaks Campground, 440 Southwest Third Street/P.O. Box 184, Otter Creek, FL 32683, 352/486-3236.

28 VILLAGE PINES CAMPGROUND

Rating: 5

On U.S. 19/98 north of Inglis

Gainesville map, grid c4, page 128

Snowbirds flock to this park each winter to find peace and shade under the pines. It is close to the Gulf Hammock Wildlife Management Area and Goethe State Forest, a 48,000-acre tract of longleaf pine flatwoods laced with roads and trails for hiking and horseback riding. For state forest information, call 352/447-2202. Groceries, restaurants, and laundry facilities are available seven miles away in Inglis.

Campsites, facilities: There are 30 RV sites with full hookups and picnic tables; half are pull-through. Three tent sites have water and electricity. On the premises are restrooms, showers, a dump station, a recreation room, horseshoe pits, and shuffleboard courts. Children are allowed. Leashed pets are permitted.

Reservations, fees: Reservations are not necessary. Sites are $9 per night for two people, plus $1 for each additional person and $2 for using air conditioners or electric heaters. Credit cards are not accepted. Long-term stays are OK.

Directions: From Inglis, on U.S. 19/98, drive seven miles north to the campground. Look for the covered wagon out front.

Contact: Village Pines Campground, 8053 Southeast 140th Lane, Inglis, FL 34449, 352/447-2777.

29 BIG OAKS RIVER RESORT AND CAMPGROUND

Rating: 7

Between Inglis and Crystal River

Gainesville map, grid b3, page 128

These wooded three acres in this new campground offer direct access to the Withlacoochee River for canoeing, fishing, and just enjoying the view. Saltwater fishing is just 7.5 miles downstream at the Gulf of Mexico.

Campsites, facilities: There are 21 full-hookup RV sites for overnighters and seasonal visitors. A tent area accommodating five tents is set apart from the recreational vehicles; they have water and electricity and a common fire pit. Restrooms, showers, laundry facilities, and cable TV are available. On the premises are a pool, a boat ramp, dock, canoe rentals, cabins, and a dog-walk area. Also for rent are kayaks, bicycles, pontoon boats, inner tubes, and johnboats. A new recreation hall was completed in 2003, offering darts, games, TV, and other entertainment. Children are welcome. Leashed pets are permitted.

Reservations, fees: Reservations are recommended. Sites are $12 to $18 per night for two people, plus $1.50 per extra person. Major credit cards are accepted. Long-term rates are available.

Directions: From Inglis, drive south on U.S. 19 to the outskirts of town. Turn west on West River Road to the park entrance.

Contact: Big Oaks River Resort and Campground, 14035 West River Road, Inglis, FL 34449, 352/447-5333, fax 352/447-4125, website: www.bigoaksriverresort.com.

30 B'S MARINA AND CAMPGROUND

Rating: 5

West of Yankeetown

Gainesville map, grid b3, page 128

The only campground in Yankeetown that fronts on the Withlacoochee River, this park is just 2.5 miles from the Gulf of Mexico. With an emphasis on kayaking and fishing, this campground is decidedly water oriented. Fishing guides and charters are available. "We want you to come back and tell us some good fish tales," say the owners.

Campsites, facilities: There are 15 RV sites for overnights and 15 for seasonal visitors. Five tent sites have water and electricity. All RV sites have full hookups. Restrooms, showers, laundry facilities, a boat ramp, dock, kayak and pontoon boat rentals, and a dog-walk area are provided. Children are welcome. Leashed pets ("good dogs only") are permitted.

Reservations, fees: Reservations are recommended. Sites are $20 per night for two people, plus $2.50 per extra person. Credit cards are not accepted. Long-term rates are available.

Directions: From Yankeetown, drive west on County Road 40 to 66th Street, where you'll see a sign for the park. Turn left on 66th Street and continue to Riverside Drive. Turn right and go one block to the park entrance on the river.

Contact: B's Marina and Campground, 6621 Riverside Drive, Yankeetown, FL 34498, 352/447-5888, fax 352/447-3177, email: marinama@svic.net.

31 CATTAIL CREEK RV PARK

Rating: 7

In Yankeetown

Gainesville map, grid c4, page 128

This friendly, well-kept campground has plenty of shade and paved roads that are great for little kids on skates and bikes. The pool is the social center of the park, although every now and then the party shifts to the recreation hall for a "Wingding" potluck supper and dance. Fishing is the favorite pastime; a nearby county boat ramp and several marinas provide access to the Gulf of Mexico and estuaries in the Gulf Hammock Wildlife Management Area, havens for redfish, sea trout, flounder, and drum. The campground has fish-cleaning tables set aside for successful anglers and holds "fish lie fabrication classes" for those who come back empty-handed. The management also sponsors community fish fries and contests.

Campsites, facilities: There are 72 RV or tent sites with full hookups, picnic tables, and cable TV (long-term only). On the premises are restrooms, showers, laundry facilities, a dump station, a pool, and a recreation hall. The restrooms are wheelchair accessible. Children and leashed pets are welcome.

Reservations, fees: Reservations are recommended. Sites are $20 per night for two people, plus $2 for each extra person. Credit cards are not accepted. Long-term stays are OK.

Directions: From U.S. 19/98 in Inglis, turn west on County Road 40 and drive three miles to the campground.

Contact: Cattail Creek RV Park, 41 Cattail Lane, Yankeetown, FL 34498, 352/447-3050, website: www.cattailcreekrvpark.com.

COURTESY OF FLORIDA STATE PARKS

Chapter 5

Jacksonville Area

Jacksonville Area

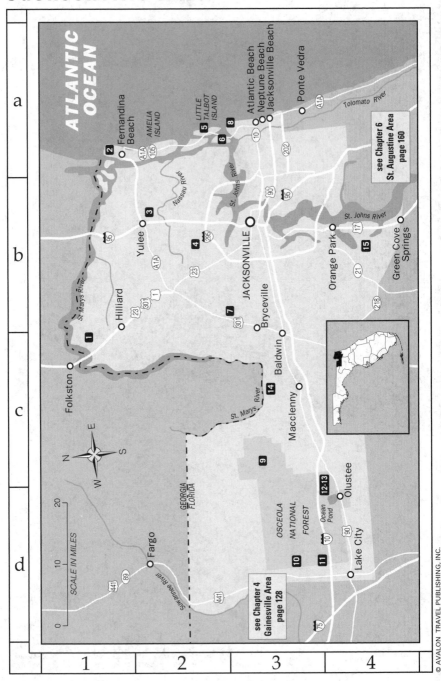

© AVALON TRAVEL PUBLISHING, INC.

1 RALPH E. SIMMONS MEMORIAL STATE FOREST

Rating: 8

North of Hilliard on the St. Marys River just south of Georgia

Jacksonville map, grid c1, page 146

One great thing about camping here is that you're likely to be very much alone, except possibly during hunting season. Part of this 3,630-acre state forest (formerly known as St. Marys State Forest) borders a six-mile stretch of the St. Marys River, the watery line between Florida and Georgia. The vehicle-accessible site is simply an oak-shaded area where the palmettos and scrub oaks have been cleared out along with the rest of the underbrush—so expect little privacy from neighbors. The oak hammock is just off the St. Marys River and Pigeon Creek, a rivulet that empties into the St. Marys. A county-maintained boat ramp is less than .25 mile away, and right next to that is a popular summer swimming spot on the St. Marys. The forest is a largely ignored, out-of-the-way spot where nature lovers who don't mind skipping a shower or two will have a blast. Look for deer, wild turkeys, and the once-endangered fox squirrel, which is now making a comeback. Early in the day, keep your eye out for otters alongside the river or the creek. That's also a good time for freshwater anglers to try their hand at the river. The forest contains some increasingly rare natural areas, such as seepage slopes and longleaf wire grass sand hills. Horseback camping is available, as are trails for horseback riding and day hikes.

Canoeists can use any of three designated primitive campsites along the St. Marys. If you need to rent a canoe, contact local liveries such as Canoeport in St. George, Georgia, at 912/843-2688, or Outdoor Adventures in Jacksonville at 904/393-9030.

If you're not hunting, then you're not allowed to camp in the forest during hunting seasons, which are periods of no more than two weeks—usually just four days or so—scattered across the calendar from late September to late February. Hunters go after deer, hogs, wild turkeys, and small game then. Unlike many places frequented by hunters, this stretch of natural Florida has been reserved for non-hunters in significant periods during the cooler winter months, which is dandy news for primitive campers.

Campsites, facilities: One primitive camping area is accessible by car, and four primitive sites are accessible by canoe or boat on the St. Marys River. The site accessible by car offers a vault toilet and is near a boat ramp on the river. No showers, dump stations, restrooms, or other facilities are provided. Groceries and other supplies can be purchased about five miles away in Hilliard or in Folkston, Georgia. Children and leashed pets are welcome.

Reservations, fees: For the drive-in site, contact either the Florida Division of Forestry or the St. Johns River Water Management District ahead of time to learn the combination for the lock that controls an access gate. Canoeists and other boaters on the St. Marys should contact the water management district to see if space is available. Campsites are first-come, first-served. Camping is free.

Directions: From Hilliard, drive seven miles north on U.S. 1 to the town of Boulogne, then turn right onto Lake Hampton Road/State Road 121. Look for an entrance less than one mile ahead on the left, just past Pigeon Creek.

Contact: Florida Division of Forestry, 3742 Clint Drive, Hilliard, FL 32046, 904/845-3597. Additional information is available from the St. Johns River Water Management District, Division of Land Management, P.O. Box 1429, Palatka, FL 32178-1429, 386/329-4500 or 800/451-7106, website: www.sjrwmd.com.

2 FORT CLINCH STATE PARK

🏃 🏊 🚣 🛶 🎣 ⛵ 🚐 ⛺

Rating: 10

**On the Atlantic Ocean at Florida's
northeastern tip**

Jacksonville map, grid a1, page 146

You can fall asleep to the sound of ocean waves crashing near your sandy campsite. The ride to the park is a study in contrasts, as you pass neat shops and Victorian homes in old-town Fernandina Beach, as well as huge power plants. But the key attraction is the park.

The campground is set where the St. Marys and Amelia Rivers come together to form Cumberland Sound, the border between Florida and Georgia. You have a choice of two camping areas: 21 unshaded, sandy sites are near the ocean, and 41 others are in a shady coastal hammock of big, beautiful oaks and cedars on the Amelia River. Both are outstanding in their own way. Fireflies might flicker like Christmas lights at dusk in the shady "river campground," where you will feel more sheltered from other campers thanks to at least some native brush providing a screen. At the beach sites, you'll be closer to other campers. But it's hard to beat waking up to feel the sea breeze and see the pink fingers of dawn reaching over the Atlantic and the nearby dunes. We found raccoons to be a manageable but irksome problem at the river sites (tip: keep food and coolers in the car).

Anglers use a fishing pier to catch whiting, red bass, and sheepshead, while windsurfers take to the Amelia River, also known as the Intracoastal Waterway. The beach is popular among sunbathers and swimmers. Nearby in town are rental canoes and kayaks, a boat ramp, tennis and volleyball courts, and saltwater fishing charters. At the park, nature lovers have two hiking trails to choose from: a loop that leads through a wooded area and around man-made Willow Pond, or a shorter path near the park's namesake fort that passes through a hammock en route to the Intracoastal Waterway.

Even if you have a passing interest in history, don't miss the centerpiece of the two-square-mile park—the fort. Named for a commander who fought in the Second Seminole War in the 1840s, Fort Clinch was only partially finished when the Civil War commenced in 1861. Because no Yankee troops were around, the Confederates quickly took over the place. By early the following year, though, with the coastal islands to the north in Federal hands, the Confederates abandoned the fort as indefensible, and Union troops moved in soon thereafter. The fort never was completed because construction of its masonry walls was outpaced by the development of new and better cannons. Almost every day now, you can watch men dressed as Union soldiers perform historical reenactments.

For the best reenactment, visit on the first weekend of each month and take a nighttime candlelight tour that conjures up images of the Union and Confederate soldiers who battled on these very grounds. During the summer, candlelight tours also are held on the second and third weekends of the month (call for reservations). In May, a special full-garrison reenactment by Union soldiers takes place, then the fort is turned over to the Confederates in October.

For a special side trip, cross the St. Marys River to get to the Cumberland Island National Seashore in Georgia. Wild horses roam the northern stretches of the island, and a couple of old mansions can still be viewed along its beaches. An eerie island attraction is the ruins of Dungeness, the stately home of the Carnegie family. "It sort of reminds you of Tara from *Gone with the Wind*—after it burned down," says a friend.

To get to Cumberland Island, use your own boat to cross the St. Marys River. An alternative is to drive 40 miles to the town of St. Marys, Georgia, and catch a ferry from there. To do this, head west on Highway A1A from Fort Clinch's campground through Fernandina Beach to northbound I-95. Cross the Florida/Georgia border. At the first exit, Highway

40, go east to the town of St. Marys. There, catch a ferry to Cumberland Island, which is just across the Cumberland Sound from Fort Clinch State Park. For more information, call the national seashore at 912/882-4335.

Campsites, facilities: Sixty-two sites for tents and RVs are available in two sections, all offering water and electric hookups and campfire rings. Restrooms, showers, a dump station, laundry facilities, firewood, and a playground are available. Groceries, LP gas, restaurants, and bait are available within five miles. Children are welcome. Leashed pets are permitted with proof of current rabies vaccination.

Reservations, fees: Reservations are recommended; call ReserveAmerica at 800/326-3521. Sites are $19 per night for four people, plus $2 per extra person, for electricity, and per pet daily. Major credit cards are accepted. Stays are limited to 14 days.

Directions: From I-95 north of Jacksonville, take Exit 373 and go 15 miles east on Highway A1A, passing through the town of Fernandina Beach along the way. Turn right at Atlantic Avenue. Proceed two miles to the park, at left.

Contact: Fort Clinch State Park, 2601 Atlantic Avenue, Fernandina Beach, FL 32034, 904/277-7274, website: www.floridastateparks.org.

3 BOW AND ARROW CAMPGROUND

Rating: 3

On U.S. 17 south of Yulee

Jacksonville map, grid b2, page 146

Back before I-95 was built, the road in front of this five-acre park, U.S. 17, was the region's main route into Florida. But today that highway is much less used, although still fairly busy. The sites—some sandy, some grassy—are set back from it quite a ways. So this park is quiet, and it's shady. Construction workers and other more-or-less permanent residents tend to dominate sites, so it's important to reserve a space.

Campsites, facilities: The park offers 56 full-hookup RV campsites, most of them pull-through. Each site has a picnic table. A laundry room, restrooms, showers, LP gas, a pool, cable TV, and telephone hookups are available. Children and leashed pets are permitted.

Reservations, fees: Reservations are recommended. Sites are $22 per night for two people, plus $5 per extra person. Major credit cards are accepted. Long-term stays are OK.

Directions: From I-95 north of Yulee at Exit 373, drive three miles east on Highway A1A to U.S. 17. Turn right and go south for two miles to the campground.

Contact: Bow and Arrow Campground, 598 U.S. 17, Yulee, FL 32097, 904/225-5577, fax 904/225-9233.

4 FLAMINGO LAKE RV RESORT

Rating: 4

**Off I-295 northwest of
downtown Jacksonville**

Jacksonville map, grid b2, page 146

Visitors at this campground, which is located a quick hop off I-295, have two places to swim: the pool at the park's eastern end or the 17-acre lake on the western end. Much of the action is at the lake. Gas grills, a pavilion, picnic tables, and a deck are near the shore, where some anglers wet a line. Kids will prefer heading to the east side, though, for the basketball courts, volleyball nets, playground, and pool.

Paved roads with a speed limit of five miles per hour pass the well-tended campsites. For the best lake views, ask about sites 10 through 22. Sites 78 through 98 form a semicircle around the playground, pool, some shaded tables, and a volleyball net on the opposite side of the park. No bicycles are allowed on the beach or sidewalks. This is one of the closest campgrounds to the Anheuser-Busch Brewery on Main Street near the Broward River (tours are available). It also offers the quickest access to the Jacksonville Zoo.

Campsites, facilities: All 152 RV sites (33 pull-through) have full hookups. Facilities include a pool, a game room, volleyball, basketball, a bonfire area, a fishing lake, an adult recreation room, a beach, a pavilion with gas grills, and nature trails. Showers, restrooms, a dump station, pay phones, cable TV, LP gas, and a laundry room are also available. Alcoholic beverages must be contained in cups. Parents need to supervise their children at all times. Leashed dogs under 30 pounds are permitted, but they must use the two dog-walk areas and refrain from barking.

Reservations, fees: Reservations are recommended. Sites are $26 per night for two people, plus $2 for each additional person. Major credit cards are accepted. Long-term rates are available.

Directions: From Jacksonville, take I-95 north to I-295 (Exit 362B). Head west to the first exit (Exit 32, Lem Turner Road), then drive north a short distance to Newcomb Road. Turn left. You'll soon see the campground.

Contact: Flamingo Lake RV Resort, 3540 Newcomb Road, Jacksonville, FL 32218, 904/766-0672, website: www.flamingolake.com.

5 LITTLE TALBOT ISLAND STATE PARK

Rating: 10

On the Atlantic Ocean in Fort George east of Jacksonville

Jacksonville map, grid a2, page 146

Ideal for nature lovers and beachgoers, sun-washed Little Talbot Island is the only place you can camp in the sprawling complex of natural areas known as the Talbot Islands State Parks. At Little Talbot, you can hike and bike through maritime forests or boat through salt-marsh areas (rental canoes are available). You also can cross the dunes that protect the island from the Atlantic Ocean to swim or fish for flounder, redfish, bluefish, striped bass, and sheepshead.

The packed-dirt campsites are fairly close together. Some are screened from neighbors by at least limited brush. Still, the island is remote, so it's not difficult to find solitude. Little Talbot's hiking trails span more than four miles and reward walkers with more solitude than found at many state parks. Try to spot otters, rabbits, or bobcats as you explore. Birdwatchers admire the bald eagles and songbirds, which are among the nearly 200 species of birds identified here.

You may be sorry if you don't leave at some point to explore other portions of the five-square-mile Talbot Islands State Parks. At Big Talbot Island State Park, huge, bleached fallen tree trunks have become improbably large pieces of driftwood that give the shore a surreal, almost spooky feel. Look for birds along the five marked hiking trails that crisscross the sprawling 2,000-acre day-use area.

A little farther north, Amelia Island State Park also offers a taste of "The Real Florida," resembling as closely as possible the Florida that European explorers found when they arrived some 500 years ago. It's a fishing spot, but some people hike along the beach or bird-watch. You can also rent horses to explore the beach. For $45 (age 13 and up only; weight limit 230 pounds), you can saddle up at the Kelly Seahorse Ranch concession in the park. Hourly rides leave at 10 A.M., noon, 2 P.M., and 4 P.M. Check in 30 minutes prior to your ride. For information, call 904/491-5166.

Finally, don't miss a visit to Florida's oldest plantation—nearby Kingsley Plantation, the former home of cotton and sugar planter Zephaniah Kingsley. Get good directions from Little Talbot Island State Park so that you can easily locate the plantation, which is tucked far back from a long dirt road where the bent arms of oak trees converge overhead to form a canopy. Kingsley was a slave trader who married a teenage slave named Anna, then freed her. She went on to own a five-acre farm on the eastern bank of the St. Johns

River. She burned it down and fled when Confederates from Georgia threatened to return her to slavery. If you tour the fancy plantation house, you'll notice it faces the river instead of the entrance road. The reason: Rivers were the highways of the day back then. The plantation is part of the National Park Service's 46,000-acre Timucuan Ecological and Historic Preserve; call 904/251-3537. Also nearby is the Fort George State Cultural Center (see next campground, Huguenot Memorial Park).

Campsites, facilities: These 40 water-and-electric sites are for tents and RVs; about one-third can fit rigs up to 38 feet long. Two sites are pull-through, and two spots are wheelchair accessible. Each site has a picnic table, grill, and fire ring. Canoe rentals, a playground, a nature trail, bike rentals, guided interpretive programs (usually Saturday afternoons), and volleyball entertain campers. Showers, restrooms, a dump station, a small boat ramp, and a laundry room are available. A bird sanctuary is located on nearby Fort George Island. Groceries, restaurants, and bait are located within five miles. Children are allowed. Leashed pets with rabies tags are permitted; no pets may go on the beach.

Reservations, fees: Reservations are recommended; call ReserveAmerica at 800/326-3521. Fees vary seasonally, with sites going for $10 to $14 per night for four people, plus $2 per extra person. Electricity fee is $2. Pet fee is $2 daily. Major credit cards are accepted. Maximum stay is two weeks from March through September; long-term stays are OK other times.

Directions: From I-95 in Jacksonville, take Exit 358A and go east on Heckscher Drive/State Road 105 for 22 miles to the park entrance at right.

Contact: Little Talbot Island State Park, 12157 Heckscher Drive, Jacksonville, FL 32226, 904/251-2320, fax 904/251-2325, website: www.floridastateparks.org.

6 HUGUENOT MEMORIAL PARK

Rating: 8

On the Atlantic Ocean east of Jacksonville
Jacksonville map, grid a2, page 146

Broad beaches seem to span as far as the eye can see at this 450-acre park surrounded by three bodies of water: Fort George Inlet, the St. Johns River, and the Atlantic Ocean, stretching to 26,000 feet of beachfront. These sandy campsites have no shade, but they're great for passing a few days if you like beach settings. There's a magical quality; while the view from many Florida beaches inevitably includes highrises or houses, here you'll see just sand and the Atlantic Ocean in the easternmost reaches of the park. Vehicles are permitted on the beach. A staffer says RVers are targeted by management, but we consider this one of the better places around for tenters as well. Bring your own gear to snorkel or windsurf.

Although lacking hookups, these campsites have the advantage of being reasonably close to some Jacksonville-area highlights. The nearest is the worthwhile Talbot Islands State Parks (see Little Talbot Island State Park in this chapter). The campground is also 10 miles from the Jacksonville Zoo and just down the road from the Fort George State Cultural Center, where you can take a 4.4-mile self-guided history tour by foot or car. Moss-draped oaks shade much of the route. Fort George Island has been continuously inhabited for some 5,000 years. Early Indian occupants shucked oysters and tossed them into piles, which today are up to 65 feet tall and are covered by sand and dirt, making this the highest coastal elevation south of North Carolina's Outer Banks.

Campsites, facilities: These 40 RV sites and 30 tent-only sites have no hookups. All sites have a picnic table and grill. Restrooms, showers, a dump station, a boat ramp, and a store are available. Campfires are permitted at all sites. The restrooms and store are wheelchair accessible. A boat ramp, boat rentals, and charter fishing are nearby. Two waterfront shelters with picnic tables and grills can be rented for $21 per day. Jet Skis, windsurfing, and kitesurfing are allowed. Laundry facilities are located eight miles away. Restaurants and bait are available within three miles. Children must be supervised by adults. Two leashed pets are allowed per campsite.

Reservations, fees: Reservations are accepted. Sites are $6 to $8 per night. Major credit cards are accepted. Stays are limited to 15 days out of any given 45 days.

Directions: From I-95 in Jacksonville, take Exit 358A and go east on Heckscher Drive/State Road 105 for 20 miles. The park is on the right side of the road, one mile past the ferry slip.

Contact: Huguenot Memorial Park, 10980 Heckscher Drive, Jacksonville, FL 32226, 904/251-3335, fax 904/251-3019, website: www.coj.net/Departments/Parks+and+Recreation.

7 CARY STATE FOREST

Rating: 7

North of Baldwin
Jacksonville map, grid b3, page 146

The three campsites here—set amid pine flatwoods that provide only moderate shade—are used mostly by Boy Scouts and people who like to ride their horses through these 3,400 wooded acres. A network of nature trails leads through the flatwoods and connects with a boardwalk that winds through a dark cypress swamp. Horseback riders and long-distance hikers may wish to range along a network of forest roads and trails stretching eight miles. There's also a 1.2-mile nature trail. Over a few weekends in the fall and winter, the forest is open to archers and hunters bearing muzzle-loading guns. A picnic pavilion sits near the camping area (campers must call ahead for a permit), along with a wildlife-observation tower and interpretive signs. Look for deer, wild turkeys, bobcats, and elusive black bears.

Campsites, facilities: An indeterminate number of campers can be accommodated at a single camping area of three primitive sites located in the forest. Drinking water, restrooms, and showers are available. Supplies and other conveniences can be obtained one mile away in Bryceville or seven miles south in Baldwin. Children are allowed. Leashed pets are permitted.

Reservations, fees: Reservations are required. Camping is $5 per night; you must obtain a permit by calling 904/266-5021. Day visitors are on the honor system and pay $2 per car.

Directions: From Baldwin, drive north on U.S. 301 for about seven miles. Look for the forest on your right, .25 mile north of the Bryceville Fire Station. The campsites are on the forest's main entrance road. From the town of Callahan, drive south on U.S. 301 for 15 miles. The entrance is 1.5 miles south of the forestry district office.

Contact: Cary State Forest, Florida Division of Forestry, 7465 Pavilion Drive, Bryceville, FL 32009. Forest district office: 904/266-5022; Cary State Forester/camping permits: 904/266-5021, website: www.fl-dof.com/state_forests/cary.html.

8 KATHRYN ABBEY HANNA PARK

Rating: 8

On the Atlantic Ocean in Atlantic Beach east of Jacksonville
Jacksonville map, grid a3, page 146

This oceanfront gem—named for a historian who served on the Florida Board of Parks and Historical Places in the 1940s—is one of Jacksonville's most popular parks, and for good reason. These 450 acres offer something for almost everyone. The more adventurous may want to trek through off-road trails on mountain bikes. Hikers and bicyclists (helmets are required) each enjoy their own narrow, woodsy nature trails that encircle a 60-acre freshwater lake, where anglers can try their luck for catfish. If you prefer saltwater fish, then head to the county-run park's 1.5-mile-long beach of grayish tan sand. Lifeguards watch over ocean swimmers from Memorial Day to Labor Day. From the beach, you're likely to see huge ships headed to nearby Mayport Naval Air Station, where ship tours are available most weekends; call 904/270-NAVY.

Several loops of campsites are set on either side of a crooked main campground road. The sandy/gravel campsites are irregularly spaced, so don't expect the manicured feel of a modern private campground. If you don't want to sleep in a tent near bathhouse traffic, skip sites 15, 16, 24, 25, 195, and 196.

For nature lovers and history buffs, this is the closest campground to the National Park Service's Fort Caroline National Memorial. There, approximately 140 French colonists were killed when Spanish soldiers swept down on their fort just after dawn in September 1565. It was the first decisive battle fought by Europeans for American soil and set into motion a chain of events that left Florida in Spanish hands for years to come. Today a replica of the fort, with French flags flying above cannons, stands on the banks of the St. Johns River. You can also hike the pretty Old French Trail, which runs through a remnant of the maritime hammock forest that once covered most riversides in northeast Florida. Just down the road from Fort Caroline is the National Park Service's Theodore Roosevelt Area of the Timucuan Ecological and Historic Preserve. There, you can hike the Willie Browne Trail (named for the former land owner who bequeathed these woods to the public), passing underneath mossy trees and a Confederate soldier's grave en route to the old Willie Browne homestead.

Hanna Park is about seven miles from Adventure Landing, a pirate-themed family entertainment center with go-carts, laser tag, a water park, and other activities.

Campsites, facilities: Fifteen tent sites are set apart from 278 full-hookup RV sites. For recreation, there's a hiking trail, 20 miles of single-track bicycle trails, a playground, and a fishing lake. Showers, restrooms, picnic areas, a dump station, log cabins (for rent), and a laundry

room are available. Groceries and restaurants are located throughout the town of Atlantic Beach, which surrounds Hanna Park. The beach, lake and six campsites are wheelchair accessible. Children under the age of eight must be supervised by adults while swimming. Two leashed pets are permitted per campsite.

Reservations, fees: Reservations are recommended but are usually not necessary. Sites are $14 to $18 per night for six people. Park admission fee is $1 per person over age six. Major credit cards are accepted. The maximum stay is 15 days within a 45-day period.

Directions: From I-95 in Jacksonville, take Exit 344 and drive east for about five miles on J. T. Butler Boulevard. Turn left at St. Johns Bluff Road and head north. In about six miles, turn right at Atlantic Boulevard/Highway 10. Continue seven miles, crossing the Intracoastal Waterway. Turn left at Mayport Road/Highway A1A. Turn right on Wonderwood Drive to enter the park, which is just south of the Mayport Naval Air Station.

Contact: Kathryn Abbey Hanna Park, 500 Wonderwood Drive, Jacksonville, FL 32233, 904/249-4700, fax 904/247-8688, website: www.coj.net/Departments/Parks+and+Recreation.

9 EAST TOWER

Rating: 7

Within Osceola National Forest
Jacksonville map, grid c3, page 146

At East Tower you'll camp amid some of the most wildlife-rich acreage in the state. It's not uncommon to come across deer and turkeys or even to hear the rat-a-tat-tat of an endangered red-cockaded woodpecker. In drier sandy areas, look for gopher tortoises lumbering home to their sandy burrows.

This campground primarily is designed for hunters, as evidenced by the sign on a caged pen here: "Lost dogs." Sometimes, people in pursuit of big hairy beasts with the aid of their own smaller hairy beasts notice that their four-legged helpers have vanished. But the dogs usually come back, and fellow hunters place the pooches in these cages to await their masters' return. East Tower is on the middle prong of the St. Marys River (which leads eventually to Jacksonville and splits Georgia from Florida), offering freshwater anglers a place to fish. Mountain bikers will enjoy the backcountry roads in these parts.

Campsites, facilities: Up to 75 tents can be accommodated at this primitive camping area. Flush toilets and drinking water are provided. Children are welcome. Leashed pets are permitted.

Reservations, fees: Reservations are not accepted. Cost is $2 per vehicle. Stays are limited to 14 days in any 30-day period, except during hunting season.

Directions: From Lake City, take U.S. 441 north to County Road 250 and turn right. Head east about 23 miles. Make a right onto Forest Service Road 202 and continue a short distance to the camp.

Contact: Osceola National Forest, U.S. 90, P.O. Box 70, Olustee, FL 32072, 386/752-2577, website: www.r8web.com/florida/forests/osceola.htm.

10 FLORIDA NATIONAL SCENIC TRAIL/OSCEOLA NATIONAL FOREST

Rating: 7

The trail runs southeast to northwest across the southern part of Osceola National Forest
Jacksonville map, grid d3, page 146
Here's your chance to enjoy totally primitive camping, with only a few places along the trail where you can get water and use backwoods privies. There are basically two kinds of terrain: wet and dry. In the swampy lower areas, you'll hike through bay and gum trees, cypress, ferns, and mosses. Other areas, elevated just a few feet, are known as ridges and have sun-dappled pines and wispy wire grass, along with the fan-shaped leaves of saw palmetto or per-

haps wax myrtle. Prepare to get your feet wet if it's been raining heavily; call the Forest Service one week to a few days before your visit to check on conditions.

The trail is marked by orange blazes, or short stripes, painted on trees. To prevent getting lost, look ahead to locate the next painted marking. If you see a double blaze, or two stripes painted next to each other, it indicates that the trail is about to make a turn. Keep a careful eye out around these double blazes to stay on course.

The trail starts at the historic site where the Battle of Olustee was fought during the Civil War. In just four hours on February 20, 1864, some 3,000 soldiers lost their lives in Florida's only major battle during the war. Stop by the worthwhile museum and walk the outdoor interpretive trail to learn how outnumbered Confederates headed off a Sherman-style invasion of Florida, which had for years provided a big chunk of the Confederacy's beef and other staples. Each February, on the second weekend of the month, hundreds of reenactors dressed in Union and Confederate garb come here to light cannons, ride cavalry horses, and the like.

From the interpretive center, it's about 3.5 miles to the Cobb Hunt Camp, at Forest Service Road 235. Look for several small ponds and sinkholes along the trail on the way to Cobb. About 1.5 miles farther, the orange-blazed Florida Trail crosses a blue-blazed trail that leads to the developed Ocean Pond Campground (see campground in this chapter). In another mile, the trail crosses under I-10 and follows a jeep road for about one mile. Soon, it crosses Forest Service Road 263B, and 1.3 miles later, State Road 250A. Another 1.8 miles brings you to a primitive campsite (10 miles total from the trail-head). One-half mile north, the trail crosses State Road 250. Parking is available here, so this is one place where you could terminate your hike. (You'll need two cars.)

If you decide to forge ahead, about 3.5 miles later the trail hooks up with an old tram road, where ties of cypress and heart pine elevate the trail and make for generally easy hiking.

One-half mile later, a boardwalk picks up, and in 1.5 miles you'll come to the West Tower campsite (see next campground). About 2.5 miles later the trail crosses Forest Service Road 237, following a jeep road for 1.2 miles to the Osceola National Forest boundary at State Road 262.

During hunting season, generally from mid-November through early January, camping is prohibited except at Ocean Pond Campground and designated hunt camps. To prevent assaults of another kind, bring bug repellent for warding off ticks and mosquitoes.

Campsites, facilities: Hikers can camp anywhere in the national forest as long as they pitch a tent more than 100 yards from a road during nonhunting months (hunting season usually runs mid-November to early January). That means there are virtually unlimited places to camp along the Florida National Scenic Trail's 20-mile section inside the forest. There also are two primitive backpacking campsites along the trail—one with a chemical toilet and shelter, and one near West Tower, which has a flush toilet and water. For more niceties, the trail passes the developed Ocean Pond Campground. But facilities are basically nonexistent. Campfires may be made using downed wood found on the ground. Pack out trash and bury human waste in a six-inch hole. Children and leashed pets are permitted.

Reservations, fees: Reservations are not accepted. Camping is free. Stays are limited to 14 days in a 30-day period.

Directions: From Lake City, drive about 10 miles east on U.S. 90, then turn left (north) onto Forest Service Road 241. To reach the north end of the trail, head north from Lake City on U.S. 441 about five miles and turn right onto State Road 262. The trailhead is less than a mile ahead.

Contact: Osceola National Forest, U.S. 90, P.O. Box 70, Olustee, FL 32072, 386/752-2577, website: www.r8web.com/florida/forests/osceola.htm. For trail details, we recommend that you contact the Florida Trail Association, which

maintains the trail, at 5415 Southwest 13th Street, Gainesville, FL 32608, 352/378-8823 or 877/HIKE-FLA, website: www.florida-trail.org.

11 WEST TOWER

Rating: 8

Western Osceola National Forest
Jacksonville map, grid d3, page 146

The national forest system of horseback-riding and bicycling trails is centered on this rustic, no-frills crash pad for outdoorsy types. If you're backpacking, then this is one stop along the Florida National Scenic Trail. It's also the main place to camp with your horse. The idea isn't to while away time at the dirt-road camping area in the shadow of a forest lookout tower. Instead, you should get out and explore.

From here you can traverse some 50 miles of horse trails, which also are open to backcountry mountain bikers. For beginning riders, the Green Trail is a quick five-mile jaunt on mostly main roads (be on the lookout for vehicles). If you're riding after heavy rains, stick to the Red Trail, a 20-miler through pine flatwoods and a few cypress sloughs. A cutoff allows you to reduce the Red Trail to just 10 miles.

Another 20-mile route is the Blue Trail, which offers the added enticement of the western border of the Big Gum Swamp Wilderness, a 13,640-acre area with no roads at the heart of the national forest that is least disturbed by humans. The Gold Trail, which is approximately 16 miles long, passes through two bay swamps. Avoid this route in wetter periods, particularly if you are an inexperienced rider. Check the bulletin board near the stables at West Tower for further information.

Hunters tend to use these campsites from mid-November to mid-January. Wear bright orange clothing while hiking to avoid being mistaken for game.

Campsites, facilities: Up to 75 people can be accommodated at this primitive camping area. The only facilities are drinking water, flush toilets, and horse stalls. Children are welcome. Leashed pets are permitted.

Reservations, fees: Reservations are not accepted. The cost is $2 per vehicle. Stays are limited to 14 days in any 30-day period, except during hunting season.

Directions: From Lake City, take U.S. 441 north about four miles. Turn right onto Forest Service Road 233 and go about 5.5 miles east until you see the camp.

Contact: Osceola National Forest, U.S. 90, P.O. Box 70, Olustee, FL 32072, 386/752-2577, website: www.r8web.com/florida/forests/osceola.htm.

12 OCEAN POND CAMPGROUND

Rating: 7

On the northeast end of Ocean Pond in Osceola National Forest

Jacksonville map, grid d3, page 146

This shady, placid campground sits right beside Ocean Pond, which, at 1,760 acres, is quite a large "pond." If you require electricity and water hookups as basic necessities, then this rustic place just won't do, but self-contained RVs will have no problem. Still, the campground is one of the most popular within Florida's national forests, and the scenery explains why.

The sites themselves are mostly screened from each other by brushy vegetation, so you're likely to enjoy some privacy. Many sites—most of them under tall, moss-draped pines—face the pretty, round pond. You can swim in a roped-off area in front of the campground.

Boating, fishing, canoeing, and water-skiing are popular at Ocean Pond. If you're into a nice day hike, follow the Florida National Scenic Trail, which passes by the campground, through the outback. Head south for 5.6 miles, passing some smaller sinkhole-like ponds along the way until you reach the trailhead at the Olustee Battlefield historic site. There, approximately 5,000 Johnny Rebs held off a larger force of Federals during the Civil War, pre-

venting a Sherman-style invasion of Florida, which served as the Confederacy's breadbasket. Hunting in the forest also is popular, although it is restricted in the area immediately around Ocean Pond. Most hunters camp nearby in the far more primitive Hog Pen Landing site (see next campground) and nine primitive hunt camps. During hunting season, camping is allowed only at Ocean Pond and at the designated hunt camps.

Campsites, facilities: Fifty sites without electricity, water, or sewer hookups serve tents and RVs. Facilities include a boat ramp, a swimming area, restrooms, a dump station, and showers. There's a convenience store in Olustee, but you'll have to drive to Lake City for major supply refills and restaurants. Children and leashed pets are permitted.

Reservations, fees: Reservations are not accepted. Sites are $8 per night for up to five people. Stays are limited to 14 days between May 1 and September 30, and to 30 days between October 1 and April 30.

Directions: From Lake City, drive east on U.S. 90 for 14 miles. After you pass the ranger's office and the convenience store in the town of Olustee, turn left onto County Road 250A. Follow this road north about four miles to the campground.

Contact: Osceola National Forest, U.S. 90, P.O. Box 70, Olustee, FL 32072, 386/752-2577, website: www.r8web.com/florida/forests/osceola.htm.

13 HOG PEN LANDING

Rating: 2

North of Ocean Pond in Osceola National Forest

Jacksonville map, grid d3, page 146

Here is a tranquil, rustic retreat on the north side of Ocean Pond, with sites set underneath pines and a few oaks. In late fall and early winter, you're likely to share the place with hunters in search of deer, wild hogs, bobcats, and other game. In the spring, turkey hunters turn up. It's possible to fish in the freshwater lake from the shore, but you'll do better if you have a boat.

Olustee Beach is worth a visit for a picnic and a walk down an interpretive boardwalk to the site of the long-gone, turn-of-the-century Russell Eppinger sawmill. The trail follows an old tram road that was used to carry trees from the forest to the sawmill. Back then, workers made about $2 per day for cutting 15 cross ties. Not far away is the Olustee Battlefield historic site. The Florida National Scenic Trail passes near here for plentiful hiking opportunities.

Campsites, facilities: This primitive camping area accommodates up to 30 people. Chemical toilets and a boat ramp are available. You won't find drinking water or any other facilities. Water can be obtained nearby at the developed Ocean Pond Campground. Children are welcome. Leashed pets are permitted.

Reservations, fees: Reservations are not accepted. The cost is $2 per vehicle. Stays are limited to 14 days in any 30-day period, except during hunting season.

Directions: From Lake City, head east on U.S. 90 about 10 miles. Turn left onto Forest Service Road 241, go about three miles north to Forest Service Road 241A, and turn right into the campground.

Contact: Osceola National Forest, U.S. 90, P.O. Box 70, Olustee, FL 32072, 386/752-2577, website: www.r8web.com/florida/forests/osceola.htm.

14 HIDDEN RIVER RESORT

Rating: 8

North of Macclenny just across the state line

Jacksonville map, grid c3, page 146

Although technically located in Georgia, this nature-oriented, nudist park on the St. Marys River is just across the water from Florida. Bring your own horse and ride on the trails that meander through the woods and along

the river. Canoes are for rent, and shuttle service is provided. The wooded campsites offer privacy. Family groups are welcome; a 60-by-30-foot pavilion provides gathering space. The "Nudie Blues" music festival is held each year in the last weekend in April.

Campsites, facilities: This is a nudist resort. There are 28 RV sites with full hookups and an unlimited number of tent sites. Picnic tables, restrooms, showers, and a dump station are available. On the premises are a pool, a hot tub, horseback-riding and hiking trails, canoe rentals, and a pavilion. The bathhouse is wheelchair accessible. Children are welcome. Leashed pets are allowed, as are horses.

Reservations, fees: Reservations are recommended. Sites are $45 per night for two people, plus $15 per extra person. Credit cards are not accepted. Stay as long as you wish.

Directions: From I-10, take Exit 335 at Macclenny northbound on State Road 121 and drive seven miles. Cross three bridges at the St. Marys River and the Georgia state line and immediately turn left on State Road 185. Drive 8.5 miles to Reynolds Bridge Road and turn left (this is the only paved road). The park entrance is ahead about 2,000 feet on the left.

Contact: Hidden River Resort, 9988 County Road 120, Sanderson, FL 32087, 912/843-2603, website: www.hiddenriverresort.com.

15 WHITEY'S FISH CAMP

Rating: 4

On Swimming Pen Creek south of Orange Park

Jacksonville map, grid b4, page 146

Diners have pulled up in everything from little boats to limousines to eat the alligator-tail appetizers and secret-recipe fried catfish at Whitey's restaurant overlooking Swimming Pen Creek. The popularity of the all-you-can-eat catfish spread is credited with spawning this three-acre campground. Here, oaks shade RV sites and campers launch boats for free to try for snook (particularly in winter) on the St. Johns River. Tenters sleep beside brackish Swimming Pen Creek, which meanders into Doctors Lake and the St. Johns. Dogs occasionally accompany their masters at the restaurant deck, and female diners have arrived in swimsuits. Don't try the latter; although Whitey's is casual, sunbathers must slip on shirts. Historic St. Augustine is about 35 miles away.

Campsites, facilities: All 44 RV sites have full hookups. Boat rentals, a boat ramp, charter fishing, a restaurant, and a snack bar are available. Showers, restrooms, picnic tables, a dump station, bait, tackle, and a laundry room are on site. An 18-hole golf course and grocery stores are located two miles away. Children are welcome. Leashed pets are permitted.

Reservations, fees: Reservations are not necessary. Sites are $22 per night for two people, plus $1 per extra person. Major credit cards are accepted. Long-term rates are available.

Directions: From I-295 in Orange Park, take exit 10 and go south on U.S. 17/Roosevelt Boulevard for about five miles. Turn west (right) at County Road 220. Proceed about two miles to the campground entrance.

Contact: Whitey's Fish Camp, 2032 County Road 220, Orange Park, FL 32073, 904/269-4198, website: www.whiteysfishcamp.com.

COURTESY OF ST. AUGUSTINE, PONTE VEDRA & THE BEACHES VISITORS & CONVENTION BUREAU

Chapter 6

St. Augustine Area

St. Augustine Area

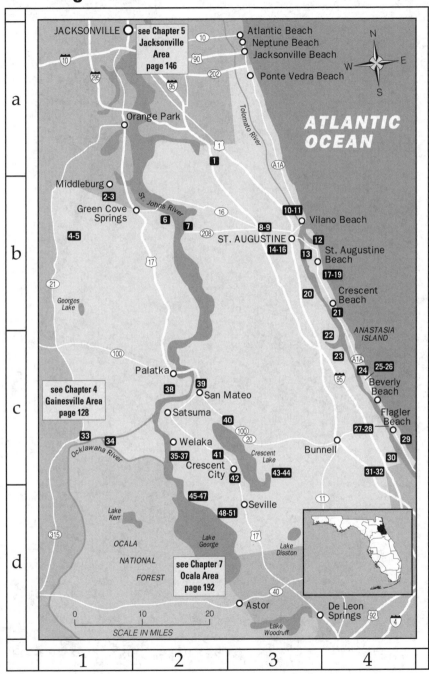

1 ST. AUGUSTINE/ JACKSONVILLE SOUTH KOA

Rating: 6

Off I-95 north of St. Augustine

St. Augustine map, grid a2, page 160

It's in a rural setting, shaded by oaks and graced with a 10-acre lake, yet the Vincent family's campground is convenient to the interstate. Anglers can try their luck at the lake, where some visitors prefer to tool around in paddleboats. Guests enjoy swimming in the pool or just hanging around the on-site Happy Daze Pub and Grille. This campground, site of many a Saturday barbecue, is about 15 miles from downtown St. Augustine (see Anastasia State Park in this chapter). Much closer, by about five miles, is the PGA Hall of Fame.

Campsites, facilities: There are 125 sites (60 pull-through). Sixty-five RV sites have full hookups, and all others—except a few tent sites—have water and electricity. Each site has a picnic table. A pool, horseshoes, miniature golf, paddleboats, a small playground, a nature walk, basketball, and darts entertain campers. Showers, restrooms, a dump station, cabins, groceries, a pizzeria pub/grille, and laundry facilities are available. Children are welcome. Leashed pets are permitted, but they must be walked in designated areas.

Reservations, fees: Reservations are recommended. Sites are $30 per night for two people, plus $3 for each additional person older than five. Major credit cards are accepted.

Directions: From I-95 at Exit 329, drive east for 200 feet on County Road 210 to KOA Road, then turn right and proceed to the campground, following the signs.

Contact: St. Augustine/Jacksonville South KOA, 9950 KOA Road, St. Augustine, FL 32095-8904, 904/824-8309 or 800/562-3433, fax 904/829-9639, website: www.koa.com/where/fl/09113.htm.

2 BLACK CREEK RAVINES CONSERVATION AREA

Rating: 6

Northwest of Green Cove Springs

St. Augustine map, grid b3, page 160

Steep ravines and hills distinguish this remote woodland with two primitive camping areas popular with hikers and equestrians. Elevations range from five feet to 90 feet above sea level—remarkable for Florida. You can canoe, fish, or boat on adjoining Black Creek on the eastern edge of the preserve. Bicyclists are forbidden, and climbing in the ravines is prohibited because of their sensitive nature. One camping area overlooks Black Creek and is accessible only by foot or boat; the other is inland at the main access point east of Middleburg.

Campsites, facilities: Tents only are permitted at the two primitive campsites. There are no facilities; bring water, supplies, mosquito repellent, and everything you'll need. Children are welcome. Leashed pets are permitted.

Reservations, fees: Sites are first-come, first-served. Camping is free. Each site accommodates up to six people. If your party has at least seven people, get a free permit and reserve at least one week ahead at 904/329-4410. Maximum stay for all campers is seven days.

Directions: The main access point is on Green Road on the southwest corner of this preserve. From Green Cove Springs, drive west on Highway 16 for five miles. Turn northwest onto County Road 218 and drive approximately one mile. At Green Road, go right .7 mile to the access point. From the town of Middleburg, drive east one mile on Highway 218. Turn north on Green Road and drive about .7 mile to the parking lot.

Contact: St. Johns River Water Management District, Division of Land Management, P.O. Box 1429, Palatka, FL 32178-1429, 386/329-4500 or 904/529-2380, website: www.sjrwmd.com.

3 JENNINGS STATE FOREST

🚶 🏊 🎣 �,🚗 🐎 ⛺

Rating: 6

West of Orange Park near Middleburg

St. Augustine map, grid b3, page 160

When it's not hunting season, this 20,885-acre state forest is a marvelous place for canoeing, hiking, bicycling, and horseback riding. Public access is restricted during hunts, so be sure to call ahead. The forest encompasses the headwaters of Black Creek and its tributaries. Ecologically speaking, forestry experts say the area is in remarkably good condition. What that means for you is that you'll see a vast array of wildlife, such as the green tree frog, hawks, foxes, deer, and rare Black Creek crayfish. There are four canoe launches, but you'll have to carry canoes over some rough terrain or use four-wheel drive to get to them. In the forest are several small historic cemeteries.

Campsites, facilities: Tents only are permitted at the three primitive campsites. There are no facilities; bring water, supplies, mosquito repellent, and everything you'll need. Children are welcome. Leashed pets are permitted.

Reservations, fees: Sites are first-come, first-served. Camping is free. Each site accommodates up to six people. If your party has at least seven people, get a free permit and reserve at least one week ahead at 904/329-4410. Maximum stay for all campers is seven days.

Directions: There are five access points; download a map from www.sjrwmd.com before making your plans. Two parking areas are on Live Oak Lane. From Middleburg, drive west on State Road 218.

Contact: Florida State Division of Forestry, 904/291-5530, or the St. Johns River Water Management District, Division of Land Management, P.O. Box 1429, Palatka, FL 32178-1429, 386/329-4500 or 800/451-7106, website: www.sjrwmd.com.

4 MIKE ROESS GOLD HEAD BRANCH STATE PARK

🚶 🚲 🏊 🎣 🐎 ♿ 🚗 ⛺

Rating: 10

Northeast of Keystone Heights

St. Augustine map, grid b1, page 160

You'll walk along rolling, sandy hills where plants are somewhat sparse and the sun can get fairly hot. But then the remote, three-square-mile park delivers its surprise: a wet mini-canyon, Florida-style. Water pours freely from a ridge, carving a ribbon of lush greenery. It slices the wilderness lengthwise and cools hikers hugging the ravine-bottom stream. It's an unusual sight for mostly griddle-flat Florida.

Among the park's three camping areas, the pine-dotted open expanse of Sandhill Camp is the sunniest. The soft hills are ancient sand dunes—that's right, the sea was much higher back then, eons ago. To the south, the gnarly branches of deep-ridged oaks provide some shade at Turkey Oak Camp. One potential drawback is that picnic tables and a public parking area for day-use visitors are near Turkey Oak, so light sleepers may be awakened by the slam of a car door. The southernmost sleeping area, Lakeview Camp, has a campfire circle at the edge of the park's largest lake, Big Lake Johnson, where anglers try for bass, speckled perch, and bream.

Five miles of hiking trails wind through this little-used gem of a park, which was built by the Civilian Conservation Corps. The circular Loblolly Trail passes beneath the sparse branches of the park's largest loblolly pines and ends at a mill site. The shortest trail, Fern Loop, starts at the precipitous ravine stairway and passes the headsprings of the Gold Head Branch stream. Long ago, the Downing & Burlington narrow-gauge railroad transported logs through the current-day park. Today, you can hike or ride a bike along the former railroad route. A swimming beach has been reopened at Gold Head so you can take a dip in Little Lake Johnson.

Campsites, facilities: The 43 RV sites have water and electric hookups, and the 31 tent sites have water only. Each campsite has a picnic table, grill, and fire ring. Recreational offerings include canoe and bicycle rentals, volleyball, and four hiking trails. Showers, restrooms, lakefront cabins, and a dump station are available. Laundry facilities, restaurants, groceries, and bait are available within six to eight miles. Children are welcome. Leashed pets are permitted with proof of vaccination.

Reservations, fees: Reservations are recommended; call ReserveAmerica at 800/326-3521. Sites are $11 per night for four people, plus $2 for each additional person, for electricity, and for pets. Major credit cards are accepted.

Directions: From I-295 at Jacksonville, take Exit 12 and drive south for about 30 miles on Blanding Boulevard/State Road 21 to the park on the left.

Contact: Mike Roess Gold Head Branch State Park, 6239 State Road 21, Keystone Heights, FL 32656, 352/473-4701.

5 MIKE ROESS GOLD HEAD BRANCH STATE PARK PRIMITIVE CAMPING

Rating: 6

Northeast of Keystone Heights on the Florida National Scenic Trail

St. Augustine map, grid b1, page 160

Look skyward for woodpeckers landing on the pointy tips of the bleached-white dead trees along the Florida National Scenic Trail. You'll pitch your tent along this car-width path. A primitive camping area with no bathrooms or other amenities is found a short walk north of Little Lake Johnson. Essentially a clearing immediately west of the pine-shaded Florida Trail, the campsite is disappointingly close to the park's established campgrounds. Although the primitive campsite requires a very short hike, you may wonder: What's the point? Why not stay in a developed campground where toilets

and water are readily available? The answer is solitude and the chance to awake closer to the fern-bordered ravine for a morning walk. You're likely to see birds in an area of burned-out pines up the trail from the campsite. The clearing and the dead trees help attract wildlife, hence the occasional soft clatter of white-tailed deer darting into the mossy woods.

Campsites, facilities: Up to 12 people can be accommodated at two primitive hike-in camping sites on the Florida National Scenic Trail. Canoe rentals, volleyball, bicycle rentals, four hiking trails, showers, restrooms, and lakefront cabins are available within the developed portion of the park. Laundry facilities, restaurants, groceries, and bait are available within six to eight miles. Children are allowed. Pets are permitted with proof of vaccination.

Reservations, fees: Reservations are recommended; call up to 60 days ahead of time to reserve a site. The fee is $3 per night per adult, $2 per child.

Directions: From I-295 at Jacksonville, take Exit 12 and drive south for about 30 miles on Blanding Boulevard/State Road 21 to the park on the left.

Contact: Mike Roess Gold Head Branch State Park, 6239 State Road 21, Keystone Heights, FL 32656, 352/473-4701.

6 BAYARD CONSERVATION AREA

Rating: 6

Near Reynolds Airpark southeast of Green Cove Springs

St. Augustine map, grid b2, page 160

Overlooking the St. Johns River, these 9,898 acres of pines and riverine bottomland hardwoods harbor turkeys, deer, gopher tortoises, and the rat-a-tat-tat of woodpeckers, yet these woods are close to metropolitan Jacksonville. One campsite, at Davis Landing, overlooks the river. Indeed, this public land offers seven miles of riverfront, providing the chance to fish from the bank, paddle a canoe (if you bring it), and spy for herons before walking inland to follow crisscrossing trails in search of warblers. One of the three campsites, reached by foot by passing a gate with a walk-through west of Highway 209 and south of Highway 226, is open to anyone most of the year, but is restricted to hunters only during hunting season. The popular Pearl's Trail and Lindsey Lane, found farther north, are off-limits to hunters at any time, and both end near an on-site security station next to a parking area.

Campsites, facilities: Tents only are permitted at the three primitive campsites, which must be reached by boat, canoe, bicycle, hiking, or horseback. There are no facilities; bring water, supplies, mosquito repellent, and everything you'll need. A boat launch is found north of Highway 16 and west of Shands Bridge. Children are welcome. Pets must be leashed.

Reservations, fees: Sites are first-come, first-served. Camping is free. Each site accommodates up to six people. If your party has at least seven people, get a free permit and reserve at least one week ahead at 904/329-4410. Maximum stay for all campers is seven days.

Directions: From Green Cove Springs, take Highway 16 east; the conservation area is about .5 mile west of the Shands Bridge, which spans the St. Johns River.

Contact: St. Johns River Water Management District, Division of Land Management, P.O. Box 1429, Palatka, FL 32178-1429, 386/329-4500 or 904/529-2380, website: www.sjrwmd.com.

7 PACETTI'S MARINA CAMPGROUND AND FISHING RESORT

Rating: 6

On the St. Johns River west of St. Augustine
St. Augustine map, grid b2, page 160

This wooded campground on the St. Johns River has lots of oak trees and is great for freshwater fishing enthusiasts who would like to spend a few days relaxing. A tackle shop, gas docks, a boat ramp, a marina, and live bait are among the 25-acre campground's most prominent amenities, but there's plenty to do onshore. The World Golf Village and PGA Tours, Jacksonville, and St. Augustine are nearby, and the ocean is just 20 minutes away. Owners Pinkham and Linda Pacetti also offer square dances, bingo, and campfires. A 200-seat restaurant has inside and outside dining and live entertainment on weekends. A recreation hall offers TV and video games, and there are motel units for the non-campers in your party. The Pacettis are the third generation of their family to own this park, which was established in 1929.

Campsites, facilities: This park has 147 full-hookup RV campsites (30 pull-through) and 25 tent sites. Some sites have picnic tables. Recreational offerings include a recreation room, a playground, a game room, shuffleboard, canoe and kayak rentals, fishing guide service, a bait and tackle shop, and horseshoes. On the premises are showers, restrooms, a dump station, rental cabins, a motel, a boat ramp and dock, groceries, a restaurant, a camp store, a large pavilion, and laundry facilities. Restrooms are wheelchair accessible. Children are welcome. Leashed pets are permitted.

Reservations, fees: Reservations are recommended. Sites are $22 to $30 per night for four people, plus $2 for each extra person over age four. Major credit cards are accepted. Long-term stays are OK.

Directions: From I-95, take Exit 318 and proceed west along State Road 16 for 12 miles to the campground.

Contact: Pacetti's Marina Campground and Fishing Resort, 6550 State Road 13 North, St. Augustine, FL 32092, 904/284-5356, fax 904/284-2369, website: www.pacettirv.com.

8 STAGECOACH RV PARK

Rating: 2

Just off I-95 west of St. Augustine
St. Augustine map, grid b3, page 160

This might make a good stopover for people

flying by on I-95, and there's even a small playground with swings and a basketball court to burn off some steam. Campsites are grassy, measuring 45 by 60 feet. The ambience is modern highway: A cluster of fast-food places and convenience stores is nearby, and two outlet malls are about .5 mile away.

Campsites, facilities: This campground offers 80 full-hookup RV sites (60 pull-through) on paved roads. A recreation room, a small playground, a basketball court, restrooms, showers, picnic tables, and a laundry room are available. Well-behaved children and small, leashed pets are permitted.

Reservations, fees: Reservations are recommended. Sites are $22 to $24 per night for two people, plus $2 per extra person age four and older. Major credit cards are accepted. Long-term stays are OK.

Directions: From I-95 and State Road 16 at Exit 318, turn left at the Denny's onto County Road 208. Drive west for .3 mile and look for the campground on your left.

Contact: Stagecoach RV Park, 2711 County Road 208, St. Augustine, FL 32092, 904/824-2319.

9 STATE PARK CAMPGROUNDS OF AMERICA
🏠 ♿ 🚐 ⛺

Rating: 2

Just off I-95 west of St. Augustine
St. Augustine map, grid b3, page 160

Contrary to its name, this private campground is not a state park. Rather, it's a convenient place for folks passing through on I-95, although a few people at this adult-oriented park stay long-term. You'll have a concrete pad and easy access to historic downtown St. Augustine (for more information, see Anastasia State Park in this chapter).

Campsites, facilities: All 50 full-hookup RV sites are pull-through; they have 30- and 50-amp service and concrete patios. A small primitive area fits a few tents. A recreation room, showers,

restrooms, picnic tables, and a laundry room are provided. Telephone service and cable TV are available from the appropriate utility company. Management says that all facilities are wheelchair accessible. Children are allowed. A dog-walk area is provided for leashed pets.

Reservations, fees: Reservations are recommended. Sites are $24 to $25 per night for two people, plus $3 per person over age 12 or $1 per younger child. Credit cards are not accepted. Long-term stays are OK.

Directions: From I-95, take Exit 318 and proceed east along State Road 16 for two miles. The campground is on the south side of the road.

Contact: State Park Campgrounds of America, 1425 State Road 16, St. Augustine, FL 32095, 904/824-4016.

10 NORTH BEACH CAMP RESORT
🏃 🏊 🏠 🚴 ♿ 🚐 ⛺

Rating: 8

On Highway A1A north of St. Augustine
St. Augustine map, grid b3, page 160

"Sunrise on the ocean, sunset on the river, and a bit of Olde Florida in between" is a slogan of this 60-acre RV-dominated campground, which extends from the ocean to the Intracoastal Waterway. Large oaks and myrtle trees give the park—home of bingo, card games, and potluck dinners—an Old Florida feel. North Beach is just about as close to the downtown historic section of St. Augustine as are the Beachcomber Outdoor Resort and Anastasia State Park campgrounds (see campgrounds in this chapter). Trees separate campsites, but campers will appreciate the pool and hot tub. Rent a boat here, or fish off a river dock.

Locals hoping to land flounder and red bass head about five miles north to the angler haven of Guana Lake, an area formed by damming the Guana River. The campground is the one of the closest available to the lake and surrounding Guana River State Park, whose 2,200 acres are spread out over hardwood hammock, salt marsh, pine flatwoods, beaches, and coastal strand. For hikers, dusk is a great time to hear the cacophony of cicadas and crickets while walking alongside the spiky, fan-shaped fronds of palmetto bushes in the state park forest. Nearly 10 miles of hiking trails lead through the diverse habitats alongside the Guana River. Native Americans lived in the current-day state park some 5,000 years ago, and the Spanish later established a mission, which was later destroyed. Look for bald eagles and osprey or some 170 other species of birds. Deer, bobcats, and other mammals live in and around the state park.

Campsites, facilities: Besides 10 tent sites, this park has 110 RV sites, most with full hookups. Each site has a picnic table. A pool, a hot tub, a recreation room, a playground, boat rentals, horseshoes, shuffleboard, volleyball, basketball, limited winter activities, and a camp circle for gatherings entertain campers. Firewood is available for use in the fire circle. Showers, restrooms, limited groceries, a boat ramp, a dock, a restaurant, a dump station, telephone hookups, bait, cable TV, and a laundry room are available. The restroom, office, ocean deck, lobby, and pool are wheelchair accessible. Children and leashed pets are welcome.

Reservations, fees: Reservations are recommended. Sites are $36 to $40 per night for two people, plus $3 for each additional person. Major credit cards are accepted.

Directions: From downtown St. Augustine, drive about five miles north on Highway A1A.

Contact: North Beach Camp Resort, 4125 Coastal Highway, St. Augustine, FL 32095, 904/824-1806 or 800/542-8316, fax 904/826-0897, website: www.northbeachcamp.com.

11 BEACHCOMBER OUTDOOR RESORT

Rating: 7

Across from the Atlantic Ocean
in Vilano Beach
St. Augustine map, grid b3, page 160

Another of the ultracivilized RV parks be-

coming popular in Florida, this pleasant Jacuzzi-equipped park is across the street from the Atlantic Ocean. A 1,015-foot pier stretches west into the Intracoastal Waterway, making it a fine place to watch a sunset and wet a fishing line. Across the street, the white-capped ocean waves lap onto the beach. There, campers swim, surfcast, and snorkel. The campground boasts "private ocean beach access," though legally speaking, all beaches in Florida are public up to the high-tide line.

Campsites, facilities: Beachcomber features 132 full-hookup RV sites (some pull-through), along with restrooms, a pool, a hot tub, shuffleboard, a playground, a barbecue area, a pier, a laundry room, two bathhouses, a clubhouse, and a dump station. Bait, tackle, and charter fishing services are available nearby. Children under 12 must be adult-supervised at the pool. At the pier, kids under 14 must be supervised. Pets should be leashed.

Reservations, fees: Reservations are required. Sites are $25 to $27 per night. Major credit cards are accepted for purchases of $100 or more. It's a private resort, so nonmembers may stay a few days as "guests." Maximum stay for members is three consecutive weeks; upon leaving for one week, they may return for another three weeks.

Directions: From downtown St. Augustine, head north on San Marco Avenue, following it about one mile before the road turns right to become the San Marco Bridge. Turn left onto Highway A1A. The campground is about one mile up the road, at left.

Contact: Beachcomber Outdoor Resort, 3455 Coastal Highway, St. Augustine, FL 32095, 904/824-9157, fax 904/829-9252.

12 ANASTASIA STATE PARK

Rating: 10

At the ocean in St. Augustine
St. Augustine map, grid b3, page 160

By far our favorite campground in these parts,

this 1,500-acre, state-run heaven seems to send just about every visitor home raving about the beach, coastal camping, and windsurfing, fishing, and swimming in the Atlantic Ocean. The sunny park has one of the nicest and least-developed stretches of beachfront around. Of course, you can take that as a clue that you won't have the place to yourself.

Moss-draped oaks help shade the camping area, which is separated from the ocean by a central park road, the slowly flowing Salt Run Lagoon (often dotted with windsurfers riding the surface), a marsh, and a barrier island. Although not located directly on the beach, you can still be lulled to sleep by the sounds of the ocean. Campfire-circle programs are offered in summer. A self-guided nature loop trail links two camping areas and leads through sand dunes covered by oaks, magnolias, and red bay trees.

This campground is the closest available to the magnificent Bridge of Lions, the impressive entrance to the historic district of downtown St. Augustine, the nation's oldest city. Spanish soldiers and missionaries were setting up housekeeping here two generations before famished Pilgrims landed at Plymouth Rock. Today, the biggest reminder of Florida's first conquerors are the massive walls of the nearby Castillo de San Marcos fort, which is still standing and open to visitors.

For a short walk, hit the .25-mile quarry trail just inside Anastasia park's entrance to see where Spaniards mined the fort's walls in the 1500s. The soft, porous limestone filled with shells and coral is known as "coquina" (or "tiny shells" in Spanish).

You can rent a canoe or sailboard for a leisurely ride on Salt Run Lagoon. While bicycling on the sun-washed park roads in summer, remember to wear sunscreen. Look for the ruby-throated hummingbird (a summer resident) or the awkwardly beautiful and endangered wood stork (which lives here year-round), among the many birds known to use the park.

All of that aside, the main reason many campers stay here is found outside the park: St. Augustine's historic district. Most tourists spend some time knocking around the sidewalk cafés and shops of the old Spanish quarter, centered on St. George Street. But the walkable district also features the nation's oldest store, house, and school, plus modern attractions such as the Alligator Farm, Potter's Wax Museum, and Ripley's Believe It Or Not Museum. Be sure to also take in the spires of nearby Flagler College. Across the street from the college at Memorial Presbyterian Church, you can see the tomb of college founder Henry Flagler, the railroad tycoon who forever transformed Florida by building a railroad that reached the Florida Keys.

Campsites, facilities: Each of the 104 RV sites and 35 tent sites has a picnic table, grill, fire ring, and piped water, and all but 35 have electricity. Several campsites are wheelchair accessible. Canoe rentals, windsurfing lessons and rentals, a playground, a 1.5-mile interpretive nature trail, horseshoes, and a camp circle for gatherings entertain campers. Showers, restrooms, a dump station, bait, beach chair and umbrella rentals, and a laundry room are available. Groceries and restaurants are located within 1.5 miles. Children are welcome. Pets are allowed with proof of vaccination; they are not permitted on the beach.

Reservations, fees: Reservations are recommended; call ReserveAmerica at 800/326-3521. Sites are $16 per night for four people, plus $2 for each additional person, for electricity, and per pet. Major credit cards are accepted. Stays are limited to 14 days.

Directions: From I-95 at Exit 311, go east on State Road 207, then turn right onto County Road 312. Turn north on Highway A1A. The park is 1.5 miles ahead on the right.

Contact: Anastasia State Park, 1340-A Highway A1A South, St. Augustine, FL 32084, 904/461-2033, fax 904/461-2006, website: www.floridastateparks.org.

13 ST. AUGUSTINE BEACH KOA

⬛ ⬛ ⬛ ⬛ ⬛ ⬛

Rating: 6

In St. Augustine Beach

St. Augustine map, grid b3, page 160

Stroll just .75 mile along a walking/biking path and you'll be enjoying the sound of ocean waves lapping the sands of St. Augustine's beaches. Fishing for bass and bream is allowed in the campground's three-acre lake without a license, but only with artificial lures and only catch-and-release. Many a camper is more interested in hopping onto the KOA's daily shuttle to St. Augustine's historic district than hanging out here to swim in the campground pool. Some campsites are sunny, but others are shaded. Try to avoid sleeping on Shark Fin Drive because it backs up onto a shopping plaza. The tent sites and RV spaces on Fisherman's Way are probably the most pleasant because they face the freshwater lake.

Campsites, facilities: Twenty tent campsites are set apart from 92 RV sites (60 pull-through). All but four of the RV sites have full hookups; others have water and electricity. Each site has a picnic table. A walking/biking path, a fishing lake, a pool, paddleboats, a playground, horseshoes, winter activities, and daily shuttle service to the city's historic area are among the amenities. Showers, restrooms, a dump station, 22 rental cabins, snacks, limited groceries, firewood, cable TV, and a laundry room are available. You can walk to restaurants, a shopping center, and tennis courts. Kids and leashed pets are welcome.

Reservations, fees: Reservations are recommended. Sites are $36 per night for two adults, plus $5 for each additional adult. Children up to 17 are not charged. Major credit cards are accepted. Long-term stays are OK.

Directions: From I-95 at Exit 311, drive three miles north on State Road 207 to State Road 312. Turn right and go four miles east to Highway A1A, then turn right, heading south. Stay in the right lane for one block. Turn right on Pope Road.

Contact: St. Augustine Beach KOA, 525 West Pope Road, St. Augustine, FL 32080, 904/471-3113 or 800/562-4022, fax 904/471-1715, website: www.koa.com.

14 INDIAN FOREST CAMPGROUND

⬛ ⬛ ⬛ ⬛ ⬛

Rating: 5

In St. Augustine

St. Augustine map, grid b3, page 160

Shaded by oak and maple trees, this park is only 3.75 miles from the St. Augustine city limits. Yet you still are likely to find deer tracks around the half-acre pond, where you can try your luck catching bass and bream. Some campsites are grassy, whereas others are gravel. Tenters enjoy a grill and fire ring at each campsite. The ocean is six miles east. St. Augustine's historic district is a little closer.

Campsites, facilities: Six tent campsites are set apart from 99 full-hookup RV sites (some pull-through). Each site has a picnic table, and all tent sites have fire rings and grills. Horseshoes, showers, a dump station, cable TV at 58 sites, wheelchair-accessible restrooms, and laundry rooms are available. Groceries can be purchased within .25 mile. Children are welcome. Leashed pets are permitted.

Reservations, fees: Reservations are essential in winter and for evening arrivals in summer. Sites are $20 to $24 per night for two people, plus $2 for each additional person. Fifty-amp electrical service and cable TV are each $2 extra. Major credit cards are accepted.

Directions: From I-95 at Exit 311, drive two miles east on State Road 207 to the campground entrance.

Contact: Indian Forest Campground, 1505 State Road 207, St. Augustine, FL 32086, 904/824-3574 or 800/233-4324.

15 SHAMROCK CAMPGROUND

Rating: 2

South of St. Augustine on U.S. 1
St. Augustine map, grid b3, page 160

Many of your neighbors will be retirees who stay at Shamrock's grassy sites on a long-term basis. Some of them use the 18-hole golf course about one mile away, whereas others favor hiking at Treaty Park, about two miles away. Shaded by magnolias, oaks, and sabal palms, Shamrock nonetheless isn't a retreat far from urban life. A Wal-Mart is just 1.5 miles away, and a trip to the convenience store simply requires walking to the front of the campground and crossing busy U.S. 1. The inland park is located some five miles from the beach and from St. Augustine's downtown historic district.

Campsites, facilities: Shamrock offers 38 full-hookup RV sites (four pull-through). Showers, restrooms, a laundry room, rental trailers, propane sales, cable TV, and telephone service are available. Limited groceries are across the street; restaurants are one mile away. Children are permitted for short stays. Leashed pets are allowed.

Reservations, fees: Reservations are advised. Sites are $20 per night for two people, plus $2 per extra adult. Credit cards are not accepted. Adults may stay long-term.

Directions: From I-95 at Exit 318, go east on State Road 16 to U.S. 1, then drive seven miles south to the campground entrance at right.

Contact: Shamrock Campground, 3575 U.S. 1 South, St. Augustine, FL 32086, 904/797-2270.

16 ST. JOHNS RV PARK

Rating: 2

Just east of I-95 south of St. Augustine
St. Augustine map, grid b3, page 160

Weekend afternoons can be a noisy affair hereabouts because this campground shares 77 acres with a flea market located next door.

Still, it's an easy detour off I-95. The park is split in two: one section is for campers; the other, dotted with pine trees, is for residents living in 50 trailers. At the park's 10-acre lake, some people fish from a gazebo. Beaches and St. Augustine's historic district are about five miles away.

Campsites, facilities: Fifteen RV sites are available for overnighters and snowbirds; the rest are full-timers. Restrooms, showers, a dump station, a laundry room, fishing lake, and limited RV supplies are available. Management says showers and laundry facilities are wheelchair accessible. A golf course is located within .5 mile. Children must be attended at all times. Leashed pets are permitted.

Reservations, fees: Reservations are recommended. RV sites are $21 to $24.50 per night. Add $2 per extra person. Major credit cards are accepted. Long-term rates are available.

Directions: From I-95 at Exit 311, head east for 200 feet on State Road 207. The campground is next to a flea market.

Contact: St. Johns RV Park, 2493 State Road 207, St. Augustine, FL 32086, 904/824-9840.

17 OCEAN GROVE RV RESORT

Rating: 8

Near the Atlantic Ocean south of
St. Augustine
St. Augustine map, grid b4, page 160

Pleasantly windy describes this barrier island campground, which backs onto the Intracoastal Waterway. On the other side, the Atlantic Ocean is just a 400-yard walk away, presenting opportunities for swimming, fishing, and snorkeling. The 20-acre resort targets families pining for a fun beach vacation. But there's plenty to do in the park, as well.

A generous three-quarters of the park is shaded by laurels and live oaks. Anglers can launch their watercraft from the campground's boat ramp leading into the Intracoastal Waterway, also known in these parts as the Matanzas River.

Downtown St. Augustine's historic district is about six miles away (see Anastasia State Park in this chapter).

Campsites, facilities: The 198 full-hookup RV sites (about 40 pull-through) are set apart from the 20 tent sites. Each site has a picnic table, and a few sites have fire rings. A pool, a hot tub, an exercise room, horseshoes, shuffleboard, a kiddie pool, a playground, a game room, cabins and park model rentals, and winter activities including basketball entertain campers. Showers, a recreation room, an outdoor pavilion, a laundry room, bait and tackle, firewood, cable TV, a boat ramp, and wheelchair-accessible restrooms are available. Groceries and a restaurant are within .25 mile. Children are welcome. Leashed pets are permitted.

Reservations, fees: Reservations are recommended. Sites are $35 to $40 per night for two people, plus $2 for each additional person and $1 for cable TV. Major credit cards are accepted. Long-term stays are OK.

Directions: Take Highway A1A south from St. Augustine for nearly seven miles to the campground.

Contact: Ocean Grove RV Resort, 4225 Highway A1A South, St. Augustine, FL 32084, 904/471-3414, fax 904/471-3590, website: www.oceangroveresort.com.

18 BRYN MAWR OCEAN RESORT

Rating: 7

On the Atlantic Ocean south of St. Augustine

St. Augustine map, grid b4, page 160

It's billed as the only RV park directly on 700 feet of beach in St. Augustine, and a sandy beach is indeed what you get. These 20 or so acres are geared toward RVers who want to camp oceanside with many of the comforts of home. A security gate controls access to the well-maintained, ownership park, where roads subject to a speed limit of five miles per hour have names like Sea Otter (closest to the beach)

and Sea Nettle. If you get tired of fishing, swimming, bodysurfing, and snorkeling in the Atlantic Ocean, you can plunge into the park pool. Don't expect rowdiness: alcoholic beverages are not allowed on the beach.

For the best ocean views, request beachfront campsites 219 through 239. In park lingo, "beachfront" campers enjoy the best view, beating out "oceanfront" (second best) or "oceanside" (third best) campsites. Other campers are more likely to see neighboring RVs but still will feel a sea breeze. If you don't want to camp near the entrance, avoid sites 67 through 69 and 239 through 241. All lots are individually owned but can be rented when not occupied. Some units in the resort are park models. The campground is about six miles south of the downtown historic district of St. Augustine (see Anastasia State Park in this chapter).

Campsites, facilities: All 144 RV sites have full hookups. A pool, an activity center, an adult center, shuffleboard, horseshoes, a playground, basketball courts, lighted tennis courts, restrooms, cable TV, snacks, ice, rental trailers, and a laundry room are available. Children are welcome, but parents are responsible for their conduct. Leashed pets are permitted and should use the dog walk north of the propane tank.

Reservations, fees: Reservations are strongly recommended, particularly in winter. Call two months ahead to reserve a park-owned trailer ($74 to $79). Regular campsites vary seasonally from $40 to $47 per night for four people, plus $2 for each additional guest or visitor, and $1 per pet. Major credit cards are accepted. Long-term stays are OK.

Directions: From I-95 at Exit 305, go east on State Road 206 for six miles to Highway A1A. Turn left, heading north. The campground is three miles ahead to the right. From St. Augustine, take Highway A1A south about six miles to the campground on the left.

Contact: Bryn Mawr Ocean Resort, 4850 A1A South, St. Augustine, FL 32080, 904/471-3353, fax 904/471-8730, website: www.brynmawr oceanresort.com.

19 PEPPERTREE BEACH CLUB RESORT

Rating: 6

On Highway A1A south of St. Augustine

St. Augustine map, grid b4, page 160

PepperTree is as much a village as it is an RV resort. Streets are paved and lighted. Lawn maintenance is available, as is cable TV, for long-term visitors. It's reminiscent of many of Florida's established retirement communities. Along with shuffleboard and horseshoes, visitors can take advantage of darts, a big-screen TV, and a fireplace, found in the clubhouse.

The wee grass lawns separating the well-tended, 30-by-80-foot campsites tend to offer only incidental shade from the sparse, bristly limbs of a singular native pine tree or other greenery. Some shady campsites are available. Catch-and-release fishing for bass and bream is available at a park lake, where you might even see otters. You can walk two blocks to the beach, and will find tennis courts about one mile away. St. Augustine's historic district is about seven miles north (see Anastasia State Park in this chapter).

Campsites, facilities: PepperTree offers 15 sites for RVs and 15 for tents, as well as rentals of park-owned homes known as "park units." Each site has a concrete patio and picnic table. A pool, a fishing deck, shuffleboard, horseshoes, basketball, darts, two fishing ponds, and a clubhouse entertain campers. Showers, restrooms, a dump station, cable TV, and a laundry room are available. Many areas are wheelchair accessible. Kids must be supervised when swimming or fishing. Leashed pets are allowed.

Reservations, fees: Reservations are recommended, particularly in February and March. Sites are $40 per night for two people, plus $3 per additional person and $1.50 for cable TV. Major credit cards are accepted. Long-term rates are available.

Directions: From I-95 at Exit 305, go east on State Road 206 for six miles to Highway A1A.

Turn left, heading north. The campground is about 1.25 miles ahead on the left. From St. Augustine, take Highway A1A south about seven miles to the campground on the right.

Contact: PepperTree Beach Club Resort, 4825 Highway A1A South, St. Augustine, FL 32084, 904/471-5263 or 800/325-2267, website: www.sabeachrentals.com.

20 MOSES CREEK CONSERVATION AREA

Rating: 6

At Moses Creek off U.S. 1 south of St. Augustine

St. Augustine map, grid b3, page 160

The concerns of campers understandably come second to the efforts to help protect the area's water supply and wildlife—the very reason this creekside wilderness was purchased by the St. Johns River Water Management District. Best left to outdoorsy types, this place is rustic with a capital R. Hiking trails run throughout the property and eventually lead to the crazily crooked Moses Creek or to the much broader stream to which the creek is linked—the Matanzas River.

The trails actually are old jeep routes that became overgrown, then were cleared again, so they may be soggy in wetter months. Bicyclists can use these pathways, but there are strict rules against going off trail. Canoeing, kayaking, and fishing are possible in Moses Creek as long as you bring your own gear. Campers can swim in the Atlantic Ocean, a short drive away at Crescent Beach. The group camping area is cool enough that staffers from the water district have been known to spend their Christmastime holidays here.

Campsites, facilities: Primitive hike-in or boat-in camping is allowed at two sites on the north side of the creek; expect no facilities. A group camp—by permit only—is found on the south side of the creek at Braddock's Point and offers a fire grill, picnic tables, and a vista overlooking the marsh and Intracoastal Waterway. Bring everything you need to either place, including food, water, camping supplies, and mosquito repellent. Pack out trash. Children are permitted. Leashed pets are allowed.

Reservations, fees: Sites are first-come, first-served. Camping is free. Each site accommodates up to six people. If your party has at least seven people, get a free permit and reserve at least one week ahead at 386/329-4410. Maximum stay for all campers is seven days.

Directions: Take U.S. 1 south from St. Augustine for about six miles to the St. Augustine Shores subdivision, which will be on your left about one mile before you cross Moses Creek. Turn left onto Shores Boulevard and work your way back to the subdivision's tennis courts. You can park there and hike in from the trailhead a short distance away.

Contact: St. Johns River Water Management District, Division of Land Management, P.O. Box 1429, Palatka, FL 32178-1429, 386/329-4500 or 800/451-7106, website: www.sjrwmd.com.

21 DEVIL'S ELBOW FISHING RESORT

🛶 🚐 🏠 ♿ 🚙

Rating: 4

On the Intracoastal Waterway south of St. Augustine

St. Augustine map, grid b4, page 160

Covering just two acres, this fishing-oriented park sits directly beside the Intracoastal Waterway and across Highway A1A from the ocean. Under family ownership for more than four decades, owners Karen and Henry Miles emphasize they are making major improvements to the park. Twenty-four fully equipped cottages, a pool, and a clubhouse are planned, with a four-phase construction schedule to begin late in 2003. Devil's Elbow is so named because of a treacherous bend in the river that existed before the U.S. Army Corps of Engi-

neers dredged it clear many years ago. Each grassy/sandy campsite has a picnic table. If you'd like to plunge into the ocean or lounge on a sunbathing beach, the Atlantic is only about .5 mile away.

From the campground boat ramp, you can pilot your boat three miles to historic Fort Matanzas (see Faver-Dykes State Park in this chapter). St. Augustine's historic district is 12 miles north (see Anastasia State Park in this chapter).

Campsites, facilities: All nine full-hookup campsites are for RVs up to 35 feet long. Each site has a picnic table, and several feature cable TV and telephone hookups; most have a view of the waterway. Boat rentals, a boat ramp and a dock, charter captains, restrooms, showers, laundry facilities, bait and tackle, and rental trailers are available. Most areas of the park are wheelchair accessible. Children are welcome. Leashed pets are permitted.

Reservations, fees: Reservations are recommended. Sites are $30 per night for two people, plus $2 per extra person. Major credit cards are accepted. Long-term rates are available.

Directions: From St. Augustine, go 12 miles south on Highway A1A to the campground. From I-95, exit at State Route 206 and drive east to Highway A1A. Turn south and go 1.5 miles to the park.

Contact: Devil's Elbow Fishing Resort, 7507 Highway A1A South, St. Augustine, FL 32056, 904/471-0398, fax 904/471-0248, website: www.devilselbowfishingresort.com.

22 FAVER-DYKES STATE PARK

🚶 🛶 🚐 🚣 ♿ 🚙 ⛺

Rating: 10

On Pellicer Creek off U.S. 1 south of St. Augustine

St. Augustine map, grid c4, page 160

In this canoeist's delight, you will discover aquatic trails leading through a landscape that has changed little since Spanish explorers first set foot here. In fact, the main body of water in the 1,608-acre park, Pellicer Creek, is named for Francisco Pellicer, who received a land grant from the king of Spain when the Spanish flag still flew over Florida.

A four-mile canoe trail, which is easy enough for beginners, can be traversed against the weak current. That way, you can make it a loop trip instead of leaving your car at one end of the creek and arranging for a ride back to camp. Call ahead to reserve a park canoe, which rents for $8 for the first two hours, plus $3 for each hour thereafter. Daily rentals are $20.

The sandy/grassy campsites aren't as picturesque as the surroundings. Landlubbers can use the short hiking trail along Pellicer Creek and Rootan Branch. A second, short nature trail leads through the high, dry pinelands near the creek. Swamps, marshes, and elevated pinelands are among the mosaic of natural Florida habitats that enrich this park with such wildlife as otters, alligators, deer, wild turkey, and a variety of birds. Look for bald eagles, which aren't uncommon.

Anglers can launch into the creek and try their luck with trout, flounder, or redfish (live shrimp are the best bait, as is true in most coastal fishing locations). The creek contains both saltwater and freshwater habitats, depending on how far you travel. Currents are mild to medium, changing with the tides.

The park, historic in itself, is only a short drive from one of Florida's more fascinating remnants of colonial history, Fort Matanzas. The name of the Spanish fort means "slaughters," recalling the two weeks in 1565 when French Protestant soldiers, wrecked along this coast by a hurricane, were systematically killed by Spanish Catholic soldiers. Later, during the struggle for northeast Florida between the Spanish and English that characterized the period leading up to the American Revolution, the inlet controlled by Fort Matanzas proved an important strategic point.

Campsites, facilities: These 30 sites for RVs or tents have water and electricity but no sewer hookups. Each site has a picnic table, grill, and fire ring. A primitive youth camping area provides simple facilities for up to 100 people. Canoe rentals, a playground, a nature trail, a boat ramp, a dump station, showers, and wheelchair-accessible restrooms are available. Children are welcome. Pets are not allowed.

Reservations, fees: Reservations are recommended; call ReserveAmerica at 800/326-3521. Sites are $9 per night for four people, plus $2 for each additional person and $2 for electricity. Credit cards are accepted. The maximum stay is 14 days, or 42 days during a six-month period.

Directions: From I-95 at Exit 298, go north on U.S. 1. On the right side of the road, you will see BP and Texaco gasoline stations. Turn right and follow the signs to the park.

Contact: Faver-Dykes State Park, 1000 Faver-Dykes Road, St. Augustine, FL 32086, 904/794-0997, fax 904/794-1378, website: www.floridastateparks.org.

23 PRINCESS PLACE PRESERVE (FORMERLY PELLICER CREEK)

Rating: 6

Northwest of Palm Coast

St. Augustine map, grid b3, page 160

This is the "crown jewel" of Flagler County Parks, featuring the oldest structure in the county—a lodge built in 1887—and 1,500 acres located at the confluence of Pellicer Creek, the Matanzas River, and Moody Creek. You'll find canoeing, horseback riding, and bicycle riding. Only primitive tent camping is allowed, and you must get a permit in person from the parks department in Bunnell. Plan accordingly. Campers are not allowed to swim in the lodge pool.

This park is part of the Pellicer Creek Corridor Conservation Area. You might spy rare species in these 3,830 acres of scattered marshes and, in four-fifths of the place, densely forested pines, shrubs, and hardwoods. Look for the Southeastern American kestrel, the cinnamon fern, and a starch-producing plant called the

East Coast coontie. The primitive camping area is near the parking lot, restrooms, the lodge house, and a loop trail of at least five miles for bicycling, hiking, or horseback riding (bring a horse).

Locals know this place for its catfish-stocked, 20-acre Pellicer Pond, which offers new fishing platforms at its opposite sides. Not just any fishing piers, these aluminum platforms are sheltered to protect anglers from the sun. The pond also has an informational kiosk, an educational display, and fish feeders for the catfish. Prefer to eat them rather than feed them? There's a six-catfish-per-day catch limit. Bring a freshwater fishing license.

Campsites, facilities: Tents can be placed overlooking the water or in the pine woods. Most sites have picnic tables and fire rings. Alcohol is prohibited, as are firearms. The gates to the campground are closed at 5 P.M., and campers may not leave or enter the park after that time. Children are welcome. Leashed pets are permitted.

Reservations, fees: Sites are free. However, you must obtain a camping permit—in person—from the Parks and Recreation office, 1200 East Moody Boulevard, Bunnell, FL 32110, 386/437-7474. Office hours are weekdays 8:30 A.M. to 5 P.M. The preserve is closed on Monday and Tuesday.

Directions: From I-95, take the exit for U.S. 1 and go east about 1.5 miles. At Old Kings Road, an unpaved highway that is nonetheless well marked, turn left. Drive 1.5 miles to Princess Place Road and to the park.

Contact: Flagler County Parks and Recreation office, 1200 East Moody Boulevard, Bunnell, FL 32110, 386/437-7474, website: www.flaglerparks.com.

24 GRANADA CAMPGROUND

Rating: 3

On Highway A1A south of St. Augustine
St. Augustine map, grid c4, page 160

These sandy and grassy campsites are sand-

wiched onto five acres between Highway A1A and the ocean for seasonal visitors to enjoy. That's a plus in terms of having a near-constant sea breeze to keep you cool. The least expensive sites, with water and electricity only, are the farthest removed from the oceanfront. Sunbathers will find a beach right at the campground, though there are some large rocks. Fishing is popular right in front of the campground, where residents sometimes hold cookouts. Bring sunblock because there is little vegetation, save a few palm trees.

Campsites, facilities: These 35 sites are for tents, RVs, or travel trailers. Of the 20 sites with full hookups, seven are pull-through. The remaining spots come with piped water and electricity. Tent campers normally opt for rustic spots on beach dunes. Facilities include restrooms, showers, a laundry room, and a dump station. For cable TV and telephone service, you must call the proper utility company. Management says all facilities are wheelchair accessible, except the beach. A restaurant is within one mile. Children and leashed pets are permitted.

Reservations, fees: Reservations are advised. Sites are $25 per night for two people, plus $2 per extra person. Credit cards are not accepted. Most folks here stay six months.

Directions: From I-95 at Exit 284, head east on State Road 100 to the dead end at Highway A1A. Turn left (north) and continue about 10 miles, passing Washington Oaks State Gardens. The campground is on the right.

Contact: Granada Campground, 6645 North Oceanshore Boulevard, Palm Coast, FL 32137, 386/445-3401.

25 FLAGLER BY THE SEA

Rating: 7

On the Atlantic Ocean north of Flagler Beach
St. Augustine map, grid c4, page 160

There's scant shade at this oceanside campground, but if you're looking for a relaxing beach experience with easy access to tourist attractions in St. Augustine (about 22 miles) or Daytona Beach (25 miles), it will do the trick. These few acres of beach also are near the residential community of Palm Coast, a place designed mostly for upscale retirees. Some campers swim and fish at the beach. For the best views, consider "oceanfront deluxe" sites, but the other sites are a short hop to the beach and sand dunes.

Campsites, facilities: There are 31 full-hookup campsites (15 pull-through) for RVs and 15 for tents. Showers, restrooms, and cable TV are available. Nearby Palm Coast has shops and restaurants. Children are allowed. Leashed pets are permitted and should use a pet walk along Highway A1A.

Reservations, fees: Reservations are recommended. Sites are $27 to $30 per night for two people, plus $5 for each additional person. Rates are higher on holiday weekends. Major credit cards are accepted. Long-term stays are OK.

Directions: From I-95 near Flagler Beach, take Exit 284 and go three miles east on State Road 100. Turn left onto Highway A1A. The campground is four miles ahead.

Contact: Flagler by the Sea, 2982 North Oceanshore Boulevard, Flagler Beach, FL 32136, 386/439-2124.

26 BEVERLY BEACH CAMPTOWN

Rating: 7

On the Atlantic Ocean in Beverly Beach
St. Augustine map, grid c4, page 160

If you're a sun worshiper, this 1,500-foot stretch of oceanfront is for you. One of few campgrounds directly on the sand, Camptown is located in one of the rare sections of relatively uncrowded beach left on the Atlantic coast, although some home subdivisions are going up around it. The RVs actually sit on top of the sea wall above the ocean, and the most choice sites are numbered 1 through 68. Other RVers who keep their windows open certainly can fall asleep to the sound of rolling waves. But outdoors, "beachview" campers are likely to be surrounded on three sides by RVs; Highway A1A is the western border. Tenters are relegated to sleeping between the beachfront and beachview sections.

Head north a few miles past the hamlet of Painter's Hill if you want to enjoy deserted oceanfront. Early morning beach walks at the campground are popular, with patrons enjoying the burnt orange and purple of the sun breaking over the Atlantic. Some campers wet a fishing line in the surf. Don't expect a rowdy scene: drunkenness is forbidden, and quiet time starts at 10 P.M. For day trips to area historic sites, St. Augustine is about a 30-minute drive away. Closer to home are the Bulow Plantation (see Bulow Resort Campground in this chapter) and Washington Oaks State Gardens (see Gamble Rogers Memorial State Recreation Area in this chapter).

Campsites, facilities: All 130 RV sites have full hookups. A few tent sites are tucked between a home and the clubhouse. A game room, a restaurant, showers, restrooms, bait, tackle, a gift shop, a convenience store, cable TV, and a laundry room are available. Shopping is available nearby. Children are welcome but must be supervised by adults. Pets must be leashed.

Reservations, fees: Reservations are recommended. Sites vary seasonally from $30 for tents to a range of $38 to $65 for RVs. Rates are for two people, plus $5 per extra person age 12 and older. Major credit cards are accepted. Long-term rates are available.

Directions: From I-95 near Flagler Beach, take Exit 284 and go three miles east on State Road 100. Turn left onto Highway A1A. Look for the campground three miles ahead to your right, on the beach.

Contact: Beverly Beach Camptown, 2816 North Oceanshore Boulevard, Beverly Beach, FL 32136, 386/439-3111 or 800/255-2706, website: www.beverlybeachcamptown.com.

27 PICNICKER'S CAMPGROUND AND SHELLTOWN

Rating: 6

On Highway A1A north of Flagler Beach

St. Augustine map, grid c4, page 160

Wednesday potluck dinners, Friday bingo, and summertime potluck barbecues help set the tone at co-owner John Van Buren's oceanfront RV park, but the waves splashing onto the beach across Highway A1A may interest anglers and swimmers more. The beach is about 100 yards from the campground. The campsites themselves are quite sunny and have concrete pads, although tenters still can find a place to pitch their temporary home. The four-acre camp is about 25 miles from the nation's oldest city, St. Augustine. To sleep closest to marshland and the Intracoastal Waterway, ask about sites 34 through 46. Sites 1 through 6 are closest to the Atlantic Ocean, but that means they're also nearest Highway A1A (not to mention the laundry room).

Campsites, facilities: The 59 full-hookup RV sites are set apart from a tent area, where sites have water and electricity. A recreation room, a pool table, a gift shop, showers, restrooms, picnic tables, a dump station, cable TV, and a laundry room are available. Restaurants are located within one mile. Groceries are three miles away. Children are welcome. Leashed pets are permitted.

Reservations, fees: Reservations are recommended. Sites are $28 per night for two people, plus $3 per extra person over age two. Major credit cards are accepted. Long-term stays are OK.

Directions: From I-95 near Flagler Beach, take Exit 284 and go three miles east on State Road 100. Turn left onto Highway A1A. The campground is 2.2 miles ahead.

Contact: Picnicker's Campground and Shelltown, 2455 North Oceanshore Boulevard, Flagler Beach, FL 32136, 386/439-5337 or 800/553-2381.

28 SINGING SURF CAMPGROUND

Rating: 6

North of Flagler Beach on Highway A1A

St. Augustine map, grid c4, page 160

Snooze away at a concrete-pad site surrounded by grass across the street from the Atlantic Ocean. The sunny camp is popular among retirees who congregate in winter on a long-term basis to share potluck suppers, bingo contests, card games, and other distractions in the recreation room. The park backs onto the Intracoastal Waterway, where anglers try their luck for redfish and trout. At a nearby marina, you can launch a boat or canoe into the waterway. The campground is a pleasant place to stop if you want access to the beach and the comforts of small-town Flagler Beach, named for railroad tycoon Henry Flagler, whose building of the Florida East Coast Railroad forever changed Florida by luring tourists and new residents. The campground is within a 30-minute drive of the nation's oldest city, St. Augustine.

Campsites, facilities: Fifty-four campsites are available for RVs or tents. Twelve RV sites are pull-through, and all have full hookups. Campers are entertained by a recreation room, a community grill used for cookouts, and wintertime activities. Showers, restrooms, limited groceries, bait and tackle, rental apartments, and a laundry room are available. Several people in wheelchairs have been happy staying at the park and all sites are accessible, according to management. A restaurant and marina are nearby. Children and leashed pets are allowed.

Reservations, fees: Reservations are required except from May to September, when they are recommended. Sites are $30 per night for two people, plus $2 for each additional person. Rates are higher during holidays. Major credit cards are accepted. Long-term stays are OK.

Directions: From I-95 near Flagler Beach, take Exit 284 and go three miles east on State Road 100. Turn left onto Highway A1A. Look for the campground two miles ahead.

Contact: Singing Surf Campground, 2424 North Oceanshore Boulevard, Flagler Beach, FL 32036, 386/439-5473 or 800/521-6133.

29 GAMBLE ROGERS MEMORIAL STATE RECREATION AREA

Rating: 10

On the Atlantic Ocean south of Flagler Beach

St. Augustine map, grid c4, page 160

A seemingly endless breeze wafts through the beachfront campsites of this 145-acre state park named for the late Gamble Rogers, the "Florida Troubadour" who chronicled the state's history and lore in folk songs before drowning in the ocean. The sun-washed campsites, composed of compressed coquina rock, overlook the beach where Rogers died.

For respite from the sun at this pretty picnic spot, a 20-minute nature trail near the park's entrance leads through a coastal scrub habitat of low-lying magnolia, oak, cedar, and sabal palms on the west side of the highway. Pick up an interpretive brochure at the entrance station to recognize the plants.

Bring your own boat or canoe to use the boat launch. Anglers go after trout, redfish, and flounder at the Intracoastal Waterway, located on the park's west side. Surfcasting at the beach may yield pompano, whiting, drum, or, at certain times of the year, bluefish.

For a pleasant day trip, the landscaped grounds of Washington Oaks State Gardens are about 13 miles north on Highway A1A. For our money, its nature trails outshine the gardens. You may be alone—or nearly so—on the Bella Vista and Mala Compra Trails. They take in a section of increasingly rare mature coastal hammock, as well as dense canopied coastal scrub and an estuarine tidal marsh. Bicyclists may join hikers on two other trails: the now-abandoned Old Highway A1A and the Jungle Road portion of the Bella Vista Trail. Call 904/446-6780. Nearby sites of interest include

St. Augustine's historic district, within a 30-minute drive of Gamble Rogers. Nine miles away is the Bulow Plantation State Historic Site (see Bulow Resort Campground below).

Campsites, facilities: Forty-four campsites are for RVs or tents; 10 sites are smaller, so they hold RVs measuring no more than 25 feet long. Each site has a picnic table, grill, and fire ring. A nature trail, a boat launch, showers, restrooms, and a dump station are available. For wheelchair users, there's an accessible campsite, picnic pavilion, grill, picnic table, and beach ramp. A public golf course is less than .5 mile away. Children are welcome. Leashed pets are permitted with proof of current rabies vaccination.

Reservations, fees: Reservations are recommended; call ReserveAmerica at 800/326-3521. Sites are $17 per night for four people, plus $2 for each additional person. Pet fee is $2 daily; electricity and an oceanfront site are each $2 additional. Major credit cards are accepted. The maximum stay is 14 days.

Directions: From I-95 near Flagler Beach, take Exit 284 and go three miles east on State Road 100. Turn right at Highway A1A and look for the campground about three miles south of Flagler Beach.

Contact: Gamble Rogers Memorial State Recreation Area, 3100 Highway A1A, Flagler Beach, FL 32136, 386/517-2086, website: www.floridastateparks.org.

30 BULOW RESORT CAMPGROUND

Rating: 8

East of I-95 and west of Flagler Beach

St. Augustine map, grid c4, page 160

While parts of this sprawling, 90-acre campground are sunny, much of it is shaded by the huge old oaks that define Florida's most beautiful woodlands. Still, the attraction isn't the sites themselves; it's getting out of your RV to experience all that the park—the scene of potluck dinners and dances in winter—has to offer. Visitors fish from canals, while others explore via rented canoes or bicycles. Under new management, this park has become popular for rallies and gatherings during Daytona's Bike Week and other festivals.

The relaxed, full-service campground is practically next door to the ruins of a worthwhile yet little-visited attraction: Bulow Plantation Ruins State Historic Site. Once one of Florida's most prosperous sugar plantations, the place was destroyed during the Seminole Indian Wars. Now all that is left of the gracious mansion and plantation are the towering coquina-rock ruins of the sugar mill, several wells, a spring house, and the crumbling foundation of the mansion. It looks sort of like a medieval castle in ruins (albeit a small one). Interpretive signs explain how the 1830s plantation functioned, and some mill machinery can be seen.

For a six-mile (one-way) day hike, follow the Florida National Scenic Trail from the plantation to Bulow Creek State Park in Ormond Beach. The route will take you through jungly forest, salt marsh, and pine flatwoods. It's real Old Florida, which is increasingly difficult for modern-day vacationers to experience. Bring mosquito repellent. Consider skipping a hike in summer.

Campsites, facilities: Nearly all 350 RV campsites (most pull-through) have full hookups; 50 tent sites also are provided. A pool, a playground, horseshoes, paddleboats, shuffleboard, canoe rentals, and a 6,000-square-foot recreation hall with raised stage entertain campers. Showers, restrooms, a dump station, a restaurant/pub, rental cabins, cable TV, a convenience store, and a laundry room are available. Most areas of the park are wheelchair accessible. Children and pets are permitted.

Reservations, fees: Reservations are recommended. They are required during special events. Sites normally are $18 to $22 per night for two people, plus $2 for each additional person. Major credit cards are accepted. Long-term stays are OK.

Directions: From I-95 near Flagler Beach, take Exit 284 and go east on State Road 100 to the traffic light. Turn right onto Old Kings Road. Proceed three miles to the campground entrance.
Contact: Bulow Resort Campground, 3345 Old Kings Road South, Flagler Beach, FL 32136, 386/439-9200 or 800/782-8569, fax 386/439-6757, website: www.bulow.com.

31 GRAHAM SWAMP CONSERVATION AREA

Rating: 6

West of Flagler Beach
St. Augustine map, grid b3, page 160

Conditions are sometimes too wet for hiking, but there is a primitive campsite here near the headwaters of Bulow Creek. This 3,084-acre conservation area is meant to preserve the ecology of an area surrounded by civilized development. You can fish and the bird-watching is great. Almost two-thirds of the land is wetland hardwood swamp; the fringes are drier.

Campsites, facilities: Tents only are permitted. There are no facilities; bring water, supplies, mosquito repellent, and everything you'll need. Children are welcome. Leashed pets are permitted.

Reservations, fees: Sites are first-come, first-served. Camping is free. Each site accommodates up to six people. If your party has at least seven people, get a free permit and reserve at least one week ahead at 904/329-4410. Maximum stay for all campers is seven days.
Directions: From I-95, take exit 284 east on State Road 100. Turn north at Old Kings Road and go 4.5 miles to the main access point on the east side of the road. An entrance from State Road 100 is planned, allowing bicycling, hiking, canoeing, and horseback riding.
Contact: St. Johns River Water Management District, Division of Land Management, P.O. Box 1429, Palatka, FL 32178-1429, 386/329-4500 or 800/451-7106, website: www.sjrwmd.com.

32 HOLIDAY TRAVEL PARK

Rating: 5

Off I-95 southwest of Flagler Beach
St. Augustine map, grid c4, page 160

You're right next to I-95, which is great if you just want a quick place to stop for the night. If you like to fish, you might ask for a spot on Marco Polo Road, which is right across from the campground lake. The busiest area of the park is near the pool, tennis courts, and bathhouse. Three spots are right next to the pool: 117, 118, and 119. For longer-term stays, you could find comparably priced campgrounds nearby in woodsier settings or directly on the beach. What you're mainly buying here is convenience, although there is a bulletin of planned activities hanging in the office to help keep campers entertained. The campground is close to the Bulow Plantation Ruins State Historic Site (see Bulow Resort Campground in this chapter). The nation's oldest city, St. Augustine, is within one-half hour's drive.

Campsites, facilities: This co-op park has 40 RV sites, about 10 of which offer full hookups; the rest have water and electricity only. Plenty of open space accommodates primitive tent camping. Some of the RV owners leave their rigs on site year-round; others allow their lots to be rented out. Recreational offerings include adult and kiddie heated pools, a playground, tennis courts, a recreation hall, shuffleboard, and fire rings. Showers, restrooms, a dump station, picnic tables, and a laundry room are available. Campers 18 and younger are welcome but must be accompanied by an adult at the pool. Leashed pets are permitted.

Reservations, fees: Reservations are advised. Nightly fee for two people normally is $22 to $28 for RV sites and $13 for tent sites, but will be higher during special events. Add $6 per extra person over age 12; $3 for kids ages six to 12. Major credit cards are accepted.

Directions: From I-95 at Exit 278, go west on Old Dixie Highway. Make an immediate right turn into the gas station. Follow its road to the back to enter the campground.

Contact: Holiday Travel Park, 2261 South Old Dixie Highway, Bunnell, FL 32110, 386/672-8122, fax 386/437-8432.

33 KENWOOD RECREATION AREA

Rating: 5

On the Rodman Reservoir south of Palatka
St. Augustine map, grid c1, page 160

This campground will be closed throughout 2003 and 2004, while the state acquires the land. When it reopens, improvements may include cabins and other niceties. Call to check the status. A Cross-Florida Greenways visitor center remains open daily except Wednesday from 9 A.M. to 5 P.M. (386/312-2273).

Like the Rodman Reservoir, this rustic place owes its existence to the ill-considered damming of the Ocklawaha River during the 1960s. Fishing is the big activity here, with most anglers going after bass and some speckled perch.

Nearby are Palatka's Ravine State Gardens (386/329-3721). The gardens are beautiful, particularly in March and April when the azaleas are in bloom. But the most interesting feature of the park is the steep ravine formed when water flowed through the sandy ridges on the west side of the St. Johns River. Created by the Depression-era Works Progress Administration, the gardens today are a favorite of joggers and bicyclists. Nature trails also are popular. Bicyclists will enjoy the ride from the Kenwood campground to the gardens and back. Another popular spot in the area is the East Palatka Fruit Market on U.S. 17 south of State Road 207, which has earned a reputation statewide for its excellent produce. The picks change with the season, but may include tomatoes, oranges, boiled peanuts, or grapefruit; call 386/325-4765.

Campsites, facilities: The campground will be closed through 2004. Call to see if it has reopened.

Reservations, fees: Call for updated information.
Directions: From Palatka, take State Road 19 south about 10 miles. Turn west onto County Road 310. Turn south when it dead-ends into County Road 315. Head south one mile or less and turn left onto Park Access Road, which leads to the campground at 300 Kenwood Boat Ramp Road.
Contact: Florida Greenways and Trails, Department of Environmental Protection, 8282 Southeast Highway 314, Ocala, FL 34470, 352/236-7143, website: www.dep.state.fl.us/gwt.

34 RODMAN RESERVOIR

Rating: 8

On the Rodman Reservoir south of Palatka
St. Augustine map, grid c1, page 160

Once the domain of only primitive campers, significant improvements were made here in 2001 and 2002. The road has been paved, a new entrance station has been constructed, and a new wheelchair-accessible bathhouse has been added. Power and water have been added to some sites. A ranger is now living on-site 24 hours a day for security.

The campground is not far from what some environmentalists refer to as "that damn dam." But don't let that deter you; there's plenty of wildlife and lots of things to do if you enjoy the outdoors. A little explanation about the controversy: In the 1960s, with the communist threat of the Cuba–Soviet Union axis lurking just 90 miles south of Florida, some bright people got the idea to cut a waterway, a la Panama Canal, across central Florida. The idea was to offer ship traffic a route sheltered from the possibly problematic Straits of Florida. And so, voila! Let's just gouge a big canal through the middle of the state, using the Ocklawaha River as part of the pathway, the engineers and hydrologists thought. Little did they know that a decades-long fight to scotch the plan would ensue, led mostly by the Gainesville-based

Florida Defenders of the Environment. The reason: It would have turned the gently meandering Ocklawaha into a series of ponds, much like the Rodman Reservoir you see here. A dam was built to stop up the river at this point, although environmentalists intervened during the Nixon administration to halt construction of the rest of the project.

Today, this big lake of a "river" is a unique place to camp. However, it remains controversial, with environmentalists trying to return it to its natural state, and bass fishers and other residents of the area fighting them bitterly every step of the way to keep it as a reservoir.

You're likely to see bald eagles soar overhead, and you'll definitely have great access to excellent bass fishing. Probably the most popular activity is fishing; there is no shortage of places to wet a line. The boat dock connects to a small island in the reservoir.

The campsites are sandy, only semishaded, and set amid pine trees. Good side trips are Ravine State Gardens or the open-air farmer's market in Palatka.

Campsites, facilities: Thirty-nine sites are for RVs and tents. Drinking water, grills, 12 picnic tables, eight picnic shelters, a dump station, a boat dock, a boat ramp, and wheelchair-accessible restrooms with showers are available. Fifteen sites now have electricity and water. Grocery stores, laundry, and other supplies are less than 10 miles away in Palatka. Children under 15 must be accompanied by an adult. Leashed pets are permitted.

Reservations, fees: Reservations are not taken. Sites are $17 per night for those with water and electricity; primitive sites are $10 per night. Credit cards are not accepted. The maximum stay is 14 days in a 30-day period but can be extended at the discretion of the gate tender or park ranger. Campers can use the boat launch free; others would pay $3.

Directions: From Palatka, take State Road 19 south about 12 miles, crossing the bridge over the Cross Florida Barge Canal, then turn right to head west for 2.5 miles on Rodman Dam

Road. Turn right onto Rodman Dam Access Road, which leads to the campground.

Contact: Florida Greenways and Trails, Department of Environmental Protection, 8282 Southeast Highway 314, Ocala, FL 34470, 352/236-7143, website: www.dep.state.fl.us/gwt.

35 SHELL HARBOUR RESORT

Rating: 6

On the St. Johns River in Satsuma
St. Augustine map, grid c2, page 160

Part of a resort complex that includes a motel, cabins, restaurant, and bar, this pretty park is set on 15 wooded acres along the St. Johns River. Don't be surprised to see at least two dozen peacocks running around the property. With an 800-foot-long dock and 1,600 feet of river shoreline, the campground can accommodate a huge number of anglers. The waterfront restaurant has banquet facilities and makes for a great spot to watch the sun set.

Campsites, facilities: Ten tent sites are set apart from the 28 RV sites (some full-hookup). On the premises are restrooms, showers, a dump station, a heated pool, a boat ramp, a dock, horseshoes, volleyball, a restaurant, snacks, a rental cabin, motel-style rooms, a laundry room, and a bar with a pool table, darts, and a big-screen TV. Groceries are about two miles away. Children and leashed pets are welcome.

Reservations, fees: Reservations are recommended. Sites are $10 to $15 per night. Major credit cards are accepted. Long-term stays are OK.

Directions: From Palatka, take U.S. 17 south about 15 miles into Satsuma. Head west (right) on County Road 309 for about two miles until you see Shell Harbour Road. Turn right. The campground is just ahead.

Contact: Shell Harbour Resort, 140 Shell Harbour Road, Satsuma, FL 32189, 386/467-2330, website: www.partyontheriver.com.

36 ACOSTA CREEK HARBOR

Rating: 4

North of Welaka
St. Augustine map, grid b3, page 160

Majestic oak trees and fragrant citrus trees shade this riverfront location on the St. Johns. Popular with anglers and boaters, the four RV sites are part of a large-boat marina and rental cottage complex built on the grounds of a turn-of-the-century home. A boat ramp is one mile away.

Campsites, facilities: There are four full hookup sites available for RVs and two tent sites with water and electricity. Each has grills, picnic tables, cable TV, and concrete pads. Restrooms, showers, and laundry facilities are available. On the premises are a heated pool, boat docks, boat rentals, and cabins, cottages, and efficiencies. Children are welcome, but most campers are adults. Leashed pets are permitted.

Reservations, fees: Reservations are recommended. Sites are $20 per night. Major credit cards are accepted. Long-term rates are available.

Directions: From the north, take U.S. 17 south to Satsuma. Turn right on County Road 309 and drive 3.5 miles to Acosta Creek Drive. Turn right and go to the end of the road. From Crescent City on U.S. 17, turn left on County Road 308 to Fruitland. Turn on County Road 309 and proceed to Welaka. Drive two more miles and turn left on Acosta Creek Drive.

Contact: Acosta Creek Harbor, 124 Acosta Creek Drive, Satsuma, FL 32189, 386/467-2229.

37 BIG RIVER RV RESORT (FORMERLY LAZY DAYS)

Rating: 5

On Little Lake George south of Palatka
St. Augustine map, grid c2, page 160

A forestry preserve is on one side of this RV resort, but the key attraction is water, not woods. These 35-by-55-foot (and bigger) paved campsites are set amid pines on the east bank of Little Lake George, which acts as sort of a wide, watery centerpiece within the narrower St. Johns River as the river wends its way south toward the more-noted Lake George. Understandably, bass fishing is popular in this laid-back part of the world. Residents report seeing animals regularly, including fox, bobcats, deer, and eagles. Each campsite has a 10-by-20-foot concrete patio.

Campsites, facilities: All 110 full-hookup sites are for RVs. Some are set overlooking the river. Restrooms, showers, picnic tables, a dump station, a pool, a dock, a boat basin, a recreation hall, horseshoes, telephone service, and a laundry room are available. Management says all facilities are wheelchair accessible. Groceries and restaurants are located nearby. Children and pets are permitted.

Reservations, fees: Reservations are recommended. Sites vary seasonally from $24 to $30 per night for two people, plus $2 for each additional person. Major credit cards are accepted. Long-term rates are available.

Directions: From Palatka, take U.S. 17 south about 15 miles into Satsuma, then continue south about five miles on County Road 309 to the town of Welaka. Turn right at the stoplight. Proceed one block to Front Street and turn left. The campground is less than one mile ahead at the end of the street, at left.

Contact: Big River RV Resort, P.O. Box 246, Welaka, FL 32193, 386/467-2100.

38 CARAVELLE RANCH WILDLIFE MANAGEMENT AREA

Rating: 6

South of Palatka
St. Augustine map, grid b3, page 160

Bald eagles love this place, seeking out hammock islands for nesting sites. You'll also see alligators, a wide variety of birds, and maybe even a Florida black bear. Stretching across

13,383 state-managed acres, Caravelle Ranch Wildlife Conservation Area is distinguished by its location at the confluence of the Ocklawaha and St. Johns Rivers. The Cross-Florida Greenway runs east-west on the northern edge. During hunting season, public access is restricted.

Campsites, facilities: Tents only are permitted at the two primitive campsites. One is on the St. Johns River and accessible only by boat. The other is inland on the Camp Branch Creek. There are no facilities; bring water, supplies, mosquito repellent, and everything you'll need. Children are welcome. Leashed pets are permitted.

Reservations, fees: Sites are first-come, first-served. Camping is free. Each site accommodates up to six people. If your party has at least seven people, get a free permit and reserve at least one week ahead at 904/329-4410. Maximum stay for all campers is seven days.

Directions: The main access point by car is the parking lot on State Route 19, six miles south of Palatka. From there, bicyclists and hikers can strike out to the nearest camping area. A boat ramp to the Ocklawaha River is just south of the main entrance on State Route 19.

Contact: Call the Florida Fish and Wildlife Conservation Commission at 352/732-1225. Additional information is available from the St. Johns River Water Management District, Division of Land Management, P.O. Box 1429, Palatka, FL 32178-1429, 386/329-4500 or 800/451-7106, website: www.sjrwmd.com.

39 HALF SHELL RESORT

Rating: 3

South of Palatka in San Mateo
St. Augustine map, grid b3, page 160

What makes this adults-only park special? Its people, say the owners. Mostly long-term seasonal visitors stay in this wooded setting on the St. Johns River.

Campsites, facilities: There are 34 RV sites with full hookups and picnic tables; three are pull-through. Rigs as long as 45 feet can be accommodated. Restrooms, showers, laundry facilities, and cable TV are available, but not phone service. A recreation hall offers planned activities. Children are not welcome. Leashed pets are permitted.

Reservations, fees: Reservations are recommended. Sites are $15 per night. Credit cards are not accepted. Long-term rates are available.

Directions: From Palatka, drive south on U.S. 17 for six miles. Turn west on Roberts Boulevard in San Mateo and go one block to the river.

Contact: Half Shell Resort, 132 Roberts Boulevard, San Mateo, FL 32189, 386/325-3166.

40 DUNNS CREEK CONSERVATION AREA

Rating: 5

Eight miles south of Palatka
St. Augustine map, grid c3, page 160

Known mainly by locals and seasonal hunters, this is a very marshy area where people comfortable with primitive backcountry camping may be rewarded with spectacular opportunities to view wildlife, particularly at dusk and dawn. You might see deer, fox, yellow-crowned night herons, red-shouldered hawks, barred owls, and more. But you'll pay for it in the comfort area because this 3,182-acre tract of land purchased by the St. Johns River Water Management District for water conservation purposes is only sparsely developed, with a few dirt roads. Hikers might share a tram road with horseback riders or bicyclists; another dry trail leads through Long Swamp. Bring a hat and sunscreen; some sparse pines provide scant shade, but this is mainly floodplain swamp bordering five miles of Dunns Creek.

Campsites, facilities: Tents only are permitted at the two primitive campsites, which must be reached on foot, bicycle, or horseback. There are no facilities; bring water, supplies, mosquito repellent, and everything you'll need. Children are welcome. Pets must be leashed.

During hunting season, the area is closed to other activities.

Reservations, fees: Sites are first-come, first-served. Camping is free. Each site accommodates up to six people. If your party has at least seven people, get a free permit and reserve at least one week ahead at 904/329-4410. Maximum stay for all campers is seven days.

Directions: From Palatka, go south on U.S. 17, turn east at Highway 100, and go about three miles to Tram Road. Turn right. Take Tram Road about .5 mile to the entrance.

Contact: St. Johns River Water Management District, Division of Land Management, P.O. Box 1429, Palatka, FL 32178-1429, 386/329-4500 or 800/451-7106, website: www.sjrwmd.com.

41 CRESCENT CITY CAMPGROUND

Rating: 6

Near Lake George on U.S. 17
south of Palatka
St. Augustine map, grid c2, page 160

Several oaks lend shade to this 10-acre country campground, located near the bass-fishing waters of Crescent Lake and Lake George. A small creek runs through the park, where some campsites have concrete pads, whereas others are gravelly or grassy. All sites have concrete patios. Although overnighters use the park, it's more likely to be filled with vacationers who stay longer and participate in potluck suppers and other planned activities.

Campsites, facilities: Ten tent sites are set apart from the 82 full-hookup RV sites (20 pull-through). Restrooms, showers, a dump station, a laundry room, a recreation room, a pool, a playground, a hiking trail, lighted shuffleboard courts, horseshoes, cable TV, telephone hookups, fire rings, LP gas sales, and campsite picnic tables are available. Groceries, a restaurant, and bait are about one mile away. Most areas are wheelchair accessible. Children and leashed pets are permitted.

Reservations, fees: Reservations are recommended in season. Sites are $23 per night for two people, plus $3 per extra person. Rates are $10 higher during Race Week (February) and Bike Week (March). Major credit cards are accepted. Long-term stays are OK.

Directions: From Palatka, take U.S. 17 south about 20 miles. Look for the campground about one mile north of Crescent City.

Contact: Crescent City Campground, Route 2, Box 25, Crescent City, FL 32112, 386/698-2020 or 800/634-3968, website: www.crescentcitycampground.com.

42 LEONARD'S LANDING LAKE CRESCENT RESORT

Rating: 6

In Crescent City

St. Augustine map, grid c3, page 160

Lake Crescent is famed for bass and crappie fishing, and most campers here are focused on angling. At 16,000 acres, the lake is one of the largest in the state and is 13 miles long and two miles wide. This campground (part of the Lake Crescent Motel and Resort) claims to offer the best lake access, with an on-site boat ramp, dock, bait and tackle, and boat and canoe rentals. Sites are sunny and have lake views.

Campsites, facilities: This 27-unit park has five sites for overnighters and 21 for seasonal visitors; tents are allowed. All sites have water and electricity (22 have full hookups), picnic tables, grills, cable TV, and optional phone service. Restrooms, showers, a dump station, a heated pool, a recreation room, a boat ramp, a dock, bait and tackle, a restaurant and pub, a snack bar, and a motel are on the premises. Children are welcome. Small leashed pets are permitted.

Reservations, fees: Reservations are recommended. Sites are $22.50 per night for two people, plus $3 per extra person. Major credit cards are accepted. Stay as long as you like.

Directions: From U.S. 17 in Crescent City, drive east on Grove Avenue when you see the sign

for Lake Crescent Motel and Resort, across the street from Miller's Supervalue grocery store.

Contact: Leonard's Landing Lake Crescent Resort, 100 Grove Avenue, Crescent City, FL 32112, 386/698-2485, website: www.lakecrescent.com.

43 BULL CREEK CAMPGROUND

Rating: 5

At Dead Lake west of Flagler Beach

St. Augustine map, grid c3, page 160

Anglers arrive by boat, car, or seaplane to sleep at these waterfront campsites that offer easy access to two lakes—Dead Lake and Crescent Lake. The focus of the rustic six-acre campground is water: A guide service helps anglers track down crappie and bass. If you prefer, rent a boat to go it alone or rent a canoe to follow a canoe trail. Water-skiing and a protected cove for boaters round out the water-oriented amenities. A new marina and boat docks were recently completed, and the owners have added 50 acres with a nature walk.

Campsites, facilities: There are 50 campsites for RVs up to 36 feet long and for tents, each with a picnic table and full hookups (but no cable TV). A boat ramp, boat rentals, a restaurant, showers, restrooms, cottages, cabins, horseshoes, bait and tackle, firewood, limited groceries, and a laundry room are available. Management says most of the park is wheelchair accessible. Children and leashed pets are permitted.

Reservations, fees: Reservations are recommended. Sites are $21 per night for two people, plus $3 for each additional person over age 12. Major credit cards are accepted. Long-term rates are offered.

Directions: From I-95 near Flagler Beach, take Exit 284 and drive about six miles west on State Road 100. Turn left at State Road 305. Proceed about four miles south to State Road 2006, turn right, and continue four miles to the campground where the road dead-ends at Dead Lake.

Contact: Bull Creek Campground, 3861 County Road 2006, Bunnell, FL 32110, 386/437-3451.

44 HAW CREEK PRESERVE (FORMERLY HAW CREEK CONSERVATION AREA)

Rating: 7

On Haw Creek in southwestern Flagler County

St. Augustine map, grid c3, page 160

The main reason the St. Johns River Water Management District bought these 4,529 acres comprising the Crescent Lake Conservation Area wasn't to please campers but to protect water quality and environmental values along the north side of Haw Creek adjacent to the Haw Creek State Preserve. Yet for outdoorsy campers who are willing to go a night or two without a shower, it's a great way to escape from your cares. You'll sleep amid riverine swamp and marshes (don't forget to bring mosquito repellent) and can spend the daylight hours hiking through higher, drier pineland and pasturelands on the short hiking trail near the campsite.

The Haw Creek Preserve camping is under the jurisdiction of the Flagler County Parks Department, which has built a boardwalk overlooking the swamp and creek. Look for bald eagles, hawklike ospreys, long-legged wading birds, and waterfowl. Motorboats and canoes can be launched at the Russell Landing boat ramp. You'll follow Haw Creek to the worthwhile freshwater-fishing spots of Crescent Lake.

Another primitive group campsite is located at the main access point for Crescent Lake Conservation Area, where you can hike and bicycle. To get there, drive from the intersection of County Road 305 and U.S. 17 in the burg of Seville and go north two miles. Turn east on North Raulerson Road and go one mile to the parking area.

Campsites, facilities: This primitive camping area accommodates an indeterminate number of campers coming as a group. Facilities are limited to restrooms, picnic tables, a hiking trail, and a boat ramp. Bring food and camping gear. Guns, motorcycles, and all-terrain vehicles are prohibited. Children and leashed pets are permitted.

Reservations, fees: Camping requires a permit from the Flagler County Parks Department; call 386/437-7490 or see www.flaglerparks.com. There is no fee.

Directions: From U.S. 1 at Bunnell, take State Road 100 west for about six miles. Turn left (south) onto State Road 305. In about three miles, turn right (west) onto County Road 2007 to the entrance in two miles.

Contact: For more information and maps of the Crescent Lake Conservation Area and Haw Creek areas, contact the St. Johns River Water Management District, Division of Land Management, P.O. Box 1429, Palatka, FL 32178, 386/329-4500 or 904/329-4404, website: sjrwmd.com.

45 HARLEY PAIUTE'S CAMPGROUND & MARINA

Rating: 7

Near Georgetown

St. Augustine map, grid b3, page 160

Located in a back-to-nature setting on the St. Johns River, this park bills itself as an "Indian camping village" with a boat ramp with river access. It attracts nature-loving campers, anglers, and snowbirds, but motorcyclists are welcome, too. Watch the sun set over the Ocala National Forest across from the riverbank. An 18-hole golf course is across the street. You'll find good hiking three miles away in the Welaka State Forest, and Daytona is about an hour's drive.

Campsites, facilities: There are 46 RV sites and 20 tent spots with water and electricity. Some sites have picnic tables, grills, cable TV, and phone service available. About half the sites are open for overnighters. Restrooms, showers, laundry facilities, a boat ramp, dock, dogwalk area, and a clubhouse are on the premises. Continuing with the Native American theme, an Indian festival is celebrated the second week in November. Children are welcome. Leashed pets are permitted.

Reservations, fees: Reservations are recommended. Sites are $17.50 per night for two people, plus $2 per extra person. Major credit cards are accepted. Long-term rates are available.

Directions: From Satsuma at U.S. 17, drive south on County Road 309 for 11 miles. The park is on the river across from the Live Oak Golf Course.

Contact: Harley Paiute's Campground & Marina, 1269 County Road 309, Crescent City, FL 32112, 386/467-7050, website: www.harley-paiute.com.

46 GEORGETOWN MARINA AND LODGE

Rating: 5

On Lake George in Georgetown
St. Augustine map, grid d2, page 160

The lure here is fishing for the big bass that inhabit 11-mile-long Lake George. In fact, this quiet, out-of-the-way campground/marina/fish camp boasts, "See what a fish camp should be!" It's located on the St. Johns River at the mouth of Lake George. Largemouth bass are the main game fish, yet some anglers also go after striped bass, bream, shellcracker, catfish, or speckled perch. It's possible to canoe and kayak on the St. Johns if you bring your own watercraft. Efficiency apartments are available, in case you grow weary of roughing it in your RV. Retirees are the main patrons of these semishaded camping sites, which are set among pines. Other parts of the park are shaded by large oaks.

Campsites, facilities: All 33 full-hookup sites are for RVs, and eight are pull-through. Each site has a concrete patio. Restrooms, showers,

a dump station, a boat ramp, boat slips, charter fishing, horseshoes, cable TV, a laundry room, and a wheelchair-accessible fishing dock are available. Groceries and a restaurant are located within one mile. Children and leashed pets are permitted.

Reservations, fees: Reservations are recommended. Sites are $20 per night for two people, plus $2 for each extra person. Major credit cards are accepted. Long-term stays are OK.

Directions: From Palatka, take U.S. 17 south about 15 miles into Satsuma. Turn right on County Road 309 and proceed about 16 miles into Georgetown. When you pass the only yield sign in Georgetown, continue about one mile. The marina and lodge are on the right.

Contact: Georgetown Marina and Lodge, P.O. Box 171, 1533 County Road 309, Georgetown, FL 32139, 386/467-2002 or 866/325-2003, email: georgetownmarina@gbso.net.

47 PORT COVE RV PARK & MARINA

Rating: 4

Near Georgetown
St. Augustine map, grid b3, page 160

This brand-new park on the St. Johns River is still being improved, but at this writing, a boat dock and 74 wooded sites were available.

Campsites, facilities: There are 74 RV sites with full hookups and concrete pads. Restrooms, showers, laundry facilities, and cable TV are available. A pool, store, and restaurants are planned. Children are welcome, but adults over age 35 are preferred. Leashed pets under 20 pounds are permitted.

Reservations, fees: Reservations are recommended. Sites are $27 per night for two people, plus $7.50 per extra person. All areas are said to be wheelchair accessible. Credit cards are not accepted. Long-term rates are available.

Directions: From Palatka, take U.S. 17 south about 15 miles into Satsuma. Turn right on County Road 309 and proceed about 16 miles into Georgetown.

Contact: Port Cove RV Park & Marina, 110 Georgetown Landing Road, Georgetown, FL 32139, 386/467-2880, email: rkoger@bellsouth.net.

48 LAKE GEORGE CONSERVATION AREA

Rating: 6

West of Seville near Lake George in the Lake George Conservation Area

St. Augustine map, grid d2, page 160

Several primitive sites are found in the Lake George Conservation Area, including one described here. It's ideal for a large party of horseback riders who want to camp out together. These 19,831 acres offer virtually unlimited opportunities for exploration along a network of dirt roads. It's about a 10-mile ride to the Jumping Gully campsite (see campground in this chapter), mostly through pine woods, if you'd like to make it a two-night affair. Look for deer and bobcats along the way.

You don't have to be saddle-bound to camp here. Mountain bikers and hikers might wish to use the forest roads in the conservation area, home to threatened and endangered species, including the Florida black bear and Sherman's fox squirrel. Skip swimming, though, because nearby Lake George is quite shallow around the edges and contains a plentiful population of alligators. Bring your own gear to canoe, boat, or fish for bass.

Campsites, facilities: This oak-shaded tent camping area is generally reserved for groups of seven or more people, but if your party is smaller, then check with the water district to see if it is available. A fire ring is provided, as is a hand-cranked well, but its water technically is not drinkable. It can be used for washing up, watering horses, and the like, and some people do drink from wells like this one because the wells are so far removed from civilization and are considered unlikely to be polluted. Two boat ramps are nearby. Laundry facilities and groceries are about 15 miles away in Crescent City. Children and leashed pets are permitted.

Reservations, fees: Permits are required for groups of seven or more and should be applied for at least one week in advance. Camping is free. The maximum stay is seven days. Camping is forbidden during the general gun season for hunters (typically in November).

Directions: Drive north on U.S. 17 from Barberville. When you reach the hamlet of Seville, head west on County Road 305/Lake George Road. The entrance to the tract is about two miles ahead and is known as Truck Trail No. 2. That's where you'll see the group camping area. For a map, check the website listed below.

Contact: St. Johns River Water Management District, Division of Land Management, P.O. Box 1429, Palatka, FL 32178-1429, 386/329-4883, website: www.sjrwmd.com. Additional information is available from Volusia County's Department of Environmental Management at 386/804-0439.

49 BARRS LANDING

Rating: 5

Near Seville on Lake George in the Lake George Conservation Area

St. Augustine map, grid d2, page 160

The Barrs Landing campsite might look like the nicest around if you're perusing a map of the conservation area because it's the only one right on Lake George. But don't be fooled. This is basically a low-lying clearing in the brush at the water's edge. It's often mosquito infested and occasionally wet. A better choice is Jumping Gully (see next campground). Or, if you're camping with a group and have a permit, try the Lake George Conservation Area Group Camping site (see previous campground).

Still, there are virtually unlimited opportunities for horseback riding, biking, and hiking along a network of dirt roads in these 25,000-plus remote acres jointly owned by the water

management district, Volusia County, and the state. Bring your own boat or canoe to fish at Lake George. Forget swimming, though. For one thing, the lake is quite shallow at the edge. For another, it boasts a fairly large population of alligators.

Look for otters, deer, bobcats, and gopher tortoises during your walks. If you're willing to do without niceties such as showers, you'll be rewarded by sleeping in woods that also are home to the Florida black bear (a threatened species), Sherman's fox squirrel (an endangered species), and a large concentration of bald eagles.

Campsites, facilities: Four rustic tent sites accommodate up to 24 people during non-hunting season but are closed during the general gun season (typically November). No facilities are available. For a vault toilet, you'll need to go to the Lake George Conservation Area Group Camping site. Laundry facilities and groceries are about 15 miles away in Crescent City. Children and leashed pets are permitted.

Reservations, fees: Reservations are not accepted, but permits are required for groups of seven or more. Camping is free. The maximum stay is seven days.

Directions: Drive north on U.S. 17 from Barberville. When you reach the hamlet of Seville, head west on County Road 305/Lake George Road. The entrance to the tract is about two miles ahead. Just inside the entrance, head north (right) about two miles on Truck Trail No. 2, a dirt road. Turn left onto another dirt road known as Barrs Road, which will take you to the lakeside camping area.

Contact: St. Johns River Water Management District, Division of Land Management, P.O. Box 1429, Palatka, FL 32178-1429, 386/329-4500 or 800/451-7106, website: www.sjr-wmd.com.

50 JUMPING GULLY

Rating: 7

At Lake George Conservation Area
south of Palatka
St. Augustine map, grid d2, page 160

These 39 square miles of remote land near Lake George are jointly owned by the water management district, Volusia County, and the state. If you're willing to do without such niceties as showers (you *could* rinse off in the lake), you'll be amply rewarded. You'll camp in the domain of endangered Sherman's fox squirrels, a large concentration of bald eagles, and Florida black bears, a threatened species. Look for alligators, otters, bobcats, deer, and gopher tortoises.

Campers sleep in a clearing set in a picturesque oak hammock with a little creek running through. There are virtually unlimited opportunities for horseback riding, biking, and hiking along a network of dirt roads. The bass haven of 11-mile-long Lake George attracts anglers, boaters, and, at times, canoeists and kayakers.

Camping isn't allowed during periods when the general gun season is in effect for hunters. The dates change slightly from year to year, but normally span from mid- to late November.

Campsites, facilities: Four primitive tent sites accommodate up to 24 people. No facilities are available, other than an artesian-well spigot for cleanup water. Bring drinking water, food, mosquito repellent, and all other supplies. Laundry and groceries are about 10 to 15 miles away in Crescent City. Children and leashed pets are permitted.

Reservations, fees: Reservations are not accepted, but permits are required for groups of seven or more. Camping is free. The maximum stay is seven days.

Directions: From Barberville, head north on U.S. 17. When you reach the hamlet of Seville, go west on County Road 305/Lake George Drive. The entrance to the tract is about two miles ahead. Turn right (north) on Truck Trail No. 2, a dirt road. Continue for about five miles, where Denver Road cuts off to the right. The camping area is off to the left in a wooded area.

Contact: St. Johns River Water Management District, Division of Land Management, P.O. Box 1429, Palatka, FL 32178-1429, 386/329-4500 or 800/451-7106, website: www.sjr-wmd.com.

51 PINE ISLAND CAMPGROUND & MARINA

Rating: 3

On Lake George west of Seville
St. Augustine map, grid d2, page 160

If you like fishing, you'll like these four rustic acres on the shores of 100-square-mile Lake George. The grassy campsites and cabins are most popular among anglers seeking bass in the 72-degree lake waters and hunters hot on the trail of deer, turkey, hogs, and ducks. An alternative: Use Pine Island as a base of operation by day for boating, and hike in the near-by Lake George Conservation Area (see campground in this chapter).

Campsites, facilities: All 29 campsites are for RVs and tents. Sixteen have full hookups; the rest have water and electricity. On the premises are showers, restrooms, cabin rentals, a boat ramp, johnboat rentals, a marina, boat slips, fishing guide services, a game room, a nature trail, horseshoes, snacks, bait and tackle, a recreation room, and laundry facilities. A convenience store is located within four miles. Children and leashed pets are allowed.

Reservations, fees: Reservations are recommended. Sites are $9.50 to $12 per night for two people, plus $1 for each additional person. Credit cards are not accepted. Long-term stays are OK.

Directions: Drive north on U.S. 17 from Barberville. When you reach the hamlet of Seville, head west on County Road 305/Lake George Road, passing through the Lake George Conservation Area. The road ends at Pine Island Marina.

Contact: Pine Island Campground & Marina, 1600 Lake George Road, Seville, FL 32190, 386/749-2818.

Chapter 7

Ocala Area

Ocala Area

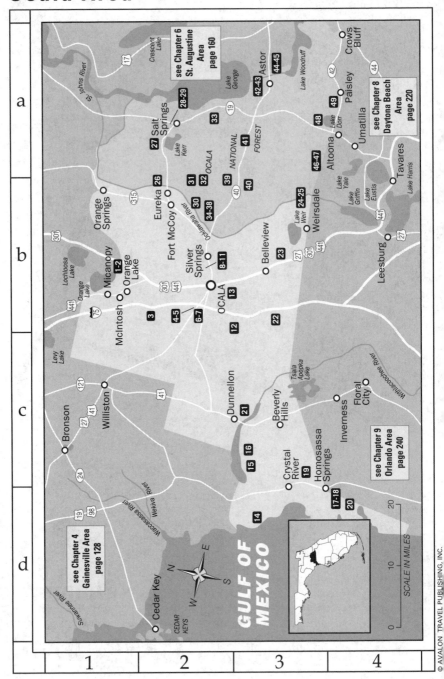

Crescent Lake
St. Johns River
17
see Chapter 6 St. Augustine Area page 160
28-29
Salt Springs
27
Lake Kerr
26
315
Eureka
Orange Springs
301
Lochloosa Lake
Micanopy
1-2
Orange Lake
McIntosh
75
301
441
Silver Springs
8-11
OCALA
13
3
4-5
6-7
12
Levy Lake
121
Williston
41
Bronson
27 41
24
19 98
see Chapter 4 Gainesville Area page 128
Wacasassa River
Waccasassa River
19
Cedar Key
CEDAR KEYS
Lake George
42-43 Astor
44-45
Lake Woodruff
19
33
OCALA
41 FOREST
NATIONAL
31 32 39
40 40
34-38
Fort McCoy
Ocklawaha River
30
Belleview
23
Lake Weir
24-25
Weirsdale
441
301
22
Dunnellon
21
Beverly Hills
Crystal River
15 16
19
Homosassa Springs
17-18 20
14
Tsala Apopka Lake
Floral City
Inverness
Withlacoochee River
see Chapter 9 Orlando Area page 240
GULF OF MEXICO
Crows Bluff
42
Paisley
44
49
48
Umatilla
Altoona
46-47
Lake Yale
Lake Griffin
Lake Eustis
Tavares
Lake Harris
441
Leesburg
27
see Chapter 8 Daytona Beach Area page 220
Lake Dorr
N E W S
SCALE IN MILES
20
10
0

© AVALON TRAVEL PUBLISHING, INC.

1 SPORTSMAN'S COVE ON ORANGE LAKE

Rating: 4

At Orange Lake in McIntosh

Ocala map, grid b1, page 192

As the name suggests, anglers use this campground as a crash pad after a day of snagging panfish and bass at Orange Lake and Lake Lochloosa. But it's convenient to the interstate for overnighters, and a good base camp for visiting Gainesville or Silver Springs. Oak trees and lake views are the reward for staying here, as well as the quiet. Instead of a monotonous blue sea that stretches hypnotically to the horizon, this scene is broken up by islands—Redbird Island is up ahead, and to the right are Hixon, Bird, and McCormick Islands. The lake levels on this side are very low these days, so the facility's boating amenities may not be available when you visit, but public boat ramps are nearby to reach deeper waters. In this retiree-oriented community of grassy canalside campsites, wintertime activities keep campers entertained.

Campsites, facilities: All 49 full-hookup campsites are for RVs or tents. Cabins, cable TV, showers, restrooms, a dump station, a boat ramp, boat slips, a recreation room, and laundry facilities are available. Children are welcome. Leashed pets are permitted but must use the dog walk on the park's east side.

Reservations, fees: Reservations are recommended. Sites are $15 per night for four people, plus $1.50 for each additional person. Long-term rates are available. Credit cards are not accepted.

Directions: From I-75 at Exit 368, take County Road 318 east for two miles to U.S. 441. Turn left. Continue three more miles north, passing State Road 320, and turn right at Avenue F, which is the second blinking light. The campground entrance is ahead.

Contact: Sportsman's Cove on Orange Lake, 5423 Avenue F, McIntosh, FL 32664, 352/591-1435, website: www.sportsman-cove.net.

2 GRAND LAKE RV & GOLF RESORT

Rating: 8

On Orange Lake in the town of Orange Lake

Ocala map, grid b1, page 192

A nine-hole championship golf course greets RVers as they drive into this super-manicured resort, which sprawls on a hill overlooking Orange Lake. If golf isn't your game, you'll find world-class bass fishing in the lake and three separate gathering places for socializing; parimutuel betting is available at the jai alai fronton (arena) next door. Shade is minimal in most of the park, but some sites have panoramic views of the lake. Be careful with children around the lake; they are not allowed near it because of alligators.

Campsites, facilities: These 239 full-hookup RV sites overlook Orange Lake. A nine-hole golf course, a driving range, a pool, a clubhouse, a TV room, shuffleboard, exercise trails, golf lessons, and fishing lessons entertain campers. Showers, restrooms, a dump station, a boat dock, a pier, a barbecue pit, park models, and laundry facilities are available. All areas are wheelchair accessible. Children must be adult-supervised when at the pool, fishing, or near the pier. Leashed pets must walk in the open field or on the edge of the road.

Reservations, fees: Reservations are recommended. Sites are $36 per night. Major credit cards are accepted. Long-term rates are available.

Directions: From I-75 at Exit 368, take County Road 318 east for about two miles, crossing U.S. 441. Turn left (north) on the road next to Ocala Jai Alai to get to the campground.

Contact: Grand Lake RV & Golf Resort, P.O. Box 370/4555 West Highway 318, Orange Lake, FL 32681, 352/591-3474 or 800/435-2291, website: www.grandlakeresort.com.

3 ENCORE RV PARK—OCALA

Rating: 10

Off I-75 between Gainesville and Ocala

Ocala map, grid b2, page 192

Set amid the sprawling ranches of horse country, this immaculate RV resort with a heated
pool is surprisingly wooded and parklike.
Paved roads wind past concrete-pad campsites with patios. Many campers stay for the
season, but the park's location near the interstate makes it a good option for overnight
travelers as well. The pool is an impressive
sight for a campground swimming hole: The
blue waters and encircling patio are surrounded
by towering moss-draped oaks that provide
some shade. Within a short drive is Orange
Lake, famed for bass fishing, and the historic
towns of McIntosh and Micanopy, which have
quaint antique shops. Supermarkets and restaurants are nearby. Planned activities include
tai chi, aerobics, and fishing outings, plus the
usual array of card games, potlucks, movies,
and so forth.

Campsites, facilities: There are 140 full-hookup
RV sites (45 pull-through). A pool, horseshoes,
shuffleboard, showers, restrooms, a dump station, firewood, cable TV, telephone hookups,
laundry facilities, and two recreation halls
with kitchens are available. Children are welcome. Leashed pets are permitted, but they
must use the wooded dog walk on the park's
east side.

Reservations, fees: Reservations are recommended. Sites are $28 per night. Major cred-
it cards are accepted. Long-term rates are
available.

Directions: From I-75 at Exit 368, turn west
onto County Road 318. Go 200 yards, turn left
(south) on Highway 225, and continue .5 mile
to the entrance on the left.

Contact: Encore RV Park—Ocala, 16905 Northwest Highway 225, Reddick, FL 32686, 352/591-
1723 or 877/267-8737, fax 352/591-2842, website:
www.rvonthego.com.

4 OAK TREE VILLAGE CAMPGROUND

Rating: 5

West of Ocala

Ocala map, grid b2, page 192

This park, a quick hop off I-75, feels almost
like a subdivision, albeit a tree-shaded one.
Row after row, street after street, campers are
lined up 14 abreast, all parked diagonally on
paved, 10 mph streets that are straight as ar-
rows. When the pool is crowded, floats and
tubes are forbidden. Most campsites at the 40-
acre park are shaded (hence the park's name).
Campsites 7 through 14 are closest to the laundry facilities, pool, and playground. Sites 104
and 105 flank the showers. Anglers, hikers,
mountain bikers, and hunters can head about
15 miles east to Ocala National Forest. For a
joyride, head west from the campground on
U.S. 27. In about one mile you'll begin to see
would-be champion horses grazing on the pretty rolling hills of some of the area's fabled horse
farms. Double Diamond Farm is one of several in the region that permits visitors (from
1 P.M. to 4 P.M. weekdays); call 352/237-3834.

Campsites, facilities: There are 137 pull-through
RV sites (70 with full hookups), plus 20 tent
campsites situated along the back two rows of
the park. A pool, a playground, horseshoes,
shuffleboard, racquetball, a party room, tennis, and winter social programs entertain
campers. Showers, restrooms, picnic tables, a
dump station, and laundry facilities are available. Management says restrooms and the recreation room are wheelchair accessible. Groceries
are within one mile, and a restaurant is .25
mile away. Children under 12 must be adult-
supervised at the pool and recreation area. All
pets—even cats—must be leashed.

Reservations, fees: Reservations are not necessary. Sites are $15.50 to $18 per night for
two people, plus $1.75 for each additional per-
son. Major credit cards are accepted. Long-
term stays are OK.

Directions: From I-75 at Ocala, take Exit 354 onto U.S. 27 heading west and turn right almost immediately at Blitchton Road. Proceed .25 mile to the campground.

Contact: Oak Tree Village Campground, 4039 Northwest Blitchton Road, Ocala, FL 34482, 352/629-1569.

5 ARROWHEAD CAMPSITES AND MOBILE HOME PARK

Rating: 4

West of Ocala

Ocala map, grid b2, page 192

This campground is a quick detour from I-75 for weary travelers on the road to Disney, but the park really prefers long-term, budget-conscious vacationers to rent their mobile home lots. The pretty rolling hills of horse farms are as close as one mile west on U.S. 27, and certainly the park borrows from that ambience in describing itself as "an oasis of quiet luxury . . . picturesque."

Campsites, facilities: Most of the 130 RV sites have full hookups; a separate tent section offers six spots with water, electricity, and cable TV. A pool, a playground, an exercise room, new laundry facilities, horseshoes, shuffleboard, a recreation room, a camp circle, and a wintertime activity schedule entertain campers. Showers, restrooms, firewood, cable TV, and laundry facilities are available. Groceries and a restaurant are within 300 feet. Children are permitted. Leashed pets are accepted.

Reservations, fees: Reservations are recommended in winter. Nightly fee for two people in an RV is $16 to $18. Add $1 per extra person and $1.75 for using air-conditioning or heaters. Tent sites are $10. Major credit cards are accepted. Long-term rates are available.

Directions: From I-75 at Ocala, take Exit 354 onto U.S. 27 heading west, then turn left onto Northwest 38th Avenue. The campground is 250 feet ahead.

Contact: Arrowhead Campsites and Mobile

Home Park, 1720 Northwest 38th Avenue, Ocala, FL 34482, 352/622-5627, website: www.arrowheadcampsites.com.

6 HOLIDAY TRAV-L-PARK

Rating: 4

Off I-75 in Ocala

Ocala map, grid b2, page 192

Snowbirds fleeing blustery northern temperatures like to park rigs up to 65 feet long at this 9.5-acre campground. They spend many a winter hour engaged in park activities such as bingo, suppers, and group barbecues. Row after row, 12 to 13 campers are parked diagonally along ruler-straight streets. Oaks shade some grassy/sandy sites, but others are sunny.

For a pleasant ride, go west along the rolling terrain of U.S. 27 to pass would-be champion thoroughbreds at some of the region's horse farms. To watch equestrian training activity at Ocala Breeders' Sales Company and Training Center, show up before 10 A.M.; call 352/237-2154. Even though some anglers, hikers, mountain bikers, and seasonal hunters come here to be just 20 miles from Ocala National Forest, perhaps the best reason to sleep in Ocala is the bread pudding and meatloaf served at the city's top restaurant, Carmichael's, located nearby at 3105 Northeast Silver Springs Boulevard.

Campsites, facilities: Five tent sites and 104 pull-through RV sites (all with full hookups) are available. A pool, a playground, a horseshoe pit, shuffleboard, a recreation room, and winter activities entertain campers. Showers, restrooms, picnic tables, a dump station, limited groceries, cable TV, telephone hookups, and laundry facilities are available. A restaurant is within walking distance. All areas of the park are wheelchair accessible. Children must be accompanied by an adult at the pool. Leashed pets should use the dog walk at the park's eastern border.

Reservations, fees: Reservations are recommended, particularly in winter. Sites are $24 per night for two people, plus $2 for each additional person and $2 for air-conditioning. Major credit cards are accepted. Long-term rates are available.

Directions: From I-75 at Exit 352, take State Road 40 west .5 mile to the park on the right.

Contact: Holiday Trav-L-Park, 4001 West Silver Springs Boulevard, Ocala, FL 34482, 352/622-5330 or 800/833-2164.

7 MOTOR INNS MOTEL AND RV PARK

Rating: 2

Off I-75 in Ocala
Ocala map, grid b2, page 192

Convenience is the main attraction here. RVs are somewhat hemmed in, with a handful of mobile homes to the north and two motel buildings and a fruit stand to the south. I-75, which leads vacationers to Disney World, Tampa, or even Michigan, is just one block west. A paved road with a 10 mph speed limit passes the partially shaded campsites.

Campsites, facilities: Most of these 104 RV sites have full hookups, and the rest have water and electricity. A pool, showers, restrooms, a dump station, and laundry facilities are available. Kids must be supervised at all times. Small, leashed animals are permitted, but pooches must use the park's dog walk.

Reservations, fees: Reservations are recommended, particularly in winter. Sites are $17 to $19 per night. Major credit cards are accepted. Long-term rates are available.

Directions: From I-75 at Exit 352, take State Road 40 east for one block to the campground.

Contact: Motor Inns Motel and RV Park, 3601 West Silver Springs Boulevard, Ocala, FL 34475, 352/629-6902.

8 THE SPRINGS RV RESORT

Rating: 5

Near the Silver Springs nature theme park in Silver Springs
Ocala map, grid b2, page 192

Although you certainly may lounge around the sunny Olympic-sized pool or in the 17,000-square-foot clubhouse, at least some campers prefer spending daylight hours three blocks away at Silver Springs, a 350-acre nature theme park with animal shows and picnic areas (see next campground). Also within blocks of here is Wild Waters, a six-acre water park. The 52-acre campground bills itself as "the land of sunshine." Stay at one of these open, unshaded concrete-pad and grassy sites and you'll probably agree, particularly in summer.

Campsites, facilities: All 618 pull-through RV sites have full hookups. For recreation, there's a pool, horseshoes, tennis, shuffleboard, social programs, a wheelchair-accessible clubhouse, a card room, and a pool room. Showers, restrooms, some cable TV hookups, some telephone hookups, and laundry facilities are available. Restaurants are located within blocks of here. Children are welcome. You must walk leashed pets outside of the park.

Reservations, fees: Reservations are recommended. Sites are $22 per night for two people, plus $2.50 for each additional person. Major credit cards are accepted. Long-term stays are OK.

Directions: From I-75 at Exit 352, take State Road 40 east for about eight miles to 52nd Court. Turn left. The campground is ahead.

Contact: The Springs RV Resort, 2950 Northeast 52nd Court, Silver Springs, FL 34488, 352/236-5250, website: www.rvresorts.com.

9 SILVER SPRINGS CAMPERS GARDEN

Rating: 5

Opposite the Silver Springs theme park in Silver Springs

Ocala map, grid b2, page 192

Tarzan swung through this neighborhood long ago. Actually, it was actor Johnny Weissmuller shooting the 1939 film *Tarzan Finds a Son* across the street at the 780-square-foot cavern of Silver Springs—Florida's original tourist attraction. Henry Ford, Thomas Edison, and thousands of others have visited the theme park, which today offers glass-bottomed boats, animals from six continents, a petting zoo, and picnic areas on its 350 acres. Also across the street is Wild Waters, a six-acre water park.

The bent branches of deep-furled oaks help shade some campsites at the 15.5-acre campground, but others are sunny and open. Just downstream at Silver River State Park, a hiking trail winds beneath fan-leafed sabal palms and shiny-leaved magnolias. If you go, look for otters in early morning along the Silver River, reached via the trail. Anglers, hikers, mountain bikers, and seasonal hunters can drive a short distance east from the campground to Ocala National Forest.

Campsites, facilities: Ten tent sites are set apart from the 191 full-hookup RV sites (pull-through). A pool, a playground, a horseshoe pit, a shuffleboard court, a wintertime activity schedule, and a wheelchair-accessible clubhouse entertain campers. Showers, restrooms, a dump station, picnic tables, cable TV, telephone hookups, and laundry facilities are available. All areas of the park are wheelchair accessible. A restaurant is located next door, and groceries are within two blocks. Children are welcome, but not for long-term stays. Leashed pets are permitted.

Reservations, fees: Reservations are recommended in winter. Sites are $23 per night for two people, plus $1.50 for each additional person and $2 for cable TV or when using air conditioners or heaters. Credit cards are not accepted. Long-term rates are available.

Directions: From I-75 at Exit 352, take State Road 40 east for about eight miles. The campground is opposite the Silver Springs nature theme park.

Contact: Silver Springs Campers Garden, 3151 Northeast 56th Avenue, Silver Springs, FL 34488, 352/236-3700 or 800/640-3733, website: www.campersgarden.com.

10 SILVER RIVER STATE PARK

Rating: 10

East of Ocala and south of Silver Springs

Ocala map, grid b3, page 192

Wow! A brand-new addition to Florida's award-winning state park system is here, and it's amazing. Dozens of springs, 14 distinct plant communities, and 10 miles of river frontage dot these 5,000 breathtaking acres. "People rave about this place," says one of the park rangers. Canoe on the Silver River; there are two launching points. One is outside the park at the foot of the Ocklawaha Bridge on State Road 40; the other is in the park at the end of the River Trail (you'll have to portage your canoe .6 mile from the parking lot). The state is still making improvements to the park, so check the website for the latest information.

Campsites, facilities: There are 59 RV and tent sites with picnic tables, water and electricity, and fire rings. Big rigs are welcome and six sites have 50-amp electrical services. Restrooms, showers, a dump station, laundry facilities, and cabin rentals are available. Children are welcome. Leashed pets are permitted.

Reservations, fees: Reservations are recommended; call ReserveAmerica at 800/326-3521. Sites are $15 per night for four people, plus $2 per extra person, $2 for electricity, and $2 for pets. Major credit cards are accepted.

Directions: From the intersection of State Road 40 and State Road 35 in Silver Springs, drive south on State Road 35 one mile.

Contact: Silver River State Park, 1425 Northeast 58th Avenue, Ocala, FL 34470, 352/236-7148, website: www.floridastateparks.org.

11 OCKLAWAHA PRAIRIE RESTORATION AREA

🏃 🚴 🛶 🐕 ⛺

Rating: 6

South of Silver Springs
Ocala map, grid b3, page 192

These 6,077 acres opened to the public when the St. Johns River Water Management District acquired the land for purposes of restoring the Upper Ocklawaha River Basin. Previously a farm, the homestead and structures have been restored as an ecotourism retreat and renamed as The Refuge at Ocklawaha. Local astronomy clubs sometimes gather here to take advantage of the dark skies overhead. Canoes and cabins are for rent at The Refuge.

For the adventurous, though, the area has appeal for mountain biking, backpacking, canoeing, and horseback riding. The Kyle Young Canal (C-212) is the man-made leg of the Ocklawaha River, and its restoration is intended to restore the surrounding flood plain. Canoeists can paddle the canal or the Ocklawaha River Channel to the west; the more natural channel rejoins the canal at the southeastern end of the property. A boat ramp is at Moss Bluff near the intersection of Country Road 464C and County Road 314A. About six miles of trails are available for biking and hiking.

Campsites, facilities: There are two primitive campsites. One is a short hike northward from The Refuge parking lot. The other is in the southern section of the area called the Chernobyl Memorial Forest. Tents only are permitted. There are no facilities; bring water, supplies, mosquito repellent, and everything you'll need. Children are welcome. Leashed pets are permitted.

Reservations, fees: Sites are first-come, first-served. Camping is free. Each site accommodates up to six people. If your party has at least seven people, get a free permit and reserve at least one week ahead at 386/329-4410. Maximum stay for all campers is seven days.

Directions: From Ocala, drive south on State Road 40 six miles to County Road 314A. Turn north on 137th Avenue/Old River Road and drive a short distance to The Refuge. For access to the Chernobyl Memorial Forest area, turn south on Country Road 314A and turn right on County Road 464C about two miles to the parking area.

Contact: St. Johns River Water Management District, Division of Land Management, P.O. Box 1429, Palatka, FL 32178-1429, 386/329-4500 or 800/451-7106, website: www.sjrwmd.com. For information about The Refuge at Ocklawaha, write to 14835 South East 85th Street, Ocklawaha, FL 32179; or call 352/288-2233.

12 OCALA/SILVER SPRINGS KOA

🏊 🏠 🏕 🚐 ⛺

Rating: 7

Off I-75 south of Ocala
Ocala map, grid c3, page 192

Ducks flapping their wings at the two park ponds and the graceful springtime sight of blooming magnolias lend atmosphere to this 20-acre wooded retreat just off I-75. The oak- and magnolia-shaded grassy/sandy campsites tend to fill up pretty quickly in winter, so call ahead. Like other KOAs, the attraction for couples and families is plunging into the pool or heading to the game room after a long day of interstate driving or taking in area attractions. The Silver Springs nature theme park is less than one-half hour east. Ocala National Forest is farther east. For a joyride, head west on U.S. 27 to pass would-be champion horses grazing on the rolling hills of some of the region's many noted horse farms.

Campsites, facilities: Most of the 140 RV sites have full hookups, including telephone availability. They are set apart from 15 tent sites. Each site has a picnic table. For recreation, there's a pool, a hot tub, a sauna, a kiddie pool, a game room, a playground, a TV lounge, a horseshoe pit, a shuffleboard court, a volleyball net, a recreation room, a basketball court, and wintertime social activities. Facilities include showers, restrooms, a convenience store, a dump station, cabins, cable TV, and a laundry room. Twenty-five restaurants are within two miles. Children are welcome. Leashed pets are permitted.

Reservations, fees: Reservations are recommended. Sites are $30 to $39 per night for two people. Add $6 for each additional adult, $4 per extra child age four and older. Major credit cards are accepted. Long-term stays are OK.
Directions: From I-75 at Exit 350, take State Road 200 west to 38th Avenue. Turn right. The campground is .5 mile ahead at left, next to the Disney Information Center.
Contact: Ocala/Silver Springs KOA, 3200 Southwest 38th Avenue, Ocala, FL 34474, 352/237-2138 or 800/562-7798, fax 352/237-9894.

13 CAMPER VILLAGE OF AMERICA

Rating: 3

Off I-75 south of Ocala
Ocala map, grid c3, page 192
With four shopping plazas, a mall, and two movie theaters within one mile of here, you have all the comforts of home. Still, to the other side of the campground, horse farms dominate. This adult-oriented, family-run campground aims to create a small-town, familiar feel by scheduling numerous wintertime activities, including dancing, musical performances, bus trips to nearby attractions, and potluck dinners. Each morning, free coffee is brewed at the office of this lighted park with paved roads. There's not a lot of landscaping, so campsites tend to be open and sunny.
Campsites, facilities: The park offers 250 full-hookup RV sites (several pull-through). About 150 sites are filled by park models or permanent residents. For recreation, there are

shuffleboard courts, horseshoe pits, winter activities, and a 400-person-capacity recreation hall. Showers, restrooms, a dump station, telephone hookups, laundry facilities, and free cable TV are available. Within one mile you'll find four supermarkets, a hospital, and nearly 40 restaurants. The recreation hall, restrooms, and office are wheelchair accessible. Children are permitted for short stays. Leashed pets are accepted.

Reservations, fees: Reservations are recommended in winter. Sites are $20 per night for two people, plus $1.50 per additional person. Use of air conditioners or electric heaters costs $1.75 each night. Credit cards are not accepted. Long-term stays are OK.
Directions: From I-75 at Exit 350, take State Road 200 west for 1,000 feet to the campground.
Contact: Camper Village of America, 3931 Southwest College Road, Ocala, FL 34474, 352/237-3236, email: campervill@aol.com.

14 ENCORE SUPERPARK— CRYSTAL RIVER (FORMERLY CRYSTAL ISLES RV RESORT)

Rating: 10

West of Crystal River
Ocala map, grid d3, page 192
Located on a canal with access to the Crystal River, this resort offers lots to do, including fishing, boating, social activities, sports, and even tennis. But the location makes it ideal as a base camp for those who want to explore local sights. Manatees are a top tourist draw, with several local tours offering trips to see the 200 lumbering sea cows that spend their winters in the spring-fed, 72-degree waters of the Crystal River. Spectacular diving springs, famous around the world for their purity and clarity, are within four miles. King Spring, near the Plantation Inn and Golf Resort (352/795-4211) down the road from the RV resort, is 75 feet across and drops 30 feet to a cavern. If you didn't bring your diving gear, you can rent

snorkel or scuba equipment from many local dive shops.

Campsites, facilities: This 30-acre RV resort has 250 full-hookup sites (six pull-through) with cable TV. Restrooms, showers, picnic tables, grills, fire rings, laundry facilities, a heated pool, a hot tub, a dump station, a recreation room, a playground, horseshoes, shuffleboard, tennis, basketball, volleyball, a boat ramp, boat docks, fishing lake, and a store are on the premises. Children and leashed pets are welcome.

Reservations, fees: Reservations are recommended. Sites are $28 to $32 per night. Major credit cards are accepted. Long-term stays are OK.

Directions: From U.S. 19 in Crystal River, drive four miles west on State Road 44/Fort Island Trail to the park, at right.

Contact: Encore SuperPark—Crystal River, 11419 West Fort Island Trail, Crystal River, FL 34429, 352/795-3774 or 888/783-6763, fax 352/795-4897, website: www.rvonthego.com.

15 QUAIL ROOST RV CAMPGROUND

Rating: 4

North of Crystal River
Ocala map, grid c3, page 192

For the retired snowbird who likes conveniences in a more natural setting, this well-maintained park may fit the bill: Some sites are set under trees, and some are out in the open. The main roads are paved. Social programs in the winter include bingo, cards, games, campfires, dinners, and Sunday breakfasts prepared and served by the owners. Pick up major supplies in Crystal River or Dunnellon, both 7.5 miles away.

Campsites, facilities: This adults-preferred park has 72 full-hookup sites with telephone and cable TV access. Half are pull-throughs and can accommodate the largest RVs, even triple slide-outs. Swim in the heated pool. Restrooms, showers, laundry facilities, picnic tables, shuffleboard, horseshoes, bocce ball, basketball, a

pool table, wintertime social programs, and a recreation room are available. Two restaurants are within walking distance. There are no facilities for children. No dogs are allowed from November through April.

Reservations, fees: Reservations are recommended. Sites are $25 per night for two people, plus $1 for each additional person. Credit cards are not accepted. Long-term stays are allowed.

Directions: In downtown Crystal River, from the intersection of U.S. 19 and County Road 495, drive northwest on the county road for 7.5 miles to the park, at right.

Contact: Quail Roost RV Campground, 9835 North Citrus Avenue, Crystal River, FL 34428, 352/563-0404, website: www.quailroostcampground.com.

16 LAKE ROUSSEAU RV PARK

Rating: 6

Between Crystal River and Dunnellon
Ocala map, grid c3, page 192

Bass fishing is primo on Lake Rousseau, but land-bound campers will also enjoy views of its sparkling waters. Nestled amid oaks draped with Spanish moss, the campground is home to a mix of year-round residents in mobile homes, travelers in all manner of rigs, and anglers. Some sites are on the water; you may share your bit of lakefront with the ducks. The park is out in the countryside but not prohibitively far from attractions such as Homosassa Springs State Wildlife Park, golf courses, beaches, Silver Springs, and Weeki Wachee Spring.

Campsites, facilities: Pitch your tent or park your RV on one of 122 grassy sites with full hookups, including telephone availability and cable TV. About 20 sites are available for overnighters, and 60 for seasonal visitors. Restrooms, showers, laundry facilities, picnic tables, a pool, a recreation room with planned activities during the winter season, boat docks, a boat ramp, boat rentals, rental trailers, a store, LP gas, and horseshoes are on site. The restrooms and recreation hall are wheelchair accessible. Children and leashed pets (no attack dogs) are welcome.

Reservations, fees: Reservations are recommended. Sites are $27 per night. Boat launches are free for campers. Boat dockage is available for an extra charge. Major credit cards are accepted. Long-term rates are available.

Directions: From the town of Crystal River, drive north on U.S. 19 for six miles. Turn east on State Road 488 and continue four miles. Turn north on Northcut Avenue (watch for the campground sign) and proceed 1.3 miles until the road dead-ends at the campground. From Dunnellon, at the intersection of U.S. 41 and State Road 488, drive five miles west on State Road 488 to Northcut Avenue and proceed as above.

Contact: Lake Rousseau RV Park, 10811 North Coveview Terrace, Crystal River, FL 34428, 352/795-6336, fax 352/564-4287, website: www.lakerousseaurvpark.com.

17 CAMP 'N' WATER OUTDOOR RESORT

Rating: 7

South of Homosassa Springs

Ocala map, grid d4, page 192

Secluded but not isolated, this 13-acre, well-shaded park is on the banks of the Homosassa River. The resort is oriented to boaters as well as campers: There are 28 boat slips in the marina, and the fishing grounds of the Gulf of Mexico are just five miles away. Anglers from all over the world flock to the Crystal River area for sportfishing. Sea trout and redfish are plentiful in nearshore waters, and the magnificent silver tarpon is abundant farther out. Don't miss a visit to nearby Homosassa Springs State Wildlife Park (352/628-2311), where you can see a manatee up close. The park, previously a private zoo and tourist attraction, is a rehabilitation center for manatees who were orphaned or injured in the wild

and for those born in captivity. It claims to be the only center in the world where you can view these gentle creatures every day of the year. An underwater observatory lets visitors observe them eye to eye. You can also see wood ducks, flamingos, birds of prey, herons, and egrets on the grounds. Alligators, snakes, hippopotamuses, black bears, white-tailed deer, and river otters are among the other residents.

Campsites, facilities: There are 81 RV sites with full hookups and cable TV; some have telephone access. Restrooms, showers, picnic tables, grills, a dump station, laundry facilities, a dining area, rental cabins, and an adult TV room are available. You'll also find a playground, a pool, basketball and shuffleboard courts, horseshoes, a boat ramp, a fish cleaning station, cabin rentals, and a marina. The bathrooms and clubhouse are wheelchair accessible. A supermarket is five miles away. Children and leashed pets are welcome.

Reservations, fees: Reservations are advised. Sites are $24 per night for four people, plus $2.50 for each additional person up to a party of six. Major credit cards are accepted. Maximum stay is six months.

Directions: From Crystal River, drive south on U.S. 19 for 7.3 miles to County Road 490A/West Halls River Road and turn west. Drive .5 mile, turn south (left) on Fishbowl Drive, and follow to Mason Creek Road. Turn left. Go one mile to Garcia Road, turn right onto Garcia. Continue .25 mile to Priest Lane. Turn right, and follow signs to the park.

Contact: Camp 'N' Water Outdoor Resort, 11465 West Priest Lane, Homosassa, FL 34448, 352/628-2000, fax 352/628-0066, email: campnwater@mindspring.com.

18 TURTLE CREEK RV RESORT

Rating: 7

South of Homosassa Springs

Ocala map, grid d4, page 192

You can cast your line into Turtle Creek from

the bank of this campground, but the wintertime action tends to take place indoors. Planned seasonal activities run the gamut, from ladies' luncheons, holiday dinners, and potluck feasts to crafts, exercise classes, card tournaments, and boat tours. There's even a bowling league, plus line dancing and country music shows performed by campers (bring your instrument). A short distance upriver is the Homosassa Springs State Wildlife Park (described in previous campground); six miles downriver is the Gulf of Mexico. Sites are oversized, big enough for large RVs. Folks are friendly; a nice widow brought us home-baked cookies one night.

Campsites, facilities: All 225 sites have full hookups, cable TV, and picnic tables. Restrooms, showers, laundry facilities, a dump station, a pool, a recreation pavilion, pool tables, fishing from the bank, horseshoes, shuffleboards, and rental units are available. The restrooms, office, recreation hall, and laundry are wheelchair accessible. Children are welcome. Leashed pets are permitted.

Reservations, fees: Reservations are recommended. Sites are $24 per night for two people, plus $2 per additional adult and $2 for children. Major credit cards are accepted. Long-term stays are OK.

Directions: From Crystal River, drive south on U.S. 19 for 7.3 miles to County Road 490A/West Halls River Road and turn west. Drive .5 mile to Fishbowl Drive, turn south, and go 1.5 miles.

Contact: Turtle Creek Campground, 10200 West Fishbowl Drive, Homosassa Springs, FL 34448, 352/628-2928 or 800/471-3722, fax 352/628-6964, email: turtlecreek@gowebco.com.

19 ROCK CRUSHER CANYON RV AND MUSIC PARK

🚶 ≋ 🏕 🚐 ⛺

Rating: 10

East of Crystal River
Ocala map, grid c3, page 192

Want to see headline artists like Willie Nelson, Hootie and the Blowfish, Pat Boone, the Oak Ridge Boys, Three Dog Night, or Faith Hill? This brand-new, 60-acre RV park is part campground, part concert venue. There's live entertainment every weekend in a garden pavilion, plus outdoor concerts in an amphitheater that seats 7,000. For show information, call 352/795-1313, website: www .rockcrushercanyon.com. However, the RV park itself has much to recommend, set in a wooded area not far from the Withlacoochee State Forest. Rallies and caravans are welcome. The park was opened in 2001, and the grounds are kept immaculate, even to the point of reseeding the RV sites when the grass gets eroded. Don't worry about noise from the concerts; they are usually over by 10 P.M.

Campsites, facilities: There are 398 full-hookup RV sites with 50-amp electrical service, cable TV, instant phone service, and grassy pads. Sites are wooded. Twenty tent sites with water and electricity are also available. Restrooms, showers, laundry facilities, a heated pool, a Jacuzzi, fitness station, a restaurant, and recreation hall are provided. The concert area is set apart from the RV park. Children are welcome. Leashed pets are permitted.

Reservations, fees: Reservations are recommended. Sites are $35 per night for two people, plus $2 per extra person. Major credit cards are accepted. Long-term rates are available.

Directions: In Crystal River, from State Road 44 and U.S. 19, drive south on U.S. 19 about two miles to the Home Depot and intersection with Venable Road. Turn left on Venable Road and go west about 3.5 miles. At Rock Crusher Road, turn south and drive .5 mile to the park.

Contact: Rock Crusher Canyon RV and Music Park, 275 South Rock Crusher Road, Crystal River, FL 34429, 352/795-3870, website: www .rccrvpark.com.

20 CHASSAHOWITZKA RIVER CAMPGROUND AND RECREATION AREA

Rating: 8

South of Homosassa Springs
Ocala map, grid d4, page 192

The shady campground gets hard use during holidays and weekends, but the location can't be beat and it's well worth a visit. Campers can launch their boats or canoes from the boat ramp near Chassahowitzka Spring. The waterway flows southwest to the Gulf of Mexico, with dozens of creeks and crystal-clear springs offering tempting side trips along the way. Be sure to rinse your boat motor and trailer thoroughly afterward to remove all weed fragments and to prevent the spread of weeds to other bodies of water. Canoes and small flat-bottomed boats can be rented at the campground. Nearby is the Chassahowitzka National Wildlife Refuge, a swampy coastal area that's popular among area anglers for both freshwater and saltwater fishing.

Campsites, facilities: There are 88 campsites for RVs, tents, and pop-up campers in this county-run campground; 40 have full hookups, 16 have electricity and water only, and the rest are primitive. Restrooms, showers, laundry facilities, a camp store, and a boat ramp are available. Canoes and johnboats are for rent. Alcoholic beverages are prohibited. Children are welcome. Leashed pets are permitted with proof of rabies vaccination.

Reservations, fees: Reservations are required for full hookup sites, but not for the primitive sites. Sites are $14 to $18 per night for two people, plus $2 for each additional person above age six. Credit cards are not accepted. Maximum stay is six months.

Directions: From the intersection of U.S. 19 and County Road 480 south of Homosassa Springs and Crystal River, drive west on County Road 480/Miss Maggie Drive for 1.7 miles until the road ends at the campground.

Contact: Chassahowitzka River Campground and Recreation Area, 8600 West Miss Maggie Drive, Homosassa, FL 34448, 352/382-2200. Citrus County Parks and Recreation Office, P.O. Box 1439, Crystal River, FL 34423-1439, 352/795-2202.

21 RAINBOW SPRINGS STATE PARK

Rating: 9

Near Dunnellon
Ocala map, grid c3, page 192

The campground is divided into two areas: A heavily wooded loop near the picturesque Rainbow River and a sprawling barren field without trees near the office. The river sites are so superior to the others that you may think you're in two different parks. But if you don't make it into the wooded section, the proximity to the river may help you endure the field camp. You can rent canoes and inner tubes to drift downstream; note that there is no shuttle service to bring you back to the campground. Strap on a snorkel mask and explore the crystalline waters near the swimming area in the campground. Rainbow Springs is the state's third largest spring, pumping 600 million gallons of sparkling water a day. The surroundings are so breathtaking that a hotel was built near the spring in the 1890s. In the 1930s, private developers made it a tourist attraction that operated for four decades. The state, in conjunction with the Marion County parks department, acquired the park in 1989, and later acquired the previously privately operated campground (ergo, the swimming pool). Today, the main part of the park has azalea gardens, an amphitheater, and picnic grounds that are popular for group events. Avoid holidays, when the park gets crowded.

Campsites, facilities: These 105 RV and tent sites have water and electricity; 40 have sewer hookups. Restrooms, showers, picnic tables, fire rings, laundry facilities, a dump station, a playground, a pool, canoe rentals, and a recreation hall are provided. Also for rent are inner tubes and diver-down flags; however, shuttle service is not provided for those who float too far down the river. The restrooms and store are wheelchair accessible. Children are welcome. Pets are permitted in the campground with proof of vaccination.

Reservations, fees: Reservations are recommended; call ReserveAmerica at 800/326-3521. Sites are $13 to $15 per night for four people, plus $3 for each additional person, $2 for electricity, $2 for sewer, and $2 for each pet. No more than eight people are permitted per site. Credit cards are accepted. Stays are limited to 120 days between October 1 and March 31; from April through September, you may stay only two weeks.

Directions: From I-75 south of Ocala, take Exit 341 onto State Road 484 west for 19 miles. At Southwest 180th Avenue Street (west of the airport), turn north. Drive 2.5 miles to the entrance, on the west side.

Contact: Rainbow Springs State Park, 18185 Southwest 94th Street, Dunnellon, FL 34432, 352/489-5201, fax 352/465-7209.

22 OCALA RANCH RV PARK (FORMERLY WATER WHEEL RV PARK)

Rating: 3

Off I-75 south of Ocala
Ocala map, grid b3, page 192

Winter-long campers and year-round residents are targeted by this park, although some of the grassy, sunny sites are set aside for overnighters. The 33-acre park has become a year-round resort community, with live concerts, entertainment, and seasonal activities geared to an active retiree clientele. Many overnighters stay once and then come back for monthly stays. Shopping and restaurants are nearby.

Campsites, facilities: Among the 160 RV sites, 60 are pull-through. All have full hookups and

telephone availability. Each has a picnic table. A modem is offered in the recreation hall. Facilities include a heated pool, a spa, walking paths, and a community center building. Showers, restrooms, and laundry facilities are available. Most areas are wheelchair accessible. Children are welcome, but most visitors tend to be retirees. Pet restrictions apply.

Reservations, fees: Reservations are recommended. Sites are $25 per night for two people, plus $2 for each additional person. Major credit cards are accepted. Long-term stays are OK.

Directions: From I-75 at Exit 341, take County Road 484 west for .5 mile to the park on the right.

Contact: Ocala Ranch RV Park, 2559 Southwest Highway 484, Ocala, FL 34473, 352/347-4008 or 877/809-1100.

23 SOUTHERN SUN RV AND MOBILE HOME PARK

Rating: 3

Just south of Belleview
Ocala map, grid b3, page 192

Call early if you want a spot at this sunny, sleepy 10-acre RV park. When contacted one November, the place already was booked up until March and had a wait list of six parties. Retirees tend to dominate the clientele. These grassy lots are sizable at 30 by 50 feet. They're set back from cars zipping by on U.S. 441 and County Road 25, and the park can't be seen from the highway.

Campsites, facilities: All 45 RV sites have full hookups and a picnic table; an additional 18 mobile homes are on the site. Horseshoes, showers, restrooms, a recreation room, cable TV, telephone hookups, and laundry facilities are available. Management says the clubhouse, showers, and laundry room are wheelchair accessible. Small, leashed pets under 15 pounds are permitted.

Reservations, fees: Reservations are recommended. Sites are $17 per night for two people,

plus $2 for each additional person. Credit cards are not accepted. Long-term rates are available.

Directions: From Belleview, go south on U.S. 441 a short distance to County Road 25A. Turn left at Southeast 69th Terrace, the first driveway on your left.

Contact: Southern Sun RV and Mobile Home Park, 1165 Southeast 69th Terrace, Belleview, FL 34420, 352/245-8070, fax 352/245-8070.

24 SUNNYHILL RESTORATION AREA

Rating: 6

East of Weirsdale and west of Ocala National Forest

Ocala map, grid b3, page 192

Just south of the Ocklawaha Prairie Restoration Area and covering a nine-mile stretch of the river lies the Sunnyhill Restoration Area, a 4,357-acre public wilderness area managed by the St. Johns River Water Management District. Like the Ocklawaha tract, this was acquired to restore the old, straightened river and return water to the wetlands. You'll see lots of wading birds, and sandhill cranes like to spend the winter here. The Blue House, which was once a farmhouse on the property, has been converted to an exhibit center and offers nature tours. Canoeists can launch at the Moss Bluff boat ramp at the corner of Country Road 314A and County Road 464. Paddle south nine miles to The Blue House. Stretching along the canoe route is a levee trail suitable for biking and hiking. There are three primitive campsites, including one at The Blue House. Access to this area may be restricted while the restoration work is going on. Get up-to-date information from the water management district before heading out.

Campsites, facilities: Tents only are permitted. There are no facilities; bring water, supplies, mosquito repellent, and everything you'll need. Children are welcome. Leashed pets are permitted.

Reservations, fees: Sites are first-come, first-served. Camping is free. Each site accommodates up to six people. If your party has at least seven people, get a free permit and reserve at least one week ahead at 386/329-4410. Maximum stay for all campers is seven days.

Directions: From Weirsdale at the intersection of County Road 42 and County Road 25, drive east six miles to The Blue House. Parking areas for the two other primitive sites are on Southeast 182nd Avenue Road/Forest Road 8, a north-south forest road accessible from the north from County Road 314A just east of Moss Bluff.

Contact: St. Johns River Water Management District, Division of Land Management, P.O. Box 1429, Palatka, FL 32178-1429, 386/329-4500 or 800/451-7106, website: www.sjr-wmd.com.

25 EMERALDA MARSH CONSERVATION AREA

Rating: 6

East of Weirsdale

Ocala map, grid b3, page 192

Migrating birds, ducks, and rare species such as the bald eagle may be spotted in this 7,089 tract about four miles south of the Sunnyhill Restoration Area. Threaded with small lakes, this area allows hunting, so call ahead to be sure hiking, canoeing, and bird-watching are safe. There are three boat ramps and one primitive site in the northern section of the property.

Campsites, facilities: Tents only are permitted. There are no facilities; bring water, supplies, mosquito repellent, and everything you'll need. Children are welcome. Leashed pets are permitted.

Reservations, fees: Sites are first-come, first-served. Camping is free. Each site accommodates up to six people. If your party has at least seven people, get a free permit and reserve at least one week ahead at 386/329-4410. Maximum stay for all campers is seven days.

Directions: To reach the campsite, hike in from the parking area on Emeralda Island Road. From Weirsdale, drive east past the Sunnyhill Restoration Area on County Road 42 and turn south on County Road 452. Drive about 1.5 miles and turn west on Emeralda Island Road, which continues about four miles, heading west and veering 90 degrees south to the parking area.

Contact: St. Johns River Water Management District, Division of Land Management, P.O. Box 1429, Palatka, FL 32178-1429, 386/329-4500 or 800/451-7106, website: www.sjrwmd.com.

26 OCKLAWAHA RV PARK AND CANOE OUTPOST

Rating: 6

On the Ocklawaha River near Ocala National Forest

Ocala map, grid b2, page 192

Canoeing beneath the moss-draped trees flanking the 110-mile-long Ocklawaha River is something bored office workers might daydream about as they wait for five o'clock to roll around. Paddlers in spring and fall wind through narrow waterways lined with gnarly cypress, swamp maple, and sabal palm—the fan-leafed state tree. Along the way, an early morning mist rises over spring-fed streams. The river widens into lily-pad-filled ponds in some places. Bobcat, deer, and Florida black bears live in the surrounding forest.

Adventure-seekers tend to be drawn to this seven-acre campground, where canoes rent for $16.50 daily per person and campsites fill up fast, except in summer. Some seasonal campers have stayed here at least three consecutive winters. Anglers can launch at the boat ramp to go after some 100 species of fish in the Ocklawaha, or take advantage of the park's catch-and-release fishing pond. RV sites are shady or sunny. Tenters set up in a pine-studded area. If you want to camp alone, the on-site canoe outfitter will tell you where you may paddle your canoe to a variety of woodsy primitive camping areas. Proprietor Larry Reiche contends there are no mosquitoes to speak of and the canopy of trees makes riverfront canoe-in camping comfortably cooler in the summer. Hikers may see deer or wild turkeys along the nearby Cross Florida Greenway, which long ago was meant to become a barge canal gouged through the belly of Florida, almost like the Panama Canal, linking the Atlantic Ocean and the Gulf of Mexico. A welcome center for the Cross Florida Greenway and Ocala National Forest is at the corner of County Road 316 and Highway 40.

Campsites, facilities: Fourteen tent sites are set apart from the 12 full-hookup RV sites. You also can paddle out to pitch a tent along nearby riverbanks. A catch-and-release fishing pond, a small playground, a recreation room, showers, restrooms, snacks, a boat ramp, limited camping and fishing supplies, a dump station, and canoe and kayak rentals are available. Children are welcome. Dogs may chase a ball in a large field but must be leashed elsewhere, including along the park's dog walk.

Reservations, fees: Reservations are recommended for canoeing or camping. Nightly fee for two people is $16.50 for RV sites, $10 for tent sites. Add $1 to $3 for each additional person. Overnight primitive canoe/camping trips are $20 per rental canoe per day, plus transportation ($20 to $45). Or bring your own canoe and just pay for the shuttle. Major credit cards are accepted. Long-term stays are OK.

Directions: From I-75 at Exit 352, take State Road 40 east about 10 miles through Ocala and Silver Springs. Turn left at County Road 315 and proceed 12 miles north to County Road 316. Turn right. The campground is about four miles ahead at the Ocklawaha River. Turn left before the bridge, and follow to the camp store, located near where the road's pavement ends.

Contact: Ocklawaha RV Park and Canoe Outpost, 15260 Northeast 152nd Place, Fort McCoy, FL 32134, 352/236-4606, email: canoeing1@aol.com, website: http://members.aol.com/ocooutpost.

27 LAKE DELANCY CAMPGROUND

Rating: 2

In northern Ocala National Forest
Ocala map, grid a2, page 192

The Florida National Scenic Trail passes through this rustic, no-frills campground, offering you an opportunity to scale the rolling, sandy, pine-studded hills that dominate the sunny northern part of the forest. You also can try your hand at fishing in the shallow freshwater lake next to the campground, which basically is little more than a clearing in the woods and is dominated by hunters during prescribed seasons.

Campsites, facilities: This primitive camping area can accommodate up to 30 RVs and 80 tents. Vault toilets, hand-pumped drinking water, fire rings, and several picnic tables are available. Children are welcome. Leashed pets are permitted.

Reservations, fees: Reservations are not accepted, nor are credit cards. Sites are $5 per night. The maximum stay is 14 days in any 30-day period.

Directions: From Ocala, take State Road 40 east about 12 miles. Turn left onto County Road 314 and continue northeast about 15 miles. Turn left (north) onto Forest Service Road 88 and go about nine miles, then turn right (east) onto Forest Service Road 75 and look for the campground on the right. If you reach State Road 19, you've gone too far.

Contact: Ocala National Forest, Lake George Ranger District, 17147 East State Road 40, Silver Springs, FL 34488, 352/236-0288 or 352/625-2520.

28 SALT SPRINGS RECREATION AREA

Rating: 9

In northeastern Ocala National Forest
Ocala map, grid a2, page 192

The big attraction here are the natural springs, called Salt Springs, but not salty the way ocean water is. Instead, it's tinged with calcium, sodium, potassium, and other minerals, yet still is clear enough to make swimming or snorkeling pleasant. Flowing at a speedy rate of 53 million gallons per day, the spring was treasured by Native Americans and was said to have medicinal value, with each of the five boils supposedly curing different ailments. It's even been said that these waters were the legendary Fountain of Youth. When President Roosevelt designated the Ocala National Forest in 1908, hardy travelers braved difficult roads to take a dip.

Canoeists follow the spring's run to Lake George (rental canoes are available nearby), while anglers snag bass at Florida's second largest lake. Motorboats can be rented at Salt Springs Marina and Landing; call 352/685-2255.

There's good hiking nearby along the Salt Springs Trail, a three-foot-wide dirt path that cuts a two-mile loop through sand pine scrub, slash pine flatwoods, bayheads, cypress, and clusters of oak trees. The trail leads to an observation platform on the Salt Springs Run, a nice place to picnic in cooler months. For a longer hiking challenge, try the sandier, more open portion of the Florida National Scenic Trail that runs nearby. The new Bear Swamp Trail boardwalk winds for 1.5 miles past some huge cypress trees.

The campground itself is sort of bowl-shaped, leading down to the springs. Big shady oaks as well as some sand pine and longleaf pine dot the grounds. The RV sites are grassy, and primitive sites are sandy. If you bring horseshoes or a basketball, you can use them at facilities here. Salt Springs is actually a small town in the woods where you can get pizza, seafood, or a square meal at various restaurants, or mail a postcard at the local post office.

Campsites, facilities: There are 106 RV sites (back-in only) with full hookups and 54 primitive sites for tents or small RVs. Each site has a picnic table, a grill, and a fire ring. On the premises are restrooms, showers, a dump station, a small store, a recreation barn, and a picic area. You can swim in the springs. All sites are wheelchair accessible. Children and leashed pets are welcome. Pets are not allowed in the day-use area (the spring). Note that check-out time is 1 P.M.; if you stay longer, you will be charged a day-use fee. You can stay as long as you like.

Reservations, fees: Reservations are recommended; call 877/444-6777 or go online at www.reserveusa.com. Full-hookup sites are $17 per night for five people and two vehicles; primitive sites are $13 for five people and two vehicles. Major credit cards are accepted. A discount of 50 percent applies to campers with Golden Age cards.

Directions: From Ocala, take State Road 40 east 11 miles. At County Road 314, turn northeast and drive 16 miles. At State Route 19, drive .25 mile and look for the campground on the right.

Contact: Salt Springs Recreation Area, Ocala National Forest, 14151 State Road 19 North, Salt Springs, FL. Mailing address: c/o American Land & Leisure, P.O. Box 5358, Salt Springs, FL 32134, 352/685-2048 or 352/685-2674.

29 ELITE RESORTS AT SALT SPRINGS

Rating: 9

In northeastern Ocala National Forest
Ocala map, grid a2, page 192

This wooded campground fronts onto Little Lake Kerr, where you can fish or rent pontoon boats from the park. It's one of the more deluxe RV-oriented parks in the Ocala National Forest and is located 300 yards from the Salt Springs. In the recreation hall, you'll find bingo twice weekly, dances on Saturday nights, and a myriad of other activities. A modem is accessible here, too, if you need to check your email.

Campsites, facilities: There are 470 RV sites available for overnighters, of which 50 can be used for seasonal stays. All have full hookups, picnic tables, and cable TV. RVs as large as 45 feet can be accommodated, and eight sites have 50-amp electrical service. Restrooms, showers, a dump station, laundry facilities, and telephone service are available. On the premises are a pool, a sandy beach, a boat ramp, a dock, a clubhouse, propane gas sales, horseshoe pits, volleyball and shuffleboard courts, tennis courts, a dog-walk area, a shopping center with two restaurants, 40 cottages for rent, nature trails, and miniature golf. Most areas are wheelchair accessible; all roads are paved. Children are welcome. Leashed pets are permitted.

Reservations, fees: Reservations are recommended but usually are not necessary. Sites are $24 per night. Major credit cards are accepted. The maximum stay is 14 days.

Directions: From Ocala, take State Road 40 east about 12 miles to County Road 314. Turn left and drive 18 miles north to the campground. At State Road 19, turn north and go one mile to the park. From I-95 in Daytona, take Exit 88 westbound 25 miles on State Road 40 to State Road 19. Turn north and drive 17 miles to the park.

Contact: Elite Resorts at Salt Springs, 25250 East County Road 316, Salt Springs, FL 32134, 352/685-1900, fax 352/685-0557, website: www.eliteresorts.com.

30 GORE'S LANDING PARK

Rating: 3

On the Ocklawaha River
Ocala map, grid b2, page 192

You might want to take a look at this little-frequented former hunting camp before deciding, sight unseen, to stop at this county park. Lacking electricity, water, and showers, Gore's Landing won't satisfy big-city sensibilities. But canoeists and anglers in pursuit of any of 100 species of fish can think of this primitive camping area as a crash pad that allows them to get on the Ocklawaha River bright and early, thanks to the on-site boat ramp. If you don't have a canoe, rentals are available at Ocklawaha Outpost on County Road 316 at the river; call 352/236-4606. The 118-acre park is a pleasant enough place to eat a picnic lunch at the no-frills concrete picnic tables shaded somewhat by trees.

Campsites, facilities: Twelve primitive camp sites are here. A restroom, picnic tables, a boat ramp, and barbecue grills are available. Children are welcome. Pets are prohibited.

Reservations, fees: Reservations are not taken. Sites are $5 per night. Credit cards are not accepted.

Directions: From I-75 at Exit 352, take State Road 40 east about 10 miles through Ocala and Silver Springs. Turn left at County Road 315. Turn right at Northeast 105th Street (a sign marks the turn). The park is ahead.

Contact: Marion County Parks and Recreation, 8282 Southeast County Road 314, Ocala, FL 34470, 352/236-7111.

31 FORE LAKE CAMPGROUND

Rating: 8

**On Fore Lake in western
Ocala National Forest**
Ocala map, grid b2, page 192

You'll while away the time amid picturesque live oak hammocks and pines beside a pretty freshwater lake. Fishing and swimming in 77-acre Fore Lake are popular pursuits here at one of the forest's most popular lake-area campgrounds (Juniper Springs, Salt Springs, and Alexander Springs are more popular). You may also launch a canoe if you bring one. The green, pleasant campground is only a 15-minute drive from the Silver Springs nature theme park (see Silver Springs Campers Garden campground in this chapter), and just minutes away from fine nature trails at Lake Eaton.

Campsites, facilities: All 31 campsites (20 for RVs and 11 for tents) have picnic tables and grills. Restrooms with flush toilets and drink-

ing water are available, as are a picnic shelter and pay phone. There are no showers, dump stations, or other facilities. Campfires are permitted inside fire rings. Children and leashed pets are welcome.

Reservations, fees: Reservations are not taken. Sites are $8 per night for five people. Credit cards are not accepted. The maximum stay is 14 days in any 30-day period.

Directions: From Ocala, take State Road 40 east about 12 miles. Turn left onto County Road 314 and continue northeast about six miles until you see the entrance on the left.

Contact: Ocala National Forest, Lake George Ranger District, 17147 East State Road 40, Silver Springs, FL 34488, 352/236-0288 or 352/625-2520.

32 LAKE EATON CAMPGROUND

Rating: 5

**On Lake Eaton in western
Ocala National Forest**
Ocala map, grid b2, page 192

Oaks and pines tower over this small campground at the southern end of idyllic Lake Eaton. The fishing pier and boat launch are pluses for those who want to stick close to camp; however, you should not miss the opportunity to explore some really interesting hiking terrain nearby. Head back out to County Road 314A and continue north approximately two miles to County Road 314. Turn right (heading east), then make another right onto the dirt road that comes up next, Forest Service Road 86. When that curves around to the left, turn right (south) onto Forest Service Road 79. Whew! All the maneuvering is worth it, though, because you will find two first-class hiking trails that are accessible, short, and interesting enough even for people who aren't into hiking for the sheer pleasure of it.

Our favorite is the Lake Eaton Sinkhole Trail, which is actually a network of trails totaling 2.2 miles. The big feature, as you might imagine, is the sinkhole. A mere one-half-mile hike brings you to an observation deck that allows you to peer into this dark, cool hole spanning 450 feet across and reaching a depth of 80 feet. By all means, take the last few steps and follow the boardwalk and stairs leading down into the sinkhole.

The other trail is the Lake Eaton Loop Trail. It provides access through a slightly inclined forest slope to the lake's northeast shore. Passing over mulch and yellow-red sand, you'll walk through an area where you will encounter odd, dwarflike oaks and the pointy fronds of saw palmetto. Altogether, you can see more than a half dozen natural communities ranging from the dry xeric hammocks filled with sand to the wet, wet lake itself. Animals of note include the osprey, deer, wild turkey, and scrub jay. People who are interested in rare plants should keep an eye out for the scrub milkwort, scrub buckwheat, and scrub morning glory.

Campsites, facilities: Thirteen primitive campsites are provided for tents or small RVs, along with picnic tables, vault toilets, hand-pumped drinking water, a boat ramp, fire rings, and a fishing pier. A few spaces will accommodate RVs up to 35 feet. Children are welcome. Leashed pets are permitted.

Reservations, fees: Reservations are not accepted, nor are credit cards. Sites are $6 per night for up to five people. The maximum stay is 14 days in any 30-day period.

Directions: From Ocala, take State Road 40 east for approximately 17 miles, turning left onto County Road 314A about five miles after entering the forest. Head north for five miles, then turn right (east) onto Forest Service Road 95. After just .5 mile or so, turn left onto Forest Service Road 96A. Drive about one mile north to the campsites.

Contact: Ocala National Forest, Lake George Ranger District, 17147 East State Road 40, Silver Springs, FL 34488, 352/236-0288 or 352/625-2520.

33 HOPKINS PRAIRIE

Rating: 4

In central Ocala National Forest
Ocala map, grid a2, page 192

Camp in an oak hammock next to a wet prairie and a shallow lake. You can try your luck fishing there. If you decide to boat, bring a canoe or craft with a motor of no more than 10 horsepower. The Florida National Scenic Trail passes near here.

Campsites, facilities: The camping area has 21 sites with fire rings, lantern posts, and picnic tables, plus some undeveloped sites for RVs or tents. Drinking water is available from a hand pump. Vault toilets are provided. Children and leashed pets are permitted.

Reservations, fees: Reservations and credit cards are not accepted. Sites are $5 per night for up to five people. The maximum stay is 14 days in a 30-day period.

Directions: From Ocala, take State Road 40 east about 32 miles. Turn left on State Route 19 and go about eight miles north to the campground entrance on the left.

Contact: Ocala National Forest, Lake George Ranger District, 17147 East State Road 40, Silver Springs, FL 34488, 352/236-0288 or 352/625-2520.

34 COLBY WOODS RV RESORT

Rating: 6

At the western edge of Ocala National Forest
Ocala map, grid b2, page 192

The meandering, tree-flanked Ocklawaha River is only steps from this 39.5-acre wooded campground, so it's no wonder that bass anglers launch boats at the nearby county boat ramp to try their luck in the sun-dappled waters. Canoeists on the lookout for deer and turkeys peer into the passing woods as they paddle along the river. For a picnic lunch, consider a takeout pork sandwich from Roger's Bar-B-

Que, down the street on East State Road 40. It's next door to an Ocala National Forest Visitor Center, where you can pick up forest maps.

Of the paved or gravelly/grassy sites at Colby Woods, some are shady, but others are sunny. Despite the presence of nature trails a short walk away, some campers prefer to stick close to their vacation home for the park's wintertime activities, such as bingo, cards, dances, and crafts. RV sites are laid out along roads like city blocks, but tenters are confined to a wooded area near the main road.

Campsites, facilities: This park has 11 tent sites and 165 full-hookup RV sites (125 pullthrough). Each site has a picnic table. A pool, a hot tub, a playground, a nature trail, a horseshoe pit, shuffleboard, a game room, a camp circle, volleyball, and winter activities entertain campers. Showers, restrooms, a dump station, cabins, laundry facilities, and canoe rentals are available. Wheelchair access is provided to showers and the meeting hall. Within .5 mile are a boat ramp, a restaurant, bait, and firewood. Groceries can be purchased six miles away. Children are welcome May through September and are subject to an 11 P.M. curfew. Leashed pets should use the dog walk in back.

Reservations, fees: Reservations are recommended in winter. Sites are $19 per night for a family of four, plus $2 for cable TV. Tenters pay $15. Credit cards are not accepted.

Directions: From I-75 at Exit 352, take State Road 40 east for about 12 miles. The park is on the left, just beyond the Ocklawaha River Bridge.

Contact: Colby Woods RV Resort, 10313 East State Road 40, Silver Springs, FL 34488, 352/625-1122 or 352/625-1911.

35 FOREST COVE CAMPGROUND

Rating: 2

In western Ocala National Forest
Ocala map, grid b2, page 192

This nine-acre, pine-dotted campground offers sun-dappled campsites near several lakes in the surrounding national forest. Juniper Springs Recreation Area, a popular picnic spot, is about 13 miles east. The Silver Springs nature theme park is about five miles west. The Atlantic Ocean and Gulf of Mexico are about one hour's drive in either direction.

Campsites, facilities: Tents are permitted in summer only, but RVers camp year-round at the 53 full-hookup sites (12 pull-through). Each site has a picnic table. A group barbecue/campfire area, a recreation hall, horseshoes, and shuffleboard entertain campers. Showers, restrooms, two dump stations, and laundry facilities are available. A convenience store is about one mile away; a supermarket is within five miles. Children are welcome. Leashed pets are permitted.

Reservations, fees: Reservations are accepted. Sites are $11 per night per site. Credit cards are not accepted. Long-term rates are available.

Directions: From I-75 at Exit 352, take State Road 40 east for 14 miles to Piney Path Road/Northeast 115th Avenue. Turn right. The campground is one mile ahead on the washboard road at right, past Ben's Hitching Post (see campground below).

Contact: Forest Cove Campground, 1700 Northeast 115th Avenue, Silver Springs, FL 34488, 352/625-1295.

36 BEN'S HITCHING POST

Rating: 4

In western Ocala National Forest
Ocala map, grid b2, page 192

This is the closest private campground to the Ocala National Forest Visitor Center Northeast. Some campsites are open and grassy, but trees help shade others. As much as picnickers like to relax at Juniper Springs Recreation Area about 13 miles west or spend the day at the Silver Springs nature theme park four to six miles to the east, this campground makes sure its guests stay busy:

Potluck dinners, bingo, and campfires are among the activities on the schedule.

Campsites, facilities: This adult-oriented park offers 46 full-hookup RV campsites (some pull-through), plus 10 for tents. For recreation there's a pool, a hot tub, shuffleboard, horseshoes, wintertime planned activities, a recreation hall with a fireplace, game tables, and exercise equipment. Showers, wheelchair-accessible restrooms, picnic tables, telephone hookups, firewood, and laundry facilities are available. Restaurants are within one mile. Children are not permitted. Pets are allowed.

Reservations, fees: Reservations are recommended. Sites are $16 per night for two people, plus $3 per extra person. Major credit cards are accepted. Long-term rates are available.

Directions: From I-75 at Exit 69, take State Road 40 east for 14 miles to Piney Path Road/Northeast 115th Avenue. Turn right. The campground is 300 feet ahead.

Contact: Ben's Hitching Post, 2440 Northeast 115th Avenue, Silver Springs, FL 34488, 352/625-4213, fax 352/625-0020.

37 LAKE WALDENA RESORT

Rating: 6

In western Ocala National Forest
Ocala map, grid b2, page 192

Check out the wintertime activities posted on the bulletin board: Exercise at 9 A.M., bowling at 10 A.M., and bingo at 7 P.M.—and that's just one day. Activities vary daily at this 35-acre campground and may include singing hymns on Sunday or going to a potluck dinner on Saturday. Campers' birthdays and anniversaries are also noted so you can pass along your best wishes.

Paved roads lead to several tree-shaded campsites that border nature preserves or Lake Waldena, where anglers, boaters, and swimmers head. Don't fish in the lake's roped-off area, though, because that's for swimmers. To sleep closest to Lake Waldena, try sites 1, 24,

25, or 37. To sleep along a nature preserve, ask about sites 1 through 13 or 62 through 64. A semitropical environment—unusual for national forests—is located 13 miles east at Juniper Springs Recreation Area. The Silver Springs nature theme park is eight miles west of the campground.

Campsites, facilities: All 100 campsites have full hookups, a concrete slab, and a picnic table. Some sites are pull-through. Two sites are for tents. Shuffleboard, horseshoes, pool tables, a television, winter activities, a playground, boat rentals, a swimming lake, and a recreation hall entertain campers. Showers, restrooms, firewood, telephone hookups, park model sites, and laundry facilities are available. Groceries and the nearest restaurant are about three miles away. Kids under 12 must be accompanied by an adult in common areas. Pets should be tied up within your campsite and leashed during walks.

Reservations, fees: Reservations are advised. Sites are $16 to $18 per night for four people, plus $2 for each additional person. Credit cards are not accepted. Long-term rates are available.

Directions: From I-75 at Exit 352, take State Road 40 east for about 17 miles through Ocala. (Lake Waldena Resort is eight miles east of the Silver Springs theme park.)

Contact: Lake Waldena Resort, 13582 East Highway 40, Silver Springs, FL 34488, 352/625-2851 or 800/748-7898, fax 352/625-7069, website: www.lakewaldena.com.

38 ROBIN'S NEST RV PARK

Rating: 4

In western Ocala National Forest
Ocala map, grid b2, page 192

This no-frills, rustic campground at the western edge of the Ocala National Forest attracts retirees who pay by the year or month and enjoy wintertime activities such as ice-cream socials and darts. The Silver Springs nature theme park is a short drive to the east. The national forest's popular Juniper Springs Recreation Area is about 10 miles east.

Campsites, facilities: Only self-contained rigs are accepted at these 50 full-hookup sites. No showers or restrooms are provided. An exercise room, wintertime planned activities, laundry facilities, and a ramp for airboats are available. Groceries and restaurants are within 1.5 miles. Snacks and bait are within .25 mile. Children are not allowed. Leashed pets are permitted.

Reservations, fees: Reservations are recommended. Sites are $13.50 per night for two people, plus $2 per extra person. Credit cards are not accepted. Long-term rates are available.

Directions: From I-75 at Exit 352, take State Road 40 east about 20 miles to enter Ocala National Forest and the town of Lynne. Turn right at the campground sign. Proceed to the hilltop and turn right. Go one block, then turn left into the park.

Contact: Robin's Nest RV Park, 13400 Northeast First Street Road, Silver Springs, FL 34488, 352/625-3090.

39 MILL DAM LAKEFRONT COMMUNITY

Rating: 4

In Ocala National Forest
Ocala map, grid b2, page 192

In summer, families vacation here. In winter, mainly retirees stay at this open and sunny mobile home/camping community on Mill Dam Lake. Anglers try for largemouth bass, bream, catfish, perch, and specks at this huge lake, which is at least 200 acres in size. Or they cross State Road 40 to fish at Halfmoon Lake. Mill Dam Beach is within walking distance. The surrounding national forest is one of the state's last bastions of the Florida black bear, although you're unlikely to see one of the nocturnal creatures. Instead, while hiking any of the 68 miles of the Florida National Scenic Trail that span the national forest, you might glimpse a wild turkey or a deer scampering away in the distance.

Campsites, facilities: All 17 sites are for RVs or tents and have water and electric hookups. Adjacent but separate is a mobile home park with 138 lots. Cabins, a screened pavilion, shuffleboard, horseshoes, laundry facilities, a gift shop, showers, restrooms, and groceries and gasoline are available. Children are welcome. Pets must stay out of the lake and be leashed at all times.

Reservations, fees: Reservations are advised. Sites are $14 per night for two people, plus $3 per additional adult. Major credit cards are accepted. Long-term rates are available.

Directions: From I-75 at Exit 352, take State Road 40 east about 21 miles through Ocala and past the Silver Springs nature theme park to the campground entrance. The campground is four miles east of County Road 314A.

Contact: Mill Dam Lakefront Community, 18975 East State Road 40, Silver Springs, FL 34488, 352/625-4500, fax 352/625-4506, website: www.milldamlake.com.

40 LAKE BRYANT PARK

Rating: 4

On Lake Bryant in Ocklawaha
Ocala map, grid b3, page 192

Dirt roads lead through this wooded campground/mobile home park, where launching at the boat ramp for a day of fishing on Lake Bryant is the focus for anglers. It's the only public boat launch in the area, the owners say. Some rustic campsites are fairly sunny, although most have at least a little shade. Forty-five mobile homes share the property, and some long-term campers spend the year here. If you want to swim, wait until summer because the lake is cold in winter.

Campsites, facilities: These 84 campsites (some pull-through) accommodate RVs and tents. Trailer rentals, a boat ramp, bait, a general store, showers, restrooms, and a dump station are available. Cable TV is on the menu for long-termers only. Families with children stay at designated family sites; kids must be attended in the campground. Small leashed pets are permitted.

Reservations, fees: Reservations are recommended. Sites are $15 per night for two people, plus $2 per extra person. Major credit cards are accepted. Long-term rates are available.

Directions: From I-75 at Exit 352, take State Road 40 east about 24 miles, passing the Silver Springs nature theme park, a high bridge, and County Road 314A. Approximately 2.5 miles past County Road 314A, turn right between the church and convenience store. The campground is 2.5 miles ahead.

Contact: Lake Bryant Park, 5000 Southeast 183rd Avenue Road, Ocklawaha, FL 32179, 352/625-2376 or 888/807-4858, fax 352/625-5676, email: glen@aiservices.com.

41 JUNIPER SPRINGS RECREATION AREA

🧍🏊🏄🐕♿🚐⛺

Rating: 9

Near Juniper Springs in central Ocala National Forest

Ocala map, grid a3, page 192

Situated beside two springs that pour forth 13 million gallons of crystal-blue water each day, this site is a contender for the most popular campground in the forest. Of course, the presence of warm showers and other amenities such as concession-stand food doesn't hurt. Be forewarned: You can't always get one of these first-come, first-served sites. So show up as early as possible on Friday, for instance, if you're planning a weekend getaway.

The campsites in general are sufficiently sheltered from one another by generous shrubs and a campground setup that utilizes paved, curving roads to help provide privacy. Hiking is available on the Florida National Scenic Trail, which runs through the campground and north into the Juniper Prairie Wilderness. A short interpretive nature trail also wends its way along the creek. Canoeing is

popular, and snorkelers love to dive in the 72-degree springwater.

Campsites, facilities: Juniper Springs features 79 campsites, about half of them pull-through. Restrooms, a concession stand, hiking trails, canoe rentals, and a dump station are available. The day-use buildings are wheelchair accessible. Children, leashed pets, and campfires are allowed.

Reservations, fees: Reservations are not taken. Sites are $13 to $15 per night for five people. Major credit cards are accepted. The maximum stay is 14 days in any 30-day period.

Directions: From Ocala, take State Road 40 east about 28 miles. Look for the entrance road on your left.

Contact: Ocala National Forest, 10863 East State Road 40, Silver Springs, FL 34488, 352/625-3147 or 352/625-2520. Mailing address: P.O. Box 5369, Salt Springs, FL 32134, 352/685-2048, website: www.camprrm.com.

42 ST. JOHNS RIVER CAMPGROUND

🐕🚐⛺

Rating: 6

West of Astor Park

Ocala map, grid a3, page 192

Large, shaded sites and centralized location make this new park a gem. Clean and modern facilities, huge oak trees, and nearby access to fishing on the St. Johns River are just part of the attraction; the campground is also fairly close to Daytona Beach. Marinas and restaurants are 200 yards away.

Campsites, facilities: Of a total of 60 sites, 30 are available for overnighters and seasonal visitors. Fifteen primitive tent sites are set apart from the RVs. All RV sites have full hookups and picnic tables; some have grills and cable TV. Restrooms, showers, laundry facilities, a clubhouse, and shuffleboard courts are available. Children are welcome. Small, leashed pets are permitted.

Reservations, fees: Reservations are recom-

mended. Sites are $20 per night for two peo-
ple, plus $2 per extra person. Major credit cards
are accepted. Long-term rates are available.

Directions: From I-95, drive west on State Road
40 for 28 miles. The park is on the right side,
.25 mile from the St. Johns River Bridge.

Contact: St. Johns River Campground, 1520
State Road 40, Astor, FL 32102, 352/749-3995,
fax 352/759-3419, website: www.stjohnsriver-
campground.com.

43 PARRAMORE'S FANTASTIC FISH CAMP AND FAMILY RESORT

Rating: 6

**On the St. Johns River south
of Lake George**

Ocala map, grid a3, page 192

As the campground's largemouth bass logo
suggests, probably the biggest draw here is the
lure of good fishing, followed closely by the
chance to see wild animals such as deer and,
if you're lucky, bobcats. The sunny, grassy
campsites provide a decent base of operations
for those who want easy access to various pursuits in this slow-paced part of the state. The
33-acre, semishady resort is across the river
from Ocala National Forest and, should you
tire of the campground pool, it is quite close
to the swimming and hiking opportunities at
Alexander Springs (see campground in this
chapter). The park is only about six miles from
the Pioneer Arts Settlement, where reenactors
of pioneer life produce arts and crafts. Festivals are held at the arts settlement twice a year
in the fall and spring. At nearby Spring Garden Ranch, restaurant patrons can look through
windows to watch trotter horses train every
morning during the winter.

Campsites, facilities: There are 72 full-hookup
sites for RVs and 10 for tents. Each site has a
picnic table and fire ring. A pool, boat and
canoe rentals, a playground, snorkeling, paddleboats, an exercise room, a game room, ten-

nis, and volleyball entertain campers. On the
premises are restrooms, showers, a boat ramp,
a dock, a dump station, groceries, bait, tackle, cabin rentals, and laundry facilities. Cable
TV, phone service, and firewood are available.
A restaurant is about two miles away. Restrooms, the store, and dock are wheelchair accessible. Children and leashed pets are welcome.

Reservations, fees: Reservations are recommended. Sites are $19 to $32 per night for two
adults, plus $2 for each additional adult and
$1 for each child. Major credit cards are ac-
cepted. Long-term stays are OK.

Directions: From I-95 at Exit 268, go west on
State Road 40. About two blocks short of the
St. Johns River, turn right (north) onto Riley
Pridgeon's Road. After one mile, turn left onto
South Moon Road, which leads west to the
park entrance.

Contact: Parramore's Fantastic Fish Camp and
Family Resort, 1675 South Moon Road, Astor,
FL 32102, 386/749-2721 or 800/516-2386, fax
386/749-9744, website: www.parramores.com.

44 ASTOR LANDING CAMPGROUND AND MARINA (FORMERLY HOLMAR MARINA)

Rating: 7

On the St. Johns River south of Astor

Ocala map, grid a3, page 192

People arrive by boat and by car to camp at
these 11 rustic acres on the west bank of the
St. Johns River and Lake Dexter, where the
owners have recently invested in a boat ramp
and other amenities. Outdoorsy folks use the
tree-shaded spot as a base for hunting, swimming, hiking, and bicycling at Ocala National
Forest, the park's neighbor across the street.
Anglers fish for bass and specks at the St.
Johns River. It's a good location for all sorts
of outdoor activities, and the park welcomes
family reunions and other groups. Houseboats
are for rent (call 352/759-3300), but there's lots
to do in this decidedly marine-oriented park.

Campsites, facilities: All 50 sites have full hookups, and an indeterminate number of tents can be accommodated. Boat slips with 30-amp and 50-amp shore power and water hookups, dockside sewage pumpout, a boat ramp, canoe rentals, a fishing pond, showers, restrooms, a picnic area, general store, laundry facilities, and a dump station are available. Groceries and a restaurant are about five miles away in Astor. Children and pets are permitted.

Reservations, fees: Reservations are not necessary. Sites are $15 per night for two people, plus $2 per extra person. Major credit cards are accepted. Long-term stays are OK.

Directions: From I-75 at Exit 352, drive about 40 miles east on State Road 40 through Ocala, Silver Springs, and Ocala National Forest. Turn right at Alco Road, one mile west of the St. Johns River. Continue four miles as the road veers left to the riverside camp.

Contact: Astor Landing Campground and Marina, 25934 Holmar Drive, Astor, FL 32102, 352/759-2121, website: www.astorlanding.com.

45 WILDWOODS CAMPGROUND
Rating: 6

Near Astor in the Ocala National Forest
Ocala map, grid b3, page 192

All travelers are welcome at this fishing-oriented park near the St. Johns River and Lake George. Practice your casting in the fishing pond on the premises. You'll find both sunny and shady spots here.

Campsites, facilities: There are 72 campsites with full hookups for RVs and tents. Restrooms, showers, laundry facilities, cable TV, and telephone service are available. On the premises are a clubhouse, shuffleboard courts, and a dog-walk area. Children are welcome. Leashed pets are permitted.

Reservations, fees: Reservations are recommended. Sites are $21 per night for two people, plus $1.50 per extra person. Credit cards

are not accepted. Long-term rates are available. Stay as long as you wish.

Directions: From I-95 in Ormond Beach, take Exit 268 and go west 30 miles on State Road 40 the park. From I-75 at Exit 352, go east on State Road 40 for 30 miles.

Contact: Wildwoods Campground, 22113 State Road 40, Astor, FL 32102, 352/759-3538.

46 ALEXANDER SPRINGS
Rating: 8

In southeastern Ocala National Forest
Ocala map, grid a3, page 192

The clear, 72-degree water flowing out of this spring at the rate of 80 million gallons daily makes this a very pleasant place to spend a hot summer day. Swimming and snorkeling are popular pursuits (equipment can be rented here), and certified divers may scuba dive. The sandy beach sets it apart from the forest's other popular springs—Juniper Springs. Canoe rentals are available, and many campers make the seven-mile trip down the spring's run. Archaeologists say the area around the springs has been inhabited for more than 1,000 years. You can hike about one mile along an interpretive trail that explains how early inhabitants, the Timucuan Indians, used native plants. A spur trail leads to a nearby section of the Florida National Scenic Trail, which leads over sandy, pine-covered hills. We spotted a baby wild hog there, just one of the wildlife species, including deer and black bear, said to abound here.

Look for otters along the spring's run and gopher tortoises in the sandy hills nearby. The campground is open, covered mostly with pines. It offers less privacy than many spots in the national forest, but it's still pleasant. Mountain bikers enjoy the Paisley Woods biking trail, a 22-mile loop that connects Alexander Springs with the Clearwater Lake campground, passing mostly through pine-dotted hills.

Campsites, facilities: All 68 campsites are for tents or RVs up to 35 feet long. No hookups are available (although some were to be added during 2000). On the premises are restrooms, showers, a dump station, a concession stand, a swimming area, hiking trails, and an amphitheater. Most areas are wheelchair accessible. Children and leashed pets are permitted.

Reservations, fees: Reservations are not taken. Sites are $15 per night for five people. Major credit cards are accepted. Stays are limited to 14 days in any 30-day period.

Directions: From Ocala, take State Road 40 east about 26 miles to State Road 19. Turn right and continue about eight miles south. Make a left, heading east, on County Road 445 (not 445A). Look for the entrance to the campground about five miles ahead on the left.

Contact: Alexander Springs Campground, Ocala National Forest, 49525 County Road 445, Altoona, FL 32702, 352/669-3522. Or write to RRM Regional Office, 26701 East Highway 40, Silver Springs, FL 34488, 352/625-0546, fax 352/625-0712, website: www.camp rrm.com.

47 OCALA FOREST CAMPGROUND

Rating: 5

In southeastern Ocala National Forest
Ocala map, grid a3, page 192

It would be hard to accidentally stumble upon the Skorski family's out-of-the-way private campground within Ocala National Forest. Area attractions are canoeing at the forest's Juniper Springs Recreation Area 12 miles away, and the antique shops of Mount Dora 17 miles away. But there's lots to do in the park, from golfing to bicycling and more. A long oval island of RVs forms the center of this thumb-shaped campground. Tenters head all the way back to the thumbnail—the park's wooded western border. To sleep closest to the pool (and dog walk), try sites 1 through 11. To border stands of trees, ask about sites 69 through 95.

Campsites, facilities: Twenty-five tent sites are separated from the 100 full-hookup RV camp-

sites (many pull-through). A nine-hole golf course, a pool, horseshoes, shuffleboard, a recreation hall, bike rentals, winter activities, a game room, a playground, and a pool table entertain campers. Showers, restrooms, a dump station, groceries, a park model section, and laundry facilities are available. The park also has a boat ramp and docks; however, a long drought has left water levels low. A restaurant is about seven miles away. Young children must be adult-supervised. Leashed pets must use the eastern-border dog walk.

Reservations, fees: Reservations are recommended. Sites are $15.50 and $16.50 per night for two people, plus $3 for each additional person and $2 for use of air conditioners or electric heaters. Credit cards are accepted. Long-term rates are available.

Directions: From Umatilla, go north on State Road 19, then turn left at County Road 42. The campground is ahead to your right.

Contact: Ocala Forest Campground, 26301 Southeast County Road 42, Umatilla, FL 32784, 352/669-3888.

48 LAKE DORR CAMPGROUND

Rating: 4

In southern Ocala National Forest
Ocala map, grid a3, page 192

Extremely tall, straight pines provide reasonable shade from the sun for these sandy campsites, which are set within a forest where fire has beaten back much of the understory of saw palmetto. That means you won't enjoy a whole lot of privacy. The following could apply to many areas of the forest, but it should be reiterated: Stay away from the clusters of saw palmetto because they can harbor rattlesnakes. Fishing is popular at nearby Lake Dorr, where you also can swim at a sandy beach. Canoes share the lake with buzzing motorboats—after all, this is one lake where there is no limit on how much horsepower your boat can pack. Hikers can pick up the Florida National Scenic

Trail a few miles up State Road 19 at Alexander Springs.

Campsites, facilities: All 34 campsites are for tents or RVs. No hookups or pull-through sites are available. Drinking water, restrooms, hot showers, picnic tables, and two boat ramps are provided. Children and leashed pets are welcome.

Reservations, fees: Reservations are not taken. Sites are $7 per night for five people. Credit cards are not accepted. Stays are limited to 14 days in any 30-day period.

Directions: From Deland, go west on County Road 42 for 24 miles. Turn right and head north on State Road 19 about three miles. Look for the entrance to your right.

Contact: Ocala National Forest, Seminole Ranger District, 40929 State Road 19, Umatilla, FL 32784, 352/669-3153, website: www.southernregion.fs.fed.us.

49 CLEARWATER LAKE CAMPGROUND

Rating: 8

In southeastern Ocala National Forest
Ocala map, grid a4, page 192

Set in an oak hammock on the shores of Clearwater Lake, this peaceful campground is less popular than the bigger campgrounds in the forest, partly because of its lack of hot showers and an isolated locale. Swimming, fishing, and canoeing are possible in the lake, but motorboats are banned. Mountain bikers can follow the Paisley Woods biking trail, a 22-mile loop that connects Alexander Springs with the Clearwater Lake campground, passing mostly through pine-dotted hills.

Hikers can stay busy for quite a while here. Consider the Florida National Scenic Trail, which passes through a section of woods that was burned out a few years ago but is now re-generating. By all means, though, don't miss the nearby St. Francis Interpretive Trail, which passes through riverine swamp, pine flatwoods, oak hammock, bayhead swamp, and open flatwoods. Keep your eye out for red-tailed hawks and pileated woodpeckers. If you're up to a seven-mile round-trip hike, consider trekking to the former town of St. Francis, once a bustling citrus and timber port on the St. Johns River. After steamboats were replaced by railroads as the main form of transport, St. Francis faded away and eventually was overtaken by the forest. With the aid of a pamphlet available at the trailhead, you can pick out markers of the onetime civilization, including an old levee built to flood a field so rice could be grown. To reach the trailhead, take County Road 42 east a few miles from the campground, turn left (north) on Forest Service Road 542, and look for signs.

Access to the forest's hiking and biking trails is restricted during hunting season, which generally runs from mid-November to early January. Check with the Forest Service for exact dates.

Campsites, facilities: All 42 campsites are for tents and RVs. Water is available, but there's no sewer or electric service. On the premises are restrooms, hot showers, a dump station, a swimming beach, and hiking trails. Children and leashed pets are permitted.

Reservations, fees: Reservations are not taken. Sites are $10 per night for five people. Credit cards are not accepted. Stays are limited to 14 days in any 30-day period.

Directions: From DeLand, take County Road 42 west about 15 miles to the hamlet of Paisley. Look for the campground entrance ahead on the left.

Contact: Ocala National Forest, Seminole Ranger District, 40929 State Road 19, Umatilla, FL 32784, 352/669-3153, website: www.southernregion.fs.fed.us.

COURTESY OF DAYTONA BEACH AREA CONVENTION & VISITOR BUREAU

Chapter 8

Daytona Beach Area

Daytona Beach Area

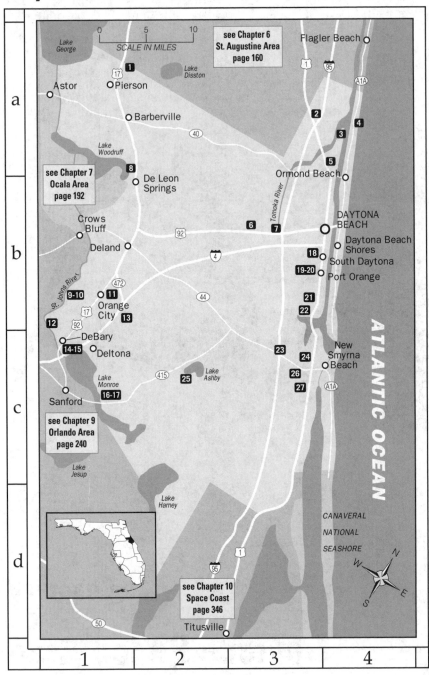

■ SUNNY SANDS NUDIST RESORT

Rating: 3

East of Pierson

Daytona Beach map, grid a1, page 220

You're way out in the boondocks here. As if that weren't enough to ensure privacy, the place is fenced and gated to boot. The park should rightfully be called a "clothing-optional" rather than "nudist" resort. You can wear clothes anywhere you'd like except the swimming pool and hot tub, and on cold days you'll find that almost everyone has a stitch of clothing on somewhere. The 45-acre park is heavily shaded with live oaks and, according to the management, features a laid-back lifestyle targeted at families. About 60 families or couples live here permanently in mobile homes. Bring your own canoe to paddle on the small lake or head a few miles away to catch bass in Lake George. Sites along Lakeshore Drive overlook tiny Crystal Lake.

Not far up the road you'll find the Lake George Conservation Area, which is chock full of hiking trails. There, nature abounds and wildlife lovers won't be disappointed. You're virtually sure to see birds and waterfowl, and if you're lucky, you might catch sight of a deer or otter. Shy and rarely seen bears are known to live in the area. At Sunny Sands, nights are generally quiet, but there are some social events such as bingo, dances, and spaghetti and chili cook-offs. Campers also have been known to throw a toga party now and again.

Campsites, facilities: This clothing-optional resort has 14 sites for RVs, 13 with full hookups. A large area is set aside for an indeterminate number of tents. Four tent sites have electricity. On the premises are restrooms, showers, laundry facilities, a nine-hole chipping course, basketball, volleyball, horseshoes, a pool, a hot tub, a one-mile-long walking trail, a restaurant and bar, and a *pétanque* court (French-style bowling). Cable TV and telephone service are available in the rental trailers. Restaurants and limited groceries are about two miles away.

The pool area is wheelchair accessible. Children are welcome, but single adults must be members of the Kissimmee-based American Association of Nude Recreation or the Naturist Society based in Oshkosh, Wisconsin. One leashed cat or dog is allowed per site.

Reservations, fees: Reservations are recommended, particularly in the winter months. Sites range from $30 to $39 per night for two people, plus $14 per extra person. Single campers are asked to phone before visiting. Cable TV costs $1. Major credit cards are accepted. Long-term stays are OK.

Directions: From I-95 at Exit 268, head west on State Road 40 for about 18 miles. In Barberville, turn right onto U.S. 17 and go about five miles north to the town of Pierson. Turn east (right) onto Washington Avenue. Follow it 1.25 miles to Turner Road, where you'll turn left. When the road curves to the right, you'll be within one block of the resort's gate. Continue, then look to the left for the resort gate and telephone.

Contact: Sunny Sands Nudist Resort, 502 Central Boulevard, Pierson, FL 32180, 386/749-2233, fax 386/749-0240, website: www.sunnysands.com.

■ ENCORE SUPERPARK— DAYTONA BEACH NORTH

Rating: 9

In Ormond Beach

Daytona Beach map, grid a4, page 220

Set in an area of pine flatwoods nine miles from the ocean, this park is ideal if you want a clean, resort-style camping experience far removed from the Spring Break atmosphere of Daytona Beach. Many campsites are at least partially shaded, thanks to a towering forest of ruler-straight pine trees. If you're just passing through, this is an excellent choice: It's just off the highway, and you'll probably find what you need right at the campground, which has 351 RV sites and 100 tent sites.

The 80-acre park is broken into two circles of campsites, one devoted to overnight guests, the other mainly for permanent residents and overflow campers. At the center of the camper-oriented circle is a swimming pool, a store, a laundry room, and a campground office. To sleep around this hub of activity (and its parking area), try sites 1 through 12. You'll pay the highest fee for these "super sites," as they're called. For canalside spots, request from among sites 384 to 390. In winter, you'll find planned activities geared toward retirees fleeing cold winters: bingo, dances, exercise classes, coffee klatches, and card parties. But bikers do show up during Daytona's famed Bike Week. A perky staff aims to adhere to the park's "fun and friendly service" mantra, and an example is their name for those giant umbrellas you see scattered around the park—they're "fun-brellas." It's convenient to Tomoka Basin Geo-Park (see campground in this chapter) and the Bulow Plantation Ruins State Historic Site (see Bulow Resort Campground in the St. Augustine chapter).

Campsites, facilities: There are 335 RV sites (250 full-hookup, 219 pull-through) and about 100 rustic tent sites. For entertainment, try the golf driving nets, *pétanque* (French-style bowling), horseshoes, miniature golf, racquetball, basketball, shuffleboard, sand volleyball, bocce ball (lawn bowling), tennis courts, the playground, the pool, or winter activities. Facilities include restrooms, showers, picnic tables, a convenience store, a dump station, cable TV hookups, and laundry facilities. Restaurants are within one mile, and groceries are about five miles away. Children and leashed pets are permitted.

Reservations, fees: Reservations are necessary from January through March and are recommended at other times of the year. Sites are $32 to $38 per night for two people, plus $2 daily if you want to hook up to cable TV. Major credit cards are accepted. Long-term stays are OK.

Directions: From I-95 at Exit 273, head north

on U.S. 1 for .5 mile to the park entrance on the right.

Contact: Encore SuperPark—Daytona Beach North, 1701 North U.S. 1, Ormond Beach, FL 32174, 386/672-3045 or 877/277-8737, fax 386/672-3026, website: www.rvonthego.com.

3 TOMOKA BASIN GEOPARK

Rating: 9

At the Halifax River north of Ormond Beach
Daytona Beach map, grid a4, page 220

Set at the confluence of the Tomoka and Halifax Rivers, this 10,000-acre state park incredibly started out as a simple sandbar between the two rivers but today is a lush forest of large oaks, shady hammocks, and saltwater marshes. Here, Timucuan Indians built a village they dubbed Nocoroco long before a wealthy Scotsman named Richard Oswald transformed it into the Mount Oswald Plantation. Oswald arrived after the American Revolution and proceeded to grow sugar, rice, and indigo, a plant used to make a blue dye popular at the time. (Visit the park museum to learn more about the history of the place.)

The sandy landlocked campsites are set along three circles. You'll enjoy at least some privacy from neighbors, thanks to the oaks and palms that help divide camping spots. For the most privacy, request a site along the "third loop," the only loop to sport a single, not double, row of campsites.

A .25-mile nature trail leads from the park museum through a shady coastal hammock to a picnic area. Rental canoes allow visitors to explore the rivers and salt marshes, which still teem with the fish that originally attracted the Timucuans. Brackish-water catches include snook, redfish, flounder, and speckled trout. Rangers say the best bait is live shrimp.

The park is a short drive from the Atlantic Ocean and is close to Bulow Creek State Park, a little-used, out-of-the-way slice of natural Florida open for day visits. At Bulow

Creek, you'll find the Fairchild Oak, which sprang up from an acorn about the time of Jesus Christ. Today its heavy, gnarly branches, covered in resurrection ferns, dip all the way to the ground. (Don't climb on them, please.) The oak is named for David Fairchild, a botanist who loomed large in Florida's history around the turn of the century. Several hiking trails lead through the gorgeous Florida backcountry, including a six-mile hike along the Florida National Scenic Trail from Bulow Creek State Park to the Bulow Plantation Ruins State Historic Site (see Bulow Resort Campground in the St. Augustine chapter).

Campsites, facilities: There are 100 sites with water and electricity for RVs (up to 34 feet long and 11 feet in height) or tents. Each site has a picnic table and fire ring. On the premises are restrooms, showers, a dump station, a recreation room, a boat ramp, firewood, canoe rentals, and a playground. Groceries, restaurants, and laundry facilities are nearby. The park's museum, docks, and picnic shelters are wheelchair accessible, as are four campsites and the restroom building in the campground. Children are welcome. Pets are permitted with proof of vaccination against rabies; there is an additional charge of $2 per night.

Reservations, fees: Reservations are recommended; call ReserveAmerica at 800/326-3521. From May 1 through Oct. 31, sites are $10 per night for one family or group up to four people, plus $2 for electricity. There is an extra-person charge of $2 for nonfamily members in groups of more than four people. From Nov. 1 through April 30, the base fee rises to $15 per night. Major credit cards are accepted. The maximum stay is 14 days year-round.

Directions: From I-95 at Exit 268, go east on State Road 40 to North Beach Street. Turn left and drive 3.5 miles north to the park entrance.

Contact: Tomoka Basin GeoPark, 2099 North Beach Street, Ormond Beach, FL 32174, 386/676-4050.

4 OCEAN VILLAGE CAMPER RESORT

Rating: 6

At the Atlantic Ocean in Ormond Beach
Daytona Beach map, grid a4, page 220

The beach is the big attraction here, and this eight-acre park plays it to the hilt with tropical lighted tiki huts lining the oceanfront. The campground is actually across Highway A1A from the beach. Yet an employee boasts of being able to throw a rock underhanded into the ocean from the office at the front of the park during high tide.

To sleep closest to the ocean (and campground entrances), ask about campsites 1 to 8 or 44 to 46. Tent sites are set back farthest from the ocean. Families as well as retired people sleep at these grassy sites with concrete patios, and social programs include bingo, card games, picnics, and potluck dinners. Anglers interested in surfcasting for whiting, bluefish, or pompano can buy frozen bait at the on-site convenience store or travel less than one mile for the fresh stuff.

Campsites, facilities: The campground offers 65 RV sites, 60 of which have full hookups. These spots are set apart from the 40 tent-only sites (some with water and electricity). Each site has a picnic table. On the premises are shuffleboard, a volleyball net you can take to the beach, a communal barbecue pit, a pool table, a pavilion, and bait sales. Facilities include restrooms, showers, a dump station, a convenience store, and laundry facilities. Cable TV and telephone service are available. Restaurants are nearby. Children are welcome. Leashed, attended pets are permitted, but guard dogs are forbidden.

Reservations, fees: Reservations are recommended during special events. Sites are $25 to $30 per night for two adults and two children, plus $5 for each additional adult. Cable TV hookup is free. Major credit cards are accepted. Long-term stays are OK.

Directions: From I-95 at Exit 268, go east on State Road 40 to Highway A1A. Turn left and drive four miles north to the campground on the left.

Contact: Ocean Village Camper Resort, 2162 Ocean Shore Boulevard, Ormond By The Sea, FL 32176, 386/441-1808.

5 HARRIS VILLAGE AND RV PARK
🏊 🎣 🐾 ♿ 🚐 ⛰️

Rating: 6

In Ormond Beach
Daytona Beach map, grid a4, page 220

Open from October through April, this sunny, over-55 park has a preference for motor homes and describes itself as "a nice little place for quiet people." Still, things can get busy during special events in the Daytona area, such as Bike Week, Speed Weeks, and Biketoberfest (bikes meaning motorcycles), so be sure to call ahead. Daytona Beach's International Speedway is 20 minutes away. RV supplies, stores, and restaurants are nearby.

Campsites, facilities: There are 20 RV sites, with 10 available for overnighters and 10 for seasonal visitors. Each site has full hookups, picnic tables, and cable TV. Restrooms, showers, and laundry facilities are available. Children are not welcome. One small leashed pet is permitted; barking dogs will not be tolerated, and the management must preapprove all pets.

Reservations, fees: Reservations are required. Sites are $25 to $36 per night for two people, plus $5 to $15 per extra person. Rates are higher during special events. Credit cards are not accepted. Long-term rates are available.

Directions: From I-95, take Exit 273 southeast four miles on U.S. 1 to the park.

Contact: Harris Village and RV Park, 1080 North U.S. 1, Ormond Beach, FL 32174, 386/673-0494, fax 386/672-5716, website: www.harrisvillage.com.

6 TIGER BAY STATE FOREST
🥾 🚲 🏊 🐴 ⛰️

Rating: 6

West of Daytona Beach
Daytona Beach map, grid a1, page 220

More than 11,000 acres of public land suitable for hiking, cycling, horseback riding, and backpacking comprise Tiger Bay State Forest, which is under joint management with the St. Johns River Water Management District. Horses and mountain bikes are allowed on forest roads only. Backpackers can access a primitive campsite on Indian Lake, and trails crisscross the tract, which stretches from U.S. 40 in the north to U.S. 92 in the south. Most of the land is wetland forest, marked by "pine islands" of trees and a pine ridge; the habitat is home to the black bear and bald eagle. Call ahead to avoid hunting season, usually in the fall and winter months. Much of the forest was burned in 1998, and you may still see damage from the wildfires. Some areas may be closed.

Campsites, facilities: Tents only are permitted. There are no facilities; bring water, supplies, mosquito repellent, and everything you'll need. Children are welcome. Leashed pets are permitted.

Reservations, fees: Permits are required; call the state forest office at 386/226-0250 for instructions and fees.

Directions: From I-95, take Exit 261 westbound on U.S. 92 for four miles. At Indian Lake Road, turn north. This will bring you to the main access point. The campsite is two miles from here. Other access points are on the north side off of U.S. 40, seven miles west of I-95.

Contact: Tiger Bay State Forest, 4316 West International Speedway Boulevard, Daytona Beach, FL 32124, 386/226-0250, fax 386/226-0251, website: www.fl-dof.com/state_forests/tiger_bay.htm. Additional information is available from the St. Johns River Water Management District, Division of Land Management, P.O. Box 1429, Palatka, FL 32178-1429, 386/329-4500 or 800/451-7106, website: www.sjrwmd.com.

7 INTERNATIONAL RV PARK AND CAMPGROUND

Rating: 6

In Daytona Beach

Daytona Beach map, grid b3, page 220

Opened in 2001, this brand-new park built on what was once vacant land is convenient to beaches, Daytona's International Speedway, and other tourist attractions. It attracts people of all ages—from snowbirds to race fans. Sites are extra large, accommodating rigs up to 40 feet long. The landscaping is new, as are the roads, pool, recreation hall, and campsites. The owners plan to double the park's size in the future. Tenters (as many as 500) can be accommodated in the wooded overflow area targeted for future expansion.

Campsites, facilities: All 137 sites have full hookups and 50-amp electrical service. At 37-by-47 feet, these are some of the largest sites we've seen in a developed campground, and they were planned that way. Restrooms, showers, laundry facilities, a pool, a clubhouse, horseshoe pits, shuffleboard courts, a dog-walk area, and a putting green are available. Children are welcome. Leashed pets are permitted.

Reservations, fees: Reservations are recommended. Sites are $25 per night for two people, plus $2 per extra person. Major credit cards are accepted. Long-term rates are available.

Directions: From I-95, take Exit 261 onto U.S. 92 and travel west 1.1 miles to the park.

Contact: International RV Park and Campground, 3175 W. International Speedway Blvd., Daytona Beach, FL 32124, 386/239-0249, website: www.internationalrvdaytona.com.

8 HIGHLAND PARK FISH CAMP

Rating: 3

Northwest of DeLand by the Lake Woodruff National Wildlife Refuge

Daytona Beach map, grid a1, page 220

We like this rustic place not for its facilities per se—they are, in fact, modest—but because of the great location. The oak-shaded and sunny campsites at this 33-acre fish camp give anglers access to the St. Johns River and Lake Woodruff (and the surrounding wildlife refuge) via the Norris Dead River. For hikers, these grassy campsites also are the closest available to two sets of trails, one at Lake Woodruff National Wildlife Refuge and another at DeLeon Springs State Park.

At the wildlife refuge (next door), there are three short nature trails and a much longer circuit of about 6.5 miles that leads bicyclists and hikers through woods and atop dikes built to hold in man-made freshwater lakes. Anglers can buy tackle and live bait at the fish camp to try their hand here. Visit in fall or winter to see abundant waterfowl and wading birds. Any time of the year, keep an eye out for otters, bobcats, deer, and other wild animals, particularly early or late in the day. Florida black bears live in the refuge but are rarely seen. To get to the refuge, head north on Grand Avenue to Mud Lake Road, where you will see refuge headquarters. Proceed down Mud Lake Road to a parking area to find the hiking trails. For refuge information, call 386/985-4673.

Don't leave this region without seeing DeLeon Springs State Park. The .5-mile nature trail there is pleasant for even the least rugged visitor. At one time, elephants, giraffes, and other circus creatures would pad down the route annually when the trail led to a railroad siding where the Clyde Beatty Circus unloaded each year for its winter respite. Monkey Island Trail, which was named for the island where a band of escaped circus monkeys lived for awhile, is among several spur trails. Or opt for the 5.2-mile-long Wild Persimmon Trail, a narrow path that is a little hard to navigate if you're not used to hiking. Bring water and insect repellent.

Swimming is the highlight at DeLeon Springs, where 19 million gallons of water bubble out of the earth every day. Native Americans began going to the springs as early as 8000 B.C., and a late-1800s advertisement extolled the health benefits of the spring water "impregnated with a deliciously healthy combination of soda and sulfur." Yum! Nature painter John James Audubon passed this way, and later a sugar mill was built on the grounds. You can still see some pieces of the now-defunct mill on display. The old sugar mill now houses a snack bar, the Old Spanish Sugar House Grill and Griddle House, where you can grill your own pancakes. A bike trip to DeLeon Springs and back, broken up by some swimming, hiking, and picnicking, makes for a pleasant day. For park information, call 386/985-4212.

In recent years, the fish camp has started attracting bluegrass music fans who, a couple times a week or so in winter, put on impromptu pickin's. Snowbirds tend to be devoted anglers, though, so the camp offers an occasional fish fry.

Campsites, facilities: There are 55 full-hookup sites, five water-and-electric sites, and an indeterminate number of primitive spots. On the premises are showers, restrooms, a dump station, firewood (at times), cabin rentals, horseshoes, a boat ramp, charter fishing services, motorboat and rowboat rentals, a limited store, bait, tackle, and a dock. Restaurants and a grocery store are located within three miles. Children and leashed pets are welcome.

Reservations, fees: Reservations are recommended but are not always necessary. Sites are $16 per night for two people, plus $2 per additional adult. If you want to turn on your air conditioner, a $2 daily fee applies. Major credit cards are accepted. Long-term stays are OK.

Directions: From central DeLand, take State Road 44/New York Avenue west to Grand Avenue. Turn right, heading north. Grand Avenue will dogleg, merging for a time with Minnesota Avenue to head west and then turn north again. Stay on Grand Avenue as you pass the landfill and Humane Society Road on the right. Not far past that, turn left onto Highland Park Road. Follow it 1.5 miles to the fish camp.

Contact: Highland Park Fish Camp, 2640 West Highland Park Road, DeLand, FL 32720, 386/734-2334 or 800/525-3477, fax 386/943-9681, website: www.hpfishcamp.com.

9 BLUE SPRING STATE PARK

Rating: 9

West of Orange City

Daytona Beach map, grid b1, page 220

At any time of year this well-used picnic spot is worth a visit, but show up when it's cold for a better shot at getting a gander at lots of manatees—maybe 60 of them, like on the day we visited. Endangered sea cows congregate generally from November through March in the 72-degree waters flowing from the spring for which the park is named. From the boardwalk above the clear blue waters it's easy to see their whiskers and the outlines of their dark, blubbery bodies.

You can't take motorboats up the Blue Spring Run, but you can swim there. Canoeing, swimming, and scuba diving may be restricted in certain areas if manatees are present, yet you always can enjoy these activities somewhere in the vicinity. Rental canoes give visitors access to the St. Johns River and Lake Beresford, where anglers with freshwater fishing licenses find bass, bluegill, shellcrackers, and specks.

Regular campsites are in a sun-dappled pine forest not far from the spring. Hikers and backpackers traverse a four-mile trail that tends to flood in summer and fall (bring hiking boots). The trail straddles pine flatwoods and marsh, ending in a lush oak hammock where four primitive campsites tend to be dry even when the trail is under water.

History-minded campers should check out the park's waterfront Thursby House, a two-story wooden house with double verandas and a real Old South feel. The pioneer Thursby family built it in 1872 atop a mound of snail shells deposited by Timucuan Indians, who made the snails a staple of their diet hundreds of years before. Union gunboat crews and U.S.

presidents are among the visitors who have arrived at the Thursby House over the years.

Campsites, facilities: This state park offers 51 sites, all with electricity. Four primitive campsites serve backpackers. Except for the primitive camping areas, all sites have water, picnic tables, and grills. On the premises are restrooms, showers, picnic tables, a dump station, rental cabins, a fishing pier, covered pavilions, and canoe rentals. A boat ramp for small boats is nearby. A park concession stand sells snacks and some groceries. Restaurants, groceries, and laundry facilities are about two miles away. Children are welcome. Leashed pets are permitted with proof of current rabies vaccination.

Reservations, fees: Reservations are recommended; call ReserveAmerica at 800/326-3521. Sites are $15 to $17 per night. Pet fee is $2 nightly. Primitive backpacking campsites are $3 per person. Major credit cards are accepted. Maximum stay is 120 days.

Directions: From I-4, take exit 114 and follow the signs south on 17-92 to Orange City, about 2.5 miles. Make a right onto West French Avenue and drive until it ends at the campground. The park is about two miles west of City Hall.

Contact: Blue Spring State Park, 2100 West French Avenue, Orange City, FL 32763, 386/775-3663, fax 386/775-7794.

🔟 HONTOON ISLAND STATE PARK

🏃 🚵 🏊 🛶 🥾 ⛺

Rating: 10

On Hontoon Island west of Orange City, via ferry or boat

Daytona Beach map, grid b1, page 220

This island between the St. Johns and Huntoon Dead Rivers holds special appeal because it is not accessible by car; you must take a boat or the free passenger ferry to get here. Of course, that means RV campers are out of luck. But if you have a tent or a boat big enough to sleep in, then you can look forward to a unique experience.

At 2.5 square miles, the island is large enough to allow some hiking or canoeing, but not so big that you'll get lost. A nature trail winds past mounds built hundreds of years ago by Timucuan Indians. In the picnic area, you'll see a replica of a 14th-century owl totem carved by the Native Americans and discovered here in 1955. You're virtually sure to see Florida's ubiquitous turkey vultures and seagulls, and perhaps deer, armadillo, otter, and wild turkeys. Before the state bought the island in 1967, the land served as a pioneer homestead, cattle ranch, and boatyard. Today much of it has been restored to a more-natural condition.

Seventy-three species of fish have been identified in the St. Johns River, although around here most anglers use live shiners or artificial bait to lure bass. Other popular targets include shellcrackers, catfish, and bluegill. To add adventure to your visit, consider renting a canoe at Blue Spring State Park (see campground in this chapter) and paddling to a campsite on Hontoon Island. Winter is the best time to camp to avoid mosquitoes because campsites sit where marsh and hammock meet (no sites are on the water). In summer, says a ranger, "we definitely got the market cornered on mosquitoes." Swimming is out of the question any time because of alligators.

Campsites, facilities: Twelve primitive tent sites and 52 slips for boat campers are available. Each tent site has a picnic table, a grill suitable for cooking or a small campfire, and nearby access to communal water spigots. Facilities in the park include restrooms, showers, boat docks, picnic tables, canoe rentals, bicycle trails, an enclosed pavilion, six rustic cabins, and a playground. Access is restricted to boats, so you have to bring all the supplies you will need. Children are permitted. Pets are not allowed. Bring your own firewood; it's against the rules to gather wood within the park.

Reservations, fees: Reservations are required; call ReserveAmerica at 800/326-3521. On weekends and holidays, there is a two-night minimum. Boat slips are available on a first-come, first-served basis. Rental cabins may be reserved (and often are, particularly at busy times such as Thanksgiving and Christmas) up to 11 months in advance. Sites are $8 per night for camping for four people, plus $2 per extra person; $10 for a boat slip, plus $2 for electricity. Major credit cards are accepted.

Directions: From DeLand, head west on State Road 44/New York Avenue, veering left on Old Route 44. Follow the well-marked route to the dock where you'll catch the free ferry, which runs on demand from 8 A.M. to sunset. Overnight campers may arrive not later than 7 P.M. A good place to launch your own boat is Blue Spring State Park.

Contact: Hontoon Island State Park, 2309 River Ridge Road, DeLand, FL 32720, 386/736-5309, website: www.hontooncso.com.

11 DELAND/ORANGE CITY KOA

Rating: 4

In Orange City

Daytona Beach map, grid b1, page 220

Birders might spy hawks, woodpeckers, or other birds in the oaks dotting this family-run park, where sandy interior roads lead to shady, sandy sites, most of them with patios. Children's activities are sometimes scheduled on holiday weekends. There's also a swimming pool, a game room, a playground, and the like. Leave the campground by day to enjoy area highlights such as nearby Blue Spring State Park, Hontoon Island State Park, and DeLeon Springs State Park. It's also close to the St. Francis Interpretive Trail.

Campsites, facilities: All 100 tent sites are set apart from the 150 RV sites (70 pull-through). Each site comes with a picnic table and water and electricity hookups; 130 have full hookups. On the premises are showers, restrooms, a dump station, a recreation room, a pool, a playground, a game room, horseshoes, volleyball,

basketball, limited groceries, a restaurant, and laundry facilities. Firewood is available. A grocery store is a five-minute drive away. Children and leashed pets are welcome.

Reservations, fees: Reservations are necessary in February and March. Sites are $23 per night for two people, plus $2.50 for each additional adult. For electricity, the fee is $3; add sewer for $2 more. Major credit cards are accepted. Long-term stays are OK.

Directions: From I-4 at Exit 114, travel west on State Road 472 for 1.5 miles to Minnesota Avenue. Turn left. The campground is about .25 mile ahead.

Contact: DeLand/Orange City KOA, 1440 East Minnesota Avenue, Orange City, FL 32763, 386/775-3996 or 800/KOA-7857, website: www.koa.com.

12 HIGHBANKS MARINA AND CAMP RESORT

Rating: 7

On the St. Johns River in DeBary

Daytona Beach map, grid b1, page 220

Like most campgrounds along the St. Johns River, this one is geared toward anglers who go after bass, shellcracker, catfish, and other freshwater prizes. Big oaks, interspersed with magnolias, shade parts of these 25 acres. The management employs a full-time recreation director year-round, so don't be surprised to find an ice-cream social on Saturday evening or bingo on weekends. Kids can fish at the park's small-fry fishing pond and take a two-hour nature cruise on the park's River Queen tour boat. "Let's go 'gator spottin'," says the manager, C. Richard Brown.

Half of the campers live permanently at the grassy/concrete-pad sites. They enjoy a pool for swimming and .5 mile of riverfront for strolling. Hiking trails are nearby. This campground is only a few miles from Blue Spring State Park and, by boat, Hontoon Island State Park. It's also pretty close to DeLeon Springs

State Park and Ocala National Forest. To camp nearest to the St. Johns River, ask about Cypress Lane sites 107 through 130. To stay beside the fish pond, request sites 38 through 64 on Hickory and Live Oak Drives.

Campsites, facilities: All 221 full-hookup sites are for RVs up to 40 feet long. Six sites are pull-through. Tents are allowed on 20 sites May 1 to October 31 only. Charter fishing services, wildlife boat tours, rental boats, billiards, a playground, a game room, horseshoes, shuffleboard, a recreation room, and a full-time recreation director entertain campers. On the premises are showers, restrooms, firewood, a 72-slip marina, a boat ramp, bait and tackle, limited groceries, picnic tables, a dump station, rental RV cabins, a snack bar, and laundry facilities. An on-site restaurant was opened recently. Management says the main bathhouse and clubhouse are wheelchair accessible. Children are welcome but may stay only two weeks. Two small- to medium-size pets are allowed per site.

Reservations, fees: Reservations are recommended and are accepted up to two months in advance. Sites are $22 to $25 per night for two people, plus $5 for each additional person. Major credit cards are accepted. Adults are welcome for long-term stays.

Directions: From I-4 at Exit 104, head north on U.S. 17/92 into DeBary. At the second light, turn left onto Highbanks Road. Go 2.5 miles west to the campground and marina.

Contact: Highbanks Marina and Camp Resort, 488 West Highbanks Road, DeBary, FL 32713, 386/668-4491, fax 386/668-5072, website: www.campresort.com.

13 SUNBURST RV PARK—ORANGE CITY (FORMERLY VILLAGE PARK RV RESORT)

Rating: 7

Off I-4 in Orange City
Daytona Beach map, grid b1, page 220
This is part of a much larger complex known

as Country Village, which is essentially a retirement village made up of mobile homes with suburban-style carports on mowed lots. Eighty percent of sites are snagged by people who live here year-round or for the winter season, taking advantage of the park's arts-and-crafts classes, dances, parties, and special outings. With euchre nights, Bible study, regularly scheduled blood pressure checks, and an on-site beauty salon, you know this is a different camping experience. This is one of the few parks we know of that lists tai chi among its planned activities. Many guests spend some time across the street sipping coffee at a diner, frequenting a shopping center, or taking in movies at a theater. Guests also have access to an 18-hole wooded golf course, which surrounds the RV parks.

Some RV sites are shaded and sandy-floored, whereas others are open and grassy. To be near the 12-foot-deep pool, try odd-numbered sites 5 through 15. The RV park is about five minutes from Blue Spring State Park (see campground in this chapter) and a 25-minute ride to the Daytona International Speedway. If you're in the mood for a palm reading or psychic consultation, this is the closest campground to Cassadaga, a small, off-the-beaten-path community favored by spiritualists.

Campsites, facilities: All 525 full-hookup spots are for RVs, with many pull-through sites available. For entertainment, try golf, miniature golf, a billiards room, a picnic pavilion, horseshoes, bocce ball (lawn bowling), a large heated pool, a Jacuzzi, a kiddie pool, planned activities, and the game room. Facilities include restrooms, showers, picnic tables, laundry facilities, and a convenience store. Groceries are within two miles. Children are welcome. Leashed pets are allowed.

Reservations, fees: Reservations are recommended. Sites are $32 per night for two people, plus $2 for each additional person. Credit cards are accepted. Long-terms stays are OK.

Directions: From I-4 at Exit 114, head west on State Route 472 (Howland Avenue) to the traffic light. Turn left on Route 4101 and drive one mile. At Graves Avenue, turn left and drive one block to the park.

Contact: Sunburst RV Park—Orange City, 2300 East Graves Avenue, Orange City, FL 32763, 386/775-2545 or 800/545-7354, fax 386/775-1517, website: www.rvonthego.com.

14 LAKE MONROE PARK AND CAMPGROUND

Rating: 6

On the St. Johns River south of DeBary
Daytona Beach map, grid c1, page 220

This small, oak-shaded campground is in a county-run park where Lake Monroe runs into the St. Johns River, a habitat for alligators (don't feed them). It's shady, and you'll often get a breeze off the lake. Saw palmettos between the sites help provide some privacy. Your neighbors may be snowbirds or construction workers who toil up the road a little way; because it's just off the interstate, this campground may make a convenient stop in a pretty spot. Although anglers catch bluegill and speckled perch from the pier, most guests use this campground as an inexpensive springboard for trips to Orlando, Disney World, Daytona Beach, or Ocala National Forest. Even closer are Blue Spring State Park and Hontoon Island State Park, as well as DeLeon Springs State Park.

Campsites, facilities: This park, just .5 mile off the interstate, offers 44 spots for RVs and 26 for tents, all with water and electricity. On the premises are restrooms, showers, a dump station, picnic tables, grills, fire rings, two boat ramps, a playground, a picnic pavilion, and a wheelchair-accessible floating dock and fishing pier. A restaurant and groceries are about one mile away. Children and leashed pets are permitted.

Reservations, fees: Reservations are recommended. From April 1 through August 31, rates are $10 per night for two people, plus $2 for each additional person and $2 for electricity. From September 1 through March 31, the rate rises to $15. Credit cards are not accepted.

Stays are limited to two weeks, or three weeks if no one is waiting for a site.

Directions: From I-4 at Exit 104, head north on U.S. 17/92. Cross the St. Johns River and you'll see the park on your right. If eastbound on I-4, take Exit 52; at the end of the ramp, turn left and proceed to U.S. 17/92, then turn north (left) on U.S. 17/92.

Contact: Lake Monroe Park and Campground, 975 South U.S. 17/92, DeBary, FL 32713, 386/668-3825. Or write to Volusia County Leisure Services, 202 North Florida Avenue, DeLand, FL 32720, 386/736-5953, website: www.volusia.org/parks/camping.htm.

15 GEMINI SPRINGS

Rating: 10

East of DeBary
Daytona Beach map, grid c1, page 220

This 200-acre park was opened by the county in 1996 after acquiring the site from private owners. The biggest attraction is Gemini Springs itself, a natural spring with waters at 72 degrees year-round, but the pristine woods and surroundings are also a draw. You can swim in the spring's 200-by-60-foot swimming hole, which is about eight feet deep, and kids can amuse themselves by jumping in from a dock. Canoes are available for rent. The park offers interpretive programs and a 1.5-mile-long nature trail. All of the campground amenities are newly built, and it's frequented mostly by locals or their tourist friends looking for a quiet getaway with no RV traffic.

Campsites, facilities: Only tents are allowed on these 40-plus sites (no hookups). Water is available near the campsites, all of which rest on elevated pads and have picnic tables and grills. Restrooms and showers are available. On the premises are a natural spring with swimming, nature trails, a playground, and a camp circle. Part of the park is wheelchair accessible, but not the campsites. Children are welcome. Leashed pets are permitted.

Reservations, fees: Reservations are recommended. Sites are $20 per night for up to eight people. The park has a $3.50 admission per car. Credit cards are not accepted. The maximum stay is two weeks.

Directions: From I-4, take Exit 108 onto Dirksen Drive westbound toward DeBary one mile. The park entrance will be on your left.

Contact: Gemini Springs, 37 Dirksen Drive, DeBary, FL 32713, 407/668-3810, fax 386/668-3812. Or contact the Volusia County Leisure Services Department, 202 North Florida Avenue, DeLand, FL 32720-4618, 386/736-5953, website: www.volusia.org/parks/camping.htm.

PARADISE LAKES TRAVEL TRAILER PARK

Rating: 4

South of Deltona
Daytona Beach map, grid c1, page 220

This family-run campground is set in an oak forest next to a small lake with a swimming beach where anglers try to catch bass. Most campsites are sandy, although a few are grassy. If you want to canoe or go out in a johnboat, bring your own; no motorized watercraft are allowed on the lake. Most campers are senior citizens who stay only during the winter months. Some weekend regulars leave their trailers on site and pay $80 to $85 for the privilege. Although campsites 1 through 40 are termed "lakeside," sunbathers may prefer sites 11 through 20 to be closest to the beach.

Campsites, facilities: The park offers 175 full-hookup sites for RVs and limited tent sites. Seven sites are pull-through. On the premises are restrooms, showers, a dump station, laundry facilities, a playground, horseshoes, and a limited convenience store. Groceries and restaurants are about two miles away. Children are permitted. Leashed pets are allowed in the camping area but are forbidden at the beach and the grassy beachfront.

Reservations, fees: Reservations are recommended from October through April but are not necessary at other times. Sites are $20 per night for two people, plus $2 for each additional person. Credit cards are not accepted. Long-term stays are OK.

Directions: From I-4 at Exit 53, head east on DeBary Avenue/Doyle Road for about four miles. You'll see the park on the right.

Contact: Paradise Lakes Travel Trailer Park, 1571 Doyle Road, Deltona, FL 32725, 386/574-2371.

17 LAKE MONROE CONSERVATION AREA

Rating: 6

On Lake Monroe and the St. Johns River east of Sanford
Daytona Beach map, grid c1, page 220

Native Americans long ago hunted and fished on these marshy 7,390 acres. Now, anglers and boaters travel down this stretch of the St. Johns River and canoeists sometimes paddle on Lake Monroe. In all, this retreat offers more than three miles of shoreline on the lake or river. The rustic, no-frills campsites are on the northern bank of the St. Johns and are well separated from each other. More than five miles of hiking trails start at the parking area off Reed Ellis Road and make three loops as they wind through floodplain marsh, swamp, and forest. Look for wood storks, sandhill cranes, turkeys, deer, and plentiful alligators. About 94 percent of this land is wetlands, so much of it is not accessible on foot. Bring a hat and sunscreen because it's an open, sunny place. American Forests' Global ReLeaf program is working to add more trees to the place, formerly known as the Kratzert Tract (named for one-time owner Minnie Beck Kratzert).

Campsites, facilities: Tents only are permitted at six primitive campsites, which are reached by boat or hiking. There are no restrooms or other facilities. Bring food, supplies, mosquito repellent, and everything else you'll need.

A nearby boat ramp providing access to the conservation area's portion of the St. Johns River is found on State Road 46, a little more than two miles east of County Road 415. Children are welcome. Pets must be leashed.

Reservations, fees: Sites are first-come, first-served. Camping is free. Each site accommodates up to six people. If your party has at least seven people, get a free permit and reserve at least one week ahead at 386/329-4404. Maximum stay for all campers is seven days.

Directions: From Sanford, go east about four miles on State Road 46 to County Road 415, where you'll turn north (left). Travel about three miles on the county road, crossing the St. Johns River, then turn into a parking area, at right. Another parking area—for better hiking, bird-watching, and for horseback riding—is farther east. To get there, continue on County Road 415 about one mile, turn left onto Reed Ellis Road, and continue .9 mile to the parking area, at left. For more details, get a map and booklet from the water district before your trip.

Contact: St. Johns River Water Management District, Division of Land Management, P.O. Box 1429, Palatka, FL 32178-1429, 407/893-3127, website: www.sjrwmd.com.

18 ORANGE ISLES CAMPGROUND

Rating: 6

In Port Orange
Daytona Beach map, grid b3, page 220

One big plus in winter is that you can pick oranges and grapefruit from the trees growing in this renovated 17-acre campground, although some visitors are more interested in jumping into the 50-foot-long swimming pool. The large, shaded campsites are about 2.5 miles from the Atlantic Ocean and just around the corner from the Port Orange Sugar Mill Ruins (see next campground, Nova Family Campground). It's close to Daytona's International Speedway and is popular during Bike Week and other festivities.

Tenters are set aside in a section between the trailer storage area and Nova Road, which is a fairly busy street. A few guests stay long-term and sleep at grassy sites farther off the main road. A bathhouse and shuffleboard court are by sites 77 to 84. If you're lucky, you'll be here when sweet-scented oranges are in bloom.

Campsites, facilities: There are 350 full-hookup sites for RVs and tents. Each site has a picnic table. On the premises are showers, restrooms, a dump station, a log cabin recreation room, a pool, a playground, shuffleboard, horseshoes, and laundry facilities. Restrooms and showers are wheelchair accessible, according to management. Groceries and restaurants are within one mile. Children are permitted. Leashed pets are allowed.

Reservations, fees: Reservations are recommended. Sites are $15 to $35 per night for two people, plus $5 for each additional person (except kids under 12). Rates are higher during special events. Major credit cards are accepted. Long-term stays are OK.

Directions: From I-95 at Exit 260A, proceed east on State Road 400 about three miles to Nova Road. Turn right and drive past three traffic lights. Look for the park on the right.

Contact: Orange Isles Campground, 3520 South Nova Road, Port Orange, FL 32119, 386/767-9170, website: www.daytonachamber.com/orangeisles/index.htm.

19 NOVA FAMILY CAMPGROUND

Rating: 5

In Port Orange
Daytona Beach map, grid b3, page 220

Amid the big oaks shrouded in Spanish moss, you'll occasionally hear owls hooting at night. Weddings and family reunions sometimes are held in the log cabin recreation hall, and special events include hayrides, pig roasts, canoe trips, and karaoke nights. If you arrive at the 18.5-acre wooded park during one of two motorcycle gatherings, Biketoberfest in October or Bike Week in March, you may see an unusual event for campgrounds—a wet T-shirt contest. "The biker-friendly place to camp," proclaims the park's pamphlet.

Tall, dense oaks shade the grassy campsites, some of which have concrete pads. Tent sites tend to be at the perimeter, but most full-hookup RV sites are within reasonable distance of the fenced pool toward the back of the campground. Although campers aged 30 and older are targeted, families with children are welcome. Aquatic activities are available fairly close by at beaches, springs, rivers, and lakes. The Daytona International Speedway is also nearby.

History buffs can travel a few blocks down Herbert Street to the ruins of a sugar mill that dates to before Florida's statehood—the Sugar Mill Ruins. Today you can see the decrepit coquina-rock and sandstone walls of the sugar mills along with some of the big vats and other machinery used by British and Bahamian settlers. During the War between the States, Confederate soldiers moved from the battle-torn beach to this inland mill to process salt, not sugar, for preserving meat for shipment to battle lines. Some 80 years later, in 1946, the site was turned into a tourist attraction. It was a kind of botanical garden featuring shade-tolerant plants such as azaleas (which still bloom in spring), as well as bromeliads, succulents, ivy, and palms. In the early 1950s it was turned into a short-lived dinosaur attraction called Bongoland, named for Bongo, a baboon that was kept here. Today you'll see large stone replicas of dinosaurs at the shady, 12-acre park, which is now maintained by a group of volunteers. In a weird sort of way, it encapsulates Florida's history from colonial days to the present.

Campsites, facilities: Two hundred tent sites are set apart from the 100 RV sites (50 full-hookup, 10 pull-through). Picnic tables and grills are available at some sites. On the premises are showers, restrooms, fire rings, a dump station, a recreation room, a pool, horseshoes, shuffleboard, a game room, limited groceries, snacks, and laundry facilities. Cable TV and telephone hookups are available, as is firewood. Children are welcome. Pets are permitted, for a daily fee.

Reservations, fees: Reservations are recommended. Sites are $25 per night for two people, plus $3 for each additional person over age 10, $1 for pets weighing less than 25 pounds, and $2 for larger animals. Rates increase during special events such as Bike Week. Major credit cards are accepted. Long-term stays are OK.

Directions: From I-95 at Exit 256, go east on State Route 421/Dunlawton Avenue through two stoplights to Clyde Morris Boulevard and turn left. Continue north through two more lights to Herbert Street, then turn right. The park is .25 mile ahead.

Contact: Nova Family Campground, 1190 Herbert Street, Port Orange, FL 32119, 386/767-0095, fax 386/767-1666.

20 DAYTONA BEACH CAMPGROUND

Rating: 6

In Port Orange

Daytona Beach map, grid b3, page 220

Although it is dubbed Daytona Beach Campground, this 17-acre park actually is in the quieter neighboring city of Port Orange. The open and shaded campsites are set in a neighborhood located just a few miles from the Daytona Beach Regional Airport and the Daytona International Speedway. Although overnighters appreciate that fact, patrons also include long-term residents who enjoy holding bingo games, potluck dinners, and dances away from the bustling throng of oceanside Daytona Beach. Like all campgrounds in the area, this place is extremely popular during certain times from February through April, starting with Bike Week and lasting through Spring Break. For day trips, drive about six miles to swim in the Atlantic Ocean instead of the park's pool, or travel about three miles to the Sugar Mill Ruins (see Nova Family Campground in this chapter).

Campsites, facilities: A section of 25 tent sites is set apart from the 180 full-hookup RV sites (25 pull-through). Around 100 sites are available for overnighters. Each site has a picnic table. On the premises are restrooms, showers, a dump station, a recreation room, a pool, a playground, shuffleboard, horseshoes, basketball, and laundry facilities. Cable TV is available. Management says the office and restrooms are wheelchair accessible. Groceries, snacks, and a restaurant are within walking distance. Children and leashed, attended pets are welcome.

Reservations, fees: Reservations are required. Sites are $27 per night for two people, plus $5 for each additional person. Major credit cards are accepted. Stay as long as six months.

Directions: From I-95 at Exit 260A, proceed east on State Road 400 for about 2.5 miles to Clyde Morris Boulevard. Turn right and continue about three miles south to the campground on the left.

Contact: Daytona Beach Campground, 4601 South Clyde Morris Boulevard, Daytona Beach, FL 32119, 386/761-2663, fax 386/761-9187.

21 ROSE BAY TRAVEL PARK

Rating: 5

At Rose Bay in Port Orange
Daytona Beach map, grid b3, page 220

Popular with Canadians who escape frigid temperatures by spending winters on Rose Bay, inland from the Atlantic beach, the 37-acre park gets crowded with all manner of folks during Bike Week in spring and Race Week in winter.

To sleep closest to the waterfront recreation area at the tip of this long, narrow, somewhat shaded campground, ask about campsites 300 to 305. To be closest to the boat launch and dock, try sites 283 to 289 or 227 to 231. The pool and recreation room are at the opposite

end of the park near campsite 78. Besides bingo and potluck dinners, some winter residents enjoy fishing in the park's small brackish lake.

Campsites, facilities: All 307 full-hookup sites can accommodate RVs up to 40 feet long, and 20 spots may be used for tents. On the premises are restrooms, showers, a dump station, laundry facilities, picnic tables, a pool, shuffleboard and *pétanque* courts, a dock, a boat ramp, and a recreation room. Cable TV and telephone service are available. Groceries and restaurants are nearby. Children are allowed on a short-term basis. Pets must be kept on three-foot leashes.

Reservations, fees: Reservations are recommended. Sites are $25 per night for two people, plus $5 for each additional person. Major credit cards are accepted. Adults are welcome for long-term stays.

Directions: From I-95 at Exit 256, take State Road 421 east for three miles to Nova Road. Turn right and head south. The campground is about five miles ahead on the right, .5 mile west of U.S. 1.

Contact: Rose Bay Travel Park, 5200 South Nova Road, Port Orange, FL 32127, 386/767-4308, fax 386/767-7060, email floridianrvresorts@aol.com.

22 SUGAR MILL MOBILE HOME PARK

Rating: 2

Off I-95 at New Smyrna Beach
Daytona Beach map, grid b3, page 220

Campers at these grassy sites are somewhat outnumbered by residents of the senior park's 40 mobile homes, so expect a residential feel. Sugar Mill's main attraction is its access—a quick hop off I-95, four miles from the Atlantic Ocean, 10 miles from the Canaveral National Seashore, and one hour from major Orlando attractions. Entertainment options at the 15-acre park are slim, highlighted by a fishing pond and wintertime organized activities such as bingo and craft-making. The namesake sugar mill actually is .5 mile away at the Sugar Mill Ruins Historic Site, a small, wooded Volusia County-run park where picnickers eat near the decrepit stone walls of a sugar mill built before the Second Seminole War.

Campsites, facilities: For campers aged 55 and older, this park has 30 full-hookup sites accommodating RVs up to 35 feet long. On the premises are showers, restrooms, laundry facilities, a recreation room, shuffleboard, a pool table, and a fishing pond. Groceries and a restaurant are .5 mile away. Bait is 1.5 miles away. Children are not permitted. Leashed pets are allowed.

Reservations, fees: Reservations are required. Sites are $20 per night for two people, plus $5 for each additional person. No credit cards are accepted. Long-term stays are OK.

Directions: From I-95 at Exit 249, head east on State Road 44 for .25 mile to the park entrance at right.

Contact: Sugar Mill Mobile Home Park, 2590 State Road 44, New Smyrna Beach, FL 32168, 386/428-9052, fax 386/428-8802.

23 DAYTONA SOUTH/ NEW SMYRNA BEACH KOA

Rating: 6

West of New Smyrna Beach
Daytona Beach map, grid c3, page 220

Swimmers have their choice of aquatic venues: the campground pool or the Atlantic Ocean five miles away, where you can drive on the hard-packed sand (except when the nests of endangered sea turtles are present). Some shell-rock or grassy campsites are sunny, whereas others enjoy shade from magnolias, oaks, or palms. Indeed, 25 acres of this 30-acre park are dotted with trees, and campsites are scattered throughout. Expect little privacy, though, because campsites are right next to each other with little or no brush to separate them. During some holiday periods, children's activities

are organized here, but retirees dominate from November to April, when activities trend toward bingo, potluck dinners, and dances. It's about 20 miles to the Merritt Island National Wildlife Refuge, heading south. Daytona International Speedway is about 20 miles north.

Campsites, facilities: A section of 60 tent sites is set apart from the 208 RV sites. Each site has a picnic table. On the premises are showers, restrooms, a dump station, a recreation room, cabin rentals, a pool, a playground, a game room, miniature golf, horseshoes, shuffleboard, limited groceries, and laundry facilities. Restaurants and bait are within five miles. The showers and store are wheelchair accessible, according to management. Children and leashed pets are welcome.

Reservations, fees: Reservations are recommended. Sites are $21 to $24 per night (higher during special events) for two people, plus $2.50 for each additional adult and $2 for cable TV. Major credit cards are accepted. Long-term stays are OK.

Directions: From I-95 at Exit 249, go east on State Road 44 to Old Mission Road. Turn right and continue 1.5 miles south to the campground on your right.

Contact: Daytona South/New Smyrna Beach KOA, 1300 Old Mission Road, New Smyrna Beach, FL 32168, 386/427-3581 or 800/562-1244, website: www.beachcamping.net.

24 SUGAR MILL RUINS TRAVEL PARK

Rating: 4

West of U.S. 1 in New Smyrna Beach
Daytona Beach map, grid c3, page 220

At this shady campground where anglers catch mullet and catfish from the banks of the brackish fishing hole, the owners have taken some pains to preserve native Florida vegetation. The full-hookup grassy campsites along Quail Hollow Drive tend to enjoy the most shade from palms, pines, and oaks. Camping spots farther from the center of the park can be quite sunny because they're in the garden section, where small hibiscus bushes dominate. Sites are lined up, as many as 21 to 25 abreast, along straight, 5 mph roads whose names conjure up natural images—Jack Rabbit Run, Raccoon Road, Armadillo Drive. To sleep nearest to the pool (and the entrance-area laundry room), ask about full-hookup sites 47 to 50.

Don't expect to see a sugar mill. The park gets its name from the nearby Sugar Mill Ruins Historic Site, a small, sleepy, wooded, Volusia County-run park. It serves as a reminder of the Second Seminole War, when Indians clashed with settlers who moved into the area to grow sugar and indigo, a plant valued for its role in making a then-popular blue dye. You can picnic at tables near the decaying stone walls of the mill, now being overcome by sabal palms and other native vegetation. Elsewhere, the quaint commercial district of New Smyrna Beach is sort of a quiet cousin of Daytona Beach. For now, at least, it's far enough removed from Daytona that it doesn't get quite the crowds, except for spillover business during the festivals in Daytona Beach.

Campsites, facilities: An area with 62 tent sites is adjacent to the 117 RV sites (most full-hookup and pull-through). On the premises are showers, restrooms, a dump station, laundry facilities, a recreation room, a convenience store, a pool, volleyball, basketball, a playground, horseshoes, and canoe rentals. Cable TV hookups are available. Children must be adult-supervised at the pool. Leashed pets must use the designated dog walk.

Reservations, fees: Reservations are recommended except in summer. Sites typically are $30 per night for two people in season, $20 other times. Add $3 for each additional adult. Major credit cards are accepted. Long-term stays are OK.

Directions: From I-95 at Exit 249, head east on State Road 44. Turn right onto Old Mission Road. In about .25 mile, look for the faux waterwheel marking the campground entrance on the right.

Contact: Sugar Mill Ruins Travel Park, 1050 Old Mission Road, New Smyrna Beach, FL 32168, 386/427-2284, fax 386/428-8521, website: www.sugarmilltravelpark.com.

25 LAKE ASHBY PARK

Rating: 8

Southwest of New Smyrna Beach

Daytona Beach map, grid c3, page 220

Located on 3,200-acre Lake Ashby, this county-run park is set in a beautiful hardwood and softwood hammock. No RVs are permitted, which is a bonus to tenters who want to get away from it all. Note that the showers are cold. The wooded park has a fishing pier and boardwalk near the lake, and there's a prehistoric archaeological site. As always around Florida lakes, be careful of alligators.

Campsites, facilities: Ten tent sites are available. Restrooms and cold showers are provided but no water or electricity hookups. A boardwalk, a pavilion, and a fishing pier are wheelchair accessible. Children are welcome. Leashed pets are permitted.

Reservations, fees: Reservations are recommended. Sites are $10 to $15 per night for up to six people. Credit cards are not accepted. Campers may stay as long as two weeks.

Directions: From I-95, take Exit 249 west on State Road 44 about five miles. At State Road 415, turn south and drive 4.5 miles to an orange TV tower. Turn east onto Lake Ashby Road and follow the signs to Boy Scout Camp Road. The park is about .5 mile ahead on the right.

Contact: Lake Ashby Park, 4150 Boy Scout Camp Road, New Smyrna Beach, FL 32764, 386/428-4589, fax 386/424-2970. Or contact the Volusia County Leisure Services Department, 202 North Florida Avenue, DeLand, FL 32720-4618, 386/736-5953, website: www.volusia.org/parks/camping.htm.

26 SPRUCE CREEK PARK

Rating: 7

South of Port Orange

Daytona Beach map, grid c3, page 220

Spruce Creek Park spells r-e-l-i-e-f for tenters weary of sharing campgrounds with trailers or motorhomes. RVs are not welcome in this county-run park, which is primarily a picnic and daytime recreation spot for locals. Located just off busy U.S. 1, you can launch your canoe onto Spruce Creek or cast a line from the fishing pier. The surroundings are wooded.

Campsites, facilities: Only tents are allowed at this 17-site campground. Each has a picnic table and grill; water is available, but electricity is not. Restrooms, showers, and firewood are available. On the premises are a campground pavilion, a fishing pier, a canoe launch, a playground, and a nature trail. The pavilion and pier are wheelchair accessible. Children are welcome. Leashed pets are permitted.

Reservations, fees: Reservations are recommended. Sites are $10 to $15 per night for up to six people. Credit cards are not accepted. The maximum stay is two weeks.

Directions: From I-95, take Exit 249 east on State Road 44 for five miles. Turn north on U.S. 1 and drive 5.5 miles. The park is located on the west side just north of the three bridges crossing Spruce Creek.

Contact: Spruce Creek Park, 6250 South Ridgewood Avenue, Port Orange, FL 32127, 386/322-5133, fax 386/304-5515. Or contact the Volusia County Leisure Services, 202 North Florida Avenue, DeLand, FL 32720-4618, 386/736-5953, website: www.volusia.org/parks/camping.htm.

27 RIVER BREEZE PARK

Rating: 7

South of New Smyrna Beach

Daytona Beach map, grid c2, page 220

No RVs are allowed into this nicely wooded, county-run campground, which makes a peaceful and relaxing stay for tenters. The campground is located on the Intracoastal Waterway, where you'll see dolphins at play and sometimes manatees lolling in the shallows. A big draw at the park is the boat ramp, but you can also fish from the dock nearby. Bird-watching is also a favorite activity.

Campsites, facilities: Seventeen tent sites are available. Each has a picnic table and grill but no water or electricity hookups. Restrooms and showers are in the campground. Two campsites, the boat ramp, dock, and restrooms are wheelchair accessible. Children are welcome. Leashed pets are permitted.

Reservations, fees: Reservations are recommended. Sites are $15 per night. Credit cards are not accepted. Campers can stay up to two weeks.

Directions: If traveling northbound on I-95, take Exit 231 east one mile to U.S. 1. Turn north on U.S. 1 and drive about eight miles to H.H. Burch Road. If southbound, take Exit 244 and drive east to U.S. 1. Turn south on U.S. 1 and drive to Oak Hill and H.H. Burch Road.

Contact: River Breeze Park, 250 H.H. Burch Road, Oak Hill, FL, 386/345-5525, fax 386/345-5526. Or contact Volusia County Leisure Services, 202 North Florida Avenue, DeLand, FL 32720, 386/736-5953, website: www.volusia.org/parks/camping.htm.

Chapter 9

Orlando Area

Orlando Area

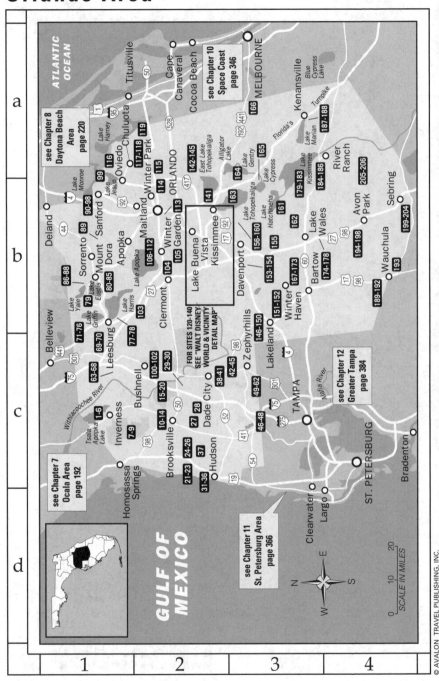

Walt Disney World & Vicinity

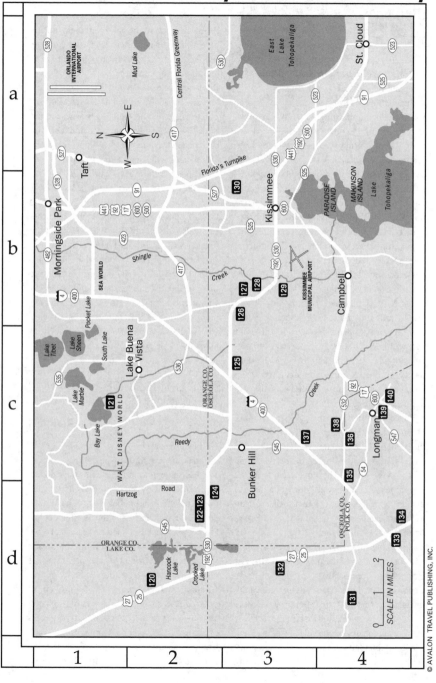

© AVALON TRAVEL PUBLISHING, INC.

1 POTTS PRESERVE

🚶 🚴 🛶 ⛺

Rating: 9

East of Inverness between Tsala Apopka Lake and the Withlacoochee River

Orlando map, grid c1, page 240

When you're approaching the 9,349-acre property, keep an eye out to the left side of the road, where you may see swallow-tailed kites soaring overhead as they search for food. The endangered scrub jay also is found in the pockets of sandhill scrub interspersed throughout this beautiful land, with riverine swamp, freshwater marsh, Florida flatwoods, and other types of habitat, including former pasturelands. Other wildlife seen here are the fox squirrel, deer, turkey, and gopher tortoises.

Hikers can use 30 miles of trails, including a four-mile walk along the Withlacoochee River and a 16-mile back-country loop. There are 12 miles of roads for horseback riders and bicycling. Formerly a ranch, this land was acquired by the state to preserve the wetlands that are so important to Florida's water purity. Canoeists and anglers can enjoy the river and paddle up to the River campsite described below.

Three campsites are accessible by car: Oak Hammock, Equestrian, and River. Probably the prettiest is Oak Hammock, set amid a cluster of the old, moss-draped oaks that define backwoods Florida. The Equestrian and Oak Hammock sites have wells, but you'll need to boil or purify the water before drinking. Chemical toilets can be found at the River and Equestrian sites. Additionally, there are two backpacking camps: the Holly Tree site in the northeast portion of the property, and the Far Point site in the northwest corner.

Campsites, facilities: There are several camping areas in this 8,507-acre preserve of forest, freshwater marshes, and oak hammocks. A few sites are near the equestrian staging area, which offers a limited number of horse stalls; water is available. The other two camping areas—one near the banks of the Withlacoochee River and one in an oak hammock—do not have water. Bring water, food, and camping supplies, and pack out trash. Children are allowed, but dogs are not.

Reservations, fees: Permits are required. Contact the district by phone, or download the application from the website (www.swfwmd.state.fl.us/recguide/permitsapps.htm) and mail or fax it back. You must allow 10 working days for processing the application. Camping is free.

Directions: From Inverness, drive west on U.S. 41 to the intersection with State Road 44. Immediately after the intersection, continue as U.S. 41 curves around. Turn right on Turner Camp Road/County Road 581. Drive about five miles to the entrance on Dee River Road. A boat ramp at Hooty Point where the county road dead-ends at the water gives access to the river hiking trail and the canoe route.

Contact: Southwest Florida Water Management District, 2379 Broad Street, Brooksville, FL 34609-6899, 352/796-7211, ext. 4470 or 800/423-1476, ext. 4470, fax: 352/754-6877, website: www.swfwmd.state.fl.us.

2 RIVERSIDE LODGE

🛶 ⛺ 🏠 ♿ 🚐

Rating: 3

East of Inverness

Orlando map, grid c1, page 240

Want to settle in for a while? This park prefers RVers who like to stay put. Sites are nestled under tall oaks and palms next to the Withlacoochee River and near the Withlacoochee State Trail, which is a good route for bicycling. Bass anglers and canoeists think the area is paradise. In the winter, social programs are held in the park's recreation hall.

Campsites, facilities: This 39-unit, adult-oriented park has 10 RV sites with full hookups. Trailers must be self-contained; no restrooms or showers are available. On the property are laundry facilities, a wheelchair-accessible recreation lodge, and a boat ramp. There are no facilities for children. Leashed pets under 20 pounds are permitted.

Reservations, fees: Reservations are recommended. Sites are $20 per night for two people. Credit cards are not accepted. Long-term stays are OK.

Directions: From I-75, take State Road 44 west 8.5 miles toward Inverness.

Contact: Riverside Lodge, 12561 East Gulf to Lake Highway, Inverness, FL 34450, 352/726-2002.

3 FORT COOPER STATE PARK

Rating: 4

East of Inverness

Orlando map, grid c1, page 240

Set in lush hardwood hammocks, these are primitive, out-in-the-woods campsites that are accessible by car. They're not right on Lake Holathlikaha, but a long drought has dropped the water level so low that swimming is no longer possible. The springs that once fed the lake have also dried up. About 10 miles of hiking trails wind mostly through shady oak hammocks and sandhill areas. Horseback riders can't use these paths, but just outside park boundaries the Rails-to-Trails network is open to them.

Lake Holathlikaha, it's said, was a welcome stopover for federal soldiers who sweated through the Florida outback during the Second Seminole War in the 1830s and 1840s, supplying them with water and sustenance. In 1836, some 380 soldiers, most of them wounded or sick, hastily built a fort near the lake. It served them for 16 days while they skirmished with the Seminoles until reinforcements arrived. Once a year, the park holds reenactments of what life was like in those days, with militiamen, Seminoles, and Army regulars acting out their duties.

Campsites, facilities: About 15 tents can be accommodated at two primitive camping areas. Each site has a picnic table, a grill, and a fire

ring. The only facilities are vault toilets and running water. The park has canoe and paddleboat rentals and hiking trails. Groceries and restaurants are within three miles. Children are welcome. Pets are prohibited.

Reservations, fees: Reservations are required. Sites are $3 per night per adult, $2 per child. Credit cards are not accepted. Stays are limited to two weeks.

Directions: From Inverness, take U.S. 41 south to the city limits and follow the signs to the park.

Contact: Fort Cooper State Park, 3100 South Old Floral City, Inverness, FL 34450, 352/726-0315, fax 352/726-5959.

4 TRAIL'S END CAMP

Rating: 6

Near Floral City

Orlando map, grid c1, page 240

This heavily wooded campground is located on the Withlacoochee River, with views of miles of undeveloped cypress-lined riverbank. Paddle your canoe, or fish from the dock. You're pretty much surrounded by wilderness. The river's headwaters are in northern Polk County at Green Swamp, the same place that gives rise to the Hillsborough, Ocklawaha, and Peace Rivers. Don't confuse it with the river of the same name in northern Florida. The waters are colored dark by the tannins and organic acids seeping from surrounding cypress swamps and pinewoods. If you brought your bicycle, don't miss the 46-mile Withlacoochee bike trail. Some nature trails are nearby in the Withlacoochee State Forest. In the campground, dancing and music hold forth on Friday and Saturday nights in the wintertime. Saturday is karaoke night. The campground's location in Floral City is ideal for exploring the nearby Withlacoochee State Forest and historic Fort Cooper State Park (see previous campground). It tends to be favored by retirees staying for the winter season, hunters, and anglers.

Campsites, facilities: This 65-acre campground

has eight RV sites for overnighters and 42 for season stays. About 100 primitive tent sites are separated from the RVs, and a water source is nearby. Restrooms, showers, picnic tables, fire rings, a dump station, a playground, a fishing pier, boat docks, a gun range, rental cabins, an archery range, rental canoes and rowboats, and horseshoe pits are available. Children and leashed pets are welcome.

Reservations, fees: Reservations are not necessary. RV sites are $16 per night for four people. Primitive sites are $8. Major credit cards are accepted. Stay as long as you wish.

Directions: From I-75, take Exit 63 and drive west on State Road 48 for 10 miles to Trail's End Road. Turn north and go four miles to the river.

Contact: Trail's End Camp, 12900 Trail's End Road, Floral City, FL 34436, 352/726-3699.

⑤ FLYING EAGLE

Rating: 7

Along the Withlacoochee River southeast of Inverness

Orlando map, grid c1, page 240

It's hard to believe as you look out over the mosaic of small lakes, marshes, and swamps with scattered forest uplands, but this was once a working ranch. The man who built the Flying Eagle ranch heard about a breed of cattle from England, known as Essex cattle, that were adapted to living in swamps. So, during wet periods back in the old days, you could look out over this terrain and see a bunch of cow heads sticking out above the water.

The land, purchased by the water management district and now being returned to a more-natural state, is part of the Tsala Apopka chain of lakes. It's an ideal setting for hiking or horseback riding; mountain bikers can follow 13 miles of forest roads but are strictly prohibited from off-trail use of the property. Some biking may be slow going; while the scenery is beautiful, some sections of the unpaved roads

are sugar-fine sand. Hikers will find more than 16 miles of foot trails. Fishing is best at the Mocassin Slough Bridge.

The most picturesque route is the Loop Road Trail. Turn right off the main road through the property about .25 mile past the entrance station. It's a serpentine road that connects a series of small "islands" that lay in the middle of a large swath of marsh. Check ahead of time if you intend to connect back with the main road and continue on toward the backpackers' campsite; the district has removed about a 100-yard section of the road near the end to improve natural water flows on the property. The best time to avoid high water and hunters is January and February. An alternative in wetter times is to stick to the main road, but it runs along a fence line, and the arrow-straight road does not foster quite the same feeling of being "out there."

Campsites, facilities: There are four primitive camping areas on this 10,720-acre preserve. Two areas, one of which is reserved for equestrian camping, are accessible by car at the front gate to the preserve. A third site is accessible only to backpackers. The fourth is for canoeists traversing the Withlacoochee River. Vehicles are prohibited, except when driving to the two sites by the front gate to offload gear. No water is available. Bring water, food, and camping supplies. Pack out trash. Camping is not allowed during hunting season. (Hunting season is scattered throughout the year and changes by a day or two each year, but generally runs September 28 to October 5, October 25 to 27, November 9 to 17, November 22 to December 15, and March 15 to 23.) No generators, RVs, or loud music. Dogs are forbidden.

Reservations, fees: Permits are required. Contact the district by phone, or download the application from the website (www.swfwmd .state.fl.us/recguide/permitsapps.htm) and mail or fax it back. You must allow 10 working days for processing the application. Camping is free.

Directions: From the intersection of U.S. 41 and State Road 44 in Inverness, go one mile south on U.S. 41. Turn east on Lakeview Drive and go one block to Old Floral City Road. Drive one block south and turn left on Eden Drive. Proceed four miles east to the gate.

Contact: Southwest Florida Water Management District, 2379 Broad Street, Brooksville, FL 34609-6899, 352/796-7211, ext. 4470 or 800/423-1476, ext. 4470, fax: 352/754-6877, website: www.swfwmd.state.fl.us.

6 MOONRISE RESORT

Rating: 6

Between Floral City and Inverness
Orlando map, grid c1, page 240

This campground is part of a quiet five-acre community of rental cabins and mobile homes on the shores of Tsala Apopka Lake. You can rent a boat or canoe and explore the 9,000-acre body of water, which is actually a chain of connected lakes. The park rents johnboats, larger motorboats, canoes, and paddleboats by the hour, day, or week. Cast your line from the dock, or sit on the benches and watch the water. Throughout the park are cypress trees and oaks hung with frilly Spanish moss that trails down from the branches. Pick up supplies in Floral City or in Inverness, which is five miles north. The Withlacoochee State Trail is nearby, and the northern terminus of this 46-mile bicycling, horseback-riding, and walking trail begins in Citrus County near Dunnellon and travels south through Hernando County and the Withlacoochee State Forest, ending in northern Pasco County. Access points are scattered along the route, which parallels U.S. 41 along the northern half and the Withlacoochee River in the southern half. The trail, formerly a railroad right-of-way, is paved; equestrians use a parallel sandy path.

Campsites, facilities: The park has 14 RV sites with full hookups; cable TV and telephone service are available for long-term campers. One site is pull-through. Restrooms, showers, picnic tables, a dump station, a recreation room, laundry facilities, shuffleboard courts, horseshoe pits, a boat ramp, fishing docks, and rental cottages are on the property. Children and leashed pets are welcome.

Reservations, fees: Reservations are recommended. Sites are $15 per night for two people, plus $1 for each additional person. Credit cards are not accepted. Long-term stays are OK. The minimum stay is two nights; on holiday weekends, it's three nights.

Directions: From I-75, take Exit 314 and drive west on State Road 48 for approximately 12 miles until you reach Floral City. One block before you arrive at the big intersection with U.S. 41, turn north on Old Floral City Road, which parallels U.S. 41. Drive 1.5 miles, turn east on Moonrise Lane, and continue .25 mile to the park entrance. Or, from the intersection of U.S. 41 and County Road 39A/Gobbler Road, drive east for one block to Old Floral City Road, then turn south and drive one mile to Moonrise Lane.

Contact: Moonrise Resort, 8801 East Moonrise Lane, Lot 18, Floral City, FL 34436, 352/726-2553 or 800/665-6701, website: www.moonriseresort.com.

7 TILLIS HILL

Rating: 8

In the Withlacoochee State Forest Citrus Tract south of Inverness
Orlando map, grid c1, page 240

Both families and organized equestrian groups enjoy this campground, which serves as a base camp for dozens of miles of horseback-riding trails through the sandy, rolling terrain of the state forest. Ride for the day on forest roads or on trails weaving through the pinewoods, which sprawl over 41,000 acres. (The Citrus Tract is the largest of the five sections of the Withlacoochee State Forest.) There's also a two-day horseback trail with a primitive camping zone called Perryman Place that can accommodate 100 people; be sure to bring water because there are no facilities. Organized groups need to have a permit for all activities in the forest.

Campsites, facilities: Targeted to horseback riders, this state forest campground has 37 sites with water, electricity, picnic tables, grills, and fire rings. There's also a 20-stall horse stable, a dining hall with a kitchen, a large open-air picnic shelter, and a barbecue pit. Restrooms and showers are provided. Children are welcome, but pets are prohibited.

Reservations, fees: Reservations are required. Sites are $13 per night for five people, plus $3 for each horse stall. Two tents or one RV are permitted on each site. The dining hall can be rented for a fee, depending on the size of the group. Credit cards are not accepted.

Directions: From Inverness, drive 10 miles south on U.S. 41 to County Road 480. Turn right and drive eight miles west. Turn north on Forest Road 13 and drive three miles to the campground.

Contact: Withlacoochee State Forest Recreation Visitors Center, 15003 Broad Street, Brooksville, FL 34601, 352/754-6896 or fire dispatch 352/754-6777. For reservations, call 352/344-4238.

8 HOLDER MINE
🚶 🛶 🚐 ⛺

Rating: 8

In the Withlacoochee State Forest Citrus Tract south of Inverness

Orlando map, grid c1, page 240

Holder Mine is so named because there were once phosphate mines in the area. In fact, a pit created by the mining operation remains near the campground, which has oversized sites in a pine forest. There's deep water at the bottom of the pit, and curious anglers have been known to catch fish here, although swimming is prohibited and probably not a good idea for scofflaws. This is also a staging area for hikers on the Florida National Scenic Trail (46 miles long) and for horseback riders exploring the forest. A watering area for horses is pro-

vided, as is a place to tie them up while riders use the restrooms.

Campsites, facilities: You'll find 27 campsites with water, picnic tables, grills, and fire rings. Restrooms, showers, and a dump station are available. Children are welcome. Pets are prohibited.

Reservations, fees: Reservations are not taken. Sites are $10 per night for five people. Credit cards are not accepted. This campground is open only on weekends (from noon Friday through noon Monday) and holidays.

Directions: From the junction of State Road 44 and State Road 581 on the west side of Inverness, drive five miles south on State Road 581 to the campground entrance.

Contact: Withlacoochee State Forest Recreation Visitors Center, 15003 Broad Street, Brooksville, FL 34601, 352/754-6896 or fire dispatch 352/754-6777.

9 MUTUAL MINE RECREATION AREA
🚶 🚐 ⛺

Rating: 9

In the Withlacoochee State Forest Citrus Tract south of Inverness

Orlando map, grid c1, page 240

Campers are well separated from their neighbors in this secluded pine flatwood forest that's remote enough to escape urban traffic and noise. The Florida National Scenic Trail can be accessed from here by walking 1.5 miles west of the campground. An abandoned mining pit is nearby; most of the water has leached out, and it's only about 10 feet deep. Nonetheless, swimming is prohibited. You'll have to pick up supplies in Inverness because there's not much in the way of civilization around here.

Campsites, facilities: There are 13 sites with water, picnic tables, grills, and fire rings. Flush toilets are available, but there are no showers. A youth camping group is also on site. Children are welcome. Pets are prohibited.

Reservations, fees: Reservations are not taken.

Sites are $10 per night for five people. Credit cards are not accepted. This campground is open only on weekends (from noon Friday through noon Monday) and holidays.

Directions: From the junction of State Road 44 and State Road 581 on the west side of Inverness, drive eight miles south on State Road 581 to the campground entrance on the west side of the highway.

Contact: Withlacoochee State Forest Recreation Visitors Center, 15003 Broad Street, Brooksville, FL 34601, 352/754-6896 or fire dispatch 352/754-6777.

10 FRONTIER CAMPGROUND

Rating: 3

West of Brooksville
Orlando map, grid c2, page 240

Near the campground office is a small, open-air gathering place called "Liar's Corner," presumably reserved for anglers bragging about their catch of the day. With little screening between the sites, however, neighbors will know the real truth. Populated by snowbirds and permanent residents, this fenced park is close to doctors' offices, auto repair outfits, and a Wal-Mart. Motorbikes are allowed in the park only for registered camper transportation to their sites—an important point to remember if the Croom Motorcycle Area campground in the Withlacoochee State Forest is full and you have visitors.

Campsites, facilities: There are 110 RV sites in this community of 66 mobile homes. Restrooms, showers, laundry facilities, a dump station, an adult recreation hall, a pool, horseshoe pits, shuffleboard courts, and a playground are provided. Children are welcome. One small dog or cat is permitted on each lot; pets must not be kept outside.

Reservations, fees: Reservations are accepted. Sites are $20 per night for two people, plus $1 for each additional person. No credit cards are accepted. Long-term stays are allowed.

Directions: From Brooksville, drive west on State Road 50 for five miles.

Contact: Frontier Campground, 15549 Cortez Boulevard, Brooksville, FL 34613, 352/796-9988.

11 BRENTWOOD LAKE CAMPING

Rating: 2

North of Brooksville
Orlando map, grid c2, page 240

Secluded from the highway on a wooded hill, the campground is perched on high ground overlooking a private lake stocked with bass, catfish, and bream. Tall oaks provide shade and atmosphere. In the center is a grassy field for tent campers or outdoor games. Grocery stores, restaurants, and a golf course are within two miles. Children are welcome, although most people staying here are retirees. "Spend a little time or a lifetime," say the owners, Laine and Elaine Brayko. "People of all ages are welcome."

Campsites, facilities: There are 100 sites with water and electricity; 61 have sewer hookups. A large area is available for primitive tent camping. Restrooms, showers, picnic tables, a dump station, laundry facilities, a recreation room, shuffleboard courts, and horseshoe pits are available. Children are welcome. Leashed pets are permitted.

Reservations, fees: Reservations are not necessary. Sites are $15 per night for two people, plus $2 for each additional person. If you use air-conditioning or electric heaters, there is an additional charge of $2 per unit. Credit cards are not accepted. Long-term stays are allowed.

Directions: From Brooksville, drive north on U.S. 41 for 3.2 miles. Turn west onto Ancient Trail, a gravel road, and go .2 mile to the campground.

Contact: Brentwood Lake Camping, 11089 Ancient Trail, Brooksville, FL 34601, 352/796-5760.

12 CLOVER LEAF FOREST RV PARK

Rating: 6

In Brooksville

Orlando map, grid c2, page 240

A sign at the entrance states: "Welcome back, winter residents. We missed you." What are they coming back to? A shaded, wooded setting of slash pines and leafy oak trees and neatly kept campsites with concrete patios. Another unusual feature is the indoor swimming pool, Jacuzzi, and sauna. Believe it or not, it can easily get too cold for outdoor swimming in upper Florida, although, of course, everything's relative. The RV park is next door to a mobile home community, and many campers stay for the season.

Campsites, facilities: All 277 RV sites have full hookups. Restrooms, showers, laundry facilities, picnic tables, an indoor and an outdoor pool, a recreation room, shuffleboard, billiards and card room, horseshoe pits, cable TV access, and telephone service are available. Some areas are wheelchair accessible. Children may stay up to two weeks in the campground but are not allowed in the adjacent adults-only mobile home park. Leashed pets are permitted.

Reservations, fees: Reservations are recommended. Sites are $27 per night for two people, plus $1 per extra person. Major credit cards are accepted. Long-term rates are available.

Directions: From I-75 at Exit 301, go west 10 miles on State Road 50, which merges into State Road 50A. Turn right (north) onto State Road 41. Look for the park one mile ahead, across the street from an elementary school.

Contact: Clover Leaf Forest RV Park, 910 North Broad Street, Brooksville, FL 34601, 352/796-8016 or 877/796-5381, fax 352/796-5381, email: cnichols@hometownamerica.net.

13 HIDDEN VALLEY CAMPGROUND

Rating: 4

East of Brooksville

Orlando map, grid c2, page 240

Enormous live oak trees provide a pretty, leafy canopy over this rustic, family-friendly campground, a long-time family operation where the owner raised his children and doesn't feel hostile toward yours. One attraction nearby in Brooksville is Roger's Christmas House Village, a garden complex of five historic houses where various vendors sell gifts. Also in Brooksville, you'll find grocery stores and plenty of fast-food restaurants, mostly on the south side of town along U.S. 41.

Campsites, facilities: All 71 RV sites have full hookups and cable TV access. Telephone service is available at 40 sites. Restrooms, showers, picnic tables, laundry facilities, a playground, a recreation hall, horseshoe pits, and shuffleboard courts are provided on the property. Families with children are welcome. Leashed pets are allowed.

Reservations, fees: Reservations are not necessary. Sites are $18 per night for two people, plus $2 for each additional person. A surcharge of $2 per day applies if you use air-conditioning or an electric heater. Credit cards are not accepted. Long-term stays are permitted.

Directions: From I-75, take Exit 301 and drive west for approximately seven miles on State Road 50 to the campground entrance. Or, from Brooksville, drive 2.5 miles east on State Road 50.

Contact: Hidden Valley Campground, 22329 Cortez Boulevard, Brooksville, FL 34601, 352/796-8710.

14 LAKESIDE MOBILE MANOR

Rating: 2

In Brooksville

Orlando map, grid c2, page 240

Coffee and doughnuts are served to guests at this RV park on Saturday mornings, but if that's not enough to get you going, cast your line in a four-acre fishing lake and try your luck. Most campers here are staying for six months in the cooler season.

Campsites, facilities: Targeting snowbirds, this 14-acre lakefront mobile home park has 73 spaces, with 40 available for RVs. Full hookups, cable TV and telephone access, and picnic tables are provided at each site. There are no showers. Campers under age 55 are not welcome. The recreation hall is wheelchair accessible. Leashed pets weighing less than 30 pounds are permitted; limit one per site.

Reservations, fees: Reservations are recommended. Sites are $20 per night for two people, plus $3 per extra person. Credit cards are not accepted. Long-term stays are OK; stay for six months and leave the RV for the rest of the year for free.

Directions: From downtown Brooksville, travel one mile north on U.S. 41. The park entrance is at the intersection of the highway and Croom Road.

Contact: Lakeside Mobile Manor, 1020 Lakeside Drive, Brooksville, FL 34601, 352/796-4600.

15 BUTTGENBACH MINE CAMPGROUND (FORMERLY CROOM MOTORCYCLE AREA)

Rating: 7

In the Croom Tract of Withlacoochee State Forest

Orlando map, grid c2, page 240

Nearby is the Croom Motorcycle Area, which is nirvana for motorcyclists, dirt bikers, and all-terrain cycle fans. The motorcycle area sets aside 2,600 acres for cyclists to rev their engines and roar around the forest. The result is a kind of dusty moonscape of denuded trails, lonely trees with all the soil eroded around their roots, and a noise level to rival the Grand Prix. Decades ago, the terrain had been damaged already by phosphate mining operations, borrow pits dug to build the interstate highway, and cyclists during a time when their activities were not regulated and they were free to roam. By setting aside this land, the state confines the motorcycles to one area. Bikers from as far north as Canada come to use the "training pit," a crater-sized sandy valley with plenty of bumps for getting airborne. An "inexperienced rider area" is near the campground. There's also a day-use area with picnic tables, water, restrooms, and parking. Bikers must purchase permits ($35 for one year, or $5 per quarter) in person at the entrance gate; credit cards are not accepted. All cycles must be trailered in; however, you are allowed to ride your vehicle in low gear from the campground to the riding area. No bicycling is allowed. If the campground is full, then try the nearby Silver Lake Recreation Complex or Tall Pines RV Park.

Campsites, facilities: All 50 sites in this state forest campground have electricity. Water, restrooms, showers, grills, fire rings, and picnic tables are available. Children are welcome. Pets are prohibited.

Reservations, fees: Reservations are not taken. Sites are $13 per night for five people. Up to five people, using two tents or one RV, are permitted per site. Larger groups need to get a permit first. Credit cards are not accepted.

Directions: From I-75, take Exit 301 westbound on State Road 50 and drive .1 mile. Turn north onto Western Way; the forest entrance is just ahead. Buttgenbach Mine Campground is four miles north of the entrance. Be sure your gear is tied securely because the dirt road is pitted and bumpy.

Contact: Withlacoochee State Forest Recreation Visitors Center, 15003 Broad Street,

Brooksville, FL 34601, 352/754-6896 or fire dispatch 352/754-6777.

16 SILVER LAKE CAMPGROUND

Rating: 9

In the Croom Tract of Withlacoochee State Forest, Silver Lake Recreation Complex
Orlando map, grid c2, page 240

Silver Lake gets much use from locals and savvy folks during the summer, but it can be nearly deserted weekdays in the winter. It's also convenient to I-75, a fact that campers on the road may not realize. Interstate noise is the only drawback; otherwise, the campground would be nearly perfect. It overlooks Silver Lake, which is really a broad area on the Withlacoochee River; your neighbors in the campground may be canoeists passing through. The woods are thick and shady, and cypress trees with peculiar-looking root knobs erupting from the ground line the bottomlands near the lake. More than 30 miles of hiking trails are in the surrounding forest. (Paved and unpaved bicycle trails are also at hand on the Withlacoochee State Trail.) Note that mountain bikes are restricted to forest roads and the approved off-road trails; hiking trails are for foot traffic only. The local health department has banned swimming in the river as a potential health hazard because of bacteria, but the truth is that people do go for dips at will.

Campsites, facilities: Twenty-three campsites have water, electricity, grills, fire rings, and picnic tables. Restrooms, showers, a dump station, and a boat ramp are available. Children are welcome. Pets are allowed.

Reservations, fees: Reservations are not taken. Sites are $13 per night for five people. Up to five people, using two tents or one RV, are permitted per site. Groups require a permit. Credit cards are not accepted.

Directions: From I-75, take Exit 309 eastbound on State Road 50 for .75 mile. Turn north at the traffic light; the highway is marked as Croom Rital Road on the north side and Kettering Road on the south side, but just follow the signs for the Withlacoochee State Trail. Drive 3.5 miles. Just before the interstate overpass, turn east into the Silver Lake complex. This is the first campground on your left.

Contact: Withlacoochee State Forest Recreation Visitors Center, 15003 Broad Street, Brooksville, FL 34601, 352/754-6896 or fire dispatch 352/754-6777.

17 CYPRESS GLEN CAMPGROUND

Rating: 9

In the Croom Tract of Withlacoochee State Forest, Silver Lake Recreation Complex
Orlando map, grid c2, page 240

Set in a mixed forest of pines and hardwoods, the campground slopes toward Silver Lake, where there's a small beach and a far-off view of the interstate bridge. Sites are generously spaced, and the forest creates lush shade. The hiking trails begin at Silver Lake Campground down the road; bicycles are allowed on forest roads. Just north of the Silver Lake area is a canoe outfitter: Nobleton Boat and Canoe Rental (352/796-7176). Anglers regularly catch all kinds of bass, panfish, and catfish in the river.

Campsites, facilities: The largest of the three campgrounds in this state forest complex, Cypress Glen has 43 sites with piped water and electricity. Restrooms, showers, picnic tables, grills, and fire rings are provided. Children and pets are welcome.

Reservations, fees: Reservations are not taken. Sites are $13 per night for five people. Up to five people, using two tents or one RV, are permitted per site. Groups need a permit. Credit cards are not accepted. This campground is open only on weekends (from noon Friday to noon Monday) and holidays.

Directions: From I-75, take Exit 309 eastbound on State Road 50 for .75 mile. Turn north at the traffic light; the highway is marked as Croom Rital Road on the north side and

Kettering Road on the south side, but just follow the signs for the Withlacoochee State Trail. Drive 3.5 miles. Just before the interstate overpass, turn east into the Silver Lake complex. This is the second campground on your left, about .8 mile from the turn.

Contact: Withlacoochee State Forest Recreation Visitors Center, 15003 Broad Street, Brooksville, FL 34601, 352/754-6896 or fire dispatch 352/754-6777.

CROOKED RIVER CAMPGROUND

Rating: 9

In the Croom Tract of Withlacoochee State Forest, Silver Lake Recreation Complex
Orlando map, grid c2, page 240

You'll find more level, open sites here than in the other campgrounds in this forest complex, making it a better choice for RVers. Many sites overlook the Withlacoochee River, which at this point becomes a narrow, winding course with coffee-colored waters. Steps lead down to the river's edge. Note the cypress tree in midstream and the stain from a long-gone highwater mark.

Campsites, facilities: All 26 sites have water, picnic tables, grills, and fire rings but no electricity. Restrooms and showers, which are wheelchair accessible, are available. Children and pets are welcome.

Reservations, fees: Reservations are not taken. Sites are $10 per night for five people. Up to five people, using two tents or one RV, are permitted per site. Groups need a permit. Credit cards are not accepted.

Directions: From I-75, take Exit 309 eastbound on State Road 50 for .75 mile. Turn north at the traffic light; the highway is marked as Croom Rital Road on the north side and Kettering Road on the south side, but just follow the signs for the Withlacoochee State Trail. Drive 3.5 miles. Just before the interstate overpass, turn east into the Silver Lake complex.

This is the third campground on your left, about 1.2 miles from the main entrance.

Contact: Withlacoochee State Forest Recreation Visitors Center, 15003 Broad Street, Brooksville, FL 34601, 352/754-6896 or fire dispatch 352/754-6777.

19 PRIMITIVE CAMPING ZONE, CROOM HIKING TRAILS (FORMERLY TUCKER HILL)

Rating: 9

In the Croom Tract of Withlacoochee State Forest
Orlando map, grid c2, page 240

As many as 100 people can be accommodated at this designated primitive camping zone that encompasses about three acres. The area is so large that even when other backpackers are staying here you're still likely to have that "alone in the woods" feeling. A water spigot is located at the fire tower one mile away. Most hikers use one of three loop trails that compose the Croom Hiking Trails, with a combined length of 31.3 miles.

Campsites, facilities: This unnamed primitive camping zone has no facilities. Bring your own water. Bury human waste six inches deep. Children are welcome. Pets are prohibited.

Reservations, fees: Reservations are not necessary, but organized groups must secure a permit. Camping is free. The area is closed during muzzle-loading and general gun seasons.

Directions: Hikers can park at the Tucker Hill Fire Tower on the west side of the forest at the intersection of Forest Road 3 and Forest Road 6/Croom Road. The camping area is about one mile north of the tower by foot trail.

Contact: Withlacoochee State Forest Recreation Visitors Center, 15003 Broad Street, Brooksville, FL 34601, 352/754-6896 or fire dispatch 352/754-6777.

20 TALL PINES RV PARK

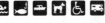

Rating: 3

Near Brooksville

Orlando map, grid c2, page 240

Under new management, this 5.5-acre park is undergoing improvements. It's right off I-75 and gets overflow use from the all-terrain-vehicle and motorbike users of the Croom Motorcycle Area in the state forest less than one mile away. Don't be concerned about the motorcyclists; they're more Nickelodeon types than Hell's Angels, with brightly colored racing silks, expensive gear, and miniature motorbikes for their kids. Nearby are all the usual interstate stops: restaurants, fast food, gas stations, and even tourist information; a big grocery store and a shopping center are within walking distance. You can stay as long as you like, and you won't find mobile homes or park models in your midst.

Campsites, facilities: Sixty-two sites accommodate RV and tent campers. Full hookups, restrooms, showers, laundry facilities, and a wheelchair-accessible recreation hall are provided. No cable TV is offered. Children are welcome. Leashed pets are permitted.

Reservations, fees: Reservations are not necessary. Sites are $17 per night during the summer and $20 per night in the winter for two people, plus $3 per extra person, and $2 for use of air conditioners or electric heaters. Credit cards are accepted. Long-term stays are OK for RVs and travel trailers.

Directions: From I-75, take Exit 301 eastbound on State Road 50 for .1 mile. Watch for the park driveway on the north side of the road, between the Waffle House and the Racetrac station.

Contact: Tall Pines RV Park, 30455 Cortez Boulevard, Brooksville, FL 34602, 352/799-5587.

21 HOLIDAY SPRINGS TRAV-L-PARK

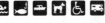

Rating: 2

Southwest of Brooksville

Orlando map, grid c2, page 240

This clean park has an eight-acre lake for fishing and boating and an unusual spring-fed natural swimming pool whose temperature stays at 75 degrees year-round. A short nature trail leads from the lake to the spring. Management works extra hard at security, parking patrol cars with dummies near the entrance and keeping doors to common areas locked at times.

Campsites, facilities: There are 40 RV sites in this 235-unit mobile home community that accommodates rigs up to 40 feet long. Full hookups, cable TV and telephone access, picnic tables, laundry facilities, a dump station, recreation rooms, a 40-by-80-foot dance hall, shuffleboard courts, a boat dock, and rental trailers are available. The park may allow families with small children for overnight stays but primarily is interested in people age 50 and over driving newer RVs. Small, leashed pets are permitted.

Reservations, fees: Reservations are not necessary. Sites are $25 per night for two people, plus $2 for each additional person. Credit cards are not accepted.

Directions: From the junction of U.S. 19 and State Road 50, drive seven miles south on U.S. 19. The park is on the northwest side of the intersection of U.S. 19 and County Road 578/County Line Road.

Contact: Holiday Springs Trav-L-Park, 138 Travel Park Drive, Spring Hill, FL 34607, 352/683-0034.

22 MARY'S FISH CAMP

Rating: 3

On the Mud River west of Weeki Wachee

Orlando map, grid c2, page 240

You'll find this quiet, secluded park tucked

into an almost junglelike thicket of trees on the Mud River, a tidal watercourse that joins the scenic Weeki Wachee River 2.5 miles away. It's ideal for canoeists, anglers, and boaters (the river has Gulf access); a few brave sailboaters have even been known to come up the river when the water is high. A boat ramp is nearby at Bayport. You can also fish from the campground docks. To keep a "nice, quiet, family atmosphere," management does not permit alcohol or use of foul language in the park.

Campsites, facilities: There are 27 sites with full hookups, and one tent site with electricity. Restrooms, showers, picnic tables, three rental cabins, and boat docks on the Mud River are available. Absolutely no alcohol or profanity are allowed. Children are welcome but not pets.

Reservations, fees: Reservations are recommended. Nightly fee for two people is $18 for RVs, $12.50 for tents. Add $1.50 to $2.50 for each additional person. Credit cards are not accepted.

Directions: From U.S. 19 and State Road 50 in Weeki Wachee, drive four miles west on State Road 50. Look for the park sign at Mary's Fish Camp Road and drive .25 mile south.

Contact: Mary's Fish Camp, 8092 Mary's Fish Camp Road, Weeki Wachee, FL 34607, 352/596-2359, fax 352/596-5562.

23 CHIEF ARIPEKA TRAVEL PARK

Rating: 2

West of Spring Hill
Orlando map, grid c2, page 240

Close to shopping and restaurants, the RV park is nonetheless secluded and far from noise and traffic. Oversized lots accommodate big rigs. There's not much to do in the park, but within a couple of miles are the deep-sea fishing charters and marinas of Hernando Beach. The community of Aripeka is a fishing village today, but in the 1920s it was quite the fashionable vacation resort.

Campsites, facilities: All 28 RV sites have full hookups. Restrooms, showers, and a dump station are provided. The park is oriented toward retirees and snowbirds. Children may visit adult campers. Pets are permitted.

Reservations, fees: Reservations are recommended. Sites are $20 per night for two people, plus $1 for each additional person. Credit cards are not accepted. Long-term stays are permitted.

Directions: From U.S. 19 and County Road 595 in Spring Hill, drive west on County Road 595 for two miles. The park is on the south side of the road.

Contact: Chief Aripeka Travel Park, 1582 Osowaw Boulevard, Spring Hill, FL 34607, 352/686-3329.

24 CAMPER'S HOLIDAY TRAVEL PARK

Rating: 6

Southeast of Brooksville
Orlando map, grid c2, page 240

This attractive, secluded countryside park with a 13-acre fishing lake offers large and shady sites set in a forest of live oak, slash pines, and other trees for overnighters, short-term vacationers, and groups. Campers stay in a section with its own pavilion. It adjoins the park's 300 retirement camper condominium lots, and campers may use all of the common areas. Don't feed or approach the alligators you may see on Sparkman Lake. Note that boat motors are limited to three horsepower. A convenience store is near the park, and a staffed guard gate keeps out curiosity seekers. It's too remote from the interstate for overnight campers who don't plan ahead, but worth the effort.

Campsites, facilities: All 66 RV sites have full hookups and cable TV and telephone access. Tents are permitted in summer on the same sites. Restrooms, showers, picnic tables, laundry facilities, a dump station, a pool, a recreation room, shuffleboard courts, and a

playground are on the premises. Families with children are welcome to camp for fewer than 30 days. One leashed pet is permitted per site.
Reservations, fees: Reservations are not necessary for short-term stays. Sites are $18 to $20 per night for two people, plus $2 for each additional person. Add $1.50 for using air-conditioning or electric heaters. Credit cards are not accepted. Campers must be vacationers or seasonal tenants; transient workers may be allowed to stay up to 30 days if space is available. Long-term visitors must be 50 and older or retired.
Directions: From I-75, take Exit 301 and drive west on State Road 50 into Brooksville. At the intersection with Emerson Road/County Road 581, turn south for 5.5 miles. Stay on that road all the way to the park; it winds around. Look for the park sign at left.
Contact: Camper's Holiday Travel Park, 2092 Culbreath Road, Brooksville, FL 34602, 352/796-3707, fax 352/796-6232.

25 TOPICS RV TRAVEL TRAILER PARK

🏊 🐕 ♿ 🚐

Rating: 4

South of Brooksville
Orlando map, grid c2, page 240

Set on a hill in the open countryside, the Topics RV park has unusually large sites at 40 by 100 feet. Loads of social activities are planned during the winter months, including golf leagues (ending the season with a competition), monthly ladies' and men's luncheons at local restaurants, a mixed bowling league, and a year-end festival with free food and drink. The Blue Tees driving range is across the street, and many golf courses are nearby. The park also is convenient to Weeki Wachee Spring, one of the longest-lived tourist attractions in Florida. In fact, no one can travel across the state without seeing the billboards for Weeki Wachee's "mermaid" theater, which, since 1947, has featured underwater ballet performed by women

wearing fishtail costumes. There's also a bird-of-prey show, a petting zoo, and a wilderness river cruise. If that's not enough, next door is Buccaneer Bay, a water park with flume and tube rides, beaches, and picnic areas. Just to the east of the park is the little Slovakian farming community of Masaryktown, founded in 1925 and named after Garrigue Masaryk, the first president of Czechoslovakia.
Campsites, facilities: The 40-acre, 231-unit, adults-only park has 93 large RV sites with full hookups, cable TV, and telephone access. Restrooms, showers, laundry facilities, a clubhouse with kitchen facilities, shuffleboard courts, and a heated pool are available. All areas are wheelchair accessible. Children are not allowed. Two leashed pets are permitted per site.
Reservations, fees: Reservations are required. Sites are $15 to $25 per night for two people, plus $2 for each additional person. Credit cards are not accepted. Seasonal visitors are preferred.
Directions: From U.S. 41, drive two miles west on County Road 578/County Line Road. Or, from U.S. 19, drive eight miles east on County Road 578/County Line Road.
Contact: Topics RV Travel Trailer Park, 13063 County Line Road, Spring Hill, FL 34609, 352/796-0625, fax 352/796-0282.

26 GULF COAST NUDIST RESORT

🏊 🐕 🚐 ⛺

Rating: 5

East of Hudson
Orlando map, grid c2, page 240

Nudists will find a relaxed, friendly, rustic setting with lots of trees, say the managers of this eight-acre, clothing-optional park. RVs up to 40 feet in length are welcome.
Campsites, facilities: There are 75 RV sites with full hookups; 15 sites are pull-through. About 24 to 40 tents can be accommodated in an area separate from the RVs for primitive camping. Cable TV and telephone service are available at the developed sites. Picnic tables, restrooms, showers, laundry facilities, a dump station, a

pool, a recreation hall, tennis courts, horseshoes, shuffleboard, *pétanque* (French-style bowling) courts, a camp circle, and rental trailers are on site. Children are welcome. Leashed pets are permitted.

Reservations, fees: Reservations are recommended. Sites are $17 to $40 per night. Credit cards are accepted. Long-term stays are OK.

Directions: From U.S. 19 in Hudson, drive two miles east on County Road 578/County Line Road. At East Road, turn south and continue two miles. Look for the campground's six-foot sign on a fence.

Contact: Gulf Coast Nudist Resort, 13220 Houston Avenue, Hudson, FL 34667, 727/868-1061, website: www.gulfcoastresort.com.

27 BIG OAKS RV PARK

Rating: 3

South of Brooksville

Orlando map, grid c2, page 240

Set in the countryside, this adult park caters to overnighters as well as snowbirds. It's within one hour's drive of Busch Gardens, Weeki Wachee Spring, Sea World, Disney World, the Gulf of Mexico, and Roger's Christmas House Village. The latter is a fanciful Victorian year-round place where six houses are each decorated with their own Christmas theme. Golf, fishing, bowling, shopping, restaurants, and flea markets are within 10 to 15 minutes. Sites are large and grassy. They're also shady, except for the two treeless sections of pull-through spaces. New owners have made improvements to the bathhouse, roads, and recreation hall.

Campsites, facilities: The park has 115 sites with full hookups. Restrooms, showers, laundry facilities, a pool, a clubhouse, shuffleboard courts, horseshoes, and a dump station are on the premises. Rental trailers are available. Children are permitted to visit only. One small leashed pet per site is permitted.

Reservations, fees: Reservations are recommended. Sites are $25 per night for two peo-

ple, plus $2 for each additional person. Credit cards are not accepted. Long-term stays are OK.

Directions: From Brooksville at State Road 50, drive south on U.S. 41 for eight miles. Or, from I-75, take Exit 285 onto County Road 52 and drive west. Turn north on U.S. 41 and drive five miles.

Contact: Big Oaks RV Park, 16654 U.S. 41, Spring Hill, FL 34610, 352/799-5533.

28 TRAVELERS REST

Rating: 7

Off I-75 west of Dade City

Orlando map, grid c2, page 240

Long-legged egrets and blue herons swoop into the three lakes of this wooded resort set in the rolling hills of Florida's citrus and cattle ranching country. But it's no shrinking violet of a place—not with wood carving, a gardening club, a motorcycle club, and several social programs planned by a full-time activities director. You'll likely sleep on a hill, where there's room for 60 rigs. The retiree-oriented resort is near the Pioneer Museum and antique malls.

Campsites, facilities: The mobile home/RV park has 671 sites, of which about 60 spots with full hookups are for RVs. A heated pool, a spa, a nine-hole golf course, three recreation buildings, two tennis courts, Ping-Pong, shuffleboard, and bocce courts (lawn bowling) are on site. Cable TV, telephone access, restrooms, showers, laundry facilities, limited supplies, propane, a dump station, and a modem hookup are available. Groceries and restaurants are nearby. Children are welcome to camp short-term only. Pets must be leashed.

Reservations, fees: Reservations are recommended. Sites are $25 per night. Major credit cards are accepted. Long-term stays are OK for adults.

Directions: From I-75, take Exit 293 and drive .24 mile west. Turn south on County Road 577 and continue one mile. At Johnston Road, turn west and go one mile to the park.

Contact: Travelers Rest, 29129 Johnston Road, Dade City, FL 33523, 352/588-2013, fax 352/588-3462.

29 SEVEN ACRES RV PARK

Rating: 1

North of Dade City on U.S. 301
Orlando map, grid c2, page 240

Although it's located on busy U.S. 301, this park is quiet and favored by long-term RVers.

Campsites, facilities: There are 160 grassy RV sites with full hookups and telephone access. Five sites are pull-through. The recreation hall is wheelchair accessible. Many sites are occupied by full-timers. Children and small pets are permitted.

Reservations, fees: Reservations are not necessary. Sites are $15 per night. Credit cards are not accepted. Long-term stays are OK.

Directions: From Dade City, drive three miles north on U.S. 301 to the park on the west side of the road.

Contact: Seven Acres RV Park, 16731 U.S. 301, Dade City, FL 33525, 352/567-3510.

30 WITHLACOOCHEE RIVER PARK

Rating: 9

East of Dade City
Orlando map, grid c2, page 240

As one of the few areas in Pasco County that has not been developed for farming or commercial uses, this park is a gem. You may see bald and golden eagles, owls, deer, wild hogs, alligators, blue indigo snakes, armadillos, and more. The campground makes a good base for hiking the 13 miles of nature trails here or for canoe trips on the Withlacoochee River. If you haven't done much primitive camping before, this is a good place for a dry run; your car is only .5 mile away. Fish off the dock on the river, not on the riverbank; it's adjacent to the canoe launch. Note that you'll have to carry your canoe 100 feet from the parking area to the launch.

The park also offers a 40-foot observation tower, picnic shelters, playground, a recreation field, and a taste of life from the 19th century—you'll see a reconstructed 1800s fort, a primitive log cabin, and Indian villages. At press time, more historic replicas were under construction, including a homestead, trading post, and school house/church building. The idea is that you'll be able to experience Florida and all its cultures extant in the 1800s. Additionally, this park is planning to host such events as the Mountain Man Rendezvous, Mother's Day Pow Wow, a Native American Music Festival, and an international multicultural festival. The campground is part of the 260-acre county-run park in the larger wilderness area operated by the Southwest Florida Water Management District, but these events are being coordinated by the Pasco County Parks and Recreation Department and the Withlacoochee American Indian Historical Society.

Campsites, facilities: You'll have to hike .5 mile to the campground in this 606-acre wilderness park. There are 10 primitive sites with picnic tables and fire rings; there's a newly added compost toilet in the camping area. Wheelchair-accessible flush toilets and running water are .5 mile from the camping area; no showers are available. The nearest groceries are five miles away in Dade City. Children are welcome. Leashed pets are permitted.

Reservations, fees: Reservations are not necessary, although you must get a permit from the park office. Camping is free. The maximum stay is seven days, but you can request an extension.

Directions: From Dade City, take State Road 533 to River Road and turn right (east). Follow the road about five miles to Auton Road, then turn right (south) and go to the park entrance.

Contact: Withlacoochee River Park, 12929 Withlacoochee Boulevard, Dade City, FL 33525, 352/567-0264 or 352/521-4104 (phone/fax line). Information is also available from the East

Pasco Parks and Recreation Department, 36620 State Road 52, Dade City, FL 33525, 352/521-4182.

31 WINTER PARADISE RV PARK

Rating: 3

North of Hudson Beach

Orlando map, grid c2, page 240

Whether for golfing, boating, fishing, visiting the beach, shopping, or relaxing by the pool, this park is centrally located, just three miles from the Gulf of Mexico in a busy suburb with plenty of entertainment. The area has many seafood and ethnic restaurants, as well as chain-operated eateries.

Campsites, facilities: Most sites at this 300-unit RV park have full hookups; a few have water and electricity only. Restrooms, showers, laundry facilities, shuffleboard courts, horseshoe pits, a pool, and a recreation building with billiard tables and a library are provided. The clubhouse, office, and laundry room are wheelchair accessible. Children are welcome. Pets are allowed; dog walks are on two sides of the park.

Reservations, fees: Reservations are recommended. Sites are $22 per night for two people, plus $1 for each additional person. Credit cards are accepted. Long-term stays are OK.

Directions: From Hudson, drive 2.5 miles north on U.S. 19 to the park, at the corner with Denton Avenue.

Contact: Winter Paradise RV Park, 16108 U.S. 19, Hudson, FL 34667, 727/868-2285 or 800/328-0775.

32 SEVEN OAKS TRAVEL PARK

Rating: 3

In Hudson

Orlando map, grid c2, page 240

Although located smack-dab in the middle of the urbanized Gulf Coast, this park has a quiet, semirural setting in an area of rolling hills and tall oaks. It's just east of the major thoroughfare at 17 feet above sea level, which means it's probably secure from high water if you leave your RV parked here long-term. Beaches are three miles away.

Campsites, facilities: This adults-only park has 100 RV sites with full hookups and 10 tent sites. Restrooms, showers, laundry facilities, a pool, shuffleboard courts, a recreation hall, and horseshoe pits are available. The clubhouse, pool, office, and bathhouse are wheelchair accessible. Children are welcome to stay two weeks at a time. Leashed pets are permitted.

Reservations, fees: Reservations are recommended. Sites are $15 to $21 per night for two people, plus $3 for each additional person. Credit cards are not accepted. Long-term stays are OK.

Directions: From Hudson, drive 1.5 miles north on U.S. 19. Turn east on Bolton Avenue in town and continue .7 mile to the park.

Contact: Seven Oaks Travel Park, 9207 Bolton Avenue, Hudson, FL 34667, 727/862-3016, website: www.7oakstravelpark.com.

33 SHADY ACRES MOBILE HOME AND RV PARK

Rating: 3

North of Hudson

Orlando map, grid c2, page 240

Old oak trees provide plenty of shade and buffer guests from traffic on the nearby six-lane highway. Head to the recreation hall for bingo, coffee, doughnuts, and potluck dinners. The beach is one mile away. Supermarkets, doctors' offices, and a hospital are conveniently close.

Campsites, facilities: This 72-unit urban mobile home community with a recreation hall, laundry facilities, and restrooms has 24 full-hookup RV sites. Cable TV and telephone access are available, and the rec hall and restrooms are wheelchair accessible. Children are welcome. Small pets are allowed.

Reservations, fees: Reservations are recommended. Sites are $20 per night. Credit cards are not accepted. Long-term stays are permitted.

Directions: From the junction of State Road 52 and U.S. 19, drive two miles north on U.S. 19.

Contact: Shady Acres Mobile Home and RV Park, 14417 U.S. 19 North, Hudson, FL 34667, 727/868-9589.

34 GULFBREEZE RV PARK

Rating: 2

North of Hudson

Orlando map, grid c2, page 240

The park targets long-term visitors for, as they say, "a week, a month, forever." It's set on a hill in a quiet residential area with plenty of trees, yet is still close to shops and restaurants.

Campsites, facilities: There are 140 RV sites with full hookups and telephone and cable TV access. Restrooms, showers, laundry facilities, picnic tables, a dump station, a pool, a wheelchair-accessible recreation hall, horseshoe pits, and shuffleboard courts are on the premises. Children are welcome. Leashed pets are permitted.

Reservations, fees: Reservations are not necessary. Sites are $15 per night for two people, plus $2 for each additional person. Credit cards are not accepted. Long-term RVers are preferred.

Directions: From the junction of State Road 52 and U.S. 19, drive five miles north on U.S. 19. Turn east at the Sprint convenience store (Bolton Avenue) and go two blocks.

Contact: Gulfbreeze RV Park, 9014 Bolton Avenue, Hudson, FL 34667, 727/862-6826.

35 LAKEWOOD TRAVEL PARK

Rating: 2

In Hudson

Orlando map, grid c2, page 240

Backing up to a country meadow and overlooking a farm pond, this suburban park contains a mix of sunny and shady spots. The atmosphere is friendly and homey, with some residents living here year-round. It may be hard to find a spot in winter, when many campers opt for the $250 monthly rate. Within a few miles are Gulf beaches, Tarpon Springs, Weeki Wachee, nature parks, and golf courses.

Campsites, facilities: There are 88 RV sites with full hookups and optional cable TV and telephone service. Restrooms, showers, laundry facilities, and an activities building are provided. The park caters to retirees staying one month at a time, but all ages are welcome. Pets are allowed.

Reservations, fees: Reservations are not necessary. Sites are $16 per night for two people, plus $2 for each additional person and $1 for pets. Rates are discounted in summer. Credit cards are not accepted.

Directions: From U.S. 19 in Hudson, drive east on State Road 52 for 4.5 miles.

Contact: Lakewood Travel Park, 11517 State Road 52, Moon Lake, FL 34654, 727/856-1306.

36 SUNBURST RV PARK— PORT RICHEY

Rating: 7

In Hudson

Orlando map, grid c2, page 240

Targeting active retirees, this RV park is centrally located to shopping and the Gulf of Mexico. Formerly known as Barrington Hills RV Resort, the park is now part of the Encore chain. During the winter, a full schedule of planned activities helps seasonal visitors socialize and get to know each other.

Campsites, facilities: There are 390 RV sites, among which 20 are pull-through. Rigs up to 45 feet long can be accommodated. All sites have full hookups, 50-amp service, picnic tables, cable TV, and telephone service available. Restrooms, showers, a dump station, laundry facilities, a pool, a clubhouse, horseshoe pits, shuffleboard courts, billiards room, and a golf net are on the premises. Children are welcome. Leashed pets are permitted.

Reservations, fees: Reservations are recommended. Sites are $20 per night. Major credit cards are accepted. Long-term rates are available.

Directions: From I-75, take Exit 285 west on State Road 52. Turn right on Little Road and head north. At New York Avenue, turn left and drive to the park on the south side of the road.

Contact: Sunburst RV Park—Port Richey, 9412 New York Avenue, Hudson, FL 34667, 727/868-3586 or 877/287-2757, fax 727/863-7259, website: www.rvonthego.com.

37 CREWS LAKE PARK

Rating: 8

On Crews Lake off U.S. 41

Orlando map, grid c2, page 240

Here's another area the bulldozers haven't touched. Operated by Pasco County, this 111-acre park is heavily wooded with large live oak trees overlooking the 750-acre Crews Lake. Urban dwellers can seek respite from city life, but the park gets little use because so few people know about it. Take a quiet walk along 2.5 miles of trails through the palmetto and pine forest. A specially planted garden is replete with flowers and plants that draw butterflies and birds. A paved bike path winds one mile through the woods; it's popular with inline skaters. However, fishing and boating are not possible; a drought has severely affected Crews Lake, and weeds have taken over much of the lakebed. The campground was originally built for Scout use but has been opened to the public because it wasn't being put to use during the week.

Campsites, facilities: The park has 10 primitive tent-only sites with picnic tables, grills, and one community water source; there is a chemical toilet but no restrooms in the campground. An outdoor cold-water shower is available. Elsewhere in the park are restrooms, nature

trails, horseshoe pits, a boat ramp, a pier, a volleyball field, two playgrounds, picnic pavilions, and an observation tower. Children are welcome. Leashed pets are allowed.

Reservations, fees: Reservations are not necessary, but call in advance to see if there are vacancies. Scout groups take priority. Camping is free. The maximum stay is seven days.

Directions: From I-75, take Exit 285 and drive 10 miles west on State Road 52 past U.S. 41. Continue two more miles, then turn north on Shady Hills Road and drive 3.5 miles to Crews Lake Road.

Contact: Crews Lake Park, 16739 Crews Lake Drive, Shady Hills, FL 34610, 727/861-3038. Reserve a pavilion at 727/861-3052. Information is also available from the Pasco County Parks and Recreation Department, 4111 Land O' Lakes Boulevard, Suite 202, Land O' Lakes, FL 34639, 352/521-4182.

38 GROVE RIDGE ESTATES

Rating: 3

South of Dade City on U.S. 98

Orlando map, grid c2, page 240

Horses graze near this neatly kept park located adjacent to an orange grove. The country setting offers plenty of wide-open spaces for those who crave the outdoors, but stores and other conveniences are nearby in Dade City.

Campsites, facilities: This adults-only RV resort accepts self-contained rigs at least 20 feet long at the 250 full-hookup sites. Laundry facilities, shuffleboard courts, horseshoe pits, a recreation hall, a pool, telephone service, and rental trailers are available. Children are not allowed except for brief visits. One pet under 25 pounds is permitted per site.

Reservations, fees: Reservations are recommended. Sites are $20 per night for two people, plus $1 for each additional person. Credit cards are not accepted. Most campers are staying for the winter season.

Directions: From I-75, take Exit 285 eastbound

10 miles on State Road 52 to Dade City. Turn south on U.S. 301/U.S. 98 and go through town. At the point where U.S. 98 veers off toward Lakeland, keep traveling on U.S. 98. Drive .5 mile southeast to the park.

Contact: Grove Ridge Estates, 10721 U.S. 98, Dade City, FL 33525, 352/523-2277, website: www.bel-aireresorts.com.

39 COUNTRY AIRE ESTATES

Rating: 4

South of Dade City
Orlando map, grid c2, page 240

Groceries and restaurants are nearby, and antique hounds will find plenty of shops to browse in Dade City. Social activities are held year-round at this park, where the vast majority of the 68 lots are owned by residents, leaving about 18 sites open to people passing through in winter. There's a two-acre pond for those anglers inclined to try their luck.

Campsites, facilities: Catering to RVers age 55 and older, this hillside park has about 18 sites with full hookups available for RVs. Restrooms, showers, picnic tables, laundry facilities, a heated pool, a clubhouse, horseshoe pits, shuffleboard courts, telephone service, and cable TV are available. Families with children are permitted to stay a couple of nights in summer; children are not accepted at other times. Pets under 15 pounds are permitted.

Reservations, fees: Reservations are recommended. Sites are $20 per night for two people. Credit cards are not accepted. Long-term rates are available.

Directions: From Dade City, drive south on U.S. 301, turn east on McDonald Road near the city limits, just before the Wal-Mart shopping center, and go .2 mile.

Contact: Country Aire Estates, 38130 McDonald Road, Dade City, FL 33525, 352/567-3630.

40 MORNINGSIDE RV ESTATES

Rating: 4

On the south side of Dade City
Orlando map, grid c2, page 240

This snowbird-oriented resort with a gated entrance is within walking distance of two large shopping centers. Shade in the RV park is minimal.

Campsites, facilities: The 55-and-older park has 400 RV sites with full hookups, free cable TV, and telephone access. Restrooms, showers, a dump station, a heated indoor pool, two clubhouses, laundry facilities, horseshoe pits, and shuffleboard courts are provided. The recreation hall, pool, and pool hall are wheelchair accessible. Pets are prohibited.

Reservations, fees: Reservations are recommended. Sites are $25 per night for two people, plus $1 for each additional person. Credit cards are not accepted.

Directions: From Dade City, drive south on U.S. 301, then turn east (left) on Morning Drive behind the Wal-Mart shopping center.

Contact: Morningside RV Estates, 12645 Morning Drive, Dade City, FL 33525, 352/523-1922.

41 MANY MANSIONS RV PARK

Rating: 3

South of Dade City
Orlando map, grid c2, page 240

Surrounded by dwindling citrus groves and open pastureland, this park is located in the country yet is just five minutes from shopping, dining, and downtown Dade City. Planned activities include bingo, cards, pokeno, and cookouts, as well as weekly evening church services. Sites are laid out neatly in subdivision style, with straight roads; most spots are not back-to-back.

Campsites, facilities: This adults-oriented RV park has 235 grassy, full-hookup sites with optional telephone service or cable TV access.

Restrooms, showers, laundry facilities, a dump station, a camp circle, and a clubhouse are available. Some trailers are available for rent. Children may camp short-term only. Small pets are permitted on a leash.

Reservations, fees: Reservations are recommended. Sites are $18 per night for two people, plus $3 for each additional person. Credit cards are not accepted.

Directions: From Dade City, drive south on U.S. 301/98. When U.S. 98 forks south on the edge of town, continue on U.S. 98 for three miles. Take the Richland exit to County Road 35A, turn right and go one mile to Stewart Road. Turn left (east) at the park entrance.

Contact: Many Mansions RV Park, 40703 Stewart Road, Dade City, FL 33525, 352/567-8667 or 800/359-0135.

42 CITRUS HILL PARK AND SALES

Rating: 3

Between Dade City and Zephyrhills
Orlando map, grid c3, page 240

As the name implies, the trailer park is on a hill in what used to be orange grove country before freezes forced the citrus industry to look south to warmer points. Activities within the park include a golf league, bingo, crafts, bunco, euchre, church services, special dinners and socials, and a weekly coffee hour. Grocery stores, restaurants, and five golf courses are within five miles. There are no facilities for children.

Campsites, facilities: This retiree-oriented park has 182 grassy RV sites with full hookups and telephone and cable TV access. Restrooms, showers, picnic tables, a dump station, laundry facilities, a recreation hall, horseshoe pits, shuffleboard courts, a post office, and planned social activities are provided. The clubhouse and restrooms are wheelchair accessible. Leashed pets are allowed.

Reservations, fees: Reservations are required. Sites are $20 per night for two people, plus

$1 for each additional person. Credit cards are not accepted. Stays of up to seven months are OK.

Directions: From Dade City, drive six miles south on U.S. 98. The park is on the east side of the road.

Contact: Citrus Hill Park and Sales, 9267 U.S. 98, Dade City, FL 33525, 352/567-6045, fax 352/567-3119, website: www.bel-airesorts.com.

43 FOREST LAKE RV RESORT

Rating: 5

North of Zephyrhills
Orlando map, grid c3, page 240

This sparkling-clean park maintains it is "your year-round vacation home," and fewer than half of the sites are open for seasonal campers. Interior street names attest to the park's affinity for Canadian campers: for example, Bruins Drive, Maple Leaf Drive, and Canadiens Drive. The location is close to Gulf of Mexico beaches and Central Florida attractions, including baseball spring training, dog and horse racing, and Seminole bingo. Planned activities make sure the residents have fun if they care to stay on site most of the time.

Campsites, facilities: The RV resort/mobile home park has 124 lots for RVers (out of a total of 274). Sites have full hookups and telephone and cable TV access. Restrooms, showers, laundry facilities, shuffleboard courts, horseshoe pits, a recreation hall, a pool, and a spa are on the premises. Children are not welcome except when visiting residents for less than two weeks. Small pets are permitted on a leash.

Reservations, fees: Reservations are recommended. Sites are $24 per night for two people, plus $1 per extra person. Major credit cards are accepted.

Directions: From I-75, take Exit 279 and drive 12 miles east on State Road 54 to the intersection with U.S. 301. The park is on the south side of the highway, east of the intersection.

Contact: Forest Lake RV Resort, 41219 Hockey Drive, Zephyrhills, FL 33540, 813/782-1058 or 800/283-9715, fax 813/788-5246, website: www.forestlake-estates.com.

44 WATERS EDGE RV RESORT

Rating: 4

North of Zephyrhills
Orlando map, grid c3, page 240

Set on 20 acres with tall oak trees, Waters Edge is located far enough away from town to enjoy a rural neighborhood setting but still be within a few minutes of shopping, restaurants, and a hospital. Paved interior roads lead to grassy back-in sites; few are shady. Social activities in winter include bingo, billiards, card games, and exercises in the pool.

Campsites, facilities: This adult park has 40 RV sites with full hookups and cable TV and telephone access. Restrooms, showers, laundry facilities, a dump station, a pool, a clubhouse, horseshoe pits, and shuffleboard courts are on site. The park caters to retirees who stay seven months out of the year and store their RVs on site the rest of the time. Children may visit park residents for up to two weeks. Leashed pets are permitted.

Reservations, fees: Reservations are recommended. Sites are $20 per night for two people, plus $2 for each additional person. Credit cards are not accepted.

Directions: From Zephyrhills, drive one mile north on U.S. 301. Turn east onto Pretty Pond Road and go .5 mile to the stop sign at Wire Road. Head north on Wire Road for .25 mile to Otis Allen Road, then turn east and continue .5 mile to the entrance.

Contact: Waters Edge RV Resort, 39146 Otis Allen Road, Zephyrhills, FL 33540, 813/783-2708 or 800/471-7875, website: www.bel-aire resorts.com.

45 BAKER ACRES RV RANCH

Rating: 4

On the north side of Zephyrhills
Orlando map, grid c3, page 240

Nondenominational church services are held each Sunday in the recreation hall. Other activities include dances, a singles club, exercise classes, ceramics, crafts, sewing, wood carving, quilting, bowling, cards, bingo, and field trips. The pool is heated. In the card room, residents play cribbage, euchre, pinochle, and more. The park is part of the Bel-Aire Resorts group.

Campsites, facilities: All 355 sites have full hookups, with telephone service and cable TV available. Restrooms (but no showers), laundry facilities, shuffleboard and bocce ball (lawn bowling) courts, horseshoe pits, a recreation hall, a card room, and a pool are on the premises. RVs must be at least 20 feet long (up to a maximum of 35 feet) and must be less than 10 years old. Management says all areas of the park are wheelchair accessible. Children are not welcome except for short visits. Leashed pets under 25 pounds are permitted.

Reservations, fees: Reservations are recommended. Sites are $20 per night for two people, plus $1 for each additional person. Credit cards are not accepted. Long-term rates are available.

Directions: From Zephyrhills, drive one mile north on U.S. 301. Turn east onto Pretty Pond Road and go .5 mile to the stop sign at Wire Road. Head north on Wire Road to the park entrance.

Contact: Baker Acres RV Ranch, 7820 Wire Road, Zephyrhills, FL 33540, 813/782-3950 or 800/741-7875, fax 813/783-3406, website: www.bel-aireresorts.com.

46 QUAIL RUN RV PARK

Rating: 6

West of Zephyrhills in the farm community of Wesley Chapel

Orlando map, grid c3, page 240

"No rig is too big," brag the managers. Tall oaks shade this campground, which is close enough to I-75 to be a practical overnight refuge. You might spot a flock of sandhill cranes on the rolling hills nearby or even in the park. A golf course, tennis courts, and a driving range are within one mile, but the park is a nice stopping place for interstate drivers.

Campsites, facilities: All 147 grassy RV sites have full hookups and telephone access. A pool, a playground, a volleyball field, horseshoes, shuffleboard, restrooms, showers, picnic tables, and a dump station are provided. Management says the bathhouse, recreation hall, laundry, and office are wheelchair accessible. Families with children are welcome, although the park tends to attract full-time RVers and retirees. Leashed pets under 35 pounds are permitted. Only two pets are allowed per site, and attack breeds are prohibited.

Reservations, fees: Reservations are recommended. Sites are $26 per night for two people, plus $2 for each additional person. Using air conditioners or heaters costs $2 a day extra. Credit cards are accepted. Long-term stays are allowed.

Directions: From I-75, take Exit 58 westbound on State Road 54 .5 mile. At Old Pasco Road, turn north and drive two miles.

Contact: Quail Run RV Park, 6946 Old Pasco Road, Wesley Chapel, FL 33544, 813/973-0999 or 800/582-7084, website: www.quailrunrv.com.

47 ENCORE RV PARK— TAMPA NORTH

Rating: 6

North of Lutz

Orlando map, grid c3, page 240

In the winter, snowbirds thaw out in the solar-heated hot tub and swimming pool and catch some rays on the pool deck. Set on 28 acres across from a Wal-Mart and near other shopping, the RV park offers comfortable amenities for those who like this style of vacation. A 17-acre fishing lake keeps anglers busy; a gazebo looks out over it. It's a bustling place in winter, when the park population swells to 550 and an activities director arranges special events, parties, tournaments, and dances. About 45 people live here year-round, conveniently close to Busch Gardens, numerous Disney-area attractions, Crystal Springs, the Hillsborough River, several lakes, and Gulf Coast beaches. Big-rig sites are available.

Campsites, facilities: All 253 sites have full hookups and paved patios, as well as telephone and cable TV availability. A heated pool, a Jacuzzi, a recreation center, horseshoes, shuffleboard, billiards, a game room, restrooms, showers, a dump station, picnic tables, propane, park model rentals, and laundry facilities are on the premises. Across the street is a shopping center with a supermarket, restaurants, a pharmacy, a Wal-Mart, and hair salons. Children are permitted. Pets must be leashed.

Reservations, fees: Reservations are recommended. Sites are $26 to $31 for two people. Add $1.50 for each additional person. Credit cards are accepted.

Directions: From I-75, take Exit 58 and drive 8.2 miles west on State Road 54. The resort is at left, near the corner of U.S. 41.

Contact: Encore RV Park—Tampa North, 21632 State Road 54, Lutz, FL 33549, 813/949-6551 or 800/879-2131, fax 813/949-4921, website: www.encoreparks.com.

48 LAKE COMO CLUB

🚶🏊🎣🛶🐕🛶♿🚐⛺

Rating: 5

On U.S. 41 north of Tampa
Orlando map, grid c3, page 240

Lake Como Club has all of the amenities of a fancy RV park: three new clay tennis courts, a heated swimming pool, a hot tub, a sauna, a golf driving range, an archery range, planned activities in the recreation hall, and fishing and boating on a 35-acre lake with a sandy beach. The major difference? This has been a nude recreation community since 1940. In fact, Pasco County claims to have more nudist resorts than any other place in Florida—even a nudist housing development.

Campsites, facilities: This nudist resort has 75 RV sites and 20 tent-only sites separate from the RV section. All have water and electricity. On the premises are restrooms, showers, a dump station, a pool, a boat ramp, a dock, a playground, a volleyball field, laundry facilities, and motel rooms. The RV sites, restrooms, and showers are wheelchair accessible. Children are welcome. Leashed pets are permitted.

Reservations, fees: Reservations are not necessary. Sites are $20 to $45 per night for two people, plus one-half the camping fee for each additional person. Major credit cards are accepted.

Directions: From I-75, take Exit 275 and drive west on State Road 56 for one mile. At State Road 54, bear west five more miles. At the intersection with U.S. 41, turn south and drive one block to Leonard Road, where you will turn west. Drive .5 mile to the park.

Contact: Lake Como Club, 20500 Cot Road, Lutz, FL 33549, 813/949-1810 or 877/TRY-LAKE, fax 813/949-4937, website: www.lakecomoresort.com.

49 SKYDIVE CITY

🐕🚐⛺

Rating: 4

East of Zephyrhills
Orlando map, grid c3, page 240

Expand your camping trip with a "blue skies" experience, if you dare. Zephyrhills is world-famous for its bottled water—and as a site for skydiving. Skydive City sees some 78,000 skydives per year, including 2,250 tandem jumps. Complete instruction is available; the staff is qualified by skydiving associations.

Campsites, facilities: The campground, part of a skydiving complex at the Zephyrhills airport, has 55 RV sites with full hookups near the drop zone and 20 tent sites. Services include restrooms, showers, laundry facilities, access to Twin Otter aircraft, a covered packing tent, student gear, a food concession, a beer bar, shuttle service to major airports, and rigging services and sales. Campers are expected to be skydiving while here. Children and pets are welcome.

Reservations, fees: Reservations are recommended. Sites are $8 per night. You must also purchase five jump tickets for each week (no refunds). Major credit cards are accepted.

Directions: From U.S. 301 just south of Zephyrhills, drive east on Chancey Road for about 3.5 miles. The entrance is on the left. Look for the "Skydive" sign.

Contact: Skydive City, 4241 Skydive Lane, Zephyrhills, FL 33542, 813/783-9399 or 800/404-9399, fax 813/782-0599, website: www.skydivecity.com.

50 SWEETWATER RV PARK

🐕🚐

Rating: 4

South of Zephyrhills
Orlando map, grid c3, page 240

Like most Zephyrhills RV parks, this one caters to retired RVers who like to spend several months at a time in Florida. It's part of a chain of nine parks in this area, including Baker Acres, Blue

Jay, Citrus Hill, Glen Haven, Grove Ridge, Rainbow Village, Southern Charm, Water's Edge, and Big Tree. Yearly rates ($1,380) are for seven months' occupancy and five months' storage, allowing residents to avoid paying sales tax on their rent. The park is surrounded by a wooden fence and has big shade trees.

Campsites, facilities: This 289-unit, snowbird-oriented mobile home and RV park offers full hookups, restrooms, showers, telephone availability, cable TV, and laundry facilities. Your RV must be self-contained. A recreation hall, shuffleboard and bocce (lawn bowling) courts, horseshoe pits, and Ping-Pong and pool tables are provided. Campers age 50 and up are preferred. Pets are permitted in the designated pet section.

Reservations, fees: Reservations are recommended. Sites are $20 per night for two people, plus $1 for each additional person. Credit cards are not accepted. Long-term rates are available.

Directions: From U.S. 301 just south of Zephyrhills, turn west on Chancey Road and drive .25 mile.

Contact: Sweetwater RV Park, 37647 Chancey Road, Zephyrhills, FL 33541, 813/788-9408, fax 813/788-3406, website: www.bel-aireresorts.com.

51 SETTLER'S REST RV PARK

Rating: 3

South of Zephyrhills
Orlando map, grid c3, page 240

Seasonal visitors flock here each winter to escape the chilly North, and most of them return year after year to this 350-unit adult community. Just 14 sites are available for overnighters.

Campsites, facilities: RVs as long as 36 feet can be accommodated at the 14 RV sites open for overnighters. The rest of the sites are for long-term visits. All have full hookups, picnic tables, cable TV, and phone service available. Restrooms, showers, a dump station, laundry facilities, and a recreation hall are in the park. Children are welcome as visitors only. Leashed pets are permitted.

Reservations, fees: Reservations are advised. Sites are $28 a night for two people, plus $2 per extra person. Credit cards are not accepted. Long-term (up to six months) or seasonal stays are encouraged.

Directions: From U.S. 301 just south of Zephyrhills, turn west on Chancey Road and drive about .25 mile.

Contact: Settler's Rest RV Park, 37549 Chancey Road, Zephyrhills, FL 33541, 813/782-2003.

52 SOUTHERN CHARM RV RESORT

Rating: 5

South of Zephyrhills
Orlando map, grid c3, page 240

Most sites are occupied by RVs parked year-round in this 48-acre, super-manicured mobile home resort. Trees are sparse, although some sites overlook a lake. Lighted, paved roads lead to sites, some with trees. If you like golf, many challenging courses are located within an easy drive. Unusual wintertime activities include pool exercises, wood carving, and a kitchen band.

Campsites, facilities: At this adults-only park, all 500 lots have full hookups, optional telephone service, and cable TV access. Facilities include a recreation hall with a large stone fireplace, shuffleboard courts, horseshoes, planned activities, laundry facilities, a post office, a pool room, a Jacuzzi, and a heated pool. RVs must be in excellent condition and at least 20 feet long. Small pets are permitted in the designated pet section.

Reservations, fees: Reservations are recommended. Sites are $20 per night for two people, plus $1 for each additional person. Credit cards are not accepted. Long-term stays are allowed.

Directions: From U.S. 301 just south of Zephyrhills, turn west on Chancey Road and drive .5 mile to Autumn Palm. The resort is just ahead, at right.

Contact: Southern Charm RV Resort, 37811 Chancey Road, Zephyrhills, FL 33541, 813/783-3477 or 800/471-7875, fax 813/783-3406, email:

bel-aire@3oaks.com, website: www.bel-aire resorts.com.

53 GLEN HAVEN RV AND MOBILE PARK

Rating: 4

South of Zephyrhills

Orlando map, grid c3, page 240

Glen Haven is one of several retirement-oriented parks along this road. Grocery stores and restaurants are nearby in Zephyrhills.

Campsites, facilities: This mobile home community/RV park has 218 concrete-pad sites with full hookups, optional telephone service, and cable TV access. Restrooms, showers, a Jacuzzi, a pool, horseshoe pits, shuffleboard courts, an exercise room, a clubhouse, and laundry facilities are provided. Activities include the usual pancake breakfasts, dances, and ice-cream socials, but also a computer club. Campers must be 55 or older. Most areas are wheelchair accessible. Leashed pets are permitted.

Reservations, fees: Reservations are recommended. Sites are $20 per night for two people, plus $1 for each additional person, and a small fee for cable TV. Credit cards are not accepted. Long-term stays are OK.

Directions: From the south side of Zephyrhills, drive south on U.S 301/County Road 41 to the intersection with Chancey Road. Turn west on Chancey Road and go one mile.

Contact: Glen Haven RV and Mobile Park, 37251 Chancey Road, Zephyrhills, FL 33541, 813/782-1856 or 800/362-5181, fax 813/783-3132, website: www.bel-aireresorts.com.

54 WHITE'S RV PARK

Rating: 4

South of Zephyrhills

Orlando map, grid c3, page 240

Set on 18 acres, this family-owned and -operated park offers lots of planned activities for its retired clientele. A golf course, grocery stores, and restaurants are close.

Campsites, facilities: This 55-and-older park has 270 concrete-pad RV sites with full hookups, picnic tables, and telephone service available. Restrooms, showers, a dump station, laundry facilities, a pool, a recreation room, billiard tables, and shuffleboard courts are on the premises. Management says all areas are wheelchair accessible. Children are permitted for short visits only. Pets are allowed.

Reservations, fees: Reservations are recommended. Sites are $18 per night for two people, plus $1 for each additional person. Credit cards are not accepted. Long-term stays are OK.

Directions: From U.S. 301 just south of Zephyrhills, turn west on Chancey Road and drive .5 mile. The park is on the south side of the road.

Contact: White's RV Park, 37400 Chancey Road, Zephyrhills, FL 33541, 813/783-1644, email: whiterv374@aol.com.

55 HUNTER'S RUN RV RESORT

Rating: 4

South of Zephyrhills

Orlando map, grid c3, page 240

Planned social activities are held during winter in the recreation hall. The RV park offers retirees a relaxing winter with lots of opportunities to make friends.

Campsites, facilities: All 309 sites have full hookups, with telephone service and cable TV access. Restrooms, showers, laundry facilities, shuffleboard and bocce (lawn bowling) courts, horseshoe pits, a recreation hall, a pool, a spa, a sauna, and an exercise room are on the premises. Campers must be 55 or older. Small pets are permitted on a leash.

Reservations, fees: Reservations are recommended. Sites are $22 per night for two people, plus $2 for each additional person. Credit cards are not accepted.

Directions: From the south side of Zephyrhills,

drive south on U.S 301/County Road 41 to the intersection with Chancey Road. Turn west and go 1.2 miles to the park, near the corner of South Allen Road.

Contact: Hunter's Run RV Resort, 37041 Chancey Road, Zephyrhills, FL 33541, 813/783-1133.

56 PALM VIEW GARDENS

Rating: 4

South of Zephyrhills
Orlando map, grid c3, page 240

This sprawling and well-manicured park on a corner of a major highway is somewhat exposed to the road. Trees are minimal, but most RVers in Zephyrhills don't seem to mind. Bench seating overlooks the stocked fishing lake, and the paved, lighted interior roads lend themselves to bicycling. Social activities are held during the season in two spacious recreation halls. The oversized pool is heated during the cooler months.

Campsites, facilities: The adults-only park has 525 RV sites with full hookups, patios, and telephone and cable TV access. Restrooms, showers, laundry facilities, a pool, two recreation halls with kitchens, horseshoes, championship shuffleboard courts, and a fishing lake are provided. Children may visit tenants for no longer than two weeks. Leashed pets are permitted.

Reservations, fees: Reservations are recommended. Sites are $20 per night for two people, plus $2.50 for each additional person. Major credit cards are accepted. Long-term stays are preferred.

Directions: From State Road 54 and U.S. 301 in Zephyrhills, turn south on U.S. 301 and drive two miles to the park. Gall Boulevard is the same as U.S. 301.

Contact: Palm View Gardens, 3331 Gall Boulevard, Zephyrhills, FL 33541, 813/782-8685, website: www.rvresorts.com.

57 HAPPY DAYS RV PARK

Rating: 5

West of Zephyrhills
Orlando map, grid c3, page 240

Churches, a shopping center, and other points of interest are close to this park. There's even a bus stop nearby. Planned activities, such as exercise and crafts classes, fashion shows, games, bingo, and Sunday church services, are held in winter. The recreation hall has a dance floor, a stage, and an electronic bingo scoreboard; the smaller lodge has a workshop area for hobbies.

Campsites, facilities: All 300 lots have full hookups; 100 sites are available for overnighters. Rigs up to 40 feet in length can be accommodated. Restrooms, showers, laundry facilities, a dump station, shuffleboard courts, horseshoe pits, a recreation hall, two pool tables, cable TV, and a heated pool are available. Children are not welcome; this is a 55-and-over park. Leashed pets under 20 pounds are permitted in one area of the park.

Reservations, fees: Reservations are recommended. Sites are $20 per night for two people, plus $2 for each additional person. Add $2 daily for use of air conditioners, electric heaters, or electric water heaters. Credit cards are not accepted. Long-term stays are permitted.

Directions: From State Road 54 and U.S. 301 in Zephyrhills, drive west on State Road 54 for about .5 mile. Turn south on Allen Road (by the Circle K store). The park is ahead within .5 mile, just past the shopping center.

Contact: Happy Days RV Park, 4603 Allen Road, Zephyrhills, FL 33541, 813/788-4858.

58 ANDY'S TRAVEL TRAILER PARK

Rating: 2

West of Zephyrhills
Orlando map, grid c3, page 240

Ready for a Saturday night bonfire? This retirement-oriented snowbird park boasts a very active social schedule, with barbecues, coffee hours, potluck dinners, bingo, cards, video nights, and more.

Campsites, facilities: Designed for the winter visitor, the park has 76 full-hookup sites for snowbirds, and six spots for overnighters. All have picnic tables. Restrooms, showers, a wheelchair-accessible clubhouse, shuffleboard courts, and a dog-walk area are on site. Children are not welcome; adults over 50 are preferred. Leashed pets under 12 pounds are permitted.

Reservations, fees: Reservations are recommended. Sites are $22 per night for two people, plus $1 per extra person. Credit cards are not accepted. Long-term rates are available.

Directions: From I-75, take Exit 279 and drive east on State Road 54 for 10 miles.

Contact: Andy's Travel Trailer Park, 37707 State Road 54, Zephyrhills, FL 33541, 813/782-3843, email: jrrenaud@3oaks.com.

59 JIM'S RV PARK

Rating: 3

West of Zephyrhills
Orlando map, grid c3, page 240

Catering to retired snowbirds who like to stay put for the season, the park has a full array of winter season activities, such as bingo, crafts, potluck suppers, dances, bowling parties, and golf outings. Within one mile are shops, restaurants, a library, banks, and video rentals. Flea markets abound in the area.

Campsites, facilities: The adults-only park has 147 sites with full hookups. Restrooms, showers, laundry facilities, shuffleboard and horseshoe courts, a recreation hall, and a pool are on the premises. Children may visit campers for up to two weeks. Small, leashed pets are permitted; one to a unit.

Reservations, fees: Reservations are recommended. Sites are $20 per night for two people, plus $1 for each additional person. Credit cards are not accepted. Long-term stays are OK.

Directions: From I-75, take Exit 279 and drive east on State Road 54 for nine miles.

Contact: Jim's RV Park, 35120 State Road 54 West, Zephyrhills, FL 33541, 813/782-5610.

60 RALPH'S TRAVEL PARK

Rating: 4

West of Zephyrhills
Orlando map, grid c3, page 240

Canadians get a warm welcome at this sprawling park, which has full-service amenities, plus a car wash area. Gas and food stores are located next door.

Campsites, facilities: There are 100 RV sites available with full hookups in this 402-lot snowbird retreat, where folks return year after year. Restrooms, showers, laundry facilities, a pool, shuffleboard courts, horseshoe pits, two recreation halls, and a workshop are available. The recreation halls, laundry room, and restrooms are accessible to wheelchairs. Campers must be 50 or older. Campers under 50 and children are permitted for visits of less than 30 days only. Pets are allowed, but they must be registered at the office.

Reservations, fees: Reservations are recommended. Sites are $17 per night for two people, plus $1 for each additional person. Cable TV costs extra, depending on your length of stay. Credit cards are not accepted. Long-term stays are the norm.

Directions: From I-75, take Exit 279 and go six miles east on State Road 54 to the park, which is on the corner of Morris Bridge Road.

Contact: Ralph's Travel Park, 34408 State Road 54 West, Zephyrhills, FL 33543, 813/782-8223 or 866/234-2056, email: ralphs33543@aol.com.

61 HILLCREST RV RESORT

Rating: 4

On the west side of Zephyrhills
Orlando map, grid c3, page 240

Extra-large lots accommodate residents in this

park-model/RV retreat favored by seasonal visitors. The management of the 40-acre resort prides itself on keeping the premises neat and orderly. RVs must be modern and well maintained; rules are strict regarding maintenance of the lots. Grocery stores and restaurants are nearby.

Campsites, facilities: There are 496 full-hookup sites with telephone and cable TV access. Restrooms, showers, two laundries, a dump station, a pool, and a clubhouse are provided; many areas are wheelchair accessible. Children are not welcome except for brief visits. Leashed pets are permitted.

Reservations, fees: Reservations are recommended. Sites are $18.50 per night for two people, plus $2 for each additional person.

Directions: From I-75, take Exit 279 eastbound on State Road 54 for 10 miles. After passing the Winn-Dixie, go .5 mile farther, turn south on Lane Road, and proceed to the park.

Contact: Hillcrest RV Resort, 4421 Lane Road, Zephyrhills, FL 33541, 813/782-1947 or 800/992-8735.

62 LEISURE DAYS RV RESORT

Rating: 3

West of Zephyrhills
Orlando map, grid c3, page 240
Staying at this sunny, landscaped, retiree-oriented park puts you close to fishing waters, tennis courts, golf courses, shopping, and Central Florida attractions. Social programs are held from November through mid-April; among them are planned campfires, bingo, crafts, card parties, pancake breakfasts, and dances. The pool is heated.

Campsites, facilities: This park has 41 RV sites with full hookups for overnighters, cable TV, and telephone access. They accommodate rigs up to 37 feet in length. Restrooms, showers, laundry facilities, a pool, an activity center, horseshoe pits, and shuffleboard courts are available. All units must be self-contained.

There are 200 additional sites for long-termers. All areas are wheelchair accessible. A 55-and-older park, Leisure Days permits children as visitors only and for short periods. Leashed pets under 25 pounds are allowed.

Reservations, fees: Reservations are recommended. Sites are $14.50 per night. Credit cards are not accepted. Long-term stays are OK.

Directions: From I-75, take Exit 279 and drive east on State Road 54 for six miles. Turn south on Morris Bridge Road and drive one block.

Contact: Leisure Days RV Resort, 34533 Leisure Days Drive, Zephyrhills, FL 33541, 813/788-2631, fax 813/715-7617.

63 CAMPERS' WORLD

Rating: 4

West of Wildwood
Orlando map, grid c1, page 240
This mostly shaded park was a logging camp back in the days when pioneers were homesteading in Florida. In fact, you'll play badminton and shuffleboard atop a former railroad bed used by loggers who moved huge cypress logs out of the area for consumption in points farther north. Another old railroad bed, eight miles away, has been converted for hiking, bicycling, and inline skating. Across the road, you'll find the old Rutland family cemetery. This park formerly had access to a canal leading to the Withlacoochee River, but no more, due to a road project.

To explore the beautiful Withlacoochee River, hop in a canoe rented from Nobleton Boat Rentals; for $30, the outfitter will drive you 10 miles upstream and you'll paddle your way back. Call 352/796-4343 or 800/783-5284, website: www.nobletoncanoes.com.

Campsites, facilities: Forty-five tent sites are set apart from 50 full-hookup RV sites (five pull-through). Each site has a picnic table and fire ring. On the premises are restrooms, showers, a dump station, laundry facilities, a pool, a recreation room, horseshoes, shuffleboard, and limited groceries Firewood is available. Restaurants and grocery stores are about seven miles away. Pets and children are allowed.

Reservations, fees: Reservations are not necessary. Sites are $13 to $15 per night for four people, plus $1 for each additional person. Credit cards are not accepted. Long-term rates are available.

Directions: From I-75 at Exit 66, travel eight miles west on State Road 44.

Contact: Campers' World, 6545 West State Road 44, Lake Panasoffkee, FL 33538, 352/748-2237.

64 ADAMS MARINA AND RV PARK

Rating: 3

On Lake Panasoffkee
Orlando map, grid c1, page 240

Once you're here, you're part of the family, say the owners. This retiree-oriented park has 29 sites for seasonal visitors and five sites for overnighters on its sunny grounds. It's located near banks, stores, and the post office. Recent drought has lowered the water level of Lake Panasoffkee, but you can fish off the dock and seawalls; the boat ramp was not usable at this writing. Most folks spend the winter, playing cards, bingo, and partaking of potluck dinners and breakfasts. The park is closed April 1 through September 15.

Campsites, facilities: Rigs up to 40 feet can be accommodated on the 34 or so full-hookup RV sites. They have picnic tables, concrete pads, cable TV, and telephone access. Restrooms, showers, laundry facilities, a dock, and shuffleboard courts are on the premises. Children are welcome for short visits. Leashed pets under 40 pounds are permitted.

Reservations, fees: Reservations are recommended. Sites are $18 per night for two people, plus $4 per extra person. Credit cards are not accepted. Seasonal rates are available.

Directions: From I-75, take Exit 321 onto

County Road 470 and drive north 3.5 miles to the park.

Contact: Adams Marina and RV Park, 1410 Northwest 21st Lane, Lake Panasoffkee, FL 33538, 352/793-6633.

65 IDLEWILD LODGE AND RV PARK

Rating: 5

At Lake Panasoffkee southwest of Wildwood
Orlando map, grid c1, page 240

A four-acre, lakeside campground, Idlewild has lots of trees and borders a wooded area. The main activity here is fishing on Lake Panasoffkee. The whole region is pretty laid-back, and this small campground is located at the even quieter north end of the lake.

The RV sites, with 12-by-30-foot concrete pads, are set behind 11 cottages that front the solar heated pool. Don't forget to pack your swimsuit; park rules forbid swimmers to wear shorts or cutoffs. Tenters are occasionally accepted as guests, but it's pretty hard to wedge any but the smallest of tents in around the concrete pads.

Campsites, facilities: All 10 full-hookup sites are for RVs. On the premises are restrooms, showers, laundry facilities, a dump station, some picnic tables, rental efficiencies, bait, tackle, a boat ramp, a pool, horseshoes, basketball, shuffleboard, and boat rentals. Cable TV and telephone service are available. Groceries and restaurants are about two miles away. Children and small leashed pets are permitted.

Reservations, fees: Reservations are recommended in winter. Sites are $15 per night for two people, plus $2 for each extra person. Credit cards are not accepted for overnight stays. Long-term stays are OK.

Directions: From I-75 at Exit 321, head west on County Road 470 for about five miles. Turn right onto County Road 400. The campground is one mile ahead.

Contact: Idlewild Lodge and RV Park, 4110

County Road 400, Lake Panasoffkee, FL 33538, 352/793-7057.

66 PANA VISTA LODGE

Rating: 3

At the Outlet River southwest of Wildwood
Orlando map, grid c1, page 240

You'll find this park at the mouth of what's known as the Outlet River, a stream that connects the popular boating and bass-fishing waters of Lake Panasoffkee to the Withlacoochee River. To canoe down the river, contact Nobleton Boat Rentals at 352/796-4343 or 800/783-5284. The campground offers some grills at the tent sites and big, wooded lots. The park sees all kinds of visitors: overnighters, snowbirds, and Floridians who leave their rigs on site to use on the weekends.

Campsites, facilities: Twenty tent sites are set apart from 70 full-hookup RV sites. Each site has a picnic table. On the premises are restrooms, showers, grills, fire rings, rental cabins, a bait and tackle shop, a boat ramp, and pontoon boat and canoe rentals. Groceries and restaurants are within two miles. Children are welcome. Small leashed pets are permitted.

Reservations, fees: Reservations are recommended. Sites are $12 to $16 per night for two people, plus $1 for each additional person. Major credit cards are accepted. Long-term stays are OK.

Directions: From I-75 at Exit 321, drive almost five miles west on County Road 470. Turn right at County Road 421 (you'll see a sign for the lodge).

Contact: Pana Vista Lodge, 3417 County Road 421, Lake Panasoffkee, FL 33538, 352/793-2061, fax 352/793-5683, website: www.qsy.com/panavista.

67 TURTLEBACK RV RESORT

Rating: 6

Off I-75 southwest of Wildwood
Orlando map, grid c1, page 240

Set on a creek that leads to the popular bass fishing waters of 27-square-mile Lake Panasoffkee, this wooded park offers campsites that are grassy and mostly shaded for its clientele, which tends to stay for the winter. Fish from the dock or from a boat. If you don't own a boat or a canoe, you can rent one here. For campers who couldn't care less that they're in bass country, try the heated pool or year-round planned activities such as bingo games, dancing, and potluck dinners.

Campsites, facilities: About 20 tent sites are set apart from 130 RV sites (100 full-hookup, 30 pull-through). Each site has a picnic table. A pool, boat and canoe rentals, a playground, a recreation hall, pool tables, horseshoes, two shuffleboard courts, and a nature trail are on the premises. Restrooms, showers, a dump station, laundry facilities, LP gas sales, rental cabins, a boat ramp, telephone service, cable TV, and social activities are available. Management says all facilities are wheelchair accessible. Groceries and restaurants are within one mile. Children and pets are permitted.

Reservations, fees: Reservations are recommended. Sites are $16 per night for two people, plus $2 for each additional person. Credit cards are not accepted. Long-term stays are OK.

Directions: From I-75 at Exit 321, head west for .75 mile to the campground on the left.

Contact: Turtleback RV Resort, 190 County Road 488, Lake Panasoffkee, FL 33538, 352/793-2501. Reserve at 800/887-8525.

68 COUNTRYSIDE RV PARK

Rating: 5

Off I-75 southwest of Wildwood
Orlando map, grid c1, page 240

This park in a quiet, rural area is good for a

quick stopover if you're traveling on I-75. It's also not far from the local focus of interest: Lake Panasoffkee, or any of the creeks leading to the watery domain of anglers and boaters. To paddle a 10-mile stretch of the nearby Withlacoochee River, try renting a canoe from Nobleton Boat Rentals; call 352/796-7176 or 800/783-5284. During the winter, park activities include bingo, potluck dinners, cards, music around the bonfire, horseshoes, shuffleboard, and a coffee house.

Campsites, facilities: The camp has 30 full-hookup RV sites and five spots for tenters. Fifteen sites are pull-through. Seasonal sites have picnic tables. On the premises are restrooms, showers, a dump station, a laundry room, a recreation hall, and a game room. Firewood is available, and a boat ramp accessing the Withlacoochee River and Lake Panasoffkee is just three miles away. Management says all buildings are wheelchair accessible. Telephone and cable TV hookups are available. Groceries and restaurants are about two miles away. Children are welcome on a short-term basis. Pets are allowed.

Reservations, fees: Reservations are recommended. Sites are $19 per night for two people, plus $2 for each additional person and $1 for using air conditioners or electric heaters. Credit cards are not accepted. Long-term stays are OK for adults.

Directions: From I-75 at Exit 321, drive west on County Road 470. In less than one mile, bear left on County Road 489, which leads to the park.

Contact: Countryside RV Park, P.O. Box 1155, Lake Panasoffkee, FL 33538, 352/793-8103.

69 WILDWOOD KOA

Rating: 6

Off I-75 in Wildwood
Orlando map, grid c1, page 240

Perhaps the best thing about this KOA is that it's right off the interstate, making it easier to get to Disney-area attractions, Ocala National Forest, or the Withlacoochee State Forest in short order. If you're tired of the pool, try the miniature golf course or hot tub. If you speak French, German, or—believe it or not—Tagalog (the language of the Philippines), then you're in luck because the proprietors do, too.

Campsites, facilities: Tent sites are set in a big area, to the side of the 108 full-hookup sites (76 pull-through). Each site has a picnic table. On the premises are restrooms, showers, a dump station, a pool, a hot tub, a playground, miniature golf, horseshoes, shuffleboard, limited groceries, and laundry facilities. Firewood is available. Restrooms and the recreation hall are wheelchair accessible. Restaurants are located within walking distance. Pets and children are allowed.

Reservations, fees: Reservations are recommended. Sites are $28 to $42 per night for two people, plus $3 for each additional person. Major credit cards are accepted. Long-term stays are OK.

Directions: From I-75 at Exit 329, drive 300 yards east on State Road 44.

Contact: Wildwood KOA, 882 East State Road 44, Wildwood, FL 34785, 352/748-2774 or 800/562-3272 (reservations only), fax 352/748-6832, website: www.floridawildwoodkoa.com.

70 LAKE DEATON RV PARK

Rating: 3

At Lake Deaton east of Wildwood
Orlando map, grid c1, page 240

At this wooded park, some campers fish in 1.5-mile-wide Lake Deaton or head for three major golf courses nearby. Others like to bicycle down the back roads to Wildwood. If you don't have any fishing luck at Lake Deaton, try wetting a line at a more noted bass fishing spot—Lake Okahumpka—on the other side of State Road 44. This campground is favored by snowbirds looking for a quiet, out-of-the-way RV park.

Campsites, facilities: This retiree-oriented park

offers 81 full-hookup RV sites (two pull-through). On the premises are restrooms, showers, a dump station, a boat ramp, a dock, a clubhouse, horseshoes, and laundry facilities. Management says the restrooms are wheelchair accessible. Groceries and restaurants are within six miles. Children are permitted only on an overnight basis. Small pets are allowed.

Reservations, fees: Reservations are recommended. Sites are $20 per night for two people, plus $2 for each additional person. Credit cards are not accepted. Long-term stays are OK.

Directions: From I-75 at Exit 329, drive eight miles east on State Road 44. Turn left onto State Road 44A, cross the railroad tracks onto County Road 145, then turn left onto County Road 146 and proceed to the park.

Contact: Lake Deaton RV Park, 4855 County Road 146, Wildwood, FL 34785, 352/748-2397, email: hstk@webtv.net.

71 RECREATION PLANTATION RV RESORT

Rating: 8

In Lady Lake

Orlando map, grid b1, page 240

As the name suggests, an active social lifestyle is what campers get in this country setting designed for adults. Events noted on the clubhouse bulletin board may range from 8:30 A.M. exercises to 7 P.M. card games or bingo in winter, so you may need your alarm clock to keep up. Some sort of activity is scheduled for most hours by the full-time winter activities director. A trio of 18-hole golf courses is located within three miles.

About half of the campsites form concentric circles around the park's central attractions—a clubhouse, a heated pool, a spa, and sports courts. The minimum 65-by-35-foot lots tend to be sunny with token, well-kept bushes and lawns that give the park a residential atmosphere. Kids may feel out of place around the middle-aged and retiree crowd, if only because rules forbid them from using the hot tub, exercise equipment, and pool tables. Full-time residents live at about 300 lots sprinkled throughout the park.

Campsites, facilities: These 850 full-hookup sites are for RVs only. Recreational offerings include a pool, a spa, two clubhouses (one is wheelchair accessible), an exercise room, billiards, planned activities, shuffleboard, bocce ball (lawn bowling), tennis, horseshoes, and table tennis. Showers, restrooms, a post office, cable TV access, telephone hookups, and laundry facilities are available. Children may camp for up to two weeks at this otherwise adult-oriented park. Leashed pets are permitted but should be walked around the retention pond and attended at all times.

Reservations, fees: Reservations are suggested. Sites are $27 per night for two people, plus $3.50 for each additional person. Major credit cards are accepted. Long-term rates are available.

Directions: From Leesburg, drive about seven miles north on U.S. 27. Turn left on County Road 466. The park is on the right, .5 mile west of the turnoff.

Contact: Recreation Plantation RV Resort, 609 County Road 466, Lady Lake, FL 32159, 352/753-7222 or 800/448-5646, website: www.recreationplantation.com.

72 BLUE PARROT CAMPING PARK

Rating: 5

In Lady Lake

Orlando map, grid b1, page 240

This place is designed for active seniors, as evidenced by the advertised slogan: "Caution—Adults at Play." Besides teeing off for free at the park's par-3, nine-hole golf course, visitors can swim in the heated pool, share potluck dinners, attend Bible studies, play bingo (in winter), learn to quilt and sew, and take part in other activities organized by a resident association.

La Plaza Grande shopping center and an RV hand-wash business are nearby, so expect a suburban experience. Most of the concrete-pad or grassy sites along the lighted, paved streets are devoted to retirees who spend months at the 80-plus-acre park. Overnighters are relegated to a small area close to County Road 25. Located in sleepy Lake County, which is marked by rolling hills and 1,400 named lakes, the camp could serve as a crash pad for bass anglers.

Campsites, facilities: All 452 full-hookup sites (17 pull-through) at this retiree-oriented park are for RVs up to 44 feet long. A golf course, a pool, billiards, a recreation room, horseshoes, shuffleboard, and social programs entertain campers. Showers, restrooms, a convenience store, a Sunday chapel, cable TV, telephone service, and laundry facilities are available. Children may camp short-term. Leashed pets must use the designated dog walks.

Reservations, fees: Reservations are recommended. Sites are $24 per night for two people, plus $2.50 for each additional person. Major credit cards are accepted. Long-term rates are available.

Directions: From County Road 466/Lemon Street in Lady Lake, drive a short distance northwest on U.S. 27/441 to the cutoff for County Road 25. Take County Road 25 north to the park entrance on your right.

Contact: Blue Parrot Camping Park, 40840 County Road 25, Lady Lake, FL 32159, 352/753-2026, fax 352/753-8383, website: www.rvresorts.com.

73 SUNSHINE MOBILE HOME PARK

Rating: 2

South of Lady Lake
Orlando map, grid b1, page 240

Campers are outnumbered by residents of the 70 mobile homes at this retiree-oriented park, but overnighters can join along in winter ac-

tivities or take a dip in the pool all the same. The grassy/concrete-pad RV sites are set on 11 acres about three miles due north of Lake Griffin State Park, where paddlers using canoes rented from the park and bass anglers with their own boats launch into 14-square-mile Lake Griffin. This sleepy region of Florida is characterized by lake-dotted countryside surrounded by grassy, rolling hills that were citrus groves before the bad freezes of the 1980s. Disney World and other Orlando-area attractions are about one hour south.

Campsites, facilities: This age-55-and-older park has 20 full-hookup RV sites (two pull-through) with picnic tables. A pool, an exercise room, horseshoes, shuffleboard, winter social programs, and a wheelchair-accessible recreation hall entertain campers. Showers, restrooms, seasonal trailer rentals, and laundry facilities are available. Children are prohibited. Leashed pets are permitted.

Reservations, fees: Reservations are suggested. Sites are $16 per night for two people, plus $1 for each additional person and $1 if you use air conditioners or electric heaters. Credit cards are not accepted. Long-term stays are OK.

Directions: From County Road 466 in the town of Lady Lake, drive south on U.S. 27/441 to Griffin View Drive. Turn left (east). The park is .5 mile ahead at Sunshine Boulevard.

Contact: Sunshine Mobile Home Park, 401 Sunshine Boulevard, Lady Lake, FL 32159, tel./fax 352/753-2415.

74 LAKE GRIFFIN STATE PARK

Rating: 8

In Fruitland Park
Orlando map, grid b1, page 240

Largemouth bass are the goal of anglers at 14-square-mile Lake Griffin, although bluegill and specks make respectable consolation prizes. Bird-watchers, on the other hand, remark that the rookery, which resounds with a cacophony of bird chatter, is their favorite part of the

427-acre park. Actually, the most unusual facet of this park may be the "floating islands." See the marsh between Lake Griffin and its uplands? Sometimes chunks break off from that marshy mat of soil and roots, and they float like icebergs toward the lake.

We have good memories of this place, where we once spent a New Year's Eve watching the stars, but the traffic getting to it can be congested. Campers sleep under oaks, and the sites are lovely. Bring mosquito repellent in summer. All sites—most sandy, some with pads—have a picnic table, a grill, and a fire ring for roasting marshmallows. As at most other state parks, campers are set apart from day-use areas such as the .75-mile nature trail. Look for otters, rabbits, and raccoons during your stay. Canoeists and boaters use a ramp at the head of a .25-mile canal leading to Lake Griffin. Ocala National Forest is nearby.

Campsites, facilities: All 40 sites are for RVs and tents, and all have water and electric hookups. Eight sites are pull-through. Each site has a picnic table, a grill, and a fire ring. On the premises are showers, restrooms, a dump station, a boat ramp, a dock, canoe rentals, a playground, a nature trail, horseshoe and volleyball areas, and laundry facilities. Two sites, the pavilion, and fishing dock have wheelchair access. A restaurant, bait, and groceries are available within one mile. Children are welcome. Pets are allowed with proof of vaccination.

Reservations, fees: Reservations are recommended; call ReserveAmerica at 800/326-3521. Sites are $10 per night for four people, plus $2 for each additional person. Add $2 for electricity or per pet. Major credit cards are accepted. The maximum stay is 120 days within six months.

Directions: From Leesburg, drive about two miles north on U.S. 441/27. The park is on the right side of the road.

Contact: Lake Griffin State Park, 3089 U.S. 441/27, Fruitland Park, FL 34731, 352/360-6760, fax 352/360-6762, website: www.floridastateparks.org.

75 PINE ISLAND CAMPGROUND AND FISH CAMP

Rating: 3

At Lake Griffin east of Lady Lake
Orlando map, grid b1, page 240

The on-site taxidermy service should be your first clue that bass is king at this remote retreat near the mouth of the Ocklawaha River at the northwestern end of Lake Griffin. Bream, catfish, and crappie also lurk in the sizable lake. Fishing guide Captain Larry Fetter uses live bait to lure (and release) the prize that some people mount on their walls—bass. If you don't like to fish or motor around in a boat, look elsewhere for a spot to set up camp. No pool, shuffleboard, or other activities are offered. Oaks shade each rustic campsite.

Campsites, facilities: Twenty-one RV sites have full hookups, and 13 tent spots come with electricity and water. For recreation, there's a fishing guide, boat rentals, 80 covered boat stalls, a boat ramp, and campfire areas. Showers, restrooms, a dump station, and laundry facilities are available. Children are welcome. Pets must be leashed.

Reservations, fees: Reservations are not taken. Sites are $17 per night for two people, plus $2 for each additional person. Major credit cards are accepted. Long-term stays are OK.

Directions: From U.S. 27 in Lady Lake, drive east on County Road 466/Lemon Street to the stop sign. Turn left and follow Lake Griffin Road about five miles to the campground entrance.

Contact: Pine Island Campground and Fish Camp, 6808 Lake Griffin Road, Lady Lake, FL 32159, 352/753-2972.

76 MORGAN'S MOBILE HOME PARK AND FISH CAMP

Rating: 2

On Lake Griffin in eastern Fruitland Park
Orlando map, grid b1, page 240

The clientele consists mostly of retirees at this

15-acre, laid-back RV park/fish camp on Lake Griffin, where anglers launch their boats to pursue bass and bream. From the deck of the camp's sightseeing sidewheel paddleboat, *The Gator Princess,* visitors try to spot alligators, herons, and the occasional otter. You can also tour a World War II–era, 65-foot PT boat. Stands of palms and deciduous trees tend to shelter the grassy RV sites. Orlando's theme parks are about one hour away.

Campsites, facilities: All 58 full-hookup sites are for RVs. Recreation options include a boat ramp and dock, sightseeing boat tours, and a recreation room. Showers, restrooms, a dump station, bait and tackle, and laundry facilities are available. All areas of the park are wheelchair accessible. Groceries can be purchased one block from here. A restaurant is one mile away. Children are permitted, but the park is geared toward retirees. Small, leashed pets are allowed.

Reservations, fees: Reservations are not necessary. Sites are $15 per night for two people, plus $1 for each additional person. Credit cards are not accepted. Long-term stays are OK.

Directions: From the intersection of U.S. 27 and U.S. 441 in Leesburg, drive north on U.S. 27. At the third stoplight, turn right. The park entrance is 1.5 miles ahead on Picciola Road.

Contact: Morgan's Mobile Home Park and Fish Camp, 04056 Picciola Road, Fruitland Park, FL 34731, 352/787-4916.

77 HOLIDAY TRAVEL RESORT

Rating: 9

In Leesburg

Orlando map, grid b1, page 240

Indoor pools are rare at Florida campgrounds, but here adult swimmers can float on their backs and gaze up at a blue sky through a row of skylights in a modern, bright-white building, or peer out the broad glass doors to see RVs parked in the distance. Outdoors, another pool is open to kids as well as adults. This 200-plus-acre park is massive: Beyond a security gate, the paved park roads lead to a sprawling resort with 935 sites, of which 185 sites are for short-term campers. The rest are for RVs planning to stay a while. A social director plans activities for not one, but three, recreational buildings.

A retired and semiretired crowd is targeted by management, but kids can take advantage of the miniature golf course and other amenities by camping short-term. Bring your own boat to launch from a campground ramp into a canal leading to the bass fishing waters of Lake Harris. A nine-hole chip-and-putt golf course has artificial turf. Palms, native pines, and other trees lend shade to portions of the park, but several gravel or grassy RV sites bear the brunt of the sun's forceful rays.

Campsites, facilities: There are 185 full-hookup, pull-through sites for RVs up to 40 feet long. All sites have picnic tables. Another 750 sites are set aside for long-term or seasonal stays. Tenters may use the park in summer only. A chip-and-putt golf course, a miniature golf course, two pools, three recreation rooms, a playground, a hot tub, billiards, a softball field, eight horseshoe pits, 14 shuffleboard courts, four tennis courts, two volleyball courts, and winter social programs entertain campers. Showers, restrooms, a marina, a boat ramp, a dock, a dump station, groceries, bait and tackle, laundry facilities, and a poolside restaurant are available. Management says all public facilities are wheelchair accessible. Children may camp up to two weeks at this otherwise adult-oriented park. Leashed pets must use the designated dog walk.

Reservations, fees: Reservations are recommended. Sites are $26 per night for two people, plus $3 per extra person and $2 for cable TV. Major credit cards are accepted. Long-term rates are available.

Directions: From Leesburg, drive south on U.S. 27 for three miles. Turn west at County Road 33 and proceed one mile to the park.

Contact: Holiday Travel Resort, 28229 County Road 33, Leesburg, FL 34748, 352/787-5151 or 800/428-5334, fax 352/787-1052, website: www.holidaytravelresort.com.

78 RIDGECREST RV RESORT

Rating: 6

South of Leesburg

Orlando map, grid b1, page 240

Half of 30-acre Ridgecrest RV Park is devoted to retirees in mobile homes, whereas the other half is set up for RV and tent campers of any age. The result is a residential feel at the oak- and palm-dotted facility, located about two miles from the bass fishing waters of Lake Harris. Some campsites are grassy, and others have concrete pads. A January antique fair and a March art festival entertain folks in the city of Leesburg, but some overnighters may be more interested in Disney World, which is 36 miles away.

Campsites, facilities: Ten tent sites are set apart from 136 full-hookup RV sites (10 pull-through). Each site has a picnic table. A heated pool, a hot tub, a recreation hall, shuffleboard, a library, a camp circle for gatherings, winter social programs, a game room, and an exercise room entertain campers. Showers, restrooms, a dump station, rental park models, telephone hookups, propane, and laundry facilities are available. Management says the office and some RV sites are wheelchair accessible. You'll find groceries one mile away and a restaurant within five miles. Children are welcome. Pets under 20 pounds are permitted.

Reservations, fees: Reservations are recommended. Sites are $17 per night for two people, plus $2 for each additional person. Credit cards are not accepted. Long-term stays are OK.

Directions: From Leesburg, travel five miles south on U.S. 27 to the park entrance.

Contact: Ridgecrest RV Resort, 26125 U.S. 27 South, Leesburg, FL 34748, 352/787-1504.

79 HAINES CREEK RV VILLAGE

Rating: 5

On Haines Creek east of Leesburg

Orlando map, grid b1, page 240

A campground gazebo and boardwalk over-look 650 feet of Haines Creek. On the banks, anglers try to snag bream and other fish—as do a few long-legged wading birds at creek-side. Paved, lighted streets curve past gravel and grassy campsites, a few sporting RVs with attached screen patios. Tent sites tend to be sunny and grassy. Cabbage palms and other trees partially shade some RV sites. Although you technically could take day trips to Disney World or other Orlando-area attractions farther south, that isn't the focus of this relaxed lake region where the action revolves around boating, fishing, and, to a lesser extent, canoeing. Tree-lined Haines Creek leads west to Lake Griffin and east to Lake Eustis, and anglers can take advantage of the camp's private docks and boat ramp to get to bass country.

Campsites, facilities: RVers can choose from 86 full-hookup sites (two are pull-through). Each site has a picnic table. The facility includes boat rentals, a boat ramp, private docks, horseshoes, and a recreation hall. Showers, restrooms, a dump station, and laundry facilities are available. The restrooms, recreation hall, and laundry room are accessible to wheelchairs. Groceries and bait can be purchased across the street. A restaurant is five miles away. Children are welcome for overnight visits only. Leashed pets are permitted.

Reservations, fees: Reservations are recommended. Sites are $18 per night for two people, plus $1 for each additional person and $1 for pets. Credit cards are not accepted. Senior citizens are welcome to stay long-term.

Directions: From U.S. 27 in Leesburg, drive south on U.S. 441 about four miles. At the traffic signal, turn left onto County Road 44. Drive five miles and turn left into the campground before you reach the Haines Creek bridge.

Contact: Haines Creek RV Village, 10121 County Road 44 East, Leesburg, FL 34788, 352/728-5939, fax 352/728-5798.

80 TRIMBLE PARK

🏊 🚣 🚤 🎣 ♿ 🚐 ⛺

Rating: 4

By Lake Beauclaire near Mount Dora
Orlando map, grid b1, page 240

Set beside serene Beauclaire and Carlton Lakes, this 71-acre, county-run park is well removed from the hustle and bustle of Orlando and technically is in the town of Tangerine (despite the Mount Dora address). It's geared toward locals, but vacationers passing through are welcome to set up camp at the grassy sites. Bird-watching and picnicking are popular pursuits, and fishing is possible from lakeside docks. A short nature trail provides about 15 minutes of diversion for hikers, threading through a forest studded with moss-covered oaks.

Campsites, facilities: All 15 sites have electricity, picnic tables, grills, and fire rings. On the premises are restrooms, showers, a dump station, a boat ramp, and a playground. Groceries, restaurants, and laundry facilities are a 15-minute drive away. Children are welcome. Pets and alcohol are prohibited.

Reservations, fees: Reservations are recommended if you want a site with electricity. Pay by cash or check when you make the reservation 45 days in advance; you must stay a minimum of two nights. Telephone reservations are not accepted. Primitive camping (tents only) is first-come, first-served. Sites are $10 to $15 per night. Add $3 for electricity and $1 for admission. Credit cards are not accepted. Stays are limited to 14 days.

Directions: From Apopka, head north on U.S. 441 about seven miles. Turn left onto Earl Wood Road, which will turn into Trimble Park Road. The campground is two miles ahead.

Contact: Trimble Park, 5802 Trimble Park Road, Mount Dora, FL 32757, 352/383-1993, website: http://parks.orangecountyfl.net.

81 FLORIDA ANGLERS RESORT

🏊 🚣 🚤 🐾 🚐 ⛺

Rating: 2

On Lake Harris east of Leesburg
Orlando map, grid b1, page 240

Sunbathers at the swimming beach can plunge into the broad waters of Lake Harris, but the lake is better known among anglers as a place to pull in some bass (bring your own boat). The eight-acre park is a rustic collection of cottages, 11 mobile homes, and 17 paved RV sites. You can pitch a tent lakeside, under an oak or palm tree, or just about anywhere you choose as long as you check with management first. Although the lake stretches about six miles at its widest point, reminders of city life aren't far behind; Lake Square Mall is across the street from the park.

Campsites, facilities: An indeterminate number of tent sites and 17 full-hookup RV sites are provided. Horseshoes, shuffleboard, a swimming beach, and a recreation room are available. Other facilities include showers, restrooms, a dump station, picnic tables, a boat ramp, a dock, boat slips, cable TV, and laundry facilities. Within .25 mile are groceries, a restaurant, and bait. Children are welcome. Leashed pets are permitted.

Reservations, fees: Reservations are recommended. Sites are $10 to $23 per night. Credit cards are not accepted. Long-term stays are OK.

Directions: From the intersection of U.S. 27 and U.S. 441 in Leesburg, head about five miles east toward Tavares on U.S. 441. When you see the Lake Square Mall on the left and the McDonald's on the right, look for the campground sign to your right. It directs you to the park entrance.

Contact: Florida Anglers Resort, 32311 Anglers Avenue, Leesburg, FL 34788, 352/343-4141, website: www.floridaanglersresort.com.

82 FISHERMAN'S COVE RV RESORT

Rating: 6

Near Lake Harris south of Tavares
Orlando map, grid b1, page 240

On Warm Mist Circle, about half the campsites back onto a par-3, nine-hole golf course that overlooks tree-lined Lake Harris. The lake provides a pretty backdrop for golfers. Still, as you might guess, Fisherman's Cove caters more to anglers who are tempted by the bass and catfish in the lake. The blue waters are reachable by boat via a canal from the campground boat ramp. Water-skiing isn't popular here because alligators and snakes tend to live in Florida lakes, and this one is no exception.

Expect little shade at the grassy campsites. To avoid sleeping closest to the park entrance gates, skip sites on Red Rose Drive and Ripple Avenue. West of the golf course are the heated pool and recreation hall, where an activities director organizes potluck dinners, three kinds of dancing classes, and other entertainment. Nearby is historic Mount Dora, home to antique shops and good restaurants. Disney World is about 45 miles away.

Campsites, facilities: All 330 full-hookup sites are for RVs; during the off-season, tenters can be accommodated on 20 sites. Recreation options include a nine-hole, par-3 golf course, a pool, horseshoes, shuffleboard, two activity lodges, and organized events. Showers, restrooms, a boat ramp, a 157-slip marina, park model rentals, a seven-unit motel, a dump station, and laundry facilities are available. The recreation hall is accessible to wheelchairs. Children under age 12 must be adult-supervised at the pool. Leashed, attended pets are permitted.

Reservations, fees: Reservations are recommended. Sites are $26 per night for two people, plus $10 per extra person. Credit cards are accepted. Long-term rates are available.

Directions: From Tavares, drive 2.5 miles south on State Road 19/Duncan Drive to the campground entrance on your right.

Contact: Fisherman's Cove RV Resort, 29115 Eichelberger Road, Tavares, FL 32778, 352/343-1233 or 800/254-9993.

83 HOLIDAY MOBILE PARK

Rating: 2

At Lake Eustis in Tavares
Orlando map, grid b1, page 240

Bicyclists follow Lake Eustis Drive northeast of the 10-acre park for a pleasant view of Lake Eustis, which spans about four miles at its widest point. But don't count on getting a camping spot: Campers are outnumbered by residents living at the 50 RV spaces and 160 mobile homes, leaving 20 or so paved lots for short-term stays. At least in winter, boat slips are hard to come by at the marina. Notwithstanding the pretty bike ride outside the boundaries, residents tend to stick close to home and pedal down park streets, if at all, or swim in the heated pool.

Campsites, facilities: This age-55-and-up park offers about 50 full-hookup sites for RVs up to 35 feet long. A pool, a clubhouse, shuffleboard, and wintertime sing-alongs entertain campers. Showers, restrooms, a marina, a dump station, and laundry facilities are available. Groceries can be purchased across the street. A restaurant and bait are available .5 mile away. Children are allowed to visit. Pets are prohibited.

Reservations, fees: Reservations are recommended in winter. Sites are $16 per night for two people. Credit cards are not accepted. Long-term rates are available.

Directions: From the intersection of State Road 19/Duncan Drive and U.S. 441/Burleigh Boulevard in Tavares, continue northeast on U.S. 441 for about one mile to the RV park.

Contact: Holiday Mobile Park, 561 East Burleigh Boulevard, Tavares, FL 32778, 352/343-2300.

84 PALM GARDENS

Rating: 4

At the Dead River north of Tavares

Orlando map, grid b1, page 240

Boating is the name of the game at this tree-dotted park on the Dead River, linking you to a chain of lakes. If you don't bring your own watercraft, rent one here ($45 and up for a half day for a 14-footer, or $85 for a half day on a 21-foot pontoon boat). Tour the Dead River, which river flows for about two miles before joining seven-mile-long Lake Eustis, then the bigger fishing waters of Lake Harris. Indeed, boaters and anglers who stay at these paved RV spots can explore thousands of acres of waters hereabouts, including Little Lake Harris and the Dora Canal, which leads to Lake Dora. Mount Dora's antique shops, boutiques, and many restaurants are close by. Disney World is about 45 miles away.

Campsites, facilities: The park offers 10 tent sites and 15 full-hookup RV sites (15 pull-through). A recreation room, a camp circle for gatherings, showers, a dump station, wheelchair-accessible restrooms, 14 rental cottages, bait, tackle, laundry facilities, snacks, a boat dock, boat rentals, a restaurant, and a lounge are available. Children are welcome. Leashed pets are permitted in the camping area but not the rental cottages.

Reservations, fees: Reservations are advised. Sites are $15 per night for two people, plus $5 for each additional person. Major credit cards are accepted. Long-term stays are OK.

Directions: From Tavares, drive one mile north on U.S. 441 to the park entrance on the right.

Contact: Palm Gardens, 11801 U.S. 441, Tavares, FL 32778, 352/343-2024, fax 352/342-5516.

85 WOODS-N-WATER TRAILS RV COMMUNITY

Rating: 4

On Lake Saunders west of Mount Dora

Orlando map, grid b1, page 240

A gazebo sits at a point stretching into tree-lined Lake Saunders, where boaters from the 17-acre adult park can tool around. From another nearby point, picnickers can look onto the calm one-square-mile lake. Campers tend to spend months at this country-atmosphere community, so it may be difficult to get a reservation if you wait to call between November 1 and March 15. Although Disney World and other Orlando-area attractions are about one hour to the south, Floridians familiar with this region and the February Mount Dora Art Festival think two words whenever Mount Dora is mentioned: "antiques" and "art."

Campsites, facilities: This adults-only park has 136 grassy, full-hookup RV sites with concrete patios and driveways. For recreation, there's a pool, horseshoes, shuffleboard and bocce ball (lawn bowling) courts, volleyball, a nature walk, an activities hall, and a boat ramp. Showers, restrooms, a dump station, and laundry facilities are available. Children are permitted with overnight campers or those staying less than two weeks. Leashed pets are permitted at designated campsites at the park's northern end and must use the bordering dog walk.

Reservations, fees: Reservations are required. Sites are $20 per night for two people, plus $1.50 for each additional person. Credit cards are not accepted. Long-term rates are available.

Directions: From Eustis, exit on U.S. 441 south to State Road 19A. At Bay Road, turn right and drive .25 mile to the park.

Contact: Woods-n-Water Trails RV Community, 1325 Bay Road, Mount Dora, FL 32757, 352/735-1009.

86 SOUTHERN PALMS RV RESORT

Rating: 7

In northern Eustis

Orlando map, grid b1, page 240

In summer, families stake out the grassy camp-sites and two swimming pools at this 100-plus-acre park, part of the Manufactured Homes Communities Inc. chain. In winter, retired Northerners predominate, attracted by bingo, pancake breakfasts, and other entertainment. Lighted, paved streets lead past the quite-sunny RV sites where mowed lawns and, in some cases, trailer skirts lend a residential touch. A handful of camping spots are near a pond where visitors catch minnows to use for bait at bass lakes found 10 minutes away in Tavares. (In fact, there are some 1,400 named lakes in sleepy Lake County.) Disney World and other Orlando-area attractions are about one hour south. Bring an umbrella or hat. Although pines and palms are scattered around the park, they provide relatively little shade.

Campsites, facilities: All 1,028 full-hookup sites are for RVs. Three clubhouses, two pools, two hot tubs, shuffleboard, horseshoes, bocce ball (lawn bowling), and winter social programs entertain campers. Showers, restrooms, a dump station, cable TV, telephone hookups, exercise rooms, and laundry facilities are available. Within one mile are groceries, bait, and restaurants. Most areas are wheelchair accessible. Children are welcome. Leashed pets are permitted.

Reservations, fees: Reservations are recommended. Sites are $27 per night for two people, plus $2 for each additional person. Credit cards are accepted. Long-term stays are the norm.

Directions: From State Road 44/Orange Avenue in Eustis, turn north on State Road 19/Grove Street. In about .5 mile, veer left onto County Road 44 and follow it nearly .5 mile. The park is on the right before the intersection with County Road 452.

Contact: Southern Palms RV Resort, 1 Avocado Lane, Eustis, FL 32726, 352/357-8882 or 800/277-9131, fax 352/357-2155, website: www.southernpalmsrv.com.

87 LAKESIDE RV PARK

Rating: 6

On Lake Smith south of Umatilla

Orlando map, grid b1, page 240

Although Lake Smith isn't large enough to be named on a state map, the bass anglers who set up camp here (mainly retirees) don't seem to mind. Neither do the visitors who skip the heated pool and paddle along the lake in a campground-furnished canoe. To the south, Eustis hosts a folk festival in December, a jazz festival in March, and April's Lake County Fair. Disney World and other Orlando-area attractions are about one hour's drive to the south.

Campsites, facilities: This 55-plus park offers 50 full-hookup RV sites (29 pull-through). Each site has a picnic table. About half the park is taken up with park models and full-timers. A pool, a hot tub, a recreation hall, and winter social programs entertain campers. Showers, restrooms, a dock, a boat ramp, a dump station, firewood, and laundry facilities are available. Management says all areas are wheelchair accessible. Groceries, bait, and a restaurant are located within 1.5 miles. Children are allowed to visit. Pets are prohibited.

Reservations, fees: Reservations are recommended. Sites are $20 per night for two people, plus $1 for each additional person. Credit cards are not accepted. Long-term rates are available.

Directions: From the intersection of State Road 44/Lakewood Avenue and State Road 19 in Eustis, drive about 2.5 miles north on State Road 19 to the park entrance. The campground is halfway between Eustis and Umatilla.

Contact: Lakeside RV Park, 38000 State Road 19, Umatilla, FL 32784, 352/669-5569, fax 352/669-5113.

88 OLDE MILL STREAM RV RESORT

≋ ᫅ ⛵ 🏕 🐕 ♿ 🚐 ⛺

Rating: 7

On Lake Pearl in Umatilla

Orlando map, grid b1, page 240

Bus trips to the Geritol Follies, the Ringling Brothers circus, gambling cruises, dinner theater, and the like aren't the main reason campers head to these 70 acres on Lake Pearl, but the plentiful winter activities on site are a real draw. A sample schedule includes the "Goldentones Show," euchre, almost-daily exercise classes, line dancing, wellness seminars, movies, dances, plus church services (the park has its own pastor) and "Gospel tellers" group on Sunday evenings. A curving, heated pool overlooks the blue waters of the 100-acre lake, where boaters search for bass. The sizable sunny sites (40 by 60 feet) are big enough so that if you have two or three slideouts, you won't feel stuck on top of your neighbor. Around 80 percent of the visitors here are staying for six months, so you'll have plenty of time to get to know one another. The sites sit diagonally along paved streets named for notable rivers—Ohio and Hudson, to name a few. To sleep closest to the 1,700 feet of lakefront, ask about campsites 2 through 18. If you get a landlocked site, take in the lake view from the clubhouse's screened-in porch. The park is sparkling clean, but don't expect a woodsy setting.

Campsites, facilities: This adults-only park offers 303 large RV sites with full hookups, concrete pads, and telephone access. Tents are permitted from April 1 to November 1. Each site has a picnic table. For entertainment, there's a pool, a driving range, miniature golf, a barbecue picnic area, horseshoes, shuffleboard, wintertime social activities, and a wheelchair-accessible, 800-square-foot recreation hall. Showers, restrooms, a dump station, and laundry facilities are available. Groceries and a restaurant are across the street. You must be at least 25 years old to camp, but children may

visit guests. Pets must be leashed and walked in the mowed field.

Reservations, fees: Reservations are recommended. Sites are $26 per night for two people, plus $2 for each additional person. Major credit cards are accepted. Long-term stays are OK.

Directions: From Orlando, drive northwest on U.S. 441 to State Road 19. Turn right, heading toward Umatilla. Continue about 10 miles to the park entrance on the right, south of State Road 42.

Contact: Olde Mill Stream RV Resort, 1000 North Central Avenue, Umatilla, FL 32784, 352/669-3141 or 800/449-3141, website: www.oldemillstreamrv.com.

89 KELLY PARK

🚶 ≋ 🏊 🎣 ♿ 🚐 ⛺

Rating: 7

At Rock Springs in Apopka

Orlando map, grid b1, page 240

Each minute, more than 26,000 gallons of cool, crystal-clear water pour out of a cave to form Rock Springs, which is the main attraction of this 245-acre county park. Swimming and snorkeling in the cool, natural springwaters are favored activities. The picnic pavilions and two miles of hiking trails also are popular. The camping sites—concrete pad and shell rock—are set in a shady forest.

Campsites, facilities: This county-run park has 21 RV sites (one pull-through) with electricity and water hookups, and three tent sites. Each has a picnic table, a fire ring, and a grill. On the premises are showers, restrooms, a dump station, a playground, a nature trail, volleyball, and snacks. Management says the restrooms, pavilions, and swimming area are wheelchair accessible. Groceries, restaurants, and laundry facilities are within five miles. Children are allowed. Pets and alcoholic beverages are prohibited.

Reservations, fees: Reservations are recommended, but you must pay in cash when you make the reservation. Telephone reservations are not accepted. Sites are $15 per night for up to four people, plus $3 for electricity. Orange County residents pay a discounted rate of $10 nightly. All campers age six and older also pay a one-time park entrance fee of $1 per person. The maximum stay is 14 consecutive days.

Directions: From Orlando, take U.S. 441 north into Apopka. Turn right on Park Avenue. Proceed six miles to the end, then bear right onto Kelly Park Road. The park is at the end of the road.

Contact: Kelly Park, 400 East Kelly Park Road, Apopka, FL 32723, 407/889-4179, fax 407/889-3523.

90 TWELVE OAKS RV RESORT

Rating: 5

Off I-4 west of Sanford
Orlando map, grid b1, page 240

The crooked branches of oaks and bristly pines help shade some of the campsites at this nearly 30-acre park that's a quick hop off I-4 but primarily caters to longer-term visitors. Other campsites are sunny. Despite the heated swimming pool and the shuffleboard court, some visitors are more interested in other things: shopping malls nearby and Disney World, which you'll find about 30 miles south of here. The park has a few sites available for overnighters or new snowbirds staying for the season.

Campsites, facilities: Among these 247 full-hookup, concrete pad RV sites (about 35 pull-through), 20 are available for overnighters and 45 are for seasonal stays. RVs as large as 45 feet can be accommodated. A pool, a recreation hall with planned activities, shuffleboard, horseshoes, a playground, long-term storage, social programs, and a picnic shelter are available. Showers, restrooms, a dump station, a small store, and two laundry facilities are on the premises. The recreation hall, office, and restrooms are wheelchair accessible. Children are allowed. Leashed pets are permitted.

Reservations, fees: Reservations are recommended. Sites are $26 per night for two people, plus $2 for each additional person. Major credit cards are accepted. Long-term stays are OK.

Directions: From Orlando, take I-4 north to State Road 46 (Exit 101BC). Drive two miles west to the park.

Contact: Twelve Oaks RV Resort, 6300 State Road 46 West, Sanford, FL 32771, 407/323-0880 or 800/633-9529, fax 407/323-0899.

91 TOWN AND COUNTRY RV RESORT

Rating: 4

Off I-4 west of Sanford
Orlando map, grid b1, page 240

Mainly snowbird retirees and motor home club members pull into this 30-acre park's paved roads to arrive at grassy campsites and concrete patios shaded by oak, palm, and pine trees. Although anglers can head three miles to the St. Johns River or two miles to Lake Monroe, some campers prefer to stay right here on two-lane Orange Boulevard and spend some time socializing. In winter, campers break bread together at numerous organized dinners and take trips to craft shows and flea markets. Nearby are several miles of hiking and canoe trails at Wekiwa Springs State Park. The Sanford Historic District is about five miles east, and Disney World is about 30 miles south.

Campsites, facilities: All 300 RV sites have full hookups and picnic tables. Six sites are pull-through with water and electricity only. Bingo, a swimming pool, a pool table, a recreation room, shuffleboard, horseshoes, and winter activities entertain campers. Showers, restrooms, a dump station, and laundry facilities are on the premises. Management says all areas are wheelchair accessible. A mall, restaurants, and bait are available two miles away, and groceries can be purchased five miles away. Six golf courses and two bowling alleys are within a 20-minute drive. Children are allowed for overnight stays or short vacations but not long-term. Leashed pets are permitted.

Reservations, fees: Reservations are required in winter. Sites are $25 per night for two people, plus $2 for each additional person. Add $2 daily for electricity. Major credit cards are accepted. Long-term stays are OK.

Directions: From Orlando, take I-4 north to State Road 46 (Exit 101C). Go west about one mile to Orange Boulevard, then turn right. The park is about one mile ahead on the right.

Contact: Town and Country RV Resort, 5355 Orange Boulevard, Lake Monroe, FL 32747, 407/323-5540, fax 407/321-4495.

92 WEKIVA FALLS RESORT

Rating: 7

On the Wekiva River east of Sorrento
Orlando map, grid b1, page 240

Swimmers plunge into the springs where prehistoric sharks and elephant-like mastodons standing nine feet tall lived thousands of years ago. It's the kind of place where your children can let their imaginations run wild: Cave divers have uncovered shark teeth dating back at least 10 million years from the caverns beneath the swimming beach area. And a mastodon jawbone with teeth was found here quite accidentally during a cleanup of the spring boil.

Campsites, facilities: All 786 RV sites offer full hookups, and 47 tent sites have water and electricity. A fishing pier, sightseeing cruises, rental canoes, a luau bandstand, and hiking trails entertain campers. On the premises are showers, restrooms, a marina, more than 200 picnic tables, a dump station, limited groceries, and laundry facilities. Children are welcome. Pets are prohibited.

Reservations, fees: Reservations are recommended. Sites are $18 per night for two people, plus $9 for each additional person older than 12 or $6 for campers aged two to 11. Electricity costs $2 extra. Credit cards are not accepted. Long-term rates are available.

Directions: From I-4 at Exit 101C, drive about six miles west on State Road 46 to Wekiva River Road. Turn left there and go 1.25 miles south to the campground entrance.

Contact: Wekiva Falls Resort, 30700 Wekiva River Road, Sorrento, FL 32776, 407/830-9828 or 352/383-8055.

93 WEKIWA SPRINGS STATE PARK

Rating: 10

At Wekiwa Springs north of Apopka
Orlando map, grid b1, page 240

This is one of the most popular and well used of Florida's state parks, and for good reason. Wekiwa Springs pumps about 42 million gallons of cool, clear water daily to the delight of swimmers and snorkelers. Its run to the Wekiva River and ultimately the St. Johns River is a wonderful route to canoe in a bit of natural Florida that is being rapidly surrounded by the creep of suburbia. Tall oaks lend shade to campsites, which give visitors a good base for seeing natural Florida. Some campers hike on the 13.5-mile Sand Lake Trail or the shadier 5.3-mile Volksmarch Trail. Bicyclists are limited to paved roads within the 10-square-mile park and some of the hiking trails. The equestrian crowd can set out on eight miles of trails set largely along backcountry roads, and stop to water horses at Camp Big Fork (where horse camping is allowed for a fee). The horse trails are divided into two loops and are used by hikers and park staff. Keep your eye out for black bears because this park not far south of Ocala National Forest is one of the bruins' southernmost outposts in the region; periodically, the shy, nocturnal mammals turn up in the backyards of suburbanites whose homes are quickly clogging this once-peaceful swath of the Sunshine State.

Campsites, facilities: Sixty sites with electricity and water can accommodate RVs or tents. Each site has a picnic table, a grill, and a fire ring. On the premises are restrooms, showers, a dump station, snacks, and canoe rentals. Horseshoes, a playground, and a volleyball court are in a picnic area. Management says all park buildings are accessible to wheelchairs. Groceries, restaurants, and laundry facilities are within four miles of the park. Two golf courses are within one mile. Children are welcome. Leashed pets with proof of rabies vaccination are permitted. Firearms and alcohol are prohibited.

Reservations, fees: Reservations are recommended; call ReserveAmerica at 800/326-3521. Sites are $17 to $19 per night for four people. Pet fee is $2 daily. Major credit cards are accepted. Maximum stay is 14 days.

Directions: From Orlando, take I-4 northeast to Exit 94. Head west on State Road 434 for about one mile to Wekiwa Springs Road. Turn right and continue 5.5 miles to the campground.

Contact: Wekiwa Springs State Park, 1800 Wekiwa Circle, Apopka, FL 32712, 407/884-2008, fax 407/884-2014.

94 LIVE OAK BACKPACKING SITE
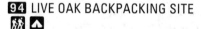

Rating: 7

In Wekiwa Springs State Park
Orlando map, grid b1, page 240

As you might gather from the name, this campsite is located in an oak hammock. It's probably the least popular primitive camping area in the 10-square-mile state park, and it is used mostly for overflow when others are full. There's a good side to that, though: You're likely to have to yourself thousands of acres of native Florida woodlands that look much as they did in Ponce de Leon's day. Or nearly so. The campsite is one of two along a 13-mile trail. You'll hike through open pine flatwoods and dark oak hammocks. The trail can be pretty soggy after heavy rains, so check with park rangers ahead of time.

Campsites, facilities: Up to 10 backpackers can be accommodated at this primitive campsite,

which requires a five-mile round-trip hike. The only facility is an in-ground fire circle. You must carry in water, food, firewood, and all supplies and pack out trash. Fires are allowed in the provided ground grill. Children are permitted. Pets, firearms, and alcohol are prohibited.

Reservations, fees: Reservations are required; call the park office at 407/884-2008. Fees are $3 per night for each person age 16 or older, $2 for younger children. At least one member of your camping party must be at least age 18. Major credit cards are accepted.

Directions: From Orlando, take I-4 northeast to Exit 94. Head west on Highway 434 for about one mile to Wekiwa Springs Road. Turn right, continue 5.5 miles to the campground parking lot, and start hiking at the trailhead near the park's popular spring area. Talk to a ranger to get instructions on finding the site.

Contact: Wekiwa Springs State Park, 1800 Wekiwa Circle, Apopka, FL 32712, 407/884-2008.

95 CAMP COZY CANOE/ BACKPACKING SITE

Rating: 8

In Wekiwa Springs State Park
Orlando map, grid b1, page 240

Although set aside primarily for hikers, this primitive campsite located about 100 yards off Rock Springs Run is sometimes opened to canoeists as well. It's an old hunting camp from a time before this area was a state park—hence the spigot, which provides water that is OK for cleaning up but is technically not designated for drinking. The campsite is on the edge of an oak hammock, so you can take your pick between a shady spot under the arching branches of oaks or a sunnier sleeping spot in the bordering pine flatwoods. Rock Springs Run, which forms the border between the state park and Rock Springs Run State Reserve, spans eight miles downstream and is covered in an easy four-mile canoe trip. The run is the headwaters of the Wekiva

River. (About the two spellings: Wekiva is Indian for "flowing water" and Wekiwa means "spring of water.")

Campsites, facilities: This primitive site can accommodate 10 backpackers or canoeists. Hikers trek about five miles round-trip. The only facilities are a fire ring and a spigot that produces nonpotable water. You must carry in drinking water, food, firewood, and all other supplies, and pack out trash. Children are permitted. Pets, firearms, and alcohol are prohibited.

Reservations, fees: Reservations are required; call the park office at 407/884-2008. Fees are $3 per night for each person age 16 or older, $2 for younger children. Major credit cards are accepted.

Directions: From Orlando, take I-4 northeast to Exit 94. Head west on Highway 434 for about one mile to Wekiwa Springs Road. Turn right and continue 5.5 miles to the campground parking lot and trailhead. Talk to a ranger to get instructions on finding the site and where to launch a canoe.

Contact: Wekiwa Springs State Park, 1800 Wekiwa Circle, Apopka, FL 32712, 407/884-2008. Canoes are rented out by the park's concessionaire; for rates, call 407/880-4110. Or, try local canoe liveries such as King's Landing, 5714 Baptist Camp Road, 407/886-0859.

96 BIG BUCK CANOE SITE

Rating: 8

On Rock Springs Run in Wekiwa Springs State Park

Orlando map, grid b1, page 240

This is the last of three primitive campsites along the popular Rock Springs Run canoe route between Wekiwa Springs and the Wekiva River. All are an easy half-day paddle—maybe two to three hours, traveling with the current. Big Buck is in a riverine swamp studded by sweet gum and cypress trees, and the campsite itself is shaded by a big live oak tree.

Pitch your tent on mowed native grasses. There are a couple of benches and a ground grill. Other than that, you're on your own. You may see other canoeists go by, but you won't hear the rumble of motorboats; they're not allowed on this part of the run.

Some canoeists opt instead for the two other primitive campsites on this run. Indian Mound is preferred by most paddlers because it's right on the river, whereas Big Buck is about 50 yards inland. The park's newest canoe-in site, called Otter Camp, is a little smaller than the rest. Yet, it may please some tentative campers because it's the newest (hence, least known) and, as the first site reached from the trailhead, it's the easiest to reach.

Campsites, facilities: Up to 10 people can sleep at this small primitive campsite, reached by canoe in two-and-one-half to three hours. Besides a ground grill, a couple of benches, and a spigot with nonpotable water, there are no facilities. Bring drinking water, food, firewood, and all the supplies you will need. Pack out trash. Children are allowed. Pets, firearms, and alcohol are prohibited.

Reservations, fees: Reservations are required; call the park office at 407/884-2008. Fees are $3 per night for each person age 16 or older, $2 for younger children. At least one member of your camping party must be age 18 or older. Major credit cards are accepted. Stays are limited to a few days.

Directions: From Orlando, drive northeast on I-4 to Exit 94. Head west on Highway 434 for about one mile to Wekiwa Springs Road. Turn right and continue 5.5 miles to the campground parking lot and trailhead. Talk to a ranger to get instructions on finding the site and where to launch a canoe.

Contact: Wekiwa Springs State Park, 1800 Wekiwa Circle, Apopka, FL 32712, 407/884-2008. Canoes can be rented from the park; for rates, call 407/880-4110.

97 INDIAN MOUND CANOE SITE

Rating: 9

On Rock Springs Run in Wekiwa Springs State Park

Orlando map, grid b1, page 240

If you've read the canoe magazines carefully or looked at the material available online, this is likely the campsite you've heard about whenever Wekiwa Springs State Park is mentioned. Indian Mound is on an S turn on Rock Springs Run by a nice white-sand beach right by the water. It's on a little raised bank overhung with huge live oaks. Notice that "hill" overgrown with palmettos next door? That's an old Indian "midden," or mound, built up by Native Americans who piled their garbage—sort of a prehistoric landfill, but cleaner than today's version. Like the Big Buck site, this is no more than a three-hour paddle, and you'll be running with the current. Here, as at Buffalo Tram, look for deer, river otters, wild turkeys, bobcats, and the secretive black bear.

Campsites, facilities: Up to 10 canoeists can sleep at this primitive campsite, reached in two-and-one-half to three hours. A fire ring is provided, but there are no other facilities. Bring drinking water, food, firewood, and all the supplies you will need. Pack out trash. Children are allowed. Pets, alcohol, and firearms are prohibited.

Reservations, fees: Reservations are required; call the park office at 407/884-2008. Fees are $3 per night for each person in your party age 16 or older, $2 for younger children. Major credit cards are accepted. Stays are limited to a few days.

Directions: From Orlando, take I-4 northeast to Exit 94. Head west on Highway 434 for about one mile to Wekiwa Springs Road. Turn right and continue 5.5 miles to the campground parking lot. Talk to a ranger to get instructions on finding the site and where to launch a canoe.

Contact: Wekiwa Springs State Park, 1800 Wekiwa Circle, Apopka, FL 32712, 407/884-2008. Canoes can be rented at the park.

98 BUFFALO TRAM BOAT/ CANOE SITE

Rating: 7

On the Wekiva River in Wekiwa Springs State Park

Orlando map, grid b1, page 240

Here, you'll camp next to remnants of the old cypress-logging operations that used to provide jobs when there weren't many to be found in this part of Florida. The pilings you see in the Wekiva River are from old mechanical logging equipment used to move logs around. They were known as "buffaloes"—hence the name of this camping site. The fairly small, mostly sunny site is considered by some to be not as pretty as Indian Mound, which is located farther south on Rock Springs Run. And you'll also chance hearing the occasional motor of a small passing skiff, whereas you won't hear motors on Rock Springs Run, where they are prohibited. This spot is set up relatively high, perhaps six feet above the water, so you're in a kind of blind: Canoeists can go past and you can see them, but they won't likely see you.

Campsites, facilities: Up to 10 people can sleep at this primitive campsite. A fire ring is provided, but there are no other facilities. Bring drinking water, food, firewood, and all other camping supplies. Pack out trash. Children are permitted. Pets, alcohol, and firearms are prohibited.

Reservations, fees: Reservations are required; call the park office at 407/884-2008. Fees are $3 per night for each person age 16 or older, $2 for younger children. At least one member of your camping party must be age 18 or older. Major credit cards are accepted. Stays are limited to a few days.

Directions: From Orlando, take I-4 northeast to Exit 94. Head west on Highway 434 for about one mile to Wekiwa Springs Road. Turn right and continue 5.5 miles to the campground parking lot. Talk to a ranger to get instructions on finding the site and where to launch.

Contact: Wekiwa Springs State Park, 1800 Wekiwa Circle, Apopka, FL 32712, 407/884-2008. Canoes can be rented from the state park.

99 LAKE JESUP CONSERVATION AREA

Rating: 6

At Lake Jesup south of Sanford
Orlando map, grid a1, page 240

Here on the north bank of the boating and fishing waters of Lake Jesup, you'll sleep within a nearly two-square-mile area that offers trails for hiking and horseback riding through wet prairie grasslands. Look for eagles, hawks, and alligators along the lakeshore. The conservation area actually is bigger than this tract in which you'll camp. It actually comprises three distinct areas totaling 3,432 acres around Lake Jesup. Bird-watching is good at a tract to the southwest, called Marl Beds Flats tract, which is reached by car by following Sanford Avenue south from State Road 46 to the road's dead end at the lake. A lakeview observation tower is at the East Lake Jesup Tract, which is found on the southern bank of Lake Jesup at the northern dead end of Elm Street, north of Oviedo. The point of the conservation area is to protect Lake Jesup, so expect a frills-free existence. It's mostly wet prairie grasslands that extend back from the lakeshore to the marl beds and thickly wooded hammocks found at Caldwell's Field, which is at the Marl Beds Flats tract.

Campsites, facilities: A primitive camping area is found in the North Lake Jesup tract and is reached via a short walk. Three nearby boat ramps provide access to Lake Jesup, but there are no facilities in the camping area. Bring food, supplies, drinking water, and mosquito repellent. Children are permitted. Pets must be leashed.

Reservations, fees: Sites are first-come, first-served. Camping is free. Each site accommodates up to six people. If your party has at least seven people, get a free permit and reserve at least one week ahead at 386/329-4410. Maximum stay for all campers is seven days.

Directions: From U.S. 17/92 in Sanford, go east about 3.5 miles, passing Sanford Airport. Turn right (south) onto Cameron Avenue, and proceed about two miles until the road deadends at the conservation area's North Lake Jesup tract.

Contact: St. Johns River Water Management District, Division of Land Management, P.O. Box 1429, Palatka, FL 32178-1429, 386/329-4500 or 800/451-7106, website: www.sjrwmd.com.

100 THE OAKS CAMPGROUND

Rating: 6

In Bushnell
Orlando map, grid c2, page 240

Most folks come for the season, enjoying music-oriented activities and all manner of dancing, bingo, exercise programs, bus tours, craft and quilting classes, and nondenominational Sunday school and Bible study. But the theme here is music. "There's always something musical going on," the owners say. Jam sessions and choir practices are held each week; a piano bar offers crooners the chance to entertain. Indoors or out, you might find a spontaneous sing-along. Tastes are eclectic, from country music and Broadway tunes to swing. Tampa, Walt Disney World, and other Central Florida attractions are within a one-hour drive.

Campsites, facilities: This 373-unit park features 300 sites for seasonal visitors and 50 for overnighters. Big rigs can be accommodated. All sites have full hookups, picnic tables, and cable TV. Restrooms, showers, a dump station, laundry facilities, a pool, a recreation and entertainment hall, horseshoe pits, and shuffleboard courts are on the premises. Most areas are wheelchair accessible. Children are welcome. Leashed pets are permitted.

Reservations, fees: Reservations are recommended. Sites are $22 per night for two people,

plus $2 per extra person. Credit cards are not accepted. Stay as long as you wish.

Directions: From I-75, take Exit 314 and drive east .25 mile on State Road 48.

Contact: The Oaks Campground, 5551 Southwest 18th Terrace, Bushnell, FL 33513, 352/793-7117, fax 352/793-7792.

101 SUMTER OAKS RV PARK

Rating: 3

South of Bushnell

Orlando map, grid c2, page 240

With planned activities keeping visitors busy from November through March, Sumter Oaks RV Park attracts seasonal visitors and those who wish to make Florida home. Bicycling, hiking, and canoeing are within 10 miles; a large flea market is just eight miles away.

Campsites, facilities: This all-ages park has 99 RV sites with concrete patios. Fifteen are pull-through. All have full hookups and telephone service availability. Restrooms, showers, laundry facilities, a pool, a clubhouse, shuffleboard courts, a snack bar, propane gas, and a store are on the premises. All areas are wheelchair accessible. Pets are permitted.

Reservations, fees: Reservations are not necessary. Sites are $22 per night for two people, plus $1 per extra person. Major credit cards are accepted. Stay as long as you wish.

Directions: From I-75, take Exit 309 and drive east 1.5 miles on County Road 673.

Contact: Sumter Oaks RV Park, 4602 County Road 673, Bushnell, FL 33513, 352/793-1333.

102 RED BARN MOBILE HOME PARK AND CAMPGROUND

Rating: 5

Off I-75 in Bushnell

Orlando map, grid c2, page 240

Hundreds of large oaks grace this Old Florida park, which targets retirees looking for a quiet but fun place to spend some time fishing at a one-acre lake or swimming in a pool. This is the closest campground to the Dade Battlefield Historic Site, where Major Francis Dade and his troops were massacred three days after Christmas in 1835 by Seminole Indians dead-set against being moved to Oklahoma. "Have a good heart. Our difficulties and dangers are over now," Dade said shortly before the battle, believing his soldiers had passed the most-likely spots for an Indian ambush. "And as soon as we arrive at Fort King you'll have three days to rest and keep Christmas gaily." You can walk along the old Fort King Military Road, the route the soldiers took from Fort Brooke (now Tampa) to Fort King (now Ocala). Make sure to stop at the visitors center that dissects the battle's action. The battle is reenacted during one weekend each December.

Campsites, facilities: This retiree-oriented camp has 397 full-hookup RV sites and 20 tent sites. Most sites are pull-through, and some have picnic tables. A pool, a recreation room, horseshoes, shuffleboard, and winter social programs entertain campers. On the premises are restrooms, showers, a recreation room, and laundry facilities. Management says all areas are wheelchair accessible. A new restaurant, a lounge, and banquet facilities accommodating up to 250 people are in the park. Groceries and restaurants are within two miles. Children are permitted, although the park targets senior citizens. Pets are allowed.

Reservations, fees: Reservations are recommended. Sites are $22 per night for two people, plus $2 per extra person and $1.75 for cable TV. Credit cards are not accepted. Long-term stays are OK.

Directions: From I-75 at Exit 314, drive east on State Road 48. You will see the park almost immediately.

Contact: Red Barn Mobile Home Park and Campground, 5923 Southwest 20th Drive, Bushnell, FL 33513, 352/793-6065 or 352/793-6220.

103 CLERBROOK RESORT

🚴 🏊 🛶 🚐 🐎 👫 ♿ 🚍 ⛺

Rating: 9

In Clermont

Orlando map, grid b2, page 240

You can't do this place justice by calling it a campground or even an RV park, not with its library, post office, beauty salon, and, oh yes, obvious devotion to golf. Osprey and long-legged wading birds sometimes look onto the 18-hole, par-67 golf course from surrounding wetlands and lakes. If golfers somehow lose a club, they can order a customized replacement from the park's pro shop and ask the golf pro for tips to try out at the putting green or driving range.

Clearly, the idea is to leave your grassy, sunny RV site at this 287-acre resort each morning and take part in everything else it offers: 13 shuffleboard courts, three pools with hot tubs, and more. Anglers try for bass and catfish at ponds and at any of the region's chain of 17 lakes including Lake Harris, a boating and water-skiing spot. A full-time activities director also keeps campers moving with square dancing lessons, bingo, and a host of events in the three clubhouses. For a day trip, try Disney World, Sea World, or other Orlando-area attractions.

Campsites, facilities: There are 1,200 sites, of which 870 full-hookup sites are for RVs up to 40 feet long. Five sites are for tents. Each site has a picnic table. For recreation, there's a golf course, three pools, three hot tubs, a playground, an exercise room, a driving range, a putting range, horseshoes, shuffleboard, volleyball, basketball, a game room, pool tables, and winter social programs. Showers, restrooms, trailer rentals, a dump station, cable TV, and laundry facilities are available. Management says all areas are wheelchair accessible. Children are welcome. Leashed pets are permitted.

Reservations, fees: Reservations are required. Sites are $24 per night for two people, plus $5

for each additional person. Major credit cards are accepted. Long-term stays are OK.

Directions: From Florida's Turnpike west of Winter Garden, take Exit 285 and drive south on U.S. 27 for about two miles. The park is on the right.

Contact: Clerbrook Resort, 20005 U.S. 27, Clermont, FL 34711, 352/394-5513 or 800/440-3801, fax 352/394-8251.

104 TORCHLITE TRAVEL TRAILER PARK

🏠 ♿ 🚍

Rating: 2

South of Clermont

Orlando map, grid b2, page 240

Owners Blanche and Doug Engates think of their park as a quiet, woodsy spot, notwithstanding its location on U.S. 27, a major thoroughfare. The 39 grassy/concrete-pad sites are set on 13 acres in a lake-dotted region of Florida. Fifty-four mobile homes are also in this park. Local bass anglers head west to Lake Louisa, one of 13 lakes linked together by an officially designated "Outstanding Florida Water"–the Palatlakaha River. To swim, fish, or canoe, try the lake's namesake state park at Louisa's southwestern corner off on U.S. 27, seven miles south of State Road 50; call 352/394-3969. Disney World and other Orlando-area attractions are less than one hour south.

Campsites, facilities: Four water and electric sites (no tenters) are set apart from 39 RV sites (35 full-hookup pull-throughs). Each site has a picnic table. Shuffleboard and a recreation room entertain campers. Showers, restrooms, a dump station, and laundry facilities are available. Groceries are .25 mile away. Bath houses, laundry facilities, and the recreation hall are wheelchair accessible. Children are welcome to camp but may not reside in mobile homes. Leashed pets are permitted.

Reservations, fees: Reservations are recommended. Sites are $15 per night for two people, plus $1 for each additional person. Credit cards are not accepted. Long-term stays are OK.

Directions: From State Road 50 in Clermont, drive 3.5 miles south on U.S. 27. You'll see the park entrance on the right.

Contact: Torchlite Travel Trailer Park, 10201 U.S. 27 South, Clermont, FL 34711, 352/394-3716.

105 THOUSAND TRAILS ORLANDO

Rating: 8

South of Clermont
Orlando map, grid b2, page 240

Part of the Thousand Trails national campground membership club, this 255-acre resort (or "preserve," as the marketing folks call it) targets Disney World and theme park destination campers, families, and full-timers. Disney World is just nine miles away, but there's plenty to do in the campground, too. On the premises is a 60-acre, spring-fed lake with fishing, row boating, and canoeing options. Teens can play video games in the game room, and playgrounds occupy the younger set. Entertainment is presented weekly in the recreation hall. Activities directors lead campers in arts and crafts, line dancing, and the like; they also plan children's activities. If you invite friends or family who don't camp, they can rent one of the 30 on-site trailers to round out your party.

Campsites, facilities: In this membership park, RVs and tents can be accommodated on 734 sites, all of which have picnic tables and grills. Restrooms, showers, a dump station, and laundry facilities are available. Amenities include a pool and spa, a boat ramp and dock, canoe rentals, miniature golf, a recreation hall, playgrounds, nature trails, shuffleboard and tennis courts, a video and game room, horseshoe pits, a campground store, rental trailers, and propane gas sales. Most areas are wheelchair accessible. Children are welcome. Leashed pets are permitted.

Reservations, fees: Reservations are recommended, especially during the busy season from December 19 through March 31. Call 90 days in advance for reservations during this high-demand period. Sites are $20 per night. Trial memberships are available for $30 for two nights. Major credit cards are accepted.

Directions: From Clermont, drive 13 miles south on U.S. 27. From Kissimmee, drive west on State Road 192 to U.S. 27; turn north on U.S. 27 and drive two miles.

Contact: Thousand Trails Orlando, 2110 U.S. 27 South, Clermont, FL 34711, 352/394-7575 or 800/723-1217, website: www.1000trails.com.

106 ORLANDO WINTER GARDEN CAMPGROUND

Rating: 5

In Winter Garden
Orlando map, grid b2, page 240

All the streets in this 30-acre campground are paved, and some grassy sites are shady. There are four bathhouses, two laundry rooms, and an adult lounge. When guests don't drive 30 minutes to Disney World or other theme parks, they enjoy swimming in the two heated pools and biking around the park. For an alternate route, head to a nearby favorite of bicyclists, joggers, and inline skaters—the West Orange Trail, two miles west of Florida's Turnpike at the Lake/Orange County line. The trail links Apopka, Clarcona, Winter Garden, and other points; for details, call West Orange Trail at 407/654-1108.

Campsites, facilities: Of the 400 sites for RVs, 350 have full hookups. Tents are no longer permitted. Cable TV and telephone service are available. Each site has a picnic table. Two pools, a hot tub, a playground, a recreation room, horseshoes, shuffleboard, an adult lounge, and winter social programs entertain campers. On the premises are restrooms, showers, a dump station, and laundry facilities. Management says the pool, laundry room, and restrooms are wheelchair accessible. A restaurant and groceries are across the street. Children and leashed pets are permitted.

Reservations, fees: Reservations are recommended. Sites are $24 per night for two people, plus $3.50 for each additional person. Major credit cards are accepted. Long-term stays are OK.

Directions: From Florida's Turnpike at Exit 267, take Colonial Drive/State Road 50 west for two miles to the campground at right.

Contact: Orlando Winter Garden Campground, 13905 West Colonial Drive, Winter Garden, FL 34787, 407/656-1415, fax 407/656-0858.

107 STAGE STOP CAMPGROUND

Rating: 6

In Winter Garden

Orlando map, grid b2, page 240

These 22 acres of grassy sites are set alongside a major highway 10 miles west of Orlando. The most heavily used recreation facility is the Olympic-sized swimming pool, although guests also can take advantage of horseshoes, shuffleboard, and badminton. Disney-area attractions are about 30 minutes away.

Campsites, facilities: These 248 full-hookup sites, some with telephone access, are for RVs and tents. Some sites are pull-through. Each has a concrete patio and picnic table. A pool, horseshoes, shuffleboard, a playground, badminton, winter activities, restrooms, showers, a limited store, and laundry facilities are available. Management says the restrooms are wheelchair accessible. Children and pets are permitted.

Reservations, fees: Reservations are recommended in winter. Sites are $22 per night for two people, plus $4 for each additional person. From May 1 through September 30, there is an additional electric fee of $1.50 per day. Major credit cards are accepted. Long-term stays are OK.

Directions: From Florida's Turnpike (northbound), take Exit 267 and travel 2.5 miles west

to the campground. If you're traveling southbound on the turnpike, get off at Exit 272 and drive 2.5 miles east to the campground.

Contact: Stage Stop Campground, 14400 West Colonial Drive, Winter Garden, FL 34787, 407/656-8000, fax 407/656-3840.

108 OUTDOOR WORLD ORLANDO CAMPGROUND

Rating: 6

South of Winter Garden

Orlando map, grid b2, page 240

Unlike many RV parks, Outdoor World Orlando does not permit seasonal stays, so your neighbors are likely to be vacationers visiting the sights of Central Florida. The maximum stay is two weeks. This park is part of a national membership chain, but trial memberships are available. Disney World is about seven miles away, and the park is located near shopping centers. Planned activities are held in the recreation hall during the winter months. There's also a lake with fishing and canoeing opportunities.

Campsites, facilities: All 117 sites are available for RV campers; 108 spots have full hookups and 25 have 50-amp service. An undetermined number of tent sites are also available. Restrooms, showers, a dump station, and laundry facilities are provided. On the premises are a pool, a clubhouse, shuffleboard and *pétanque* (French-style bowling) courts, miniature golf, canoe rentals, and a dog-walk area. All areas are wheelchair accessible. Children are welcome. Leashed pets are permitted.

Reservations, fees: Reservations are recommended. Sites are $25 per night. Trial memberships are available. Major credit cards are accepted. The maximum stay is two weeks.

Directions: Traveling southeast, take I-4 to Exit 64B and drive onto U.S. 192 westbound. Proceed west five miles to State Road 545 North (Avalon Road), and turn right. The campground is ahead one mile on the left. If traveling northwest, take Florida's Turnpike to Exit

244. Drive west on State Road 192 for 23 miles to State Road 545 and turn north. Drive one mile to the campground.

Contact: Outdoor World Orlando Campground, 13800 State Road 545 North, Winter Garden, FL 34787, 407/239-8774 or 800/446-0229, fax 407/239-1776.

109 WOODLANDS LUTHERAN CAMP

Rating: 6

In Montverde
Orlando map, grid b2, page 240

No, you don't have to be of the Lutheran faith to camp in these 180 acres of woods and horse pastures. Your religion isn't an issue. That's why the park is known also as Woodlands Camp, attracting retirees for winter-long visits and families for shorter vacations spent around the heated pool and along wooded trails for hikers, mountain bikers, and horseback riders. Indeed, some of the 30 resident horses are made available for rides from September through May. Still, the campground's double-duty purpose as a destination for Lutherans explains why after-hours callers may hear a recorded schedule for family Bible events and the like.

Trees help shade the sandy campsites, but the true attraction is the surroundings: Guests enjoy free use of canoes in which they can paddle around two small park lakes, stopping now and then to fish. For better-known bass waters, travel about 10 miles north to Little Lake Harris and adjoining seven-mile-wide Lake Harris. East of the little community of Montverde looms eight-mile-long Lake Apopka, a popular place to watch sunsets from the eastern lakeshore. (Early risers might consider viewing sunrises from Lake Apopka's western border.) Disney World is about a one-half-hour drive away.

Campsites, facilities: All 200 sites have full hookups and a picnic table. Although RVs up to 35 feet long can be accommodated, tents and small campers generally use a separate area for units up to 23 feet long. A pool, a playground, horseback trails, horseshoes, shuffleboard, tennis, bocce ball (lawn bowling), basketball, volleyball, a softball field, a chip-and-putt golf course, and winter social programs are available. Showers, restrooms, a dump station, a recreation room, four rental cabins, snacks, firewood, and laundry facilities are on the premises. A 24-hour supermarket is within five miles. Families with children usually stay short-term. Leashed pets are permitted.

Reservations, fees: Reservations are recommended, particularly in winter. Sites are $20 per night for two people, plus $2 per extra adult and $2 for using air conditioners. Credit cards are not accepted. Season-long stays are OK.

Directions: The campground is on County Road 455, two miles north of State Road 50/West Colonial Drive. From Florida's Turnpike at Exit 272, go west 2.5 miles to County Road 455. Turn right. Continue less than two miles to the campground.

Contact: Woodlands Lutheran Camp, 15749 County Road 455, Montverde, FL 34756, 407/469-2792, fax 407/469-4742, email: woodlands@woodlandscamp.com, website: www.woodlandscamp.com.

110 MAGNOLIA PARK

Rating: 4

On Lake Apopka west of Apopka
Orlando map, grid b2, page 240

Orange County promotes this 56-acre park/campground as a place that features spectacular sunsets on the county's largest lake. And that much is true; the sunsets over Lake Apopka are simply gorgeous. What they don't tell you is that Lake Apopka is dead, having been fouled by runoff from nearby vegetable farms. Years of legal controversy ensued, and environmental regulators are still working to bring the lake back to a healthful state. But take a look at a satellite picture of Florida and you'll see they have a long way to go. Lake Apopka stands out on a satellite shot not because of its size—Lakes Okeechobee and George, for instance, are far bigger—but because of its fluorescent green color. Anglers who bring a boat can make a run down toward Winter Garden and try their luck, or work their way up into the canals on the lake's north side to fish for specks or catfish before returning to the gravel campsites. A recent drought has reduced water levels so only small boats can be used.

Campsites, facilities: All 18 sites at this county-run park have electricity, picnic tables, and fire rings. On the premises are restrooms, showers, a dump station, a boat ramp, and a playground. Groceries, restaurants, and laundry facilities are within five miles. Children are welcome. Pets are permitted in the camping area, but not the general park or playground. Alcohol is prohibited.

Reservations, fees: Reservations are recommended; they must be made in person. Sites are $10.50 to $18 per night, depending on your age and county residency. Credit cards are not accepted. Maximum stay is 21 days.

Directions: From Apopka, head south on County Road 437/Ocoee-Apopka Road. Turn right onto Binion Road, which leads to the campground.

Contact: Magnolia Park, 2929 Binion Road, Apopka, FL 32703, 407/886-4231, website: http://parks.orangecountyfl.net.

111 SUN RESORTS

Rating: 8

West of Apopka

Orlando map, grid b2, page 240

Targeted to families and adult visitors, this park does a nice job of mixing overnighters, seasonal vacationers, and permanent residents in a 110-acre wooded park. It has also emphasized a balance of maintaining a mix of shaded areas, especially in the tenting area, with tree-limb clearance in the RV area. The Y-shaped pool is one of the larger we've seen in an RV park, with 110,000 gallons of water and a poolside stage for entertainment and shows. A kiddie pool is next to the big pool. A park model area is set apart from the overnighters so you have more of an RV park feel. Shopping and restaurants are nearby, but Walt Disney World is a 25-mile ride. You can make a day trip out of it.

Campsites, facilities: There are 140 full-hookup RV sites (45 pull-through) and an undetermined number of tent sites with water and electricity in a separate area. Rigs up to 40 feet can be accommodated. All sites have picnic tables; some have cable TV. Restrooms, showers, laundry facilities, a pool, trading post/store, snack bar, miniature golf, LP gas sales, and a recreation hall with planned activities, dog-walk area, and shuffleboard courts are on the premises. Entertainment includes volleyball, basketball, billiards, video rentals, a kiddie pool, and a playground. The trading post areas are wheelchair accessible. Children are welcome. Leashed pets are permitted.

Reservations, fees: Reservations are recommended. Sites are $22 to $27 per night for two adults and three children, plus $5 per additional person. Major credit cards are accepted. Long-term rates are available.

Directions: From the Florida Turnpike, take Exit 267A to 429 North. Turn right on West Road (Exit 26). At Clarcona-Ocoee Road, turn left and go 3.2 miles. Turn north on Apopka Vineland Road and drive 1.8 miles to the park on the left. From I-4, take Exit 92 onto Semoran Boulevard and drive west 6.5 miles. Turn south on Sheeler Road and proceed 2.8 miles. At Clarcona-Ocoee Road, turn left and drive .2 mile to the resort.

Contact: Sun Resorts, 3000 Clarcona Road, Apopka, FL 32703, 407/889-3048, fax 407/889-0887, website: www.sunrvresorts.net.

112 CLARCONA HORSEMAN'S PARK

🐴 🚐 ⛺

Rating: 6

In Apopka

Orlando map, grid b2, page 240

Saddle up! This 40-acre park with access to the 22-mile West Orange Trail equestrian path was created for horseback riders, but anyone can camp here if space is available. The campground primarily accommodates equestrians participating in a myriad of competitions and shows, or those who want to take their mounts on the adjoining trail. Operated by Orange County, the park also has a go-cart track for Quarter Midget Racing. A manager lives on the property; office hours are 7 A.M. to 6 P.M. seven days a week, but the park is open 24 hours. Since it's on the show circuit, you may hear your neighbors leaving at 3 A.M. to get to the next stop.

Campsites, facilities: There are 28 campsites for RVs or tents; each has water and electricity. Restrooms, showers, horse barns, bleacher seating, judging towers, and dressage show rings are on the premises. Children are welcome. Leashed pets are permitted.

Reservations, fees: All sites are first-come, first-served. Sites are $15 per night for two people, plus $3 for electrical service. Credit cards are not accepted. The maximum stay is two weeks.

Directions: From I-4, take Exit 80B onto U.S. 441/Orange Blossom Trail and drive northbound to Apopka, about 13 miles. Turn west on Apopka-Vineland Road/County Road 435 and drive four miles. Turn right on McCormick Road and proceed .5 mile. Turn right on Damon Road to the park.

Contact: Clarcona Horseman's Park, 3535 Damon Road, Apopka, FL 32703, 407/886-6255 or 407/886-9761 if horse shows are in progress, fax 407/886-2142, website: http://parks.orangecountyfl.net.

113 TURKEY LAKE PARK

Rating: 7

In west Orlando

Orlando map, grid b2, page 240

A very unusual addition to this city-run park is the Cracker Farm, which re-creates a nostalgic look at Florida's rural life. Kids of all ages can meet and pet farm animals at a 100-year-old barn donated by the Presbyterian Church of Apopka. Seven miles of nature trails meander through the live oak hammock and cattail marshes, and bicyclists can cover three miles of trails before returning to their asphalt campsites.

This occasional wedding spot is a local favorite for weekend picnics, as families stake out the 125 picnic tables, 77 barbecue grills, and 15 picnic shelters. Swimmers plunge into a pool overlooking Turkey Lake. A 200-foot-long fishing pier aids freshwater anglers. What's remarkable is that this little nature spot is just about one mile from Universal Studios, five miles from International Drive, and 15 miles from Disney-area attractions.

Campsites, facilities: An indeterminate number of tent sites are set apart from 36 RV sites (12 full-hookup). Each RV site has a picnic table and a grill. The tent sites have no water or electricity. A pool, three playgrounds, a nature trail, disc golf, volleyball, cabins, restrooms, showers, a dump station, and laundry facilities are on the premises. Groceries and restaurants are about one mile away. Children are welcome. Dogs are permitted in RVs and may be walked on leashes.

Reservations, fees: Reservations are recommended and required during holidays. Nightly fee for two people is $18 for an RV site, $7 for a tent site. Add $2 for each additional person. Credit cards are accepted. Stays are limited to 29 days.

Directions: Head west from downtown Orlando on the East-West Expressway/State Road 408. Exit at Hiawassee Road. Go south to the campground.

Contact: Turkey Lake Park, 3401 South Hiawassee Road, Orlando, FL 32835, 407/299-5594 or 407/299-5581, website: www.city oforlando.net/public_works/parks/cityparks /turkeylake/turkeyLake.htm.

114 HAL SCOTT REGIONAL PRESERVE AND PARK

🏃 🚵 ⛵ 🐕 ⛺

Rating: 6

On the Econlockhatchee River
southeast of Orlando

Orlando map, grid b2, page 240

The Econlockhatchee River divides these 8,427 acres of untamed country preserved by the county and the St. Johns River Water Management District to the benefit of resident bald eagles, gopher tortoises, bobcats, and river otters. Look up—maybe you'll see a sandhill crane while following the several miles of trails available for hiking, bicycling, bird-watching, or horseback riding. Trails crisscross the property, leading past the old Yates Homestead to a creek called Cowpen Branch, and on to more distant points in these sun-dappled prairie and flatwoods. Anglers have a short walk from the parking lot to reach a 17-acre lake named for Hal Scott. Campsites, found farther in the preserve, are on the river and well separated from each other.

Campsites, facilities: The park offers four primitive backpacking tent sites. From the parking area, the nearest campsite requires about a one-mile hike. Bring drinking water, food, mosquito repellent, and all supplies that you'll need. Pack out trash. Children are welcome. Pets must be leashed.

Reservations, fees: Sites are first-come, first-served. Camping is free. Each site accommodates up to six people. If your party has at least seven people, get a free permit and reserve at least one week ahead at 386/329-4410. Maximum stay for all campers is seven days.

Directions: From Orlando, go east on State Road 50 to State Road 520. Turn right (south).

A few miles down, turn right again into the Wedgefield subdivision on Maxim Parkway. Turn left at Bancroft Street, right at Meredith Avenue, and left onto Dallas Boulevard, then follow signs. The park entrance is 1.6 miles from the intersection of Meredith and Dallas, on the right. There is also an exit for Dallas Boulevard from the Bee-Line Expressway eastbound.

Contact: St. Johns River Water Management District, Division of Land Management, P.O. Box 1429, Palatka, FL 32178-1429, 386/329-4500 or 800/451-7106, website: www.sjrwmd.com. Or, contact Orange County Parks and Recreation, 407/836-6200, website: http://parks.orangecountyfl.net.

115 HIDDEN RIVER RV PARK

🏃 ⛵ 🐕 🚐 ⛺

Rating: 4

At the Econlockhatchee River east
of Orlando

Orlando map, grid a2, page 240

This tiny RV park offers just a few grassy tent sites and concrete-pad RV spots shaded by big oaks next to the Econlockhatchee River. The Big Econ is a primitive, rain-fed stream that winds through ancient cypress and hardwood forests. The park rents canoes for two very different trips on the river: a challenging nine-mile, twisting route that is cool and shady (and sometimes unavailable because of low water levels) and an easier 10-mile trip along an open section of the river with high, sandy banks. Landlubbers can hike on the Florida National Scenic Trail, which passes through these parts, too. This five-acre campground is about 20 miles from Cape Canaveral and about 40 miles from Disney-area attractions.

Campsites, facilities: Four tent sites are set apart from 18 RV sites (all full-hookup, two pull-through). Many sites are occupied by full-timers, so call ahead. Each site has a picnic table, a grill, and a fire ring. On the premises are restrooms, showers, a boat ramp, canoe and kayak rentals, horseshoes, and laundry facilities. Groceries and restaurants are about one mile away. Children may camp short-term. Small, leashed pets are allowed.

Reservations, fees: Reservations are recommended. Sites are $20 to $25 per night for two people, plus $5 for each additional person. No credit cards are accepted. The maximum stay is one week for tents, unlimited for RVs.

Directions: From Orlando, take Colonial Drive/State Road 50 east. The park will be on your right, just before the highway crosses the Econlockhatchee River.

Contact: Hidden River RV Park, 15295 East Colonial Drive, Orlando, FL 32026, 407/568-5346, email: hiddenriverpark@aol.com.

116 MULTI LAKE PARK

Rating: 3

East of Sanford on Mullet Lake
Orlando map, grid a1, page 240

The blue waters of Mullet Lake beckon anglers and boaters who stay at this 151-acre county-operated campground. Access to the St. Johns River is the main attraction, but you can camp here with a permit to overlook the 631-acre lake, or enjoy the picnicking area for day use. Swimming is not allowed. There is no staff on site.

Campsites, facilities: There are no designated campsites, and camping is primitive. However, restrooms, showers, grills, water, a boat ramp, and a picnic pavilion are available. Children are welcome. Pets are not allowed.

Reservations, fees: A camping permit is required; call the Seminole County Parks and Recreation Department for details. The park is open 24 hours a day. Sites are $5 per night for four people. Credit cards are not accepted. The maximum stay is seven days.

Directions: From Sanford, drive south on U.S. 17/U.S. 92 for nearly one mile. Turn east onto State Road 46 and drive 6.3 miles. Turn left onto West Osceola Road and proceed 1.5 miles. Turn left onto Mullet Lake Park Road. The park is ahead 1.7 miles.

Contact: Mullet Lake Park, 2368 Mullet Lake Road, Geneva, FL 32732. Or contact the Seminole County Parks and Recreation Department, 1101 E. First Street, Sanford, FL 32771, 407/788-0405, website: www.co.seminole.fl.us/parks/mullet.asp.

117 FLORIDA NATIONAL SCENIC TRAIL/CHULUOTA

Rating: 7

In Chuluota
Orlando map, grid a2, page 240

You'll need to hike in with a tent, water, and other supplies strapped to your back because no facilities are available at this campsite on a woodsy stretch of the Florida Trail. It's simply a wild retreat from urban Orlando. Amy Gagnon, a dog trainer in Oviedo, Florida, says she likes to take her Yorkie and three Labrador retrievers camping in the remote wilderness here.

Campsites, facilities: Primitive camping for backpackers is permitted along the trail. There are no facilities, so bring food, water, a tent, and other camping gear. Bury all human waste, and pack out garbage. Children are allowed. Leashed pets are tolerated.

Reservations, fees: No permission is needed to camp, and sites are taken on a first-come, first-served basis. Camping is free.

Directions: From Highway 419 in Chuluota, turn left at Langford Drive. After about .25 mile, look to the right for a wide dirt road with no houses; it leads to the marked Florida National Scenic Trail entrance. The trailhead is off Langford Drive and Washington Avenue.

Contact: Florida Trail Association, 5415 Southwest 13th Street, Gainesville, FL 32608, 352/378-8823 or 877/HIKE-FLA, website: www.florida-trail.org. For help with directions, call the Greater Sanford Chamber of Commerce, 407/322-2212.

118 LAKE MILLS PARK

Rating: 6

East of Casselberry near Chuluota
Orlando map, grid a2, page 240

Towering oak trees said to be 150 years old, pine forests, and a mixed hardwood swamp remind you of how Florida used to look. You can fish or boat on Mills Lake. This pretty 50-acre county park also has a day-use area with volleyball, a playground, and jogging trail.

Campsites, facilities: There are 12 primitive sites with picnic tables for RVs and tents. Restrooms and showers are provided. In the park are a boardwalk, playground, jogging and fitness trail, sand volleyball courts, an amphitheater, and picnic pavilions. Children are welcome. Pets are not allowed.

Reservations, fees: A camping permit is required; call the park at 407/788-0609 for details. The fee is $5 per person, or $20 for the park's single group site. Credit cards are not accepted. The maximum stay is seven days.

Directions: From County Road 415/Chuluota Road in the town of Chuluota, drive east on Lake Mills Road about .25 mile. Turn north on Tropical Avenue and proceed a short distance to the park.

Contact: Lake Mills Park, 1301 Tropical Avenue, Chuluota, FL 32766, 407/788-0609. Or, contact the Seminole County Parks and Recreation Department, 1101 E. First Street, Sanford, FL 32771, 407/788-0405, website: www.co.seminole.fl.us/parks/mills.asp.

119 CHRISTMAS AIRSTREAM PARK

Rating: 5

In Christmas east of Orlando
Orlando map, grid a2, page 240

Although the name might mislead you, you don't have to arrive in one of those now-fashionable orbs of silver known as an Airstream to camp at the concrete pad/gravel sites in this rustic 18-acre park. Any RV will do, although tenters are not allowed. The flat, wooded park is only a few miles from the St. Johns River and the St. Johns River National Wildlife Refuge. You can hike through the wildlife refuge or tour it by car. Also close by is the Fort Christmas Historical Park and Museum, where you can see how early settlers lived in this part of Florida during the Second Seminole War of the 1830s and 1840s. A replica fort and other displays are featured. Generally speaking, this sleepy part of Florida is skipped by out-of-towners except at Christmastime when people travel for hours to the post office here to have their greeting cards postmarked "Christmas, FL." The campground is about 20 miles from the Kennedy Space Center, and about 50 miles from Disney-area attractions.

Campsites, facilities: Of the 176 available RV sites, all have full hookups and many are pull-through. A pool, a playground, a recreation room, a camp circle for gatherings, winter recreation programs, restrooms, showers, dump stations, telephone service, and laundry facilities are available. Two meeting halls are offered for camper rallies. Management says all areas are wheelchair accessible. Children are welcome. Two leashed pets are permitted per site. Aggressive breeds are prohibited.

Reservations, fees: Reservations are necessary in winter. Sites are $20 per night for four people, plus $2 for each additional person. Credit cards are not accepted. Long-term stays are OK.

Directions: From I-95, take Exit 215 and drive eight miles west on State Road 50 to the park. If you're traveling on I-4, use exit 83B and drive 18 miles east on State Road 50 to the park.

Contact: Christmas Airstream Park, 25525 East Colonial Drive, Christmas, FL 32709; 407/568-5208, fax 407/568-5207, email: jsuncamp@aol.com.

120 CITRUS VALLEY CAMPGROUND

🏊 🐕 🏕️ 🚐 ⛺

Rating: 5

In Clermont within 10 miles of Disney World
Walt Disney World map, grid d2, page 241

Proximity to Disney World—less than 10 miles away—may be the biggest selling point of this place for overnighters. Sure, retirees flee icy Northern temperatures by plunging into the park's pool and dominating its grassy campsites in winter. And about 30 spots are taken by year-round residents. But Mickey Mouse beckons. This is the quieter, less-touristy part of the greater Disney area. Anglers may prefer to head to little Hancock Lake, perhaps the closest of the region's plentiful (mostly small) lakes. Local bass anglers prefer 3,634-acre Lake Louisa, located about six miles north of the campground as the crow flies. Picnicking and swimming at Lake Louisa State Park requires a longer drive, yet you may get to see alligators and deer at the 1,790-acre parcel of land, which is home to 10 types of biological communities, including scrubland, blackwater stream, and upland hardwoods. Call the state park at 352/394-3969.

Campsites, facilities: Of the 312 sites available for RVs and pop-ups, most have full hookups and the rest have water and electricity. Each site has a picnic table. There are 22 sites for tents. A pool, a playground, horseshoes, shuffleboard, a pool table, a recreation hall, and seasonal planned activities entertain campers. Showers, restrooms, a dump station, trailer rentals, limited groceries, cable TV, telephone hookups, and laundry facilities are available. A restaurant is one mile away. Children are welcome. Pets must be leashed.

Reservations, fees: Reservations are recommended. Sites are $17 to $24 per night for two people, plus $2 for each additional person. Major credit cards are accepted. The maximum stay is two weeks for kids and tent campers; otherwise, unlimited stays are OK.

Directions: From I-4 at Exit 64B in Kissimmee, take U.S. 192 west. Turn north onto U.S. 27 and continue 2.5 miles to the park on your right.

Contact: Citrus Valley Campground, 2500 U.S. 27 South, Clermont, FL 34711, 352/394-4051, fax 352/394-4101.

121 DISNEY'S FORT WILDERNESS CAMPGROUND

🚶 🚴 🏊 🐕 🏕️ ♿ 🚐 ⛺

Rating: 10

On the grounds of Walt Disney World
Walt Disney World map, grid c1, page 241

At this gem of a park, the 700 acres of lush wilderness stand out as the sole campground located on the Disney resort property, with full access to Disney World by land, water, or monorail. Guests enjoy complimentary transportation throughout the Walt Disney World Resort. For a campground, the recreational opportunities are mind-boggling: Swimming, fishing, water-skiing, and canoeing are popular at lakes on the property, and golf courses are nearby. Biking, tennis, horseback riding, and hiking on a two-mile nature trail are available. Children's activities include a nightly campfire visit by Disney characters, Disney movies, a petting farm, and pony rides.

One author who camped as a child at these paved sites with separate gravel sitting areas highly recommends it to parents. This is camping with a very polished feel, including air-conditioned bathrooms and heated swimming pools. Of course, you pay for the amenities. Still, the price is no more than you'd expect to pay to stay in most of the mid- to low-priced motels in the area. Plan on waiting quite awhile if you're checking in at a busy time. An hour-long wait is not unusual, but arriving early in the day helps. The busy times of year are generally in the summer and around major holidays, although things can get busy at any time.

Campsites, facilities: The 694 full-hookup RV sites are set apart from the 90 tent sites. Each site has a picnic table and a grill. A pool, a charter fishing, boat and canoe rentals, paddleboats, a playground, game rooms, a nature trail, golf, miniature golf, a driving range, horseshoes, shuffleboard, tennis, volleyball, hayrides, horseback riding, a petting farm, dinner shows, and pony rides entertain campers. On the premises are restrooms, showers, a dump station, groceries, laundry facilities, and restaurants. Management says the restrooms and transportation to other facilities on the Disney property are wheelchair accessible. Cable TV is available at some RV sites. Children are welcome. Leashed pets are restricted to full-hookup sites.

Reservations, fees: Reservations are recommended. Sites are $34 to $80 per night for two people, plus $2 for each additional adult and $3 per pet. Major credit cards are accepted. Long-term stays are OK.

Directions: From I-4, take Exit 67 onto State Road 536 westbound and follow signs to the campground entrance.

Contact: Disney's Fort Wilderness Campground, 4510 North Fort Wilderness Trail, Lake Buena Vista, FL 32830, 407/824-2900 or for reservations, 407/939-6244, fax 407/824-3508, website: www.disney.com.

122 ENCORE SUPERPARK— ORLANDO

Rating: 10

Four miles west of Disney World
Walt Disney World map, grid d2, page 241
Just four miles from Walt Disney Resort, this park is convenient to shopping and restaurants. You won't have to leave the park to enjoy yourself; it's a self-contained recreation place in itself for all ages. Pools, tennis courts, planned activities, and views of 160-acre Lake Davenport offer relaxation after a day in the theme parks. It's all done in the first-class manner that Encore SuperParks are known for.

Campsites, facilities: There are 467 RV sites (70 pull-through). Tents are allowed. RVers have picnic tables, paved pads, and patios with 30- and 50-amp electrical service available, plus cable TV and telephone service. Rigs up to 45 feet long can be accommodated. Restrooms, showers, laundry facilities, two heated pools, a Jacuzzi, a playground, tennis courts, sand volleyball, a basketball court, horseshoe pits, shuffleboard courts, a recreation center, fitness center, mail enter, and golf nets are on the premises. Children are welcome. Leashed pets are permitted.

Reservations, fees: Reservations are recommended. Sites are $36 to $38 per night. Major credit cards are accepted. Long-term rates are available.

Directions: From I-4 at Exit 64B, drive west about five miles on U.S. 192/Irlo Bronson Highway to the campground.

Contact: Encore SuperPark—Orlando, 9600 Irlo Bronson Highway, Clermont, FL 34711, 863/420-1300 or 888/558-5777, fax 863/420-1400, website: www.rvonthego.com.

123 RACCOON LAKE CAMP RESORT

Rating: 7

Four miles west of Disney World
Walt Disney World map, grid d2, page 241
This campground is somewhat west of the really crazy portions of U.S. 192. It's about four miles from Disney World, yet still within easy driving distance of major attractions and restaurants. You can rent boats, canoes, or Jet Skis to go out on Raccoon Lake, play miniature golf, or ride bikes to tool around the park. Forget motorbikes and skateboards, though, because they're forbidden.

Campsites, facilities: Fifty-nine tent sites are set apart from 454 RV sites (371 full-hookup, 157 pull-through). Each site has a picnic table. A pool, a wading pool, a recreation room, boat and canoe rentals, a playground, a game room, miniature golf, basketball, horseshoes, shuffleboard, and organized activities in winter and on summer holiday weekends entertain campers. On the premises are restrooms, showers, a dump station, a boat ramp, a dock, rental cabins and cottages, limited groceries, a restaurant, and laundry facilities. Children under 10 must be adult-supervised at the pool. Leashed pets should be walked on the park's west side.

Reservations, fees: Reservations are recommended. Sites are $15 to $35 per night for two people, plus $3 for each additional person over age 18. Major credit cards are accepted.

Directions: From I-4 at Exit 64B, head west on U.S. 192/Irlo Bronson Highway for 5.5 miles to the campground.

Contact: Raccoon Lake Camp Resort, 8555 West Irlo Bronson Highway, Kissimmee, FL 34747, 407/239-4148 or 800/776-9644, fax 407/239-0223, email: information@raccoonlake.com, website: www.raccoonlake.com.

124 SECRET LAKE RESORT

Rating: 7

On U.S. 192 near Disney World

Walt Disney World map, grid d2, page 241

This mega-RV resort is situated on gently rolling terrain about five miles from the Disney World entrance. The idea is to accommodate everyone from overnighters to people who live here for one year or longer, so the 100-acre campground has been split into sections—some devoted to overnighters, some for monthly guests, and so on.

The way this park advertises itself says a lot: "With so much to do here, you may not even care that we're minutes from Walt Disney World." You can swim in two heated pools (there's a wading pool for the kids) and fish or boat at a small lake known to hold some big catfish. Considering the additional opportunities for recreation, such as a hot tub, an exercise room, and volleyball, it's clear that not every camper heads to the great Disney palace every day but stays right here. In winter, you'll find a lot of snow-

birds and families on extended vacations. In summer, the clientele is mostly people going to Disney World and other local attractions. Tenters may be disappointed by the lack of shade, but some sites offer lake views. Restaurants are across the street, but you'll want to drive there rather than cross the busy, multilane road on foot.

Campsites, facilities: The camp has 675 full-hookup RV sites, most pull-through. Tenters are welcome. Two pools (one adults-only), a wading pool, a hot tub, a dock, an exercise room, a game room, horseshoes, shuffleboard, volleyball, and pool tables entertain campers. Restrooms, showers, rental trailers, limited groceries, snacks, a cafe, LP gas sales, laundry facilities, cable TV, and telephone service are available. The pool and restrooms are wheelchair accessible. Children and pets are welcome.

Reservations, fees: Reservations are recommended. Sites are $30 to $36 per night for eight people, plus $1.60 for cable TV. Major credit cards are accepted. Long-term stays are OK.

Directions: From I-4 at Exit 64B, drive west about five miles on U.S. 192/Irlo Bronson Highway to the campground on the south side.

Contact: Secret Lake Resort, 8550 West Irlo Bronson Highway, Kissimmee, FL 34747, 407/396-6101, 888/352-2267, or 888/352-2267, fax 407/396-2958, website: www.secretlakeresort.com.

125 ENCORE SUPERPARK— TROPICAL PALMS RESORT

Rating: 9

Off U.S. 192 near Disney World

Walt Disney World map, grid c3, page 241

A fair supply of palms, pines, and other trees shade the sites at this lush resort, but you can get a sunny spot if that's what you're after. These 60 acres are shared by campers and people renting villas, bungalows, and cabanas. A full-sized, somewhat Y-shaped heated pool is open 24 hours, and sunbathers lounging around its patio can gaze at a pleasant green backdrop of palms, tall pines, and shade trees. But the main benefit of staying here is that you're within a few minutes of the major Central Florida attractions. You can even walk to the Old Town entertainment district, which has 70 shops, restaurants, and rides. Two championship golf courses, Pirate's Cove adventure golf, and Watermania, a water theme park, are nearby.

Campsites, facilities: Twenty-five tent sites are set apart from 525 RV sites (425 full-hookup, 200 pull-through). Each site has a picnic table. A pool, kiddie pool, a playground, a café, basketball hoops, a game room, shuffleboard, a recreation room, horseshoes, and a sand volleyball court entertain campers. A shuttle bus, limited groceries, snacks, laundry facilities, restrooms, showers, a dump station, cable TV, telephone hookups, a business center, discounted attraction tickets, rental cottages, rental suites, rental park models, and a poolside café are available. Restaurants and shops are located within walking distance. Children and leashed pets are welcome.

Reservations, fees: Reservations are recommended. Sites are $24 to $35 per night. Major credit cards are accepted. Stays are limited to 30 days.

Directions: From I-4 at Exit 64A, head east one mile on U.S. 192/Irlo Bronson Highway, then turn right on Holiday Trail. Follow it south to the campground, which is located behind Old Town.

Contact: Encore SuperPark—Tropical Palms Resort, 2650 Holiday Trail, Kissimmee, FL 34746, 407/396-4595 or 800/64-PALMS (800/647-2567), fax 407/396-8938, website: www.encorerv.com or www.tropicalpalmsrv.com.

126 SHERWOOD FOREST RV RESORT

Rating: 7

On U.S. 192 near Disney World

Walt Disney World map, grid b3, page 241

Like numerous campgrounds in the area, the big attraction of Sherwood Forest is its prox-imity to the many Disney-area attractions. Staying here puts you about four miles from the main gate to Disney World. Parts of the manicured, residential-feel community are shaded by oaks and pines. Paved roads lead from the security gate to the campsites—most grassy, some sunny. Parents are welcome to bring the kids; they can send them to the playground while they head to the small on-site fishing lake or heated pool. Overnighters outnumber seasonal visitors here, a testament to the park's proximity to Mickey Mouse. The clubhouse is big enough to seat at least 400.

Campsites, facilities: All 512 full-hookup sites (all pull-through) are for RVs and tents. Overnighters can usually choose from 350 sites; only 165 are set aside for seasonal visitors. Most sites have a picnic table. A pool, a hot tub, horseshoes, tennis, shuffleboard, a clubhouse, and winter social programs entertain campers. On the premises are restrooms, showers, a dump station, laundry facilities, trailer rentals, a pavilion, and limited groceries. Management says the restrooms and camp store are wheelchair accessible. Restaurants are nearby. Children are welcome. Two pets under 30 pounds each are permitted per site.

Reservations, fees: Reservations are recommended. Sites are $33.50 to $37.50 per night for two people, plus $1.50 for each extra person. Major credit cards are accepted. Long-term rates are available.

Directions: From I-4 at Exit 64A, head east on U.S. 192/Irlo Bronson Highway nearly three miles to the campground.

Contact: Sherwood Forest RV Resort, 5300 West Irlo Bronson Highway, Kissimmee, FL 34746, 407/396-7431 or 800/548-9981, fax 407/396-7239.

127 KISSIMMEE/ORLANDO KOA (FORMERLY KISSIMMEE CAMPGROUNDS AND MOBILE HOME)

🏊 🐕 🚶 ♿ 🚐 ⛺

Rating: 6

Off U.S. 192 in Kissimmee, east of Disney World

Walt Disney World map, grid b3, page 241

This KOA is tucked just off the busy main drag—U.S. 192—about five miles from Walt Disney World. The eight-acre park has a pool and grassy sites with shade.

Campsites, facilities: The camp has 51 full-hookup RV sites and one tent site. Each has a picnic table. On the premises are restrooms, showers, a dump station, rental trailers, a pool, a playground, and laundry facilities. Most areas of the park are said to be wheelchair accessible. Groceries and restaurants are within one mile. Children and pets are welcome.

Reservations, fees: Sites are $26 to $35 for two people. Add $3 to $5 for each additional person. Major credit cards are accepted. Stays are limited to six months for RVers, two weeks for tenters.

Directions: The campground is off U.S. 192, between mile markers 12 and 13. From I-4, take exit 129 five miles east on U.S. 192/Irlo Bronson Highway, passing Highway 535. Turn left near Sam's Club on Cecile Drive, then left on Alligator Lane.

Contact: Kissimmee/Orlando KOA, 2643 Alligator Lane, Kissimmee, FL 34746, 407/396-2400 or 800/562-7791, fax 407/396-7577, website: www.koa.com.

128 ORANGE GROVE CAMPGROUND

🏊 🐕 🚶 🚐 ⛺

Rating: 6

Off U.S. 192 in Kissimmee, east of Disney World

Walt Disney World map, grid b3, page 241

Imagine waking up on a brisk winter morn-ing, walking a few feet from your paved or grassy campsite, and plucking fresh oranges off a tree for breakfast. You can do it at this former orange grove, where campers can savor tangerines, grapefruits, lemons, and oranges for free. One-time grove or not, trees—and therefore shade—are sparse. Play miniature golf on the premises, or drive a short distance to get in a round of the real thing.

The 14-acre park is behind the Value Outlet Shops in the heart of Disney-area shopping and entertainment attractions. It's essentially around the corner from the Medieval Times dinner show and about five miles from the main gate to Disney World.

This is not camping in the get-back-to-nature sense. Your eyes will be assaulted whenever you venture far from the campground by the electric signs of T-shirt shops, restaurants, and the rest of the tourist traps packed chock-a-block along U.S. 192. But it is one of the more convenient spots to camp if you're making the rounds at Disney World.

Campsites, facilities: Twenty-two tent sites are set apart from 177 full-hookup RV sites. Each site has a picnic table. A pool, miniature golf, a playground, horseshoes, shuffleboard, and winter social programs entertain campers. On the premises are restrooms, showers, a dump station, laundry facilities, and limited groceries. Golf and restaurants are within one mile; groceries are two miles away. Children are welcome. Leashed, attended pets are permitted.

Reservations, fees: Reservations are recommended in winter. Sites are $17 to $28 per night for two people, plus $2 for each additional person over the age of three. Major credit cards are accepted. Long-term stays are OK.

Directions: From I-4 at Exit 64A, head east on U.S. 192/Irlo Bronson Highway. After you pass mile marker 14, look for the Wal-Mart ahead. Turn left at that intersection onto Old Vineland Road (not Vineland Road). Proceed to the campground 100 yards ahead, behind the Kissimmee Manufacturers Outlet Mall.

Contact: Orange Grove Campground, 2425 Old Vineland Road, Kissimmee, FL 34746, 407/396-6655 or 800/3-CAMPIN.

129 GREAT OAK RV RESORT

Rating: 6

In Kissimmee, six miles east of Disney World
Walt Disney World map, grid b3, page 241

If you want to sleep closest to the well-used swimming pool or the restrooms, ask for a spot in section C. Although some families vacation here (a pediatric clinic is conveniently located next door), the typical campers at Great Oak RV Resort are snowbird couples who might like to take part in bingo, potluck suppers, or trips to the bowling alley during the winter months. Disney World is about six miles from these grassy campsites with concrete patios—some with shade and others in the sunshine. About four miles away is a Kissimmee city park on 11-mile-long Lake Tohopekaliga, where fishing, boating, and picnicking are popular pursuits.

Campsites, facilities: The park offers 196 full-hookup RV sites (10 pull-through) and three tent sites, though tents can be accommodated at the RV sites if space allows. Each site has a picnic table. On the premises are restrooms, showers, a dump station, a pool, horseshoes, shuffleboard, and laundry facilities. Management says the office and recreation hall are wheelchair accessible. Groceries and restaurants are within two miles. Children and pets are permitted.

Reservations, fees: Reservations are recommended. Sites are $25 per night for two people, plus $2 for each additional person. Sites for camping in tents, vans, or pick-up trucks are $20 to $23. Major credit cards are accepted. Long-term stays are OK.

Directions: From I-4, take Exit 64A and proceed east on U.S. 192/Irlo Bronson Highway for five miles. Turn right on Bass Road (the first street past the Wal-Mart). Continue about

.75 mile to Yowell Road. Turn right. You'll soon see the campground.

Contact: Great Oak RV Resort, 4440 Yowell Road, Kissimmee, FL 34746, 407/396-9092, fax 407/396-9093.

130 MILL CREEK RV RESORT

Rating: 1

In Kissimmee, east of Disney World
Walt Disney World map, grid b3, page 241

This may not be the ideal vacation spot, with 95 percent of its occupants being full-time campers, families, and students attending the Motorcycle and Marine Institute of Orlando. But if you needed a place to stay, it's about 13 miles from the entrance to Disney World and about three miles from the bass fishing waters of 11-mile-long Lake Tohopekaliga. In spring, the Houston Astros play exhibition games a short drive away at 5,130-capacity Osceola County Stadium, 1000 Bill Beck Boulevard. For tickets, call 407/839-3900.

Campsites, facilities: This park offers 155 full-hookup RV sites (three pull-through). Restrooms, showers, laundry facilities, a pool, a recreation hall, shuffleboard, horseshoes, cable TV, and telephone service are available. Management says showers and restrooms are wheelchair accessible. Groceries and restaurants are within two miles. Children are allowed. Small pets under 20 pounds are OK.

Reservations, fees: Reservations are recommended. Sites are $27 per night for two people, plus $1 for each additional person. Credit cards are not accepted. Long-term rates are available.

Directions: From I-4 at Exit 64A, head east on U.S. 192/Irlo Bronson Highway about 10 miles to Michigan Avenue/Highway 531. At the bowling alley, turn left (north). Proceed about two miles to the park.

Contact: Mill Creek RV Resort, 2775 Michigan Avenue, Kissimmee, FL 34744, 407/847-6288.

131 WALLABY RANCH FLIGHT PARK

Rating: 6

Southwest of Disney World

Walt Disney World map, grid d4, page 241

We include this hang-glider park as an inducement for those free spirits out there who might want to try something completely new while camping their way across Florida. To camp here, you must have the urge to soar above the earth. "The Best Place on Earth to Fly Hang Gliders" is how the 200-acre former cattle ranch bills itself. And darned if it doesn't attract hang gliders from all over.

The focus of the ranch is a 45-acre, level field of green grass, which is free of debris and power lines. With four "aerotugs" available, veteran hang gliders won't have to wait long to get in the air. Novices are welcome, too. The park promises a safe, enjoyable training session. Back on the ground, members of your party who are not interested in hang gliding can swim in a pool, enjoy woodsy hiking or mountain biking trails, scale the climbing wall, or take out four-wheelers to run around the property. RVers can be accommodated, but it's mostly a place where hang gliders set up their tents and "hang" out on a Saturday night drinking beer under the stars.

Campsites, facilities: An indeterminate number of campsites are available, but only for hang-gliding enthusiasts who come here to do their thing. If you're not a hang glider, you should find another campground. However, the occasional curious adventurer wanders in now and then and makes new friends (and discovers a new hobby along the way).

Reservations, fees: Reservations are not accepted nor are they necessary for hang gliders using the park's facilities. Camping is free. Hang-gliding rides are $15 each. Novices can go up with an instructor in a tandem flight and learn to hang glide for $80 a flight.

Directions: From Kissimmee, take I-4 south

to U.S. 27 (Exit 55). Head north for 1.5 miles. Turn left at Dean Still Road. Look for the ranch 1.7 miles ahead on the left.

Contact: Wallaby Ranch Flight Park, 1805 Dean Still Road, Wallaby Ranch, FL 33837-9358, 863/424-0070, website: www.wallaby.com.

132 FLORIDA CAMP INN

Rating: 6

Southwest of Disney World on U.S. 27, north of Davenport

Walt Disney World map, grid d3, page 241

Bring sunscreen if you plan to lounge around the patio of the heated pool or spend a lot of time outdoors at this sun-baked community of 800 sites located about a nine-mile drive from Disney World. A few bushes and trees separate the grassy campsites—meaning you'll be certain to meet your neighbor, even if you don't attend the organized winter dances, sing-alongs, and musical entertainment gigs advertised on the park's Florida Camp Inn cable station (channel 2).

From the air, this grid-pattern park appears to be a sea of white RVs with clumps of shade trees at the center. Beyond its borders, broad expanses of dirt fields are broken up by green dots of citrus trees planted in straight rows. Campers tend to spend months here and are asked to follow the 33 park rules. Among them: Follow the 9.75 mph speed limit on park roads, use power tools between 10 A.M. and 3 P.M. only, and ride your bike during daylight hours.

Campsites, facilities: There are 800 sites, 777 (most full-hookup) are for RVs, and 23 are for tents. A pool, a recreation hall, shuffleboard, a dump station, grills, showers, restrooms, cable TV, limited groceries, and laundry facilities are available. Children are permitted. Leashed pets are permitted for overnight, but not monthly, stays and must use the dog walk between the fence and the highway.

Reservations, fees: Reservations are recommended. Monthly and seasonal campsites are first-come, first-served, although reservations can be made for stays of four months or more. Sites are $20 per night for two people, plus $1 for each additional person and $2 for cable TV. Credit cards are not accepted. Long-term rates are available.

Directions: From I-4 at Exit 55, drive 4.5 miles north on U.S. 27 to the park on your left.

Contact: Florida Camp Inn, 9725 U.S. 27 North, Davenport, FL 33837, 863/424-2494, fax 863/424-3599.

133 FORT SUMMIT CAMPING RESORT

Rating: 8

Off I-4 south of Disney World

Walt Disney World map, grid d4, page 241

Don't be confused by the name. This is not Disney World's famed Fort Wilderness Campground, but Disney World is definitely the focus for staying here. Set behind a motel, this sunny, palm-dotted campground nonetheless caters to the theme-park crowd by offering free shuttle rides to Disney World, which is seven miles northeast. The grassy sites with concrete patios are large. Expect to have a good view of neighboring RVs (which is par for the course this close to Disney). Scattered native palms provide token shade. Grass, not privacy hedges, is the preferred landscaping.

In a region often dominated by retirees, parents may breathe a sigh of relief here. A fenced low-impact playground, video games, a wading pool, a heated pool, and Kansas City Royals spring training baseball games played across the street keep young campers entertained. So can the park's car rentals, if you want to drive the family to Sea World or Universal Studios, about 20 minutes away. You can buy tickets to most attractions, including Disney World, either at the park's front desk or at the motel lobby (which means you don't need to wait in line for tickets later at those destinations).

Campsites, facilities: Thirty-eight tent sites are set apart from 249 full-hookup RV sites (80 pull-through). Each site has a picnic table, and some have grills. A large heated pool, a wading pool, a sundeck, a recreation room, a playground, a game room, an exercise room, basketball, volleyball, pool tables, and social programs entertain campers. Showers, restrooms, rental cabins, a dump station, a "fully stocked" store, snacks, laundry facilities, car rentals, cabins, cable TV, telephone hookups, and free Disney World shuttles are available. Planned activities are on tap in the winter months. The store and restrooms are wheelchair accessible. A restaurant is within walking distance. Children are welcome. Leashed pets are permitted.

Reservations, fees: Reservations are not necessary. Sites are $32 per night for two people, plus $4 for each additional person. Major credit cards are accepted. Long-term rates are available.

Directions: From I-4 at Exit 55, go south on U.S. 27 and turn right after a short distance on Frontage Road. The park is between a Best Western Motel and a Texaco station.

Contact: Fort Summit Camping Resort, 2525 Frontage Road, Davenport, FL 33837, 941/424-1880 or 800/424-1880, fax 863/420-8831, website: www.fortsummit.com.

134 DEER CREEK RV GOLF RESORT

Rating: 8

Off I-4 south of Disney World

Walt Disney World map, grid d4, page 241

With names like Arnold Palmer Drive and Jack Nicklaus Lane in one of the park's lot-ownership sections, it's clear that the most unusual amenities aren't the two-story poolside clubhouse or even the five heated pools. Instead, golf is king. It would be hard to find a Florida RV destination more focused on golf than this one, with a lighted driving range, a pro shop, a putting green, and a hilly, 18-hole golf course.

You'll sleep in the RV portion of this manicured, multifaceted, residential-style retirement community that comprises more than 200 acres. The mostly sunny campsites sit about 35 to 40 feet apart on what is known as the Lake Wales Ridge (elevation 150 feet above sea level, once a long island in a much deeper ancient sea). As you drive through this complex of park models and RVs to get to your paved campsite, you'll go up one major hill to approach the RV section. Some sites are on one side of the hill; others are on the descent. In the afternoon, some campers stop for happy hour at the poolside tiki bar. Disney World is about 10 miles north. The Kansas City Royals play their spring training exhibition games down the street.

Campsites, facilities: One-hundred of the 861 sites are for RVs and have picnic tables and full hookups. A golf course, a driving range, a pool, a spa, a playground, a game room, horseshoes, shuffleboard, basketball, tennis, volleyball, billiards, and organized activities (usually in winter) entertain campers. Showers, restrooms, park model rentals, snacks, a tiki bar, a restaurant/lounge, cable TV, LP gas sales, and laundry facilities are available. Groceries are within .5 mile. The clubhouse and bathhouse are wheelchair accessible. Children are welcome. Pets are permitted.

Reservations, fees: Reservations are recommended in winter. The winter rate (November 1 through May 1) is $35 per night for two people, plus $1.50 per extra person. The rest of the year, sites are $30 per night for two people. Major credit cards are accepted. Long-term stays are OK.

Directions: From I-4 at Exit 55, drive one mile south on U.S. 27 to the park on your left.

Contact: Deer Creek RV Golf Resort, 42049 U.S. 27 North, Davenport, FL 33837, 863/424-2839 or 800/424-2931, fax 836/424-3336, email: deercreekfl@gocampingamerica.com.

135 MOUSE MOUNTAIN RV CAMPING RESORT

Rating: 7

South of Disney World

Walt Disney World map, grid c4, page 241

Many campers here are planning to go to Disney World, which is located a mere six-mile drive north past citrus groves and tiny Reedy Lake (at left). The sunny or somewhat shaded, grassy campsites and accompanying paved patios are set on a hill, which in flat Florida passes for a "mountain" (hence the park's name). A plus: The family-managed spot is set a respectable distance from the neon signs and multiple lanes of U.S. 192, where many bargain-hunting, Disney-bound motel guests end up.

Campsites, facilities: Nineteen tent sites are set apart from 260 full-hookup RV sites (20 pull-through). A heated pool, a playground, horseshoes, shuffleboard, practice putting greens, a new recreation hall, and winter activities entertain campers. Restrooms, showers, a dump station, limited groceries, propane, some cable TV hookups, and laundry facilities are available. You can hook up your laptop in the office to pick up your email. Children and leashed pets are permitted.

Reservations, fees: Reservations are recommended. Sites are $25 per night for two people, plus $1 for each additional person. Major credit cards are accepted.

Directions: From I-4, take Exit 58 onto State Road 532/Osceola Polk Line Road. Drive east 1.6 miles just past the light. The park is on the right.

Contact: Mouse Mountain RV Camping Resort, 7500 State Road 532/Osceola Polk Line Road, Davenport, FL 33837, 863/424-2791 or 800/347-6388, fax 863/420-9104, website: www.mousemountainrv.com.

136 LAKEWOOD RV RESORT

Rating: 6

South of Disney World

Walt Disney World map, grid c4, page 241

For tree fans, this park is easier on the eyes than some sun-baked alternatives equally close to Disney World (six miles). As you follow the gentle curve of the paved, 10 mph road through tree-canopied section C, note the slightly bent trunks of the sun-filtering trees. Many campers leave their rig on site when they head home for the spring and summer, and on about half the sites are mobile homes.

The grounds actually support 482 sunny or shady sites—221 in a park-model section and most others used by long-term residents accustomed to the routine of 3 P.M. daily garbage pickups (except Sundays). The 30-by-40-foot pool sits closest to campsites A6 through A8 in the grid-pattern portion of the park, where every street is accorded an alphabetical letter. So to sleep near the pool, ask for a site in the lower end of the alphabet; section R is farthest away, at the back of the park.

Campsites, facilities: About 175 full-hookup sites (many pull-through) are for RVs. For recreation, there's a pool, a playground, horseshoes, shuffleboard, a recreation hall, and wintertime planned activities. Restrooms, showers, a dump station, and laundry facilities are available. Children under 12 must be adult-supervised at the pool. Leashed, attended pets under 30 pounds are permitted and must use the designated dog walk.

Reservations, fees: Reservations are recommended. Sites are $26 per night for two people, plus $1.50 for each additional person. Credit cards are not accepted. Long-term rates are available.

Directions: From I-4 at Exit 58, go east on State Road 532/Osceola/Polk Line Road less than one mile to the park on the right side. The park is just beyond a traffic light.

Contact: Lakewood RV Resort, 7700 Osceola/Polk Line Road, Davenport, FL 33896, 863/424-2669, fax 863/424-6229, email: lakewoodfl@earthlink.net.

137 PARADISE RV RESORT

Rating: 4

Four miles west of Disney World

Walt Disney World map, grid c3, page 241

This park has an unusual amenity for its denizens: an underground shelter in case of tornadoes or threatening weather. The RV spots aren't shaded, although the grassy tent sites are. RV sites are set diagonally on 20-by-40-foot concrete pads separated by grass. Many campers stay for extended periods in the winter, and some live at the nine-acre park year-round, congregating at the TV and card room to socialize.

Campsites, facilities: Fifteen tent sites are set apart from 115 full-hookup RV sites (five pull-through). Each site has a picnic table. For recreation, there's a recreation room, horseshoes, a campfire area, a playground, and basketball hoops. Restrooms, showers, a dump station, LP gas sales, limited groceries, a laundry room, cable TV, telephone hookups, and an underground storm shelter are available. Management says the restrooms and showers are wheelchair accessible. Restaurants are about four miles away. Children and leashed pets are welcome.

Reservations, fees: Reservations are recommended. Sites are $20 per night for two people, plus $1.50 for each additional person over age three. Credit cards are not accepted. Long-term stays are allowed for RVers; tenters are limited to two weeks.

Directions: From I-4 at Exit 64B, head west on U.S. 192/Irlo Bronson Highway. Turn left onto County Road 545/Old Lake Wilson Road and proceed 3.5 miles south, passing under I-4. The campground is on the left.

Contact: Paradise RV Resort, 725 South Old Lake Wilson Road, Kissimmee, FL 34747, 407/396-2506, website: www.snowfresh.com/page26.html.

138 21 PALMS RV RESORT

Rating: 6

Seven miles south of Disney World

Walt Disney World map, grid c4, page 241

A small alligator in the fish pond certainly intrigues out-of-state visitors, but an even bigger attraction of these 30 secluded acres is the short seven-mile drive to Disney World. Not only for campers who want to lounge around a solar-heated pool, this park offers a free Nautilus fitness center with an unusual pitch: "Take a healthy break. Relax and enjoy our facilities while you strengthen, firm, and tone your body." Paved roads lead to the level RV sites and concrete patios. Precious few trees dot the lots, although the surrounding land is woodsy.

Campsites, facilities: This all-ages park has 94 paved RV sites with full hookups. A pool, a fitness center, horseshoes, shuffleboard, a pool table, a recreation hall, and planned activities keep campers entertained. Restrooms, showers, a dump station, picnic tables, TV hookups, propane, rental park models, and air-conditioned laundry facilities are available. Children are welcome. Inquire about pet restrictions.

Reservations, fees: Reservations are recommended. Sites are $18 per night for two people, plus $5 per extra person. Major credit cards are accepted.

Directions: From Orlando, take I-4 to U.S. 192 (Exit 64B). Go west nearly three miles, passing the Disney World entrance, to State Road 545. Turn left. Continue five miles to Polk County Road. Turn left. The park is two miles ahead. From Tampa, take I-4 to Polk County Road (Exit 24) and go about two miles east to the park.

Contact: 21 Palms RV Resort, 6951 Polk County Road, Davenport, FL 33837, 407/397-9110.

139 RV CORRAL

Rating: 2

South of Disney World on U.S. 17/92

Walt Disney World map, grid c4, page 241

All ages are welcome at this 25-acre rural park, now under new ownership. It's located about 11 miles south of Disney World.

Campsites, facilities: There are 27 full-hookup RV sites (two pull-through); most have picnic tables. Wheelchair-accessible showers, restrooms, and laundry facilities are available. A supermarket and restaurant are about seven miles away in Haines City. Small children are unwelcome. Leashed, attended pets are allowed.

Reservations, fees: Reservations are recommended. Sites are $17 per night for two people, plus $1 for each additional person. Credit cards are not accepted. Long-term stays are OK.

Directions: From I-4 at Exit 58, go left on Osceola Polk Line Road. Turn right on U.S. 17/92 and drive four miles south. The park is ahead at right.

Contact: RV Corral, 4141 U.S. 17/92 North, Davenport, FL 33837, 863/420-2181, email: conrad20015@cs.com.

140 THREE WORLDS RV AND MOBILE HOME RESORT

Rating: 6

On U.S. 17/92 south of Disney World

Walt Disney World map, grid c4, page 241

Country living is the catchphrase at this 120-acre rural home of preserved wooded areas and three small fishing lakes, yet the park is not far from two major tourist attractions: Sea World is about 18 miles away, while the I-4 exit to Disney World is 11 miles off. (Also about 18 miles away, Cypress Gardens, a 67-year-old park best known for its water-ski exhibitions and beautiful grounds, closed in April 2003, a victim of dwindling visitors in the wake of the September 11, 2001, tragedy and long declines in attendance; the state of Florida is attempting to purchase the property and reopen it someday to the public.) Many retirees treat the place like a second home and spend entire winters at the grassy/concrete-pad sites.

The typically sunny campsites sit along curvy roads in an amoeba-shaped section dotted with pines and sabal palms. To sleep apart from most RVs, ask for one of the 12 lakeview spots at the northwest corner of the RV recreational area. Farther east, campsites east of the heated pool also enjoy the relative seclusion of having no neighbors to the back. You'll just need to walk a couple of blocks to attend dances and other activities at the 5,000-square-foot lakeside clubhouse, which you will share with residents of the park's 64 mobile homes (situated to the east of RVs) and 66 park models (set to the west).

Campsites, facilities: This park has 247 full-hookup sites for RVs (five pull-through). A pool, a recreation hall, shuffleboard, horseshoes, social programs, billiards, and a miniature golf course entertain campers. Showers, restrooms, a dump station, trailer rentals, cable TV, a country store, and laundry facilities are available. Management says the showers, bathhouse, recreation hall, and pool area are wheelchair accessible. A supermarket and restaurant are about seven miles away in Haines City. Families with small children may camp up to two weeks. Leashed pets under 20 pounds are permitted.

Reservations, fees: Reservations are not necessary. Sites are $18 to $20 nightly for two people, plus $2 for each additional person. Major credit cards are accepted. Adults may stay long-term.

Directions: From I-4 at Exit 55, drive 1.5 miles north on U.S. 27 to Loughman Road/County Road 54. Turn right and go about six miles to U.S. 17/92. Turn right. The park is ahead at left.

Contact: Three Worlds RV and Mobile Home Resort, 3700 U.S. Highway 17/92 North, Davenport, FL 33837, 863/424-1286.

141 PONDEROSA RV PARK

Rating: 7

Off U.S. 192 east of Kissimmee
Orlando map, grid b2, page 240

The Houston Astros' spring training home is across the street from this snowbird and family-oriented park, where the sparse needles of pine trees partially shade some camping spots (other sites are sunny). The 15-acre park is about three miles northeast of a Kissimmee city park, where you can fish, boat, and picnic, at the north end of 11-mile-long Lake Tohopekaliga. It's also close to the four-mile-wide bass fishing waters of East Lake Tohopekaliga. But to answer the kids' question, the campground is about 15 miles northeast of Disney World.

Campsites, facilities: Of the 180 RV sites, all have full hookups, two are pull-through, and most have concrete pads. Six tent sites with water and electricity are set somewhat apart from the RV section. Each site has a picnic table. For recreation, there's a heated pool, a recreation room, a playground, horseshoes, shuffleboard, basketball, and winter social programs. Restrooms, showers, a dump station, laundry facilities, cable TV access, telephone hookups, and an office modem to retrieve email are available. Management says the restrooms, recreation hall, and other buildings are wheelchair accessible. Children and pets (no pit bulls) are permitted. Campfires are forbidden.

Reservations, fees: Reservations are recommended. Sites are $26 per night for two people, plus $2 for each additional person. Major credit cards are accepted. Stay as long as you like.

Directions: From I-4 at Exit 64A, head east on U.S. 192/Irlo Bronson Highway to Boggy Creek Road. Turn left and proceed about one mile north to the park.

Contact: Ponderosa RV Park, 1983 Boggy Creek Road, Kissimmee, FL 34744, 407/847-6002, fax 407/847-2400.

142 ORLANDO SOUTHEAST/ LAKE WHIPPOORWILL KOA

Rating: 7

On Lake Whippoorwill east of Orlando
Orlando map, grid a2, page 240

These mostly grassy sites are set amid pine trees alongside fishable 350-acre Lake Whippoorwill in the rural eastern section of Orange County. A hairdresser is available in winter, when the place fills up with snowbirds who enjoy pancake breakfasts, potluck dinners, and bingo at the 40-acre park. Swimming, boating, fishing, and water-skiing are popular. The management says it's about a 20-minute drive to Disney-area attractions and 35 minutes to Cape Canaveral.

Campsites, facilities: Five tent sites are set apart from 120 RV sites (all full-hookup). Each site has a picnic table. Cable TV and telephone service are available. A pool, a recreation hall, a hot tub, canoe rentals, a playground, horseshoes, shuffleboard, and volleyball entertain campers. On the premises are restrooms, showers, a boat ramp, a dock, a dump station, cabin rentals, laundry facilities, limited bait and tackle, and a gift shop and store. The recreation hall, pool, and convenience store are wheelchair accessible. A restaurant is within walking distance. Children and leashed pets are welcome.

Reservations, fees: Reservations are recommended. Sites are $35 to $47 per night for two people, plus $2 to $3 for each additional person. Major credit cards are accepted. Long-term stays are OK.

Directions: From Orlando, take State Road 528/the Bee Line Expressway east to State Road 15/Narcoossee Road, then go south for 3.5 miles to the park.

Contact: Orlando Southeast/Lake Whippoorwill KOA, 12345 Narcoossee Road, Orlando, FL 32827, 407/277-5075 or 800/999-5267, email: www.whippoorwillkoa@piorl.com.

143 MOSS PARK

Rating: 7

Near Lake Hart southeast of Orlando
Orlando map, grid a2, page 240

Boating, hiking, and wildlife observation are the most popular activities at this little-publicized, 2.5-square-mile county campground, which is favored by locals. The heavily wooded shell-rock sites, each with a picnic table, a grill, and a fire ring, are nestled between Lake Hart and Lake Mary Jane, both of which are popular for swimming and fishing. It's adjacent to the 1,800-acre Split Oak Forest Mitigation Park, where you'll find several hiking trails. During 2003, a new campground is being built with 56 sites. The older sites will be available until the new campground is completed; after that the old campground will be converted to a day-use area.

Amid the majestic old oaks and freshwater marshes, look for sandhill cranes, deer, wild turkeys, wood storks, and fox squirrels—a remarkable array when you consider how close you are to Orlando. When the Moss family donated the land to Orange County in 1930, it was known as "Bear Island," but you won't see any bears today. Canoeing, kayaking, waterskiing, and windsurfing are possible on the lakes if you bring your own equipment. A three-mile nature trail and several more miles of hiking trails will please day hikers. This park is 25 miles from Disney-area attractions.

Campsites, facilities: The county-run campground offers 52 sites. Of these, 16 RV sites have electricity and water hookups. The remaining 39 primitive sites are for RVs or tents and are set aside from the others. Each site has a picnic table, a grill, and a fire ring. Facilities include restrooms, showers, a dump station, two boat ramps, a beach, hiking trails, playgrounds, pavilion rentals, softball field, and volleyball. Management says the restrooms are wheelchair accessible. Children are welcome. Pets are prohibited. Absolutely no alcohol is allowed; the rule is enforced with a $500 fine and/or six months in jail.

Reservations, fees: Reservations are recommended if you want a site with electricity. Pay by cash or check when you make the reservation 45 days in advance, and you must stay a minimum of two nights. Telephone reservations are not accepted. Primitive camping (tents only) is first-come, first-served. Sites are $10 to $15 per night. Add $3 for electricity and $1 for admission. Credit cards are not accepted. Stays are limited to 14 days.

Directions: Take State Road 528/Bee Line Expressway east from Orlando International Airport about three miles. At Exit 13, head south on Narcoossee Road/State Road 15 for 2.5 miles, then turn left onto Moss Park Road. From State Road 417/Greenway Expressway, take Exit 13 onto Narcoossee Road and go north a short distance to the Moss Park Road.

Contact: Moss Park, 12901 Moss Park Road, Orlando, FL 32812, 407/273-2327, fax 407/249-4498, website: http://parks.orangecountyfl.net.

144 EAST LAKE FISH CAMP
🏊 🛶 🚐 🐕 ♿ 🚙 ⛺

Rating: 3

On East Lake Tohopekaliga south of Orlando
Orlando map, grid a2, page 240

Not for nothing is the main road through the park known as Big Bass Road. This place on four-mile-wide East Lake Tohopekaliga is designed for anglers. But it's more than a fish camp, with airboat rides, a kidney-shaped pool, and even a barnyard with cattle and goats. Some families camp here even if they're not after bass, specks, or shellcrackers. You may be able to get a shady spot, but about one-third of the sites are sunny. The place is favored by snowbirds and permanent residents, who take up about half the spots.

Campsites, facilities: Twenty-three tent sites are set apart from 263 full-hookup RV sites (about 35 pull-through). Facilities include restrooms, showers, a dump station, gasoline and LP gas sales, laundry facilities, picnic tables, cabin rentals, a pool, a restaurant, boat rentals, fishing guide services, bait and tackle sales, a boat ramp, and tennis courts. Management says the entire park is wheelchair accessible. Children and pets are permitted.

Reservations, fees: Reservations are not accepted. Nightly fee for two people is $20 for an RV site, $18 for a tent site. Add $1 per extra person. Major credit cards are accepted. Long-term stays are OK.

Directions: From the Central Florida Greenway/Highway 417, take Exit 17 and drive south on Boggy Creek Road for about five miles. Turn right onto Fish Camp Road and continue south to Big Bass Road, which leads through the park.

Contact: East Lake Fish Camp, 3705 Big Bass Road, Kissimmee, FL 34744, 407/348-2040, fax 407/348-7797.

145 THE FLORIDIAN RV RESORT
🏊 🛶 🚐 🐕 🥾 ♿ 🚙 ⛺

Rating: 7

South of Orlando on the Orange/
Osceola County line
Orlando map, grid a2, page 240

This large, 140-acre gated park with paved roads has lots of oak trees providing shade. It's next to a mobile home park run by the same folks who manage the campground. Increasingly, families live in the campground; fewer retirees head here than in the past. Still, during the busy winter season, campers enjoy dances, play bingo and card games, organize tennis teams, and attend periodic on-site health fairs. A new clubhouse was recently added. If you bring a boat or canoe, you can launch from the park into Fells Cove, which leads to East Lake Tohopekaliga. Bathrooms are within easy walking distance on lighted paths from the water-and-electric sites. The campground is about 20 miles from Walt Disney World.

Campsites, facilities: The campground offers 457 RV sites (about 350 full-hookup). Tenters can use 70 RV sites in an area with water and electric hookups only. On the premises are restrooms, showers, a dump station, laundry facilities, picnic tables, a playground, a recreation hall, a hot tub, a boat ramp and dock, volleyball, shuffleboard, and tennis courts. The new clubhouse has an atrium seating area, TV and card rooms, and billiards. Many areas have wheelchair access. Children and small pets are allowed.

Reservations, fees: Reservations are recommended in January, February, and March. Sites are $18.50 per night for two people, plus $1 for each additional person age six and older. Major credit cards are accepted. Long-term stays are OK.

Directions: From Orlando, take State Road 15/Narcoossee Road south to State Road 530. The campground is to the left of the intersection.

Contact: The Floridian RV Resort, 5150 Boggy Creek Road, St. Cloud, FL 34771, 407/892-5171, email: floridianrv@aol.com.

146 LAKELAND RV RESORT

Rating: 7

Off I-4 in Lakeland
Orlando map, grid b3, page 240

This tree-shaded spot off I-4 is near little Lake Deeson, which is stocked with bass, catfish, and bluegill. A heated pool and wintertime activities such as bingo, card nights, and arts classes entertain campers. It's not unusual for visitors to sleep at this 24-acre campground simply because of its location: Theme parks in Tampa and Orlando are about 30 minutes from the grassy and paved sites (most with patios). The Detroit Tigers play spring training games down the road off State Road 33; call 863/686-8075 for game information. Tickets are available at the stadium an hour before games begin.

Campsites, facilities: There are 227 full-hookup sites (75 pull-through) for RVs, and about 40 sites can be used by tenters. Each has a picnic table. For recreation, there's a pool (a spa was added in 2002), a kiddie pool, a clubhouse, paddle boats, a stocked lake, a playground, horseshoes, miniature golf, Ping-Pong, basketball, seasonal activities, shuffleboard, and a children's playroom. Also on the premises are showers, restrooms, LP gas sales, a dump station, a screened pavilion, rental cabins, a camp store, an on-site video/book library, a 3,000-square-foot screened pavilion, two kitchens, a modem hookup to check email, and laundry facilities. Ditto for a dog-washing station (you do the washing). Management says most areas are wheelchair accessible. Groceries, a restaurant, and bait are available within a five-minute drive. Children are welcome. Leashed pets are permitted.

Reservations, fees: Reservations are not required. Sites are $18 to $28 per night for two people, plus $2 for each additional person and $2 for 50-amp electrical service. Major credit cards are accepted. Long-term stays are OK.

Directions: From I-4, take Exit 33 and drive about one mile northeast on State Road 33/County Road 582 (Socrum Loop) to Old Combee Road. Turn right and proceed .25 mile to the campground, on the right.

Contact: Lakeland RV Resort, 900 Old Combee Road, Lakeland, FL 33805, 863/687-6146 or 888/622-4115, email: lakelandrv@aol.com, website: www.lakelandrvresort.com.

147 TIKI VILLAGE CAMPGROUND

Rating: 5

Off I-4 in Lakeland
Orlando map, grid b3, page 240

An RV dealer and one of Florida's largest malls (Lakeland Mall) are within walking distance when you stay at Tiki Village, a fast stop off I-4. Still, you may see tigers, as in the Detroit Tigers, play spring training games nearby at Joker Marchant Stadium, 2301 Lakeland Hills Boulevard; call 863/686-8075 for game information. Despite the winter social programs and the swimming pool, you're getting convenience here: Tampa and Orlando theme parks are only about 30 minutes away by car. The two fish ponds are a plus, especially for families with kids in tow.

Campsites, facilities: All 210 full-hookup sites are for RVs up to 45 feet long. Twenty are pull-through. A pool, a recreation room, a play area, horseshoes, shuffleboard, and winter activities entertain campers. On the premises are showers, restrooms, snacks, LP gas sales, and laundry facilities. Groceries and a restaurant are within walking distance. Children are welcome. Two small pets are permitted per site.

Reservations, fees: Reservations are recommended. Sites are $25 per night for two people, plus $2 for each additional person. Major credit cards are accepted. Yearly rates are available.

Directions: From I-4, take Exit 32 and drive one block north on U.S. 98 to Crevasse Street. Turn right and proceed about .25 mile to the entrance, on the left.

Contact: Tiki Village Campground, 905 Crevasse Street, Lakeland, FL 33809, 863/858-5364 or 863/858-8217, fax 863/853-9446, website: www.tikivillagecampground.com.

148 LELYNN RV RESORT

Rating: 3

In Polk City

Orlando map, grid b3, page 240

Although children are allowed, this RV park is decidedly retiree- and snowbird-oriented, with planned activities during the winter months. The park boasts of a quiet setting, where campers can watch the sun set over Lake Agnes. Fishing and boating are options, too.

Campsites, facilities: Of the 365 sites, 350 are available for seasonal visitors and 15 for overnighters. Nine are pull-through. All have full hookups, 50-amp service, and picnic tables. Restrooms, showers, a dump station, laundry facilities, and, for long-termers, telephone service are available. On the premises are a pool, a boat ramp, a dock, propane gas

sales, shuffleboard courts, a dog-walk area, and a recreation room. All areas are wheelchair accessible. Children and small pets are permitted.

Reservations, fees: Reservations are recommended. Sites are $25 per night for two people, plus $2 per extra person. Credit cards are not accepted. Long-term or seasonal stays are allowed.

Directions: From I-4, take Exit 44 and drive north on State Road 559 for one block to the park.

Contact: LeLynn RV Resort, 1513 State Road 559, Polk City, FL 33868, 863/984-1495, fax 863/984-0257.

149 SCENIC VIEW MOBILE HOME PARK

Rating: 1

In Lakeland

Orlando map, grid b3, page 240

One-half-mile-long Lester Lake is down the street to the west, and citrus groves to the south and northwest fill the air with the heady scent of blooming fruit. Yes, several oaks do lend shade at this retiree-oriented, residential park, but chances are that your grassy/concrete-pad campsite will be sunny. For every RV, there are nearly two mobile homes (75 total).

Campsites, facilities: At this age-55-and-up park, all 44 full-hookup sites are for RVs. There are no showers or restrooms. A recreation pavilion, horseshoes, shuffleboard, wintertime social programs, and drinking water are available. Groceries, a restaurant, and laundry facilities are within one mile. Children are prohibited. Leashed pets are permitted.

Reservations, fees: Reservations are recommended. Sites are $18 per night for two people, plus $1 for each additional person. Credit cards are not accepted.

Directions: From I-4, take Exit 32 and drive 2.25 miles north on U.S. 98 to West Daughtery Road. Turn left. The park is one mile ahead on the right.

Contact: Scenic View Mobile Home Park, 2025 West Daughtery Road, Lakeland, FL 33810, 863/858-2262, fax 863/858-4700.

150 LAKE JULIANA BOATING AND LODGING

Rating: 4

At Lake Juliana north of Auburndale
Orlando map, grid b3, page 240

In a region normally focused on retirees, families can take solace in knowing that this five-acre park has a swimming beach, pool, volleyball net, and toddler-oriented play center to entertain the kids. Bass fishing nonetheless remains the key attraction for campers at these grassy/concrete-pad sites. A canal links nearly two-mile-long Lake Juliana with smaller Lake Mattie, giving anglers and water-skiers 2,100 watery acres to explore.

Campers are somewhat outnumbered by mobile home residents at this small complex, where the family atmosphere comes with rules that Mom and Dad would approve of: Eat in the picnic area, not at the pool; and no foul language, please. Disney World, Sea World, and Busch Gardens are within 45 miles.

Campsites, facilities: All 10 full-hookup sites are for RVs. On the premises are a pool, an adult swing, a wheelchair-accessible recreation room, a volleyball net, a playground, restrooms (no showers), a dump station, rental cottages, cabins, a boat ramp, covered boat slips, boat rentals, a tanning bed, a toddler play area, limited groceries, a picnic area, bait, tackle, cable TV, and laundry facilities. Restaurants are three miles away. Children must be adult-supervised at the pool and pier. Leashed, attended pets are permitted.

Reservations, fees: Reservations are recommended. Sites are $27.50 per night for two people, and $5 per extra person. Major credit cards are accepted. Long-term stays are OK.

Directions: From I-4, take Exit 44 and drive south less than one mile on State Route 559.

Turn right onto Lundy Road and proceed to the complex at Lake Juliana.

Contact: Lake Juliana Boating and Lodging, 600 Lundy Road, Auburndale, FL 33823, 863/984-1144.

151 VALENCIA ESTATES

Rating: 2

On U.S. 98 south of Lakeland
Orlando map, grid b3, page 240

Palm trees dot this 55-and-older park, where residents of the 86 mobile homes outnumber folks sleeping at the 30 grassy/concrete-pad campsites. The full schedule of winter activities includes Bible study, crafts, card nights, bingo, bowling, golf and pool leagues, as well as weekly coffees, monthly potlucks, and twice-monthly pancake and sausage breakfasts.

Lakeland doesn't usually jump to mind when one considers Florida's prime tourism spots, but this way station of a city between Tampa and Orlando hosts the Detroit Tigers for spring training games in March. It's a good home base for the Florida Aquarium or pier in St. Petersburg, as well as Disney World and Historic Bok Sanctuary in Lake Wales. For a pretty walk, park four miles away at Florida Southern College, whose buildings at Ingraham Avenue and Lake Hollingsworth Drive were designed by Frank Lloyd Wright. Then circle the lake fronting the college—Lake Hollingsworth. You'll pass the Lakeland Yacht and Country Club along the way.

Campsites, facilities: At this age-55-plus park, all 30 full-hookup sites will accommodate RVs up to 40 feet long. A dump station and laundry facilities are provided. Showers and restrooms are now available in the clubhouse. A pool, three lighted shuffleboard courts, winter programs, and a clubhouse entertain campers. Cable TV and telephone hookups are available. A restaurant and groceries are within two miles. Children are prohibited. Leashed pets up to 45 pounds are allowed.

Reservations, fees: Reservations are recommended, and they are a must for the winter season because most tenants return year after year. Sites are $22 per night for two people, plus $10 per extra person. Credit cards are not accepted. Long-term stays are welcome.

Directions: From East Main Street in Lakeland, drive 3.5 miles south on U.S. 98. The park entrance is on the right. From I-4, take Exit 27 to State Road 570 (Polk Parkway) west. Exit on U.S. 98 at Bartow and drive .5 mile north to the first left turn.

Contact: Valencia Estates, 3325 Bartow Road/U.S. 98, Lakeland, FL 33803, 863/665-1611 or 800/645-9033, fax 863/667-3698.

152 SANLAN RANCH CAMPGROUND

Rating: 9

On U.S. 98 south of Lakeland
Orlando map, grid b3, page 240

More than 90 types of birds have been spotted at this notable private recreation area, which covers more than one square mile. Still, golfers tend to prefer walking from their grassy campsites to the adjacent Bramble Ridge Golf Course, where the driving range was voted best in the county by locals. A private camper entrance leads to the par-72, 18-hole course, where Sanlan guests receive a discount.

Look for alligators and ducks while paddling along the park's canoe trails or walking along three wooded hiking trails (a total of seven miles). A cacophony of bird chatter in winter enlivens a pensive stop along the two-mile-long Rookery Trail, near Banana Lake. A boat ramp provides access to Banana Lake, one of three park lakes. The park isn't only about wilderness activities, though; bingo games and potluck dinners are held in the winter at the 200-person-capacity recreation hall, and aquacize sessions are sometimes offered at one of the three solar-heated pools. Joggers follow a three-mile shady trail around the golf course.

Lakefront campsites have no utilities, just tables. At sites along the camping circle, there are no sewer hookups. If you prefer big sites, note that the "ranch view" sites are smaller than regular full-hookup sites.

Campsites, facilities: More than 500 sites and a primitive group camping area are for RVs up to 50 feet long or tents. Two pools, a wading pool, 18 lighted shuffleboard courts, a lighted golf driving range, a playground, horseshoes, a recreation hall, three nature trails, and winter activities entertain campers. Facilities include restrooms, showers, a dump station, a modem hookup to check email, and laundry facilities. Children are permitted. Two pets are allowed per site.

Reservations, fees: Reservations are recommended. Sites are $14 to $28 per night for two people, plus $2.50 for each additional person. Pet fee is 50 cents daily. Major credit cards are accepted.

Directions: From East Main Street in Lakeland, drive 3.5 miles south on U.S. 98 to the park, which is on the right side of the road. Or, from the Polk County Parkway (State Road 520), take Exit 10 southbound on U.S. 98. Drive .25 mile to the park on the west side of U.S. 98.

Contact: Sanlan Ranch Campground, 3929 U.S. 98 South, Lakeland, FL 33813, 863/665-1726 or 800/524-5044, website: www.sanlan.com.

153 OAK HARBOR

Rating: 6

On Lake Lowery west of Haines City
Orlando map, grid b3, page 240

You'll pass citrus groves—and perhaps the aroma of sweet blossoms—on the approach to this off-the-beaten-path lakefront park, where clumps of tall, lanky palms and brushy oaks lend a woodsy feel. Bass anglers, water-skiers, and swimmers share the calm blue waters of nearly two-mile-long Lake Lowery here. Many campers spend entire winters at these grassy campsites with concrete patios, while other folks live in the 65-acre park's 70 mobile homes. Although the private park enjoys admirable shade from its overstory of trees, there is comparatively little eye-level brush separating camping spots. This is a gathering spot for seaplane and float plane rallies.

Campsites, facilities: While 110 RV sites have full hookups, 10 others have water and electricity only. A recreation room, winter social programs, showers, restrooms, picnic tables, a dump station, a boat ramp, and laundry facilities are available. A restaurant and bait shop are three miles away. Groceries are within five miles. Children and leashed pets under 40 pounds are permitted.

Reservations, fees: Reservations are recommended. Sites are $22 per night for two people, plus $2 for each additional person. Prices include your own boat dock. Credit cards are not accepted. Long-term stays are OK.

Directions: From U.S. 27 in Haines City, drive 4.5 miles west on U.S. 17/92. Turn right at Experiment Station Road. Cross the railroad tracks, then turn right at Old Haines City/Lake Alfred Road. Continue 1.5 miles. Turn left on Lake Lowery Road. The park is ahead at right.

Contact: Oak Harbor, 100 Oak Harbor, Haines City, FL 33844, 863/956-1341, fax 863/956-1341.

154 CENTRAL PARK OF HAINES CITY

Rating: 7

Off U.S. 27 in Haines City
Orlando map, grid b3, page 240

With morning newspaper delivery and daily garbage pickup service, snowbirds don't escape civilization—they embrace it. Campers are encouraged to plant landscaping, add driveways, put in sidewalks, and attach screen rooms to their concrete-pad RV sites to make them feel at home. Many retirees spend entire winters in this lake-dotted region of rolling hills, some taking advantage of health screenings,

bingo, exercises, and Sunday church services in the park's recreation hall. Oaks shade some campsites, which are set block-style in single and double rows.

Campsites, facilities: The 354 full-hookup sites are for tents or RVs. Twenty-six sites are pull-through. For recreation, there's a pool, a recreation hall, horseshoes, shuffleboard, bocce (lawn bowling) courts, and winter activities. Showers, restrooms, and laundry facilities are available. A shopping center is .25 mile away. An 18-hole golf course is one mile away. Children are permitted. Leashed pets may use two pet walks at park boundaries.

Reservations, fees: Reservations are not necessary. Sites are $21 to $23 per night for two people, plus $1 for each additional person. Credit cards are not accepted. Long-term stays are OK. Group camping is available.

Directions: From I-4 at Exit 55, go south about 12 miles on U.S. 27. Turn right at Commerce Avenue, which is the second stoplight in Haines City (if you hit U.S. 17/92, you've gone too far). The park is ahead at left.

Contact: Central Park of Haines City, 1501 Commerce Avenue, Haines City, FL 33844, 863/422-5322, website: www.centralpark.home.att.net.

155 GREENFIELD VILLAGE RV PARK

Rating: 3

Off U.S. 27 in Dundee
Orlando map, grid b3, page 240

In this region of rolling, citrus-dotted hills, the bigger towns of Lake Wales and Winter Haven (with their antique shops) are better known than Dundee, a sleepy, wide spot in the road where these 104 concrete-pad RV sites are set. Swimming in the heated pool is a highlight at the grassy, flat park, which is kept neat as a pin. Oaks and palms provide some shade for campers, who often stay at least three months. Elsewhere, an 18-hole golf course is .2 mile away and locals fish at area lakes. The boat ramp to the biggest nearby body of water, Lake Hamilton, is up U.S. 27 about 3.5 miles northwest of the park. Historic Bok Sanctuary, an estate and gardens where 45-minute carillon recitals are held daily at 3 P.M., is in Lake Wales; call 863/676-1408.

Campsites, facilities: This age-55-and-up park offers 92 full-hookup sites with picnic tables for long-staying RVs and 12 with full hookups for overnighters. Rigs up to 45 feet in length can be accommodated. A pool, shuffleboard, a recreation hall, winter social programs, showers, restrooms, and trailer rentals are available. Free local calls and computer hookups are available in the laundry room. Management says the pool, laundry facilities, bathhouse, and recreation hall are wheelchair accessible. Groceries, a restaurant, and laundry facilities are within .25 mile. Children are not allowed. Large dog breeds like rottweilers, pit bulls, and Doberman pinschers are prohibited; otherwise, pets are permitted.

Reservations, fees: Reservations are recommended. Sites are $30 per night, plus $2 per extra person. Credit cards are not accepted. Long-term stays are OK.

Directions: From U.S. 27 at Dundee, drive west .1 mile on State Road 542. Turn left almost immediately into the park.

Contact: Greenfield Village RV Park, P.O. Box 1807, Dundee, FL 33838, 863/439-7409.

156 MERRY D RV SANCTUARY

Rating: 6

Southeast of Disney World
Orlando map, grid b3, page 240

This 54-acre rural park bills itself as a "back-to-nature" campground where most sites are shaded and people who want a peaceful, quiet night after a hectic day at Disney World will be happy. Some folks stay here long-term, too. Paved interior roads lead to large sites—at least 50 by 80 feet for pull-through spots. In the busy winter season, campers can enjoy arts-and-crafts classes, card games, ice-cream socials, Bible study nights, and periodic group trips to casinos and other places. Fishing is possible in a small lake, but you'll have to travel about eight miles to get bait and tackle. The park is within a few miles of the main gate to Walt Disney World.

Campsites, facilities: Nine tent sites are set apart from 91 full-hookup sites with cable TV access and telephone availability. Forty-two sites are pull-through. Each site has a picnic table. On the premises are restrooms, showers, a dump station, rental trailers, a recreation room, a playground, a nature trail, horseshoes, laundry facilities, and a long, narrow field that some campers have used as a golf driving range. Management says the restrooms and showers are wheelchair accessible. Groceries and restaurants are within two miles. Children and pets are permitted.

Reservations, fees: Reservations are required. Sites are $14 to $25 per night for two people, plus $2 for each additional person. Major credit cards are accepted. Long-term stays are OK.

Directions: From U.S. 192 in Kissimmee, go south on U.S. 17/92 about three miles. Turn left at County Road 531/Pleasant Hill Road. Continue seven miles to the campground, at left.

Contact: Merry D RV Sanctuary, 4261 Pleasant Hill Road, Kissimmee, FL 34746-2933, 407/870-0719 or 800/208-3434, fax 407/870-0198, website: www.merryd.com.

157 ALOHA RV PARK

Rating: 1

Southwest of Kissimmee
Orlando map, grid b3, page 240

In the winter, you can pick oranges at this park, located within 15 miles of Disney World. Anglers may want to head about five miles east to fish for bass, specks, or catfish in 11-mile-long Lake Tohopekaliga. A good portion of these paved campsites are taken by full-time or seasonal residents rather than overnighters, although campers may choose to spend only one night. Park rules tend to be geared toward full-time residents. Also, campers are asked to use the restrooms in their rigs. Winter residents take part in bingo games, shuffleboard, pancake breakfasts, and spaghetti dinners.

Campsites, facilities: Self-contained rigs are accepted at this adult-oriented park with 112 full-hookup RV sites (35 pull-through). On the premises are restrooms, showers, a dump station, laundry facilities, picnic tables, a pool, and a game room. Groceries and restaurants are about five miles away. Children may camp on a short-term basis. Small pets are welcome.

Reservations, fees: Reservations are recommended. Sites are $20 per night for two people. Credit cards are not accepted. Long-term stays are OK.

Directions: From Kissimmee, take U.S. 17/92 south about seven miles.

Contact: Aloha RV Park, 4648 South Orange Blossom Trail, Kissimmee, FL 34746, 407/933-5730.

158 RICHARDSON'S FISH CAMP

Rating: 2

On Lake Tohopekaliga south of Kissimmee
Orlando map, grid b3, page 240

The main reason to stay at this six-acre camp is to venture out onto 23,000-acre Lake Tohopekaliga to fish for trophy bass, specks, and panfish. This off-the-beaten-path spot on the lake's northeast shore emphasizes a laid-back lifestyle in a quiet setting shaded by large oak trees. Many patrons stay in air-conditioned rental cabins. A plus: One boat slip is included in the price of the campsites, which are sandy or grassy with concrete pads. The park also offers airboat rides.

Campsites, facilities: Four tent sites are set apart from 16 full-hookup, pull-through RV sites. On the premises are restrooms, showers, a dump station, a boat ramp, charter fishing

services, a dock, bait and tackle, covered slips, snacks, and laundry facilities. Management says the dock behind the bait shop and office are wheelchair accessible. Children and pets are permitted.

Reservations, fees: Reservations are recommended. Sites are $19.50 to $25 per night for two people, plus $1 for each additional person and $1 for pets. Credit cards are not accepted. Long-term stays are OK.

Directions: From Kissimmee, take State Road 525/Neptune Road east. Turn right (south) onto King's Highway. Turn right onto Pine Island Road, then right again onto Scotty's Road. You'll be heading north at this point. Follow signs and take the road to the end.

Contact: Richardson's Fish Camp, 1550 Scotty's Road, Kissimmee, FL 34744, 407/846-6540.

159 GATOR RV RESORT

Rating: 4

East of St. Cloud
Orlando map, grid b3, page 240

At these rates, this countryside campground with a mix of sunny and shady sites is a bargain for anyone willing to bear the traffic to get to Walt Disney World about 20 miles to the west. The Atlantic Ocean (at Melbourne) is just under one hour's drive east. But most folks here are passing the winter or passing through, not yearning for Mickey Mouse.

Campsites, facilities: This 110-unit park sets aside 20 sites for overnighting RVs and 30 for seasonal campers; four sites are available for tents. All RVers have full hookups, concrete pads, picnic tables, cable TV, and telephone service available. Restrooms, showers, a dump station, laundry facilities, a restaurant, a snack bar, a well-stocked fishing pond, and propane gas sales are on the premises. Restrooms, the laundry room, and the restaurant are wheelchair accessible. Children and leashed pets are permitted.

Reservations, fees: Reservations are not necessary except during the winter. Sites are $16 per night. Credit cards are not accepted. Long-term stays are available.

Directions: From Florida's Turnpike, exit eastbound on U.S. 192/441 and drive through the town of St. Cloud. Continue east two miles; the park is on the north side east of State Road 15.

Contact: Gator RV Resort, 5755 East Irlo Bronson Highway, St. Cloud, FL 34771, 407/892-8662, fax 770/645-4629.

160 SOUTHPORT RV PARK, CAMPGROUND AND MARINA

Rating: 7

**South of Kissimmee on West
Lake Tohopekaliga**

Orlando map, grid b3, page 240

While this newly refurbished, 25-acre park is plenty close to Disney World, most folks here are more interested in the boating, fishing, and wooded atmosphere on West Lake Tohopekaliga, which is known for world-class bass fishing. You get a free boat slip with each camp site. The clientele is a mix of families, anglers, and retirees.

Campsites, facilities: There are 53 full-hookup RV sites and 10 tent sites with water and electricity set apart from the RV area. All have picnic tables and grills. Some sites (number 28 through 37) overlook the lake, and two are wheelchair accessible. The campers' fishing area is separated from the boat slips so you're not apt to snag your line or tangle with a neighbor's boat lines. Restrooms, showers, a dump site, and laundry facilities are available. On the premises are a boat ramp, dock, a fish-cleaning station, a clubhouse with planned activities in season, bait and tackle, a store, snack bar, horseshoe pit, volleyball net, and pavilion. Airboat tours leave every 30 minutes, and fishing guide service is available. Children are welcome. Leashed pets are permitted.

Reservations, fees: Reservations are recom-

mended. Sites are $12 to $15 per night for two people, plus $2 per extra person. Credit cards are not accepted. Long-term rates are available.

Directions: From I-4, take Exit 64A east onto U.S. 192. Turn right on Poinciana Boulevard. Follow Poinciana Boulevard until it crosses Pleasant Hill Road and dead-ends into Southport Park.

Contact: Southport RV Park, Campground and Marina, 2001 East Southport Road, Kissimmee, FL 34746, 407/933-5822, website: www.southportpark.com.

161 CAMP MARY MOBILE HOME AND RV PARK

Rating: 1

**On Lake Hatchineha southeast
of Haines City**

Orlando map, grid b3, page 240

Bass fishing is big at this little park, which is home to only five paved campsites and 10 mobile homes on sprawling Lake Hatchineha. Although you may water-ski or swim in the six-mile-long lake, the calm waters seem to be the domain of bass boats. Elsewhere, bicyclists enjoy pedaling about five miles west of here past citrus groves on Jennings Road, south of State Road 542, and past groves farther northwest on State Road 544. Disney World is within 35 miles.

Campsites, facilities: All five full-hookup RV sites have picnic tables. Showers, restrooms, trailer rentals, a boat ramp, boat slips, and laundry facilities are available. Across the canal are a restaurant, snacks, and bait. Groceries are nine miles away. Children and small leashed pets are permitted.

Reservations, fees: Reservations are recommended. Sites are $20 per night. Credit cards are not accepted.

Directions: From Alternate U.S. 27 south of Haines City, drive 11 miles east on State Road 542. Turn left on Bass Street, then right on Catfish Street, and continue to the road's end.

Contact: Camp Mary Mobile Home and RV Park, 151 Catfish Street, Haines City, FL 33844, 863/439-4666.

162 LAKE PIERCE ECO RESORT

Rating: 10

Between Haines City and Lake Wales on the north side of Lake Pierce

Orlando map, grid b3, page 240

Fed up with big-city life, Frank Wezyk in 1999 sold his assets to create this 20-acre paradise on the north side of 4,000-acre Lake Pierce. Once a dilapidated trailer park, the place today is a jewel, where you can see wildlife close at hand (his feeding of the birds and fish, though of course not alligators, is something to see, and visitors are invited to join in), and just enjoy the outdoors. In fact, that's the kind of traveler Wezyk wants to visit the park, and he's worked hard to create an "ecological park." For example, a series of lights and mirrors under the 200-foot dock illuminate the fish and watery denizens. You can canoe, fish, hike, and bike around the area. The only thing you can't do: Bring pets. They'll scare away the wildlife. A Vietnam veteran, Wezyk offers special rates for veteran's groups, car clubs, and Harley Davidson clubs.

Campsites, facilities: There are 15 RV sites with full hookups and 50 tent sites. Ten tent sites have water and electricity. All developed sites have picnic tables, grills, and cable TV. Restrooms, showers, laundry facilities, a nature trail, fishing dock, canoe rentals, and shuffleboard courts are on the premises. Most areas are wheelchair accessible. Children are welcome. No pets, please.

Reservations, fees: Reservations are recommended. Sites are $20 to $25 per night for two people, plus $3 per extra person. Credit cards are not accepted. Long-term rates are available.

Directions: From the intersection of State Road 60 and U.S. 27 in Lake Wales, drive east on State Road 60 one mile. Turn north on U.S. Alternate 27/U.S. 17 and proceed 15 miles.

Turn right on Tindel Camp Road and go one mile. At Lake Mabel Road, turn left and proceed to Canal Road one mile.

Contact: Lake Pierce Eco Resort, 3500 Canal Road, Lake Pierce, FL 33853, 863/439-2023, fax 863/439-6166, website: www.lakepierce.com.

163 LAKE TOHO RESORT

Rating: 2

On Lake Tohopekaliga south of Kissimmee

Orlando map, grid b3, page 240

This place was once known as Red's Fish Camp, which is why they sometimes answer the phone, "Reds!" Lacking amenities such as a pool or other diversions for children, Lake Toho Resort is favored mostly by a crowd interested in fishing or taking airboat rides on the lake. About half the residents live here year-round. Sites are grassy, and shade is fairly sparse unless you manage to get a site in the back row. You can fish from the bank of 11-mile-long Lake Tohopekaliga, but you'll probably have better luck if you bring your own boat (no rentals are available) and use the park boat ramp.

Campsites, facilities: This park has 250 full-hookup RV sites; tents are not allowed. Each site has a picnic table. Facilities include restrooms, showers, a dump station, laundry facilities, a boat ramp, and a restaurant that serves breakfast, lunch, and dinner. Management says all public areas are wheelchair accessible. Groceries are seven miles away. Children are welcome. Pets must be leashed.

Reservations, fees: Reservations are recommended in the winter. Sites are $20 for two people, plus $2 per extra person. Credit cards are not accepted. Long-term stays are OK.

Directions: From I-4 at Exit 64A, head east on U.S. 192/Irlo Bronson Highway. Turn right at Kissimmee Park Road, at the first stoplight on the east side of town. The road dead-ends into the campground at Lake Tohopekaliga.

Contact: Lake Toho Resort, 4715 Kissimmee Park Road, St. Cloud, FL 34772, 407/892-8795.

164 CANOE CREEK CAMPGROUND

Rating: 5

South of St. Cloud

Orlando map, grid a3, page 240

Although it's called Canoe Creek Campground, there is no creek and no place to canoe. You can camp, though. Some sites are grassy; others have concrete pads. Compared with other parks closer to Disney World, this one has a quieter, more rural feel, with oaks shading part of the 26-acre park. For the most part, the place (and its four-foot-deep screened and heated pool) attracts senior citizens, but families are welcome. As for the puzzling name, Canoe Creek simply is the moniker of a creek that connects two nearby lakes—Cypress and Gentry. Disney-area attractions are about 25 miles away.

Campsites, facilities: These 178 full-hookup sites with picnic tables are for RVs. Tenters may use the RV sites in spring, summer, and fall. A therapy exercise pool, horseshoes, shuffleboard, and winter social programs entertain campers. On the premises are restrooms, showers, a dump station, trailer rentals, and laundry facilities. The recreation hall, pool area, and laundry facilities are accessible to wheelchairs. Children and pets are permitted.

Reservations, fees: Reservations are recommended. Sites are $27 per night for two people, plus $2 for each extra person. Credit cards are not accepted. Long-term stays are OK.

Directions: From St. Cloud, drive about six miles south on State Road 523 to the campground.

Contact: Canoe Creek Campground, 4101 Canoe Creek Road, St. Cloud, FL 34772, 407/892-7010 or 800/453-5268.

165 CYPRESS LAKE RV AND SPORTS CLUB

Rating: 6

On Lake Cypress south of St. Cloud

Orlando map, grid a3, page 240

Lake Cypress makes this remote RV park a picturesque place to stay where you're sure to see some interesting wildlife, including sandhill cranes, otters, and bald eagles.

The main thing to do here is fish for bass. Some people also go after specks or bream. You don't have to be an angler to appreciate the place—just gazing out at the pretty blue waters of Lake Cypress is a treat. The proprietors will give you an airboat tour of the lake where you're likely to see bald eagles, alligators, and other wildlife. A boat launched here can make its way all the way to Lake Okeechobee and back, but it's not a trip we would attempt in one day. The sites are grassy and right near the lake's edge; most are sunny, but some are shaded by giant cypress trees. Disney World is about 30 miles north.

Campsites, facilities: All 45 RV spaces (tents are no longer allowed) have full hookups. On the premises are restrooms, showers, laundry facilities, a recreation room, rental cabins, a boat ramp, bait and tackle, snacks, gasoline sales, and basketball. Management says the sites and restrooms are wheelchair accessible. Telephone service is available. The on-site restaurant serves breakfast, lunch, and dinner. You'll find groceries and restaurants within 10 miles. Kids and small pets are permitted.

Reservations, fees: Reservations are recommended, particularly in winter. Sites are $23 for two people. Major credit cards are accepted.

Directions: From St. Cloud, take Highway 523/Canoe Creek Road south about 10 miles. Just after you pass under Florida's Turnpike, turn right onto Lake Cypress Road. Follow it to the end, where you'll find the campground.

Contact: Cypress Lake RV and Sports Club,

3301 Lake Cypress Road, Kenansville, FL 34739, 407/957-3135.

166 BULL CREEK WILDLIFE MANAGEMENT AREA

Rating: 6

Eight miles east of Holopaw on Bull Creek and Billy Lake, south of U.S. 192

Orlando map, grid a3, page 240

Marsh rabbits hop about and sandhill cranes nest in spring in the wet prairies of this 23,504-acre wilderness. Look for deer at dawn or dusk while exploring the oak hammocks and while following the 8.6-mile loop trail that encircles the heart of these varied woods of sun-dappled pine flatwoods, cypress hardwoods, and wetlands of seasonal lilies and pitcher plants. More than 17 miles of the Florida National Scenic Trail runs the length of the area and connects to the Three Lakes Wildlife Management Area to the southwest (see campground in this chapter). The three camping areas could hardly be farther apart from each other. One, near the northern boundary, is at Crabgrass Creek; reach it by walking about one mile from the parking area located immediately south of U.S. 192, about two miles west of Highway 419. Another campsite is along a spur of the loop trail and is near the hunt-check station and informational kiosk at the western entrance of the conservation area; pick up a brochure at this entrance for a self-guided tour, whose stops include one at a historic railroad tram. The third campsite is at the southwestern boundary near the canoeing waters of Billy Lake.

Campsites, facilities: Three primitive camping areas are reached by foot. Two are one mile or less from parking areas. Camping is allowed at the designated campground only during hunting season and throughout the year at designated campsites on the Florida National Scenic Trail (as long as you hike to the site via the trail). A well with a pitcher pump providing nonpotable water is available at each camp-ing area, but there are no other facilities. Bring food, drinking water, supplies, and mosquito repellent. Pack out trash. Children are permitted. Pets must be leashed.

Reservations, fees: Sites are first-come, first-served. Camping is free. Each site accommodates up to six people. If your party has at least seven people, get a free permit and reserve at least one week ahead at 386/329-4410. Maximum stay for all campers is seven days. For ground conditions and hunting dates, contact the Florida Fish and Wildlife Conservation Commission at 352/732-1225.

Directions: From I-95 at Exit 180 (Melbourne), go west on U.S. 192. Drive 21.6 miles west to Crabgrass Road. Turn left. Proceed six miles south to the entrance.

Contact: St. Johns River Water Management District, Division of Land Management, P.O. Box 1429, Palatka, FL 32178-1429, 386/329-4500 or 800/451-7106, website: www.sjrwmd.com.

167 PEACE RIVER VILLAGE MOBILE RV PARK

Rating: 2

Near the Peace River east of Bartow

Orlando map, grid b3, page 240

The phosphate-mining town of Bartow isn't a likely tourist destination, but some people live in this park's 90 mobile homes (outnumbering campers three to one). Canals surround these 23 wooded acres with grassy and paved RV sites. Local anglers launch boats at a nearby ramp just south of State Road 60. Disney World is one hour north of here.

Campsites, facilities: All 30 full-hookup RV sites are pull-through. Showers, restrooms, a dump station, a wheelchair-accessible recreation room, shuffleboard, cable TV, laundry facilities, and a nearby boat ramp are available. Groceries and a restaurant are 1.5 miles away. Children are welcome. Small pets are permitted.

Reservations, fees: Reservations are recommended. Sites are $20 per night for two people,

plus $2 per extra person. The rate drops to $15 per night in the summertime. Credit cards are not accepted. Long-term stays are OK.

Directions: From Bartow, drive east on State Road 60, passing U.S. 98. The park is .5 mile east of the city limits.

Contact: Peace River Village Mobile RV Park, 2405 State Road 60 East, Bartow, FL 33830, 863/533-7823, fax 863/938-7868.

168 GOOD LIFE RV RESORT

Rating: 5

At Lake Garfield east of Bartow
Orlando map, grid b3, page 240

Located along a divided highway east of the phosphate-mining town of Bartow, this un-shaded, retiree-oriented park on one-mile-wide Lake Garfield won't satisfy forest fans. But it can tempt freshwater anglers looking for bass and bream. Locals use a boat ramp off Highway 60 to fish. There's a nine-hole golf course between the RV section and the lake, but there is no on-site boat ramp or beach. Swimmers use a heated pool instead. The lakeview sites are taken by full-timers.

Mobile homes and long-term residents nearly dominate the 397 sites (about 150 are for RVs). Ruler-straight streets are laid out in a grid pattern and are named after states that are close to retirees' hearts: Ohio, North Carolina, New York, and so on. To avoid sleeping nearest to State Road 60, skip sites 101 to 199 and 140 to 150. Disney World is one hour north.

Campsites, facilities: This retiree-oriented park offers 150 RV sites. A pool, a recreation hall, golf course, shuffleboard, horseshoes, and winter activities entertain campers. Showers, restrooms, a dump station, and laundry facilities are available. Children under 17 must be adult-supervised at the pool, and their length of stay may be restricted. Leashed pets are allowed.

Reservations, fees: Reservations are recommended. Sites are $22 per night. Credit cards are not accepted. Long-term rates are available.

Directions: From U.S. 98 in Bartow, drive east on State Road 60, passing U.S. 17 and the Peace River. The park is ahead on the right.

Contact: Good Life RV Resort, 6815 State Road 60 East, Bartow, FL 33830, 863/537-1971, fax 863/537-2687.

169 CYPRESS GARDENS CAMPGROUND

Rating: 5

East of Winter Haven
Orlando map, grid b3, page 240

"Lots of trees and wonderful people" is how the owners describe their RV park in this lake-dotted region west of Walt Disney World. Most visitors are snowbirds here for the winter months, but all ages are welcome. Shopping and restaurants are close by.

Campsites, facilities: There are 226 RV sites for overnighters and seasonal visitors. All have full hookups and picnic tables. Restrooms, showers, laundry facilities, and telephone service are available. On the premises are a pool, a recreation hall with planned activities during the winter, shuffleboard courts, and a dog-walk area. Most areas are wheelchair accessible. Children are welcome. Leashed pets are permitted.

Reservations, fees: Reservations are recommended. Sites are $20 per night for two people, plus $10 per extra person. Credit cards are not accepted. Long-term rates are available.

Directions: From the intersection of U.S. 17 and State Road 542 in Winter Haven, go east on State Road 542 about 5.5 miles. When you reach the burg of Eastwood, turn right on Lake Daisy Road and go about one mile to the park.

Contact: Cypress Gardens Campground, 1951 Lake Daisy Road, Winter Haven, FL 33884, 863/324-3136, fax 863/318-9806, email: spierce4@tampabay.rr.com.

170 CYPRESS MOTEL AND TRAILER COURT

Rating: 1

South of Winter Haven
Orlando map, grid b3, page 240

This tiny, one-acre park has three RV sites and lies in the shadow of a 21-unit motel. To swim, try the motel's heated pool.

Campsites, facilities: Three full-hookup sites are for RVs up to 30 feet long. A pool, a playground, restrooms, showers, a dump station, and laundry facilities are available. Children and pets are permitted.

Reservations, fees: Reservations are recommended. Sites are $17.50 per night. Major credit cards are accepted.

Directions: From U.S. 27, drive 1.7 miles west on State Road 540 to the 7-11 store at the traffic light. Turn right onto Cypress Gardens Road to the park.

Contact: Cypress Motel and Trailer Court, 5651 Cypress Gardens Road, Winter Haven, FL 33884, 863/324-5867 or 800/729-6706, fax 863/324-5867, website: www.cypressmotel.com.

171 HOLIDAY TRAVEL PARK

Rating: 7

South of Winter Haven
Orlando map, grid b3, page 240

Scrub oaks shade some sites at this 22-acre park, where half of the campers stay short-term, and the rest spend the entire winter. All campsites have 8-by-10-foot patios and are set diagonally along paved, typically ruler-straight, 5 mph roads. To sleep farthest from State Road 540, ask about spots along Palm Drive. But that means you'll need to walk to the opposite side of the park for potluck dinners, arts and crafts, and a dip in the 25-by-50-foot pool near the entrance. Disney World is 25 miles to the north.

Campsites, facilities: Eighty RV sites for overnighters and 120 for seasonal visitors are available. Many are pull-through, and all have full hookups, concrete pads, patios, and a picnic table. Twenty tent sites with water and electricity are set apart from RVs. A heated pool, a game room, miniature golf, a playground, horseshoes, tennis, bocce ball (lawn bowling), shuffleboard, a recreation hall, and winter social programs entertain campers. Showers, restrooms, a dump station, firewood, a limited store, cable TV access, a kitchen, and laundry facilities are available. A restaurant is across the street, and groceries are one mile away. Children are welcome. Leashed pets under 20 pounds are OK.

Reservations, fees: Reservations are recommended. Sites are $22 per night, plus $2 for each additional person. Major credit cards are accepted. The maximum stay is six months.

Directions: From U.S. 27, drive one mile west on State Road 540 to the park entrance.

Contact: Holiday Travel Park, 7400 Cypress Gardens Boulevard, Winter Haven, FL 33884, 863/324-7400 or 800/858-7275 (for reservations), website: www.holidaytravelpark.com.

172 A-OK CAMPGROUND

Rating: 2

Near Eagle Lake south of Winter Haven
Orlando map, grid b3, page 240

A citrus grove abuts this three-acre, adults-only park, where permanent residents live in 11 mobile homes and at some of the grassy RV sites equipped with concrete patios. Across the street to the north, Eagle Lake stretches about 1.5 miles. Not far south from the sun-dappled park is one-half-mile-wide Millsite Lake. You can fish for bass in this lake-dotted region.

Campsites, facilities: All 21 full-hookup sites are for RVs up to 40 feet long. Showers, restrooms, and a dump station are available. All areas are wheelchair accessible, according to management. One mile away are groceries, a restaurant, and laundry facilities. Children are not permitted, but they can visit campers here. Leashed pets are allowed.

Reservations, fees: Reservations are recommended in winter. Sites are $17 per night for two, plus $2 for each additional person. Credit cards are not accepted. Long-term stays are OK for adults.

Directions: From Winter Haven, go south on U.S. 17, passing Highway 559. At Bartow Municipal Airport, turn right onto Spirit Lake Road. Continue less than two miles to Thornhill Road. Turn right. The campground is on the right at the junction with Crystal Beach Road.

Contact: A-OK Campground, 6959 Thornhill Road, Winter Haven, FL 33880, 863/294-9091.

173 LAKESHORE PALMS TRAVEL PARK

Rating: 2

South of Winter Haven

Orlando map, grid b3, page 240

From Lakeshore Palms you can see the distant, towering spindle of Cypress Gardens' "Island in the Sky" sightseeing ride, which is vaguely akin to Seattle's Space Needle. Best known for its water-ski shows and beautiful grounds, Cypress Gardens closed in April 2003 but is expected to reopen to the public after the state of Florida purchases it under a land preservation program. About two miles north of the historic tourist attraction, this little snowbird travel park offers 40 grassy campsites fitted onto about two acres. A fence and hedges enclose the property.

Although the park sits on 100-acre Lake Grassy, don't use that as a directional guide. At least one map shows another body of water in this lake-dotted region sharing that name. Instead, look for one-mile-wide Lake Eloise, located north of the park. Bass anglers and water-skiers find fun in the region's lakes. Bicyclists pedal past orange groves and lakes east of the park on County Road 540A. Disney World is 33 miles north.

Campsites, facilities: Forty RV sites (32 full-

hookup) and two tent sites are provided (two have water and electricity). Among all of these, 15 are available for overnighters and 10 for seasonal visitors. Shuffleboard and winter programs keep campers entertained. Showers, restrooms, picnic tables, a screened picnic pavilion, a dump station, a boat ramp, boat rentals, telephone hookups, and laundry facilities are available. Cable TV is reserved for monthly campers. Groceries and a restaurant are two miles away. Children may camp short-term. Quiet, leashed pets are allowed.

Reservations, fees: Reservations are required from October to April and are recommended at other times. Sites are $22 per night for two, plus $2 for each additional person and a small fee for using electric heaters or air-conditioning. Credit cards are not accepted. Long-term stays are OK for adults.

Directions: Follow highway signs to Cypress Gardens; the campground is about two miles north of the park entrance. Or, from Winter Haven, take U.S. 17 south over the bridge past the Cleveland Indians spring training ballpark and go to the next stoplight. Turn left onto County Road 655. Travel about two miles to the next stoplight. Turn left by the convenience store onto Eagle Lake Loop Road, which becomes Eloise Loop Road/County Road 540A. The campground is about two miles ahead on your right.

Contact: Lakeshore Palms Travel Park, 4800 Eloise Loop Road, Winter Haven, FL 33884, 863/324-1339.

174 PARAKEET PARK

Rating: 2

On South Scenic Highway (State Road 17) south of Lake Wales

Orlando map, grid b4, page 240

On your approach to this 20-acre park, don't be surprised if you need to slow your speed to follow a truck laden with a heap of oranges. You're in the northern portion of Florida's fabled citrus belt. Surrounded by orange groves, the park nonetheless has a residential feel: Campers are outnumbered by residents of the 103 mobile homes.

Retirees flock to this lake region in winter to escape blustery northern temperatures and wade in the sun-dappled pool. Nearby is the Historic Bok Sanctuary. Orlando's theme parks are about 45 minutes north.

Campsites, facilities: All 25 full-hookup sites are for RVs up to 36 feet long and have picnic tables. A pool, a game room, shuffleboard, and winter activities in the wheelchair-accessible clubhouse entertain campers. Showers, restrooms, a dump station, cable TV, telephone hookups, and laundry facilities are available. Groceries and a restaurant are within two miles. Children may camp only on a short-term basis. Small pets are permitted. The campground is closed during the summer.

Reservations, fees: Reservations are recommended. Sites are $15 per night for two people, plus $1 for each additional person and $2 for using electric heaters or air-conditioning. Credit cards are not accepted. Long-term rates are available.

Directions: From Lake Wales, drive 2.4 miles south on South Scenic Highway/State Road 17 to the park.

Contact: Parakeet Park, 2400 South Scenic Highway/State Road 17, Lake Wales, FL 33859, 863/676-2812.

175 LAKE WALES CAMPGROUND

Rating: 6

South of Lake Wales
Orlando map, grid b4, page 240

Oaks and the sparse needles of pine trees lend shade to some grassy campsites at this busy winter spot, but other sites are sunny. A shaded walkway leads through a flower garden, and a small natural pond adds to the scenery of the 14-acre park. The new owners have brought in lots to do. Nearby are the Historic Bok Sanc-

tuary, a hilly garden spot perfect for picnics at its 3 P.M. carillon recitals; and Le Chalet Suzanne, where more than a few diners have landed private planes at the on-site airstrip to feast by candlelight on six-course gourmet dinners. Orlando-area theme parks are one hour north.

Campsites, facilities: Eight tent sites and 108 RV sites (60 pull-through, 100 full-hookup) are provided. Each site has a picnic table. Shuffleboard courts, horseshoe pits, a playground, wintertime activities, and a wheelchair-accessible recreation room entertain campers. The recreation hall has a raised stage, dance floor, kitchen, and entertainment center. Coffee is served every morning, and on Sundays, there are church services. Showers, restrooms, trailer rentals, and laundry facilities are provided on the grounds. The recreation room is also wheelchair accessible, and the park's roads are paved. Groceries and a restaurant are within 1.5 miles. Children may camp for up to two weeks. Leashed pets are permitted.

Reservations, fees: Reservations are recommended. Sites are $17 per night for two people, plus $2 for each additional adult and $1 per child. Major credit cards are accepted. Long-term stays are OK.

Directions: From State Road 60 at Lake Wales, drive three miles south on U.S. 27 to the park entrance.

Contact: Lake Wales Campground, 15898 U.S. 27, Lake Wales, FL 33859, 863/638-9011, fax 863/638-2873, email: lakewalesrv@surfbest.net.

176 LAKEMONT RIDGE HOME AND RV PARK

Rating: 4

In Frostproof
Orlando map, grid b4, page 240

Retirees flock here to partake of a very busy social schedule planned by an activities director, such as exercises, dances, dinners, crafts, live entertainment, bingo, and seasonal events like luaus and holidays parties. There are even community campfires and church services. A computer with Internet access is available in the recreation hall. The park has ambitious development plans to add several hundred more sites. A park model section lies just west of the RV section.

Campsites, facilities: Among 55 available RV sites, 45 are for seasonal visitors and 10 for overnighters. All have full hookups, picnic tables, and cable TV. Phone service is available for long-staying visitors. Restrooms, showers, laundry facilities, a pool, a recreation hall, shuffleboard courts, and a large dog-walk area are on site. Children are allowed. Leashed pets are permitted.

Reservations, fees: Reservations are recommended. Sites are $24 per night for two people, plus $2 per extra person. Credit cards are not accepted. Long-term rates are available.

Directions: From the intersection of U.S. 98 and U.S. 27 in Frostproof, drive east on U.S. 98 about two miles. The park is just past County Road 630 on the right.

Contact: Lakemont Ridge Home and RV Park, 2000 Maine Street, Frostproof, FL 33843, 863/635-4472, fax 863/635-1627, email: lakemontrv@cs.com.

177 LILY LAKE GOLF RESORT

Rating: 7

South of Frostproof

Orlando map, grid b4, page 240

This really can't be considered a campground at all, and maybe even the term RV park is stretching it a little. RV campers are welcome to rent a limited number of sites from owners of the existing lots, but the emphasis is on selling "RV portes" and park models. Of course, the amenities are spectacular. You can fish on Lily Lake and guests have free use of boats. The golf course is a major draw for the mostly retirement-age clientele.

Campsites, facilities: A limited number of RV sites (around 15) are available for rent from owners of lots at this new, sprawling manufactured home community. Full hookups, cable TV, full security, and a clubhouse are available. (Pop-up campers and truck campers are prohibited.) On the premises are a heated pool, a golf course, a fishing lake, billiards, a dog-walk area, tennis and shuffleboard courts, and a recreation hall. All areas are wheelchair accessible. Children are not welcome. Leashed pets are permitted (limit of two).

Reservations, fees: Reservations are recommended. Sites are $30 per night for two people. Major credit cards are accepted. Long-term stays are available.

Directions: From the intersection of U.S. 98 and U.S. 27, drive south a few miles on U.S. 27. The resort is on the east side.

Contact: Lily Lake Golf Resort, 500 U.S. 27 South, Frostproof, FL 33843, 863/635-3685 or 800/654-5177, website: www.lilylake.com.

178 CAMP INN RESORTS

Rating: 7

In Frostproof

Orlando map, grid b4, page 240

Located down the road from the small Lake Wales Municipal Airport, an RV dealer, and other commercial establishments, this 85-acre park is big: Indeed, 45 campsites line up side by side at its widest point (Evergreen Circle). And the place has not one, but three, laundry rooms. Paved roads pass the grassy RV sites, where some campers spend months or even years.

Near the entrance on busy U.S. 27 are a handful of water- and electricity-equipped sites, as well as two pools—one heated, the other not. Beyond that, a section of pull-through camping spots leads to eight shuffleboard courts and an 8,000-square-foot recreation hall at the park's center. Farther back, you'll find the bulk of the campsites—meaning most RVs are insulated from U.S. 27. To overlook an oval meadow, ask about sites on Laurel or Seagrape. For pull-through spots closest to a small lake (across a park road), consider sites B1, C1, D1, E5, E6, or E7. Frostproof isn't exactly a tourism mecca, but Orlando theme parks are about one hour away.

Campsites, facilities: Nearly all 796 RV sites have full hookups; 190 are pull-through. Tenters can make camp at 23 sites. There are picnic tables at each site. Two pools, a whirlpool, a game room, a recreation hall, shuffleboard, horseshoes, and winter social programs entertain campers. Showers, restrooms, a dump station, LP gas sales, and laundry facilities are available. Management says all areas are wheelchair accessible. A restaurant and groceries are within two miles. Children may camp on a short-term basis. Leashed pets should use the entrance-area dog walk.

Reservations, fees: Reservations are recommended. Sites are $22 per night for two people, plus $1 for each additional person and $2 for cable TV. Major credit cards are accepted. Long-term stays are OK for adults, preferably age 50 and up.

Directions: From State Road 60 in Lake Wales, turn south onto U.S. 27. The campground is eight miles ahead on the right side of the road.

Contact: Camp Inn Resorts, 10400 Highway 27, Frostproof, FL 33843, 863/635-2500, website: www.chateaucommunities.com.

179 LAKE KISSIMMEE STATE PARK
🚶 🚲 ⛴ 🚐 🏕 🐕 🏕 ♿ 🚙 ⛺

Rating: 10

At Lake Kissimmee east of Lake Wales
Orlando map, grid b3, page 240

This nearly eight-square-mile remote state park is famous for its weekend living-history demonstrations of an 1876 "cow camp." Just walk 50 yards from the parking lot to the 200-acre pen of scrub cows to swap stories around a campfire with a costumed ranger posing as a "cow hunter." Don't make reference to modern-day things such as MP3 players or cell phones, though, because the cowpoke will claim to not understand you. He'll instead hearken back to simpler days—when frontier cowboys herded cattle and, earlier, provided the Confederacy with much of its beef.

Campers sleep north of the cow camp along two loops near an observation tower, where visitors climb three landings to gaze onto an expanse of prairielike pasture. Each shell-rock campsite is equipped with a grill, a picnic table, and a fire ring handy for building campfires to roast marshmallows by. Plentiful picnic tables sit at creekside or beneath the twisted branches of oaks elsewhere in the park.

Look for turkeys, bald eagles, deer, and a sea of pickerelweed stretching toward the horizon during walks along 13 miles of hiking trails. A short nature loop and two long loop trails that encompass much of the park—one north of Zipper Canal, the other south of it—are reachable from the marina-area concession stand north of the cow camp. Notice the park's varied landscape: wide-open wet prairies, sun-dappled pine flatlands, and shady hammocks with orchids and mosses. Bring mosquito repellent for a more pleasant walk.

A launch ramp leads boaters a short distance east to the park's namesake, Lake Kissimmee, where anglers try for specks, bass, and shellcrackers in Florida's third largest lake. Canoeists who bring their own craft can paddle five to seven miles along a pretty loop starting at Zipper Canal and heading west (counterclockwise) to Lake Rosalie, Rosalie Creek, Tiger Lake, Tiger Creek, and the eastern corner of 47-square-mile Lake Kissimmee, before returning to the boat ramp. The placid waters you'll see here eventually flow south down the Kissimmee River to the Everglades and Florida Bay at the state's southern tip, some 200 miles distant. At night, you'll listen to the croaking of frogs, but on busy fishing weekends, the roar of far-off boat engines can also be heard.

Campsites, facilities: All 60 sites have water, electricity, a picnic table, a grill, and a fire ring for RVs, tents, and other campers. A playground, nature trails, showers, restrooms, a dump station, and a 50-person-capacity youth camping area are available. Two campsites, the fishing pier, and restrooms are wheelchair accessible. Laundry facilities, a restaurant, snacks, and bait are within five miles, and groceries are 15 miles away. Kids and pets are welcome.

Reservations, fees: Reservations are recommended; call ReserveAmerica at 800/326-3521. Sites are $8 to $14 per night for four people, plus $2 for each additional person. Major credit cards are accepted. The maximum stay is two weeks.

Directions: From U.S. 27 at Lake Wales, travel about nine miles east on State Road 60. Turn left at Boy Scout Road. After three miles, turn right at Camp Mack Road. The park is five miles ahead.

Contact: Lake Kissimmee State Park, 14248 Camp Mack Road, Lake Wales, FL 33853, 863/696-1112.

180 CAMP MACK'S RIVER RESORT

Rating: 8

At Lake Kissimmee east of Lake Wales
Orlando map, grid b3, page 240

Fish camps are usually not known for their amenities, but this one is pretty deluxe. A new pool and clubhouse were recently built, and the park has large sites for big rigs while retaining a wooded atmosphere. But the main deal is fishing, airboat rides, and boating on Lake Kissimmee and the nearby other waters famed for bass. Lake Kissimmee State Park is nearby.

Campsites, facilities: There are 100 RV sites and three tent sites. Park models are being sold on the property, and cabins are for rent. All sites have full hookups, concrete pads, picnic tables, and cable TV. Restrooms, showers, laundry facilities, a pool, a boat ramp, a fish-cleaning station, a clubhouse, bait and tackle, a store, and boat rentals are available. Most areas are wheelchair accessible. Children are welcome. Leashed pets are permitted.

Reservations, fees: Reservations are recommended. Sites are $30 per night for four peo-

ple, plus $10 per extra person and $5 for cable TV. Major credit cards are accepted. Long-term rates are available.

Directions: From U.S. 27 at Lake Wales, travel about nine miles east on State Road 60. Turn left at Boy Scout Road. After three miles, turn right at Camp Mack Road. The park is six miles ahead.

Contact: Camp Mack's River Resort, 14900 Camp Mack Road, Lake Wales, FL 33898, 863/696-1108 or 800/243-8013, fax 863/696-1500, website: www.campmack.com.

181 FALLEN OAK PRIMITIVE CAMPGROUND

Rating: 6

In Lake Kissimmee State Park
east of Lake Wales
Orlando map, grid b3, page 240

The name of this campground is your first clue that these primitive sites are at the edge of an old oak hammock. One of the biggest oak trees has fallen over, providing food and shelter for lots of small critters. The approximately six-mile loop trail on which these campsites are located is part of a 13-mile stretch of the Florida National Scenic Trail that runs through the state park. Be forewarned that the trail may be very muddy during the June-to-September rainy season; be sure to check with park rangers ahead of time. This campsite is not too far from the main camp road but is still far removed from the most-used parts of the park, where you'll find plenty of recreation opportunities, including canoeing, fishing, boating, and bicycling. On cooler weekends, expect to have some company here. If you wind up alone, consider yourself lucky.

Campsites, facilities: Primitive camping areas accommodate about 12 people, but you must hike three to 3.5 miles to reach your tent site. A picnic table and campfire area are provided. There is no piped water, no toilet, and no other facilities. Bring water, food, mosquito repellent, and all other supplies. Children are welcome. Pets, firearms, and alcoholic beverages are prohibited.

Reservations, fees: Reservations are recommended. Camping costs $6 per night for two people and $3 per extra person. Major credit cards are accepted. Stays are limited to two weeks.

Directions: From U.S. 27 at Lake Wales, travel approximately nine miles east on State Road 60, then turn left onto Boy Scout Road. In three miles, turn right at Camp Mack Road. The park entrance is five miles ahead.

Contact: Lake Kissimmee State Park, 14248 Camp Mack Road, Lake Wales, FL 33853, 863/696-1112.

182 BUSTER ISLAND PRIMITIVE CAMPGROUND

Rating: 6

In Lake Kissimmee State Park east of Lake Wales

Orlando map, grid b3, page 240

Secluded Buster Island is surrounded on six sides by water, including Lakes Tiger, Kissimmee, and Rosalie. But you'd be hard-pressed to know you're on an island because creeks, not lakes, border three of its six sides. The campsites are part of the six-mile Florida National Scenic Trail loop. You'll pass through oak hammocks and scrubby flatwoods of pine and oak. Be aware that the trail may be very muddy during the June-to-September rainy season, so check with park rangers ahead of time. If you want to take advantage of the canoeing, boating, fishing, and biking opportunities here, do it before or after your hike because they are accessible only at the main portion of the park.

Campsites, facilities: Primitive camping areas accommodate about 12 people, but you must hike three to 3.5 miles to reach your tent site. A picnic table and campfire area are provided. There is no piped water and no other

facilities. Bring water, food, mosquito repellent, and all other supplies. Children and pets are welcome.

Reservations, fees: Reservations are recommended. Camping costs $6 per night for two people, plus $3 per extra person. Major credit cards are accepted. Stays are limited to two weeks.

Directions: From U.S. 27 at Lake Wales, travel about nine miles east on State Road 60. Turn left at Boy Scout Road. In three miles, turn right at Camp Mack Road. The park is five miles ahead.

Contact: Lake Kissimmee State Park, 14248 Camp Mack Road, Lake Wales, FL 33853, 863/696-1112.

183 THE HARBOR RV RESORT AND MARINA

Rating: 6

On Lake Rosalie east of Lake Wales

Orlando map, grid b3, page 240

If the boat ramp on seven-square-mile Lake Rosalie isn't enough to convince you, then the bass logo makes it clear: Fishing is popular at this 13-acre marina and RV park set in a relaxed, lake-dotted region. Many campers enjoy this park's tranquillity and the bright glow of the sun rising over the lake. For a lakeside camping spot, request sites 37, 54, 55, or 56. Lots 99 through 104 are secluded spots near the woods.

Paved, 5 mph streets pass the grassy/concrete-pad sites, most of which are shaded by oaks. Outside the park, much of the land bordering the lake is undeveloped, making it easy on the eyes. Three miles away is the 1800s-style cow camp at Lake Kissimmee State Park (see campground in this chapter). Orlando-area theme parks are about 45 minutes north.

Campsites, facilities: RVs and tents can be accommodated at 55 full-hookup sites (10 pull-through). The park caters to mix of seasonal visitors, baby boomers, and first-time RVers. A pool, shuffleboard, and a recreation hall entertain campers. Showers, restrooms, a marina, and laundry facilities are available. Planned activities get started in November, with fishing and shuffleboard tournaments, dinners, art classes, church services, and day tours, to name just a few. Children are welcome. Pets are permitted.

Reservations, fees: Reservations are recommended in winter. Sites are $19 to $30 per night for two people, plus $2 for each additional person, $2 for using heaters or air conditioners, and $1.50 for cable TV. Major credit cards are accepted. Long-term stays are OK.

Directions: From U.S. 27 at Lake Wales, travel about 9.9 miles east on State Road 60. Turn left at Boy Scout Road. In 3.5 miles, turn right at Camp Mack Road. Continue 1.7 miles to the park entrance.

Contact: The Harbor RV Resort and Marina, 10511 Monroe Court, Lake Wales, FL 33898, 863/696-1194, fax 863/696-4000, website: www.harbor-rv-marina.com.

184 GRAPE HAMMOCK RV PARK AND MARINA

Rating: 3

On the Kissimmee River east of Lake Wales
Orlando map, grid b4, page 240

Fishing is the lure at this relaxed spot on the Kissimmee River. In bad weather, die-hard anglers can cast lines from the riverbanks, but the usual routine is to head a short distance to the broad waters of Florida's third largest lake—Lake Kissimmee. Campers have been known to bring back some big bass. Also known as Grape Hammock Fish Camp, these 21 acres are rustic. Cabins sit beneath a canopy of oaks. Campsites are sandy or grassy, with some situated near the canal. Three-wheelers may ride slowly through the park to get to the main road, and dogs may walk leash-free unless they cause trouble.

Professional guides Johnny Doub and Mike Gruber consider the odds of catching a 10-pound bass best from January until summer's

end; call them at 800/826-0621. Campground motorboats rent for $40. Fun-loving houseboaters have prompted the implementation of a park rule: Parties must move indoors at 10 P.M.; any offending houseboater must leave if "noise, arguing, fighting, etc., continues, and the law is called again."

Campsites, facilities: Seven no-hookup tent sites are set apart from 59 full-hookup RV sites (10 pull-through). A pool, shuffleboard, a recreation room, showers, restrooms, a dump station, cabin rentals, a boat ramp, a dock, boat rentals, airboat tours, houseboat moorings, bait, tackle, and laundry facilities are on the premises. Management says the recreation room, restrooms, and telephone are wheelchair accessible. A restaurant and golf course are within three miles. Children under 12 must be adult-supervised at the pool. Pets are welcome, but disruptive animals should be leashed.

Reservations, fees: Reservations are recommended. Sites are $14 to $22 per night for two adults and two children, plus $1 per extra person and $2 for cable TV. Major credit cards are accepted. Long-term stays are OK.

Directions: From Lake Wales, travel 22 miles east on State Road 60. Turn left at Grape Hammock Road. The entrance is 1.25 miles ahead.

Contact: Grape Hammock RV Park and Marina, 1400 Grape Hammock Road, Lake Wales, FL 33853, 863/692-1500, website: www.grapehammock.com.

185 RIVER RANCH RV RESORT

Rating: 10

On the Kissimmee River between Lake Wales and Yeehaw Junction
Orlando map, grid b4, page 240

Families like this spot. The buffet is a popular choice at this spectacular resort's restaurant, which is located across the driveway from the on-site airstrip. Kids stop to buy candy at the snack bar between bouts of combat in the game room, and a guard stands posted at the resort's long entranceway. In short, this is the civilized, "front country" companion to the KICCO Wildlife Management Area next door (see next campground), and it's for RVs and motel guests only.

It's a special spot. The setting is rustic and woodsy, right next to the Kissimmee River in a rural section of Florida, but don't even think about roughing it. Choose from a campsite in a shady Old Florida oak hammock or a sunny site next to the canal where you can dock your boat. Fish from a riverbank, or try for bass from your own johnboat or canoe. Fishing guide services are available nearby; inquire at the registration desk. Don't miss taking at least a short hike down the Florida National Scenic Trail next door at KICCO Wildlife Management Area. Or, take a drive over to Lake Kissimmee State Park and check out the historic cow camp.

Campsites, facilities: All 367 RV sites have electricity, water, and cable TV access. Facilities include restrooms, showers, a dump station, an airstrip, a restaurant, laundry facilities, a boat dock, hiking trails, a game room, a snack bar, limited bait and tackle sales, guided horseback rides on weekends, golf, tennis courts, and meeting rooms. Other entertainment includes rodeos, "gunslinger" shows, trap shooting and gun range, a petting zoo, boat tours, airboat rides, and more. Many areas are wheelchair accessible. Children and pets are permitted in the camping area but not in the resort's motel rooms.

Reservations, fees: Reservations are recommended. Sites are $35 to $45 per night for four people, plus $2 for each extra person. Major credit cards are accepted.

Directions: From Florida's Turnpike at Yeehaw Junction, take Exit 193 and travel west on State Road 60 about 25 miles, crossing the Kissimmee River, and look for the entrance ahead on the left. From Lake Wales, head east on State Road 60 about 25 miles and look for the entrance on the right before you reach the Kissimmee River.

Contact: River Ranch RV Resort, 24700 State Road 60/P.O. Box 30421, River Ranch, FL 33867, 863/692-1321; fax: 863/692-9707, website: www.riverranchrv.com.

186 KICCO WILDLIFE MANAGEMENT AREA

🚶 🚴 🏊 🐕 🏕

Rating: 8

On the Kissimmee River between Lake Wales and Yeehaw Junction

Orlando map, grid b4, page 240

Three remote and little-used camping spots along the Florida National Scenic Trail are just right for the backpacker who wants to get away from it all. And yet you're within an easy walk of showers, hot food, running water, and the rest of the amenities offered at the River Ranch RV Resort complex, located at the northern end of this wildlife management area.

The hiking trail stretches about eight miles along the length of this one-mile-wide green ribbon. The 12-square-mile area features deep, dark hammocks of oak trees covered with moss and resurrection ferns, as well as pine flatwoods, scrub, and some marshy areas and stands of cypress. The hiking trail runs parallel to the Kissimmee River. The U.S. Army Corps of Engineers straightened the gently meandering stream into a big, angular ditch in the 1960s. Now, the Corps is working with the South Florida Water Management District, owner of the KICCO property, on a restoration plan for the river.

The name KICCO (pronounced KISS-oh) comes from the 1920s-era Kissimmee Island Cattle Company, which grazed cattle here. Now the tract is managed jointly by the water district and the Florida Fish and Wildlife Conservation Commission. Check with the game commission's Lakeland office at 863/648-3203 for hunt dates. Be sure to wear orange-blaze clothing if you're camping during those times, which are generally around Thanksgiving and in the spring turkey season.

The first campsite is within one mile of the trailhead. Another is about three miles farther, and the third is another three miles past that. None of the sites is actually on the riverbank, but all three are very close to it.

Bicycling is allowed along the hiking trails only. You also can launch a canoe or boat at River Ranch RV Resort and travel downstream, although you might have a rough time finding a place to dock. To explore, hiking is your best bet.

Campsites, facilities: An indeterminate number of tenters can be accommodated at three sites along the Florida National Scenic Trail. No facilities are available. Bring water, food, mosquito repellent, and supplies. Pack out trash and bury human waste in a six-inch hole. Children and pets are permitted.

Reservations, fees: Reservations are not required to backpack and camp on the Florida National Scenic Trail, although you are advised to call the water management district ahead of time to check on conditions. Camping is free. (As for camping anywhere except on the trail, camping is allowed at designated sites only during hunting season.)

Directions: From Florida's Turnpike at Yeehaw Junction, take Exit 193 and travel west on State Road 60 about 25 miles, crossing the Kissimmee River, and look for the River Ranch RV Resort entrance ahead on the left. From Lake Wales, head east on State Road 60 about 25 miles and look for the resort entrance on the right before you reach the Kissimmee River. When you reach the security kiosk at River Ranch RV Resort, tell the guard you're headed to the Florida National Scenic Trail to hike.

Contact: Florida Trail Association, 5415 Southwest 13th Street, Gainesville, FL 32608, 352/378-8823 or 877/HIKE-FLA, website: www.florida-trail.org. For hunting or general information, try Florida Fish and Wildlife Conservation Commission, 941/648-3205.

187 LAKE MARIAN PARADISE

Rating: 3

On Lake Marian south of St. Cloud
Orlando map, grid a4, page 240

The definition of "paradise" may be debated by anyone who doesn't enjoy the main activity here—fishing, fishing, and more fishing. This is the classic fish camp, way out in the boonies near the sprawling hunting and hiking domain of the Three Lakes Wildlife Management Area (see campground in this chapter) and the Lake Marian Creek Management Area. Some retirees and a number of working people live at these sunny and shady sites full-time or at least long-term. The camp is set on Lake Marian, a 5,800-acre unspoiled lake. Besides fishing, you can hike in the wildlife management area, which seems to burst at the seams with critters compared with nearby urban Florida. Amenities are sparse, and you're a good 30-minute drive from the closest groceries. A small restaurant is located in the nearby hamlet of Kenansville.

Campsites, facilities: All 45 full-hookup sites are for RVs, and cable TV is available. On the premises are restrooms, showers, a dump station, picnic tables, a boat ramp, efficiency motel rentals, laundry facilities, bait and tackle, and boat rentals. Children may stay short-term. Pets are permitted, although management reserves the right to turn away pets that are troublesome.

Reservations, fees: Reservations are advised. Sites are $19.50 per night for two people, plus $5 for each additional person. Major credit cards are accepted. Adults are welcome for long-term stays.

Directions: From St. Cloud, take Highway 523/Canoe Creek Road south about 32 miles. When you see Arnold Road, turn right, heading southwest. It leads to the fish camp. If you reach the point where Highway 523 passes under Florida's Turnpike west of Kenansville, you've gone too far and should turn around. If you're coming from southern Florida, take

Florida's Turnpike to the Yeehaw Junction exit. Head north on U.S. 441 about 14 miles to Highway 523, turn left (west), and go about three miles to Arnold Road, where you'll turn left. **Contact:** Lake Marian Paradise, 901 Arnold Road, Kenansville, FL 34739, 407/436-1464.

188 THREE LAKES WILDLIFE MANAGEMENT AREA

Rating: 7

South of St. Cloud near Kenansville
Orlando map, grid a4, page 240

Turkeys scared by the sound of footsteps rush into tall grasses for camouflage at this relatively wildlife-packed, 53,000-acre tract. Improbably located within a reasonable drive from the big city lights of Disney World, this haven of hunters and hikers requires some pre-planning by getting all the current maps and regulations. The area is called Three Lakes because it sits between Lakes Kissimmee, Jackson, and Marian. After a rain, muddy trails are likely to sport more deer tracks and turkey prints than signs of humans. Look for bobcats or deer darting from a wooded area into the prairies.

You may camp only at hunter-designated campsites during hunting season, which varies from year to year. The rest of the time you can camp at all designated backpacking campsites on the Florida Trail. Call 352/378-8823 or see www.florida-trail.org for more information. These various backpacking sites include one that is a 1.5-mile walk from Parker House to Dry Pond, and a more-remote camping area that is about 75 yards across and features maybe a little more underbrush. The hiking trail winds through dry pine flatwoods and scrub communities as well as lusher hardwood hammocks.

It helps to have a four-wheel-drive vehicle in Three Lakes, and we would consider it more or less mandatory if you're hauling an RV when it's been raining. For day use, the roads are well suited for horseback riding and mountain biking. Anglers can head to the end of Road 16 to launch onto Lake Jackson.

Campsites, facilities: Three primitive camping areas accommodate an indeterminate number of RVs or tents during hunting season only. Three other primitive camping areas are accessible only to hikers on the Florida Trail. There are no facilities, so bring drinking water. In a few places you will find water pumps, but the water is not certified as safe for human consumption, although it is usable for washing off, watering animals, and so forth. Children and pets are permitted.

Reservations, fees: Sites are first-come, first-served and require a free permit from the Florida Fish and Wildlife Conservation Commission. When requesting a permit, ask for a map.

Directions: From St. Cloud, take Highway 523/Canoe Creek Road south about 25 miles. The wildlife management area sprawls over nearly 80 square miles. One entrance to the Florida Trail is on State Road 60, 14.5 miles west of the town of Yeehaw Junction. Others are 25 miles south of St. Cloud on Canoe Creek Road, off County Road 523 west off U.S. 441 near Kenansville, off U.S. 441 13.5 miles south of Holopaw.

Contact: Florida Fish and Wildlife Conservation Commission, Ocala Regional Office, 1239 Southwest 10th Street, Ocala, FL 34474, 352/732-1225, website: www.floridaconservation.org.

189 PIONEER CREEK RV PARK

Rating: 7

Off U.S. 17 south of Bowling Green
Orlando map, grid b4, page 240

A retirement lifestyle—not backwoods cookouts with Smokey the Bear—is what you'll get at Pioneer Creek RV Park, which offers paved, lighted streets and clean RV sites where outdoor clotheslines are forbidden. From golf at 8:30 A.M. to pinochle in the smoke-free clubhouse at 7 P.M., the rotating schedule of winter activities can keep visitors busy in case the heated pool and woodworking shop aren't enough. Many retirees spend months at the oak-shaded RV sites, whose small mowed lawns and, in some cases, attached screen rooms lend a residential feel to the park. Campers on Drum Drive and the northern portion of Arrowhead Loop back onto a conservation area that divides the park. Nearby is the Paynes Creek State Historic Site, where a Seminole Indian trading post once stood. Although life in this region of Florida is slow paced, you'll find that a Ford dealership, a citrus stand, a pet supply store, and other businesses down a ways on U.S. 17, in Wauchula, are reminders of urban life.

Campsites, facilities: This park offers 377 full-hookup sites for retirees in RVs. A pool, a clubhouse, a woodworking shop, shuffleboard, horseshoes, pool tables, bocce (lawn bowling) courts, and planned wintertime activities entertain campers. Showers, restrooms, a dump station, picnic areas, winter church services, cable TV (long-term campers only), and laundry facilities are available. All areas are wheelchair accessible. Children are not allowed. Campers with pets sleep in a designated section; one leashed pet is permitted per site.

Reservations, fees: Reservations are suggested. Sites are $21 per night for two people, plus $2.50 per extra person. Major credit cards are accepted. Long-term rates are available. The park's office is closed in the summer.

Directions: From Main Street/State Road 64A in Wauchula, go north about six miles on U.S. 17 to Broward Street (just south of the Polk County line) to the park, on the right.

Contact: Pioneer Creek RV Park, 138 East Broward Street, Bowling Green, FL 33834, 863/375-4343, website: www.rvresorts.com.

190 WAGON WHEEL RV PARK

Rating: 5

Off U.S. 17 north of Wauchula
Orlando map, grid b4, page 240

Located 50 miles from the beach in a citrus-dotted portion of the state often overlooked by tourists, the 20-acre, adults-only park is .5 mile off the main drag, U.S. 17. Retirees take part in wintertime social programs before retiring to their grassy RV sites with concrete patios. Three miles to the northeast is the Paynes Creek State Historic Site, where a Seminole Indian trading post once stood. Wauchula, a thriving agricultural community, is three miles south.

Campsites, facilities: This adults-only park has 265 full-hookup sites for RVs up to 40 feet long. Showers, restrooms, laundry facilities, a recreation room, horseshoes, shuffleboard, and winter social programs are available. Management says facilities are wheelchair accessible. Children are only permitted to visit park residents; campers must be at least 18. Leashed pets under 30 pounds are allowed; management must preapprove the breed.

Reservations, fees: Reservations are not necessary. Sites are $14 per night for two adults, plus $3 per extra person. Credit cards are not accepted. Long-term stays are encouraged.

Directions: From the junction of U.S. 17 and State Road 62 north of Wauchula, travel .5 mile north on U.S. 17 to Bostick Road. Turn left and continue .5 mile west to the park, on the right.

Contact: Wagon Wheel RV Park, 2908 Red Barn Lane, Bowling Green, FL 33834, 863/773-3157.

191 CRYSTAL LAKE VILLAGE RV AND MOBILE HOME PARK

Rating: 7

Off U.S. 17 north of Wauchula
Orlando map, grid b4, page 240

Orange groves flank three sides of this 37-acre community, set in the sleepy inland region of Florida. Retirees escape cold northern winters by spending six months here, passing the time with square dances, arts and crafts, trips on the park's 29-passenger bus, and fishing at a three-acre stocked lake. Lighted streets and paved driveways lead up to the plentiful park models and the RV sites, some of which are shaded. If the 18-hole golf course located about 1.25 miles away doesn't fit the bill, then try another course six miles distant. Disney World is a long day trip to the northeast.

Campsites, facilities: Open to campers age 55 and over, this 360-site mobile home/RV park offers more than 50 full-hookup sites with paved driveways and patios for RVs up to 35 feet (some 40 feet) long. Showers, restrooms, a pool, a hot tub, trailer rentals, horseshoes, shuffleboard, a recreation hall, billiards, planned activities, a fishing lake, and laundry facilities are provided. Management says all facilities are wheelchair accessible. A restaurant, groceries, and an 18-hole golf course are within 1.5 miles. Leashed pets are permitted.

Reservations, fees: Reservations are recommended. Sites are $14 per night for two people, plus $3 for each additional person and an additional charge for cable TV. Credit cards are accepted. Long-term stays are OK.

Directions: From Wauchula, travel three miles north on U.S. 17 to Maxwell Drive, which is .25 mile south of State Road 62. Turn right onto Maxwell and continue east to the park.

Contact: Crystal Lake Village RV and Mobile Home Park, 237 Maxwell Drive, Wauchula, FL 33873, 863/773-3582 or 800/661-3582, fax 863/773-0410.

192 LITTLE CHARLIE CREEK RV PARK

Rating: 5

At the Peace River north of Wauchula
Orlando map, grid b4, page 240

Household garbage must be placed in dark-colored bags and recyclables in clear or white bags for the twice-weekly curbside pickup—a hint that this park prizes cleanliness and neatness. The attraction at this adult park is mixing with your neighbors at potluck dinners and organized games of pokeno, bingo, shuffleboard, and pool. For anglers, the lure is the Peace River, which is located just west of the RV park. Little Charlie Creek passes by here, too, to intersect with the Peace River. Keeping the peace is a good idea at the RV park, set in a sleepy section of Florida. Among the 31 park rules: Anything hung on a clothesline must be removed by 4 P.M., and lawn watering must be done early in the morning or late in the evening, and in moderation. Most people are staying for the winter, though there are a few full-timers.

Campsites, facilities: The adult-oriented park has 188 full-hookup sites for RVs. Showers, restrooms, laundry facilities, shuffleboard, horseshoes, planned activities, and a recreation hall are provided. Visiting children must be accompanied by an adult while in the recreation center or other common areas. Leashed, immunized pets are permitted.

Reservations, fees: Reservations are suggested but overnighters are welcome. Sites are $20 per night for two people. Major credit cards are accepted. Long-term stays are OK.

Directions: From the intersection of U.S. 17 and Main Street in Wauchula, drive north on U.S. 17 about one mile. Turn right at REA Road at the Wal-Mart. Soon after, turn left onto Heard Bridge Road. Travel north about two miles, crossing the Peace River. The campground is to your right.

Contact: Little Charlie Creek RV Park, 1850 Heard Bridge Road, Wauchula, FL 33873, 863/773-0088, fax 863/773-2274.

193 RIVER VALLEY RV RESORT

Rating: 10

South of Wauchula
Orlando map, grid b4, page 240

With the Peace River running alongside and a campground boat ramp, anglers and boaters find this resort just their style, but so will families and campers with pets. Part of the park has a lovely wooded canopy, and children are now welcomed year-round. Recently added were a playground, sand and grass volleyball areas, and a basketball court. A separate area of the park is set aside for older snowbirds. Owners Randy and Barb Perry invite you to relax on their "famous verandas" overlooking the river and oak trees. This park has much to offer for the camper who likes a nature-oriented setting with civilized amenities and lots of sports.

Campsites, facilities: This sprawling, 73-acre, all-ages resort has 454 sites laid out in neat suburb-style. About 226 tents can be accommodated in a large field, as well. RV sites have full hookups and picnic tables; big rigs can be accommodated. Restrooms, showers, a dump station, laundry facilities, a heated pool, a snack bar, an activity center/lodge, a boat ramp, shuffleboard courts, propane gas sales, and a nature trail are on the premises. Many areas are wheelchair accessible. Children are welcome. Leashed pets are permitted.

Reservations, fees: Reservations are recommended. Sites are $23.50 to $33.50 per night for two people, plus $4 per extra person. Major credit cards are accepted. Stay as long as you wish.

Directions: From Wauchula, drive two miles south on U.S. 17 to the resort, which is on the east side.

Contact: River Valley RV Resort, 2555 U.S. 17 South, Wauchula, FL 33873, 863/735-8888 or 888/977-7878, fax 863/753-8691, website: www.rivervalleyrvresort.com.

194 ADELAIDE SHORES RV RESORT (FORMERLY GOLDEN SUNSET)

Rating: 7

North of Avon Park
Orlando map, grid b4, page 240

This lakeside retirement community offers social programs for residents and guests; they enjoy bingo, cards, parties, shows, trips, and cruises. Many campers are seasonal; Avon Park's population swells from 9,000 to 13,000 in the winter. The RV resort is on a 96-acre lake, affording opportunities for fishing. The swimming pool (heated to 85 degrees) and tennis courts are also popular. In the area, numerous golf courses are located within a 10-minute drive.

Campsites, facilities: This adults-only park offers 200-plus full-hookup sites for RVs; the other 200 sites are being sold for RVs or park models. On the premises are restrooms, showers, a dump station, two laundry facilities, a 5,000-square-foot clubhouse, trailer rentals, an Olympic-sized pool with tiki bar, a dock with boat slips, an exercise room, a dance floor, tennis courts, bocce ball (lawn bowling) courts, shuffleboard, horseshoes, pool table, and a putting green. Cable TV (free) and telephone service are available. Sites are 45 feet by 65 feet with concrete pads. All areas are said to be wheelchair accessible. Groceries and restaurants are within one mile. Pets are permitted.

Reservations, fees: Reservations are recommended. Sites are $27 per night. Major credit cards are accepted. Stay as long as you like.

Directions: From Avon Park, travel north four miles on U.S. 27 to the park.

Contact: Adelaide Shores RV Resort, 2881 U.S. 27 North, Avon Park, FL 33826, 863/453-2226 or 800/848-1924, website: www.adelaide shores.com.

195 ORANGE BLOSSOM FELLOWSHIP COMMUNITY

Rating: 2

In Avon Park
Orlando map, grid b4, page 240

Visitors to this Christian community are subject to certain restrictions: no alcohol, no tobacco, no immodest clothing. Each February and March there is an old-style "camp meeting." People of various Christian faiths have chosen to retire here. In fact, the RV sites basically are an adjunct to the more-permanent mobile homes. Some residents like to fish at a small on-site lake. Unsurprisingly for this area of Florida, the park borders orange groves. Campers have a choice of sandy, concrete pad, and grassy sites. Shade is sparse. Most folks stay two to three months in the winter.

Campsites, facilities: All 15 full-hookup sites are for RVs. On the premises are restrooms, showers, shuffleboard, and a recreation room with regularly scheduled church services. Groceries, a restaurant, and laundry facilities are about three miles away. Leashed pets under 30 pounds and children are allowed.

Reservations, fees: Reservations are recommended. Sites are $10 per night for two people, plus $5 for each additional person. Credit cards are not accepted. Long-term stays are OK.

Directions: From U.S. 27, take State Road 64/Main Street east through the town of Avon Park. After about two miles, turn left onto County Road 17A. drive about three miles and look for the park ahead on the left

Contact: Orange Blossom Fellowship Community, 1400 County Road 17A North, Avon Park, FL 33825, 863/453-6052, fax 863/453-0301.

196 STEWARTS MOBILE VILLAGE

Rating: 1

On U.S. 27 in Avon Park
Orlando map, grid b4, page 240

RVs and tents are outnumbered by mobile homes at this small roadside park located down the street from Avon Park Municipal Airport. It's within walking distance of a shopping center, and RV repairs and service are on site. You also can cross the street to fish from the piers at .25-mile-wide Lake Onaka.

Campsites, facilities: Two tent sites are set apart from seven full-hookup sites for RVs up to 40 feet long. On the premises are restrooms, showers, a dump station, picnic tables, laundry facilities, rental trailers, and horseshoes. The

restrooms are wheelchair accessible. Children and pets are welcome.

Reservations, fees: Reservations are recommended. Sites are $20 per night for two people, plus $2.50 for each extra person. Major credit cards are accepted. Long-term rates are available.

Directions: Take U.S. 27 south from Avon Park to the campground.

Contact: Stewarts Mobile Village, 1116 U.S. 27 South, Avon Park, FL 33825, 863/453-3849 or 800/724-7502, email: stewarts@tmni.net.

197 REFLECTIONS ON SILVER LAKE

Rating: 6

South of Avon Park
Orlando map, grid b4, page 240

A "winter destination community" for the over-55 crowd, this family-owned park is divided into three areas: RVs, park models, and mobile homes. A full-time activities coordinator fills the hours for RVers who come from all over the country and Canada to spend the season here. The park fronts onto Silver Lake for pretty views and fishing.

Campsites, facilities: There are 338 RV sites, of which eight are available for overnighters. All have full hookups. Restrooms, showers, laundry facilities, a heated pool, fishing lake, a boat dock, two recreation halls, shuffleboard, *pétanque* and bocce courts, and a dog-walk area are on-site. Children are allowed as guests visiting campers. Leashed pets are permitted.

Reservations, fees: Reservations are recommended. Sites are $20 per night for two people, plus $2 per extra person. Major credit cards are accepted. Long-term rates are available.

Directions: From the intersection of U.S. 27 and State Road 64, drive south on U.S. 27 1.5 miles. The park entrance is across the street from South Florida Community College.

Contact: Reflections on Silver Lake, 1850 U.S. 27 South, Avon Park, FL 33825, 863/453-5756, fax (863)453-9468, email: rosl@strato.net.

198 LAKE BONNET VILLAGE

Rating: 7

At Lake Bonnet south of Avon Park
Orlando map, grid b4, page 240

This combination campground and mobile home park is in a quiet, woodsy setting overlooking spring-fed 260-acre Lake Bonnet. Many sites are shaded by large oaks, and the view of the lake is pretty. Favored by retirees, this is a nice option for those who prefer a more nature-oriented setting. The RV sites have concrete pads, whereas the three tent sites are grassy. Nearly one-half the sites are occupied by people who live here year-round, and a good portion of the rest stay here on a long-term basis. You can swim in the heated pool, relax in a hot tub, or go boating, fishing, or water-skiing on Lake Bonnet. Highlands Hammock State Park is about 15 miles away (see next campground). If you're feeling adventurous, check out the secluded hiking trails at the 106,000-acre Avon Park Air Force Range (see campground in this chapter), approximately 12 miles away.

Campsites, facilities: The 209 full-hookup RV sites are set apart from three tent sites. Five RV sites are pull-through. On the premises are restrooms, showers, a dump station, laundry facilities, picnic tables, a wheelchair-accessible recreation room, a pool, a hot tub, a boat ramp, a dock, boat and canoe rentals, a playground, horseshoes, shuffleboard, volleyball, and limited groceries. Children are welcome for up to one month. Pets are permitted.

Reservations, fees: Reservations are recommended. Sites are $20 per night for two people, plus $2 for each extra person. Major credit cards are accepted. Long-term rates are available.

Directions: From Avon Park, take State Road 17 south about four miles to Lake Bonnet Road. Turn left and go about one mile east to the park.

Contact: Lake Bonnet Village, 2900 East Lake Bonnet Road, Avon Park, FL 33825, 863/385-7010, website: www.lakebonnetvillage.com.

199 HIGHLANDS HAMMOCK STATE PARK

Rating: 10

West of Sebring
Orlando map, grid b4, page 240

An occasional white-tailed deer may be seen munching in open fields at dusk here at one of Florida's oldest state parks—one of our favorite campgrounds in the state. During the winter, you're nearly guaranteed to see large groups of deer at the historic homestead/grove area snacking on the still-producing citrus trees! The scenery is worth the somewhat-cramped-together official camping spots. This park offers nearly 10,000 acres of virgin hardwood forest with a cypress swamp, pine flatwoods, sand pine scrub, scrubby flatwoods, and marsh.

You're almost certain to see an alligator during your stay, and the lucky camper could encounter more elusive wildlife such as bobcats, otters, and owls. Opened in 1931, this gem was one of the four original parks in the state parks system, which was organized in 1935. A museum here recounts how the Civilian Conservation Corps helped build Florida's park system during the Great Depression.

Guided walks and tram tours offered by rangers are your best bet for viewing wildlife, but you also can choose from eight nature and mountain-biking trails that cover 11 miles. Horseback-riding trails are available, too. Riding rented bikes along a loop road is popular. Some nature trails traverse boardwalks in a gorgeous old cypress swamp and other wet areas, and dirt paths elsewhere lead through woods. To help avoid seeing a neighbor eye to eye, ask about a few of the 16 drive-up primitive camping spots located in pine flatwoods. RVs and tents in the regular campground are pretty much squeezed together.

Campsites, facilities: The campground has 112 RV sites with water and electric hookups, picnic tables, and grills. Twenty-six sites for tents, with water only, are set aside from the RVs.

Tenters can also stay in 16 sites in a primitive camping area. On the premises are restrooms, showers, a dump station, laundry facilities, grills, a convenience store, a recreation hall, playgrounds, nature trails, horseshoes, shuffleboard, bicycle rentals, and mountain-bike trails. The Hammock Inn, run by a concessionaire, offers breakfast, lunch, and dinner. Try the locally famous "wild orange" pies and milkshakes. In the winter months, campground hosts provide morning coffee socials, potluck dinners, and music around the campfire. Management says the museum, restrooms, camp store, and some trails have wheelchair access. Groceries and restaurants are about five miles away. Children and groups are welcome. Pets are allowed with proof of vaccination.

Reservations, fees: Reservations are recommended; call ReserveAmerica at 800/326-3521. Sites are $8 to $13 per night for four people, plus $2 per extra person and $2 for electricity. Major credit cards are accepted. Stays are restricted to two weeks.

Directions: From U.S. 27 near Sebring, drive west on County Road 634/Hammock Road to the park.

Contact: Highlands Hammock State Park, 5931 Hammock Road, Sebring, FL 33872, 863/386-6094, fax 863/386-6095, email: hammock@strato.net.

200 HIGHLAND WHEEL ESTATES RV/MOBILE HOME PARK

Rating: 3

Near Lake Jackson in Sebring
Orlando map, grid b4, page 240

These shady oak- and pine-dotted lots are located across from 3,000-acre Lake Jackson, where locals scuba dive, snorkel, windsurf, fish, water-ski, and swim. The lake is a spectacular sight as you drive through Sebring, and on windy days, you'll see whitecaps whipping up across the waters. Catering to snowbirds age 50 and older, the park is close to historic downtown Sebring. There, you'll find a small community theater, an arts complex, a library, a civic center, and a new YMCA. The campground is about one mile from a mall and not much farther from Highlands Hammock State Park.

Campsites, facilities: This adult-oriented park has 100 full-hookup RV sites with picnic tables, and five tent sites. A new heated swimming pool, clubhouse, horseshoes, billiards, and winter social programs entertain campers. On the premises are restrooms, showers, a dump station, laundry facilities, and trailer rentals. Be sure to bring your own spoon and dish for the Sunday ice-cream socials. Other activities are water aerobics, arts and crafts, Bible study and church services, bunco, ladies billiards, and more. Management says the clubhouse is wheelchair accessible. Groceries are one mile away, and a restaurant is within walking distance. Visiting children are welcome. Pets are not allowed.

Reservations, fees: Reservations are recommended. Sites are $15 for tenters; and $20 per night for two people in an RV, plus $2 for each additional person. Credit cards are not accepted.

Directions: From the corner of U.S. 27 and Hammock Road in the center of Sebring, travel west on Hammock Road for a short distance.

Contact: Highland Wheel Estates RV/Mobile Home Park, 1004 Hammock Road, Sebring, FL 33872, 863/385-6232, email hwe@strato.net.

201 LAKESIDE STABLES

Rating: 3

In Sebring on Arbuckle Creek
Orlando map, grid b4, page 240

Equestrians will like this campground, which is part of a horse stable operation. It's located on Arbuckle Creek, and you can launch a canoe here or fish. But the emphasis is on horses, with breaking and training available, and mounts for sale. You can fish in the creek.

Campsites, facilities: There are 10 RV sites with

full hookups and a primitive tenting area. Restrooms, showers, horse stables, canoe rentals, and a dog-walk area are available. Children are welcome. Leashed pets are permitted.

Reservations, fees: Reservations are recommended. Sites are $25 per night for two people, plus $5 per extra person. Credit cards are not accepted.

Directions: From the intersection of U.S. 27 and U.S. 98 in Sebring, drive east on U.S. 98 to the park.

Contact: Lakeside Stables, 5000 U.S. 98, Sebring, FL 33876, 863/655-2252, fax 863/655-9525, email: styrell@strato.net.

202 SEBRING GROVE RV RESORT
🏊 🎣 🚤 🐴 ♿ 🚐

Rating: 5

South of Sebring

Orlando map, grid b4, page 240

Just .5 mile from Lake Jackson's swimming, fishing, and boating activities, Sebring Grove is convenient to shopping and restaurants. Planned activities keep folks busy in the recreation room. Sebring is a flourishing retirement community with one of the finest state parks in Florida nearby, Highlands Hammock State Park (see campground in this chapter).

Campsites, facilities: There are 20 full-hookup sites for overnighters in this 114-unit RV park. Eight sites are pull-through. RVs up to 40 feet in length can be accommodated. Restrooms, showers, laundry facilities, telephone hookups, a pool, a clubhouse, shuffleboard courts, and a dog-walk area are available. Most areas are wheelchair accessible. Children may stay for short visits. Leashed pets are permitted; only one pet per lot.

Reservations, fees: Reservations are recommended. Sites are $23 per night for two people, plus $2 per extra person. Credit cards are not accepted. Long-term (up to six months) or seasonal stays are preferred.

Directions: From Sebring, drive south on U.S. 27 about two miles. Do not pass U.S. 98; you will have gone too far.

Contact: Sebring Grove RV Resort, 4105 U.S. 27 South, Sebring, FL 33870-5599, 863/382-1660, fax 863/382-2565.

203 WHISPERING PINES VILLAGE
🛶 🚤 ♿ 🚐 ⛺

Rating: 5

In Sebring

Orlando map, grid b4, page 240

This place is one-third mobile homes and two-thirds RV sites, but the feeling is more residential than campground. Shaded by some palms and pines, it is one of the closest places to camp near notable Highlands Hammock State Park (see campground in this chapter). The park tends to attract people staying for the winter, with just 10 sites available for overnighters. Boating and fishing are possible one mile away at 3,000-acre Lake Jackson. Many activities are planned in the recreation hall; a mall and theaters are nearby, and downtown Sebring is three miles away.

Campsites, facilities: This retiree-oriented park has 155 full-hookup RV sites, of which about 100 have picnic tables. Three tent sites are available. On the premises are restrooms, showers, laundry facilities, a wheelchair-accessible recreation room, trailer rentals, and horseshoes. You will find groceries and restaurants within one mile. Children are allowed, but the park is geared toward retirees. Pets are prohibited, unless you are an overnight visitor staying with friends camped in the park.

Reservations, fees: Reservations are recommended. Sites are $25 per night for two people, plus $2 daily for each additional person. Credit cards are not accepted. Long-term stays are OK.

Directions: From U.S. 27 near Sebring, drive west on County Road 634/Hammock Road for one mile to Brunn's Road. Turn right, heading north, and look for the campground .5 mile ahead on the left.

Contact: Whispering Pines Village, 2323 Brunn's Road, Sebring, FL 33872, 863/385-8806, website: http://sebring-florida.com/wpines.

204 HIGHLAND OAKS RV RESORT

Rating: 5

Off U.S. 27 south of Sebring
Orlando map, grid b4, page 240

Winter visitors flock to this park in Central Florida to thaw out in the sun and get to know each other and the surrounding area. It doesn't have a pool, but it does have shuffleboard courts and a horseshoe pit. Fishing and water-skiing are possible at area lakes, and Highlands Hammock State Park is a short drive away.

Campsites, facilities: This adults-only park has 106 full-hookup RV sites with picnic tables. On the premises are restrooms, showers, laundry facilities, a recreation room, horseshoes, and shuffleboard. There is no dump station. Management says all facilities are wheelchair accessible. Cable TV and telephone service are available. Groceries can be purchased within five miles. One restaurant is across the road, and others are in town, about seven miles away. Children are welcome only to visit park residents. Pets are permitted.

Reservations, fees: Reservations are recommended. Sites are $17.50 per night for two people, plus $2 for each extra person. Credit cards are not accepted. Long-term stays are OK.

Directions: From the intersection of U.S. 27 and U.S. 98/State Road 66, turn onto U.S. 98 and drive about .25 mile. Turn left on County Road 17 North and drive about .5 mile. Turn left on Sixth Street South and follow the paved road to the park entrance.

Contact: Highland Oaks RV Resort, 7001 Seventh Avenue West, Sebring, FL 33876, 863/655-1685.

205 AVON PARK AIR FORCE RANGE

Rating: 9

Northeast of Avon Park
Orlando map, grid b4, page 240

Yes, this is a bombing range and training area for Air Force pilots with 82,000 acres open for public access. While that may sound like an odd destination for those who seek to escape their worries, this remote, wooded domain of bobcats, deer, squirrels, and wild turkeys makes a pretty retreat for outdoorsy types who don't mind Port-O-Lets and cold showers. Day or night, you may see jets flying overhead as they head back and forth to the restricted areas for strafing runs and bomb practice. The size of a small county, the range encompasses everything from deep, dark forests to desertlike scrub areas that are subject to occasional flooding. Gnarly oaks shade the camping areas, which are big enough for most campers to find a sleeping spot away from strangers. You'll like the privacy.

Hunting season is the exception, when about 2,000 people descend on these lands for weekend hunts, collectively bagging a gaggle of turkeys (110 of them, for instance, from mid-March to mid-April of 2002). The park is closed to campers during the main hunting season, principally for deer and hogs. These dates typically fall between mid-September and January, so be sure to call ahead.

Hikers can pad along a 27-mile-long section of the Florida National Scenic Trail from here. Head north and you'll eventually reach the KICCO Wildlife Management Area (see campground in this chapter). Head south and you'll eventually pass through South Florida Water Management District lands to reach Bluff Hammock Road, which, on detailed maps, can be found at the Kissimmee River and S-65B Access Road. The Lake Arbuckle National Recreation Trail (16 miles long) originates at Willingham Campground, one of the three camping areas. From the Outdoor Recreation Office, a 1.2-mile boardwalk nature trail leads to the edge of Lake Arbuckle and a 30-foot observation tower. Starting at Austin Hammock Campground, the Sandy Point Wildlife Refuge Trail makes several loops adding up to 6.2 miles so you can adjust your hike to your energies and abilities. All hikers must get a permit.

Bring your own boat to fish for bass, bream, and catfish in the Kissimmee River or stocked catfish ponds. Some day visitors simply take joyrides on designated roads through the 128 square miles that are open to the public. They just want to get a taste of a real bombing range. Don't get too excited: All you'll really see is woods; 24,000 military-sensitive acres are off-limits to the public. Undetonated bombs were occasionally found over the years, although today the area has been thoroughly cleaned; still, you are warned not to touch anything that resembles ordnance.

Campsites, facilities: Three primitive camping areas are open to the public some Friday and Saturday nights; two of the three also are open on some Sunday nights. Camping areas also are open to hunters chosen through a lottery process during limited hunting seasons. Facilities include Port-O-Lets and hand pumps to provide water for cleaning up; bring your own drinking water. All three camping areas have cold showers. Most sites have picnic tables. There are no other amenities, so bring food and all other supplies. A convenience store is two miles from the main entrance. Laundries and a restaurant are seven miles away. Children are permitted. Pets must be leashed.

Reservations, fees: Very important: Call Thursday afternoon before your weekend trip to see whether the bombing range will be open to campers that weekend; it's closed when military activities are ongoing. Hunters need to obtain a highly coveted permit by calling during February to get an application. Camping costs $5 per person per weekend, or $7 per family per weekend. Credit cards are not accepted.

Directions: From the Orlando area, drive south for about one hour on U.S. 27 to the town of Avon Park, then head left (east) on Highway 64 for about 10 miles. The road dead-ends at the bombing range. A guard will direct you to

the Outdoor Recreation Office, where you must purchase a permit and sign a waiver releasing the federal government from liability should you fall into a shell hole or gun emplacement. **Contact:** Outdoor Recreation, 347 RQW, DET1, OLA/CEVN, 29 South Boulevard, Avon Park Air Force Range, FL 33825-5700, 863/452-4254 or a recorded message at 863/452-4119, ext. 5.

206 LAKE GLENADA RV PARK

Rating: 3

South of Avon Park

Orlando map, grid a4, page 240

Adults are preferred at this lakeside RV park in citrus and cattle country. You'll see huge trucks loaded with oranges driving past the park on their way to the citrus processing plants. The park has a boat ramp and access to fishing and boating on Lake Glenada.

Campsites, facilities: Out of a total of 202 RV sites with full hookups, about 150 are available for overnighters and 50 for seasonal visitors. Rigs up to 36 feet can be accommodated. Sites have concrete pads, picnic tables, and cable TV. Restrooms, showers, laundry facilities, a pool, a boat ramp, dock, recreation hall with planned activities, shuffleboard courts, and a dog-walk area are available. Children are not welcome. Small, leashed pets are permitted.

Reservations, fees: Reservations are recommended. Sites are $24 per night for two people, plus $2 extra person. Credit cards are not accepted. Long-term rates are available.

Directions: From the intersection of State Road 64 and U.S. 27 in Avon Park, drive south on U.S. 27 about three miles to the park, on the east side.

Contact: Lake Glenada RV Park, 2525 U.S. 27 South, Avon Park, FL 33825, 863/453-7007.

COURTESY OF PETER TRITLEY

Chapter 10

Space Coast

Space Coast

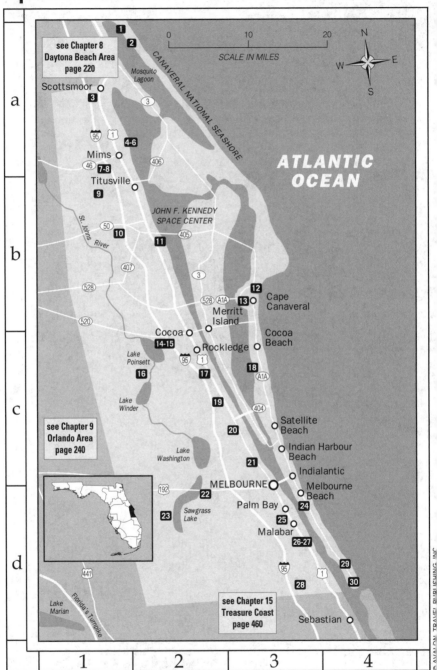

SCALE IN MILES
0   10   20

see Chapter 8
Daytona Beach Area
page 220

see Chapter 9
Orlando Area
page 240

see Chapter 15
Treasure Coast
page 460

ATLANTIC OCEAN

CANAVERAL NATIONAL SEASHORE

Mosquito Lagoon

Scottsmoor

Mims

Titusville

JOHN F. KENNEDY SPACE CENTER

St. Johns River

Lake Poinsett

Cocoa

Rockledge

Cape Canaveral

Merritt Island

Cocoa Beach

Lake Winder

Lake Washington

Satellite Beach

Indian Harbour Beach

Indialantic

MELBOURNE

Melbourne Beach

Palm Bay

Sawgrass Lake

Malabar

Lake Marian

Florida's Turnpike

Sebastian

1 CANAVERAL NATIONAL SEASHORE BEACH CAMPING

Rating: 8

On unspoiled Atlantic beach between Cape
Canaveral and New Smyrna Beach
Space Coast map, grid a1, page 346

Wow. If you're lucky enough to snag one of
these sites during the half-year this beach is
open, consider yourself blessed. This is the
largest stretch of undeveloped beach left between Miami and Daytona Beach. Don't think
of this as car camping because you may have
to slog .75 mile to reach the farthest site. Think
of it as a backpacking trip, and you'll be there
in no time. Your reward is awakening to the
sight of the sun coming up over the Atlantic
as you listen to the waves lapping at the shore.
Bring plenty of sunscreen, even in the winter.

Campsites, facilities: Two beach sites accommodate as many people as you like. No facilities are provided. You must bring everything,
including water and stove. A chemical toilet is
located at the parking lot. Trash must be packed
out. Children are OK. No pets are allowed.
The camping area is closed from April 30
through October 31.

Reservations, fees: Reservations and a permit
are required in advance of your trip. Get a
backcountry permit from the visitor information center at 7611 South Atlantic Avenue, New
Smyrna Beach, FL 32169, or call 386/428-3384
to see if a site is available. Fees are $10 per
night for the first six people, and another $10
fee if your party exceeds six people. Permits
are issued, in person only, at the visitor center before 4 P.M. on the day before your camping trip begins. The visitor center is open from
9 A.M. to 4:30 P.M.

Directions: From Exit 249 on I-95, head east
on State Road 44 to A1A. Turn south. The
visitor center is about 10 miles ahead.

Contact: Canaveral National Seashore, 308 Julia
Street, Titusville, FL 32796, 386/428-3384, ext.
10, website: www.nps.gov/cana/index.htm.

2 CANAVERAL NATIONAL SEASHORE ISLAND CAMPING

Rating: 8

In the Mosquito Lagoon between Cape
Canaveral and New Smyrna Beach
Space Coast map, grid a1, page 346

If you love backcountry camping by boat, you
have to try this. You get your own island, and
it's in an area known for great fishing and bird-
watching. You'll want to obtain a detailed nautical chart and bring along your compass —
and know how to use them. Some of the sites
require you to navigate into some fairly intri-
cate waterways. Because of the lack of development along its edges, the Mosquito Lagoon
is one of the most productive estuaries in Florida, and the fishing is nearly always good. There's
a good reason this is called the Mosquito Lagoon. Even in the winter, you'll want to bring
along plenty of bug dope.

Campsites, facilities: Eleven sites accommodate from six to 40 people. The only facilities
are a picnic table at each site and fire containers of some form at most sites. You must
bring everything, including water, stove, and
firewood. No bathroom facilities are provided; you must dig a cathole or pack out waste.
Trash must also be packed out. Download a
small map of the island campsites at the website listed below (not useful for navigation).
Children and pets are OK.

Reservations, fees: Reservations are required.
Get a backcountry permit from the visitor information center at 7611 South Atlantic Avenue, New Smyrna Beach, FL 32169, or call
386/428-3384 to see if a site is available. Permits are issued up to seven days in advance
for lagoon camping. Fees are $10 per night for
the first six people, and another $10 fee if your
party exceeds six people.

Directions: From Exit 249 on I-95, head east
on State Road 44 to A1A. Turn south. The visitor center is about 10 miles ahead. There are
several options for putting in your watercraft;

these are explained to you when you pick up your permit.

Contact: Canaveral National Seashore, 308 Julia Street, Titusville, FL 32796, 386/428-3384, ext. 10, website: www.nps.gov/cana/index.htm.

3 CRYSTAL LAKE RV PARK

Rating: 4

Off I-95 in Scottsmoor

Space Coast map, grid a1, page 346

A quick hop off I-95, this family-owned park's main attraction is looking skyward to watch NASA's thunderous space shuttle liftoffs. (While the space shuttle program was suspended temporarily in the wake of the *Columbia* tragedy, unmanned space launches are still taking place. Call 321/867-4636 for dates and times.) At other times, the key on-site entertainment is fishing at a three-acre lake, where you can catch bass and catfish, although you also may wet a line for saltwater species in the Indian River, three miles away. Under new management that is making improvements to the park, it's probably the closest private campground to the isolated beaches of the Canaveral National Seashore. During special events at Daytona Beach, such as Bike Week and Speed Weeks, the management says there's room here for a quiet night's sleep. It's also fairly close to the Merritt Island National Wildlife Refuge (see Titusville KOA in this chapter). Kennedy Space Center, 321/452-2121, is about 30 miles from these grassy campsites, which are surrounded by a few maples, palms, and cedar trees.

Campsites, facilities: This park offers 60 full-hookup RV sites (45 pull-through). As many as 45 tents may use RV sites or camp in a separate small primitive area. A convenience store is 1.5 miles away. On the premises are restrooms, showers, laundry facilities, picnic tables, a pool, a recreation hall, horseshoes, and shuffleboard. Children and leashed pets are welcome.

Reservations, fees: Reservations are recommended in winter. Sites are $12 to $20 per night for two people, plus $3 for each additional person and $3 for electricity. Credit cards are not accepted. Long-term stays are OK.

Directions: From I-95, take Exit 231 and drive east 1,000 feet on State Road 5A/Stuckway Road. Look for the campground on the left behind Stuckey's.

Contact: Crystal Lake RV Park, 4240 Stuckey Road (or P.O. Box 362), Scottsmoor, FL 32775, 321/268-8555 or 888/501-7007, website: www.nbbd.com/crystallake.

4 BUCK LAKE CONSERVATION AREA

Rating: 5

West of Mims on Buck Lake in northwestern Brevard County

Space Coast map, grid a1, page 346

Bring binoculars because this wilderness area is home to otters, fox, gopher tortoises, turkey, and deer. Also bring skeeter repellent; the campsite overlooking Buck Lake is basically in marshy floodplain, as is a nearby camping spot. Formerly used for grazing cattle and harvesting timber, these 9,291 acres of backcountry are found on the opposite side of State Road 46 from another woodsy alternative—Seminole Ranch Conservation Area (see campground in this chapter). A small ridge in the eastern part of the Buck Lake property provides conditions dry enough that you might see the rare scrub jay. Two campsites in the middle of the conservation area are near a freshwater fishing lake and require a bit of a trek from either of the two provided parking areas; some campers might prefer to bicycle the three-plus miles. Boaters can use a ramp on State Road 46 at Six Mile Creek, then travel up the creek to explore a small part of the conservation area or travel south to Salt Lake and the fishing waters of Loughman Lake, both in the Seminole Ranch Conservation Area, and continue on to the St. Johns River. Camping is prohibited during hunting season.

Campsites, facilities: Tents only are permitted at the five primitive campsites, reached by foot, bicycle, or horseback. Two sites are within .75 mile from a parking area; the next-closest spot requires a trek that is twice as far. There are no restrooms, showers, or supplies. Bring water, food, mosquito repellent, and everything you'll need. A boat ramp is nearby. Children are permitted. Pets must be leashed.

Reservations, fees: Sites are first-come, first-served. Camping is free. Each site accommodates up to six people. If your party has at least seven people, get a free permit and reserve at least one week ahead at 386/329-4410. Maximum stay for all campers is seven days.

Directions: From I-95 at Exit 223, go west on State Road 46 about one mile. To explore the eastern end of the tract, continue about 4.5 miles and look for the western entrance, which leads to the closest parking area for campsites by Buck Lake.

Contact: St. Johns River Water Management District, Division of Land Management, P.O. Box 1429, Palatka, FL 32178-1429, 386/329-4500 or 800/451-7106, website: www.sjrwmd.com.

5 NORTHGATE TRAVEL PARK

Rating: 3

North of Titusville in Mims

Space Coast map, grid a1, page 346

More mobile home park than campground, this big, retiree-oriented place offers little shade and is directly on busy U.S. 1. Sites are mostly grassy, although a few have concrete pads. A plus: You can swim in the pool, as well as be relatively near the site of NASA's space shuttle launches. Campers sometimes watch launches from Northgate's parking lot. (While the space shuttle program was suspended temporarily in the wake of the *Columbia* tragedy, unmanned space launches are still taking place.) Kennedy Space Center is about 20 miles away.

Campsites, facilities: This campground has 111 full-hookup RV sites (about 10 pull-through) with picnic tables; about 40 are available for overnighters. Fifteen tent sites are also provided. On the premises are restrooms, showers, laundry facilities, a recreation hall, a pool, shuffleboard, and limited groceries. Wintertime activities are offered. Management says the recreation hall is wheelchair accessible. Restaurants are within two miles. Children are allowed, but this is primarily a 55-and-older park that boasts a lot of activities to keep them busy, from quilting, card games, monthly dinners, weekly coffee breaks, and Bible study classes. One small (under 25 pounds), leashed pet per campsite is permitted.

Reservations, fees: Reservations are accepted. Sites are $20 per night for two people, plus $2 for each additional person. Credit cards are accepted. Long-term stays are allowed.

Directions: From I-95, take Exit 223. Drive east on State Road 46 to U.S. 1. Turn left and proceed about two miles north to the campground, on left.

Contact: Northgate Travel Park, 3277 First Avenue, Mims, FL 32754, 321/267-0144, fax 321/267-0501.

6 WILLOW LAKES RV AND GOLF RESORT

Rating: 6

In Titusville

Space Coast map, grid a2, page 346

With its first phase just opened, Willow Lakes plans eventually to have more than 400 sites. This new gated park that targets 55-plus RVers now offers 140 lots, some of which have already been sold for park models or seasonal visitors. Phase 2 will be for Class A motorhomes. All the facilities are new. Some lots are waterfront, and you can watch space launches from the park. Your RV must be at least 22 feet long.

Campsites, facilities: All sites are full hookup. Restrooms, showers, a dump station, laundry facilities, and telephone service are available. On the premises are a heated pool, a recreation hall, golf course, shuffleboard courts, *pétanque* courts, and bocce ball. This is an adults-only park. Leashed pets are permitted.

Reservations, fees: Reservations are recommended. Sites are $30 to $32 per night. Major credit cards are accepted. Long-term rates are available.

Directions: From I-95, take Exit 223 eastbound on State Road 46 to U.S. 1. Turn south and drive .5 mile to the park.

Contact: Willow Lakes RV and Golf Resort, 2199 North U.S. 1, Titusville, FL 32796, 321/269-7440 or 877/787-2751, website: www.willowlakes.com.

◼ SEASONS IN THE SUN MOTORCOACH RESORT

Rating: 10

In Mims

Space Coast map, grid a1, page 346

Opened in summer 2002, this brand-new big-rig resort has 232 sites in a sunny, landscaped area of citrus trees and shady old oak hammocks. Some sites are for sale, and the park has plans for further enlargement. The owners say you can see space shuttle launches from within the park (while the space shuttle program was suspended temporarily in the wake of the *Columbia* tragedy, unmanned space launches are still taking place), and most tourist attractions are within easy driving distances. **Campsites, facilities:** All 232 sites have full hookups, picnic tables, grills, cable TV, and telephone service connections. Restrooms, showers, a dump station, and laundry facilities are available. On the premises are a heated pool, lap swimming pool, whirlpools, lakes, recreation hall with a fully equipped kitchen, exercise equipment, tennis courts, bocce ball, a reading library, shuffleboard courts, a dog-walk area, and a nature trail. Most areas are wheelchair accessible. Children are welcome. Leashed pets are permitted.

Reservations, fees: Reservations are recommended. Sites are $27 to $35 per night for two people, plus $3 to $5 per extra person. Major credit cards are accepted. Long-term rates are available.

Directions: From I-95, take Exit 223 westbound on State Road 46 for .5 mile to the park.

Contact: Seasons in the Sun Motorcoach Resort, 2400 Seasons in the Sun Boulevard, Titusville, FL 32754, 877/687-7275, fax 321/385-0450, website: www.seasonsinthesunrvresort.com.

◼ TITUSVILLE KOA

Rating: 5

Off I-95 west of Mims

Space Coast map, grid a1, page 346

The names of the paved streets at this 14-acre park—Michigan Avenue, Iowa Avenue, and Ontario Boulevard, for example—are a clue that the place is popular among snowbirds. These mostly shady, grassy spots, more than a dozen of which are occupied by permanent residents, are within one mile of an 18-hole golf course. Temperatures can dip to an average low of 48 degrees Fahrenheit in winter, which explains the fireplace in the adult recreation room, where potluck dinners and bingo entertain visitors during the busy winter.

The campground is less than 20 miles from Kennedy Space Center, so periodically you'll hear the roar of NASA shuttle shots. But another big draw is that this is one of the closest parks to the Merritt Island National Wildlife Refuge—219 square miles of mostly unspoiled Florida backcountry that will please hikers or vacationers who prefer a casual walk in the woods. Try the .5-mile Oak Hammock Interpretive Trail, the two-mile Palm Hammock Loop Trail, or the five-mile Allan D. Cruickshank Loop Trail, which features an observation tower and leads to the Indian River. For a self-guided driving tour, pick up a pamphlet at the visitors center. Keep your eye out for birds—at least 310 species of winged creatures have been spotted. If you show up in January or February, you're likely to see tens of thousands of ducks and coots stopping to dine there. Call the refuge at 321/861-0667.

Campsites, facilities: Thirty tent sites are set slightly apart from 210 RV sites. Most sites have full hookups, and all have picnic tables. A pool, a playground, a game room, shuffleboard, horseshoes, a pool table, video games, and wintertime social programs entertain campers. On the premises are restrooms, showers, a dump station, laundry facilities, LP gas sales, a camp store, a picnic pavilion, rental cabins, and a lodge where functions are held. Cable TV and telephone service are available on most sites. Children must be adult-supervised at the pool and play in designated areas. Leashed, attended, vaccinated pets are permitted and must use the perimeter dog walk.

Reservations, fees: Reservations are recommended. Sites are $20 to $27 per night for two people, plus $2 for each additional child and $3 per adult. Major credit cards are accepted. Long-term stays are OK.

Directions: From I-95, take Exit 223 and drive west on State Road 46 for .25 mile to the campground, on your left.

Contact: Titusville KOA, 4513 West Main Street, Mims, FL 32754, 321/269-7361 or 800/KOA-3365, fax 321/267-2417, website: www.koa.com.

9 SEMINOLE RANCH CONSERVATION AREA

🚶 🚲 🛶 🐴 🐕 ⛺

Rating: 6

East of Orlando at the convergence of Orange, Brevard, Volusia, and Seminole Counties

Space Coast map, grid b1, page 346

Set along 12 miles of the St. Johns River, there are 28,785 acres of marshy wilderness best left to fans of primitive camping, horseback riders, bird-watchers, and canoeists. There's also a mountain bike trail. This land was the first purchase made under the state's Save Our Rivers land acquisition program, which is intended to protect water quality by preserving the land from development. Except for the two boat ramps, there are no facilities. The rewards are occasional sightings of roseate spoonbills, white pelicans, and sandhill cranes, and hiking along 4.3 miles of the Florida National Scenic Trail. Seasonal hunting is permitted in a nearly 6,000-acre southern section, which is not near the campsites. One campsite overlooks little Silver Lake; another, right off Hatbill Road, is near the fishing grounds of Loughman Lake. A fairly convenient parking area is between the two sites. A camping spot overlooking the St. Johns River is within a short walk of the park's information kiosk and another parking area. You've certainly left the city life behind—neighbors of this wilderness include the Tosahatchee State Reserve, Little-Big Econ State Forest, and the St. Johns National Wildlife Refuge.

Campsites, facilities: Tents only are permitted at the four primitive campsites, which require a short walk or trip by bicycle, horseback, boat, or canoe. The only facilities are two boat launches. There are no restrooms or showers. Bring water, food, mosquito repellent, and everything you'll need. Children are permitted. Pets must be leashed.

Reservations, fees: Sites are first-come, first-served. Camping is free. Each site accommodates up to six people. If your party has at least seven people, get a free permit and reserve at least one week ahead at 386/329-4410. Maximum stay for all campers is seven days.

Directions: From I-95 at Exit 223, go west on State Road 46. Before you reach the Brevard/Volusia county line, turn left (south) onto Hatbill Road to enter the conservation area. Drive about three miles to the parking area. If you arrive by boat, there is boat access at the junction of State Road 50 and the St. Johns River (Midway Fish Camp) and an Orange County public boat ramp. Follow the river north to the Hatbill Park boat ramp, which is near the campsites at the center of the conservation area. For more detailed directions, contact the water district.

Contact: St. Johns River Water Management District, Division of Land Management, P.O. Box 1429, Palatka, FL 32178-1429, 386/329-4500 or 800/451-7106, website: www.sjrwmd.com.

🔟 THE GREAT OUTDOORS RESORT
🚶 🚴 🏊 🎣 🐕 ♿ 🚐

Rating: 10

Off I-95 west of Titusville

Space Coast map, grid b1, page 346

To call this a campground is a major understatement. Actually, it's a sprawling retirement community, complete with post office, beauty shop, and golf cart showroom. It's also one of the few RV parks we know of that markets itself through a videotape.

Located across the street from the St. Johns National Wildlife Refuge, the complex is huge—about 4.5 square miles. Facilities range from back-in RV sites to a full-scale retirement home for the non-RVer. An interesting innovation between those two extremes is the RV "porte," which looks sort of like a garage or carport. You can park your RV under its roof and feel more or less like you're in a regular home. Some have decks and screened porches. Others have three-bedroom homes with full kitchens built around them. Instead of adding a garage to the home, these folks have added homes to the garage.

The range of available activities is astounding: golfing at a par-71 course, playing tennis at four lighted courts, swimming in two pools, getting in a game of darts or billiards, participating in year-round organized activities such as arts-and-crafts classes, bicycling around the park, relaxing at the restaurant and lounge, exercising at the health club, or hiking on nature trails. Anglers try for catfish, bass, and panfish in at least 20 stocked freshwater lakes on

the property. The park emphasizes its array of resident wildlife, including deer, wild turkeys, bald eagles, quail, rabbits, and waterfowl. Kennedy Space Center is about 12 miles away.

Campsites, facilities: The campground has 110 full-hookup RV sites for mobile campers. All are for self-contained rigs at least 18 feet long. On the premises are restrooms, showers, a dump station, laundry facilities, two pools, two hot tubs, a recreation room, an exercise room, shuffleboard, a golf course, tennis courts, groceries, and a restaurant. Cable TV is available. All areas are wheelchair accessible. This park permits children, but it targets older campers. Two dogs per site are allowed.

Reservations, fees: Reservations are recommended. Sites are $30 to $50 per night for two adults, plus $3 for each additional adult. Major credit cards are accepted.

Directions: From I-95, take Exit 215 and head west on State Road 50 for .5 mile.

Contact: The Great Outdoors Resort, 125 Plantation Drive, Titusville, FL 32780, 321/269-5004 or 800/621-2267, fax 321/269-0694, website: www.tgoresort.com.

🔟🔟 MANATEE HAMMOCK
🏊 🎣 🚗 🐕 ♿ 🚐 ⛺

Rating: 7

On the Indian River in Titusville

Space Coast map, grid b2, page 346

This lovely 26-acre spot on the Indian River is probably the closest, more nature-oriented campground from which to feel the ground rumble beneath your feet as you look skyward at the space shuttle blasting off from Kennedy Space Center less than 10 miles away. (While the space shuttle program was suspended temporarily in the wake of the *Columbia* tragedy, unmanned space launches are still taking place.) It's a wooded park, a pleasant piece of Old Florida preserved by the county government. The grassy or compacted-dirt campsites sit along narrow 5 mph roads marked by occasional tight turns that can challenge big rigs. Near the park's center sit many of its entertainment options: shuffleboard, a pool, and horseshoe pits. To the northeast, windsurfing and fishing are possible in the Indian River. You also can canoe or kayak (bring your own watercraft). Campfires are forbidden at individual campsites, so use the public fire ring across the road from the east bathhouse if you're up for telling ghost stories late at night. Nearby is the Enchanted Forest Nature Center, which opened in November 2002 (321/264-5192).

Campsites, facilities: Thirty tent sites are set apart from 147 RV sites (most full-hookup, 12 pull-through). Rigs up to 40 feet long can be accommodated. Each site has a picnic table. On the premises are restrooms, showers, a dump station, laundry facilities, a grill area, a pool, a small boat ramp, horseshoes, shuffleboard, volleyball, and a recreation hall. Management says the restrooms are wheelchair accessible. Children are welcome but must be adult-supervised. Two leashed, attended pets are permitted per RV.

Reservations, fees: Reservations are recommended up to one year in advance but are not accepted for some spots. Sites are $20 to $22 per night for six people. Major credit cards are accepted. Long-term stays are OK.

Directions: From I-95, take Exit 215 and drive east on State Road 50 for three miles to U.S. 1. Turn right, heading south. Look for the park on your left, four miles beyond the turnoff.

Contact: Manatee Hammock, 7275 U.S. 1 South, Titusville, FL 32780, 321/264-5083, fax 321/264-6468, website: www.brevardparks.com.

12 JETTY PARK CAMPGROUND

Rating: 7

In Cape Canaveral

Space Coast map, grid b3, page 346

This 30-acre park is best known as one of the great places to stand at a 500-foot-long fishing pier to watch NASA's space shuttle rumble into the heavens from Kennedy Space Center,

about 10 miles away. (While the space shuttle program was suspended temporarily in the wake of the *Columbia* tragedy, unmanned space launches are still taking place.) Other days, campers can watch the Disney and Carnival cruise ships sail in on the jetty from Cape Canaveral. Dolphins and manatees travel the waterway at times. In the summer, you might notice sea turtles lumbering onto the beach to dig holes and plop as many as 200 eggs in their earthen "nests" at night.

The campsites—mostly sandy and grassy with precious little shade—are set back from the beach alongside the channel into Port Canaveral. Most spots are along two loops; restrooms, showers, and laundry facilities are at the center of each loop. To be closest to the beach, ask for sites 87 to 117.

Campsites, facilities: The camp has 117 RV sites (32 full-hookup), plus an overflow area. In addition, an indeterminate number of tents can be accommodated in an area set apart from the RVs. Each regular RV site has a grill and picnic table. On the premises are restrooms, showers, laundry facilities, a playground, a fishing pier, horseshoes, volleyball, bait and tackle, snacks, picnic pavilions, a dump station, and limited groceries. Management says the jetties and fishing pier are accessible to wheelchairs. A restaurant is within three miles. Kids are welcome. Pets and campfires are forbidden.

Reservations, fees: Reservations are recommended; a two-day minimum stay is required for reserved sites. Sites are $19 to $26 per night for six people. Major credit cards are accepted. The maximum stay is 21 days.

Directions: From I-95, take Exit 205 and follow the Bee Line Expressway/State Road 528 east. Exit at mile marker 54, enter Port Canaveral's South Cruise Terminal, then turn right onto George King Boulevard. Follow the signs to the campground, at 400 East Jetty Park Road.

Contact: Jetty Park Campground, 400 East Jetty Road, Cape Canaveral, FL 32920, 321/783-7111, fax 321/783-5005.

13 OAK MANOR MOBILE PARK/MANGO MANOR

Rating: 2

In Cape Canaveral

Space Coast map, grid b3, page 346

True to its name, a few oak and mango trees grow in Oak Manor Mobile Park, a quiet, no-frills place, but it's in an industrial section not particularly geared toward recreation. Much of the 20-acre facility is occupied by people (many of them retirees) who live year-round in mobile homes. Kennedy Space Center is about 10 miles from the sites—most paved, some grassy. A plus for water lovers: Ocean swimming and fishing spots are a little under one mile away.

Campsites, facilities: All 71 full-hookup sites in this park are for self-contained RV units. There are no restrooms, showers, or cable TV; however, laundry facilities and a dump station are provided. Children are welcome. One leashed pet per site is permitted.

Reservations, fees: Reservations are recommended; the park fills up early in winter. Sites are $22 per night for two people, plus $1 per extra person. Credit cards are not accepted. Long-term stays are OK.

Directions: From I-95, take Exit 205 and follow the Bee Line Expressway/State Road 528 east to Port Canaveral. At the port, go right (south) on Highway A1A over the bridge to the traffic light. Turn left onto Central Avenue. Look for the park to your left, just past the lumberyard, at 8705 North Atlantic Avenue.

Contact: Oak Manor Mobile Park/Mango Manor, 190 Oak Manor Drive, Cape Canaveral, FL 32920, 321/799-0741, fax 321/783-8671.

14 SON RISE PALMS CHRISTIAN RV PARK (FORMERLY TEEN MISSIONS)

Rating: 5

Off I-95 west of Cocoa

Space Coast map, grid c2, page 346

Many people stay long-term at the grassy sites in this sunny and open park—a convenient place to pull off the highway for a night's rest. Despite the name, you don't have to be Christian to stay here. Geared to families and retirees, the campsites are relatively close to a nearly one-mile-long nature trail and a 20-acre lake. Under new management, the park was previously known as Teen Missions RV Park.

Campsites, facilities: The 83 full-hookup RV sites are set apart from six tent sites, which have water and electricity. Each site has a picnic table. On the premises are restrooms, showers, laundry facilities, a nature trail, horseshoes, and a pool. Management says the showers and toilets are wheelchair accessible. A supermarket is two miles away; restaurants are within three miles. Children are welcome. Nonaggressive, leashed pets under 35 pounds are permitted.

Reservations, fees: Reservations are recommended, particularly in winter. Sites are $27 per night for four people, plus $2 per additional adult, $1 per extra child. Credit cards are not accepted. Maximum stay is six months.

Directions: From I-95, take Exit 201 and head west one short block on State Road 520 to Tucker Lane. Turn left, heading south for about .7 mile. The park is just ahead.

Contact: Son Rise Palms Christian RV Park, 660 Tucker Lane, Cocoa, FL 32926, 321/633-4335, email: sonrisepalmsrvpark@hotmail.com.

15 F. BURTON SMITH REGIONAL PARK

Rating: 7

West of Cocoa and Titusville
Space Coast map, grid c2, page 346

Tents only are permitted at this 1,360-acre county park, which is primarily a day-use area for nature walks, canoeing, picnicking, and fishing in a small lake (no swimming is allowed). There's also a large pavilion that seats 600 people for group outings. The campground, which overlooks a pond, is used mostly by Scout groups, but anyone can camp here with a permit if there's room.

Campsites, facilities: There's a one-half acre primitive tent area with a fire ring. Restrooms and showers are provided, and water is available. On the premises are two lakes for fishing and canoeing, a playground, nature trail, picnic pavilions, and group pavilion. Children are welcome. Pets are prohibited.

Reservations, fees: Camping is by reservation only, and a permit is required. You can download a permit from the website or obtain one in person from the parks and recreation department, which is open weekdays 8 A.M. to 5 P.M.

Directions: From I-95, take Exit 201 and head west on State Road 520 for five miles to the park.

Contact: F. Burton Smith Regional Park, 7575 West State Road 50, Cocoa, FL. For information, contact the Brevard County Parks and Recreation Department, 8400 Forrest Avenue, Cocoa, FL 32922, 321/633-1874, fax 321/633-1850, website: www.brevardparks.com.

16 RIVER LAKES CONSERVATION AREA

Rating: 6

On the St. Johns River west of Rockledge
Space Coast map, grid c2, page 346

An isolated getaway within easy driving distance for Space Coast boaters and canoeists, this 19,536-acre conservation area straddles a stretch of the St. Johns River. The stretch is dotted by a few lakes that feel like a short strand of pearls—the northernmost pearl is Lake Poinsett, Lake Winder is at the center, and southernmost are the fishing waters of Lake Washington. The conservation area is a prized spot for boaters, anglers, seasonal hunters, and bird-watchers. The latter are on the lookout for rare Florida sandhill cranes and endangered wood storks. Bald eagles and river otters may be seen in this floodplain, where saw grass, maidencane, and arrowhead are among the tell-tale wetland plants. Wetlands mean airboat country in these parts, so don't be surprised if an airboat rumbles past your campsite. You'll sleep around Lake Winder, which is near the center of this elbow-shaped conservation area. A fixed-crest weir, which helps ensure Melbourne's water supply, is just north of Lake Washington.

Campsites, facilities: Tents only are permitted at the 11 boat-in or canoe-in primitive campsites, all scattered around Lake Winder and a bit south of the lake. The nearest campsite is about four miles from the Lake Florence trailhead. There are no facilities. Bring water, food, mosquito repellent, and everything you'll need. Five boat ramps provide access to the conservation area. Two shelters have been built on the east side of the river, to be used for daytime recreation or weather protection. Children are permitted. Pets must be leashed.

Reservations, fees: Sites are first-come, first-served. Camping is free. Each site accommodates up to six people. If your party has at least seven people, get a free permit and reserve at least one week ahead at 386/329-4410. Maximum stay for all campers is seven days.

Directions: From I-95 in Cocoa, take Exit 201 west less than one mile on State Road 520, turn left (south) onto Tucker Lane, and follow the road about two miles to a parking area and boat/canoe launch at Lake Florence. Alternatively, you could enter the conservation area via four other boat ramps. For detailed directions and a map showing all campsites, contact the water district before your trip.

Contact: St. Johns River Water Management District, Division of Land Management, P.O. Box 1429, Palatka, FL 32178-1429, 386/329-4500 or 800/451-7106, website: www.sjrwmd.com.

17 SPACE COAST RV RESORT

Rating: 6

Off I-95 south of Rockledge
Space Coast map, grid c2, page 346

Maybe the main attribute of this 22-acre park is that it's very convenient to I-95 if you happen to be passing through and need a place to spend the night, or want to stay somewhat near a space launch. Some sites are occupied by people who live year-round amid the oaks, maples, palms, and Australian pines that offer shade. Fishing is possible in two small on-site ponds and in the nearby Indian River. If you're too pooped to drive nine miles to the Atlantic Ocean, you can swim in the park's heated pool or walk across the street to a golf course. Tent sites and cabins are closest to a small lake (and the park entrance). To sleep nearest to a long pond, ask for full-hookup sites E15 through E24. Kennedy Space Center is about 12 miles away.

Campsites, facilities: Two tent sites are set apart from 267 full-hookup RV sites (74 pull-through). On the premises are restrooms, showers, a dump station, LP gas sales, laundry facilities, rental cabins, a pool, a unisex beauty shop, a TV lounge, and shuffleboard. All areas of the park are said to be wheelchair accessible. Children are welcome. Small, leashed, attended pets are permitted but must be transported to and from the designated pet-walk area.

Reservations, fees: Reservations are recommended in winter. Sites are $35 per night, plus $3 per extra person and a small fee for electricity. Major credit cards are accepted. Long-term stays are OK.

Directions: From I-95, take Exit 195 and head north on Fiske Boulevard to Barnes Boulevard. Turn right (east). The campground is about .5 mile ahead.

Contact: Space Coast RV Resort, 820 Barnes Boulevard, Rockledge, FL 32955, 321/636-2873 or 800/982-4233, fax 321/636-0275, website: www.spacecoastrv.net.

18 OCEANUS MOBILE VILLAGE AND RV PARK

Rating: 4

Near the Banana River south
of Cocoa Beach
Space Coast map, grid c3, page 346

This small park has a coastal location with an on-ocean fishing pier just about one mile north of Patrick Air Force Base, removed from the relative hustle and bustle of the beaches in Cocoa Beach. You're not right on the ocean, but it's just a 200-foot walk to the beach. A county-run boat ramp nearby allows campers to launch into the Banana River, west of the 2.2-acre park.

From the the 240-foot fishing pier, anglers pull in trout, whiting, and redfish. If they don't catch anything, they can eat at the on-site restaurant, the Old Fisherman's Wharf, which is known for seafood. Kennedy Space Center is 30 minutes away from this open and sunny park, where paved roads lead to concrete (mostly) sites with patios.

Campsites, facilities: The mobile home park has 38 full-hookup sites for RVs. Some are pull-through. On the premises are restrooms, showers, a dump station, laundry facilities, picnic tables, a pool, a restaurant, boat slips, and a fishing pier. Children and leashed pets are welcome.

Reservations, fees: Reservations are recommended in winter and on holiday weekends. Sites are $30 to $32 per night for two people, plus $2 for each additional person. Credit cards are not accepted. Long-term stays are OK.

Directions: From Highway 520 in Cocoa Beach, follow Highway A1A south for 5.5 miles. Look for the park to your right, across the street from the beach.

Contact: Oceanus Mobile Village and RV Park, 152 Crescent Beach Drive/23rd Street, Cocoa Beach, FL 32931, 321/783-3871, email: oceanuscb@aol.com.

19 CASA LOMA ESTATES

Rating: 2

At the Indian River north of Melbourne
Space Coast map, grid c2, page 346

At this 55-plus mobile home park located 300 yards from the Indian River, retirees count bingo, exercise classes, and potluck dinners among the highlights of a wintertime visit. A good many visitors stay for the winter or are retired military personnel who want to be near the base exchange and social milieu of Patrick Air Force Base. The grassy sites have concrete patios and asphalt driveways; shade trees are quite young, so expect little sun protection. The 21-acre park is on busy U.S. 1 and is a good 35-minute drive from the Kennedy Space Center. The ocean is about four miles away, across the nearby Pineda Causeway.

Campsites, facilities: This adults-only park has 24 full-hookup RV sites, each with a picnic table. On the premises are restrooms, showers, a dump station, a recreation hall, a pool table, an indoor shuffleboard table, table tennis, horseshoes, shuffleboard, and laundry facilities. Management says the recreation room is wheelchair accessible. A convenience store is next door. Restaurants are within .5 mile. Children are prohibited, except when visiting older family members. Pets are permitted.

Reservations, fees: Reservations are advised in winter. Sites are $20 per night. Credit cards are not accepted. Long-term rates are available.

Directions: From I-95, take Exit 191 and head east on Highway 509/Wickham Road. As soon as the road angles right to head south, turn left onto Suntree Boulevard. At U.S. 1, turn right and proceed less than one mile to the park, at right.

Contact: Casa Loma Estates, 6560 North Harbor City Boulevard/U.S. 1, Melbourne, FL 32940, 321/254-2656.

20 PALM SHORES RV PARK

Rating: 3

North of Melbourne
Space Coast map, grid c3, page 346

Location, location, location. From here, you can go fishing or boating in the nearby Indian River, and you're only a few minutes from the beach. Kennedy Space Center is within a 45-minute drive. Paved interior roads lead to sunny and shady sites, each with a concrete patio. Boat and RV storage are available, and a boat ramp is one mile away.

Campsites, facilities: This campground offers 36 full-hookup RV sites and eight RV sites with water and electricity. On the premises are restrooms, showers, laundry facilities, a dump station, and a recreation hall called The Hen House. A supermarket is within two miles. Children and leashed pets are permitted.

Reservations, fees: Reservations are recommended. Sites are $15 per night for two people, plus $1 for each additional person over age three. Credit cards are not accepted. Long-term stays are OK.

Directions: From I-95, take Exit 191 and head east on Highway 509/Wickham Road to the Pineda Causeway. Instead of getting on the causeway, turn right on U.S. 1. Travel .7 mile south to the park on the right.

Contact: Palm Shores RV Park, 5090 North Harbor City Boulevard, Melbourne, FL 32940, 321/254-4388, website: www.palmshoresrv-park.com.

21 WICKHAM PARK

Rating: 7

West of U.S. 1 in Melbourne

Space Coast map, grid c3, page 346

Not only can you horse around at Wickham Park, but you also likely will see horses in the stalls or along horse trails at the 400-acre local landmark. In far-flung Brevard County, this popular county-run picnic spot stands out because of its size and all that it offers, including archery, disc golf, a horse exercise area, and a 20-station, 1.5-mile-long workout trail. Visitors can jump into two sand-bottomed fishing lakes for a swim. They can hike through a honeycomb of nature trails on the park's east side or ride their own horses along trails on the west side. Bicyclists and inline skaters take advantage of the wide, paved streets that circle the open, airy park.

The grassy campsites are not too far removed from major streets, giving the place a suburban feel. The water- and electricity-equipped grassy sites are set along two loops—Campground A (with about 55 sites) and smaller Campground B. To tell ghost stories or roast marshmallows around a campfire, head to the fire pit in Campground A. Brush screens some of the 35-by-35-foot sites from neighboring campsites. The campground is busy in winter; the park's separate day-use areas are most popular in summer. The fishing waters of the Indian River are five miles away. Kennedy Space Center is about 35 miles distant.

Campsites, facilities: All 88 RV sites have water and electricity and are set apart from 22 primitive tent sites. Two man-made swimming lakes, a nature trail, an archery range, horseshoes, volleyball, a horse trail, ball fields, disc golf, a playground, restrooms, showers, a dump station, an amphitheater, picnic pavilions, horse stalls, a horse show ring, grills, picnic tables, and laundry facilities are available. Campground A has a fire pit. Management says the restrooms are wheelchair accessible. Groceries and restaurants are within one mile. Children must be adult-supervised. Two leashed pets are permitted per site.

Reservations, fees: Reservations are accepted with a two-night minimum stay. Sites are $13 to $16 per night for six people. Major credit cards are accepted. The maximum stay is 180 days per year.

Directions: From I-95, take Exit 183 and head east on State Road 516/Eau Gallie-Sarno Road to the third traffic light. Turn left on Wickham Road. Travel about 2.5 miles north to Parkway Drive, then turn right. The entrance is ahead on the left.

Contact: Wickham Park, 2500 Parkway Drive, Melbourne, FL 32935, 321/255-4307, fax 321/255-4343. Or contact the Brevard County Parks and Recreation Department, 8400 Forrest Avenue, Cocoa, FL 32922, 321/633-1874, fax 321/633-1850, website: www.brevardparks.com.

22 CAMP HOLLY

Rating: 2

At the St. Johns River west of Melbourne

Space Coast map, grid d2, page 346

It's a fish camp, and a small one at that—2.5 acres. Airboat rides are the highlight, but fishing-boat and canoe rentals also keep folks entertained at this laid-back spot at the headwaters of one of Florida's largest rivers, the St. Johns. You can even take an airboat tour at night. The open and sunny camp has a view of the river and the old U.S. 192 bridge. Sites are hard to come by, so call ahead for availability.

Campsites, facilities: A few sites are available for tents and RVs; they have electricity and water only. On the premises are showers, restrooms, a boat ramp, a dock, boat and canoe rentals, a bar with a pool table, and snacks. Management says that the camp store is wheelchair accessible. Groceries and a restaurant are within three miles. Children and leashed pets are permitted.

Reservations, fees: Reservations are necessary. Sites are $9 per night. Credit cards are not accepted. Long-term stays are OK.

Directions: From I-95, take Exit 180 and head west for three miles on U.S. 192 to the bridge over the St. Johns River. You'll see the fish camp there.

Contact: Camp Holly, 6901 U.S. 192 West, Melbourne, FL 32904, 321/723-2179, website: www.campholly.com.

23 THREE FORKS MARSH CONSERVATION AREA

Rating: 5

West of Melbourne in southwestern
Brevard County

Space Coast map, grid d2, page 346

Alligators sun themselves along the banks of this floodplain, and river otters, wading birds, and shorebirds are the expected beneficiaries of an ongoing restoration effort. These 52,000 acres had been severely impacted by diking and draining for farms, so the water management district bought the land to ultimately help the St. Johns River; here, the channels of the St. Johns arise in the marsh south of Lake Hell 'n' Blazes. You'll traverse those channels—called Three Forks Run—to get to the rustic campsite at Lake Hell 'n' Blazes. Anglers and canoeists favor the narrow waters that connect that lake to Sawgrass Lake, about four miles northeast, where another campsite is found. It's a rustic experience; some visitors opt for day visits, following the looped rectangular hiking trail found far from the campsites and southeast of the parking area (south of Malabar Road) or riding their own airboats up the C-40 canal, which runs down the middle of the long conservation area. Hiking also is possible at the southern boundary along the C-54 canal, which doubles as the Brevard/Indian River county line, and at the eastern neighbor, T.M. Goodwin Waterfowl Management Area. If that's not enough,

just across the C-54 canal is the Blue Cypress Conservation Area (see listing in the Treasure Coast chapter).

Campsites, facilities: Tents only are permitted at the two boat-in or canoe-in primitive campsites, which are about two to four miles from the nearest boat ramps. There are no facilities at the campsites, but there are restrooms and picnic tables by the recreation area's parking lot. Bring water, food, mosquito repellent, and all other necessities. Three boat ramps provide access to the conservation area. Children are permitted. Pets must be leashed.

Reservations, fees: Sites are first-come, first-served. Camping is free. Each site accommodates up to six people. If your party has at least seven people, get a free permit and reserve at least one week ahead at 386/329-4410. Maximum stay for all campers is seven days.

Directions: From I-95 in Melbourne at Exit 173, go west about eight miles on Malabar Road/State Road 514 to the Thomas O. Lawton Recreation Area, the main entry point into the Three Forks Marsh Recreation Area. A boat ramp/canoe launch is at a man-made lake near the parking lot, picnic tables, and restrooms. From here, the nearest campsite (at Lake Hell 'n' Blazes) is about four miles beyond the water retention area, up Three Forks Run. Another boat ramp is at Camp Holly (see previous campground) on the northern end of the tract off of U.S. 192/State Road 500. The other two boat ramps are off of Kenansville Road on the southern side of the conservation area; enter from Kenansville Road/Fellsmere Grade. For detailed directions and a map, contact the water district before your trip.

Contact: St. Johns River Water Management District, Division of Land Management, P.O. Box 1429, Palatka, FL 32178-1429, 386/329-4500 or 800/451-7106, website: www.sjrwmd.com.

24 OUTDOOR RESORTS MELBOURNE BEACH

Rating: 8

On Highway A1A in Melbourne Beach
Space Coast map, grid d3, page 346

One of the best things about this luxury RV resort is its proximity to the ocean and beach, which is just across Highway A1A, and to the Indian River nearby. You'll often feel a sea breeze here. The paved RV sites—with patios and a few sabal palms—are across the highway from a nicely landscaped beachside recreation complex that includes a 3,000-square-foot activity center and palm-flanked oceanview pool.

The 40-acre park isn't exactly a place for shrinking violets. You can swim in the ocean or in one of three pools, choose from six tennis courts or eight lighted shuffleboard courts, use the boat ramp to access the Indian River for boating or fishing, or drop a line off the 300-foot fishing pier. Bicyclists tool around the park or on a path that runs along Highway A1A. On summer nights, some guests watch sea turtles nest on the nearby beach. Kennedy Space Center is within a 45-minute drive.

Campsites, facilities: Amid this 576-unit community, there are a varying number of full-hookup sites available for overnight or seasonal RVs. Each site has a picnic table. On the premises are restrooms, showers, three pools, lighted tennis courts, a hot tub, an activities center, a health club, two clubhouses, boat ramp, a dock, shuffleboard, and a laundry room. Planned activities are held during the winter months. Management says the buildings, bathhouse, and pool areas are wheelchair accessible. Children are welcome. Leashed, attended pets are permitted.

Reservations, fees: Reservations are recommended. Sites are $38 to $49 per night for four people, plus $2 for each additional person. Major credit cards are accepted. Long-term stays are OK.

Directions: From I-95, take Exit 180 and travel east on State Road 192 to Highway A1A. Turn right (south). Look for the campground on the right in four miles.

Contact: Outdoor Resorts Melbourne Beach, 3000 Highway A1A South, Melbourne Beach, FL 32951, 321/724-2600 or 800/752-4052, fax 321/727-0175.

25 LAZY K RV PARK

Rating: 2

On U.S. 1 in Palm Bay
Space Coast map, grid d3, page 346

Located right beside busy U.S. 1, this sunny, five-acre park is open and airy. It is across from great fishing on the Indian River. Native sabal palm trees are scattered around the park, where paved streets pass grassy sites and concrete patios. Kennedy Space Center is about 30 minutes away.

Campsites, facilities: All 62 full-hookup sites are for RVs, with cable TV, telephone service, and 30-amp or 50-amp electrical service available. Each site has a concrete patio and a picnic table. On the premises are restrooms, showers, horseshoes, shuffleboard, a recreation room, and laundry facilities. Management says that the restrooms and laundry are wheelchair accessible. Children are discouraged from staying here. Pets are allowed.

Reservations, fees: Reservations are recommended. Sites are $22 to $26 per night, plus $3 for each additional person. Major credit cards are accepted. Long-term rates are offered.

Directions: From I-95, take Exit 173 and travel 4.5 miles east on State Road 514/Malabar Road to U.S. 1. Turn left and proceed north to the campground.

Contact: Lazy K RV Park, 5150 Dixie Highway Northeast, Palm Bay, FL 32905, 321/724-1639, email: ttrevellin@aol.com.

26 ENCHANTED LAKES ESTATES

Rating: 3

In Malabar

Space Coast map, grid d3, page 346

Mention the obscure town of Malabar and many Floridians will scratch their heads. But bring up the nearby Indian River, and they'll certainly know what you're talking about. A popular boating and fishing destination, the river is two miles east of the grassy/concrete-pad sites at this 28-acre park. The ocean is just two miles farther east as the crow flies, but you should expect to drive six miles north to a Melbourne causeway first to get there. This neatly kept, sunny RV park's "enchanted lake" has fountains and lush tropical landscaping.

Campsites, facilities: Of the 75 full-hookup RV sites, 60 are pull-through. Each site has a concrete patio and a picnic table. On the premises are showers, restrooms, a recreation hall, a heated pool, an exercise room, a pool table, laundry facilities, and planned activities. Cable TV and telephone service are available. Management says the recreation hall is wheelchair accessible. A restaurant, groceries, and bait are available within .5 mile. Children are allowed. Leashed pets are permitted.

Reservations, fees: Reservations are recommended. Sites are $28 per night for two people, plus $2 for each additional person. Credit cards are not accepted. Long-term stays are OK.

Directions: From I-95, take Exit 173 and travel east on State Road 514/Malabar Road for two miles. The park is next to Palm Bay Hospital.

Contact: Enchanted Lakes Estates, 750 Malabar Road, Malabar, FL 32950, 321/723-8847, fax 321/724-1102, website: www.enchanted-lakes.net.

27 CAMELOT RV PARK

Rating: 6

On U.S. 1 in Malabar

Space Coast map, grid d3, page 346

Finding out what activities are scheduled to take place at the recreation hall is as simple as turning on the free 35-plus-channel cable TV service and tuning to Channel 5, the park's information station. Yes, this is camping in the civilized sense of the word. Beyond the entrance gates of the family-run campground, paved roads lead to shady or sunny spots equipped with concrete patios and picnic tables. Anglers and boaters can cross the street—well-traveled U.S. 1—to get to a dock on the Indian River. Many of the usual RV-park rules apply at this 20-acre RV/mobile home destination, with two perhaps-welcome exceptions: You may wash your RV or car; and two vehicles, not one, may be parked at each site. Channel 15 on the cable TV service delivers information about NASA so you can monitor space launches at the Kennedy Space Center, about a 45-minute drive northeast. The park overlooks the Indian River Lagoon.

Campsites, facilities: Many of the 130 full-hookup sites with concrete pads are available for overnighting RVs, and two of three are taken by seasonal visitors. Rigs up to 45 feet long can be accommodated. A recreation hall, a craft center, a fishing dock, shuffleboard, basketball, and winter activities entertain campers. Restrooms, showers, picnic tables, laundry facilities, and a dog-walk area are on site. Cable TV and telephone service are available. Most areas are wheelchair accessible. Children are allowed to visit, but this is primarily a 50-plus age park. Leashed, attended pets are permitted.

Reservations, fees: Reservations are recommended. Sites are $22 to $30 per night for two people, plus $2 for each additional person and $1 for using 50-amp electrical service. Cable TV is free. Major credit cards are accepted. Long-term rates are available.

Directions: From I-95, take Exit 173 and travel 4.5 miles east on State Road 514/Malabar Road to U.S. 1. Turn right. The park entrance is about two blocks ahead at right.

Contact: Camelot RV Park, 1600 U.S. 1, Malabar, FL 32950, 321/724-5396, fax 321/724-9022, website: www.camelotrvpark.com.

28 ST. SEBASTIAN RIVER STATE BUFFER PRESERVE

Rating: 7

Between Fellsmere and Sebastian on the C-54 Canal

Space Coast map, grid d3, page 346

Bring a camera to preserve memories of seeing turkey, deer, bald eagles, and otters, among other critters, at this 21,951-acre preserve. Wildlife is abundant. Indeed, a wheelchair-accessible platform serves as a manatee viewing area. This place aims to protect manatees, red-cockaded woodpeckers, and Florida scrub jays by providing an upland buffer to the creek (hence, the park's "buffer" name). You'll sleep near a hiking trail north of the C-54 Canal, which divides the preserve in two. Look for white pelicans along the canal. Hikers, bicyclists, and horseback riders can follow more than seven miles of trails that ribbon the preserve and are named for colors—Blue Trail, Red Trail, Yellow Trail, Green Trail. Two short spur trails (less than one mile each) lead to the north prong of the St. Sebastian River. If that's not enough, a looped walking path is behind the Visitors Center. Bring sunscreen and a hat; it's an open and sunny place with seasonal wetlands, hardwood swamp, and pines that provide little in the way of sun protection. Get maps from the St. Johns River Water Management District before heading out.

Campsites, facilities: Tents only are permitted at the five primitive hike-in campsites. You'll walk .1 mile to Storytelling Camp or .5 mile to the other site, called Horseman's Headquarters. There are no facilities in the camping area, except for the paddock and water for horses at Horseman's Headquarters. On the opposite end of the preserve, there are restrooms at the wheelchair-accessible visitors center, which is open weekdays only. Bring water, food, and supplies. Children are permitted. Pets must be leashed.

Reservations, fees: Reservations are advised at least three days ahead, preferably earlier. Camping is free. Each site accommodates about 15 people.

Directions: From I-95 at Exit 173, go west on Malabar Road/State Road 514, then south (right) onto Babcock Road/County Road 507. Continue 11.5 miles and turn east onto Buffer Preserve Drive. The south entrance can be reach by driving 1.8 miles east of I-95 on Fellsmere Road/County Road 512.

Contact: St. Sebastian River State Buffer Preserve, 1000 Buffer Preserve Drive, Fellsmere, FL 32948, 321/953-5004 or 321/676-6614. Additional information and maps are available from the St. Johns River Water Management District, Division of Land Management, P.O. Box 1429, Palatka, FL 32178-1429, 386/329-4500 or 800/451-7106, website: www.sjrwmd.com.

29 LONG POINT PARK

Rating: 7

At the Indian River in Melbourne Beach

Space Coast map, grid d4, page 346

Long Point is actually on an island, not a point. But that probably makes it all the more popular. Surrounded by the Indian River, this 60-acre, county-run camping park draws boaters, anglers, canoeists, and kayakers bound for the Indian River.

Most of the grassy campsites are set around the park perimeter. Full-hookup sites are located at the center. As a brochure puts it, this place has two little lakes—one for swimming, and one for wildlife. To be closest to the swimming lake, ask about the water- and electricity-equipped sites numbered 14 to 22.

Full-hookup sites are near the other lake. Tenters who want to get away from it all may want to get away from the on-site bait and tackle sales, located near tent sites 30 to 40; ask for a camping spot in the other two rustic areas instead. The park is just 1.5 miles from the quiet, slow-paced Sebastian Inlet State Park, on the Indian River.

Campsites, facilities: Many tents can be accommodated in a primitive tenting overflow area set apart from 170 RV sites. Fifteen sites have full hookups; others have water and electricity only. On the premises are showers, restrooms, a dump station, picnic tables, grills, fire rings (at waterfront sites), a boat ramp, a fishing pier, a playground, horseshoes, volleyball, and a laundry room. Management says the restrooms, pavilions, swimming pond, and playground are wheelchair accessible. Children are welcome. Two leashed, well-attended pets are permitted per site.

Reservations, fees: Reservations are accepted; but if you make a reservation, you are required to stay for at least two nights. There is a $12.50 cancellation charge if you change your mind 72 hours prior to check-in date. No refunds are given if you cancel within 72 hours. Sites are $14 to $21 per night, depending on the campsite services you need. Major credit cards are accepted. The maximum stay is 180 days.

Directions: From U.S. 192 in Melbourne, go south approximately 17 miles on Highway A1A. Look for the turnoff to the park on the right about 1.5 miles north of Sebastian Inlet State Park.

Contact: Long Point Park, 700 Long Point Road, Melbourne Beach, FL 32951, 321/952-4532, website: www.campingspacecoast.com.

30 SEBASTIAN INLET STATE PARK

Rating: 10

On the Indian River in Melbourne Beach
Space Coast map, grid d4, page 346

Surfers are fond of this popular state-run park, which boasts three miles of natural beaches and an inlet connecting the ocean and Indian River Lagoon. And it's paradise for anglers who take out their own boats, rent them from the park, or use the jetties to catch any of a vast array of fish attracted to the inlet.

Actually, the 379-acre park is different things to different people. Sunbathers favor a dip in the ocean. Picnickers stake out their favorite sun-washed spots (bring caps and sunscreen). Bicyclists who desire something more challenging than the park roads can head north for 14 miles along Highway A1A, stopping to enjoy numerous access points to the ocean. Snorkeling is also possible, but you should avoid the inlet itself, which has wicked currents. Instead, rangers recommend heading to the southern portion of the park to snorkel in the ocean; reefs are about 50 feet offshore.

Campsites overlook the Sebastian Inlet. You will enjoy relative peace away from the madding daytime crowds because you'll camp at the Indian River side of the park, not near the concession stand, ocean swimmers, surfers, or showers on the Atlantic side across Highway A1A.

Don't neglect the park's Sebastian Fishing Museum, which highlights the area's history of commercial fishing, or the McLarty Treasure Museum, recollecting the days hundreds of years ago when treasure-laden Spanish galleons would crash along this coast. The museum commemorates a Spanish fleet that was wrecked near here by a hurricane in 1715 while carrying gold and silver from Peru to Spain.

If you arrive in summer, sign up for a ranger-guided nighttime turtle walk to watch sea turtles lumber onto the beach to dig holes and lay as many as 200 eggs each. This park is one of our favorite campgrounds in Brevard County, but it's WAY down at the southeastern corner. Expect at least a 30-minute drive to Kennedy Space Center and Cocoa Beach. Still, if you want to see a slice of southern oceanside Brevard in a more or less natural state, this is probably your best bet.

Campsites, facilities: All 51 sites are for RVs and tents, and all have water and electricity. Each site has a picnic table, a grill, a fire ring, and a pad made of stabilized fill. On the premises are restrooms, showers, a dump station, a boat ramp, boat and canoe rentals, a nature trail, a breakfast-and-lunch snack bar, and laundry facilities. Management says that restrooms, parking lots, both museums and jetties, and the concession area are wheelchair accessible. Groceries are two miles away. Children are welcome. Pets are allowed in designated areas. **Reservations, fees:** Reservations are recommended; call ReserveAmerica at 800/326-3521.

Sites are $19 per night for four people, plus $2 for each additional person. Electricity costs $2 extra, and the pet fee is $2. Major credit cards are accepted. The maximum stay is 14 days.

Directions: From U.S. 192 in Melbourne, travel about 22 miles south on Highway A1A. Look for the park about 1.5 miles south of Long Point Park. If you're traveling from Vero Beach, drive about 12 miles north on Highway A1A to the park entrance.

Contact: Sebastian Inlet State Park, 9700 Highway A1A South, Melbourne Beach, FL 32951, 321/984-4852, website: www.floridastate parks.org.

Chapter 11

St. Petersburg Area

St. Petersburg Area

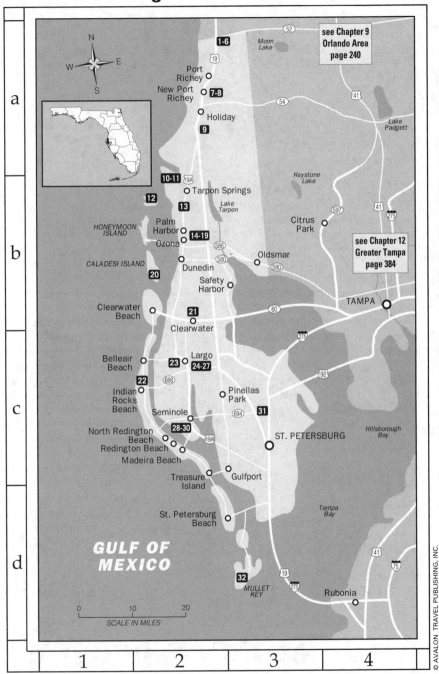

see Chapter 9
Orlando Area
page 240

see Chapter 12
Greater Tampa
page 384

Moon Lake

Port Richey
New Port Richey
Holiday
Tarpon Springs
Palm Harbor
Ozona
Dunedin
Safety Harbor
Clearwater Beach
Clearwater
Belleair Beach
Largo
Indian Rocks Beach
Seminole
North Redington Beach
Redington Beach
Madeira Beach
Treasure Island
Gulfport
St. Petersburg Beach

HONEYMOON ISLAND
CALADESI ISLAND

Lake Tarpon
Keystone Lake
Lake Padgett

Citrus Park
Oldsmar
TAMPA

Pinellas Park
ST. PETERSBURG

Hillsborough Bay

Tampa Bay

GULF OF MEXICO

MULLET KEY

Rubonia

0   10   20
SCALE IN MILES

© AVALON TRAVEL PUBLISHING, INC.

1 SUNDANCE LAKES RV RESORT

Rating: 3

In Port Richey

St. Petersburg map, grid a2, page 366

This sunny and open park, which can accommodate rigs up to 40 feet long, is set back one block from a busy six-lane highway. Shopping centers are within walking distance and a flea market is next door. Five major golf courses are a short drive away. Tarpon Springs, Busch Gardens, Weeki Wachee Spring, Disney World, Epcot, the Salvador Dali Museum, and Homosassa Springs are easy day trips from the park. Hudson Beach is two miles away, and the beach at Green Key is four miles away. Complete medical facilities and churches are close by.

Campsites, facilities: This manicured RV community has 523 concrete-pad sites with full hookups and cable TV and telephone access. Restrooms, showers, laundry facilities, a heated pool, tennis, a pool hall, a recreation hall with sitting porch, shuffleboard, horseshoes, and four lakes are on the premises. Children are welcome for short stays, but there is no playground and management prefers campers 55 and older. Leashed pets under 25 pounds are permitted.

Reservations, fees: Reservations are recommended. Sites are $22 per night for two people, plus $2.50 for each additional person. Major credit cards are accepted. The resort targets northerners age 55 and over who stay for the season, although overnighters are welcome.

Directions: From the junction of U.S. 19 and State Road 52, drive 300 yards south on U.S. 19. Turn west on Hachem Drive and continue into the park.

Contact: Sundance Lakes RV Resort, 6848 Hachem Drive, Port Richey, FL 34668, 727/862-3565, website: www.rvresorts.com.

2 TROPIC BREEZE RV AND MOBILE HOME PARK

Rating: 3

In Port Richey

St. Petersburg map, grid a2, page 366

"Only friendly people allowed here," says the park literature. "Others must go home." The management's advice continues: "Talk to other people. Go places together. Socialize." Like most RV parks aimed at snowbirds, all that socializing takes place in the recreation hall, though malls, restaurants, golf courses, and other entertainment options are nearby.

Campsites, facilities: This 114-unit mobile home community has 39 sites for RVers over the age of 55, with full hookups, cable TV, and telephone service available. Restrooms, showers, and a recreation room are on the property. Children are allowed for short-term visits. Leashed pets under 30 pounds are permitted.

Reservations, fees: Reservations are recommended. Sites are $18 per night for two people, plus $3 for each additional person. Credit cards are not accepted. Long-term stays are OK.

Directions: From the junction of U.S. 19 and State Road 52, drive .5 mile south on U.S. 19. The park is on the east side of the road.

Contact: Tropic Breeze RV and Mobile Home Park, 11310 U.S. 19, Port Richey, FL 34668, 727/868-1629.

3 JOURNEY RV PARK

Rating: 1

In Port Richey

St. Petersburg map, grid a2, page 366

Snowbirds like the convenience of having grocery stores, restaurants, and laundry facilities nearby. An RV dealership is part of the park, as well as propane sales. Jay B. Starkey Wilderness Park (see campground in this chapter), where all the camping is primitive, is close enough to give them a taste of nature if they have such a hankering.

Campsites, facilities: The park has 17 RV sites, all with full hookups. Cable TV and telephone access are available. An RV dealership is on site. Most residents are year-round or seasonal, but families with children are welcome. Leashed pets are permitted.

Reservations, fees: Reservations are recommended. Sites are $10 per night for two people, plus $1 per extra person. Credit cards are not accepted. Long-term stays are OK.

Directions: From the junction of U.S. 19 and State Road 52, drive one mile south on U.S. 19. The park is on the west side of the road.

Contact: Journey RV Park, 11113 U.S. 19, Port Richey, FL 34668, 727/862-0003 or 888/331-0003.

▣ SUNCOAST RV RESORT

Rating: 4

North of New Port Richey
St. Petersburg map, grid a2, page 366

With tall pines casting sun-dappled shadows, you can hardly tell this RV resort is next to a mall and on a major highway. The managers guarantee in writing that restrooms will be clean, staff will be courteous, and the pool will be sparkling. It's near shopping, restaurants, and fishing and boating on the Gulf of Mexico. Planned activities are held in the winter months, with everyone pitching in to offer ideas or help. Choose between sunny and shady sites.

Campsites, facilities: There are 165 RV sites with full hookups and 30 sites for tents. A pool, shuffleboard courts, horseshoe pits, a recreation hall, a pavilion with a fireplace, and laundry facilities are available. The laundry room and pavilion are wheelchair accessible. Children and leashed pets are welcome.

Reservations, fees: Reservations are recommended. Sites are $25 per night for two people, plus $1.50 for each additional person and

$3 for using electrical service. Major credit cards are accepted.

Directions: From the junction of U.S. 19 and State Road 52, drive 1.8 miles south on U.S. 19 to the park, on the east side of the road.

Contact: Suncoast RV Resort, 9029 U.S. 19, Port Richey, FL 34668, 727/842-9324 or 888/922-5603.

▤ OAK SPRINGS TRAVEL PARK

Rating: 3

North of New Port Richey
St. Petersburg map, grid a2, page 366

Several small lakes are scattered throughout this huge adult travel resort, which is so big it has bicycle parking near the recreation hall to accommodate guests who want to cover a lot of ground on wheels. In the winter, snowbirds pass the time with social activities such as line dancing, potluck dinners, ice-cream socials, exercise classes, parties, arts-and-crafts classes, and bingo. Church services are held here, too.

Campsites, facilities: For adults only, this 528-unit park has 200 RV sites with full hookups. Facilities include restrooms, showers, a pool, a horseshoe pit, a game room, shuffleboard courts, and a laundry room. Children are not welcome. Leashed pets are allowed.

Reservations, fees: Reservations are recommended. Sites are $22 per night for two people, plus $2 for each additional person. Major credit cards are accepted. Long-term rates are available.

Directions: From the junction of U.S. 19 and State Road 52 in New Port Richey, drive two miles south on U.S. 19. At Jasmine Boulevard, turn west and go one block to the park entrance on Scenic Drive.

Contact: Oak Springs Travel Park, 10521 Scenic Drive, Port Richey, FL 34668, 727/863-5888, website: www.rvresorts.com.

6 JA-MAR TRAVEL PARK

🏊 🎣 🏠 ♿ 🚐

Rating: 3

In Port Richey

St. Petersburg map, grid a2, page 366

Actually two resorts located 1,800 feet apart, this mobile home/RV park welcomes overnighters, even though most people here are seasonal visitors. Planned activities—as many as 10 daily—include everything from Bible study to line dancing and euchre games. Bus trips are arranged to nearby attractions. Stores and restaurants are close by. Two ponds line the entrance drive; be careful when entering the park at night. One of the lakes is stocked for fishing.

Campsites, facilities: There are 400 lots with full hookups, with about half available for overnighters. Rigs up to 38 feet in length can be accommodated. Restrooms, showers, laundry facilities, a recreation hall, shuffleboard courts, lakes, and a pool are on the premises. All areas are wheelchair accessible. This is a 55-and-older park, but children may stay short-term. Leashed pets are permitted.

Reservations, fees: Reservations are recommended. Sites are $20 per night for two people, plus $2 for each additional person, $2 for 30-amp electrical service, and $3.50 for 50-amp service. Credit cards are not accepted. Long-term stays are allowed.

Directions: From U.S. 19 near Hudson, drive south to State Road 52. The park is on the west side of the road, just south of the intersection.

Contact: Ja-Mar Travel Park, 11203 U.S. 19, Port Richey, FL 34668, 727/863-2040, fax 727/862-8882, website: www.ja-mar-travelpark.com.

7 JAY B. STARKEY WILDERNESS PARK

🚶 🚴 🎣 ♿ 🚐 ⛺

Rating: 10

On the east side of New Port Richey

St. Petersburg map, grid a2, page 366

Set on the edge of an urban area and upscale housing developments, this 8,700-acre public preserve is part of a wilderness tract originally owned by Jay B. Starkey, who bought the land in 1937 for cattle grazing. A new environmental education center was recently built for meetings, exhibits, and nature training. Almost all the sites are for tents; only two can accommodate pop-up trailers. Picnic areas, pavilions, shelters, a paved bike trail, and 13 miles of hiking trails are in the park. Limited freshwater fishing is available along the Anclote and Pithlachasotee Rivers. The following are not allowed: alcoholic beverages, guns or trapping devices, collecting or removing plants or animals, swimming, canoeing or boating, digging, motorcycles, and all-terrain vehicles. The park has 10 miles of marked bridle paths designated for equestrian use. Horses must be trailered into the park, and each rider must carry proof of a current negative Coggins test.

Campsites, facilities: The main campground has 16 primitive sites for tents, including two for pop-up campers. Larger RVs and generators are not allowed. Facilities include restrooms, showers, picnic tables, grills, and fire rings. Large cabins are available for rent for $15 per night for eight persons; smaller cabins are $10 per night for four people. One cabin and the environmental education center are wheelchair accessible. A backcountry camping area has been designated for equestrian use. Supplies and provisions must be packed into those sites because vehicles are not allowed. All ground fires must be contained. Three backpacking campsites are located near the foot trails; each has a picnic table, a grill, and a fire ring. Children are welcome. Pets are prohibited in the campground, though you may walk a dog on a six-foot leash elsewhere in the park.

Reservations, fees: Reservations are required for the main campground and are recommended for equestrian sites; they may be made up to 30 days in advance in person. For backpacking, sites can be reserved up to 90 days in advance, and campers must register at the kiosk in person for their own safety. Tent sites in the main area are $5 per night (a site accommodates up to eight people and two tents). Credit cards are not accepted. Camping is free for backpacking and equestrian sites. Stays are limited to seven days.

Directions: From I-75, take Exit 285 and drive west on State Road 52 for 21 miles. At Little Road, turn south and go six miles. Turn east onto River Crossing Boulevard and drive three miles to the park entrance. The drive winds through a residential development until it deadends at Wilderness Road. When coming from U.S. 19 in New Port Richey, take State Road 54 east for 2.5 miles to Little Road, then head north to River Crossing Boulevard. Drive three miles east to the park entrance.

Contact: Jay B. Starkey Wilderness Park, 10500 Wilderness Road, New Port Richey, FL 34656, 727/834-3247 or 727/834-3262, fax 727/834-3277. Or write to Pasco County Parks and Recreation Department, 7750 North Congress Street, New Port Richey, FL 34653.

8 ORCHID LAKE TRAVEL PARK

Rating: 3

In New Port Richey
St. Petersburg map, grid a2, page 366

This quiet park is located on Orchid Lake near orange groves, upscale homes, shopping, and many golf courses. Social programs are held in the winter months.

Campsites, facilities: The 55-and-older, retiree-oriented park has 406 RV sites with full hookups and telephone and cable TV access. Restrooms, showers, a recreation hall, a card room, laundry facilities, a pool, horseshoe pits, and shuffleboard courts are provided. Visiting grandchildren are welcome. Indoor cats are permitted.

Reservations, fees: Reservations are recommended. Sites are $23 per night for two people, plus $1 for each additional person. Credit cards are not accepted.

Directions: From I-75, take the exit to State

Route 52 and go west to Little Road and proceed one mile to Arevee Drive. Turn west; the park is near the corner.

Contact: Orchid Lake Travel Park, 8225 Arevee Drive, New Port Richey, FL 34653, 727/847-1925, website: www.flrvresorts.com.

9 HOLIDAY TRAVEL PARK

Rating: 3

In Holiday north of Tarpon Springs
St. Petersburg map, grid a2, page 366

This is a convenient base for exploring Gulf Coast attractions, such as the sponge docks of Tarpon Springs four miles south. Rigs up to 40 feet long can be accommodated. At 7,000 square feet, the clubhouse has a seating capacity of 400, a pool room, a card room, and a library. For those cool winter days, the pool is heated.

Campsites, facilities: The 613-unit park has 85 full-hookup RV sites (some pull-through). Wheelchair-accessible restrooms, plus showers, laundry facilities, a dump station, a pool, pet areas, and a recreation hall are provided. Rental trailers are available. The resort caters to 50-and-older travelers, but all ages are welcome. Leashed pets are permitted.

Reservations, fees: Reservations are not necessary. Sites are $23 per night for two people, plus $2 for each additional person. Credit cards are not accepted. Long-term stays are OK.

Directions: From the intersection of U.S. 19 and State Road 54, drive 3.5 miles south on U.S. 19. The park is on the east side of the junction of U.S. 19 and Alternate U.S. 19.

Contact: Holiday Travel Park, 1622 Aires Drive, Holiday, FL 34690, 727/934-6782.

10 LINGER LONGER RESORT

Rating: 4

In Tarpon Springs
St. Petersburg map, grid b2, page 366

Get out your tackle box: Fish caught within

small-boat range of this park include snook, redfish, tarpon, trout, cobia, flounder, snapper, and grouper. A mix of shady and sunny sites is located on the Anclote River, which provides boaters five-minute access to the Gulf of Mexico. Just across the river are the sponge-fishing docks of Tarpon Springs and numerous restaurants serving great seafood and Greek dishes. Early in the century, many Greeks immigrated here and found work diving to the depths of the Gulf in search of natural sponges; they built an industry that thrived until bacteria contaminated the sponge beds in the 1940s. Sponge diving has made a comeback in recent years, but the real business of Tarpon Springs is tourism. You'll find sponge-diving exhibitions, sponge museums (including the aptly named Sponge-o-rama), and sponges for sale.

Campsites, facilities: This mobile home park offers a separate section of 150 grassy RV-only sites with full hookups. Restrooms, showers, picnic tables, laundry facilities, a boat dock, horseshoe pits, shuffleboard courts, rental cottages, and a recreation hall are available. Electric heaters are prohibited, but air conditioners are allowed. Although it's an adult-oriented park (with wintertime activities), children are permitted in camping areas. One leashed pet under 25 pounds is allowed per site.

Reservations, fees: Reservations are recommended. Sites are $24 per night for two people, plus $1 per extra person. Major credit cards are accepted. Long-term stays are OK.

Directions: From Alternate U.S. 19 in Tarpon Springs, just north of the Anclote River Bridge, drive west on Anclote Road for approximately .75 mile to the park.

Contact: Linger Longer Resort, 355 Anclote Road, Tarpon Springs, FL 34689, 727/937-1463 or 800/958-8899.

11 HICKORY POINT MOBILE HOME AND RV PARK

Rating: 4

In Tarpon Springs
St. Petersburg map, grid b2, page 366

Here is a park with that quaint "Old Florida" feel that the brochures promise. It's a parklike setting with 650 feet of river frontage; you easily can see the Gulf of Mexico and enjoy pretty sunsets, as well as fish for redfish and snook. Watch manatees, dolphins, and anglers stream by the place. Large hickory trees lend shade. A horse farm is across the street, which is indicative of the rural setting.

Campsites, facilities: There are 26 grassy RV sites with full hookups tucked into this six-acre, 35-unit mobile home court on the Anclote River. On the premises are restrooms, showers, picnic tables, a dump station, a boat ramp, a dock, and laundry facilities. Restaurants, a beach, and three county parks are within walking distance. Children are permitted for short-term visits. Leashed, well-behaved pets are accepted.

Reservations, fees: Reservations are recommended. Sites are $25 per night for two people, plus $3 extra for each additional person. Credit cards are not accepted. Stay as long as you like.

Directions: From Alternate U.S. 19 in Tarpon Springs, just north of the Anclote River Bridge, drive west on Anclote Road for about 2.5 miles to the park entrance.

Contact: Hickory Point Mobile Home and RV Park, 1181 Anclote Road, Tarpon Springs, FL 34689, 727/937-7357.

12 ANCLOTE KEY STATE PRESERVE BOAT-IN SITES

Rating: 10

On Anclote Key three miles west of Tarpon Springs
St. Petersburg map, grid b2, page 366

The deserted white-sand beach is an amazing

four miles long, and camping here is a real Robinson Crusoe experience. No ferry service is available; you'll have to come in your own boat. Furthermore, there are no docks, so you'll have to anchor offshore and wade in or beach your boat on the sand. The effort is worthwhile, though. On the southern shore is a lighthouse built in 1887 that once guided shipping traffic with its 101-foot-high beacon. The island is a bird-watcher's delight; more than 43 species have been spotted, including the bald eagle. Rangers say the swimming is great, but they advise using caution because of boat traffic.

Campsites, facilities: Primitive camping is permitted on the north side of the island. A chemical toilet is available, but there are no other facilities. Bring everything you need, including water. There are several picnic shelters on the island for day use. All litter must be carried out. Children are welcome. Pets are forbidden.

Reservations, fees: Reservations are not necessary. Camping is free.

Directions: Boaters will need to use nautical chart 11411.

Contact: Anclote Key State Preserve, c/o Honeymoon Island State Park, 1 Causeway Boulevard, Dunedin, FL 34698, 727/469-5942.

13 PALM HARBOR RESORT

Rating: 3

In Palm Harbor
St. Petersburg map, grid b3, page 366

With just a few spots for overnighters, this trailer park and fish camp overlooks the Sutherland Bayou. Most folks here are anglers, and the park fills up fast for the entire winter.

Campsites, facilities: There are 28 RV sites with full hookups and picnic tables. About half have concrete pads. Restrooms, showers, laundry facilities, and telephone service are available. On the premises are a pool, a boat ramp, a fish-cleaning station, a clubhouse, and a bait

and tackle store. Children are welcome. Leashed pets are permitted.

Reservations, fees: Reservations are recommended. Sites are $28 per night for two people. Major credit cards are accepted. Long-term rates are available.

Directions: From Palm Harbor, drive north on Alternate 19 North to the Crystal Beach area. Look for the park on the big curve between Tampa Road and Alderman Road.

Contact: Palm Harbor Resort, 2119 Alternate 19 North, Palm Harbor, FL 34683, 727/785-3402.

14 BAY AIRE RV PARK

Rating: 5

In Palm Harbor
St. Petersburg map, grid b2, page 366

Like most Florida RV campgrounds, this park wears two coats: In the wintertime, retirees migrate south to renew old acquaintances and participate in planned activities in the recreation hall. In the off-season, the demographics are more mixed, and the place is less crowded. Either time, the grassy park has a friendly, homey feel, with a blend of Australian pines, palm trees, tropical shrubs, and grass lawns and a gate for security. Across the street is the Pinellas Trail, a 42-mile paved biking and walking path converted from an old railway. This park also makes a good stopover for those who want to explore Tarpon Springs and its Greek village.

Campsites, facilities: This park has 151 RV sites, all with full hookups, plus cable TV and telephone access. Tents are allowed only from May through October. A limited number of sites are available for 40-foot rigs and slide-out trailers. On the premises are restrooms, showers, a recreation hall, a pool, shuffleboard courts, horseshoe pits, and laundry facilities. The recreation hall and restrooms are wheelchair accessible. This is primarily an adult park. Children are welcome only in the summer months up to October 1; after that, they can visit campers. Leashed pets are welcome.

Reservations, fees: Reservations are recommended from November through April. Sites are $30 per night for two people, plus $1.50 for each additional person over the age of three. Cable TV, telephone, and 50-amp electrical service cost extra. Major credit cards are accepted. RVers can stay as long as they like.

Directions: From the intersection of Alternate U.S. 19 and State Road 584/Tampa Road, drive 1.4 miles north on Alternate U.S. 19. The park is on the east side of the road.

Contact: Bay Aire RV Park, 2242 Alternate U.S. 19, Palm Harbor, FL 34683, 727/784-4082, fax 727/784-9698 or 888/241-9090.

15 SHERWOOD FOREST RV RESORT

Rating: 4

In Palm Harbor

St. Petersburg map, grid b2, page 366

Beach lovers will appreciate the campground's proximity to Caladesi Island State Park and Honeymoon Island State Park. Ferry service is available to Caladesi Island from Honeymoon Island. The sponge docks of Tarpon Springs and the antique stores of downtown Dunedin are only minutes away. You can ride your bike on the Pinellas Trail, which passes within 100 feet of the campground. Tent sites overlook the little lake, which has canoeing and fishing.

Campsites, facilities: Campers will find 104 grassy RV sites with full hookups and seven primitive tent sites. On the premises are restrooms, showers, a clubhouse, a pool, and laundry facilities; all areas are said to be wheelchair accessible. Children are welcome. Cats and dogs under 35 pounds are permitted in a separate section.

Reservations, fees: Reservations are recommended. All sites are $29 per night for two people, plus $2.50 for each additional person and $1.50 for use of air conditioners. Tent sites are $20 to $25 without hookups. Credit cards are accepted. Long-term stays are OK.

Directions: From the intersection of Alternate U.S. 19 and State Road 586/Curlew Road, drive .8 mile north on Alternate U.S. 19 to the park on the west side of the road.

Contact: Sherwood Forest RV Resort, 251 Alternate U.S. 19 North, Palm Harbor, FL 34683, 727/784-4582.

16 CLEARWATER–TARPON SPRINGS KOA

Rating: 6

In Palm Harbor

St. Petersburg map, grid b2, page 366

If you like KOA-style camping and plan on doing a lot of sightseeing, then this park may be for you. It's on a busy six-lane highway and is convenient to Tarpon Springs, the beaches at Dunedin, and Central Florida attractions such as Busch Gardens, Weeki Wachee, St. Petersburg museums and aquariums, and Ybor City. The pool is heated.

Campsites, facilities: There are 92 RV sites with full hookups and cable TV, and a separate area for 24 tents with water and electricity. Restrooms, showers, laundry facilities, a dump station, a pool, and a recreation hall are on the property. A separate wheelchair-accessible restroom is provided, and all other areas of the park are navigable for wheelchairs. Children are welcome. Leashed pets are permitted.

Reservations, fees: Reservations are recommended. Sites are $30 per night for two people, plus $1.50 for extra children under 17 and $5 for each additional adult. Use of air conditioners and electric heaters costs $4 per day. Major credit cards are accepted. Long-term stays are OK.

Directions: From U.S. 19 and State Road 584/Tampa Road, drive 2.9 miles north on U.S. 19 to the park on the east side of the road.

Contact: Clearwater–Tarpon Springs KOA, 37061 U.S. 19 North, Palm Harbor, FL 34684, 727/937-8412 or 800/KOA-8743, website: www.koa.com.

17 CYPRESS POINT RV RESORT

Rating: 7

In Palm Harbor
St. Petersburg map, grid b2, page 366

Set on 35 acres overlooking Lake Tarpon, this park is minutes from public beaches and other attractions. Spanish moss hangs from some of the oaks near the marsh at water's edge. The location is convenient to the Tarpon Springs tourist area, restaurants, and Gulf beaches, but there's so much to do here, including swimming, boating, fishing, and tennis, that you may not want to leave. You can see the lake from the heated pool while you're swimming.

Campsites, facilities: The 402 sites have full hookups; telephone and cable TV service are available. On the premises are restrooms, showers, a clubhouse, a heated pool, a boat ramp, two playgrounds, a family recreation room, an adults-only card room, horseshoe pits, shuffleboard and tennis courts, a convenience store, and laundry facilities. The bathhouses, office, and recreation areas are wheelchair accessible. Children are allowed during the summer. Pets are permitted; a dog walk is available.

Reservations, fees: Reservations are recommended. Sites are $25 per night for two people, plus $2.50 for each additional person. Major credit cards are accepted. Long-term rates are available.

Directions: From the intersection of U.S. 19 and State Road 584/Tampa Road, drive north on U.S. 19 for three miles. The park is north of Alderman Road.

Contact: Cypress Point RV Resort, 37969 U.S. 19 North, Palm Harbor, FL 34684, 727/938-1966, website: www.rvresorts.com.

18 CALADESI RV PARK

Rating: 3

In Palm Harbor
St. Petersburg map, grid b2, page 366

Some shaded lots are available in this quiet park. It is near beaches, golf courses, the Pinellas walking and cycling trail, and Gulf fishing. Groceries and restaurants also are close by.

Campsites, facilities: This adults-oriented park has 85 grassy RV sites with full hookups. Three sites are pull-through; rigs up to 35 feet long can be accommodated. Restrooms, showers, picnic tables, a dump station, a pool, and laundry facilities are provided. Leashed small pets are permitted.

Reservations, fees: Reservations are recommended. Sites are $25 per night for two people, plus $2 for each additional person. Major credit cards are accepted.

Directions: From the intersection of Alternate U.S. 19 and State Road 586/Curlew Road in Dunedin, drive one mile north on Alternate U.S. 19 to Tampa Road. The park is on the northwest corner of the intersection.

Contact: Caladesi RV Park, 205 Dempsey Road, Palm Harbor, FL 34683, 727/784-3622, email: caladesi@yahoo.com.

19 DUNEDIN RV RESORT

Rating: 7

In Dunedin
St. Petersburg map, grid b2, page 366

Targeted to the "active and adventurous," this immaculate park is near everything civilized, but also very nature oriented. You can watch blue herons and egrets stalk their dinner in salt marshes on either side of the park. Oak trees provide shade for campers and homes for squirrels. The park is near the ocean and beaches. For guests who enjoy biking and walking, the Pinellas Trail passes right by the park. You're just three miles from the Caladesi Island ferry and Honeymoon Island State Park, the Toronto Blue Jays spring training facilities, Tarpon Springs sponge docks, antique shops, flea markets, deep-sea fishing, and restaurants.

Campsites, facilities: This 233-unit park has 100 RV sites with full hookups; 18 are pull-through. Cable TV and telephone service are available.

Restrooms, showers, a dump station, a recreation hall with big-screen TV and modem hookup, a heated pool, a playground, laundry facilities, and a clubhouse are provided. You'll also find shuffleboard courts, Ping-Pong, Foosball, volleyball, bocce ball, and a playground. The mobile homes are separated from the RV area. All sites, one bathhouse, the laundry room, and the recreation room are wheelchair accessible. Children and leashed pets are welcome.

Reservations, fees: Reservations are recommended. Sites are $33 to $40 per night for two people, plus $3 for each additional person and $2 for 50-amp electrical service. Major credit cards are accepted. Long-term rates are available.

Directions: From the intersection of Alternate U.S. 19 and State Road 586/Curlew Road in Dunedin, drive .5 mile north on Alternate U.S. 19 to the park.

Contact: Dunedin RV Resort, 2920 Alternate U.S. 19 North, Dunedin, FL 34698, 727/784-3719 or 800/345-7504, website: www.go-campingamerica.com/dunedinbeach.

20 CALADESI ISLAND STATE PARK

Rating: 10

On Caladesi Island west of Dunedin

St. Petersburg map, grid b2, page 366

You can't really camp here in the official sense of the word because you have to sleep on your boat. But since the island is accessible only by boat, we assume you'll love the 650 dry acres and 1,800 acres of mangrove flats and submerged lands—walk the four miles of unspoiled beach in search of the perfect seashell or hike the island's nature trails. The beach is so beautiful that it's been ranked as one of the top 10 in the United States for nearly a decade. A new floating concrete dock that is wheelchair accessible and a marine pump-out station were built a couple of years ago. In addition, the marina, seawalls, and boardwalk system were overhauled. If you don't have access to a boat, then you can make a day trip out of it by boarding the ferry that leaves from the Honeymoon Island State Park Marina on the hour between 10 A.M. and 4 P.M. For ferry information, call 727/442-7433, website: www.dolphinencounter.org.

Campsites, facilities: Boaters are welcome for overnight stays on this barrier island, although camping on the shore is not allowed. There are 100 boat slips at a dock located on the bay side of the island; electricity and water are available. Restrooms, cold-water showers, a picnic area with grills, and a concession stand are on the island. The marina, floating dock, concession stand, restrooms, and boardwalk to the beach are wheelchair accessible. Children are welcome, as are pets.

Reservations, fees: Reservations are recommended; call ReserveAmerica at 800/326-3521. Major credit cards are accepted. The fee is $9 per night for four people, plus $2 per extra person, $2 for electricity and $2 for pets with proof of rabies vaccine.

Directions: Boaters should use nautical chart 11411. Day visitors taking the ferry should drive west from U.S. 19 in Dunedin on State Road 586/Curlew Road until it ends at Honeymoon Island State Park. The ferry leaves from the state park's marina. It costs $4 to enter the park; the ferry fees are $7 for adults and $3.50 for children (round-trip).

Contact: Caladesi Island State Park, c/o Gulf Islands GEOPark, 1 Causeway Boulevard, Dunedin, FL 34698, 727/469-5918 or 727/469-5942, website: www.floridastateparks.org.

21 TRAVEL TOWNE RV RESORT

Rating: 5

In Clearwater

St. Petersburg map, grid b2, page 366

This Wilder RV Resorts–owned park targets retirees and full-timers who want to be close to shopping centers, golf, boat ramps, charter fishing services, and other attractions. Executive and PGA golf courses are within five minutes.

Campsites, facilities: This adults-only park has 360 RV sites with full hookups and patios, plus optional cable TV and telephone service. On the premises are restrooms, showers, picnic tables, a heated pool, a recreation hall with planned activities, shuffleboard courts, horseshoe pits, and laundry facilities. Children are welcome. Leashed pets are allowed.

Reservations, fees: Reservations are recommended. Sites are $23 per night for two people, plus $2.50 for each additional person. Major credit cards are accepted. Long-term stays are permitted.

Directions: From the intersection of State Road 60 and U.S. 19, travel north on U.S. 19 for 5.5 miles. The park is on the west side of the road.

Contact: Travel Towne RV Resort, 29850 U.S. 19 North, Clearwater, FL 33761, 727/784-2500, fax 727/784-7999, website: www.rvresorts.com.

22 INDIAN ROCKS BEACH RV RESORT

Rating: 7

In Indian Rocks Beach

St. Petersburg map, grid c2, page 366

A few coveted sites overlook the Intracoastal Waterway (and usually are taken), but others have lots of shade. The lure is that the powder-white, gulf-front beach is just 100 yards away, across the street from the park, which is set on a narrow barrier island. Shops, boating, and fishing are nearby. Keep your restroom key handy; bathrooms are locked around the clock. You'll get your key upon check-in.

Campsites, facilities: Among 54 sites, 30 RV overnight sites have full hookups. Picnic tables, restrooms, showers, laundry facilities, and a heated pool are available. For cable TV and phone service, you must call the appropriate utility company. Four restaurants are within a three-block walk. Most areas are wheelchair accessible. Children are welcome. Two leashed pets are permitted per site, although rottweilers, pit bulls, and Doberman pinschers are forbidden.

Reservations, fees: Reservations are advised. Sites are $30 to $50 per night for two people, plus $3 for each additional person. There is a $5 deposit for a bathroom key. Major credit cards are accepted. Long-term stays are OK.

Directions: From I-275, take Exit 31B and drive west on State Road 688/Ulmerton Road about 16 miles until it dead-ends at State Road 699/Gulf Boulevard. Turn north (right) and proceed less than one block to the park at right.

Contact: Indian Rocks Beach RV Resort, 601 Gulf Boulevard, Indian Rocks Beach, FL 33785, 727/596-7743.

23 INDIAN ROCKS TRAVEL PARK

Rating: 2

In Largo

St. Petersburg map, grid c2, page 366

An 18-hole golf course is within walking distance of this RV park. Best of all, though, this open and sunny park is just 1.5 miles east of the beach. The place is oriented to retirees who spend the winter in Florida, so expect organized activities.

Campsites, facilities: There are 30 RV sites with full hookups and access to cable TV and telephone service in this 175-unit retirement trailer park. On the premises are restrooms, showers, a dump station, a pool, a recreation room, shuffleboard courts, and laundry facilities. Families with small children may stay only for short visits. Pets are not welcome.

Reservations, fees: Reservations are recommended. Sites are $21 to $24 per night for two people, plus $3 for each additional person. Major credit cards are accepted. Long-term stays are OK.

Directions: From the intersection of U.S. 19 and State Road 688/Ulmerton Road, drive west on State Road 688 for 11 miles. At Vonn Road, turn right and continue .3 mile north to the park at right.

Contact: Indian Rocks Travel Park, 12121 Vonn Road, Largo, FL 33774, 727/595-2228.

24 SUN SEAIR MOBILE HOME AND RV PARK

Rating: 3

In Largo

St. Petersburg map, grid c2, page 366

Many snowbirds leave their RVs here during the summer when they return north. Spacious sites accommodate rigs up to 40 feet long at this 142-unit mobile home park set on 11 acres. Shade is minimal, but the park is neat and clean. Modern, self-contained units are the norm. St. Petersburg and Tampa attractions are conveniently close.

Campsites, facilities: This adult-oriented park offers 60 full-hookup sites for self-contained, modern RVs. Cable TV, telephone service, showers, a dump station, a heated pool, a clubhouse, shuffleboard courts, and laundry facilities are available. A supermarket, restaurants, and Kmart are within two miles. Children may visit for short periods. Pets under 15 pounds are permitted in a separate section.

Reservations, fees: Reservations are recommended. Sites are $20 per night for two people, plus $1 for each additional person. Credit cards are not accepted. Long-term rates are available.

Directions: From I-275, take Exit 30 and drive 1.5 miles northwest on State Road 686/Roosevelt Boulevard. At State Road 688/Ulmerton Road, turn west and drive three miles. Turn south on Haines Road and drive one block to 126th Avenue North. Go east to the park.

Contact: Sun Seair Mobile Home and RV Park, 6372 126th Avenue, Largo, FL 33773, 727/531-3644 or 800/451-4181.

25 YANKEE TRAVELER RV PARK

Rating: 7

In Largo

St. Petersburg map, grid c2, page 366

A maintenance crew works daily to keep up the park's neat appearance, and the managers live on site to ensure that older RVers have everything they need for a relaxing vacation. The pool is heated, and social programs are held in winter. Public parks, malls, and restaurants are close by. The park is undergoing major improvements to its infrastructure—with some sites offering up to 100-amp electrical service. The recreation hall was recently remodeled, and planned activities keep everyone busy during the high season. Under family ownership for 22 years, this park intends to stay in the big leagues of snowbird destinations. As the owners say, "Luxury at your front door—the best of Florida in your back yard." Lake Seminole is three miles away for the anglers in the group.

Campsites, facilities: There are 30 RV sites with full hookups for overnighters and 175 for seasonal visitors; telephone and cable TV service are available. Rigs up to 40 feet can be accommodated. All sites have picnic tables, grills, and cable TV. On the premises are restrooms, showers, a dump station, a pool, a Jacuzzi, a wheelchair-accessible recreation hall, horseshoe pits, shuffleboard courts, dog-walk area, and laundry facilities. Campers must be over 55; children may visit them for short periods. Pets under 15 pounds are permitted.

Reservations, fees: Reservations are recommended. Sites are $24 per night for two people, plus $1.50 for each additional person. Major credit cards are accepted. Long-term rates are available.

Directions: From I-275 southbound, take Exit 31B on Ulmerton Road west for 6.6 miles. The campground is on the left. Northbound, take Exit 30. Drive 1.5 miles northwest on State Road 686/Roosevelt Boulevard. At State Road 688/Ulmerton Road, turn west and drive 5.1 miles to the park on the south side of the road.

Contact: Yankee Traveler RV Park, 8500 Ulmerton Road, Largo, FL 33771, 727/531-7998, fax 727/373-0084, website: www.yankeetraveler.net.

26 SUNBURST RV PARK— ST. PETERSBURG

Rating: 6

In Largo

St. Petersburg map, grid c2, page 366

Bingo, billiards, card games, and trips to the dog track entertain RVers at this park, part of the Encore chain. Stores, hair salons, an 18-hole golf course, restaurants, and shopping are nearby.

Campsites, facilities: There are 288 full-hookup RV sites with cable TV. Rigs up to 45 feet long can be accommodated. Restrooms, showers, a dump station, laundry facilities, and telephone service are available. On the premises are a pool, a recreation hall with planned activities, horseshoe pits, shuffleboard courts, billiards room, and a golf net. Children are welcome. Leashed pets are permitted.

Reservations, fees: Reservations are recommended. Sites are $20 and up per night. Major credit cards are accepted. Long-term rates are available.

Directions: From I-275 southbound, take Exit 31B on Ulmerton Road west. The park is just past Roosevelt Road on the left.

Contact: Sunburst RV Park—St. Petersburg, 6900 Ulmerton Road, Largo, FL 33771, 727/531-5589 or 877/297-2757, fax 727/531-0160, website: www.rvonthego.com.

27 BRIARWOOD TRAVEL VILLA

Rating: 5

In Largo

St. Petersburg map, grid c2, page 366

You may forget you're in the city; when we were there, we were stunned to find such a pretty RV spot in an urban setting. Even though there's a bus stop at the front, this peaceful community is heavily wooded with hundreds of tall oak trees and winding paved roads that encircle little Lake Kathleen. "Sometimes I feel like I have my own little cabin out in the woods," says one resident, whose remarks are printed in the park brochure, and we concur. Some lots overlook the one-acre lake, and all sites have shade trees. Golf courses, groceries, a mall, and laundry facilities are nearby; the Pinellas Trail bike path is .5 mile away. RV and boat storage is available.

Campsites, facilities: This adults-only park has 138 RV sites, most with full hookups, and 18 tent sites. Cable TV and telephone service are available. On the premises are a dump station, a picnic shelter, horseshoe pits, shuffleboard courts, and a restaurant. Campers must be self-contained; there are no showers or restrooms. Children are permitted for short stays only; the park prefers campers who are over 55. Dogs are not welcome, but cats are.

Reservations, fees: Reservations are not taken. Sites are $25 per night. Credit cards are not accepted. Long-term rates are available.

Directions: From the intersection of State Road 688/Ulmerton Road and Alternate U.S. 19/Seminole Boulevard in Largo, drive two blocks north on Seminole Boulevard. The park is on the west side.

Contact: Briarwood Travel Villa, 2098 Seminole Boulevard, Largo, FL 33778, 727/581-6694.

28 HOLIDAY CAMPGROUND

Rating: 6

In Seminole

St. Petersburg map, grid c2, page 366

This park is located on a saltwater bayou with access to the Gulf of Mexico. You can fish from the pier in the waters of Long Bayou or ride your bike around the sprawling complex. The swimming pool, shuffleboard courts, and horseshoe pits are near the main highway, which can carry quite a bit of traffic. If you're tent camping with kids, you'll like the fact that the playground is close by.

Campsites, facilities: This park has 650 RV sites, most with full hookups and cable TV service, and a separate tent camping area that can accommodate up to 25 or more tents. Waterfront sites have water and electricity only. On the premises are restrooms, showers, picnic tables, shuffleboard and bocce (lawn bowling) courts, horseshoe pits, a pool, a spa, a recreation hall, a fishing pier, a playground, laundry facilities, and a store. Children are allowed. Two small, leashed pets are welcome per site; Dobermans, rottweilers, and pit bulls are prohibited.

Reservations, fees: Reservations are recommended. Sites are $17 to $23 per night for two people, plus $2 for each additional person. Major credit cards are accepted. Long-term stays are permitted.

Directions: From I-275, take Exit 28 and drive 7.5 miles west on State Route 694 (Gandy Boulevard) to the park at left.

Contact: Holiday Campground, 10000 Park Boulevard, Seminole, FL 33777, 727/391-4960 or 800/354-7559.

29 BICKLEY PARK

Rating: 3

In Seminole
St. Petersburg map, grid c2, page 366

Concrete-pad sites accommodate rigs up to 35 feet long at this park set beside a busy highway. It's 1.5 miles from the beach and near golf courses, fishing, shopping, and churches. Bay Pines Veterans Hospital is one mile away. But what really keeps the same folks coming back winter after winter are the planned activities, such as potluck dinners, bingo, crafts, and parties. "We're just a friendly mom-and-pop place," says the manager.

Campsites, facilities: The 186-unit adults-only park has 154 RV sites available, with full hookups, cable TV, and telephone service. Restrooms, showers, shuffleboard courts, a clubhouse, and laundry facilities are provided. Most of the park is wheelchair accessible. Children are not welcome. Leashed pets under 35 pounds are permitted.

Reservations, fees: Reservations are recommended. Sites are $25 to $30 per night for two people, plus $3 per extra person. Major credit cards are accepted. Long-term rates are available.

Directions: From I-275, take Exit 28 and drive nine miles west on County Road 694 (Gandy Boulevard/Park Boulevard) to Alternate U.S. 19 (Seminole Boulevard). Turn south and drive 1.5 miles to the park, which is on the west side between 54th and 57th Streets.

Contact: Bickley Park, 5640 Seminole Boulevard, Seminole, FL 33772, 727/392-3807.

30 ST. PETERSBURG RESORT KOA

Rating: 6

In St. Petersburg
St. Petersburg map, grid c2, page 366

A secluded family resort, this KOA offers large sites in a quiet oak- and palm-shaded setting adjacent to Boca Ciega Bay and two miles from Gulf of Mexico beaches. The bay provides boat access to the gulf waters. Among the activities for kids are video games, bike rentals, and miniature golf. Sites of interest nearby include the Pinellas Trail bike path, Busch Gardens, Sunken Gardens, the municipal pier, John's Pass Boardwalk, the Great Explorations Hands-on Museum, and the Florida Aquarium. Of special note is the Salvador Dali Museum (727/823-3767), the world's largest collection of the artist's surrealist works, including several huge "masterwork" canvases. Originally a private collection, the art was moved from Cleveland to St. Petersburg by the owners in 1982.

Campsites, facilities: The campground has 379 RV sites (87 pull-through) with full hookups; it also has nine tent-only sites with no hookups, separated from the RVs. Restrooms, showers, picnic tables, a dump station, a pool, a Jacuzzi, a boat ramp, docks, a playground, a game room, walking trails, horseshoe pits, shuffleboard and volleyball courts, laundry facilities, and a store are on the property. The stores, restrooms, recreation hall, pool, and pier are

wheelchair accessible. Rental cabins are available. Children and leashed pets are welcome.
Reservations, fees: Reservations are recommended. Sites are $30 to $70 per night for two people, plus $6 for each additional adult and $4 for children. Major credit cards are accepted. RV campers can stay as long as they like.
Directions: From I-275, take Exit 25 and drive 5.5 miles west on 38th Avenue North. Veer right onto Tyrone Boulevard/Bay Pines Boulevard and drive 1.5 miles to 95th Street, then turn north and continue .5 mile.
Contact: St. Petersburg Resort KOA, 5400 95th Street North, St. Petersburg, FL 33708, 727/392-2233 or 800/562-7714, fax 727/398-6081, website: www.koa.com.

31 ROBERT'S MOBILE HOME AND RV RESORT

Rating: 4

In St. Petersburg
St. Petersburg map, grid c3, page 366

This 624-unit, neatly manicured mobile home park draws older campers who appreciate the large RV sites shaded by oaks and pines. Social programs are held in winter; you can also play tennis or relax in the pool's spa.
Campsites, facilities: There are 427 RV sites with full hookups, cable TV, and available telephone service. On the premises are restrooms, showers, a dump station, a recreation room, a pool, a Jacuzzi, horseshoe pits, shuffleboard, volleyball and tennis courts, and laundry facilities. All areas are wheelchair accessible. Older travelers are preferred. Pets under 40 pounds are permitted.
Reservations, fees: Reservations are recommended. Sites are $25 per night for two people, plus $3 for each additional person. Credit cards are not accepted.
Directions: From I-275, take Exit 28 and drive 1.3 miles west on County Road 694 (Gandy Boulevard/Park Boulevard) to the park.
Contact: Robert's Mobile Home and RV Re-

sort, 3390 Gandy Boulevard North, St. Petersburg, FL 33702, 727/577-6820, website: www.robertsrv.com.

32 FORT DE SOTO PARK CAMPGROUND

Rating: 10

On Pinellas Bayway South in Tampa Bay
St. Petersburg map, grid d3, page 366

Not only is this park heavily wooded and shady, but it also has great water views and abundant foliage screening campers from their neighbors. The branches hang so low over the road that some RVers have complained about it being difficult to drive through. Alcoholic beverages are prohibited. You are not allowed to swim in the waters off the campground, but there are two swimming beaches within the park. A pet beach is a new addition. Like most great parks so close to a city, Fort De Soto draws a crowd on weekends, and you cannot stay here unless you make reservations in person.
Campsites, facilities: This 235-site county campground is divided into two areas: one along a spit of land surrounded by water, the other fronting on the bay. Among them are 149 RV sites and 86 tent sites. Almost all sites are waterfront, and some have good views of St. Petersburg and the Gulf of Mexico. Most areas are wheelchair accessible. Sites 1 through 85 are designated for tent, van, and pop-up campers; the good news is that these are beautifully situated on the waterfront. The RV sites are excellent, too. Water, electricity, picnic tables, grills, restrooms, showers, a dump station, laundry facilities, a store, and two play areas are provided. A boat ramp is in the park. Children are welcome. Previously prohibited, pets are now allowed.
Reservations, fees: Reservations are recommended and must be made in person no more than 30 days in advance of stay; you cannot reserve by phone or by mail. The minimum stay is two nights. You can make reserva-

tions at the campground, or at two other offices: 631 Chestnut Street in Clearwater, 727/464-3347; or at 501 First Avenue North, Room A116, St. Petersburg, 727/582-7738. Sites are $23 per night for six people from August through December; the rest of the year, the base fee is $33. Credit cards are not accepted. The maximum stay is 14 days during any 30-day period between January and April; the rest of the year, you may extend your visit by 14 days depending on availability of campsites.

Directions: From I-275, take Exit 17 and drive two miles west on State Road 682, also known as U.S. 19 North/54th Avenue South/Pinellas Bayway. At Pinellas Bayway South, turn south and continue about three miles to the park.

Contact: Fort De Soto Park Campground, 3500 Pinellas Bayway South, Tierra Verde, FL 33715, 727/582-2267, website: www.fortdesoto.com.

Chapter 12

Greater Tampa

Greater Tampa

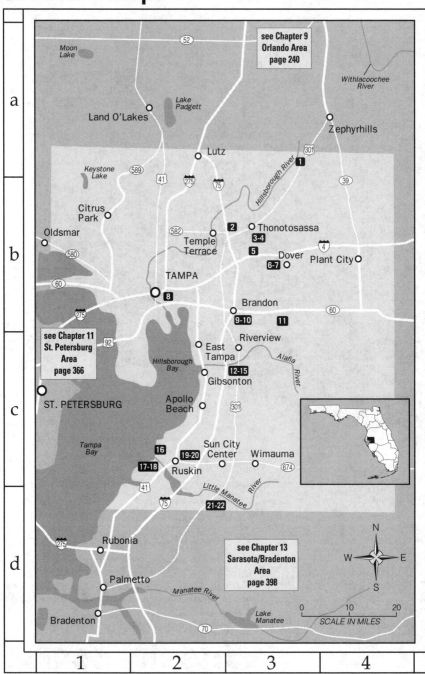

Moon Lake

52

see Chapter 9
Orlando Area
page 240

Withlacoochee River

Lake Padgett

a

Land O'Lakes

Zephyrhills

Lutz

301

1

Keystone Lake

589

41

275

75

39

Hillsborough River

Citrus Park

2

Thonotosassa

3-4

Oldsmar

582

Temple Terrace

5

4

Dover

Plant City

580

6-7

60

TAMPA

8

Brandon

60

b

see Chapter 11
St. Petersburg Area
page 366

92

9-10

11

Riverview

East Tampa

Alafia River

Hillsborough Bay

12-15

Gibsonton

ST. PETERSBURG

Apollo Beach

301

c

Tampa Bay

16

Sun City Center

Wimauma

19-20

674

17-18

Ruskin

Little Manatee River

41

75

21-22

see Chapter 13
Sarasota/Bradenton Area
page 398

Rubonia

N

275

W   E

Palmetto

S

Manatee River

Bradenton

70

Lake Manatee

0   10   20

SCALE IN MILES

◘ HILLSBOROUGH RIVER STATE PARK

Rating: 10

North of Thonotosassa and south of Zephyrhills

Greater Tampa map, grid a3, page 384

Like most of the Florida parks developed by the Civilian Conservation Corps during the 1930s, Hillsborough River State Park is a jewel. The river flows through a lush forest of pines and oaks, its waters dark with tannin. Canoeing is great because this is one of the few rivers in the state with Class II rapids. There are eight miles of nature trails, and a huge man-made, spring-fed swimming pool draws crowds of bathers on hot summer days. You can also tour Fort Foster (by reservation only); sometimes, volunteers clad in period dress enact what life was like in the fort in the 1830s when its role was to protect a military road during the Indian wars. Bicycles and canoes are available for rent; you're not allowed to take rental canoes on the rapids. The campground is thoughtfully arranged in three loops, so there's a feeling of privacy and seclusion. Pick up supplies in Thonotosassa or Zephyrhills.

Campsites, facilities: There are 106 sites, all with water and 84 with electricity, all available for both RVers and tent campers. Picnic tables, grills, fire rings, restrooms, showers, a dump station, a pool, canoe rentals, hiking trails, a historic fort, horseshoe pits, a snack bar, and laundry facilities are available. Campsites, picnic areas, and the pool are wheelchair accessible. Children are welcome. Leashed pets are permitted in the Hammock Circle camping area with proof of vaccination.

Reservations, fees: Reservations are recommended; call ReserveAmerica at 800/326-3521. Sites are $13 per night for four people, plus $2 for each additional person and $2 for electricity. Pets cost $2 extra. Major credit cards are accepted. The maximum stay is 14 days in winter, 120 days at other times.

Directions: From I-75, take Exit 265 and drive east on State Road 582/Fowler Avenue for 1.2 miles. At U.S. 301, turn north and drive 12 miles to the park. From I-4, take Exit 7 onto U.S. 301 and drive 13 miles north to the park.

Contact: Hillsborough River State Park, 15402 U.S. 301 North, Thonotosassa, FL 33592, 813/987-6771, fax 813/987-6773, website: www.floridastateparks.org.

◙ HAPPY TRAVELER RV PARK

Rating: 6

East of I-75 in Thonotosassa

Greater Tampa map, grid b3, page 384

Leafy trees shadow many of the sites in this RV-oriented park, which claims to be the closest campground to Busch Gardens, the zoo and roller coaster attraction. The Big Top Flea Market is across the street, and plenty of shops and restaurants are nearby. But what really puts the 28-acre park on the map is its next-door neighbor, Canoe Escape (813/986-2067). Campers can get discounts to paddle rental canoes on the peaceful Hillsborough River. Paved interior roads lead to sites that are grassy or dirt; a few are concrete. Although you're only 12 miles from downtown Tampa, you'll see lots of birds and wildlife.

Campsites, facilities: This adult park has 224 full-hookup sites for RVs or tents. On the premises are restrooms, showers, a dump station, a pool, a clubhouse, tennis, shuffleboard, horseshoes, table tennis, and laundry facilities. All ages are welcome, but no one under age 21 can stay longer than two weeks. Leashed, nonaggressive pets are allowed.

Reservations, fees: Reservations are recommended. Sites are $23.50 per night for two people, plus $1 for each additional person. Major credit cards are accepted. Long-term stays are OK.

Directions: From I-75, take Exit 265 onto Fowler Avenue and go .5 mile east to the park, at the corner of Walker Road.

Contact: Happy Traveler RV Park, 9401 East

Fowler Avenue, Thonotosassa, FL 33592, 813/986-3094 or 800/758-2795, fax 813/986-9077, email: htrvpk@aol.com.

3 CAMP LEMORA RV PARK

Rating: 6

In Thonotosassa

Greater Tampa map, grid b3, page 384

Much of the park is open to the sun, with plenty of space for big RVs, and a little creek runs down the back of the property. The owners describe the place as a quiet, relaxing nature park close to springs, a river, and a lake, with an area for hiking nearby.

Campsites, facilities: This 302-slot RV park has 130 sites available for overnight campers. Full hookups, plus telephone service and picnic tables are available. On the premises are restrooms, showers, a dump station, a pool, horseshoe pits, shuffleboard courts, a general store, and laundry facilities. Most areas are wheelchair accessible. Children are welcome. Leashed pets are allowed.

Reservations, fees: Reservations are recommended. Sites are $21 per night for two people, plus $2 for each additional person. Credit cards are not accepted. Long-term stays are OK.

Directions: From I-75, take Exit 265 and drive east on State Road 582/Fowler Avenue for 1.2 miles. At U.S. 301, turn north and drive eight miles to the park. From I-4, take Exit 7 onto U.S. 301 and drive north for 1.5 miles. Or, from I-4 at Exit 6, drive north on U.S. 301 for 12.5 miles.

Contact: Camp Lemora RV Park, 14910 Dead River Road, Thonotosassa, FL 33592, 813/986-4456.

4 SOUTHERN AIRE

Rating: 6

In Thonotosassa

Greater Tampa map, grid b3, page 384

Rigs up to 40 feet long can be accommodated

on the manicured grounds of this countryside park. A sunny, Olympic-sized, heated pool, neatly tended shuffleboard courts, and a large private lake keep snowbirds busy during the season.

Campsites, facilities: This park has 450 sites with full hookups, plus cable TV, picnic tables, and telephone service. On the premises are restrooms, showers, a recreation hall, a pool, a Jacuzzi, horseshoe pits, shuffleboard courts, and laundry facilities. Children and pets are permitted.

Reservations, fees: Reservations are not necessary. Sites are $21 per night for two people, plus $2.50 for each additional person. Major credit cards are accepted. Long-term rates are available.

Directions: From I-4, take Exit 10 and drive north on County Road 579 for four miles. Turn right on Florence Avenue and drive .1 mile east to the park.

Contact: Southern Aire, 10511 Florence Avenue, Thonotosassa, FL 33592, 813/986-1596, website: www.rvresorts.com.

5 RALLY PARK (FORMERLY LAZY DAYS RV RESORT)

Rating: 4

Northeast of Tampa

Greater Tampa map, grid b3, page 384

This RV park is part of a 104-acre RV-oriented shopping center, the Lazy Days Super Center, with more than 800 new and used rigs on display and a Camping World store where you can pick up needed supplies. Overnighters and rally groups are welcome, and there's a full-time coordinator to help plan group events. The banquet kitchen can serve as many as 600 people. Of course, if you want to kick the tires of a new RV, this is the place.

Campsites, facilities: There are 300 RV sites with full hookups, concrete pads, and picnic tables. Rigs up to 45 feet can be accommodated. Restrooms, showers, laundry facilities, a dump station, a screened and heated pool, a

12,000-square-foot recreation hall, a computer room with Internet access, tennis courts, and horseshoe and shuffleboard courts are on the premises. A Cracker Barrel restaurant is part of the complex. All areas are wheelchair accessible. Included with the price of your site is breakfast and lunch Monday through Saturday, cable TV, and the morning newspaper. Children are welcome. Leashed pets are permitted.

Reservations, fees: Reservations are recommended. Sites are $25 per night. Major credit cards are accepted. The maximum stay is two weeks.

Directions: From I-4 north of Tampa, take Exit 10 northbound on County Road 579 for .2 mile to the Lazy Days Super Center.

Contact: Rally Park, 6210 County Road 579, Seffner, FL 33584, 813/246-4777 or 800/905-6627, fax 813/246-5504, website: www.lazydays.com

6 SUNBURST SUPERPARK—TAMPA EAST (FORMERLY GREEN ACRES RV RESORT)

Rating: 7

Near Dover

Greater Tampa map, grid b3, page 384

Convenient to the interstate and to Tampa attractions 12 miles west, the park attracts retirees and families on vacation. Some visitors head to Busch Gardens theme park, one of the nation's largest zoos. It has more than 2,700 animals, lots of children's educational activities, and a petting zoo, as well as the world's two tallest inverted roller coasters. In winter, the RV park largely becomes a snowbird park, and social programs include music jamborees, dances, line dancing, potlucks, and parties. RVs up to 45 feet long can be accommodated. This is a good place to stay when attending RV shows nearby. Interior paved roads lead to a mixture of sites, some grassy and sunny, others shell-carpeted and shaded by palms. Some sites have patios.

Campsites, facilities: All but 23 of the 428 RV sites have full hookups; the rest have water and electricity. Thirty tent sites have water and electricity. Most sites have picnic tables. Restrooms, showers, laundry facilities, a dump station, two heated pools, a spa, a fishing pond, horseshoes, shuffleboard, volleyball, card rooms, and a recreation hall are available. A convenience store is across the street. Children are welcome. Leashed pets are permitted.

Reservations, fees: Reservations are recommended. Sites are $31 to $39. Major credit cards are accepted. Long-term stays are OK.

Directions: From I-4, take Exit 14 and drive south on McIntosh Road for .25 mile. At the first traffic light, turn west (right). Proceed about 200 yards to the park.

Contact: Sunburst SuperPark—Tampa East, 12870 U.S. 92, Dover, FL 33527, 813/659-0002 or 877/917-2757, fax 813/659-2026, website: www.rvonthego.com.

7 ENCORE RV PARK—TAMPA EAST

Rating: 8

Near Dover

Greater Tampa map, grid b3, page 384

This place is part of Encore's new brand of high-end parks designed for active, older RVers who want to spend one month or longer in a resort community that boasts: "Park your wheels. Kick up your heels!" Yet tourists, overnight travelers, and camping clubs are welcome, too. The pool is heated, and kids have a playground to keep them occupied. Kids can also fish in the pond on the property. A couple of sites are "CyberSites," meaning they provide modem hookups.

Campsites, facilities: All 262 full-hookup sites accommodate tents or RVs. Picnic tables, restrooms, showers, laundry facilities, a dump station, a pool, a playground, horseshoes, meeting halls, a fishing pond, propane, cable TV, phone hookups, and shuffleboard are available. Restaurants and shops are a 10-minute drive away. Children are welcome. Leashed pets are permitted.

Reservations, fees: Reservations are recommended. Sites are $32 to $38 per night; higher during special events. Major credit cards are accepted. Long-term stays are OK.

Directions: From I-4, take Exit 14. Drive south about one-eighth of a mile to the park at right.

Contact: Encore RV Park—Tampa East, 4630 McIntosh Road, Dover, FL 33527, 813/659-2504 or 800/454-7336, fax 813/659-2171, website: www.rvonthego.com.

8 BAY BAYOU RV RESORT

Rating: 5

West side of Tampa

Greater Tampa map, grid b2, page 384

Free coffee and snacks are served each morning to wintertime campers, who also enjoy a full menu of planned activities, including ice-cream socials, potluck dinners, bingo, card games, poker, and special outings. Sites are grassy, oversized, and shady with paved access roads. Some even overlook a creek. The modern, free-form pool is heated during the cooler months, and the Jacuzzi is kept at the same temperature as the pool. Tampa Bay Downs, a thoroughbred racetrack, is nearby.

Campsites, facilities: All 240 RV sites in this adult-oriented park have full hookups, and many come with optional telephone service. On the premises are picnic tables, restrooms, showers, a dump station, a pool, a Jacuzzi, shuffleboard courts, and laundry facilities. All areas are wheelchair accessible. Children are permitted for a maximum of 30 days. One leashed dog under 30 pounds is allowed per site.

Reservations, fees: Reservations are recommended. Sites are $27 to $29 per night for two people, plus $2 for each extra person. Major credit cards are accepted. Long-term rates are available.

Directions: From I-275, take Exit 50 and drive west on Busch Boulevard for .1 mile. At Florida Avenue, turn left and drive .5 mile south. At Waters Avenue, turn and travel west for 10 miles to Country Way Boulevard. Turn south and drive .25 mile. Turn west on Memorial Highway and drive .8 mile to the park.

Contact: Bay Bayou RV Resort, 12622 Memorial Highway, Tampa, FL 33635, 813/855-1000, fax 813/925-0815, email: baybayourv@aol.com.

9 CITRUS HILLS RV PARK

Rating: 3

East of Brandon

Greater Tampa map, grid b3, page 384

This quiet, shady park recently tripled its number of spaces to 220. A swimming pool is planned for the future. About half of the sites are sunny; oaks lend shade to the rest. It's a retiree magnet in winter, when bingo and potluck dinners are among activities. The park is close to several Tampa attractions, including Ybor City, a worthwhile stop. At the turn of the century, Ybor City was home to more than one hundred cigar factories that employed Cuban, Spanish, and Italian immigrants. Today, the National Historic Landmark District is celebrated for its charm and its vibrant nightlife featuring blues cafés, rock clubs, a microbrewery, and restaurants—the most famous being the Columbia, which serves authentic Spanish cuisine. Explore the area's past as the "cigar capital of the world" at the Ybor City State Museum (813/247-6323), housed in an old bakery with a restored cigar worker's home on the grounds. Now you know where "Hav-a-Tampa" came from.

Campsites, facilities: All 220 RV sites have full hookups with cable. Seventy have telephone hookups. More than half are permanent resident. No sites are pull-through. On the premises are picnic tables, restrooms, and showers. Restaurants and a supermarket are one mile away. The park targets retired travelers, but there are no age restrictions. Small pets are allowed.

Reservations, fees: Reservations are not necessary. Sites are $20 per night for two people, plus $3 for each additional person. Credit cards are not accepted. Long-term stays are OK.

Directions: From I-75, take Exit 257 and drive east on State Road 60 about two miles to the park on the east side of Brandon.

Contact: Citrus Hills RV Park, 5311 East State Road 60, Dover, FL 33527, 813/737-4770.

10 LITHIA SPRINGS PARK

Rating: 9

Southeast of Brandon

Greater Tampa map, grid b3, page 384

Camping is a first-come, first-served deal at this popular 160-acre Hillsborough County park, so you'll have to register early on holiday weekends. The oversized sites are shaded by a jungle of scrub oak trees. Each year, some 200,000 people come from all over to swim in the 72-degree spring, which has been fenced off and resembles a municipal pool. A lifeguard is on duty on winter weekends, and everyone is ordered out of the water every hour or two for safety checks. You can canoe and fish in the Alafia River, but swimming is banned by the health department. Improvements are planned at this county park by 2004. Call ahead to be sure the park is open.

Campsites, facilities: There are 40 RV and tent sites with water, electricity, picnic tables, grills, and fire rings. Some sites will not fit RVs because of low-hanging trees. Restrooms, showers, a dump station, horseshoe pits, and a playground are on the property. Children are welcome. Leashed pets are permitted.

Reservations, fees: Reservations are not taken. Campsites are $12 per night. Credit cards are not accepted. The maximum stay is 14 days.

Directions: From I-75, take Exit 257 and drive east on State Road 60 for two miles. At County Road 640/Lithia Road, turn right and drive south to the park.

Contact: Lithia Springs Park, 3932 Lithia Springs Road, Lithia, FL 33547, 813/744-5572. Hillsborough County Parks and Recreation Administrative Office: 1101 East River Cove Street, Tampa, FL 33604, 813/975-2160, website: www.hillsboroughcounty.org/parks.

11 EDWARD MEDARD PARK AND RESERVOIR

Rating: 9

East of Brandon

Greater Tampa map, grid b3, page 384

Improvements are planned at this county park by 2004. Call ahead to be sure the park is open. Once a phosphate mine, this 1,284-acre tract near the Alafia River includes a 700-acre reservoir with a white-sand swimming beach. The emphasis is on fishing. Bream, speckled perch, and catfish are plentiful, but officials are trying hard to increase the population of the coveted largemouth bass. Paradoxically, to encourage bigger, better bass, anglers are urged to harvest those under 14 inches; that's so the older fish can mature and grow. And to really get the frenzy going, two fish feeders have been placed in the lake near the Burnt Stump dock and a footbridge. You're invited to bring commercial fish food, dry dog food, oatmeal, and even bread to use as chum. Boaters are instructed to anchor away from four fish attractors in deeper water and to cast toward them. The state's regulations on largemouth bass don't apply here, where it's a whole different ball game. For more angling tips, get a copy of the park's fishing brochure.

The heavily wooded campsites are arranged in two loops near the lake, and horseback-riding trails wind through the park. Allow four hours for a round-trip ride on the bridle paths. (You can rent horses by the hour at the stable just north of the park.) Because no reservations are accepted and the park receives about 500,000 visitors a year, try to time your visit for the middle of the week and on nonholiday weekends.

Phosphate, used to manufacture agricultural fertilizer, is dug from enormous earth-scarring pits, and it's interesting to see how land used for such a purpose can be reclaimed for public recreation. The soil around the so-called Sacred Hills play and picnic area was dug from the mine.

Campsites, facilities: This Hillsborough County park has 40 sites with water, electricity, picnic tables, and grills. Restrooms, showers, a dump station, a boat ramp, a fishing pier, a playground, nature trails, horseshoe pits, and horseback-riding trails are available. Groceries, restaurants, and laundry facilities are nearby. Children and pets are welcome.

Reservations, fees: Reservations are not accepted. Sites are $12 per night. Credit cards are not accepted. Campers must register one-half hour before sunset. If the sign says the campground is full, drive through and check, then go back and tell the ranger about any empty spots. The maximum stay is 14 days.

Directions: From I-75, take Exit 257 and drive east on State Road 60 through Brandon. Continue six miles farther. At Turkey Creek Road, turn and drive one mile south to the park.

Contact: Edward Medard Park and Reservoir, 5276 Panther Loop, Plant City, FL 33567, 813/757-3802, fax 813/757-3939. Hillsborough County Parks and Recreation Administrative Office: 1101 East River Cove Street, Tampa, FL 33604, 813/975-2160, website: www.hillsboroughcounty.org/parks.

12 HIDDEN RIVER TRAVEL RESORT

Rating: 7

In Riverview

Greater Tampa map, grid c3, page 384

The quiet, peaceful Alafia River runs the length of the resort. Fish from the docks on the river, swim in the heated pool, relax by the one-acre lake, or drive a few golf balls on the three-hole course. There's also a 2.5-mile nature trail. Planned activities are held November through April.

Campsites, facilities: All 350 RV sites have full hookups, plus cable TV and telephone service. On the premises are picnic tables, restrooms, showers, laundry facilities, a dump station, a pool, a boat ramp, boat docks, a playground, a nature trail, a small golf course, horseshoe pits, a volleyball area, a game room, rental trailers, a camp circle, and a one-acre lake. The common areas are wheelchair accessible. Adults are preferred, but children are welcome for short stays. Pets are permitted. Annual residents are especially welcome.

Reservations, fees: Reservations are recommended. Sites are $23 per night for two people, plus $2 for each additional person. Credit cards are not accepted.

Directions: From I-75, take Exit 250 and drive east on Gibsonton Drive/Boyette Road for 2.5 miles. At McMullen Loop Road, turn north and drive .8 mile to the park.

Contact: Hidden River Travel Resort, 12500 McMullen Loop Road, Riverview, FL 33569, 813/677-1515.

13 ALAFIA RIVER RV RESORT

Rating: 7

In Riverview

Greater Tampa map, grid c3, page 384

Swim in the heated pool or launch your fishing boat from the boat ramp on the Alafia River. Shade trees and river views give the park a natural atmosphere, even though it's conveniently close to the interstate.

Campsites, facilities: All 203 RV sites (four pull-through) have full hookups; cable TV and telephone service are available for long-term visitors. Restrooms, showers, laundry facilities, a dump station, a pool, a clubhouse, horseshoe pits, shuffleboard courts, and a boat ramp are provided. The restrooms and clubhouse are wheelchair accessible. Children are welcome. Leashed pets under 25 pounds are permitted.

Reservations, fees: Reservations are recommended. Sites are $22 per night for two people, plus $2.50 for each extra person and $1.50 for electricity. Major credit cards are accepted. Long-term stays are OK.

Directions: From I-75, take Exit 250 east and drive .25 mile to the park.

Contact: Alafia River RV Resort, 9812 Gibsonton Drive, Riverview, FL 33569, 813/677-1997 or 800/555-4384, website: www.alafia riverrvresort.com.

14 RICE CREEK RV RESORT

Rating: 7

In Riverview

Greater Tampa map, grid c3, page 384

The park attracts snowbirds with its paved, lighted streets, a mix of sunny and shady sites with concrete patios, and a tree canopy of massive oaks. All sorts of recreational facilities are available, including craft and pool rooms and a lounge. Entertainers are booked into the 15,000-square-foot clubhouse. Groceries, restaurants, and golf courses are nearby.

Campsites, facilities: The RV resort has 573 full-hookup sites. Cable TV, telephone service, restrooms, showers, laundry facilities, a heated pool, a Jacuzzi, a clubhouse, an exercise room, a library, horseshoe pits, and shuffleboard courts are available. Campers over age 55 are preferred. Leashed pets are permitted.

Reservations, fees: Reservations are required during winter and recommended the rest of the year. Sites are $23 per night for two people, plus $2.50 for each additional person. Major credit cards are accepted. Long-term rates are available.

Directions: From I-75, take Exit 250 and drive east on Gibsonton Drive/Boyette Road for one mile to U.S. 301. Turn south and drive .25 mile to the park, which is on the left.

Contact: Rice Creek RV Resort, 10714 U.S. 301 South, Riverview, FL 33569, 813/677-6640, fax 813/677-1373, website: www.rvresorts.com.

15 ALAFIA RIVER STATE PARK

Rating: 10

East of Riverview

Greater Tampa map, grid c3, page 384

These 6,879 acres were once a phosphate mine. Today, this land is becoming famed as the site of some of the best mountain bike trails in Florida. But the news for everyone else is that campers, equestrians, and canoeists will find a home here, too. The park was originally opened for day use only in 1998, but recently a campground was completed. There is a ranger station on site and a picnic area. The park has 14 miles of off-road biking for users of varying skills (in the parlance of one biker, the red markers for advanced users really do mean "advanced"). Horseback riders can meander around on 16 miles of trails, and there are four miles of hiking paths. The park fronts onto 12 miles of the Alafia River's south prong, and the canoeing is considered quite good.

Campsites, facilities: Thirty campsites with water and electricity have recently been completed. Facilities include restrooms, showers, and paved roads. Call ahead to see if wheelchair-accessible areas have opened yet. Children are welcome. Leashed pets are permitted.

Reservations, fees: Reservations are recommended; call ReserveAmerica at 800/326-3521. Sites are $13 per night for up to six people, plus $2 per pet and $2 for electricity. Admission with a horse costs $5 per horse up to $12 for four horses in the same trailer. Major credit cards are accepted. Long-term rates are available.

Directions: From southbound I-75, take Exit 257 to State Road 60 and drive east 12 miles to County Road 39. Turn south on County Road and drive 13 miles until you reach the park. If traveling north, take Exit 250 and drive east on Gibsonton Drive/Boyette Road for one mile to U.S. 301. Turn north on U.S. 301 and proceed north to County Road 672. Turn east on County Road 672. Continue to County

Road 39 and turn north. The park entrance is on County Road 39.

Contact: Alafia River State Park, 14502 S. County Road 39, Lithia, FL 33547, 813/672-5132, website: www.floridastateparks.org.

16 E. G. SIMMONS PARK

Rating: 5

West of Ruskin

Greater Tampa map, grid c2, page 384

Views of sparkling-blue Tampa Bay are marvelous from several places in this 469-acre park, but the camping areas are set in mangroves and overlook a bayou. There's a swimming beach about one mile away from the campsites. Fish from the piers or launch your boat at the ramp. Like many Florida parks so close to urban areas, the spot gets a lot of use on weekends and holidays. You can camp in two separate loops. Shade and privacy are minimal. Improvements are planned at this county park by 2004. Call ahead to be sure the park is open.

Campsites, facilities: All 88 sites in this Hillsborough County park have water; 70 have electricity. Picnic tables, grills, fire rings, restrooms, showers, a dump station, a boat ramp, and a playground are provided. Children are welcome. Leashed pets are permitted.

Reservations, fees: Reservations are not accepted. Sites are $12 per night. Credit cards are not accepted. The maximum stay is 14 days.

Directions: From I-75, take Exit 240 and drive west on State Road 674 for three miles. At U.S. 41, turn north and go one mile. Head west on 19th Avenue Northeast about two miles to the park.

Contact: E. G. Simmons Park, 2401 19th Avenue Northwest, Ruskin, FL 33570, 813/671-7655. Hillsborough County Parks and Recreation Administrative Office: 1101 East River Cove Street, Tampa, FL 33604, 813/975-2160, website: www.hillsboroughcounty.org/parks.

17 RIVER OAKS RV RESORT

Rating: 5

South of Ruskin

Greater Tampa map, grid c2, page 384

Campers over 55 and retirees are welcome at this small, quiet park on the Little Manatee River. "It's like being in the country, away from traffic and noise," says the manager. Bingo, fish fries, and community dinners in the recreation hall are counterpoints to fishing in the river and boating. Lots of live oak trees shade the park.

Campsites, facilities: Twenty-nine RV sites are available for overnighters, plus 70 for seasonal visitors. None are pull-through, and rigs must be no longer than 30 feet. All have concrete pads, full hookups, picnic tables, and grills. Restrooms, showers, laundry facilities, a boat ramp, a recreation hall, horseshoe pits, shuffleboard courts, and a dog-walk area are on site. Children are not welcome. Small, leashed pets are permitted.

Reservations, fees: Reservations are recommended. Sites are $20 per night for two people, plus $2 per extra person. Credit cards are not accepted. Long-term stays are permitted.

Directions: From I-75, take Exit 240 and drive west on State Road 674 for three miles. At U.S. 41, turn south and drive six miles to Stephens Road. Turn left on Stephens Road and take the first right. Follow the drive to the end; the park will be on your left.

Contact: River Oaks RV Resort, 201 Stephens Road, Ruskin, FL 33570, 813/645-2439 or 800/645-6311.

18 HAWAIIAN ISLES

Rating: 7

Outside of Ruskin on Bay Road

Greater Tampa map, grid c2, page 384

The Hawaiian mystique sells, even in tropical Florida. Yep, the lighted, paved roads in this RV park boast names like Aloha Boulevard, Waiki-ki Way, and Leilani Lane, but don't look too closely for hula girls except on the park brochure. The Wilder Resort Parks chain understands its market—snowbirds who want a resort experience combined with all-American luxuries. (Other Florida properties include Blue Parrot Camping Park in Lady Lake, Palm View Gardens in Zephyrhills, Travel Towne Resort in Clearwater, Cypress Pointe in Palm Harbor, Rice Creek RV Resort in Riverview, Southern Aire in Thonotosassa, Fort Myers RV Resort in Fort Myers, Sundance Lakes RV Resort in Port Richey, Oak Springs RV Resort in Port Richey, Pioneer Creek RV Resort in Bowling Green, and The Springs RV Resort in Silver Springs.)

Hawaiian Isles scores with an Olympic-sized swimming pool (heated, of course), a two-story cabana overlooking the pool, a whopping 33-unit laundry room, two huge recreation halls with card and billiard rooms, a one-mile nature trail, 16 championship shuffleboard courts, and many waterfront campsites. The park overlooks Cockroach Bay and canals. Golf courses and tennis courts are a short distance away. Reserve early because campers tend to reserve for next winter before they leave at season's end.

Campsites, facilities: This mobile-home/RV park has 805 full-hookup sites for recreational vehicles. Cable TV, telephone service, restrooms, showers, recreation halls, a pool, a whirlpool, horseshoe pits, shuffleboard courts, and laundry facilities are available. Adult campers are preferred. Pets under 25 pounds are permitted.

Reservations, fees: Reservations are recommended. Sites are $23 per night for two people, plus $2.50 for each additional person. Major credit cards are accepted. Long-term stays are OK.

Directions: From I-75, take Exit 240 and drive west on State Road 674 for three miles. Turn south on U.S. 41 and drive two miles to the park.

Contact: Hawaiian Isles, 4120 Cockroach Bay Road, Ruskin, FL 33570, 813/645-1098, website: www.rvresorts.com.

19 SUN LAKE RV RESORT

Rating: 4

In Ruskin

Greater Tampa map, grid c2, page 384

Fish in the 35-acre lake or rent a boat to get closer to the action in this retiree-oriented park. The sunny, grassy landscape is friendly to even the biggest RVs. Social programs are held in the recreation hall. Some sites are occupied by park models.

Campsites, facilities: The park has 47 RV sites and 10 spots for tents. All have full hookups and cable TV; telephone service is available at 25 sites. Picnic tables, restrooms, showers, a recreation hall, a pool, a dock, boat and canoe rentals, horseshoe pits, shuffleboard courts, and laundry facilities are provided. All areas are wheelchair accessible. Children are welcome for short stays. Leashed pets are permitted.

Reservations, fees: Reservations are recommended. Sites are $21 per night for two people, plus $2 for each additional person and $1 for cable TV Major credit cards are accepted. Campers over 55 are welcome for long-term stays.

Directions: From I-75, take Exit 240 and drive west on State Road 674 for .5 mile. At 33rd Street Southeast, turn south and drive .6 mile to the park.

Contact: Sun Lake RV Resort, 3006 14th Avenue Southeast, Ruskin, FL 33570, 813/645-7860, email: sunlakerv@aol.com.

20 HIDE-A-WAY RV RESORT

Rating: 7

In Ruskin

Greater Tampa map, grid c2, page 384

Set on the Little Manatee River, the park is laid out lengthwise to take maximum advantage of the waterfront. At the heart of the park is a pool, a recreation room, a fishing pier, and a campfire circle. There's room for 34 boats to tie up at the docks, and the river offers access to Tampa Bay and the Gulf of Mexico. Golfing, flea markets, and Sun City Center are nearby.

Campsites, facilities: All 307 RV sites have full hookups. On the premises are picnic tables, restrooms, showers, a dump station, recreation hall, a boat ramp, docks, a pool, a Jacuzzi, horseshoe pits, shuffleboard courts, and laundry facilities (most areas are wheelchair accessible). Children are welcome. A maximum of two pets are permitted, provided they stand no taller than 18 inches at the shoulder.

Reservations, fees: Reservations are required. Sites are $22 per night for two people, plus $2 for each additional person and $1.50 if you use air-conditioning. Credit cards are accepted. Long-term stays are OK.

Directions: From I-75, take Exit 240B and drive west on State Road 674 for three miles. Turn south on U.S. 41 and drive 2.5 miles to Chaney Road, then go east on Chaney to the park.

Contact: Hide-A-Way RV Resort, 2206 Chaney Road, Ruskin, FL 33570, 813/645-6037 or 800/607-2532.

21 MASONIC PARK AND YOUTH CAMP

Rating: 5

South of Wimauma

Greater Tampa map, grid d2, page 384

Masons and their families come from all over the United States and Canada to stay at this shady, forested, 202-acre campground, the only Masonic-affiliated RV park in Florida. Many guests are seasonal visitors, and the park is often filled during the winter. Your neighbors could also be Boy Scout troops and church youth groups permitted to stay in the nearby group tent camping area. A 2.5-mile hiking trail runs along the Little Manatee River. Paddlers can canoe on a small lake (use of park canoes is free). For less-rustic pursuits, head to the large recreation hall, with

a seating capacity of 125 and a communal kitchen seating 300.

Campsites, facilities: Open to members of the Masonic fraternity nationwide (there are 80,000 in Florida alone), this park has 73 RV sites with water, electricity, and picnic tables. Facilities include restrooms, showers, laundry facilities, a dump station, a playground, horseshoe pits, shuffleboard courts, nature trails, a recreation hall, and a camp circle. Children are welcome. Leashed pets are allowed.

Reservations, fees: Reservations are not taken. Sites are $12 per night. Credit cards are not accepted. The maximum stay is six months.

Directions: From I-75, take Exit 240 and drive east on State Road 674 for four miles. At U.S. 301, turn south and drive 3.5 miles to the park entrance.

Contact: Masonic Park and Youth Camp, 18050 U.S. 301 South, Wimauma, FL 33598, 813/634-1220 or 813/933-9010.

22 LITTLE MANATEE RIVER STATE PARK

Rating: 10

South of Wimauma

Greater Tampa map, grid d2, page 384

Opened in 1987, this little-known state park has modern facilities on the Little Manatee River, a narrow, tannin-stained tributary that widens as it flows southwest to the Gulf of Mexico. Rent canoes from Canoe Outpost just north of the park on U.S. 301, or bring your own. The campsites are nestled in a sand pine scrub forest, with lush screening from your neighbors. There's plenty to do here: In addition to canoeing, check out the 6.5-mile hiking trail (part of the Florida National Trail), which skirts the park's northern wilderness area, or explore on horseback. Ten miles of horseback trails wind through the rest of the park. You might see bobcats roaming remote areas in the 2,416-acre park.

Campsites, facilities: This park has 34 RV or

tent sites with water, electricity, picnic tables, grills, and fire rings. Restrooms, showers, a dump station, a canoe ramp, a playground, a nature trail, and horse stalls are available. The campground, picnic area, and restrooms are wheelchair accessible. Children are welcome. Pets are permitted with proof of vaccination. A primitive backpacking site is also available; hikers must obtain a permit at the ranger station. In addition, four campsites are set aside for equestrians.

Reservations, fees: Reservations are recommended; call ReserveAmerica at 800/326-3521.

Sites are $13 per night for four people, plus $2 for each extra person and $2 for electricity. Major credit cards are accepted. The maximum stay is 120 days.

Directions: From I-75, take Exit 240 and drive east on State Road 674 for six miles. In Wimauma, turn south on U.S. 301 and drive five miles. At Lightfoot Road, turn west and go .2 mile to the park.

Contact: Little Manatee River State Park, 215 Lightfoot Road, Wimauma, FL 33598, 813/671-5005, fax 813/671-5009, website: www.floridastateparks.org.

Chapter 13

Sarasota/Bradenton Area

Sarasota/Bradenton Area

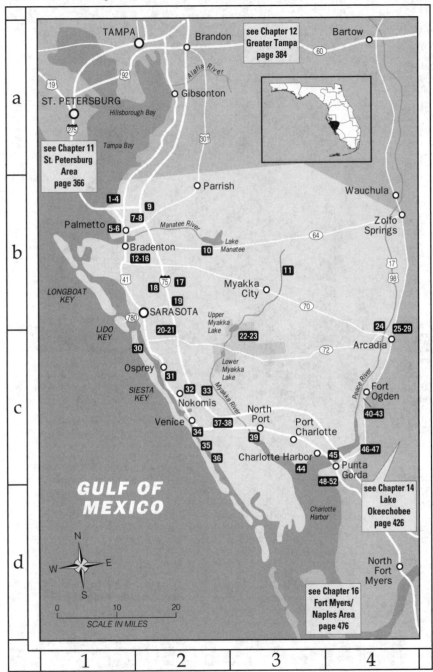

1 FROG CREEK CAMPGROUND AND RV PARK

Rating: 6

In Palmetto

Sarasota/Bradenton map, grid b1, page 398

Steady improvements have been made to this park over the past few years. A heated pool has been built, and new restrooms and landscaping were completed recently. A fishing stream runs through the park, which is a short drive from the beaches, deep-sea fishing, museums, and other attractions.

Campsites, facilities: RVers can choose from 180 lots with concrete pads and picnic tables, and there are 15 tent sites. On the premises are restrooms, showers, laundry facilities, a dump station, shuffleboard courts, horseshoe pits, and a recreation hall. The restrooms, laundry, and recreation hall are wheelchair accessible. Children under 16 are welcome, but they must be supervised by an adult in public areas. Leashed pets are permitted.

Reservations, fees: Reservations are recommended. Sites are $24 per night for two people, plus $1 for each additional person, $2 for air-conditioning or heater use, and $1 for pets. Major credit cards are accepted. Long-term stays are OK.

Directions: From I-75, take Exit 228 and drive one mile west on I-275. Exit northbound on U.S. 41 and continue .5 mile to Bayshore Road. Turn west and drive .6 mile.

Contact: Frog Creek Campground and RV Park, 8515 Bayshore Road, Palmetto, FL 34221, 941/722-6154 or 800/771-3764, website: www.frogcreekrv.com.

2 FIESTA GROVE RV RESORT

Rating: 6

In Palmetto

Sarasota/Bradenton map, grid b1, page 398

This park, once a citrus grove, is dotted with orange trees, and guests are welcome to pick and eat the fruit. Activities in the recreation hall include aerobics, line dancing, card games, bingo, ice-cream socials, bowling, bicycle rides, bus trips, and coffees. The location is near the Sunshine Skyway Bridge (I-275), a spectacular, almost dizzying drive that takes motorists 150 feet above the waters of Tampa Bay. Also nearby is the site where explorer Hernando de Soto and 600 soldiers landed in 1539 with a mandate to colonize Florida for Spain. The National Park Service, which says that the effort was the first large-scale European mission into North America, commemorates this spot at the De Soto National Memorial in Bradenton (941/792-0458).

Campsites, facilities: Most of the 220 lots are taken by park models, but about one-third are RV sites. The RVers have full hookups and cable TV, except for in 15 sites that have water and electricity only. Restrooms, showers, laundry facilities, a heated pool, shuffleboard, bocce ball, a wheelchair-accessible recreation hall, and a dump station are available. Children under 17 must be supervised in public areas. Pets are permitted.

Reservations, fees: Reservations are recommended. Sites are $24 per night for two people, plus $1.50 for each additional person and $1 for cable TV. Credit cards are not accepted. Long-term stays are OK.

Directions: From I-75, take Exit 228 and drive one mile west on I-275. Exit northbound on U.S. 41 and continue .5 mile to Bayshore Road. Turn west and drive .5 mile.

Contact: Fiesta Grove RV Resort, 8615 Bayshore Road, Palmetto, FL 34221, 941/722-7661.

3 TERRA CEIA VILLAGE RV RESORT

Rating: 4

In Palmetto

Sarasota/Bradenton map, grid b1, page 398

Oak trees and lush landscaping enhance the park grounds, which also contain a stocked pond for fishing. It's an adult-oriented, 15-acre resort that is 12 miles from the beach and is close to golf courses, Indian Mound Park, and the Sunshine Skyway Bridge.

Campsites, facilities: Seventy of the 203 RV lots are available to travelers and offer full hookups, including cable TV and telephone access. Eight sites are pull-through. On the premises are restrooms, showers, laundry facilities, a dump station, a heated pool, a stocked pond, horseshoes, shuffleboard, bocce ball (lawn bowling), and a clubhouse, which is wheelchair accessible. A convenience store is at the corner. The nearest restaurant is about 1.5 miles away; a supermarket is about five miles away. Children are not welcome as campers but may visit. Leashed pets are permitted.

Reservations, fees: Reservations are required. Sites are $20 per night for two people, plus $1.50 for each additional person. Major credit cards are accepted. Year-round stays are OK.

Directions: From I-75, take Exit 228 and go west to U.S. 41 (Exit 1). Go north on U.S. 41 for .75 mile to the park, at left.

Contact: Terra Ceia Village RV Resort, 9303 U.S. 41 North, Palmetto, FL 34221, 941/729-4422.

4 WINTERSET PARK

Rating: 4

In Palmetto

Sarasota/Bradenton map, grid b1, page 398

Frog Creek, a fishing stream, borders the property. Several golf courses and driving ranges are within a few minutes' drive. Nearby is the Gamble Plantation State Historic Site (941/723-4536), the last surviving antebellum mansion in the southern half of the state. It was originally the home of Major Robert Gamble, an early settler who built a 3,500-acre sugar plantation on the banks of the Manatee River. The home is also notable for providing refuge to the Confederate secretary of state, Judah P. Benjamin, after the fall of the Confederacy.

Today, the house is furnished in the manner of the mid-19th century and depicts the lifestyle of the times.

Campsites, facilities: Out of a total of 213 RV sites, about half are available for overnighters and seasonal guests. Sites have full hookups. Facilities include restrooms, showers, laundry facilities, shuffleboard courts, two pools, a wheelchair-accessible recreation room, tennis courts, and a dog-walk area. Grocery stores and restaurants are nearby. This is an adults-only park. Pets under 20 pounds are allowed.

Reservations, fees: Reservations are recommended. Sites are $19.50 per night for two people. Credit cards are not accepted. Long-term stays are OK.

Directions: From I-75, take Exit 228 and drive one mile west on I-275. Exit northbound on U.S. 41 and continue .5 mile to the park.

Contact: Winterset Park, 8515 U.S. 41 North, Palmetto, FL 34221, 941/722-4884, fax 941/722-5820, website: www.nhms.com.

5 FISHERMAN'S COVE RESORT

Rating: 4

Near Palmetto

Sarasota/Bradenton map, grid b1, page 398

Don't forget to pack your racquet because this is one of the few RV parks in Florida to have tennis courts right on the property. If that's not your game, then launch your boat from the campground boat ramp and you'll be right on Terra Ceia Bay, which has access to Tampa Bay and the Gulf of Mexico. St. Petersburg is a quick ride away over the spectacular Sunshine Skyway Bridge, which soars 150 feet above the water. Golf courses are within easy driving distance, and groceries and restaurants are close. Social programs are held in the recreation hall year-round. Campsites are grassy with concrete pads and are large enough to accommodate even bigger rigs; however, there are no pull-through sites.

Campsites, facilities: All 82 RV lots have full

hookups with cable TV and telephone access. On the premises are restrooms, showers, a dump station, laundry facilities, a heated pool with Jacuzzi, a boat ramp, tennis courts, a clubhouse, exercise and game rooms, and a tiki hut for camp gatherings. All areas are wheelchair accessible. Children may visit for short periods. Pets are permitted.

Reservations, fees: Reservations are recommended. Sites are $35 per night for two people, plus $2 for each additional person. Major credit cards are accepted. Long-term stays are OK.

Directions: Southbound on the Sunshine Skyway Bridge (I-275/U.S. 19), continue two miles south from the toll plaza to the park, set on the east side of U.S. 19 after you cross Terra Ceia Bay. Northbound on I-275, turn south at U.S. 41 and drive 2.3 miles. At U.S. 19, drive north one mile. The park is just before the Sunshine Skyway Bridge toll plaza.

Contact: Fisherman's Cove Resort, 100 Palmview Road, Palmetto, FL 34221, 941/729-3685, fax 941/721-0614.

6 TROPIC ISLES MOBILE HOME PARK

🏊 🎣 🚤 🐕 🚐

Rating: 4

In Palmetto

Sarasota/Bradenton map, grid b1, page 398

As a camper at Tropic Isles Mobile Home Park, you automatically earn the privilege of using the permanent boating facilities and marina, just as long-term residents do. Boaters will appreciate the location: access to the Gulf of Mexico and its fishing grounds is first-rate. The open and sunny park overlooks Terra Ceia Bay, and many sites are waterfront. During the winter, the clubhouse buzzes with activity, with weekly social hours (coffee and doughnuts are served), potluck suppers, game nights, bingo, and card parties. There's even an auditorium with a stage for large functions. The park has a bus that takes residents out for weekly shopping trips; group outings to local at-

tractions are also available. Note that bicycles have the right-of-way on the park's paved roads.

Campsites, facilities: All 103 grassy RV sites in this adults-only, 362-unit mobile home park have full hookups and concrete patios. RVs must be self-contained; there are no showers or restrooms. On the premises are a heated pool, 12 championship shuffleboard courts, horseshoe pits, a clubhouse, a wheelchair-accessible auditorium and yacht club, a boat ramp, docks, a marina, a grocery store, laundry facilities, and a beauty parlor. For cable TV and telephone service, you must call the proper utility. Only people age 55 and older are welcome as campers, but children may visit for short periods. Small, leashed pets are permitted but must not be tied outside units.

Reservations, fees: Reservations are recommended. Sites are $40 per night. Credit cards are not accepted. Long-term stays are OK.

Directions: From I-75, take Exit 224 westbound on U.S. 301 and drive 10.5 miles to the park, at right.

Contact: Tropic Isles Mobile Home Park, 3100 10th Street West, Palmetto, FL 34221, 941/721-8888, fax 941/729-0687.

7 ELLENTON GARDENS TRAVEL RESORT

🏊 🎣 🐕 ♿ 🚐

Rating: 3

In Ellenton

Sarasota/Bradenton map, grid b2, page 398

For people who like to shop, this 16-acre park is a find. Factory outlets, malls, and all manner of other stores are nearby. Even doctors' offices, a hospital, and a library are within one mile. A small fishing lake lies at the center of the park, which is home to a lot of semipermanent trailers and manufactured homes. Activities held in the recreation hall include exercise and arts-and-crafts classes, line dancing, and bingo. Campsites have concrete pads fronting paved roads.

Campsites, facilities: All 196 sites have full

hookups with optional telephone service and cable TV. RVs must be self-contained. Restrooms, showers, laundry facilities, a heated pool, shuffleboard courts, a lake, a dump station, and a recreation hall are on site. All areas are wheelchair accessible. Children are welcome. Small dogs and cats are permitted on a leash.

Reservations, fees: Reservations are recommended. Sites are $27 per night for two people, plus $2 for each additional person. Credit cards are not accepted. Long-term stays are OK.

Directions: From I-75, take Exit 224 and head northeast on U.S. 301 for 1.4 miles to the park entrance on the left side of the road.

Contact: Ellenton Gardens Travel Resort, 7310 U.S. 301 North, Ellenton, FL 34222, 941/722-0341, fax 941/723-6121.

8 PALM BAY RV PARK

Rating: 3

North of Bradenton
Sarasota/Bradenton map, grid b2, page 398

A private walk provides pedestrian access from this adult-oriented park to a large shopping center. Churches and the Manatee Memorial Hospital are within one mile. Park management must approve RVs in advance of stay; 12-foot-wide, 40-foot-long RVs are permitted where lot size allows. This park is geared toward senior citizens who are staying three to four months at a time.

Campsites, facilities: These 78 full-hookup RV spots are set inside a 164-unit, adult-oriented mobile home park. Facilities include restrooms, showers, a laundry room, a pool, a billiard and card room, shuffleboard courts, and a clubhouse. Children may stay a maximum of two weeks. Pets aren't allowed, not even with visitors.

Reservations, fees: Reservations are recommended. Sites are $18 to $24 per night for two people, plus $2 for each additional person. Credit cards are not accepted. Long-term stays are OK.

Directions: From I-75, take Exit 224 and drive west on U.S. 301 for 3.1 miles. The park is .25 mile west of U.S. 41.

Contact: Palm Bay RV Park, 751 10th Street East, Palmetto, FL 34221, 941/722-7048.

9 ENCORE RV RESORT— SARASOTA NORTH

Rating: 9

Near Bradenton
Sarasota/Bradenton map, grid b2, page 398

Spotless campsites with concrete pads and patios are arranged in a circle around 17-acre Lake Mohoina, which is stocked with fish. Two spots are pull-through, and unlike many private RV parks in Florida, this 70-acre alternative has picnic tables at each site. An activities director keeps campers busy during the winter with games and other recreation in the two-story clubhouse. Among the more unusual planned activities are stained-glass classes and woodworking. The small boat ramp puts you on the Manatee River, which accesses the Gulf of Mexico. Restaurants, shops, and a golf course are within one to two miles.

Campsites, facilities: All 409 RV sites have picnic tables and full hookups, with cable TV and telephone availability. On the premises are two heated pools, a spa, a clubhouse, picnic area, restrooms, showers, a small boat ramp, an exercise and game room, horseshoes, billiards, limited supplies, a lake, a dump station, and golf nets. Children are permitted. Leashed pets are permitted.

Reservations, fees: Reservations are recommended. Sites are $32 to $39 per night. Major credit cards are accepted. Long-term stays are OK.

Directions: From I-75, take Exit 220 westbound .5 mile on State Road 64 to Kay Road. Turn northeast and drive .9 mile to the park entrance on the left.

Contact: Encore RV Resort—Sarasota North, 800 Kay Road Northeast, Bradenton, FL 34212, 239/745-2600 or 800/678-2131, fax 239/748-8964, website: www.rvonthego.com.

10 LAKE MANATEE STATE PARK

Rating: 10

On the south shore of Lake Manatee

Sarasota/Bradenton map, grid b2, page 398

The thickly landscaped camping area is within walking distance of Lake Manatee's swimming area and a playground. Although the shrubs are not tall enough to provide shade, they form a dense screen between each site, so you'll feel secluded from your neighbor. There are 30 sites on each of two campground loops, further promoting a sense of privacy. Groceries and laundry facilities are nine miles away. The 2,400-acre lake, which is part of the reservoir that supplies drinking water to Manatee and Sarasota Counties, is ideal for canoeing and fishing. Note that boat motors are limited to 20 horsepower. A grassy beach slopes gently down to the water in the swimming area. Watch out for alligators, the park rangers warn. The gators are monitored but not fenced. If you see one near the beach, report it to the office, and, of course, don't harass it. A one-mile-long nature trail offers a chance to learn more about the park's biological communities: flatwoods and sand pine scrub. Among the animals regularly seen in the park are cottontail and marsh rabbits, cotton rats, and gray squirrels. Occasionally, you may see bobcats, gray foxes, and deer.

Campsites, facilities: There are 60 sites with water and electricity for RVs or tents. Restrooms, showers, picnic tables, fire rings, grills, a playground, a boat ramp, a dock, a nature trail, and a dump station are provided. The campground, picnic areas, and boat docks are wheelchair accessible. Boats are available for rent. Children are welcome. Pets are permitted with proof of vaccination.

Reservations, fees: Reservations are recommended; call ReserveAmerica at 800/326-3521. Sites are $8 to $10 per night for four people, plus $2 for each additional person and $2 for electricity. Major credit cards are accepted.

Stays are limited to 120 days in the off-season (May 1 through November 30) and two weeks at other times.

Directions: From I-75, take Exit 220 eastbound nine miles on State Road 64 to the park on the left.

Contact: Lake Manatee State Park, 20007 State Road 64, Bradenton, FL 34212, 941/741-3028 (between 3 P.M. and 5 P.M.), fax 941/741-3486, website: www.floridastateparks.org.

11 WISHFUL THINKIN' FARMS

Rating: 8

Northeast of Myakka City

Sarasota/Bradenton map, grid b3, page 398

Doug "Donny" Jones, a lifelong rancher who'll admit to being "as old as dirt," opens 240 acres of pine woods on his working cattle spread to campers. Most guests come to ride his 42 horses ($12 per hour for guided trail rides) or explore the woods on foot or on their own mountain bikes. Skilled equestrians can go for moonlight rides, but expert riders get invited to test the limits of their ability on pitch-dark nights. There's a pond for swimming, and Jones says the alligators know to stay in the swamp—or wind up in his frying pan. Twice a year, "black powder shoots" are held for groups who dress in Daniel Boone–style gear and reenact the days of the mountain men of yore. Riding and roping lessons are offered. One thing's for sure at Wishful Thinkin' Farms, says Jones: "Everyone has a blast."

Campsites, facilities: As many as 1,000 people in tents and self-contained RVs can be accommodated in a pine forest on this 600-acre cattle and horse ranch. A chemical toilet and a hand pump for well water are located near the ranch house. There are no other facilities for campers; it's wise to bring your own water. Horses are available for rent. Children are welcome. Pets are prohibited.

Reservations, fees: Reservations are required. Sites are $3 per night per person if you ride a horse during your stay. Otherwise, camping is $5 nightly per person. Credit cards are not accepted.

Directions: From I-75, take Exit 217 and drive east on State Road 70 for 23 miles. In Myakka City, at the caution light for the town's main intersection, turn and drive north on Myakka-Wauchula Road for 7.5 miles. When the road narrows to one lane, watch for three houses on the right. Turn east between the second and third houses onto Juel Gill Road. Follow the dirt road for 1.5 miles to the ranch.

Contact: Wishful Thinkin' Farms, 5815 Juel Gill Road, Myakka City, FL 34251, 941/322-1074.

12 SARASOTA BAY TRAVEL TRAILER PARK

Rating: 4

In Bradenton

Sarasota/Bradenton map, grid b2, page 398

A sign at the trailer-park entrance warns campers: "Slow. Grandparents at play." And do they ever play, at least in the winter. The park's Friendship Hall offers pool tables, Ping-Pong, and a full schedule of social activities—but, notably, no pool (a public beach is one mile away). Campers can build things in the woodworking shop, tinker with their boats, or work out in the exercise room, which is stocked with Nautilus equipment. The park overlooks Sarasota Bay, where pelicans and seagulls wheel and turn in the breeze. Follow the bay by boat, and it leads to the ocean. Most guests leave their rigs here year-round, and many have added carports, porches, and screened rooms to their trailers. Located in a suburban neighborhood on a main road leading to the beach, the neatly kept park is near shops and restaurants. Its roads are paved, and Norfolk pines and queen palms provide a little greenery. If you hail from the Midwest and come to escape the frigid winters, you'll find plenty of fellow campers from your neck of the woods.

Campsites, facilities: There are 240 spots in this park, with about 60 full hookup sites available for overnighters and seasonal visitors. Most folks stay for the winter and leave their rigs on site during the summer; around 25 people live in the park year-round. Additionally, there is an overflow area for self-contained RVs; these have water and electricity only. Restrooms, showers, laundry facilities, a recreation hall, shuffleboard courts, horseshoe pits, boat ramps, a boat repair area, docks, an exercise room, and a woodworking shop are available. Children may visit for up to two weeks for $2 per person per night. No dogs are permitted; indoor cats, birds, and fish are allowed.

Reservations, fees: Reservations are recommended. Sites are $32 per night for two people, plus $2 for each additional person. Credit cards are not accepted. Long-term stays are OK.

Directions: From I-75, take Exit 217 and drive west on State Road 70 for about 11 miles to State Road 684/Cortez Road. Turn left. Drive two miles west to the park entrance, at left.

Contact: Sarasota Bay Travel Trailer Park, 10777 Cortez Road West, Bradenton, FL 34210, 941/794-1200 or 800/247-8361, fax 941/761-0629.

13 HOLIDAY COVE RV RESORT

Rating: 5

In Cortez

Sarasota/Bradenton map, grid b2, page 398

Set in a stand of Australian pines and palm trees, this resort has water access to Sarasota Bay and the Intracoastal Waterway. Boat slips are available, and you can fish from the docks in the park. The long white-sand beaches of Anna Maria Island and Longboat Key are nearby, and you can walk to restaurants, shops, and the beachfront less than a mile away.

Campsites, facilities: All 112 sites have full hookups and cable TV. Restrooms, showers, picnic tables, a heated pool, shuffleboard courts, horseshoe pits, laundry facilities, a recreation hall, and a boat ramp are provided. Groceries and a restaurant are across the street. Children are welcome. Pets are permitted.

Reservations, fees: Reservations are recommended. Sites are $30 to $38 per night for two people, plus $2 for each additional person. Major credit cards are accepted.

Directions: From I-75, take Exit 217 and drive west on State Road 70 for 13 miles to Cortez Road. Turn left and drive five miles. The park entrance is on the north side.

Contact: Holiday Cove RV Resort, 11900 Cortez Road West/P.O. Box 713, Cortez, FL 34215, 941/792-1111 or 800/346-9224, website: www.holidaycoverv.com.

14 PLEASANT LAKE RV RESORT

Rating: 4

In Bradenton

Sarasota/Bradenton map, grid b2, page 398

In the center of this sunny park is a rectangular man-made lake, which is stocked for bass fishing and has grassy slopes where campers pull ashore their johnboats. You'll have to confine your swimming to the pool, however. Like most bodies of freshwater in Florida, there's always a possibility that an alligator may be lurking nearby. Suitable for big RVs, the park has large sites with concrete pads and few trees to get in the way. A guardhouse and golf-cart patrols provide a feeling of security. Down the street is a large shopping plaza with a grocery store, restaurants, banks, and a gas station. Tourist attractions in the area include Gulf beaches, the Ringling Museum of Art, the Gamble Plantation Historic Site, the Lionel Train Museum, Jungle Gardens, a dog-racing track, Sunken Gardens, and Busch Gardens.

Campsites, facilities: All 343 sites have full hookups; only self-contained units are welcome. Telephone and cable TV service are available. On the premises are restrooms, showers, laundry facilities, a pool, shuffleboard courts, horseshoe pits, bocce ball (lawn bowling) courts, a

fishing lake, and a recreation room. The restrooms, laundry, and recreation room are wheelchair accessible. This is an adults-only park, but families with children may stay for up to two weeks. Leashed pets are permitted.

Reservations, fees: Reservations are recommended. Sites are $25 to $35 per night for two people, plus $2 for each additional person. Major credit cards are accepted. Stays up to six months are allowed.

Directions: From I-75, take Exit 217 and drive west on State Road 70 for .3 mile to the park, which is on the north side of the road.

Contact: Pleasant Lake RV Resort, 6633 53rd Avenue East, Bradenton, FL 34203, 941/756-5076 or 800/283-5076, website: www.pleasantlakervresort.com.

15 TROPICAL GARDENS RV PARK

Rating: 2

In Bradenton

Sarasota/Bradenton map, grid b2, page 398

Although many of the units in this suburban park are mobile homes or permanent trailers, overnighters are welcome at the 48 available spaces. Sites are small with concrete pads. During the winter, planned social activities in the clubhouse keep residents entertained, and church services are held on Sundays. The security gate is locked at night. The location is convenient for exploring nearby tourist attractions, such as the Gamble Plantation Historic Site. Within a couple hours' drive are Sea World, Disney World, and Silver Springs.

Campsites, facilities: Adults are preferred at this park's 155 full-hookup RV sites. Telephone and cable TV access are available. On the premises are restrooms, showers, a screened pool, shuffleboard, a dump station, laundry facilities, and a recreation hall. The restrooms and recreation hall are wheelchair accessible. Within two blocks are a supermarket, a drug store, a medical center, and a restaurant. Leashed pets are permitted.

Reservations, fees: Reservations are recommended. Sites are $30 per night for two people, plus $2 for each additional person. Credit cards are not accepted. Long-term stays are OK.

Directions: From I-75, take Exit 217 (if you're southbound) or 217B (northbound) and drive west on State Road 70 for about six miles to the park, which is on the south side of the road, just past 15th Street East/Old 301 Boulevard.

Contact: Tropical Gardens RV Park, 1120 53rd Avenue East, Bradenton, FL 34203, 941/756-1135.

16 HORSESHOE COVE RESORT

Rating: 7

In Bradenton
Sarasota/Bradenton map, grid b2, page 398

At the heart of this all-ages park is a lovely 12-acre island with a nature trail, picnic areas with barbecue grills, lighted fishing docks, boating facilities, and a gazebo. During the winter, there's plenty to do in the 2,000-square-foot recreation hall, including square dancing, quilting, wood carving, billiards, bingo, and social activities. In the summer, kids can catch fish off the docks, swim in the pool, or ride bikes on the paved road. Some sites overlook the Braden River. Unlike many parks with security gates, this park's gate is secured 24 hours a day, not just at night.

Campsites, facilities: This all-ages park has 476 full-hookup sites, where 125 are available for RVs (no tents are permitted). For cable TV and telephone service, call the appropriate utility company. Restrooms, showers, laundry facilities, a recreation hall, a game room, a pool, a spa, shuffleboard, horseshoes, two fishing docks, boat docks, a picnic shelter and separate picnic area, and a nature trail are on the property. Shopping is nearby. Children are welcome. Leashed pets are allowed if you get an RV spot in the pet section.

Reservations, fees: Reservations are recommended during winter. Sites are $38.50 per

night for two people, plus $3 for each additional person. Major credit cards are accepted. Long-term stays are OK.

Directions: From I-75, take Exit 217 westbound on State Road 70 for 1.1 miles to the first traffic light at Caruso Road/60th Street East. Turn north and proceed to the park on the west side of the road.

Contact: Horseshoe Cove Resort, 5100 60th Street East, Bradenton, FL 34203, 941/758-5335 or 800/291-3446, website: www.horseshoecove.zzn.com.

17 LINGER LODGE RV RESORT

Rating: 5

Near Bradenton
Sarasota/Bradenton map, grid b2, page 398

Linger Lodge borders the Braden River, a peaceful stream where you'll see blue herons wading on the banks and other birds roosting in low overhanging branches. Anglers regularly hook bass, bluegill, crappie, and catfish. A few campsites are near the river, but travelers passing through tend to sleep at upland sites and have standard views of other trailers and park models. Fried "local farm-raised" alligator is the big seller at the unusual restaurant, which also offers seafood, sandwiches, and indoor and screened outdoor seating overlooking the river; it draws crowds on weekends, and you'll hear cars coming and going from 11 A.M. until closing time at 9 P.M. (8 P.M. on Sundays; the restaurant is closed on Mondays). The 10-acre park also contains a small aviary, which is home to peacocks and other exotic birds. The showers, restrooms, and laundry facilities are toward the back of the building that houses the restaurant. Park owner Frank Gamsky entertains people with magic tricks and tales; a self-taught taxidermist, he keeps a display of rattlesnakes near the restaurant. He also exhibits a "short-horned deer," which has a story behind it: In 1992, a hurricane picked up a Florida deer and swept it off to Texas, where it bred with a long-horned steer. A Texas tornado then allegedly blew the rare offspring back into the hands of Frank. **Campsites, facilities:** Ninety-five sites have full hookups and cable TV access; most have concrete pads. The number of sites available for overnighters varies. Rigs up to 38 feet can be accommodated. Restrooms, showers, laundry facilities, a dump station, a boat ramp, and a restaurant are on the premises. A recreation hall is to open in the owners' previous residence after they complete their new home on the riverfront. Some sites have picnic tables. This is an adults-only park, but children are allowed to stay 15 days up to twice per year. Small, leashed pets are permitted in one section.

Reservations, fees: Reservations are recommended. Sites are $22 per night for two people, plus $2 for each extra person. Cable TV, garbage pickup, and electricity are included. Major credit cards are accepted. Long-term rates are available.

Directions: From I-75, take Exit 217 and drive west on State Road 70 for .2 mile to Tara Boulevard. Turn south and drive four miles. Note that the road changes names to Linger Lodge Road, then turns sharply east and crosses I-75. At the stop sign at Oak Hammock Road, turn south and drive .3 mile into the park.

Contact: Linger Lodge RV Resort, 7205 Linger Lodge Road, Bradenton, FL 34202, 941/755-2757, fax 941/758-0758.

18 ARBOR TERRACE RV RESORT

Rating: 4

In Bradenton

Sarasota/Bradenton map, grid b2, page 398

Located between Bradenton and Sarasota, this park has easy access to local attractions. Groceries and restaurants are within .5 mile. Road warriors can relax; lots of spaces are pull-through. You'll also find some well-shaded spots.

Campsites, facilities: Set on 40 acres, the 402-unit resort has 189 available RV sites with full hookups; telephone service is available at most spots. Fifteen tent sites have water and electricity. On the premises are restrooms, showers, a dump station, horseshoe pits, shuffleboard courts, a pool, two recreation rooms, and laundry facilities. Campers of all ages are welcome. Pets are accepted.

Reservations, fees: Reservations are recommended. Fee for two people is $35 per night for RV sites, $21 nightly for tent spots. Add $3 for each additional person. Major credit cards are accepted. Long-term stays are OK.

Directions: From I-75, take Exit 217 and drive west on State Road 70 for 10 miles. Turn south on U.S. 41 and continue one mile. At 57th Avenue West, turn left by the Red Lobster and drive east for about .25 mile.

Contact: Arbor Terrace RV Resort, 405 57th Avenue West, Bradenton, FL 34207, 941/755-6494 or 800/828-6992, fax 941/755-8177, website: www.suncommunities.com.

19 SUN-N-FUN RV RESORT

Rating: 7

In Sarasota

Sarasota/Bradenton map, grid b2, page 398

As the name implies, the emphasis here is on fun. A full-time activities director coordinates dozens of programs each day for guests, most of whom are snowbirds and retired people. They have plenty to choose from, including swimming in a heated Olympic-sized pool with two Jacuzzis, exercising in the fitness center, fishing in the private lake, playing at the nine-hole miniature golf course, or lobbing tennis balls on the three lighted courts. Also offered are crafts classes, theme parties and dances, and a singles club. The park has a total of 1,600 sites, many of them shaded by oaks, and is close to some RV service centers. Beaches are eight miles to the west, and shopping and outlet malls are within a 15-minute drive.

Campsites, facilities: The 1,600-unit resort park with park models and rental units has an unspecified number of RV sites with full hookups and cable TV. Restrooms, showers, laundry facilities, a dump station, several recreation rooms, a lake, two Jacuzzis, a pool, an exercise room, horseshoe pits, courts for shuffleboard, volleyball, bocce ball (lawn bowling), tennis, rental trailers, and The Sandbar Grill restaurant (open during the season) are on site. All ages are welcome. Pets are allowed.

Reservations, fees: Reservations are recommended. Sites are $23 to $57 per night. Major credit cards are accepted. The maximum stay is nine months.

Directions: From I-75, take Exit 210 eastbound on Fruitville Road and drive one mile. The park is on the north side.

Contact: Sun-n-Fun RV Resort, 7125 Fruitville Road, Sarasota, FL 34240, 941/377-8250 or 800/843-2421, fax 941/378-4810, website: www.sun-n-funfl.com.

20 WINDWARD ISLE RV PARK

Rating: 2

In Sarasota

Sarasota/Bradenton map, grid c2, page 398

The open and sunny park is convenient to the interstate for overnighters, but note that there is no bathhouse or dump station. Next door is a Waffle House, plus three fast-food joints. A golf course is across the street. A supermarket is about .25 mile away.

Campsites, facilities: This mobile home park has 99 grassy, full-hookup sites for self-contained RVs. Just 17 are available for overnighters; the rest of the sites are taken by people who stay year-round or choose to leave their rigs during the hot summer months. There are no showers or restroom facilities. A pool, horseshoe pits, shuffleboard courts, laundry facilities, picnic tables, social programs, and a recreation room are available. A three-hole golf course was added in 2001, and electrical service was upgraded from 30 amps to 50 amps throughout the park.

Children may stay a maximum of 15 days, twice a year. Pets are prohibited.

Reservations, fees: Reservations are recommended. Sites are $30 to $40 per night for two people, plus $2 for each additional person. Credit cards are not accepted. Long-term stays are OK.

Directions: From I-75, take Exit 205 westbound on State Road 72. Drive .1 mile to the park on the north side of the road.

Contact: Windward Isle RV Park, 1 Catamaran Drive, Sarasota, FL 34233, 941/922-3090.

21 PINE SHORES TRAILER PARK

Rating: 3

In Sarasota

Sarasota/Bradenton map, grid c2, page 398

During its 40 years of existence, Pine Shores Trailer Park has seen plenty of changes as urban sprawl and "progress" enveloped it on the well-traveled Tamiami Trail. Some folks favor it because of its proximity to beaches, fishing, and boating. This is a 55-plus park, and children are welcome to visit only for short periods of time.

Campsites, facilities: About 40 full-hookup spaces with concrete pads and picnic tables are available for overnighters and seasonal visitors in this 300-unit mobile home park. Restrooms, showers, laundry facilities, and telephone service are available. On the premises are a recreation room with planned activities during the winter and shuffleboard courts. Children are not welcome for long-term stays. Pets are prohibited.

Reservations, fees: Reservations are recommended. Sites are $18 to $30 per night. Credit cards are not accepted. Long-term rates are available.

Directions: From I-75 at Exit 205, drive west on Clark Road (State Route 72) for 4.8 miles. Turn north on Tamiami Trail (U.S. 41) and drive .4 mile to the park.

Contact: Pine Shores Trailer Park, 6450 South Tamiami Trail, Sarasota, FL 34231, 941/922-1929.

22 MYAKKA RIVER STATE PARK

🏃 🚴 🛶 🚤 ⛺ ♿ 🚐 ⛰️

Rating: 10

Outside of Sarasota on the Myakka River
Sarasota/Bradenton map, grid c3, page 398

One of only two rivers in Florida designated as Wild and Scenic, the Myakka River is the centerpiece of this 28,875-acre state park, one of Florida's largest. Bird-watchers, canoeists, anglers, hikers, backpackers, horseback riders, and tourists flock here year-round to experience nature close at hand. The park is especially noted for its wide variety and large number of birds, especially turkeys and hawks, although many other forms of wildlife abound, including alligators, deer, bobcats, and cottontail rabbits. In fact, one-fourth of the park is a wilderness preserve open to a limited number of users.

Because it's so popular, the two main campgrounds seem to squeeze everyone together, but the park does provide fast, easy access to canoeing, mountain biking and hiking trails, the boat basin, tram tours of the hammocks and river floodplain, and airboat tours. An elevated, 125-foot walkway allows a good view of the forest tree canopy. The river flows 34 miles through the park and widens into two large lakes. Don't think about taking a dip, though, because no swimming is permitted anywhere. You'll understand why when you realize that the "log" right next to your canoe is actually a huge alligator.

Anglers routinely catch bass, bream, and catfish. There's a boat ramp on Upper Myakka Lake, but the water is shallow and your keel should not have draw. A new wheelchair-accessible fishing pier has been built recently. It's best to pick up supplies before you arrive; a snack bar operates within the park, but groceries and restaurants are 10 to 15 miles away. Wildlife tours are offered by tram and boat.

Campsites, facilities: The two campgrounds have a total of 76 sites for RVs and tents: 48 with electricity and water, and 28 with water only. The Old Prairie Campground, the smallest of the two with 25 sites, also has five cabins for rent. The other campground, Big Flats, is about three miles from the main gate. Each campsite has a picnic table and a grill or fire ring/grill combination. Restrooms, showers, laundry facilities, a dump station, a playground, a boat ramp, and rental cabins are available. The visitor center, restrooms, fishing pier, nature trail, picnic areas, and concession building are wheelchair accessible. Children are welcome, but pets are prohibited.

Reservations, fees: Reservations are recommended; call ReserveAmerica at 800/326-3521. Sites are $13 to $16 per night for four people, plus $2 for each additional person. Electricity costs $2 per night. Major credit cards are accepted. The maximum stay is 14 days, with extensions available upon approval of the park manager.

Directions: From I-75, take Exit 205 eastbound on State Road 72 and drive nine miles to the park.

Contact: Myakka River State Park, 13207 State Road 72, Sarasota, FL 34241, 941/361-6511, fax 941/361-6501, website: www.myakkariver.org.

23 MYAKKA RIVER TRAIL PRIMITIVE BACKPACKING SITES

🏃 🚴 ⛰️

Rating: 9

In Myakka River State Park
Sarasota/Bradenton map, grid c3, page 398

You'll likely see deer, turkey, wild hogs, otters (if you're lucky), armadillos, a bobcat, or even a bald eagle while hiking along the 39-mile Myakka River Trail, which meanders in four loops through oak and palm hammocks, pine flatwoods, and dry prairies. With lots of small marshes on the trail, too, rangers say you can expect to have wet feet during the rainy summer months. Driest conditions are from late fall through early spring. Always carry water with you; although pitcher-pump wells are available at teach campsite, they may be dry in the spring. The Mossy Hammock camping area is the closest to the parking area; it's 2.2 miles away on the Bee Island loop. Continue hiking south and west to the Bee Island site about 2.9 miles away. You can complete the loop and end at the parking area.

But if you're not ready to return to civilization, the Honore, Deer Prairie, and East loops continue farther east. Four other primitive campgrounds, each with three campsites, are also available. Distance from the trailhead varies, with Panther Point 8.6 miles away; Honore, 8.7 miles; Oak Grove, 9.5 miles; and the Prairie site, 14.1 miles. The path, maintained by the Florida Trail Association, is marked with orange and blue blazes. You may encounter day hikers and horseback riders at various points. Bicycles are not permitted on the hiking trails, but all are allowed on most of the dirt roads that crisscross the park. Hikers and backpackers visiting the park in the summertime will find themselves almost completely alone—their reward for braving the heat.

Campsites, facilities: There are six primitive camping zones, each suitable for a maximum of 12 backpackers. Bring your own water—a well pump is available at each area, but all water should be purified by boiling or chemical means, and the well may run dry during the spring. Bury human waste six inches deep, away from the campsite and water supply. Use camp stoves, if possible. Pets are not allowed.

Reservations, fees: Reservations are recommended; call ReserveAmerica at 800/326-3521. Camping costs $3 per night per adult and $2 for anyone aged 6 to 17. All backpackers must register at the ranger station and obtain instructions.

Directions: From I-75, take Exit 205 eastbound on State Road 72 and drive nine miles to the park.

Contact: Myakka River State Park, 13207 State Road 72, Sarasota, FL 34241, 941/361-6511, fax 941/361-6501.

24 ARCADIA'S PEACE RIVER CAMPGROUND

Rating: 10

In Arcadia

Sarasota/Bradenton map, grid b4, page 398

Ready for something amazing? You get the best of both worlds at this 151-acre private campground: primitive camping amid vast acres of wild beauty of the Peace River and the conveniences of full-service RV camping. In addition to the RV section, which has a selection of shady and sunny sites, a whopping two-thirds of the park is set aside for primitive tent campers. Just pick a spot; there are no formal campsites along a winding, hilly dirt road that meanders through 100 acres of hardwood forest. You might be able to get a pop-top trailer on this road, but taller rigs will be impeded by low-hanging branches, and they are not allowed. Some spots are on the oxbows of the river. Small campfires are permitted. At the center of the park are the mysterious-looking ruins of a chautauqua, an open-air stadium that burned down in the 1930s.

The park also is laced with nature trails and dirt roads for walking and biking, and there's a dock on the river that offers a scenic overlook. Other recreational amenities include fishing, paddleboat rentals, and an 18-hole miniature golf course. An unusual feature is a paintball course and fields. Two large playing fields in the wilderness let aficionados run free with paint-laced projectiles. There's also a 30,000-square-foot paintball course for tournaments so people can watch without getting "painted." Less-energetic folks who want to ramble around the grounds can rent golf carts.

For the more adventurous, canoe outfitters provide shuttle transportation and equipment for exploring and camping expeditions along the Peace River Canoe Trail, a popular 67-mile waterway that once marked the boundary between Indian territory on the east and pioneer settlements on the west. The river trail has swift-flowing narrows and occasional rapids, and is bordered by dense forests teeming with wildlife: wild hogs, armadillos, egrets, and the like. For more information and reservations, call Canoe Outpost at 863/494-1215 or Canoe Safari at 863/494-7865.

Campsites, facilities: The campground has 176 RV sites with full hookups. On the premises are restrooms, showers, laundry facilities, a dump station, a convenience store, a pool, a playground, a fishing pond, a miniature golf course, a recreation room, horseshoe pits, shuffleboard courts, and two paintball fields. There are also a large number of wilderness sites without water, electricity, or other facilities (RVs are not allowed on these sites). The office, store, recreation hall, and restrooms are wheelchair accessible; in addition, you can rent golf carts to drive anywhere in the 150 acres. Children are welcome. Leashed pets are permitted.

Reservations, fees: Reservations are recommended. Sites are $33 per night for two people, plus $5 for each additional person over age 12, and $3 for using air conditioners or electric heaters. Major credit cards are accepted. Long-term stays are OK.

Directions: From southbound I-75, take Exit 217 onto State Road 70 and drive 38 miles east to the park, at the junction of State Road 72. From northbound I-75, take Exit 164 onto U.S. 17 and drive north for 24 miles to State Road 70 in Arcadia. Turn west and drive two miles to the park at the State Road 72 junction.

Contact: Arcadia's Peace River Campground, 2998 Northwest Highway 70, Arcadia, FL 33821, 863/494-9693 or 800/559-4011, fax 863/494-9110, website: www.peacerivercampground.com.

25 PEACE RIVER PRIMITIVE CANOE SITES

Rating: 10

On the Peace River

The slow-moving Peace River winds past cat-tle farms and walls of moss-draped oaks near the west-central Florida town of Arcadia. Once in a while, a cow, normally hidden within the green backdrop, can be spotted munching grass at water's edge. You may also see alligators and wading birds. Your mission: Fritter away a morning by paddling a canoe to a primitive camping spot. Start staking out a secluded place on the west side of the river after passing the cabins about eight miles into the 23-mile, two-day trip. You'll probably enjoy more privacy the farther south you go; besides, the sunnier, open clearings that make obvious camping spots farther north tend to be snagged early. Choose a camping spot before you pass the main recognizable landmark—a bridge at mile 13. Otherwise, your canoe trip the next day may seem too short.

Paddling nine hours during a long weekend on the Peace River belies the waterway's warring history; many Seminole War battles occurred on its banks. Nowadays, you may occasionally hear gunfire—from hunters stalking wild hogs and deer in winter. Normally, the river lives up to its peaceful name, and it's a favorite getaway for Floridians from all over.

Campsites, facilities: Primitive campers may pitch tents at various locations on the right side of the river. You can download a map of permitted campsites from www.dep.state.fl.us/gwt/guide/regions/westcentral/trails/peace_riv.htm. There are no facilities, so bring water, tents, a food-packed cooler, and camping supplies. Piped water is not available. Children are allowed. Pets are permitted.

Reservations, fees: Making reservations through a canoe outfitter is recommended. Fees for two people run around $65 overnight, including canoe rental and a ride to the canoe launch; you'll essentially paddle back to your parked car. Camping is free if you have your own canoe and arrange for a friend to pick you up downriver.

Directions: From Arcadia, drive west on State Road 70, then turn right at County Road 661 to get to Canoe Outpost or Canoe Safari. If you own a canoe, you can have an outfitter drive you to the canoe launch. Or you can launch on your own from Pioneer Park at the intersection of U.S. 17 and State Road 64 in Zolfo Springs, then have someone pick you up downriver.

Contact: Canoe Outpost, 2816 Northwest County Road 661, Arcadia, FL 34266, 863/494-1215, fax 863/494-4391, website: www.canoeoutpost.com. Canoe Safari, 3020 Northwest County Road 661, Arcadia, FL 34266, 863/494-7865, website: www.canoesafari.com. If you own a canoe and have questions about launching from Pioneer Park, call the park at 863/735-0330. Additional information about canoeing on the Peace River can be obtained from the Office of Greenways & Trails, 3900 Commonwealth Boulevard, MS 795, Tallahassee, FL 32399, 850/488-3701 or 877/822-5208.

26 BIG TREE RV PARK

Rating: 4

East of Arcadia
Sarasota/Bradenton map, grid c4, page 398
Big Tree attracts active senior citizens by offering a busy schedule of social activities and crafts sessions. Aside from a pool and a huge spa, the largely open and sunny park has pool tables. There's a bowling alley one mile down the street and a Wal-Mart shopping center practically next door; it's connected to the park by a paved bicycle path. Down the road is historic Arcadia with its bounty of antique shops and restaurants.

Campsites, facilities: All 390 full-hookup RV sites are for people age 55 and older. On the premises are restrooms, showers, laundry facilities, a recreation hall, a heated pool and spa, a billiards hall, shuffleboard courts, and horseshoes. Children may visit for a few days but not camp. Dogs are not allowed; cats are permitted, but they must be confined.

Reservations, fees: Reservations are recommended. Sites are $28 per night. Credit cards are not accepted. Long-term rates are available.

Directions: From southbound I-75, take Exit 217 onto State Road 70 and drive 42 miles east to the intersection of U.S. 17 in Arcadia. Continue 1.8 miles on State Road 70 to the park. From northbound I-75, take Exit 164 onto U.S. 17 and drive north for 24 miles to State Road 70. Turn right and drive 1.8 miles east to the park, at left.

Contact: Big Tree RV Park, 2626 Northeast Highway 70, Arcadia, FL 34266, 863/494-7247 or 800/741-7875, email: bel-aire@3oaks.com, website: www.bel-aireresorts.com.

27 TOBY'S RV RESORT

Rating: 6

On the east side of Arcadia
Sarasota/Bradenton map, grid c4, page 398
Targeted to retirees seeking a "home away from home," the park is within bicycling distance to Wal-Mart and a grocery store. (Free loaner bikes are available.) Much of the infrastructure was built in the past few years, so everything feels new and well maintained. In the clubhouse, campers can socialize and take part in all kinds of planned activities, including computer classes, arts and crafts, bingo, and line dancing. "We have any activity under the sun," say the managers. Campers can use the park's computer to get online. Sites are large enough to fit any size RV, and they're nice and sunny, the better to thaw out snowbirds weary from the cold up North.

Campsites, facilities: Of 379 total RV sites at this 50-and-older park, 60 are available for overnighters and 319 for seasonal guests. Sites have full hookups and 50-amp service; all have concrete pads, picnic tables, and phone service availability. On the premises are restrooms, showers, a dump station, laundry facilities, a heated pool and spa, a driving range, miniature golf, a nature trail, a lake with a dock, propane gas sales, a dog-walk area, and courts for *pétanque* (French-style bowling), bocce (lawn bowling), shuffleboard, and horseshoes. All areas are wheelchair accessible. Children are not welcome. Leashed pets under 35 pounds are permitted.

Reservations, fees: Reservations are recommended. Sites are $28 per night for two people, plus $1 per extra person. Credit cards are not accepted. Long-term stays are permitted.

Directions: From I-75, take exit 217 eastbound on State Road 70 for 45 miles through Arcadia. The park is one mile east of the Wal-Mart on the north side of the road.

Contact: Toby's RV Resort, 3550 Northeast Highway 70, Arcadia, FL 34266, 800/307-0768 (reservations only) or 863/494-1744, fax 863/494-2944, website: www.tobysrv.com.

28 LITTLE WILLIE'S RV RESORT

Rating: 3

North of Arcadia

Sarasota/Bradenton map, grid c4, page 398

This adults-only park overlooks wide-open farm country and is convenient for passersby on U.S. 17. Most sites are on an open field. There's not a whole lot to do beyond swimming in the new heated pool, but canoeing, boating, and golf are nearby.

Campsites, facilities: All 331 RV sites have full hookups and concrete patios. Facilities include restrooms, showers, laundry facilities, a clubhouse, a heated pool, horseshoes, and shuffleboard. A convenience store is across the street. Children are not welcome as campers but may visit short-term. Leashed pets are allowed; no aggressive breeds.

Reservations, fees: Reservations are recommended. Sites are $22 per night for two people. Credit cards are not accepted. The park traditionally is closed May 15 through September 15.

Directions: From southbound I-75, take Exit 217 onto State Road 70 and drive 42 miles east to the intersection of U.S. 17 in Arcadia. Turn north and drive five miles to the park. From

northbound I-75, take Exit 164 onto U.S. 17 and drive north for 24 miles into Arcadia at State Road 70. Continue north on U.S. 17 for five miles to the park.

Contact: Little Willie's RV Resort, 5905 Northeast U.S. 17, Arcadia, FL 34266, 863/494-2717.

29 CRAIG'S RV PARK

Rating: 4

North of Arcadia

Sarasota/Bradenton map, grid c4, page 398

The 65-acre park caters to snowbirds, offering bus tours of the area, daily exercise programs, weekend socials, church services, bingo, golf putting greens, and a driving range. It's near the Peace River, which is a good spot for fishing and boating. Close by is the historic village of Arcadia, whose downtown is dotted with restored turn-of-the-century buildings and antique stores. This is also cowboy country: rodeos are a highlight in March and July.

Campsites, facilities: The park has 328 RV sites with full hookups. On the premises are restrooms, showers, laundry facilities, a dump station, a pool, a recreation hall, a golf driving range, horseshoe pits, and shuffleboard courts. All areas are wheelchair accessible. Children are allowed to visit during the winter. Pets are allowed on a leash in a separate section of the park.

Reservations, fees: Reservations are required in winter. Sites are $25 per night for two people, plus $1 for each additional person. Major credit cards are accepted. Long-term stays are OK.

Directions: From southbound I-75, take Exit 205 onto State Road 72 and drive 40 miles east to Arcadia, then travel seven miles north on U.S. 17 to the park. From northbound I-75, take Exit 164 onto U.S. 17 and drive north. The park is seven miles north of Arcadia.

Contact: Craig's RV Park, 7895 Northeast U.S. 17, Arcadia, FL 34266, 863/494-1820 or 877/750-5129, fax 863/494-1079, website: www.craigsrv.com.

30 GULF BEACH CAMPGROUND

Rating: 8

On Siesta Key
Sarasota/Bradenton map, grid c2, page 398

At these prices you should expect something special, and Gulf Beach Campground delivers. This park is on the much-lauded beaches of Siesta Key on the Gulf of Mexico. Siesta Key's sand is considered among the whitest and most powdery stuff in the world. From a bench at the edge of the campground, you can watch the pelicans skim inches above the surface of the water. Or, down on the beach, you can play in the surf, build a sand castle, or work on your tan. The campground is next to a county park, so on one side, at least, you're not hemmed in by buildings. Waves are gentle most of the time, perfect for little kids, but don't bring your surfboard. Australian pines provide relief from the sun. Sites are a bit close together and are laid out in two long rows stretching perpendicular from the street to the beach, with a driveway in the middle. Nearby is a bike path; you'll find restaurants, stores, and beach supplies two miles north in Siesta Village.

Campsites, facilities: RVs and tents can be accommodated on 48 campsites with full hookups, cable TV, and picnic tables. Restrooms, showers, and laundry facilities are available. Children are welcome. Call for current pet policy.

Reservations, fees: Reservations are recommended. The fee for two people varies seasonally from $25 nightly for tents in summer to a high of $52 nightly for RVs in winter. Rates vary according to how close you are to the beach. Add $2 for each additional person. There are also $2 surcharges each for use of cable TV, air conditioners, and electric heaters, or $1 for 50-amp service. Major credit cards are accepted. Seasonal rates are available.

Directions: From I-75, take Exit 205 west for about seven miles to the dead end at Midnight Pass Road. Turn left (south) and travel 2.3 miles to the park, at right.

Contact: Gulf Beach Campground, 8862 Midnight Pass Road, Sarasota, FL 34242, 941/349-3839.

31 OSCAR SCHERER STATE PARK

Rating: 10

In Osprey midway between Sarasota and Venice
Sarasota/Bradenton map, grid c2, page 398

The seclusion and natural beauty of this park will surprise you. After battling traffic on busy U.S. 41, which is lined with strip shopping centers, auto dealerships, and commercial chaos, you'll enter 1,384 acres of woods and tranquility. Home to many endangered animals, notably the Florida scrub jay, the park has a freshwater swimming lake and a tidal creek for canoeing. Canoes are available for rent at the ranger station ($5 per hour or $25 per day); you are not permitted to pull boats or canoes on the creek bank because they cause erosion. Here's a paradox: You may catch bass, bream, or catfish above the dam on South Creek if you have a freshwater fishing license; however, if you fish below the dam for snook, redfish, or snapper, then a saltwater license is a must. Two nature trails run along the creek. Got a hankering for beaches on the Gulf of Mexico? They're three miles west of the park. You'll just have to face that traffic again.

Campsites, facilities: There are 104 campsites with water, electricity, picnic tables, grills, and fire rings; among these, 90 are for RVs. Restrooms, showers, a dump station, a playground, a lake, and canoe rentals are available. Wheelchair-accessible areas include some sites and the picnic areas. Children are welcome. Pets are permitted with proof of vaccination.

Reservations, fees: Reservations are recommended; call ReserveAmerica at 800/326-3521. Sites are $11 to $16 per night for four people, plus $2 for each additional person, for electricity, and per pet. Major credit cards are accepted. The maximum stay is 14 days.

Directions: From I-75 traveling north, take Exit 195 westbound on Laurel Road for two miles. At U.S. 41, turn north and drive two miles. The park is on the east side. If you're traveling south, use Exit 200.

Contact: Oscar Scherer State Park, 1843 South Tamiami Trail, Osprey, FL 34229, 941/483-5956.

32 ENCORE SUPER PARK— SARASOTA SOUTH

Rating: 10

East of Nokomis

Sarasota/Bradenton map, grid c2, page 398

This deluxe park on Dona Bay is a huge hit with retired snowbirds who spend the cooler months in Florida, but it has plenty of things to do keep people of all ages occupied: Golf, two pro sand volleyball courts, four tennis courts, and basketball, for example. The heated, 120,000-gallon pool is big enough for laps and water aerobics. But it's not all about sports; opportunities to socialize run the gamut from theme parties (Germanfest, lobster feasts, country-and-western dinner shows) to bingo, card games, arts and crafts, and auctions. Professional shows and concerts are held in an outdoor amphitheater. There's even a business center with fax, copier, Internet access, and computers. "We're kind of like a small town all to ourselves," say the managers.

Campsites, facilities: There are 167 sites for RVs. Full hookups, cable TV, telephone service, and picnic tables are available. Also on site are restrooms, showers, laundry facilities, a dump station, a pool, a recreation hall, an outdoor amphitheater, a model train room, a nature walk, a clubhouse, a game arcade, four tennis courts, a golf practice complex, a miniature golf course, a volleyball area, a fitness center, a kid's pirate ship play fort, a library with children's room, a basketball court, horseshoe pits, shuffleboard courts, a tool and craft shop, boat storage, and a bocce ball (lawn bowling) park. Most areas are wheelchair ac-

cessible. Children are welcome. Leashed pets are permitted.

Reservations, fees: Reservations are recommended. Sites are $48 per night for two people, plus $2 for each additional person. Major credit cards are accepted. Long-term stays are OK.

Directions: From I-75, take Exit 195 westbound on Laurel Road for one mile. Look for the park to your left.

Contact: Encore Super Park–Sarasota South, 1070 Laurel Road East, Nokomis, FL 34275, 941/488-9674 or 800/548-8678, fax 941/485-5678, website: www.rvonthego.com.

33 STAY-N-PLAY RV RESORT

Rating: 8

East of Nokomis

Sarasota/Bradenton map, grid c2, page 398

This sprawling park is both a convenient stop for overnight travelers and a destination park. Among the 362 sites are 20 "luxury super sites" that feature personal amenities, such as private hot tubs, barbecue grills, patio furniture, tanning tables, boat docks with electric boats, and privacy fences. At the center of the 404-acre complex are three large lakes. All sites overlook the lakes, which are stocked with largemouth bass, crappie, specks, and bluegill. The 12,000-square-foot clubhouse has a wooden dance floor and a wide veranda that opens onto the pool deck.

Campsites, facilities: There are 362 RV sites with full hookups, cable TV, and telephone service. Restrooms, showers, laundry facilities, a dump station, tennis courts, a pool with a Jacuzzi, a 12,000-square-foot clubhouse with large-screen TV and fireplace, a miniature golf course including water wheel, a driving range, a post office, volleyball courts, shuffleboard, and an exercise room are available. Children are welcome. Leashed pets are permitted.

Reservations, fees: Reservations are recommended. Sites are $25 to $35 per night for two people, plus $2 for each additional person. Major credit cards are accepted. Long-term stays are OK.

Directions: From I-75, take Exit 195 and drive east on Laurel Road to the bottom of the ramp. At Knight's Trail, turn north and drive 1,000 feet to the park.

Contact: Stay-N-Play RV Resort, 899 Knight's Trail, Nokomis, FL 34275, 941/485-1800 or 800/437-9397, fax 941/488-1813.

COUNTRY CLUB ESTATES

Rating: 2

In Venice

Sarasota/Bradenton map, grid c2, page 398

Advertisements for the park tout it as being in the "best location in the nation," and some campers might agree. The Intracoastal Waterway borders the community on the east, and Gulf of Mexico beaches are less than one mile to the west. Shopping centers, restaurants, banks, doctors' offices, and a hospital are all within two blocks. There's even a golf course nearby, which is fitting because the park itself is a former golf course, as hinted by street names such as Bogie and Turf. Dock your boat for an additional fee; a lagoon in the park provides access to the Intracoastal Waterway. RVers have access to the common areas of the mobile home park, including a heated pool and a recreation hall with an auditorium, a stage, a card room, and a ceramics room. The place also has a bowling league, tennis groups, and golf leagues for men and women.

Campsites, facilities: A 509-unit mobile home community for adults only, Country Club Estates has 10 RV sites for travelers with full hookups and cable TV. Restrooms, showers, a pool with a spa, boat docks, shuffleboard courts, bocce (lawn bowling) courts, and a recreation hall are available. You must be 55 or older to camp. Pets are prohibited in the RV section.

Reservations, fees: Reservations are recom-mended. Sites are $27 to $35 per night. Credit cards are not accepted. Six-month stays are permitted.

Directions: From the intersection of U.S. 41 and Business Route 41 on the north side of Venice, drive south on the business route for 1.5 miles and turn into the park, which is behind the Publix supermarket. The park entrance is located directly off the main highway.

Contact: Country Club Estates, 700 Waterway, Venice, FL 34285, 941/488-2111, fax 941/483-4958.

FLORIDA PINES MOBILE HOME COURT

Rating: 2

In Venice

Sarasota/Bradenton map, grid c2, page 398

Social programs are held for residents between October 15 and April 15 in this clean, well-landscaped mobile home and RV community for retirement living near the Gulf of Mexico. Shopping, restaurants, and supplies are available .25 mile away.

Campsites, facilities: There are 30 paved RV sites with cement patios in this mobile home community for retirees. Full hookups, cable TV, restrooms, showers, laundry facilities, a dump station, horseshoe pits, shuffleboard courts, and a wheelchair-accessible recreation room are available. Big rigs can be accommodated. You must be 55 or older to stay here. Pets are prohibited.

Reservations, fees: Reservations are recommended. Sites are $18 to $32 per night for two people, plus $1.50 for each additional person and for air-conditioning usage, and $2.50 for using electrical heaters. Credit cards are not accepted.

Directions: From I-75, take Exit 193 southwest for 6.5 miles. At State Road 776, turn right and drive two blocks.

Contact: Florida Pines Mobile Home Court, 150 Satulah Circle, Venice, FL 34293, 941/493-0019.

36 BAY PALMS RV PARK

Rating: 3

In Englewood

Sarasota/Bradenton map, grid c2, page 398

For an urban location, the setting is very Floridian: A dozen century-old live oaks and 85 palm trees shade this park, which fronts on Lemon Bay. Twelve boat slips are available; they accommodate boats up to 18 feet long. Gulf beaches are 1.7 miles away. Golf courses, grocery stores, restaurants, and laundry facilities lie within two miles. About 10 miles south of the park is Gasparilla Island State Park, a beachfront park with a lighthouse built in 1890 and some great shelling. Gasparilla Island, named for pirate José Gaspar, who used the island as a hiding place in the 1700s, also offers great fishing on Boca Grande Pass, which is famed for tarpon.

Campsites, facilities: This 2.8-acre adult park has 33 sites, 17 of which are available for transient stays (not overnight). Sites have full hookups with 30-amp service, cable TV, and telephone access. Also on the grounds are park models rented year-round. Restrooms, showers, and laundry facilities are on site. Quiet pets (no pit bulls) are allowed in one section of the park; all dogs are walked outside the park and owners must clean up after them.

Reservations, fees: Reservations are recommended. Sites are $500 to $900 per month during the season (January through April), and a three-month minimum stay applies. Only two people are permitted per lot. Credit cards are not accepted. Long-term stays are encouraged.

Directions: From I-75, take Exit 193 (Jacaranda Boulevard) heading west until it dead-ends into State Road 776. Turn south (left) and drive about seven miles. The park is on the right, just past Travis Marina and the Radio Shack.

Contact: Bay Palms RV Park, 1000 South McCall Road, Englewood, FL 34223, 941/474-1446, email: rnmgarms@cs.com.

37 VENICE CAMPGROUND

Rating: 8

East of Venice

Sarasota/Bradenton map, grid c2, page 398

Want to get out of the sun? Set on the scenic Myakka River, Venice Campground is tucked into an old-growth oak hammock that casts shady relief. Some RV sites overlook an inlet off the river, and the tent area is on the waterfront, separated from the trailer section. Three miles of nature trails offer views of the river, which is popular with canoeists and anglers. A restaurant is next door, but there's not much else in the way of development; the park has a secluded, back-to-nature ambience. A security gate keeps out the curious. The campground sells some groceries—ice, soda, and even a few RV supplies—but you'll have to drive into Venice three miles west for most items. Venice, like its Italian namesake, is laced with canals and waterways, but it's best known for an unusual beachcombing sport: Instead of shells, people look for fossilized shark teeth. North of Venice is a popular surfing spot at North Jetty Park.

Campsites, facilities: This 25-acre campground has 104 RV sites with full hookups and 30 tent sites with water; some have electricity. Picnic tables, restrooms, showers, laundry facilities, a dump station, a pool, a boat ramp, boat and canoe rentals, cabin rentals, a playground, a game room, horseshoe pits, shuffleboard courts, a volleyball field, and a limited store are available. A supermarket is about 3.5 miles away. Children are welcome. Leashed pets are permitted at RV sites only.

Reservations, fees: Reservations are recommended. RV sites are $26 to $38. Prices are for four people; add $2.75 for each additional person over age six. Major credit cards are accepted. The maximum stay is nine months.

Directions: From I-75, take Exit 191 southbound on River Road and drive one mile. Turn left on Venice Avenue (a dirt road) and continue .5 mile east to the campground.

Contact: Venice Campground, 4085 East Venice Avenue, Venice, FL 34292, 941/488-0850, fax 941/485-1666, website: www.campvenice.com.

38 RAMBLERS REST RESORT CAMPGROUND

Rating: 6

East of Venice

Sarasota/Bradenton map, grid c2, page 398

Towering slash pines welcome campers to this 100-acre park on the Myakka River in an area little touched by development. Many of the sites are occupied by retirees in park models. Bingo, arts and crafts, choir singing, wood carving, and square dancing are among the activities held in the recreation hall. Fish from the riverfront dock or launch your boat and head south for the Gulf of Mexico. The swimming pool is heated. Within 20 miles are Sarasota-area attractions such as the John and Mable Ringling Museum of Art (941/359-5700), which displays contemporary pieces and Baroque works from the Old Masters. Although the name of John Ringling, who lived in Sarasota, is synonymous with the circus, he was also an avid art collector; his Italianate mansion and formal gardens are open to the public. Sarasota considers itself the state's center of all things cultural, with an opera house, theaters, and art galleries concentrated downtown. Other attractions in Sarasota are the Mote Marine Science Aquarium (941/388-1385), which has a shark tank among other exhibits, and the Pelican Man Bird Sanctuary (941/388-4444), a rehabilitation center for injured birds.

Campsites, facilities: There are 589 RV sites, 563 of which have full hookups. Water and electricity are available at the remaining spots, which can accommodate 18 tenters. On the premises are picnic tables, restrooms, showers, a dump station, a clubroom, a pool with a Jacuzzi, a boat ramp, a dock, a playground, an exercise room, horseshoe pits, shuffleboard courts, a convenience store, and laundry fa-

cilities. Most areas are wheelchair accessible. Children are welcome. Pets under 18 pounds are allowed; they may be walked in remote areas only.

Reservations, fees: Reservations are recommended. Sites are $29 per night for two people, plus $2 for each additional person. Credit cards are not accepted. Long-term rates are available for seasonal visitors.

Directions: From I-75, take Exit 191 southbound on River Road and drive three miles. The campground is on the east side.

Contact: Ramblers Rest Resort Campground, 1300 North River Road, Venice, FL 34293, 941/493-4354, fax 941/496-9520, website: www.ramblersrest.com.

39 MYAKKA RIVER RV PARK

Rating: 3

West of North Port

Sarasota/Bradenton map, grid c3, page 398

This park is located at the delta of the Myakka River, in an area overlooking the river floodplain. The location is good for bird-watching if you can get a site on the south side of the 40-acre park. The sites are big enough for 40-foot rigs; two sites even accommodate 46-footers. Nearby is North Port, which has seen less development than many of the fast-growing cities on Florida's west coast. The town is home to Warm Mineral Springs (941/426-1692), a health spa where the water stays at 87 degrees year-round. You can swim there for $6.50 a day.

Campsites, facilities: You'll find 15 grassy RV or tent sites with full hookups, picnic tables, and concrete patios, as well as 58 park-model sites. Restrooms, showers, laundry facilities, shuffleboard, a pool, rental units, picnic tables, a patio with a barbecue, a newly remodeled clubhouse, and a canoe launch are available. A public boat ramp for bigger vessels is three miles away. Two supermarkets are a 10-minute drive away. Children are welcome. Leashed pets are permitted.

Reservations, fees: Reservations are recommended. Sites are $24 to $30 per night for two people, plus $3 for each additional person over the age of six. Major credit cards are accepted. Long-term stays are OK.

Directions: From I-75, take Exit 191 southbound on River Road and drive six miles to U.S. 41. Turn left and drive .5 mile. The park is on the right side of the road, just beyond the bridge.

Contact: Myakka River RV Park, 10400 Tamiami Trail, Venice, FL 34287, 941/426-5040, fax 941/426-5712.

40 RIVERSIDE RV RESORT & CAMPGROUND

Rating: 9

South of Arcadia

Sarasota/Bradenton map, grid c4, page 398

More than 70 acres in size, this park is convenient to I-75 travelers. It caters to young families—some weekend activities are specifically for children—but it also offers river canoeing, kayaking, and fishing, which appeal to teenagers and adults. There's a video arcade, and the proximity of the playground to the swimming pools—one designed for water volleyball—was established with parental supervision in mind. These oak-shaded and sunny sites are large, buffered by a wildlife area and the Peace River, near its mouth on the Gulf of Mexico. A new boat ramp was recently added.

Campsites, facilities: This park offers 235 full-hookup RV sites with picnic tables, as well as a small primitive tent camping area. There are restrooms, showers, laundry facilities, a dump station, a canoe launch, canoe and kayak rentals, a recreation hall, a playground, horseshoes, shuffleboard, a volleyball field, two pools (one heated), a spa, a limited store with propane and RV supplies, and a boat dock on the Peace River. Children are welcome. Leashed cats and dogs are permitted; a pet walking area is provided.

Reservations, fees: Reservations are recommended. Fee for two people is $36 for RV sites and $30 for primitive tent sites; rates are lower in summer. Add $2.50 for each extra person. Major credit cards are accepted. Long-term stays are OK.

Directions: From I-75, take Exit 170 onto Kings Highway/County Road 769 and drive five miles east to the park.

Contact: Riverside RV Resort & Campground, 9770 Southwest County Road 769, Arcadia, FL 34266, 863/993-2111 or 800/795-9733, fax 863/993-2021, website: www.riversidervresort.com.

41 LETTUCE LAKE TRAVEL RESORT

Rating: 5

Near Fort Ogden

Sarasota/Bradenton map, grid c4, page 398

Greeted by Canadian flags, campers at this manicured park tend to stay for the winter or even longer in their RVs or park models. The big attraction is a county boat ramp that gives anglers and boaters access to Lettuce Lake, a wide spot on the Peace River as it flows into the Gulf of Mexico. The campground has a dock on the "lake" and a pretty wooded area on the banks where you can sit at picnic tables with a drink in hand and while away the hours. It's a rural spot; it's out there with the orange groves and cattle, and it has shell-rock roads, as well as oaks, palms, and hibiscus. That rural flavor is part of its appeal.

Campsites, facilities: There are 247 sites with full hookups and picnic tables; about half of the sites have concrete pads. Restrooms, showers, laundry facilities, a pool, a recreation center, a lakefront dock, horseshoes, and shuffleboard courts are available. A public boat ramp is next door. A supermarket is 7.5 miles away. Children are permitted if they are well supervised. Leashed, supervised pets under 20 pounds are allowed.

Reservations, fees: Reservations are recommended. Sites are $24 per night for two people,

plus $2.50 for each additional person. Credit cards are not accepted. Long-term stays are OK.

Directions: From southbound I-75, take Exit 170 onto Kings Highway/County Road 769 and drive northeast for six miles to County Road 761. Turn southeast, go two miles, then take Lettuce Lake Avenue to the park. From northbound I-75, take Exit 164 onto U.S. 17 and drive north 10 miles to County Road 761. Turn west, go two miles, then take Lettuce Lake Avenue to the park, which is right next to Oak Haven Park.

Contact: Lettuce Lake Travel Resort, 8644 Southwest Reese Street, Arcadia, FL 34269, 863/494-6057, fax 863/494-4254.

42 OAK HAVEN PARK

Rating: 4

Near Fort Ogden
Sarasota/Bradenton map, grid c4, page 398

Heavily wooded Oak Haven Park is adjacent to Lettuce Lake Park, which has a public boat ramp. A small golf course is down the block. The park is on the same street as Lettuce Lake Travel Resort (see previous campground). Says the management: "We are country. You come here to rest."

Campsites, facilities: All 119 RV sites have full hookups; about 22 are available for overnighters and new seasonal visitors. On the premises are restrooms, showers, laundry facilities, a pool and spa, shuffleboard, horseshoes, and a small library for guests. A supermarket and restaurants are eight miles away. The park is senior-oriented, but children may visit. Leashed pets under 20 pounds are permitted in a separate section.

Reservations, fees: Reservations are recommended. Sites are $25 per night for two people, plus $2 per extra person. Credit cards are not accepted. Long-term stays are the norm.

Directions: From southbound I-75, take Exit 170 onto County Road 769 and drive northeast for six miles to County Road 761. Turn

southeast, go two miles, then take Lettuce Lake Avenue to the park. From northbound I-75, take Exit 164 onto U.S. 17 and drive north for 10 miles to County Road 761. Turn west, go two miles, then take Lettuce Lake Avenue to the park.

Contact: Oak Haven Park, 10307 Southwest Lettuce Lake Avenue, Arcadia, FL 34266, 863/494-4578.

43 LIVE OAK RV RESORT

Rating: 6

South of Arcadia, off I-75
Sarasota/Bradenton map, grid c4, page 398

This 80-acre park with a security gate is nestled in an area of horse ranches, farms, and fruit groves along the Peace River near historic Punta Gorda. The park caters to upscale retirees, with a chipping green on the property and plenty of recreational activities. During the winter season, the park hosts dances, dinners, other social events, choir singing, and religious services.

Campsites, facilities: The resort has 399 RV sites, most with full hookups and concrete pads. Pop-up trailers, pickup-truck campers, and tenters will be turned away; RVs must be at least 23 feet long. On the premises are showers, restrooms, laundry facilities, a pool and Jacuzzi, a poolside snack bar, a recreation hall, an exercise room, a game room, a golf putting and chipping green, horseshoe pits, shuffleboard courts, and bocce ball (lawn bowling) courts. A supermarket and restaurants are eight miles away. Children may visit but not camp. Leashed pets are permitted.

Reservations, fees: Reservations are taken. Sites are $25 per night. Major credit cards are accepted. Long-term stays are OK.

Directions: From I-75, take Exit 164 onto U.S. 17 and drive 10 miles north to the entrance.

Contact: Live Oak RV Resort, 12865 Southwest Highway 17, Arcadia, FL 34269, 863/993-4014 or 800/833-4236, fax 863/993-0940.

44 ENCORE SUPER PARK— PORT CHARLOTTE

Rating: 8

In the community of El Jobean near the Myakka River

Sarasota/Bradenton map, grid c3, page 398

About half of the 528 concrete-pad sites in this well-manicured mobile home community are available for RVs, although none are pull-through. Lots are roomy, measuring 30 by 80 feet. You won't find much shade in the camping area, but there is a view of pine trees near the lakes. A path winding through the complex has mile markers so joggers and bicyclists can keep track of their exercise progress. The park is minutes from the Texas Rangers' winter training camp, the Charlotte Towne Center mall, Englewood Beach, Gasparilla Island State Park, the Thomas Edison Home, and the Ringling Brothers and Barnum & Bailey Circus and Museum.

Campsites, facilities: The adults-only resort has 268 RV sites with full hookups and telephone access. The property contains four spring-fed lakes, shuffleboard courts, a pool, horseshoe pits, laundry, and a recreation hall used for dances, exercise classes, and other activities. Leashed pets are allowed.

Reservations, fees: Reservations are recommended. Sites are $32 to $37 per night for two people, plus $3 for each additional person. Credit cards are accepted. Long-term stays are permitted.

Directions: From I-75, take Exit 179 onto Toledo Blade Boulevard heading southwest. Go 6.5 miles to State Road 776/El Jobean Road and turn south. The park is 3.3 miles ahead on the right.

Contact: Encore Super Park–Port Charlotte, 3737 El Jobean Road, Port Charlotte, FL 33953, 941/624-4511 or 800/468-5022, fax 941/624-5238, website: www.rvonthego.com.

45 CHARLOTTE HARBOR RV PARK

Rating: 1

On U.S. 41 in Charlotte Harbor

Sarasota/Bradenton map, grid c4, page 398

This park is tiny, with just 1.5 acres available, and most folks are parked full-time. But a narrow waterway provides access (for small boats only) to the Peace River and Charlotte Harbor, where the big fish swim. A shopping center, beaches, a public pool, and laundry facilities are close by; indeed, you can walk to eight restaurants and a supermarket. You can also walk to a fishing bridge on the Peace River.

Campsites, facilities: Thirty sites with full hookups, concrete pads, and picnic tables are available for RVs. Tents are prohibited. Restrooms, showers, and a dump station are provided. Children are welcome. Small, leashed pets are permitted.

Reservations, fees: Reservations are recommended. Fee for two people is $22 per night for RV sites. Add $2 for each additional person. Credit cards are not accepted. Long-term stays are OK.

Directions: From I-75, take Exit 170 westbound on Kings Highway to U.S. 41. Turn south on U.S. 41/Tamiami Trail and drive .5 mile. The park is just north of the bridge crossing the Peace River.

Contact: Charlotte Harbor RV Park, 4838 Tamiami Trail, Charlotte Harbor, FL 33980, 941/625-5695.

46 PALMS AND PINES RIVERSIDE RESORT

Rating: 2

On the south side of the Peace River east of Punta Gorda

Sarasota/Bradenton map, grid c4, page 398

Palms and Pines Riverside Resort, primarily a residential trailer park, faces the scenic Peace River. Some lots have boat docks; however, swimming is not permitted because of the presence of alligators. Close by are boat ramps, fishing piers, a golf course, and shopping. Life in Charlotte

County revolves around boating, so you'll find plenty of marinas and boating supply stores nearby. In the wintertime, manatees are commonly seen along the Peace River and in the harbor.

Campsites, facilities: Overlooking the Peace River, this 114-unit, adults-only mobile home park offers overnighters 25 concrete-pad RV sites with full hookups, cable TV, and telephone access. On the premises are a boat ramp, fishing paddleboats, a wheelchair-accessible recreation room, horseshoe pits, and shuffleboard courts. There are no restrooms, so rigs must be self-contained. Pets are welcome.

Reservations, fees: Reservations are recommended in winter. Sites are $26 per night for two people, plus $5 for each additional person. Credit cards are not accepted. Long-term stays are encouraged.

Directions: From I-75, take Exit 164 and drive 1.8 miles north on U.S. 17 to Cleveland Avenue. Turn west and drive .3 mile to Riverside Drive, then head north for one-half block.

Contact: Palms and Pines Riverside Resort, 5400 Riverside Drive, Punta Gorda, FL 33982, 941/639-5461, email: manage@palmsandpinesinc.net.

⁴⁷ SHELL CREEK RESORT

Rating: 6

East of Punta Gorda

Sarasota/Bradenton map, grid c4, page 398

Set far from urban sights, this open and sunny park overlooks scenic Shell Creek, a tributary of the Peace River. Also nearby is the Fred C. Babcock/Cecil M. Webb Wildlife Management Area, a 65,000-acre hunting park famous for its doves, quail, deer, and wild hogs and for freshwater fishing and frog gigging. But frankly, this adult-oriented park welcomes visitors for more civilized fun. During the winter months, visitors can keep in shape with an aquacise program in the heated pool, and anglers will delight in the great fishing. Bands entertain at holiday dances held five times a year.

Campsites, facilities: RVers over age 55 are welcome at the 185 full-hookup RV spots. Cable TV access, wheelchair-accessible restrooms, showers, laundry facilities, a pool and spa, a billiards room, tournament shuffleboard courts, a boat ramp, a marina, and a store are on the grounds. A supermarket and pizza parlor are within seven miles. Children can visit for up to 30 days. Leashed pets are permitted and must use the designated dog-walk area.

Reservations, fees: Reservations are recommended. Sites are $30 per night for two people, plus $3 per extra person. Major credit cards are accepted. Long-term stays are OK.

Directions: From I-75, take Exit 164 northbound on U.S. 17 and go four miles. At County Road 764, turn east and drive 4.5 miles to the park.

Contact: Shell Creek Resort, 35711 Washington Loop Road, Punta Gorda, FL 33982, 941/639-4234, fax 941/639-2801.

⁴⁸ PUNTA GORDA RV RESORT

Rating: 6

Off U.S. 41 in Punta Gorda

Sarasota/Bradenton map, grid c4, page 398

Does your rig or boat need a wash? This palm-dotted park offers well water so you can do the job. That's only one of many features that attract the primarily Midwestern clientele. A canal behind the nearly 30-acre property offers boaters direct access to Alligator Creek and the Gulf of Mexico for fishing; even sailboats can cruise right out to the open water without encountering bridges. A bait and tackle store is next door. A par-three golf course is across the street, and a restaurant is within walking distance. A monthly activity calendar and newsletter keep campers apprised of the on-site social programs.

Campsites, facilities: The adult-oriented RV park has 223 sites with full hookups, cable TV, and telephone access. Restrooms, showers, picnic tables, a clubhouse, two spas, a boat ramp, an exercise room, horseshoes, shuffleboard, a convenience store, a beauty/barber shop, laundry facilities, and both city water and well water are available. There's also a pool with a tiki hut. The recreation hall and pool area are accessible to wheelchairs. Children are not welcome as campers, but grandkids can visit for short stays. Small, leashed pets (one per site) are permitted.

Reservations, fees: Reservations are recommended in summer and required in the winter season. Sites are $23 per night for two people, plus $3.50 for each additional person. Credit cards are not accepted. Long-term stays are OK.

Directions: From I-75, take Exit 164 and drive 2.3 miles west on U.S. 17 to U.S. 41. Go south for two miles, turn west onto Rio Villa Drive, and take the second left at the sign.

Contact: Punta Gorda RV Resort, 3701 Baynard Drive, Punta Gorda, FL 33950, 941/639-2010, fax 941/637-4931, website: www.isni.net/~pgrv.

49 ALLIGATOR MOBILE HOME AND RV PARK

Rating: 3

South of Punta Gorda

Sarasota/Bradenton map, grid c4, page 398

In the cool of the evening you'll see a few tenants gather outside their trailers to exchange news, but the center of activity is a large two-story recreation hall in the middle of the grounds. Catering to retirees who are staying for the season, this ownership and site-share park is on a quiet side road five miles south of downtown Punta Gorda with good access to local attractions. A golf course, restaurants, and groceries are within two miles. Although the park is age-restricted (one person must be at least 55, the spouse at least 45), grandchildren may visit.

Campsites, facilities: This mobile home park has 166 sites available for RVs, offering full hookups, 30-amp and 50-amp electrical service, cable TV, and telephone access. On the premises are restrooms, showers, a dump station, a wheelchair-accessible clubhouse, a pool, shuffleboard courts, a pool table, and laundry facilities. Families with children are not welcome. Leashed pets are permitted.

Reservations, fees: Reservations are recommended. Sites are $22 per night for two people, plus $3 for each additional person. Major credit cards are accepted.

Directions: From I-75 take Exit 161 onto Jones Loop Road and drive .5 mile west. Turn south onto County Road 765A/Taylor Road and drive one mile to the park.

Contact: Alligator Mobile Home and RV Park, 6400 Taylor Road, Lot 112, Punta Gorda, FL 33950, 941/639-7000 or 941/639-7916, website: www.alligatorpark.com.

50 WATER'S EDGE RV RESORT

Rating: 5

East of Punta Gorda

Sarasota/Bradenton map, grid c4, page 398

A 1,500-square-foot recreation room adjacent to the pool is the hub of activity, hosting pancake breakfasts, potlucks, wine and cheese parties, ice-cream socials, and crafts classes. The campsites, which are big enough to accommodate RVs up to 45 feet long, form a half-circle around a 20-acre fishing lake. Canoes and paddleboats are available for rent. A few pine trees provide a touch of greenery, but there isn't much shade.

Campsites, facilities: This resort has 174 sites (some full-hookup) for RVs, slide-outs, trailers, and campers. A separate area offers water-and-electric sites for six tenters. Restrooms, showers, picnic tables, a dump station, laundry facilities, a pool with a spa, a playground, horseshoes, a volleyball field, a small camp store, and paddleboat rentals are available. Children are welcome. Leashed pets are permitted.

Reservations, fees: Reservations are recommended. RV sites are $31 and tent campers pay $22 per night for two people, plus $3 for each additional adult. Children are $2 extra. Major credit cards are accepted. Maximum stay is six months.

Directions: From I-75, take Exit 161 onto Jones Loop Road and drive east for 500 feet. Turn north onto Piper Road and drive 2.7 miles. Piper Road becomes Golf Course Boulevard; the campground is just .5 mile past the four-way stop sign at Airport Road.

Contact: Water's Edge RV Resort, 6800 Golf Course Boulevard, Punta Gorda, FL 33982, 941/637-4677 or 941/637-1188 or 800/637-9224, fax 941/637-9543, website: www.watersedge rvresort.com.

51 ENCORE RV PARK— PUNTA GORDA

Rating: 8

South of Punta Gorda
Sarasota/Bradenton map, grid c4, page 398

Brown pelicans rest atop dock posts here, taking a break after their latest round of fishing. Campers, too, can fish at this well-kept, boating-oriented resort with a stream running past. That is, if they're not busy with the golf outings, movies, dancing, potlucks, and weekly bingo games offered in winter. The campground is screened from the road by lots of greenery, and the sites are a cut above those at most RV parks. A few rigs up to 40 feet long can be accommodated.

Campsites, facilities: All 182 RV sites have full hookups. Restrooms, showers, picnic tables, laundry facilities, a boat ramp, a heated pool with a spa, a game room, shuffleboard courts, horseshoes, and propane are available. For cable and telephone service, call the appropriate utility company. Children may stay a few days or visit; the typical camper at this retiree-oriented park is around age 70, a staffer says. Leashed pets are permitted.

Reservations, fees: Reservations are recommended. Sites are $29 and up per night for two people. Major credit cards are accepted. Long-term stays are OK.

Directions: From I-75, take Exit 161 onto Jones Loop Road and drive west for .75 mile to U.S. 41. Cross U.S. 41 and continue .5 mile to the park, at right.

Contact: Encore RV Park—Punta Gorda, 10205 Burnt Store Road, Punta Gorda, FL 33950, 941/639-3978 or 877/237-2757, fax 941/639-8073, website: www.rvonthego.com.

52 SUN-N-SHADE CAMPGROUND

Rating: 6

South of Punta Gorda
Sarasota/Bradenton map, grid c4, page 398

Mostly sunny, this campground is favored by retirees and snowbirds seeking to get out of the cold from the long winter up north. A few trees provide shade and landscaping. Planned activities keep folks busy in the recreation hall.

Campsites, facilities: Of the total 201 full-hookup RV sites, 25 are available for overnighters. All sites have picnic tables, concrete pads, cable TV, and phone service availability. Restrooms, showers, a dump station, and two laundry facilities round out the basic facilities. Amenities are a pool, a recreation hall, shuffleboard courts, two dog-walk areas, and a nature trail. In season, planned activities include bingo, games, cards, parties, dinners, and breakfasts. The clubhouse, pool area, and restrooms are wheelchair accessible. Children are allowed. Leashed pets are permitted.

Reservations, fees: Reservations are recommended. Sites are $29 per night for two people, plus $3.50 per extra person and $2 if air conditioners are used. Major credit cards are accepted. Long-term or seasonal stays are preferred.

Directions: From I-75, take Exit 158 and drive one mile west on Tucker's Grade/State Road 762. At U.S. 41, turn south and go 3.5 miles.

Contact: Sun-n-Shade Campground, 14880 Tamiami Trail, Punta Gorda, FL 33955, 941/639-5388, fax 941/639-0368, website: www.sunnshade.com.

COURTESY OF PETER TRITLEY

Chapter 14

Lake Okeechobee

Lake Okeechobee

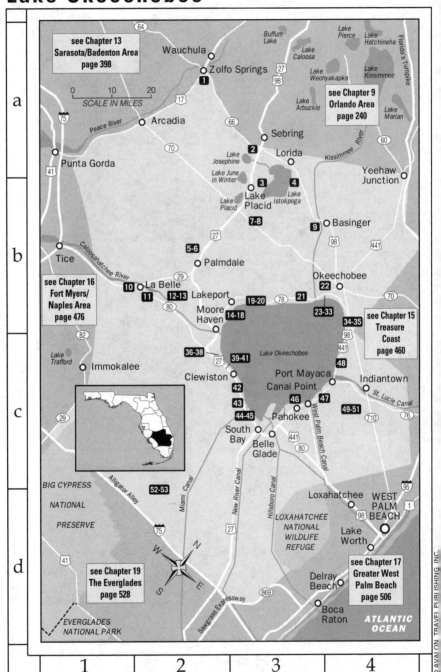

■ PIONEER PARK OF HARDEE COUNTY

🏊 ⛗ 🐕 ⛤ 🚌 ⛺

Rating: 7

On the Peace River in Zolfo Springs

Lake Okeechobee map, grid a2, page 426

You won't soon forget this focal point of Hardee County, if only for its wildlife refuge near the campground in Pioneer Park. In 2001, the county made major improvements to the refuge that allow the animals to move freely in a natural habitat while visitors watch from an elevated boardwalk. The animals include cougars and two black bears. All the denizens of this refuge cannot be returned to the wild for one reason or another, and they had been previously kept in a caged, zoolike environment here. One of the bears? A retired professional wrestler (declawed). The cougar? Given up by its owners when the pet—once fist-sized—grew too big. Each has its own personality, and of course, a name. The refuge is open daily from 10 A.M. to 4 P.M., except Wednesdays, Thanksgiving, and Christmas Day. Admission of $1 to $2 per person helps contribute to support the animals and their habitat.

The campground offers grassy sites in this 115-acre public park for tenters and RVers. A dike and a handful of short walking trails are by the Peace River, where anglers try for panfish. This sleepy region also attracts weekend canoeists who launch here and paddle past cattle farms and moss-draped hardwoods on the slow-moving river, ending the overnight journey 23 miles downstream in Arcadia, or closer to home for half-day trips. Among the area canoe outfitters is Canoe Outpost, 2816 Northwest County Road 661 in Arcadia, 863/494-1215. If your dog will be joining you, try Canoe Safari, 3020 Northwest County Road 661 in Arcadia, 863/494-7865. Other outfitters typically nix pets.

Primitive camping only is available at Pioneer Park in late February through early March (call 863/773-2161 for exact dates) during the county's Pioneer Park Days, celebrated by an old-fashioned parade through downtown Wauchula and displays of antique farm equipment, entertainers, and a 500-booth flea market in the park.

Campsites, facilities: There are 62 campsites for RVs and 25 for tents. Most sites have water and electricity. Showers, restrooms, a small museum, a playground, nature trails, fishing ponds, an entertainment pavilion, a picnic area, and a dump station are available. A restaurant, a convenience store, a bank, and bait are within .25 mile. Children and leashed pets are permitted. Pets must be kept under control at all times; pet "disturbances" will not be tolerated "at any time." Alcohol is forbidden.

Reservations, fees: Reservations are not accepted. Sites are $7 per night for two people, plus $2 per extra person and $4 for electricity. Credit cards are not accepted. Stays are limited to 14 days consecutive days.

Directions: The park is at the intersection of U.S. 17 and State Road 64 in Zolfo Springs.

Contact: Pioneer Park of Hardee County, c/o Hardee County Public Works Department, 205 Hanchey Road, Wauchula, FL 33873, 863/735-0330 or 863/773-9430. Contact the wildlife refuge at 650 Animal Way, Zolfo Springs, FL 33890, 863/735-9531.

■ BUTTONWOOD BAY

🚶 🚲 🏊 ⛵ 🚌 🐕 ♿ 🚐

Rating: 5

On Lake Josephine south of Sebring

Lake Okeechobee map, grid a3, page 426

"A great place to live" and "your fun-filled winter home" are two of the ways this 130-acre RV resort describes itself. Geared to the retired set (but you can stay if you are 19 or older), the park is set in the middle of orange groves on 1,300-acre Lake Josephine. A small stream runs through the property as well.

Paved, lighted streets lead to two pools and two recreation centers, where bingo, cards, and dancing entertain snowbirds from more than half of the U.S. Golf aficionados can warm up at an on-site driving range before heading to any of the 15 golf courses within 15 miles. If the 1.5-mile-long nature trail gets to be old hat, try the trails at Highlands Hammock State Park.

Campsites, facilities: This adults-only park has 535 full-hookup RV sites. Two recreation centers, two pools, an exercise room, a nature trail, miniature golf, a driving range, horseshoes, tennis, a bocce (lawn bowling) court, snacks (in winter), a woodworking shop, pool tables, shuffleboard, and organized activities entertain campers. On the premises are restrooms, showers, a dump station, laundry facilities, a boat ramp, and a dock. Management says the buildings and common areas are wheelchair accessible. Groceries are five miles away. Restaurants are about two miles away. Children may visit only for short stays. Pets are welcome.

Reservations, fees: Reservations are recommended. Sites are $25 to $40 per night for two people, plus $4 for each additional person. Credit cards are not accepted. Long-term stays are OK.

Directions: From Sebring, take U.S. 27 five miles south and look for the RV resort on the right.

Contact: Buttonwood Bay, 10001 U.S. 27 South, Sebring, FL 33870, 863/655-1122 or 800/289-2522.

🖪 CYPRESS ISLE RV PARK AND MARINA

Rating: 3

On Lake Istokpoga in Lake Placid
Lake Okeechobee map, grid b3, page 426

Fishing is the name of the vacation game at Cypress Isle. Wild shiners and lake access are the amenities the proprietors mention first when asked about their park. Eleven-mile-long Lake Istokpoga is well known for its bass, bream, and crappie fishing. Boating is a popular pursuit, and each campsite has a covered boat slip. Fish fries and other cookouts keep the campers occupied when they're not wet-

ting a line. A fair number of cypress trees shade the grassy sites.

Campsites, facilities: Of the 17 sites for RVs or tents, seven have full hookups. All sites have water and electricity. Some of the campsites have the lake at their back doors. On the premises are restrooms, showers, a dump station, laundry facilities, a recreation room, rental cabins, trailer rentals, a boat ramp, boat rentals, charter fishing services, covered boat slips, a convenience store, and bait and tackle. Children and leashed pets are permitted.

Reservations, fees: Reservations are recommended but drive-ins are usually available. Sites are $15 to $25 per night for two people, plus $3 for each additional person. Credit cards are not accepted. Long-term stays are welcomed.

Directions: From U.S. 27 in Lake Placid, take County Road 621 for 7.5 miles east to Cypress Isle Road. Turn left. Go to the end of the road and turn right.

Contact: Cypress Isle RV Park and Marina, 2 Cypress Isle Lane, Lake Placid, FL 33852, 863/465-5241, email: cypressisle@htn.net, website: www.geocities.com/cypressislesrv.

🖪 MOSSY COVE FISH CAMP

Rating: 2

East of Lake Istokpoga
Lake Okeechobee map, grid b3, page 426

These seven acres are on the quiet, scenic, little-used eastern side of cypress-ringed Lake Istokpoga. You may spot wildlife along the shore, although most visitors turn their attention toward the fish in the 43-square-mile lake. The campsites are grassy.

Campsites, facilities: This fish camp offers 39 full-hookup RV spots and four tent sites. On the premises are restrooms, showers, a dump station, laundry facilities, rental cottages, a boat ramp, wheelchair-accessible dock, a convenience store, and bait and tackle. Children and pets are welcome.

Reservations, fees: Reservations are recom-

mended. Sites are $20 per night for two people, plus $3 for each additional person. Credit cards are not accepted. Long-term stays are OK.

Directions: From Lorida, drive about three miles east on U.S. 98. Turn right (south) on County Road 621. In about five miles, turn right (west) on Godwin Road and proceed to the fish camp.

Contact: Mossy Cove Fish Camp, 3 Mossy Cove Drive, Lorida, FL 33857, 863/655-0119 or 800/833-2683.

⑤ FISHEATING CREEK CAMPGROUND

Rating: 10

On Fisheating Creek in Palmdale
Lake Okeechobee map, grid b2, page 426

Fisheating Creek is one of Florida's prettiest natural areas and has attracted generations of picnickers, swimmers, and canoeists. Bring or rent a canoe at the campground, and you can paddle through marshes and past raised banks where you'll sometimes see rope swings that kids once used to jump into the water (despite the presence of alligators). Enjoy a picnic on riverbanks fringed by moss-draped oaks and cypress trees. Wildlife abounds along the creek, particularly wading birds, alligators, otters, and turtles. Back in the woods, you'll sometimes see deer, wild hogs, and armadillos. The swimming beach is a delight, located on a normally breezy, oak-shaded, five-acre spring-fed lake. Astronomists come here because it is one of the few places where city lights won't blot out the stars.

Improvements are being made to this once rustic getaway, now under control of the state game commission and run by concessionaire Ellen Peterson. A new full-hookup RV area was opened in 2003. The park is part of 18,000 acres of wilderness.

The previous campground owners—the Lykes brothers of hot dog and bacon fame—kicked up quite a controversy a few years ago when they started reserving the creek for campground guests only, claiming unauthorized visitors were littering and causing other problems. The slow-flowing creek traditionally had been used by locals and visitors for fishing, canoeing, and swimming. The state attorney general and others quickly countered that the meat company was illegally trying to keep folks off a public waterway. In the end, the controversy was resolved by the state taking over this camping area.

Campsites, facilities: About 60 primitive tent and RV sites with fire rings and picnic tables are available along the creek and near the swimming lake. Another 50 full-hookup RV sites were recently built. Restrooms, showers, laundry facilities, a boat ramp, canoe and kayak rentals, and a campground store are available. A supermarket is located within 15 miles. Swim in the lake, but it's against the rules to swim in the creek. Children are permitted. Leashed pets are allowed, but must be kept under control at all times. If you plan an overnight canoe trip, call the park first to determine if the water is high enough. Transportation is available to your starting point, and you can leave your car at the campground. Primitive sites are available along the river for trips as long as two days.

Reservations, fees: Reservations are recommended. Tent camping costs $15 to $25 per night; RV sites with full hookups are $25. Major credit cards are accepted.

Directions: From Moore Haven, go north on U.S. 27 for 16 miles to the entrance. The wildlife management area is one mile north of State Road 29 at Fisheating Creek.

Contact: Fisheating Creek Campground, 7555 North U.S. 27, Palmdale, FL 33944, 863/675-7855, fax 863/675-7845, website: www.fisheatingcreek.com. Or contact the Florida Fish and Wildlife Conservation Commission, 3900 Drane Field Road, Lakeland, FL 33811-1299, 863/648-3203.

⑥ HENDRY'S SABAL PALMS CAMPGROUND

Rating: 4

Southwest of Okeechobee

Lake Okeechobee map, grid b3, page 426

What makes this park special? Answered the owners: It's "secluded." Seasonal visitors are the norm at this 70-unit park in Glades County, south of Lake Placid. It's located just two miles from the beauties of Fisheating Creek. Four bluegrass festivals are held here each year, as well as lawn mowing races. Say, what? Lawn mower racing is a sport using vehicles that look like combination go-carts and riding lawn mowers.

Campsites, facilities: There are 10 sites available for overnighters, and 60 for winter visitors. Ten are pull-through. All but 10 sites have concrete pads. In an area set apart from the RVs, 25 tents can be accommodated (no water or electricity). Picnic tables, restrooms, showers, and laundry facilities are available. On the premises are a fishing pond, recreation room, shuffleboard courts, and boat and canoe rentals. Children are allowed, but this is an adults-preferred park, generally speaking. Leashed pets are permitted.

Reservations, fees: Reservations are recommended. Sites are $18 per night for two people, plus $2 per extra person. Credit cards are not accepted. Long-term rates are available.

Directions: From Palmdale, drive east on County Road 733 (at the country store) and go to the end of the road. Turn north and drive 1.5 miles to the campground entrance on the left.

Contact: Hendry's Sabal Palms Campground, P.O. Box 298, Palmdale, FL 33944. Physical location: 9505 Maine Street Northwest. 863/675-1778, fax 863/675-4689, email: dwhendry42 @aol.com.

⑦ SUNBURST RV RESORT— LAKE PLACID (FORMERLY PINE RIDGE RV RESORT)

Rating: 6

South of Lake Placid

Lake Okeechobee map, grid b3, page 426

This home of wintertime dances, crafts, bingo, and special events is geared toward retirees who spend months or years at these RV sites and mobile homes. Managed by Encore Properties, the resort has its own activities director, which is a bit unusual for these parts. Campers who want to go it alone can bicycle past surrounding orange groves. Of the 27 area lakes, perhaps two are most famous for fishing and water-skiing—Lake Placid, about three miles northwest, and 43-square-mile Lake Istokpoga, farther northeast.

Campsites, facilities: At this 322-site mobile-home/RV park, about 125 sites are available for RVs. A recreation hall, a heated pool, bocce (lawn bowling) courts, billiards, horseshoes, shuffleboard, tennis, and winter social programs entertain campers. Restrooms, showers, a dump station, laundry facilities, park-model rentals, cable TV hookups, and telephone service are available. Groceries are within walking distance. Restaurants are about three miles away. Children and leashed pets are accepted.

Reservations, fees: Reservations are recommended. Sites are $20 to $23 per night. Major credit cards are accepted. Long-term stays are OK.

Directions: From Lake Placid, drive south on U.S. 27 for 6.5 miles to State Road 70. Turn left. The park is .5 mile ahead, at right.

Contact: Sunburst RV Resort–Lake Placid, 303 State Road 70 East, Lake Placid, FL 33852, 863/465-4815 or 877/317-2757, fax 863/465-1077, website: www.rvonthego.com.

8 CAMP FLORIDA RESORT

Rating: 8

South of Lake Placid

Lake Okeechobee map, grid b3, page 426

This brand-new, all-ages resort employs an unusual circular layout—a nice change from the rectangular sameness of other RV parks. Set on Lake Grassy, everything is brand-new, from the landscaping to the infrastructure. Lots are sort of pie-shaped, giving you breathing space from your neighbors, and each circle is separated from the next one by a road. Nearby are 27 lakes for fishing and boating, 12 golf courses, and historical attractions, but there's more than enough to do in the park, including tennis, a nature trail, marina, and docks. A grocery story and many restaurants are nearby.

Campsites, facilities: There are 180 full-hookup RV sites, all available for overnighters and seasonal visitors. Most sites have concrete pads and picnic tables. Restrooms, showers, laundry facilities, and telephone service are available. On the premises are a pool, a boat ramp, a clubhouse, shuffleboard courts, a dog-walk area, and miniature golf. Children are welcome. Leashed pets under 20 pounds are permitted.

Reservations, fees: Reservations are recommended. Sites are $27.50 per night. Major credit cards are accepted. Long-term rates are available.

Directions: From Lake Placid, drive south on U.S. 27 about five miles to the park. From the intersection of U.S. 27 and State Road 70, drive north on U.S. 27 about six miles.

Contact: Camp Florida Resort, 1525 U.S. 27 South, Lake Placid, FL 33852, 863/699-1991 or 800/226-5188; fax: 863/699-1995; website: www.campfla.com.

9 NINE MILE GRADE CAMPGROUND

Rating: 6

East of Lorida on the Kissimmee River

Lake Okeechobee map, grid b3, page 426

In exchange for the longer trips you'll have to make for such conveniences as groceries and laundry facilities, you'll get a secluded, quiet campground alongside the Kissimmee River. It's the kind of place where you can roast marshmallows at campfire rings for a relaxing, old-style camping experience.

The campground is set in one of the old oak hammocks that mark the edge of the historic floodplain of the Kissimmee River, where fishing, boating, and canoeing are popular. The once-meandering stream has been straitjacketed by federal engineers into a big, angular ditch. But the U.S. Army Corps of Engineers and the South Florida Water Management District are working to restore the river to its natural state, in which it overflows and drenches the marshy areas along its banks, providing a home for waterfowl and other creatures. The restoration project is one of the most ambitious in the world.

Canoeists in particular might enjoy exploring some of the river's old oxbows, which are set to be reinvigorated during the restoration. Bring your own watercraft or make plans to rent a boat in the area. Near the campground are eight miles of hiking and biking trails. You also can cross the river north of here to hike along the Florida National Scenic Trail.

Campsites, facilities: This campground offers four RV sites with water and electricity, and eight primitive sites for tents or RVs. Each site has a picnic table, a fire ring, and a grill. On the premises are restrooms, showers, a dump station, a boat ramp, and a playground. All areas are wheelchair accessible. Groceries and restaurants are six miles away. The nearest laundry facilities are 20 miles away. Children and pets are permitted.

Reservations, fees: Reservations are not accepted. Sites are $8 per night for six people. Credit cards are not accepted. Long-term stays are OK.

Directions: From Okeechobee, take State Road 70 west 16 miles to County Road 721 north. Turn right and go 4.5 miles to Boat Ramp Road (on the right). Turn left. Proceed to the end of the road.

Contact: Nine Mile Grade Campground, 992 Boat Ramp Road, Lorida, FL 33857, 863/763-3113.

10 WHISPER CREEK RV RESORT

Rating: 4

Near the Caloosahatchee River in La Belle
Lake Okeechobee map, grid b1, page 426

Besides a little lake and the surrounding woods, this 57-acre, adults-only park has the advantage of being just one mile north of the Caloosahatchee River, which is a plus for some anglers. If that won't do, head one-half hour east to the bass mecca of Lake Okeechobee. Don't worry if fishing is not your only interest: The owners say 75 percent of guests are snowbirds here for the winter, and there are plenty of scheduled activities for landlubbers. Want shade? Request a spot in the oak-and-palm-dotted section up front. Sunny sites will warm your bones in the winter.

Campsites, facilities: All 396 sites in this wheelchair-accessible, adults-only park have full hookups, including telephone and cable TV. Lots are 40-by-50 feet, with 10-by-30 foot concrete patios. Facilities include a solar-heated pool, horseshoes, shuffleboard, and a 5,000-square-foot clubhouse, which has a large auditorium with an elevated stage, community kitchen, a game room with pool tables, and a library. Socialize with fellow campers at dances, bingo, potluck suppers, arts and crafts, shuffleboard tournaments, and nondenominational church services on Sunday mornings. Showers, restrooms, a dump station, and laundry facil-

ities also are available. Grocery stores, a restaurant, bait, and tackle are located one mile away. All the public areas, including the pool, laundry, recreation hall, and restrooms, are readily accessible to the physically challenged—an amenity in which the owners take pride. Two leashed pets per household are permitted.

Reservations, fees: Reservations are recommended. Sites are $21 per night. Credit cards are not accepted. Long-term stays are encouraged.

Directions: From State Road 80 in the town of La Belle, turn north onto State Road 29. Continue for about one mile to the park entrance.

Contact: Whisper Creek RV Resort, 1980 Hickory Drive/State Road 29 North, La Belle, FL 33975, 863/675-6888, fax 863/675-2323, website: www.whispercreek.com.

11 GRANDMA'S GROVE RV PARK

Rating: 4

Near the Caloosahatchee River in La Belle
Lake Okeechobee map, grid b2, page 426

Guests can pluck free fruit off orange trees in the surrounding 40-acre grove during the citrus season. A walking trail passes by the fragrant grove and circles much of the 18-acre, adults-only RV park. Anglers tend to strike out for the nearby Caloosahatchee River or farther east for Lake Okeechobee, about one-half hour away. Potluck dinners and street names like Grandma's Boulevard and Feather Bed Lane lend a folksy air. Like other grandmothers, this Grandma lays down some strict rules: No converted school buses are permitted, clotheslines must be hung at the rear of units, and quiet hours begin at 10 P.M.

Campsites, facilities: All 190 RV sites at this wheelchair-accessible, adults-only park offer full hookups. Each site has a picnic table and a concrete patio. A pool, dances, arts and crafts, exercises, shuffleboard, horseshoe pits, a social club, and a walking trail entertain guests. Showers, restrooms, a campfire ring, a barbecue grill, laundry facilities, and on-site cable

TV and telephone service (for long-term campers) are available. Families with children may be accepted short-term; call ahead to inquire. Pets should use the designated dog walk near an orange grove.

Reservations, fees: Reservations are recommended. Sites are $20 per night for two people, plus $2 per extra person. Credit cards are not accepted. Long-term rates are available.

Directions: From Fort Myers, drive 22 miles east on State Road 80 to the campground on the left.

Contact: Grandma's Grove RV Park, 2250 State Road 80 West, La Belle, FL 33935, 863/675-2567.

12 ORTONA LOCK AND DAM CAMPGROUND

Rating: 8

On the Caloosahatchee River east
of La Belle

Lake Okeechobee map, grid b2, page 426

Visitors tend to fall into one of two groups: The first set adores this remote and peaceful 25-acre recreation area with a view of cow pastures and the off chance of hearing a distant rooster crow. The other likes the quick access to boating and fishing from this U.S. Army Corps of Engineers campground on the Caloosahatchee River. Ortona's faithful fans (many of them retirees) normally keep the 51 sites filled through winter. Don't count on finding an open spot in time to hear bluegrass music at the one-day Ortona Cane Grinding Festival, which is held each February. The sun-washed campsites are lined up in rows, creating sort of a parking-lot feel. Tenters need free-standing tents; all sites have concrete pads. A pair of bald eagles nests nearby, to the delight of birders. Don't miss the drama of walking across the narrow, steel-grate footbridge directly over the rushing waters of the Caloosahatchee River lock and dam.

Campsites, facilities: All 51 sites for RVs and tents have water and electric hookups, picnic tables, grills, fire rings, and concrete pads surrounded by gravel. Besides two fishing piers and a boat ramp, the campground offers showers, restrooms, a dump station, and laundry facilities. Three wheelchair-accessible campsites are near restrooms; other accessible areas are the laundry room and one fishing pier. A convenience store is nearby. Bait, tackle, and a restaurant are available nine miles away in La Belle. Children are allowed. Leashed pets are permitted.

Reservations, fees: Reservations are accepted by calling 877/444-6777; website: www.reserve usa.com/nrrs/fl/orto. The fee is $16 per night during the season and $8 from May 1 to September 30. Major credit cards are accepted. Stays are limited to 14 days in a 30-day period.

Directions: From La Belle, go east on State Road 80 for 10 miles to Dalton Lane. Turn north and follow the signs to the campground. From Clewiston, drive nine miles north on U.S. 27. At State Road 80, turn west and drive 14 miles to Dalton Lane.

Contact: Ortona Lock and Dam Campground, 1660 South Franklin Lock Road, Alva, FL 33920, 239/694-2582, website: www.saj.usace .army.mil/recreation/index.html. For more information, contact the U.S. Army Corps of Engineers, South Florida Operations Office, 525 Ridgelawn Road, Clewiston, FL 33440-5399, 863/983-8101.

13 MEADOWLARK CAMPGROUND

Rating: 4

On the Caloosahatchee River
in Moore Haven

Lake Okeechobee map, grid b2, page 426

Regulars escape the snowy Midwest, Canada, and the Northeast to winter at this unadvertised, off-the-beaten-path park on the Caloosahatchee River, and they routinely clinch the top prize in area horseshoe championships. The laid-back place allows boats to be parked on the oversized lots. With rabbits, birds, and even alligators in the woodsy surroundings, owner Kim Christy believes the 13-acre park lends more of a feel of camping than many of her competitors do. Besides fishing, folks busy themselves with winter activities: Bible study, weekly potluck dinners, twice-weekly bingo, dancing, crafts, and exercises. "There are people who have been coming here for 30 years," Christy says.

Campsites, facilities: This adults-only park has 152 heavily wooded full-hookup sites (two pull-through) for RVs up to 40 feet long; about half are available for overnighters and seasonal visitors. A game room, horseshoes, shuffleboard, quilting classes, and wintertime activities entertain campers. Showers, restrooms, picnic tables, cable TV, a dump station, a new pool, propane gas sales, and laundry facilities are available. Groceries can be purchased 12 miles away. Leashed pets are permitted but may not be tied up outside.

Reservations, fees: Reservations are recommended. Sites are $28 per night for two people, plus $3 for each additional person. Credit cards are not accepted. Long-term rates are available.

Directions: From La Belle, take State Road 29 north. Turn right (east) at State Road 78. Turn right at Ortona Road. The campground is two miles ahead (stay straight at the fork in the road).

Contact: Meadowlark Campground, 12525 Williams Road Southwest, Moore Haven, FL 33471, 863/675-2243, email meadowlark1@earthlink.net.

14 LAKE OKEECHOBEE SCENIC TRAIL—CULVERT 5A

Rating: 7

On southwestern Lake Okeechobee near Moore Haven

Lake Okeechobee map, grid b3, page 426

You're virtually certain to see alligators, birds, and furry critters while hiking or bicycling along this remote stretch of the 110-mile-long Herbert Hoover Dike. You'll sleep in marsh country. The site is on the rim canal and is easily accessible by boat. To the east, a broad expanse of reeds leads to the far-off open waters of Lake Okeechobee. To the west, you should be able to make out the fuzzy outlines of Nicodemus Slough, a meandering waterway working its way slowly through lots of marsh.

Mosquitoes may drive you crazy in summer here. But officials say that the birds, fish, and animals that lure thousands of people to the Big O each year wouldn't be so numerous if it weren't for the three- to eight-mile-wide littoral zone bordering the lake's southern and western shores. Just bring your DEET. Some consider western Lake Okeechobee the prettiest part of the Southeast's largest lake. If you're continuing on to the next rustic campsite by foot or bicycle, travel 12 miles southeast to Lake Okeechobee Scenic Trail—Liberty Point. If you're northbound, it's about six miles to Lake Okeechobee Scenic Trail—Lakeport.

Campsites, facilities: This primitive tent-camping area is accessible by foot, boat, and bicycle. A fire ring and a shelter with a picnic table are provided. There are no toilets, piped water, or other facilities. Bring water, food, camping supplies, sunscreen, and mosquito repellent. Children and leashed pets are permitted.

Reservations, fees: Camping is first-come, first-served. There is no fee.

Directions: The campsite is on the rim canal on the lakeside of the levee, two miles south of the intersection of Highway 78 and the Herbert Hoover Dike. For detailed directions and a map, contact the U.S. Army Corps of Engineers.

Contact: U.S. Army Corps of Engineers, South Florida Operations Office, 525 Ridgelawn Road, Clewiston, FL 33440, 941/983-8101, website: www.sfwmd.gov.

15 LAKEPORT RV PARK

Rating: 5

Near Lake Okeechobee in Lakeport
Lake Okeechobee map, grid b3, page 426

Under new ownership that expects to expand amenities here by 2004, this over-55 park has sunny spots overlooking the Rim Canal; some lots are on the waterfront. Campers (mostly retirees) escape blustery winters in Michigan, New York, Ohio, and other snowy parts of the country by sleeping here. Bass anglers can head out of the canal to get to Florida's largest lake—Okeechobee. Hike or cycle on the dike above the lake.

Campsites, facilities: There are about 92 full-hookup RV sites, of which most are available for season-long stays. Six sites are available for overnighters. Facilities include showers, restrooms, laundry, a hot tub, boat ramp, dock, shuffleboard courts, and a recreation building where bingo, cards, and organized dinners are held. The restrooms and recreation hall are wheelchair accessible. Tents are prohibited. Children may stay no longer than one month. Leashed pets under 25 pounds are permitted.

Reservations, fees: Reservations are recommended. Sites are $25 per night for four people, plus $5 per extra person. Credit cards are not accepted. Long-term rates are available.

Directions: From Moore Haven, drive about nine miles north on State Road 78 to Lakeport. Turn left at State Road 74. In .5 mile, turn left by the water tower onto Ted Beck Road, which curves into Milum Drive. The campground is the first RV park on Milum Drive.

Contact: Lakeport RV Park, 2800 Milum Drive, Moore Haven, FL 33471, 863/946-1415, email: lakeportrv@yahoo.com.

16 ARUBA RV RESORT

Rating: 4

Near Lake Okeechobee in Lakeport
Lake Okeechobee map, grid b3, page 426

Fishing is popular here. A boat launch and moorings, plus two fish-cleaning areas, make this obvious. Anglers hoping for bass and speckled perch use the campground boat ramp for access to 467,000-acre Lake Okeechobee, but you can also fish from a bank. You must spend at least two months at the 14-acre RV park to get a waterfront site in winter. Like most RV parks circling Lake Okeechobee, this place is mostly flat and sunny with a relatively sparse sprinkling of palms, oaks, and towering Australian pines. A nearby trailhead leads hikers and bicyclists to the top of the Herbert Hoover Dike encircling the fabled lake. The views in the Big O region are often rewarding: Boaters are said to have spotted as many as 32 types of birds during an outing on the lake. If you tire of roughing it, drive about 15 minutes to use the video games and poker tables at Brighton Seminole Bingo (863/467-9998) located at the Indian tribe's reservation off Highway 721, west of Lake Okeechobee.

Campsites, facilities: All 150 RV sites have full hookups and picnic tables; most have access to cable TV. The sites are exceptionally large at 40 by 52 feet. A heated pool and exercise room, fishing guide services, bank fishing, pontoon-boat fishing or sightseeing, a dance floor, shuffleboard, a clubhouse, horseshoes, and a community fire ring entertain campers. Moorings are available for most boats. Showers, restrooms, a boat ramp, on-water fuel pumps, tackle, bait, a dump station, and laundry facilities are on the premises. Children are permitted. Dogs should use the pet walk next to the dump station.

Reservations, fees: Reservations are recommended. Sites are $20 per night for two people, plus $5 for each additional adult and $3 per child. Major credit cards are accepted. Long-term stays are OK.

Directions: From Okeechobee, take Highway 78 west about 25 miles to County Road 74 in Lakeport, then turn right. The park is ahead at left.

Contact: Aruba RV Resort, 1825 Old Lakeport Road, Lakeport, FL 33471, 863/946-1324, fax 863/946-1270, website: www.okeedirect .com/arubarv.htm.

⓱ NORTH LAKE ESTATES RV RESORT

Rating: 6

Near Lake Okeechobee in Lakeport
Lake Okeechobee map, grid b3, page 426
The paved, lighted streets at this 36-acre RV community have names like Mallard Drive and Perch Lane—a reflection of its visitors' interest in fishing and duck hunting on nearby Lake Okeechobee. Boaters launch from North Lake Marina adjacent to the park. Don't expect to rough it. This may be the neatest, cleanest, most manicured RV park on this side of the lake. With trash pickup, a $325,000 clubhouse, resident managers, and concrete pads that extend to the streets, the RV park feels like a residential community. Many people stay at least two months. Nearly all campers are retirees. For a view of the park's ornamental lake, request a waterfront site on Bass Drive or Widgeon Lane. Alternatively, most Pintail Lane sites back onto a canal. Campers on Mallard Drive and Widgeon Lane have the shortest walk to the pool.

Campsites, facilities: This 300-unit, adult-oriented park accepts RVs at all 100 full-hookup sites, each with a 700-square-foot concrete pad. A boat ramp, clubhouse (with a deck and pool), horseshoes, shuffleboard, a game room, an exercise room, a crafts room, and wintertime activities entertain guests. Showers, restrooms, picnic tables, on-site park-model sales, and laundry facilities are available. Management says buildings are wheelchair accessible. Convenience stores, restaurants, and a public boat ramp are within two miles. Children tend to visit long-term campers for a week or so, then leave. Leashed pets are permitted.

Reservations, fees: Reservations are recommended. Sites are $23 per night for two people, plus $2.50 per extra person. Credit cards are not accepted. Long-term rates are available.

Directions: From Moore Haven, go north for nine miles on State Road 78 to the campground, at right.

Contact: North Lake Estates RV Resort, 765 East State Road 78, Moore Haven, FL 33471, 863/946-0700.

⓲ GATOR'S RV

Rating: 2

Near Lake Okeechobee in Lakeport
Lake Okeechobee map, grid b3, page 426
Devoted to this casual spot, retirees and snowbirds come to snag easy-to-catch speckled perch at Lake Okeechobee and fry up dinners of the flaky white meat. Boaters launch from Harney Pond Canal one block from the campground to fish or hunt ducks at the nation's second largest natural lake.

Campsites, facilities: At this 27-unit park, 15 full-hookup sites (eight pull-through) are for RVs, and about 10 tents can be set up just about anywhere for primitive camping. Showers, restrooms, a dump station, cable TV access, and limited laundry facilities are available. Most campers use a laundry business one block away. Boat launches, a convenience store, restaurants, and bait are also one block away. There's a supermarket within 16 miles. Children are permitted, although there is little for them to do; management says kids usually visit long-term campers for a week or so, then leave. Leashed pets are permitted.

Reservations, fees: Reservations are recommended in winter but are not necessary in summer. Sites are $18 per night. Credit cards are not accepted. Long-term rates are available.

Directions: From Okeechobee, go south on U.S. 441. Turn right at State Road 78 and continue about 27 miles to the entrance. The campground is one block west of Harney Pond Canal.

Contact: Gator's RV, 900 East State Road 78, Lakeport, FL 33471, 863/983-9155.

19 LAKE OKEECHOBEE SCENIC TRAIL—LAKEPORT

Rating: 7

On the western bank of Lake Okeechobee

Lake Okeechobee map, grid b3, page 426

Awakening to a pastel sun rising over Florida's largest lake is an experience you're unlikely to get at a motel room or an established campground, no matter what you pay. Here you can get it for free.

The Herbert Hoover Dike rises an average of 34 feet to hold in Lake Okeechobee and avoid a repeat of the massive hurricane-spawned floods that killed nearly 2,000 people in the early 20th century. Although the dike irritatingly blocks views of the lake for anyone driving around it, hikers and mountain bikers making their way along the top of the sun-washed dike will see the lake all day long and sleep at the water's edge on somewhat uneven ground (bring an air mattress). This western side of Lake Okeechobee is the most scenic. Look for ducks and long-legged wading birds. If you're continuing your trek around the lake, it's about six miles south to the next rustic campsite, Lake Okeechobee Scenic Trail-Culvert 5A. To the north, it's 12.2 miles to Indian Prairie.

Campsites, facilities: This primitive tent-camping area is reached by foot or bicycle; boats can access the area from the lake by going through the lock at Lakeport. A fire ring and a shelter with a picnic table are provided. There is no restroom or piped water. Bring water, food, a hat, sunscreen, camping supplies, and mosquito repellent. Children and leashed pets are OK.

Reservations, fees: Camping is first-come, first-served. There is no fee.

Directions: The campsite is .75 mile north of the intersection of Highway 78 and the Herbert Hoover Dike at Lakeport. The camping spot is on the borrow canal, which is on the land side of the levee. For detailed directions and a map, contact the U.S. Army Corps of Engineers.

Contact: U.S. Army Corps of Engineers, South Florida Operations Office, 525 Ridgelawn Road, Clewiston, FL 33440-5399, 863/983-8101, website: www.sfwmd.gov.

20 INDIAN PRAIRIE CANAL PRIMITIVE SITES

Rating: 6

On Lake Okeechobee

Lake Okeechobee map, grid b3, page 426

Duck hunters flock to this primitive campground in one of the prettiest regions of Lake Okeechobee, so don't count on solitude. What you will get is a campground host and no-frills campsites with shell-rock pads. Look for birds that are commonly found in the Everglades—for instance, the black-headed, white-feathered, gawky-looking wood stork, and the brown, goose-sized, white-spotted limpkin, whose eerie wail may give you a start the first time you hear it. The camping area is part of the Lake Okeechobee Scenic Trail (LOST), which allows hikers or bicyclists with at least one week to spare to encircle the huge lake by camping at nine rustic camping areas and four more-developed campgrounds located no more than 10 miles apart. If you're fishing, bring a fishing license and check current regulations. When we last checked, all black bass between 13 inches and 18 inches had to be released immediately—all other lengths were keepers.

The LOST trail is one of Florida's jewels and one of the more unusual trails in the nation. The trail is on top of the berm around the lake, and it's possible to hike or bike the complete circle of 110 miles, or access the trail at various points around the lake. Three trail-head information shelters showing the full map of sites have recently been built. You'll find them at the Clewiston office of the U.S. Army Corps of Engineers, adjacent to the Okee-Tantie Campground, and at Nubbins Slough Access Area (see campgrounds in this chapter). You can also download the map of shelters and access points at www.sfwmd.gov.com. In addition to the campsites, about 30 shade shelters have been recently built around the lake; each is about 2.5 to three miles apart. The gates at the top of the levee have been replaced to allow a two-foot gap for bikers (fat tires only), and much exotic, non-native vegetation has been removed to allow vistas of the pretty lake.

Campsites, facilities: Ten primitive campsites and a group camping area are available for tents and RVs. There are no hookups and there is no shade. Facilities include a vault toilet, a fire ring, a boat ramp, trash receptacle, and picnic tables. There is no piped water, so bring plenty of your own, plus food and camping supplies. Pack out trash. Children and leashed pets are permitted. If you crave shade and are hardy, hike to the LOST campsite about .5 mile south of here. There's a shade shelter, fire ring, and mowed area to set up one tent.

Reservations, fees: Sites are first-come, first-served. Camping is free.

Directions: The campsite is .5 mile south of the Indian Prairie Canal, on the land side of the levee. From the town of Okeechobee, go south on State Road 78. Cross over the Kissimmee River and pass through the settlement of Buckhead Ridge. The Indian Prairie Canal is the next major canal. Go over the bridge to the canal, then turn left into the campground.

Contact: U.S. Army Corps of Engineers, South Florida Operations Office, 525 Ridgelawn Road, Clewiston, FL 33440, 863/983-8101, website: www.sfwmd.gov.

21 BUCKHEAD RIDGE MARINA

Rating: 4

At Lake Okeechobee in Buckhead Ridge

Lake Okeechobee map, grid b3, page 426

Some down-home anglers cotton to Buckhead Ridge, a small, backwoods town that hasn't been ruined yet by overdevelopment. At sunny Buckhead Ridge Marina, the flat campground has a smattering of palms and other native trees. Some campsites overlook a canal. Tenters are likely to hear the rumble of RV air conditioners because the small, grassy area for tents is near some RV sites.

Folks tend to be here for one thing: to go out onto the lake, found beyond a set of locks farther down the canal rimming the campground. Veteran bass guide Captain Mac Russell can tell you whether you should use a June Bug Worm for bass or if bluegills are biting at the mouth of the campground-area canal; call 863/467-4516. Boat rentals are $55 daily, $45 half day.

Campsites, facilities: All 86 full-hookup campsites are for RVs, and 10 tents can be set up in a grassy area. Each site has a picnic table. Recreational offerings include fishing guide services, a recreation hall, and boat rentals. You'll also find a restaurant, a snack bar, gas, bait, tackle, a boat ramp, boat storage, waterfront mobile home rentals (starting at $55), a dump station, and laundry facilities. Most areas are wheelchair accessible. Children are welcome. Pets are permitted.

Reservations, fees: Reservations are recommended. Sites are $15 to $25 per night. Major credit cards are accepted. Long-term stays are OK.

Directions: From Okeechobee, turn right onto State Road 78 and continue about 10 miles. Turn left on State Road 78B and drive 1.5 miles to the marina/campground on the left. The campground is one mile past the Kissimmee River.

Contact: Buckhead Ridge Marina, 670 State Road 78B, Okeechobee, FL 34974, 863/763-2826 or 800/367-1358.

22 LAKE OKEECHOBEE SCENIC TRAIL—KISSIMMEE RIVER

Rating: 7

On the northern bank of Lake Okeechobee

Lake Okeechobee map, grid b4, page 426

You'll sleep near the Kissimmee River, which, along with Lake Okeechobee and the Everglades, is part of an ecosystem that stretches north to Disney World and south to the tip of Florida. The Kissimmee, a ruler-straight river-turned-canal, once was a shallow, meandering stream about 100 miles long. Now straightened and deepened by dozens of feet, its course runs only about 50 miles. Ecologically speaking, this alteration has meant trouble. All of the perimeter marsh that needs to be flooded with fresh, clean water—once provided by the river—now doesn't get flushed out. So where you used to see tens of thousands of ducks and wading birds along the Kissimmee, you'll see fewer today in the slow-moving and impeded waterway. Federal engineers and state biologists are working to return the Kissimmee to a more natural state. Many more birds have returned since, and it now counts as part of a great birding trail.

Look for wading birds and other creatures as you hike along the levee that holds in "the liquid heart of South Florida," as the lake is called. Indeed, birders consider the northwestern lake region one of the best birding areas in Florida. If you're making the trip around the entire lake by foot or bicycle, the next rustic camp spot is 9.9 southwest at Indian Prairie. Heading east, it's nine miles to Lake Okeechobee Scenic Trail—Nubbin Slough.

Campsites, facilities: This primitive tent-camping area is reached by foot or bicycle. A fire ring and a shelter with a picnic table are provided. There is no restroom or piped water. Bring water, food, a hat, sunscreen, camping supplies, and mosquito repellent. Children and leashed pets are OK.

Reservations, fees: Camping is first-come, first-served. There is no fee.

Directions: The campsite is off Highway 78, just southwest of the Kissimmee River. Specifically, the campsite is .5 mile south of Highway 78 on the lakeside of the levee. For detailed directions, a map, and a brochure, contact the U.S. Army Corps of Engineers before your trip.
Contact: U.S. Army Corps of Engineers, South Florida Operations Office, 525 Ridgelawn Road, Clewiston, FL 33440-5399, 863/983-8101, website: www.sfwmd.gov.

23 OKEE-TANTIE CAMPGROUND AND MARINA

Rating: 7

At Lake Okeechobee and the Kissimmee River, 4.5 miles west of Highway 441

Lake Okeechobee map, grid b4, page 426

This county-owned, peninsular park is a local landmark on the north shore of Lake Okeechobee at the mouth of the Kissimmee River, with boat ramps providing direct access to both bodies of water. It's a first-rate base camp for fishing, as well as a chance to enjoy the outdoors and view wildlife. Hikers, equestrians, and bicyclists can get a rare view of Lake Okeechobee from atop the 34-foot-high, 107-mile-long Herbert Hoover Dike, which is also part of the Lake Okeechobee Scenic Trail and the Great Florida Birding Trail. Campsites range from sunny to shady, but a hat and sunscreen are always recommended. Paved roads lead to the gravel/grassy sites. The park has a popular restaurant and serves as tournament headquarters for various bass fishing contests. But the campground is gated and secured from the public use areas. Seaplanes can pull up on the shore of the river; on a recent Saturday, we counted 13 parked on the banks.

Campsites, facilities: There are 271 RV sites (164 full hookup, with 42 pull-through, and 107 with water and electricity). Additionally, 38 primitive tent sites are available. All sites have a picnic table and a grill. You'll find showers, restrooms, laundry facilities, a day-use picnic area and playground, public boat ramps and fish-cleaning stations, boat rentals, a marina and fuel dock, bait and tackle with limited groceries and firewood, and a seafood restaurant. Children are welcome. Leashed pets are permitted.

Reservations, fees: Reservations are recommended. From May 1 through October 31, sites are $16 per night for two people, plus $5 for each additional adult and $3 per child (under age six is free). The base rate from November 1 through April 30 is $24.50 to $28. Major credit cards are accepted. Long-term rates are available.

Directions: From State Road 70 and U.S. 441/Parrott Avenue in the town of Okeechobee, go south on U.S. 441/Parrott Avenue. Turn right on Highway 78 West and continue about 4.5 miles to the campground entrance on the left, just before the Kissimmee River bridge.

Contact: Okee-Tantie Campground and Marina, 10430 Highway 78 West, Okeechobee, FL 34974, 863/763-2622, fax 863/763-8136, email: okeetantie@yahoo.com.

24 ELITE RESORTS BIG "O"

Rating: 6

Southwest of Okeechobee
Lake Okeechobee map, grid b3, page 426

With lake access, a boat ramp, and a fish-cleaning station, the name of the game at this condominium park is fishing, but when the fish aren't biting, there are plenty of other things to do. From October through April, the park's activities director plans live entertainment, special dinners, bingo, line dancing, and more. On Sundays, church services are held. Some sites overlook the Rim Canal. Shopping and golf courses are nearby in the town of Okeechobee.

Campsites, facilities: This 55-and-older, wheelchair-accessible park has 320 full-hookup RV or park model spots with picnic tables and concrete pads; many sites have been sold for condominium ownership, so call ahead to see if an overnight spot is free. Restrooms, showers, a dump station, laundry facilities, and telephone service are available. On the premises are a heated pool, a boat ramp, a fish-cleaning station, a clubhouse, horseshoe pits, shuffleboard courts, a dog-walk area, and a putting green. Children are not welcome. Leashed pets are permitted.

Reservations, fees: Reservations are recommended. Sites are $36 per night for two people during the winter, and $25 from April 1 through November 1. Major credit cards are accepted. Long-term (up to six months) or seasonal stays are preferred.

Directions: From the intersection of U.S. 441 and State Road 78, continue southwestbound on State Road 78 for about 3.5 miles. The resort will be on your left. From Moore Haven, drive toward the town of Okeechobee on State Road 78 for about 35 miles; the park will be on your right.

Contact: Elite Resorts Big "O," 7950 Southwest Highway 78, Okeechobee, FL 34974, 863/467-5515, fax 863/467-1183, website: www.eliteresorts.com.

25 BIG LAKE LODGE AND RV PARK

Rating: 7

Southwest of Okeechobee
Lake Okeechobee map, grid b3, page 426

Want to keep your boat close by? This well-maintained, all-ages fishing resort has a boat dock at almost every campsite, making it easy to carry out those cleaning, loading, and maintenance chores. You'll overlook the wide blue waters of the rim canal leading to Lake Okeechobee and catch glimpses of the fantastic variety of birds that make this area their home. Under new management, the park attracts anglers and bird-watchers, and brags that it's only 40 miles east of the Atlantic Ocean, making it convenient for snowbirds visiting the Fort Pierce or West Palm Beach area. Owner Betty Arrington describes the park as "down to earth, in a country atmosphere . . . We don't compete with Holiday Inn or the Joneses."

Campsites, facilities: There are 37 RV sites for rigs up to 37 feet long; eight sites are pull-through. Four tents can be accommodated in an area separate from the RVs; these sites have water and electricity. Each RV site has concrete pads, full hookups with 50-amp electrical service, grills, and cable TV, and 32 are waterfront with boat docks. Restrooms, showers, laundry facilities, and telephone service are available. On the premises are a boat ramp, a fish-cleaning station, rental units, and planned activities, such as fish fries, barbecues, and potluck suppers. Children are welcome. Leashed pets under 20 pounds are permitted.

Reservations, fees: Reservations are recommended. Sites vary by the season and by location, but range between $20 to $35 per night for two people, plus $5 per extra person. Major credit cards are accepted. Long-term rates are available.

Directions: From the town of Okeechobee, drive south on U.S. 441 to the park at the intersection with County Road 15A.

Contact: Big Lake Lodge and RV Park, 8680 Highway 441 Southeast, Okeechobee, FL 34974, 863/763-4638 or 866/256-5566.

26 HUTTONS TRAILER PARK

Rating: 3

In Okeechobee

Lake Okeechobee map, grid b4, page 426

A flower-bordered, stucco "Huttons" entrance sign is illuminated by a floodlight. The main attraction is the rim canal leading to the bass haven of Lake Okeechobee, but the exercise classes, weekly bingo, sing-alongs, and monthly craft activities also entertain adults. Part of the park is laid out with park models; the rest caters to RVs. To sleep closest to the rim canal and shuffleboard courts, ask about lots 30 through 36A, 49, and 74 through 84. Many sites are booked year after year, so you may vie for few available spaces in winter.

Campsites, facilities: This adults-only park has about 25 full-hookup sites for RVs. Shuffleboard, horseshoes, a small putting green, a pool table, a recreation hall, and scheduled activities keep campers busy. Showers, restrooms, two enclosed fish-cleaning houses, and laundry facilities are provided. Small dogs are permitted.

Reservations, fees: Reservations are advised and require a $100 deposit. Sites are $20 per night for two people, plus $1 for each additional person. Credit cards are not accepted. Long-term rates are available.

Directions: From State Road 70 and U.S. 441/Parrott Avenue in the town of Okeechobee, go south on U.S. 441/Parrott Avenue to Lake Okeechobee. Turn right at Highway 78 and continue about two miles west to the campground entrance on the left, just past the Big O timeshare resort.

Contact: Huttons Trailer Park, 9100 Highway 78 West, Okeechobee, FL 34974, 863/763-5627, email: huttons@okeechobee.com.

27 WINDSOR MANOR RV PARK

Rating: 6

Southwest of Okeechobee

Lake Okeechobee map, grid b3, page 426

Open from October 15 through May 1, this sunny park attracts boaters and anglers who are allowed to leave their rigs on the premises year-round to avoid the hassle of hauling them back home at the end of the season. A boat ramp leading to Lake Okeechobee is across from the park entrance, and plenty of boat trailer storage is available.

Campsites, facilities: There are 42 sites for RVs, two of them pull-through. All have full hookups and concrete pads. Restrooms, showers, a dump station, laundry facilities, and telephone service are available. On the premises are a fish-cleaning station, a recreation hall, horseshoe pits, shuffleboard courts, a gazebo, and planned social activities. Campers must be 55 years and older. Pets are not welcome.

Reservations, fees: Reservations are recommended. Sites are $20 per night for two people. Credit cards are not accepted. Long-term rates are available.

Directions: From Okeechobee, head south on Highway 78 West for six miles to the park.

Contact: Windsor Manor RV Park, 10000 Highway 78 West, Okeechobee, FL 34974, 863/467-2307, fax 863/763-0201, email: windsormanor @ictransnet.com.

28 LAKE OKEECHOBEE RESORT KOA

Rating: 9

In Okeechobee

Lake Okeechobee map, grid b4, page 426

Beyond the security gate sits the continent's largest KOA, covering 117 acres. Here you won't find a simple recreation hall but a 20,000-square-foot "convention center and RV rally site" where dances, bingo, meetings, and the clatter of Ping-Pong balls bring the place alive. And there's not just a pool. Instead, one heated pool serves families, and a separate adults-only pool has a tiki-style bar set in a fountain-filled pond.

The horseshoe-shaped park is built around the putting greens and fairways of a nine-hole golf course. From the big windows of the park's 80-seat restaurant, diners overlook the golf course from behind the first tee. Wintertime campers have been known to show up from every state east of the Mississippi River to camp at the grassy, paved sites. Some coastal urbanites use the place as a weekend fishing or boating getaway. One-quarter mile south is Lake Okeechobee, where several largemouth bass tournaments are held each year. Disney World is less than two hours north.

Campsites, facilities: All 748 full-hookup sites are for RVs up to 40 feet long. A separate area is set aside for 20 tents. Recreational facilities include two pools, a kiddie pool, a hot tub, a nine-hole golf course, a game room, a playground, horseshoes, tennis courts, volleyball,

shuffleboard, pool tables, a recreation hall, and wintertime social programs. Showers, restrooms, a restaurant, cable TV, telephone hookups, limited groceries, park-model sites, and laundry facilities are available. Management says bathhouses and laundry facilities are wheelchair accessible. Children are welcome. Leashed pets are permitted.

Reservations, fees: Reservations are recommended. RV sites are $32 to $48 per night for two people, plus $4 to $6 per extra person. Tent sites are $28 to $38. Major credit cards are accepted.

Directions: If you're traveling south on Florida's Turnpike, exit at Yeehaw Junction. Follow U.S. 441 south for 33 miles to the park. If you're traveling north on Florida's Turnpike, exit at PGA Boulevard. Go west to the Beeline Highway/State Road 710. Turn right and follow this road to the town of Okeechobee. Turn left (west) onto State Road 70, then turn left (south) on U.S. 441. The park is ahead, near the junction with State Road 78.

Contact: Lake Okeechobee Resort KOA, 4276 U.S. 441 South, Okeechobee, FL 34974, 863/763-0231 or 800/562-7748, fax 863/763-0531, website: www.koa.com.

29 LAKESIDE RV PARK

Rating: 3

Southwest of Okeechobee

Lake Okeechobee map, grid b3, page 426

Year after year, seasonal visitors return to this small park south of Okeechobee for "great fishing and even better fishing stories." The town of Okeechobee has dozens of these semi-permanent RV parks, set jowl to jowl on U.S. 441.

Campsites, facilities: Anglers and outdoors lovers occupy these 76 sites with concrete pads. Rigs up to 35 feet in length can be accommodated. All have full hookups. Restrooms, showers, laundry facilities, and telephone service are available. The park is partially shaded and close to restaurants, boating supply stores, and other conveniences. Children and leashed pets are permitted.

Reservations, fees: Reservations are recommended. Sites are $15 per night for two people, plus $3 per extra person. Credit cards are not accepted. Long-term rates are available.

Directions: From the intersection of State Road 70 and U.S. 441, head south to the park.

Contact: Lakeside RV Park, 4074 U.S. Highway 441 Southeast, Okeechobee, FL 34974, 863/467-1530.

30 ZACHARY TAYLOR CAMPING RESORT

Rating: 6

South of Okeechobee

Lake Okeechobee map, grid b4, page 426

This green place offers more shade than many Lake Okeechobee–area campgrounds, which may explain why it can't guarantee a site preference at reservation time. In fact, the park is now encouraging year-long lot leases, rather than overnight stays or short-term vacations.

Cypress trees and native palms shade these 20 acres set along 1,500 feet of lazy Taylor Creek, and some campers end up becoming equity owners. Although a heated pool and planned activities at the waterfront recreation hall are provided, fishing remains the god of all activities here in the shadow of the nation's second largest inland freshwater lake. An on-site concrete boat ramp leads to the Big O.

Campsites, facilities: These 250 full-hookup sites are for RVs or tents. For recreation, there's a pool, a recreation hall, horseshoes, shuffleboard, and planned activities. Showers, a boat ramp, a dock, rental units, picnic tables, bait, and laundry facilities are available. Trips with fishing guides can be arranged. Cable TV and phone service are available if you stay at least one month. The recreation hall and restrooms are wheelchair accessible. Children are permitted for short stays. Leashed pets are accepted for $2 daily.

Reservations, fees: Reservations are preferred. Sites are $29 to $34 per night for two people, plus $2 per extra person. Major credit cards are accepted. Long-term stays are preferred.

Directions: From State Road 70 and U.S. 441/Parrott Avenue in the town of Okeechobee, go south on U.S. 441/Parrott Avenue to Lake Okeechobee. Turn left to continue east on U.S. 441. Turn left at Southeast 30th Terrace. The campground is ahead.

Contact: Zachary Taylor Camping Resort, 2995 U.S. 441 Southeast, Okeechobee, FL 34974, 863/763-3377 or 888/282-6523, fax 863/763-6301, website: www.campfloridarv.com.

31 TAYLOR CREEK LODGE

Rating: 2

South of Okeechobee

Lake Okeechobee map, grid b4, page 426

Don't confuse this park with the bigger, greener Zachary Taylor Camping Resort (see previous campground). For the most part, campsites here bake in the sun. Some have water views, but most are inland. Many waterview sites are reserved for residents of the park's 48 mobile homes, which are squeezed together.

Still, catching speckled perch, bass, bluegill, and catfish at Taylor Creek and nearby 467,000-acre Lake Okeechobee is the driving ambition of campers here, as it is at other parks in the shadow of the Big O. That's made obvious by the angler-oriented amenities: boat slips, a fish-cleaning station, bait, tackle, and a nearby fishing guide service. Those who want to go it alone can rent a boat for $80 daily or $45 for a half day. Light sleepers should avoid the inland row of sites that back onto busy U.S. 441. Tent campers normally sleep in their own waterview section informally called "the Point."

Campsites, facilities: All 102 sites have water and electricity. Restrooms, showers, cabins, boat rentals, boat slips, snacks, and bait and tackle are available. Children are welcome except for permanent stays. Small pets are permitted.

Reservations, fees: Reservations are advised. Sites are $15 to $18 per night for two people, plus $5 for each additional person; kids under age six stay free. Credit cards are not accepted. Long-term rates are available.

Directions: From State Road 70 and U.S. 441/Parrott Avenue in the town of Okeechobee, go south on U.S. 441/Parrott Avenue to Lake Okeechobee. Turn left to continue east on U.S. 441 and proceed about four miles to the campground.

Contact: Taylor Creek Lodge, 2730 U.S. 441 Southeast, Okeechobee, FL 34974, 863/763-4417.

32 LAKE OKEECHOBEE SCENIC TRAIL—NUBBIN SLOUGH

Rating: 6

At northeastern Lake Okeechobee
east of Okeechobee
Lake Okeechobee map, grid b4, page 426

Beautiful sunsets and good access by powerboat from the lake are what set this rustic campsite apart. This part of Lake Okeechobee doesn't get as much visitation as some parts that are more convenient to modern facilities, but that's why we like it. You can still find some increasingly rare xeric hammocks on this end of the lake, although you may have to go afar to see them. If you're spending several days hiking or bicycling along the Herbert Hoover Dike, the next campsite south is 10.3 miles away at Lake Okeechobee Scenic Trail–Chancy Bay. To the west, travel about nine miles, just passing the Kissimmee River, to reach Lake Okeechobee Scenic Trail–Kissimmee River.

Until not that long ago, Nubbin Slough was one of the traditional routes for cow poop to get into Lake Okeechobee. Now, the South Florida Water Management District has launched a cleanup of the dairies to the north, which has included paying dairy farmers to move their herds north into other drainage basins.

Campsites, facilities: This primitive tent-camping area is accessible by foot or bicycle; power-

boats also have good access from the lake. A fire ring and a shelter with a picnic table are provided. There is no toilet, no water, and no other facilities. Bring water, food, sunscreen, a hat, camping supplies, and mosquito repellent. Children and leashed pets are permitted.

Reservations, fees: Camping is first-come, first-served. There is no fee.

Directions: The campsite is .5 mile north of the Nubbins Slough recreation area on the lakeshore, east of the town of Okeechobee and off U.S. 98/441. For detailed directions, a map, and a brochure, contact the U.S. Army Corps of Engineers before your trip.

Contact: U.S. Army Corps of Engineers, South Florida Operations Office, 525 Ridgelawn Road, Clewiston, FL 33440-5399, 863/983-8101, website: www.sfwmd.gov.

33 PRIMROSE RV PARK

Rating: 4

South of Okeechobee
Lake Okeechobee map, grid b4, page 426

One of a dozen or so adults-preferred RV parks on the northern side of Lake Okeechobee, Primrose RV Park is easily accessible from both the west and east coast of Florida. It overlooks the deep blue water of the rim canal leading to the lake, and tends to attract anglers and snowbirds staying for the mild Florida winter. About half the sites are occupied year-round.

Campsites, facilities: Of the 59 sites in this community, 27 are available for overnighters and seasonal visitors in rigs up to 36 feet. Two sites are pull-through, and 14 have concrete pads. The park also offers five tent sites with water and electricity. All RV sites have full hookups and picnic tables. Restrooms, showers, a dump station, laundry facilities, and telephone service are available. On the premises are a boat ramp, dock, fish cleaning station, and wheelchair-accessible clubhouse, where planned activities include potluck suppers and bingo. Children are not welcome. Small leashed pets are permitted.

Reservations, fees: Reservations are recommended. Sites are $20 a night for two people, plus $5 for each additional person. Credit cards are not accepted. Long-term stays are the norm.

Directions: From the intersection of U.S. 98 and U.S. 441 with State Road 78 in Okeechobee, drive 4.3 miles south to the park.

Contact: Primrose RV Park, 6070 Highway 441 Southeast, Okeechobee, FL 34974, 863/763-8711, email: primrose@okeechobee.com.

34 FIJIAN RV PARK

Rating: 4

South of Okeechobee

Lake Okeechobee map, grid b4, page 426

Sitting on the northern end of 740-square-mile Lake Okeechobee, this 3.5-acre park has an understandable focus—the lake. Campers (mostly retirees) launch boats from a park ramp to follow a canal to the watery home of bass and specks. Some campers fish from the bank; the open and sunny park has 850 feet of waterfront. With no swimming pool, playground, or shuffleboard, these grassy sites with concrete patios are best left to grown-up anglers and boaters. But in the wintertime, live entertainment in the 5,000-square-foot recreation building does provide another way to pass time.

Campsites, facilities: Campers age 55 and older are welcome at the 40 full-hookup RV sites in this 77-unit park. Winter social programs, a game room, a recreation room, showers, restrooms, a dump station, a boat ramp, a dock, cable TV, telephone hookups, and laundry facilities are available. Children are permitted for short-term stays or to visit long-term campers. Small, leashed pets are accepted; use the designated dog walk.

Reservations, fees: Reservations are recommended. Sites are $30 per night for two people, plus $5 per extra person. The park is open from October 1 to May 1. Credit cards are not accepted. Long-term rates are available.

Directions: From State Road 70 and U.S. 441/Parrott Avenue in the town of Okeechobee, go south on U.S. 441/Parrott Avenue to Lake Okeechobee. Turn left to continue east on U.S. 441. Proceed about five miles, past Nubbin Slough, to the park entrance at right.

Contact: Fijian RV Park, 6500 U.S. 441 Southeast, Okeechobee, FL 34974, 863/763-6200 or 888/646-2267, fax 863/763-6973, email: fijian-rv@aol.com.

35 BOB'S BIG BASS RV PARK

Rating: 2

Southeast of Okeechobee

Lake Okeechobee map, grid b4, page 426

The name is a hint that bass fishing at nearby 740-square-mile Lake Okeechobee is popular among campers. With only a recreation room for entertainment, it's best to bring along fishing rods and a motorboat to traverse the two miles from the park's rim canal to locks leading to the Big O.

Campsites, facilities: This adults-only park has an "unlimited" area set apart for tents and 48 full-hookup RV sites (10 pull-through). Each site has a picnic table. A recreation room, showers, restrooms, a boat ramp, a camp circle for campfires, firewood, and laundry facilities are available. Groceries, bait, and restaurants are nearby. Adults are preferred, but children are allowed for short-term stays. Leashed pets are permitted.

Reservations, fees: Reservations are recommended. The camping fee is $18 per night for two people, plus $2 to $5 per extra person. Credit cards are not accepted. Long-term rates are available.

Directions: From State Road 70 and U.S. 441/Parrott Avenue in the town of Okeechobee, go south on U.S. 441/Parrott Avenue to Lake Okeechobee. Turn left to continue east on U.S. 441 and proceed about eight miles to the entrance.

Contact: Bob's Big Bass RV Park, 12766 U.S. 441 Southeast, Okeechobee, FL 34974, 863/763-2638.

36 UNCLE JOE'S FISH CAMP

Rating: 3

South of Moore Haven

Lake Okeechobee map, grid c2, page 426

If you love fishing for bass or hunting for ducks at Lake Okeechobee, then you'll like these grassy or concrete-pad campsites. (You can also use this as an access point for bicycling and hiking on the dike.) A fish camp is just what the name implies—a place to sleep so you can rise early the next day to catch finned critters. Forget swimming pools or shuffleboard; you won't find such amenities here. During the season, planned activities include weekly fish fries. Boaters will be glad that the boat ramp has direct access to Lake Okeechobee, meaning they won't face the hassle of waiting to get past a lock. We happened to stop by on the first day of duck-hunting season, and the boat ramp was a beehive of activity. Hunters clad in green camouflage waited in line to launch their watercraft, some of which were edged with frilly dried plant matter the better to fool the ducks.

Some folks stay at this five-acre camp for months, earning a free, reserved boat dock after a four-month stay. Motorboats rent for $50 daily. If someone in your party is dying for a hot meal in front of a TV after so much solitude on the lake, then the cabins with kitchenettes (renting for $35 and up) will provide a little extra comfort.

Campsites, facilities: All 18 full-hookup sites are for RVs up to 38 feet long, while the occasional tenter who comes through can set up across the street on 10 primitive sites in a field. Fishing guides and boat rentals are available. Showers, restrooms, a dump station, cabin rentals, a boat ramp, limited groceries, snacks, sandwiches, firewood, bait, boat gas, dock space, and laundry facilities are on the premises. Most areas are wheelchair accessible. Restaurants and a supermarket are 10 minutes away. Families with small children and pets are welcome.

Reservations, fees: Reservations are not necessary. Sites are $20 per night, plus $5 if your party has more than two people. Credit cards are not accepted. Stay as long as you like.

Directions: From Clewiston, take U.S. 27 west to State Road 720 and turn right. Continue four miles, then turn right at the Uncle Joe's sign.

Contact: Uncle Joe's Fish Camp, 2005 Griffin Road Southeast, Moore Haven, FL 33471, 863/983-9421, email: unclejoefishcamp@aol.com.

37 LAKE OKEECHOBEE SCENIC TRAIL—LIBERTY POINT

Rating: 7

On the land side canal bordering the dike along Lake Okeechobee

Lake Okeechobee map, grid c2, page 426

At dawn, a gorgeous burnt-orange and purple glow rises over the 740-square-mile expanse of Lake Okeechobee. The view is your reward for skipping conveniences like showers and toilets.

People who take the trouble of following the tire ruts along the sun-washed, shell-rock Herbert Hoover Dike tend to rave about the experience. Wading birds stand like statues in the shallow marsh to the east before pouncing on meals of fish. Otters sometimes scurry into the lake early in the morning. And you're almost certain to see some alligators. Places to fish from shore are hard to find here because of the plentiful water plants sticking up from the surface of Florida's largest lake; fishing lines are bound to get caught in the weeds. If this stop is part of a bicycle or hiking trip along the entire 110-mile-long levee, then the next rustic campsite to the southeast is 10.8 miles away (see Lake Okeechobee Scenic Trail—Lake Harbor in this chapter). It's a 12-mile trek northwest to Lake Okeechobee Scenic Trail—Culvert 5A (see campground in this chapter).

Campsites, facilities: This primitive tent-camping area is accessible by foot; long-distance trekkers circling the lake might arrive by bicycle or foot. Boaters can dock nearby at Uncle Joe's Fish Camp. A fire ring and a shelter with a picnic table are provided. There are no toilets or piped water. Bring plenty of water, food, camping supplies, and mosquito repellent. Children and leashed pets are OK.

Reservations, fees: Camping is first-come, first-served. There is no fee.

Directions: The campsite is just east of Uncle Joe's Fish Camp (see campground in this chapter), so park at Uncle Joe's; you may be asked to pay $3. To get there from Clewiston, take U.S. 27 to State Road 720, turn right, then go to the Uncle Joe's entrance. From Uncle Joe's levee gate, hike atop the dike in a southeastern direction about .5 mile to the Florida Trail campsite.

Contact: U.S. Army Corps of Engineers, South Florida Operations Office, 525 Ridgelawn Road, Clewiston, FL 33440-5399, 863/983-8101, website: www.sfwmd.gov.

38 THE MARINA RV RESORT

Rating: 7

Southwest of Okeechobee
Lake Okeechobee map, grid b3, page 426
This renovated park is on federal lands adjacent to the Moore Haven Lock that connects eastern Lake Okeechobee to the Caloosahatchee River leading to Fort Myers and the Gulf Coast. Under new management, the campground is popular with boaters, anglers, and hunters, but also offers access to the dike for bicycling and hiking. A new swimming pool and recreation buildings were recently added. There is a gated security entrance and plenty of parking for boat trailers. Managers live on site.

Campsites, facilities: Among 73 sites, 59 have full hookups and the rest have water and elec-

tric. Tent sites are available along Duck Hunter's Circle near the clubhouse. For sites along the water, ask for lots 82 through 98 on Fisherman's Lane. Restrooms, showers, a dump station, laundry facilities, and rental units are available. On the premises are a swimming pool, a boat ramp, a fish-cleaning station, a clubhouse, gazebo, horseshoe pits, shuffleboard courts, bait house, and gas pumps. Children are welcome. Leashed pets are permitted.

Reservations, fees: Reservations are recommended. Sites are $18 per night. Major credit cards are accepted. Long-term rates are available.

Directions: From the intersection of U.S. 27 and State Road 78, go north on 78 for about a mile. Turn right on Canal Road and drive through a residential area until the road ends at the park.

Contact: The Marina RV Resort, 900 County Road 720, Moore Haven, FL 33471, 863/946-2255; reservations 904/824-7063.

39 HOLIDAY TRAV-L-PARK

Rating: 4

West of Clewiston
Lake Okeechobee map, grid c3, page 426
"Have you checked? Antenna down? Step up? Drain cap on? Wife on board? Have a good trip," advises a sign as you exit this park. Formerly a KOA, this is a convenient place to sleep if you want to walk or cycle along the lake's 107-mile-long dike the next morning or take your boat out to fish for largemouth bass. Within three miles are a golf course, tennis and racquetball facilities, a Lake Okeechobee boat launch, shopping, and a hospital. The park boasts a smattering of exotic trees; request site 2 in February or March if you'd like to sample a tasty loquat plucked from a low-hanging tree branch.

Campsites, facilities: There are 124 pull-through RV sites with full hookups, plus a separate area with six tent sites in a corner near the entrance. Facilities include restrooms, showers, a dump station, a store, cabin rentals, and laundry facilities. There's also a hot tub, a pool, a horseshoe pit, a game room, a playground, a shuffleboard court, and an adult activity room. Movies, bingo, potluck suppers, and crafts also keep guests entertained. All areas are wheelchair accessible. Children are permitted; parents are responsible for the safety of their kids at the pool. Leashed dogs must use a pet walk near the entrance.

Reservations, fees: Reservations are required December through March. Sites are $26 per night for two people, plus $4 for each additional person over age 11. Major credit cards are accepted. Long-term rates are available.

Directions: From Clewiston, travel about two miles west on U.S. 27 and then turn right at County Road 720. The campground entrance is located about 700 feet ahead on the right.

Contact: Holiday Trav-L-Park, 194 County Road 720, Clewiston, FL 33440, 863/983-7078 or 877/983-7078.

40 ROBIN'S NEST RV RESORT

Rating: 3

North of Moore Haven

Lake Okeechobee map, grid b3, page 426

This park is so fresh that the trees have not grown in yet, but it targets seasonal visitors who are looking for a convenient base for Lake Okeechobee's charms that is also near citylike amenities (Wal-Mart, restaurants, and other shopping). Open from October 1 through April 30, the park lies neatly under the sun along U.S. 27. This park has affiliations with The Marina RV Resort on Lake Okeechobee (see campground in this chapter).

Campsites, facilities: There are 248 RV sites with full hookups, concrete pads, and picnic tables. Restrooms, showers, laundry facilities, and telephone service are available. On the premises are a heated pool, two clubhouses, a three-hole golf course, shuffleboard courts, and a snack bar. Live music is scheduled every

weekend from December through the end of March. Planned activities include music, games, group meals, and karate classes. Children are welcome for short stays only at this 50-plus preferred park. Leashed pets are permitted. Stay here and get full-day use of the owners' boat and recreational facilities at The Marina RV Resort on Lake Okeechobee.

Reservations, fees: Reservations are recommended. Sites are $18 per night. Major credit cards are accepted. Long-term rates are available.

Directions: From Moore Haven, drive nine miles north on U.S. 27 to the park, which is on the west side.

Contact: Robin's Nest RV Resort, 2365 North U.S. 27, Moore Haven, Fl 33471, 863/946-3782, fax 863/946-3883.

41 OKEECHOBEE LANDINGS

Rating: 3

In Clewiston

Lake Okeechobee map, grid c3, page 426

Purchasers of park models, trailer lots, and seasonal visitors in big RVs people this 27-acre community, which attracts anglers and retirees. Nonetheless, tenters are welcome at 25 spots. Speckled perch, bluegill, largemouth bass, and catfish tempt them from nearby Lake Okeechobee. It may be hard to believe that this sunny, landscaped suburb of RVs is set—like all other trailer parks and land on the southern end of Lake Okeechobee—in what was once a forbidding, dense, custard apple swamp. Early settlers chopped down those trees. In the 1930s, the state and U.S. Army Corps of Engineers built a towering levee to encircle the lake after hurricane-spawned floods killed nearly 2,000 people, mostly in nearby Belle Glade. You won't be able to see the "Big O" from here or, for that matter, from most places around the lake, because the levee is so high. If you'd like a water view, request a campsite near the park's seven-acre lake.

Campsites, facilities: All 270 large RV sites set

on paved streets have full hookups, including cable TV. Tenters sleep at 25 sites that are not set apart from RVs. A pool, a Jacuzzi, shuffleboard, horseshoes, a tennis court, a game room, bingo, special events, and a wintertime snack bar entertain guests. Showers, restrooms, picnic tables, a dump station, and laundry facilities are available. You can store your boat, car, or RV when necessary. Management says the office, bathhouse, and clubhouse are wheelchair accessible. Groceries can be purchased one mile away; a restaurant and bait shop are within .5 mile. Children are welcome. Leashed pets are permitted.

Reservations, fees: Reservations are recommended. Sites are $24.50 per night. Major credit cards are accepted. Long-term stays are OK.

Directions: From downtown Clewiston, go east on U.S. 27 to the park entrance. Signs on the highway mark the turnoff to the park, which is at the eastern end of town.

Contact: Okeechobee Landings, 420 Holiday Boulevard, Clewiston, FL 33440, 863/983-4144, email: info@okeechobeelandings.com.

42 LAKE OKEECHOBEE SCENIC TRAIL—LAKE HARBOR

Rating: 6

On Lake Okeechobee four miles east of Clewiston

Lake Okeechobee map, grid c3, page 426

Look for bald eagles, turkeys, deer, bobcats, and hawklike ospreys as you hike along this portion of the 107-mile-long, semigrassy berm that holds in Lake Okeechobee. Former park ranger Tambour Eller once counted about 10 types of birds while strolling the short distance from the U.S. Army Corps of Engineers office to the lake. "I see more wildlife and birds here than I actually have at the Everglades," Eller says.

Most South Floridians aren't aware that they can hike, bicycle, and camp along the sun-washed, shell-rock hiking trail atop the Herbert Hoover Dike. It's one of the few ways to see Florida's largest lake, which, for motorists, is hidden from view by the 34-foot-high dike. For the squeamish, this campsite may present a good introduction to experiencing the lake. It is fairly close to amenities in Clewiston as well as the Army Corps office that oversees the trail. If you're going the distance around the lake, it's 10.8 miles northwest to the next rustic campsite, Lake Okeechobee Scenic Trail—Liberty Point (see campground in this chapter). Need a hot shower? It's about nine miles southeast to tent-permissible South Bay RV Park (see campground in this chapter).

Campsites, facilities: This primitive tent-camping area is accessible by foot or bicycle. A fire ring and a shelter with a picnic table are provided. There is no toilet, water, or other facilities. Bring water, food, sunscreen, a hat, camping supplies, and mosquito repellent. Children and leashed pets are permitted.

Reservations, fees: Camping is first-come, first-served. There is no fee.

Directions: The campsite is on the lakeside of the Herbert Hoover Dike, about four miles east of Clewiston. You could park at the U.S. Army Corps of Engineers (with permission) or at the nearby Clewiston city boat ramp, then hike about 5.2 miles south. A better bet is to ask for a shortcut, as well as a map and a brochure, from the U.S. Army Corps of Engineers before your trip.

Contact: U.S. Army Corps of Engineers, South Florida Operations Office, 525 Ridgelawn Road, Clewiston, FL 33440-5399, 863/983-8101, website: www.sfwmd.com.

43 CROOKED HOOK RV RESORT

Rating: 6

East of Clewiston

Lake Okeechobee map, grid c3, page 426

One of the cleanest private parks around Lake Okeechobee, anglers seek Crooked Hook out for its proximity to the bass haven. But seasonal visitors fill up the park fast in the wintertime for line dancing, bowling outings, or other daily activities, and it is close to shopping and restaurants in Clewiston. In a region where sun-baked RV sites tend to be the norm, this 30-acre, retiree-oriented place offers something different: It has some shaded campsites and greenery that make it feel tropical and relaxing. The levee is across the highway, hiding the big blue waters of the lake.

Campsites, facilities: An area that holds about 35 tents is set apart from 175 full-hookup RV sites (10 pull-through). A heated pool, a recreation room, a playground, an exercise room, horseshoes, shuffleboard, *pétanque* (French-style bowling), and wintertime daily activities entertain campers. Showers, restrooms, picnic tables, and laundry facilities are available. Three miles away are restaurants, groceries, an 18-hole golf course, and bait. Children are welcome, although the park mainly attracts retirees. Small, leashed pets are permitted.

Reservations, fees: Reservations are required. Sites are $18 to $25 per night for two people, plus $3 per extra person. Major credit cards are accepted. Long-term stays are the norm, though a few sites are available for overnighters during the winter.

Directions: From Clewiston, go three miles east on U.S. 27 to the campground entrance.

Contact: Crooked Hook RV Resort, 51700 U.S. Highway 27, Clewiston, FL 33440, 863/983-7112, email: crhrv@onearrow.net.

44 SOUTH BAY RV CAMPGROUND

Rating: 6

In South Bay

Lake Okeechobee map, grid c3, page 426

The town of South Bay is routinely ignored by guidebooks and tourists, but its proximity to Lake Okeechobee fishing, hiking, cycling, and bird-watching give cause to recommend it. A 24-hour on-site manager lives within footsteps

of the county-run campground's office. The large paved campsites are sunny and are set along two elongated loops named Shellcracker Circle and Bluegill Circle. For the most popular sleeping spots at Shiner Lake, request sites 6 through 23. An adjacent city boat ramp/day-use picnic area leads to the fishing mecca of Lake Okeechobee. There's also a screened-in picnic area with large grills for gathering, and an air-conditioned recreational hall with pool table, card tables, and color TV. A campfire ring offers socializing opportunities.

Campsites, facilities: The 72 campsites have water, electricity, and cable TV. Showers, restrooms, a playground, a game room, a dump station, laundry facilities, horseshoes, and pool tables are available. A boat ramp is nearby. Nearly 20 campsites are wheelchair accessible. Children are welcome. Leashed, attended pets (no pit bulls) are permitted.

Reservations, fees: Reservations can be made up to 90 days in advance, unless reserving by phone, which requires 14 days' notice. Sites are $16.50 to $17.50 per night for five people, plus $2.12 for each additional person. Major credit cards are accepted. Monthly rates are available.

Directions: From U.S. 27 and State Road 80 in South Bay, follow U.S. 27 northwest about 2.5 miles. Turn right at Levee Road, then turn right into the campground.

Contact: South Bay RV Campground, 100 Levee Road, South Bay, FL 33493, 561/992-9045 or 877/992-9915. Additional information: Palm Beach County Parks and Recreation Department, 561/992-9045, website: www.pbc-gov.com/parks.

45 BELLE GLADE MARINA CAMPGROUND

Rating: 4

On Lake Okeechobee's Torry Island

Lake Okeechobee map, grid c3, page 426

If you're coming from eastern Palm Beach County, this is probably the closest place to pitch a tent or hook up a rig at Lake Okeechobee, particularly if you want a golf course practically on the premises. The Belle Glade Country Club is across the levee from the campground, which is popular with bass anglers and boaters who seek to experience the nation's second largest inland freshwater lake. Many sites have personal docking facilities with lake access.

Calling the farming-dominated community of Belle Glade a logical tourism spot would be stretching things. In the largest city on Lake Okeechobee, the town's impoverished areas have drawn comparisons to the Third World. But this city-owned campground is on 75-acre Torry Island, well removed from the poverty. Meanwhile, county tourism promoters are laboring mightily to attract vacationers to the communities rimming the lake.

Campsites, facilities: There are 350 campsites for RVs and 45 for tents. Most have electricity, water, and sewer hookups. For recreation, there's a miniature golf course, horseshoes, shuffleboard, organized activities, and fishing guides. Some sites have boat docks or overlook lagoons dotted with lily pads. Tenters are usually placed overlooking the rim canal that leads to the lake. Near the entrance to the campground are pavilions for rent, and you might spy a birthday party or baby shower going on. Eight public boat ramps, plus showers, restrooms, barbecue/picnic areas, and laundry facilities are available. Within walking distance are a golf course, boat rentals, a restaurant, bait, and tackle. Children and pets are permitted.

Reservations, fees: Camping is first-come, first-served. Sites are $16 per night for two people, plus $2 for each additional person. Credit cards are not accepted. Long-term stays are allowed.

Directions: From U.S. 27 and State Road 80 in South Bay, go east nearly two miles on State Road 80. Turn left at State Road 715 and proceed about 2.25 miles. Turn left at West Canal Street North/State Road 717. Continue about two miles west to the campground entrance

on Torry Island. (On Torry Island, State Road 717 is known as Chosen–Torry Island Road.) **Contact:** Belle Glade Marina Campground, 110 Southwest Avenue E, Belle Glade, FL 33430, 561/996-6322. Or contact the City of Belle Glade Office of Parks and Recreation, Municipal Complex, Belle Glade, FL 33430, 561/996-0100.

46 EVERGLADES ADVENTURES RV AND SAILING RESORT

Rating: 6

At Lake Okeechobee

Lake Okeechobee map, grid c3, page 426

Formerly known as Pahokee Marina and Campground, this park on city-owned land is undergoing improvements and renovations through 2004. New managers are doubling the size of the complex, adding a swimming pool and recreation center, and further developing its deep-water harbor for sailboats. But don't wait for the completion of this work. This park boasts the only developed lakefront campsites on the eastern shore of Lake Okeechobee. The grassy campsites are directly on the banks of Lake Okeechobee, providing a pretty sunset view. The berm that surrounds the lake is behind the park, so you'll actually drive up and over the dike and then down to the campground. It's also convenient to the small shops of little Pahokee, a farming community. Although the park has some trees, expect plenty of sunshine. Fishing and boating are the main attraction, but access to the hiking and bicycling options on the dike is excellent. All ages are welcome.

Campsites, facilities: RVs and tents can use these level, grassy 119 sites with full hookups. Shuffleboard, horseshoes, a playground, restrooms, showers, cabin rentals, a dump station, a boat ramp, bait, tackle, and limited groceries are available. When complete, the park will have 84 deep-water slips in its marina, two fishing piers, three boat ramps, and trailer storage. Already available is a new boat rental fleet of pontoon boats and Boston Whalers fully equipped for fishing. Bicycle, canoe, and kayak rentals are on site. Children and pets are permitted.

Reservations, fees: Reservations are recommended. Sites are $23 per night for four people (rates are subject to change without notice). Major credit cards are accepted. Stay as long as you like.

Directions: The park is on Lake Okeechobee in the heart of Pahokee. Head west over the levee from the intersection of U.S. 441 and State Road 715.

Contact: Everglades Adventures RV and Sailing Resort, 190 North Lake Avenue, Pahokee, FL 33476, 561/924-7832 or 800/335-6560; fax 561/924-7271, website: www.evergladesadventuresresort.com.

47 LAKE OKEECHOBEE SCENIC TRAIL—CHANCY BAY CAMPSITE

🚶 🚴 🐕 ⛺

Rating: 6

On Lake Okeechobee
Lake Okeechobee map, grid c3, page 426

Creamy pastels light the sky above Lake Okeechobee at dusk. This lakeshore campsite has a beautiful westward view over the lake. Ranger Jerre Killingbeck planted the cluster of palm trees and dragged a picnic table to this spot, as he did at the eight other Lake Okeechobee Scenic Trail (LOST) sites he developed around the lake. Expect to walk about .5 mile from the boat ramp to the site. That's not too far, by design. "This would allow even folks with small kids to 'hike' and 'camp' away from developed parks," says Killingbeck. If you're going the distance around the lake, the next rustic campsite to the north—Nubbin Slough—is 10.3 miles away. If you're southbound, it's nine miles to the next sleeping spot, Lake Okeechobee Scenic Trail—South Nubbin Slough (see campground in this chapter).

Campsites, facilities: This primitive tent-camping area accommodates several tents and is accessible by foot; long-distance trekkers circling the lake might arrive by bicycle. A fire ring and a shelter with a picnic table are provided. There are no toilets and no piped water. Bring plenty of water, food, camping supplies, and mosquito repellent. Children and leashed pets are OK.

Reservations, fees: Sites are first-come, first-served. Camping is free. Stays are limited to five consecutive days.

Directions: From the junction of Highway 76 and U.S. 98/441 at Port Mayaca, go north on U.S. 98/441 about seven miles to the Chancy Bay boat ramp, at left. Park your car. Walk to the campsite, which is just over the levee and maybe .5 mile north, on the lake side of the Herbert Hoover Dike. The area is hidden in a tree canopy and isn't visible from the trail. Look for the Scenic Trail sign and follow the path to the campsite. For detailed information, contact the U.S. Army Corps of Engineers before your trip or study the website.

Contact: U.S. Army Corps of Engineers, South Florida Operations Office, 525 Ridgelawn Road, Clewiston, FL 33440-5399, 863/983-8101, website: www.sfwmd.gov.

48 LAKE OKEECHOBEE SCENIC TRAIL—SOUTH PORT MAYACA

🚶 🚴 🐕 ⛺

Rating: 5

At eastern Lake Okeechobee
Lake Okeechobee map, grid c4, page 426

This part of the trail is a lot more scenic since the removal of vegetation, allowing first-rate views of the lake from atop 34-foot-high Herbert Hoover Dike. Still, so few people hike along the sun-parched, shell-rock road atop the Herbert Hoover Dike that you'll feel like you're getting away from it all. You'll see miles of water stretching ahead of you like an ocean; to the land side are marshy areas and tiny farms of banana groves or ranches.

Listen to the waves lapping against the rough shoreline; on windy days, they may sound more like a roar. Birds are plentiful. Stop for a picnic on the swath of mowed grass along the dike during your hike or bike ride. Bicyclists have been known to circle the sun-washed, 110-mile-long dike in as little as two days, seeing first hand why the Seminole tribe dubbed the lake "big water" (Okeechobee). If you're going the distance along the entire lake, the next rustic campsite is seven miles north at Lake Okeechobee Scenic Trail—Chancy Bay (see previous campground). Want a shower and civilization? Go to Everglades Adventure RV and Sailing Resort (formerly Pahokee Campground) about 10.3 miles south in Pahokee for a reprieve (see campground in this chapter).

Campsites, facilities: This primitive tent-camping area is accessible by foot or bicycle. A fire ring/grill and a newly built shelter with a picnic table are provided. There is no toilet or other facilities. Bring water, food, sunscreen, a hat, camping supplies, and mosquito repellent. Children and leashed pets are OK.

Reservations, fees: Camping is first-come, first-served. There is no fee.

Directions: The campsite is on the lakeside of the levee, about two miles south of the Port Mayaca lock, at the base of the berm overlooking the water. The lock is on U.S. 441/U.S. 98 at the Okeechobee Waterway and the intersection with State Road 76. You'll park at the Port Mayaca levee gate, then hike or bike two miles south to the campsite. You can also access this site from the Canal Point picnic area on U.S. 441/98, approximately 3.4 miles north of the town of Pahokee. It's a seven-mile trek to the site. For detailed directions and a map, contact the U.S. Army Corps of Engineers.

Contact: U.S. Army Corps of Engineers, South Florida Operations Office, 525 Ridgelawn Road, Clewiston, FL 33440, 941/983-8101, website: www.sfwmd.gov.

49 DUPUIS MANAGEMENT AREA

Rating: 8

East of Port Mayaca

Lake Okeechobee map, grid c4, page 426

Before it was purchased by the South Florida Water Management District to help conserve some of the cleanest water remaining in this part of the world, this remote spot was known as the White Belt Ranch. Why? It was cattle country, and the moo-heads who grazed here were black with a big white stripe down their sides. The 21,875 acres of oaks, pines, and marshes has an equestrian camping area and a separate family camping area. Set in pine flatwoods, the general campground is a getaway from urbanity—here, you're two miles east of angler-haven Lake Okeechobee, and the armadillos scurrying through the palm thickets are a reminder that you're many miles west of urban South Florida. The campsites encircle a little pond, and if you're well prepared for roughing it, this is a nice place to stay.

Backpackers hike a little more than two miles to reach the first primitive camping area, a cleared area with fire rings. If the site has been taken, then hikers are expected to continue another four miles or so to get to the next rustic camping area.

This is great country for hiking and mountain biking in South Florida. It's especially pleasant if you arrive in winter when the weather's cool and bugs are bearable. Don't be surprised to spot deer, turkey, wild hogs, and small mammals at dawn or dusk. Bald eagles nest here. Wood storks and white ibis, in search of food, stalk the marshes close to the road during the rainy season. More than 35 miles of the Florida Trail wind through the forest. Four loop trails—measuring 4.3 miles, 6.8 miles, 11.5 miles, and 15.6 miles—were developed by the Florida Trail Association, and begin in pine flatwoods. The terrain varies throughout the reserve and includes wet prairie, lots of cypress domes, and some scrub. A connector trail leads to J.W. Corbett Wildlife Management Area (see campground in this chapter). Together, Corbett and the Dupuis Management Area offer the biggest swath of pine flatwoods remaining in Palm Beach County. In some places, you'll notice little ponds; they're former watering holes for the cattle that lived here when the late John Dupuis Jr. owned this land.

Fat-tired bicycles are permitted only on named and numbered forest roads. Camping is permitted during hunting season, but this is a time to be careful and wear orange or bright colors. Hunters are warned to watch out for hikers and horseback riders. They tend to be a hospitable bunch; one friendly hunter freely offered us his orange vests when we expressed concern about mountain biking on the property during the bird-hunting season. But he also recommended that it would not be such a great idea to bike around here during ground hunts when people are shooting low to the surface. Although the hunting season dates change from year to year, hunting for deer and small game tends to occur most weekends in September, October, November, most of December, and early January. March weekends are reserved for turkey hunters. Another warning is in order about the wild hogs on the property. They can be dangerous, particularly if they feel cornered. The hogs are pests and are the only animal hunted here with no bag limit. Remember also that the place was bought by the government because it helps store clean water. Some of that water may make the trails impassable if you're not up to getting your feet wet.

Campsites, facilities: A drive-up primitive family camping area of 20 sites with picnic tables is provided, as well as three hike-in backcountry campsites along portions of the Florida National Scenic Trail. A portable toilet and a fire ring are offered in the family camping area. No facilities are provided in the backcountry. Bring plenty of water, plus food, camping gear, and mosquito repellent. Children are welcome, but not dogs. At the family campground, only tents

and pop-top campers are allowed. Generators are prohibited. Call 561/924-5310, ext. 3333, to check on conditions before you head out.

Reservations, fees: Sites are first-come, first-served. A day-use fee of $3 per person per day is included in the camping fees. Camping is $4 per person at backcountry sites, $5 per person at the family campground, and $7 at the equestrian site. Registration is on the honor system.

Directions: From I-95, take Exit 101 west on State Road 76 for about 20 miles. For the drive-up family camping area, enter Gate 1, which is the main entrance, and drive about one mile on the dirt road to the campground. For backcountry camping, enter the reserve at Gate 2 and park. Follow the hiking trail to the backcountry campsites. For more details and a map, contact the water management district.

Contact: South Florida Water Management District DuPuis Reserve Field Office, 23500 Southwest Kanner Highway, Canal Point, FL 33438, 561/924-5310. Additional information is available from the headquarters office of the South Florida Water Management District, 3301 Gun Club Road, West Palm Beach, FL 33406, 561/686-8800 or 800/432-2045, website: www.sfwmd.gov.

50 DUPUIS MANAGEMENT AREA EQUESTRIAN CENTER AND CAMPGROUND

Rating: 8

East of Port Mayaca

Lake Okeechobee map, grid c4, page 426

Horses in the DuPuis Management Area are limited to this equestrian campsite, roads, and designated horse trails developed by the Dupuis Horsemen's Association. Still, you'll find plenty of places to ride in this 34-square-mile forest of oaks, pines, and marsh. Four looped horseback-riding trails range from 7.2 to 17.5 miles. Be aware of the presence of some wild hogs on the property. You can see the gouged terrain where they have rooted around in the ground for grubs and such; make sure to steer your steed away from those potentially injuring holes.

Campsites, facilities: A basically unlimited number of primitive sites accommodate tenters on horseback. Restrooms, about 20 horse stalls, and a fenced exercise area for horses are provided. There is no drinkable water, so bring plenty of water, plus food, camping gear, mosquito repellent, and other supplies. Children are welcome. Dogs are prohibited.

Reservations, fees: Sites are first-come, first-served. Camping is $7 per person per night without a horse, or $9 per night for one person and one horse housed in a stall.

Directions: From I-95, take Exit 101. Go west on State Road 76 for a little over 20 miles to the forest, at left. Enter at Gate 3, which is the equestrian center entrance.

Contact: South Florida Water Management District DuPuis Reserve Field Office, 23500 Southwest Kanner Highway, Canal Point, FL 33438, 561/924-5310. South Florida Water Management District, 3301 Gun Club Road, West Palm Beach, FL 33406, 561/686-8800 or 800/432-2045, website: www.sfwmd.gov.

51 J. W. CORBETT WILDLIFE MANAGEMENT AREA

Rating: 7

West of West Palm Beach

Lake Okeechobee map, grid c4, page 426

At 94 square miles, this chunk of backwoods stands out for outdoorsy types in largely suburban and agricultural Palm Beach County. At certain wet times of year, the muddy roads tend to be fresh with the tracks of resident creatures, such as deer, turkeys, bobcats, raccoons, and occasionally, ill-tempered wild hogs. No wonder that a portion of the Florida National Scenic Trail slices east-west through the southern portion of these 60,224 acres, from Seminole Pratt Whitney Road to northwest of

Big Gopher Canal, crossing abandoned tomato fields (east of the canal) along the way.

You can drive into this mosaic of wetlands, pines, and hardwoods for a somewhat rough-and-tumble windshield tour down dirt roads. It's best to use a four-wheel-drive vehicle. Most campsites are found alongside canals. Two others are near the northern entrance on either side of the main dirt road, called North Grade. Even near the entrance you may see endangered wood storks—black-headed, white-bodied, goose-sized birds—fishing for dinner. You're certainly out in the woods here. Twenty-five miles to the east, West Palm Beach, the nearest major city, seems light years away. Yet the power lines crossing diagonally through parts of this wilderness are reminders that the place isn't untouched.

Campsites, facilities: These 16 primitive camping areas for tents, trailers, and RVs are open during hunting season (generally winter and spring) and on Fridays, Saturdays, and Sundays after the close of the wintertime hunting season through the Sunday two weeks prior to the next hunting season in spring. There is no piped water, so bring plenty of your own. Bring food and camping supplies, including mosquito repellent. There are no toilets or other facilities. Children and pets are allowed.

Reservations, fees: Sites are first-come, first-served. Backpacking requires a permit, so contact the Florida Fish and Wildlife Conservation Commission. Camping is free.

Directions: From I-95 (Exit 77), go west on Northlake Boulevard. Turn right at State Road 710/Beeline Highway and continue about 20 miles. Look for the entrance to your left after passing the Pratt Whitney/United Technologies plant. If you reach the Martin County line, you've gone too far.

Contact: Florida Fish and Wildlife Conservation Commission, South Regional Office, 8535 Northlake Boulevard, West Palm Beach, FL 33412, 561/625-5122. Or contact its state headquarters at 850/488-4676, website: www.floridaconservation.org.

52 BIG CYPRESS CAMPGROUND

🌊 🏊 🐕 🚴 ♿ 🚗 ⛺

Rating: 5

In the Everglades on Seminole Indian land
Lake Okeechobee map, grid d2, page 426

Back when Native American tribes were forced to follow the Trail of Tears to reservations out West, the resistant Seminoles had the distinction of never surrendering to federal troops. Eventually, three wars with U.S. soldiers forced the Seminoles southward through the length of Florida to vanish into the mysterious Everglades. There they lived for decades until they struck peace, but did not sign a treaty, with the federal government. Today, of the two local camping alternatives on the Big Cypress Seminole Indian Reservation, these 54 mowed acres are the citified choice. The well-tended lawn encircling the basketball and shuffleboard courts could be mistaken for suburban parkland if it weren't for the campground's native thatched-roof shelters (called "chickees"), which shade some of the picnic tables.

Oaks and cabbage palms dot the landscape and help separate RV campsites, although trees don't totally block views of neighbors. Primitive tenters can set up camp in their own area far from the rumble of RV generators. In summer, the sun will fry you at the pool and the miniature golf course. Free buses will take you to one of the tribe's gambling casinos, and there are ice-cream socials, potluck dinners, and other planned activities in the recreation room.

Within one mile, the tribe's Kissimmee Billie Swamp Safari offers airboat rides and swamp buggy eco-tours. Frog legs and alligator-tail nuggets are served at the safari's Swamp Water Cafe. Hunters can track such animals as trophy boars and red stag deer year-round at the tribe's 3,000-acre Big Cypress Hunting Adventures hunting preserve; call 800/689-2378 for reservations. Also nearby is the Ah-Tah-Thi-Ki Museum, which tells the story of the tribe's history and culture.

Campsites, facilities: There are 110 RV campsites and 100 sites for tents. RV sites have concrete pads; 60 have full hookups, and the rest have water and electricity. Facilities include a clubhouse, a pool, miniature golf, basketball courts, shuffleboard, horseshoes, a playground, and a weight room. Showers, restrooms, cabins, and laundry facilities are available. All areas are wheelchair accessible. Children are welcome. Leashed pets are permitted.

Reservations, fees: Reservations are suggested but aren't crucial for tent sites. Sites are $22 per night for two people, plus $5 for each extra person. Major credit cards are accepted. Seasonal rates are available, but no long-term stays are allowed.

Directions: From Fort Lauderdale, take I-75 west to Exit 49, then head north for about 22 miles to the campground. From Naples, take I-75 east for 52 miles to Exit 49, then go north to the campground.

Contact: Big Cypress Campground, HC 61, Box 54-A, Clewiston, FL 33440, 863/983-1330 or 800/437-4102, website: www.seminole tribe.com/campground.

53 KISSIMMEE BILLIE SWAMP SAFARI

🚶 🌊 ⛺

Rating: 6

In the Everglades on Seminole Indian land
Lake Okeechobee map, grid d2, page 426

Today's Seminole Indians sleep in modern houses instead of the thatched-roof chickee huts of yore. But visitors here can get a taste of the past. You won't actually be camping in a traditional sense: Beds surrounded by mosquito netting are provided in these waterfront huts that look like tiny wood cabins with plentiful slatted, screened windows. Still, this qualifies as roughing it for most people because there is no electricity, no air-conditioning, no sink, and no in-hut bathroom. Lanterns provide light. Outside, torches light pathways. In short, campers can imagine time-traveling back to the days when the tribe settled in this remote land to escape federal troops in the Seminole War.

What attracts Miami regulars, foreigners, and the curious to this remote wilderness is the overall experience. Campers can sit around a fire and hear Indian folklore after gliding across the grassy Everglades waters in an airboat. They can kick back on a porch rocking chair at the park's Swamp Water Cafe after trying Indian fry bread and frog legs, or explore the surrounding wilderness by horse. Guided hiking tours are $20 per person. Rides in a swamp buggy—a pickup truck with massive wheels—are $20 for adults, $10 for ages six to 12. At the Gum Slough, panthers, American bison, antelopes, and hogs may be seen. Hunters with at least $285 to spare can take home a hog or other game at the tribe's 3,000-acre Big Cypress Hunting Adventures preserve, accessed here; call 800/689-2378.

Campsites, facilities: Thirty thatched-roof native Indian shelters called "chickees" sleep two people each, and the nine dormitory-style chickees sleep eight to 12 people each. Indian gift shops, a restaurant, guided hiking tours, airboat rides, swamp buggy eco-tours, safari hunting trips, alligator pits, and reptile shows entertain visitors. Showers, restrooms, and laundry facilities are provided. Chickees have no electricity or plumbing. Children are permitted. No pets, please.

Reservations, fees: Reservations are suggested. Two-person chickees are $35 per night; dorm-style chickees are $65 per night. Major credit cards are accepted. Long-term stays are allowed.

Directions: From Fort Lauderdale, take I-75 west to Exit 49. Go north for about 22 miles to the park entrance.

Contact: Kissimmee Billie Swamp Safari, HC 61, Box 46, Clewiston, FL 33440, 863/983-6101 or 800/949-6101, website: www.seminole tribe.com/safari.

Chapter 15

Treasure Coast

Treasure Coast

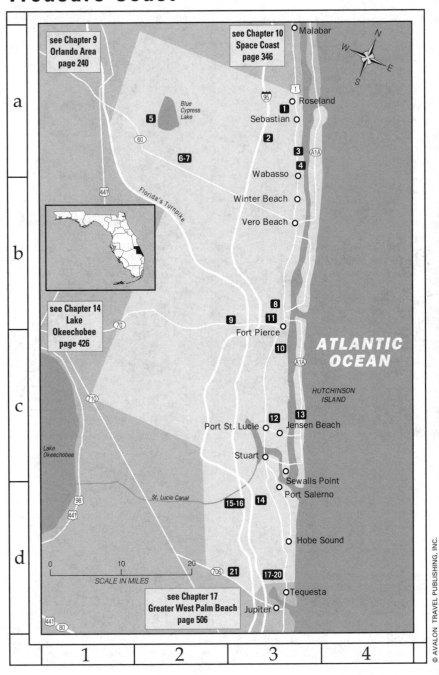

see Chapter 9
Orlando Area
page 240

see Chapter 10
Space Coast
page 346

Malabar

Blue
Cypress
Lake

Roseland

1

Sebastian

2

3

4

Wabasso

Winter Beach

Vero Beach

5

6-7

Florida's Turnpike

see Chapter 14
Lake
Okeechobee
page 426

8

9

11

Fort Pierce

10

ATLANTIC
OCEAN

HUTCHINSON
ISLAND

Lake
Okeechobee

12

13

Port St. Lucie

Jensen Beach

Stuart

Sewalls Point

Port Salerno

St. Lucie Canal

15-16

14

Hobe Sound

0   10   20

SCALE IN MILES

21

17-20

see Chapter 17
Greater West Palm Beach
page 506

Tequesta

Jupiter

© AVALON TRAVEL PUBLISHING, INC.

❶ DONALD MACDONALD PARK

🏃 ⛵ 🚐 🏕 ♿ 🚍 ⛺

Rating: 5

In Roseland

Treasure Coast map, grid a3, page 460

Tall pines, scraggly oaks, sabal palms, and southern red cedars shield the rustic campsites from each other and give a raw, wild flavor to this primitive, heavily wooded, county-run campground located near civilization. Each camping spot does have some shade, a picnic table, and a ground grill. Anglers, canoeists, and boaters use the boat ramp to launch onto the Sebastian River. For a short walk, try the interpretive nature trail and observation boardwalk. The campground is close to the Sebastian Inlet State Park.

Campsites, facilities: There are 28 primitive tent campsites with no hookups and one RV site with electricity. Water faucets are located randomly around the campground. The tent sites can also be used for self-contained RVs. Showers, restrooms, a fire pit, a boat ramp, a short nature trail, and an observation boardwalk are available. Site No. 2 and restrooms are wheelchair accessible. Children are welcome. Pets are permitted.

Reservations, fees: Sites are first-come, first-served and cost $15 per night for tent sites and $20 for the single RV site. Credit cards are not accepted.

Directions: From I-95 at Exit 156, drive east on County Road 512/Fellsmere Road, then turn north (left) on Roseland Road/County Road 505. The entrance is on your left, beyond Dale Wimbrow Park.

Contact: Donald MacDonald Park, 12315 Roseland Road, Roseland, FL 32957, 772/589-0087, website: http://indian-river.fl.us/playing/parks/macdon.html.

❷ ENCORE RV RESORT— VERO BEACH

Rating: 7

Off I-95 north of Vero Beach

Treasure Coast map, grid a3, page 460

This 35-acre RV resort is so civilized that garbage is picked up at your campsite by the concrete-paved road at 10 A.M. daily, and loud radios are forbidden. It's an Encore park, so expect professional landscaping and services. Encore RV Parks are designed for RVers looking to spend one month or longer in a resort community, but overnight travelers also show up at the large sites and plunge into the 22-by-36-foot, kidney-shaped heated pool.

King Palm Drive is the closest to nearby I-95. On the other side of the park is a pine forest. The Los Angeles Dodgers have played spring training baseball games since 1953 eight miles to the south at 4101 26th Street, Vero Beach; for tickets, call 772/569-4900.

Campsites, facilities: All 300 sites have full hookups and cable TV. Some sites are pull-through. For recreation, there's a heated pool, a game room, horseshoes, miniature golf, a playground, shuffleboard, bocce ball (lawn bowling), croquet, table tennis, a lending library, two recreation halls (one with a kitchen), and scheduled winter activities. Showers, restrooms, a general store, picnic tables, rental park models, and laundry facilities are available. Restaurants are nearby. Children are welcome. Leashed pets are permitted.

Reservations, fees: Reservations are advised. Sites are $32 to $38 per night for two people, plus $2 per extra person. Major credit cards are accepted. Long-term stays are OK.

Directions: From I-95 at Exit 156, drive east for one block on County Road 512/Fellsmere Road to the park entrance on your right at 108th Avenue. The park is behind McDonald's.

Contact: Encore RV Resort—Vero Beach, 9455 108th Avenue, Vero Beach, FL 32967, 772/589-7828, fax 772/628-7081. Toll-free: 800/628-7081, website: www.rvonthego.com.

3 WHISPERING PALMS RV PARK

Rating: 5

On U.S. 1 in Wabasso

Treasure Coast map, grid a3, page 460

Retirees escaping frosty northern winters are targeted by this sprawling 35-acre home of not one, but two, heated pools and two recreation rooms, located four miles west of Atlantic Ocean beaches. The sunny, concrete-pad RV sites are outnumbered by the 328 mobile homes. The nicely kept park is set in a sleepy area and is bordered by U.S. 1 and FEC Railroad tracks. Anglers often travel a few miles northeast to the Indian River/Brevard County line to crowd the jetty at the 500-acre Sebastian Inlet State Park.

Campsites, facilities: This adult-oriented park has 250 full-hookup RV sites. A pool, horseshoes, shuffleboard, winter social programs, two recreation rooms, and two tennis courts entertain campers. Showers, restrooms, a dump station, and laundry facilities are available. The pull-through sites are wheelchair accessible. Groceries, snacks, and restaurants are one mile away. Children are allowed for short-term visits only. Leashed pets under 25 pounds are permitted.

Reservations, fees: Reservations are recommended. Sites are $33.50 per night for two people, plus $3 for each additional person. Major credit cards are accepted. Long-term stays are OK.

Directions: From I-95 at Exit 156, drive east for six miles on County State Road 512 to U.S. 1. Turn right and continue 2.1 miles south to the campground.

Contact: Whispering Palms RV Park, 10305 U.S. 1, Sebastian, FL 32958, 772/589-3481.

4 VERO BEACH KAMP

Rating: 6

On U.S. 1 north of Vero Beach

Treasure Coast map, grid a3, page 460

A hair salon, a ceramics shop, and other businesses set a commercial tone for the road that fronts this campground—U.S. 1. Still, the region focuses on its pretty outdoor attributes, with Atlantic Ocean beaches two miles east, a boat ramp on the Indian River .5 mile from the campground, deep-sea fishing at offshore reefs, and shelling and clamming nearby.

Five rows of grassy RV slots line up campers side by side, about 20 sites per row. Tenters sleep farthest from U.S. 1 in the back of the 14-acre campground. Some roads are paved, but others aren't. This woodsy park is bordered to the north and south by orange groves, and about two-thirds of the grounds are shaded by oaks, Australian pines, and sabal palms. You might hear a woodpecker squawk in midafternoon, as we did. The restrooms and laundry are by sites 319, 320, 414, 415, 514, and 515.

Campsites, facilities: These 120 full-hookup RV sites are set apart from a tent camping area. Each site has a picnic table. For recreation, there's a pool, a playground, shuffleboard, winter social programs, and a recreation room. Showers, grills, fire rings, a dump station, cabins, a convenience store, a deli, a gift shop, cable TV, and laundry facilities are available. Restrooms, the office, and activity building are wheelchair accessible. Children are welcome. Leashed, attended pets are permitted.

Reservations, fees: Reservations are required in winter and recommended at other times. Sites are $30 per night for two people, plus $3 for each additional person and $1.75 for cable TV. Major credit cards are accepted. Long-term rates are available.

Directions: From I-95 at Exit 156, drive east for two miles on County Road 512 to County Road 510 and turn right. Continue six miles, following the curve to the left, to U.S. 1. Turn left. The campground is .25 mile ahead, to your right.

Contact: Vero Beach Kamp, 8850 U.S. 1, Sebastian, FL 32958, 772/589-5665 or 877/589-5643, fax 561/388-5722.

5 MIDDLETON'S FISH CAMP

🏕 🎣 🚐 🐕 ♿ 🚙 ⛺

Rating: 4

At Blue Cypress Lake west of Vero Beach

Treasure Coast map, grid a2, page 460

Even though serious anglers try for speckled perch and bass at 6,500-acre Blue Cypress Lake, this wild region holds promise for bird-watchers, wildlife admirers, duck hunters, and anyone who doesn't mind giving up niceties like electric hookups for a night. Some Mid-westerners return to this rustic campground year after year, lured by 80-plus-degree winter temperatures and the call of the outdoors. The primitive camp is surrounded by huge, government-owned lands set aside for wildlife.

At dusk, deer cross the five-mile dirt road that leads to cypress-lined Blue Cypress Lake, which is named for the trees' blue appearance at sunrise. Alert campers may see otters, ea-gles, hawks, alligators, and osprey. Yet, as the name suggests, fishing is the highlight at the only camp on the lake, which is the headwa-ters to the St. Johns River. Fishing guides charge $225 daily or $150 a half day for two people. To go it alone, motorboats start at $35 for four hours. You can also rent pontoon boats and kayaks.

Campsites, facilities: This primitive, county-owned camping area offers approximately 10 RV and 15 tent sites. There are no hookups, but showers, restrooms, a boat ramp, boat and canoe rentals, fishing guides, cabins, and rental trailers are available. Most areas are said to be wheelchair accessible. Children and leashed pets are permitted.

Reservations, fees: Sites are first-come, first-served, and there is no fee. Credit cards are accepted for cabin and boat rentals. The max-imum stay is one week.

Directions: From I-95 at Exit 147, drive west for 18 miles on State Road 60, veering around a bend known as 20 Mile Bend and passing a waterway called Padgett Branch. Signs will in-struct you to turn right at Blue Cypress Lake Road. If you pass a microwave tower on State Road 60, then you've missed the turn to the lake. Follow Blue Cypress Lake Road for five miles to its end to reach the fish camp.

Contact: Middleton's Fish Camp, 21704 73rd Manor, Vero Beach, FL 32966, 772/778-0150.

6 BLUE CYPRESS CONSERVATION AREA

🏕 🎣 🚐 ⛺

Rating: 6

At Blue Cypress Lake west of Fellsmere and Vero Beach

Treasure Coast map, grid a2, page 460

Airboaters thunder through the area in their private craft and duck hunters sleep here in sea-son, but these 52,671 wild acres also hold allure for hikers and bird-watchers. Look for alliga-tors, bald eagles, osprey, long-legged wading birds, and a few of the nation's 500 to 1,000 en-dangered snail kites—dark, hawklike birds with tightly curled, reddish orange beaks that some-times nest in the conservation area's southeastern portion. There are several access points, so be sure to get a map before planning your trip.

Duck Camp is at the southern end of a four-mile-long, diked, man-made lake. From the camp, marshland stretches about one mile west to the angler-haven of Blue Cypress Lake. Watch fiery orange sunsets there. Farther south-east, North Camp abuts marshland that spreads about one mile west to another diked, artifi-cial lake on the west side of County Road 512. Marsh means mosquitoes, so bring repellent or you'll be sorry.

Hikers can follow a network of about 20 miles of foot trails. For a casual stroll, an un-shaded, car-width hiking path runs west from the parking lot off County Road 512. From atop the levee, you'll see a mosaic of wetland communities dominated by maidencane, saw grass, and willows. The trail can be a little mo-notonous, but the occasional unexpected squeaks from coots and the roar of approaching air-boats (usually on weekends) help enliven the walk. A 10-mile-long hiking trail starts at one of several conservation-area parking lots; this one is located on the north side of State Road 60, just west of a short bridge located nine miles west of I-95. The trail goes north along Levee 77, passing a primitive campsite about 2.5 miles down, then west along Levee 76; the last four miles are considered by state staffers to be among the most scenic. You can take a break at two benches before the trail ends at a water control structure. Boating is best at Blue Cypress Lake, which is reached by a ramp west of the lake at Middleton's Fish Camp (see previous campground). You also may fish and paddle your own canoe around a man-made lake that is reachable from the boat ramp just west of County Road 512.

Campsites, facilities: Six primitive camping areas offer no hookups; most require at least a short hike to reach. A boat ramp, restrooms, and canoe launch are at the main access point on the north side of State Road 60 at North Camp. Bring water, sunscreen, insect repellent, bright orange clothing during hunting season, and rain gear from May through September.

Reservations, fees: Sites are first-come, first-served. Camping is free. Each site accommodates up to six people. If your party has at least seven people, get a free permit and reserve at least one week ahead at 386/329-4410. Maximum stay for all campers is seven days.

Directions: To reach the eastern camping area—North Camp—from I-95 (Exit 147), go west on State Road 60, then travel 7.5 miles to County Road 512, where you'll turn right (north). Continue about 3.5 miles, passing a parking area along the way, and turn left into the closest parking area to North Camp. For a map, directions, and other details about campsites, contact the water management district before your trip, or see the website.

Contact: St. Johns River Water Management District, Division of Land Management, P.O. Box 1429, Palatka, FL 32178-1429, 386/329-4500 or 800/451-7106, website: www.sjrwmd.com.

▪ FORT DRUM MARSH CONSERVATION AREA

Rating: 6

10 miles east of Yeehaw Junction and west of Vero Beach between State Road 60 and Florida's Turnpike

Treasure Coast map, grid b3, page 460

Just south of the Blue Cypress Conservation Area you'll find 20,862 acres of mostly marshy, impassable wetlands. You can hike or bike three of the perimeter edges of this square-shaped plot as the trail parallels man-made canals. On the west side, where land is higher and drier than the center section, are a couple of little lakes and the Fort Drum Creek. Horseback riding, bird-watching, and boating are favored activities, but avoid hunting season, when camping is closed. The Florida Trail Association has developed the trails and three primitive campsites.

Campsites, facilities: Tents only are permitted. There are no facilities; bring water, supplies, mosquito repellent, and everything you'll need. Children are welcome. Leashed pets are permitted.

Reservations, fees: Sites are first-come, first-served. Camping is free. Each site accommodates up to six people. If your party has at least seven people, get a free permit and reserve at least one week ahead at 386/329-4410. Maximum stay for all campers is seven days.

Directions: From I-95, take Exit 147 westbound on State Road 60 to the "20 Mile Bend." Pass the intersection with County Road 512 and continue west 10.9 miles to the access area on the north side.

Contact: St. Johns River Water Management District, Division of Land Management, P.O. Box 1429, Palatka, FL 32178-1429, 386/329-4500 or 800/451-7106, website: www.sjrwmd.com.

8 PORT ST. LUCIE RV RESORT

Rating: 7

In Port St. Lucie

Treasure Coast map, grid b3, page 460

Port St. Lucie RV Resort fills a void for campers with large motorhomes and trailers who want to explore the Treasure Coast. Just five miles from the ocean, the park opened in 2000 with a brand-new pool and all new facilities. Within one block are several shopping centers, two groceries, and many restaurants; visitors can access a Wal-Mart behind the park through a side gate.

Campsites, facilities: The park has 117 sites with full hookups, picnic tables, cable TV, optional telephone service, and concrete pads. Four sites are pull-through, and there are no size restrictions. Restrooms, showers, laundry facilities, a pool, and a recreation hall are available. All areas are wheelchair accessible. Children are welcome, but adults are preferred. Leashed pets are permitted.

Reservations, fees: Reservations are recommended. Sites are $30 nightly for two people, plus $2 per extra person. A one-time fee of $2 is charged for pets. Major credit cards are accepted. Seasonal stays are permitted.

Directions: From the intersection of Port St. Lucie Boulevard and U.S. 1, drive north about .5 mile. Turn right on Jennings Road; the park will on your right about 2,000 feet ahead.

Contact: Port St. Lucie RV Resort, 3703 Jennings Road, Port St. Lucie, FL 34952, 772/337-3340 or 877/405-2333 or fax 772/337-7347, website: http://portstlucievresort.com.

9 ROAD RUNNER TRAVEL RESORT

Rating: 6

West of Fort Pierce

Treasure Coast map, grid b3, page 460

This 38-acre blend of citified amenities in a wooded, rural setting lures some people to live here and others to visit. Besides the campground's heated pool and unusual offerings such as a *pétanque* (French-style bowling) court and three recreation halls, owners Jim and Marilyn Minix's park rules aim to satisfy urban sensibilities: Keep your campsite neat. Overnighters should place garbage bags at the paved road in front of their campsite before checking out. Long-term campers should rake lawn debris into a pile in front of their lots to be picked up. Still, the park won't soon be mistaken for a suburban subdivision, if only for its pines and sabal palms. Roads are paved. And how many suburbs boast a fishing pond by a general store? A par-three golf course has recently been completed.

For fun, boaters and anglers can drive five to six miles to Atlantic Ocean beaches, the Indian River, or the St. Lucie Inlet. Back at the campground, the packed winter activities schedule keeps visitors busy. A sample day: 7 A.M. walk, 8 A.M. flea market trip, 9 A.M. exercises, 2 P.M. water exercises, 7 P.M. cards. To sleep beside the park's lake, ask about the sunny, nearly treeless campsites on Lincoln Circle. For a canopy of shade trees, ask about campsites on Madison and Eisenhower Drives (although several other streets have at least some shade). The park is near the small St. Lucie County Airport.

Campsites, facilities: These 452 full-hookup campsites are for RVs and tents. A pool, a tennis court, a *pétanque* court, shuffleboard, horseshoes, winter activities, and three recreation halls keep campers entertained. Showers, restrooms, a restaurant, groceries, a dump station, rental park models, rental villas, the on-site Coyote convenience store, and laundry facilities are available. Most areas are wheelchair accessible. Children under 12 must be adult-supervised at the pool and other public areas. Leashed pets are permitted.

Reservations, fees: Reservations are advised. Sites are $30 per night for two people, plus $2 for each additional person. Major credit cards are accepted. Long-term rates are available.

Directions: From I-95 at Exit 131B, go west on Orange Avenue/State Road 68 a short distance to the first light. Turn right at Kings Highway/State Road 713. Turn right in 2.5 miles at St. Lucie Boulevard. The campground is one mile ahead on your left.

Contact: Road Runner Travel Resort, 5500 St. Lucie Boulevard, Fort Pierce, FL 34946, 772/464-0969 or 800/833-7108, website: www.roadrunnertravelresort.com.

SUNNIER PALMS NUDIST CAMPGROUND

Rating: 5

Off I-95 west of Fort Pierce
Treasure Coast map, grid c3, page 460

A visit to this former KOA may come as a shock to anyone who hasn't plunged into its heated pool lately. Everyone at this 24-acre park is expected to participate in the nudist lifestyle and must be nude in the pool or hot tub. But there is a definite nature orientation, and even activism: The park helped save a rare plant and a butterfly species that lost their habitat to development by allowing the colonies to be moved to the park land. Foot trails lead through a sun-dappled forest of pines and spiky palmettos interspersed with shady oaks. Some campers at this private, flat, fenced park hike or take blankets out to lie naked in the 12 acres or so of woods. The tent area is in a field set aside from the concrete-pad RV sites; some sites are shady, but others are grassy and open. You'll get a taste of both worlds here: The reasonably close highway and fast-food joints are reminders of city life. Yet streetside country mailboxes and neighboring orange groves lend a rural feel to the park.

Campsites, facilities: This nudist resort has 50 full-hookup sites and 12 spots with water and electricity for RVs. Perhaps 100 tents can be accommodated in a field. A pool, a hot tub, organic gardening, nature trails, a playground, and a butterfly exhibit entertain campers. A certain amount of decorum is expected: "Your behavior is your passport." Part of the park is a 12-acre nature sanctuary. Showers, restrooms, a dump station, a grocery store, rental villas, and laundry facilities are available. A restaurant is within two miles. Children are welcome. Pets are prohibited.

Reservations, fees: Reservations are necessary in winter. Sites are $29 to $39 per night, plus $11 per extra adult. Credit cards are not accepted. Long-term stays are permitted.

Directions: From I-95 at Exit 129, drive west on Okeechobee Road/State Road 70 for about 1.5 miles to the campground. The park is one mile west of Florida's Turnpike (Exit 152).

Contact: Sunnier Palms Nudist Campground, 8800 Okeechobee Road, Fort Pierce, FL 34945, 772/468-8512, website: www.sunnier.com.

⓫ OUTDOOR RESORTS AT ST. LUCIE WEST

Rating: 10

West of Port St. Lucie between I-95 and Florida's Turnpike
Treasure Coast map, grid b3, page 460

This brand-new resort is for Class A Motorhomes 25 feet or longer—which gives you an expectation of the kinds of amenities to expect: several swimming pools, lighted tennis courts, golf course, and deluxe paved sites on which to park that expensive rig. It's three miles from the famous PGA Golf Club, but already has nine holes of its own on site. When fully built out, the resort will have 510 sites (many for ownership), five swimming pools, four tennis courts, 18 holes of golf, a fitness center and owner's lounge, and more.

Campsites, facilities: There are 259 campsites completed so far, each with cement pads, picnic tables, full hookups, telephone and cable TV. By early 2003, three pools were open, as were two lighted tennis courts, a nine-hole golf course, and a large clubhouse. Security and on-site staff are available 24 hours. Restrooms, showers, a dump station, a dog-walk area, and laundry facilities are also provided. Most areas are wheelchair accessible. Children are welcome. Leashed pets are permitted.

Reservations, fees: Reservations are recommended. Sites are $39 to $49 per night for two people, plus $5 per extra person. Major credit cards are accepted. Long-term rates are available.

Directions: From I-95, take Exit 121 onto St. Lucie West Boulevard in an eastbound direction. Drive .3 mile, and turn left on Northwest Peacock Boulevard. Continue 1.3 miles to the park entrance on the left. From Florida's Turnpike, take Exit 152 at Fort Pierce. Follow the signs to I-95 and proceed with the directions above.

Contact: Outdoor Resorts at St. Lucie West, 800 Northwest Peacock Boulevard, Port St. Lucie, FL 34986, 772/336-1136, fax 772/336-1193, website: www.outdoor-resorts.com.

12 THE SAVANNAS RECREATIONAL AREA

Rating: 5

East of U.S. 1 in southeastern Fort Pierce
Treasure Coast map, grid c3, page 460

Some people rave about the rustic Savannas, a 550-acre county park/camping getaway where boaters snag bass and visitors lazily paddle rental canoes. Inside the gate, in day-use area No. 2, you can eat a picnic lunch, then walk along the Everglades-like marsh on a hiking trail shaded by shaggy Australian pines. The trail leads to a sort of makeshift observation tower, where you can peer out over the saw grass and cattails. You'll hear frogs croaking—after all, this is a wild retreat. Rent a canoe for $4 hourly for an up-close view of the marsh.

Although the park is large, it feels fairly small if you don't head out into the marsh. The limited dry land is hemmed in by the watery prairie. Expect to see neighboring RVs and tents from your no-frills, grassy campsite. To help minimize that, spring for a waterview site.

County promoters say the Savannas is Florida's last freshwater lagoon system. The preserve actually extends outside this campground to take in about eight square miles of marsh and uplands between White City Road/State Road 172 and Jensen Beach Boulevard/State Road 707A. From the campground, Atlantic Ocean beaches are nine miles east, for those who want to swim or sunbathe.

Campsites, facilities: There are 33 campsites for RVs and 13 for tents. All sites have water, and some have full hookups. Canoe rentals, nature trails, a playground, a dump station, showers, restrooms, a boat ramp, a picnic shelter, and laundry facilities are available. Groceries can be purchased within two miles. A restaurant is within 10 miles. Children are welcome. Leashed dogs are permitted.

Reservations, fees: Reservations are accepted. Sites are $13 to $20 per night for four people, plus $1 to $2 for each extra person. There is an additional admission fee of $1 per car. Credit cards are accepted. RVers can stay as long as two months; for tenters, the stay is limited to a maximum of 14 consecutive days.

Directions: From I-95 at Exit 131A, drive east for about four miles on Orange Avenue/State Road 68. Turn right (south) at South Fourth Street/U.S. 1. Continue almost five miles to Midway Road/County Road 712. Turn left and proceed east to the park entrance, about 1.5 miles ahead.

Contact: The Savannas Recreational Area, 1400 East Midway Road, Fort Pierce, FL 34982, 772/464-7855 or 800/789-5776, fax 772/464-1765, website: www.stlucieco.gov/leisure/savanna.htm.

13 THE VILLAGE AT NETTLES ISLAND

Rating: 7

On the Atlantic Ocean on Hutchinson Island
Treasure Coast map, grid c3, page 460

This 130-acre, ocean-to-river island resort feels

like a residential community. Before you pull into the concrete driveway beside your RV site and personal patio, you'll follow paved roads that pass park models with attached Florida rooms, lots with docks on the Intracoastal Waterway, and maybe even a retirement-ready, double-wide mobile home with a front porch and garden. Tents, of course, are not allowed. It seems like every square inch of this sun-washed barrier island is covered with villas, RVs, and park models, although roads and green ribbons of lawn separate sleeping spots. At the resort's center is its hub of activity—a clubhouse, a pool, and sports courts. From the marina (bring your own boat), you can embark on a day of boating or fishing in the Intracoastal Waterway, the Atlantic Ocean, or the Indian River Lagoon.

The Intracoastal Waterway stretches one mile from the wee backyards of western waterfront lots. RV sites are scattered throughout this barrier island off Florida's Treasure Coast. Although the island technically has 1,578 sites, only 50 to 125 at any given time may be open to campers who bring their own rigs. The other sites here at this condominium-concept park largely are devoted to vacation rentals. February is the busiest time of the year, so call early if that's when you'll be coming.

Campsites, facilities: All 1,578 sites have full hookups, but only 50 or so are available at any given time for short-term stays. For recreation, there's a pool, miniature golf, a clubhouse, horseshoes, a playground, tennis, shuffleboard, and volleyball. Showers, restrooms, a café, a dump station, a grocery store, cable TV, park models, a marina, and laundry facilities are available. Children are permitted. Leashed pets are allowed on park streets and in a dog walk in front.

Reservations, fees: Reservations are advised. Sites are $31 to $47 per night, plus $2 for electricity. Major credit cards are accepted. Long-term stays are OK.

Directions: From Stuart, drive north on Highway A1A/Ocean Drive to Hutchinson Island

past the county line. Nettles Island is located just ahead, on the left side of the road.

Contact: VNI Realty, 9803 South Ocean Drive, Jensen Beach, FL 34957, 772/229-1300, website: www.vnirealty.com.

14 SOUTH FORK ST. LUCIE RIVER MANAGEMENT AREA

Rating: 6

West of Stuart

Treasure Coast map, grid b3, page 460

Here's a nice new spot near urban South Florida, but it's only accessible by canoe or on foot. Eventually, these 180 acres may become part of the planned Atlantic Ridge State Park, but until public road access issues are resolved through a neighboring residential area, you'll have to get here under your own steam. A canoe and kayak livery (South River Outfitters) is located near the highway, but the campground and official trailhead are 20 miles south, and there are no public roads to this particular spot. You will need a permit from the South Florida Water Management District to sleep at the campsite. The canoe and kayak livery offers guided trips, as well as boat rentals.

Campsites, facilities: Campsites accommodate 20 persons at a canoe landing at the sound end of the tract. Tents only are permitted. There are no facilities; bring water, supplies, mosquito repellent, and everything you'll need. Children are welcome. Leashed pets are permitted.

Reservations, fees: Permits are required. Contact the water management district by phone at 561/682-6635 or 561/682-6649, or download the application from the website. Camping is free.

Directions: From I-95, take Exit 101 eastbound .25 mile on State Road 76/Kanner Highway. Turn south on Lost River Road. You'll immediately see South River Outfitters located opposite the Wendy's Restaurant. Do not keep driving toward the Halpatiokee Regional Park, which is a Martin County-operated day-use area for baseball, skating, and soccer.

Contact: For camping permits, contact the South Florida Water Management District, 3301 Gun Club Road, West Palm Beach, FL 33406, 561/686-8800 or 800/432-2045 (toll-free in Florida), website: www.sfwmd.gov. For boat launching or rentals, contact South River Outfitters, 7645 Lost River Road, Stuart, FL 34996, 772/223-1500.

15 PHIPPS PARK

Rating: 4

On the St. Lucie Canal west of Stuart
Treasure Coast map, grid d3, page 460

This 57-acre, grassy, county-operated park on the St. Lucie Canal has huge spaces and lots of room for big rigs on its grassy camping spots. Shade comes from palm trees and native scrub, so the sunniness depends on the time of day. Boats under 20 feet can launch from Phipps Park, whereas campers with bigger boats should opt for the nearby St. Lucie Lock and Dam. Feel free to keep your boat at your site. Locals and out-of-towners alike camp at the park, which is on the saltwater side of the St. Lucie Lock and Dam. Anglers take boats out to try for snook and bass. The park restrooms are not real modern, but there's lots of room for everyone in the park and you won't feel crowded, even in the high winter season. A locked gate nightly and on-site manager provides a feel of security.

Campsites, facilities: The 43 officially numbered campsites and open field of about 17 overflow sites are for RVs or tents, but no hookups are offered. Each site has a picnic table, a grill, and a fire ring. A playground, a nearby boat launch, showers, a dump station, and wheelchair-accessible restrooms are available. Restaurants, laundry facilities, a bank, and a supermarket are five or six miles away. Children are welcome. Pets are forbidden.

Reservations, fees: Reservations are not ac-

cepted. Sites are $6 per night. Martin County residents pay half price. Credit cards are not accepted. You may stay up to 30 days per year.

Directions: From I-95, take Exit 101 and go west on State Road 76. Pass Florida's Turnpike. Turn right at Locks Road. Proceed one mile to the park entrance at right.

Contact: Phipps Park, 2175 Southwest Locks Road, Stuart, FL 34997, 772/287-6565.

16 ST. LUCIE LOCK RECREATION AREA

Rating: 8

On the St. Lucie Canal west of Stuart
Treasure Coast map, grid d3, page 460

This 154-acre area run by the U.S. Army Corps of Engineers combines the opportunity to commune with nature and marvel at the ingenuity of the human mind. The drama of standing above the massive lock system and watching boats travel beneath your feet is one attraction of this restful, sunny spot on the St. Lucie Canal. Daytime picnickers and campers alike stop to watch the action. As boats spend 15 to 20 minutes passing through the lock, the curious look downward to read the home ports on the boat transoms to get an idea of just how far the vessels have traveled. It's an awesome sight to behold. A one-mile nature trail is available for hikers on the north side of the lock/dam with an observation area overlooking Hog Creek. You may spot alligators and gopher tortoises near the trail and on Killingbeck Island. To the east of the campground is a 2,500-square-foot visitor center with a free lending library, a movie, and exhibits on the Okeechobee Waterway.

If you're lucky enough to snag one of the three waterfront RV sites, you may warm your bones in the sunshine, at least in winter. In summer, a nice breeze normally wafts from the canal. The three grassy canal-view tent sites sit just beyond the RVs, with shaded picnic tables and fences around them. Tall Australian pines provide some shade for the remaining concrete-pad RV sites. Meanwhile, boaters can motor up to this camping area and sleep aboard their vessels at the eight boat campsites. Anglers can launch from the camping area to go up the canal for bass. Others catch mullet and catfish from the lock's pier. Tip: Cross the lock if you want to try for snook. This campground is another example of the U.S. Army Corps of Engineers' taste for precision, from its immaculate sites to its attention to detail.

Campsites, facilities: Eight boat campsites, eight RV sites with electricity and water hookups, and three tent sites are offered. Each site has a picnic table, a grill, and a fire ring. A playground, a boat ramp, showers, a dump station, and wheelchair-accessible restrooms are available. A convenience store and a deli are two miles away; a laundry and a supermarket are six miles away. Children are welcome. Leashed pets are permitted.

Reservations, fees: Reservations are accepted. Tent sites are $12 per night; RVers and boaters pay $16. Major credit cards are accepted. You may stay 14 days in a 30-day period. If you're lucky and plan ahead, you can get a free campsite in exchange for 24 to 30 hours weekly volunteer service; these opportunities are naturally limited during the popular winter months.

Directions: From I-95, take Exit 101 and go west on State Road 76. Pass Florida's Turnpike. Turn right at Locks Road. Continue 1.5 miles to the end of the road, then turn left at Canal Street and proceed to the campground.

Contact: St. Lucie Lock Recreation Area, 2170 Southwest Canal Street, Stuart, FL 34997, 772/219-4575. For reservations, call 877/444-6777 or see www.reserveusa.com/nrrs/fl/stlu/stlu.htm.

17 JONATHAN DICKINSON STATE PARK

Rating: 10

Near the Atlantic Ocean in Hobe Sound
Treasure Coast map, grid d3, page 460

This place is excellent for a family outing be-cause something will please almost everyone in your party. You can hike to the top of piney hills and, if you stand and look toward the Indian River in the distance, imagine how these were once huge sand dunes at the edge of Florida, eons ago when the oceans were much deeper. Much of the hiking here is easy, level, and suited to a day excursion with the kids. Horseback riding is popular, as is canoeing in the Loxahatchee River, fishing, nature study, and side trips to nearby beaches. Mountain biking trails complete the picture; ask about "Camp Murphy." You're likely to see deer, Florida sandhill cranes, wading birds, and other wild animals throughout the park.

The park is named for a Quaker merchant who shipwrecked nearby in 1696. But probably the most colorful of the historic figures is a 20th-century addition to the local lore known as Trapper Nelson. We highly recommend taking a canoe or narrated riverboat tour up to the site of Trapper Nelson's old camp on the Loxahatchee River. Nelson was a hermit who came to live on the banks of the beautiful Loxahatchee during the Great Depression, eking out an existence by trapping animals for their fur. Before dying under mysterious circumstances more than three decades later, he built a small zoo at his place and added to his living by charging tourists who were passing by on the river a fee to see the menagerie. After his death the site was preserved, complete with the animal pens, his cabin, a Seminole-style "chickee" shelter, and exotic trees, including wild almond, bamboo, sausage tree, guava, and java plum.

If you're handy with a canoe or kayak, try an all-day paddle down the Loxahatchee, which is designated by the federal government as the only Wild and Scenic River in this part of the state. From the spot where Indiantown Road crosses the Loxahatchee, you'll paddle seaward, past dark, brooding cypress forests to where the freshwater turns salty and mangroves appear on the banks. Some parts of the trip are achingly beautiful and serene, although you will pass underneath I-95 and Florida's Turnpike at one point. You're virtually certain to see alligators (in fact, one of the few documented cases of an alligator attacking a human occurred here a few years ago when an old, sick gator attacked and killed a young boy). If you're lucky, you might even see a manatee, that lumbering but lovable endangered mammal also known as the sea cow. Bald eagles, once endangered but now on the upswing, also are sighted sometimes, along with the hawk-like osprey. The park rents canoes, but the area's most popular canoe livery is Canoe Outfitters of Florida, which charges $50 for three people in a canoe and $40 for a kayak, with shuttle service; call 772/746-7053.

Fishing is good, both in the Loxahatchee River and the nearby Indian River. Redfish, trout, and snook are among the favored game fish. Some anglers prefer surfcasting in the nearby Atlantic Ocean for whiting, pompano, and jack, while other members of the family sunbathe.

Also consider two other side trips: At the Jupiter Lighthouse and Museum, a short drive away, you can learn how Confederate soldiers captured the light and doused it—without firing a shot—to aid ships running the Yankee blockade. Also, don't miss a trip to Blowing Rocks Preserve, where water jets up through blowholes in an intriguing rock formation in what's known as Anastasia limestone. The wave action has worn the relatively soft stone into fascinating and beautiful shapes. At high tide, watch water spout through the blowholes. At low tide, explore the caves and tidal pools. It's within a 30-minute drive. Guided nature walks are offered Thursday at 2 P.M. and Sunday at 11 A.M. Call 772/747-3113.

Campsites, facilities: All 135 RV and tent sites have water and electric hookups. Boat tours, canoe rentals, a playground, horseback-riding trails, four nature trails, and a bicycling trail entertain campers. Showers, a boat ramp, limited groceries, and rental cabins are available. About two miles away are restaurants, bait, and laundry facilities. Some areas of the park are wheelchair accessible. Children are welcome. One pet is permitted in the campground with proof of vaccination.

Reservations, fees: Reservations are recommended; call ReserveAmerica at 800/326-3521. Sites are $17 per night for four people arriving in one vehicle, plus $2 for each additional person. Use of electricity costs $2. If no campsites are available, people with self-contained rigs can arrange to stay one night for an $8 parking fee. Major credit cards are accepted. The maximum stay is 14 nights.

Directions: From I-95, take Exit 87A and go east on State Road 706. Turn left at U.S. 1. Look for the park entrance on the left.

Contact: Jonathan Dickinson State Park, 16450 Southeast Federal Highway, Hobe Sound, FL 33455, 772/546-2771.

18 KITCHING CREEK BACKCOUNTRY SITE

Rating: 9

In Jonathan Dickinson State Park

Treasure Coast map, grid d3, page 460

This primitive campground on the Florida National Scenic Trail is great if you want to get away from all the trappings of modern society, but there is a price to pay—you have to hike approximately 9.5 miles from the trailhead. The first third or so runs through the ancient beach dunes that once protected this part of Florida from the Atlantic Ocean, back when the earth was warmer and the seas much higher than today. Now you'll find stunted scrub oaks and pines along these ridges, which will make the early going a little difficult if you're used to Florida flatlands. After about three miles, though, the trail flattens out into the pine woods that mark many a Florida backcountry site and provide the setting for this campground. You'll recognize the place because there's a fire ring on the ground.

You have to show up at least 3.5 hours before sundown, but we recommend a much earlier start, even if you're a fast hiker. That headstart will ensure that you'll get here before others do, particularly on fall and winter weekends. Kitching Creek itself is a fairly small freshwater stream at this point. It's way upstream of the Loxahatchee River, but dedicated freshwater anglers may want to try their luck for fish.

Campsites, facilities: No more than eight backpackers may share these three primitive campsites. There is a pit toilet. Water is available, but you'll have to treat it before drinking. You must bring everything you'll need, including extra water, food, mosquito repellent, camping supplies, and bags to pack out trash. Human waste must be packed out as well. Children are welcome. Pets are prohibited.

Reservations, fees: Reservations are not accepted. Campsites are claimed on a first-come, first-served basis at the park entrance station. Fees are $3 per night per adult and $2 per child. Major credit cards are accepted.

Directions: From I-95, take Exit 87A and go east on State Road 706. Turn left at U.S. 1. Look for the park entrance on the left.

Contact: Jonathan Dickinson State Park, 16450 Southeast Federal Highway, Hobe Sound, FL 33455, 772/546-2771.

19 SCRUB JAY BACKCOUNTRY SITE

Rating: 9

In Jonathan Dickinson State Park
Treasure Coast map, grid d3, page 460

Of the two backcountry sites reserved for hikers at one of Florida's loveliest state parks, this is the closest to the trailhead. Show up by the mandated deadline of 2 P.M. (preferably much earlier) to begin your 5.6-mile hike. You'll make your way through about three miles of gently rolling ancient beach dunes that are now covered by stunted scrub oaks and pine trees. Go another two miles or so through pine flatwoods to reach the campsite. It's on the same trail as the Kitching Creek site in this chapter.

Campsites, facilities: No more than eight backpackers may share these three primitive campsites. There are no facilities. Water is available, but you'll have to treat it before drinking. You must bring everything you'll need, including extra water, food, mosquito repellent, camping supplies, and bags to pack out trash. Human waste must be packed out as well. Children are welcome. Pets are prohibited.

Reservations, fees: Reservations are not accepted. Campsites are claimed on a first-come, first-served basis at the park entrance station. Fees are $3 per night per adult and $2 per child. Major credit cards are accepted.

Directions: From I-95, take Exit 87A and go east on State Road 706. Turn left at U.S. 1. Look for the park entrance on the left.

Contact: Jonathan Dickinson State Park, 16450 Southeast Federal Highway, Hobe Sound, FL 33455, 772/546-2771.

20 EAGLE VIEW EQUESTRIAN SITE

Rating: 8

In Jonathan Dickinson State Park
Treasure Coast map, grid d3, page 460

Here is a site designed specifically for people with horses. At one time there was an old stable house, a remnant of the time when this land was privately owned. Bring some kind of portable fencing to keep your horses contained, although using a system of ground stakes is permissible. The land is part of a multiuse area studded with sable palmettos, wax myrtles, and tall pines. Some pockets will get muddy at wetter times of the year.

Campsites, facilities: Three equestrian campsites accommodate up to three parties. No facilities are provided except for fire rings and picnic tables. You must bring everything you'll need, including water, food, mosquito repellent, camping gear, and bags to pack out trash. RVs should be self-contained; there are no toilets. Children are welcome. Pets are prohibited.

Reservations, fees: Call ahead to make arrangements to bring your horse. Fees are $3 per night per adult and $2 per child; additional fees are required for horses. Major credit cards are accepted.

Directions: From I-95, take Exit 87A and go east on State Road 706. Turn left at U.S. 1. Look for the park entrance on the left.

Contact: Jonathan Dickinson State Park, 16450 Southeast Federal Highway, Hobe Sound, FL 33455, 772/546-2771.

21 WEST JUPITER WETLANDS MANAGEMENT AREA

Rating: 2

West of Jupiter

Treasure Coast map, grid b3, page 460

Part of the state's continuing Save Our Rivers (SOR) program of purchasing and preserving wetlands, this 1,922-acre tract provides hiking and canoeing within easy distance of the urban areas of Palm Beach and Martin counties. You can camp anywhere along the south side of the canal that crosses this rectangular-shaped property (but not elsewhere). You are allowed to canoe in the interior ponds, but not in the canal. Swimming and boating are prohibited. Eventually, this area (sometimes known as Pal Mar) may be developed and opened to hunting.

Campsites, facilities: There are no facilities, and this area is accessible only on foot from designated access points on State Road 706 (Indiantown Road). Bring water, food, and everything you need. Children are welcome. Leashed pets are permitted.

Reservations, fees: Permits are required. Contact the water management district by phone at 561/682-6635 or 561/682-6649, or download the application from the website. Camping is free.

Directions: From I-95, drive west from Exit 87A on State Road 706. After the intersection with State Road 711, continue west about two miles. The management area is on your right. If you reach State Road 710, you're gone too far.

Contact: For camping permits, contact the South Florida Water Management District, 3301 Gun Club Road, West Palm Beach, FL 33406, 561/686-8800 or 800/432-2045 (toll-free in Florida), website: www.sfwmd.gov.

Chapter 16

Fort Myers/Naples Area

Fort Myers/Naples Area

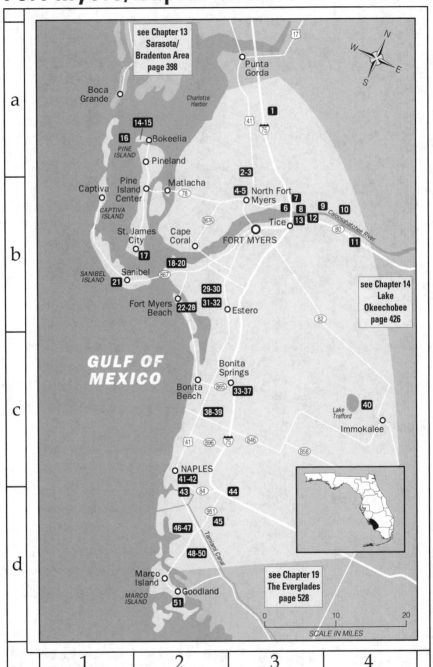

1 FRED C. BABCOCK/ CECIL M. WEBB WILDLIFE MANAGEMENT AREA

Rating: 8

Overlooking Webb Lake

Fort Myers/Naples map, grid a3, page 476

Hunters from as far away as Jacksonville show up to participate in the frenetic nine-day deer and three-day hog hunts, taking home 65 deer and 139 hogs one recent winter. But this 103-square-mile pine-dotted wilderness is better known among locals for its quail hunting, with about 2,500 birds snagged yearly. Regulars also fish for the bluegill, catfish, and bass that are stocked in the 5.25-mile-long lake, or ride their horses or mountain bikes through the mostly sunny wilderness (all-terrain vehicles are prohibited). There are no official campsites—just head to Loop A or Loop B on the west side of Webb Lake to stake out your own primitive spot. A thicker stand of pines shades the camping area than elsewhere. Hikers won't find official trails and instead walk along the many elevated or unimproved roads that slice the landscape; wear orange during hunting season. After hunting season, only about 15,000 acres of the wildlife management area are freely accessible, but you may climb fences to continue walking or riding a bike around the entire 65,770 acres during open hours after hunting season.

Campsites, facilities: Forty-one tents, trailers, or self-propelled campers can be accommodated at this primitive camping area daily during the hunting season, which generally runs from mid-October through mid-January. At other times, camping is permitted from 5 P.M. Fridays to 9 P.M. Sundays, and on Memorial Day, Independence Day, Martin Luther King Day, and Labor Day. There are no hookups and no piped water, so bring all the water you'll need. A portable toilet is available during hunting season only; bury human waste six inches deep at other times. Small campfires are per-

mitted, as long as you ring your fire with rocks. A boat ramp and a lake for fishing are available. Children are welcome. Dogs should be caged or leashed in the camping area.

Reservations, fees: Camping is first-come, first-served. If you are not hunting, a recreational use permit is $3 daily per person or $6 per carload; keep it in your possession. Alternatively, camping is free if you buy a $27 annual hunting permit (also known as a wildlife management area stamp) at any county tax collector's office around Florida or from the sporting goods department at stores such as Wal-Mart and Kmart. You can also order a license by phone by calling 888/347-4356 (fishing) or 888/486-8356 (hunting).

Directions: From I-75, take Exit 158 and drive east for .5 mile on Tuckers Grade to the entrance on the right.

Contact: Fred C. Babcock/Cecil M. Webb Wildlife Management Area, 239/575-5768. Alternatively, Florida Fish & Wildlife Conservation Commission, 863/648-3203.

2 TAMIAMI RV PARK

Rating: 3

North of Fort Myers

Fort Myers/Naples map, grid a3, page 476

Across the street from this sun-drenched park is the Shell Factory, a 70,000-square-foot store that claims to have the largest collection of seashells and coral in the world (for sale, of course). Next door is an enormous mobile home community (a sister park, Tamiami Village, with 700 sites) and a barber shop. Speaking of shells, it's illegal to collect live shells from the beach; those are the ones with the little critters still inside them. When you find an empty one, try soaking it in a bucket of water with bleach to remove algae and make it look nearly as perfect as those for sale at the Shell Factory. Another method for cleaning shells is to leave them outside in the Florida rain and sun for a few days.

Campsites, facilities: This park has a total of 241 full-hookup RV sites with cable TV and telephone service available. About half are taken by visitors who stay six months and then store their trailers, and 15 are permanent residents. The rest are available for shorter-term campers. Restrooms, showers, laundry facilities, shuffleboard courts, a recreation hall, a pool, horseshoe pits, and two pool tables are on site. The restrooms, laundry room, and recreation hall are wheelchair accessible. Children are welcome for short visits. One small pet under 25 pounds is allowed.

Reservations, fees: Reservations are recommended. Sites are $20 to $24 per night for two people, plus $3 for each additional person. Credit cards are not accepted. Long-term stays are OK.

Directions: From I-75, take Exit 143 westbound on State Road 78 eight miles to new U.S. 41. Turn north at Cleveland Avenue and drive two miles. Don't be fooled into turning north on Business Route 41, one mile before you reach new U.S. 41.

Contact: Tamiami RV Park, 16555 North Cleveland Avenue, North Fort Myers, FL 33903, 239/995-7747, 239/997-2697, or 888/609-9697, website: www.tamiamirvpark.com.

3 GARDEN RV PARK

Rating: 2

Near North Fort Myers

Fort Myers/Naples map, grid a3, page 476

Quiet and well-tended, this park draws mostly retirees. It's one mile from the Shell Factory and near other attractions. Card games, weekly bingo, and potluck suppers provide action during the winter. Maximum length of stay? "Forever."

Campsites, facilities: This adults-only park has 34 full-hookup RV sites for rigs as long as 48 feet (12 pull-through). Restrooms, showers, picnic tables, a dump station, a recreation room, shuffleboard courts, and laundry facilities are

on the premises. All areas are wheelchair accessible. Children are not permitted. Small, well-behaved pets are OK.

Reservations, fees: Reservations are required. Sites are $20 per night for two people, plus $3 for each additional person. Credit cards are not accepted. Long-term visitors and small, well-behaved pets are welcome.

Directions: From I-75, take Exit 158 and drive 10 miles west to U.S. 41. Turn south and drive .5 mile to Laurel Drive. Turn east and go .5 mile to Garden Street, then head north to the park.

Contact: Garden RV Park, 2830 Garden Street, North Fort Myers, FL 33917, 239/995-7417, fax 239/995-1481.

4 SWAN LAKE VILLAGE & RV RESORT

Rating: 5

In North Fort Myers

Fort Myers/Naples map, grid b3, page 476

Snowbirds who patronize this park are so devoted that one woman even wrote a poem about the place. What sets Swan Lake apart is that, unlike many campgrounds married to a mobile home park, here the RV area is removed from highway noise and separate from the manufactured homes. It even has its own clubhouse with an adjacent pool. Slash pines and palm trees shade the 60-acre park, which has two fishing lakes and a citrus grove. Shopping, the Shell Factory, and Fort Myers attractions are close by. Fort Myers is a popular vacation spot for many reasons: broad, sugar-white beaches, abundant fishing in both saltwater and on rivers, undeveloped barrier islands where nature still reigns, and wildlife ranging from the endangered manatee to all manner of wading birds.

Campsites, facilities: This 156-unit mobile home community has an attached RV park with 104 full-hookup sites that accommodate RVs up to 40 feet long, plus six tent sites. Each site has a picnic table. Restrooms, showers, laundry facilities, a pool, a clubhouse, two lakes, a recreation room, horseshoes, shuffleboard, daily wintertime activities, and an open field (where some campers hit golf balls) are available. For cable TV and telephone service, you must call the proper utility. A supermarket is one mile away. Adults over 50 are preferred; children are not permitted. Leashed pets that weigh under 20 pounds are permitted, and you can walk your dog in a special pooches area.

Reservations, fees: Reservations are recommended. Sites are $22 per night for two people, plus $3 per extra person. Credit cards are not accepted. Long-term stays are OK.

Directions: Take I-75 to Exit 143 and go west on State Road 78 for 5.2 miles to Business Route 41. Turn north (right) and drive a little over one mile to the park, at right.

Contact: Swan Lake Village & RV Resort, 2400 North Tamiami Trail, North Fort Myers, FL 33903, 239/995-3397, fax 239/995-7879, website: www.swanlakevillage.com.

5 SWIFT'S TRAILER PARK
Rating: 2

In North Fort Myers

Fort Myers/Naples map, grid b3, page 476

This wooded, quiet, and friendly seven-acre park is near the Caloosahatchee River and other attractions, public swimming pools, a library, and shopping. Indeed, a shopping center at the south side of the park offers a video-rental shop, a post office, a grocery store, a restaurant, and a credit union, while another shopping center is two blocks away on the west side of Business Route 41. Board game tournaments, coffee klatches, craft nights, and monthly potluck dinners are held during winter.

Campsites, facilities: This adult-oriented park has 38 full-hookup sites, about 20 of which are available to travelers. Additionally, there are 45 mobile homes in the park. Restrooms, showers, two shuffleboard courts, a small laundry room, and a recreation room with a pool table are provided. For telephone service, you must

call the phone company. Campers must be 55 and older. Leashed pets are permitted only for short-term camping in the RVs.

Reservations, fees: Sites typically are first-come, first-served, but reservations may be accepted if you plan to stay at least three months. Fee is $22 per night for two people, plus $1 per extra person. Credit cards are not accepted. Long-term stays are OK.

Directions: From I-75, take Exit 143 and go west on State Road 78 for 5.5 miles, then north on Business Route 41 for one block. At Powell Drive, turn right. The park is less than one block ahead.

Contact: Swift's Trailer Park, 1846 Powell Drive, Lot 44, North Fort Myers, FL 33917, 239/997-4636, fax 239/997-2305.

6 SUNBURST RV PARK— NORTH FORT MYERS (FORMERLY PIONEER VILLAGE)
Rating: 7

In North Fort Myers

Fort Myers/Naples map, grid b3, page 476

RVers may not want to leave if they stay overnight in this 80-acre deluxe snowbird resort, where more than half the sites go to visitors who stay for the season. It's plenty close to the local attractions, but so many sports facilities and other activities are available on site that you may want to stay a month or more. Under the direction of an activities director during the high season from November 15 through April 15, residents can compete in tennis, horseshoe, and shuffleboard tournaments, and the recreation hall is Action Central for arts-and-crafts classes, bingo, card games, square dancing, quilting, ice-cream socials, and potluck dinners. A few mature oaks shade some sites, but many spots are sunny. Not too far away is the Edison Winter Home and Laboratory (239/334-3614), where inventor Thomas A. Edison, who gave us, among other things, the light bulb and the phonograph, spent his winters.

Next door is the home of auto magnate Henry Ford, which is also open to the public and reached at the same phone number. Six-Mile Cypress Slough Preserve (239/432-2004) is a 2,000-acre wetland northeast of Fort Myers. It features a self-guided nature boardwalk and an opportunity to see alligators in the wild.

Campsites, facilities: This community has 470 RV sites (no size restrictions, and most are pull-through) with full hookups; 200 are available for overnighters, along with 20 tent sites. A heated, oversized swimming pool with whirlpool and cabana, an 8,700-square-foot clubhouse, and a putting and chipping green are available. Volleyball, billiards, tennis, shuffleboard, basketball, horseshoes, a library, laundry facilities, showers, and restrooms also are on the premises. The park is oriented to active retirees, but families with children are permitted for short-term stays. Leashed animals are permitted, and there's a dog-walk area.

Reservations, fees: Reservations are recommended. Sites are $30 and up per night for two people, plus $2.50 for each extra person. Major credit cards are accepted. Long-term stays are the norm.

Directions: From I-75, take Exit 143 westbound on Bayshore Road for one mile. At Samville Road, turn south and go .2 mile.

Contact: Sunburst RV Park—North Fort Myers, 7974 Samville Road, North Fort Myers, FL 33917, 239/543-3303 or 877/897-2757, fax 239/543-3498, website: www.rvonthego.com.

7 SEMINOLE CAMPGROUND

Rating: 1

Near North Fort Myers
Fort Myers/Naples map, grid b3, page 476
Set on 20 shaded acres, this wooded, rustic campground is near the interstate, which is convenient for overnighters. A small creek runs through the campground, and the thick woods are beautiful. Tents are set apart from the RVs, and you may request an adults-only or family-

only area. Take a look around before you decide. The clientele varies; one day, you may see a tenter with a full-sized refrigerator in front of his site, whereas on other days, you may see vacationers. Beaches are 30 minutes away.

Campsites, facilities: The park has 129 RV sites and 10 spots set apart for tents. RV sites have full hookups, satellite cable TV, and telephone availability. Tenters have a community water source but no electricity. Restrooms, showers, picnic tables, a dump station, a pool, a playground, a game room, laundry facilities, and rental trailers are on site. Children are welcome, but not pets.

Reservations, fees: Reservations are not necessary. Sites are $11 to $15 per night for two people, plus $1 to $2 for each additional person. Credit cards are not accepted. Long-term stays are OK.

Directions: From I-75, take Exit 143 eastbound on State Road 78/Bayshore Road for .25 mile. Turn north on Wells Road and go .25 mile. At Triplett Road, turn west and proceed to the park.

Contact: Seminole Campground, 8991 Triplett Road, North Fort Myers, FL 33917, 239/543-2919, fax 239/731-2598.

8 UPRIVER CAMPGROUND RV RESORT

Rating: 8

In North Fort Myers on the Caloosahatchee River
Fort Myers/Naples map, grid b3, page 476
Some sites overlook a short inlet leading to the Caloosahatchee River, so you can feed pelicans from your own private dock or look for a manatee trying to stay warm in the river during the cooler months. A full-time activities director makes sure campers are entertained in the winter. This campground is exceptional in that it is set back from the road with a huge open golf chipping range in front; it also has lots of mature oaks, pines, sabal palms, and even a few orange trees. The surrounding area

is quiet and rural. Still, there's plenty to do (fishing and boating on the river, swimming in the pool), and the park is a popular destination for snowbirds and retirees. Fifty large pull-through sites are to be added, as well as a new recreation hall.

Campsites, facilities: Catering to campers 55 and older, the park has 300 RV sites with full hookups, cable TV, and telephone availability. Restrooms, showers, picnic tables, a boat ramp, an exercise and game room, a golf chipping course, laundry facilities, a pool, and tennis courts are provided. The restrooms, laundry room, and recreation hall are wheelchair accessible. Children are welcome for short periods in the summer. One small pet is allowed per site.

Reservations, fees: Reservations are recommended. Sites are $26 to $33 per night for two people, plus $2 for each additional person. Major credit cards are accepted.

Directions: From I-75, take Exit 143 eastbound on State Road 78 for 1.5 miles. The campground is on the south side.

Contact: Upriver Campground RV Resort, 17021 Upriver Park, North Fort Myers, FL 33917, 239/543-3330 or 800/848-1652, fax 239/543-6663, website: www.upriver.com.

9 W. P. FRANKLIN LOCK AND DAM CAMPGROUND

Rating: 8

East of Fort Myers

Fort Myers/Naples map, grid b4, page 476

This is the westernmost campground run by the U.S. Army Corps of Engineers on the 152-mile Okeechobee Waterway, which crosses Lake Okeechobee and ends on the east coast of Florida near Stuart. This section on the Caloosahatchee River is the most scenic because it still has the old river oxbows outside of the main boating channel. You can ski in the channel, but at that speed you'll likely miss seeing wildlife such as alligators, river otters, bobcats, eagles, ospreys, hawks, and black vul-

tures. The endangered West Indian manatee swims upstream to warmer waters in the winter; sometimes, manatees get penned in with boats going through the locks and hitch a ride farther upstream. Campsites are paved and shade is minimal, although all sites overlook the river and a small inlet where boat campers can tie up their craft.

Campsites, facilities: There are 30 sites for RVs, tents, and drive-in campers, as well as eight boat-in spots. Showers, restrooms, laundry facilities, a dump station, and a boat ramp are provided. A supermarket is 12 miles away. Children and leashed pets are welcome.

Reservations, fees: Reservations are recommended; call ReserveAmerica at 800/326-3521. Sites are $16 per night. Major credit cards are accepted. Maximum stay is 14 days in a 30-day period.

Directions: From I-75, take Exit 143 eastbound on State Road 78 for 10 miles. While driving, you will come to a stop sign after five miles; turn north and continue on State Road 78 as it winds around south again and west. The campground is on the south side of the road.

Contact: W. P. Franklin Lock and Dam Campground, 17850 North Franklin Lock Road, Alva, FL 33920, 239/694-8770; visitor center: 239/694-2582. Or, call the U.S. Army Corps of Engineers headquarters at 863/983-8101 (weekdays).

10 CALOOSAHATCHEE REGIONAL PARK

Rating: 8

East of North Fort Myers on the Caloosahatchee River

Fort Myers/Naples map, grid b4, page 476

Tent campers, rejoice. This new 768-acre park is for you, and also mountain bikers, horseback riders, hikers, and nature lovers. And let's not forget canoeists and kayakers. Opened recently by Lee County, the park has palmetto prairies and cypress domes, as well as three other kinds of habitats to explore. Five miles of dedicated hiking trails let you get back to the wilderness; 10 miles of shared hiking, mountain biking and equestrian trails offer another option. During the first weekend in December, this is the site of a re-enactment of the Battle of Fort Myers, and rangers hold campfire programs periodically throughout the year. There's a fishing dock and kayak rentals on the river.

Campsites, facilities: There are 27 tent sites with picnic tables and grills. Water is available at eight sites, and two are wheelchair accessible. Restrooms and showers are provided, but not electricity. Children are welcome. Pets are prohibited.

Reservations, fees: Reservations are recommended; they can be made online at www.leeparks.org. Sites are $10 per night, or $15 for group sites of six tents, and $20 for horse camping. Major credit cards are accepted. Maximum stay is two weeks.

Directions: From I-75, take Exit 143 onto State Road 78 and drive northeast 3.2 miles. At State Road 31, turn left and drive one mile. Turn right on County Road 78/North River Road and proceed eight miles to the park.

Contact: Caloosahatchee Regional Park, 19130 North River Road, Alva, FL 33920, 239/693-2689, fax 239/693-8248, website: www.leeparks.org.

11 RIVERBEND MOTORCOACH RESORT

🏊 ⛴ 🚐 🐕 ♿ 🚙

Rating: 9

North of Fort Myers on the Caloosahatchee River

Fort Myers/Naples map, grid b4, page 476

Open for its first season in 2002–2003, this brand-new luxury resort welcomes Class A motorcoaches only. About 50 of the sites are available for rent; the rest are condominium lots. The park has 1,000 feet of frontage on the Caloosahatchee River northern shore. East of here in the town of Alva is the Eden Harbor Winery, where you can observe the wine-making process and taste the homegrown product, which is reminiscent of sweet German wines.

Campsites, facilities: All sites have full hookups, satellite TV, and phone service available. Lots are fully landscaped, and the developers have kept some natural preserve areas on the site, including an oak grove along the river. Restrooms, showers, laundry facilities, a pool, a boat ramp, dock, boat rentals, a clubhouse, horseshoe pits, shuffleboard courts, snack bar, store, and nature trails are available. All areas are wheelchair accessible. Children are welcome, but no more than four people are allowed per coach. Leashed pets are permitted.

Reservations, fees: Reservations are recommended. Sites are $35 to $70 per night for two people. Major credit cards are accepted. Long-term rates are available.

Directions: From I-75, take Exit 141 and go east on State Road 80 for 17 miles. The park will be on your left.

Contact: RiverBend Motorcoach Resort, 5800 West State Road 80, Alva, FL, 33920, 866/RVRIVER, fax 863/674-0089, website: www.riverbendflorida.com.

12 ORANGE HARBOR MOBILE HOME AND RV PARK

🚲 🏊 ⛴ 🚐 ♿ 🚙

Rating: 4

In Fort Myers

Fort Myers/Naples map, grid b3, page 476

As you cross the soaring bridge over the Caloosahatchee River, you can see this sprawling mobile home and RV park on the south bank. It's near a manatee haven and bird sanctuary on the Caloosahatchee and Orange Rivers. The open and sunny RV area is separate from the 364-unit mobile home community, where there seems to be a golf cart parked in every driveway; campers may use the pool and common areas there. Near this park at Coastal Marine Mart is Manatee World (239/693-1434), where you can book a river cruise through one of the state's most populated manatee sanctuaries. The endangered manatees (or sea cow, as this gentle animal is sometimes called) are often injured or killed by speeding boats; many bear the scars of past encounters with propellers because they stay close to the surface to breathe. On this cruise, the captain shuts off the engines so you can float quietly among the creatures. Reservations are recommended.

Campsites, facilities: Overnighters are not allowed. Long-term visiting senior citizens are the preferred campers at this park, which offers 130 full-hookup sites for RVs. Restrooms, showers, a pool, laundry facilities, a boat ramp, boat docks, and a recreation room are provided. A supermarket is .5 mile away. Children are not accepted, except to visit campers. Pets are forbidden.

Reservations, fees: Reservations are recommended. Sites are $1,000 for two months or $1,435 for three months, plus the cost of electricity. Add $50 per month for 50-amp service. Credit cards are not accepted. Minimum stay is two months.

Directions: From I-75, take Exit 141 eastbound on State Road 80/Palm Beach Boulevard for .5 mile, then turn north into the park.

Contact: Orange Harbor Mobile Home and RV Park, 5749 Palm Beach Boulevard, Fort Myers, FL 33905, 239/694-3707, website: www.orangeharbor.com.

13 CYPRESS WOODS RV RESORT

Rating: 8

East of Fort Myers

Fort Myers/Naples map, grid b3, page 476

Opened in 1999, this is among the new breed of luxury resorts targeted to motorcoaches, fifth wheels, and travel trailers—"one of the most beautiful and private outdoor resorts ever created," according to the color brochure. Sites have space for two cars and 50-foot concrete pads and a patio. The 6,500-square-foot main recreation hall is big enough for any manner

of entertainment. The property is architecturally planned to incorporate nature preserves and open spaces. Besides RV spots, lots are being sold for homes.

Campsites, facilities: This new luxury campground has 290 RV sites large enough to accommodate the biggest of rigs. Each site has concrete pads, full hookups, and cable TV; telephone service is available. Restrooms, showers, and laundry facilities are available. On the premises are a heated pool and spa, a lake, a recreation hall, and a dog-walk area. All areas are wheelchair accessible. Children are allowed for stays up to 30 days. Leashed pets are permitted; limit of two per site.

Reservations, fees: Reservations are recommended, and require a 25 percent deposit. No refunds are allowed if you cancel within 30 days of your arrival date, nor are they permitted for early checkouts. Sites are $36 per night from May 1 to September 30. From October 1 to April 30, the fee is $60 per night for two people, plus $5 for each additional person. Major credit cards are accepted. Long-term stays are OK.

Directions: From I-75, take Exit 139 eastbound about .5 mile to the resort entrance on the left.

Contact: Cypress Woods RV Resort, 5551 Luckett Road, Fort Myers, FL 33905, 239/694-2191, fax 239/694-4969, website: www.cypresswoodsrv.com.

14 TROPIC ISLE RV RESORT

Rating: 7

In Bokeelia on Pine Island

Fort Myers/Naples map, grid a2, page 476

Set on 15 acres at the northern tip of Pine Island in a small community of vacation homes and condominium complexes, this park makes a good base camp for those interested in fishing and exploring the nearby islands by boat. A dock and boat ramp are nearby. Sites are open and sunny, and a big lake is at the back of the laid-back park. Bokeelia is home to the

Sunburst Tropical Fruit Company (239/283-1200), where, depending on how well it is staffed at the moment, you may be able to tour a working mango grove that was planted in the 1920s. Sample fresh fruit in season after the tour; at other times of the year, you can taste mango chutney.

Campsites, facilities: This adult-oriented park has 145 concrete-pad, full-hookup sites with cable TV and telephone links. Restrooms, showers, laundry facilities, a pool, a Jacuzzi, shuffleboard courts, a clubhouse, a pool table, horseshoe pits, a dump station, and wintertime entertainment are available. A driving and putting range also is on the grounds. A supermarket is seven miles away. Children may visit campers short-term. Leashed pets are permitted.

Reservations, fees: Reservations are advised. Sites are $42 per night for two people, plus $5 per extra person. Major credit cards are accepted. No camping-club discounts are honored. Long-term stays are OK.

Directions: From I-75, take Exit 143 westbound on State Road 78 for about 20 miles to Pine Island. When you reach the dead end of the road at Pine Island Center, turn north on Stringfellow Road/State Road 767, and drive five miles.

Contact: Tropic Isle RV Resort, 15175 Stringfellow Road Northwest, Bokeelia, FL 33922, 239/283-4456.

15 BOCILLA ISLAND SEAPORT AND CHARLOTTE HARBOR RESORT

🏊 🎣 🏕 🐕 ♿ 🚐

Rating: 7

In Bokeelia on Pine Island

Fort Myers/Naples map, grid a2, page 476

Although you can kayak, canoe, or hike in this area, the real attraction is boating and fishing. The wheelchair-accessible pier stretches 300 feet, and charter fishing guides are available. Nearby is the 200-acre, county-owned Bocilla Island Preserve. The RV park is part of a cluster of properties offering vacation rentals and quiet island experiences. Dock your boat at the private boat slips, or rent one from the resort. Minor boat repairs are made on site. A private beach is available for landlubbers, as is the pool and the clubhouse with planned activities.

Campsites, facilities: This 55-and-older park has 26 RV sites with full hookups; one site has 50-amp service. Restrooms, showers, laundry facilities, and telephone service are available. On the premises are a tiki hut for socializing, a clubhouse, a heated pool, horseshoe pits, shuffleboard courts, a fishing pier, a boat ramp, boat slips, and boat rentals. Also for rent are efficiency apartments, mobile homes, and "cracker" cottages. Children are welcome but most campers are anglers and nature lovers over 55. Small, leashed pets under 20 pounds are permitted; messes must be cleaned up immediately, and pets are not allowed on the fishing pier.

Reservations, fees: Reservations are recommended. Sites are $45 per night; you'll be charged extra for electricity after seven days. Credit cards are not accepted. Long-term stays are allowed.

Directions: From I-75, take Exit 143 westbound on State Road 78 for about 20 miles to Pine Island. When you reach the dead end of the road at Pine Island Center, turn north on Stringfellow Road/State Road 767, and drive to the end of the road where it changes names to Main Street and veers to your left. The park will be on your left across from the fishing pier.

Contact: Bocilla Island Seaport and Charlotte Harbor Resort, 8421 Main Street, Bokeelia, FL 33922, 239/283-2244, fax 239/283-8283, website: www.bokeelia.net.

16 CAYO COSTA STATE PARK BOAT-IN SITES

🥾 🏊 🎣 🚐 ⛺

Rating: 10

On Cayo Costa Island 12 miles west of Pine Island

Fort Myers/Naples map, grid a1, page 476

Play Robinson Crusoe on this nearly deserted

island, which is accessible only by boat. The 2,300-acre Cayo Costa State Park is one of the state's largest unspoiled barrier islands, with extensive dunes and white-sand beaches on the Gulf side and protected waters and mangroves on the east side. In the middle are pine flatwoods and oak hammocks; the island is big enough to accommodate six miles of hiking trails. If you don't have your own boat, the *Tropic Star* shuttle boat (239/283-0015, website: www.tropicstarcruises.com) runs from Pineland Marina in Bokeelia. Reservations are required, and the fare is $25 round-trip for adults and $20 for children. The ferry leaves Bokeelia at 9:30 A.M. daily and at 2 P.M. on some days, with return trips departing from Cayo Costa at 3 P.M. A park ranger meets the ferry on the island with a tram so you can load your camping gear. The tram (50 cents per person) takes you one mile west to the camping area and the cabins. Of course, you can hike it, too.

As you walk across the island from the boat docks to the Gulf of Mexico, you'll see a tiny pioneer cemetery, a legacy of the small settlement that was here through the 1950s. Earlier, the Calusa Indians lived on this land. The north end of the island at Boca Grande Pass is acclaimed for its tarpon fishing, but you may also catch the much-prized snook, flounder, redfish, trout, and sheepshead.

Campsites, facilities: There are 25 primitive tent sites and 12 rustic cabins with bunks. Bring all supplies. No water or electricity is available at the boat docks. The campground is one mile west of the docks on the Gulf side; restrooms, water, cold showers, picnic tables, and grills are provided. Although drinking water is available on the island, you may want to carry in better-tasting stuff. The really big luxury here? Once a day, the park ranger sells ice made with a generator. Pets are prohibited.

Reservations, fees: Reservations are recommended; call ReserveAmerica at 800/326-3521. Sites are $13 per night for four people. Reservations are required for cabins, which are $20 per night for six people. Boaters who

want to tie up at the dock and sleep overnight pay the regular camping fee. Major credit cards are accepted.

Directions: From I-75, take Exit 143 westbound on State Road 78 for 20 miles. When you reach the dead end at Pine Island Center, turn north on Stringfellow Road/State Road 767 and drive 10 miles to Four Winds Marina in Bokeelia. By boat, use nautical chart 25E.

Contact: Cayo Costa State Park, P.O. Box 1150, Boca Grande, FL 33921, 239/964-0375, fax 239/964-1154, website: www.floridastateparks.org.

17 FORT MYERS/ PINE ISLAND KOA

Rating: 7

On the southern end of Pine Island

Fort Myers/Naples map, grid b2, page 476

Lapped by the warm waters of the Gulf of Mexico, Pine Island's climate is so tropical that fruit is grown here commercially. The island has seen little development until recently. Nearby is the Matlacha fishing village, site of the "fishing-est bridge" in the United States. Of course, the fishing is great in all the waters nearby. The two-wheeled set can take their bikes for a spin around the quiet town of St. James City.

If you don't have a boat, then call one of the many local marinas to rent one so you can see all the interesting islands around Bokeelia. Among them, Cabbage Key is home to a little restaurant and inn where patrons over the decades have made wallpaper out of dollar bills. Supposedly, this is where Jimmy Buffett was inspired to write "Cheeseburger in Paradise," although his former neighbors in Key West would surely dispute that claim. Or cruise by Useppa Island, where wealthy people from all over the world have constructed the kind of fabulous getaways we all would build (in even better taste, of course) if we ever won the lottery.

Campsites, facilities: This 370-unit KOA offers RV sites with full hookups, cable TV, and telephone service. Choose also from primitive tent-camping spots or sites with water and electricity. Restrooms, showers, picnic tables, a playground, shuffleboard courts, a pool, a spa, tennis courts, three fishing lakes, horseshoe pits, a pool table, a clubhouse with a kitchen and a stage, saunas, laundry facilities, a store, and a gift shop are available. Children and leashed pets are welcome.

Reservations, fees: Reservations are recommended. Sites are $20 to $45 per night for two adults. Kids camp free; the charge for extra adults is $5. Major credit cards are accepted.

Directions: From I-75, take Exit 143 westbound on State Road 78 for 20 miles to Pine Island. When you reach the dead end at Pine Island Center, turn south on Stringfellow Road/State Road 767 and drive 10 miles to the park.

Contact: Fort Myers/Pine Island KOA, 5120 Stringfellow Road, St. James City, FL 33956, 239/283-2415 or 800/562-8505, website: www.koa.com.

18 THE IONA RANCH

Rating: 5

In Fort Myers

Fort Myers/Naples map, grid b2, page 476

Very residential and quiet, this RV park has many fruit and palm trees and a pond with fish and turtles, but no fishing is permitted. Sites are 32 by 55 feet and have concrete patios. Feel free to pick oranges from the scattered trees, except where posted signs state otherwise. The Sanibel Factory Shops are close by.

Campsites, facilities: Catering to people 55 and older, this 166-unit mobile home community offers 66 RV sites with full hookups and telephone access. Restrooms, showers, laundry facilities, shuffleboard courts, a recreation hall, a pool, and a dump station are available. Children are not accepted, except to visit campers. Cats and birds are permitted, but dogs are forbidden.

Reservations, fees: Reservations are recommended. Sites are $30 per night for two people, plus $2.50 for each extra person. Credit cards are not accepted. Long-term stays are OK.

Directions: From I-75, take Exit 131 west on Daniels Parkway for 5.5 miles to State Road 869/Summerlin Road. Turn left on State Road 869 and drive eight miles to State Road 867/McGregor Boulevard. Turn right onto State Road 867, then immediately left (north) onto Davis Road. The park is .75 mile ahead on the right.

Contact: The Iona Ranch, 16295 Davis Road, Fort Myers, FL 33908, 239/466-0440, fax 239/466-6619, email: Ionaranch1@aol.com.

19 THE GROVES RV RESORT

Rating: 7

In Fort Myers

Fort Myers/Naples map, grid b2, page 476

This park boasts it is the closest RV park to Sanibel Island, which is saying something since the fabled isle houses only one campground and hundreds of luxury condos and homes. Social activities are planned during the winter. The Sanibel Factory Shops outlet mall is nearby. To get to Sanibel Island beaches, located just across the causeway, you'll have to pay a toll of $3. Many people park their RVs or cars just off the causeway and then go fishing, swimming, or windsurfing; they don't beat the toll, but these wide spots in the road have Australian pines, a modicum of privacy, and vistas of water, water everywhere.

Campsites, facilities: All 306 grassy RV sites have full hookups, picnic tables, cable TV, and telephone availability. Restrooms, showers, picnic tables, concrete patios, laundry facilities, a pool, a library, a game room, shuffleboard, horseshoes, bocce ball, an exercise room, wintertime social programs, and a dump station are available. Management says the clubhouse is wheelchair accessible. An 18-hole golf course is nearby; a supermarket is about five miles away. Children are welcome. Leashed pets under 35 pounds are permitted.

Reservations, fees: Reservations are recommended. Sites are $36 per night for two people, plus $3 for each additional person. Major credit cards are accepted. Long-term stays are OK.

Directions: From I-75, take Exit 131 west on Daniels Parkway for 5.5 miles to State Road 869/Summerlin Road. Turn southwest on State Road 869 and drive 6.6 miles to John Morris Boulevard. Turn north and go .8 mile to the park.

Contact: The Groves RV Resort, 16175 John Morris Road, Fort Myers, FL 33908, 239/466-5909, 239/466-4300, or 800/828-6992, fax 239/466-6310, website: www.suncommunities.com.

20 SIESTA BAY RV RESORT

Rating: 5

East of Sanibel Island on the mainland

Fort Myers/Naples map, grid b2, page 476

Favored by busy, busy wintering retirees who like lots of activity, this sparkling clean park is three miles from the beach on Sanibel Island. There are more double-wide mobile homes here than RVs, and a sense of permanence and community holds forth, at least in the wintertime when everyone is here. Sabal palms and two lakes give a touch of greenery. Don't feed the swans on the lake, although you are welcome to watch them float lazily on the water. The broad, smooth concrete roadways are perfect for bicycling; plenty of residents have adult tricycles parked in front of their units.

Campsites, facilities: The sprawling mobile home/RV park has 162 RV sites with full hookups and concrete pads available for overnighters and seasonal visitors. Restrooms, showers, two pools, a Jacuzzi, horseshoe pits, shuffleboard and three lighted tennis courts, volleyball, a putting green and driving range, laundry facilities, fishing lakes, two recreation halls, library, card room, and fitness center are available. Tours, field trips, theme parties,

dances, clubs, classes, music groups and competitive sports keep visitors more than occupied. Management says all buildings are wheelchair accessible. Golf is two miles away. Children are permitted for short visits only. Pets are forbidden.

Reservations, fees: Reservations are required. Sites are $40 per night for two people, plus $3 for each additional person. Major credit cards are accepted. Long-term stays are OK.

Directions: From I-75, take Exit 131 west on Daniels Parkway for 5.5 miles to State Road 869/Summerlin Road. Turn southwest on State Road 869 and drive 6.5 miles to the park.

Contact: Siesta Bay RV Resort, 19333 Summerlin Road, Fort Myers, FL 33908, 239/466-8988 or 800/828-6992, website: www.suncommunities.com.

21 PERIWINKLE PARK

Rating: 8

On Sanibel Island

Fort Myers/Naples map, grid b1, page 476

Periwinkle Park is the only campground on Sanibel Island, which is famed around the world for its wonderful shelling beaches. If you camp here instead of on the mainland, you'll at least avoid paying the $3 toll each time you cross the causeway to experience Sanibel. The island has expensive vacation homes, fancy resort hotels, and quaint boutiques selling pastel-colored vacation clothing and knickknacks made of shells, but it retains much of its junglelike lushness and small-town atmosphere. A two-lane road winds north to the J. N. "Ding" Darling National Wildlife Refuge, where camping is not permitted. Hike the nature trails in this 5,030-acre sanctuary (closed on Fridays) or paddle your canoe; less adventurous types or those in a hurry can see much of the refuge on the five-mile road that winds through it.

Also on Sanibel is a historic village and museum, a lighthouse built in 1884, and several shell and marine life attractions. More great beaches are farther north on Captiva Island, so named because the pirate Jose Gasparilla had a camp there and kept captives on it. The campground stays in island character with shady trees and roads built of crushed shells and gravel. It's .5 mile from the beach; from the back of the campground, you can ride a fat-tired bike on an unpaved access road or walk to the Gulf of Mexico. Some sites overlook a little pond next to an aviary filled with exotic birds.

Campsites, facilities: Eighty RVs can be accommodated on tropical wooded sites with full hookups in this 326-unit park; 50 sites have telephone access. Seven sites are pull-through. Tenters can choose from among 11 sites set apart from the RV area. Restrooms, showers, a dump station, laundry facilities, and a recreation room are on the premises. Children are allowed. Dogs are forbidden.

Reservations, fees: Reservations are recommended January through March and on holiday weekends. Sites are $35 per night for two people, plus $2 for each additional person. Credit cards are not accepted. Long-term stays are OK.

Directions: From I-75, take Exit 131 west on Daniels Parkway for 5.5 miles to State Road 869/Summerlin Road. Turn left on State Road 869 and drive 9.5 miles to the Sanibel Island Causeway. Continue over the causeway to the four-way intersection, then turn north on Periwinkle Way and go .25 mile. The park is on the left.

Contact: Periwinkle Park, 1119 Periwinkle Way, Sanibel, FL 33957, 239/472-1433.

22 RED COCONUT RV RESORT

Rating: 9

On Estero Island at Fort Myers Beach
Fort Myers/Naples map, grid b2, page 476
How close do you want to be to the beach? This is the only Fort Myers campground that is directly on the Gulf of Mexico. The best (and most expensive) sites are on the beach side and enjoy shade from tall Australian pines.

Less pricey sites are across the street; they're also less crowded, are shaded by Norfolk pines and coconut trees, and put you within walking distance of the beach. Nine-hole golf courses and boat/canoe rentals are close by. When you tire of beachside fun, ride your bike north to the Times Square area clustered around the bridge to the mainland. It's great for people-watching, even if you're not interested in the honky-tonk T-shirt shops, pizzerias, and ice-cream parlors.

Campsites, facilities: All 176 full-hookup sites have cable TV. Tents are now allowed; they'll be placed on the same spots as the RVs. Restrooms, showers, picnic tables, a dump station, horseshoe pits, shuffleboard courts, laundry facilities, and a recreation room featuring a six-foot TV screen and movies are on the premises. Rental trailers are available. Children are welcome. Leashed pets are permitted.

Reservations, fees: Reservations are recommended. Sites are $40 to $60 per night for two people, depending on location of the site and time of year, plus $5 for each additional person in your party. Major credit cards are accepted. The minimum stay is three nights, and long-term stays are allowed. Daytime guests pay $3 each.

Directions: From I-75, take Exit 131 west on Daniels Parkway for 5.5 miles to State Road 869/Summerlin Road. Turn southwest on State Road 869 and drive 5.5 miles to San Carlos Boulevard. Turn south (left) on that road and go one mile until it ends on Estero Island. Turn left on Estero Boulevard and drive 1.5 miles.

Contact: Red Coconut RV Resort, 3001 Estero Boulevard, Fort Myers Beach, FL 33931, 239/463-7200, ext. 200, or 888/262-6226, fax 239/463-2609, website: www.redcoconut.com.

23 EBB TIDE RV PARK

Rating: 2

In Fort Myers Beach
Fort Myers/Naples map, grid b2, page 476
This sleepy mobile home and RV park shares

the street with the big local commercial fishing fleet. Boats rigged with enormous nets trawl the Gulf of Mexico for their catch, returning with loads of shrimp, lobster, and fish. If you want fish, you probably can't buy it any fresher than from their seafood markets, some of which sell retail. The streets in the little park are narrow, so be careful with big trailers. Nearby is another retirement-oriented RV park named Oyster Bay, at 1711 Main Street (239/463-2171); it has 101 sites for snowbirds and three for overnighters.

Campsites, facilities: The park has 148 RV-only sites with full hookups. Restrooms, showers, laundry facilities, a pool, a boat ramp, shuffleboard courts, and a recreation room are on the premises. The recreation hall is wheelchair accessible. Most campers are retired, but small children are welcome. Leashed pets are permitted.

Reservations, fees: Reservations are advised as early as one year ahead. The camping fee is $25 per night for two people, plus $2 per extra person. Credit cards are not accepted. Long-term stays are permitted.

Directions: From I-75, take Exit 131 west on Daniels Parkway for 5.5 miles to State Road 869/Summerlin Road. Turn southwest on State Road 869 and drive 5.5 miles to San Carlos Boulevard. Turn south on that road and go three miles to Main Street, just before the bridge, then turn left. The park is .25 mile ahead on the left.

Contact: Ebb Tide RV Park, 1725 Main Street, Fort Myers Beach, FL 33931, 239/463-5444.

24 GULF WATERS RV RESORT

Rating: 8

In Fort Myers Beach

Fort Myers/Naples map, grid b2, page 476

Just minutes from the beach, this is one of the newest parks in the area. Big rigs up to 40 feet long can be accommodated on huge lots measuring 30 by 100 feet.

Campsites, facilities: There are 320 full-hookup RV sites, all with picnic tables, cable TV, and telephone service availability. Restrooms, showers, laundry facilities, a computer room with six modem hookups, a pool, spa, poolside tiki bar, a clubhouse, horseshoe pits, shuffleboard courts, basketball, and a dog-walk area are available. Most areas are wheelchair accessible. Children are welcome. Leashed pets are permitted.

Reservations, fees: Reservations are recommended during winter. Sites are $22 to $32 per night. Major credit cards are accepted. Long-term rates are available.

Directions: From I-75, take Exit 131 west on Daniels Parkway for 5.5 miles to State Road 869/Summerlin Road. Turn southwest on Summerlin Road and drive 5.5 miles to Pine Ridge Road. Turn left, and then make an immediate right on Summerlin Square. The park will be on your left.

Contact: Gulf Waters RV Resort, 17500 Pine Ridge Road, Fort Myers Beach, FL 33931, 239/437-5888, fax 239/437-5922, website: www.gulfwatersrv.com.

25 FORT MYERS BEACH RV RESORT

Rating: 5

In Fort Myers Beach

Fort Myers/Naples map, grid b2, page 476

This 15-acre park is centrally located near Gulf beaches, the Thomas Edison and Henry Ford homes, Sanibel Island, and Fort Myers Beach. Paved interior roads lead to grassy sites with concrete patios.

Campsites, facilities: RVs up to 40 feet in length and tents are accommodated at the 305 full-hookup sites with cable TV and telephone access. Restrooms, showers, picnic tables, a dump station, a pool, a Jacuzzi, an exercise room, shuffleboard courts, laundry facilities, rental trailers, and winter entertainment are available. Families with children are welcome. Leashed pets are permitted.

Reservations, fees: Reservations are required. Sites are $25 to $31 per night for two people, plus $5 for each additional person. Major credit cards are accepted. Campers can stay as long as seven months.

Directions: From I-75, take Exit 131 west on Daniels Parkway for 5.5 miles to State Road 869/Summerlin Road. Turn southwest on State Road 869 and drive 5.5 miles to San Carlos Boulevard. Turn north (right) on that road and go .7 mile to the park on the right.

Contact: Fort Myers Beach RV Resort, 16299 San Carlos Boulevard, Fort Myers, FL 33908, 239/466-7171 or 800/553-7484, fax 239/466-6544.

26 SUNBURST RV PARK— FORT MYERS BEACH (FORMERLY GULF AIR)

Rating: 7

In Fort Myers Beach
Fort Myers/Naples map, grid b2, page 476

A nest for snowbirds, this mobile home/RV park dotted with queen palms hosts coffee hours for its campers along with many other social activities, including bingo, potluck dinners, dances, and arts and crafts. The park is central to the Minnesota Twins spring training camp, golf courses, dog racing, shelling, a bird sanctuary, marinas, deep-sea fishing charters, and miles of white-sand beaches. A shopping center is located next door.

Campsites, facilities: The adult-oriented park has 55 full-hookup sites for RVs. Restrooms, showers, picnic tables, laundry facilities, shuffleboard courts, a recreation hall, a pool, a dump station, and horseshoe pits are available. Activity programs run from November 15 through April 15. Children are welcome for short-term stays only. Leashed pets are allowed.

Reservations, fees: Reservations are recommended. Sites are $29 per night for two people. Major credit cards are accepted. Long-term stays are OK.

Directions: From I-75, take Exit 131 west on Daniels Parkway for 5.5 miles to State Road 869/Summerlin Road. Turn southwest on State Road 869 and drive 5.5 miles to San Carlos Boulevard. Turn south and go .5 mile to the park on the left.

Contact: Sunburst RV Park—Fort Myers Beach, 17279 San Carlos Boulevard Southwest, Fort Myers Beach, FL 33931, 239/466-8100 or 877/937-2757, fax 239/466-4044, website: rvonthego.com.

27 SAN CARLOS RV PARK AND ISLANDS

Rating: 5

Near Fort Myers Beach
Fort Myers/Naples map, grid b2, page 476

Fish from some of the campsites at this seven-acre boating-oriented campground, which extends off a causeway onto a peninsula surrounded by mangroves. You may see a porpoise, manatee, or mullet and numerous tropical birds. If you're into deep-sea fishing, this is a great location: Charter boats are within walking distance, and you can tie up your own boat at the docks. There's a one-mile bicycling and walking path to the beach; restaurants are close by. The campground, which is shaded by Australian pines, lies at the base of the busy Matanzas Pass Bridge, the only access road to the Gulf of Mexico and Estero Island. Sometimes traffic backs up at this spot in front of the park. The tent area overlooks the water, and RV sites have concrete pads.

Campsites, facilities: RV and tent campers can stay at the 122 full-hookup sites, which have telephone service available. Restrooms, showers, picnic tables, a dump station, a pool, a Jacuzzi, a boat ramp, kayak rentals, shuffleboard and horseshoe areas, laundry facilities, and a recreation room are on site. Management also rents out 19 mobile homes to vacationers. The office and recreation hall are wheelchair accessible. Children and leashed pets are welcome.

Reservations, fees: Reservations are recommended. Sites are $33.50 per night for two people, plus $2 for each additional person and $2 for using air-conditioning. Major credit cards are accepted.

Directions: From I-75, take Exit 131 west on Daniels Parkway for 5.5 miles to State Road 869/Summerlin Road. Turn southwest on State Road 869 and drive 5.5 miles to San Carlos Boulevard. Turn south and go two miles.

Contact: San Carlos RV Park and Islands, 18701 San Carlos Boulevard, Fort Myers Beach, FL 33931, 239/466-3133 or 800/525-7275, website: www.gocampingamerica.com/sancarlos.

28 INDIAN CREEK PARK

Rating: 8

In Fort Myers Beach

Fort Myers/Naples map, grid b2, page 476

In the winter, people from Michigan, Ohio, New York, Massachusetts, and Quebec flock to this sprawling but immaculate RV park, which is one of the largest in Florida if you count the number of sites. Many visitors leave their rigs here year-round; they've built Florida rooms (typically with windows on all sides) onto their trailers and added utility sheds. On the scale of a small city's recreation department, the park offers three swimming pools, 16 shuffleboard courts, three tennis courts, a year-round recreation director, and a tournament-sized pool hall. Nineteen small lakes dot the park, which is two miles from the beach and next door to a miniature golf course. Social activities, needless to say, are ubiquitous.

Campsites, facilities: Set on 200 acres, this senior-oriented park has a whopping 1,202 RV sites (plus another 300 mobile home sites) with full hookups, cable TV, telephone service, and picnic tables. On the premises are restrooms, showers, a dump station, three pools, Jacuzzis, 19 lakes, three clubhouses, horseshoe pits, shuffleboard, three tennis courts, and laundry facilities. An 18-hole golf course is two miles

away. Children are not welcome. Small pets are permitted at certain sites only.

Reservations, fees: Reservations are required. Sites are $37 to $39 per night for two people, plus $3 for each additional person. Major credit cards are accepted. Long-term stays are allowed.

Directions: From I-75, take Exit 131 west on Daniels Parkway for 5.5 miles to State Road 869/Summerlin Road. Turn southwest (left) on State Road 869 and drive 5.5 miles to San Carlos Boulevard. Turn left onto San Carlos Boulevard. The park is .2 mile ahead.

Contact: Indian Creek Park, 17340 San Carlos Boulevard, Fort Myers Beach, FL 33931, 239/466-6060 or 800/828-6992, fax 239/466-7475, website: www.suncommunities.com.

29 FORT MYERS RV RESORT

Rating: 6

In Fort Myers

Fort Myers/Naples map, grid b2, page 476

"We pamper the camper," insist the owners of neatly kept Fort Myers RV Resort, and they've certainly included nearly every amenity seen in an RV park, from an 18-hole miniature golf course to a post office and beer sales. What you won't find is a beach, so drive about eight miles to Sanibel Island or Fort Myers Beach if you pine for sand. Although part of the park fronts on busy U.S. 41, the place is so large that campers toward the back won't be conscious of much noise. Some spots are on a creek where you can fish. Greenery includes slash pine, queen palms, and Australian pines. Shopping centers are close by.

Campsites, facilities: All 345 grassy RV sites offer full hookups and telephone service. Ask about cable TV. Restrooms, showers, some picnic tables, a dump station, a playground, a pool, a boat ramp, a dock, horseshoes, shuffleboard, a miniature golf course, a recreation hall, a pool table, a volleyball field, a store, and laundry facilities are on site. Children and pets are welcome.

Reservations, fees: Reservations are required from October to April. Sites are $28 per night for two people, plus $2.50 for each additional person. Major credit cards are accepted. Long-term stays are OK.

Directions: From I-75, take Exit 128 westbound on Alico Road for three miles. Turn north (right) on U.S. 41. Drive .6 mile to the park on the west side of the highway.

Contact: Fort Myers RV Resort, 16800 South Tamiami Trail, Fort Myers, FL 33908, 239/267-2141 or 239/267-2211.

30 WOODSMOKE CAMPING RESORT

Rating: 7

South of Fort Myers

Fort Myers/Naples map, grid b2, page 476

Slash pines, melaleucas, and lakeside cypress trees cast shade throughout the park. Resist the temptation to feed the ducks, but feel free to watch their antics. Hike on a short boardwalk nature trail. Two miles away is the Koreshan State Historic Site (see campground in this chapter). The park is within easy driving distance of beaches, deep-sea fishing charters, Sanibel Island and nature preserves, the Henry Ford and Thomas Edison homes, the Shell Factory, and the Corkscrew Swamp Sanctuary. Most visitors here are staying for the season.

Campsites, facilities: You'll find 300 sites, nearly all with full hookups. Seventy-five are pull-through. For cable TV and telephone, you must call the appropriate utility company. Restrooms, showers, a heated pool, a spa, a recreation hall, three lakes, a large pavilion, shuffleboard, horseshoes, and laundry facilities are available. Children are welcome. Leashed pets are permitted, except for Doberman pinschers, pit bull terriers, German shepherds, and rottweilers.

Reservations, fees: Reservations are recommended, particularly in winter. Sites are $28 to $40.50 per night for two people, plus $3.50

for each additional adult. Major credit cards are accepted. Long-term stays are OK.

Directions: From I-75, take Exit 123 westbound on Corkscrew Road for two miles. Turn north on U.S. 41 and drive two miles. The park is between Hickory Street and Sanibel Boulevard.

Contact: Woodsmoke Camping Resort, 19551 U.S. 41 South, Fort Myers, FL 33908, 239/267-3456 or 800/231-5053, fax 239/267-6719, website: http://woodsmokecampingresort.com/index.html.

31 SHADY ACRES RV PARK

Rating: 7

South of Fort Myers

Fort Myers/Naples map, grid b2, page 476

On cool nights, folks gather around the community campfire for socializing in this well-shaded, lushly landscaped park. Orange-colored flame vine and purple bougainvillea add color. Watch squirrels scramble up the sabal palms. During winter, a restaurant and snack bar is open on the grounds, and social activities, such as crafts, bingo, dances, pool parties with live entertainment, exercise classes, and singing, are available. A golf course is within two miles. Some sites overlook a pond and a creek. Although U.S. 41 is a congested highway, this park is nicely secluded from the road. Shopping centers and tourist attractions are nearby. Just down the road at 19701 North Tamiami Trail is a similar adult-oriented RV park called Sunseekers (239/731-1303); it offers 190 seasonal sites and 35 overnight spots.

Campsites, facilities: The retiree-oriented park has 270 full-hookup RV sites and 14 tent sites set aside from the motor homes. Two sites are pull-through. Restrooms, showers, picnic tables, a dump station, a pool, laundry facilities, cable TV, a playground, horseshoe pits (tournaments during winter), shuffleboard courts, propane sales, and a recreation room with pool and Ping-Pong tables are provided. Children may camp for two weeks only. Leashed pets are permitted, except for rottweilers, pit bulls, German shepards, and Doberman pinschers.

Reservations, fees: Reservations are recommended. Sites are $29 per night for two people, plus $3 for each additional person. Major credit cards are accepted.

Directions: From I-75, take Exit 128 westbound for three miles on Alico Road. Turn south on U.S. 41 and go three miles. At the campground sign, turn west and drive .25 mile to the park.

Contact: Shady Acres RV Park, 19370 South Tamiami Trail, Fort Myers, FL 33908, 239/267-8448, fax 239/267-7026, website: www.shady-acresfl.com.

32 KORESHAN STATE HISTORIC SITE

Rating: 10

In Estero

Fort Myers/Naples map, grid b2, page 476

Adjoining the Estero River, the campground is part of a state historic site that memorializes a Utopian communal religious settlement founded in 1870 by a New York doctor who planned to construct a "New Jerusalem" here to follow the religion of "Koreshanity." No, this man had nothing to do with David Koresh and the tragic conflagration at Waco, Texas, during the 1990s. Cyrus Teed was inspired by the Bible to take the name Koresh, a Hebrew transliteration of Cyrus, which was the name of the Persian king who allowed the Jews held captive in Babylon to return to Israel.

Tours of the Koreshan communal settlement are held regularly, including views of the founder's house, the bakery, outbuildings, and the "planetary court." Followers believed that the earth was a hollow sphere with the planets inside. The governing council consisted of seven women who ran the day-to-day operations of the settlement; leaders of the religion were celibate. Many of the followers came from Chicago with all their furnishings, much of which still can be seen. Teed thought he was immortal, but he died in 1908. Even his tomb has not lasted; it was destroyed in a hurricane in the 1920s. When the settlement dwindled to four members, they donated this land in 1961 to the state; however, the Koreshan Unity Foundation still runs a library and museum near the state park. Don't miss touring the historic site while you're camped here, and imagine what it would be like if Teed's plans for settling 8 to 10 million people had come to fruition. The campground is shady and cool—a real treat in itself. Swimming is not permitted in the Estero River; canoeing, cycling, boating, and fishing are the things to do. Canoes are for rent on the river, which is part of a state-designated canoe trail.

Campsites, facilities: The 156-acre state park has 48 sites with water and electricity for either RVs or tents, plus another 12 sites for tents only. The sites are well buffered from each other by scrub and trees. Restrooms, showers, picnic tables, grills, a dump station, laundry facilities, a playground, rental canoes, a camp circle, and a boat ramp are available. Some camp sites, the tour areas, and the restrooms are wheelchair accessible, and the shell roads are wide and level. The park has made extra effort to provide access for persons with disabilities but you can contact a park ranger for special needs. Children are welcome. Pets are allowed for $2 daily with proof of vaccination.

Reservations, fees: Reservations are recommended; call ReserveAmerica at 800/326-3521. Sites vary seasonally from $12 to $20 per night for a family of eight, plus $2 for electricity. Major credit cards are accepted. The maximum stay is 14 days.

Directions: From I-75, take Exit 123 westbound on Corkscrew Road for two miles. Cross U.S. 41 and continue .25 mile west to the park.

Contact: Koreshan State Historic Site, P.O. Box 7, Estero, FL 33928, 239/992-0311, fax 239/992-1607, website: floridastateparks.org and www.koreshanshs.tripod.com.

33 BONITA BEACH TRAILER PARK

Rating: 4

In Bonita Springs

Fort Myers/Naples map, grid c3, page 476

Tall slash pines, scarlet bougainvillea blossoms, and perfectly formed Norfolk pines give campers a sense of being sheltered from the busy road that leads to the beach nearby. You'll find pool tables and—in winter—dances, bingo, and card games in the recreation hall. A miniature golf course is across the street. Ride your bicycle to Barefoot Beach Preserve two miles west or take a free trolley. The Gulf of Mexico is 1.25 miles away, and Lover's Key State Park (239/463-4588) is seven miles distant.

Campsites, facilities: The 12.5-acre park has 30 RV sites with full hookups. Four sites can accept rigs up to 40 feet long. Restrooms, showers, picnic tables, a dump station, a clubhouse, shuffleboard, a pool, winter activities, and telephone service are available. A supermarket is two blocks away. Children are allowed. Only one leashed pet under 20 pounds is permitted per site.

Reservations, fees: Reservations are recommended. Sites are $32 per night for two people, plus $3 for each additional person. Credit cards are not accepted. Long-term stays are OK.

Directions: From I-75, take Exit 116 westbound on Bonita Beach Road for five miles. The park is two blocks west of U.S. 41. Turn north on Meadowlark Lane, and go one block to the park entrance.

Contact: Bonita Beach Trailer Park, 27800 Meadowlark Lane, Bonita Springs, FL 34134, 239/498-1605 or 800/654-9907, fax 239/498-1605.

34 IMPERIAL BONITA ESTATES

Rating: 4

In Bonita Springs

Fort Myers/Naples map, grid c3, page 476

Located on the Imperial River, the park has social activities year-round, although winter is the more active season. Grocery stores and restaurants are within three miles, and beaches are close by. Many of the barrier island beaches at this end of the county are government-owned and protected from development. Lover's Key State Park (239/463-4588), a 434-acre collection of islands, canals, tidal lagoons, and mangroves, is accessible by road or by water for fishing, boating, canoeing, and swimming. You can't swim in the canals, but why would you want to when there are sugar-white beaches on Lover's Key? A footbridge connects some of these little islands, so you'll have more of an opportunity to spot wildlife, including several species of woodpeckers and shorebirds. Look for roseate spoonbills and egrets as they hunt for food. You may also see porpoises and manatees near shore.

Campsites, facilities: There are 312 RV sites with full hookups available in this 696-unit, 81-acre mobile home community, which is wheelchair accessible. Restrooms, showers, picnic tables, a dump station, two laundry facilities, a large heated pool, horseshoe pits, shuffleboard courts, and a recreation room are on site. Visitors should be age 55 or older, but children may visit, and those under 10 must be accompanied outside the RV. House pets are permitted; be sure to clean up after them and keep them leashed.

Reservations, fees: Reservations are recommended. Sites are $35 to $42 per night from January through March; and $31 to $36 from April through December. Major credit cards are accepted. Long-term visits are OK.

Directions: From I-75, take Exit 116 westbound on Bonita Beach Road for 1.1 miles. Turn north on Imperial Street and drive .3 mile. At Dean Street, turn east and go two blocks. The park is on the left.

Contact: Imperial Bonita Estates, 27700 Bourbonniere Drive, Bonita Springs, FL 34135, 239/992-0511 or 800/690-6619, fax 239/992-6126, website: www.imperialbonitaestates.com.

35 CITRUS PARK

Rating: 5

In Bonita Springs

Fort Myers/Naples map, grid c3, page 476

This new park offers 968 sites for vacationers, seasonal visitors, and full-timers. Its claim to fame: More activities than you can shake a stick at. The roster of things to do fills four pages of the park's monthly newsletter. For example: astronomy classes, tea with a Collier County pioneer, flu shots, movies, Dixieland and German music bands, choral groups, line dancing, and the usual potlucks, bingo, cards, and so forth.

Campsites, facilities: Nearly all 968 sites have full hookups and cable TV. Picnic tables are available upon request. Twenty-five sites are pull-through. Restrooms, showers, laundry facilities, and telephone service are available. On the premises are two pools, a recreation hall, several lakes, horseshoe pits, shuffleboard courts, a dog-walk area, and *pétanque* and bocce courts. All areas are wheelchair accessible. Children are allowed for short visits only; this is a 55-plus park. Leashed pets are permitted.

Reservations, fees: Reservations are recommended. Sites are $33 per night for two people, plus $1 per extra person. Credit cards are not accepted. Long-term rates are available.

Directions: From I-75, take Exit 116 eastbound on Bonita Beach Road a short distance. Turn north on Bonita Grande Road and proceed to East Terry Drive. Turn left on East Terry Drive and proceed to Trost Boulevard. Turn north on Trost Boulevard and drive to the park.

Contact: Citrus Park, 25501 Trost Boulevard, Bonita Springs, FL 34135, 239/992-3030, fax 239/992-4130.

36 GULF COAST CAMPING RESORT

Rating: 3

In Bonita Springs

Fort Myers/Naples map, grid c3, page 476

At Christmastime, at least one camping couple has been known to set out baskets of grapefruit for their neighbors to take—a sign of both friendliness and the abundance of winter citrus yields among the slowly dwindling fruit trees. Set in a neighborhood of small, warehouse-based businesses, this park has a little pond and an undeveloped jungly area behind. It tends to attract boaters and snowbirds. As more people buy lots here, the number of spots for overnighters shrinks, but most sites still cater to people passing through or looking to spend a few winter months in a warm retreat.

Campsites, facilities: Catering to people age 55 and older, this 260-unit park offers 175 full-hookup grassy sites for RVs up to 37 feet long. Three sites are set aside for tents. For cable TV and telephone service, call the appropriate utility company. Restrooms, showers, a pool, a recreation hall, shuffleboard courts, horseshoe pits, and wintertime social programs are available. Children may visit campers. Small, leashed dogs are allowed.

Reservations, fees: Reservations are recommended in winter or any time for stays of three months or longer. Sites are $26 per night for two people, plus $2 for each additional person. Credit cards are not accepted. Long-term rates are available.

Directions: From the intersection of Old U.S. 41 and U.S. 41 in North Bonita Springs, drive .25 mile north on U.S. 41. Turn east at the sign and go two blocks.

Contact: Gulf Coast Camping Resort, 24020 Production Circle, Bonita Springs, FL 34135, 239/992-3808.

37 BONITA LAKE RV RESORT

Rating: 5

In Bonita Springs
Fort Myers/Naples map, grid c3, page 476

Most campers here are retired folks spending the winter in the sunshine, and there's plenty of that. A few fruit trees offer greenery; the pool is heated in the winter, and the whirlpool is open year-round for soothing weary muscles. A fishing lake might yield hours of relaxation. Some people eat lunch at what is considered a small picnic island. Everglades Wonder Gardens, an old-time tourist attraction with birds, alligators, otters, snakes, and other wildlife, is nearby.

Campsites, facilities: The 167 grassy sites at this 10-acre park have full hookups and are for RVs up to 40 feet long. All sites have picnic tables. Telephone service is available. Restrooms, showers, a dump station, a pool, a Jacuzzi, horseshoe pits, shuffleboard courts, laundry facilities, a recreation hall, and wintertime social programs are available. An 18-hole golf course is five miles away. Children are allowed. Small, leashed pets are permitted.

Reservations, fees: Reservations are recommended. Sites are $34 per night for two people, plus $3 for each additional person. Major credit cards are accepted. Long-term stays are permitted.

Directions: From I-75, take Exit 116 westbound on County Road 865/Bonita Beach Boulevard for two miles. At County Road 887/Old U.S. 41, turn north and drive 1.7 miles to the park.

Contact: Bonita Lake RV Resort, 26325 Old U.S. 41, Bonita Springs, FL 34135, 239/992-2481 or 800/828-6992, fax 239/992-2357, website: www.suncommunities.com.

38 LAKE SAN MARINO RV PARK

Rating: 6

North of Naples
Fort Myers/Naples map, grid c2, page 476

Visitors to this over-55 park keep a keen edge: Shuffleboard is so competitive that the courts are surrounded by bleachers for spectator seating. The pastime seems to be taken as seriously as a Wimbledon tennis match. Campsites are grassy with adjoining concrete patios. Lake San Marino RV Park is strategically poised for enjoying Greater Naples, close to shopping and restaurants, near the Naples–Fort Myers greyhound track and several golf courses, and two miles from the spectacular beachfront Delnor–Wiggins Pass State Park (239/597-6196). The state park, south from here on U.S. 41, then east on County Road 846, is open for day use only. There's gulf-front swimming and shelling, fishing, a boat ramp, and an observation tower. West on County Road 846 is the National Audubon Society's Corkscrew Swamp Sanctuary, a unique forest of towering 500-year-old bald cypress bisected by a two-mile boardwalk. The refuge teems with nearly 200 species of birds, including nesting wood storks, plus alligators, deer, and bobcat. For details, call 239/657-3771.

Campsites, facilities: The 35-acre park has 415 sites with full hookups and picnic tables. About half are available for new seasonal visitors; the rest are taken by folks who leave their rigs on site in the summer. Restrooms, showers, laundry facilities, a pool, horseshoe pits, shuffleboard courts, a clubhouse, telephone service, wintertime social programs, a camp circle for gatherings, and a small fishing lake with a pier are available. Management says the pool area and bathhouse are wheelchair accessible. Two miles away are groceries, a restaurant, bait, and LP gas. Children are permitted, but in winter the park is predominantly retiree oriented. One leashed pet under 35 pounds is permitted per site.

Reservations, fees: Reservations are required. Sites are $37 per night for two people, plus $3 for each additional person. Major credit cards are accepted. Long-term stays are OK.

Directions: From I-75 Exit 111, go west to U.S. 41, then north (right) to Wiggins Pass Road. Turn right onto Wiggins Pass. The park is .25 mile ahead at right. Alternatively, from U.S. 41 in Bonita Springs, drive two miles south to Wiggins Pass Road. Turn east and go .25 mile.

Contact: Lake San Marino RV Park, 1000 Wiggins Pass Road, Naples, FL 34110, 239/597-4202 or 800/828-6992, fax 239/592-0790, website: www.suncommunities.com.

39 PALM RIVER MOBILE HOME PARK

Rating: 2

North of Naples

Fort Myers/Naples map, grid c2, page 476

Set on the Cocohatchee River, this senior-oriented park hosts potluck dinners, pancake breakfasts, cards, bingo, and crafts during the winter season. Campers can fish from the docks, which accommodate boats up to 20 feet long for an extra charge. Paved, lighted roads lead to concrete sites at this open and sunny park. Shopping, medical facilities, churches, and restaurants are nearby. At least one camper in your party must be over the age of 55.

Campsites, facilities: This 68-unit condominium mobile home park is targeted to people over age 55. There are 10 RV sites with full hookups, a clubhouse, and boat docks. Groceries are .5 mile away. Children and pets are not allowed.

Reservations, fees: Reservations are recommended. Sites are $25 per night. Credit cards are not accepted. Long-term stays are OK.

Directions: From U.S. 41 in Bonita Springs, drive three miles south to Walker Bilt Road, which intersects with the highway on the south side of the Cocohatchee River. Turn west on Walker Bilt Road and drive a short distance to the park.

Contact: Palm River Mobile Home Park, 793 Walker Bilt Road, Naples, FL 34110, 239/597-3639.

40 LAKE TRAFFORD MARINA AND CAMPGROUND

Rating: 5

In Immokalee

Fort Myers/Naples map, grid c4, page 476

Immokalee—meaning "my home" in the Seminole Indian tongue—is home to sprawling cattle ranches, citrus and vegetable farms, and anglers, which makes it an offbeat destination for campers. This fishing camp is nestled on the shores of Lake Trafford, a 1,600-acre basin described as "infested" with largemouth bass, as well as crappie, bluegill, and shellcracker. Children are welcome, although parents should be sure to keep an eye on them: "Too many alligators!" warns the camp's management. The park also offers boat tours, fishing guides, and airboat rides. Fishing is the main draw, but there are other attractions: a Cinco de Mayo festival in May celebrating the culture of Mexican migrant farm workers who flock here from September through June; the Immokalee Harvest Festival in April; and the Immokalee Horse Trails equestrian competition in February.

Campsites, facilities: There are 32 RV sites with full hookups and 10 sites for tents in this 64-unit park. The tent policy may change, so call ahead. On the premises are restrooms, showers, a dump station, a boat ramp, a lakeside pier, and a marina with a bait and tackle store, boat rentals, and fishing guides. Children and pets are welcome.

Reservations, fees: Reservations are taken. Sites are $18 per night for two people, plus $1 for each additional person. Major credit cards are accepted. Long-term stays are OK.

Directions: From I-75, take Exit 111 east onto County Road 846 and drive 30 miles to Immokalee. Turn west on State Road 29 and drive about two miles to County Road 890/Lake Trafford Road. Continue three miles west to the campground.

Contact: Lake Trafford Marina and Campground, 6001 Lake Trafford Road, Immokalee, FL 34142, 239/657-2401, fax 239/658-2401.

41 ROCK CREEK RV RESORT AND CAMPGROUND

Rating: 6

In Naples

Fort Myers/Naples map, grid c2, page 476

Overnight visitors need luck to get into this suburban park, but it's worth a try to sleep so close to Naples attractions. Despite being in the heart of the city, the place is shady and jungly with sabal palms, bougainvillea, oaks, and flowering hibiscus. The 17-acre park sits on the banks of pretty Rock Creek, which flows into the Gulf of Mexico. Seasonal guests don't seem to mind the noise of traffic from the small airport next door. A short 2.5-mile drive away are downtown Naples' quaint but pricey marketplaces, such as Tin City, a trendy enclave of restaurants and shops on the city's old fishing wharves. From there, charter boats are waiting to embark on Gulf fishing excursions. Tour boats are available as well. Also near the park are the Collier County Museum, a big regional mall, and Caribbean Gardens, formerly known as Jungle Larry's, a tourist zoo famous for its boat tours of islands inhabited by monkeys and apes. For more information, call 239/262-5409.

Campsites, facilities: The 225-unit park has 70 RV sites with picnic tables, full hookups, and cable TV. Park models are for sale. Restrooms, showers, laundry facilities, a dump station, a large heated pool, two recreation halls, a boat ramp, horseshoe pits, shuffleboard courts, wintertime planned activities, and a chickee hut for gatherings are available. Children and overnighters are welcome only in the summer for short periods; in the winter months, this is an adults-only park. Call for current pet policy.

Reservations, fees: Reservations are required for the few campsites available in the winter season; they are not necessary in the summer. Sites are $40 to $47 per night for two people, plus $2 for each additional person. Credit cards are not accepted. Long-term stays are OK.

Directions: From I-75, take Exit 107 and turn right onto Pine Ridge Road. Drive two miles, then turn left onto Airport Pulling Road. Continue south for 4.5 miles, then turn right onto North Road. The park entrance sign is 100 yards ahead. The park is just south of Naples Municipal Airport.

Contact: Rock Creek RV Resort and Campground, 3100 North Road, Naples, FL 34104, 239/643-3100, fax 239/643-3101, website: www.rockcreekrv.com.

42 ENDLESS SUMMER RV ESTATES

Rating: 2

In Naples

Fort Myers/Naples map, grid c2, page 476

This is an older, somewhat congested park in a suburban area that's under pressure from sprawling development. It's convenient to shopping and has a heated, screened-in pool. (Many pools in this area have screen rooms called lanais built over them to keep out mosquitoes, a real plus in buggy Florida.) Bingo and social activities are held November through April at this nine-acre, open and sunny park, where paved roads lead to concrete pads.

Campsites, facilities: The park has 120 RV sites with full hookups. Restrooms, showers, laundry facilities, picnic tables, a heated pool, shuffleboard courts, a clubhouse, and horseshoe pits are on the premises. Restaurants and a supermarket are one mile away. Children are welcome. Leashed pets are permitted.

Reservations, fees: Reservations are recommended. Sites are $32 per night for two people, plus $2 to $3 for each extra person. Major credit cards are accepted. Long-term stays are OK.

Directions: From I-75, take Exit 101 south onto County Road 951, then drive west on State Road 84 for one mile. Turn west onto Radio Road and go 1.5 miles to Tina Lane. Turn north (right) into the RV/mobile home park.

Contact: Endless Summer RV Estates, 2 Tina Lane, Naples, FL 34104, 239/643-1511.

43 ENCHANTING ACRES RV PARK

Rating: 1

Just south of Naples

Fort Myers/Naples map, grid d2, page 476

"Enchanting" may be overstating the ambience of this sun-scorched campground located across from a shopping center. Except for a few scraggly palms, there's little landscaping. The park is along traffic-congested U.S. 41, with easy access for weary travelers who need an overnight parking spot and aren't looking for a lot of amenities.

Campsites, facilities: This adult-oriented park offers 62 full-hookup sites for self-contained RVs; a neatly kept mobile home community adjoins the park. There are no restrooms, showers, or other facilities. Across the street are a supermarket, a restaurant, and shopping. Children are not permitted. Small pets are accepted.

Reservations, fees: Reservations are recommended. Sites are $20 per night for two people, plus $3 for each additional person. Credit cards are not accepted. Long-term stays are OK.

Directions: From downtown Naples, take U.S. 41/Tamiami Trail south to Enchanting Boulevard and turn left into the park. Landmark: the Naples Towne Center shopping mall is across the highway.

Contact: Enchanting Acres RV Park, 1 Enchanting Boulevard, Naples, FL 34112, 239/793-0091.

44 CLUB NAPLES RV RESORT

Rating: 5

Southeast of Naples

Fort Myers/Naples map, grid d3, page 476

To eastbound travelers on I-75, Exit 101 is the last opportunity for easy-on, easy-off camping before reaching Greater Fort Lauderdale, which typically takes two hours. This well-kept campground, with paved roads and grassy sites set on 20 acres, is the first of several near the interstate along Collier Boulevard (County Road 951) and is convenient to fast-food restaurants, gas stations, and Naples-area tourist attractions. South on Collier Boulevard, about a 20-minute drive, is Marco Island, a resort town with plenty of golfing, fishing, boating, fine dining, and shopping options, plus Tigertail Beach on the Gulf of Mexico, which is open to the public. This is also the way to reach U.S. 41/Tamiami Trail, the eastbound route to Big Cypress National Preserve and Everglades National Park.

Campsites, facilities: There are 309 sites with full hookups, cable TV, and picnic tables. On the premises are restrooms, showers, laundry facilities, a dump station, propane supply, a small general store, a swimming pool and whirlpool, a playground, activity rooms, rental park models, a miniature golf course, volleyball, *pétanque,* basketball, horseshoe pits, shuffleboard courts, and modem hookup for computers. The restrooms, clubhouse, and office are wheelchair accessible. Children are welcome. Leashed pets are permitted.

Reservations, fees: Reservations are recommended. Sites are $38 per night for two people, plus $2.50 for each extra person. Major credit cards are accepted. Long-term stays are OK.

Directions: From I-75, take Exit 101 south on Collier Boulevard (County Road 951). Turn east on Beck Boulevard and drive one mile to the resort.

Contact: Club Naples RV Resort, 3180 Beck Boulevard, Naples, FL 34114, 239/455-7275 or 888/795-2780, fax 239/455-7271, website: www.clubnaplesrv.com.

45 KOUNTREE KAMPINN RV RESORT

♨ 🐾 🚐

Rating: 6

South of Naples

Fort Myers/Naples map, grid d2, page 476

Shade, glorious shade. A tropical forest canopy of pines and palms envelops this campground near Everglades National Park, Marco Island, the Ten Thousand Islands, and Naples. A gun range and golf courses are nearby. Pick up supplies three miles away at shopping centers on the corner of County Road 951/Collier Boulevard and U.S. 41/Tamiami Trail. Within a short hike from the park, you'll find a flea market and a rustic county-owned sports complex that has a go-cart track and spectator bleachers for swamp buggy races.

Campsites, facilities: All 161 RV sites have full hookups, cable TV, and telephone availability; tents are not allowed. Restrooms, showers, picnic tables, laundry facilities, a pool, horseshoe pits, a recreation room, bocce (lawn bowling), shuffleboard courts, and wintertime social programs are available. Children are welcome. Leashed pets under 30 pounds are permitted.

Reservations, fees: Reservations are recommended. Sites are $35 per night for two people, plus $3 per extra person. Cable TV is free, but a $2 fee applies if you need to hook up to 50-amp electrical service. Major credit cards are accepted. Long-term stays are OK.

Directions: From I-75, take Exit 101 and head south on County Road 951/Collier Boulevard for five miles to the park. To enter the park, you must pass the campground and make a U-turn .25 mile past Edison College. From U.S. 41/Tamiami Trail, turn north on County Road 951 and drive three miles.

Contact: Kountree Kampinn RV Resort, 8230 Collier Boulevard, Naples, FL 34114, 239/775-4340, fax 239/775-2269, website: www.kountreekampinn.com.

46 MARCO-NAPLES HITCHING POST TRAVEL TRAILER RESORT

♨ 🐾 ♿ 🚐

Rating: 4

South of Naples

Fort Myers/Naples map, grid d2, page 476

These sun-drenched pull-through sites measure a roomy 30 by 60 feet with 8-by-20-foot concrete patios. The park is within seven miles of two beaches and close to "U-pick" vegetable and fruit farms, shopping centers, bowling alleys, golf courses, grocery stores, and restaurants. But the park's recreation hall activities may keep campers close to home, with an action-packed schedule that includes blood pressure checks every other week, Jazzercise, water aerobics in the pool, a library, square dances, cookouts, and outings such as cruises. There's even a ladies' horseshoe-throwing group.

Campsites, facilities: This wheelchair-accessible park has 300 sites with full hookups and picnic tables. About 236 are available for seasonal visitors, and 50 for vacationers. Restrooms, showers, laundry facilities, a dump station, a recreation building, a pool, shuffleboard and handball courts, and horseshoe pits are available. Children are permitted for short stays only. Leashed pets are allowed.

Reservations, fees: Reservations are recommended. Sites are $28 per night for two people, plus $2.50 for each additional person. Credit cards are not accepted. The maximum stay is seven months. The park is open October 1 through May 1.

Directions: From I-75, take Exit 101 and head south on County Road 951 for 6.8 miles. Turn north at U.S. 41/Tamiami Trail and drive 1.3 miles to Barefoot Williams Road. Turn south and continue to the park entrance.

Contact: Marco-Naples Hitching Post Travel Trailer Resort, 100 Barefoot Williams Road, Naples, FL 34113, 239/774-1259 or 800/362-8968, fax 239/774-9552, website: www.hitchingpostrv.com.

47 NAPLES/MARCO ISLAND KOA KAMPGROUND

Rating: 6

South of Naples

Fort Myers/Naples map, grid d2, page 476

This KOA and the Silver Lakes RV Resort (see next campground) are best situated for campers who want all the amenities of a developed park plus convenient access to Marco Island. For tenters and those with pop-tops, this is the only close option because Silver Lakes won't open its gate to these campers. The sites are fairly crowded but designed for easy parking, and planned activities entertain folks during the season. The boat ramp provides access to the Gulf of Mexico and for canoeing in Henderson Creek and the Audubon Society's Rookery Bay Wildlife Sanctuary, which is a short paddle downstream. The mangroves offer good saltwater fishing grounds for snapper, sheepshead, redfish, and—albeit rarely—snook. A license is required, and you must be sure to follow the rules and season restrictions, as well as boating speed limits, because Florida Marine Patrol enforcement is strict.

Campsites, facilities: There are 172 sites with full hookups, cable TV, and picnic tables. RVs can pull through half the sites. On the premises are restrooms, showers, laundry facilities, a dump station, a pool and hot tub, a playground, a game room, shuffleboard and bocce ball (lawn bowling) courts, canoe and banana bike rentals, a boat ramp, cabin rentals, and two pet walks. The restrooms, recreation hall, and some campsites are wheelchair accessible. Children are welcome. Leashed pets are permitted.

Reservations, fees: Reservations are recommended. Sites are $35 to $70 per night for two people, plus $4 for each additional child and $6 per extra adult. Major credit cards are accepted. Long-term stays are OK.

Directions: From I-75, take Exit 101 and drive eight miles south on County Road 951. At the intersection with U.S. 41/Tamiami Trail, continue south on County Road 951 for .5 mile. Turn west on Tower Road, then drive one more mile to the park entrance.

Contact: Naples/Marco Island KOA Kampground, 1700 Barefoot Williams Road, Naples, FL 33962, 239/774-5455.

48 SILVER LAKES RV RESORT AND GOLF CLUB

Rating: 10

North of Marco Island

Fort Myers/Naples map, grid d2, page 476

Their slogan: "An Invitation to the Good Life!" The emphasis is on "the good life" because this park is marketed to older adults who've made significant investments in their RVs and are willing to spend $60 a night—among the higher prices we've seen. Of course, you get what you pay for: The gated park has spent awesome bucks on amenities, from a pristinely maintained nine-hole executive golf course to two swimming pools. Lots (measuring 45 by 90 feet, with 24-by-40-foot concrete pads) are for sale for those who want to return each winter, but owners are permitted to rent them to overnighters. Worried about the lawn in your absence? Automatic sprinklers make sure the grass stays green. The park, which is close to Marco Island, is two miles from a public boat ramp with direct access to the Gulf of Mexico and the Ten Thousand Islands. A factory outlet shopping mall is next door, and department and grocery stores are within five minutes' drive. About two miles south on County Road 951 at Shell Island Road is the Stephen F. Briggs Memorial Nature Center at Rookery Bay, a nature exhibit and interpretive boardwalk through a mangrove estuary ecosystem. Here's where you can see how Southwest Florida looked before development: low-lying foliage that's home to an array of birds, lizards, snakes, and the almost-extinct Florida panther. For information, call 239/775-8569.

Campsites, facilities: This ultradeluxe, adult-oriented condominium RV resort has 520 full-hookup lots with telephone service, cable TV, restrooms, showers, and laundry facilities available. Three stocked freshwater fishing lakes, a nine-hole golf course, two heated swimming pools, two spas, three tennis courts, six shuffleboard courts, six regulation horseshoe pits, a fitness center, two clubhouses, pool tables, and a pro shop are on site. The "Diamond Club House" has banquet facilities, a dance floor, library, and TV room. RV and boat storage is available so you can leave your stuff in the spring. All areas are wheelchair accessible. Converted trailers, tents, pop-up campers, and truck campers are prohibited. Children are welcome for short stays. Two pets are permitted per site.

Reservations, fees: Reservations are recommended. Sites are $60 per night. Major credit cards are accepted. Long-term stays are OK.

Directions: From I-75, take Exit 101 southbound on County Road 951 for seven miles to the intersection with U.S. 41/Tamiami Trail. Continue on County Road 951 for 1.5 miles to the park entrance on the south side.

Contact: Silver Lakes RV Resort and Golf Club, 1001 Silver Lakes Boulevard, Naples, FL 33114, 239/775-2575 or 800/843-2836, fax 239/775-9989, website: www.silverlakes.com.

49 GREYSTONE PARK

Rating: 3

North of Marco Island

Fort Myers/Naples map, grid d2, page 476

On the highway between Naples and Everglades City, Greystone Park also is midway between the primitive wonders of Big Cypress Swamp and the luxurious, manicured ambience of Marco Island. The sun-swept park is landscaped with Norfolk Island pines and sabal palms, and borders on Henderson Creek, which at high tide allows small boats (18 feet long or smaller) access to the Gulf

of Mexico. The adjacent grocery store sells Latin American specialties.

Campsites, facilities: The 200-unit mobile home park has 65 concrete-pad RV sites with full hookups for overnighters and seasonal visitors; cable TV is available on a monthly basis. Fifteen sites are available for tenters. Restrooms, showers, picnic tables, laundry facilities, a store, a recreation hall, shuffleboard courts, pool tables, horseshoes, wintertime social programs, and a pool are provided. Supermarkets and Kmart are .25 mile away. The pool area, recreation hall, and laundry are wheelchair accessible. This is an age 55-plus park; children may visit residents only. Small, leashed pets under 30 pounds are allowed, and a dog-walk area accommodates their needs.

Reservations, fees: Reservations are accepted. Sites are $35 per night for two people, plus $2 for each additional person. Major credit cards are accepted. Long-term stays are encouraged.

Directions: From I-75 Exit 101, go south on County Road 951 for nine miles to U.S. 41/Tamiami Trail. Turn left. The park is .25 mile ahead at right.

Contact: Greystone Park, 13300 East Tamiami Trail, Naples, FL 34114, 239/774-4044, fax 239/774-0105, website: www.greystonervpark.com.

50 PARADISE POINTE RV RESORT

Rating: 8

North of Marco Island

Fort Myers/Naples map, grid d2, page 476

Paradise Pointe is the younger sister of Greystone Park and was developed by the same investors. The new facility, however, targets the upscale RV crowd: RVs must be at least 24 feet long, and pop-up campers and camping vans are not welcome. The sites have huge concrete pads for easy parking. The relatively young landscaping is growing in, adding an increasing lushness to the grounds. The park, built around five lakes, has a luxurious air-conditioned clubhouse with pool tables, a TV room, and a large gathering hall for parties. The other amenities are resort-class: tennis courts, a large swimming pool and Jacuzzi, and a fully equipped health spa.

Campsites, facilities: The 56-acre park offers 383 full-hookup sites, including cable TV and telephone access. Restrooms, showers, a pool, a spa, tennis and shuffleboard courts, horseshoe pits, a clubhouse with a kitchen, a TV room, game room, laundry facilities, a small putting green, and a health spa with a massage therapist and weights are on the premises. RVs must be at least 24 feet long; pop-up campers and vans are not welcome. A supermarket and restaurants are two miles away. Children are allowed for two weeks. Pets are permitted.

Reservations, fees: Reservations are recommended. Sites are $40 to $45 per night. Major credit cards are accepted. Long-term stays are allowed.

Directions: From the intersection of U.S. 41/Tamiami Trail and County Road 951, drive east on U.S. 41 for 2.5 miles.

Contact: Paradise Pointe RV Resort, 14500 East Tamiami Trail, Naples, FL 34114, 239/793-6886 or 877/4-NAPLES.

51 MAR-GOOD RV PARK

Rating: 2

In Goodland on Marco Island

Fort Myers/Naples map, grid d2, page 476

This is the only RV camp on Marco Island, so it's often filled up during the winter season. The park was founded some 40 years ago, and owner Elhannon Combs is a history buff who displays an eclectic mix of archaeological finds and antiques here. The park's restaurant was once a movie theater, and a back room houses a "museum" with Calusa Indian artifacts dug up on the property every time a new tree was planted. The park can be jammed bumper

to bumper with RVs parked at just 40 sites, but don't worry: Combs says, "I'll put you someplace." He adds that the best time for overnighters to visit is from April to May and from July to September.

The park is in the heart of Goodland, a laidback village with a few good seafood restaurants and an old inn. The other side of Marco is upscale, with plenty of shopping and a variety of restaurants, plus public Tigertail Beach on the Gulf of Mexico. Marco's evolution from a sleepy hamlet hidden in mangroves began in the 1960s with development by three brothers: Elliott, Robert, and Frank Mackle, members of a wealthy family. The Mackles' ambition to transform this former Indian fishing ground hit a roadblock in the 1970s when the government, under pressure from environmental groups, refused to issue more dredging permits. The Mackles' dreams were dashed, and the paving of Marco slowed.

Campsites, facilities: There are 40 RV or tent sites with picnic tables, full hookups, and cable TV. On the premises are restrooms, showers, laundry facilities, a boat ramp, boat charters, a small grocery store, cottages, and a restaurant. This is an adults-only park, where families with children are welcome only on holidays. Leashed pets are permitted.

Reservations, fees: Reservations are recommended. Sites are $30 per night for two people, plus $2 for each additional person. Credit cards are not accepted. Long-term stays are OK.

Directions: From Naples, take U.S. 41/Tamiami Trail south to State Road 92. Turn west and cross the bridge to Marco Island. After the bridge, immediately turn south on State Road 92A toward Goodland. Turn east on Pear Tree Avenue. The park is about two blocks from the intersection, at 321 Pear Tree.

Contact: Mar-Good RV Park, 321 Pear Tree Avenue, P.O. Box 248, Goodland, FL 33933, 239/394-6383, fax 239/394-4845, website: www.goodlandfl.com.

Chapter 17

Greater West Palm Beach

Greater West Palm Beach

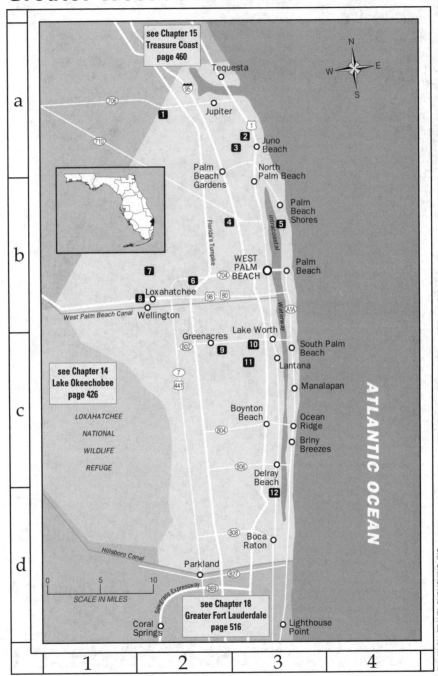

1 WEST JUPITER CAMPING RESORT

Rating: 5

West of Jupiter

Greater West Palm Beach map, grid a2, page 506

Fan-shaped palm fronds and the long needles of Florida slash pine trees shade portions of this remote, 10-acre campground, but odds are that the paved roads will lead you to a sunny RV campsite. Tenters sleep in their own section along a tree-dotted fence line near the playground and 84-degree heated pool. Some campers pluck their own breakfasts of grapefruits and oranges from the park's fruit trees in winter. Video games are found in a large tiki hut, and monthly entertainment may bring a band, a magician, or a disc jockey to the campground. The beach is about a 10-minute drive east, and the St. Louis Cardinals play spring training games one highway exit south at Roger Dean Stadium, 4751 Main Street, in Jupiter; for baseball tickets, call 561/775-1818. Within a 30-minute drive are Lion Country Safari and fishing charters at Lake Okeechobee. In Jupiter, the oldest lighthouse in Palm Beach County is open for tours Sunday through Wednesday and has a small museum at its base; call 561/747-6639.

Campsites, facilities: The 74 full-hookup RV sites in this resort are set apart from a large tent section. A pool, a playground, tennis, volleyball, horseshoes, shuffleboard, monthly entertainment, a basketball court, catch-and-release fishing pond, and a game room with video games and pool tables entertain campers. Showers, restrooms, picnic tables, concrete pads and patios, a convenience store, deli foods, cable TV, telephone hookups, rental RVs, LP gas, and laundry facilities are available. Nearby are canoe rentals, a golf course, and a theater. Most areas are wheelchair accessible. Children are permitted. Pets are allowed, but small dogs are preferred.

Reservations, fees: Reservations are recommended. Fees for two people are $25 to $33 per night for RVs, $19 to $26 nightly for tents. Add $5 per additional adult and $3 for cable TV. Major credit cards are accepted. Long-term stays are OK.

Directions: From I-95, take Exit 87B and go west about five miles on State Road 706/Indiantown Road. Turn left (south) at 130th Avenue North and proceed to the campground entrance at the first right.

Contact: West Jupiter Camping Resort, 17801 130th Avenue North, Jupiter, FL 33478, 561/746-6073 or 888/746-6073, fax 561/743-3738, website: www.westjupitercampingresort.com.

2 JUNO BEACH RV PARK

Rating: 6

Off U.S. 1 in Juno Beach

Greater West Palm Beach map, grid a3, page 506

The lapping waves of the Atlantic Ocean are within walking distance of this sunny 25-acre park, where paved streets (maximum speed of 10 mph) pass two rectangular fishing lakes, a playground, and a heated pool with hot tub. If the place feels like a residential community, the park's condominium concept explains why: A monthly maintenance fee for the condo owners includes niceties such as lawn upkeep and underground sprinklers, and some campers opt to buy their concrete-pad RV sites at about half the cost of monthly rental rates. (The fee does not apply for overnighters or seasonal visitors.)

Most campsites are sun-baked, but a line of tall trees borders the back of sites A29 through A48. To avoid feeling like a sardine in a sea of RVs, don't sleep in section C, where rigs are packed together in groups of 10. Anglers need to walk only a few steps to cast a line into a fishing lake if they snag campsites A59 through A68 or any in section B. For another fishing option, head to a pier east of the campground.

Campsites, facilities: Among the 264 sites in

this condominium resort, 100 full-hookup spots are for transient RVs up to 45 feet long and have a picnic table and a fire ring. A pool with a sundeck and a hot tub, a recreation room, a playground, horseshoes, shuffleboard, two fishing lakes, and social programs keep campers busy. Restrooms, a dump station, rental trailers, and two laundry facilities are available. Management says most areas are wheelchair accessible. Groceries and restaurants are nearby. Young children must be adult-supervised, and everyone under 18 is subject to a 10 P.M. curfew. Leashed pets (a maximum of two are allowed) must walk in designated areas.

Reservations, fees: Reservations are recommended. Sites are $28 to $40 per night for two people and one pet, plus $2 for each additional person or extra pet. Add $3 for electrical service; cable TV is included in the base rate. Major credit cards are accepted. Long-term stays are OK.

Directions: From I-95, take Exit 87A and go east a little over four miles on Indiantown Road to U.S. 1. Turn right (south). In about three miles, you'll see a shopping center called The Bluffs on the left side. Turn right at the corner of SunTrust Bank. The RV park is one block ahead to your right.

Contact: Juno Beach RV Park, 900 Juno Ocean Walk, Juno Beach, FL 33408, 561/622-7500, fax 561/627-6595.

3 PALM BEACH GARDENS RV PARK

Rating: 4

In Palm Beach Gardens
Greater West Palm Beach map, grid a3, page 506

Plunging into the heated pool, tossing horseshoes, or playing a wintertime game of bingo at the recreation room are the main activities for folks at these grassy and gravel RV sites, but they may wish to venture out of the 10-acre park for more action. Within 2.5 miles are the

PGA National Resort and Spa and the full-service yacht harbor of Soverel Harbour. More down to earth, the big rolling dunes and fairly wide stretch of sand at Juno Beach are about three miles east of this former KOA. In spring, the St. Louis Cardinals play practice games at nearby Roger Dean Stadium, 4751 Main Street in Jupiter; for tickets, call 561/775-1818. Farther west, drag racers and racing school students attend more than 150 events per year at the 200-acre Moroso Motorsports Park; call 561/622-1400. Most visitors to this park stay for a month or two or the entire winter.

Campsites, facilities: All 106 full-hookup RV sites (most of them pull-through) have picnic tables. A pool, a recreation room, horseshoes, propane gas sales, showers, restrooms, limited RV parts, and a dump station are available. A supermarket, restaurants, and Palm Beach Gardens Mall are about one mile away. Children are allowed for short-term stays, and leashed pets are permitted.

Reservations, fees: Reservations are not necessary. Sites are $30 to $32 per night for two people, plus $5 for each additional adult and $2 per child. Credit cards are not accepted. Long-term stays are allowed.

Directions: From I-95, take Exit 83 and go east about 1.5 miles on Donald Ross Road to Military Trail. Turn right. Proceed less than 1.5 miles to Hood Road. Turn left (east). The park is about .25 mile ahead.

Contact: Palm Beach Gardens RV Park, 4063 Hood Road, Palm Beach Gardens, FL 33410, 561/622-8212, fax 561/622-3419.

4 VACATION INN RESORT

Rating: 6

West of West Palm Beach
Greater West Palm Beach map, grid b3, page 506

Major William Lauderdale and his Tennessee Volunteers cut their way through a jungly subtropical forest during the Second Seminole

War of the mid-1800s to create the now-busy thoroughfare that fronts this campground. Continue farther south to Fort Lauderdale, and you'll see how Major Lauderdale's trail has been transformed into an asphalt street crammed with neon lights and strip shopping centers with too-small parking lots. But we digress.

Beyond the security gate sits a manicured campground tailored to the resort crowd vacationing in what sometimes is called the state's wealthiest (per capita) county—Palm Beach. Ask for a brochure and you'll be able to choose from four campsite designs, all with lighted patios, automatic lawn sprinklers, paved sites, and cable TV. Some people buy their lots, so the number of spaces available to campers varies.

To reach the ocean, drive about five miles east on Blue Heron Boulevard, passing through some dingy neighborhoods, and cross a bridge to Singer Island, the one-time winter playground of the late industrialist John D. MacArthur. You can use one of three municipal beaches in the small town of Palm Beach Shores. For a more woodsy oceanfront experience, head north a few miles on Highway A1A to swim in the ocean or wade in the Intracoastal Waterway at the state park named for MacArthur. Fishing is also popular there.

Campsites, facilities: All 400 full-hookup sites are for self-contained RVs. Facilities include restrooms, showers, picnic tables, cable TV, and laundry. Two pools, a TV lounge, racquetball, tennis, a clubhouse, billiards, an exercise room, horseshoes, and two hot tubs entertain campers. Children and leashed pets are permitted.

Reservations, fees: Reservations are advised. Sites are $50 per night for two people, plus $3 for each additional person. Major credit cards are accepted for daily rates. Long-term rates are available.

Directions: Exit I-95 at Blue Heron Boulevard (Exit 76). Head west a few blocks to Military Trail. Turn left and look for the park about .5 mile ahead on the east side of the road.

Contact: Vacation Inn Resort, 6500 North Military Trail, West Palm Beach, FL 33407, 561/848-6166 or 800/262-9681.

5 PEANUT ISLAND

Rating: 10

Near the town of Riviera Beach between Singer Island and Palm Beach

Greater West Palm Beach map, grid b3, page 506

Can it get much better than this? You have (almost) your own wooded private island, accessible only by boat, yet so close to civilization and there's a fascinating historic hook. Peanut Island is a Palm Beach County park with 20 primitive tent sites, but you can only get there by ferry or private boat. Just east of the island is the Port of Palm Beach, where cruise and cargo ships sail past to their docks; on the west side is the barrier island protecting this lovely spot from Atlantic Ocean waves. All around you are waterways and sailboat anchorages. You'll have to make an effort, and definitely reservations, but it's worthwhile.

This 86-acre "spoil island," formed from sand dredged from the ocean in 1919 when developer Henry Flagler decided he needed ocean access for his yachting customers, became a historical hot spot in 1961 during the Cuban Missile Crisis. The U.S. Navy Seabees secretly built an emergency fallout shelter here for President John F. Kennedy, who often spent winter weekends at the Kennedy compound in the ritzy town of Palm Beach nearby. Today, the bunker and what would have been a command center for the president in case of a nuclear attack is part of the tour offered by the Palm Beach Maritime Museum onsite (561/842-8202). The island also served as a Coast Guard station, and the ecologically oriented park service plans to reforest the island with native vegetation. Australian pines are pretty, but they are a non-Florida native tree and are considered a nuisance because of their brittleness in high winds. Meantime, kayakers and boaters use the island during the day, either beaching their craft on the shore or anchoring nearby and swimming to or walking on the shallow sandbars to the island. A paved path of pretty blocks encircles the isle so you can have the panoramic experience.

Campsites, facilities: There are 20 primitive tent sites set on this oval-shaped island wooded with Australian pines and palm trees. Beaches are on the east side of the island. Wheelchair-accessible restrooms, showers, picnic tables and a communal fire ring are available. The island is closed after dark for campers' use only. Children are welcome. Leashed pets are permitted. A 170-foot fishing pier, boat dock, and slips for 19 boats are provided.

Reservations, fees: You must have reservations. Camping is $16.50 per night. Check-in is 1 P.M. and check-out is 11 A.M. Only six people are allowed per site. Call the park office at 561/845-4445 for information or 561/966-6600. The campground/dock office also monitors VHF channel 16. For ferry service, call 561/339-2504 or stop by Phil Foster Park across from the island on Blue Heron Boulevard.

Directions: From I-95, take Exit 76 eastbound onto Blue Heron Island Boulevard. Drive 3.5 miles east to Phil Foster Park for the ferry service. Marinas and boat services are nearby for private boaters, including the Riviera Beach Marina on Blue Heron Boulevard.

Contact: Palm Beach County Parks and Recreation Department, 2700 Sixth Avenue South, Lake Worth, FL 33461, 561/582-7992, fax 561/588-5469, website: www.pbcgov.com/parks/locations/parks/peanuts.htm.

6 PINE LAKE CAMP RESORT

Rating: 4

West of West Palm Beach
Greater West Palm Beach map, grid b2, page 506

Don't plunge into the park's little Pine Lake, or you may have a chance encounter with an occasional summer visitor—an alligator. Instead, you can swim in the heated pool near the playground. Tuesday and Saturday mean bingo time in winter at this flat campground about 10 miles east of the Lion Country Safari wildlife park. On Sunday morning, coffee and doughnuts are served at the park pavilion. To sleep farthest from busy Okeechobee Boulevard, ask about the campsites rimming Pine Lake, although only five have full hookups. Full-hookup sites start at a canal lining Okeechobee Boulevard and move farther inland.

Campsites, facilities: All 194 RV campsites have water and electricity. Fewer than half have sewer hookups. A pool, a playground, shuffleboard, horseshoes, and limited winter activities entertain campers, most of whom are retirees staying for the winter. Showers, restrooms, a dump station, pavilions, a camp store, LP gas, and laundry facilities are available. Outlet shops are 1.5 miles away. Children are allowed. One dog under 25 pounds is accepted per site, but pit bulls are forbidden.

Reservations, fees: Reservations are recommended during the winter. Sites are about $14 to $20 per night for two people, plus $2 per extra person. Major credit cards are accepted. Long-term stays are OK.

Directions: From I-95, take Exit 70B and go west on Okeechobee Boulevard about five miles to Skees Road. Turn left, then immediately turn right into the campground. If instead you're traveling on Florida's Turnpike, take Exit 99 and go west one mile to the campground.

Contact: Pine Lake Camp Resort, 7000 Okeechobee Boulevard, West Palm Beach, FL 33411, 561/686-0714.

7 SUNSPORT GARDENS

Rating: 6

In Loxahatchee west of West Palm Beach
Greater West Palm Beach map, grid b2,
page 506

At Hugo Forester's family-targeted nudist retreat located in rural Loxahatchee, everyone is expected to be in the altogether while swimming in the pool or the hot tub, although exceptions are made in other areas of the resort. The bent trunks of palm trees may lean away from your pop-up or RV at the grassy campsites. Some sites are shadier than others, but the 42-acre park proudly displays its greenery. At least some RV campers will sleep near a lake flanked by arrow-straight, sparse-needled pines. Tenters may set up primitive campsites wherever they'd like. For afternoon shade, duck into the screened pavilion for a game of darts or cards. The restaurant serves breakfast, lunch, and dinner, and every February, this park is the home of the Midwinter Naturist Festival. Lion Country Safari, golf courses, and shopping are nearby. Prince Charles has climbed onto polo ponies at the nearby 125-acre Palm Beach Polo and Country Club, where matches are held in winter; call 561/798-7000.

Campsites, facilities: This 40-acre family nudist retreat has innumerable tent sites and 58 RV sites, 40 sites with full hookups and 18 with water and electricity. A heated pool, a hot tub, a sauna, a playground, a Kidz Club, a game room, two lighted tennis courts, regulation volleyball courts, two new *pétanque* (French-style bowling) courts, paddleboats, horseshoe pits, a game room with Ping-Pong and pool tables, a sundeck, and a .25-mile nature trail keep campers busy. Dances are held Saturday nights in the pavilion. Showers, restrooms, two dump stations, rental trailers and cabins, firewood, laundry facilities, snacks, and a restaurant are on premises. Groceries are six miles away. Children are welcome. Leashed pets are OK.

Reservations, fees: Reservations are recommended; they are a must November through April. Sites are $30 per night for two people; $25 for singles. Major credit cards are accepted.

Directions: From I-95, take Exit 70B and go west on Okeechobee Boulevard about 14 miles, passing through Royal Palm Beach. At D Road, turn right. Continue 2.5 miles until it dead-ends into North Road. Turn right, then take the first left to enter the campground.

Contact: Sunsport Gardens, 14125 North Road, Loxahatchee, FL 33470, 561/793-0423 or 800/551-7217, fax 561/793-6370, website: www.sunsportgarden.com.

8 LION COUNTRY SAFARI KOA

Rating: 7

In Loxahatchee west of West Palm Beach
Greater West Palm Beach map, grid b2,
page 506

Wake to the roar of lions. No kidding. The kings of the jungle tend to express their opinions around their 6:30 A.M. feeding time next door at the 500-acre Lion Country Safari wildlife park, where tourists drive within inches of the freely roaming cats, 2.5-ton white rhinos, and more than 1,000 other creatures. In the afternoon, monkeys get into the verbal act. You'll hear them from your partially shaded or sunny shell-rock campsite.

Although a heated pool and social activities can keep campers busy, sleeping next to the nation's first drive-through cageless zoo (opened in 1967) is the prime reason to stay at the remote 20-acre campground. There is precious little else to do in this fairly rural region, where roadside vegetable stands sometimes can be found along State Road 80. So campers understandably head next door to the safari's amusement park rides and drive-through zoo, where they stop to let elephants cross in front of their cars.

Elsewhere, hikers who travel about four miles west of the KOA can see the northern Everglades by visiting one of the largest water-pumping stations in the world—the S5-A, which is bigger than most houses. Walk down the little-explored levee separating sugarcane fields from the Everglades. To your left, you'll probably see alligators, wading birds, and waterfowl such as ducks and coots. Within the first mile, you'll see an experimental project aimed at cleaning dirty sugarcane water before it reaches the Everglades, and maybe get a glimpse of more wildlife. To get to the S5-A pump station, turn right from the KOA onto State Road 80/Southern Boulevard. Head west about four miles to where the road bends (called 20 Mile Bend). Instead of taking the main road to the right, make a left across the metal bridge crossing the canal, then immediately turn left. Take that road east to the dead end by a picnic area and then park. Look to the southwest and you'll see a gate preventing vehicular access to the levee. Just walk around the gate and hike as far south as you'd like.

Campsites, facilities: Twenty-two tent sites are set apart from 211 full-hookup RV sites (158 pull-through). For recreation, there's a pool, a playground, a game room, volleyball, basketball, shuffleboard, horseshoes, miniature golf, winter and summer social programs, rental cabins, and a recreation room. Showers, restrooms, a dump station, picnic tables, limited groceries, LP gas sales, and laundry facilities are on the premises. Management says wheelchairs have access to the store, showers, restrooms, pool, and laundry room. Children are welcome. Leashed pets are OK.

Reservations, fees: Reservations are recommended. Sites are $27 to $36 per night for two people, plus $3 for each additional person and $3 for using air-conditioning or electrical heaters. Major credit cards are accepted. The maximum stay is three months.

Directions: From I-95, take Exit 68 and go west on U.S. 98/Southern Boulevard for 15 miles to the campground at right.

Contact: Lion Country Safari KOA, P.O. Box 16066, 2000 Lion Country Safari Road, Loxahatchee FL 33470, 561/793-9797 or 800/562-9115, fax 561/763-9603, website: www.koa.com.

9 CAMPING RESORT OF THE PALM BEACHES

Rating: 4

Near Florida's Turnpike west of Lake Worth
Greater West Palm Beach map, grid c2, page 506

Potluck dinners are a year-round institution at this fairly urban campground fronting busy four-lane Lake Worth Road. In winter, bowling, bingo, bonfires, evening card games, Saturday night coffee, and other activities help round out the action, which may be a good thing, considering the distance from South Florida's tourist hot spots. Atlantic Ocean beaches and a fishing pier are about six miles east. Lion Country Safari is 16 miles to the northwest.

Activities are concentrated at the front portion of the respectably shady campground, so you won't sleep right next to well-traveled Lake Worth Road. A strip of scattered parking spaces separates campers from the hub of campground activities. RVs are lined up, two deep and about 20 abreast, along three long oval islands. A single line of campers in Section D perhaps enjoy the most privacy, with a smattering of trees to one side and a park road at another.

Campsites, facilities: These 134 full-hookup sites are for RVs or tents. A pool, a recreation hall, shuffleboard, horseshoes, a game room, a playground, and basketball keep campers busy. Showers, a fire ring, a barbecue area, a camp store, a dump station, and laundry facilities are provided. Children and leashed pets are permitted.

Reservations, fees: Reservations are recommended. Sites are $18 to $37 per night for three people, plus $4 for each additional person. Major credit cards are accepted. Long-term rates are offered.

Directions: From Florida's Turnpike at Exit 93, drive nearly three miles east on Lake Worth Road to the park entrance at right.

Contact: Camping Resort of the Palm Beaches,

5332 Lake Worth Road, Lake Worth, FL 33463, 561/965-1653 or 800/247-9650, fax 561/965-9095, website: www.camppalmbeaches.com.

10 JOHN PRINCE PARK CAMPGROUND

Rating: 6

On Lake Osborne west of Lake Worth

Greater West Palm Beach map, grid c3, page 506

The placid waters of Lake Osborne provide a pleasant backdrop for joggers and bicyclists following the shady five-mile exercise path that winds through 726-acre John Prince Park, a county-run recreation complex big enough to merit three entrances. The 48-acre campground is set in the southern portion of the shady park. Within the park outside the campground, banyan trees and shaggy Australian pines shade scattered picnic tables near tennis courts and two volleyball nets. Golfers can take their pick of a driving range, 18-hole miniature golf, or a par-3 golf course. At the park's focal point—Lake Osborne—you can boat, water-ski, or fish for bass (just bring the gear).

Some waterview campsites are shady; inland campsites tend to have little or no brush separating neighbors. Inquire about waterview sites on Explorer Lane or Allegro Road if you don't plan to camp for more than two weeks (the limit at those sites). For the best lakeview spots on a loop drive with a central community campfire circle, try sites 38 through 41. Fifty-three sites are paved; the rest have a shell rock surface. Don't expect a manicured feel at this tree-dotted park. Rules clearly state that alligators and snakes are considered residents that should be respected and left alone. You needn't worry, though, because alligators and snakes pose little threat if you don't bother them. Just don't feed the gators. A security gate is closed 24 hours a day.

Campsites, facilities: All 265 campsites have water, electricity, and picnic tables. Restrooms, fire rings, a boat ramp, a dump station, and four playgrounds are on site. At the park beyond the entrance gate are a fitness trail, a golf course, a driving range, a nature area, and picnic areas. Several areas are wheelchair accessible. Children are welcome. Leashed, attended pets (no pit bulls) are permitted.

Reservations, fees: Reservations are recommended. Sites are $16.50 to $20 per night for five people, plus $2 for each additional person. Credit cards are not accepted. Camping is limited to 100 days per year. The maximum stay at waterfront sites with the best views is 14 days.

Directions: From I-95, take Exit 63 and go west on Sixth Avenue South to Congress Avenue. Turn left. The campground entrance is about .5 mile ahead on the left. From the Florida Turnpike, take the Lake Worth Road exit and turn left. Drive 5.2 miles to Congress Avenue and turn right. Drive .9 mile to the park.

Contact: John Prince Park Campground, 4759 South Congress Avenue, Lake Worth, Florida 33461. Or contact the Palm Beach County Parks and Recreation Department, 2700 Sixth Avenue South, Lake Worth, FL 33461, 561/582-7992 or 877/992-9925, fax 561/588-5469, website: www.co.palm-beach.fl.us/parks.

11 PALM BEACH TRAVELER PARK

Rating: 1

In Lantana

Greater West Palm Beach map, grid c3, page 506

This 7.5-acre suburban home of wintertime bingo games and potluck dinners attracts a 50-50 mix of permanent residents and travelers. The paved park roads, which have a 10 mph speed limit, form a rough figure eight through the grounds, passing staggered, instead of rigidly side-by-side, sleeping spots. Atlantic Ocean beaches are four miles east. A few minutes away is Lake Worth, which is ignored by many tourists. Still, head that way for some bright spots: a 1,000-foot ocean fishing pier, a beach where early birds get the best parking spots, and free concerts at the Bryant Park band shell on the Intracoastal Waterway.

Campsites, facilities: This adult-oriented park has 100 full-hookup sites for RVs. Each rig must have its own bathroom and shower. A pool, shuffleboard, a clubhouse, horseshoes, rental trailers, laundry facilities, and wintertime social programs are available. The pool and clubhouse are wheelchair accessible. Children may visit a registered camper for no more than two weeks per year. Pets are forbidden.

Reservations, fees: Reservations are recommended. Sites are $25 per night for two people, plus $2 per additional person. Credit cards are not accepted. Long-term stays are OK.

Directions: From I-95, take Exit 61 and go west a little more than two miles on Lantana Road/County Road 812. Turn left at Lawrence Road. The park is .5 mile ahead on the right.

Contact: Palm Beach Traveler Park, 6159 Lawrence Road, Lantana, FL 33462, 561/967-3139, email: jerryrv@msn.com.

12 DEL-RATON TRAVEL TRAILER PARK

Rating: 2

On U.S. 1 in Delray Beach
Greater West Palm Beach map, grid d3, page 506

If you want to camp near the beach in southern Palm Beach County, this is pretty much your only choice. Tourists sometimes are astounded by the seemingly endless stream of strip shopping centers spanning almost the length of U.S. 1 in South Florida, and this neck of the woods is no exception. Car dealerships, shops, eateries, and more hubs of commerce line the street on the approach to the five-acre park. Once you pass the security gate, the straight, paved roads (with 5 mph speed limits) pass tree-dotted yet largely sunny concrete-pad campsites separated from each other by grassy lawns. The park is the closest to the tony shops at Mizner Park in Boca Raton. The Atlantic Ocean is a short drive east.

Campsites, facilities: All 60 full-hookup sites (25 pull-through) are for RVs up to 38 feet long. Showers, restrooms, a dump station, a recreation room, LP gas sales, and laundry facilities are available. Groceries and a restaurant are across the street. Children are welcome short-term but not as monthly residents. Pets are forbidden.

Reservations, fees: Reservations are recommended, except in summer. Sites are $27 to $33 per night for two people, plus $1 per extra person. Credit cards are not accepted. Long-term stays are permitted for adults.

Directions: From I-95, take Exit 51 and go east one mile on Linton Boulevard to U.S. 1/South Federal Highway. Turn right. Proceed one mile to the trailer park.

Contact: Del-Raton Travel Trailer Park, 2998 South Federal Highway, Delray Beach, FL 33483, 561/278-4633, email: delraton@aol.com.

COURTESY OF VISIT FLORIDA

Chapter 18

Greater Fort Lauderdale

Greater Fort Lauderdale

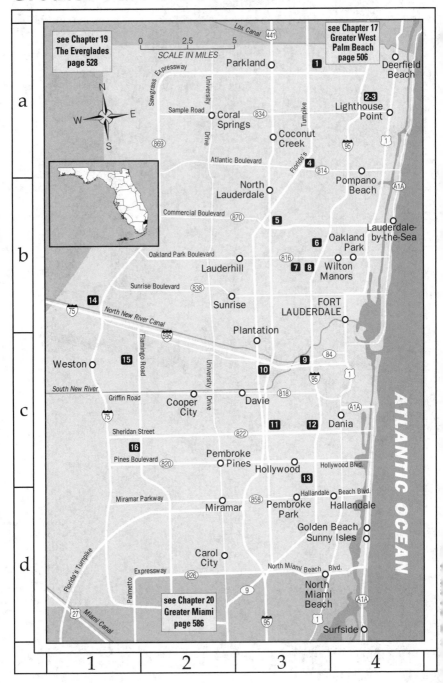

see Chapter 19
The Everglades
page 528

see Chapter 17
Greater West
Palm Beach
page 506

0   2.5   5
SCALE IN MILES

Lox Canal 441

Parkland

Deerfield
Beach

1

2-3
Lighthouse
Point

Sawgrass Expressway

University Drive

Sample Road

Coral
Springs

834

Coconut
Creek

Florida's Turnpike

95

1

869

Atlantic Boulevard

4
814

North
Lauderdale

Pompano
Beach

A1A

Commercial Boulevard

870

5

Lauderdale-
by-the-Sea

Oakland Park Boulevard

6

Oakland
Park

Lauderhill

816

7 **8**

Wilton
Manors

Sunrise Boulevard

838

Sunrise

FORT
LAUDERDALE

14
75

North New River Canal

595

Plantation

9
84

15

Flamingo Road

10

95

1

Weston

South New River

Griffin Road

University Drive

Cooper
City

Davie

818

11

12

Dania

A1A

75

Sheridan Street

822

16

Pines Boulevard

820

Pembroke
Pines

Hollywood

Hollywood Blvd.

13

Miramar Parkway

Miramar

858

Pembroke
Park

Hallandale

Beach Blvd.

Hallandale

Golden Beach

Sunny Isles

Carol
City

Expressway

826

North Miami Beach Blvd.

9

North
Miami
Beach

A1A

Florida's Turnpike

Palmetto

27

Miami Canal

see Chapter 20
Greater Miami
page 586

95

1

Surfside

ATLANTIC OCEAN

N
W   E
S

a

b

c

d

1   2   3   4

1 QUIET WATERS PARK

Rating: 8

In Pompano Beach

Greater Fort Lauderdale map, grid a3, page 516

Tall Australian pines shade the campsites, which overlook a fjordlike lake. You almost could forget you're in the city if it weren't for the park's noisy public beach and nearby water playground. (Swimming at the campsites is prohibited.) If you're camping with friends who don't have their own equipment, tell them about "rent a camp," a package deal that includes a sleeping pad for each person, a cooler, and use of a canoe. On weekends, the park tends to be chaotic, so try to arrange your stay during quieter times. Site 23 is the most secluded, although it's also farthest from the bathhouse. An unusual feature of the park is a "cable skiing" concession near the swimming beach: Instead of a boat, a mechanized cable pulls you across the water on skis. You can also try your luck in the fishing lake, paddle a canoe, catch a breeze on a sailboard, or ride your bike. This park has one of South Florida's few mountain bike trails. Ten minutes from the park is Butterfly World, a tourist attraction where thousands of butterflies flutter freely about you.

Campsites, facilities: This 430-acre county park offers 16 "rent a camp" sites with permanent canvas tents mounted on 8-by-10-foot wooden platforms. Seven additional tent-only sites accommodate campers with their own gear. Restrooms, showers, picnic tables, grills, and fire rings are provided; water is available only at a central source. The park has a camp store, an 18-hole miniature golf course, two lakes, a swimming area, and a playground. The campsites, water playground, and walking paths are wheelchair accessible. Children and one leashed pet are welcome.

Reservations, fees: Prepaid reservations are required. Sites are $25 per night for two people,

plus $2 for each extra person up to a group of six. Two pets are permitted; the extra fee is $1 per pet. Major credit cards are accepted. The maximum stay is two weeks.

Directions: From I-95, take Exit 42B and drive 2.8 miles west on Hillsboro Boulevard. Turn south at Powerline Road and continue .5 mile to the park entrance on the west.

Contact: Quiet Waters Park, 6601 North Powerline Road, Pompano Beach, FL 33073, 954/360-1315, website: www.broward.org/parks.

2 BREEZY HILL RV RESORT

Rating: 3

In Pompano Beach

Greater Fort Lauderdale map, grid a4, page 516

Security gates and concrete-block walls guard this neatly kept RV park and mobile home community. It's preferred by French Canadians, many of whom leave their rigs here year-round. During the winter, campers keep busy by taking English classes, reading a newsletter in French, bowling, playing bocce (lawn bowling), *pétanque* (French-style bowling), or shuffleboard, and participating in other activities. All sites have concrete pads and accommodate RVs up to 42 feet long. This is one of three well-established snowbird refuges within two blocks of each other.

Campsites, facilities: Among the 764 full-hookup sites, about seven for overnighters and the rest are available for seasonal RVs. More than 200 are permanent residents. Restrooms, showers, laundry facilities, a billiard hall, horseshoes, and shuffleboard are available. There are two pools (one heated) and two recreation halls. A convenience store is one block away. A supermarket and the ocean are three miles distant. You must be 55 or older to stay here, and pop-up campers are not allowed. Pets are prohibited, as are children.

Reservations, fees: Reservations are recommended. Sites are $25 to $29 per night for two people, plus $3 per additional person. Major credit cards are accepted. Long-term stays are permitted.

Directions: From I-95, take Exit 39 east on Sample Road and drive .25 mile. At Northeast Third Avenue, turn north and go 1.5 miles to Northeast 48th Street. Turn east and use the second park entrance.

Contact: Breezy Hill RV Resort, 800 Northeast 48th Street, Pompano Beach, FL 33064, 954/942-8688, website: www.mhchomes.com.

3 HIGHLAND WOODS TRAVEL TRAILER PARK

Rating: 2

In Pompano Beach
Greater Fort Lauderdale map, grid a4, page 516

If you have business in the area or are visiting relatives, then this place might do. The quiet park is geared to people over 45 and families who like a homey atmosphere. Paved interior roads lead to the concrete sites, each offering a grassy area in back and to the side. Fort Lauderdale's famous sandy beaches are four miles away.

Campsites, facilities: This 147-site adult-oriented RV park offers full hookups, restrooms, showers, a swimming pool, a recreation room, *pétanque* (French-style bowling), horseshoes, shuffleboard, pool tables, two laundry rooms, and wintertime activities such as bingo. Groceries, restaurants, movies, and a flea market require about a five-minute drive. Children are allowed. Pets are permitted in a designated area.

Reservations, fees: Reservations are recommended. Sites are $22 to $27 per night for two people, plus $3 per extra person. Credit cards are accepted. Long-term stays are OK.

Directions: From I-95, take Exit 39 east on Sample Road and drive .25 mile. At Northeast Third Avenue, turn north and go 1.5 miles to Northeast 48th Street. Turn east; the park is on the south side of the road.

Contact: Highland Woods Travel Trailer Park, 900 Northeast 48th Street, Pompano Beach, FL 33064, 954/942-6254, website: www.mhchomes.com.

4 GOLF VIEW ESTATES

Rating: 3

In Pompano Beach
Greater Fort Lauderdale map, grid a3, page 516

An immaculate walled mobile home community wedged between a busy highway and a warehouse area, this resort has the feel of a permanent neighborhood. Many travel trailers are parked here year-round, and their owners have built on "Florida rooms" (screened porches). An adult tricycle is parked in almost every well-tended driveway. Nightly security patrols, a heated swimming pool with Jacuzzi, saunas for men and women, and a sundeck complete the picture.

Campsites, facilities: Open to campers 55 and older, this RV park/mobile home community offers 120 RV sites with full hookups. About 30 additional lots are occupied by full timers. Shuffleboard courts, a pool, a Jacuzzi, saunas, and a large wheelchair-accessible clubhouse are provided. Children and pets are prohibited.

Reservations, fees: Reservations are recommended. Sites are $33 per night for two people. Credit cards are accepted. Long-term rates are available.

Directions: From I-95, take Exit 36 and drive 2.5 miles west on Atlantic Boulevard to Northwest 31st Avenue. Turn north; the entrance to the park is on the west side. From Florida's Turnpike, take Exit 67 and go .5 mile south on Northwest 31st Avenue.

Contact: Golf View Estates, 901 Northwest 31st Avenue, Pompano Beach, FL 33069, 954/972-4140, fax 954/972-3041, website: www.golfviewestates.com.

5 KOZY KAMPERS TRAVEL TRAILER PARK

🐕 🚐

Rating: 2

In Fort Lauderdale

Greater Fort Lauderdale map, grid b3, page 516

Despite its urban locale, this pine-needle-blanketed park is notable for its forest of 100-foot-tall Australian pines. You can park even the biggest rig under towering trees that shelter many of the concrete-pad sites. Shopping centers and restaurants are nearby, and the location offers good access to local attractions, such as the *Jungle Queen* riverboat cruise, the Sawgrass Mills outlet mall, Pompano Harness Racing, and Dania Jai Alai. Although kids are permitted, parents are warned that they must assume financial responsibility for any damage or injury caused by their children "regardless of age."

Campsites, facilities: All 104 sites have full hookups with 30-amp and 50-amp service, cable TV, and telephone availability. Fourteen are pull-through. Restrooms, showers, a laundry room, a dump station, and a recreation hall are provided. Children are welcome but must be supervised by an adult in all areas of the park. Leashed dogs are permitted; a small dog-walk area has been set aside.

Reservations, fees: Reservations are recommended. Sites are $28 to $35 per night for two people, plus $3 for each additional person. Major credit cards are accepted. Long-term stays are OK.

Directions: From I-95, take Exit 32 on Commercial Boulevard and drive west three miles to the park, which is on the north side. From Florida's Turnpike, take Exit 62 and go east on Commercial Boulevard .5 mile.

Contact: Kozy Kampers Travel Trailer Park, 3631 West Commercial Boulevard, Fort Lauderdale, FL 33309, 954/731-8570, fax 954/731-3140, website: www.kozykampers.com.

6 JOHN D. EASTERLIN PARK

🚶 🚴 🛶 🐕 ⛵ 🚐 ⛺

Rating: 7

In Oakland Park

Greater Fort Lauderdale map, grid b3, page 516

It's hard to believe you're still in urban Fort Lauderdale. Some cypress trees are 250 years old and stand 100 feet tall. A magnificent canopy of cypress, cabbage palms, and oaks shades the grassy sites. Don't miss the winding nature trail, where you'll see ferns, wild coffee bushes, red maple trees, and cabbage palms in a .75-mile walk. This Designated Urban Wilderness Area was acquired by the county in 1944 by foreclosure and originally named Cypress Park; it was renamed after a county commissioner in 1965. You can fish in the lake, but you're encouraged to release your catch; swimming is not allowed. The winding paved road is good for leisurely cycling.

Campsites, facilities: The 46-acre county park has 45 paved RV sites and 10 tent sites with electricity, water, restrooms, showers, picnic tables, and grills. Also in the park are a lake, nature trail, two playgrounds, horseshoe pits, shuffleboard courts, and a volleyball field. Children are welcome. Pets are permitted with proof of vaccination.

Reservations, fees: Reservations are recommended. Sites are $17 to $23 per night for four people, plus $2 to $2.50 for each additional person. Credit cards are not accepted. The maximum stay is 14 days; if you pay by the month, you can stay up to six months.

Directions: From I-95 southbound, take Exit 32 and head west on Commercial Boulevard for .1 mile. Turn south at Powerline Road and go .9 mile. Turn west at Northwest 38th Street; you'll see the park entrance on the south side of the road. From I-95 northbound, take Exit 31 and go east to Powerline Road. Go north on Powerline Road to Northwest 38th Street. Turn west and drive under the interstate and across the railroad tracks. The entrance is just past the tracks.

Contact: John D. Easterlin Park, 1000 North-west 38th Street, Oakland Park, FL 33309, 954/938-0610, fax 954/938-0625, website: www.broward.org/parks.

▉7 SUNSHINE HOLIDAY RV RESORT (FORMERLY LAKESHORE ESTATES RV RESORT)

Rating: 2

In Fort Lauderdale

Greater Fort Lauderdale map, grid b3, page 516

Most of the tenants stay year-round in this trailer park, which has a security gate that requires you to punch in an entrance code. Some sites on the east side are shaded by mature oaks, but much of the park is sunny. A shopping center is across the street. A majority of the visitors and mobile home residents are from Quebec; you'll hear plenty of French spoken here.

Campsites, facilities: There are 100 full-hookup RV sites in this 212-unit adults-only community, which offers restrooms, two heated pools, a recreation hall, laundry facilities, a 33-acre lake, and shuffleboard courts. Activities include bingo, parties, dances, potlucks, horse-shoes, various outings, and a *pétanque* court. Children are welcome. Pets are permitted.

Reservations, fees: Reservations are recommended. Sites are $30 per night for two people, plus $5 for each additional person. Major credit cards are accepted. Long-term stays are permitted.

Directions: From I-95, take Exit 31B and drive 1.5 miles west on Oakland Park Boulevard. The park entrance is on the south side.

Contact: Sunshine Holiday RV Resort, 2802 West Oakland Park Boulevard, Fort Lauderdale, FL 33311, 954/731-1722 or 877/327-2757, fax 954/731-0451, website: www.rvonthego.com.

▉8 PARADISE ISLAND RV RESORT (FORMERLY BUGLEWOOD)

Rating: 4

In Fort Lauderdale

Greater Fort Lauderdale map, grid b3, page 516

This is a homey kind of place where campers grow potted geraniums in their front yards and hang little wooden signs with their names on their rigs. A high ficus hedge surrounds the clean, manicured RV resort, cutting it off from city sights. Mature oaks and palm trees shade some campsites. A security gate offers peace of mind.

Campsites, facilities: There are 150 RV sites with full hookups in this 232-unit park. Restrooms, showers, laundry facilities, a pool, a recreation hall, two adults-only lounges, a barbecue pavilion, and shuffleboard, bocce (lawn bowling), and *pétanque* (French-style bowling) courts are available. Children under 16 must be accompanied by an adult in the clubhouse, pool, bathrooms, and laundry. Two leashed pets per site are permitted.

Reservations, fees: Reservations are recommended. Sites are $36 per night for two people, plus $3.50 for each additional person. Major credit cards are accepted. Long-term stays are OK.

Directions: From I-95, take Exit 31B and drive .25 mile west on Oakland Park Boulevard. Turn south onto Northwest 21st Avenue; the park entrance is on the west side of the street.

Contact: Paradise Island RV Resort, 2121 Northwest 29th Court, Fort Lauderdale, FL 33311, 954/485-1150 or 800/487-7395, fax 954/485-5701.

▉9 YACHT HAVEN PARK MARINA

Rating: 7

In Fort Lauderdale

Greater Fort Lauderdale map, grid c3, page 516

For a taste of the "Venice of America," as

Fort Lauderdale is often called, this RV resort and marina has much to offer. About half the sites are on the New River; you might find a CEO's yacht or an oceangoing sailboat parked at the dock near your site. Try to get a spot on Perry Street or Magellan Drive, which overlook the river and the trees of the Secret Woods Nature Center, a county park. Other sites offer postcard-quality vistas of expensive waterfront homes. There's a security gate, and most sites have a raised concrete patio next to the RV pad. The pool is heated in winter. The New River leads to the fishing grounds of the Gulf Stream. Follow the driving directions carefully; this is a tricky park to enter from the west, but it's well worth the effort.

Campsites, facilities: All 250 sites have full hookups. Restrooms, showers, laundry facilities, a dump station, a pool, a spa, a recreation hall, shuffleboard courts, boat docks, and a boat ramp are available. Children are welcome. Leashed pets are permitted.

Reservations, fees: Reservations are recommended. Sites are $33 to $45 per night for two people, plus $5 for each additional person. You can moor your boat for an extra charge. Credit cards are not accepted. Long-term stays are OK.

Directions: From I-95, take Exit 25 on State Road 84 westbound; the entrance is .1 mile from the exit ramp, on the north side of the highway. If you miss the entrance, you can drive west another .5 mile and make a U-turn heading east. Immediately after the U-turn, follow the signs for Marina Bay Resort and for the service road, which returns you to State Road 84 westbound.

Contact: Yacht Haven Park Marina, 2323 State Road 84, Fort Lauderdale, FL 33312, 954/583-2322 or 800/581-2322, website: www.yachthaven-park.com.

10 TWIN LAKES TRAVEL PARK

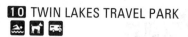

Rating: 3

In Fort Lauderdale

Greater Fort Lauderdale map, grid c3, page 516

Tucked into an industrial neighborhood in a web of major highways, Twin Lakes is a peaceful, sunny campground dotted with tabebuia and mature shade trees. A sign at the entrance announces *"Il est imposible de parquer ici"* ("It is impossible to park here"), evidence of the French-Canadian clientele. About 95 percent of the visitors here are from Canada. Besides being a good base from which to explore the Everglades, it's convenient to Sawgrass Mills, the world's largest outlet mall; Blockbuster Golf and Games entertainment park; and the Old West-theme town of Davie, where even the McDonald's has hitching posts.

Campsites, facilities: All 374 sites have full hookups; about 100 available for seasonal visitors. Restrooms, showers, a pool, laundry facilities, *pétanque* (French-style bowling) and shuffleboard courts, horseshoe pits, and a recreation hall are on site. Children are welcome. Small leashed pets are permitted.

Reservations, fees: Reservations are recommended. Sites are $35 per night for two people, plus $3 per additional person. Major credit cards are accepted. Long-term stays are allowed.

Directions: From I-595, or Florida's Turnpike, exit onto U.S. 441 and go .4 mile south. Turn west (right) on Southwest 36th Court/Oakes Road and drive two blocks, then turn north on Burris Road. Continue .5 mile to the park.

Contact: Twin Lakes Travel Park, 3055 Burris Road, Fort Lauderdale, FL 33314, 954/587-0101 or 800/327-8182, fax 954/587-9512.

11 SEMINOLE PARK

Rating: 3

In Hollywood

Greater Fort Lauderdale map, grid c3, page 516

This private campground on land leased from the Seminole Indian tribe welcomes older travelers, many of whom return year after year. Bingo, potluck dinners, and dances keep people busy in the wintertime. Some sites are paved, but others are grassy. Stores are within walking distance, but be careful because the highway carries heavy traffic.

Campsites, facilities: All 102 RV sites have full hookups, plus cable TV and telephone access. Amenities include restrooms, showers, a pool, a recreation hall, and *pétanque* (French-style bowling) and shuffleboard courts. The office, recreation hall, and pool are wheelchair accessible. Adult campers are preferred. Only pets under 10 pounds are permitted.

Reservations, fees: Reservations are recommended. Sites are $32 per night for two people, plus $2 per extra person. Credit cards are not accepted. Long-term rates are available.

Directions: From I-95, take Exit 25 westbound for 2.8 miles on Stirling Road. Turn south at U.S. 441/State Road 7 and drive .2 mile to the park, on the east side of the road.

Contact: Seminole Park, 3301 North State Road 7, Hollywood, FL 33021, 954/987-6961.

12 T. Y. PARK

Rating: 5

In Hollywood

Greater Fort Lauderdale map, grid c3, page 516

Bring a fishing pole to try your luck in the well-stocked lake that is the centerpiece of this 150-acre oak-shaded park in the middle of the metropolitan area. (You'll also need a Florida fishing license.) A two-mile path around the lake is a favorite with joggers and bicyclists. On weekends, the park is jammed with local kids and families picnicking on the grounds and swimming in the lake. Art fairs and community festivals are sometimes held here, too, adding to the crowds. What does T. Y. stand for? "Topeekeegee Yugnee" is what the Seminoles called "the gathering place."

Campsites, facilities: There are 48 campsites, including 12 for tents, in this county park. Water, electricity, grills, picnic tables, and patios are provided at RV sites. Two tent sites have electricity and water hookups. Restrooms, showers, laundry facilities, a trading post, bicycle and boat rentals, a swimming lagoon with a water slide, and basketball and volleyball courts are available. Children are welcome. Leashed pets are permitted at campsites and in the park but may not be taken on the beach; they must be preregistered at the park office. Twenty-four-hour security is provided.

Reservations, fees: Reservations are recommended. Sites are $17 to $22 per night for four people, plus $2 for each additional person. Credit cards are accepted. The maximum stay is 14 consecutive days, or six months for extended stays, depending on availability.

Directions: From I-95 in Hollywood, take Exit 21 west on Sheridan Street for .7 mile. Turn north at Park Road and drive .2 mile to the entrance.

Contact: T. Y. Park, 3300 North Park Road, Hollywood, FL 33021, 954/985-1980, fax 954/961-5950, website: www.broward.org/parks.

13 LAKE TRINITY ESTATES (FORMERLY TRINITY TOWERS RV PARK)

Rating: 4

In Pembroke Park

Greater Fort Lauderdale map, grid c3, page 516

This 11-acre park is ingeniously slipped underneath a Christian TV station's towering antenna and studios, which broadcasts live religious programming. A lake borders the south side of the property, and the campsites are well landscaped. Each winter, campers, many of them French Canadians, compete in *pétanque* (French-style bowling) and shuffleboard contests. The beach is about six miles east, and the Miami Dolphins play pro football about a 10-minute drive west; for tickets, call 305/620-2578.

Campsites, facilities: This 290-unit community hosts 117 RV-only sites, of which 78 have full hookups. Most sites fit rigs up to 40 feet. Water, electricity, restrooms, showers, a swimming pool, shuffleboard, and *pétanque* (French-style bowling) are available. Most areas are wheelchair accessible. Children are welcome. Dogs are not permitted, but cats and birds are allowed.

Reservations, fees: Reservations are recommended in winter. Sites are $27 to $29 per night for two people, plus $1 for each additional person. Major credit cards are accepted. Long-term stays are OK.

Directions: From I-95, take Exit 19 westbound on Pembroke Road for .5 mile to the park, which is on the south side.

Contact: Lake Trinity Estates, 3300 Pembroke Road, 1 Lake Trinity Estates, Pembroke Park, FL 33021, 954/962-7400, email: laketrinityestates@tbn.org.

14 MARKHAM PARK

Rating: 10

Near the Everglades

Greater Fort Lauderdale map, grid b1, page 516

You'd have to spend weeks at this 665-acre county park before you could sample everything there is to do here. For one, there's a gnarly off-road mountain-biking trail with sharp turns and what passes for altitude in flat South Florida. (The other two popular mountain biking parks are Oleta State Park in North Miami

and Amelia Earhart Park in Hialeah, both in Miami-Dade County south of here. Markham Park is said to be the most technical, requiring more skill than the others.) You can also bicycle on paved roads that wind through the park and in the campground clusters. Forgot your bike? The park rents them for children and adults. If your tastes run to the cosmic, there's stargazing in the observatory every Saturday. Gun enthusiasts come from all over to take aim on the 50-yard and 100-meter target ranges, which are said to be Florida's best.

From the concrete boat ramps, you can launch your craft into the L-35A Canal, which stretches along the eastern edge of the Everglades, or the New River Canal, which runs east to west. Hike through the Australian pine forest to the levee that separates the vast watery prairie of the Everglades from civilization; from atop the levee, you can see for miles. When you get hot, cool down in the oversized pool (swimming is not allowed in the lake or the canals). The pool is open from February to September. On weekends, the campground fills up fast, so be sure to make reservations. Also, be aware that parties can sometimes disturb campers on Friday and Saturday nights. But during the week, you can relax at your large, wooded campsite in peace and quiet.

Campsites, facilities: Split among 12 campground clusters are 80 RV and tent spots with water and electricity. Eight sites have full hookups. An additional 10 tent sites have no water or electricity. All have picnic tables, grills, and fire rings. Restrooms and showers are available. For fun, take your pick from: the pool, the lake, two boat ramps, boat rentals, racquetball and tennis courts, mountain-biking trails, playgrounds, gun ranges, horseshoe pits, volleyball and basketball courts, an observatory, private Jet Ski lake, a biking/jogging path, a one-mile-long equestrian trail, and a model airplane field. Most areas are wheelchair accessible, including some paved campsites. Children and leashed dogs are welcome.

Reservations, fees: Reservations are recommended, especially on weekends. Reservations are accepted up to one year in advance. Sites are $17 to $19 per night for four people, plus $2 for each additional person. Major credit cards are accepted.

Directions: From Fort Lauderdale, take I-595 west eight miles to Exit 1A at State Road 84. Continue on State Road 84 west to the second traffic light, then turn north into the park entrance.

Contact: Markham Park, 16001 State Road 84, Sunrise, FL 33326, 954/389-2000, website: www.broward.org/parks.

15 SEMINOLE HEALTH CLUB

Rating: 3

In Davie

Greater Fort Lauderdale map, grid c1, page 516

Coconut palms, orchids, and banana and mango trees give this wooded 11-acre naturist park a tropical feel, even though it's rapidly being surrounded by housing subdivisions. Horses and a goat or pig (or two) will make you think of the farm. In the center of the park's pond is Monkee Island where real primates run loose—a treat for children. As at most nudist campgrounds, the managers are careful to screen out curiosity-seekers and to protect the privacy of their guests. If you pass muster, you'll get the ultimate tan. A plus for those who travel with their pets: there's also a free-roaming area for dogs.

Campsites, facilities: This nudist resort offers 50 RV slots and five tent sites with water and electricity hookups. Restrooms, showers, two laundry rooms, an outdoor gym, a game room, a dance floor, a restaurant, motel rooms with color TVs but no bathrooms, a large swimming pool, and courts for tennis, shuffleboard, and *pétanque* (French-style bowling) are available. Families with children are welcome. Leashed pets are permitted. Visitors are asked

to spend the day here before camping to make sure everyone is comfortable with each other.

Reservations, fees: Reservations are required. Sites are $30 to $35 per night for two people or a family. Beyond that, add $10 per extra person. Credit cards are not accepted. Long-term stays are OK.

Directions: From Fort Lauderdale, take I-595 west for seven miles to Southwest 136th Avenue. Drive three miles south to Southwest 26th Street. Turn west and continue 1.6 miles to Southwest 142nd Avenue, then turn left. At 37th Court, turn left, then immediately turn right onto a paved road that leads to the park entrance. From I-75, take the Griffin Road exit eastbound about three miles to the first traffic light that allows you to cross the canal to Orange Drive, which parallels Griffin Road. On Orange Drive, turn west and drive to Southwest 142nd Avenue. Go north past the dump (which is being developed into a county park), and the park will be on your right.

Contact: Seminole Health Club, 3800 Southwest 142nd Avenue, Davie, FL 33330, 954/473-0231, fax 954/476-7042, email: sonshiners@aol.com.

16 C. B. SMITH PARK

Rating: 7

In Pembroke Pines

Greater Fort Lauderdale map, grid c1, page 516

Kids flop down a water slide on inner tubes at this 320-acre county park, but you won't be able to hear their gleeful shouts from the sunny, palm-dotted campground on the park's other side. The lake is the focus of attention. For fun, try the water slide, sunbathe at the beach, tool around in a paddleboat, play racquetball, tennis, or volleyball, visit the playground, or toss a few horseshoes at the horseshoe pits.

Campsites, facilities: Sixty full-hookup RV sites (30 pull-through) and 12 tent sites overlook an 80-acre lake. Restrooms, showers, picnic tables, grills, and laundry facilities are available. Children are welcome. Leashed pets are permitted.

Reservations, fees: Reservations are recommended. Sites are $19 per night for four people, plus $2 for each additional person. Major credit cards are accepted. Unlike most public parks, this one permits long-term stays of up to six months.

Directions: From I-75, take Exit 9A east on Pines Boulevard for one mile to Flamingo Road. Turn north and go to the park at 900 North Flamingo Road.

Contact: C. B. Smith Park, 900 North Flamingo Road, Pembroke Pines, FL 33028, 954/437-2650, website: www.broward.org/parks.

Chapter 19

The Everglades

The Everglades

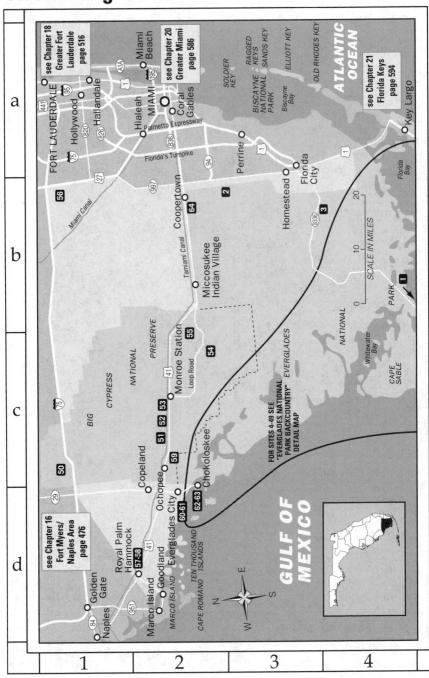

see Chapter 18 Greater Fort Lauderdale page 516

see Chapter 20 Greater Miami page 586

see Chapter 21 Florida Keys page 594

see Chapter 16 Fort Myers/Naples Area page 476

ATLANTIC OCEAN

FORT LAUDERDALE
Hollywood
Hallandale
Hialeah
MIAMI
Miami Beach
Coral Gables
Palmetto Expressway
Florida's Turnpike
Perrine
Homestead
Florida City
Key Largo

SOLDIER KEY
RAGGED KEYS
SANDS KEY
ELLIOTT KEY
OLD RHODES KEY
BISCAYNE NATIONAL PARK
Biscayne Bay
Florida Bay

Coopertown
Miccosukee Indian Village
Monroe Station
Loop Road
Chokoloskee
Copeland
Ochopee
Everglades City
Royal Palm Hammock
Goodland
Golden Gate
Naples
Marco Island

BIG CYPRESS NATIONAL PRESERVE

EVERGLADES NATIONAL PARK

Whitewater Bay
CAPE SABLE
TEN THOUSAND ISLANDS
MARCO ISLAND
CAPE ROMANO

Miami Canal
Tamiami Canal

FOR SITES 4-49 SEE "EVERGLADES NATIONAL PARK BACKCOUNTRY" DETAIL MAP

SCALE IN MILES
0 10 20

GULF OF MEXICO

N E S W

Everglades National Park Backcountry

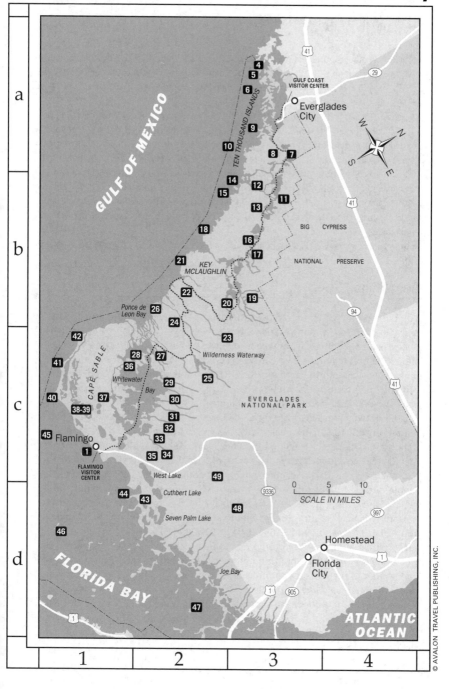

The Everglades

More than any other natural feature, the Everglades define South Florida. They are, in the true sense of the word, unique. Author Marjory Stoneman Douglas recognized this in her 1947 classic, *The Everglades: River of Grass,* when she penned these famous words: "There are no other Everglades in the world."

The river of grass she referred to was the 50-mile-wide band of wispy saw grass that looks from afar like a dry prairie, until your soggy boots sink knee-deep in the watery bottom. The broad expanse is punctuated by small rises covered with trees (known as tree islands) and stretches from Lake Okeechobee nearly to Florida Bay. Water levels in the river fluctuate naturally, from ankle- to chest-deep. Modern drainage efforts have thrown that hydrologic equilibrium out of whack, but much of the Everglades' original appeal still can be enjoyed by modern-day visitors; meanwhile, the state and federal governments are working overtime to restore what remains of the original wilderness. It's a good thing: More than 1.5 million people per year visit the Everglades.

In this chapter, we catalog camping opportunities throughout much of the greater Everglades

Boat/Canoe Sites

You'll need nautical charts to help you access these sites within the national park. Obtain them from the Marina Store near the Flamingo Visitor Center, Everglades National Park Boat Tours at the Gulf Coast Ranger Station, or at area bait shops. Helpful materials also can be ordered from the Florida Parks and Monuments Association, 10 Parachute Key #51, Homestead, FL 33034, 305/247-1216.

If you don't have your own boat, canoe, or kayak, several outfitters are available. Canoes rent for $21 daily at Everglades National Park Boat Tours (239/695-2591), located downstairs from the Gulf Coast Ranger Station in Everglades City. Rentals are $30 to $35 for the first day, $25 to $35 thereafter, at North American Canoe Tours (239/695-4666) in Everglades City. Kayaks are $35 to $55 for the first day, $30 to $50 for the second and third days, $20 to $40 for each day thereafter. At Flamingo Marina, canoes rent for $8 hourly, $32 daily, and $40 overnight. Single-person kayaks rent for $11 hourly, $43 daily, and $50 overnight. Two-person kayaks rent for $16 hourly, $54 daily, and $60 overnight. For motorized trips into the backcountry, 16-foot fishing skiffs rent for $22 hourly, $65 half day, and $90 daily. Reserve at 239/695-3101 or 800/600-3813.

More than a dozen other outfitters offer expeditions into the Everglades, as well as canoe or kayak rentals and other services. Ask an Everglades National Park ranger to mail you a current list of outfitters, along with a free backcountry trip planner; call 305/242-7700.

The listings that follow are separated into four categories: Everglades National Park campgrounds with facilities, Everglades National Park backcountry sites, Big Cypress National Preserve camping areas, and campgrounds outside National Park Service management.

ecosystem, including the Big Cypress National Preserve, the Everglades water conservation areas, and points nearby. If you have the time, we urge you to check out those spots. Most visitors to South Florida never see all of them.

The place that most tourists visit and the one that offers the most opportunities for campers who really want to get away from the megalopolis we call South Florida is Everglades National Park, considered by the United Nations to be as significant as the Egyptian pyramids and Australia's Great Barrier Reef. It is twice the size of Rhode Island and offers 2,356 square miles to explore.

You're virtually certain to see an alligator sunning itself. (Don't worry, though, because the gator is unlikely to hurt you.) For bird-watchers, thousands of winged visitors head to the park, one of the largest migrations in the nation, each winter. The winter months are the best time to visit because you'll have less trouble with the 40-odd types of resident mosquitoes (still, bring repellent, preferably one containing DEET). From muggy May to November, temperatures reach the high 80s to high 90s, and lightning storms and torrential local downpours are common. From January to mid-March, temperatures usually are moderate and skies tend to be clear.

Most of the national park is underwater, so many of the following campsites can be reached only by boat, canoe, or kayak, and a few others only by trail. But overland, there are several sites where you can see what makes the Everglades special. You can also camp in places that offer the standard comforts, places where you can bring a mountain bike as well as your hiking boots. Check the Other Everglades Parks section toward the end of this chapter if you're not into totally roughing it. We'll handle the wilderness experience first.

For the total Everglades experience, camping in backcountry areas requires special preparation and precautions. First, bring all the water you'll need, generally one gallon per person per day. Also, be wary of raccoons, which will make their way into your food and drinking water if they can. Carry a hard-bodied cooler, put your food inside, and tie it shut. In brackish and saltwater areas, raccoons seem perpetually thirsty and will go after your freshwater. They're crafty, so take some time to figure out how you're going to preserve your sustenance. Discuss other precautions with backcountry rangers when you pick up a camping permit. Know your capabilities and watch the weather carefully. If you can afford one, a global positioning system will help keep you from getting lost but is no substitute for a good grasp of orienteering. If you're canoeing or kayaking, consider transporting some of your dry clothes and other valuables in a waterproof bag. Dry Bag is one well-known brand name.

There are three types of backcountry campsites in the park. At a ground site, you pitch your tent on the ground. An equal number of sites are on so-called chickees. Although named after the thatched-roof huts of the Seminole Indians, chickee campsites in the park are 10-by-12-foot wooden platforms raised above the water and covered by a flat roof. At chickee sites, you'll need a free-standing tent; no stakes can be driven into the platform. Chickees are equipped with chemical toilets. The third type of site is the beach site. The shelly beaches of the Everglades won't remind you of Miami Beach, but they have a beauty all their own. Most beach sites and a few ground sites do not have toilets. You'll have to dig a hole at least six inches deep to bury waste or, better yet, pack out waste.

Raccoons and bugs are worst at ground and beach sites. Many beach sites also have biting gnats known as no-see-ums. This is another reason to come when it's cold or at least cool—meaning in the winter. Do not underestimate the mosquitoes or other biting bugs: Bring lots of repellent and mosquito netting, even in the winter. These items are not optional. For all practical purposes, the skeeters make camping in the Everglades backcountry impossible from about April to October.

We like beach sites best because that's also where you'll want to build a campfire, which is not allowed at chickee or ground sites but is permitted at most beach sites.

Die-hard adventurers can paddle a canoe or kayak 99 miles through the western length of Everglades National Park to sample many campsites on a trail called the Wilderness Waterway. It takes a lot of planning—and supplies—to make the seven- to 10-day trip. Some people rave about the trek's solitude and the challenge of maneuvering through a maze of red mangroves. Park ranger Steve Robinson calls the monotonous mangrove trail "the world's largest sensory-deprivation tank."

Don't expect an Amazonian jungle that is alive with critters and adventure at every turn. In television terms, this is more like the dull parts of *Survivor,* versus the enthusiastic pursuits undertaken by the Australian star of *The Crocodile Hunter.* Says park ranger Robinson: "You really have to like the solitude," telling most visitors to try loop trails instead. "I don't need that much Zen." In short, consult a ranger about which overnight camping trips are best for you.

Fishing is excellent throughout Everglades National Park. Be aware that even though you're in a national park, you'll need a Florida fishing license.

A note of caution about alligators: Do not feed them. They become acclimated to human company, expect food from us, and will eventually chomp off someone's hand or foot. If an alligator approaches you, assume that it has been improperly fed and try to get away.

Also, don't throw your fish-cleaning remains into the water near your campsite. We once were shaken up as we watched an alligator make a beeline for the dock where we stood in front of the Canepatch backcountry site, a spot that is favored by backcountry fishermen. Previous anglers must have been tossing out their leavings, which apparently made the gator start associating people with food. When we later told a backcountry ranger about this close encounter, she advised us that if a future alligator encounter ever got any closer—say, within whacking distance—we should smack the alligator on its head with a canoe paddle. The idea is to make gators uncomfortable around people, as nature intended.

Something to consider if you're taking a backcountry trip: Occasionally, a canoeing party will show up at a backcountry site when their permit is technically for another site. Perhaps they fell behind, got held up by weather, or had some other unfortunate circumstances. That's one thing; however, we've also seen some parties who simply prefer a particular site and show up there even though they have a permit for another destination. If they're traveling under muscle power and it's late in the day, or if the weather is turning bad, there's little you can do but smile and tolerate the crowding. But if it's relatively early in the day, or they're in a power-boat, and the weather is OK, you may want to call their bluff and ask them to produce a permit. If they're in the wrong place, you are within your rights to ask interlopers to go to the correct campsite. Use your judgment. Whatever you decide to do, make it a point to report such invaders to backcountry rangers.

The national park entrance fees are $10 at the main entrance in Homestead, $8 at Chekika Campground (which may be closed due to high water, so call ahead), and free at Everglades City. Website: www.nps.gov/ever.

Everglades Field Guide

Solitude and star-studded night skies are the main draw here, but observant campers also are sure to see alligators and long-legged wading birds during their stay at Everglades National Park, the first U.S. National Park preserved primarily for its variety and abundance of wildlife. Here's what to look for each month:

January
Lumbering manatees swimming in the boat basin at Flamingo Marina. Plentiful wading birds at Mrazek Pond.

February
Manatees on cool mornings at Flamingo Marina. Red-shouldered hawks, which are starting to nest. At Eco Pond, nesting moorhens.

March
Hundreds of roseate spoonbills and their young at Eco Pond.

April
The bellow of alligators (it's mating time).

May
Deer fawns with their mothers. Brown pelican chicks.

June
Barn swallows swarming to eat dragonflies.

July
Six-inch baby alligators in ponds. Turtles nesting along road's edge. Snook and tarpon in the Florida Bay flats.

August
Loggerhead turtles hatching from eggs.

September
White-crowned pigeons flying south from here to the tropics.

October
Wintering ducks, peregrine falcons, shorebirds, and turkey vultures starting to rise in numbers.

November
Bald eagles building nests. Manatees swimming on the freshwater side of Flamingo Marina.

December
Recently hatched Great Southern white butterflies. Increasing numbers of ducks in ponds and on Florida Bay.

Source: Everglades National Park

Everglades National Park

■ FLAMINGO CAMPGROUND

🚶 🚴 🛶 🎣 🏊 🐴 🚐 ⛺

Rating: 9

On Florida Bay in Everglades National Park
Everglades map, grid b4, page 528;
Everglades Backcountry map, grid c1,
page 529

When a tourist acquaintance told wildlife photographer/biologist Nicole Duplaix that he wanted to see within one day a manatee, the goose-sized limpkin bird, and two other Everglades animals, she knew to try Flamingo Marina, east of this campground. You're sure to spot some sort of wildlife near there—maybe alligators, wading birds, or the occasional American crocodile. Be sure to venture to the end of the 38-mile main park road to see this area, which is the prettiest spot reachable by car.

The campground overlooks the smooth, blue-green waters of Florida Bay. Fifteen walk-in sites are near water's edge, providing tenters with a view of far-off mangrove islands jutting from glassy bay waters. West of the open, grassy field for tents, RVers are grouped closer together but enjoy more shade. Some tenters drag canoes to their campsites or tie them near the water in anticipation of a morning launch to sightsee or fish for snook, snapper, jacks, trout, redfish, and sheepshead. A huge hole in the bay floor, scooped out to provide fill when Flamingo was a tiny fishing village (pre-national park status), is often overlooked by anglers. But toss in a line and you may well be surprised. Motorboaters launch to the east at the marina to fish for big-game tarpon or cross the bay to the Florida Keys.

Canoes, single-person kayaks, motorized skiffs, and bicycles are available for rent at the marina. Tickets to a tram tour and the worthwhile Bald Eagle and Pelican sightseeing boats also are sold there. A 12-hour advance reservation is required for the Cape Sable beach and birding cruise; call 239/695-3101.

If someone in your party hates campout meals, partake of the pizza, seafood, and picture-window bay views nearby at the park's sole restaurant. Some patrons consider the rum runners at the companion bar among the best. At the nearby Flamingo Visitor Center, 25 cents buys a telescopic view of bald eagles nesting in a mangrove island. Campers also have the advantage of being first in line at Flamingo's concession stand, where sometimes-scarce bicycles and canoes are rented on a first-come, first-served basis.

Don't be surprised if the masked face of a raccoon peeks into your tent screen door at dusk. Tie rope around your cooler to protect food and water from the critters, or store edibles in your vehicle. If you forget to bring DEET, several brands of insect repellent are sold at the marina store. Ask rangers about any other precautions.

Campsites, facilities: This is the biggest campground in Everglades National Park. It offers 234 drive-up campsites for tents, trailers, or RVs and 64 walk-up tent sites. There are no hookups, but you will find cold showers, restrooms, picnic tables, grills, a pay phone, two dump stations, an amphitheater for winter programs, and two hiking trails. Within walking distance are limited groceries, camping supplies, bicycle rentals, canoe and skiff rentals, and sightseeing cruise boats. A bayview restaurant, lounge, gas station, and boat ramp also are nearby. Several mountain biking trails can be started from here; ask the park office for maps. Children and leashed pets are permitted.

Reservations, fees: Reservations are accepted up to five months in advance at 800/365-CAMP (2267) or 301/722-1257. Sites are $14 per night for up to eight people. Group sites are $28 nightly for up to 15 people. Campers also pay a $10 park entrance fee, which is good for seven days. Major credit cards are accepted. The maximum stay is 14 days between November 1 and April 30, or 30 days per year.

Directions: From Miami, take Florida's Turnpike to its southern terminus at U.S. 1. In about one block, turn right at Palm Drive. Cross the railroad tracks and pass the Circle K. At the traffic light at Southwest 192nd Avenue/State Road 9336, turn left by the Robert Is Here fruit stand. Proceed south about two miles. When State Road 9336 veers right, follow it to the right instead of going straight toward the alligator farm. The park entrance is four miles ahead. Follow the main park road about 38 miles to the campground on the left, beyond the marina.

Contact: Everglades National Park, 40001 State Road 9336, Homestead, FL 33034, 305/242-7700. For questions about Flamingo, contact the Flamingo Visitor Center at 239/695-2945. Website: www.nps.gov/ever.

❷ CHEKIKA CAMPGROUND

Rating: 8

In Everglades National Park
Everglades map, grid b3, page 528

This campground is closed when water is high in the Everglades, and it may be further affected by plans to restore a higher water flow to nearby Shark River Slough as part of a bit Everglades restoration programs being carried out by the state and federal governments. Be sure to call ahead. At this writing, it is closed indefinitely. Still, it's worth the visit if you can find it open. It's the national park's closest campground to Miami and Homestead. About 10 miles north of here, the ferocious and independent Seminole warrior for whom the campground is named—Chekika—was killed. Invading U.S. soldiers paddled 16 canoes through the seemingly inaccessible Everglades to get to his hideout during the Second Seminole War in the 1840s. Later, on the grounds now visited by campers, prospectors in 1943

hoped to strike oil. They dug a well but found water instead. For half a century the well spewed cool, sulfurous water from the Biscayne Aquifer, located hundreds of feet below, to the surface. Locals flocked here, believing that the springs had healing powers.

Today, campsites are at the edge of a jungly, tropical hardwood hammock that rises like a bump in the vastness of the sun-splashed saw grass. Picnic pavilions with grills are near a swimming area, which was made by diking and directing the once-fabled artesian well into a natural depression. Dab on bug repellent before you check out the nature trails—or camp, for that matter. Otherwise, you'll be sorry. What sets this one-square-mile former state recreation area apart from the rest of Everglades National Park is that it's the only place where you can get a hot shower, unless you rent a motel room at Flamingo Lodge.

Campsites, facilities: Each of the 20 drive-up campsites for tents, trailers, or RVs accommodates eight people. There are no hookups, but you will find hot showers, restrooms, a dump station, two hiking trails, a pond for swimming and fishing, and water basins for filling water jugs. The boardwalk to the picnic area is wheelchair accessible. You can buy supplies in Homestead. Children and leashed pets are permitted.

Reservations, fees: Camping is first-come, first-served. Sites are $14 per night plus an $8 entrance fee, which is good for seven days. If no ranger is at the gate, then register yourself and pay on the honor system. Credit cards are not accepted. The maximum stay is 14 days between December 1 and May 31, or 30 days per year. Call ahead to see if the water is high; if so, the campground will be closed.

Directions: From Miami, go west on U.S. 41/Tamiami Trail. Turn left at Krome Avenue/State Road 997. Proceed south about 10 miles and turn right at Richmond Drive/Southwest 168th Street. Seven miles ahead, the road dead-ends into Southwest 237th Avenue. Turn right (north) and go about .5 mile until you see the park entrance on the left.

Contact: Everglades National Park, 40001 State Road 9336, Homestead, FL 33034, 305/251-0371. Website: www.nps.gov/ever.

3 LONG PINE KEY CAMPGROUND

Rating: 7

In Everglades National Park
Everglades map, grid b4, page 528

The pine-dotted campground is the closest to the most-popular walking trails and the main park entrance. You can view plentiful birds along the nearby Anhinga Trail boardwalk in winter, and you will still see, among the spindly young trees, a few pine trunks snapped in two by 1992's Hurricane Andrew along the Long Pine Key Trail leading west from the campground. Rangers speak at the amphitheater in winter and answer questions year-round at the visitors center to the east. There's a great six-mile, one-way bike trail just across the road from the campground, leading fat-tire bikes through a double-track dirt road in a winding pine forest and more. You can make it a 12-mile loop by exiting the trail onto the main highway, turning north and heading back on the road to the campground. Another little-used biking trail is the Old Ingraham Highway, built in the 1920s; it's a 21-mile trip out and back on an old rutted road where alligators will flee your approach and you'll spook blue herons and other birds from their hiding places.

For a woodsy walk from this pine-dotted campground, drive west along the sole road to reach the thicker canopy of Mahogany Hammock (bring mosquito repellent). Its parking area is at the first turnoff after Pa-hay-okee Overlook, one of several stops along the 38-mile park road leading to Flamingo. Although the beauty of Pa-hay-okee's sea of saw grass typically is described as subtle, even a first-time visitor might notice the huge white clouds—sometimes described as "Florida's mountains"—building over the pancake-flat prairie.

Campsites, facilities: All 108 drive-up campsites are for tents, trailers, or RVs. There are no hookups. You will find restrooms, cold showers, picnic tables, grills, a pay phone, a dump station, an amphitheater for winter programs, several nearby hiking trails, and a fishing pond. Children and leashed pets are permitted.

Reservations, fees: Reservations are accepted up to five months in advance at 800/365-CAMP (2267) or 301/722-1257. Sites are $14 per night for up to eight people. Group sites are $28 for up to 15 people. Campers also must pay a $10 entrance fee, which is good for one week. Major credit cards are accepted. The maximum stay is 14 days between November 1 and April 30, or 30 days per year.

Directions: From Miami, take Florida's Turnpike to its southern terminus at U.S. 1. In about one block, turn right at Palm Drive. Cross the railroad tracks and pass the Circle K. At the traffic light at 192nd Avenue/State Road 9336, turn left by the Robert Is Here fruit stand. Proceed south about two miles. When State Road 9336 veers right, follow it to the right instead of going straight toward the alligator farm. The park entrance is four miles ahead. The campground is on the left about four miles beyond the entrance.

Contact: Everglades National Park, 40001 State Road 9336, Homestead, FL 33034, 305/242-7700. Website: www.nps.gov/ever.

Everglades National Park Backcountry

4 TIGER KEY BOAT/CANOE SITES

Rating: 10

At the Gulf of Mexico in the Ten Thousand Islands, Everglades National Park

Everglades Backcountry map, grid a3, page 529

Great sunsets reward campers at this quiet, breezy, secluded beach, which features a broad unobstructed view of the Gulf of Mexico. Horseshoe crabs the size of a thumbnail scamper on the beach at low tide, and the clicking sound you hear may be from the shrimp spending their youth in the Gulf of Mexico. Sleeping at the beach instead of deep within the national park's woodsy bowels is the best alternative for anyone who likes campfires (permitted only at beach campsites) and who are adverse to the park's 40-odd types of mosquitoes. Even so, bring DEET for insurance and visit in winter. "Of course, that's when the people are here," notes Lisa Andrews, a former seasonal park ranger. Tip: To try to beat other winter visitors to the punch, show up as early as 7:30 A.M. the day before your intended campout to obtain the necessary permit.

Occasionally, bald eagles and raccoons make an appearance. Keep water in locked coolers to protect it from thirsty masked marauders. Be aware of shallow water and limited access at low tides. The place is accessible only by canoe, kayak, or small powerboat (at low tide, the three-foot beach waters present trouble for some boats). Although the official campsite is on the west side of the island, some friends of ours have bent the rules and slept on the spit of land at the north end of the island. They tell us a channel running in front of this spit of land provides good fishing when the tides run. No-see-ums may bug you at dusk; if you retreat to your tent to escape them, be sure to return outside when they subside an hour or two later. That way, you'll enjoy a black sky filled with stars.

Campsites, facilities: Three beach tent sites accommodate a total of 12 people. You must use a canoe or kayak to travel eight miles from the Gulf Coast Ranger Station in Everglades City. You can use a motorboat to reach the northwest side, although you might have a problem at dead low tide if your boat has a deep draft. No piped water is available, so bring plenty. There is no toilet; bury human waste six inches deep. Dead and downed wood may be used for campfires below the high tide line. Trash must be packed out. Children are OK. No pets, please. If you're under human power, it's best to plan this trip far ahead so that you can ride out to the site on an outgoing tide and ride the incoming tide back in another day. Trying to paddle against the tide is virtually pointless.

Reservations, fees: Get a backcountry permit in person up to 24 hours before the day of your intended campout at the Gulf Coast Visitor Center. They are not issued by phone or mail. Camping permits for any length of stay are $10 for parties of up to six people, $20 for groups of seven to 12, and $30 for 13 or more. Major credit cards are accepted. There's a three-night stay limit.

Directions: From the intersection of U.S. 41/Tamiami Trail and State Road 29 east of Naples, drive about five miles south on State Road 29 to the Everglades National Park Gulf Coast Visitor Center, on your right by Chokoloskee Bay. A ranger will explain the Tiger Key route. To avoid getting lost, obtain nautical chart 11430 at area bait stores, the ranger station, or downstairs from the ranger station at Everglades National Park Boat Tours.

Contact: Everglades National Park, 40001 State Road 9336, Homestead, FL 33034, 305/242-7700. For backcountry questions, contact the Gulf Coast Visitor Center at 239/695-3311. Website: www.nps.gov/ever.

5 PICNIC KEY BOAT/CANOE SITES

Rating: 10

On the Gulf of Mexico in the Ten Thousand Islands, Everglades National Park

Everglades Backcountry map, grid a3, page 529

People once headed to the long, white-sand beach of Picnic Key in the Ten Thousand Islands for big picnic dinners. The unobstructed view of the Gulf of Mexico and the broad, thin beach of this mangrove-covered island continue to win fans. To Sandee and David Harraden, it was the perfect place to marry. In 1996, they brought inflatables for floating lazily on the water and set up a volleyball net and a campfire to entertain their wedding guests, who arrived by powerboat. With the westward view at sunset, the fiery disc of the sun "sits onto the water," says Sandee, who, along with her husband, rents canoes and arranges trips from the local outfitter North American Canoe Tours. "It's a really pretty sunset."

Besides a fishing pole and bait for surfcasting, bring bug repellent. Mosquitoes and no-see-ums have a field day here when winds subside. Camp well above the high tide line of the narrow beach. In storms, westerly winds can pummel the shore. As some of our party learned on one stormy night here, make sure you stake down your tent well. Beach your boat securely; the deep offshore channel is swift, and the sharp underwater oyster bars aren't kind to feet. The camping area on the southwest side of Picnic Key—just east of the small mangrove island in the channel between Picnic and Tiger Keys—is accessible to canoes and small boats at all tides. Only the northern beach has water deep enough to accommodate powerboats.

Campsites, facilities: Three beach tent sites accommodate a total of 16 people. You must use a kayak, canoe, or powerboat to travel seven to eight miles from the Gulf Coast Visitor Center in Everglades City. No piped water is available, so bring plenty. A vault toilet is provided. Dead and downed wood may be used for campfires below the high tide line. Trash must be packed out. Children are OK. No pets are allowed.

Reservations, fees: Get a backcountry permit in person up to 24 hours before the day of your intended campout at the Flamingo Visitor Center or Gulf Coast Visitor Center. They are not issued by phone or mail. Camping permits for any length of stay are $10 for parties of up to six people, $20 for groups of seven to 12, and $30 for 13 or more. Major credit cards are accepted. There's a three-night stay limit.

Directions: From the intersection of U.S. 41/Tamiami Trail and State Road 29 east of Naples, drive five miles south on State Road 29 to the Everglades National Park Gulf Coast Visitor Center, located on your right by Chokoloskee Bay. A ranger will explain the Picnic Key route. To avoid getting lost, obtain nautical chart 11430 at area bait stores, the ranger station, or downstairs from the ranger station at Everglades National Park Boat Tours. If you're under human power, it's best to plan this trip far ahead so that you can ride out to the campsite on an outgoing tide and ride the incoming tide back in another day. Paddling against the tide is arduous.

Contact: Everglades National Park, 40001 State Road 9336, Homestead, FL 33034, 305/242-7700. For backcountry questions, contact the Flamingo Visitor Center at 239/695-2945 or the Gulf Coast Visitor Center at 239/695-3311. Website: www.nps.gov/ever.

6 KINGSTON KEY BOAT/ CANOE SITES

Rating: 7

At the Gulf of Mexico in the Ten Thousand Islands, Everglades National Park

Everglades Backcountry map, grid a3, page 529

This front-row view of fiery sunsets on the broad Gulf of Mexico requires only a six-mile trip from the Gulf Coast Visitor Center. It's one of the park's newer backcountry sites (opened in 1996). Behind you, a shady mangrove island provides contrast. The roofed, elevated wooden chickee platform was built on a sand point at the mouth of Indian Key Pass to replace the nearby storm-damaged Comer Key campsite (although day-trippers may stop at Comer Key). Some consider Kingston a second-rate replacement, but supporters coo at its Gulf view and the many visible stars that pepper the night sky. Dolphins occasionally swim by. A pelican sometimes hangs out on a nearby piling.

The wee would-be "beach" is swamped at high tide. It can be noisy with boats passing by, including diesel-powered crab boats that sometimes thunder past as early as 4 A.M. Bring a free-standing tent; no stakes may be pounded into the platform.

Campsites, facilities: Two tent sites on elevated wooden platforms accommodate three people each. You must use a canoe, kayak, or motorized boat to travel about six miles from the Gulf Coast Ranger Station in Everglades City to this chickee and dock. No piped water is available, so bring plenty. Bring a portable stove because campfires are prohibited. A vault toilet separates the two sites. Trash must be packed out. Children are OK. No pets, please.

Reservations, fees: Get a backcountry permit in person up to 24 hours before the day of your intended campout at the Gulf Coast Visitor Center. They are not issued by phone or mail. Camping permits for any length of stay are $10 for parties of up to six people, $20 for groups of seven to 12, and $30 for 13 or more. Major credit cards are accepted. There's a one-night stay limit.

Directions: From the intersection of U.S. 41/Tamiami Trail and State Road 29 east of Naples, drive five miles south on State Road 29 to the Everglades National Park Gulf Coast Visitor Center, on your right by Chokoloskee Bay. A ranger will explain the Kingston Key route. To avoid getting lost, obtain nautical chart 11430 at area bait stores, the ranger sta-

tion, or downstairs from the ranger station at Everglades National Park Boat Tours. If you're under human power, it's best to plan this trip far ahead so that you can ride out to the site on an outgoing tide and ride the incoming tide back in another day. Trying to paddle against the tide through Indian Key Pass is difficult.
Contact: Everglades National Park, 40001 State Road 9336, Homestead, FL 33034, 305/242-7700. For backcountry questions, contact the Gulf Coast Visitor Center at 239/695-3311. Website: www.nps.gov/ever.

◼ SUNDAY BAY BOAT/ CANOE SITES

Rating: 7

On Sunday Bay in Everglades National Park
Everglades Backcountry map, grid a3, page 529

Look for dolphins as you paddle or motor to this roof-covered chickee, set in a shallow bay and tucked behind a little mangrove-covered island. Other than Lopez River (see next campground), this is the closest site on the Wilderness Waterway to the outpost of civilization you'll find at Chokoloskee and nearby Everglades City. It's a decent first stop if you're planning a three- or four-day canoe or kayak loop, say to Watson's Place and Rabbit or Pavilion Key and then back to Chokoloskee. You'll get your arms limbered up without paddling all that far.

Canoeists and kayakers will also find this spot to be a good choice for an overnighter if the wind kicks up and makes a trip across Chokoloskee Bay or "outside" in the Gulf of Mexico difficult. Of course, bugs are likely to be worse if it's the least bit warm (so come in winter). Even Sunday Bay itself can get kicked up by a decent wind. The fishing here is usually excellent. Snook travel the backwater creeks during winter. That attracts anglers who arrive by boat, and the possible occasional buzz of motors may annoy paddlers who want absolute solitude.

Campsites, facilities: Two tent sites on elevated wooden platforms accommodate up to six people each. You must use a kayak, canoe, or powerboat to travel 11.5 to 12 miles from the Gulf Coast Visitor Center in Everglades City or 8.5 to nine miles from Chokoloskee. No piped water is available, so bring plenty. Bring a portable stove because campfires are prohibited. Pack out trash. A dock and a vault toilet are provided. Children are OK. No pets, please.

Reservations, fees: Get a backcountry permit in person up to 24 hours before the day of your intended campout at the Flamingo Visitor Center or Gulf Coast Visitor Center. They are not issued by phone or mail. Camping permits for any length of stay are $10 for parties of up to six people, $20 for groups of seven to 12, and $30 for 13 or more. Major credit cards are accepted. There's a one-night stay limit.

Directions: From the intersection of U.S. 41/Tamiami Trail and State Road 29 east of Naples, drive five miles south on State Road 29 to the Everglades National Park Gulf Coast Visitor Center, on your right by Chokoloskee Bay. A ranger will explain the route to Sunday Bay. Obtain nautical chart 11430.

Contact: Everglades National Park, 40001 State Road 9336, Homestead, FL 33034, 305/242-7700. For backcountry questions, contact the Flamingo Visitor Center at 239/695-2945 or the Gulf Coast Visitor Center at 239/695-3311. Website: www.nps.gov/ever.

8 LOPEZ RIVER BOAT/ CANOE SITES

Rating: 7

On the Lopez River along the Wilderness Waterway in Everglades National Park

Everglades Backcountry map, grid a3, page 529

If you want to admire stars in an ebony sky but have only enough time or energy for the shortest possible overnight trip from the Chokoloskee boat ramp, this is it. These ground sites on the southern bank of the Lopez River sit five miles from the Chokoloskee boat ramp and eight miles from Everglades City, making this the closest camping option on the fabled Wilderness Waterway—an inland water route and adventurist's dream spanning 99 miles from Everglades City to Flamingo. Because these shady campsites are near civilization, you may hear the buzz of powerboat motors; vessels pass closely to avoid oyster bars in the river. The Lopez family lived here for two generations up until the 1940s, and as you approach from the tea-colored river you can't miss the tree-shaded concrete cistern that marks the turn-of-the-century family homestead. To Marie Lopez and her beau, Walter Alderman, it was a pretty (and unique) setting for tying the knot.

The downside of the thick tangle of buttonwood trees and mangroves is mosquitoes, which can be ravenous even in winter. Meanwhile, hungry raccoons can rip into Styrofoam coolers and plastic gallon water jugs. They also can get into backpacks of food hanging in trees. Tip: Wrap rope several times around a locked plastic cooler containing your edibles and water, then tie the rope to keep critters out. Because of these drawbacks, some people prefer to stop at this campsite only to picnic or stretch the legs, then spend the night elsewhere.

Campsites, facilities: Three ground tent sites accommodate a total of 12 people. You must use a kayak, canoe, or powerboat to travel five miles from the Chokoloskee boat ramp or eight miles from the Gulf Coast Visitor Center in Everglades City. No piped water is available, so bring plenty. Bring a portable stove because campfires are prohibited. Pack out trash. A vault toilet and tables are provided. Children are OK. No pets are allowed.

Reservations, fees: Get a backcountry permit in person up to 24 hours before the day of your intended campout at the Flamingo Visitor Center or Gulf Coast Visitor Center. They are not issued by phone or mail. Camping permits for any length of stay are $10 for parties of up to six people, $20 for groups of seven to 12, and $30 for 13 or more. Major credit cards are accepted. There's a two-night stay limit.

Directions: From the intersection of U.S. 41/Tamiami Trail and State Road 29 east of Naples, drive five miles south on State Road 29 to the Everglades National Park Gulf Coast Visitor Center, on your right by Chokoloskee Bay. A ranger will explain the Lopez River route. Use nautical chart 11430.

Contact: Everglades National Park, 40001 State Road 9336, Homestead, FL 33034, 305/242-7700. For backcountry questions, contact the Flamingo Visitor Center at 239/695-2945 or the Gulf Coast Visitor Center at 239/695-3311. Website: www.nps.gov/ever.

9 RABBIT KEY BOAT/CANOE SITES

Rating: 8

On the Gulf of Mexico in the Ten Thousand Islands, Everglades National Park

Everglades Backcountry map, grid a3, page 529

This beach is a favorite because it's one of the closest sandy sleepover spots to Chokoloskee and nearby Everglades City. If you're in a motorboat, getting here is a cinch—just nine miles from Everglades City, six from Chokoloskee. And if fishing, you'll have your choice of the oyster bars in Chokoloskee Bay, the tide-influenced comings and goings of redfish and the like in Chokoloskee Pass, and, of course, the Gulf of Mexico.

Dolphins may occasionally swim by. Shorebirds flutter along the sandy strip. You'll sleep on the western end of the island at the mouth of Rabbit Key Pass. Unlike ground or chickee campsites within the park, here you can enjoy a campfire. Some people know this beach as the place where early 20th century murder suspect Ed Watson was buried for a short time; outraged Chokoloskee residents shot him and dragged his body here to ensure he no longer

hurt anyone (see Watson's Place campsite for a fuller story).

For paddlers, the key to getting here is careful timing. We knew a guy who would scour the tide charts for weeks ahead to prepare for this trip. (It's worth it, though, to get a beach where you can watch a fabulous Everglades sunset alone, or virtually so.) Here's the thing: Pick a day when the tide is going out at the time you want to head out for the site, and then coming back in the next day about when you want to. For example, if the high tide is at, say, 6 A.M. on Saturday, you can start going out any time after that (there will be an hour or so of slack time). The next day, wait until low tide about midday, then start paddling in. It makes for a good, quick, fun overnighter with plenty of time for fishing. If you ignore the tides, you do so at your own peril. Trying to paddle against the tide through one of the passes in the Ten Thousand Islands is misery.

The island has a fairly narrow beach. Beware of prickly pear near the toilet, and pitch your tent up on the grasses off the beach.

Campsites, facilities: Two beach tent sites accommodate a total of eight people. You must use a kayak, canoe, or powerboat to travel six miles from Chokoloskee or nine miles from the Gulf Coast Visitor Center in Everglades City. No piped water is available, so bring plenty in raccoon-proof containers. A vault toilet is provided. Dead and downed wood may be used for campfires below the high tide line. Trash must be packed out. Children are OK. No pets, please.

Reservations, fees: Get a backcountry permit in person up to 24 hours before the day of your intended campout at the Flamingo Visitor Center or Gulf Coast Visitor Center. They are not issued by phone or mail. Camping permits for any length of stay are $10 for parties of up to six people, $20 for groups of seven to 12, and $30 for 13 or more. Major credit cards are accepted. There's a two-night stay limit.

Directions: From the intersection of U.S. 41/Tamiami Trail and State Road 29 east of

Naples, drive five miles south on State Road 29 to the Everglades National Park Gulf Coast Visitor Center, on your right by Chokoloskee Bay. A ranger will explain the Rabbit Key route. To avoid getting lost, obtain nautical chart 11430.

Contact: Everglades National Park, 40001 State Road 9336, Homestead, FL 33034, 305/242-7700. For backcountry questions, contact the Flamingo Visitor Center at 239/695-2945 or the Gulf Coast Visitor Center at 239/695-3311. Website: www.nps.gov/ever.

10 PAVILION KEY BOAT/ CANOE SITES

Rating: 8

On the Gulf of Mexico in Everglades National Park

Everglades Backcountry map, grid a3, page 529

Walk ashore this cacti-dotted island to see nary a footprint in the sand. "You are alone," says Joe Podgor, Miami Springs environmental activist. Bird-watching, fishing, and collecting seashells are popular, as is watching the orange glow of the sunset on the horizon. Stake out a private shoreline campsite at the northern end of the island (the southern end is closed to landings). Legend has it that pirates once camped along this long sandy beach and that their tents resembled a pavilion—hence the island's name. Pirates are said to have captured prisoners from a schooner, including one young woman who died tragically and still walks the beach at night. Today, raccoons, not pirates, are more resemblant of a platoon of flag-waving soldiers as they approach docked canoes and boats in search of water and food. Store water and edibles in locked, thick-plastic coolers; wrap and tie rope tightly around the coolers. Raccoons have been known to bite through plastic water jugs. If you're planning to spend several days in the Everglades, you may reach

Pavilion Key from such places as Rabbit Key (four miles), Watson's Place (eight miles), Lopez River (10 miles), or the Chokoloskee boat ramp (10 miles).

Campsites, facilities: Four beach tent sites accommodate five people each. You must use a kayak, canoe, or powerboat to get here from other campsites or to travel 13 miles here from the Gulf Coast Visitor Center in Everglades City. Boats must land on the northernmost sand spit only, not elsewhere, per park rules. No piped water is available, so bring plenty. Pack out trash. A vault toilet is provided. Dead and downed wood may be used for campfires below the high tide line. Children are OK. No pets, please.

Reservations, fees: Get a backcountry permit in person up to 24 hours before the day of your intended campout at the Flamingo Visitor Center or Gulf Coast Visitor Center. They are not issued by phone or mail. Camping permits for any length of stay are $10 for parties of up to six people, $20 for groups of seven to 12, and $30 for 13 or more. Major credit cards are accepted. There's a three-night stay limit.

Directions: From the intersection of U.S. 41/Tamiami Trail and State Road 29 east of Naples, drive about five miles south on State Road 29 to the Everglades National Park Gulf Coast Visitor Center, on your right by Chokoloskee Bay. A ranger will explain the Pavilion Key route. To avoid getting lost, obtain nautical chart 11430 at area bait stores, the ranger station, or downstairs from the ranger station at Everglades National Park Boat Tours.

Contact: Everglades National Park, 40001 State Road 9336, Homestead, FL 33034, 305/242-7700. For backcountry questions, contact the Flamingo Visitor Center at 239/695-2945 or the Gulf Coast Visitor Center at 239/695-3311. Website: www.nps.gov/ever.

11 DARWIN'S PLACE BOAT/CANOE SITES

Rating: 8

On the Wilderness Waterway in Everglades National Park

Everglades Backcountry map, grid b3, page 529

Basically a clearing found at water's edge along the Wilderness Waterway, Darwin's Place is preferred over more-famous Watson's Place by some campers. That's because it's a smaller site—and odds are you'll share it with fewer people. Also, picnic tables are provided, which makes mealtime more pleasant.

A man named Arthur Darwin moved to this island between Chevalier and Cannon Bays just as World War II was ending. Some old nautical charts still refer to it as Opossum Key, yet by the time Darwin left his homestead in 1971 (park officials let him stay on after the park was established in 1947), everyone knew it as Darwin's Place. Like the famous Charles Darwin who wrote *The Origin of Species,* the grandfatherly Arthur Darwin was a naturalist. But he was self-taught and got lots of practice living on his Everglades homestead.

Today, you can see the shell-and-concrete foundation of Darwin's cistern at this elevated, partly shady campsite. Walk inland a bit, and you also may notice mounds as tall as five feet high; they're oyster shell middens created by earlier residents, the Calusa Indians. Mosquitoes can be atrocious (as at any ground site), so bring DEET, mosquito coils, and, if possible, a hat with mosquito netting. Darwin's Place is accessible to powerboats as well as canoes—hence the frequent buzz of boats passing by on the Wilderness Waterway. Tie your craft securely; there's no dock.

Campsites, facilities: Two ground tent sites accommodate a total of eight people. You must use a kayak, canoe, or powerboat to travel to this location, which sits 20.5 miles from Everglades City's Gulf Coast Visitor Center. No piped water is available, so bring plenty. Pack out trash. Bring a portable stove because campfires are prohibited. A vault toilet and two picnic tables are provided. Children are OK. No pets, please.

Reservations, fees: Get a backcountry permit in person up to 24 hours before the day of your intended campout at the Flamingo Visitor Center or Gulf Coast Visitor Center. They are not issued by phone or mail. Camping permits for any length of stay are $10 for parties of up to six people, $20 for groups of seven to 12, and $30 for 13 or more. Major credit cards are accepted. There's a three-night stay limit.

Directions: From the intersection of U.S. 41/Tamiami Trail and State Road 29 east of Naples, drive five miles south on State Road 29 to the Everglades National Park Gulf Coast Visitor Center, on your right by Chokoloskee Bay. A ranger will explain the route to Darwin's Place. To avoid getting lost, obtain nautical chart 11430 at area bait stores, the ranger station, or downstairs from the ranger station at Everglades National Park Boat Tours.

Contact: Everglades National Park, 40001 State Road 9336, Homestead, FL 33034, 305/242-7700. For backcountry questions, contact the Flamingo Visitor Center at 239/695-2945 or the Gulf Coast Visitor Center at 239/695-3311. Website: www.nps.gov/ever.

12 WATSON'S PLACE BOAT/CANOE SITES

Rating: 9

On the Chatham River in Everglades National Park

Everglades Backcountry map, grid b3, page 529

If you bring plenty of DEET and a vivid imagination to this large wooded campsite on the north side of the Chatham River, hiking around the stomping grounds of turn-of-the-century murder suspect Ed Watson will be a treat. A hulking, bearded man, Watson settled here in a two-story house built on a native shell mound (the house's concrete cistern still stands). He supposedly moved here to flee pursuers who believed he had killed, among others, the famous female outlaw Belle Star. Soon, Watson's hired hands began to disappear—funny, right around payday. Nervous neighbors suspected the boss had killed them. After the body of Hannah Smith was seen floating nearby in 1910, frightened townsfolk took matters into their own hands and shot Watson to death at postmaster Ted Smallwood's store (now a museum), 16 miles away in Chokoloskee.

Today, hikers still may see the ruins of Watson's sugarcane syrup cauldron and farm machinery, as well as several exotic plants (picking them is prohibited). To add dimension to your stay, bring along Peter Matthiessen's book *Killing Mr. Watson,* a fictionalized yet largely historical account of the secretive man's exploits. The family of alligator hunter and marijuana smuggler Loren "Totch" Brown moved to this same outpost in the 1930s, inspiring his autobiography, *Totch: A Life in the Everglades.*

You'll likely share this site with others since it can accommodate far more tents than most Everglades backcountry spots. The long distance from Everglades City makes popular Watson's Place impractical for many weekend kayakers and canoeists. Consider spending at least three nights in the national park, camping at Lopez River (eight miles from Everglades City), then Watson's Place (19 miles from Everglades City), before doubling back for a campout at Sunday Bay (8.5 miles from Watson's Place) and awaking to an 11.5-mile paddle back to Everglades City. To get to Watson's Place from the Wilderness Waterway, leave the well-marked water route at marker 99 and head 1.5 miles down the Chatham River. The campsite is accessible to paddlers and powerboats at all tides.

Campsites, facilities: Five ground tent sites accommodate a total of 20 people. You must use a kayak, canoe, or powerboat to travel 16 miles from the Chokoloskee boat ramp or 19 miles from the Gulf Coast Visitor Center in Everglades City. No piped water is available, so bring plenty in raccoon-proof containers. Pack out trash. Bring a portable stove because campfires are prohibited. A vault toilet, long dock, and canoe ramp are provided. Children are OK. No pets, of course.

Reservations, fees: Get a backcountry permit in person up to 24 hours before the day of your intended campout at the Flamingo Visitor Center or Gulf Coast Visitor Center. They are not issued by phone or mail. Camping permits for any length of stay are $10 for parties of up to six people, $20 for groups of seven to 12, and $30 for 13 or more. Major credit cards are accepted. There's a two-night stay limit.

Directions: From the intersection of U.S. 41/Tamiami Trail and State Road 29 east of Naples, drive five miles south on State Road 29 to the Everglades National Park Gulf Coast Visitor Center, on your right by Chokoloskee Bay. A ranger will explain the route to Watson's Place. To avoid getting lost, obtain nautical chart 11430.

Contact: Everglades National Park, 40001 State Road 9336, Homestead, FL 33034, 305/242-7700. For backcountry questions, contact the Flamingo Visitor Center at 239/695-2945 or the Gulf Coast Visitor Center at 239/695-3311. Website: www.nps.gov/ever.

13 SWEETWATER BOAT/ CANOE SITES

Rating: 7

On Sweetwater Creek in Everglades National Park

Everglades Backcountry map, grid b3, page 529

Relatively few people take the two-mile detour from the 99-mile-long Wilderness Waterway (spanning Everglades City to Flamingo) to sleep on this double chickee set off the north end of a small island on Sweetwater Creek. Solitude is your reward. "Sweetwater" is colloquial for the fresh, drinkable water that falls from the sky. You must bring your own drinking water on the long trip here, so every drop you conserve may very well seem sweet.

The buckets of water that fall during the summer rainy season help explain the site's name. The campsite also is near the transition zone between brackish and fresh water.

Look for alligators. The bordering mangroves are alive with herons and other birds. Fish splash in the shallow water. If you're paddling, set aside about three nights to get to and from Everglades City, making two sleepover stops at Lopez River (eight miles from Everglades City) or at other sites suggested by a ranger. Only low-profile powerboats under 18 feet in length and with shallow draft should attempt docking at Sweetwater. Bring extra rope to tie a free-standing tent to the wooden, roof-covered platform that will serve as your campsite. No stakes or nails may be used.

Campsites, facilities: Two parties of up to six people each may stay at this elevated roof-covered wooden platform; a vault toilet separates the two sites. You must use a kayak, canoe, or powerboat to travel 16.5 miles from the Chokoloskee boat ramp or 19.5 miles from the Gulf Coast Visitor Center in Everglades City. No water is available. Pack out trash. Bring a portable stove because campfires are prohibited. A dock is provided. Children are OK. Pets are prohibited.

Reservations, fees: Get a backcountry permit in person up to 24 hours before the day of your intended campout at the Flamingo Visitor Center or Gulf Coast Visitor Center. They are not issued by phone or mail. Camping permits for any length of stay are $10 for parties of up to six people, $20 for groups of seven to 12, and $30 for 13 or more. Major credit cards are accepted. There's a one-night stay limit.

Directions: From the intersection of U.S. 41/Tamiami Trail and State Road 29 east of Naples, drive five miles south on State Road 29 to the Everglades National Park Gulf Coast Visitor Center, on your right by Chokoloskee Bay. A

ranger will explain the route to Sweetwater. To avoid getting lost, obtain nautical chart 11430. **Contact:** Everglades National Park, 40001 State Road 9336, Homestead, FL 33034, 305/242-7700. For backcountry questions, contact the Flamingo Visitor Center at 239/695-2945 or the Gulf Coast Visitor Center at 239/695-3311. Website: www.nps.gov/ever.

14 MORMON KEY BOAT/ CANOE SITES

Rating: 8

On the Gulf of Mexico in Everglades National Park

Everglades Backcountry map, grid b3, page 529

This is one of those odd pieces of real estate in the national park to which individual landowners still lay claim. Even half a century after the park was dedicated in 1947, some persistent souls continue to cite problems with the deed transfers. The legal wrangling won't interfere with your enjoyment of a long, shelly beach, where you can sit around a campfire or collect a handful of seashells (look for old conchs).

The beach is low but long—more than 100 yards, which is a rarity hereabouts. That affords pretty views of the sun setting on the Gulf of Mexico's broad horizon. The sun can bear down hard on this open beach at high noon, making it uncomfortably hot. Beyond the beach, you'll find the area's ubiquitous vegetation: mangroves. Bring a fishing rod; you'll be close to good angling spots near the mouth of the Huston and Chatham Rivers. Canoes can access Mormon Key at all tides. Powerboats, cautiously driven, should also be able to get close to the beach; check with rangers for tide information. It's best to land on the west side, facing Chatham Bend. The key is a miserable place to land during a storm, when north-northwest winds pummel it.

Campsites, facilities: Two beach tent sites accommodate a total of 12 people. You must use a canoe, kayak, or powerboat to get here. Travel distances vary by the route chosen; the sites are 14.5 miles to 20 miles from the Chokoloskee boat ramp or 17.5 miles to 20.5 miles from the Gulf Coast Visitor Center in Everglades City. No piped water is available, so bring plenty in raccoon-proof containers. There is no toilet, electricity, table, or dock. Human waste must be buried at least six inches deep or packed out with the trash. Dead and downed wood may be used for campfires below the high tide line. Children are welcome, but not pets.

Reservations, fees: Get a backcountry permit in person up to 24 hours before the day of your intended campout at the Flamingo Visitor Center or Gulf Coast Visitor Center. They are not issued by phone or mail. Camping permits for any length of stay are $10 for parties of up to six people, $20 for groups of seven to 12, and $30 for 13 or more. Major credit cards are accepted. There's a three-night stay limit.

Directions: From the intersection of U.S. 41/Tamiami Trail and State Road 29 east of Naples, drive five miles south on State Road 29 to the Everglades National Park Gulf Coast Visitor Center, on your right by Chokoloskee Bay. A ranger will explain the route to Mormon Key. Use nautical chart 11430.

Contact: Everglades National Park, 40001 State Road 9336, Homestead, FL 33034, 305/242-7700. For backcountry questions, contact the Flamingo Visitor Center at 239/695-2945 or the Gulf Coast Visitor Center at 239/695-3311. Website: www.nps.gov/ever.

15 NEW TURKEY KEY BOAT/CANOE SITES

Rating: 7

On the Gulf of Mexico in Everglades National Park

Everglades Backcountry map, grid b2, page 529

Secluded New Turkey Key and its sister campsite, Turkey Key, feature small beaches facing the fine sunsets of the Gulf of Mexico. The beach sand is actually a shelly mix, but it's the best you'll see in these parts. There's a large open, grassy area, perhaps 75 feet by 50 feet, where you can pitch a tent in the middle of the key.

Campsites, facilities: Two beach tent sites accommodate 10 people. You must use a canoe, kayak, or powerboat to get here. Travel distance varies by the route you choose; expect to travel 16.5 to 22 miles from the Chokoloskee boat ramp or 19.5 to 25 miles from the Gulf Coast Visitor Center in Everglades City. No piped water is available, so bring plenty in raccoon-proof containers. Pack out trash. A vault toilet is provided. Dead and downed wood may be used for campfires below the high tide line. Children are allowed, but not pets.

Reservations, fees: Get a backcountry permit in person up to 24 hours before the day of your intended campout at the Flamingo Visitor Center or Gulf Coast Visitor Center. They are not issued by phone or mail. Camping permits for any length of stay are $10 for parties of up to six people, $20 for groups of seven to 12, and $30 for 13 or more. Major credit cards are accepted. There's a two-night stay limit.

Directions: From the intersection of U.S. 41/Tamiami Trail and State Road 29 east of Naples, drive about five miles south on State Road 29 to the Everglades National Park Gulf Coast Visitor Center, on your right by Chokoloskee Bay. A ranger will explain the route to New Turkey Key. Use nautical chart 11430.

Contact: Everglades National Park, 40001 State Road 9336, Homestead, FL 33034, 305/242-7700. For backcountry questions, contact the Flamingo Visitor Center at 239/695-2945 or the Gulf Coast Visitor Center at 239/695-3311. Website: www.nps.gov/ever.

16 PLATE CREEK BAY BOAT/CANOE SITE

Rating: 8

On Plate Creek Bay along the Wilderness Waterway in Everglades National Park

Everglades Backcountry map, grid b3, page 529

If you want a camping retreat all to yourself, you're certain to get it here. This single tent site, which was built before the national park was established in 1947, is nirvana to adventurists tired of "wilderness" outings that pack strangers' tents together like sardines. At this former base camp for Joseph Cotton's real estate sales operations and his hunting/fishing parties, breezes and a southeastern exposure help make insects less of a problem. Fans love the clear water, pretty sunsets and sunrises, and a star-filled sky. On the downside, weekend boat traffic tends to be heavy. You'll be sleeping along the sole inland route between Chokoloskee and the good fishing holes down south. Bring extra rope to tie a free-standing tent to the chickee hut that serves as a tent site. No stakes or nails may be used.

Anyone relying on muscle power to get here should set aside five days or so to paddle a canoe or kayak to and from Everglades City, making sleepover stops at perhaps Lopez River (eight miles from Everglades City) and Sweetwater (19.5 miles from Everglades City) along the way. Outdoors enthusiasts also stop here during trips along the Wilderness Waterway, a well-marked inland water route that runs from Everglades City to Flamingo. Tides aren't a big issue at Plate Creek; it's accessible to canoes and powerboats up to 21 feet in length at all tides. But overhanging branches of mangroves may snag boats with T-tops.

Campsites, facilities: One tent site on an elevated wooden platform accommodates up to six people. You must use a kayak, canoe, or powerboat to travel 23 miles from the Chokoloskee boat ramp or 26 miles from the Gulf Coast

Visitor Center in Everglades City. No water is available. Pack out trash. Bring a portable stove. Campfires are prohibited. A vault toilet and a dock are provided. Children are allowed, but no pets.

Reservations, fees: Get a backcountry permit in person up to 24 hours before the day of your intended campout at the Flamingo Visitor Center or Gulf Coast Visitor Center. They are not issued by phone or mail. Camping permits for any length of stay are $10 for parties of up to six people, $20 for groups of seven to 12, and $30 for 13 or more. Major credit cards are accepted. There's a one-night stay limit.

Directions: From the intersection of U.S. 41/Tamiami Trail and State Road 29 east of Naples, drive five miles south on State Road 29 to the Everglades National Park Gulf Coast Visitor Center, on your right by Chokoloskee Bay. A ranger will explain the route to Plate Creek Bay. To avoid getting lost, obtain nautical chart 11430 at area bait stores, the ranger station, or downstairs from the ranger station at Everglades National Park Boat Tours.

Contact: Everglades National Park, 40001 State Road 9336, Homestead, FL 33034, 305/242-7700. For backcountry questions, contact the Flamingo Visitor Center at 239/695-2945 or the Gulf Coast Visitor Center at 239/695-3311. Website: www.nps.gov/ever.

17 LOSTMAN'S FIVE BAY BOAT/CANOE SITES

Rating: 5

On Lostman's Five Bay in Everglades National Park

Everglades Backcountry map, grid b3, page 529

Because this camping area involves a two- to three-day paddle from Everglades City and can accommodate a large number of campers, it gets a fair amount of use by people completing the Wilderness Waterway, a 99-mile route from Everglades City to Flamingo. But it's a ground site, and thus is buggier than chickee campsites. Among other drawbacks: It tends to flood during extreme high tides or heavy rains and is usually windy and sun-baked. Only a few palms shade the clearing of high ground where you'll pitch a tent. For a more pleasant night's sleep, opt instead for Broad River or the nearby Plate Creek Bay chickee, if you can.

Campsites, facilities: Two ground tent sites accommodate a total of 10 people. You must use a canoe, kayak, or powerboat to travel 24 miles from the Chokoloskee boat ramp or 27 miles from the Gulf Coast Visitor Center in Everglades City. No piped water is available, so bring plenty. Bring a portable stove because campfires are prohibited. A toilet is provided, as is a large dock that can fit several medium-sized boats. Trash must be packed out. Children are OK. No pets, please.

Reservations, fees: Get a backcountry permit in person up to 24 hours before the day of your intended campout at the Flamingo Visitor Center or Gulf Coast Visitor Center. They are not issued by phone or mail. Camping permits for any length of stay are $10 for parties of up to six people, $20 for groups of seven to 12, and $30 for 13 or more. Major credit cards are accepted. There's a two-night stay limit.

Directions: From the intersection of U.S. 41/Tamiami Trail and State Road 29 east of Naples, drive five miles south on State Road 29 to the Everglades National Park Gulf Coast Visitor Center, on your right by Chokoloskee Bay. A ranger will explain the route to Lostmans Five. To avoid getting lost, obtain nautical charts 11430 and 11432 at area bait stores, the ranger station, or downstairs from the ranger station at Everglades National Park Boat Tours.

Contact: Everglades National Park, 40001 State Road 9336, Homestead, FL 33034, 305/242-7700. For backcountry questions, contact the Flamingo Visitor Center at 239/695-2945 or the Gulf Coast Visitor Center at 239/695-3311. Website: www.nps.gov/ever.

18 HOG KEY CANOE/KAYAK SITES

Rating: 7

On the Gulf of Mexico in Everglades National Park

Everglades Backcountry map, grid b2, page 529

Powerboats can't approach this remote getaway because the water surrounding the island is quite shallow; in addition, a history of strong winds and rough seas makes landing dicey even for canoes and kayaks (if you must, use two anchors). Even canoeists and kayakers may have to anchor a good distance from the island and wade across shallow mudflats to the campsite. Although small, the site is well liked by many paddlers because it's right on the Gulf of Mexico. Bring a fishing pole; prime spots are minutes away to the north and south. What's more, this is a good way station for kayakers and canoeists to camp and shorten their paddling days—seas usually are rough between Turkey Key and Lostman's River. Downsides include a northern view—lousy for taking in sunsets or sunrises—and the fact that no signs mark the campsite, making it all the more difficult to find. Look for the campsite's namesake; resident wild hogs occasionally make appearances.

Campsites, facilities: Two beach tent sites accommodate a total of eight people. You must use a canoe or kayak. Travel distance varies; the shortest distance is 22.5 miles from the Chokoloskee boat ramp and 25.5 miles from the Gulf Coast Visitor Center in Everglades City. Powerboats are no use, as you can't dock here. No piped water is available, so bring plenty. There is no toilet; bury human waste or pack it out with the trash. Dead and downed wood may be used for campfires below the high tide line. Children are OK. No pets are allowed.

Reservations, fees: Get a backcountry permit in person up to 24 hours before the day of your intended campout at the Flamingo Visitor Center or Gulf Coast Visitor Center. They are not issued by phone or mail. Camping permits for any length of stay are $10 for parties of up to six people, $20 for groups of seven to 12, and $30 for 13 or more. Major credit cards are accepted. There's a two-night stay limit.

Directions: From the intersection of U.S. 41/Tamiami Trail and State Road 29 east of Naples, drive five miles south on State Road 29 to the Everglades National Park Gulf Coast Visitor Center, on your right by Chokoloskee Bay. A ranger will explain the route to Hog Key. To avoid getting lost, obtain nautical charts 11430 and 11432.

Contact: Everglades National Park, 40001 State Road 9336, Homestead, FL 33034, 305/242-7700. For backcountry questions, contact the Flamingo Visitor Center at 239/695-2945 or the Gulf Coast Visitor Center at 239/695-3311. Website: www.nps.gov/ever.

19 WILLY WILLY BOAT/ CANOE SITES

Rating: 7

On Rocky Creek Bay in Everglades National Park

Everglades Backcountry map, grid b3, page 529

Nobody likes mosquitoes, so it's understandable that Calusa Indians hundreds of years ago used the remains of the shellfish they ate to build this ground higher to help them get away from blood-sucking skeeters (and floods). Today, tropical hardwood trees—not ever-present mangroves—shade tenters just as they did Indians.

This site is favored by serious anglers, who venture into area waters to go after snook and mangrove snapper, then sleep here. The formidable distance makes Willy Willy impractical for weekend kayakers or canoeists. Consider a week-long vacation with campouts along the way at Lopez River (eight miles from Everglades City), Sweetwater (19.5 miles from Everglades City), and Plate Creek Bay (26 miles

from Everglades City). Adventurists sometimes make a two-mile northeastward detour to sleep here during trips along the Wilderness Waterway, a well-marked inland water route that runs from Everglades City to Flamingo. Early settlers are said to have burned smudge pots of dead black mangrove to try to keep bugs away, and were said to have lived entirely in smoke. Tip: Bring mosquito netting and DEET. Also, protect your food and water from raccoons. Fortunately, tides aren't a big issue at Willy Willy; it's accessible to canoes and powerboats at all tides.

Campsites, facilities: Three ground tent sites accommodate a total of 10 people. You must use a kayak, canoe, or powerboat to travel 32.5 miles from the Chokoloskee boat ramp or 35.5 miles from the Gulf Coast Visitor Center in Everglades City. No piped water is available, so bring plenty. Bring a portable stove because campfires are prohibited. A vault toilet, small dock, and picnic table are provided. Trash must be packed out. Children are OK. No pets, please.

Reservations, fees: Get a backcountry permit in person up to 24 hours before the day of your intended campout at the Flamingo Visitor Center or Gulf Coast Visitor Center. They are not issued by phone or mail. Camping permits for any length of stay are $10 for parties of up to six people, $20 for groups of seven to 12, and $30 for 13 or more. Major credit cards are accepted. There's a three-night stay limit.

Directions: From the intersection of U.S. 41/Tamiami Trail and State Road 29 east of Naples, drive about five miles south on State Road 29 to the Everglades National Park Gulf Coast Visitor Center, on your right by Chokoloskee Bay. A ranger will explain the route to Willy Willy. To avoid getting lost, obtain nautical charts 11430 and 11432 at area bait stores, the ranger station, or downstairs from the ranger station at Everglades National Park Boat Tours. It pays to get a new chart 11432; older versions misplace Willy Willy. After going north on Rocky Creek, turn left—not right—on Rocky Creek Bay, then go southwest for .1 mile, looking for the narrow dock on the uncharted creek flowing north of the bay. A sign marks the campsite.

Contact: Everglades National Park, 40001 State Road 9336, Homestead, FL 33034, 305/242-7700. For backcountry questions, contact the Flamingo Visitor Center at 239/695-2945 or the Gulf Coast Visitor Center at 239/695-3311. Website: www.nps.gov/ever.

20 RODGERS RIVER BAY BOAT/CANOE SITES

Rating: 8

On Rodgers River Bay in Everglades National Park

Everglades Backcountry map, grid b2, page 529

Tarpon fishing is considered good in the surrounding bays, and bass waters are nearby, so camping at this site set in a small, protected cove is popular. Here, you'll sleep closest to a traditional nesting site for Everglades wading birds, which are considered an important barometer of the ecosystem's overall health. Consider this description from the 1940s: "The whole scene fairly swamped, seethed and crawled with running, flapping young birds. . . . Overhead, constantly arriving and departing, wheeling, circling, were squadrons of adults, which pitched and dived into the general melee on whistling, rushing wings."

Alas, the birds' numbers have been greatly reduced by disruptions in the natural Everglades water flows caused by development and farming. Still, in some good years when enough water courses through the 'Glades, you'll find this nesting site alive with birds, albeit fewer.

From the campsite, you'll notice egrets and herons flying overhead. Look for alligators and possibly a small crocodile. The site is a typical Everglades National Park backcountry chickee. It is close to the halfway point on the 99-mile-long Wilderness Waterway from Everglades

City to Flamingo, which takes about 10 days by canoe or one to two days by motorboat. Bring extra rope to tie a free-standing tent to the chickee hut that serves as a tent site. No stakes or nails may be used.

Campsites, facilities: Two tent sites on elevated wooden platforms accommodate up to six people each. You must use a powerboat, kayak, or canoe to travel 36 miles from the Chokoloskee boat ramp or 39 miles from the Gulf Coast Visitor Center in Everglades City. No piped water is available, so bring plenty. Bring a portable stove because campfires are prohibited. A vault toilet and dock are provided. Trash must be packed out. Children are OK. No pets, please.

Reservations, fees: Get a backcountry permit in person up to 24 hours before the day of your intended campout at the Flamingo Visitor Center or Gulf Coast Visitor Center. They are not issued by phone or mail. Camping permits for any length of stay are $10 for parties of up to six people, $20 for groups of seven to 12, and $30 for 13 or more. Major credit cards are accepted. There's a one-night stay limit.

Directions: From the intersection of U.S. 41/Tamiami Trail and State Road 29 east of Naples, drive about five miles south on State Road 29 to the Everglades National Park Gulf Coast Visitor Center, on your right by Chokoloskee Bay. A ranger will explain the route to Rodgers River. To avoid getting lost, obtain nautical charts 11430 and 11432 at area bait stores, the ranger station, or downstairs from the ranger station at Everglades National Park Boat Tours.

Contact: Everglades National Park, 40001 State Road 9336, Homestead, FL 33034, 305/242-7700. For backcountry questions, contact the Flamingo Visitor Center at 239/695-2945 or the Gulf Coast Visitor Center at 239/695-3311. Website: www.nps.gov/ever.

21 HIGHLAND BEACH BOAT/CANOE SITES

Rating: 7

On the Gulf of Mexico in Everglades National Park

Everglades Backcountry map, grid b2, page 529

This large site is heavily used, despite its remoteness. The reason: It features a beach on the Gulf of Mexico framed by coconut palms. Sunsets can be gorgeous, with the feel of a tropical paradise in this subtropical wilderness. The vegetation, a kind of low brush, is set back about 50 feet from the water, allowing campers a beach that is nice and wide, if a little low-slung. The shoreline's low profile can be a problem when a west wind kicks up because the tides can rush in fairly fast and far, so check the weather forecast. In any case, pitch your tent a healthy distance from where the waves are breaking.

Birds abound in winter, including ibises, herons, and egrets. Wild boars occasionally make appearances. The sand consists of broken shells and marl mud. Be mindful of tides when approaching camp; if you arrive at low tide, you may be cut off by huge, exposed mudflats. In that case, prepare to wade. And wear old sneakers. You never know when you might trod on an errant oyster shell that can cut you badly. Unless you have a motorboat, you'll need more than one day to make it to Highland Beach. Consult with rangers about other stops to make along the way.

Campsites, facilities: Four beach tent sites accommodate a total of 24 people. You must use a powerboat, kayak, or canoe to travel a minimum of 29.5 miles from the Chokoloskee boat ramp or 32.5 miles to 39 miles from the Gulf Coast Visitor Center in Everglades City, depending on the route chosen. There is no piped water, so bring your own. Trash must be packed out. No toilet is available; bury human waste six inches deep. Dead and downed wood may be used for campfires below the high tide line. Children are OK. No pets, please.

Reservations, fees: Get a backcountry permit in person up to 24 hours before the day of your intended campout at the Flamingo Visitor Center or Gulf Coast Visitor Center. They are not issued by phone or mail. Camping permits for any length of stay are $10 for parties of up to six people, $20 for groups of seven to 12, and $30 for 13 or more. Major credit cards are accepted. There's a three-night stay limit.

Directions: From the intersection of U.S. 41/Tamiami Trail and State Road 29 east of Naples, drive about five miles south on State Road 29 to the Everglades National Park Gulf Coast Visitor Center, on your right by Chokoloskee Bay. A ranger will explain the route to Highland Beach. To avoid getting lost, obtain nautical charts 11430 and 11432 at area bait stores, the ranger station, or downstairs from the ranger station at Everglades National Park Boat Tours.

Contact: Everglades National Park, 40001 State Road 9336, Homestead, FL 33034, 305/242-7700. For backcountry questions, contact the Flamingo Visitor Center at 239/695-2945 or the Gulf Coast Visitor Center at 239/695-3311. Website: www.nps.gov/ever.

22 BROAD RIVER BOAT/ CANOE SITES

Rating: 7

On the Broad River in Everglades National Park

Everglades Backcountry map, grid b2, page 529

This is the campsite closest to the halfway point on the Wilderness Waterway, which runs 99 miles from Flamingo to Everglades City. The trip will generally take about 10 days by kayak or canoe, although it's possible to complete in a day or two by powerboat. If you're trying to save time or avoid the waves of the Gulf of Mexico, you can take a cutoff just south of here known as "The Nightmare." This moniker did not come from nowhere. Although The Nightmare shaves a few miles off your trip, it's also nearly impossible, even for kayaks and canoes, during low tide. Luckily, though, the Broad River campsite is usually accessible at low tide, even to big boats. Just be ready for strong river currents and up to a three-foot tidal differential when mooring at this site on the south bank of the Broad River. Mosquitoes and other bugs can be a big problem in any season. The ground campsite can get quite muddy when it's been raining.

Campsites, facilities: Three ground tent sites accommodate a total of 10 people. You must use a powerboat, kayak, or canoe to get here. Travel distance varies by route chosen; expect to travel a minimum of 33.5 miles from the Chokoloskee boat ramp, 36.5 miles from the Gulf Coast Visitor Center in Everglades City, or 39.5 miles from the Flamingo Visitor Center. No piped water is available, so bring plenty. Bring a portable stove because campfires are prohibited. A vault toilet, table, small dock, and canoe ramp are provided. Trash must be packed out. Children are OK. No pets, please.

Reservations, fees: Get a backcountry permit in person up to 24 hours before the day of your intended campout at the Flamingo Visitor Center or Gulf Coast Visitor Center. They are not issued by phone or mail. Camping permits for any length of stay are $10 for parties of up to six people, $20 for groups of seven to 12, and $30 for 13 or more. Major credit cards are accepted. There's a two-night stay limit.

Directions: From the intersection of U.S. 41/Tamiami Trail and State Road 29 east of Naples, drive five miles south on State Road 29 to the Everglades National Park Gulf Coast Visitor Center, on your right by Chokoloskee Bay. A ranger will explain the route to Broad River. To avoid getting lost, obtain nautical charts 11430 and 11432 at area bait stores, at the ranger station, or downstairs from the ranger station at Everglades National Park Boat Tours. If you're approaching from Flamin-

go, buy charts 11432 and 11433 at the Flamingo Visitor Center.

Contact: Everglades National Park, 40001 State Road 9336, Homestead, FL 33034, 305/242-7700. For backcountry questions, contact the Flamingo Visitor Center at 239/695-2945 or the Gulf Coast Visitor Center at 239/695-3311. Website: www.nps.gov/ever.

23 CAMP LONESOME BOAT/CANOE SITES

Rating: 7

On the Broad River in Everglades National Park

Everglades Backcountry map, grid c2, page 529

They don't call this place Lonesome for nothing. It's about three miles east of the Wilderness Waterway, which itself is sparsely populated. To find the campsite, you have to look for a narrow dock jutting out of thick brush. When you get closer to it, you'll see the campsite sign. This old Calusa Indian mound was built up from oyster shells and other leavings, and is shaded by sabal palms and relatively rare tropical hardwoods such as red-barked gumbo-limbo.

It is one of the few campsites in the park where you can catch sight of the sawgrass prairies that earned the Everglades its nickname, "River of Grass." Another plus: Picnic tables will make meals easier.

There are, however, lots of mosquitoes, so come during a winter cold snap, if possible. The site is next to a large fork in the Broad River. Look for the dock on the north bank. Camp Lonesome can be done as an overnight trip only if you have a motorboat. Otherwise, plan an outing of several days or even a week.

Campsites, facilities: Three ground tent sites accommodate a total of 10 people. You must use a powerboat, kayak, or canoe to get here. Travel distances vary by route chosen; it's a minimum of 41 miles from the Chokoloskee boat ramp, 44 miles from the Gulf Coast Visitor Center in Everglades City, or 49 miles from the Flamingo Visitor Center. The site is accessible at all tides. No piped water is available, so bring plenty. Bring a portable stove because campfires are prohibited. Pack out trash. A vault toilet, two picnic tables, and a dock are provided. Children are OK. No pets, please.

Reservations, fees: Get a backcountry permit in person up to 24 hours before the day of your intended campout at the Flamingo Visitor Center or Gulf Coast Visitor Center. They are not issued by phone or mail. Camping permits for any length of stay are $10 for parties of up to six people, $20 for groups of seven to 12, and $30 for 13 or more. Major credit cards are accepted. There's a three-night stay limit.

Directions: From the intersection of U.S. 41/Tamiami Trail and State Road 29 east of Naples, drive about five miles south on State Road 29 to the Everglades National Park Gulf Coast Visitor Center, on your right by Chokoloskee Bay. A ranger will explain your route to Camp Lonesome. To avoid getting lost, obtain nautical charts 11430 and 11432 at area bait stores, the ranger station, or downstairs from the ranger station at Everglades National Park Boat Tours. If you're approaching from Flamingo, buy charts 11432 and 11433 at the Flamingo Visitor Center.

Contact: Everglades National Park, 40001 State Road 9336, Homestead, FL 33034, 305/242-7700. For backcountry questions, contact the Flamingo Visitor Center at 239/695-2945 or the Gulf Coast Visitor Center at 239/695-3311. Website: www.nps.gov/ever.

24 HARNEY RIVER BOAT/ CANOE SITE

Rating: 6

On the Broad River in Everglades National Park

Everglades Backcountry map, grid b2, page 529

For one researcher of this book, the Harney River chickee will forever have a special significance. This is the place where—after coming down the Shark River Slough and unmarked routes through the mangroves, and spending two nights quite lost in the Everglades—Robert McClure and his partner saw the sign "Harney River" on the chickee. Finally, they knew where they were. Their destination was Flamingo. But if they'd gone just another three or four miles, they would have entered the Gulf of Mexico. It just goes to show how handy a global positioning system can be. The chickee is nothing special by Everglades standards, but it is out in wild country where the fishing is great.

Of course, Lt. Colonel William Harney wasn't looking for a fishing hole when he was said to have discovered the river in 1840. Instead, he was coming back from leading 90 soldiers in 16 canoes on a successful December raid against Seminole leader Chief Chekika's camp to avenge the deaths of seven people. Bring extra rope to tie your free-standing tent to the chickee platform that serves as a tent site. No stakes or nails may be used.

Campsites, facilities: One tent site on an elevated wooden platform accommodates up to six people. You must use a powerboat, kayak, or canoe to travel 31 miles from the Flamingo Visitor Center, a minimum of 42 miles from the Chokoloskee boat ramp, or at least 45 miles from the Gulf Coast Visitor Center in Everglades City. No piped water is available, so bring plenty. Bring DEET to combat bugs and any supplies you'll need, including a portable stove (campfires are prohibited). A vault toilet and dock are provided. Trash must be packed out. Children are OK. No pets, please.

Reservations, fees: Get a backcountry permit in person up to 24 hours before the day of your intended campout at the Flamingo Visitor Center or Gulf Coast Visitor Center. They are not issued by phone or mail. Camping permits for any length of stay are $10 for parties of up to six people, $20 for groups of seven to 12, and $30 for 13 or more. Major credit cards are accepted. There's a one-night stay limit.

Directions: To avoid getting lost, obtain nautical charts 11432 and 11433 at the Flamingo Visitor Center or area bait stores. If you're approaching from Everglades City, buy charts 11430 and 11432 within the Gulf Coast Visitor Center.

Contact: Everglades National Park, 40001 State Road 9336, Homestead, FL 33034, 305/242-7700. For backcountry questions, contact the Flamingo Visitor Center at 239/695-2945 or the Gulf Coast Visitor Center at 239/695-3311. Website: www.nps.gov/ever.

25 CANEPATCH BOAT/ CANOE SITES

Rating: 8

East of Tarpon Bay on Squawk Creek in Everglades National Park

Everglades Backcountry map, grid c2, page 529

It's called Canepatch because some misguided soul once tried to eke out a living here raising cane. Sugarcane, that is—the very crop grown across an 1,100-square-mile swath two counties northeast of here that environmentalists say is a threat to the Everglades. This little cane patch never really worked out, though. Today, there's no remnant of it except for an elevated clearing where you can pitch a tent. You may see wild bananas, limes, and papayas. Although remote, this former Seminole Indian site gets used a fair bit by locals, largely because small motorboats can easily reach the dock leading to it. Expect to see birds and alligators in winter. In summer, mosquitoes make camping here impractical; even in winter they can swarm mercilessly. Bring mosquito netting and mosquito coils.

These waters are popular among anglers looking for snook in winter; the snook head up into the backcountry to keep warm when cold fronts blow through Florida Bay. If you continue northeast one mile or two from this site, you'll come to Rookery Branch, where freshwater flows into brackish water. It's a spot favored by anglers looking for bass and snook. The formidable distance makes it impractical for weekend kayakers or canoeists. Consider making it a stop on a week-long vacation.

Worthy of note here: Canepatch has a lot of poison ivy. Really a lot. Know what it looks like before you come here, or you could end up very uncomfortable. Also, ask a ranger whether any problem alligators frequent these waters now. Last time we camped here, an alligator alarmed us by approaching our canoe just about as soon as we docked; it was clear that fishermen had been throwing fish scraps into the water.

Caution to canoeists: Boaters sometimes speed through narrow Avocado Creek, so keep alert while paddling there. Once you reach the Canepatch site, you may want to continue north about one mile so you can look for a small batch of banana trees on the west side of Rookery Branch. They're delicious, sweet, plump little things. There are also banana trees at Canepatch, but they usually have been picked clean by previous campers.

Campsites, facilities: Four ground tent sites accommodate a total of 12 people. You must use a canoe, kayak, or powerboat to travel 29.5 miles from the Flamingo Visitor Center, a minimum 51.5 miles from the Chokoloskee boat ramp, or at least 54.5 miles from the Gulf Coast Ranger Station in Everglades City. No piped water is available, so bring plenty. Bring a portable stove because campfires are prohibited, although you shouldn't be surprised to find remainders of illicit campfires here. A toilet, table, and dock are provided. Trash must be packed out. Children are OK. No pets, please.

Reservations, fees: Get a backcountry permit in person up to 24 hours before the day of your intended campout at the Flamingo Visitor Center or Gulf Coast Visitor Center. They are not issued by phone or mail. Camping permits for any length of stay are $10 for parties of up to six people, $20 for groups of seven to 12, and $30 for 13 or more. Major credit cards are accepted. There's a three-night stay limit.

Directions: From Miami, take Florida's Turnpike to its southern terminus at U.S. 1. In about one block, turn right at Palm Drive. Cross the railroad tracks and pass the Circle K. At the flashing traffic light at 192nd Avenue/State Road 9336, turn left by the Robert Is Here fruit stand. Proceed south about two miles. When State Road 9336 veers right, follow it to the right instead of going straight toward the alligator farm. The park entrance is four miles ahead. Follow the main park road 38 miles to Flamingo Marina on the left to launch. To avoid getting lost, obtain nautical charts 11432 and 11433 at the Flamingo Visitor Center or area bait stores. If you're approaching from Everglades City, buy charts 11430 and 11432 within the Gulf Coast Visitor Center.

Contact: Everglades National Park, 40001 State Road 9336, Homestead, FL 33034, 305/242-7700. For backcountry questions, contact the Flamingo Visitor Center at 239/695-2945 or the Gulf Coast Visitor Center at 239/695-3311. Website: www.nps.gov/ever.

26 GRAVEYARD CREEK BOAT/CANOE SITES

Rating: 7

On the Gulf of Mexico in Everglades National Park

Everglades Backcountry map, grid b2, page 529

Once upon a time, there was a graveyard somewhere along this creek, but it has long since been obliterated by hurricanes or covered over by the encroaching mangroves. As legend has it, feuding hunters who were supplying pelts for the popular raccoon coats of the 1920s had it out here.

Spectacular sunsets and fine fishing are the payoff for staying at this ground site, where bugs sometimes swarm thickly—so much so, in fact, that some discouraged campers retreat into their tents at dusk (reminder: go in winter). If you retreat at dusk, be sure to return outdoors an hour or two later to admire the terrific stars, advises park ranger Steve Robinson, who also likes the nighttime sounds of fish splashing in these waters.

You'll sleep on a somewhat-shady sand ridge that is subject to limited southwesterly winds. It's surrounded by red mangroves. Getting to the site, at the mouth of Graveyard Creek, can be a little tricky. You actually go to the east of the main mouth of the creek and circle counterclockwise to find the spot where you can land your boat or canoe. (Use your nautical chart.) What's more, the fast current that lures game fish to this area also has been known to sink boats that weren't moored properly at the dock. Check with rangers about tide conditions because the flats around here can be left high and dry during a particularly low tide.

Campsites, facilities: Four ground tent sites accommodate a total of 12 people. You must use a canoe, kayak, or powerboat to get here. Travel distances vary by route chosen; expect to travel 28 miles from the Flamingo Visitor Center, a minimum of 38.5 miles from the Chokoloskee boat ramp, or a minimum of 41.5 miles from the Gulf Coast Ranger Station in Everglades City. No piped water is available, so bring plenty. Bring a portable stove because campfires are prohibited. Pack out trash. A toilet and table are provided. Children are OK. No pets, please.

Reservations, fees: Get a backcountry permit in person up to 24 hours before the day of your intended campout at the Flamingo Visitor Center or Gulf Coast Visitor Center. They are not issued by phone or mail. Camping permits for any length of stay are $10 for parties of up to six people, $20 for groups of seven to 12, and $30 for 13 or more. Major credit cards are accepted. There's a three-night stay limit.

Directions: To avoid getting lost, obtain nautical chart 11432 at the Flamingo Visitor Center or area bait stores. If you're approaching from Everglades City, buy charts 11430, 11432, and 11433 within the Gulf Coast Visitor Center.

Contact: Everglades National Park, 40001 State Road 9336, Homestead, FL 33034, 305/242-7700. For backcountry questions, contact the Flamingo Visitor Center at 239/695-2945 or the Gulf Coast Visitor Center at 239/695-3311. Website: www.nps.gov/ever.

27 SHARK RIVER BOAT/ CANOE SITE

Rating: 6

On the Shark River in Everglades National Park

Everglades Backcountry map, grid c2, page 529

The origin of the name Shark River is a little obscure, and you're unlikely to see many sharks today. For that you'd probably have to head out to nearby Ponce de Leon Bay or beyond to the Gulf of Mexico. You're much more likely to spot birds and perhaps a porpoise or two playfully swimming along the mangrove-flanked Shark River. Or maybe you'll see a raccoon trying to get into your water jug. Bring a freestanding tent; no stakes can be pounded into the chickee platform, which sits against a thick stand of mangroves (and, hence, can be buggy). For us, this site is more than a full day's paddle from Flamingo, but it's easily reachable by motorboat. It's best used as a stopover on your way to Canepatch or points farther north on the Wilderness Waterway.

Campsites, facilities: One tent site on an elevated wooden platform accommodates up to six people. You must use a canoe, kayak, or boat to travel 21 miles from the Flamingo Visitor Center or, depending on the route chosen, a minimum of 45 miles from the Chokoloskee boat ramp or 48 miles from the Gulf Coast Ranger Station in Everglades City. No piped water is available, so bring plenty. Bring a portable stove because campfires are prohibited. Pack out trash. A vault toilet and dock are provided. Children are OK. No pets, please.

Reservations, fees: Get a backcountry permit in person up to 24 hours before the day of your intended campout at the Flamingo Visitor Center or Gulf Coast Visitor Center. They are not issued by phone or mail. Camping permits for any length of stay are $10 for parties of up to six people, $20 for groups of seven to 12, and $30 for 13 or more. Major credit cards are accepted. There's a one-night stay limit.

Directions: From Miami, take Florida's Turnpike to its southern terminus at U.S. 1. In about one block, turn right at Palm Drive. Cross the railroad tracks and pass the Circle K. At the flashing traffic light at 192nd Avenue/State Road 9336, turn left by the Robert Is Here fruit stand. Proceed south about two miles. When State Road 9336 veers right, follow it to the right instead of going straight toward the alligator farm. The park entrance is four miles ahead. Follow the main park road 38 miles to Flamingo Marina to launch your vessel. Ask a ranger for directions to Shark River. To avoid getting lost, obtain nautical chart 11433 at the Flamingo Visitor Center or area bait stores. If you're approaching from Everglades City, buy charts 11430, 11432, and 11433 within the Gulf Coast Visitor Center.

Contact: Everglades National Park, 40001 State Road 9336, Homestead, FL 33034, 305/242-7700. For backcountry questions, contact the Flamingo Visitor Center at 239/695-2945 or the Gulf Coast Visitor Center at 239/695-3311. Website: www.nps.gov/ever.

28 OYSTER BAY BOAT/ CANOE SITES

Rating: 7

On Oyster Bay in Everglades National Park

Everglades Backcountry map, grid c2, page 529

If the weather is turning nasty, you should consider staying in this double chickee that is tucked behind an island. By the same token, you'll have to follow your nautical chart closely to find the place, which is located in a cove about one mile southwest of Wilderness Waterway marker No. 2. This stopover is not obvious from Oyster Bay and has been missed by more than one canoeing party. Two researchers of this book, Robert McClure and Sally Deneen, learned this the hard way one trip, when their canoe was half-swamped in Oyster Bay. Several boats have sunk near here because of the oyster bars—hence the campsite's name. The area is known for good fishing. Bottlenosed dolphins sometimes make appearances. Also, look skyward as you paddle; you may see an osprey flying toward its sizable nest atop a snag. Lucky anglers just might pull in a redfish near one of the bay's oyster bars.

Campsites, facilities: Two tent sites on an elevated wooden platform accommodate up to six people each. A vault toilet separates the two sites. You must use a boat, canoe, or kayak to travel 18 miles from the Flamingo Visitor Center or, depending on the route chosen, a minimum 48.5 miles from the Chokoloskee boat ramp or a minimum 51.5 miles from the Gulf Coast Ranger Station in Everglades City. No piped water is available, so bring plenty. Bring a portable stove because campfires are prohibited. Pack out trash. A dock is provided. Children are OK. No pets, please.

Reservations, fees: Get a backcountry permit in person up to 24 hours before the day of your intended campout at the Flamingo Visitor Center or Gulf Coast Visitor Center. They are not issued by phone or mail. Camping permits for any length of stay are $10 for parties of up to six people, $20 for groups of seven to 12, and $30 for 13 or more. Major credit cards are accepted. There's a one-night stay limit.

Directions: To avoid getting lost, obtain nautical chart 11433 at the Flamingo Visitor Center or area bait stores. If you're approaching from Everglades City, buy charts 11430, 11432, and 11433 within the Gulf Coast Visitor Center.

Contact: Everglades National Park, 40001 State Road 9336, Homestead, FL 33034, 305/242-7700. For backcountry questions, contact the Flamingo Visitor Center at 239/695-2945 or the Gulf Coast Visitor Center at 239/695-3311. Website: www.nps.gov/ever.

29 WATSON RIVER BOAT/ CANOE SITES

Rating: 7

On the Joe River in Everglades National Park

Everglades Backcountry map, grid c2, page 529

This is the least-used chickee in the southern end of the park, even though the fishing around here is excellent. Go figure. Despite the name, the site is not actually on the river. As you head north toward the mouth of the river, follow your nautical chart carefully. The chickee is on the northern tip of a big island behind some mangroves, which should help protect you from winds and rough seas. Look for manatees and alligators from your campsite. Only one party of campers per night is allowed, so you'll have privacy.

Campsites, facilities: One tent site on an elevated wooden platform accommodates up to six people. You must use a boat, canoe, or kayak to get here; expect to trek 16 miles from the Flamingo Visitor Center or, depending on the route chosen, a minimum of 56 miles from the Chokoloskee boat ramp or 59 miles from the Gulf Coast Ranger Station in Everglades City. No piped water is available, so bring plenty. Bring a portable stove because campfires are prohibited. Pack out trash. A toilet and dock are provided. Children are OK. No pets, please.

Reservations, fees: Get a backcountry permit in person up to 24 hours before the day of your intended campout at the Flamingo Visitor Center or Gulf Coast Visitor Center. They are not issued by phone or mail. Camping permits for any length of stay are $10 for parties of up to six people, $20 for groups of seven to 12, and $30 for 13 or more. Major credit cards are accepted. There's a one-night stay limit.

Directions: From Miami, take Florida's Turnpike to its southern terminus at U.S. 1. In about one block, turn right at Palm Drive. Cross the railroad tracks and pass the Circle K. At the flashing traffic light at 192nd Avenue/State Road 9336, turn left by the Robert Is Here fruit stand. Proceed south about two miles. When State Road 9336 veers right, follow it to the right instead of going straight toward the alligator farm. The park entrance is four miles ahead. Follow the main park road 38 miles to Flamingo Marina to launch your vessel. Ask a ranger for directions to Watson River. To avoid getting lost, obtain nautical chart 11433 at the Flamingo Visitor Center or area bait stores. If you're approaching from Everglades City, buy charts 11430, 11432, and 11433 within the Gulf Coast Visitor Center.

Contact: Everglades National Park, 40001 State Road 9336, Homestead, FL 33034, 305/242-7700. For backcountry questions, contact the Flamingo Visitor Center at 239/695-2945 or the Gulf Coast Visitor Center at 239/695-3311. Website: www.nps.gov/ever.

30 NORTH RIVER BOAT/ CANOE SITE

Rating: 8

On the North River in Everglades National Park

Everglades Backcountry map, grid c2, page 529

There is no marked canoe trail leading here, so you'll need to be extremely handy with a map and compass. The North River chickee is set amid a maze of islands off the north edge of Whitewater Bay. You'll likely head here from the Roberts River or Watson River campsites, both of which are three miles away. It's brackish water, and during the wintertime the snook fishing is quite good. Look for manatees in winter.

Campsites, facilities: One tent site on an elevated wooden platform accommodates up to six people. You must use a boat, canoe, or kayak to travel 17 miles from the Flamingo Visitor Center, a minimum of 59 miles from the Chokoloskee boat ramp or at least 62 miles from the Gulf Coast Ranger Station in Everglades City. No piped water is available, so bring plenty. Bring a portable stove because campfires are prohibited. Pack out trash. A toilet and dock are provided. Children are OK. No pets, please.

Reservations, fees: Get a backcountry permit in person up to 24 hours before the day of your intended campout at the Flamingo Visitor Center or Gulf Coast Visitor Center. They are not issued by phone or mail. Camping permits for any length of stay are $10 for parties of up to six people, $20 for groups of seven to 12, and $30 for 13 or more. Major credit cards are accepted. There's a one-night stay limit.

Directions: Ask a ranger for directions to North River. To avoid getting lost, obtain nautical chart 11433 at the Flamingo Visitor Center or area bait stores. If you're approaching from Everglades City, buy charts 11430, 11432, and 11433 within the Gulf Coast Visitor Center.

Contact: Everglades National Park, 40001 State Road 9336, Homestead, FL 33034, 305/242-7700. For backcountry questions, contact the Flamingo Visitor Center at 239/695-2945 or the Gulf Coast Visitor Center at 239/695-3311. Website: www.nps.gov/ever.

31 ROBERTS RIVER BOAT/ CANOE SITES

Rating: 7

On the Roberts River in Everglades National Park

Everglades Backcountry map, grid c2, page 529

Like the North River and Lane Bay chickees, Roberts River is snuggled way up into the maze of mangrove islands that marks the transition from freshwater to saltwater Everglades northeast of Whitewater Bay. This is a decent choice if you expect a strong wind to be blowing because it's tucked against the north side of the river in a crook, affording some protection. Be sure to keep a map and compass handy and ask a ranger for great directions; it can be easy to get lost on the way here.

Campsites, facilities: Two tent sites on an elevated wooden platform accommodate up to six people each; a vault toilet separates the two sites. You must use a boat, canoe, or kayak to travel 13.5 miles from the Flamingo Visitor Center. If you're arriving from the north, Roberts River is a minimum of 62 miles from the Chokoloskee boat ramp or 65 miles from the Gulf Coast Visitor Center in Everglades City. No piped water is available, so bring plenty. Bring a portable stove because campfires are prohibited. Pack out trash. A dock is provided. Children are OK. No pets, please.

Reservations, fees: Get a backcountry permit in person up to 24 hours before the day of your intended campout at the Flamingo Visitor Center or Gulf Coast Visitor Center. They are not issued by phone or mail. Camping permits for any length of stay are $10 for parties of up to six people, $20 for groups of seven to 12, and $30 for 13 or more. Major credit cards are accepted. There's a one-night stay limit.

Directions: From Miami, take Florida's Turnpike to its southern terminus at U.S. 1. In about one block, turn right at Palm Drive. Cross the railroad tracks and pass the Circle K. At the flashing traffic light at 192nd Avenue/State Road 9336, turn left by the Robert Is Here fruit stand. Proceed south about two miles. When State Road 9336 veers right, follow it to the right instead of going straight toward the alligator farm. The park entrance is four miles ahead. Follow the main park road 38 miles to Flamingo Marina to launch your vessel. Ask a ranger for directions to Roberts River. To avoid getting lost, obtain nautical chart 11433 at the Flamingo Visitor Center or area bait stores. If you're approaching from Everglades City, buy charts 11430, 11432, and 11433 within the Gulf Coast Visitor Center.

Contact: Everglades National Park, 40001 State Road 9336, Homestead, FL 33034, 305/242-7700. For backcountry questions, contact the Flamingo Visitor Center at 239/695-2945 or the Gulf Coast Visitor Center at 239/695-3311. Website: www.nps.gov/ever.

32 LANE BAY BOAT/CANOE SITE

Rating: 7

On Lane Bay in Everglades National Park
Everglades Backcountry map, grid c2,
page 529

It could be said for almost any of the campsites in the remote Everglades, but it goes doubly so for Lane Bay and, perhaps to a lesser degree, Hell's Bay and Pearl Bay (see campgrounds in this chapter): Don't attempt this canoe route unless you are at least moderately skilled with a map and compass. The maze of passageways that leads to these campsites is truly mind-boggling, and even experienced canoeists know to watch every twist and turn on the nautical chart to avoid getting lost. A global positioning system, and knowledge of how to use it, can help make up for a lack of experience in the Everglades backcountry but will NOT replace basic orienteering skills.

Now that we've scared the bejeesus out of you, there is an upside: You're likely to be alone on the water much of the day and probably won't have any company at night. Unlike Pearl Bay and Hell's Bay, there is no marked canoe trail leading to Lane Bay. On the other hand, unlike her sisters to the south, Lane Bay features pretty straightforward access by motorboat. You'll feel sun and wind from the south—and itchiness all over if you don't avoid the abundant poison ivy and poisonwood around the site, which abuts mangroves. Bring extra rope to tie a free-standing tent to the chickee hut that serves as a tent site. No stakes or nails may be used. Try to spot manatees in the wintertime. At night, stars fill an ebony sky.

Campsites, facilities: One tent site on an elevated wooden platform accommodates up to six people. You must use a boat, canoe, or kayak to travel about 13 miles from the Flamingo Visitor Center. If you're arriving from the north, Lane Bay is a minimum 63 miles from the Chokoloskee boat ramp or 66 miles from the Gulf Coast Ranger Station in Everglades City, depending on which route you choose among the various possibilities. No piped water is available, so bring plenty. Bring a portable stove because campfires are prohibited. Pack out trash. A toilet and dock are provided. Children are OK. No pets, please.

Reservations, fees: Get a backcountry permit in person up to 24 hours before the day of your intended campout at the Flamingo Visitor Center or Gulf Coast Visitor Center. They are not issued by phone or mail. Camping permits for any length of stay are $10 for parties of up to six people, $20 for groups of seven to 12, and $30 for 13 or more. Major credit cards are accepted. There's a one-night stay limit.

Directions: From Miami, take Florida's Turnpike to its southern terminus at U.S. 1. In about one block, turn right at Palm Drive. Cross the railroad tracks and pass the Circle K. At the flashing traffic light at 192nd Avenue/State Road 9336, turn left by the Robert Is Here fruit stand. Proceed south about two miles. When State Road 9336 veers right, follow it to the right instead of going straight toward the alligator farm. The park entrance is four miles ahead. Follow the main park road 38 miles to Flamingo Marina to launch your vessel. To avoid getting lost, obtain nautical chart 11433 at the Flamingo Visitor Center or area bait stores.

Contact: Everglades National Park, 40001 State Road 9336, Homestead, FL 33034, 305/242-7700. For backcountry questions, contact the Flamingo Visitor Center at 239/695-2945 or the Gulf Coast Visitor Center at 239/695-3311. Website: www.nps.gov/ever.

33 HELL'S BAY BOAT/ CANOE SITES

Rating: 8

On Hell's Bay in Everglades National Park
Everglades Backcountry map, grid c2, page 529

Wickedly meandering Hell's Bay is a canoeist's delight—or bane, if you don't enjoy bumping periodically into the branches and thick roots of mangrove trees. Like Lane Bay, Hell's Bay, and Pearl Bay (see campgrounds in this chapter) should be avoided by those who aren't skilled with a map and compass. The passageways that lead to these sites are a veritable maze. Even experienced canoeists know to watch every twist and turn on the nautical chart to avoid getting lost. A global positioning system, and knowledge of how to use it, can help make up for a lack of experience in the Everglades backcountry but should never be used to replace basic orienteering skills. Still, the journey is worth the effort because you're likely to be alone—or nearly so—on the water all day and, if you're lucky, won't have any company at night. Anglers make day trips to try for snook and bass, and at times pull out nuisance Mayan cichlids one after another. The trail got its name from a ranger who happened upon a fine fishing hole back here and found it was "hell to get into and hell to get out of" from Whitewater Bay, so he built the Hell's Bay Canoe Trail. Bring extra rope to tie a freestanding tent to the chickee hut that serves as a tent site. No stakes or nails may be used.

A saving grace for Hell's Bay and Pearl Bay: Both are on a canoe trail marked by white, numbered PVC pipes sticking up above the water; however, the meandering trail makes sharp turns, and sometimes you'll find that a marker has disappeared for one reason or another.

To use the canoe trail, you'll need to find a way to strap a canoe to the top of your vehicle and head north from Flamingo Marina along the main park road about eight miles to the canoe trailhead. If you're renting a canoe, try to beat the rush by arriving early on winter mornings. We do not recommend trying to reach these sites by motorboat. You can't use a boat on the Hell's Bay Canoe Trail, so you'd have to circle in from Whitewater Bay to get here. Find another spot instead.

Campsites, facilities: Two tent sites on an elevated wooden platform accommodate up to six people each. You must canoe or kayak six miles from the Hell's Bay Canoe Trailhead or take a boat up to 20 feet long via the East River and Whitewater Bay. From Everglades City, Hell's Bay is a minimum of 69.5 miles away. From the Chokoloskee boat ramp, it's at least 66.5 miles. No piped water is available, so bring plenty. Bring a portable stove because campfires are prohibited. Pack out trash. A toilet and dock are provided. Children are OK. No pets, please.

Reservations, fees: Get a backcountry permit in person up to 24 hours before the day of your intended campout at the Flamingo Visitor Center or Gulf Coast Visitor Center. They are not issued by phone or mail. Camping permits for any length of stay are $10 for parties of up to six people, $20 for groups of seven to 12, and $30 for 13 or more. Major credit cards are accepted. There's a one-night stay limit.

Directions: From Miami, take Florida's Turnpike to its southern terminus at U.S. 1. In about one block, turn right at Palm Drive. Cross the railroad tracks and pass the Circle K. At the flashing traffic light at 192nd Avenue/State Road 9336, turn left by the Robert Is Here fruit stand. Proceed south about two miles. When State Road 9336 veers right, follow it to the right instead of going straight toward the alligator farm. The park entrance is four miles ahead. Follow the main park road for 29 miles to the Hell's Bay Canoe Trailhead on the right to launch. To avoid getting lost, obtain nautical chart 11433 at the Flamingo Visitor Center or area bait stores.

Contact: Everglades National Park, 40001 State Road 9336, Homestead, FL 33034, 305/242-

7700. For backcountry questions, contact the Flamingo Visitor Center at 239/695-2945 or the Gulf Coast Visitor Center at 239/695-3311. Website: www.nps.gov/ever.

34 PEARL BAY BOAT/ CANOE SITES

Rating: 8

On Pearl Bay in Everglades National Park
Everglades Backcountry map, grid c2, page 529

Pearl Bay is a worthwhile destination, a place to sit back and admire the scenery of the mangrove-bordered bay after a morning spent paddling through a meandering route to get here. The paddle is just right for some tastes—not too long so as to be overly taxing, yet curvy enough to present some challenge. Don't be too alarmed if you look across the calm bay from your chickee at dusk and see the red, glowing eyes of an alligator. Gators often get a bum rap; more people around the country die from bee stings and encounters with pigs than from alligators. The reptiles rarely attack people. The sharply curving canoe route to Pearl Bay is the same as for Hell's Bay; just leave the trail at marker No. 165. During your paddle, which will take about three hours from the trailhead, look skyward for the snag with the osprey nest along the way. No motorized craft are allowed on this canoe trail, which adds to the wilderness experience. For more on Hell's Bay, see previous campground.

Note: We once experienced an overly friendly alligator here. Be sure not to drop remains of fish cleaning or other odiferous goodies in the water.

Campsites, facilities: Two tent sites on an elevated wooden platform accommodate up to six people each. You must canoe or kayak four miles from the Hell's Bay Canoe Trailhead or take a boat up to 20 feet long via the East River and Whitewater Bay. From

Everglades City, Pearl Bay is a minimum 71.5 miles away. From the Chokoloskee boat ramp, it's a minimum 68.5 miles, depending on the route chosen. No piped water is available, so bring plenty. Bring a portable stove because campfires are prohibited. Pack out trash. Kids are welcome. No pets, please. Management says the accessible chemical toilet, handrails, and canoe dock make this the park's sole wheelchair-accessible backcountry site.

Reservations, fees: Get a backcountry permit in person up to 24 hours before the day of your intended campout at the Flamingo Visitor Center or Gulf Coast Visitor Center. They are not issued by phone or mail. Camping permits for any length of stay are $10 for parties of up to six people, $20 for groups of seven to 12, and $30 for 13 or more. Major credit cards are accepted. There's a one-night stay limit.

Directions: From Miami, take Florida's Turnpike to its southern terminus at U.S. 1. In about one block, turn right at Palm Drive. Cross the railroad tracks and pass the Circle K. At the flashing traffic light at 192nd Avenue/State Road 9336, turn left by the Robert Is Here fruit stand. Proceed south about two miles. When State Road 9336 veers right, follow it to the right instead of going straight toward the alligator farm. The park entrance is four miles ahead. Follow the main park road 29 miles to the Hell's Bay Canoe Trailhead on the right to launch. To avoid getting lost, obtain nautical chart 11433 at the Flamingo Visitor Center or area bait stores.

Contact: Everglades National Park, 40001 State Road 9336, Homestead, FL 33034, 305/242-7700. For backcountry questions, contact the Flamingo Visitor Center at 239/695-2945 or the Gulf Coast Visitor Center at 239/695-3311. Website: www.nps.gov/ever.

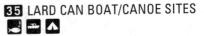

35 LARD CAN BOAT/CANOE SITES

Rating: 4

Along the Hell's Bay Canoe Trail in Everglades National Park

Everglades Backcountry map, grid c2, page 529

What sets Lard Can apart from Hell's Bay is that it is somewhat easier to reach—the first stop on the wickedly meandering canoe trail (just depart the trail at marker No. 156); however, it is a ground site set amid towering mangroves and buttonwoods, so it's easily missed by canoeists not paying close attention to their maps. Also, because it's a low-lying ground site, the ground is often damp and the bugs are likely to be a lot worse than at a chickee, even in winter. We'd steer clear of the site except on the coldest days. This is a fitting place to stop for a bathroom break, but we'd try to avoid it as a nighttime respite. It's also not nearly as picturesque as Hell's Bay (three miles away) or Pearl Bay (one mile). For more on Hell's Bay, see campground earlier in this chapter.

Campsites, facilities: Four ground tent sites accommodate a total of 10 people. You must canoe or kayak three miles from the Hell's Bay Canoe Trailhead or take a boat up to 20 feet long via the East River and Whitewater Bay. From Everglades City, Lard Can is a minimum 72.5 miles. From the Chokoloskee boat ramp, it's at least 69.5 miles. No piped water is available, so bring plenty. Bring a portable stove because campfires are prohibited. Pack out trash. A toilet is provided. Children are OK. No pets, please.

Reservations, fees: Get a backcountry permit in person up to 24 hours before the day of your intended campout at the Flamingo Visitor Center or Gulf Coast Visitor Center. They are not issued by phone or mail. Camping permits for any length of stay are $10 for parties of up to six people, $20 for groups of seven to 12, and $30 for 13 or more. Major credit cards are accepted. There's a two-night stay limit.

Directions: From Miami, take Florida's Turnpike to its southern terminus at U.S. 1. In about one block, turn right at Palm Drive. Cross the railroad tracks and pass the Circle K. At the flashing traffic light at 192nd Avenue/State Road 9336, turn left by the Robert Is Here fruit stand. Proceed south about two miles. When State Road 9336 veers right, follow it to the right instead of going straight toward the alligator farm. The park entrance is four miles ahead. Follow the main park road 29 miles to the Hell's Bay Canoe Trailhead on the right to launch. To avoid getting lost, obtain nautical chart 11433 at the Flamingo Visitor Center or area bait stores. If you're approaching from Everglades City, buy charts 11430, 11432, and 11433 within the Gulf Coast Visitor Center.

Contact: Everglades National Park, 40001 State Road 9336, Homestead, FL 33034, 305/242-7700. For backcountry questions, contact the Flamingo Visitor Center at 239/695-2945 or the Gulf Coast Visitor Center at 239/695-3311. Website: www.nps.gov/ever.

36 JOE RIVER BOAT/CANOE SITES

Rating: 7

On the Joe River in Everglades National Park

Everglades Backcountry map, grid c1, page 529

One of this book's researchers, Robert Mc-Clure, spent many a happy childhood afternoon fishing for redfish and snapper around here. Like nearby Oyster Bay and South Joe River, this campsite, with a pair of chickee platforms, is one of the most easily accessible from Flamingo by canoe. As such, it's heavily used. Joe River is good for winter canoeists: It's calm back here compared to the rough waters and gusty winds out on Whitewater Bay. The chickee is tucked back into a crook along the north bank of the Joe River just east of where it empties into Mud Bay. Because of its

out-of-the-wind location, it's fairly buggy for a chickee site.

Campsites, facilities: Two tent sites on an elevated wooden platform accommodate up to six people each. You must use a boat, canoe, or kayak to travel a minimum of 17 miles from the Flamingo Visitor Center. If you're arriving from the north, it's a minimum of 52.5 miles from the Chokoloskee boat ramp or at least 55.5 miles from the Gulf Coast Ranger Station in Everglades City, depending on the route chosen. No piped water is available, so bring plenty. Bring a portable stove because campfires are prohibited. Pack out trash. A toilet and dock are provided. Children are OK. No pets, please.

Reservations, fees: Get a backcountry permit in person up to 24 hours before the day of your intended campout at the Flamingo Visitor Center or Gulf Coast Visitor Center. They are not issued by phone or mail. Camping permits for any length of stay are $10 for parties of up to six people, $20 for groups of seven to 12, and $30 for 13 or more. Major credit cards are accepted. There's a one-night stay limit.

Directions: From Miami, take Florida's Turnpike to its southern terminus at U.S. 1. In about one block, turn right at Palm Drive. Cross the railroad tracks and pass the Circle K. At the flashing traffic light at 192nd Avenue/State Road 9336, turn left by the Robert Is Here fruit stand. Proceed south about two miles. When State Road 9336 veers right, follow it to the right instead of going straight toward the alligator farm. The park entrance is four miles ahead. Follow the main park road 38 miles to Flamingo Marina to launch your vessel. Ask a ranger for directions to Joe River. To avoid getting lost, obtain nautical chart 11433 at the Flamingo Visitor Center or area bait stores. If you're approaching from Everglades City, buy charts 11430, 11432, and 11433 within the Gulf Coast Visitor Center.

Contact: Everglades National Park, 40001 State Road 9336, Homestead, FL 33034, 305/242-7700. For backcountry questions, contact the

Flamingo Visitor Center at 239/695-2945 or the Gulf Coast Visitor Center at 239/695-3311. Website: www.nps.gov/ever.

37 SOUTH JOE RIVER BOAT/CANOE SITES

Rating: 7

On the Joe River in Everglades National Park

Everglades Backcountry map, grid c1, page 529

This is the closest backcountry site to Flamingo, and as such it sees heavy use from canoeists who want to get somewhere in one (albeit long) day and don't want to travel the whole 99-mile-long Wilderness Waterway spanning the watery innards of the national park. Some anglers motor up for snapper, snook, and other game fish. The raised wooden chickee platforms are set in a small bay away from Whitewater Bay, so they afford some protection against bad weather. Bring a free-standing tent; no stakes may be pounded into the wooden platform. Look for manatees in nearby Hidden Lake.

Campsites, facilities: Two tent sites on an elevated wooden platform accommodate up to six people each. You must use a boat, canoe, or kayak to travel about 11.5 miles from the Flamingo Visitor Center. From Everglades City, South Joe River is a minimum 62 miles, depending on the route chosen. From Chokoloskee, it's at least 59 miles. No piped water is provided, so bring plenty. Bring a portable stove because campfires are prohibited. Pack out trash. A toilet and dock are available. Children are OK. No pets, please.

Reservations, fees: Get a backcountry permit in person up to 24 hours before the day of your intended campout at the Flamingo Visitor Center or Gulf Coast Visitor Center. They are not issued by phone or mail. Camping permits for any length of stay are $10 for parties of up to six people, $20 for groups of seven to 12, and $30 for 13 or more. Major credit cards are accepted. There's a one-night stay limit.

Directions: From Miami, take Florida's Turnpike to its southern terminus at U.S. 1. In about one block, turn right at Palm Drive. Cross the railroad tracks and pass the Circle K. At the flashing traffic light at 192nd Avenue/State Road 9336, turn left by the Robert Is Here fruit stand. Proceed south about two miles. When State Road 9336 veers right, follow it to the right instead of going straight toward the alligator farm. The park entrance is four miles ahead. Follow the main park road 38 miles to Flamingo Marina to launch your vessel. Ask a ranger for directions to South Joe River. To avoid getting lost, obtain nautical chart 11433 at the Flamingo Visitor Center or area bait stores. If you're approaching from Everglades City, buy charts 11430, 11432, and 11433 within the Gulf Coast Visitor Center.

Contact: Everglades National Park, 40001 State Road 9336, Homestead, FL 33034, 305/242-7700. For backcountry questions, contact the Flamingo Visitor Center at 239/695-2945 or the Gulf Coast Visitor Center at 239/695-3311. Website: www.nps.gov/ever.

38 EAST CLUBHOUSE BEACH HIKE-IN OR BOAT/CANOE SITES

Rating: 8

On Florida Bay in Everglades National Park

Everglades Backcountry map, grid c1, page 529

You're likely to be alone in this vast wilderness, giving you the feeling that you could walk around nude if you wanted (except for the mosquitoes that come out at dusk and hang around until dawn). If you paddle out for a little fishing, don't be surprised if a spider has spun a web on your cooler by the time you return. The threat of raccoons getting into your cooler is a reminder that this is wilderness. Stars sparkle in a black nighttime sky untouched by city lights. The sand/marl beach camping area is fairly level and backed by mangroves and buttonwoods. East Clubhouse Beach and Clubhouse Beach to the west are the only places on Florida Bay where backpackers can hike for an overnight stay. Forget hiking in wet, muddy, skeeter-happy summer, when six inches of standing water isn't uncommon. Indeed, the sea can rise high enough in winter that it can be difficult to figure out where to stake a single tent to keep it dry, let alone four tents, which this site supposedly accommodates.

Campsites, facilities: Four beach tent sites theoretically accommodate a total of 24 people, but, for practical purposes, this site is best left to one tent party due to the rising seas that shrink the beach. You must hike or use a boat, canoe, or kayak to travel about four miles from the Flamingo Visitor Center. No piped water is available on site, so bring plenty of your own. There is no dock, nor a toilet; bury human waste six inches deep. Dead and downed wood may be used for campfires below the high tide line. Pack out trash. Children are allowed. No pets, please.

Reservations, fees: Get a backcountry permit in person up to 24 hours before the day of your intended campout at the Flamingo Visitor Center or Gulf Coast Visitor Center. They are not issued by phone or mail. Camping permits for any length of stay are $10 for parties of up to six people, $20 for groups of seven to 12, and $30 for 13 or more. Major credit cards are accepted. There's a three-night stay limit.

Directions: From Miami, take Florida's Turnpike to its southern terminus at U.S. 1. In about one block, turn right at Palm Drive. Cross the railroad tracks and pass the Circle K. At the flashing traffic light at 192nd Avenue/State Road 9336, turn left by the Robert Is Here fruit stand. Proceed south about two miles. When State Road 9336 veers right, follow it to the right instead of going straight toward the alligator farm. The park entrance is four miles ahead. Follow the main park road 38 miles to Flamingo Marina to launch your vessel. Ask a ranger for directions to East Clubhouse Beach. To avoid getting lost, obtain

nautical chart 11433 at the Flamingo Visitor Center or area bait stores.

Contact: Everglades National Park, 40001 State Road 9336, Homestead, FL 33034, 305/242-7700. For backcountry questions, contact the Flamingo Visitor Center at 239/695-2945 or the Gulf Coast Visitor Center at 239/695-3311. Website: www.nps.gov/ever.

39 CLUBHOUSE BEACH HIKE-IN OR BOAT/CANOE SITES

🚶 🛶 ⛵ ⛺

Rating: 8

On Florida Bay in Everglades National Park
Everglades Backcountry map, grid c1,
page 529

Clubhouse Beach and East Clubhouse Beach (see previous campground) are the only places on Florida Bay where backpackers can hike and camp. The seven-mile Coastal Prairie Trail starts near Flamingo Marina and can be a miserable experience in summer, when a half-foot of water may be standing in the then-muddy, buggy trail; try winter instead. Canoeists and kayakers love the place because it's quite close to Flamingo and easy to reach. You'll sleep on a sand/marl beach backed by mangroves and buttonwoods. Skeeters and sand fleas can be trouble if the wind is coming from the north. When the water is quite low, exposed mudflats may make the place inaccessible to boaters. Check with a ranger on tide and wind conditions beforehand to time your trip so you won't face a tough boat trip or paddle in either direction. It's not as breathtaking as the campsites at nearby Cape Sable (see campgrounds in this chapter), but you'll be in a coastal prairie area, so look for birds.

Campsites, facilities: Four beach tent sites technically accommodate a total of 24 people, but rising seas can make it difficult to figure out where to pitch a tent where it's certain to stay dry during high tide (ask a ranger for pointers). You must hike or use a boat, canoe, or kayak to travel about seven miles from the

Flamingo Visitor Center. No piped water is available, so bring plenty. There is no dock, nor toilet; bury human waste six inches deep. Dead and downed wood may be used for campfires below the high tide line. Pack out trash. Children are OK. No pets, please.

Reservations, fees: Get a backcountry permit in person up to 24 hours before the day of your intended campout at the Flamingo Visitor Center or Gulf Coast Visitor Center. They are not issued by phone or mail. Camping permits for any length of stay are $10 for parties of up to six people, $20 for groups of seven to 12, and $30 for 13 or more. Major credit cards are accepted. There's a three-night stay limit.

Directions: From Miami, take Florida's Turnpike to its southern terminus at U.S. 1. In about one block, turn right at Palm Drive. Cross the railroad tracks and pass the Circle K. At the flashing traffic light at 192nd Avenue/State Road 9336, turn left by the Robert Is Here fruit stand. Proceed south about two miles. When State Road 9336 veers right, follow it to the right instead of going straight toward the alligator farm. The park entrance is four miles ahead. Follow the main park road 38 miles to Flamingo Marina to launch your vessel. Ask a ranger for directions to Clubhouse Beach. To avoid getting lost, obtain nautical chart 11433 at the Flamingo Visitor Center or area bait stores.

Contact: Everglades National Park, 40001 State Road 9336, Homestead, FL 33034, 305/242-7700. For backcountry questions, contact the Flamingo Visitor Center at 239/695-2945 or the Gulf Coast Visitor Center at 239/695-3311. Website: www.nps.gov/ever.

40 EAST CAPE SABLE BOAT/CANOE SITES

Rating: 8

In Everglades National Park

Everglades Backcountry map, grid c1, page 529

The Cape Sable sites—East Cape Sable, Mid-

dle Cape Sable, and Northwest Cape Sable (see campgrounds in this chapter)—are some of the most beautiful in the park. Set on a high shelly, sunny, breezy beach some six feet above Florida Bay, the sites mark the place where the Florida Peninsula turns to head north. Fires are allowed below the high tide line; use only driftwood or limbs that are already dead and downed. Try to reach your campsite by midafternoon so you can sit and contemplate the exceptional sunsets. Look for pink flamingos—the real thing, not the plastic lawn ornament.

Cape Sable can be a very long paddle from Flamingo when conditions are not right, so check with rangers ahead of time and keep a close eye on the weather. The short, steep, breaking waves create downright hazardous conditions for canoeists who try to go against the tide and winds. The cape tends to be dominated by motorboaters. In all, the three Cape Sable camping areas can hold a total of 156 people, making them by far the largest backcountry sites in the park. Rangers seem to discourage it, but you can swim here. One of this book's researchers, Robert, was sure to take a dip every time he visited as a boy.

Even in winter, be prepared for an onslaught of mosquitoes. Repellant and netting are a must.

Campsites, facilities: Fifteen beach tent sites accommodate a total of 60 people. You must use a boat, canoe, or kayak to travel about 10 miles from the Flamingo Visitor Center. No piped water is available, so bring plenty. There is no dock, nor toilet; bury human waste six inches deep. Dead and downed wood may be used for campfires below the high tide line. Pack out trash. Children are permitted. No pets, please.

Reservations, fees: Get a backcountry permit in person up to 24 hours before the day of your intended campout at the Flamingo Visitor Center or Gulf Coast Visitor Center. They are not issued by phone or mail. Camping permits for any length of stay are $10 for parties of up to six people, $20 for groups of seven to 12, and

$30 for 13 or more. Major credit cards are accepted. There's a seven-night stay limit.

Directions: From Miami, take Florida's Turnpike to its southern terminus at U.S. 1. In about one block, turn right at Palm Drive. Cross the railroad tracks and pass the Circle K. At the flashing traffic light at 192nd Avenue/State Road 9336, turn left by the Robert Is Here fruit stand. Proceed south about two miles. When State Road 9336 veers right, follow it to the right instead of going straight toward the alligator farm. The park entrance is four miles ahead. Follow the main park road 38 miles to Flamingo Marina to launch your vessel. Ask a ranger for directions to East Cape Sable. The campground can be approached by way of Florida Bay or, when conditions are right, inland through the Bear Lake Canoe Trail. To avoid getting lost, obtain nautical chart 11433 at the Flamingo Visitor Center or area bait stores. If you're approaching from Everglades City, buy charts 11430, 11432, and 11433 within the Gulf Coast Visitor Center.

Contact: Everglades National Park, 40001 State Road 9336, Homestead, FL 33034, 305/242-7700. For backcountry questions, contact the Flamingo Visitor Center at 239/695-2945 or the Gulf Coast Visitor Center at 239/695-3311. Website: www.nps.gov/ever.

41 MIDDLE CAPE SABLE BOAT/CANOE SITES

Rating: 9

On the Gulf of Mexico in Everglades National Park

Everglades Backcountry map, grid c1, page 529

Sunsets are pretty at this breezy, sun-washed, shelly sand beach, but don't expect to have the place to yourself. Nearly five dozen other campers might show up at the popular spot. To ranger Steve Robinson's way of thinking, Cape Sable is a fine runner-up to his favorite canoeing destination, Carl Ross Key (see campground in this chapter). Tip: Canoeists should hug the protective coastline and try to paddle with the winds and tides between Cape Sable and Flamingo, particularly in windy winter—something easier said than done. "If you're like me," Robinson says, "you get the winds both ways. The winds shift on you."

Even in winter, be prepared for an onslaught of mosquitoes. Repellant and netting are a must.

Read the trip notes for East Cape Sable (see previous campground).

Campsites, facilities: Fifteen beach tent sites accommodate a total of 60 people. You must use a boat, canoe, or kayak to travel about 13.5 miles from the Flamingo Visitor Center. No piped water is available, so bring plenty. There is no dock, nor toilet; bury human waste six inches deep. Dead and downed wood may be used for campfires below the high tide line. Pack out trash. Children are OK. No pets, please.

Reservations, fees: Get a backcountry permit in person up to 24 hours before the day of your intended campout at the Flamingo Visitor Center or Gulf Coast Visitor Center. They are not issued by phone or mail. Camping permits for any length of stay are $10 for parties of up to six people, $20 for groups of seven to 12, and $30 for 13 or more. Major credit cards are accepted. There's a seven-night stay limit.

Directions: From Flamingo, ask a ranger for directions to Middle Cape Sable. To avoid getting lost, obtain nautical chart 11433 at the Flamingo Visitor Center or from area bait stores. If you're approaching from Everglades City, buy charts 11430, 11432, and 11433 within the Gulf Coast Visitor Center.

Contact: Everglades National Park, 40001 State Road 9336, Homestead, FL 33034, 305/242-7700. For backcountry questions, contact the Flamingo Visitor Center at 239/695-2945 or the Gulf Coast Visitor Center at 239/695-3311. Website: www.nps.gov/ever.

42 NORTHWEST CAPE SABLE BOAT/CANOE SITES

Rating: 9

On the Gulf of Mexico in Everglades National Park

Everglades Backcountry map, grid c1, page 529

The sun pounds this shelly beach, where a breeze blows from all sides and sunsets are characteristically pretty. The other Cape Sable camping areas are more popular, but this one has the advantage of fewer potential neighbors—eight other parties, tops. Anchor your boat from the bow if the weather is dicey, and pull canoes way up onto the beach, lest they float out to sea. Be prepared for skeeters, sand fleas, and marauding raccoons. Review the trip notes for East Cape Sable (see campground in this chapter).

Campsites, facilities: Nine beach tent sites accommodate a total of 36 people. You must use a boat, canoe, or kayak to travel about 18.5 miles from the Flamingo Visitor Center. No piped water is available, so bring plenty. There is no dock, nor toilet; bury human waste six inches deep. Dead and downed wood may be used for campfires below the high tide line. Trash must be packed out. Children are permitted. No pets, please.

Reservations, fees: Get a backcountry permit in person up to 24 hours before the day of your intended campout at the Flamingo Visitor Center or Gulf Coast Visitor Center. They are not issued by phone or mail. Camping permits for any length of stay are $10 for parties of up to six people, $20 for groups of seven to 12, and $30 for 13 or more. Major credit cards are accepted. There's a seven-night stay limit.

Directions: From Miami, take Florida's Turnpike to its southern terminus at U.S. 1. In about one block, turn right at Palm Drive. Cross the railroad tracks and pass the Circle K. At the flashing traffic light at 192nd Avenue/State Road 9336, turn left by the Robert Is Here fruit stand. Proceed south about two miles. When State Road 9336 veers right, follow it to the right instead of going straight toward the alligator farm. The park entrance is four miles ahead. Follow the main park road for 38 miles to Flamingo Marina to launch your vessel. Ask a ranger for directions to Northwest Cape Sable. To avoid getting lost, obtain nautical chart 11433 at the Flamingo Visitor Center or from area bait stores. If you're approaching from Everglades City, buy charts 11430, 11432, and 11433 within the Gulf Coast Visitor Center.

Contact: Everglades National Park, 40001 State Road 9336, Homestead, FL 33034, 305/242-7700. For backcountry questions, contact the Flamingo Visitor Center at 239/695-2945 or the Gulf Coast Visitor Center at 239/695-3311. Website: www.nps.gov/ever.

43 ALLIGATOR CREEK CANOE SITES

Rating: 8

On Alligator Creek in Everglades National Park

Everglades Backcountry map, grid d2, page 529

A relatively new backcountry campground set amid huge mangroves awaits paddlers at the end of the meandering West Lake Canoe Trail, which is accessible off the main park road not far north of Flamingo. Despite the easy access, it's relatively remote. Your reward may be seeing Everglades wading birds or crocodiles—North America's only crocs, which are not dangerous.

You'll sleep on slightly higher ground along a canal section of Alligator Creek, but the surrounding, somewhat-shady buttonwood forest blocks views (and wind). The place was used as a wilderness camping area long ago, which explains the abandoned, overgrown foot trail and many visible former campsites in the area.

Only small boats with motors under 5.5 horsepower can make it to today's official camping area, which is at the junction of Garfield Bite and Alligator Creek. The vegetation in Long Lake at low tide can pose a problem even for small motors. Bring mosquito repellent; skeeters make extreme pests of themselves most times of the year.

Campsites, facilities: Three ground tent sites accommodate a total of eight people. You must canoe or kayak 8.5 miles from the West Lake Canoe Trailhead. No piped water is available, so bring plenty. There is no dock, nor toilet. Dead and downed wood may be used for campfires below the high tide line. Pack out trash. Children are allowed. No pets, please.

Reservations, fees: Get a backcountry permit in person up to 24 hours before the day of your intended campout at the Flamingo Visitor Center or Gulf Coast Visitor Center. They are not issued by phone or mail. Camping permits for any length of stay are $10 for parties of up to six people, $20 for groups of seven to 12, and $30 for 13 or more. Major credit cards are accepted. There's a two-night stay limit.

Directions: From Miami, take Florida's Turnpike to its southern terminus at U.S. 1. In about one block, turn right at Palm Drive. Cross the railroad tracks and pass the Circle K. At the flashing traffic light at 192nd Avenue/State Road 9336, turn left by the Robert Is Here fruit stand. Proceed south about two miles. When State Road 9336 veers right, follow it to the right instead of going straight toward the alligator farm. The park entrance is four miles ahead. The West Lake Canoe Trailhead is 31 miles ahead on the left.

Contact: Everglades National Park, 40001 State Road 9336, Homestead, FL 33034, 305/242-7700. For backcountry questions, contact the Flamingo Visitor Center at 239/695-2945 or the Gulf Coast Visitor Center at 239/695-3311. Website: www.nps.gov/ever.

44 SHARK POINT BOAT/ CANOE SITE

Rating: 8

On Florida Bay in Everglades National Park
Everglades Backcountry map, grid d1,
page 529

Ahhh. Your party is sure to be alone at this secluded site alongside mangrove-lined Garfield Bite. You'll camp on a sand spit that can be reached by powerboats only during extremely high tides. Shark Point also is close to Snake Bite, where you are likely to see wading birds and other wildlife in the winter. And it's quite convenient to Flamingo. You'll want to check wind and tide information carefully if you're planning to head straight here from Flamingo by way of Florida Bay; the wrong conditions can ruin a trip. For that reason, canoeists tend to arrive via West Lake. Should you hear about a big wind blowing up or some other problem, ask about heading down the West Lake Canoe Trail to reach this site.

Campsites, facilities: One ground tent site accommodates up to eight people. You must use a boat, canoe, or kayak to travel eight miles from Flamingo Marina. No piped water is available, so bring plenty. There is no dock, nor toilet; rangers recommend bringing a portable toilet. Dead and downed wood may be used for campfires below the high tide line. Pack out trash. Children are OK. No pets, please.

Reservations, fees: Get a backcountry permit in person up to 24 hours before the day of your intended campout at the Flamingo Visitor Center or Gulf Coast Visitor Center. They are not issued by phone or mail. Camping permits for any length of stay are $10 for parties of up to six people, $20 for groups of seven to 12, and $30 for 13 or more. Major credit cards are accepted. There's a three-night stay limit.

Directions: From Miami, take Florida's Turnpike to its southern terminus at U.S. 1. In about one block, turn right at Palm Drive. Cross the railroad tracks and pass the Circle K. At the flashing traffic light at 192nd Avenue/State Road 9336, turn left by the Robert Is Here fruit stand. Proceed south about two miles. When State Road 9336 veers right, follow it to the right instead of going straight toward the alligator farm. The park entrance is four miles ahead. Follow the main park road 38 miles to Flamingo Marina to launch into Florida Bay. To avoid getting lost, obtain nautical chart 11451 at the Flamingo Visitor Center or area bait stores.

Contact: Everglades National Park, 40001 State Road 9336, Homestead, FL 33034, 305/242-7700. For backcountry questions, contact the Flamingo Visitor Center at 239/695-2945 or the Gulf Coast Visitor Center at 239/695-3311. Website: www.nps.gov/ever.

45 CARL ROSS KEY BOAT/ CANOE SITES

Rating: 9

On western Florida Bay in Everglades National Park

Everglades Backcountry map, grid c1, page 529

Paradise—that's how park ranger Steve Robinson describes his favorite breezy campsite, located on the northernmost of two islands that were joined together until a storm divided them. Hearing the cacophony of birds on the once-adjoining rookery island to the south, Sandy Key, and gazing toward its convention of ospreys, eagles, herons, cormorants, and other winged creatures searching for food in the mudflats inspires awe in Robinson. Every winter, a few hundred roseate spoonbills roost in Sandy Key's biggest trees. And during his canoe treks from Flamingo to this island, he has admired eight-foot sharks skimming across huge, shallow-water mudflats. Look for "fins cruising over the flats," says the fourth-generation Floridian.

High, shelly sand surrounds the campsite, where mosquitoes are rarely a problem. Expect limited shade. Although the lure of sleeping on an island in the middle of Florida Bay is hard to resist, keep in mind that the beach here is tiny and at least one ranger we talked to says it's not a great place for swimming, although swimming is possible. This is an area where Florida Bay's "Dead Zone" sometimes appears, meaning the water is murky and the fishing experience may be less than pleasant. Still, many a motorboater has hung out here overnight, and some consider it very pretty (check out the sunsets). It's a bit of a haul across open water for canoeists, although kayakers have been known to make the trip.

To avoid getting in the path of high-speed boaters, canoeist Robinson takes a direct route, paddling straight from Flamingo to Carl Ross, crossing shallows along the way and sometimes getting marooned on the flats until the tides rise again. He passes time by staying put, admiring the terns, gulls, and herons hunting for meals. Expect an all-day paddle. Under ideal conditions, it takes four to six hours to attempt a beeline route from Flamingo to the key. Add time if you hug the wind-protective coastline, then cross the windy bay in an L-shaped route. In winter, winds howl from the north, which makes it easier to get to the island but a devil to paddle back from it. Be prepared to face even 10 straight days of small-craft weather advisories due to high winter winds; the park concessionaire wisely refuses to rent craft under those conditions. Kayaks, not canoes, are best bets for wintertime paddlers. Bring an anchor so you can take rest breaks.

Campsites, facilities: Three beach tent sites accommodate a total of nine people. You must use a boat, canoe, or kayak to travel about eight or 10 miles. No piped water is available, so bring plenty. There is no dock, nor toilet; bury waste six inches deep. Dead and downed wood may be used for campfires below the high tide line. Pack out trash. Children are permitted. No pets, please.

Reservations, fees: Get a backcountry permit in person up to 24 hours before the day of your intended campout at the Flamingo Visitor Center or Gulf Coast Visitor Center. This is one of the few sites in the park for which you can obtain a permit over the phone by calling Flamingo. If you intend to call for a permit, prepare to be insistent because some park employees are unaware that phone permits are available for remote Florida Bay sites, including this particularly far-off one. Camping permits for any length of stay are $10 for parties of up to six people, $20 for groups of seven to 12, and $30 for 13 or more. Major credit cards are accepted. There's a two-night stay limit.

Directions: From Miami, take Florida's Turnpike to its southern terminus at U.S. 1. In about one block, turn right at Palm Drive. Cross the railroad tracks and pass the Circle K. At the flashing traffic light at 192nd Avenue/State Road 9336, turn left by the Robert Is Here fruit stand. Proceed south about two miles. When State Road 9336 veers right, follow it to the right instead of going straight toward the alligator farm. The park entrance is four miles ahead. Follow the main park road 38 miles to Flamingo Marina to launch into Florida Bay. To avoid getting lost, obtain nautical chart 11451 at the Flamingo Visitor Center or area bait stores.

Contact: Everglades National Park, 40001 State Road 9336, Homestead, FL 33034, 305/242-7700. For backcountry questions, contact the Flamingo Visitor Center at 239/695-2945 or the Gulf Coast Visitor Center at 239/695-3311. Website: www.nps.gov/ever.

46 LITTLE RABBIT KEY BOAT/CANOE SITES

Rating: 7

On Florida Bay in Everglades National Park
Everglades Backcountry map, grid d1, page 529

Sorry, canoe fans. Realistically, this spot is best reserved for motorboaters and the hardiest of kayakers because you have to cover so much open water. The beach campsite is situated on the west side, where the sunsets are pretty, but getting there can be a little tricky. Approach the island from the east, keeping your eye out for PVC pipes with orange flags that mark a channel. As you approach the island, watch to see where a moat, perhaps eight to 10 feet deep, has been trenched around the north side of the island. Bear right to follow it around to the small dock on the west side.

Campsites, facilities: Four ground tent sites accommodate a total of 12 people. You must use a boat, canoe, or kayak to travel about 11 miles from Flamingo. No piped water is available, so bring plenty. Bring a portable stove because campfires are prohibited. A chemical toilet, picnic table, and dock are provided. Trash must be packed out. Children are OK. No pets, please.

Reservations, fees: Get a backcountry permit in person up to 24 hours before the day of your intended campout at the Flamingo Visitor Center. Or, if you're leaving from the Keys, call the Flamingo Visitor Center for a permit; this is one of the few places for which permits are commonly issued by phone. If you intend to call for a permit, prepare to be insistent because some park employees are unaware that phone permits are available for remote Florida Bay sites, including this particularly far-off one. Camping permits for any length of stay are $10 for parties of up to six people, $20 for groups of seven to 12, and $30 for 13 or more. Major credit cards are accepted. There's a two-night stay limit.

Directions: From Miami, take Florida's Turnpike to its southern terminus at U.S. 1. In about one block, turn right at Palm Drive. Cross the railroad tracks and pass the Circle K. At the flashing traffic light at 192nd Avenue/State Road 9336, turn left by the Robert Is Here fruit stand. Proceed south about two miles. When State Road 9336 veers right, follow it to the right instead of going straight toward the alligator farm. The park entrance is four miles ahead. Follow the main park road about 38 miles to Flamingo Marina to launch. From there, follow nautical chart 11451. You can also launch from Lower Matecumbe Key in the Florida Keys.

Contact: Everglades National Park, 40001 State Road 9336, Homestead, FL 33034, 305/242-7700. For backcountry questions, contact the Flamingo Visitor Center at 239/695-2945. Website: www.nps.gov/ever.

47 NORTH NEST KEY BOAT/CANOE SITES

Rating: 7

On eastern Florida Bay in Everglades National Park

Everglades Backcountry map, grid d2, page 529

This island with white beaches surrounded by blue water in northeastern Florida Bay often has a sort of Caribbean feel about it—at least when the water stays clear. It's one of only three keys in the Florida Bay section of Everglades National Park where visitors are allowed to land, so it gets a fair amount of day use by motorboaters. They generally come to the crescent-shaped beach on the northwest part of the island. If you're in a canoe (actually, kayaks make more sense because you'll be covering a lot of open water), opt instead for the southwest side, where there is no dock, and you'll have at least a little more privacy. There is room for seven groups of people, and the place is quite popular, especially on weekends, so count on company.

A note on navigation: Even with a nautical chart, some powerboaters have been known to navigate their way from Blackwater Sound into Florida Bay (through a passage known as "The Boggies") and then cut directly southwest for North Nest Key. Some of these same boaters also have been known to run aground or worse, so avoid the temptation. Look due west and you'll see Duck Key. Head for that until your chart shows you've cleared the shallows off your port before you turn to head for North Nest Key. (Canoeists and kayakers, of course, won't have this problem.)

Campsites, facilities: Seven beach tent sites accommodate a total of 25 people. You must use a boat, canoe, or kayak to travel about eight miles from launch sites in the Upper Florida Keys. No piped water is available, so bring plenty. Bring a portable stove because campfires are prohibited. A toilet and dock are provided. Pack out trash. Children are OK. No pets, please.

Reservations, fees: Get a backcountry permit in person up to 24 hours before the day of your intended campout at the Flamingo Visitor Center or Gulf Coast Visitor Center. Or, if you're leaving from the Keys (which makes sense if you're coming here), call the Flamingo Visitor Center for a permit; this is one of the few places for which permits are commonly issued by phone. If you intend to call for a permit, prepare to be insistent because some park employees are unaware that phone permits are available for remote Florida Bay sites, including this particularly far-off one. Camping permits for any length of stay are $10 for parties of up to six people, $20 for groups of seven to 12, and $30 for 13 or more. Major credit cards are accepted. There's a seven-night stay limit.

Directions: From Miami, take Florida's Turnpike to its southern terminus at U.S. 1 in Florida City. Check there to make sure you have gas, because there will be none until you reach Key Largo, some 20 miles farther south. Once you get to Key Largo, you need to launch your boat on the Florida Bay side. There are several places from which to launch. Probably the most convenient is Florida Bay Outfitters (305/451-3018) at mile marker 104. You can obtain nautical chart 11451 and other supplies there, and they'll probably let you launch and park for free. Also ask Everglades National Park rangers for recommended launch sites in the Upper Florida Keys.

Contact: Everglades National Park, 40001 State Road 9336, Homestead, FL 33034, 305/242-7700. Flamingo Visitor Center rangers, 239/695-2945. Website: www.nps.gov/ever.

48 ERNEST COE HIKE-IN/ BICYCLE-IN SITE

🚶 🚵 ⛰️

Rating: 7

In Everglades National Park

Everglades Backcountry map, grid d3, page 529

This is one of three campsites in Everglades National Park suited for backpackers and one of two suitable for cyclists. The others are Ingraham (see campground in this chapter; OK for cycling), about six miles down the trail, and Clubhouse Beach (see campground in this chapter), near Flamingo. Do not attempt this trip except in the winter. It's just too buggy and humid otherwise. Unlike most backcountry backpacking and bicycling adventures in national parks, this one follows an old road. Decades ago, the hard limestone roadbed led to what was then the fishing village of Flamingo, at the south end of the mainland. The road has since been abandoned for vehicle traffic and runs along a canal that angles southwest toward the campsite from the trailhead. You'll rarely have company when traveling along this road. Still, don't pitch your tent where it will block access to intersecting roads used occasionally by wilderness firefighters.

The camp is in an open, grassy area inside a hardwood hammock—the relatively rare collection of thick-trunked gumbo-limbos and tropical mahogany trees that dot the southern Everglades. You'll be surrounded by a carpet of saw grass interrupted in places by scattered hammocks. The road can be a little slick when wet. Before you hit the trail, learn about poisonwood, a cousin of poison ivy and poison oak. You're likely to encounter it out here.

Campsites, facilities: One primitive ground tent site accommodates up to eight people. You must hike or bicycle about five miles to get here from the Royal Palm area—less if you travel from the gate at the park's sole road (ask rangers for directions). No piped water is available, so bring plenty. There is no toilet; bury

human waste. Pack out trash. Children are allowed. Sorry, no pets or campfires.

Reservations, fees: Get a backcountry permit in person up to 24 hours before the day of your intended campout from the entrance station at the Homestead main park entrance. They are not issued by phone or mail. Camping permits for any length of stay are $10 for parties of up to six people, $20 for groups of seven to 12, and $30 for 13 or more. Major credit cards are accepted. There's a three-night stay limit.

Directions: From Miami, take Florida's Turnpike to its southern terminus at U.S. 1. In about one block, turn right at Palm Drive. Cross the railroad tracks and pass the Circle K. At the flashing traffic light at 192nd Avenue/State Road 9336, turn left by the Robert Is Here fruit stand. Proceed south about two miles. When State Road 9336 veers right, follow it to the right instead of going straight toward the alligator farm. The park entrance is four miles ahead. Once inside the park, drive toward the Royal Palm Visitor Center. Park at the entrance to Ingraham Highway, near Hidden Lake.

Contact: Everglades National Park, 40001 State Road 9336, Homestead, FL 33034, 305/242-7700. For backcountry questions, contact the Flamingo Visitor Center at 239/695-2945 or the Main Visitor Center at 305/242-7700. Website: www.nps.gov/ever.

49 INGRAHAM HIKE-IN/ BICYCLE-IN SITE

🚶 🚵 ⛰️

Rating: 6

In Everglades National Park

Everglades Backcountry map, grid c2, page 529

For what to expect, review the trip notes for Ernest Coe (see previous campground). The distinction here is that you will have to hike or bicycle another five to seven miles through the park's officially designated Pinelands area to sleep at the end of the old roadbed. You'll be rewarded by isolation that is hard to match in bustling South Florida, with a view of sweeping saw grass plains dotted by hardwood hammocks. Unless you just like the feeling of carrying a pack on your back, this place is best suited for bicyclists. Backpackers should opt for Ernest Coe if it's available. It offers more shade, and you won't have to hike as far.

Campsites, facilities: One primitive ground tent site accommodates up to eight people. You must hike 11 miles one-way from the trailhead to get here. No piped water is available, so bring plenty. There is no toilet; bury human waste. Trash must be packed out. Children are allowed. Sorry, no pets or campfires.

Reservations, fees: Get a backcountry permit in person up to 24 hours before the day of your intended campout from the entrance station at the Homestead main park entrance. They are not issued by phone or mail. Camping permits for any length of stay are $10 for parties of up to six people, $20 for groups of seven to 12, and $30 for 13 or more. Major credit cards are accepted. There's a three-night stay limit.

Directions: From Miami, take Florida's Turnpike to its southern terminus at U.S. 1. In about one block, turn right at Palm Drive. Cross the railroad tracks and pass the Circle K. At the flashing traffic light at 192nd Avenue/State Road 9336, turn left by the Robert Is Here fruit stand. Proceed south about two miles. When State Road 9336 veers right, follow it to the right instead of going straight toward the alligator farm. The park entrance is four miles ahead. Once inside, drive toward the Royal Palm Visitor Center. Park at the entrance to Ingraham Highway, near Hidden Lake.

Contact: Everglades National Park, 40001 State Road 9336, Homestead, FL 33034, 305/242-7700. For backcountry questions, contact the Flamingo Visitor Center at 239/695-2945 or the Main Visitor Center at 305/242-7700. Website: www.nps.gov/ever.

Big Cypress National Preserve

50 BEAR ISLAND CAMPGROUND

Rating: 4

North of I-75 in Big Cypress National Preserve

Everglades map, grid c1, page 528

Turkey hunters in winter flock to this northern part of 1,138-square-mile Big Cypress National Preserve. Found way out in the boonies, this place tends to be lively in winter—alive with campers using swamp buggies, all-terrain vehicles, and any sort of off-road vehicle, and is growing ever more popular with mountain bikers and hikers. The no-frills camping area is little more than a road with campsites to either side. A campground host resides here at certain points in the year.

Campsites, facilities: Only tent campers may sleep at this primitive camping area. There are no hookups. A portable toilet is provided, but there are no other facilities. Bring mosquito repellent, food, water, and any supplies you'll need. Children are welcome. Pets must be on a six-foot leash and restrained at all times.

Reservations, fees: Reservations are not accepted, and there is no fee to camp. A $35 off-road-vehicle annual permit is required. Get it at the Big Cypress Visitor Center.

Directions: From Naples, drive east on U.S. 41/Tamiami Trail to the intersection of State Road 29. Continue on U.S. 41 for about six miles, then turn left (north) onto Highway 839, which borders the little H. P. Williams Roadside Park. Continue north 22 miles, passing under I-75, to the camping area.

Contact: Big Cypress National Preserve, HCR 61, Box 110, Ochopee, FL 34141, 239/695-1201 or 239/695-2000. For hunting information, call 239/695-2040. Website: www.nps.gov/bicy.

51 BURNS LAKE CAMPGROUND

Rating: 3

On the Tamiami Trail in Big Cypress National Preserve

Everglades map, grid c2, page 528

This free campground is open only during hunting season, basically September 1 through January 1. It never has been more than a spartan base for exploring 728,000-acre Big Cypress National Preserve. Expect a low-brow place of sunny, rustic campsites surrounding a small lake, which is off-limits to swimmers. No sites are marked; just stake out a spot in the clearing. Bring everything, including drinking water. The only camper comforts are a couple of port-a-johns.

Campsites, facilities: At this clearing set around a lake, there is room for about 55 tents or RVs. There are no hookups. The campground has two chemical toilets, but the nearest source of drinking water is Dona Drive, four miles west on U.S. 41. Bring mosquito repellent, food, water, and any supplies you'll need. Children are welcome. Pets must be on a six-foot leash and restrained at all times.

Reservations, fees: Reservations are not accepted, and there is no fee. Stays are limited to 14 days.

Directions: From Naples, drive east on U.S. 41/Tamiami Trail to the intersection of State Road 29. Continue on U.S. 41 for seven miles, then turn north on Burns Road. Drive one mile on gravel to the campground. From Florida's Turnpike in Miami, exit at U.S. 41 and drive west for 52 miles. Turn north on Burns Road.

Contact: Big Cypress National Preserve, HCR 61, Box 110, Ochopee, FL 34141, 239/695-1201 or 239/695-2000. For hunting information, call 239/695-2040. Website: www.nps.gov/bicy.

52 MONUMENT LAKE CAMPGROUND

Rating: 6

On the Tamiami Trail in Big Cypress National Preserve

Everglades map, grid c2, page 528

The preserve's managers have upgraded this site to offer niceties you won't find at other public camping spots within 728,000-acre Big Cypress National Preserve. Here, you'll find actual restrooms with running water and an outdoor shower. Monument Lake otherwise is a rustic, bare-bones place where sunny sites surround a lake. Swimming is prohibited, lest you encounter an alligator. Winter is the best time to camp: Mosquitoes are bearable, the weather is cool, and the ground is unlikely to be sodden by summer-style rains. One of our favorite things about Big Cypress is listening to the building crescendo of sounds at night—the croaking frogs, the maracas music of cicadas. It feels a world away from urban Miami, yet it's within easy reach for a quick weekend getaway.

Near the campground is Monroe Station, a roadhouse dating back to the building of U.S. 41, or the Tamiami Trail. The Herculean effort was launched in 1917 and took 11 years to finish, with progress stymied by labor shortages during World War I and the difficulties encountered when dynamiting limestone for the roadbed. Cranes on giant barges dredged up the rock, creating the canal as they built up the roadbed.

Behind Monroe Station is the Loop Road Scenic Drive, a 26-mile single lane leading deep into the preserve's southern reaches. The dirt road can be hiked or driven with two-wheel-drive vehicles, but watch out for potholes and flooding. Along the road is the Tree Snail Hammock Nature Trail, with signs explaining the preserve's plants and animals. The loop passes through two more primitive campgrounds, Pinecrest and Mitchell's Landing (see campgrounds in this chapter), before connecting with U.S. 41 at Forty Mile Bend.

Campsites, facilities: At this clearing set around a lake, there is room for about 36 tents or recreational vehicles. There are no hookups, but there are restrooms with running water and sinks, plus an outdoor shower that can be used if you wear a bathing suit. The Oasis Visitor Center is five miles east on U.S. 41/Tamiami Trail. Bring water, food, mosquito repellent, and any supplies you'll need. Children are welcome. Pets must be on a six-foot leash and restrained at all times.

Reservations, fees: Reservations are not accepted. Fee is $14 a site per night. The campground often is filled on weekends in January and February. Stays are limited to 10 days in winter, 14 days the rest of the time.

Directions: From Florida's Turnpike in Miami, exit on U.S. 41/Tamiami Trail and drive 46 miles west to the campground on the north side of the highway. From Naples, drive east on U.S. 41 to the intersection of State Road 29, then continue east on the same road for 13 miles.

Contact: Big Cypress National Preserve, HCR 61, Box 110, Ochopee, FL 34141, 239/695-1201 or 239/695-2000. For hunting information, call 239/695-2040. Website: www.nps.gov/bicy.

53 MIDWAY CAMPGROUND

Rating: 5

On the Tamiami Trail in Big Cypress National Preserve

Everglades map, grid c2, page 528

Midway is closest to the Oasis Visitor Center, which is valuable to Big Cypress campers not only for information but also as a crucial source of drinking water. From here, backpackers can pick up the Florida National Scenic Trail and hike deep into the preserve. The sometimes-flooded path meanders for 31 miles. Oasis is a nerve center for activities in the preserve: ranger-led bicycling, hiking, and canoe trips;

group campfires; and nature talks. Inside the center are films and exhibits detailing the preserve's rich environment. For program information, call 239/695-1201. Note that this campground is open from early January until May only. Camping is no-frills. It's basically a place for motorists on U.S. 41 to pull off, stop, and pitch a tent or park an RV alongside a little lake. The reward is getting away from it all: The croaks of frogs, the chirps of cicadas, and panther-crossing signs are reminders that you're far from the city. Lots of alligators tend to hang out near the visitor center.

Campsites, facilities: At this clearing around a lake, there is room for about 30 tents or RVs. There are no hookups. Two chemical toilets are provided, but the nearest source of drinking water is three miles east on U.S. 41 at the Oasis Visitor Center. Children are welcome. Pets must be on a six-foot leash and restrained at all times.

Reservations, fees: Reservations are not accepted, and there is no fee. The campground often is filled on weekends in January and February. Stays are limited to 10 days in winter, 14 days at other times.

Directions: From Florida's Turnpike in Miami, exit on U.S. 41/Tamiami Trail and drive 41 miles west to the park on the north side of the highway. From Naples, drive east on U.S. 41 to the intersection of State Road 29. Proceed east on U.S. 41 for about 22 miles, then turn north into the campground.

Contact: Big Cypress National Preserve, HCR 61, Box 110, Ochopee, FL 34141, 239/695-1201 or 239/695-2000. For hunting information, call 239/695-2040. Website: www.nps.gov/bicy.

54 MITCHELL'S LANDING

Rating: 5

Off Loop Road in Big Cypress National Preserve

Everglades map, grid c2, page 528

Airboats occasionally launch from here, so you periodically may hear the rumble of their engines as the craft roar off into the distance. The road leading to this remote clearing is too rough for RVs, so tents only are found in this part of 1,138-square-mile Big Cypress National Preserve. For some tastes, campers sometimes may seem rougher than normal, and no park volunteer is stationed here to keep an eye on things. On weekdays, you may be lucky enough to have the place to yourself. Winter is the best time to camp anywhere in otherwise-buggy Big Cypress, which offers many miles of hiking trails, seasonal hunting, and fishing in scattered areas. Bring a mountain bike to follow trails in the northern part of the preserve. You're virtually certain to see an alligator during your visit to the preserve. Wrap bungee cord around your cooler or store it in your vehicle to protect your food from another common critter—the raccoon.

Campsites, facilities: At this clearing outfitted with a portable toilet, about 20 tents can be accommodated. There are no hookups. An airboat launch is provided, but there are no other facilities. Bring water, food, mosquito repellent, a hat, and everything else you'll need. Children are welcome. Pets must be on a six-foot leash and restrained at all times.

Reservations, fees: Reservations are not accepted, and there is no fee.

Directions: From Florida's Turnpike in Miami, exit on U.S. 41/Tamiami Trail and drive about 28 miles west, passing the Shark Valley entrance to Everglades National Park and the Miccosukee tribe cultural center. Don't veer right when the road jogs north. Instead, bear a tad left onto a little road called Loop Road; it's marked by a sign that reads "Hunters Must Check In." Follow Loop Road a little more than 10 miles to the Mitchell's Landing primitive camping area on the south side of the road. You'll see a brown tent sign instead of the posted name of the site; drive onto a rough-grade road to reach the camping area.

Contact: Big Cypress National Preserve, HCR 61, Box 110, Ochopee, FL 34141, 239/695-1201 or 239/695-2000. For hunting information, call 239/695-2040. Website: www.nps.gov/bicy.

55 PINECREST CAMPGROUND

🚶 🚴 🎣 🐕 🚐 ⛺

Rating: 7

Off Loop Road in Big Cypress National Preserve

Everglades map, grid c2, page 528

Peace. Quiet. Remoteness. That's what you get at this open and sunny clearing in 1,138-square-mile Big Cypress National Preserve. It's not suitable for large rigs, so tenters hoping to get away from it all won't hear the rumble of RV generators here. Daytime visitors to the preserve travel slowly down Loop Road by car, motorcycle, or bicycle, in hopes of catching glimpses at resident critters, including deer, alligators, birds, and the occasional bobcat or bear. Very rarely, long-time locals catch sight of an endangered Florida panther hurrying across Loop Road. Many miles of hiking trails can be accessed from right here. Trails suitable for mountain bikes are found in the northern part of Big Cypress; get a map from a ranger. Fishing is possible in the canals along Tamiami Trail, Turner River Road, and other spots. Campers here tend to be seasonal hunters and users of off-road vehicles, but you might bring a canoe if you want to paddle the Turner River and Halfway Creek south to Chokoloskee Bay. The Turner River is just west of H. P. Williams Roadside Park, which is at U.S. 41 and Highway 839. Halfway Creek is about five miles west, just beyond the intersection of U.S. 41 and Highway 841.

Campsites, facilities: At this clearing outfitted with a portable toilet, about 20 tents can be accommodated. Some smaller RVs may be able to reach the camping area during the dry season (typically winter); call about conditions. There are no hookups. Bring water, food, mosquito repellent, a hat, and everything else you'll need. Children are welcome. Pets must be on a six-foot leash and restrained at all times.

Reservations, fees: Reservations are not accepted, and there is no fee.

Directions: From Florida's Turnpike in Miami, exit on U.S. 41/Tamiami Trail and drive about 28 miles west, passing the Shark Valley entrance to Everglades National Park and the Miccosukee tribe cultural center. Don't veer right when the road jogs north. Instead, bear a tad left onto a little road called Loop Road; it's marked by a sign that reads "Hunters Must Check In." Follow Loop Road about five to six miles to the Pinecrest primitive camping area on the north side of the road. You'll see a brown tent sign instead of the posted name of the site; drive into that driveway and follow it to a clearing that serves as the camping area.

Contact: Big Cypress National Preserve, HCR 61, Box 110, Ochopee, FL 34141, 239/695-1201 or 239/695-2000. For hunting information, call 239/695-2040. Website: www.nps.gov/bicy.

Other Everglades Parks

56 EVERGLADES HOLIDAY PARK

Rating: 6

West of Fort Lauderdale in the Everglades
Everglades map, grid b1, page 528

Favored by locals for weekend getaways, this rustic bass fishing haven and gateway to the Everglades is known by tourists for its narrated one-hour-long airboat rides. Fishing is the big thing here—you can be out on the water at daybreak if you use this 15-acre park as your base camp. You can rent fishing rods and boats, or hike or cycle atop the levee for miles. You're sure to see an alligator or two and some long-legged wading birds hunting for their dinner. The mosquitoes aren't as plentiful in the cooler winter months, but they'll eat you alive in the summer if you're not prepared. Pick up groceries and other items in Fort Lauderdale because there's nothing much around here. Some supplies are sold at the general store, souvenir shop, and bait shop.

Campsites, facilities: There are 36 tent sites and 90 RV sites (many of them full-hookup) for RVs up to 40 feet long. Piped water, electricity, restrooms, showers, and picnic tables are provided. In the tent section, fire rings are at each site. Alligator-wrestling shows, airboat tours, fishing charters, a two-acre lake, a tackle shop, and boat rentals are available. You can also rent a rod and reel. The bathhouses and laundry are wheelchair accessible. All ages are welcome. Pets must be on hand-held leashes, which is wise because alligators live in the nearby saw grass.

Reservations, fees: Reservations are recommended for November through May (reserve no later than August). Sites are $14 to $20 per night. Major credit cards are accepted. Long-term stays are OK.

Directions: From I-95 in Fort Lauderdale, drive west on I-595 for eight miles until the road becomes I-75. Continue six miles west on I-75 to U.S. 27. Go south on U.S. 27 for 6.5 miles. Turn west on Griffin Road and drive .5 mile to the park.

Contact: Everglades Holiday Park, 21940 Griffin Road, Fort Lauderdale, FL 33332, 954/434-8111 or 800/226-2244, website: www.everglades holidaypark.com.

57 COLLIER SEMINOLE STATE PARK

Rating: 9

South of Naples
Everglades map, grid d2, page 528

A gateway to the Ten Thousand Islands, this park is a showcase for South Florida's unique landscape of mangrove and cypress swamps, salt-marshes, and pine flatwoods. Common to the park are royal palms, tropical hammock trees typical of the West Indies; and wildlife ranging from pelicans, wood storks, and bald eagles to the American crocodile and black bear. Be warned: Also too common are ferocious mosquitoes, which tend to be less bothersome in the cooler months but rarely disappear completely.

Think of what it must have been like here before the advent of mosquito repellent. When the Tamiami Trail (the road linking Tampa and Miami, hence the name) was built in the 1920s, crews labored in chest-deep water under nearly impossible conditions. An enormous piece of their equipment, known as a "walking dredge," is on display in the state park, which was named for Barron Collier (the developer of much of Naples) and for the Seminole Indians who lived on these lands.

Adventurers can get a taste of those difficult days (as well as a sense of the abundant birds and other wildlife that were present then, including the wood stork, brown pelican, osprey, and roseate spoonbill) by canoeing the

13.6-mile tidal creek into the park's 4,760-acre wilderness preserve. One primitive camping area, Grocery Place, is along the canoe trail; campers must register with the park ranger and file a float plan first. You'll often have the camping area to yourself. By land, another backcountry camping area is accessible to hikers, who must register with the ranger, along a 6.6-mile trail. There you'll sleep amid oaks and palms, so bring mosquito repellent. It can be buggy, which explains why the camping area is rarely used in summer. There is no water at either site; bring four quarts per person per day. Bury human waste six inches deep. Food must be suspended away from bears. All boaters and canoeists must file a float plan with the ranger station before departure.

Pick up supplies in Naples or on Marco Island. From here, you can explore Everglades City, Corkscrew Swamp Sanctuary, and the Fakahatchee Strand State Preserve.

Campsites, facilities: Part of a 6,243-acre state park and wilderness preserve, the campground offers 137 sites for RVs or tents; 91 sites have electricity, and all have water. Nineteen sites suitable for tents are in a woodsy area separate from the main campground. Two primitive camping areas are accessible by canoe or from a hiking trail; bring water because no facilities are available in those areas. Restrooms, showers, grills, picnic tables, a dump station, a playground, a boat ramp, a canoe trail, and hiking trails are within the park, which is mostly wheelchair accessible. Canoes are available for rent, and a one-hour pontoon boat tour is available. Children are welcome. Pets are allowed with proof of vaccination; however, they are not permitted on trails or in park-owned canoes.

Reservations, fees: Reservations are recommended; call ReserveAmerica at 800/326-3521. Sites in the main campground are $13 per night for four people, plus $2 for each additional person, $2 per pet, and $2 for electricity. Rates are subject to change. Backcountry camping costs $3 per adult, $2 per child. Major credit cards are accepted. The maximum stay is 14 days.

Directions: From Naples, travel 14 miles east on U.S. 41/Tamiami Trail. The campground entrance is just east of the junction with County Road 92.

Contact: Collier Seminole State Park, 20200 East Tamiami Trail, Naples, FL 34114, 239/394-3397, fax 239/394-5113, website: www.floridastateparks.org.

58 PORT OF THE ISLANDS RV RESORT

Rating: 5

On the Tamiami Trail
Everglades map, grid d2, page 528

This is a mecca for RVers who want to wander through the vast swampland and saw grass prairies of the Everglades. The RV park is no longer part of the Port of the Islands resort hotel, which has pools, tennis courts, and a marina on the south side of U.S. 41/Tamiami Trail. But campers are free to stop by the hotel restaurant and lounge if they get hungry; otherwise, there's nothing commercial near here. The campground, which is on the north side of the road, is surrounded by a million acres of federal preserves. Within the campground, pontoon tour boats are available for a two-hour cruise through the Everglades and the Ten Thousand Islands, or you can launch a canoe and explore the area on your own. There's also a full-service skeet, trap, and sporting clays gun club. This camping resort is packed December through March, but the crowds ebb as the weather warms. The management keeps mosquitoes at bay with regular ground spraying.

Campsites, facilities: All 99 RV sites have full hookups. On the premises are restrooms, showers, laundry facilities, two boat ramps, bike paths, hiking trails, and a fish-cleaning station. Most areas are wheelchair accessible. Children are welcome. Pets must be leashed.

Reservations, fees: Reservations are recom-

mended. Sites are $25 to $30 per night for two people, plus $3 per extra person and $1 for electricity. Rates are lowered during the summer. Major credit cards are accepted. Long-term stays are OK.

Directions: From Miami, take U.S. 41/Tamiami Trail west for 80 miles. The campground is on the north side of the highway when you reach Port of the Islands. From Naples, travel 25 miles east on U.S. 41.

Contact: Port of the Islands RV Resort, 12425 Union Road, Naples, FL 34114, 239/642-5343 or 800/319-4447, website: www.portoftheislands.com.

59 BIG CYPRESS TRAIL LAKES CAMPGROUND

Rating: 7

On the Tamiami Trail in Big Cypress National Preserve

Everglades map, grid c2, page 528

Keep an eye out for the giant concrete panther sitting out front, along with a sign that says: "Alligators, snakes, ice cream." For Big Cypress campers in search of full hookups, this is the only fully developed campground around. The sunny campsites surround two ponds. The world's smallest post office—a tiny little building about the size of a parking lot attendant's booth—is just down the road and draws the occasional tour bus.

Campsites, facilities: There are 50 RV sites with full hookups and picnic tables, with a separate area for 50 tents. On the premises are restrooms, showers, a dump station, laundry facilities, and a store for groceries and souvenirs. An activities house and the restrooms are wheelchair accessible. Children are welcome. Leashed pets are permitted.

Reservations, fees: Reservations are recommended. Sites are $12 to $14 per night for two people, plus $2 for each additional person. Major credit cards are accepted. Long-term stays are OK.

Directions: From Naples, drive east on U.S. 41/Tamiami Trail to the intersection of State Road 29. Continue on U.S. 41 for six miles to the campground, on the south side of the highway. From Florida's Turnpike in Miami, exit at U.S. 41 and drive west for 53 miles.

Contact: Big Cypress Trail Lakes Campground, U.S. 41, Ochopee, FL 33943, 239/695-2275 or 239/695-3063, email: traillakes@netscape.net.

60 BARRON RIVER RESORT

Rating: 6

In Everglades City

Everglades map, grid d2, page 528

Watch the sun set with a cool drink at Larry's Famous Chickee Bar and Restaurant, then feast on shrimp and stone crab pulled fresh from the Gulf of Mexico. Barron River Resort captures the easy mood of Everglades City, a picturesque fishing village that draws thousands of people to its annual Seafood and Music Festival in late January. About half of the campsites overlook the water at this open and sunny resort, and there's quick access to fishing in Gulf waters. Landlubbers can hop on a bicycle and pedal around town; a bicycle path stretches across the causeway to Chokoloskee Island. Everglades City has a colorful, if somewhat checkered, past as a refuge for fugitives and smugglers. In the 1980s, nearly half the menfolk were hauled to Miami in handcuffs for using their local knowledge of the mazelike Ten Thousand Islands to smuggle in marijuana and cocaine.

The most notorious resident was "Emperor" Ed Watson, a red-bearded rogue who fled here in the 1890s after killing three men in Georgia. Watson established a sugar plantation manned by other fugitives—who, legend has it, were rewarded for their labor with a bullet. He was gunned down by a posse in 1910 for his participation in a double murder and was buried in a shallow trench with a hangman's rope running from the grave to a tree—a symbol that shooting was too good for him.

Everglades City boomed briefly during construction of the Tamiami Trail in the 1920s and gained fame as a sportsman's paradise. The Rod and Gun Club, which opened in 1925, was a magnet for rich and famous fishermen, President "Ike" Eisenhower among them. It remains a favorite spot to swap fish tales and hoist a few while savoring the seafood.

Campsites, facilities: There are 60 sites with concrete pads, full hookups, and picnic tables; two are pull-through. Twenty-five tents can be set up in a grassy field or another area; they also may use a full-hookup site. On the premises are restrooms, showers, a boat ramp, a full-service marina, fishing charters, horseshoe pits, a chickee bar and restaurant, laundry facilities, a dump station, and motel rooms. Groceries are within three blocks. The park welcomes children and leashed pets.

Reservations, fees: Reservations are recommended. Full-hookup sites are $24 to $38 per night for two people. Primitive tent sites are $18 for two people. Add $4 for each additional person. Major credit cards are accepted. Long-term stays are OK.

Directions: From Naples, take U.S. 41/Tamiami Trail east to State Road 29. Turn south and drive about three miles to the entrance to the island of Everglades City. Cross the bridge, and look for the campground at right.

Contact: Barron River Resort, 803 Collier Avenue, Everglades City, FL 34139, 239/695-3591 or 800/535-4961, website: www.everglades park.com.

61 GLADES HAVEN

Rating: 7

In Everglades City
Everglades map, grid d2, page 528

Nestled between Everglades City and Chokoloskee Island, this campground is an ideal base camp for exploring the Wilderness Waterway, a backwater route flush with fish and feathered wildlife that meanders along the edge of Everglades National Park. From the causeway bridge, it takes two to five hours, depending on the tide and wind, to reach Comer Key, once home to hermit/mangrove philosopher Robert Osmer. He holed up here a half century ago with his favorite books and a coffeepot ready for strangers and friends who were welcome to drop by for a cup and some conversation. For information, call Kitty Hawk Kayaks (800/948-0759). Everglades National Park Boat Tours rents canoes and conducts nearly two-hour scenic boat rides for the less adventuresome. Boats leave the center every 30 minutes. For information, call 239/695-2591.

Campsites, facilities: All 51 sites have full hookups and picnic tables. On the premises are restrooms, showers, laundry facilities, a dump station, a boat ramp, a full-service marina, boat and canoe rentals, a restaurant, a delicatessen, cabins, a chickee bar, and a general store. Children are welcome. Leashed pets are permitted.

Reservations, fees: Reservations are recommended October through April. Sites are $20 to $30 per night for two people, plus $5 for each additional person. Major credit cards are accepted. Long-term stays are OK.

Directions: From Naples, take U.S. 41/Tamiami Trail east to State Road 29. Turn south and drive about three miles to Everglades City. The park is on the south side of town, across from the Everglades National Park Gulf Coast Visitor Center.

Contact: Glades Haven, P.O. Box 580 (or 800 Copeland Avenue), Everglades City, FL 34139, 239/695-2746, fax 239/695-2091, website: www.gladeshaven.com.

62 CHOKOLOSKEE ISLAND PARK

Rating: 4

On Chokoloskee Island south of Everglades City
Everglades map, grid d2, page 528

This mobile home park has the rustic charm of an old seaside motor court, although it's a bit cluttered with boat trailers and the like. The setting is right on the water, with boat and canoe rentals available, as well as charter fishing services. There's a busy social schedule during the winter, including potluck dinners, bingo, and crafts.

Campsites, facilities: The 80-unit park has 20 grassy sites for RVs and tents. Full hookups, wheelchair-accessible restrooms, showers, picnic tables, a dump station, a boat ramp, horseshoe pits, shuffleboard courts, and laundry facilities are available. RVs up to 25 feet long can be accommodated. Children are welcome. Leashed pets are permitted.

Reservations, fees: Reservations are recommended. Sites are $30 per night for two people, plus $2 for each additional person and $1.50 for electricity during summer months. Major credit cards are accepted. Long-term stays are OK.

Directions: From Naples, take U.S. 41/Tamiami Trail east to State Road 29. Turn south and drive about three miles to Everglades City, then continue about three miles to Chokoloskee Island. Turn west (right) at the post office and follow the signs to the park at 1175 Hamilton Lane.

Contact: Chokoloskee Island Park, P.O. Box 430, Chokoloskee, FL 34138, 239/695-2414, website: http://chokoloskee.com/cip.html.

63 OUTDOOR RESORTS OF CHOKOLOSKEE ISLAND

Rating: 8

On Chokoloskee Island south of Everglades City

Everglades map, grid d2, page 528

Tiny, secluded Chokoloskee Island, linked to the mainland by a causeway, is the snook fishing capital of the world. It's within one hour's drive of most Naples and Everglades attractions, but the focus is on canoeing, boating, and fishing—and with good reason. These waters are great for teaching little ones to fish; just about any persistent kid or novice can pick up enough skills in a few hours to hook a small snapper or sheepshead right from the dock. For bigger fish, you bigger anglers in search of game fish such as snook should venture into the mangroves or to the fishing holes a short distance offshore. There's nothing like heading toward a spot where you see the gulls circling. Pop your line into the middle of a school of blue runner or amberjack; they're fun to catch, practically jumping into the boat, although not great to eat. Boat and canoe rentals are available in the park, and many fishing guides and charter boats can be hired close by. More than 160 campsites have docks available; 86 are on canals or gulfside. Shade is minimal, but, hey, you're on the water, which is presumably what you came for.

Campsites, facilities: This condominium park has 283 full-hookup RV sites with cable TV. Restrooms, showers, laundry facilities, and groceries are on the premises. In addition, the park has three recreation centers, three pools, three hot tubs, a health club, shuffleboard courts, lighted tennis courts, a marina, boat docks, motel rooms, bait, tackle, canoe and kayak rentals, and wintertime activities. For telephone service, you must contact the phone company. Children are welcome. Two leashed pets are permitted per site, as long as they do not annoy other guests.

Reservations, fees: Reservations are recommended. Sites are $35.40 to $45 per night for two people; these rates are subject to change. The maximum number of people per site is four. Some lots are available for resale, but overnighters can rent sites from the park. Major credit cards are accepted.

Directions: From Naples, take U.S. 41/Tamiami Trail east to State Road 29. Turn south and drive about three miles to Everglades City, then continue about three miles to Chokoloskee Island. Look for the park at left.

Contact: Outdoor Resorts of Chokoloskee Island, P.O. Box 39, Chokoloskee Island, FL 34138, 239/695-3788, fax 239/695-3338, website: www.outdoor-resorts.com.

64 GATOR PARK

Rating: 4

On the Tamiami Trail west of Coopertown

Everglades map, grid b2, page 528

Gator-headed mannequins welcome visitors from the front porch, an eye-catching gimmick designed to lure motorists off the Tamiami Trail. Gator Park is a tourist stop with a campground out back, offering airboat tours of the Everglades, an Indian village, and a gator pen. This is the last campground with electric and water hookups before entering the Everglades. The last chance for groceries and gas is six miles east at Dade Corners, the intersection of U.S. 41 and State Road 997, also known as Krome Avenue.

Campsites, facilities: Self-contained rigs are accepted at these 21 sites with water and electric hookups. On the premises are a dump station, cooking grills, chickee huts, an airboat concession, a souvenir shop, and a restaurant. Children are welcome. Leashed pets are permitted.

Reservations, fees: Reservations are not necessary. Sites are $25 per night. Major credit cards are accepted. Long-term stays are OK.

Directions: From Florida's Turnpike in Miami, exit on U.S. 41/Tamiami Trail and drive west for 12 miles. The park is on the south side of the road, behind a tourist shop.

Contact: Gator Park, 24050 Southwest Eighth Street, Miami, FL 33187, 305/559-2255 or 800/559-2205, website: www.gatorpark.com.

COURTESY OF VISIT FLORIDA

Chapter 20

Greater Miami

Greater Miami

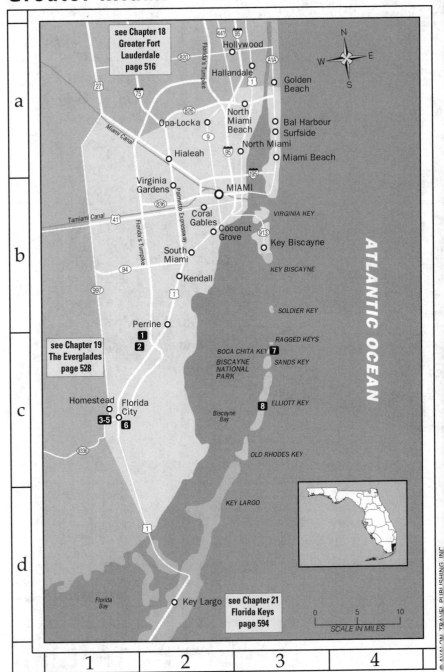

see Chapter 18
Greater Fort
Lauderdale
page 516

Hollywood

Hallandale

Golden
Beach

Opa-Locka

North
Miami
Beach

Bal Harbour

Surfside

Hialeah

North Miami

Miami Beach

Virginia
Gardens

MIAMI

VIRGINIA KEY

Coral
Gables

Coconut
Grove

Key Biscayne

South
Miami

KEY BISCAYNE

Kendall

SOLDIER KEY

Perrine

1

2

RAGGED KEYS

7

see Chapter 19
The Everglades
page 528

BOCA CHITA KEY

BISCAYNE
NATIONAL
PARK

SANDS KEY

Homestead

Florida
City

8 ELLIOTT KEY

3-5

6

Biscayne
Bay

OLD RHODES KEY

KEY LARGO

ATLANTIC OCEAN

Florida
Bay

Key Largo

see Chapter 21
Florida Keys
page 594

0   5   10

SCALE IN MILES

1 LARRY AND PENNY THOMPSON MEMORIAL PARK AND CAMPGROUND

Rating: 7

West of Perrine near Metrozoo

Greater Miami map, grid c2, page 586

With 240 RV sites and 30 tent spots, you might expect this urban campground to have a more crowded feel, but the sites are thoughtfully laid out in spoke-and-wheel groups of 20 to 30 spots each. The tenting area is set apart from the RV spots but is convenient to a bathhouse and play area. Trees are plentiful in the campground, with mango and avocado orchards nearby (no picking allowed). It's part of a busy county park that once boasted a 275-acre pine forest that was destroyed by Hurricane Andrew in 1992. Bicyclists can see the recovery firsthand by using an extensive network of trails, or they can ride on the paved roads. The fishing lake and swimming beach get crowded on weekends with day-trippers and locals using the picnic shelters for birthday parties and other festivities. When Miami's only county-run water slides reopen for the summer (from Memorial Day to Halloween), platoons of kids each weekend climb up a wooden platform to reach the top of a rocky palm-dotted hill, then plunge down slides into the 72- to 75-degree clear waters of a well-fed lake. Wednesday is the slowest day at the slides. Miami Metrozoo is next door, and the Florida Keys are one hour away.

Campsites, facilities: All 240 sites have full hookups. Ten sites are pull-through. Restrooms, showers, picnic tables, laundry facilities, a dump station, horseshoes, and a store are available. Within the county park are a lake, a swimming beach, three water slides, a fishing pier, a concession stand, bridle trails, and picnic pavilions. A supermarket is one mile away. The laundry, restrooms, and playground are wheelchair accessible. Children are welcome. Leashed pets may camp but are forbidden in the rest of the county park. All pets must be properly licensed and are welcome if kept under control and quiet. Pets may not be tied to trees or left unattended.

Reservations, fees: Reservations are taken. Sites are $10 to $19 per night for two people, plus $1 for each extra person over age four. Major credit cards are accepted. Stays are limited to three months, but an extension is available for another three months.

Directions: From Florida's Turnpike, exit west on Eureka Drive/Southwest 184th Street. Continue one mile to the park entrance at 12451 Southwest 184th Street on the north side of the road.

Contact: Larry and Penny Thompson Memorial Park and Campground, 12451 Southwest 184th Street, Miami, FL 33177, 305/232-1049, website: www.metrodade.com.

2 MIAMI/EVERGLADES KOA

Rating: 5

In southern Dade County on Southwest 162nd Avenue between Quail Roost Drive and Hainlin Mill Road

Greater Miami map, grid c2, page 586

Pick free avocados and mangoes right off the trees at this farm country campground, which is convenient to such attractions as Monkey Jungle, Metrozoo, Parrot Jungle, the Everglades, and the Florida Keys. Nearby is the Redland, Dade County's agricultural area, where much of the nation's limes are grown, as well as tropical crops, including yuca and malanga. These tubers are often cooked like potatoes and served with "mojo," a mixture of vinegar, spices, and olive oil. Staples of the Cuban-American diet, yuca and malanga have become trendy with chefs of the "New World" cooking school. In these parts, think tree farm and what you get are acres and acres of palm trees, soon to be planted outdoors in Florida subdivisions and inside Midwestern shopping malls.

Campsites, facilities: This KOA has 257 RV sites and 20 tent spots. It offers full hookups, picnic tables, restrooms, showers, laundry facilities, a circular pool with hot tub, horseshoe pits, shuffleboard and basketball courts, an adult lounge, and a convenience store. The bathhouses, store, and recreation hall are wheelchair accessible. Children and leashed pets are welcome.

Reservations, fees: Reservations are recommended. Sites are $34 to $39 per night for two people, plus $3 for each additional person. Major credit cards are accepted. Long-term stays are permitted.

Directions: From Florida's Turnpike, exit west on Quail Roost Drive and proceed five miles to Southwest 162nd Avenue, then turn south. The park entrance is .5 mile ahead on the east side of the road. From U.S. 1, drive 4.5 miles west on Southwest 216th Street to Southwest 162nd Avenue, then turn north and continue to the park.

Contact: Miami/Everglades KOA, 20675 Southwest 162nd Avenue, Homestead, FL 33187, 305/233-5300 or 800/562-7730, website: www.miamicamp.com.

🖸 THE BOARDWALK

Rating: 6

In Homestead

Greater Miami map, grid c1, page 586

This mobile home and RV park is a gated community close to city amenities, Everglades National Park, the Florida Keys, and Biscayne Bay. About two-thirds of the park is dedicated to park models, but you'll also find plenty of RV spaces available for overnighters and seasonal visitors. Everything is new—from the swimming pool and landscaping to the clubhouse and social areas.

Campsites, facilities: There are 164 RV sites with concrete pads, full hookups, and picnic tables. Restrooms, showers, and laundry facilities are available. On the premises are a heated pool, a clubhouse with a billiards and card room, planned activities in the winter, lighted shuffleboard courts, horseshoe pits, and a bar-

becue area. Children are welcome. Leashed pets of small and medium size are permitted.

Reservations, fees: Reservations are recommended. Sites are $35 per night for two people, plus $3 per extra person. Major credit cards are accepted. Long-term rates are available.

Directions: From the Florida Turnpike, take Exit 2 west on Campbell Drive and proceed to U.S. 1. Turn left on U.S. 1 and drive .3 mile to Northeast Sixth Avenue.

Contact: The Boardwalk, 100 Northeast Sixth Avenue, Homestead, FL 33030, 305/248-2487 or 888/233-9255, fax 305/248-2075.

🖸 GOLDCOASTER MOBILE HOME AND RV PARK

Rating: 3

In Homestead

Greater Miami map, grid c1, page 586

Part of the Sun Communities mobile home and RV park chain that owns dozens of parks across the nation, Goldcoaster Mobile Home and RV Park is a squeaky-clean, professionally landscaped and managed destination for snowbirds and retirees. A concrete wall encircles the park, and there's a security gate. Four miles of paved roads are ideal for bicycling and strolling. Big rigs are welcome, and a full-time recreation director is in charge of the social program. It's convenient to the Florida Keys and Biscayne Bay, and 15 minutes from the main entrance to Everglades National Park. Nearby is a large outlet mall, as well as the Homestead motorsports racing complex. Surrounding this area is the South Dade farming area, where vegetables—including tomatoes, green beans, and more—flourish in the winter sun. For a fun and different experience, drive to one of the "you-pick" strawberry fields and gather your own harvest of sweet berries.

Campsites, facilities: This 548-site manufactured home community offers 231 full-hookup sites for travelers, who can use the restrooms, showers, craft and card room, laundry facilities, deluxe shuffleboard courts, heated pool, and Jacuzzi. Children and leashed pets are welcome.

Reservations, fees: Reservations are taken. Sites are $35 per night for two people, plus $3 for each additional person. Major credit cards are accepted.

Directions: From U.S. 1 in Florida City, turn west at Palm Drive/Southwest 344th Street and proceed 1.5 miles to Southwest 187th Avenue/Redland Road, then turn south. The park entrance is on the west side.

Contact: Goldcoaster Mobile Home and RV Park, 34850 Southwest 187th Avenue, Homestead, FL 33034, 305/248-5462 or 800/828-6992, fax 305/248-5467, website: www.sun communities.com.

5 CITY OF FLORIDA CITY CAMP SITE AND RV PARK

Rating: 2

In Florida City

Greater Miami map, grid c1, page 586

Parts of this park are little more than an open, grassy field, but some shady old oaks can be found on the west side. Converted school buses are not allowed, and all RVs must have up-to-date inspections, tags, and insurance. A manager lives on the property. The tent area is set apart from the RV sites.

Campsites, facilities: This city-owned urban campground has 300 campsites, 30 of which are for tents. Full hookups, restrooms, showers, picnic tables, laundry facilities, and shuffleboard courts are available. Children are welcome. Leashed pets are permitted, except for dogs weighing more than 40 pounds.

Reservations, fees: Reservations are not necessary. Sites are $22 per night for two people, plus $2.25 for each additional person. Major credit cards are accepted. Long-term stays are OK for RVers; for tents, there's a three-day limit.

Directions: From Florida's Turnpike, take Exit 1 and drive straight two blocks to North-

west Second Avenue. The park entrance is 500 feet on the right.

Contact: City of Florida City Camp Site and RV Park, 601 Northwest Third Avenue, Florida City, FL 33034, 305/248-7889.

6 SOUTHERN COMFORT RV RESORT

Rating: 6

In Florida City

Greater Miami map, grid c1, page 586

With its swaying royal palms, fruit trees, and a rainbow of hibiscus flowers, the park displays a Caribbean mood. It's convenient to the Florida Keys, national parks, and other attractions; a discount shopping mall, the Florida Keys Factory Shops, is across the street. If you're driving to the Florida Keys, this is the last resort-style overnight campground near U.S. 1—something to note if there's an accident on the highway between Florida City and Key Largo. Often, the road is completely shut down in both directions and you're stuck for hours. Traffic may be rerouted on Card Sound Road, but that can be slow-going in a crowd.

Campsites, facilities: There are 338 full-hookup RV sites (50 pull-through) and 10 tent-only sites with water and electricity. Picnic tables, restrooms, showers, laundry facilities, a pool, a recreation room, shuffleboard, and a tiki bar are on the premises. Organized activities are offered, including aerobic exercises, bingo, and dances in winter. Rigs up to 45 feet long can be accommodated. Children are welcome. Leashed pets, except rottweilers and pit bulls, are permitted.

Reservations, fees: Reservations are recommended. Sites are $20 to $28 per night for two people, plus $2 for each additional person. Major credit cards are accepted. Long-term stays are OK.

Directions: From U.S. 1 in Florida City, turn east at Palm Drive and proceed one block to the park entrance on the south side.

Contact: Southern Comfort RV Resort, 345 East Palm Drive, Florida City, FL 33034, 305/248-6909, fax 305/245-1345, website: www.gzinc.com/comfortrv.

⁊ BOCA CHITA KEY BOAT-IN SITES
🏃 🏊 🛶 🚤 ♿ ⛺

Rating: 10

In Biscayne National Park east of Homestead

Greater Miami map, grid c3, page 586

For a taste of Robinson Crusoe–style living, camping on Boca Chita can't be beat. The only way to get here is by boat, canoe, or kayak (and that's a nine-mile paddle from the visitor center). If you don't have a vessel, call the park concessionaire to see if boat transportation to the island is available. The company also rents canoes and kayaks and conducts glass-bottom boat, snorkel, and dive trips. All trips are dependent on weather conditions. The camping area overlooks a small harbor and an ornamental lighthouse, and a hiking trail encircles the island. Be prepared for mosquitoes and other insects throughout the year. The best time to camp here is January through April.

Campsites, facilities: There are 30 primitive campsites with picnic tables and grills. Saltwater flush toilets are available, but there is no freshwater on the island, so bring your own. Pack out all trash, and lock anything edible in a hard-sided cooler to foil raccoons. Children are welcome. Pets are prohibited. The mainland park areas and restroom on the island are wheelchair accessible.

Reservations, fees: Reservations are not accepted. The fee is $15 per boat, covering six people and two tents. The maximum stay is 14 days. If a boat drops you off for camping only, the fee is $10 per site for two tents.

Directions: To reach the island in your own boat, you must use nautical chart 11451, which includes all of Biscayne National Park. Charts can be ordered from the Florida National Parks

and Monument Association, 10 Parachute Key, #15, Homestead, FL 33034, 305/247-1216, website: www.nps.gov/ever, or may be purchased at the visitor center or local bait and marine stores. To get to the Dante Fascell Visitor Center and the park concessionaire, drive south on Florida's Turnpike to Homestead. Take Exit 6 onto Speedway Boulevard and drive 4.5 miles south. At Southwest 328th Street, turn east and drive five miles to the entrance. From U.S. 1, drive south toward Homestead and turn east on Southwest 328th Street, also called North Canal Drive. Drive nine miles to the entrance.

Contact: Biscayne National Park, 9700 SW 328th Street, Homestead, FL 33033, 305/230-7275, website: www.nps.gov/bisc. For information about boat service to the island, contact the park concessionaire, Biscayne National Underwater Park Inc., 9710 SW 328th Street, Homestead, FL 33033, 305/230-1100, fax 305/230-1120, email: dive970@aol.com.

⒏ ELLIOTT KEY BOAT-IN SITES
🏃 🏊 🛶 🚤 🐕 ⛺

Rating: 9

In Biscayne National Park east of Homestead

Greater Miami map, grid c3, page 586

On weekends, Elliott Key is a popular destination for local boaters, most of whom sleep aboard their craft tied up at the dock or anchored just offshore, leaving the campground to tougher folks. The raccoons are even hardier; park rangers advise you to bring hard-sided coolers that you can lock tight. Those raccoons have even been known to open water jugs. Resist the temptation to string a hammock because hammocks are not permitted. There's a large fire pit for group campers, but ground fires are prohibited elsewhere. Backcountry camping is not permitted. The park concessionaire sometimes provides boat service to Elliott Key for campers. By canoe or kayak, expect a seven-mile paddle. January through April is the best time to camp and avoid bugs.

Campsites, facilities: Accessible only by boat, this island harbors a 40-site campground with saltwater flush toilets, cold showers, grills, picnic tables, boat slips, and a nature trail. Drinking water is available. Pack out your trash. Children are welcome. Pets are permitted on a six-foot leash.

Reservations, fees: Reservations are accepted. The fee is $15 per boat, covering six people and two tents. The maximum stay is 14 days. The fee for campers being dropped off by a boat is $10.

Directions: To reach the island in your own boat, you must use nautical chart 11451 (for details, see the previous entry for Boca Chita). To get to the Dante Fascell Visitor Center and the park concessionaire, drive south on Florida's Turnpike to Homestead. Take Exit 6 onto Speedway Boulevard and drive 4.5 miles south. At Southwest 328th Street, turn east and drive five miles to the entrance. From U.S. 1, drive south toward Homestead and turn east on Southwest 328th Street, also called North Canal Drive. Drive nine miles to the entrance.

Contact: Biscayne National Park, 9700 SW 328th Street, Homestead, FL 33033, 305/230-7275, website: www.nps.gov/bisc. For information about boat service to the island, contact the park concessionaire, Biscayne National Underwater Park Inc., 9710 SW 328th Street, Homestead, FL 33033, 305/230-1100, fax 305/230-1120, email: dive970@aol.com.

Chapter 21

Florida Keys

Florida Keys

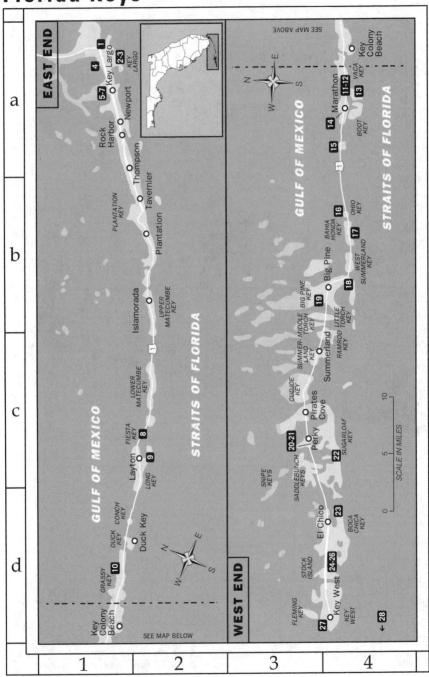

Mile Markers

As you approach the Keys, note the mile marker posts along U.S. 1, also known as the Overseas Highway, a ribbon of road that continues south for 113 miles and across 43 bridges. The numbers start at 0 in Key West, and all addresses along U.S. 1 coincide with the mile marker posts. For instance, a campground at 106003 Overseas Highway is near mile marker 106. Addresses often are further described as "ocean side" (on the Atlantic Ocean side of the road) or "bay side" (on the north side of U.S. 1, generally on Florida Bay).

1 FLORIDA KEYS RV RESORT

Rating: 7

In Key Largo on U.S. 1/Overseas Highway
Florida Keys map, grid a1, page 594

This is the first campground you'll encounter in the Florida Keys on the way south to Key West, and considering how scarce space is around here, this is a gem. Oak trees shade much of the attractive, sprawling, 10-acre campground, which attracts families, retired folks, and vacationers. The peaceful park accommodates RVs up to 45 feet long, as well as tenters. A dozen campsites overlook a picturesque man-made fishing lake (no swimming is allowed there, but there's a pool on the property). It's close to snorkeling and other water fun at nearby John Pennekamp Coral Reef State Park (see campground below).

Campsites, facilities: There are 139 RV or tent sites with water, electricity, picnic tables, cable TV, and telephone access. Only 39 sites are available for long-term visitors; 100 are set aside for overnighters and 15 are for tents. Eighty sites have full hookups. Restrooms, showers, laundry facilities, a pool, a spa, horseshoe pits, a playground, a picnic area, and courts for shuffleboard, basketball, and volleyball are provided. The bathhouse and pool area are wheelchair accessible. Children are welcome. Leashed pets are permitted.

Reservations, fees: Reservations are recommended. Sites are $40 per night for two people, plus $5 for each additional person over age 12. Major credit cards are accepted. Long-term stays are permitted.

Directions: From Florida City, drive south on U.S. 1 to Key Largo. The campground is located on the ocean side near mile marker 106, just south of the junction with Card Sound Road.

Contact: Florida Keys RV Resort, 106003 Overseas Highway, Key Largo, FL 33037, 305/451-6090, fax 305/451-4615, email: flkeysrvresort@spottswood.com.

2 JOHN PENNEKAMP CORAL REEF STATE PARK

Rating: 10

In Key Largo on U.S. 1/Overseas Highway
Florida Keys map, grid a1, page 594

This, the first underwater state park in the United States, is also one of the finest parks in Florida, with direct access to coral reef formations from a sandy beach, as well as via charter service to diving or snorkeling reefs offshore. It's a rare setting of hardwood hammocks, mangroves, and crystal-clear water bordering the Key Largo Coral Reef National Marine Sanctuary, which covers 178 nautical square miles. Paddle a canoe or visit the interpretive center. The park gets a lot of traffic from international and U.S. tourists and locals alike, and the gates often close by midday when crowds reach capacity. It has been called the world's most-traveled-to dive destination, and the cars of daytime visitors may stretch for 200 yards waiting to get into this home of brain coral and barracuda. Don't forget mosquito repellent in the hot months. And bring an air mattress or sleeping pad if you'll be tent camping, because the sites are made of gravel and limestone rock.

This is the perfect place for novice snorkelers, and especially children. The gently sloping swimming beach near the visitors center lets them try out their skills without worries. Once proficient, they can swim farther out. Just 130 feet from the water's edge lies a reconstruction of an early Spanish shipwreck. You'll see 14 cannons, an anchor, and ballast stones recovered from a ship lost in a 1715 hurricane.

Campsites, facilities: This state park has 47 sites for tents and RVs with water, electricity, picnic tables, and grills. Restrooms, showers, and laundry facilities are provided. In the main part of the park are two beaches, two nature trails, a playground, a visitors center with a 30,000-gallon saltwater aquarium, a marina, a dive shop, boat and canoe rentals, and a snack shop. Scuba instruction, snorkeling, and glass-bottom boat tours are available. Children are welcome. Pets are not allowed in the campground.

Reservations, fees: Reservations are recommended; call ReserveAmerica at 800/326-3521. Sites are $24 to $26 per night for four people, plus $2 for each additional person and $2 for electricity. Major credit cards are accepted. The maximum stay is 14 days. Reservations are advised for snorkeling trips, which cost $25 to $30 per person, plus $5 to rent a snorkel and mask; reserve at 305/451-1621.

Directions: Follow U.S. 1/Overseas Highway to mile marker 102.5 in Key Largo. The park is on the ocean side.

Contact: John Pennekamp Coral Reef State Park, P.O. Box 487, Key Largo, FL 33037, 305/451-1202, website: www.floridastate parks.org.

❸ KEY LARGO KAMPGROUND AND MARINA

Rating: 9

In Key Largo south of U.S. 1/
Overseas Highway
Florida Keys map, grid a1, page 594

One of the nicest campgrounds in the Florida Keys, this resort reflects thoughtful planning designed to please nearly everyone. Three shady tent areas are nestled against a jungly mangrove hammock on the property line; some sites have water and electricity, whereas others share a community water source. RVs are accommodated under shade trees or on waterview sites with private docks. The best waterfront sites have been sold as condominium spaces but are often rented to tourists during the summer. Spring for a site with your own private dock overlooking the long boat channel. Isolated from the beaten track, the waters don't get as stirred up as they do at other places. You'll see stingrays, tarpon, and snapper when you're snorkeling over the grassy sea bottom off the two beaches. The surrounding woods and uninhabited mangrove islands give this deluxe campground a secluded feeling, even though it's close to shopping and Key Largo attractions.

Campsites, facilities: There are 171 full-hookup slots for RVs and 32 tent sites. Cable TV, restrooms, showers, a pool, a boat ramp, two recreation halls, chickee huts (Seminole Indian thatched-roof dwellings), horseshoe pits, two sandy beaches, and volleyball, basketball, and shuffleboard courts are available. A gate provides security. Children are welcome. Leashed pets are permitted.

Reservations, fees: Reservations are recommended. Sites are $22.50 to $52.50 per night for two adults and two children under 12, plus $3 for each additional person. No more than six people are allowed per site. Major credit cards are accepted. Long-term stays are OK.

Directions: From U.S. 1/Overseas Highway at mile marker 101.5 in Key Largo, turn south at Samson Road, which dead-ends at the park entrance, on the ocean side.

Contact: Key Largo Kampground and Marina, 101551 Overseas Highway, Key Largo, FL 33037-4596, 305/451-1431 or 800/526-7688, fax 305/451-8083, website: http://members.tripod.com/klkamp.

4 KING'S KAMP AND MARINA

Rating: 1

In Key Largo on U.S. 1/Overseas Highway
Florida Keys map, grid a1, page 594

A boat ramp and a small swimming beach provide good access to Blackwater Sound and Florida Bay; the pull-up RV sites are said to accommodate rigs as long as 40 feet. Most people are here to stay, rooted nearly as strong as the lush royal poinciana and gumbo-limbo trees that shade the park. But the location is worth the effort to see if a site is available. Motel rooms and rental units are also available, and you can dock your boat in the marina.

Campsites, facilities: The park has 60 sites, of which only four are available for RVs and nine for tents. Water, electricity, restrooms, showers, picnic tables, and fire grills are available. Children and leashed pets are permitted.

Reservations, fees: Reservations are recommended. Sites are $20 to $30 per night for two people, plus $5 for each additional person. Major credit cards are accepted. Long-term stays are permitted.

Directions: Follow U.S. 1/Overseas Highway to mile marker 103.5 in Key Largo. The park is on the bay side.

Contact: King's Kamp and Marina, 103620 Overseas Highway, Key Largo, FL 33037, 305/451-0010, website: www.kingskamp.com.

5 THE RIPTIDE

Rating: 5

In Key Largo on U.S. 1/Overseas Highway
Florida Keys map, grid a1, page 594

This well-kept campground has great views of Florida Bay and pretty coconut palms. It's a quiet place that mixes seasonal residents with travelers. Sites line a hairpin drive that leads to Florida Bay, a dock, and picnic tables by the water.

Campsites, facilities: Of the 30 trailer sites, seven are set aside for RV travelers. Full hookups, cable TV, picnic tables, restrooms, showers, a dock, and rental units are available; waterfront sites have water and electricity only (no sewer hookups). The campground caters primarily to retirees. Pets are not permitted.

Reservations, fees: Reservations are recommended. Sites are $45 per night for two people, plus $10 for each additional person. Major credit cards are accepted. Long-term stays are OK. The park is open October 1 through May 1.

Directions: Follow U.S. 1/Overseas Highway to Key Largo. The park is at mile marker 97.6 on the bay side.

Contact: The Riptide, 97680 Overseas Highway, Lot 1, Key Largo, FL 33037, 305/852-8481.

6 BLUE FIN-ROCK HARBOR

Rating: 7

In Key Largo
Florida Keys map, grid a1, page 594

With just four sites for overnighters and 14 for seasonal visitors, you'll have to reserve ahead to stay at this tiny, sunny park on the ocean side of the highway. You'll park on a spit of land near this park's large marina operation and docks filled with expensive fishing boats. Ocean-view sites are naturally in high demand. Big rigs can be accommodated. There's also primitive camping on Dove Island, five minutes from the docks; the park will provide water taxi service and a radio for your use. Twenty minutes away by boat is Molasses Reef, known for great snorkeling and diving. Boat rentals and charter services are available.

Campsites, facilities: There are 18 sites in this boating- and fishing-oriented park. Sites have full hookups and cable TV. Restrooms, showers, laundry facilities, a dog-walk area, and telephone service are available. On the premises are a restaurant, a boat ramp, docks, and boat slips. Most areas are wheelchair accessible. Children are welcome. Leashed pets are permitted.

Reservations, fees: Reservations are required. Sites are $40 to $65 per night for two people. Major credit cards are accepted. Long-term rates are available.

Directions: Follow U.S. 1/Overseas Highway to Key Largo. When you reach mile marker 97 on the ocean side, turn left at First State Bank onto First Avenue. Look for Second Street on your left.

Contact: Blue Fin-Rock Harbor, P.O. Box 888, 36 East Second Street, Key Largo, FL 33037, 305/852-2025, fax 305/852-0227, website: www.milemarker97.com.

■ AMERICA OUTDOORS
🏊 🛶 🍴 🏠 🐕 ♿ 🚐 ⛺

Rating: 6

In Key Largo on U.S. 1/Overseas Highway
Florida Keys map, grid a1, page 594

This family campground strives to offer something for everyone, and it gets so crowded on holiday weekends that a security guard will be on hand to wave you in and direct traffic. The tree canopy of native hardwoods is lush and junglelike, and there's a 600-foot sandy swimming beach and a 170-foot-long T-shaped pier on Florida Bay. Campsites are sandy and well shaded, but small. The smooth waters of the bay are a favorite spot for windsurfers, ocean kayakers, and snorkelers. When snorkeling, remember that you must use a floating dive flag buoy to alert boaters to your position. Tip: Tie a long string to the dive flag and loop the other

end around your wrist; that will allow you to swim safely without being encumbered. Your pet is allowed in the water at the boat ramp but not on the beach. Canoes, paddleboats, windsurfers, sailboats, and even fishing rods are for rent at the marina.

Campsites, facilities: There are 151 full-hookup sites (20 pull-through). Three tent sites have water and electricity. Each RV site comes with free cable TV and a picnic table; telephone service is available. Restrooms, showers, laundry facilities, a dump station, a dockside restaurant, a snack bar, bait and tackle, a boat ramp, boat rentals, boat slips, a volleyball field, shuffleboard courts, horseshoes, an adult recreation hall, a beach, and a game room are available. The marina, dock, store, and bathhouses are wheelchair accessible. Children are welcome. Leashed pets are allowed.

Reservations, fees: Reservations are accepted. Sites are $45 to $90 per night for four people, plus $7 for each additional person over age six. Major credit cards are accepted. The maximum stay is six months.

Directions: Follow U.S. 1/Overseas Highway to mile marker 97 in Key Largo. The park is on the bay side.

Contact: America Outdoors, 97450 South Overseas Highway, Key Largo, FL 33037, 305/852-8054, fax 305/853-0509, email: camperr@aol.com, website: www.aokl.com.

■ FIESTA KEY RESORT KOA KAMPGROUND AND MOTEL
🏊 🛶 🍴 🏠 🐕 🚴 🚐 ⛺

Rating: 7

On Fiesta Key near Layton
Florida Keys map, grid c2, page 594

This 28-acre KOA is a self-contained resort designed to please all ages. Favored by anglers and boaters, the campground gets busy on summer weekends and during the winter. Many Miami residents park their trailers here all summer long so they can get away quickly for the weekend. The views of Florida Bay are breathtaking, and you can snorkel off the seawall near the swimming beach. Fishing in these parts for the wily bonefish is world-famous. The park organizes parties for special events like New Year's.

Campsites, facilities: There are 300 RV sites (204 full-hookup) and a shaded section for 50 tents. Ninety-six RV sites have water and electricity only. A separate "tent village" has six roofed structures with electricity, a storage compartment, and a grassy area for tents. Picnic tables, grills, restrooms, showers, LP gas, a convenience store, and two laundry rooms are available. Other features include a playground, a game room, a store, an air-conditioned recreation hall, 20 motel units, a heated pool, two hot tubs, a beach, a marina, a boat ramp, boat rentals, bicycle rentals, horseshoes, basketball, beach volleyball, and a waterfront restaurant and bar. Children are welcome. Leashed pets are permitted.

Reservations, fees: Reservations are recommended. Sites are $42 to $95 per night for two people, plus $7 for each additional child and $9 per extra adult. Major credit cards are accepted. Long-term stays are OK.

Directions: Follow U.S. 1/Overseas Highway to the resort at mile marker 70 on the bay side of Fiesta Key.

Contact: Fiesta Key Resort KOA Kampground and Motel, P.O. Box 618, Long Key, FL 33001, 305/664-4922 or 800/562-7730, fax 305/664-8741, website: www.koa.com.

⑨ LONG KEY STATE PARK

🚶 🏊 🛶 🎣 🚐 ⛺

Rating: 10

On Long Key south of Layton
Florida Keys map, grid c2, page 594

With so few sites, the campground in this 980-acre state park is often filled, but don't let that deter you from trying. The camping area has a gently curving natural shoreline and all sites are beachfront. Get up in the morning and walk a few feet right into the water. There's

almost always a breeze (sometimes too much of one!). The Australian pines and several of the trees of Caribbean origin that shaded most spots were blown down during a series of hurricanes, so campsites are now sunny. Expect little in the way of natural vegetative buffers; without the pines, many campsites and even the pedestrians on the park's beloved walking path are now visible to cars passing by on U.S. 1. A few campsites are big enough, however, to give the illusion of being far from neighbors. And vegetation in Florida grows back quickly, so by the time you read this, some of the landscaping may be back.

At low tide, kids can look for fiddler crabs and minnows in rocky tidal pools at the east end of the campground. The sea level was 20 to 30 feet higher 100,000 years ago, but today the water is so shallow that you can wade a half mile out to sea and only get waist deep. That makes it a great place to learn to snorkel, although you won't see dramatic coral formations and big fish unless you go far offshore in a boat. The Long Key Lakes Canoe Trail winds through mangrove flats and a shallow lagoon. Nearby is the Golden Orb Trail, a 40-minute nature walk. On the bay side (across U.S. 1 and east of the campground) is the Layton Trail, a meandering path through a dark, almost impenetrable hardwood hammock.

Campsites, facilities: This state park has 60 sites for tents and RVs. Water and electricity are available at all. Picnic tables, grills, restrooms, and showers are provided. There's a canoe trail, a 1.25-mile nature trail, and an interpretive program. Children are welcome. Pets are prohibited.

Reservations, fees: Reservations are recommended; call ReserveAmerica at 800/326-3521. Sites are $24 per night for four people, plus $3 for each additional person (only eight people per site) and $2 for electricity. Major credit cards are accepted. The maximum stay is 14 days.

Directions: From the town of Layton on Long Key, drive south on U.S. 1/Overseas Highway to mile marker 67. Turn south at the park sign.

Contact: Long Key State Park, P.O. Box 776, Long Key, FL 33001, 305/664-4815, website: www.floridastateparks.org.

10 JOLLY ROGER TRAVEL PARK

Rating: 7

On Grassy Key

Florida Keys map, grid d1, page 594

Primitive campers will sleep nearly surrounded by water if they book one of the six sunny sites on a tiny triangle of land jutting into Florida Bay. Concrete-paved RV sites handle rigs up to 40 feet long; 15 are pull-through. Part of the park houses 100 mobile homes. A convenience store is within walking distance. Wintertime activities include bingo, kayak trips, bus tours to the Wal-Mart in Florida City, dances, ice-cream socials, and live music in the recreation pavilion. You can swim or snorkel off the dock. There's little shade in this boating-oriented campground.

Campsites, facilities: Eighty RV sites have full hookups and cable TV, 14 tent sites have water and electricity, and six sites are primitive. Picnic tables, restrooms, showers, horseshoes, and laundry facilities are available. The park is family-oriented but tends to attract older people. Leashed pets are permitted.

Reservations, fees: Reservations are recommended. Sites are $32 per night for two tent campers and $40 to $50 for two RVers, plus $5 for each additional person over age five. Major credit cards are accepted. Long-term stays are OK for RVers. Only four occupants are allowed per tent site, and tenters can stay no more than two weeks. RV occupancy limit is six persons.

Directions: On Grassy Key, follow U.S. 1/Overseas Highway to mile marker 59.5. The park is on the bay side.

Contact: Jolly Roger Travel Park, 59275 Overseas Highway, Marathon, FL 33050, 305/289-0404 or 800/995-1525, fax 305/743-6913, website: www.jrtp.com.

11 LION'S LAIR RV PARK

Rating: 4

In Marathon

Florida Keys map, grid a4, page 594

Sites are shady at this quiet park catering to seasonal visitors. Set across the highway from a dolphin research center, the location is convenient to Marathon's shopping centers, restaurants, and boating-oriented businesses.

Campsites, facilities: Twenty RV sites and 15 tent spots are set aside for overnighters at this adults-only (35 years old and up) park. Most have full hookups, water and electricity, picnic tables, grills, and concrete pads. Restrooms, showers, a dump station, laundry facilities, and telephone service are available. On the premises are a pool, a boat ramp, a dock, and a recreation room. Most areas are wheelchair accessible. Children are not welcome. The only pets permitted are cats that are always kept indoors.

Reservations, fees: Reservations are recommended. Sites are $38 per night for two people, plus $4 for each additional person. Major credit cards are accepted. Seasonal campers (up to six months) are preferred.

Directions: Follow Overseas Highway to mile marker 59; the park is on the ocean side.

Contact: Lion's Lair RV Park, 58950 Overseas Highway, Marathon, FL 33050, 305/289-0606.

12 PELICAN MOTEL AND TRAILER PARK

Rating: 6

On Grassy Key near Marathon

Florida Keys map, grid a4, page 594

In wintertime, you'll find senior citizens enjoying boating, fishing, water sports, and activities in the recreation room, and relaxing in the sheltered picnic area next to the water. This trailer park/motel complex on the Gulf side is next door to a full-service marina and near a dolphin research center.

Campsites, facilities: A varying number of RV sites (usually around 10) are available for overnighters and seasonal visitors in this 85-unit trailer park. All sites have full hookups, picnic tables, cable TV, and optional telephone service. Restrooms, showers, a dump station, and laundry facilities are available. On the premises are a pool, a boat ramp, a dock, a clubhouse with planned activities during the winter, shuffleboard courts, a dog-walk area, and a picnic area. Children are welcome, but adults and senior citizens are preferred. Small, leashed pets are permitted.

Reservations, fees: Reservations are recommended. Sites are $25 to $35 per night for two people, plus $3 per extra person. Major credit cards are accepted. Long-term (up to six months) stays are allowed.

Directions: From Follow Overseas Highway to mile marker 59; the park is on the Gulf side.

Contact: Pelican Motel and Trailer Park, 59151 Overseas Highway, Marathon, FL 33050, 305/289-0011.

13 KEY RV PARK

Rating: 3

In Marathon

Florida Keys map, grid a4, page 594

This well-kept park caters to boaters who want ocean access near their campsite and visitors who stay for the season. Shade is minimal. A small lighthouse and park benches overlook the water. Sites line a paved road around a narrow boat channel; about half are on the canal. The park is within two blocks of restaurants and shopping, and convenient to an 18-hole, par-3 golf course, public tennis courts, groceries, and miniature golf.

Campsites, facilities: There are 200 RV-only sites, most with full hookups. Water, electricity, restrooms, showers, a boat ramp, a boat dock ($4-a-day charge), picnic tables, three laundry rooms, a recreation hall, and wintertime social programs are available. Children

are allowed. Dogs are forbidden, but other pets are accepted.

Reservations, fees: Reservations are recommended. Sites are $55 per night for two people, plus $4 for each additional person. Major credit cards are accepted. Long-term rates are available.

Directions: The park is in Marathon, on U.S. 1/ Overseas Highway between mile markers 50 and 51, on the ocean side.

Contact: Key RV Park, 6099 Overseas Highway, Marathon, FL 33050, 305/743-5164 or 800/288-5164.

14 GULFSTREAM TRAILER PARK AND MARINA

Rating: 2

In Marathon

Florida Keys map, grid a4, page 594

Favored by full-timers, this park sometimes has vacancies for travelers. Watch the sunset from a waterfront site or a poolside tiki hut with picnic tables used for social gatherings. A boat ramp is nearby, and the park has a marina with 32 slips. Mobile home parks and a commercial fishing operation are your neighbors if you stay in this boating-oriented park. The owner's motto, printed on his business card, is "Think Fish."

Campsites, facilities: There are 23 grassy RV sites with full hookups, cable TV, and telephone access in this 80-unit park. Restrooms, showers, laundry facilities, a pool, and a marina are provided. Rental units are sometimes available. Some areas are wheelchair accessible; call ahead to see what's available at the time. Children are welcome. Leashed pets are permitted.

Reservations, fees: Reservations are recommended. Sites are $40 per night for two people, plus $4 per extra person. Credit cards are not accepted. Long-term stays are OK.

Directions: In Marathon, on U.S. 1/Overseas Highway at mile marker 49, turn north toward the bay side on 37th Street.

Contact: Gulfstream Trailer Park and Marina, 880 37th Street, Marathon, FL 33050, 305/743-5619 or 800/360-5619.

15 KNIGHT'S KEY PARK CAMPGROUND AND MARINA

Rating: 7

On Knight's Key

Florida Keys map, grid a4, page 594

Mature banyan, olive, and gumbo-limbo trees shade the grassy, 19-acre campground (owned by the same family since 1962), which has some nice sites near the water. There's a small swimming beach with picnic tables and tiki huts for shade. A big plus: the old Seven Mile Bridge span, favored by inline skaters and bicyclists, is close by. Sites are oversized, some 30 feet wide and big enough to accommodate slide-out trailers. Other sites are as long as 69 feet. The Kyle Inn Restaurant, open from December 15 to April 1, offers live entertainment.

Campsites, facilities: There are 192 RV sites with water and electricity, and 17 tent sites. Picnic tables, restrooms, showers, laundry facilities, a swimming beach, a marina, a boat ramp, shuffleboard courts, pool tables, and a modem hookup to check email are available. There's also a snack bar and a restaurant. Boat and trailer storage is available. Children are welcome. You may bring pets only if you have an air-conditioned RV.

Reservations, fees: Reservations are recommended, especially on holiday weekends and during lobster season (which changes every year but generally runs for a week in August, with a "mini" season of three days in late July). Sites are $28 to $72 per night for two people, plus $8 for each additional person. Major credit cards are accepted. Campers may stay for up to six months.

Directions: The park is on the ocean side of U.S. 1/Overseas Highway at mile marker 47 and the last turnoff before the Seven Mile Bridge.

Contact: Knight's Key Park Campground and Marina, P.O. Box 525, Marathon, FL 33050, 305/743-4343 or 800/348-2267, fax 305/743-2907, website: www.keysdirectory.com/knights keycampground.

16 SUNSHINE KEY FUNRESORT

Rating: 8

On Ohio Key

Florida Keys map, grid b4, page 594

At 75 acres, this is one of the largest campgrounds in the Keys. Surrounded by crystal-clear seas, the park bills itself as a water sports wonderland, with a 172-slip marina for anglers and a narrow swimming beach. From the marina, scuba divers, snorkelers, sailors, canoeists, and ocean kayakers have access to both bay and ocean waters. But there are plenty of activities on land, too—even a game arcade for teens who feel they're too grown-up to hang out with the parental units. Coconut palms give the campground that tropical island feel. There are walking trails on 35 acres. RVs up to 12 feet wide can be accommodated, and a remarkable 325 sites are pull-through.

Campsites, facilities: All 400 grassy or gravel sites are for RVs or tents; all sites have full hookups. Picnic tables, restrooms, showers, a pool, a boat ramp, two recreation halls, a horseshoe pit, shuffleboard and basketball courts, tennis, wintertime planned activities, cable TV, a dive shop, boat ramp, boat rentals, a fishing pier, and diving and snorkeling trips are on the premises. Also on site are groceries, a snack bar, bait and tackle, laundry facilities, and rental cottages. Children are welcome. Leashed pets are permitted; a dog kennel is provided.

Reservations, fees: Reservations are recommended. Sites are $54 to $64 per night. Major credit cards are accepted. Six-month stays are allowed.

Directions: The park is on Ohio Key, on U.S. 1/Overseas Highway at mile marker 39 on the bay side.

Contact: Sunshine Key FunResort, 38801 Overseas Highway, Big Pine Key, FL 33043, 305/872-2217 or 800/852-0348, fax 305/872-3801, website: rvonthego.com. Reserve campsites or dive and snorkel trips at 800/852-0348.

17 BAHIA HONDA STATE PARK
🏊 🎣 🚤 ♿ 🚐 ⛺

Rating: 10

On Bahia Honda Key

Florida Keys map, grid b4, page 594

This beautiful state park's two swimming beaches, routinely named among the top 10 in the nation, are spectacular. One overlooks the Bahia Honda bridge, and the other is on the ocean. You can spend hours lazing on a raft and imagine yourself floating across the Atlantic, or toss a beach ball around on the shore. Hike up to the old roadbed that once served as Henry Flagler's original rail line to Key West; on the top deck is the old highway. It juts eerily into space because the state removed the central span when the new road was built. Although recent hurricanes, including Hurricane Georges in 1998, caused at least $4 million in damage to the park, trees are rejuvenating nicely in the hardwood hammock where you may choose to sleep.

Campsites, facilities: The two camping areas have a total of 80 sites with piped water, electricity, picnic tables, and nearby restrooms and showers. On the south side of the park, smaller sites are tucked into a lush hardwood hammock. On the north side, campers stay on a sun-drenched gravel promontory suitable for RVs. Some sites and the restrooms are wheelchair accessible. A snack bar, a gift shop, snorkeling tours, ocean kayak and beach bike rentals, and diving equipment are provided by a concessionaire. In addition, 19 boat slips (where you can also stay overnight) are available (reservations are recommended). Children are welcome, but pets are not permitted.

Reservations, fees: Reservations are recommended; call ReserveAmerica at 800/326-3521.

Sites are $24 per night for four people, plus $2 for each additional person and $2 for electricity. Boat slips cost $1 per linear foot (minimum charge is $22) and include water, electricity, and use of the park facilities. Major credit cards are accepted. The maximum stay is 14 days.

Directions: The park is on Bahia Honda Key, at mile marker 37 on U.S. 1/Overseas Highway, on the ocean side.

Contact: Bahia Honda State Park, 36850 Overseas Highway, Big Pine Key, FL 33043, 305/872-2353.

18 BIG PINE KEY FISHING LODGE
🏊 🎣 🚤 🏕 🐾 ♿ 🚐 ⛺

Rating: 8

On Big Pine Key

Florida Keys map, grid b4, page 594

A sprawling motel/campground resort on 10 acres, Big Pine Key Fishing Lodge is paradise for anglers. The complex has a spectacular location, bordering on Looe Key National Underwater Marine Sanctuary and the ocean. An unusually well-developed canopy of shade trees creates a natural ambience even in the interior of the campground. Swimmers can bask on the beach or at the pool. Kids will find lots of things to keep them busy, and boaters have all the amenities they could need on hand, from fishing guides to a full-service marina. The boat ramp has an immediate drop-off from the seawall edge, however, and you're advised to launch with caution. When you come home with your catch, you must use the fish-cleaning tables near the boat basin.

Campsites, facilities: There are 97 RV sites with full hookups (accommodating rigs up to 35 feet) and 58 primitive tent-only sites with community water spigots and grills. Picnic tables, restrooms, showers, laundry facilities, docks, a boat ramp, boat rentals, charter fishing and diving services, a pool, a beach, horseshoe pits, shuffleboard courts, a playground, a recreation room, and a game room are available. A convenience store, a bait and tackle shop, and rental units are on the premises. Most areas are wheelchair accessible. Children are welcome. Dogs are prohibited because they are likely to scare the endangered key deer; other pets are welcome.

Reservations, fees: Reservations are required during holidays and recommended at other times. Sites are $30 to $41 per night for two people, plus $2 for each additional child and $5 per adult. Major credit cards are accepted. Long-term stays are OK.

Directions: From U.S. 1/Overseas Highway at mile marker 33 on Big Pine Key, turn south at the park entrance on the ocean side.

Contact: Big Pine Key Fishing Lodge, 33000 Overseas Highway, P.O. Box 430513, Big Pine Key, FL 33043, 305/872-2351, fax 305/872-3868.

19 BREEZY PINES RV ESTATES

Rating: 4

On Big Pine Key

Florida Keys map, grid b3, page 594

Trees, tropical flowers, and shrubs dot this 4.5-acre inland park with shady sites. Rigs up to 34 feet long can be accommodated; none of the sites are pull-through. Heavy traffic makes it difficult to turn in and out of the park onto U.S. 1. Boating, fishing, charter services, scuba diving, and snorkeling are available nearby. Also nearby is the National Key Deer Refuge, home of the elusive, endangered miniature deer, and a bicycle path along U.S. 1.

Campsites, facilities: The 90 RV sites have full hookups and cable TV, and the six tent spots come with water and electricity. Restrooms, showers, a pool, shuffleboard, a recreation room, wintertime planned activities, a small laundry facility, and a rental unit are available. A supermarket and restaurants are within .5 mile. Children are welcome. Leashed pets under 30 pounds are permitted.

Reservations, fees: Reservations are required in winter. Sites are $25 to $35 per night for two people, plus $3 for each additional per-

son. Credit cards are not accepted. Long-term stays are OK.

Directions: From U.S. 1/Overseas Highway near mile marker 30 on Big Pine Key, turn north into the park entrance.

Contact: Breezy Pines RV Estates, 29859 Overseas Highway, Big Pine Key, FL 33043, 305/872-9041.

20 SUGARLOAF KEY RESORT KOA KAMPGROUND

Rating: 8

On Sugarloaf Key

Florida Keys map, grid c3, page 594

The southernmost KOA in North America has much to offer families who want a resort-style vacation along with the waterfront necessities that define the Florida Keys experience. Ficus, sea grape, and palm trees and ocean vistas enhance the campsites. Fifteen sites are waterfront; the tent area is in a large, shady, grassy clearing. There are plenty of amenities, including a private sandy beach with tiki huts for sunning and playing, plus the Crews Nest social pavilion, and planned activities. Boaters and anglers can use the campground's full-service marina, which has 25 boat slips. An inlet leads from the marina to either Florida Bay or the Atlantic Ocean. Canoes and other boats are available for rent. Like everywhere on the waterfront in the Keys, the waters are crystal-clear for snorkeling.

Campsites, facilities: There are 300 sites with full hookups, or water and electricity, or primitive tent spots. All have picnic benches and grills. Restrooms, showers, a sandy beach, a heated pool with a hot tub, a restaurant, a marina, a boat ramp, a convenience store, a game room, miniature golf, laundry facilities, trailer rentals, basketball, volleyball, horseshoe pits, a bar with wintertime live entertainment, and rentals of bicycles, boats, and canoes are available. Children are welcome. Leashed pets are permitted.

Reservations, fees: Reservations are recommended. Sites are $42 to $95 per night for two people, plus $7 for each additional child and $9 per adult. Cable TV costs $4; 50-amp electrical service is $5. Major credit cards are accepted. Long-term stays are allowed.

Directions: From U.S. 1/Overseas Highway at mile marker 20 on Sugarloaf Key, turn south and drive .2 mile to the park entrance.

Contact: Sugarloaf Key Resort KOA Kampground, 251 County Road 939, Sugarloaf Key, FL 33042, 305/745-3549 or 800/562-7731, fax 305/745-9889, website: www.koa.com.

21 SUNBURST RV PARK— FLORIDA KEYS

Rating: 6

On Sugarloaf Key

Florida Keys map, grid c3, page 594

The six-acre artificial lake, an almost perfect rectangle nearly split in two by a promenade that ends in a swim ladder, is the focus of this campground. Go ahead and climb into one of the park's paddleboats or kayaks; their free use is a perk of staying here. Snorkeling, swimming, windsurfing, and fishing are popular camper activities. If you get a waterfront site, be careful with children; the man-made lake is 20 feet deep (even at the shoreline in some places). In fact, children under 14 must be accompanied by an adult when near the lake, the pool, or the bathhouse. Scuba divers are welcome, but they're not allowed to use spears or guns in the lake. Motorboats are forbidden. Coconut palms and Australian pines are counterpoints to the rather barren terrain, but many sites have no shade and little vegetation. Some tent sites are gravel, whereas others are "sandboxes." Cool off in the pool, or work off some calories while line dancing. In the recreation hall, where planned activities take place in the wintertime, you can curl up with a good book or relax in front of the TV.

Campsites, facilities: Full hookups, cable TV, and telephone access are available at 80 RV sites, which accommodate rigs up to 40 feet long. There are 10 tent spots—some primitive, others with water and electricity. Picnic tables, restrooms, showers, a pool, a lake, boat docks, rental units, laundry facilities, a basketball court, and a recreation hall are available. Most areas are wheelchair accessible. Children are welcome. Two leashed pets are permitted per site.

Reservations, fees: Reservations are recommended. Sites are $28 to $51 per night for two people, plus $5 for each additional person and $2 for cable TV. Major credit cards are accepted. Long-term stays are OK.

Directions: From U.S. 1/Overseas Highway at mile marker 19.8 on Sugarloaf Key, turn south on Johnson Road. Drive .25 mile to the park.

Contact: SunBurst RV Park—Florida Keys, 3000 Johnson Road, Sugarloaf Key, FL 33044, 305/745-4129 or 800/354-5524, fax: 305/745-1680, website: www.rvonthego.com.

22 BLUEWATER KEY RV PARK

Rating: 10

On Sugarloaf Key

Florida Keys map, grid c4, page 594

You can park your big rig at poolside, on a canal lot, or on the bayfront in this deluxe park, which has a three-story clubhouse and resort-style pool. The park is set in a quiet, residential neighborhood. Key West is only 10 miles away. Waterfront sites have their own docks and tiki huts.

Campsites, facilities: Rigs up to 45 feet can be accommodated at this 81-site ownership park, which opened in 1996. Your RV must use full hookups and be at least 26 feet long; tents are not permitted. Picnic tables, restrooms, showers, and laundry facilities are provided. Waterfront sites have swimming, docks, tiki huts, and coconut palms. There's also a boat ramp, a pool, a clubhouse, and a security gate. Children are welcome. Two leashed pets are permitted per site.

Reservations, fees: Reservations are required. Sites are $42 to $88 per night for four people; no additional persons are permitted per site. Cable TV is included. Telephone service is available at $2 per night. Rates are higher during Fantasy Fest and holidays. Major credit cards are accepted. Long-term stays are OK.

Directions: On Sugarloaf Key, from U.S. 1/Overseas Highway at mile marker 14.5, turn on Bluewater Drive toward the ocean side and proceed to the park entrance.

Contact: Bluewater Key RV Park, 2950 U.S. Highway 1, Key West, FL 33040, 305/745-2494 or 800/237-2266, fax 305/745-2433, email: bluekeyrv@aol.com, website: www.bluewaterkey.com.

23 GEIGER KEY MARINA AND RV PARK

🛥️ 🚐 🐕 🚗 ⛺

Rating: 3

On Geiger Key
Florida Keys map, grid d4, page 594

Waterfront lots "on the back side of paradise" are the draw here. This secluded campground overlooks Saddlehill and Bird Keys, both uninhabited, and it has good access to the water, especially for canoes and kayaks. Some campers fish from the seawall or explore the area in kayaks or snorkel fins (bring your own gear). Campsites are gravel, so bring a sleeping pad if you're tenting. You'll probably see jets from the nearby Key West Naval Air Station streak across the sky in formation.

Campsites, facilities: There are 32 RV sites (26 full-hookup) and a small area for about four tents. Water, electricity, restrooms, showers, a recreation room, a restaurant, bait, tackle, laundry facilities, and weekend live entertainment are available. Boat slips are for rent. Children are welcome "if they're quiet and considerate." Leashed pets are permitted.

Reservations, fees: Reservations are required. In-season (October through May) sites are $40 to $65 per night; off-season, sites are $25 to $45 per night for two people, plus $5 for each additional person over age 12. Major credit cards are accepted. Long-term stays are OK.

Directions: From U.S. 1/Overseas Highway at mile marker 10.5 on Geiger Key, turn south at the Circle K onto Boca Chica Road. Go 1.5 miles, then turn east onto Geiger Road. Drive two blocks to the park entrance.

Contact: Geiger Key Marina and RV Park, 5 Geiger Road, Key West, FL 33040, 305/296-3553, fax 305/293-9319, website: www.geigerkeymarina.com.

24 LEO'S CAMPGROUND

🐕 🚐 ⛺

Rating: 2

On Stock Island
Florida Keys map, grid d4, page 594

Set on two wooded acres, this quiet, shady campground is convenient to Key West's historic area, beaches, dive shops, and fishing charters. From here, you could ride your bicycle into town or catch a bus. Parking in Key West is notoriously difficult, and a lot of visitors rent moped scooters to get around. Some sights you shouldn't miss: the buoy marking the southernmost point in the United States, only 90 miles from Cuba; sunset at Mallory Square; the Audubon House and Tropical Gardens; the Hemingway Home and Museum; and the Mel Fisher Maritime Heritage Society Museum. Fisher is a modern-day treasure salvor who discovered the wreck of a gold-laden Spanish galleon and brought his booty ashore.

Campsites, facilities: The 32 campsites come with picnic tables. RV sites have water and electricity. A separate tent section offers 12 sites overlooking a small lake; two have electricity, six have grills, and all have water. Restrooms, showers, a dump station, and a laundry facility are available. A bus stop is on the corner and serves Key West–bound passengers. Children are welcome. Leashed pets under 30 pounds are permitted in RVs only.

Reservations, fees: Reservations are not necessary. Sites are $23 to $28 per night for two people, plus $5 for each extra person and $1 per pet. Hookups for tents are $3 additional and $6 extra for RVs. Rates are higher during Fantasy Fest, Christmas, and New Year's. Major credit cards are accepted. Long-term stays are OK.

Directions: On Stock Island, from U.S. 1/Overseas Highway at mile marker 4.5, turn south at Cross Street and drive one block to the campground on Suncrest Road.

Contact: Leo's Campground, 5236 Suncrest Road, Key West, FL 33040, 305/296-5260.

25 BOYD'S KEY WEST CAMPGROUND

Rating: 5

On Stock Island

Florida Keys map, grid d4, page 594

Although set in a busy urban area just outside the Key West city limits, this 12-acre campground manages to sustain a tropical ambience, with a swimming beach, water views, and coconut palms (providing precious little shade, alas). Like Key West, it attracts all kinds of people. Here, you might see a tent cooled by a room air conditioner on concrete blocks, as well as luxury-loving campers parked in $150,000 RVs. Sites are either sandy or grassy; the longest RV that can be accommodated is 40 feet. This is the largest park close to Key West, a city celebrated by songwriters (Jimmy Buffett's "Margaritaville"), authors (Ernest Hemingway, Tennessee Williams), artists (John James Audubon), and even presidents (Harry S. Truman, who started the Hawaiian shirt craze here). Today, Key West is so far from the mainland that it's hard to believe this was once a major Florida trading port, bustling with early settlers from the Bahamas, pirates, treasure salvors, and rumrunners. Many of the gingerbread houses that were home to these early residents have been restored. Modern-day "Conchs" (pronounced "konks"), as Keys na-

tives call themselves, now make their living from art galleries, boutiques, souvenir and T-shirt shops, or by giving circus-style performances on Mallory Square.

Campsites, facilities: There are 150 full-hookup RV sites and 53 spots set apart for tents. Water and electricity are provided at all sites. Restrooms, showers, picnic tables, laundry facilities, a heated pool, a beach, a game room, a boat ramp, telephone service, cable TV, limited supplies, and a dock are available. All areas are wheelchair accessible. Children are welcome. Pets under 20 pounds are permitted on leashes.

Reservations, fees: Reservations are recommended. Sites are $36 to $45 per night for two people, plus $10 for each additional person. Add $10 for water and electricity, $15 for 50-amp service, and $20 for sewer hookups. Major credit cards are accepted. Long-term stays are OK.

Directions: From U.S. 1/Overseas Highway, turn south at mile marker 5 onto Third Street. Drive one block and turn east onto Maloney Avenue/State Road 941. The park is at 6401 Maloney Avenue.

Contact: Boyd's Key West Campground, 6401 Maloney Avenue, Key West, FL 33040, 305/294-1465, fax 305/293-9301, email: boyds camp@aol.com.

26 EL MAR RV RESORT

Rating: 6

On Stock Island

Florida Keys map, grid d4, page 594

Modeling itself as "upscale," El Mar RV Resort has waterfront sites for self-contained RVs that are 26 feet or longer. No tents are allowed. Indeed, expensive motor coaches and fifthwheelers are the norm at this sunny, sparsely landscaped park that offers eastward views of the beautiful Keys waters. Adults are the preferred visitors.

Campsites, facilities: There are seven waterfront sites and seven inland. All have full hookups and are available for overnighters or snowbirds. Picnic tables, cable TV, and phone availability are at each site, which measure 30 by 75 feet with concrete patios. RVs must be self-contained; no restrooms or showers are provided. Children are discouraged. Leashed pets under 25 pounds are permitted.

Reservations, fees: Reservations are recommended. Sites are $65 to $85 per night for two people, plus $10 per extra person. Major credit cards are accepted. Long-term rates are available.

Directions: From U.S. 1/Overseas Highway, turn south at mile marker 5 onto Third Street. Drive one block and turn east onto Maloney Avenue/State Road 941. The park is .5 mile away at 6700 Maloney Avenue.

Contact: El Mar RV Resort, 6700 Maloney Avenue, Key West, FL 33040, 305/294-0857 or 315/524-8687, fax 603/880-8187, website: www.elmarrvresort.com.

27 JABOUR'S TRAILER COURT

Rating: 1

In Key West

Florida Keys map, grid d4, page 594

An astounding number of campsites for RVs and tents are packed into this 1.5-acre campground; however, there are so many long-term campers that spots available for travelers are few and far between. The emphasis is on renting cottages, trailers, and mobile homes that are already on the property. You certainly can't get closer to Key West's main attractions than Jabour's, which is near the historic Old Town area in the center of the city.

Campsites, facilities: All 90 sites have full hookups, cable TV, and picnic tables. Restrooms, showers, and mobile-home rentals are available. Within a short walking distance is a marina where fishing charters, snorkel trips, sunset sightseeing cruises, diving excursions, and day trips to the Dry Tortugas can be arranged. Within a few blocks are restaurants, groceries, bars, and shopping. Children are welcome. Leashed pets are permitted only in self-contained RVs that have air-conditioning. If your pet is over 20 pounds, call for prior approval.

Reservations, fees: Reservations are recommended. Sites are $40 to $69 per night for two people, plus $6 for each additional child and $10 per extra adult. Major credit cards are accepted. Stays of up to six months are permitted.

Directions: When you enter Key West on U.S. 1/Overseas Highway, bear right and follow U.S. 1 southwest about two miles to Palm Avenue (at City Marina, Garrison Bight). Turn right onto Palm Avenue and continue over the Palm Avenue bridge. Cross White Street onto Eaton Street. Proceed on Eaton for .4 mile, then turn right in one and a half blocks onto Elizabeth Street. The park is at right.

Contact: Jabour's Trailer Court, 223 Elizabeth Street, Key West, FL 33040, 305/294-5723, website: www.kwcamp.com.

28 DRY TORTUGAS NATIONAL PARK/FORT JEFFERSON BOAT-IN OR FLY-IN SITES

Rating: 10

About 70 miles west of Key West in the Straits of Florida

Florida Keys map, grid d4, page 594

The 13 sun-washed camping sites on Garden Key aren't much—really just an open grassy area with a little shade from coconut palms, buttonwood trees, and steady, cooling sea breezes. But, wow, just look around you. The most imposing presence is that of the six-sided, brick-walled Fort Jefferson, built beginning in 1846 to enable the United States to protect ship traffic between the mouth of the Mississippi River and the Atlantic Ocean.

Fort Jefferson, which offers a visitors center with interpretive exhibits detailing the fort's history, is open daily. It served as a Union outpost during the War between the States and at one time housed four men suspected of trying to help bring about President Lincoln's assassination after the war's conclusion.

Garden Key is one of a cluster of islands known as the Dry Tortugas. The "dry" part of the name comes from the fact that there is no freshwater here; it can't be emphasized enough that you must bring all the water you'll need for your entire stay. "Tortugas" (meaning "turtles") dates to 1513, when Spanish explorer Ponce de Leon, who discovered Florida, spied the green, loggerhead, and hawksbill sea turtles that came ashore to nest. Today the green turtle is endangered, and the loggerhead and hawksbill are classified as threatened. But, if you're lucky, you can still watch them arrive to lay eggs in spring and summer.

Summer and spring are also the time to see the annual spectacle of 100,000 sooty terns nesting on nearby Bush Key. The sooties show up as early as mid-January and begin nesting in March. They stick around until September or so. You're also likely to see brown noddy terns, frigate birds with seven-foot wingspans, masked and brown boobies, roseate terns, double-breasted cormorants, and brown pelicans.

In the aquamarine waters between these spots of land, snorkeling is popular. Divers delight to the sight of schools of vividly colored small fish, such as the neon yellow and sky blue smallmouth grunt, making their way among multicolored sea fans and staghorn coral. Scuba divers also see sharks and barracuda. Anglers make the Dry Tortugas a frequent stop, coming back with amberjack, grouper, wahoo, and snapper, among others. If you tire of the water and Garden Key, you can make a day trip to Loggerhead Key and picnic beneath a towering lighthouse (provided you have your own boat or kayak).

A few words of caution: Watch your step in the fort because the uneven walkways and loose bricks have been known to trip up more than one visitor. In the water, you'll want to be familiar with—and carefully avoid—sea urchins, fire coral, and jellyfish.

The first-come, first-served policy can be a little intimidating, particularly if you're paying in the neighborhood of $80 per head for boat service or $150 for an air taxi; however, the ferry services will call ahead to make sure there's room for you, and one operator told us he has never seen anyone turned away. The park service also says there is an overflow area available. Things can get a little tight in March and April when bird-watchers show up. Unofficially, more than 10 parties usually are accommodated. Still, this place is so remote that crowds are rarely an issue.

Rules are strict at Dry Tortugas: Prohibited are water-skiing, personal watercraft, anchoring on or otherwise harming coral, taking lobster or conchs, spearfishing, and possession of more than one day's bag limit of fish as determined by State of Florida fishing regulations. Firearms must be unloaded and cased at all times and may not be brought ashore. All historic and archaeological material, including such items as bricks, bottles, glass, and metal, must be left undisturbed.

Campsites, facilities: Ten primitive tent sites and three sites in an overflow area are available to boaters or others who arrange to fly or boat to the island. A historic fort, a visitors center, saltwater flush toilets, and some picnic tables and grills are provided. You must bring everything else, including water, fuel, food, and other camping supplies. There is no piped water. A portable grill is recommended. Trash must be packed out. Personal watercraft and water-skiing are prohibited. Leashed pets are permitted. The long list of other rules boils down to this: Take only pictures, leave only footprints. The campground, visitors center, bookstore, and the lower level of the fort are wheelchair accessible.

Reservations, fees: Reservations are required for groups of 10 or more. Otherwise, camping is first-come, first-served. Sites are $3 per person per night. Credit cards are not accepted. Note: The campground was closed during much of 2002 and 2003 after rains ruined the septic system; call to be sure it has reopened.

Directions: To get to the island, you'll need a ferry boat, an air taxi service, or your own boat (consult nautical chart 11438). Most campers depart from Key West. There, air taxi operators include Seaplanes of Key West (305/294-0709, website: www.seaplanesofkeywest.com). Ferry boats serve the Dry Tortugas from the Florida Keys, including: Yankee Fleet (305/294-7009, website: www.yankeefleet.com) and Sunny Days (305/296-2042). Ask the ferry operators if they can accommodate your kayak. It's also possible to leave from Naples, Key Largo, Marathon, Fort Myers, or St. Petersburg. Ask the park for details.

Contact: Dry Tortugas National Park, P.O. Box 6208, Key West, FL 33041. Everglades National Park, 305/242-7700, website: www.nps.gov/drto.

COURTESY OF FLORIDA STATE PARKS

Resources

Resources

U.S. National Forests

For further information about National Forests in Florida, write, call, or visit the websites of the following forests:

USDA Forest Service
Southern Region
1720 Peachtree Road NW
Atlanta, GA 30367
404/347-4177
website: www.r8web.com

Florida Forest Supervisor's Office
325 John Knox Road, Suite F-100
Tallahassee, FL 32303
850/532-8500
TDD: 850/942-9351

Apalachicola National Forest
website: www.r8web.com/florida/
   forests/apalachicola.htm
Divided into two ranger districts:
Apalachicola Ranger District
P.O. Box 579
Bristol, FL 32321
850/643-2282
Wakulla Ranger District
57 Taft Drive
Crawfordville, FL 32327
850/926-3561

Ocala National Forest
website: www.r8web.com/florida/forests/
   ocala.htm
Divided into two ranger districts:
Seminole Ranger District
40929 State Road 19
Umatilla, FL 32784
352/669-3153
Lake George Ranger District
17147 East Highway 40
Silver Springs, FL 34488
352/625-2520

Osceola National Forest
P.O. Box 70
Olustee, FL 32072
386/752-2577
website: www.r8web.com/florida/forests/
   osceola.htm

U.S. National Parks

For further information about National Park units in Florida, write, call, or visit the websites of the following:

Reservations service
800/365-CAMP (800/365-2267)
website: http://reservations.nps.gov

Southeast Region
National Park Service
100 Alabama Street SW, 1924 Building
Atlanta, GA 30303
404/562-3100
website: www.nps.gov

Big Cypress National Preserve
HCR61, Box 110
Ochopee, FL 34141
239/695-1201
website: www.nps.gov/bicy

Biscayne National Park
9700 SW 328th Street
Homestead, FL 33033-5634
305/230-1144 or 305/230-7275
email: bisc_information@nps.gov
website: www.nps.gov/bisc

Canaveral National Seashore
Park Headquarters
308 Julia Street
Titusville, FL 32796
407/267-1110
email: cana_superintendent@nps.gov
website: www.nps.gov/cana

Castillo de San Marcos National Monument
One South Castillo Drive
St. Augustine, FL 32084
904/829-6506
email: casa_ranger_activities@nps.gov
website: www.nps.gov/casa

De Soto National Memorial
P.O. Box 15390
Bradenton, FL 34280
941/792-0458
fax 941/792-5094
email: eso_superintendent@nps.gov
website: www.nps.gov/deso

Dry Tortugas National Park
P.O. Box 6208
Key West, FL 33041
305/242-7700
email: drto_information@nps.com
website: www.nps.gov/drto
At this writing, the campground was closed
until further notice.

Everglades National Park
40001 State Road 9336
Homestead, FL 33034-6733
305/242-7700
email: ever_information@nps.gov
website: www.nps.gov/ever

Fort Caroline National Memorial/
Timucuan Preserve
12713 Fort Caroline Road
Jacksonville, FL 32225
904/641-7155
email: timu_interpretation@nps.gov
website: www.nps.gov/foca

Fort Matanzas National Monument
8635 Highway A1A South
St. Augustine, FL 32080
904/471-0116
email: FOMA_Site_Supervisor@nps.gov
website: www.nps.gov/foma

Gulf Islands National Seashore Florida District
1801 Gulf Breeze Parkway
Gulf Breeze, FL 32561
850/934-2600
email: terry_colby@nps.gov
website: www.nps.gov/guis

Timucuan Ecological and Historic Preserve
13165 Mount Pleasant Road
Jacksonville, FL 32225
or write to
12713 Fort Caroline Road
Jacksonville, FL 32225
904/221-5568
email: timu_interpretation@nps.gov
website: www.nps.gov/timu

U.S. Fish and Wildlife Service

For further information about U.S. Fish and Wildlife Service units, including National Wildlife Refuges in Florida, visit the websites of the following:

National Wildlife Refuges directory
website: http://refuges.fws.gov

Southeast Regional Office
website: http://southeast.fws.gov

U.S. Army Corps of Engineers

The U.S. Army Corps of Engineers regulates, among other things, recreational activities at several sites in Florida. For more information, contact:

Jacksonville District
P.O. Box 4970
Jacksonville, FL 32232-0019
Public Affairs Office:
904/232-2568
fax 904/232-2237
website: www.saj.usace.army.mil/recreation/
  index.html
Governs Lake Okeechobee and most of
  Florida.
South Florida Operations Office:
525 Ridgelawn Road
Clewiston, FL 33440-5399
863/983-8101

Mobile District
P.O. Box 2288
Mobile, AL 36628-0001
334/471-5966
website: www.sam.usace.army.mil/op/rec/
  seminole
Governs Lake Seminole on the Florida-
  Georgia state border.
Lake Seminole Resource Management Office:
P.O. Box 96
Chattahoochee, FL 32324
229/662-2001

Florida State Parks

Almost 150 parks are part of the award-winning Florida State Parks system.

Florida State Parks guide is available from:
Florida Department of Environmental
  Protection, Parks Information
Mail Station #535
3900 Commonwealth Boulevard
Tallahassee, FL 32399-3000
850/245-2157
website: www.floridastateparks.org

Order the guide online or download park information and park maps at www.dep.state
.fl.us/parks/communications/guide.html. You
can search for individual Florida State Parks
at www.dep.state.fl.us/parks/parksby.htm.

Florida Division of Forestry

For a trailwalker's guide to exploring Florida's state forests, visit www.trailwalker.fl-ag.com, which lists individual trails throughout the state.

For information about Florida's 30 state forests, contact the following:

Florida Division of Forestry
3125 Conner Boulevard
Tallahassee, FL 32399-1650
850/488-4274
fax 850/488-0863
website: www.fl-dof.com
Download state forest maps in Adobe Acrobat
format at www.fl-dof.com/Pubs/index.html.

Florida Division of Forestry field unit/district offices

Blackwater Forestry Center
11650 Munson Highway
Milton, FL 32570
850/957-6140
fax 850/957-6143

Bunnell District Office
5001 U.S. Highway 1
North Bunnell, FL 32110
904/446-6785
fax 904/446-6789

Caloosahatchee District Office
10941 State Road 80
Fort Myers, FL 33905
239/690-3500
fax 239/690-3504

Everglades District
3315 Southwest College Avenue
Davie, FL 33314
954/475-4120
fax 954/475-4126

Jacksonville District
7247 Big Oaks Road
Bryceville, FL 32009
904/266-5001
fax 904/266-5018

Lakeland District Office
5745 South Florida Avenue
Lakeland, FL 33813
863/648-3163
fax 863/648-3169

Myakka District Office
4723 53rd Avenue East
Bradenton, FL 34203
941/751-7627
fax 941/751-7631

Orlando Office
8431 South Orange Blossom Trail
Orlando, FL 32809
407/856-6512
fax 407/856-6514

Perry District Office
618 Plantation Road
Perry, FL 32348
850/838-2299
fax 850/838-2284

Suwannee District Office
Route 7, Box 369
Lake City, FL 32055
386/758-5700
fax 386/758-5725

Tallahassee District
865 Geddie Road
Tallahassee, FL 32304
850/488-1871
fax 850/922-2107

Waccasassa Forestry Center
1600 Northeast 23rd Avenue
Gainesville, FL 32609
352/955-2005
fax 352/955-2125

Withlacoochee Forestry Center
15019 Broad Street
Brooksville, FL 34601-4201
352/754-6777
fax 352/754-6751

Selected Individual State Forests

Big Shoals State Forest
7620 133rd Road
Live Oak, FL 32055
904/208-1460

Blackwater River State Forest
11650 Munson Highway
Milton, FL 32570
850/957-6140
fax 850/957-6143

Cary State Forest
Route 2, Box 60
Bryceville, FL 32009
904/266-5021 or 904/266-5022

Etoniah Creek State Forest
390 Holloway Road
Florahome, FL 32140
386/329-2552
fax: 386/329-2554

Goethe State Forest
8250 Southeast County Road 336
Dunnellon, FL 34431
352/447-2202
fax 352/447-1358

Jennings State Forest
1337 Longhorn Road
Middleburg, FL 32068
904/291-5530
fax 904/291-5537

Lake George State Forest
5460 North Hwy 17
DeLeon Springs, FL 32120
386/985-7820

Lake Talquin State Forest
865 Geddie Road
Tallahassee, FL 32304
850/488-1871
fax 850/922-2107

Lake Wales Ridge State Forest
452 School Bus Road
Frostproof, FL 33843
941/635-7801
fax 941/635-7837

Little Big Econ State Forest
1350 Snow Hill Road
Geneva, FL 32732
407/971-3500

Myakka State Forest
4723 53rd Avenue East
Bradenton, FL 34203
941/255-7653

Picayune Strand State Forest
2121 52nd Avenue Southeast
Naples, FL 34117
239/348-7557
fax 239/348-7559

Pine Log State Forest
715 West 15th Street
Panama City, FL 32401
850/747-5639
fax 850/872-4879

Point Washington State Forest
715 West 15th Street
Panama City, FL 32401
850/747-5639
fax 850/872-4879

Ralph E. Simmons State Forest
Route 3, Box 299
Hillard, FL 32046
904/845-3597

Seminole State Forest
Leesburg Forestry Station, 9610 CR 44
Leesburg, FL 34788
352/360-6675 or 352/360-667.

Tate's Hell State Forest
1621 Highway 98 East
Carrabelle, FL 32322
850/697-3734
fax 850/697-2892

Tiger Bay State Forest
4316 W. International Speedway Boulevard
Daytona Beach, FL 32124
386/226-0250
fax 386/226-0251

Twin Rivers State Forest
7620 133rd Road
Live Oak, FL 32060
386/208-1460
fax 386/208-1465

Welaka State Forest
P.O. Box 174
Welaka, FL 32193-0174
386/467-2388
fax 386/467-2740

Withlacoochee State Forest
15003 Broad Street
Brooksville, FL 34601
352/754-6896

Florida Fish and Wildlife Conservation Commission

The Florida Fish and Wildlife Conservation Commission supervises hunting and fishing activities, as well as wildlife conservation. For more information, contact:

Florida Fish and Wildlife Conservation Commission
620 South Meridian Street
Tallahassee, FL 32399-1600
850/488-4676

For recreation use permits, hunting season information, freshwater and saltwater fishing licenses, and information about wildlife management area regulations, see www.florida conservation.org.

Florida Fish and Wildlife Conservation Commission district offices

Northwest Region
3911 Highway 2321
Panama City, FL 32409-1658
850/265-3676

Southwest Region
3900 Drane Field Road
Lakeland, FL 33811-1299
863/648-3203

North Central Region
Route 7, Box 440
Lake City, FL 32055-8713
386/758-0525

South Region
8535 Northlake Boulevard
West Palm Beach, FL 33412
561/625-5122

Northeast Region
1239 Southwest 10th Street
Ocala, FL 34474-2797
352/732-1225

Florida Water Management Districts

In addition to managing the quality and quantity of water throughout Florida, five water management districts provide recreational opportunities on lands they control. Contact the following:

Northwest Florida Water Management District
81 Water Management Drive
Havana, FL 32333
850/539-5999
fax 850/539-4380
website: http://sun6.dms.state.fl.us/nwfwmd

Southwest Florida Water Management District
2379 Broad Street
Brooksville, FL 34609-6899
352/796-7211
website: www.swfwmd.state.fl.us

South Florida Water Management District
3301 Gun Club Road
West Palm Beach, FL 33406
561/686-8800
website: www.sfwmd.gov

Suwannee River Water Management District
9225 County Road 49
Live Oak, FL 32060
386/362-1001
website: www.srwmd.state.fl.us

St. Johns River Water Management District
P.O. Box 1429
Palatka, FL 32178-1429
386/329-4500 or 800/451-7106
website: http://sjr.state.fl.us

Florida has a rapidly growing program for the development of new trails. For more information, contact:

Office of Greenways & Trails
Florida Department of
Environmental Protection
3900 Commonwealth Boulevard, MS 795
Tallahassee, FL 32399-3000
850/245-2052 or 877/822-5208
website: www.dep.state.fl.us/gwt/index.htm

Cross Florida Greenway Field Office
8282 SE Highway 314
Ocala, FL 34470
352/236-7143

Active Volunteering

All outdoors-oriented civic groups need money, but some also want your energy. The following organizations want volunteer help or hands-on support:

Florida Trail Association
5415 SW 13th Street
Gainesville, FL 32608
352/378-8823
email: fta@florida-trail.org
website: www.florida-trail.org

Friends of Florida State Forests
3125 Conner Boulevard, Ste. C-21
Tallahassee, FL 32399-1650
850/414-9974
email: ffsf@doacs.state.fl.us

Acknowledgments

This third edition expands the work I did on the first and second editions with Tom Dubocq, Sally Deneen, and Robert McClure. Sally and Robert provided research on this edition's Everglades National Park chapter. Additionally, Joanne S. Moore, my mother, provided valuable assistance in the preparation of all editions.

Index

About the Author

© PETER TRITLEY

Marilyn A. Moore has been camping and fooling around in the outdoors most of her life. During the years of research on this book, she covered 10,000 miles without ever leaving the state, burned out a Chevy Suburban's transmission, and wore out the axle on a camper. Children Andrea and T. J. announced at one point that they never wanted to see another campground for as long as they lived. They've gotten over it.

Moore is editor of special projects for Miami-based *Latin Trade* magazine and a longtime contributor to nationally published travel guides, business publications, newspapers, and magazines. She lives in Miami Springs, Florida.

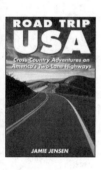